THE OXFORD COMPANION TO THE YEAR

THE OXFORD

COMPANION
TO THE YEAR

Bonnie Blackburn
& Leofranc Holford-Strevens

OXFORD
UNIVERSITY PRESS

OXFORD

UNIVERSITY PRESS

Great Clarendon Street, Oxford OX2 6DP

Oxford University Press is a department of the University of Oxford
and furthers the University's aim of excellence in research, scholarship,
and education by publishing worldwide in

Oxford New York

Athens Auckland Bangkok Bogotá Buenos Aires Calcutta
Cape Town Chennai Dar es Salaam Delhi Florence Hong Kong Istanbul
Karachi Kuala Lumpur Madrid Melbourne Mexico City Mumbai
Nairobi Paris São Paulo Singapore Taipei Tokyo Toronto Warsaw

with associated companies in Berlin Ibadan

Oxford is a trade mark of Oxford University Press
in the UK and in certain other countries

Published in the United States
by Oxford University Press Inc., New York

British Library Cataloguing in Publication Data

Data available

Library of Congress Cataloging in Publication Data

Data available

0-19-214231-3

1 3 5 7 9 10 8 6 4 2

Typeset in Centaur MT
by Alliance Phototypesetters, Pondicherry, India
Printed in Great Britain
on acid-free paper by
Biddles Ltd
Guildford and King's Lynn

PREFACE

This book is intended at once to entertain and to inform. It was first conceived by Rob Scriven, then Senior Editor in the Arts and Reference Division of Oxford University Press, as a modern-day version of Robert Chambers's *Book of Days* (1864), that quintessentially nineteenth-century gathering of useful and amusing lore on calendar customs, filled out with whatever popped into the author's mind when the days ran thin, and described in his subtitle as 'A miscellany of popular antiquities in connection with the calendar, including anecdote, biography, & history, curiosities of literature, and oddities of human life and character'. But whereas Chambers covered 366 days in two volumes of some 800 pages each in small print and double column, we were required to accommodate 367 days (including 30 February, a day acknowledged thrice in human history) within a single volume, of more generous typography, while leaving room for a second part that should treat of calendars in general, review the history of the modern Christian or international calendar, and give some account of the chief non-Christian calendars. We were therefore required to exclude, except in rare instances, birth and death dates of famous people, more particularly since there are many such books of dates in existence. Part I was written jointly by both authors; Part II is the exclusive work of Leofranc Holford-Strevens, who is also responsible for all translations throughout the book unless otherwise stated on the page or in the Bibliography.

We have adhered quite closely in Part I to our instructions, that we should list only events and people commemorated on a certain day. History is all too likely to overtake us on national days; that is the hazard of all such time-bound compilations. We have not listed the many World or National This-and-That Days proclaimed by institutions and corporations that serve as nothing but copy for desperate feature-writers; the humour would soon wear off, nor have we the political authority to decide the relative or absolute merits of causes called good, promoted on a particular day that they may be forgotten for the rest of the year. Apart from British and US holidays and commemorations, we have not made any effort to be comprehensive; our descriptions of holidays in other countries were chosen as the fancy moved us, and since they are often taken from historical sources may no longer reflect current customs.

Some holidays that now seem quite secular are based on the Christian calendar; in many cases this only returns them to their original status, as pagan celebrations which the Church attempted to extirpate. It will not please all readers to be reminded (even in our use of the traditional abbreviations BC and AD) that the calendar of ancient Rome has become the modern international standard as a result of Christianity; those to whom these facts are offensive may care to devise, and then persuade the human race to use, a truly non-sectarian and politically neutral calendar with an era whose epoch shall be equally auspicious for all the world (and not merely its secularist liberals). Failing such a calendar, and such an era, we see no virtue in evading manifest facts; nor can we apologize for the overwhelmingly Christian content of Part I (certain references to ancient Rome apart). Festivals of other religions, which are mostly based on the lunar calendar and can rarely be accommodated to specific Roman days, are described in Part II.

Calendar customs can be deceptive; though their origins sometimes seem lost in the mists of time, not infrequently they are in fact quite modern, or deliberate revivals. This is particularly true in our own age, where tourist opportunities have become the glint in the eye of communities with changing economies. Because so much of our material is based on historical sources, it would not surprise us if enterprising councils were to discover interesting possibilities. On the other hand, calendar-based holidays are difficult to fit on their proper days in an industrial society; indeed, many holidays, once calendrical, have been moved to the nearest Monday to afford a longer weekend, with a concomitant decline in the day's original significance.

Many of the commemorations included in this book will arouse different responses in different readers. More than one religion, sect, cause, or nation has its heroes and its martyrs, who may not be revered by those against whom they contended; however much one may admire their personal qualities, one can no more promiscuously approve their principles than simultaneously endorse the intentions of all national leaders or political prisoners. Even more embarrassing are miracle stories, less because modern readers cannot believe in them than because, though narrated in more than one interest, they imply unique possession of divine favour: only Elijah, and not the priests of Baal, could call down fire on Mount Carmel. Yet there was a time when miracles were accepted as undoubted fact, even when performed by the other side: not only Aaron, but the wise men of Egypt could turn rods into serpents; St Luke may speak of Simon Magus' sorceries and St Philip's miracles, but—a fact his translators disguise—he uses the same Greek word for the amazement caused by both. Neither early Christians nor their pagan enemies denied that the other party could 'make signs', as they called it; to be sure its signs might be belittled as wrought through evil spirits, or temporary in their effect, but in the last resort they had to be admitted as facts and discounted as proofs. Ancient credulity joins modern scepticism against medieval faith.

In any case, belief or disbelief, though vital to the historian, is of little or no relevance for commemorations. Let us imagine an Italian village preparing to celebrate the feast-day of its patron saint in the 1960s. We may suppose, especially if we are in one of the former papal states, that the mayor is a Communist and therefore, at least officially, an atheist; the doctor, a man of science and *laico* as few Anglo-Saxons know how to be, has little time for the Church and none at all for miraculous cures; the schoolmaster reserves his position on miracles, but dismisses the non-miraculous portion of the *vita* as a farrago of anachronisms; the priest has heard from his cousin, who works at the Vatican, that the saint is about to be struck off the calendar for being totally fictitious.

Yet we may be sure that none of them will take part any the less wholeheartedly in the communal celebrations. Perhaps some celebrations inspired by our book will be individual rather than communal; nevertheless, it is in that spirit of not so much suspended as transcended disbelief that we commend our not always pious legends.

Moreover, while some celebrations are particular and hardly to be understood in other cultures or societies, others illustrate concerns that recur from tale to tale and cult to cult; above all the harvest and the weather. It is said that a Roman once asked the great rabbi Yohanan ben Zakkai: 'We have festivals and you have festivals; we have the New Year, Saturnalia, and the Emperor's accession-day; you have Passover, the Feast of Weeks, and Tabernacles; which is the day on which we both rejoice alike?' The rabbi answered: 'It is the day when rain falls.'

Weather proverbs have a surprisingly long life; many people will recall that associated with St Swithun, though they know nothing of the saint himself. In earlier times, mnemonic rhymes attached to a saint's day reminded farmers of the time to plant or to harvest, and we all know that April showers bring May flowers. But do birds really mate in the middle of February, on St Valentine's Day? Does the cuckoo first appear around the 3rd of April? It must be remembered that all such proverbs are based on the Julian calendar, which was kept in Britain and the colonies until September 1752, when eleven days were dropped from the year to bring it in line with the Gregorian reform of 1582; thus, with the centennial leap days that have accrued since then, all weather proverbs are now out of date by thirteen days, and from 2100 will be out by fourteen.

The days are grouped by month, each month being introduced by proverbs, an account of its names in some other West European languages, with etymologies where possible, a list of holidays and anniversaries not fixed on a particular date, and excerpts from various writers, notably Spenser (*The Faerie Queene*) and Nicholas Breton (*Fantasticks*), on the nature of the month. The entry for each day begins, under the heading, with its Roman name on the left and its Sunday Letter on the right, followed (where appropriate) by proverbs relating to that day, a list of holidays and anniversaries, and an account of the day's significance in ancient Rome. Next come the holy days and saints' days. A heading lists, in bold type, any red-letter days of the Church of England, as recognized in the Book of Common Prayer (BCP) or the calendar of 1997, *The Christian Year* (CY), any Solemnity or Feast in the General Calendar of the Roman Catholic Church, or a major Orthodox feast, and in normal type any other holy days recorded in a current calendar. All these saints and holy days, unless cross-referred to another day, are discussed in the text beneath the heading.

Besides these saints, we have added (but not included in the heading) other saints who appealed to us on historical or legendary grounds; although some were admitted for their attractive personality, sanctity as such is not the pre-eminent quality of the majority, many of whom were the great historical figures of their day and politicians of the first order. The entry ends with any other matter relating to the day outside the foregoing categories, including poetry, none of it taken from Chambers's stock of minor nineteenth-century verse, which we have left for the twenty-first century to rehabilitate as the twentieth century has rehabilitated the poetry of the eighteenth.

Saints' days bring with them a complexity that is at once a problem and an opportunity: the variation in the day on which a saint is culted, both between Churches—especially between the Orthodox and the Western—and within the same Church over time, in particular after the liturgical reforms that both the Church of England and the Roman Catholic Church have in the last generation undergone. Our general principle has been to use the Western date except for those saints whose chief importance lies in the East; and to accept current dates in the West except when their former days were significant outside the Church, for instance in festivals or weather proverbs. Since we are publishing in England, we have in cases of perplexity allowed the Church of England a casting vote. However, we have occasionally exploited the choice of dates to register a saint on the day for which we had less material otherwise; in any event we have cross-referred from one date to the rest.

We make no apology for including saints of very doubtful authenticity, simply because their legends have proved so enduring a legacy in history and art. St George, though derided in the sixteenth century as no more than a tavern sign, is still the patron saint of England; his day has now been raised by the national church to a principal feast. Some will no doubt seem obscure, but none more so than some of the saints in Chambers, such as the fourth-century virgin martyr St Syncletica on 5 January. Readers suffering from a surfeit of saintliness will find relief under 12 June.

Following 31 December, we have treated the other divisions of the year, from weekdays to seasons, drawing our material from folklore as well as historical documents. The church holidays dependent on the date of Easter—the moveable feasts—have been placed in a separate section; too many books make the mistake of fitting them on the days in the year in which the book was written. Other secular holidays not fixed as to day, such as Thanksgiving, are found in the final section of Part I. Our first part is admittedly eclectic and idiosyncratic, and we hope it will enlighten as well as amuse.

Part II is the reference side of the *Companion*. Here we explain calendars of many kinds, both contemporary and historical, and the organization of time in various ways. We have included many explanations that will be useful to historians, such as how to find the date of Easter for any given year (App. H) and how to find the day of the week for any known date (App. G). We believe this to be the first book to notice within the same covers both Otto Neugebauer's non-Westernized account of the Alexandrian Easter that both Rome and Constantinople adopted without fully understanding its principles, and the definitive account by Dáibhí Ó Cróinín and Dan McCarthy of the Celtic Easter whose defeat at the Synod of Whitby in 664 secured the Roman orientation of the English church. We list important dates in the Christian, Jewish, and Muslim calendars to 2020 in Appendix K, and provide tables of regnal years of English and British Sovereigns (App. A) and of Popes (App. B), which are often used in dating. The conversion of dates between various systems is treated in Appendix F.

No doubt some readers will find Part II distressingly mathematical, others not nearly mathematical enough. The latter will find grist to their mill in the works by Nachum Dershowitz and Edward M. Reingold, and by E. G. Richards cited in our Bibliography; to the former we can offer no redress beyond the tables offered to save the need for calculation. In particular, the account of the computus by which the date of Easter is determined, and the lunar calendar on which it rests, is complicated both by the nature of the subject (even more so since Pope Gregory's reform) and by the conflicting principles and divergent methods employed in the earlier Christian centuries; those who wish to understand as well as know (if in defiance of Plato we admit the difference) must not be afraid of a long march. We have done our best to level the route, but we can no more abridge it than Euclid could offer King Ptolemy I a royal short cut to geometry.

In the early eleventh century Byrhtferth, a monk of Ramsey, devoted much of his bilingual *Enchiridion*, or handbook of necessary knowledge, to expounding the calendar; especially but not only in the English portions, he adopts the manner of the expansive schoolmaster, attempting to infect the boys in his monastic school with his own enthusiasm for the subject. 'We divide the days of the year by seven, and so we arrive joyfully at the understanding of a very great mystery.' Even leap day, which superstitious persons regarded as unlucky, becomes 'venerable'; and another topic is introduced by the assertion that 'we seek to enter the vineyard of labour with beautiful feet', like those of them that preach the gospel of peace. No doubt there were suppressed giggles, as there were when the headmaster of a Victorian public school, addressing the Classical Sixth, rubbed his hands and declared: 'Boys, this term you will be privileged to study the *Oedipus Coloneus* of Sophocles, a play absolutely brimming with grammatical difficulties.' Nevertheless, there are those who relish the study of grammatical difficulties, and computus too has its fascinations for those who appreciate structures and systems.

Throughout the book, an asterisk prefixed to a date or a word serves as a cross-reference for further information; when it is prefixed to a word, the relevant matter will be found in the same Part, whether I or II, unless the other is specified. This has not been done in Part II for dates, since they will all be found in Part I.

Those brought up to believe in the unique and inexhaustible wealth of English vocabulary, without considering how that wealth has been acquired, will be dismayed by the technical terms imported from other languages; but in relation to days and time we found not wealth but poverty, and a dearth of conceptual precision. Danes and Russians have words in common use to denote a period of twenty-four hours irrespective of its starting-point; English has no such word, but must borrow the Greek *nychthemeron*. A date comprises a day, a month, and frequently a year; but there is no English word with the specific sense of the day, excluding the month and year, like the French *quantième*, which it seemed better to borrow than to loan-translate 'how-manyeth'. Likewise, for the year, considered as a number rather than a period, we have adopted *millésime*, which so far from being abstruse is the regular term for the year stamped on a coin or printed on a wine-label.

In complex expositions, words are more convenient than phrases: we may ask what day of the week it is without feeling the need for a single word, but for explaining the mode of calculation 'day of the week' cannot compete in handiness with 'feria'. To be sure, in liturgical use a feria is a day that is neither a Sunday nor a feast; nevertheless, to the computist the word denotes the day of the week, which 'weekday' has long since refused to do. Nor could English provide a word for 'day of the lunar month', expressed in both classical and medieval Latin by *luna*; in particular, Easter is defined as the Sunday following *luna XIV*. This cannot be translated '14th moon', which would mean the fourteenth month; we have therefore allowed 'lune', already used in geometry, to take on this meaning too. For the rest, we refer readers to our Glossary, but warn them now that we call the period of daylight not the natural but the artificial day, following Bede and Chaucer. The Glossary also includes a few terms relating to the theological controversies in which some of our saints were embroiled.

Many people have given us the benefit of their expertise in various areas, ranging from calendar customs in Brazil to the intricacies of the Celtic calendar. We gratefully acknowledge the contributions of Hazel Allsop, Gráinne Bourke, Jonas Carlqvist, William Clemmell, Joseph Connors, Richard Copsey OCarm., Frank D'Accone, Warren Drake, Maureen Fant, George Ferzoco, Peter Foden, Paula Garner, David Howlett, Petrus Kaartinen, Martin Kauffmann, Richard Landes, Michael Linck, Alexander Lingas, Dan McCarthy, Paul Meyvaert, Carolyn Muessig with (all unknowing) members of the medieval-religion e-list, Helen Conrad O'Briain, Dáibhí Ó Cróinín, Vivian Ramalingam, Joshua Rifkin, Jenni Scott, Janos Simon, Barry Smith, Claus Tondering, Jens Ulff-Møller, John Waś, and Connie and Jonathan Webber. Our two very knowledgeable readers, Ronald Hutton and Jeremy Marshall, provided the ideal mix of correction, encouragement, and suggestions for improvement, both in content and focus. Alison Jones, our editor when the volume reached press, skilfully guided the book through production. Sarah Barrett, our copy-editor, took on a daunting task with fortitude and good humour. George Tulloch proved invaluable as a proofreader and fresh pair of eyes.

We spent a very profitable month at the beginning of our work as holders of a short-term fellowship at the Newberry Library in Chicago, where books and scholars happily coexist. Most of our research, however, has been conducted in the British Library and above all in the Bodleian Library, whose resources continue to surprise and delight. We looked at much more than we could use, as the staff of Duke Humfrey and the Upper and Lower Reading Rooms will readily recognize; we owe them a particular debt for their labours in our behalf.

Given on the tenth day before the Ides of May, on the Feast of St John at the Latin Gate, in the forty-seventh year of the reign of Queen Elizabeth II.

B.J.B.

L.A.H.-S.

6 May 1998 (*Old St George's Day*)
Oxford

ACKNOWLEDGEMENTS

We gratefully acknowledge permission to quote the following copyright material:

Laurence Binyon, from *Collected Poems of Laurence Binyon: Lyrical Poems* (Macmillan, 1931). By permission of The Society of Authors on behalf of the Laurence Binyon Estate.

The Bourgeois of Paris, from *A Parisian Journal 1405–1449*, trans. Janet Shirley (Oxford University Press, 1968). Reprinted by permission of the publishers.

Marquis de Chastellux, from *Travels in North America in the Years 1780, 1781 and 1782 by the Marquis de Chastellux*. A revised translation and notes by Howard C. Rice, Jr. Published for the Institute of Early American History and Culture. Copyright © 1963 by the University of North Carolina Press, renewed 1991 by Mrs Howard C. Rice, Jr. Used by permission of the publisher.

John Clare, from *The Later Poems of John Clare 1837–1864*, edited by Eric Robinson and David Powell (Oxford University Press, 1984), copyright Eric Robinson 1984; from *John Clare: Poems of the Middle Period 1822–1837*, edited by Eric Robinson, David Powell, and P. M. S. Dawson (Oxford University Press, 1996), copyright Eric Robinson. Reproduced by permission of Curtis Brown Ltd, London.

Samuel Curwen, from *The Journal of Samuel Curwen, Loyalist*, ed. Andrew Oliver (Harvard University Press, 1972). Reprinted by permission of Phillips Library, Peabody Essex Museum, Salem, Massachusetts.

Emily Dickinson, from *The Poems of Emily Dickinson*, ed. Thomas H. Johnson. Cambridge, Mass.: The Belknap Press of Harvard University Press, Copyright © 1951, 1955, 1979, 1983 by the President and Fellows of Harvard College. Reprinted by permission of the publishers and the Trustees of Amherst College.

John Evelyn, from *The Diary of John Evelyn*, ed. E. S. de Beer (Oxford University Press, 1955). Reprinted by permission of the publishers.

Rodulfus Glaber, from *Historiarum libri quinque*, ed. and trans. John France (Clarendon Press, 1989). Reprinted by permission of the publishers.

Johann Wolfgang von Goethe, from *Italian Journey*, trans. Robert R. Heitner, ed. Thomas P. Saine and Jeffrey L. Sammons (1994). Copyright © 1989 by Suhrkamp Publishers New York Inc. Reprinted by permission of Princeton University Press.

Anthony Hecht, from *The Transparent Man*. Copyright © 1990 by Anthony Hecht. Reprinted by permission of Alfred A. Knopf Inc.

Gerard Manley Hopkins, from *The Poems of Gerard Manley Hopkins*, 4th edn., ed. W. H. Gardner and N. H. MacKenzie (Oxford University Press, 1970). Reprinted by permission of Oxford University on behalf of The Society of Jesus.

Elizabeth Jennings, from *A Way of Looking*, reprinted in *Collected Poems 1953–1985* (Carcanet Press Ltd., 1986). Reprinted by permission of the author and the publishers.

Kate Jennings, from *Cats, Dogs, and Pitchforks* (William Heinemann, 1993). Reprinted by permission of the author c/o Margaret Connolly & Associates Pty Limited.

Evan Jones, from *Inside the Whale* (Addison Wesley Longman, 1960). Reprinted by permission of the author.

Francis Kilvert, from *Kilvert's Diary*, ed. William Plomer (Jonathan Cape, 1969). Reprinted by permission of the Estate of the author.

Phyllis McGinley, from *Times Three* (Secker & Warburg). Copyright 1938–42, 1944, 1945, 1958, 1959 by The Curtis Publishing Co. Used by permission of Secker & Warburg Ltd. and Viking Penguin, a division of Penguin Books USA Inc.

Philip Martin, from *New and Selected Poems* (Longman Cheshire, 1988) and *A Flag for the Wind* (Longman Cheshire, 1982). Reprinted by permission of the author.

Edna St. Vincent Millay, from *Collected Poems* (HarperCollins). Copyright 1923, 1951 by Edna St. Vincent Millay and Norma Millay Ellis. All rights reserved. Reprinted by permission of Elizabeth Barnett, literary executor.

Ogden Nash, from *Collected Verse from 1929 on* (J. M. Dent & Sons Ltd, 1961). Copyright © 1935 by Ogden Nash; first appeared in the *New York American*. By permission of Little, Brown and Company, and Curtis Brown Ltd.

Humphrey O'Sullivan, from *The Diary of Humphrey O'Sullivan*, ed. and trans. Michael McGrath, SJ (Irish Texts Society, 1936–7). Reprinted by permission of the publishers.

John Pintard, from *Letters from John Pintard to his Daughter*, ed. Dorothy C. Barck (New-York Historical Society, 1940). Reprinted by permission of The New-York Historical Society.

Penelope Shuttle, from *The Lion from Rio* (Oxford University Press, 1986). Reprinted by permission of the author and the publishers.

Sir Gawain and the Green Knight, trans. by T. Silverstein (University of Chicago Press, 1974). Reprinted by permission of the translator.

Dylan Thomas, from *A Child's Christmas in Wales*. Copyright © 1954 by New Directions Publishing Corp. Reprinted by permission of New Directions Publishing Corp.

Brian Turner, from *Ladders of Rain* (John McIndoe Ltd., 1978). Reprinted by permission of the author.

Vernon Watkins, from *The Ballad of Mari Lwyd* (Faber & Faber, 1941). © Gwen Watkins. Reprinted by permission of Mrs Gwen Watkins.

Permission to reproduce photographs was kindly given by:
AKG London (Pl. 2); Ashmolean Museum, Oxford (Pl. 13); Biblioteca Apostolica Vaticana (Pl. 11); Bodleian Library, Oxford (Pls. 1, 6, 7, 8, 10, 14, 15, 16, and jacket); British Library (Pl. 3); British Museum (Pls. 4, 9); Österreichische Nationalbibliothek: Bildarchiv (Pl. 5); St John's College, Oxford (Pls. 12, 17).

CONTENTS

PART II: *Calendars and Chronology*

LIST OF ILLUSTRATIONS

ABBREVIATIONS

AC	Anno Christi	Diocl.	(year of) Diocletian
AD	Anno Domini	*DNB*	*Dictionary of National*
AH	Anno Hegirae		*Biography*
AM	Anno Mundi	GMT	Greenwich Mean Time
AP	Anno Passionis	GN	Golden Number
AS	Anno Seleuci	Inc.	Incarnation (Alexandrian)
ASB	Alternative Service Book	ind.	indiction
AUC	Anno urbis conditae	JD	Julian Day
AY	Anno Yezdegirdae	JP	(year of) Julian Period
BC	Before Christ	*N & Q*	*Notes and Queries*
BCE	Before Common Era	NS	New Style
BCP	Book of Common Prayer	*OED*	*Oxford English Dictionary*
BL	British Library	Ol.	Olympiad
CE	Common Era	Orth.	Orthodox
CofE	Church of England	OS	Old Style
commem.	commemoration	RC	Roman Catholic
CY	*The Christian Year: Calendar,*	SE	Saka Era
	Lectionary and Collects (1997)		

PART I

CALENDAR
CUSTOMS

JANUARY

He that will live another yeare
Must eate a hen in Januvere.

The blackest month in all the year
is the month of Janiveer.

(NAMES FOR THE MONTH Latin *Ianuarius*, French *janvier*, Spanish *enero*, Portuguese *Janeiro*, Italian *gennaio*, German (in Germany and Switzerland) *Januar*, (in Austria) *Jänner*, Welsh *Ionawr*, Scots Gaelic *an Faoilteach*, Irish *Eanáir*

The name *Ianuarius* is derived from *ianua*, 'door', and is associated with the two-headed god Janus (see Pl. 1); it is therefore apt for the first month, which January was despite the evidence that the honour had once belonged to March. It is possible that the dead days of winter were not at first counted: the legendary founder of Rome, the bluff soldier-king Romulus (purported dates 753–715 BC), was said to have devised a ten-month calendar from March to December, and his no less legendary successor, the pious intellectual Numa (715–673 BC), to have added January and February.

Many Scots Gaelic names now assigned in standard usage to Roman months are reported in older dictionaries with other senses: thus *faoilteach* or *faoilleach*, from *faol*, 'wild' (or in compounds 'wolf'), is properly a time of wild winter weather, and was sometimes defined as the last fortnight of winter and the first of spring (which began on 1 Feb. OS). For the corresponding term *faoilli*, see *1 Feb. Other names on record are *am Míos Marbh*, 'the dead month', and *Deireadh-Geamhraidh*, 'the end of winter', in accordance with a system of month names most fully preserved in Manx that counted each month the beginning, middle, or end of its season.

(HOLIDAYS AND ANNIVERSARIES

First Monday Handsel Monday, when gifts were given to servants and children. Anything received on that day is supposed to bring luck for the coming year. (See *Other Holidays.)

Third Monday USA: Martin Luther King, Jr.'s Birthday (public holiday)
　　Virginia: Lee–Jackson Day
　　Alabama and Mississippi: Robert E. Lee's Birthday

Last Tuesday Shetland: Up-Helly-Aa, a festival marking the end of Christmas or rather Yule, the emphasis being laid on Norse ancestors; 'Vikings' parade in Lerwick.

Then came old *Ianuary*, wrapped well
  In many weeds to keep the cold away;
  Yet did he quake and quiuer like to quell,
  And blowe his nayles to warme them if he may:
  For, they were numbd with holding all the day
  An hatchet keene, with which he felled wood,
  And from the trees did lop the needlesse spray:
  Vpon an huge great Earth-pot steane he stood;
From whose wide mouth, there flowed forth the Roman floud.

Spenser, The Faerie Queene, VII. vii. 42

It is now Ianuary, and Time beginnes to turne the wheele of his Reuolution, the Woods begin to lose the beauty of their spreading boughes, and the proud Oke must stoop to the Axe: the Squirrell now surueyeth the Nut and the Maple, and the Hedgehogge rowles vp himselfe like a football: an Apple and a Nutmeg make a Gossips cup: and the Ale and the Fagot are the Victuallers merchandise: the Northerne black Dust is the during Fuell, and the fruit of the Grape heats the stomake of the Aged: Downe beds and quilted Cappes are now in the pride of their seruice, and the Cooke and the Pantler are men of no meane office: the Oxe and the fat Weather now furnish the market, and the Coney is so ferreted, that she cannot keepe in her borough: the Currier and the Lime-rod are the death of the fowle, and the Faulcons bels ring the death of the Mallard: the trotting gelding makes a way through the mire, and the Hare and the Hound put the Huntsman to his horne: the barren Doe subscribes to the dish, and the smallest seed makes sauce to the greatest flesh: the dryed grasse is the horses ordinary, and the meale of the beanes makes him goe through with his trauell: Fishermen now haue a cold trade, and trauellers a foule iourney: the Cook room now is not the worst place in the Ship, and the Shepheard hath a bleake seat on the Mountaine . . . To conclude, I hold it a time of little comfort, the rich mans charge, and the poore mans misery. Farewell.

Breton (1626)

In this Moneth abstain from bleeding as much as may be, and beware you take not cold after bleeding, if necessity compel, walk not abroad in the night, use to eat the best Confections, and to drink often white Wine in this Moneth, because Flegm is very predominant, and to fast long is very hurtful to the body, but to eat Winter Sallets well prepared with Oyl and Spices is much commended; a Bath or Hot-house is good, and to take Vomits is not hurtful, also take once every morning (throughout this Moneth) for three hours before dinner a little quantity of Honey of Roses, for that the same doth much comfort the Stomack, and cleanse the body of choler and flegm, and to drink also these Spices with either Wine or Ale, as Grains, Ginger, Nutmegs, Cloves, and such like, are greatly commended this Moneth.

Saunders (1665)

January is Nature's spoilt-child: all her gifts are laid under contribution by a cook of genius. Beef, veal, mutton, pork, venison, hare, pheasant, plover, the black cock, partridge, wild goose, duck, woodcock, &c., troop up to the great city, dead or alive; and in battalions that serve only to entrance with delight the assembled forces of *bon-vivans*, to whom gold will render them an easy and immediate sacrifice. Cauliflowers and celery rear their tender and delicately juicy heads, merely for the pleasure of being decapitated. At this period, truffles are poetry. And now it is, that a householder must either give good and frequent dinners, or permit himself to be thrown without the pale of society, with, to use an animating figure, the pitchfork of universal resentment. When the appetite is both excellent and discriminating, the dinner must be abundant and admirable,—anything short of these qualities, is at all times a fault, but, in January, it is a moral assassination!

    Talk not to me about presents at this time of the year: there are gifts which are to be valued more, than gold, silver, or precious stones,—I mean good dinners.

Gunter, 132–3 (1830)

In Scottish folklore, the eleven days lost in 1752 were supposed to have been taken from January, and recovered by the sorcerer Michael Scott.

> Long ago a man of the name of Michael Scott volunteered to go in search of the eleven missing days. His offer having been accepted, he took a halter and waved it three times in the air, and thereupon a handsome black steed made its appearance. Michael mounted the horse and rode through the air across the straits of Dover and landed in a town in France. He intimated the object of his visit, demanding of the people the days of which he was in search, but they said they knew nothing of them. Not satisfied with their reply he, with the aid of his horse, destroyed the town. He then went on to another town and demanded of its inhabitants that they should restore to him the lost eleven days. They refused. 'One neigh and kick of a horse I have got', said Michael, 'will send your town to destruction.' The people only laughed at him, for they saw no horse. Then Michael waved the halter in the air as he had done before leaving Scotland, and the black horse appeared breathing fire. The people trembled at the sight and gave up the missing days, when Michael returned home in triumph, and ever since Scotland has possessed 'full time'.
>
> Islay tale, quoted in Banks, 141

The real Michael Scott (*c*.1175–*c*.1236) was court magician and astrologer to the emperor Frederick II.

I JANUARY

Kalendae Ianuariae A

❧ HOLIDAYS AND ANNIVERSARIES Cuba: Liberation Day (end of Spanish rule, 1899) or Anniversary of the Triumph of the Revolution (overthrow of Batista government by Fidel Castro, 1959)

Haiti: Independence Day (end of French rule, 1804)

Philippines (Manila): Black Nazarene Fiesta, 1–9 January (in honour of the patron saint of Quiapo district)

Slovakia: Establishment of Slovak Republic (1993) (national holiday)

Sudan: Independence Day (Anglo-Egyptian Condominium until 1956)

USA: Anniversary of President Lincoln's proclamation of 1863, emancipating all slaves in the rebel states

Philadelphia: Mummers New Year's Day Parade

Pasadena: Tournament of Roses Parade and Rose Bowl football game (Big Ten vs. Pacific-10), annual since 1890

❧ ANCIENT ROME New Year's Day (see below). Dedication of temples on the Insula Tiberina to the ancient Roman god Vediovis and to the Greek god Asclepius, in Latin called Aesculapius, introduced in 291 BC after a prolonged plague.

❧ HOLY DAYS **Circumcision of Our Lord** (BCP); **Naming and Circumcision of Jesus** (CY); **Solemnity of Mary, Mother of God** (RC) (as of 1970; formerly Circumcision of Christ); Name of Jesus (Lutheran); Basil the Great (Orth.; 2 Jan. RC)

Feast of the Circumcision. According to the Law of Moses 'he that is eight days old shall be circumcised among you, every man child in your generations . . . and my covenant shall be in your flesh for an everlasting covenant' (Gen. 17: 12–13). Accordingly, 'when eight days were accomplished for the circumcising of the child, his name was called Jesus' (Luke 2: 21). Circumcision was not required of Christians, and the feast did not become established in Rome until the eleventh century.

Circumcision, or Christ submitting to the Law in that early and painfull piece of Service; this was so great a Day amongst the Heathens, that the Christians would not observe it for 1000 years, and well it was for the Christians, that this was such a Gaudy day with them, for they would not sully the joy of it with Martyring the Christians, so that whereas there were in *Constantines* time, the Feasts of 5000 Saints for every day in the year, there were none for this.   Dove (1700)

Basil the Great (Orth.). This day commemorates the death on 1 January 397 of the great theologian Basil, one of the three Cappadocian Fathers (see *10 Jan.), from 370 till his death bishop of Caesarea in Cappadocia (now Kayseri in Turkey), where he established hospitals and poor relief, the author of sermons on the Six Days of Creation (the *Hexaemeron*) and many other important works, who championed the faith of Nicaea, that the Son is consubstantial with the Father, at the Council of Constantinople in 381. A round 'Basil-cake' (*Vasiliópitta*) of milk, eggs, butter, and sugar is baked in his honour; a coin is added to the cake. In the countryside he was regarded not as a scholar but as a farmer; he inspects farm animals and asks them how they have been treated. His RC date, 14 June till 1969, is now 2 January.

New Year's Day. Although the Romans knew that their year had originally begun with *March, the name *Ianuarius* is not appropriate to an eleventh month; the New Year festivities seem too well entrenched to have been moved in historical times, and if the first written account of the Roman calendar, put on public display in the temple of Hercules and the Muses *c.*179 BC (see *30 June), had indicated a March beginning, our sources must have told us, such was the Romans' interest in their calendar (see II: *Roman Calendar). Although it was not till in 153 BC that the consuls, who gave their names to the civil year, entered office on 1 January (having done so on 15 March since 222 BC, and before that on various other dates), and then only because of a military crisis, this must have been the true day of New Year, as in medieval Europe, irrespective of the dating system.

The Kalends of January, *Kalendae Ianuariae*, were observed by Romans both publicly with games given by the consuls for the year, who came into office on that day, and privately with the giving of presents (*strenae*) and with general revelry. So well entrenched and so popular were the celebrations that in other languages of the empire the Latin name of *Kalendae* was applied to them without qualification; Christian preachers disapproved, but not their flocks, who as St Augustine testifies stoutly resisted the Church's attempt to proclaim a fast. The day's most prominent martyr, St Almachius, is not the conventional victim of pagan persecution, but an agitator who attempted to disrupt the New Year's games in Rome in the early 390s under the Christian emperor Theodosius I; the prefect Alypius, himself a Christian, averted a riot by having the gladiators behead him there and then. (Not till the next reign were gladiatorial shows suppressed; another version of the story has them stopped after one 'Telemachus' was stoned to death by the crowd for interrupting them. However, even then revivals are attested.)

In the sixth century, the churches of Gaul and Spain co-opted the 'Octave of Christmas' as the feast of the Lord's Circumcision, on the eighth day from his birth according to Jewish law; the Roman Church eventually admitted the feast to its calendar in an attempt at supplanting the persistent pagan celebrations, which included not only giving presents but drinking deep, wearing masks, and keeping one's table laden all night in order to ensure sufficiency of food all year. Indeed, it is clear that churchmen objected to these revelries, not only as good fun but as a vehicle of heathen ritual and divination; nevertheless, they were not easy to suppress, as the English missionary St Boniface (see *5 June) found. Early in 742 Boniface complained to the new pope, Zacharias (see *15 Mar.), that when his German converts (and the local Christians on whom he sought to impose Roman ways) observed the Kalends of January being celebrated at Rome and about St Peter's with dancing in the streets, heathenish cries, sacrilegious songs, tables laden with food, and women wearing amulets and offering them for sale, they inferred that this was permitted by the local clergy and reacted with scorn to his attempts at changing their behaviour. The Pope replied in due course, on 1 April 743, declaring that he had forbidden all such activities; his prohibition was confirmed by a synod later in the year.

Partly because of these Roman customs, the Church was long reluctant to count the year from 1 January; nevertheless, the day retained the title of New Year's Day and its counterpart in other languages irrespective of the day on which the number of the year changed. In England, this was not officially 1 January till 1752; moreover, many documents were dated by the sovereign's regnal year, which was reckoned from the date of accession (down to Henry III's time, of coronation); but in the thirteenth century Orm, the author of a long didactic poem called the *Ormulum*, said of the Circumcision:

7 tatt daȝȝ iss New ȝeress daȝȝ
Mang Engleþeode nemmnedd

[and that day is called New Year's Day amongst the English people]. Moreover, in calculating leap year or the date of Easter the year always began with 1 January; Irish annalists identified years by the day of the week and age of the moon on this day even when they counted years of the Christian era from 25 March; almanacs regularly began with 1 January. An eighteenth-century Florentine poet, writing two decades before Grand Duke Francesco Stefano of Tuscany imposed the modern or 'Circumcision' style, expressed the notion 'throughout the year' as 'Dal dì di capo d'anno a san Silvestro', from New Year's Day on 1 January to St Sylvester's Day on 31 December.

In Scotland the 1 January style was adopted in 1600; by then it was normal in continental Western Europe outside Italy. The Scottish entrepreneur and secret agent John Macky took note of the English dating system in a description of English life through fictitious letters to a foreigner: having dated letter ix 'January 1st, 1714', he begins:

I begin this Letter with wishing you a Happy *New-Year*, though the Year does not begin in this Kingdom till the 25th Day of *March*. I have asked several Learned Men the Reason why they do here differ from all Kingdoms of *Christendom* in the beginning their Year; but I could never have any tolerable Account given, except, that the 25th of *March* being the Day of the Blessed Virgin's Conception, they Date the *Æra* of our Lord from thence.   Macky, i. 106

Subsequent letters are dated '1713–14' or '171¾'. The 1 January reckoning had been sporadically attested from the mid-sixteenth century: Thomas Wilson's book *The Arte of Rhetorique*, dated by its printer Richard Grafton 'M.D.LIII. Mense Ianuarij', belongs, as personal, political, and religious reasons combine to prove, to 1553 not 1554. By the early eighteenth century private usage was wavering: the same periodical may, between 1 January and 24 March, use indiscriminately the higher year, the lower year, and the combined form. Eventually, the Act of Parliament introducing the New Style into Great Britain also laid down that from 1752 the year should begin on 1 January in England and her American colonies, as it did in Scotland.

Which year was longer, 1751 or 1752, in (*a*) England, (*b*) Scotland, (*c*) France? Answer: (*a*) 1752, (*b*) 1751, (*c*) 1752. In England, 1751 ran only from 25 March to 31 December, which outweighs the loss of eleven days in September 1752 (see II: **Modern Calendar: Gregorian Reform*); in Scotland, 1751 had its full complement of 365 days, but 1752 was deprived of the same eleven days; in France, where no reform was needed, both years ran their full length, but 1752, being leap year, was one day longer.

'Happy New Year'
The antient, friendly, and benevolent custom of
𝔚𝔦𝔰𝔥𝔦𝔫𝔤 𝔞 𝔥𝔞𝔭𝔭𝔶 𝔑𝔢𝔴 𝔜𝔢𝔞𝔯,
is so generally exploded, that a person must be blessed with the favours of fortune, or well known as a man of talent, to venture his consequence by now offering so familiar an address: Few, therefore, above the lowest class of society, attempt to obtrude any good wishes for the happiness, or success of his neighbour; lest, if they escape the imputation of unlicensed freedom, they be deemed vulgar, and ignorant of what is termed *fashionable life*. Even the modern expression of the
ℭ𝔬𝔪𝔭𝔩𝔦𝔪𝔢𝔫𝔱𝔰 𝔬𝔣 𝔱𝔥𝔢 𝔖𝔢𝔞𝔰𝔬𝔫,
which was long substituted for the former more expressive and better understood mode of salutation, has given way before universal refinement, real or affected; and is now sanctioned only in family circles, among intimate friends, or from a person who is either an acknowledged superior, or at least upon equality with the one whom he addresses. In like manner,
𝔑𝔢𝔴 𝔜𝔢𝔞𝔯'𝔰 𝔊𝔦𝔣𝔱𝔰
have fallen into such disuse, that they are scarcely known except in some trifling instances, where such marks of affection are offered to children emerging from the nursery.

                                                Brady, i. 142–3 (1815)

At this time, Christmas too seemed on the decline; its nineteenth-century revival did little for the New Year, though the exchange of good wishes recovered its respectability. One might stay up on New Year's Eve for a midnight toast, or make resolutions for self-improvement; revellers gathered in Trafalgar Square to see in the New Year and frolic in the fountains (a pleasure now forbidden on grounds of safety), but 1 January was an ordinary working day. However, in Scotland, which for long paid little or no attention to Christmas, the New Year was and remains a great occasion, being completely untainted by popery. By the Bank Holiday Act 1871 (34 Vict. c. 17) New Year's Day was recognized as a Bank Holiday in Scotland, but in England it did not attain that status till 1974. Since then, however, many companies have determined that it is not worth their while to resume work during the intervening week, much to the disgust and envy of journalists, who enjoy no such extended holiday.

Gift-giving. It was on 1 January that New Year gifts were given, which in earlier times had the importance that Christmas presents have with us. Romans exchanged *strenae*, which in French are still called *étrennes*; the English term 'handsels', now better known in Scotland, is attested as 'hondeselle' in the fourteenth-century poem *Sir Gawain and the Green Knight*:

> And syþen riche forth runnen to reche hondeselle,
> ȝeȝed ȝeres-ȝiftes on hiȝ, ȝelde hem bi hond,
> Debated busyly aboute þo giftes;
> Ladies laȝed ful loude, þoȝ þay lost haden,
> And he þat wan watz not wrothe, þat may ȝe wel trawe.

> The guests then go about exchanging gifts,
> Hold their presents on high and hand them out,
> Gleefully compare the gifts they get;
> Ladies laugh though losers in the game
> (A kiss!), no gainer glum, as you may guess.
>
> trans. Theodore Silverstein

New Year tokens (a politer term than 'gifts') were bestowed on and by monarchs and nobles till the time of James II; Bishop Latimer gave Henry VIII a New Testament with a cloth bearing a quotation from Hebrews 13: 4, *Fornicatores et adulteros judicabit Dominus*, 'whoremongers and adulterers the Lord shall judge'.

Public officials also received their rewards:

The mere possibility of a suspicion of prejudice in a judge ought, no doubt, to be avoided, and, so, wisely thought the great, but unfortunate Sir Thomas More.—When Mrs. Croaker had obtained a decree in Chancery against Lord Arundel, she availed herself of the *first new-year's-day* after her success, to present to Sir Thomas, then the Lord Chancellor, a PAIR OF GLOVES, containing forty pounds in angels [ten-shilling pieces], as a token of her gratitude; the gloves he received with satisfaction; these could not perhaps, as the offering of the heart, be refused, but the gold he peremptorily, though politely returned: 'It would be against good manners to forsake a gentlewoman's new-year's-gift,' said that eminent man, 'and I accept the gloves; their lining you will be pleased *otherwise* to bestow.'

Brady, i. 148

Not all Lord Chancellors were so upright. Mary Countess Cowper reports the following anecdote when her husband was Lord Chancellor:

1716. Jan. 17. This Month used to be ushered in with New Year's Gifts from the Lawyers, which used to come to near 3,000*l*. to the Chancellor. The Original of this Custom was, Presents of Wine and Provisions, which used to be sent to the Chancellor by the People who practised in his Court. But in process of Time a covetous Chancellor insinuated to them that Gold would be more acceptable; so it was changed into Gold, and continued so till the first Time my Lord had the Seals: Everyone having blamed it that ever had the Seals, but None forbidding it.

The Earl of *Nottingham* [Heanage Finch], when Chancellor, used to receive them standing by a Table; and at the same Time he took the Money to lay it upon the Table, he used to cry out, 'Oh, tyrant Cuthtom!' (for he lisped)—my Lord forbade the bringing them.

Cowper, 63

This heathenish custom and the whole jollity of the Christmas season were severely criticized by William Prynne in his *Histrio-Mastix* of 1633 (p. 755):

If wee now parallell our grand disorderly Christmasses, with these Roman Saturnals and heathen Festivals; or our New-yeares day (a chiefe part of Christmas) with their Festivity of *Ianus*, which was spent in Mummeries, Stage-playes, dancing, and such like Enterludes, wherein Fidlers and others acted lascivious effeminate parts, and went about their Towns and Cities in womens apparell; whence the whole Catholicke Church (as Alchuvinus [Alcuin], with others write) appointed a solemn publike fast upon this our New-yeares day, (which fast it seemes is now forgotten) to bewaile those heathenish Enterludes, sports, and lewd idolatrous practises which had beene used on it: prohibiting all Christians under paine of excommunication, from observing the Kalends or first of Ianuary (which wee now call New-yeares day) as holy, and from sending abroad New-yeares gifts upon it, (a custome now too frequent;) it being a meere relique of Paganisme and idolatry, derived from the heathen Romans feast of two-faced Ianus; and a practise so execrable unto Christians, that not onely the whole Catholicke Church; but even the 4 famous Councels . . . have positively prohibited the solemnization of New-yeares day, and the sending abroad of New-yeares gifts, under an anathema & excommunication, as unbeseeming Christians, who should eternally abolish, not propagate, revive, or recontinue this pagan festivall, and heathenish ceremonie, which our God abhors.

It is only fair to record that Prynne, who combined horror of jollity with horror of rebellion, had even more to complain of than other people in that contentious age.

First-footing customs. In many countries there is a custom of first-footing (Scots: first-fit). In Scotland this is done by a tall dark man, who strides silently into the house bearing whisky, coal, and black bun for the household, who reward him with food and drink of their own; in Greece, where the New Year's wish is 'old age, beauty, and great prosperity', by the master of the house or by a 'lucky' boy, meaning one whose parents are both alive (such children played a significant part in ancient Greek and Roman ritual). In Albania too the first-footer must lay a log upon the fire. In 1790 President Washington inaugurated a custom of opening his house and standing to receive visitors that lasted until 1934, Franklin Roosevelt being unable to stand.

He should be dark-haired, and should pass through the house entering at the back and leaving by the front-door.   Hampson, i. 98

It's not lucky for . . . a red-haired man to come in to your house first on a New Year's Day; there'll be a death in it afore the year's out.   *N & Q*, 5th ser., ii (1875), 465

Mummers' parade in Philadelphia. The Philadelphia mummers, though not formally recognized by the city till 1901, continued a colonial tradition of celebrating this day with a play mutated from that of St George and the Dragon. The patron saint of England was displaced by the national hero of America, who entered with the lines:

> Here am I, great Washington!
> On my shoulder I carry a gun.

Whereupon he was interrupted by a clownish character, who declared:

> Here comes I, old Cooney Cracker!
> I swear to God my wife chews terbacker!
> A pipe is good, cigars are better;
> When I get married I'll send you a letter.

The Devil was also represented. The mummers were given hospitality in every house, etiquette requiring them to be addressed only as the characters whom they played; it was remembered that a little girl burst out: 'Oh, I know thee, Isaac Simmons! Thee is not George Washington.'

Superstitions at the beginning of New Year
Alle that takun hede to dysmole dayis and vsyn nyse observauncys in the newe mone, or in the newe yeer, as settynge of mete or drynke be nyght on the benche, to fedyn Al-holde, ledyng of the plow abowtyn the fer, as for good begynnynge of the yeer that they schulde fare the bettere al the yeer folwynge . . .   *Dives and Pauper*

The superstition that the occupation of New Year's Day was representative of the year following is exemplified in Swift's *Journal to Stella*, letter xii, dated 31 December 1710:

> Would you answer M.D.'s letter,
> On New Year's Day you will do it better;
> For when the year with M.D. 'gins,
> It without M.D. never lins.

(These Proverbs have always old words in them, *lins* is leaves off.)

Bad luck

> Pray don't 'ee wash on New Year's day,
> or you'll wash one of the family away.
>
> Cast Holy Water all about,
> And have a care no fire goes out.

> Robert Herrick (1591–1674), 'The New-yeeres Gift'

Those who have not the common materials of making a fire, generally sit without one, on New Year's Day; for none of their neighbours, although hospitable at other times, will suffer them to light a candle at their fires. If they do, they say that some one of the family will die within the year.   *Gentleman's Magazine*, 81 (1811), pt. 1, 424 (North Riding of Yorkshire)

It would be considered a most grievous affair were the person who first sweeps the floor on New Year's morning to brush the dust to the door, instead of beginning at the door and sweeping the dust to the hearth, as the good fortune of the family individually would thereby be considered to be swept from the house for that year.   J. Train, ii. 115 (Isle of Man, 1845)

Good luck
If the carol-singer who first comes to your door (in Worcestershire) on New Year's morning is admitted at the front door, conducted all through the house, and let out at the back door, you will have good luck all through the year.   *N & Q*, 2nd ser., iii (1857), 343

The first day of this yeir, being Thursday, the pepill observit the old, ancient, bot beggerlie, custome, in seiking, craving, and begging handsell; mony superstitiouslie beleving that thai could not thryve all that yeir except thai haid gottin a New yeirs gift.   Nicoll, 191 (1657)

Bringing in the New Year
31 [Jan. 1664]. As soon as ever the clock struck one, I kissed my wife in the kitchen by the fireside, wishing her a merry New year, observing that I believe I was the first proper wisher of it this year, for I did it as soon as ever the clock struck one.   Pepys, v. 359

Monday, 31 December [1877]
I sat up till after midnight to watch the Old Year out and the New Year in. The bells rang at intervals all the evening, tolled just before the turn of the night and the year and then rang a joy peal,

and rang on till one o'clock. After I had gone to bed I saw from where I lay a bright blaze sprung up in the fields beyond the river and I knew at once that they were keeping up the old custom of Burning the Bush on New Year's Day in the morning. From the Knap, the hill above the village masked by the two clumps of trees, the whole valley can be seen early on New Year's Morning alight with fires. Burning the Bush, as it can be seen also from the hill at Bettws, Clyro, on which the old Chapel stands.   Kilvert, iii. 344

Divination with Bible
Happening to pass by a cottage where an old woman lived whom I knew well, I stepped in and wished her a happy new year. Instead of replying to my salutation, she stared wildly at me, and exclaimed in a horrified tone: 'New Year's Day! and I have never dipped.' . . . I gathered from her that it was customary to *dip* into the Bible before twelve o'clock on New Year's Day, and the first verse that meets the eye indicates the good or bad fortune of the inquirer through the ensuing year. My old friend added: 'Last year I dipped, and I opened on Job; and, sure enough, I have had nought but trouble ever since.'   N & Q, 2nd ser., xii (1861), 303

Last glass
The last glass of wine or spirits drained from the last bottle on New Year's Eve or Day is called the 'lucky glass'. It brings good fortune to whoever comes in for it, and if an unmarried person drinks it, he will be the first to marry among the company.   Henderson, 55

Drawing first water from the well in the Highlands. On New Year's Eve 'some carefull person is also dispatched to the *dead and living ford*, who draws a pitcher of water, observing all the time the most profound silence'. It is used on New Year's Day as follows:

The first course, consisting of the *Usque-Cashrichd*, or water from the *dead and living ford*, by its sacred virtues, preserves the Highlander, until the next anniversary, from all those direful calamities proceeding from the agency of all infernal spirits, witchcraft, evil eyes, and the like. And the second course, consisting of the fumes of juniper, not only removes whatever diseases may affect the human frame at the time, but it likewise fortifies the constitution against their future attacks. . . . Light and fire being kindled, and the necessary arrangements having been effected, the high priest of the ceremonies for the day, and his assistants, proceed with the hallowed water to the several beds in the house, and, by means of a large brush, sprinkles upon their occupants a profuse shower of the precious preservative, which, notwithstanding its salutary properties, they sometimes receive with jarring ingratitude.   Grant Stewart, 250–1 (1823)

Needle and thread ceremony at Queen's College, Oxford. This ceremony, which takes place on New Year's Day in Queen's College, Oxford, is still held. Celia Fiennes observed it in the 1690s:

There is a very odd custom in Queen Coll. for every new-years-day there is a certain sum laid out in Needles and Thread which was left by the founder, and every Gentleman of that Colledge has one given him with these words: Take this and be thrifty.   Fiennes, 38

A German visitor in 1761 explains the origin:

A curious custom exists here; on New Year's Day every member receives a needle and thread from the housekeeper, with these words, 'Take this and be chary of it'—in allusion to the name of the founder of the college, Robert Egglefield (*aiguille fil*).   Kielmansegge, 106

Wassailing. A traditional wassailing song:

Here we come a wassailing,
Among the leaves so green,
Here we come a wandering,
So fair to be seen.

Chorus.
> Love and joy come to you,
> And to your wassel too,
> And God send you a happy New Year,
>> A New Year,
> And God send you a happy New Year!
> Our wassel cup is made of rosemary-tree,
> So is your beer of the best barley.

We are not daily beggars,
> That beg from door to door;
But we are neighbours' children,
> Whom you have seen before.

Call up the butler of this house,
> Put on his golden ring,
Let him bring us up a glass of beer
> And the better we shall sing.

We have got a little purse,
> Made of stretching leather skin,
We want a little of your money
> To line it well within.

Bring us out a table,
> And spread it with a cloth;
Bring us out a mouldy cheese,
> And some of your Christmas loaf.

God bless the master of this house,
> Likewise the mistress too,
And all the little children,
> That round the table go!

Good master and mistress,
> While you're sitting by the fire,
Pray think of us poor children,
> Who are wandering in the mire.
>> Chambers, 1 Jan.

Recipe for making a wassail bowl:

Simmer a small quantity of the following spices in a teacupful of water, viz.:—Cardamums, cloves, nutmeg, mace, ginger, cinnamon, and coriander. When done, put the spice to two, four, or six bottles of port, sherry, or madeira, with one pound and a half of fine loaf sugar (pounded) to four bottles, and set all on the fire in a clean bright saucepan; meanwhile, have yolks of 12 and the whites of 6 eggs well whisked up in it. Then, when the spiced and sugared wine is a little warm, take out one teacupful; and so on for three or four cups; after which, when it boils, add the whole of the remainder, pouring it in gradually, and stirring it briskly all the time, so as to froth it. The moment a fine froth is obtained, toss in 12 fine soft roasted apples, and send it up hot. Spices for each bottle of wine:—10 grains of mace, 46 grains of cloves, 37 grains of cardamums, 28 grains of cinnamon, 12 grains of nutmeg, 48 grains of ginger, 49 grains of coriander seeds. Chambers

(In grams the spices come to: 3 g. mace, 12 g. cloves, 10 g. cardamom; 7.5 g. cinnamon; 3 g. nutmeg; 12.5 g. ginger; 13 g. coriander seed. Use whole spices.)

New Year's Day in Dumfries, 1808
Friday 1st. New Year's day. As usual a number of people going about the streets drunk. Attended the hospital at breakfast, dinner and supper. The poor people were treated by some benevolent individuals with a breakfast of tea, loaf bread, butter and eggs, dinner of roast beef, potatoes, bread and cheese with beer and toddy and a supper of cheese and bread and beer. The poor were much pleased with the day's entertainment, such as I suppose never was given in the house before.

Grierson, 199

New Year's Day as experienced by a French traveller in Albany, NY, 1781
I had traveled far enough during the day to hope for a quiet sleep, and expected a good night; but at four in the morning I was awakened by a musket fired close to my windows: I listened but heard not the smallest noise or motion in the street, which made me imagine it was some musket which had gone off by itself without causing any accident. So I attempted to go back to sleep. A quarter of an hour later a fresh musket or pistol shot interrupted my repose: this was followed by several others; so that I no longer had any doubt that it was some rejoicing or feast, like our village christenings. The hour indeed struck me as unusual, but at length a number of voices mingled with musketry, shouting 'New Year,' reminded me that it was the first of January, and I concluded that it was thus that *Messieurs les Américains* celebrated the beginning of the new year. Though this manner of proclaiming it was not, I must own, especially pleasing to me, there was nothing to do but be patient; but at the end of half an hour I heard a confused noise of upwards of a hundred persons, mostly children or young people, assembled under my windows. Soon I was even better warned of their proximity, for they fired several musket shots, knocked rudely at the door, and threw stones against my windows. Cold and indolence still kept me in bed, but M. Lynch got up, and came into my chamber to tell me that these people certainly meant to do me honor and to ask me for some money. I requested him to go down and give them two louis; he found them already masters of the house and drinking my landlord's rum. In a quarter of an hour they went off to visit other streets and continued their noise until daylight.

On rising, I learned from my landlord that it was the custom of the country for the young folks, the servants, and even the Negroes, to go from tavern to tavern, and to many other houses, to wish a happy new year and ask for drink. So that there was no particular compliment to me in this affair, and I found that, after the example of the Roman emperors, I had made a largess to the people. In the morning, when I went out to take leave of General Clinton, I met nothing but drunken people in the streets, but what astonished me most was to see them not only walk, but run upon the ice without falling or making a false step, while it was with the utmost difficulty that I kept on my feet.

Chastellux, 222–3

New Year's Day in New York City. At the end of 1827, John Pintard lamented the decline of 'many of our antient usages':

New Year was a most boisterous, & when manners were simpler & this city but an overgrown Village, began at Midnight, Drums beating Firing of Guns, huzzas, & calling at friendly doors, to congratulate the family & get a New Years dram & cookey. Visits still kept up were made after Church, but cookies begin to disappear, & altho the dram & hot punch appear on the sideboard, it is more for parade than use for few partake. Indeed since staggering thro' the streets on New Years day is out of fashion, it is impossible to drink drams at every house as of old. Children were universally sent to visit the family relations, which served to keep up acquaintance with kindred branches. The remotest, were all Uncles, Aunts & Cousins on that jovial day. Well do I recollect coming home loaded with sixpences (a great sum) & honey cookies, enough to last for months.

Pintard, ii. 382

In the Soviet Union people were encouraged to celebrate New Year's Day, and expect gifts from Grandfather Frost (*Ded-moroz*), in order to diminish appetites for Christmas, whose NS date is 7 January.

Weather proverbs. The weather in January was a favourite prognosticator for the remainder of the year. It often turns very cold at this time in the northern hemisphere. Aubrey (*Remaines*, 7) quotes an ancient Welsh proverb, *Haf hyd galan, gaeaf hyd Fai*, 'Summer till the New Year, winter till May', or, as he translates it: 'That is, if it be somerly weather till the Kalends of January, it will be winterly weather to the Kalends of May.'

In the yeere that Ianuary shall enter on the Sunday, that winter shall bee cold and moist, the Summer shall be hot, and the time of Harvest shall be windie and rainy, with great aboundance of corn, of wines, and other grains, & of all garden fruits, & hearbs, there shall be little Oyle, abundance shal be of all manner of flesh, some great newes shal men heare spoken of Kings and Prelats of the Church, and also of great Princes, great warres and robberies shall be made, and many yong people shall dye.   Erra Pater (1602)

A saying ascribed to Tsar Nicholas I is that the two generals in whom Russia could trust were Janvier and Février; he was thinking of Napoleon's experience, but the remark would still hold true when Hitler invaded the Soviet Union. Spanish variants: 'Enero y febrero comen más que Madrid y Toledo' (January and February devour more than Madrid and Toledo); 'enero y febrero desviejadero' (January and February eliminate the old folk; proverb in the state of Jalisco, Mexico).

2 JANUARY

a.d. IIII Nonas Ianuarias   B

This daye sheweth the nature and state of September. (Lloyd)

❦ HOLIDAYS AND ANNIVERSARIES Haiti: Ancestors' Day (Hero's Day) (public holiday)
  Switzerland: Berchtoldstag (Duke Berchtold V founded the city of Berne in the twelfth century)
  USA, Georgia: Ratification Day (fourth state to ratify the Constitution, 1788)

❦ HOLY DAYS Basil the Great (CY, RC; *1 Jan. Orth.); Gregory of Nazianzus (CY, RC; *25 Jan. Orth.); Sylvester (Orth.; see *31 Dec.); Serafim of Sarov (Orth., CY commem.)

Serafim of Sarov (1759–1833), Russian monk who became a hermit, a holy man sought out by visitors from all over Russia, outstanding both for personal asceticism and for gentleness towards others. He was canonized in 1903; in Russia his day is the 15th by the New Style, but his commemoration in CY is fixed for the Old Style date. The Russian Church also celebrates the Invention of his relics on 19 July OS = 1 August NS.

Washington's first flag run up, 1776: the thirteen stripes, with the Union Jack in the corner.

Eighth day of Christmas:

Weds. 2 Jan. (1760). At home all day, but little to do. Joseph Fuller Jr. and Mr. Thornton smoked a pipe with me in the even. Oh, how pleasant has this Christmas been kept as yet, no revelling nor tumultuous meetings where there too often is little else but light and trifling discourse, no ways calculated for improvement; and it's well if it's not intermixed with some obscene talk and too often with vile and execrable oaths. Not that I am anyways an enemy to innocent mirth, but what I protest is that which is not so.   T. Turner, 197

In Scotland this day was made a Bank Holiday, so that people might recover from the New Year celebrations; in 1997 it was replaced by Easter Monday, not without public indignation.

3 JANUARY

a.d. III Nonas Ianuarias   C

This day doth shew the nature and state of October. (Lloyd)

❦ HOLIDAYS AND ANNIVERSARIES   USA, Alabama: Admission Day (49th state, 1959)

❦ ANCIENT ROME   In the later Roman empire, 3–5 January were the normal days for holding the Compitalia, which technically fell at whatever point between 17 December and 5 January the magistrates might decide from year to year. Such annual but variable festivals were known as *feriae conceptivae*, in contrast to *feriae stativae* of fixed date and *feriae imperativae* such as thanksgivings for victories decreed occasion by occasion. The Compitalia were a very ancient festival, originally like the Saturnalia kept by free and slave together, but by Cicero's time left to the slaves, who on behalf of the household sacrificed a honey-cake to the crossroad gods or Lares Compitales; a woollen effigy was hung up for every free person in the household, and a ball of wool for every slave.

❦ HOLY DAYS
Genevieve (*c*.420–*c*.500), patron saint of Paris. Consecrated at the age of 7 by St Germanus of Auxerre (see *31 July), she devoted herself to charitable works, often against great opposition. Legend has made her the protectress of Paris who in 451 by the power of prayer deflected Attila the Hun from the city and during the Frankish siege of 460 brought back grain by boat from Troyes. Having been buried in the church of SS Peter and Paul built by Queen Clothilda (*3 June), she was assigned the latter's role in converting King Clovis and made his counsellor; the church was renamed after her. Her *vita* makes her cure a Goth who prayed at her tomb when his hands were crippled as a

punishment for working on Sunday; it neglects to make him do the decent thing by turning Catholic. (Goths were Arians; no contemporary hagiographer would have failed to take that point.) She acquired more fame from her intercession in 1129 (see *26 Nov.). By the eighteenth century her church had fallen into decay; its replacement was secularized by the revolutionaries, who burnt her relics, as the Panthéon. Genevieve was invoked in every necessity, especially against drought and flooding, and therefore was appropriately named patron of the French security forces by John XXIII in 1962.

The Prophet Malachi (Orth.). The last of the Twelve Prophets, in the West called Minor; *mal'ākhī* in Hebrew means 'My messenger', and was probably so intended, rather than as a name. In his prophecy (Mal. 4: 2) come the words 'But unto you that fear my name shall the Sun of righteousness arise with healing in his wings', referred by Christians to Christ. For another prophet Malachy, see *3 Nov.

Birthday of Cicero, *a.d. III Nonas Ianuarias Q. Servilio Caepione C. Atilio Serrano coss.*, literally 'on the third day before the January Ides, Quintus Servilius Caepio and Gaius Atilius Serranus being consuls', conventionally translated as 3 January 106 BC; but dates before Caesar's reform of the calendar need not coincide with the same nominal days in the Julian calendar extrapolated backwards.

Battle of Princeton, 1777: Washington expelled the British from New Jersey.

Pushkin, *Eugene Onegin* (ch. 5, stanza 1), recounts freak weather:

That year autumnal weather remained for a long time; nature waited and waited for winter: snow did not fall till January, on the night of the second to third. Awaking early, Tatiana caught sight from the window that morning of the whitened courtyard, flower-beds, roofs, and fence; delicate traceries on the panes; trees in their winter silver, merry magpies, and hills softly overlaid with the glistening carpet of winter. All around is bright, all is white.

Russians learn this passage at school, but in real life often feel uncomfortable when winter is slow to come.

The Quadrantids, an annual meteor-shower, peak about this day.

4 JANUARY

pridie Nonas Ianuarias   D

This day doth forshew the nature and state of November. (Lloyd)

❧ HOLIDAYS AND ANNIVERSARIES Myanmar (Burma): Independence Day (from Great Britain, 1948)
USA, Utah: Admission Day (45th state, 1896)

(HOLY DAYS

Elizabeth Ann Bayley Seton (1774–1821), first native saint of the USA, canonized 1975. She founded the Daughters of Charity of St Joseph, for relief of the poor and teaching in parochial schools.

Synaxis of the Seventy Disciples (Orth.), collectively honouring the 'other seventy' (or seventy-two; the manuscripts vary) whom Jesus sent ahead of Him in Luke 10: 1. Their names are not preserved, though widely differing lists were in time concocted; Eusebius in the fourth century already identifies five, namely Barnabas (*11 June), Sosthenes (co-sender of 1 Cor.), Cephas (resisted by Paul at Gal. 2: 11; in fact none other than St Peter, see *29 June), Matthias (see *24 Feb.), and Thaddaeus (see *21 Aug.).

New Year's vows, better late than never:

4 [Jan. 1664]. Home—and at my office till 12 at night, making my solemn vowes for the next year, which I trust in the Lord I shall keep. But I fear I have a little too severely bound myself in some things and in too many, for I fear I may forget some. But however, I know the worst and shall by the blessing of God observe to perform or pay my forfeits punctually. So home and to bed— with my mind at rest.   Pepys, v. 4–5

5 JANUARY

Nonae Ianuariae   E

This day doth shew the nature and state of December. (Lloyd)

(HOLIDAYS AND ANNIVERSARIES Twelfth Eve (Vigil of the Epiphany, Paramone of the Theophany)

(ANCIENT ROME In Rome, the Nones of January had no special significance; but when the Greek island of Andros had adopted a calendar calibrated to the Roman, it was on this day, called the Theodosia or Gift of the God, that the water of a spring by the temple of Dionysos tasted like wine; it continued to do so for a week, though the taste was lost if the water was taken out of sight of the temple. On a perhaps imaginary painting of this miracle described by Philostratus Titian based his *Bacchanal of the Andrians*. In the evening, during the later Roman empire, there began at Alexandria a festival that continued into the next day, celebrating the birth at cockcrow of Aiōn (Eternity), to Korē (the Maid), at which water was ceremonially drawn from the Nile and stored; since Aiōn was closely associated with Sarapis, who in turn was associated with Dionysus, the suggestion has been made that the god was meant to turn the water into wine. This would explain why the Christian Epiphany (see *6 Jan.) was associated with Christ's performance of this miracle at the wedding-feast in Cana. (It is also associated with the miracle of the loaves and fishes.)

¶ HOLY DAYS

Edward the Confessor, the last king of England in the West Saxon line of the Cerdingas, died on this day in 1066. Having been canonized in 1161, he is commemorated in some Roman Catholic countries on this day; England, however, both Anglican and Roman, keeps his translation on *13 October.

John Nepomucene Neumann (1811–60); canonized 1977. A native of Bohemia, he became a New World missionary in 1836, first as member of the Redemptorists. Appointed Bishop of Philadelphia in 1852, he was renowned for his pastoral work and his strengthening of parochial schools.

Old Christmas Day (1753–1800)
Southampton, January 12
On the 25th. of last Month, many people went into the New Forest to observe whether the Oak (which is said to blow every Christmas Day) conform'd to the New-Style, or not, but finding no Buds or any Appearance of green Leaves, came away greatly dissatisfied with the Alteration of the Day: And on Friday last, being old Christmas, they went again, and to their great Joy found the Oak blown, and several branches almost covered with green Leaves; some of which they brought away with them. This Circumstance has served to convince Abundantly that the new Christmas-Day is wrong, and they are henceforth determined to keep only the old.

The Salisbury Journal, 15 Jan. 1753 (quoted in Morsley, 24)

Old Christmas Eve (1801–1900)
Saturday, 5 January [1878]
Speaking of the blowing of the Holy Thorn and the kneeling and weeping of the oxen on old Christmas Eve (to-night) Priscilla said, 'I have known old James Meredith 40 years and I have never known him far from the truth, and I said to him one day, "James, tell me the truth, did you ever see the oxen kneel on old Christmas Eve at the Weston?" And he said, "No, I never saw them kneel at the Weston but when I was at Hinton at Staunton-on-Wye I saw them. I was watching them on old Christmas Eve and at 12 o'clock the oxen that were standing knelt down upon their knees and those that were lying down rose up on their knees and there they stayed kneeling and moaning, the tears running down their faces." '   Kilvert, iii. 354

(See also *24 Dec.)

Twelfth Eve divinations
Lay a greene Ivye leafe in a dishe, or other vessell of fayre water on Newyeeres euen at night, and couer the water in the said vessell, set it in a sure or safe place, untill Twelfe euen next after, either for your selfe or for anye other, (which will be the fifth day of January,) and then . . . marke well if the sayde leafe be faire and greene as it was before: for then you or the party for whom you laid it into the water, will be whole and sound and safe from any sicknesse all the next yeere following. But if you finde any blacke spots theron, then you or the partye for whom you laid it into the water, will be sicke the same yeere following.   Lupton, x § 87 (1579)

In Russia, various forms of divination were practised throughout the Twelve Days of Christmas, known as *svyátki*; several are described by Pushkin in the fifth chapter of *Eugene Onegin*. Traditional songs were sung, each regarded as foretelling a particular event such as bereavement or marriage; after every song a ring would be removed at random from the dish and its owner's fortune judged according to the omen. The servant-girls of the Larin household prophesied every year that the young mistresses would marry soldiers (as they do). The elder daughter, Tatiana (see *12 Jan.), holds her mirror to the moon, vainly hoping to see her future husband in it, and asks the first passing stranger his name, but he is a rustic called Agafon (Agathon), which to contemporary Russian ears sounded uncouth, Greek names having come down in the world.

Wassailing fruit trees and cattle
Memorandum that non obstante the Change of Religion, the Ploughboies, and also the Schooleboies will keep-up and retaine their old Ceremonies and Customes and priviledges, which in the west of England is used still (and I believe) in other parts. So in Somersetshire when they Wassaile (which is on . . . [lacuna] I thinke Twelfe-eve) the Plough-men have their Twelve-cake, and they goe into the Ox-house to the oxen, with the Wassell-bowle and drink to the ox w. the crumpled horne that treads out the corne; they have an old conceived Rythme; and afterwards they goe with their Wassel-bowle into the orchard and goe about the Trees to blesse them, and putt a piece of Tost upon the Rootes, in order to it.   Aubrey, 40

The Herefordshire Wassailing, as reported in the *Gentleman's Magazine*, 61 (Feb. 1791), 116:

On the eve of Twelfth-day, at the approach of evening, the farmers, their friends, servants, &c. all assemble, and near six o'clock, all walk together to a field where wheat is growing. The highest part of the ground is always chosen, where 12 small fires and one large one are lighted up. The attendants, headed by the master of the family, pledge the company in old cyder, which circulates freely on these occasions. A circle is formed round the large fire, when a general shout and hallooing takes place, which you hear answered from all the villages and fields near . . . This being finished, the company return to the house, where the good housewife and her maids are preparing a good supper, which on this occasion is always plentiful. A large cake is always provided, with a hole in the middle. After supper, the company all attend the bailiff (or head of the oxen) to the Wain-house, where the following particulars are observed: the master, at the head of his friends, fills the cup (generally of strong ale), and stands opposite the first or finest of the oxen . . . he then pledges him in a curious toast; the company then follow his example with all the other oxen, addressing each by their name. This being over, the large cake is produced, and is, with much ceremony, put on the horn of the first ox, through the hole in the cake; he is then tickled to make him toss his head: if he throws the cake behind, it is the mistress's perquisite; if before (in what is termed the boosy) the bailiff claims this prize. This ended, the company all return to the house, the doors of which are in the mean time locked, and not opened till some joyous songs are sung. On entering, a scene of mirth and jollity commences, and reigns thro' the house till a late, or rather an early, hour, the next morning.

Chambers remarks: 'The fires are designed to represent the Saviour and his apostles, and it was customary as to one of them, held as representing Judas Iscariot, to allow it to burn a while, and then put it out and kick about the materials.' This was a symbolic interpretation often bestowed on the thirteen days from Christmas to Epiphany. In some places the ceremony was conducted on Christmas Eve or Epiphany.

6 JANUARY

At twelfth-day the days are lengthened a cock's stride.

❅ HOLIDAYS AND ANNIVERSARIES USA, New Mexico: Admission Day (47th state, 1912)

Twelfth Day (but in some languages called 'thirteenth day': Swedish *trettondag jul*)

❅ HOLY DAYS **Epiphany of Our Lord** (CofE, RC); **Theophany, Baptism of Christ in the Jordan** (Orth.)

Epiphany, a term denoting the earthly manifestation of a deity (the Seleucid King Antiochus IV styled himself Epiphanes, 'Manifest', adjusted by his enemies to Epimanes, 'Mad'); the prophet Isaiah declares that the Messiah shall be called Immanuel, 'God with us'. The Orthodox more often say Theophany ('Manifestation of God') or the Lights (an image of baptism). This day properly celebrates the baptism of Christ, in his early 30s, by John the Baptist, after which 'he saw the heavens opened, and the Spirit like a dove descending upon him; and there came a voice from heaven, saying, Thou art my beloved Son, in whom I am well pleased'. Some Egyptian Christians in the second century dated this event to 11 Tybi in the 15th year of Tiberius, or 6 January AD 29; the 11th was the second day of the pagan festival by the Nile celebrating the birth of Eternity to the Maid (see *5 and *19 Jan.). The festival became popular in the East, being also taken to commemorate Christ's birth, which remained the custom at Jerusalem till the sixth century. Even now the Armenians still maintain the single feast (*Haymuʿiwn*, Epiphany) on 6 January celebrating Nativity and Baptism; on the eve one eats fried fish, lettuce, and boiled spinach, supposedly the Virgin's meal on the night before Christ's birth.

In the West, which adopted the solar festival of 25 December as its Christmas, Epiphany was slower to establish itself: the Donatists of Africa, who broke with the rest of Christendom in the early fourth century, kept Christmas on 25 December but not Epiphany. During the fourth and fifth centuries most Eastern churches accepted the separate Christmas on 25 December, and the West accepted Epiphany.

The Orthodox commemorate Christ's baptism by the Blessing of the Waters; a cross is thrown in the water, young men dive in, and he who recovers it carries it in triumph. Sailors try to be in home port; in days of sail they sought to be home at Christmas and stay there till the waters had been blessed. Some people wait till then to open barrels of new wine. This Blessing of the Waters is celebrated as the Blessing of the Sponge-Divers in Tarpon Springs, Fla., where there is a large Greek community engaged in that trade.

The festival also celebrated the visit to the 2-year-old Christ child in the reign of King Herod by oriental Magi (see *28 Dec.), which in the West has so far obscured the association with Christ's baptism that the latter is now kept on the following Sunday by

RCs and the first Sunday after 1 January by the Lutherans; contrariwise, the Orthodox have transferred the celebration of the Magi to Christmas (but see *30 Dec.). Although in the earliest Christian art they sometimes number two or four, tradition settled on three, matching their three gifts; they are identified as Caspar (who brings frankincense for Christ's divinity), Melchior (who brings gold for His royalty), and Balthazar (who brings myrrh for His sorrows), names found in the sixth-century mosaic at Sant'Apollinare Nuovo in Ravenna. Their portrayal in Persian dress caused the conquering army of the Zoroastrian shah Khosraw II, zealously destroying the churches of Jerusalem in 614, to exempt the Church of the Holy Sepulchre, where a mosaic represented them. As early as the third century they are taken for kings fulfilling the prophecy at Isa. 60: 3; a subsequent notion of their descent from the three sons of Noah caused Balthazar to be depicted as a black descendant of Ham. They are said to have arrived in Jerusalem with a suite of 1,000 men, leaving a 7,000-strong army on the left bank of the Euphrates. On their return they devoted themselves to prayer and contemplation; when St Thomas arrived in Parthia they were baptized and became missionaries. Their remains were discovered by the empress Helena and translated to Constantinople, thence in turn to Milan and Cologne. In the West they are patrons of travellers.

In many countries this, not Christmas, is the day for children to receive presents; in Italy they are distributed by Befana (a corruption of *Epifania*), an old woman who was cleaning her house when the Magi passed by. Having ascertained their errand, she asked them to wait till she had finished, but they would not tarry; by the time that she was ready, they were out of sight, and she has been searching for the Christ child ever since, descending every chimney with her gifts in case he is in the house. In Belgium children dress up as the Three Kings and sing a begging song from door to door. In Mexico colourful and beautifully made *nacimientos*—far more elaborate than our Christmas cribs, with tableaux of biblical, historical, or national scenes—are set up in churches. In Spain children are visited by the Magi, having left their shoes full of straw or grain on the balcony or by the front door. In the morning the shoes are filled with small gifts; children who find a charcoal mark on their face know they have been kissed by Balthazar. In many Spanish cities and towns the Magi progress through the streets on the evening before.

There is a popular belief that Christ is not happy during the Twelve Days from birth to baptism, and that evil spirits, such as the Greek *kalikátzari*, roam the earth; in Livonia it was said that werewolves abounded during this time. Means were devised to keep the spirits away; in much of Central Europe, by chalking the Three Kings' initials C. or K. (in Hungary G.), B., and M. on one's door at Epiphany; in Upper Bavaria, masked peasant boys with whips frighten off the witch Frau Percht. In the Netherlands, boys beat the *rommelpot* during the Twelve Days to drive them away with the din.

On this day Edward the Confessor was buried in 1066, and Richard II born in 1367; Richard regarded the Baptist as his patron saint, but was also devoted to St Edward. Both saints appear with him in the Wilton Diptych besides the royal martyr Edmund (*20 Nov.).

Twelfth-night cake. In France, as formerly in England, a special cake known as the *galette des Rois* (in English 'Twelfth cake') is made of marzipan and flaky pastry, containing a bean, sometimes now replaced by a pottery figure from the Christmas crib, called *santon* ('saintlet'); the person finding this in his or her portion is king or queen for the night, with the right to crown a consort. By ancient custom, when the king raised his cup, the cry went up 'Le roi boit', and anyone who failed to drink had his face blackened (see Pl. 2). (For similar kings of the feast, see *17 Dec.) Medieval kings of Navarre would personally appoint a 'king of the bean', at first a boy, later an adult; this custom spread elsewhere. Sometimes, as in Herrick's poem, there was also a pea, the drawer of which becomes the queen.

> *Twelfe Night, or King and Queene*
>
> Now, now the mirth comes
> With the cake full of plums,
> Where Beane's the King of the sport here;
> Beside we must know,
> The Pea also
> Must revell, as *Queene*, in the Court here.
>
> Begin then to chuse,
> (This night as ye use)
> Who shall for the present delight here,
> Be a *King* by the lot,
> And who shall not
> Be Twelfe-day *Queene* for the night here.
>
> Which knowne, let us make
> Joy-sops with the cake;
> And let not a man then be seen here,
> Who unurg'd will not drinke
> To the base from the brink
> A health to the King and the Queene here.
>
> Next crowne the bowle full
> With gentle lambs-wooll;
> Adde sugar, nutmeg and ginger,
> With store of ale too;
> And thus ye must doe
> To make the wassaile a swinger.
>
> Give then to the King
> And Queene wassailing;
> And though with ale ye be whet here;
> Yet part ye from hence,
> As free from offence,
> As when ye innocent met here.
>
> Robert Herrick (1591–1674)

The young Scot James Boswell, newly arrived in London, where he was to spend two years in fruitless search of a commission in the Guards, made the following entry in his journal in 1763:

Thursday 6 January. My brother breakfasted with me. This was Twelfth-day, on which a great deal of jollity goes on in England, at the eating of the Twelfth-cake all sugared over. I called at Gould's. Mrs Gould chid me for not being oftener there, and said jestingly that if she did not see me more, she would write to my father that I was idle. I then walked into the City. I took a whim that between St Paul's and the Exchange and back again, taking the different sides of the street, I would eat a penny Twelfth-cake at every shop where I could get it. This I performed most faithfully.

I then dined comfortably at Dolly's Beefsteak-house. I regretted much my not being acquainted in some good opulent City family where I might participate in the hearty sociality over the ancient ceremony of the Twelfth-cake. I hope to have this snug advantage by this time next year.   Boswell, 120–1

St Baddeley's Cake

The eating of the Baddeley cake, or, as it is sometimes facetiously called, St. Baddeley's Cake, is an annual ceremony performed at the greenroom of Drury Lane Theatre in London on the evening of the 6th of January. Its history is as follows. Robert Baddeley, originally a cook, afterwards a valet, and lastly an actor, died in 1794, and by will set apart one hundred pounds as a fund whose income should be used to furnish a cake and a bowl of punch every Twelfth-Night to the Drury Lane greenroom, which by long custom had been annually given over on that night to feasting and merriment.

Baddeley's bequest has been faithfully carried out, with the exception of one provision, that whenever the cake was eaten some commemoration should be made of his conjugal infelicity. In his lifetime his wife was better known than himself. She sang well and danced charmingly, was beautiful and vivacious, and was said to have been the cause of more duels than any other woman of her time. Baddeley himself was an indifferent actor, though noteworthy in histrionic annals as the original Moses in 'The School for Scandal'.

The present proprietor of Drury Lane has added a few hundred pounds of his own to the Baddeley gift, increased the bill of fare so that it includes a large number of delicacies, and reserved the privilege of inviting distinguished outsiders, both lay and professional, to join in the ceremonials. The *pièce de résistance* is still the large, round white cake, with red and green icing in the centre, which is known as St. Baddeley's Cake, and no guest goes away without securing a portion of it.   Walsh, 86–7

Twelfth Day balls. In Colonial Virginia, it was customary to hold a ball on Twelfth Day. Nicholas Creswell reports on one such in Alexandria in 1775:

Saturday, January 7th, 1775. Last night I went to the Ball. It seems this is one of their annual Balls supported in the following manner: A large rich cake is provided and cut into small pieces and handed round to the company, who at the same time draws a ticket out of a Hat with something merry wrote on it. He that draws the King has the Honor of treating the company with a Ball the next year, which generally costs him Six or Seven Pounds. The Lady that draws the Queen has the trouble of making the Cake. Here was about 37 ladies dressed and powdered to the life, some of them very handsome and as much vanity as is necessary. All of them fond of dancing, but I do not think they perform it with the greatest elegance. Betwixt the Country dances they have what I call everlasting jigs. A couple gets up and begins to dance a jig (to some Negro tune) others comes and cuts them out, and these dances always last as long as the Fiddler can play. This is sociable, but I think it looks more like a Bacchanalian dance than one in a polite assembly. Old Women, Young Wives with young children in the lap, widows, maids and girls come promiscuously to these assemblies which generally continue till morning. A cold supper, Punch, Wines, Coffee and Chocolate, but no Tea. This is a forbidden herb. The men chiefly Scotch and Irish. I went home about two o'clock, but part of the company stayed, got drunk and had a fight.

Creswell, 10–11

Twelfth Day plays. Christmas carols were sung throughout the twelve days of Christmas, and the last day was often marked with a play. In 1519 William More, Prior of Worcester, entered the following payment in his account-book:

Item to syngars of carralls 20*d*. Item rewarded to iiij pleyers a pon ye Epiphani Day belongyng to sir Edward beltenop 3*s*. 4*d*. More, 77

Twelfth Day with the Pepyses
6 [Jan. 1663]. *Twelfth-day.* And after dinner to the Dukes house and there saw *Twelfth night* acted well, though it be but a silly play and not relating at all to the name or day. Pepys, iv. 6

6 [Jan. 1669]. *Twelfth day.* . . . very merry we were at dinner, and so all the afternoon, talking and looking up and down my house; and in the evening I did bring out my cake, a noble cake, and there cut into pieces, with wine and good drink; and after a new fashion, to prevent spoiling the cake, did put so many titles into a hat and so drow cuts; and I was Queene and The Turner, King; Creed, Sir Martin Marrall; and Betty, Mrs. Millicent. And so we were mighty merry till it was night; and then, being moonshine and fine frost, they went home, I lending some of them my [newly acquired] coach to help to carry them; and so my wife and I spent the rest of the evening in talk and reading, and so with great pleasure to bed. Pepys, ix. 409

Twelfth Day at Court. Gambling at Court began on Epiphany until 1772, when it was suppressed. John Evelyn reports in 1662:

6 Jan. 1662. *Epiphanie* . . . This evening (according to costome) his Majestie opned the Revells of that night, by throwing the Dice himselfe, in the Privy Chamber, where was a table set on purpose, & lost his 100 pounds: the yeare before he won 150 pounds: The Ladys also plaied very deepe: I came away when the Duke of *Ormond* had won about 1000 pounds & left them still at passage, Cards &c.: at other Tables, both there and at the *Groome-porters*, observing the wicked folly vanity & monstrous excesse of Passion amongst some loosers, & sorry I am that such a wretched Custome as play to that excesse should be countenanc'd in a Court, which ought to be an example of Virtue to the rest of the kingdome. Evelyn, *Diary*, iii. 308

Haxey Hood Game (in Humberside, near Epworth). Legend has it that this game dates back some 600 years, when the lady of the manor, Lady Mowbray, lost her red hood in the wind. Thirteen labourers ran after it; the two who returned it were dubbed 'Lord' and 'Fool', and rewarded with a piece of land. Today thirteen red-clad Boggans, Lord and Fool included, preside over the battle for the Sway Hood, a coil of rope encased in leather, between residents of Haxey and Westwoodside. The game is over when one side succeeds in getting the Hood to its local pub.

A suggestion for an extravagant feast on Twelfth Day. Robert May, in *The Accomplisht Cook* (1665), begins his section on 'Triumphs and Trophies in Cookery, to be used at Festival Times, as Twelfth-Day, &c.' as follows:

Make the likeness of a Ship in paste-board, with flags and streamers, the guns belonging to it of Kickses [odds and ends], binde them about with packthred, and cover them with course paste proportionable to the fashion of a Cannon with Carriages, lay them in places convenient, as you see them in Ships of War; with such holes and trains of powder that they may all take fire; place your Ship firm in a great Charger; then make a salt round about it, and stick therein egg-shells full of sweet water; you may by a great pin take out all the meat out of the egg by blowing, and then fill it with the rose-water. Then in another Charger have the proportion of a Stag made of course paste, with a broad arrow in the side of him, and his body filled up with claret wine. In another Charger at the end of the Stag have the proportion of a Castle with Battlements, Percullices, Gates, and Draw-bridges made of pasteboard, the Guns of Kickses, and covered with course paste as the former; place it at a distance from the Ship to fire at each other. The Stag being plac't betwixt them with egg-shells full of sweet water (as before) placed in salt. At each side of the Charger wherein is the Stag, place a Pie made of course paste, in one of which let there be some live Frogs, in the other live Birds; make these pies of course paste filled with bran, and yellowed over with saffron or yolks of eggs, gild them over in spots, as also the Stag, the Ship, and Castle; bake them, and place them with gilt bay-leaves on the turrets and tunnels of the Castle and Pies; being baked, make a hole in the bottom of your pies, take out the bran, put in your Frogs and Birds, and close up the holes with the same course paste; then cut the lids neatly up, to be taken off by the Tunnels: being all placed in order upon the Table, before you fire the trains of powder, order it so that some of the Ladies may be perswaded to pluck the Arrow out of the Stag, then will the Claret wine follow as blood running out of a wound. This being done with admiration to the beholders, after some short pawse, fire the train of the Castle, that the peeces all of one side may go off; then fire the trains of one side of the Ship as in a battle; next turn the Chargers, and by degrees fire the trains of each other side as before. This done, to sweeten the stink of the powder, let the Ladies take the egg shells full of sweet waters, and throw them at each other. All dangers being seemingly over, by this time you may suppose they will desire to see what is in the pies; where lifting the first the lid off one pie, out skips some Frogs, which makes the Ladies to skip and shreek; next after the other pie, whence comes out the Birds; who by a natural instinct flying at the light, will put out the candles: so that what with the flying Birds, and skipping Frogs, the one above, the other beneath, will cause much delight and pleasure to the whole company: at length the candles are lighted, and a banquet brought in, the musick sounds, and every one with much delight and content rehearses their actions in the former passages.

The following Monday is Plough Monday, on which agriculture resumed after the Christmas festivities (see *Western Church Year*).

7 JANUARY

a.d. VII Idus Ianuarias   G

❨ HOLIDAYS AND ANNIVERSARIES Japan: *Nanakusa no sekku*, Seven (Medicinal) Herbs Festival: originally on 7th of 1st lunar month

❨ HOLY DAYS Raymund of Peñafort (RC); Synaxis of John the Precursor (Orth.)

Raymund or Ramón of Peñafort, in Catalan 'Ramon de Penyafort' (*c.*1180–1275); canonist, commissioned by Pope Gregory IX to compile the official collection of papal rulings on points of canon law, the so-called *Liber Extra*, promulgated in 1234, and valid in the Roman Catholic Church till 1918; elected third Master-General of the Dominican Order in 1238, he promptly produced revised constitutions that remained in force till 1924. He also compiled a penitential, the *Summa de casibus* (*c.*1238), and encouraged Aquinas to write the *Summa contra Gentiles*. At his death in 1275 the kings of Aragon and Castile attended his funeral. Feast-day formerly 23 January. He is a patron saint of lawyers.

Synaxis of John the Precursor. The Orthodox commonly call the Baptist the Prodromos ('Forerunner' or 'Precursor'). At Anchialos, new bridegrooms would be ducked in the sea, their brides sprinkled with seawater. (The medieval West also had a feast of the Lavacrum, or Font, on this day, in honour of the Baptist.)

In those Orthodox countries like Russia that keep all feasts by the Julian calendar, 7 January NS is Christmas, and will remain so down to 2100; from 2101 Christmas will be the 8th, from 2201 the 9th.

Reinhold of Cologne, allegedly murdered in 960 for excessive strictness by workmen building the old cathedral; nevertheless he is patron, not of overseers, but of sculptors and stonecutters, as well as of Hanseatic merchants and the city of Dortmund. He is portrayed as a monk with a hammer in his hand or as an armoured knight with a sword, for as one of the four legendary Sons of Haimo he had been a brave warrior before he took the cowl.

Knud Lavard (son of King Erik the Good of Denmark, 1095–1103), Duke of Slesvig, murdered by his nephew Mogens or Magnus in 1131. His day marks the end of festivities and resumption of work; Worm cites a rhyme *sankt Knud genner jul ud* ('St Knud drives Christmas out'; but see *13 Jan.).

The traditional English equivalent of modern Danish *Knud* and Norwegian and Swedish *Knut* is 'Canute', from a Latin form *Canutus* used by those who had difficulty in pronouncing initial *kn*; even so do the French call a pen-knife a *canif*. It immediately reminds the English reader of the great king who conquered England 50 years before Duke William and unlike William won his subjects' love; but above all it recalls the tale that he commanded the incoming tide to retreat and, when it did not, proclaimed the worthlessness of all kingship but God's. This king was known to his Scandinavian subjects as *Knútr*, in England as *Cnut*, by which name he is now called in academic history, perhaps to avoid suggesting the throne by the sea. Other namesakes are best given their modern vernacular names; for another St Knud, see *10 July.

In Norway *eldbjørgdagen* (the fire-saving day), from heathen rituals; but a St Eldberga was invented to explain the name. In 1786 it is reported that at Seljord the mistress of the house would celebrate the return of the sun by drinking a draught of ale before the hearth, throw something into the fire, and exclaim: 'So high be my fire that hell is no higher or hotter.' The family would then sit on the floor around the bowl with their hands behind their backs; each in turn they would lift the bowl in their mouths, drink the ale, and cast the bowl behind them with a toss of the head; if it landed face down, one would die within the year; if not, one would have the fortune to drink 'Eldberga's mind' another year. There were variations in which toasts were drunk to those in the house, and to the king. In Skedsmo they said that on that day the bear turned over in his sleep.

Millard Fillmore, President of the USA 1850–3, was born on this day in 1800; the event is sometimes celebrated in a spirit of jovial irony, for Americans of all political persuasions agree on his lack of distinction. He was never elected President: having as

Zachary Taylor's Vice-President succeeded on his death in mid-term, he found no one to nominate him in the election of 1852, and four years later was the candidate of the anti-Irish 'American Party', commonly called the 'Know-Nothing party' from its cult of secrecy. Nevertheless he deserves some commendation, less for having shaken the hand of Heinrich Schliemann, the future discoverer of Troy, than for having refused, in 1855, the doctorate of civil laws offered him by Oxford University, on the ground that he had no literary or scientific attainments that could justify accepting it.

Rock Day or St Distaff's Day. Women resumed spinning after the Christmas season (the Monday after Twelfth Day was Rock Monday); rock = distaff.

Saint Distaffs day, or the morrow after Twelfth day

Partly worke and partly play
Ye must on S. *Distaffs* day:
From the Plough soone free your teame;
Then come home and fother them.
If the Maides a spinning goe,
Burn the flax, and fire the tow:
Scorch their plackets, but beware
That ye singe no maiden-haire.
Bring in pailes of water then,
Let the Maides bewash the men.
Give S. *Distaffe* all the right,
Then bid Christmas sport *good-night*.
And next morrow, every one
To his owne vocation.

Robert Herrick (1591–1674)

8 JANUARY

a.d. VI Idus Ianuarias   A

This day before noone declareth the nature of June, and after noone the nature of May. (Lloyd)

❆ HOLIDAYS AND ANNIVERSARIES Greece: Midwife's Day or Women's Day
USA, Louisiana and Massachusetts: Battle of New Orleans Day (General Andrew Jackson inflicted a crushing defeat on British forces in 1815; both sides were unaware that the Peace of Ghent had been signed on 24 December 1814)

❆ HOLY DAYS Lucian, bishop of Beauvais (BCP)
Lucian, bishop of Beauvais (3rd c.), martyr, together with his companions Maximian and Julian, of uncertain authenticity; his cult flourished after the discovery of relics in the seventh century.

Gudule (d. 712), patron saint of Brussels, whose lamp was extinguished by the Devil and relit by an angel, or as some say by the Virgin Mary herself.

In Greece St Domnike, a fifth-century deaconess at Constantinople. On this day women of childbearing age bring the village midwife presents, pour out water for her, and kiss a phallic *schema* ('shape') made from a large leek or sausage proffered by her attendants, over which they weep; adorned with gilded flowers, onion and garlic tresses, and necklaces of dried figs, currants, and carob-beans, with a large onion in lieu of a watch, she proudly presides from a makeshift throne, revered as if she were Genetyllis, the goddess of childbirth. After a bibulous banquet she is led through the streets on a carriage like a bride and sprinkled with water at the fountain; the women sing, dance, and tell lewd jokes, the men stay indoors.

Jackson Day (legal holiday in Louisiana, and also Massachusetts), celebrating the battle of New Orleans. In much of America it became a Democratic beanfeast; in 1911 the previous year's congressional victories were celebrated at Baltimore by speeches and a banquet of 7,000 oysters, 75 gallons (US) of terrapin, 1,500 lb of capon, 500 canvas-back ducks, 45 Smithfield hams, 3,000 cigars, and 500 bottles of champagne.

9 JANUARY

a.d. V Idus Ianuarias B

> *This daye openeth the nature of August before noone, and after noone dooth shew the state of July.*
> (Lloyd)

❧ ANCIENT ROME Agonia or Agonalia: as often, the Romans themselves did not know what the word meant, but it appears in the official calendar or *fasti* four times in the year for a sacrifice in honour of a particular god. On this day the god was Janus; the other occasions were 17 March (Mars), 21 May (Vediovis?), and 11 December (Sol Indiges).

❧ HOLY DAYS

Hadrian or Adrian of Canterbury (d. 709); native of Africa, abbot near Naples; chosen archbishop of Canterbury by Pope Vitalianus, he declined the honour, but accompanied Theodore of Tarsus (*19 Sept.) and became abbot of SS Peter and Paul's (later St Augustine's), where he organized the school. Many future bishops and abbots were educated there in Latin, Greek, Roman law, theology, and plainchant.

Fillan or Foelan, an eighth-century Irish immigrant to Scotland, together with his mother, St Kentigerna; he died at Strathfillan. Robert the Bruce invoked his aid before the battle of Bannockburn, 1314:

All the nycht afore the battall [Bannockburn], kyng Robert . . . rolland all ieoperdeis and chance of fortoun in his mynd, and sumtymes he went to his devoit contemplatioun, makand his

orisoun to god and sanct Phillane, quhais arme (as he belevit) set in silver wes closit in ane cais
within his palyeon [= pavilion, tent].   Boece, fo. 212ᵛ

On this day in 1799 an income tax of two shillings in the pound was first introduced in
Great Britain to finance the war against Napoleon; modern readers may better understand the rate as 10 per cent. The tax was a wartime expedient, and became permanent
only in the later nineteenth century; at that date one still spoke of 'the income tax', in
contrast to the modern 'income tax', constructed without the article as if it were a force
of nature.

10 JANUARY

a.d. IIII Idus Ianuarias   C

This daye sheweth the nature of October before noone and after noone, the state of September. (Lloyd)

❦ HOLY DAYS

Agatho, pope 678–81, champion of orthodoxy against heresy. Successive Byzantine emperors had sought to win over the Syrian and Egyptian Monophysites, who denied that
Christ had a human as well as a divine nature; in 634 Heraclius attempted, through
Patriarch Sergius of Constantinople, to accommodate them by asserting that in his two
natures he had only one Energy. The formula was accepted by Pope Honorius I, who
added that Christ had only one Will; this 'Monothelete' doctrine was promulgated by
Heraclius in 638, but repudiated by subsequent popes. The rift was not healed until
Constantine IV summoned the Sixth Oecumenical Council (Constantinople, 680–1) to
decide the matter. The Pope arranged a series of local synods from Hatfield to the
Lateran, at which a uniform Western position was achieved for transmission to Constantinople; the Council not only upheld the existence in Christ of two Energies and
two Wills, but anathematized Honorius for 'following in all things his [Sergius'] mind
and ratifying his impious doctrines' (see too *3 July). For Agatho's interest in the English Church, see *12 January.

Gregory of Nyssa (*c.*330–*c.*395), younger brother of Basil the Great (Orth.; 9 Mar. RC,
19 July CY), one of the three great fourth-century theologians known as the
'Cappadocian Fathers': Basil, Gregory of Nyssa, and Gregory of Nazianzus. Consecrated bishop of Nyssa *c.*371, he was deposed and exiled under the Arian emperor
Valens; he was later briefly bishop of Sebaste, and under the emperor Theodosius was
a notable preacher of Nicene orthodoxy. His fame, however, rests on his writings, which
for all their debt to Platonism and to Origen (from whom he took the notion that
the Devil and the damned would ultimately be saved) also exhibit original thought; it
seems to be he who first likened the Atonement to the baiting of the Devil with a
fishhook.

II JANUARY

a.d. III Idus Ianuarias   D

> *Before noone, this daye declareth the nature of December, and after noone the nature of*
> *November.* (Lloyd)

❨ HOLIDAYS AND ANNIVERSARIES Albania: Proclamation of the Republic Day
(1946)
Nepal: National Unity Day (in honour of King Prithvinarayan, 1773–5, who established the kingdom)
Puerto Rico: De Hostos' Birthday

❨ ANCIENT ROME This day was the festival of the water-nymph Juturna, being the
dedication-day of her temple in the Campus Martius; she also had a spring at the door
of the Capitol in the south-west corner of the Forum, water from which was used in
official sacrifices. Vergil made her the sister of Turnus, the excessively warlike champion
of native Italian resistance to Aeneas' Trojans. It was also the first day of the Carmentalia, honouring the prophetic goddess of childbirth Carmentis, later made the mother
of Aeneas' ally the Arcadian immigrant Evander, who ruled in Rome before it was
Rome; the second day of the festival was the 15th. Animal skins were taboo at her shrine.

❨ HOLY DAYS In Norway and Iceland this was St Brictiva's day (*brettemesse, Brættifu-*
messa), though no one knew who she was; it was said that a farmer warned by his neighbour that it was unlucky to work on *Brette*'s day retorted that *Brette* or no *Brette* he would
cart (*brette*) home a load of hay, 'but on the way his horse hurt its foot'. The name also
took the form *brykkesmesse* or *brokkesmesse*, understood to mean that something would
break; this was sometimes interpreted as breaking up the Christmas leavings and
putting them into the pot, with the consequence that any leftover ale was to be
drunk up. In some places fresh ale was brewed, and a party held for friends and neighbours.

On Old New Year's Eve in Burghead, on the shore of the Moray Firth, near Elgin, the
ancient ceremony of the burning of 'the Clavie' takes place. A contraption made of a
tar-barrel and herring-cask attached with a large nail, filled with burning peat, is constructed, then carried through the town to a small hill, where it is placed on a pillar, allowed to burn for half an hour, and then thrown down the hill, a mass of flame. All
scramble for the embers, which bring good luck.

On this day in 1859 was born George Nathaniel Curzon, viceroy of India, husband of
two American heiresses, foreign secretary, and first Marquess Curzon of Kedleston;
known from his bearing even in youth as 'a most superior purzon', he once commented
on a proposed menu at Buckingham Palace that 'Gentlemen do not take soup at

luncheon'. The seventeenth Earl of Derby complained that Curzon made one feel 'so terribly plebeian'; nevertheless, as an able and intelligent man with a very creditable record of achievement he was a candidate for the post of Prime Minister in 1923, but George V, against the advice of his private secretary, chose Stanley Baldwin. His chief reason was that Curzon was a peer, an argument seconded by the former Prime Minister Arthur Balfour, who regarded Curzon with a disdain manifested later that evening at a house party (as reported by Blake, 213):

LADY. And will dear George be chosen?
BALFOUR. No, dear George will not.
LADY. Oh, I am so sorry. He will be terribly disappointed.
BALFOUR. I don't know. After all, even if he has lost the hope of glory he still possesses the means of Grace.

Grace Duggan was Curzon's second wife.

12 JANUARY

pridie Idus Ianuarias   E

This daye being the twelfe, dooth foreshowe the nature and condition of the whole yeare, and dooth confirm the eleven dayes going before. (Lloyd)

❦ HOLY DAYS Aelred of Rievaulx (CY); Benedict Biscop (CY commem.)

Aelred of Rievaulx (1109–66), a priest's son from Hexham, whose name, also spelt 'Ailred' and in many other ways, is a corruption of 'Æthelred', spent his youth at the court of David king of Scots (1124–53), who offered him a bishopric; preferring to be a monk, he entered the Cistercian abbey of Rievaulx in the North Riding of Yorkshire, where in 1147 he became abbot. By then, at St Bernard's request, he had already written his *Speculum caritatis* ('Mirror of Charity'); his other works include a hagiography of Edward the Confessor, at whose translation he was present (see *13 Oct.), and *De spiritali amicitia*, a Christian recasting of Cicero's dialogue on friendship. His sanctity is illustrated by the stories that, as a boy, he predicted the death of a bad archbishop of York, and as an old man near death, troubled with a cough, forgave a monk who threw him on the fire for malingering. The RC feast-day is this day or 3 March.

Benedict Biscop (628–89); founder and first abbot of Wearmouth (674); founder of the monastery of Jarrow (682). Patron of English Benedictines. He visited Rome six times, returning with relics, liturgical books, sacred images, and the archcantor John, sent by Pope Agatho (see *10 Jan.), who taught uncial script, and the order and manner of singing, to monks throughout England. Biscop's library was invaluable for Bede's studies. This day is also his RC memorial.

Marguerite Bourgeoys, b. Troyes 1620, d. Montreal 1700, who played her part in the French penetration of North America; in 1653 tutor to the children of the French garrison at Ville-Marie (Montreal); in 1688 founded the Sœurs de la Congrégation de Notre-Dame. Her life is exhibited with the utmost piety at the Chapelle Notre-Dame de Bon-Secours in Old Montreal.

Tatiana, supposed deaconess at Rome and virgin martyr, *c.*230; much honoured in the East, along with a St Eupraxia. The heroine of Pushkin's *Eugene Onegin* is called Tatiana (a lowly name in his day); her grotesque and fateful name-day party is described in ch. 5. (In the twentieth and twenty-first centuries her New Style day in Russia is 25 Jan.)

According to some calendars, it was on this day that the child Jesus returned from Egypt.

In Norway counted midwinter, as halfway between 14 October and 14 April.

Old New Year's Eve in Scarp. In the evening of this day, corresponding to Old Hogmanay or New Year's Eve in the nineteenth century, the boys of Scarp (in the Western Isles of Scotland), having forgathered at a chosen house, would tour the island in procession; at each house, after the recitation of a traditional rhyme, they would beat a hide by the fire and hold out bags for gifts of food ('a little summer produce', *beagan de thoradh an t-Samhraidh*); the procession over, they would go back to feast, and to make shinty sticks for a game to be played the next day (Old New Year's Day). The rhyme included a reference to an already obsolete custom of singeing a strip of skin from a sheep's breast as a charm against illness. The girls of Scarp played no part in the Hogmanay celebration; their great day was 12 November (Old Hallowe'en), which in turn was no business of the boys.

13 JANUARY

Idus Ianuariae   F

❦ HOLIDAYS AND ANNIVERSARIES Norway: *Tyvendedagen* or *tjugandedagen* ('twentieth day': end of Christmas season)
  Sweden: Knut's Day (end of Christmas season; see *7 Jan.)
  Togo: National Liberation Day (*coup of 1967*)

❦ HOLY DAYS Hilary of Poitiers (CofE; RC, but on 14 Jan. 1602–1969); Kentigern (RC Scotland; CY commem.); George Fox (CY commem.)

Hilary (*c.*315–*c.*368), bishop of Poitiers; a convert to Christianity, he became bishop of Poitiers *c.*353, championing orthodoxy against Arianism above all in his treatise *De Trinitate*. His name is derived from *hilaris*, 'cheerful', 'joyful'. Hilary Term at the University of Oxford and the law courts begins about this time:

This ioy, when God speakes peace to the Soule, giues end to all iarres, doubts, and differences, ouercomes the world, non-sutes the deuill; and makes a man keepe Hillary Terme all his life.

Thomas Adams, *Heaven Made Sure* (*Workes*, 1630), 905

Kentigern, alias Mungo, evangelist of Strathclyde and Cumbria, d. 612, reportedly at the age of 185. We read that before his birth his mother Taneu was thrown off a cliff in a wagon and set adrift in a coracle, and that when the ring bestowed by the queen of Strathclyde upon her lover was retrieved by the king and thrown out to sea with the command that she should find it within three days, one of Kentigern's monks discovered it in a salmon. The latter tale is commemorated by the ring and the fish in the arms of Glasgow.

George Fox (1624–91), founder of the Society of Friends (Quakers). Son of a weaver, and destined to be a shoemaker, in 1643 he left home, searching for enlightenment, and gradually forming a conviction that an institutional church was irrelevant and that the individual should seek truth by communing with God in his soul. Many joined with him and were known as 'Children of the Light' or 'Friends of the Truth', suffering persecution because they refused to take oaths or pay tithes. After the Toleration Act of 1688 the movement spread widely.

Elian (6th c.), Welsh saint, one of many saints to whom a well is dedicated. Thomas Pennant visited the well of St Elian in 1781:

The well of St. *Ælian*, a parish not far from *Llandrillo* in *Caernarvonshire*, has been in great repute for the cures of all diseases, by means of the intercession of the saint; who was first invoked by earnest prayers in the neighboring church. He was also applied to on less worthy occasions, and made the instrument of discovering thieves, and of recovering stolen goods. Some repair to him to imprecate their neighbors, and to request the saint to afflict with sudden death, or with some great misfortune, any persons who may have offended them. The belief in this is still strong; for three years have not elapsed since I was threatened by a fellow (who imagined I had injured him) with the vengeance of St. *Ælian*, and a journey to his well to curse me with effect.

Pennant, *Snowdon*, 337

In Sweden and much of Norway, this was the end of the Christmas festivities, and therefore took over St Knud from the 7th; a Norwegian variant of the rhyme cited on his day is *Tjugandedags-Knut jagar jula ut*. If it snowed on Twentieth Day, there would be twenty snowstorms before the beginning of summer on 14 April.

Feast of Fools. The Feast of Fools, also known as Feast of Sticks, was variously celebrated on this day, 1, 6, or 28 December; it was sometimes combined with the Feast of Asses, also found on 14 January and at Christmas (in honour of the ass in the stable), at which an ass was led into church to the conductus 'Orientis partibus'. A Bishop (or even Pope) of Fools was elected to celebrate mass and speak the blessing; the clergy sang bawdy songs; the subdeacons ate sausages on the altar, diced, played cards, and put old shoes and even excreta in the censer; after mass the congregation ran riot in the church, then went into town on dung-carts from which they pelted the crowd. At Antibes, lay-folk occupied the priest's seat, dressed in ragged vestments turned inside out, held the liturgical books upside down, recited gibberish, and made animal noises. The French love of puns reinterpreted *la fête des sous-diacres* ('the feast of the subdeacons') as *la fête des saouls diacres* ('the feast of the drunken deacons'). This frolic was particularly characteristic of northern France and the Low Countries, which did not observe carnival; at Cambrai, where a medieval record notes that 'today [13 Jan.] the hours of the Blessed Mary are not said because of the Feast of Fools', it was still celebrated with the cry 'L'abbé boit' in the nineteenth century. It was also known in England; Bishop Grosseteste suppressed it at Lincoln Cathedral *c*.1236, and in 1238 throughout the diocese (its day being 1 Jan.), as 'full of vanity and foul with pleasures, hateful to God and delightful to devils'.

14 JANUARY

a.d. XIX Kalendas Februarias   G

❡ HOLY DAYS

Felix of Nola (d. 260), confessor, known for conversions and miracles. His cult was strong from the fourth century, when the church dedicated to him at Nola became a place of pilgrimage.

Mallard Day at All Souls College, Oxford. On this day, in the first year of every century (hence last in 1901 and next in 2001), the fellows proceed by torchlight over the roof of the Codrington Library in search of a mallard, supposedly discovered in a drain when the college was founded in 1438, and singing a song in its honour. The full text, combining the six stanzas recorded by the seventeenth-century antiquarian Antony Wood with the refrain known from other sources, runs:

> The Griffin, Bustard, Turkey, and Capon
> Let other hungry mortals gape on,
> And on their bones with stomachs fall hard,
> But let All Souls men have the Mallard.
>
> [Chorus]
>   O by the blood of king Edward,
>   O by the blood of king Edward,
> It was a swapping, swapping Mallard!
>
> The Romans once admired a gander
> More than they did their best Commander,
> Because he saved, if some don't fool us,
> The place named from the skull of Tolus.
>
> The poets feigned Jove turned a Swan,
> But let them prove it if they can;
> To make't appear it's not at all hard,
> He was a swapping, swapping Mallard.

Some stories strange are told, I trow,
By Baker, Holinshed, and Stow,
Of Cocks and Bulls and such queer things
That happened in the reigns of their kings.

He was swapping all from bill to eye,
He was swapping all from wing to thigh,
His swapping tool of generation
Outswappèd all the wingèd nation.

Then let us drink and dance a galliard
In the remembrance of the Mallard,
And as the Mallard doth in pool,
Let's dabble, dive, and duck in bowl.

However, the fourth and fifth stanzas were subsequently suppressed, or replaced by topical satires; in the third stanza, 'To make't appear' has become the more euphonious 'As for our proofs'. Which King Edward is intended is not known.

In Stuart times Mallard Night was an annual rite of passage in which the candidates elected on or near All Souls Day the previous November became probationer fellows; they were roused from their beds by the existing probationer fellows (who were about to become full fellows) and led around the college. Since in those days fellows of Oxford colleges were often no older than modern undergraduates, and tended to behave accordingly, it is not surprising that the first record of the ceremony should be an indignant letter written in 1632 by the Archbishop of Canterbury, George Abbot, the College Visitor, denouncing

the great outrage which, as I am informed, was the last year committed in your College, where, although matters had formerly been carried with distemper, yet men did never break forth into that intolerable liberty as to tear off the doors and gates which are the fences of the College, and so to disquiet their neighbours as if it had been in a camp or town of war, to the great disgrace of the government of that University. Civil men should never so far forget themselves under pretence of a foolish Mallard as to do things barbarously unbecoming, from which I advise men warily to abstain, lest otherwise they make themselves unworthy of any habitation in the house of the Muses, which I forewarn will be the issue of those who hereafter transgress that way.

Burrows, 126–7

In 1658 the noise of Mallard Night alarmed the soldiers stationed in Oxford, who were ready to force open the gate and put down the trouble. Later the mallard hunt was restricted to the first year of the century; in other years fellows content themselves by singing the song.

The Revd John Pointer, a learned antiquarian, was thought in the college to have impugned the honour of this bird by calling it a goose in his *Academia Oxoniensis* of 1749; in fact he was guilty of no more than supposing that goose and duck 'may be both rank'd in the same Class', but next year one of the fellows, Benjamin Buckler, published anonymously a mock-learned squib, *A Complete Vindication of the Mallard of All-Souls College, Against the injurious Suggestions of the Rev. Mr. Pointer, Rector of Slapton in the County of Northampton and Diocese of Peterborough.*

In a mounted and annotated copy of Antony Wood's *History and Antiquity*, vol. ii (now Bodleian Library, MS Top. Oxon. c. 18, fo. 269ᵛ), Alderman William Fletcher of Oxford inserted the 'Impression of a Seal found by some Workmen in digging a drain, on the site of All Souls College, eastward off of the Warden's Lodgings'; it dates from the thirteenth century, displaying the emblem of a griffin and the legend 'S. Guill. Malardi cl(er)ici', the seal of William Mallard, clerk. Burrows (pp. 436–7) saw in this a possible origin for the tradition; indeed, it would account very well for the opening words of the song, for while capon and bustard are attested at a college feast in 1618 and turkey had been known for some time, not even the keenest gourmet could have dined on that mythical bird the griffin.

In Armenia this day is Circumcision, being the octave of Christmas/Epiphany.

15 JANUARY

a.d. XVIII Kalendas Februarias   A

> *The Slug makes its appearance, and commences its depredations on garden plants and green wheat.* (Forster)

❨ HOLIDAYS AND ANNIVERSARIES Guatemala: Feast of Christ of Esquipulas, or Black Christ Festival
Japan: Coming of Age Day (*Seijin no Hi*) (national holiday)
USA: Martin Luther King, Jr.'s Birthday (observed third Monday in January)

❨ ANCIENT ROME The second day of the Carmentalia (see *11 Jan.).

❨ HOLY DAYS
Paul the Hermit (d. *c.*345), also known as Paul of Thebes, hero of a romance by St Jerome but otherwise unknown; said to be the first Christian hermit, having the honour of being buried by Antony of Egypt (see *17 Jan.). He is represented in art with the two lions who allegedly dug his grave; minor characters in the tale include centaurs, satyrs, and a raven.

Ita (d. 570) founded a nunnery known in Old Irish as Clúain Creadail ('holy meadow') at a site now called Cill Íde ('Ita's church') or Killeedy, in Co. Limerick; the subject of great veneration and many legends. She excelled in the care she lavished on her pupils, but also (it was said) possessed second sight and could determine the outcome of a battle by her prayers.

The Irish Free State, *Saorstát Éireann*, was established on this day in 1922, and was immediately plunged into a civil war between those who accepted the treaty establishing it and those who had wished to fight on.

Martin Luther King, Jr., civil rights leader, born 1929, murdered 1968. On 29 August 1963, during the campaign against racial segregation in the Southern states, he addressed

American blacks who had marched on Washington in an inspirational and incantatory speech with the refrain 'I have a dream':

I have a dream that one day on the red hills of Georgia the sons of former slaves and the sons of former slave owners will be able to sit down together at the table of brotherhood . . .

I have a dream that my four little children will one day live in a nation where they will not be judged by the color of their skin but by the content of their character.

16 JANUARY

a.d. XVII Kalendas Februarias   B

(HOLY DAYS

Marcellus, bishop of Rome 306(?)–308(?), whose resistance to persecution accompanied intolerance of those less intransigent than himself, yet who was later accused by Donatists precisely of such weakness. Some scholars identify him with Marcellinus (*26 Apr.), others suggest that Marcellus struck Marcellinus off the list of popes as an apostate.

On this day in 1809, during the Peninsular War, an outnumbered British army under Sir John Moore, having reached La Coruña in fighting retreat from a bold but unsuccessful mission, beat off a French attack by Marshal Soult. Moore was killed in the action, and buried by his officers immediately after the battle; the army embarked safely.

> *The Burial of Sir John Moore at Corunna*
> Not a drum was heard, not a funeral note,
>   As his corse to the rampart we hurried;
> Not a soldier discharged his farewell shot
>   O'er the grave where our hero we buried.
>
> We buried him darkly at dead of night,
>   The sods with our bayonets turning;
> By the struggling moonbeam's misty light,
>   And the lantern dimly burning.
>
> No useless coffin enclosed his breast,
>   Not in sheet or in shroud we wound him;
> But he lay like a warrior taking his rest,
>   With his martial cloak around him.
>
> Few and short were the prayers we said,
>   And we spoke not a word of sorrow;
> But we steadfastly gazed on the face that was dead,
>   And we bitterly thought of the morrow.
>
> We thought, as we hollowed his narrow bed,
>   And smoothed down his lonely pillow,
> That the foe and the stranger would tread o'er his head,
>   And we far away on the billow!

Lightly they'll talk of the spirit that's gone,
  And o'er his cold ashes upbraid him,—
But little he'll reck, if they let him sleep on
  In the grave where a Briton has laid him.

But half of our heavy task was done,
  When the clock struck the hour for retiring;
And we heard the distant and random gun
  That the foe was sullenly firing.

Slowly and sadly we laid him down,
  From the field of his fame fresh and gory;
We carved not a line, and we raised not a stone—
  But we left him alone with his glory!

Charles Wolfe (1791–1823)

If this poem were not memorial enough, a monument was raised to Moore by the chivalry of Marshal Soult.

17 JANUARY

a.d. XVI Kalendas Februarias   C

❧ HOLIDAYS AND ANNIVERSARIES Philippines: Constitution Day (national holiday, commemorating ratification of the amended constitution in 1935)
Poland: Liberation Day (liberation of Warsaw from the Nazis by Soviet troops, 1945)

❧ HOLY DAYS Antony of Egypt, abbot (CY, RC)

Antony of Egypt (251–356). According to a Life written by Athanasius (in order to claim him for his own theological point of view), Antony lived in complete solitude from 286 to 306 and was assailed by a series of temptations, vividly depicted by later artists such as Bosch and Grunewald. The Order of the Hospitallers of Saint Antony was founded in his honour *c.*1100, and Vienne, in the Dauphiné, which claimed his relics, became a centre of pilgrimage in the Middle Ages. He was credited with curing visitors to his shrine during an outbreak of erysipelas in 1089; the disease is consequently known as 'St Antony's fire'. He is commonly portrayed with a tau-cross (i.e. T-shaped), a bell, and a pig; whence the phrase 'tantony pig' for the runt of a litter, or an obsequious follower; 'tantony' is also the smallest bell in a church tower. (For the reduction of 'St' to a *t* attached to the following vowel, cf. 'tawdry' from St Audrey, and the local pronunciation of St Osyth in Essex as 'Toozi'.) Having occupied his time in solitude with making baskets, he is patron saint of basket-makers, and from having buried St Paul the Hermit (see *15 Jan.), he is also patron saint of gravediggers. He is also patron saint of domestic animals, who are blessed in church on his feast-day. In Italy some priests are so obliging as to include automobiles, the modern beasts of burden.

The Temptations of Saint Anthony

Off in the wilderness bare and level,
Anthony wrestled with the Devil.
Once he'd beaten the Devil down,
Anthony'd turn his eyes toward town
And leave his hermitage now and then
To come to grips with the souls of men.

Afterward, all the tales agree,
Wrestling the Devil seemed to be
Quite a relief to Anthony.

Phyllis McGinley (1905–78)

Sant'Antonio gran fredura,	Great cold on St Antony's day,
San Lorenzo gran caldura,	Great heat on St Laurence's day:
L'uno e l'altro poco dura.	Neither lasts long.

(Venetian saying)

In Italy the *Festa del Porco*, where the slaughtering of the communal pig, carefully fattened up throughout the year, leads to gargantuan feasts. In Milan and Padua, St Antony is the patron saint of bakers; after blessing the animals the priest distributes a special bread, the *pane di Sant'Antonio.*

The simile 'like a tantony pig', according to the London chronicler John Stow, arose as follows:

The officers charged with oversight of the markets in this city, did divers times take from the market people, pigs starved, or otherwise unwholesome for man's sustenance; these they slit in the ear. One of the proctors for St. Anthony's tied a bell about the neck, and let it feed on the dunghills; no man would hurt or take them up, but if any gave to them bread, or other feeding, such would they know, watch for, and daily follow, whining till they had somewhat given them; whereupon was raised a proverb, 'Such an one will follow such an one, and whine as it were an Anthony pig.'   Stow, 195

In Greece, St Antony's Day is often treated as the beginning of carnival season; women begin visiting each other in the evenings, playing games and telling jokes of an uninhibited nature.

Old Twelfth Night
Ten years ago the old custom of Wassailing the apple trees in the tiny village of Carhampton [Som.] was just celebrated by a family and their friends. Today, as for centuries, men with shot guns go out into the orchard behind the village pub, and the trees are toasted in cider and are urged, in song, to bring forth a good crop of apples. . . . 'Apples, hatfuls, capfuls, three bushel bagfuls, And a little heap under the stairs' . . . Once the apple tree has been blessed, the evil spirits and witches are warded off by firing shots through the boughs of the trees. Nowadays, the custom has become a popular entertainment for the commercially interested people in the South West of England. There is the queue of photographers and television cameramen—and a few hopeful preservationists.   *English Dance and Song*, 32 (1970), 138

18 JANUARY

a.d. XV Kalendas Februarias   D

❦ HOLIDAYS AND ANNIVERSARIES Pooh Day (birthday of A. A. Milne, 1882)

❦ HOLY DAYS Prisca (BCP)

Prisca, said to have been a Roman virgin martyred in AD 47, to whom a church on the Aventine was dedicated by the fourth century; since the ninth she has been identified with the Priscilla mentioned in Acts 18 as the wife of Aquila, Jews converted by Paul.

Athanasios and Cyril, patriarchs of Alexandria (Orth.; see *2 May; *27 June), honoured in northern Greece by communal sacrifice of oxen and sheep, and individual sacrifice of a cock. It is considered unlucky to start any work; women do not bake or sew.

St Peter's Chair in Rome. A Frankish feast of Peter's pastorate, instituted in the sixth or seventh century, was later adopted in Rome, duplicating that on *22 February; in consequence, his consecration at Antioch was celebrated on the latter and that at Rome on 18 January. The feast was suppressed in 1960, but some Anglican communities observe the 'Confession of St Peter' on this day.

Francis Mortoft gives the following account of the ceremonies in Rome in 1659:

January the 17 [*sic*]. wee went to Sᵗ Peters Church in yᵉ Vattican where we saw another Ceremony; on this Day it is held that Sᵗ Peter came first to Rome, for which cause, his Chaire, which stands vpon an altar on yᵉ left hand as one goes into yᵉ Church, and was exposed to publicke view, where all Persons that came into yᵉ Church, were very Ambitious to haue their Beads and Chaplets touch yᵉ side of yᵉ Chaire, which was two or 3 persons worke to doe from Morning to night. And I dare affirme truely, there were more Beads touchd yᵉ side of yᵉ Chaire this day then would load a Cart.

There were also, the more to Honour Sᵗ Peter. about 25 Cardinals to heare Masse. and also very excellent Musicke. made by at least 20 Eunuchs. whose voyces made such melody, that ones eares receiued farr more contentment with hearing this Melodious and harmonious Musicke, then one does with beholding Sᵗ Peters pretended Chaire.   Mortoft, fos. 46ᵛ–47ʳ

Lady Morgan, in *Italy* (1821), described the ceremony in St Peter's as follows:

At the extremity of the great nave of St. Peter's, behind the altar, and mounted upon a tribune designed or ornamented by Michael Angelo, stands a sort of throne, composed of precious materials, and supported by four gigantic figures. A glory of seraphim, with groups of angels, sheds a brilliant light upon its splendours. This throne enshrines the real, plain, worm-eaten wooden chair, on which St. Peter, the prince of the Apostles, is said to have pontificated; more precious than all the bronze, gold, and gems, with which it is hidden, not only from impious, but from holy eyes, and which once only, in the flight of ages, was profaned by mortal inspection. The Festa di Cattedra is one of the very few functions, as they are called (funzioni), celebrated in St. Peter's. The splendidly dressed troops that line its nave, the variety and richness of vestments which clothe the various church and lay dignitaries, abbots, priests, canons, prelates, cardinals, doctors, dragoons, senators, and grenadiers, which march in procession, complete, as they proceed up the vast space of this wondrous temple, a spectacle no where to be equalled within the pale of European civilization. In the midst of swords and crosiers, of halberds and crucifixes, surrounded by banners, and bending under the glittering tiara of three-fold power, appears the aged, feeble, and worn-out Pope, borne aloft on men's shoulders, in a chair of crimson and gold, and environed by slaves (for such they look), who waft, from plumes of ostrich feathers mounted on ivory wands, a cooling gale, to refresh his exhausted frame, too frail for the weight of such honours. All fall prostrate, as he passes up the church to a small choir and throne, temporarily erected beneath the chair of St Peter . . . A solemn service is then performed, hosannas arise, and royal votarists and diplomatic devotees parade the church, with guards of honour and running footmen, while English gentlemen and ladies mob and scramble, and crowd and bribe, and fight their way to the best place they can obtain.   Morgan, iii. 14–16

In Brussels, there was a *vrouwenavond* or *veillée des dames* when wives had the right to their husbands' company in bed.

Earliest possible date for Septuagesima when Easter falls on 22 March in a common year.

19 JANUARY

a.d. XIV Kalendas Februarias   E

❡ HOLIDAYS AND ANNIVERSARIES USA, Texas: Confederate Heroes Day (observed on Robert E. Lee's birthday)

❡ HOLY DAYS Wulfstan (CY)

Wulfstan (*c*.1008–95), Benedictine monk, bishop of Worcester from 1062. His entire career was passed at Worcester, where he was master of the boys, then cantor, sacristan, prior, and finally bishop. The first English bishop to have systematically visited his diocese, he encouraged the building of churches. Under his direction the cathedral was rebuilt, and he made Worcester a centre of learning. An early opponent of slavery, he abolished the practice of sending slaves from Bristol to Viking Ireland. After the Norman Conquest, overcoming Archbishop Lanfranc's disdain for the English Church as he found it (see *28 May), he was one of three Saxon bishops not to be deposed. The RC commemorates him on this date as well.

Henrik (Henry), of English birth, came to Sweden with his compatriot Nicholas Breakspear, cardinal bishop of Albano (later Pope Hadrian IV), and became bishop of Uppsala; he advised Erik IX, took part in his Finnish crusade of 1157, and preached the Gospel. He was murdered in Finland on the frozen Köyliöjärvi (*järvi* = 'lake') by the wicked heathen peasant Lalli, who resented his missionary work; or, in another version, the poor and quick-tempered peasant Lalli was provoked by the bishop's excessive demands for hospitality for himself and his retinue. He was buried in Nousis; his relics are in Turku Cathedral. He is patron saint of Finland, also honoured in Nordic countries and (through the Swedish connection) Poland.

Knud IV of Denmark was sometimes honoured on this day (see *10 July).

Earliest possible date for Septuagesima when Easter falls on 22 March in a leap year. In Roman Catholic countries, and the Dutch provinces of Holland and Zeeland, this last happened in 1136, in England and other Protestant countries in 1668; it will not happen again till 2872, but the Orthodox, who still regulate the moveable feasts by the Julian calendar, will keep their 'Sunday of the Prodigal Son' on 19 January OS (= 2 February NS) 2200.

In the Coptic and Ethiopian churches, which use the Egyptian calendar as reformed by Augustus, this day corresponds in three years out of four to the Julian Epiphany, and is celebrated as the Baptism of Christ; the Christians of Egypt maintain the great festival beside the Nile from which Epiphany first developed (see *6 Jan.). In Julian leap year, the corresponding day is 20 January.

20 JANUARY

a.d. XIII Kalendas Februarias   F

❦ HOLIDAYS AND ANNIVERSARIES Brazil (Rio de Janeiro): St Sebastian Day (founding of Rio de Janeiro)
  USA: Inauguration Day (beginning of term of newly elected President and Vice-President, at noon)

❦ HOLY DAYS Fabian (BCP); Fabian and Sebastian (RC)
Fabian (d. 250), pope and martyr. Created pope in 236, despite being a layman, Fabian was martyred under the persecution of Decius. He is buried in the basilica of St Sebastian.

Sebastian, fourth-century Roman martyr whose fictitious Acts describe him as a soldier, condemned to be killed by archers for protecting martyrs, an image that captured the imagination of later painters. Nevertheless he survived his ordeal, was healed by St Castulus' widow Irene, and was finally beaten to death with cudgels. His earliest cult was a function of his status as a martyr and primarily limited to Rome; the first references to him as a protector against the plague seem to date from the late eighth century, but his cult became especially popular with the outbreak of the bubonic plague in 1348. Sebastian is patron saint of archers and athletes, Italian town police, and also of Rio de Janeiro.

Traditional day in Norway for forming fishing crews.

St Agnes' Eve

> St. Agnes' Eve—Ah, bitter chill it was!
> The owl, for all his feathers, was a-cold;
> The hare limp'd trembling through the frozen grass,
> And silent was the flock in woolly fold:
> Numb were the Beadsman's fingers, while he told
> His rosary, and while his frosted breath,
> Like pious incense from a censer old,
> Seem'd taking flight for heaven, without a death,
> Past the sweet Virgin's picture, while his prayer he saith . . .
>
> John Keats (1795–1821), 'The Eve of St. Agnes'

'Tis their only desire, if it may be done by art, to see their husbands picture in a glasse, they'le give any thing to know when they shall be married, how many husbands they shall have, by *Crom-nyomantia*, a kind of Divination with onions laid on the altar on Christmas Eve, or by fasting on St Annes eve or night, to know who shall bee their first husband.

Robert Burton, *Anatomy of Melancholy*, III. ii. iii. 1

St. Agnes' Fast is thus practised throughout Durham and Yorkshire. Two young girls, each desirous to dream about their future husbands, must abstain through the whole of St. Agnes' Eve from eating, drinking, or speaking, and must avoid even touching their lips with their fingers. At night they are to make together their 'dumb cake', so called from the rigid silence which attends its manufacture. Its ingredients (flour, salt, water, &c.) must be supplied in equal proportions by their friends, who must also take equal shares in the baking and turning of the cake, and in drawing it out of the oven. The mystic viand must next be divided into two equal portions, and each girl, taking her share, is to carry it upstairs, walking backwards all the time, and finally eat it and jump into bed.   Henderson, 70 (1866)

21 JANUARY

a.d. XII Kalendas Februarias   G

> *Sant'Agnese,*
> *El fredo va per le ciese* (Venetian saying: 'The chill passes through the hedges')

☾ HOLY DAYS Agnes (CofE, RC)

Agnes, Roman virgin martyr 301, aged 13, patron saint of girls, alleged to have sung hymns while the executioner was hacking at her neck. The similarity in sound between *Agnes* and *agnus* led to an association with lambs, furthered by notions of sweetness and innocence; in Rome lambs are presented on this day and blessed at her altar at Sant' Agnese fuori le Mura, then cared for by the nuns of Santa Cecilia in Trastevere. Their wool is used for the white cloth in the pallia granted to archbishops.

Blessing of lambs in Rome by the Pope

> Then commes in place saint Agnes day, which here in Germanie,
> Is not so much esteemde, nor kept with such solemnitie:
> But in the Popish Court it standes in passing hie degree,
> As spring and head of wondrous gaine, and great commoditee.
> For in saint Agnes Church upon this day while Masse they sing,
> Two Lambes as white as snowe, the Nonnes do yearely use to bring:
> And when the Agnus chaunted is, upon the aultar hie,
> (For in this thing there hidden is a solemne mysterie)
> They offer them. The servaunts of the Pope when this is done,
> Do put them into Pasture good till shearing time be come.
> Then other wooll they mingle with these holy fleeses twaine,
> Whereof being sponne and drest, are made the Pals of passing gaine:
> Three fingars commonly in bredth, and wrought in compasse so,
> As on the Bishops shoulders well they round about may go.
> These Pals thus on the shoulders set, both on the backe and brest,
> Have labels hanging something lowe, the endes whereof are drest,
> And typte with plates of weightie lead, and vesture blacke arayde,
> And last of all to make an ende, with knots are surely stayde.

Naogeorgus, fos. 46ᵛ–47

A divination

On St Agnes Day. Take a Sprigg of Rosemary, and another of Time, sprinkle them with Urine thrice; and in the Evening of this Day, put one into one Shooe, and the other into the other; place your Shooes on each side your Beads-head, and going to Bed, say softly to your self: St. Agnes, that's to Lovers kind, Come ease the Troubles of my Mind. Then take your Rest, having said your Prayers; when you are asleep, you will dream of your Lover, and fancy you hear him talk to you of Love. *Aristotle's Last Legacy*, 50 (1711)

22 JANUARY

a.d. XI Kalendas Februarias A

❦ HOLIDAYS AND ANNIVERSARIES New Zealand (Wellington): Anniversary Day
  St Vincent: Discovery Day

❦ HOLY DAYS Vincent of Saragossa (CofE, RC; 11 Nov. Orth.)

Vincent of Saragossa or Zaragoza (d. 304), deacon and first Spanish martyr, widely venerated in the Middle Ages. Readers of Prudentius would have learnt of a martyr who underwent imprisonment, semi-starvation, being racked, grilled, cast into prison, and clamped in stocks. He is portrayed as holding a palm or being roasted on a gridiron (more usually associated with St Laurence). His relics, preserved at Cape St Vincent from the eighth century, were translated to Lisbon in 1173, allegedly escorted up the

Tagus by the two ravens represented on the city's arms. He is patron saint of wine-growers.

St Vincent's Day serves for weather-prognostication. Take a lighted resin torch up a high hill, say the Portuguese: if the wind blows it out you will have a bumper crop and need an extra hand, but if it burns the harvest will be poor and you will have to let a man go. In Stavanger it was said that sun on his day betokened a good year; a French rhyme stated that if his day was sunny and clear, there would be more wine than water.

23 JANUARY

a.d. X Kalendas Februarias   B

❦ HOLIDAYS AND ANNIVERSARIES Bulgaria: Babin Den (Grandmother's Day)

❦ HOLY DAYS Formerly Raymund of Peñafort (see *7 Jan.)

John the Almsgiver (*c*.620), patriarch of Alexandria. Near-contemporary sources relate his extraordinary generosity (made possible by a very wealthy see), towards not only the poor but also refugees, victims of the sack of Jerusalem by the Persians, and individuals, Christian or not. He founded hospitals and monasteries and crusaded against corruption in city officials, reforming the system of weights and measures. He is patron of the Knights of Malta.

Ildefonsus, archbishop of Toledo. In Mexican towns of which he is patron his feast is celebrated with much enthusiasm; the most notable ritual is the chicken-race (*carrera de pollo*), in which riders race in pairs, one rider in each pair trying to snatch a live chicken from the other's hand.

24 JANUARY

a.d. IX Kalendas Februarias   C

❦ HOLY DAYS Francis de Sales (CY, RC); formerly Timothy (see *26 Jan.)

Francis de Sales (1567–1622), bishop of Geneva. Ordained priest in 1593, he undertook to convert Calvinist adherents in the Chablais, surviving assassins and wolves. He was appointed bishop of Geneva in 1602. Known for his gentle persuasion (more flies are attracted by honey than by vinegar, he liked to say) though firm doctrine, he was the author of a *Treatise of the Love of God* and an *Introduction to the Devout Life*, and contributed to the revival of French Catholicism. Together with Jane Frances de Chantal he founded the Order of the Visitation in 1610. His works were published in twenty-six volumes; in

1923 Pope Pius XI named him patron saint of journalists and other writers; he is also patron saint of the deaf. His feast-day was formerly 29 January.

The Great Frost of 1684 in London, as reported by John Evelyn under the date 24 January 1684:

The frost still continuing more & more severe, the Thames before London was planted with bothes in formal streetes, as in a Citty, or Continual faire, all sorts of Trades & shops were furnished, & full of Commodities, even to a Printing presse, where the People & Ladys tooke a fansy to have their names Printed & the day & yeare set downe, when printed on the *Thames*: This humour tooke so universaly, that 'twas estimated the Printer gained five pound a day, for printing a line onely, at six-pence a Name . . . There was likewise Bull-baiting, Horse & Coach races, Pupet-plays & interludes, Cookes & Tipling, & lewder places; so as it seem'd to be a bacchanalia, Triumph or Carnoval on the Water, whilst it was a severe Judgement upon the Land: the Trees not onely splitting as if lightning-strock, but Men & Cattell perishing in divers places, and the very seas so locked up with yce, that no vessells could stirr out, or come in. The fowle, Fish & birds, & all our exotique Plants & Greenes universaly perishing; many Parks of deere destroied, & all sorts of fuell so deare that there were greate Contributions to preserve the poore alive; nor was this severe weather much lesse intense in most parts of *Europe* even as far as *Spaine*, & the most southern tracts: London, by reason of the excessive coldnesse of the aire, hindring the ascent of the smoke, was so filld with the fuliginous steame of the Sea-Coale, that hardly could one see crosse the streete, & this filling the lungs with its grosse particles exceedingly obstructed the breast, so as one could scarce breath: There was no water to be had from the Pipes & Engines, nor could the Brewers, and divers other Tradesmen work, & every moment was full of disastrous accidents &c: Evelyn, *Diary*, iv. 361–3

25 JANUARY

a.d. VIII Kalendas Februarias   D

❨ HOLY DAYS **Conversion of St Paul** (CofE, RC); Gregory of Nazianzus (Orth.)

Paul (d. *c*.65), apostle of the Gentiles. Saul, a Jew born in Tarsus, educated in Jerusalem among the Pharisees, became a dedicated persecutor of Christians, and participated in the stoning of St Stephen. On the road to Damascus, blinded by a sudden bright light, he heard a voice saying: 'Saul, Saul, why persecutest thou me?' He answered: 'Who art thou, Lord?' The Lord replied: 'I am Jesus whom thou persecutest: it is hard for thee to kick against the pricks' (Acts 9: 4–5). He recovered his vision after a visit from Ananias, was baptized forthwith, and soon began to preach Christ. (See also *29 June.) This is a purely Western feast; in early sources it is called 'St Paul's translation'. *Red-letter day.

In symbolic calendars (see II: *Calendars as Written Objects*) this day is commonly marked with a weapon, to signify that St Paul was martyred (though not on this day). In Norway, where the weapon was frequently a bow, the peasants who saw this weapon on their primestaves assumed he had wielded it himself, being a mighty warrior in the morning and a saint in the afternoon.

Gregory of Nazianzus (329–89), the Theologian, son of the bishop of Nazianzus in Cappadocia; a great divine and eloquent preacher, who adopted the monastic life but was ordained priest against his will and consecrated bishop first of a Cappadocian village, then in 381 of Constantinople; after a few months he resigned, unequal to the bitter church politics of the day. His writings include theological poems, in which the thought is of considerably higher quality than the scansion. RC date formerly 9 May, now 2 January.

Dwyn or Dwynwen (*fl. c.*500), when sought in marriage by one Maelon, prayed to be free of love, but on dreaming that he was turned to ice prayed that he should be thawed, that all lovers should either succeed or be cured, and that she herself should never wish to wed. She took the veil; her church of Llanddwyn (Ynys Môn) became one of the richest in medieval Wales from the offerings made at her shrine and at the well, where visitors read their fortunes in the movements of the fish. Sick animals were brought for her to cure, but her cult was greatest among lovers, for whom the bubbling of the well was a favourable omen; her day became in Wales what St Valentine's Day is in England.

Petrarch noted in his copy of Vergil (now among the treasures of the Biblioteca Ambrosiana in Milan) that a sequence sung at mass on this day included lines in which St Paul (implausibly for a Greek-speaker) visits the poet's tomb:

Ad Maronis mausoleum	Led to Vergil's monument,
ductus fudit super eum	he poured over him
piae rorem lacrimae:	the dew of a pitying tear;
'Quem te' inquit 'reddidissem,	'What a man should I have made you
si te vivum invenissem,	had I found you alive,
poetarum maxime!'	greatest of poets!'

A doe (and a buck on 29 June) was formerly offered at the high altar of St Paul's on the patronal feast-day:

In the Third year of King Edward the First Sir William le Baud Knight made a signal Grant to the Dean and Canons of St. Pauls London, of a Doe yearly on the feast of the Conversion of Saint Paul, and of a fat Buck upon the Commemoration of the same Saint, to be offered at the high Altar in St. Pauls by the said Sir William and his household-family, and then to be distributed among the Canons resident.   Blount, 105

At St Paul's Chapel, the corner of Broadway and Fulton St., New York, the footpath through the graveyard is reopened on the eve after two days' closure to forestall a legal right of way. The rector reads four verses of Ps. 68 and the whole of Ps. 91, then proclaims: 'Open the gates that the people may enter in.'

Weather proverbs

> If the day of Saint Paule be cleere,
> Then shall betide an happie yeare:
> If it doe chaunce to snow or raine,
> Then shall bee deare all kinde of graine,

> But if the winde then bee a loft,
> Warres shall vex this realme full oft:
> And if the cloudes make dark the Skie,
> Both Neate and Fowle this yeere shall dye.
>
> Erra Pater

Similar prognostications to Erra Pater's are attested from France and Denmark. In nearly all Scandinavia this day was said to presage both weather and harvest; it was far more important than the Christmas predictions. In Norway, farmers gave themselves a chance, during the short days of winter, by redefining their terms: St Paul's day counted as sunny if the sun shone long enough to harness and unharness a horse three times, or if fair weather lasted long enough for the rider to mount or dismount.

Burns Night. Birthday of Robert Burns (1759–96). The celebrations were foreseen by Burns himself, who on 7 December 1786 wrote to Gavin Hamilton, his early patron:

For my own affairs, I am in a fair way of becoming as eminent as Thomas a Kempis or John Bunyan; and you may expect henceforth to see my birthday inserted among the wonderful events, in the Poor Robin's and Aberdeen Almanacks, along with the black Monday, & the battle of Bothwel bridge.   Burns, *Letters*, i. 70

The evening is festively celebrated with haggis boiled together with tatties and neeps (that is to say, potatoes and turnips), brought in to the sound of bagpipes and washed down with whisky:

Also this small Oate-meale mixed with blood, and the liver of either Sheepe, Calfe or Swine, maketh that pudden which is called the Haggas or Haggus, of whose goodnesse it is in vaine to boast, because there is hardly to bee found a man that doth not affect them.

'Of the excellency of Oates', Markham, 222 (1623)

> Fair fa' your honest, sonsie face,
> Great Chieftain o' the Puddin-race!
> Aboon them a' ye tak your place,
>   Painch, tripe, or thairm:
> Weel are ye wordy of a *grace*
>   As lang 's my arm. . . .
>
> Ye Pow'rs who mak mankind your care,
> And dish them out their bill o' fare,
> Auld Scotland wants nae skinking ware
>   That jaups in luggies;
> But, if ye wish her gratefu' pray'r,
>   Gie her a *Haggis*!
>
> Robert Burns, 'To a Haggis'

26 JANUARY

a.d. VII Kalendas Februarias　　　　　　　　　　　　　　　　　E

❦ HOLIDAYS AND ANNIVERSARIES Australia: Australia Day, commemorating the landing of Captain Arthur Phillip with 11 ships carrying the first European settlers, 1788. The national flag is formally raised; new citizens are officially welcomed. (National day; on this day if a Monday, otherwise first Monday thereafter.)
　India: Basant Pancami or Republic Day (national holiday; anniversary of proclamation of the Republic, 1950)
　USA, Arkansas: Douglas MacArthur Day
　Michigan: Admission Day (26th state, 1837)

❦ HOLY DAYS Timothy and Titus (CY, RC); formerly Polycarp in the West, now *23 February as in the East

Timothy (d. 97), disciple and companion of Paul, bishop and martyr, stoned to death for opposing a pagan festival. Feast-day formerly 24 January.

Titus (1st c.). Also a disciple and companion of Paul, later his secretary; he organized the Church in Crete under Paul's direction, becoming its first bishop. Feast-day formerly 4 January, then 6 February.

Paula (347–404). Widowed at the age of 32 with five children, she found solace and strength with a group of Roman women who were being instructed by St Jerome. Paula became so devoted to him that she followed him to the Holy Land, where she founded a monastery and a hostel for pilgrims. We owe much of the knowledge of her life to Jerome himself, who admits shame at having rebuked her for her prodigal almsgiving. She is buried in the Church of the Nativity at Nazareth. Paula is the patron saint of widows.

27 JANUARY

a.d. VI Kalendas Februarias　　　　　　　　　　　　　　　　　F

❦ ANCIENT ROME Dedication day in 484 BC of temple of Castor and Pollux, the Heavenly Twins, who had helped Rome to victory over the Latins twelve years earlier at Lake Regillus.

❦ HOLY DAYS Translation of John Chrysostom (Orth.; see *13 Sept.); Angela Merici (RC)

Angela Merici (Angela of Brescia) (1474–1540), foundress of the Ursuline nuns. A Franciscan tertiary, in 1535 she formed an uncloistered sisterhood, named after St Ursula, dedicated to teaching poor girls. The Congregation was formalized in 1565.

Devota, executed under Diocletian; her remains were borne to Monoecus, now called Monaco, where she is the patron saint of Monte Carlo.

Nino the Illuminatrix (14 Jan. OS), said by her preaching and miracles to have converted King Mirian III (284–361) of Kartli (eastern Georgia, also known as Iberia), in 334; three years later he and his family were baptized, and Christianity was made the state religion. Much in her written lives is legendary, but the conversion of the Iberian royal family by a female slave was recorded by Rufinus *c*.402 on the information of a prominent Iberian.

Sava Nemanjić (14 Jan. OS), the patron saint of Serbia; born in 1175 the son of the local ruler Stevan Nemanja and baptized Rastko, he was appointed at the age of 15 provincial governor of Hum (later called Hercegovina), but slipped away to become a monk on Mount Athos, where he took the name of the great hermit-saint Sabas (see *5 Dec.). His father, who had sent his soldiers after him too late, himself turned monk in 1196, with the name Symeon; together they were granted authority by the emperor Alexius III over the monastery of Hilandar, then being rebuilt for Serbian monks. Symeon died in 1199 and was canonized as a saint in 1207; Sava, by this time abbot of Studenica, to which his relics had been translated, composed the office in his honour, and also wrote his life. Thereafter he played an important part in every branch of national life, both religious and secular; in 1219 he was consecrated archbishop at the head of an autocephalous Serbian church, which he organized while also serving his brother Stevan, the first crowned king of Serbia, on diplomatic missions. In 1229–30 he made a pilgrimage to Palestine, to which he returned in 1234 after resigning his archbishopric; he died on the way back at Tŭrnovo as the guest of the Bulgarian Tsar. Ever since he has been the most beloved saint of both Church and people: his footprints are still displayed, healing springs are named after him, and a modern poet has turned him into the lord of the wolves, who symbolize the Serbian people as in pagan times; churchmen have summed up the virtues of Serbian Orthodoxy in the term *Svetosavlje*, 'St-Sava-ness'.

News of the Boston Tea Party reaches England:

Thursday, January 27th [1774]
Letters from Boston complain much of the taste of their fish being altered: Four or five hundred chests of tea may have so contaminated the water in the harbour, that the fish may have contracted a disorder not unlike the nervous complaints of the human body. Should this misfortune extend itself as far as the banks of Newfoundland, our Spanish and Portugal fish trade may be much affected by it. *Public Advertiser*, 27 Jan. 1774, quoted in Hampden, 16

On this day in 1945 the concentration camp at Auschwitz was liberated; on 3 January 1996 it was proclaimed in Germany an annual commemoration for the victims of Nazism—not a holiday, but a day on which schoolchildren should study the Holocaust.

28 JANUARY

a.d. V Kalendas Februarias   G

❨ HOLY DAYS Thomas Aquinas (CY, RC); James the Ascetic (Orth.)

Thomas Aquinas (c.1225–74), Dominican friar and theologian, the 'Doctor Communis' and the 'Doctor Angelicus'. Determined to join the Dominicans after university study, he was captured and imprisoned for a year by his parents, who objected to their son becoming a mendicant. Undeterred, he joined the Order in 1244, studying in Paris under Albert the Great, who foresaw the future greatness of 'the dumb Sicilian ox'. He progressed rapidly, becoming a lecturer in 1252 and a Master of Theology in 1256. From these early years date his Commentary on the Sentences of Peter Lombard, the *De ente et essentia*, and a number of commentaries on Aristotle and biblical commentaries. Returning to Italy in 1259, he wrote the *Summa contra Gentiles*, applying Aristotelian argument to theology, and in his 40s began his great work, the *Summa theologica*. Though it was left unfinished (after a revelation in 1272 he wrote no more), his vast output, largely dictated to secretaries (with good reason, since his handwriting is nearly illegible), remained immensely influential, and forms the basis of Roman Catholic theology. Pius V named him a Doctor of the Church in 1567. In 1880 he was declared patron of universities, colleges, and schools by Leo XIII, and is more generally patron saint of students and theologians. Feast-day formerly 7 March; moved in 1969 to avoid Lent.

James the Ascetic spent twenty years in a cave at a village called Porphyriane, in the course of which he converted a harlot. One day a man brought his sister to be cured of demonic possession; James, having driven out the devils, seduced her, murdered her and her brother, and threw their bodies into the river in order to conceal his crime. After doing so, he was overwhelmed with remorse, and shut himself up in a tomb to weep and pray. Eventually God took pity on him: when the land was smitten by drought, the bishop, conducted by a dream, found James in his tomb and revealed that God willed the penitent to pray for rain; when his prayer was answered, James perceived that God had pardoned him, and practised rigorous austerities until he died.

On this day in 814 died Charlemagne, the mighty ruler who had zealously promoted religion and learning throughout his reign; he was canonized in 1166 by Rainald of Dassel, archbishop of Cologne, chancellor of the emperor Francis Barbarossa and champion of the antipope Paschal III, but the cult did not become general.

Annual celebration in state of Jalisco (Mexico) of Battle of Zapopán (1873), in which General Ramón Corona defeated the bandit Manuel Lozada.

29 JANUARY

a.d. IIII Kalendas Februarias   A

❦ HOLIDAYS AND ANNIVERSARIES USA, Kansas: Admission Day (34th state, 1861)

❦ HOLY DAYS Formerly St Francis de Sales (now *24 Jan.)

Gildas (*c*.500–*c*.570), abbot. Born near the Clyde, he became a monk in South Wales, having probably studied under St Illtud (see *6 Nov.). His *De excidio Britanniae* ('On the ravage of Britain') of *c*.540 inveighs against the current state of British society, a prey to warlordism and disorder. He wrote forty-three years and one month after the siege of 'Mount Badon' (location disputed), which halted the Saxon advance; this was to become in Welsh tradition King Arthur's twelfth great victory, in which he carried the Cross on his shoulders for three days and three nights, and personally slew 960 of the enemy in a single charge, but Gildas neither mentions nor alludes to him. Believers in the legend say that that is because Arthur (who fought fellow Britons as well as Saxons) had killed his kindred; others prefer a simpler explanation. He states that despite the ruin of the country those who had fought in the war maintained good order, but that it had broken down under their successors: 'Britain has kings, but they are tyrants; it has judges, but they are cruel'; they plunder the innocent, defend the guilty, have many unfaithful wives, swear many oaths but break them, and so on. Some thirty years later, the English were able to break out of their areas of settlement and overrun most of what is now England; Gildas by then was dead, having emigrated to Brittany, where he gave his name to Saint-Gildas-de-Rhuys (Morbihan). He inspired a mass movement of monasticism, not only in Britain; many of his houses later became Benedictine. Among fragments of letters that he wrote on monastic matters, in one he declares that charity and a pure heart are preferable to the asceticism of those who think their self-denials make them superior to others; 'death has come into them through the windows of their pride'. He is also credited with a monastic rule (*De paenitentia*).

In some parts of Mexico a festival featuring Moorish dancers takes place on this day: a mock battle between *santiagueros*, with St James's banner and a flower in their hats, and Moors, with a black banner, masks, and tin crowns; there is a *diálogo* with drum and *flautín*.

30 JANUARY

a.d. III Kalendas Februarias   B

❦ HOLIDAYS AND ANNIVERSARIES USA, Kentucky: F. D. Roosevelt's Birthday

❦ HOLY DAYS King Charles the Martyr (CY); The Three Great Hierarchs (Orth.);
Hippolytos (Orth.; see *13 Aug.)

King Charles the Martyr was executed on this day in 1649 after a show trial instituted by
the leaders of the New Model Army through a House of Commons purged of their
opponents. Convinced by bitter experience not only that Charles would never sincerely
acquiesce in a constitutional monarchy or a church without bishops, but that he would
consider himself justified in making and breaking promises as might suit his purpose
of setting his various enemies off against one another, they were resolved, as a matter of
political necessity, to kill him; since execution without trial was repugnant, and there
was no basis in English law for trying him, they brought against him the newfangled
offence of treason against the Commonwealth of England, and declined to let him challenge the legality of their proceedings. The appearance of injustice was heightened by
the conduct of soldiers who blew smoke in his face and shouted 'Justice'; in short,
Charles, whose conduct as king had driven so many of his subjects to rebellion, was assisted by his enemies in his campaign to present himself as a martyr. This part the
'Royal Actor', as Andrew Marvell called him, played to perfection:

> *He* nothing common did or mean
> Upon that memorable Scene:
>   But with his keener Eye
>   The Axes edge did try:
> Nor call'd the *Gods* with vulgar spight
> To vindicate his helpless Right,
>   But bow'd his comely Head,
>   Down as upon a Bed.
>   'An Horatian Ode upon Cromwel's Return from Ireland'

The fast on this day instituted in 1660 (and also enacted by Virginia in 1662) was suppressed in 1859; a lesser festival was reinstated in 1980, but without the solemn services
of earlier time, though CY provides a Collect.

30 Jan. 1661. Was the first Solemn Fast & day of humiliation to deplore the sinns which so long
had provoked God against this Afflicted Church & people: ordered by *Parliament* to be annualy
celebrated, to expiate the Gilt of the Execrable Murder of the late *King Charles* I, our *Viccar* preaching on 21. *Deut*: 7. 8 on which he made a very pious, & proper discourse.

Evelyn, *Diary*, iii. 269

The verses in question run: 'And they shall answer and say, Our hands have not shed this
blood, neither have our eyes seen it. Be merciful, O LORD, unto thy people Israel,

whom thou hast redeemed, and lay not innocent blood unto thy people of Israel's charge. And the blood shall be forgiven them.'

30 [Jan. 1663]. *A solemne Fast for the King's murther.* And we were forced to keep it more then we would have done, having forgot to take any victuals into the house.   Pepys, iv. 29

An American's jaundiced view of the day at Exeter in 1778:

This being in Church of England language Charles Martyrdom 'tis farcically observed as a fast day. The Churches are open and service suitable to the solemn occasion read, to complete the absurdity here the Cathedral pulpit was covered with black cloth, the tip staves Sword and mace carried before the Maior in the same grim garb. Being desirous to hear what could be said on this ridiculous occasion I attended but was agreeably disappointed, Chancellor Quick the preacher gave the Audience a modest decent discourse from '*Every Kingdom divided against itself is brought to desolation.*' . . . To save appearances some of the shops are almost ½ darkened, Churches are opened, in other respects like as on all other working days business is going on as usual, streets are walked in, carts carriages &c running.   Curwen, i. 428–9

Radicals indulged in the counter-observation of eating calf's head at the tavern. A pamphlet published in a second edition in 1703 purports to give *The Secret History of the Calves-Head Club; or, the Republican unmask'd,* with anniversary songs dating back to 1693. The 1713 edition describes a recent festivity:

an Axe was hung up in the *Club-Room,* and was reverenced as a principal Symbol in this Diabolical Sacrament. Their Bill of Fare, was a large Dish of *Calves-Heads,* dressed several ways, by which they represented the King and his Friends, who had suffer'd in his Cause; a large *Pike* with a small one in his Mouth, as an Emblem of Tyranny; a large *Cod's-Head,* by which they pretended to represent the Person of the King singly; a *Boar's-Head* with an Apple in its Mouth, to represent the King, by this, as Beastial, as by their other Hieroglyphicks they had done Foolish and Tyrannical. After the Repast was over, one of their Elders presented an *Ikon Basilike,* which was with great Solemnity burn'd upon the Table, whilst the *Anthems* were singing.   Ward, 8

In chapter 14 of *David Copperfield,* Dickens introduces the amiable Richard Babley, known as 'Mr. Dick', whose attempts at recording his ill-treatment by his relations were continually foiled by his obsession with Charles I's execution, and his belief that some of the trouble in the king's head had been put into his own:

In fact, I found out afterwards that Mr. Dick had been for upwards of ten years endeavouring to keep King Charles the First out of the Memorial; but he had been constantly getting into it, and was there now.

From this comes the phrase 'King Charles's head' to denote a topic to which a person constantly returns for no discernible reason.

The Three Great Hierarchs SS Basil the Great (see *1 Jan.), *Gregory the Theologian* (see *25 Jan.), *and John Chrysostom* (Orth.) (see *13 Sept.); school and university holiday in Greece.

Baldhild or Bathildis, an Anglo-Saxon slavegirl who was sold into Frankland at the age of 5; there she rose to marry King Clovis II of Neustria and Burgundy in 649. She bore him three sons, who all became kings, and on his death in 657 acted as regent for the eldest, Clothar III, in whose name she attempted to unite the two kingdoms with the aid of her formidable mayor of the palace, Ebroin. In order to consolidate their power, they imposed churchmen loyal to themselves on sees previously occupied by local grandees; this aroused much opposition, requiring (we are told) the execution of nine bishops. Nevertheless, she is remembered as a saint, having formed important relationships with leading ecclesiastics such as Ouen (*24 Aug.) and Philibert (*20 Aug.), and founded the monastery of Corbie and the nunnery of Chelles, whereas Ebroin fulfils in French history the same function that Penda of Mercia does in English, of conferring sanctity on his victims (*20 Aug., *17 Sept., *2 Oct.). Among these was Baldhild herself, forced into retirement at Chelles *c.*665; her churchmen promptly joined Ebroin's opponents (see *2 Oct.). She is portrayed as a crowned nun, ascending a ladder (*échelle*) from Chelles to heaven; she should be considered as a suitable patron for the upwardly mobile.

On this day in 1540 (1539 English style) Evesham Abbey was dissolved; a monk wrote at the end of the newly installed Great Bible:

Deposicio Sancti Egwyny Episcopi fuit tercio kalendas Ianuarii Anno Domini 717 [see *30 Dec.] et Translacio eius fuit quarto Idus Septembris [10 Sept.] Anno Domini 1039. And the yere of our lorde 1539 the monastery of Evesham was suppressyd by kynge henry the viij, the xxxj yere of his raygne the xxx day of Januer at evensonge tyme the covent beyng in the quere [choir] at this verse: Deposuit potentes [from the Magnificat: He hath put down the mighty from their seat] And wold not suffur them to make an ende phillypp ballard beyng abbot at that tyme: and xxxv relygius menne at that day a lyve in the seyde monastery. The steyres and the towre wer xj schore yerdes in lenth the towre iiij^xx and ten and the spyre vij^xx.

31 JANUARY

pridie Kalendas Februarias   C

Nauru: Independence Day (from Australia, 1968)

(HOLY DAYS John Bosco (RC, CY commem.)

John Bosco (1815–88), founder of the Salesian Order. Having himself come from a very poor family, he found his vocation ministering to working-class boys in Turin, eventually setting up a residence and providing training in various workshops. A parallel order of nuns, Daughters of Our Lady, Help of Christians, was founded in 1872. Mexican youth came under his protection in 1935, at the height of official anticlericalism. Pius XII declared him patron of Catholic editors in 1946, and of Italian apprentices in 1958; John XXIII extended his patronage to Colombian and Spanish apprentices.

Birth in 1830 of James G. Blaine, a leading figure in the Republican Party after the Civil War and its defeated presidential candidate in 1884; he was described by a friend as 'the Plumed Knight' and by an enemy as 'the Continental Liar from the State of Maine'.

Eve of St Brigid (*Oíche Fhéile Bríde*), in Irish tradition the last day of winter; also known as *Lá na mBrídeog* (as it were, the Day of the Bridelets) from the little image of her set up in the house.

St Bride's Eve in Ireland

St. Bride's Eve (that is, the afternoon and night of the day before St. Bride's Feast Day), Brideóga (that is, images of St. Bride bedecked with magnificent apparel) being carried by the little girls of the town, as they go from door to door asking for halfpence, and getting them too, to make a feast for themselves, just as the urchins have the wren holly-bush, on St. Stephen's Day.

O'Sullivan, i. 217, 219 (1828)

No longer in the Roman calendar is the translation of St Mark, commemorating the transfer (by theft) of the saint's body from Alexandria to Venice in the early ninth century. It was a major feast-day in Venice.

FEBRUARY

February fill-dike be it black or be it white
but if it be white it's the better to like.

As the Day lengthens the Cold strengthens.

❆ NAMES FOR THE MONTH Latin *Februarius*, French *février*, Spanish *febrero*, Portuguese *Fevereiro*, Italian *febbraio*, German *Februar*, older *Feber*, Welsh *Chwefror*, Scots Gaelic *an Gearran*, Irish *Feabhra*

Februarius is derived from *februa*, 'means of cleansing', i.e. the purificatory and expiatory rituals of the month; but Isidore of Seville, or some unknown source, invented a god Februus, whom he equated with Pluto, god of the underworld; this new deity had quite a career in medieval authors (see *2 Feb.). The rituals are appropriate to the last month of the year, as is its shortness; moreover, before Julius Caesar's reform it was the only month with an even number of days (odd numbers being more auspicious; as Vergil put it, *numero deus impare gaudet*, 'God rejoices in the odd number'). It was also the month cut short every few years for the addition of an embolism (see *23 Feb.).

Down to the nineteenth century February was also called *Hornung* in German, properly 'the bastard begotten in the corner', and therefore (according to folk wisdom) of stunted growth; the Scots Gaelic name means 'the gelding', and an alternative Welsh name is *y mis bach*, 'the little month'. In Irish we also find *Mí na Féile Bríde*, 'the Month of Bridget's Feast' (see *1 Feb.).

February, the shortest month of the year, is reputed to have the worst weather: 'Feburier le court, Est le pire de tout.' Yet 'All the months in the year curse a fair Februeer', for rain and snow fill the reservoirs and ensure good crops: 'A Welshman had rather see his dam on her bier than see a fair Februeer' and 'Much February snow a fine summer doth show.' 'The Shepheards, and vulgar people in South Wilts call Februarie Sowlegrove: and have this proverbe of it: viz. Sowlegrove sil lew, February is seldome warme' (Aubrey, 9).

Lent begins during February in any year in which Easter falls earlier than 17 April.

❆ HOLIDAYS AND ANNIVERSARIES
First Monday
  USA, Delaware, Oregon: Lincoln's Birthday

Second Monday
 USA, Arizona: Lincoln Day

Third Monday
 USA: Presidents Day, commemorating birthdays of President Abraham Lincoln (12
  Feb.) and President George Washington (22 Feb.) (public holiday)
 Arizona: Washington Day

> And lastly, came cold *February*, sitting
> In an old wagon, for he could not ride;
> Drawne of two fishes for the season fitting,
> Which through the flood before did softly slyde
> And swim away: yet had he by his side
> His plough and harnesse fit to till the ground,
> And tooles to prune the trees, before the pride
> Of hasting Prime did make them burgein round:
> So past the twelue Months forth, and their dew places found.
>
> Spenser, *The Faerie Queene*, VII. vii. 43

It is now February, and the Sun is gotten up a Cocke-stride of his climbing, the Valleyes now are painted white, and the brookes are full of water: the Frog goes to seeke out the Paddocke, and the Crow and the Rooke begin to mislike their old Makes: forward Connies begin now to kindle, and the fat grounds are not without Lambes: the Gardiner fals to sorting of his seeds, and the Husbandman falls afresh to scowring of his Ploughshare: the Terme trauellers make the Shooemakers haruest, and the Chaundlers cheese makes the chalke walke apace: The Fishmonger sorts his ware against Lent: and a Lambe-skinne is good for a lame arme: the waters now alter the nature of their softnes, and the soft earth is made stony hard: The Ayre is sharp and piercing, and the winds blow cold: the Tauernes and the Innes seldome lack Guests, and the Ostler knows how to gaine by his Hay: the hunting Horse is at the heeles of the Hound, while the ambling Nagge carrieth the Physitian and his footcloth: the blood of Youth begins to spring, and the honour of Art is gotten by Exercise: The trees a little begin to bud, and the sap begins to rise vp out of the root: Physick now hath work among weake bodies, and the Apothecaries drugges are very gainfull: There is hope of a better time not farre off, for this in it selfe is little comfortable: and for the small pleasure that I find in it, I will thus briefly conclude of it: It is the poor mans pick-purse, and the misers cut-throat, the enemy to pleasure, and the time of patience. Farewell.   Breton (1626)

In foreign countries, February is remarkable for its time of Carnival, wherein the Genius of Good-cheer descends among his votaries, and stimulates them to continued exertions for the honour of his reign. Then it is, that the veteran cook must prepare for a long and arduous campaign. He must be as indomitable as another Charles XII., for he will have to stand under a *hot fire* for thirty consecutive days. But then during the hissing of stew-pans and roast mutton, he is permitted to cast a sheep's eye towards Lent, wherein he will be comparatively at rest. February is rich in excellent things, but we are sorry to say, that the demon EXCESS is then but too busy;— not so much at family parties, as at those scourges of every domestic tie, *club-dinners*, which admit, of course, the untender sex alone. It is then that *Koenig Gout*, and the *feu Abbé Apoplex*, make rapid advances over our destinies, and happy is he who comes off without a token of their presence.
 Yet how impossible, is it not, to resist the temptations to drive away the gloom of this season of the year, by even extraordinary enjoyments of the table, when, with a sharp appetite, we behold beef, veal, and ham, in their prime; game retaining its odour; and ducks, hens, chickens, and pigeons, with geese at their head, crying out lustily for the spit and the stew-pan!

This is truly *the* month of dinners, indigestions, suppers, balls, fun and confectionery. In this month, old, young, and middle-aged, all *sup*,—a ball without a supper is a fiddle without catgut.

The true hero of this month is the HOG. He appears in all forms, and protean as he is, is the admired of all beholders: *en boudin, à l'andouille, au cervelas, à la rezille de saucisse,*—and in a dozen other disguises, is charming; in short, he is the most solid, and, at the same time, the tenderest of friends!   Gunter, 134–6 (1830)

1 FEBRUARY

Kalendae Februariae   D

(HOLIDAYS AND ANNIVERSARIES USA: National Freedom Day, commemorating Lincoln's (legally immaterial) signature on the Thirteenth Amendment, abolishing slavery, proposed by Congress the day before; ratification was completed on 18 December

(ANCIENT ROME Juno Sospita ('Saviour'), goddess of Lanuvium, to whom Roman consuls made annual sacrifice. Girls took barley-cakes as offering to the sacred snake in her grove; if it accepted them, their virginity was confirmed and the year's fertility assured. In the late Republic temples were built to her at Rome, which by Ovid's day were in ruins.

(HOLY DAYS Brigid (RC Ireland; CY commem.); Ignatius of Antioch (RC before 1969; see *17 Oct.); Tryphon (Orth.)

Brigid (Brigit, Bridget, Bride, in modern Irish *Bríd*, formerly *Brighid*) of Ireland (d. *c.*525), abbess of Kildare. Brigid is one of the many saints of whose lives legend and folklore have far more to say than history. Having become a nun at an early age, she founded the monastery of Kildare (meaning 'Church of the Oak') for both sexes and ran it with hospitable (one might say housewifely) compassion, changing her bath-water into beer for the benefit of unexpected visitors, multiplying butter, and producing milk three times a day from miraculously obliging cows (her emblem is a cow). Her name means 'the exalted one', akin to the British tribal name *Brigantes* and the Welsh *brenin*, 'king'. A twelfth-century martyrology calls her *ard-ogh Erenn*, 'the high maid of Ireland'; legend represents her as a rich man's daughter, so supremely self-confident as to give away his wealth to beggars without his consent. She was also a friend of learning, for in her previous life she had been the Celtic goddess of art and wisdom whom Julius Caesar equated with Minerva.

Brigid is revered as Ireland's second patron saint; but until the late seventh century her fame outstripped St Patrick's. When in 680 St Wilfrid (*12 Oct.), exiled from Northumbria but present at the Lateran synod of Pope Agatho (see *10 Jan.), inserted in its acts a profession of orthodoxy on behalf of all northern parts of Britain and Ireland, he was recording a claim to metropolitan authority that the Irish needed to counter with alacrity; accordingly the hagiographer Cogitosus, finding a report that Brigid had been consecrated bishop 'by mistake', substituted an equal partnership in church government with the bishop to claim the metropolitanate of all Ireland for Kildare. However, Armagh recalled what little it knew about its own founder St Patrick, and wrote down a whole lot more, trumping a woman with a man, and a quasi-bishop with a real one (in the process also asserting superiority over the 'Columban family' of houses dependent on Iona). Nevertheless, St Brigid retained an honoured place in the new order, Patrick being said to have baptized her parents. She is the patron of dairy-maids, poets, scholars, blacksmiths, and healers; St Bride's in Fleet Street is the printers' church. Over her holy well in the City of London was built a royal palace that under Edward VI became a house of correction for vagrants (a serious social problem after the dissolution of the monasteries) and unruly apprentices; from this has come the generic name of 'Bridewell'.

Her cult has so completely displaced the Old Irish festival of *Imbolc* (later spelt *Oímelc*) that no memory of its ritual survived into medieval times, in contrast to the other three season-markers (see *1 May, *1 Aug., *1 Nov.), only the conception of this day as the first of spring, at which ewes were milked.

Tryphon, protector of vines and fields, killer of rats and caterpillars; his icons commonly depict him with a pruning-knife. On his day, the vineyards and fields are sprinkled with holy water and in some places blessed by the priest; in some places it is considered un-lucky to work, or even to pick up a pruning-knife. The prohibition is reinforced with the warning tale of a man who went to work on St Tryphon's day and came back hav-ing cut off his nose. (Cf. Pl. 3.)

Candlemas Eve, formerly considered the last day of the Christmas revels. *Poor Robin's Almanack* (1702) noted:

> When once is come Candlemass day
> Leave off at Cards and Dice to play.

Candlemas Eve, not Twelfth Night, was of old the time to take down the holiday green-ery. Robert Herrick (1591–1674) commemorated the ceremony as a time of renewal:

> *Ceremonies for Candlemasse Eve*
> Down with the Rosemary and Bayes,
>   Down with the Misleto;
> In stead of Holly, now up-raise
>   The greener Box (for show).
>
> The Holly hitherto did sway;
>   Let Box now domineere;
> Untill the dancing Easter-day,
>   Or Easters Eve appeare.
>
> Then youthfull Box which now hath grace,
>   Your houses to renew;
> Grown old, surrender must his place,
>   Unto the crisped Yew.

> When Yew is out, then Birch comes in,
>   And many flowers beside;
> Both of a fresh, and fragrant kinne
>   To honour Whitsontide.
>
> Green Rushes then, and sweetest Bents,
>   With cooler Oken boughs;
> Come in for comely ornaments,
>   To re-adorn the house.
> Thus times do shift; each thing his turne do's hold;
> *New things succeed, as former things grow old.*

Even as late as the nineteenth century superstition attached to the failure to remove every last twig:

If every remnant of Christmas decoration is not cleared out of church before Candlemas-day, there will be a death that year in the family occupying the pew where a leaf or berry is left. An old lady (now dead) whom I knew, was so persuaded of the truth of this superstition, that she would not be contented to leave the clearing of her pew to the constituted authorities, but used to send her servant on Candlemas-eve to see that her own seat at any rate was thoroughly freed from danger.   Chambers (13 July)

2 FEBRUARY

a.d. IIII Nonas Februarias   E

❨ HOLIDAYS AND ANNIVERSARIES Scotland: Candlemas Term Day (till 1990)
USA and Canada: Groundhog Day
Candlemas Day

❨ HOLY DAYS **Purification of the Blessed Virgin** (BCP); **Presentation of the Lord** (RC); **Presentation of Christ in the Temple** (CY); **Meeting of Our Lord** (Orth.); red-letter day

In accordance with Mosaic law Mary came to the Temple forty days (inclusively reckoned) after bearing Jesus both to be purified and to present him, as a male firstborn, to the Lord (Luke 2: 22 ff.). The commemoration began *c.*350 at Jerusalem, where it took place on 14 February, the fortieth day of Epiphany, combining Christ's Nativity and Baptism (see *6 Jan.), as still in Armenia; in 542, after the end of a plague, the emperor Justinian proclaimed it for 2 February, the fortieth day of the separate Christmas, in honour of the Christ child's encounter (in Greek *Hypapantē*) with Simeon and Anna. This remains its significance in the East; but when it spread to the West it was understood as the Purification of the Virgin and, like the other great Marian feasts of Annunciation (*25 Mar.), Dormition or Assumption (*15 Aug.), and Nativity (*8 Sept.), was enriched by Pope Sergius I (687–701) with a solemn procession. More recently emphasis has shifted to the Presentation, as the churching of women—their ceremonial readmission to church after childbirth—fell into disuse; the name of Presentation, not in itself new, was given official preference in both RC and CofE.

The popular name, however, still recognized in CY, is neither Purification nor Presentation but Candlemas (Latin *Candelaria*, French *Chandeleur*, German *Lichtmesse*, Irish *Féile Muire na gcoinneal*), from the candles carried during the procession and blessed to commemorate Simeon's description of the child Jesus as 'a light to lighten the Gentiles' (Luke 2: 32 from Isa. 42: 6); his canticle, the Nunc Dimittis, is sung during the procession around church before Mass. Preachers likened the wax, wick, and flames to Jesus' body, soul, and Godhead. The blessing was supposed to confer on the candles the power of warding off evil; even in the twentieth-century USA a maid asked her mistress one stormy Candlemas for permission to light a candle, which, having been blessed in church, would preserve her against harm (Douglas, *American Book of Days*). In pre-Reformation England women often carried lighted tapers at their churching; but the blessing of candles was forbidden on 6 February 1548 by proclamation of the Protestant Edward VI.

Catherine de' Ricci (1522–90). Born to a prominent Florentine family, she entered the Dominican convent at Prato at age 13, becoming prioress in 1552. During Lent in 1542 she began having ecstasies every week from noon on Thursday to 4 p.m. on Friday in which she recreated the events of the Passion; this went on for twelve years and caused great comment. At her urging, earnest prayers by the sisters finally brought the ecstasies to an end. Famed for her holiness and wisdom, she was visited by many, high and low, and corresponded with St Philip Neri (*26 May).

....

Candlemas Day. Many Christian feasts coincide with pagan ones, sometimes accidentally, sometimes deliberately, in an effort to suppress them. Starting from Bede's assertion that Candlemas was a Christian transformation of the month's pagan rituals, medieval writers invented a goddess Februa, mother of Mars, honoured by a torchlight parade that was changed for the better by Pope Sergius; or as Thomas Becon, *The Reliques of Rome* (London, 1563), has it (fo. 164ᵛ): 'Pope Sergius, otherwise called, Pope Swinesnoute, commaunded, yᵗ al the people shuld go on procession upon Candelmasse day, and cary candels about with them brenning in their handes.' Alas, Pope Swinesnout was not Sergius I, the institutor of this procession, but Sergius IV (1009–12), the cobbler's son Peter, nicknamed *Bocca di Porco*, who on being elected Pope changed his name from Peter to Sergius so as not to claim equality with the Prince of the Apostles (see *19 Apr.). Another fiction related this day to the abduction of Ceres' daughter Proserpine by Pluto, or 'Februus', through recollection of the torches used in searching for her. In fact, the Romans honoured Ceres not in February but in April; we may suspect a learned fantasy based on a false association with *cereus*, 'wax taper', and Ovid's story that at the Cerialia (*19 Apr.) foxes were let loose with burning torches tied to them. More recent writers have suggested that the feast was intended to supplant the Lupercalia on *15 February.

Candlemas is particularly rich in weather proverbs. It is widely believed that a fine Candlemas portends a prolongation of winter, a rainy one an early spring. This belief is found as far east as Crete, though elsewhere in the Greek world the Swithun principle applies: as the weather is on Hypapante, so it will be for the next forty days, or at least till the end of February. The day is known as the Miller's Holiday, *Miliarghoúsa*: the windmills stand idle, and in Crete it is said they will refuse to turn even if the miller tries to start them.

John Skelton alluded to the custom of weather prediction in 1523: 'How men were wonte for to discerne | By candlemes day, what wedder shuld holde.' From Whitby in Yorkshire comes:

> If Cannlemas day be lound and fair,
> yaw hawf o' t' winter's to come and mair;
> if Cannlemas day be murk an' foul,
> haw hawf o' t' winter's geean at Yule.

In Germany it was said that the shepherd would rather see the wolf enter his stable on Candlemas Day than the sun.

Groundhog Day. In the United States, a German belief about the badger (applied in Switzerland to the wolf) has been transferred to the woodchuck, better known as the groundhog: on Candlemas he breaks his hibernation in order to observe the weather; if he can see his shadow he returns to his slumbers for six weeks, but if it rains he stays up and about, since winter will soon be over. This has earned Candlemas the name of 'Groundhog Day'. In Quarryville, Lancaster County, Pa., a Slumbering Groundhog Lodge was formed, whose members, wearing silk hats and carrying canes, went out in search of a groundhog burrow; on finding one they watched its inhabitant's conduct and reported back. Of twenty observations recorded, eight prognostications proved true, seven false, and five were indeterminate. The ritual is now carried on at Punxsutawney, Pa., where the weather prophet has been named Punxsutawney Phil.

Snowdrops begin to come up about Candlemas, a harbinger of the early spring.

> *On the Snowdrop*
> Already now the Snowdrop dares appear,
> The first pale blossom of the unripened year:
> As Flora's breath, by some transforming power,
> Had changed an icicle into a flower:
> Its name and hue the scentless plant retains
> And Winter lingers in its icy veins.
> Anna Laetitia Barbauld (1743–1825)

Candlemas was formerly a Scottish term day, kept of old with much gaiety, including a football match; since 1990 it has been displaced to the 28th.

3 FEBRUARY

a.d. III Nonas Februarias   F

❦ HOLIDAYS AND ANNIVERSARIES Japan: Setsubun ('Season-boundary'; last day of
winter)
Switzerland: Homstrom; end of winter

❦ HOLY DAYS Blaise (BCP, RC); Ansgar (CY, RC)

Blaise (Blasius), possibly bishop of Sebaste (Sivas) in Armenia, martyred *c.*316. Till the
eleventh century he was culted on the 15th, but he was moved to the day after Candlemas because, while in prison for his faith, he was said to have been given food and light
by the mother of a boy whose life he had saved by removing a fishbone stuck in his
throat; the blessing of St Blaise (recorded in modern times) consists of placing two candles (gifts of the boy's mother) against a sore throat. In addition, he is said to have
healed and blessed sick animals while hiding in a cave to escape persecution. He is also
invoked against wolves, having forced a wolf to return a pig he had snatched from a
poor widow. One of the Fourteen Auxiliary Saints.

It is said that his tortures included laceration with iron combs; hence his emblem is
the wool-comb, and he is patron of wool-combers. One town in Italy, Taranta Peligna
in Abruzzo, still celebrates his memory annually by making 'panicelle di San Biagio',
which are stamped with the image of St Blaise, the child whose throat he cured, and the
mother. The production of the bread is a four-day affair, ending on the saint's day when
throats are anointed with oil by the priest, and the bread (by then largely inedible) is
handed out at the door.

A charm to extract items from throats:

Hold the diseased party by the throat, and pronounce these words, Blaise the martyr and servant
of Christ commands thee to pass up and down.

Advice on sore throats from *The Kalendar of Shepheards* (1604):

Good for the throat: Honey, sugar, butter with a little salt, liquorice, to sup soft eggs, hyssop, a
mean manner of eating and drinking, and sugar candy. Evil for the throat: Mustard, much lying
on the breast, pepper, anger, things roasted, lechery, much working, too much rest, much drink,
smoke of incense, old cheese and all sour things are naughty for the throat.

In Lombardy a more pleasant and much more readily available concoction is at hand
on St Blaise's Day. Eating a slice of panettone is firmly believed to protect against a sore
throat. All Christmas panettone being long gone, or too stale, the bakers have obligingly
responded to the demand and the shops are full of the festive bread.

Among the Orthodox (who cult St Blaise on *11 Feb.), this day is the Synaxis of Simeon
the God-Receiver and Anna the Prophetess; since in modern Greek *Simeón* suggests the
verb *simióno*, 'I mark', pregnant women in Greece avoid actions (such as use of sharp or
edged tools) that may mark the child.

Ansgar (Anskar) (801–65). Born in northern France near Amiens, after professing as a Benedictine, he was sent to Saxony and then brought to Denmark by King Harald I (himself baptized in 826) to convert the heathens. At first archbishop of Hamburg, his responsibility eventually extended from northern Germany to Sweden and Norway. His early successes in conversion did not withstand pagan invasions from the north. In 1914 he was named patron of Denmark (then including Iceland) and of Germany.

Werburg (Werburga, Werburgh), daughter of Wulfhere, King of Mercia, became a nun at Ely; subsequently she founded nunneries herself. She died *c.*700 at Trentham in Shropshire, but her relics were translated to Chester (see *21 June), of which she is the patron.

4 FEBRUARY

pridie Nonas Februarias   G

❮ HOLIDAYS AND ANNIVERSARIES Sri Lanka: Independence Commemoration Day (from Great Britain, 1948)

❮ HOLY DAYS Gilbert of Sempringham (CY commem.)

Gilbert of Sempringham, son of a Norman knight called Jocelyn and an unnamed English mother, founder of the only religious order to originate in England, the Gilbertine Order, at first for nuns, to whom were successively added lay sisters, lay brethren, and canons regular. The two sexes lived in separate enclosures with a sealed window between them, and used a common church with two aisles separated by a wall running from west to east. Having seen his Order through a crisis precipitated by lay brethren rebelling against their harsh conditions, he died on 4 February 1189, over 100 years old; canonization by Pope Innocent III followed in 1202 according to the new procedure of rigorous papal inquiry. The Order spread over the diocese of Lincoln, but not much outside it; a Scottish foundation failed, an invitation to Rome was languidly received. In consequence the Order, in steady decline after the Black Death, had no foreign branches to perpetuate its existence after the Dissolution of the Monasteries. The RC Church commemorates him on this day as well.

Veronica, legendary possessor of a towel bearing the face of Christ. Her name is a corruption of 'Berenice', the name bestowed by legend on the woman with an issue of blood cured at Capernaum (see *12 July); the story was blended in the West with that of the *mandelion* bearing an image 'not made by hands' supposedly sent to King Abgar V at Edessa (see *16 Aug.). Further legends were created, as that Veronica was dissatisfied with the portrait of Christ she had commissioned from a painter (some said St Luke), till Christ Himself appeared and imprinted His face on the canvas, which she then used to heal the emperor Tiberius of a grave sickness (in the oldest version, she is said to have painted the image herself). The most familiar story, however, is that she offered Him her veil as a towel on the way to the Crucifixion; the imprinted veil was itself called *veronica* (in English 'vernicle'; the name was observed to be an anagram of *vera icon*, 'true image'). From the eighth century an image of Christ as on a cloth was kept at the Oratory of Sancta Maria ad Praesepe at Rome. In 1216 the vernicle, later transferred to St Peter's, was authenticated, and an office of the Holy Face instituted; among its later devotees was Pope Alexander VI, who though a debauchee was by no means the atheist he is commonly taken for. It was lost in the sack of 1527, but recovered in the following year.

Michel de Montaigne, in Rome during Holy Week in 1581, was present at an unveiling of the relic at St Peter's:

This is a countenance wrought in needlework, of a dark and sombre tint, and framed after the fashion of a mirror. It is shown with great ceremony from a high pulpit, five or six paces in width, and the priest who holds it wears on his hands red gloves, while two or three other priests assist him in displaying it. No spectacle provokes such great show of reverence as this, the people all prostrate themselves on the ground, the greater part of them weeping and uttering cries of pity. A woman, whom they declared to be possessed, made a great uproar at the sight of this effigy, and began to screech, and twist her arms, and throw them about. . . . This display is made several times during the day, and the crowd which comes to witness the same is so vast that, as far as the eye can reach from the pulpit aforesaid outside the church, there is nought to be seen but an endless crowd of men and women. Here is the true papal court; the pomp of Rome and its chief grandeur lies in the outward show of religion: and it is a fine sight in these days, this unbounded ardour of the people for their faith.   Montaigne, *Journal*, ii. 150–1

Hrabanus Maurus, d. 856; the epithet *Maurus*, 'Black', was bestowed on him by Alcuin, whose favourite pupil he was, to match his name, 'Raven'. Having returned to teach at the Benedictine monastery of Fulda, he became its abbot in 822, and made it one of the greatest schools in Europe, becoming known as the instructor of Germany (*praeceptor Germaniae*); his pupils included the poet and theologian Walahfrid Strabo, abbot of Reichenau, the theologian and collector of classical manuscripts Servatus Lupus, abbot of Ferrières, and Otfried of Weissenburg, who composed an Old High German poem on the Gospel narrative. Hrabanus himself wrote many works of instruction, chief amongst them a twenty-two-volume encyclopedia, *De rerum naturis* ('On the Natures of Things'), together with poems perhaps including the hymn 'Veni creator spiritus'. At the turn of the century Fulda had possessed only thirty-five manuscripts; by the time Hrabanus had been driven to resign his abbacy in 842 for backing the wrong side in a struggle for the throne, the number was approaching 2,000, including texts in the vernacular. Having made his peace with the emperor, Hrabanus was created archbishop of Mainz in 847; in that capacity he held three important synods. In 1515 his remains were brought to Halle; but his more important relics, the books of the Fulda library, were mostly scattered in the sixteenth century or destroyed in the Thirty Years War.

On this day in 1475 died the papal librarian Giovanni Andrea Bussi, known in Latin as Joannes Andreas de Buxis (b. Vigevano, 24 July 1417). A learned man, he won the favour of successive popes, who unfortunately rewarded him with nominations to dignities that the powerful Sforza dukes of Milan were determined to reserve for their own supporters; unable to take possession, and therefore to enjoy the income, he was so short of money that he could not (he tells us) even afford a shave, despite becoming secretary to the scholarly philosopher Cardinal Nicholas Cusanus. His poverty made him quick to exploit the possibility afforded by the printing press of mass-producing classical and ecclesiastical Latin texts, and translations from the Greek. To be sure, the accuracy of the texts (taken from whatever manuscripts were closest to hand), as in other early editions, often leaves much to be desired; this afforded an excuse for rival scholars to deplore his commercial enterprise. Nevertheless, Bussi saw and met a need; the bibliographies of several Latin authors record his edition as the first, for which he well deserves his tomb north of the door of San Pietro in Vincoli, across the north-west corner from Cusanus.

This is the earliest date on which Ash Wednesday, beginning the Western Lent, can fall, when Easter is on 22 March.

5 FEBRUARY

Nonae Februariae   A

❡ HOLIDAYS AND ANNIVERSARIES Finland: Runeberg's Day (birthday of Johan Ludvig Runeberg, national poet of Finland)
  Mexico: Constitution Day (of 1857 and 1917); Felipe de Jesús, patron saint of Mexico City

❡ ANCIENT ROME Dedication-day of the temple on the Capitol vowed to Concordia in 218 BC by the praetor Lucius Manlius after he had crushed a mutiny and dedicated two years later; it overlooked her other temple in the Forum (see *22 July). Long afterwards, when civil war had been narrowly avoided, emperors would strike coins proclaiming the Concord of the Armies, *concordia exercituum*, perhaps in the hope of inspiring it among the soldiers paid with them.

❡ HOLY DAYS Agatha (BCP, RC)

Agatha (date unknown), virgin martyr at Catania in Sicily. One of the many martyrs who preferred death to seduction or marriage, her legendary fate, after suffering beating, the rack, and fire, was to have her breasts cut off. She is often portrayed with her two breasts on a platter, which, resembling bells, have caused her to be adopted as patron by bellfounders. She is invoked against diseases of the breast and is also patron of firefighters; her veil is imprudently asserted to protect Catania from earthquakes and eruptions of Mount Etna.

> Saint Agatha defendes thy house, from fire and fearefull flame,
> But when it burnes, in armour all doth Florian quench the same.
>
> Naogeorgus, fo. 38ᵛ (see also *4 May)

An Italian sweet, called Virgins' cakes, puts Don Fabrizio in mind of St Agatha:

He disdained the drinks table, glittering with vessels of crystal and silver on the right, and turned left towards the sweet table. Huge *babas* the colour of bay horses, like so many Mont Blancs with a snow-cap of whipped cream; *beignets Dauphine* speckled white from almonds and green from pistachio, hillocks of chocolate profiteroles, brown and rich as the top soil of the Catanian plain from which, indeed, by a long circuitous route they had come, pink *parfaits* [water-ices], champagne *parfaits*, dark *parfaits* that split open with a crackle as the spatula sliced them, airs for violin in the major of crystallized cherries, acid notes of yellow pineapples, and 'Triumphs of Gluttony', with the thick green of ground pistachios, and indecent 'Virgins' cakes'. Don Fabrizio asked for two of these, and as he held them on his plate he looked like a profane caricature of Saint Agatha displaying her own sliced-off breasts. 'Why ever didn't the Holy Office forbid these sweets when it had the chance? "Triumphs of gluttony" (gluttony, a mortal sin!), Saint Agatha's breasts sold by convents, devoured at dances. Bah!'

Giuseppe Tomasi di Lampedusa, Il gattopardo (The Leopard)

American Baptists celebrate the arrival in the New World of Roger Williams, who with four companions was subsequently expelled from Massachusetts and settled in Rhode Island; the five families formed the first Baptist community there.

6 FEBRUARY

a.d. VIII Idus Februarias   B

❦ HOLIDAYS AND ANNIVERSARIES   New Zealand: Waitangi Day (signing of Treaty of Waitangi, 1840, between the Maori and European settlers)
    USA, Arizona: Arbor Day

Accession of HM Queen Elizabeth II, 1952; red-letter day; the Union flag is flown

❦ HOLY DAYS   Paul Miki and companions (RC; CY commem. 'Martyrs of Japan'); formerly St Titus (now *26 Jan.)

Paul Miki and companions (d. 1597), first martyrs of the Far East. Miki, a Japanese Jesuit priest and prominent preacher, and his twenty-six companions, Jesuits, Spanish Franciscans, and laymen, were crucified during the persecution of Christians by the shōgun Hideyoshi.

Dorothy, martyred at Caesarea in Cappadocia (Kayseri) *c.*310. According to legend, on her way to be executed she was jeered by the lawyer Theophilus, who asked her to send him some fruits and flowers from paradise when she got there. To his shocked surprise, an angel brought him a basket containing three apples and three roses, whereupon he converted and was also martyred.

7 FEBRUARY

a.d. VII Idus Februarias   C

❦ HOLIDAYS AND ANNIVERSARIES   Grenada: Independence Day (from Great
   Britain, 1974)

❦ HOLY DAYS

Mel (formerly on 6 Feb.). Bishop of Ardagh, he was a disciple, possibly a nephew, of
St Patrick, by whom he was consecrated. He died *c.*490.

Richard of England, said to have died at Lucca in 720 on a pilgrimage to Rome; relics were
brought to Eichstädt *c.*1154. By the tenth century he had been wrongly supposed a king
of the Anglo-Saxons, though even the name seems strange for pre-Norman England.
For his children, see *25 February, *7 July, and *15 December.

The Great Frost of 1814 came to an end on this day. By then one of the traditions when
the River Thames froze was to set up printing shops on the ice. The publisher of
Frostiana kept a running account of the daily activities, printing up the book on the day
the ice started to thaw:

Tuesday, Feb. 1.—The floating masses of ice with which we have already stated the Thames to
be covered, having been stopped by London Bridge, now assumed the shape of a solid surface
over that part of the river which extends from Blackfriars' Bridge to some distance below Three
Crane Stairs, at the bottom of Queen-street, Cheapside. The watermen taking advantage of this
circumstance, placed notices at the end of all the streets leading to the city side of the river, announcing a safe footway over the river, which, as might be expected, attracted immense crowds
to witness so novel a scene. Many were induced to venture on the ice, and the example thus
afforded, soon led thousands to perambulate the rugged plain, where a variety of amusements
were prepared for their entertainment.

   Among the more curious of these was the ceremony of roasting a small sheep, which was
toasted, or rather burnt, over a coal fire, placed in a large iron pan. For a view of this *extraordinary*
spectacle, *sixpence* was demanded, and willingly paid. The delicate meat when *done*, was sold at
a shilling a slice, and termed *Lapland mutton*. Of booths there were a great number, which were
ornamented with streamers, flags, and signs, and in which there was a plentiful store of those
favourite luxuries, *gin, beer*, and *gingerbread*.

   Opposite Three Crane Stairs there was a complete and well frequented thoroughfare to Bank-
side, which was strewed with ashes, and apparently afforded a very safe, although a very rough
path. Near Blackfriars' Bridge, however, the path did not appear to be equally safe; for one young
man, a plumber, named *Davis*, having imprudently ventured to cross with some lead in his hands,
he sank between two masses of ice, to rise no more. Two young women nearly shared a similar
fate, but were happily rescued from their perilous situation by the prompt efforts of two watermen. Many a fair nymph indeed was embraced in the *icy arms* of old Father Thames;—three prim
young Quakeresses had a sort of *semi-bathing*, near London Bridge, and when landed on *terra firma*,
made the best of their way through the Borough, and amidst the shouts of an admiring populace, to their residence at Newington. . . .

Monday, Feb. 7. Large masses of ice are yet floating, and numerous lighters, broken from their moorings, are seen in different parts of the river; many of them complete wrecks. The damage done to the craft and barges is supposed to be very great. From London-bridge to Westminster, Twenty Thousand Pounds will scarcely make good the losses that have been sustained. While we are now writing, (half past 2 p. m.) *a printing press has been again set up on a large* ICE-ISLAND, between Blackfriars and Westminster-bridges. At this *new printing-office,* the remainder of a large impression of the *Title-page* of the present work is now actually being printed, so that the purchasers of FROSTIANA, will have this additional advantage.   *Frostiana,* 17–19, 24

8 FEBRUARY

a.d. VI Idus Februarias   D

❨ HOLY DAYS Jerome Emiliani (RC)

Jerome Emiliani (Girolamo Miani) (1481–1537), priest and founder of the order of the Somaschi. Defender of Venetian territory as an army officer during the war of the League of Cambrai, he turned to religious life, was ordained priest in 1518, succoured the needy, and *c.*1532 founded the Congregation of the Somaschi, devoted to the care of orphans; the name comes from Somasca, a village between Milan and Bergamo. Pius XI declared him patron of orphans and abandoned children in 1928. Feast-day formerly 20 July.

Mary, the former Queen of Scots, was executed at Fotheringay Castle in Northamptonshire on this day in 1587, after nearly twenty years of captivity and intrigue; much of Europe was horrified, much of England thought it should have happened sooner.

Then the said Queen kneeled downe upon the cushion, at which time, and very resolutely, and without anie token of feare she spake aloude this psalme in lattin: *In te domine confido, ne confundar in aeternum . . .*
   Then she laide herself upon the blocke most quietlie, and stretching out her armes and legges cryed out *In manus tuas domine* three or foure times and at the laste while one of the executioners helde her slightlie with one of his handes, the other gave her two strookes with an axe before he cutt off her head.   from Richard Wingfield's narrative, quoted in Murison, 26

9 FEBRUARY

a.d. V Idus Februarias   E

❨ HOLIDAYS AND ANNIVERSARIES Lebanon: St Maron's Day

❨ HOLY DAYS Teilo (RC Wales); formerly Cyril of Alexandria (RC; see *27 June)

Teilo (Elidius, Eliud) (6th c.), Welsh monk and bishop, founder of a monastery. He was widely popular in Wales, so much so that a miracle of multiplication was invoked to explain the existence of three bodies. His acknowledged tomb is in Llandaff Cathedral.

Apollonia, deaconess of Alexandria, martyred 249 under Decius. It is said in the Golden Legend that her tormentors first knocked out all her teeth, after which she leapt into the pyre prepared for her, much to their dismay 'that a woman was found readier for death than the persecutor for the torment'. Often portrayed with a pair of pincers, she was extremely popular in the Middle Ages—toothaches being no doubt a common occurrence—and is now the patron saint of dentists.

> Saint Appolin the rotten teeth doth helpe when sore they ake.
>
> Naogeorgus, 38

10 FEBRUARY

a.d. IV Idus Februarias   F

❦ HOLIDAYS AND ANNIVERSARIES   Malta: St Paul's Shipwreck (off the coast of Malta, AD 60)

❦ HOLY DAYS Scholastica (RC; CY commem.)

Scholastica (*c.*480–*c.*543), sister of St Benedict, the first Benedictine nun. Her abbey was at Plombariola, five miles from Benedict's, Montecassino. Gregory the Great reports that they used to meet once a year at a house outside the monasteries and converse on holy matters; on what she perceived to be the last visit, she asked Benedict to continue through the night, but he refused, for it would break the rule of his order; she prayed to God for the favour, whereupon a violent storm prevented the monks from leaving. She is commemorated in CY, and also in the Oxford Almanack. Scholastica is patron saint of convulsive children.

Charalambos (Orth.); protects against the plague. He is offered an apron or shirt woven in one night with magical spells by women gathered in a single house.

On St Scholastica's Day in 1355 a quarrel between the vintner of the Swindlestock tavern at Carfax in Oxford and some students who complained of his wine led to a three-day rampage of town against gown in which the rioters, abetted by the town authorities and reinforced by rustics, killed sixty-three students. Relations had always been tense, for the rise of the university had coincided with the decline of the cloth trade in Oxford as in other English towns; it is to this trade that the name of the tavern alludes, a swindlestock, or swinglestock, being the block on which flax is dressed. Up till the riot the Crown had attempted to balance the two interests, but thereafter the town suffered the consequence of having put itself so grievously in the wrong: not only do royal charters, in their tone and substance, show exclusive favour to the university, but until the nineteenth century the mayor and burgesses were compelled to attend a penitential service at the university church, St Mary's, on this day every year and present the oblation of 5s. 3d. (i.e. 63 pence) in memory of the murdered scholars.

II FEBRUARY

a.d. III Idus Februarias   G

❦ HOLIDAYS AND ANNIVERSARIES   Japan: National Foundation Day (commemorates founding of Japanese nation with accession of Emperor Jimmu in 660 BC) (national holiday)

Vatican City: Anniversary of the Lateran Pact (1929; independence of Vatican City and recognition of sovereignty of Holy See)

❦ HOLY DAYS   Our Lady of Lourdes (RC), commemorating the day in 1858 when Bernadette Soubirous had her first vision (see *16 Apr.)

Pope Gregory II (715–31), who won popularity by resisting imperial tax demands. When in 729 the Byzantines and Lombards combined against him, he entered the Lombard camp and startled the king into abandoning the siege and depositing his regalia at St Peter's tomb. He condemned the iconoclastic doctrine then rising into favour at Byzantium, commissioned St Boniface (see *5 June) to preach among the Frisians, and through his good relations with the Frankish Mayor of the Palace, Charles Martel, caused the Roman forms of service to be adopted by the German Church. He himself was an innovator in this regard, among other things supplying mass propers for the Thursdays in Lent.

Cædmon. At Whitby, this is the feast of Cædmon, who despite his Welsh name (Cadfan) was the first English poet whose name we know and the first to write religious poetry; he is said by Bede to have been an uneducated lay brother who looked after the monastery's cattle in the time of Abbess Hilda (see *19 Nov.), and would desert the party rather than take his turn to sing a song, until one night he dreamt that he was being ordered to sing about the Creation. He at once sang a brief hymn. On awaking, he remembered the verses; having reported his dream to the overseer, he was taken to Abbess Hilda, who ordered him to tell the whole story before a committee of learned men. All agreed that he was divinely inspired, and gave him a text to versify, which he did; Hilda thereupon persuaded him to become a monk and learn the whole course of sacred history. In due course he produced poems on Genesis, Exodus, the New Testament, and the Last Judgement; none survives, though later Old English poems on Genesis and Exodus exist. Having a premonition of his death, he made the end, according to Bede's narrative, that a good Christian should: cheerful, at peace with his companions, having made the sign of the Cross, with his last thoughts fixed upon God.

Among the Orthodox this is the day of St Blasius, pronounced 'Vlásios' in Byzantine Greek, who as in the West (see *3 Feb.) gives protection against sore throats and wolves. If in Greece one is obliged to work on his day, one should first sew a little cloth bag behind one's back and get a neighbour to ask what one is sewing; the reply, given three times, is 'I am sewing stone and whetstone, I am sewing up the wolf's jaw.' However, St Blasius has also taken over the duties of the Slavonic god of farm animals, called Vlas in South Slavonic languages, Volos in Russian; this is so not only in the modern Slav countries, but in Greece as well (much of which was formerly inhabited by Slavs). Villagers gather to eat communal dishes of goat or mutton, from beasts slaughtered in public in front of the church, and wheat cooked in butter and honey (on Corfu, watermelon as well). In Aetolia, women must not carry firewood on his day, and any beast of burden with a load will be drowned in the river by Vlasios Cattlestrangler.

There was an old folk-belief in Norway that Christ's Cross was hewn on this day, and therefore the axe should not be used.

George Washington born, 1732; until 1796, this day was often celebrated as his birthday instead of its New Style equivalent (see *22 Feb.).

Birthday of Richard Allen (1760), who in 1816 founded the African Methodist Episcopal Church.

In Iran this is the usual equivalent of 22 Bähmän, Islamic Revolution Day, commemorating the collapse of the Shah's government in 1979 (see II: *Muslim Calendar: Iran).

12 FEBRUARY

If the sun shines on St. Eulalie's day
it is good for apples and cider, they say.

❦ HOLIDAYS AND ANNIVERSARIES   USA: Lincoln's Birthday (observed on different days: see *February: Holidays and Anniversaries*)
　　USA, Georgia: Georgia Day

❦ HOLY DAYS   Formerly Seven Founders of the Servite Order (see *17 Feb.)

Julian the Hospitaller, patron of innkeepers, boatmen, and travellers (formerly on this day, now 29 Jan.). Probably fictitious, he is better represented in stained-glass windows than in liturgical calendars, but his cult was widespread by the thirteenth century. While hunting, the young Julian gave chase to a stag that turned round and spoke to him: 'Pursuest thou me, that shalt be the slayer of thy father and thy mother?' Horrified, he left home, and in a distant land served a prince, who gave him a widow in marriage with a castle for dowry. One day Julian's parents, long in search of their son, arrived at the castle. His wife, recognizing from their story who they were, settled them in the master's chamber and then went to church. Julian, upon returning home and finding a man in bed with, as he thought, his wife, drew his sword and killed them both. As penance he and his wife left the castle and set up a hospice near a wide river, providing transport across the water. One evening he admitted a half-frozen leprous beggar and, failing to warm him, put him in his own bed; thereupon the beggar rose in mid-air and announced that God had accepted Julian's penance. The legend was given classic literary expression by Flaubert in *La Légende de saint Julien l'Hospitalier*. Although Julian's wife, Basilisse, shared in his penance, she is rarely accounted a saint, perhaps because she had not shared in his sin.

> An housholdere, and that a greet, was he;
> Seint Julian he was in his countree.
>
> Chaucer, *Canterbury Tales*, General Prologue: The Franklin, I (A) 339–40

Eulalia of Barcelona, virgin martyr, reputedly crucified at 14 *c*.305; commonly taken for a figment based on Eulalia of Mérida (see *10 Dec.), but none the less patron of travellers and pregnant women, with relics in Barcelona and Wrocław.

In medieval calendars from Durham, 12 February is the day on which the birds begin to sing; but see *13 February.

13 FEBRUARY

Idus Februariae   B

❦ HOLIDAYS AND ANNIVERSARIES USA, Florida: Fiesta de Menéndez (founder of city of St. Augustine)

❦ ANCIENT ROME On this, the first day of the Parentalia, the senior Vestal Virgin performed ceremonies in honour of the dead. The festival extended to 21 February; each family gave private honour to its dead, and brought gifts to their graves. Marriages were forbidden, the temples were closed, fire did not burn on altars, magistrates did not wear official dress.

There was also a sacrifice to Faunus on the Isola Tiberina; but this day was best remembered as the *dies Cremerensis*. In 477 BC, when the Romans, at war with the Etruscan city of Veii, were being harassed by enemy guerrillas, the members of the Fabian clan had undertaken to pacify the border with their own manpower, by establishing a blockhouse on the river Cremera; after initial successes, they were led into an ambush and all 306 killed, leaving only a boy in Rome to perpetuate the line. However, a variant speaks of a great battle lost by the Romans, in which the many casualties included 'the 300 Fabii'; it is likely that the Fabii themselves were responsible for the usual story, which in retrospect contrasted the rashness of their forebears with the wariness of Quintus Fabius Maximus Cunctator, 'the Delayer', whose extreme caution, much criticized at the time, was credited with having saved Rome in the war against Hannibal.

According to some medieval calendars, on this day 'the birds begin to sing, and Hell was made'.

St Valentine's Eve

Last Friday . . . was *Valentine's* Day; and I'll tell you what I did the night before. I got five bay-leaves, and pinned four of them to the four corners of my pillow, and the fifth to the middle; and then if I dreamt of my sweetheart, *Betty* said we should be married before the year was out. But to make it more sure, I boiled an egg hard, and took out the yolk, and filled it up with salt; and when I went to bed, eat it shell and all, without speaking or drinking after it . . . We also wrote our lovers names upon bits of paper, and rolled them up in clay, and put them into water; and the first that rose up, was to be our Valentine. Would you think it?—Mr. *Blossom* was my man: and I lay a-bed and shut my eyes all the morning, till he came to our house; for I would not have seen another man before him for all the world.   *The Connoisseur*, 1 (20 Feb. 1755)

On the Eve of the 14th of *Feb.* St. *Valentine's* Day, a Time when all living Nature inclines to couple, the young Folks in *England*, and *Scotland* too, by a very ancient Custom, celebrate a little Festival that tends to the same End: An equal Number of Maids and Batchelors get together, each writes their true or some feign'd Name upon separate Billets, which they roll up, and draw by way of Lots, the Maids taking the Mens Billets, and the Men the Maids; so that each of the young Men lights upon a Girl that he calls his Valentine, and each of the Girls upon a young Man which she calls hers . . . Fortune having thus divided the Company into so many Couples, the Valentines give Balls and Treats to their Mistresses, wear their Billets several Days upon their Bosoms or Sleeves, and this little Sport often ends in Love.   Misson de Valbourg, 330–1

In Burns's song of 'Tam Glen', the maiden sings:

> Yestreen at the Valentines' dealing,
> My heart to my mou gied a sten;
> For thrice I drew ane without failing,
> And thrice it was written, Tam Glen.

Even married bishops had valentines:

13 [Feb. 1687]. I preached in the cathedral at Chester, being the first Sunday in Lent, to the greatest congregation that ever I saw, a sermon of Repentance. God give a blessing to it! Mrs. Chomondeley and her sister and his [*sic*] daughter my Valentine, and Mr. Warburton and his wife, and Major Car dined with me, and visited me again after prayers. I rebuked, as they deserved, Mrs. Brown, Mrs. Crutchley, Mrs. Eaton, and her sister, for talking and laughing in the church: and they accused Mr. Hudleston for being as guilty as themselves.   Cartwright, 32

14 FEBRUARY

a.d. XVI Kalendas Martias C

❡ HOLIDAYS AND ANNIVERSARIES   Bulgaria: Viticulturists' Day (Trifon Zarezan, 'Tryphon the Stabbed') (= Old St Tryphon's Day; see *1 Feb.)
USA, Arizona: Admission Day (48th state, 1912)

❡ HOLY DAYS   Valentine (CofE); Cyril and Methodius, Apostles of the Slavs (RC, CY; *11 May Orth.).

Valentine (3rd c.), martyr. In the fourth century, two martyrs of the name were honoured on the Via Flaminia, one at the second milestone, later identified as a Roman priest martyred on 14 February 269, the other at the sixty-third, near Terni, where he was later said to have been bishop. The two martyrs may be the same man, the bishop's cult having spread from Terni to the capital. They have no obvious connection with lovers, though in 1998 the Irish tourist board, *Bord Fáilte*, wishing to promote Dublin as the international capital of romantic love, asserted that 'St Valentine' had conducted weddings for Roman soldiers against an order of Claudius II (268–70) forbidding them to marry (such a prohibition had been imposed by Augustus but repealed by Septimius Severus) and when condemned to death cured the judge's daughter of blindness and sent her a letter signed 'your Valentine'. The tradition that birds began to sing about this time gave rise in the late fourteenth century to a belief, attested by Chaucer and contemporaries both English and French, that they chose their mates on 14 February; the association of this time of year with the spring renewal of fertility goes back to the Roman festival of Lupercalia (see *15 Feb.). This amorous behaviour passed from birds to human beings; in modern times it has been exported to other countries, even Japan, where it has mutated into a requirement for women to give chocolates to men, in particular their superiors at work. However, in 1994 the Holy Synod of the Greek Orthodox Church, observing that Valentine was a Western saint not recognized in the Eastern calendar, denounced his recently imported day and declared that if such celebrations of love were needed they should take place on St Hyacinthus' day (see *3 July); and in Germany, where St Andrew is the patron of lovers (see *29 Nov.), *Sankt Velten* is a euphemism for the Devil.

Birds mate on St Valentine's Day

> Oft have I heard both Youths and Virgins say,
> Birds chuse their Mates, and couple too, this day:
> But by their flight I never can divine,
> When I shall couple with my Valentine.
> Robert Herrick (1591–1674), 'To his Valentine, on S. Valentine's Day'

Choosing a Valentine

Traditionally, a valentine might be chosen for the coming year in one of three ways: according to true desire, by the drawing of names on the day before (see *13 Feb.), or as the first person of the opposite sex encountered on the day. The exchange of love-tokens came to be obligatory.

> Saynt Valentyne, of custume yeere by yeere,
> Men haue an vsavnce in this Regyoun
> To looke and serche Cupydes Kalundere,
>   And cheese theyre choys by gret affeccioun;—
> Suche as beon pricked by Cupydes mocion,
>   Taking theyre choyse, as theyre soort dothe falle
> But I loue oon whiche excellithe alle.

John Lydgate (?1370–1449)

> Tomorrow is Saint Valentine's day
>   All in the morning betime,
> And I a maid at your window
>   To be your Valentine.
>
> Then up he rose and donned his clothes,
>   And dupped the chamber door;
> Let in the maid, that out a maid
>   Never departed more . . .
>
> By Gis, and by Saint Charity,
>   Alack, and fie for shame!
> Young men will do't if they come to't,
>   By Cock, they are to blame.
>
> Quoth she 'Before you tumbled me,
>   You promised me to wed'.
> So would I 'a' done, by yonder sun,
>   An thou hadst not come to my bed.

Ophelia, in *Hamlet*, IV. v. 47–54, 58–65

Jesuit valentines, as explained in John Gee's 'Hold Fast Sermon' (1624):

Some Jesuites . . . upon S. *Valentines* day, chusing some female *Saint* for their *Valentine*; one takes *Saint Agatha*, another *S. Clare*, another *S. Lucie*, another *S. Catherine*, another *S. Cicely*, &c. I asked them what they meant to chuse such *Valentines*. They answered mee, that in respect of their *Vow*, they could have no *Valentine* that lived here upon earth: and in regard of their *Angelicall life*, they were to chuse *Valentines* in heaven. I asked them, whether they thought those *Saints* knew that they had chosen them for their *Valentines*. Oh yes, say they, we shall be honoured all this yeare by that *Valentine* wee make choice off, and she will intercede for us, and to some of us our *Valentine* doth appear in visible bodily shape, telling us what to doe all the yeare after.   Gee, 43–4

Valentine's Day in the Pepys family
14 [Feb. 1661]. *Valentine's day*. Up earely and to Sir W. Battens. But would not go in till I had asked whether they that opened the doore was a man or a woman. And Mingo [Batten's black servant], who was there, answered 'a Woman;' which, with his tone, made me laugh.

So up I went and took Mrs. Martha [Batten's unmarried daughter] for my Valentine (which I do only for complacency), and Sir W. Batten, he go[es] in the same manner to my wife. And so we were very merry.   Pepys, ii. 36

14 [Feb. 1662]. *Valentine's day*. I did this day purposely shun to be seen at Sir W. Battens—because I would not have his daughter to be my Valentine, as she was the last year, there being no great

friendship between us now as formerly. This morning in comes W. Bowyer, who was my wife's Valentine, she having (at which I made good sport to myself) held her hands all the morning, that she might not see the paynters that were at work in gilding my chimny-piece and pictures in my dining-room.

Pepys, iii. 28–9

St Valentine's Day Ball in New York City, 1832
This is S⁺ Valentines day, more like January midwinter than the genial days of Spring when the feathered creation pair. The Bachelors of this city give their annual Ball this evening being Bissextile or Leap Year, it will be Ladies own fault if they do not match themselves, for it is their turn, by courtesy to make advances to the Gentlemen. It is said that many suits are the results of this festive Ball, & many happy, I trust, marriages before the close of the year.   Pintard, iv. 14

Sending Valentine's cards
By the early nineteenth century the love-token had turned into a card, preferably with hearts and lace and sentimental verse, a fashion that has not quite worn out. Charles Lamb pities the poor postman staggering under his load:

This is the day on which those charming little missives, ycleped Valentines, cross and intercross each other at every street and turning. The weary and all forspent twopenny postman sinks beneath a load of delicate embarrassments, not his own. It is scarcely credible to what an extent this ephemeral courtship is carried on in this loving town, to the great enrichment of porters, and detriment of knockers and bell-wires. In these little visual interpretations, no emblem is so common as the *heart*,—that little three-cornered exponent of all our hopes and fears,—the bestuck and bleeding heart; it is twisted and tortured into more allegories and affectations than an opera hat. What authority we have in history or mythology for placing the head-quarters and metropolis of God Cupid in this anatomical seat rather than in any other, is not very clear; but we have got it, and it will serve as well as any other.

'Elia' (Charles Lamb), 'Valentine's Day' (1819)

In Armenia this day, not the 2nd, is the Lord's Encounter (*Teařnəndaraċʿ*), being forty days inclusive from *6 January. Like some other Armenian festivals, it Christianizes a pagan celebration: people leap over fires, divine the weather from the direction of the smoke, and take embers home, as formerly in honour of Mihr, the Persian god of light.

15 FEBRUARY

a.d. XV Kalendas Martias   D

❦ HOLIDAYS AND ANNIVERSARIES USA: Susan B. Anthony Day. Susan Brownell Anthony (1820–1906), having in 1852 reacted to her exclusion, as a woman, from a temperance meeting by founding the Woman's State Temperance Society of New York, became a lifelong campaigner for female suffrage; from 1870 the Anthony Woman Suffrage Amendment was introduced in Congress every year. She was also a radical abolitionist before the Civil War.

USA, Maine and Massachusetts: Maine Memorial Day (sinking of USS *Maine* and beginning of Spanish–American War)

❦ ANCIENT ROME Lupercalia, a festival of fertility and purification at which men, naked but for a wolf-mask and a loincloth, ran through the city carrying strips of goat's hide, with which they struck at passers-by; women hoping for children positioned themselves to receive the blows. At the end of the fifth century Pope Gelasius attempted to suppress it; the senate refused to comply, claiming it to be a harmless ancient custom with no pagan overtones. The stricter view was perpetuated in the Collect for the Third Sunday after Easter (BCP: 'Grant unto all them that are admitted into the fellowship of Christ's religion, that they may eschew those things that are contrary to their profession, and follow all such things as are agreeable to the same').

On this day in 44 BC the consul Mark Antony, who was one of the runners, offered Julius Caesar the diadem of royalty; only a few people clapped, whereas general applause followed Caesar's refusal. A second offer was also refused, to loud cheers; Caesar ordered the laurel wreath wound round the diadem to be dedicated on the Capitol. It was then seen that his statues had all been adorned with diadems; two of the tribunes removed them and imprisoned those who had acclaimed Caesar as king. They were hailed as new Brutuses, after the Lucius Junius Brutus who according to legend had liberated Rome from her Etruscan kings; at this Caesar dropped the mask, deprived the tribunes of office, and called them *bruti* indeed, meaning 'blockheads'. These events increased the pressure on the praetor Marcus Junius Brutus, the liberator's supposed descendant, to join the conspiracy against Caesar that came to fruition on the Ides of March, and to learn too late, when the Roman masses drove the murderers from the city, that the title of king had been more offensive than the fact of monarchy.

❦ HOLY DAYS Sigfrid (CY commem.)

Sigfrid, in Swedish Sigurd (d. *c.*1045), bishop of Växjö, apostle of Sweden. This English monk of Glastonbury, with two companions, was a missionary in Norway and Sweden; in the latter country he founded a community at Växjö and the first Swedish bishopric at Sakara, north-east of Göteborg. He is said to have been archbishop of York, which is not true, and to have baptized the Swedish king Olov Skötkonung, which seems impossible on chronological grounds. His relics were preserved in the cathedral at Växjö until their destruction in the sixteenth century. The RC Church commemorates him on this date as well.

On this day some calendars note: 'the Devil left the Lord' after the forty days' and forty nights' temptation following his baptism on 6 January.

This is currently the earliest date (corresponding to 2 Feb. OS) for the first day of the Orthodox Great Lent, when Easter falls on 4 April (22 Mar. NS), as it will next in 2010.

16 FEBRUARY

a.d. XIV Kalendas Martias E

❦ HOLIDAYS AND ANNIVERSARIES Lithuania: Independence Day (from Russia, 1918)

❦ HOLY DAYS Flavian (Orth.; see *18 Feb.)

Onesimus (1st c.); martyr. The Phrygian slave for whom Paul wrote the Epistle to Philemon, perhaps identical with the bishop of Ephesus.

Julian of Egypt, supposedly martyred along with 5,000 companions (*cum quinque milibus*) or with five soldiers (*cum quinque militibus*).

> The Snow that never drifts—
> The transient, fragrant snow
> That comes a single time a Year
> Is softly driving now—
>
> So thorough in the Tree
> At night beneath the star
> That it was February's Foot
> Experience would swear—
>
> Like winter as a Face
> We stern and former knew
> Repaired of all but Loneliness
> By Nature's Alibi—
>
> Were every storm so spice
> The Value could not be—
> We buy with contrast—Pang is good
> As near as memory—
>
> Emily Dickinson (1830–86)

17 FEBRUARY

a.d. XIII Kalendas Martias F

❦ ANCIENT ROME Quirinalia, in honour of Quirinus, the god that Romulus became when he was snatched up from earth during a sudden thunderstorm or solar eclipse while addressing the people at the Nannygoat's Marsh (*Lacus Caprae*) in the Campus Martius (commonly taken to be the site of the Pantheon).

Early Rome had been divided into thirty *curiae*, each of which had its own day in early February for performing the Fornacalia, or first-fruit offering to Ceres of toasted emmer-wheat. As the city expanded, the *curiae* were displaced by the new divisions known as *tribus* (commonly rendered 'tribes', but the Latin word has no implication of kinship, being related to Welsh *tref*, 'town'); as a result, many people did not know which *curia* they belonged to. They were allowed to make the sacrifice on the Quirinalia, which was therefore called the Feast of Fools (*feriae stultorum*).

❦ HOLY DAYS The Seven Founders of the Order of Servites (RC); Janani Luwum (CY)

Servites. The Servites or Servants of Mary (13th c.) grew out of a Florentine confraternity devoted to Mary. Originally monks, they adopted a rule derived from the Augustinians and Dominicans and became friars; the Order was recognized in 1259 and approved in 1304, and has a special devotion to the Seven Sorrows of Mary. Feast-day formerly 12 February.

Janani Luwum (1924–77), Archbishop of Uganda. His father was one of the first converts from the Acholi tribe. Having had no schooling till he was over 10, he proved himself a brilliant pupil, but being too poor for secondary education became an unlicensed teacher, saving enough of his low salary to enter a teacher-training college; here he discovered his vocation and was accepted at the diocesan theological college, being ordained in 1955. He studied for a year at St Augustine's, Canterbury; having successively been Associate of the London College of Divinity and Provincial Secretary of the Church of Uganda, in 1968 he was elected Bishop of Northern Uganda, and in 1974 Archbishop and Metropolitan of Uganda, Rwanda, and Boga-Zaïre. By this time Uganda was ruled by the increasingly unstable dictator Idi Amin, whose despotism was especially harsh towards Christians and murderous towards the Acholi. The Archbishop's attacks on the tyrant led to his death, and that of two cabinet ministers, ostensibly in a car crash; other reports indicated that the victims had been shot. In granting him a feast within fifty years of his death, the Church of England has acknowledged that his merits, and his martyrdom, are securely established without need of historical reassessment.

Theodore the Recruit (Orth.), who was executed in 306 for setting fire to the temple of Cybele, Mother of the Gods, at Euchaita near Amasea; also celebrated on the first Saturday of Lent. Promoted to general, he is also venerated on the 7th or the 8th. The RC date is 9 November.

In his *Memoirs*, under the date 17 February 1776, Edward Gibbon records his wonderment at the success of the first volume of the *Decline and Fall of the Roman Empire*:

I am at a loss how to describe the success of the work, without betraying the vanity of the writer. The first impression was exhausted in a few days; a second and third edition were scarcely adequate to the demand; and the bookseller's property was twice invaded by the pirates of Dublin. My book was on every table and almost on every toilette; the historian was crowned by the taste or fashion of the day; nor was the general voice disturbed by the barking of any *profane* critic. The favour of mankind is most freely bestowed on a new acquaintance of any original merit; and the mutual surprise of the public and their favourite is productive of those warm sensibilities, which, at a second meeting, can no longer be rekindled. If I listened to the music of praise, I was more seriously satisfied with the approbation of my judges.   Gibbon, *Memoirs*, 159–60

English copyrights were not enforced in Ireland, hence the reference to the pirates of Dublin.

18 FEBRUARY

a.d. XII Kalendas Martias   G

❨ HOLIDAYS AND ANNIVERSARIES   Gambia: Independence Day (from Great Britain, 1965)
   Nepal: National Democracy Day (anniversary of 1952 Constitution) (national day)

❨ HOLY DAYS   Bernadette Soubirous (RC, in France; see *16 Apr.); Pope Leo the Great (Orth.; see *10 Nov.)

Flavian, patriarch of Constantinople 446–9. Out of his depth in politics, he fell foul of the powerful court eunuch Chrysaphius and the Monophysite faction (which held that Christ had only one, divine, nature) led by Dioscorus, patriarch of Alexandria, and Eutyches, godfather to Chrysaphius. Deposed in 449 at a council in Ephesus, he was imprisoned for a time and died in exile; these proceedings, denounced by Pope Leo the Great (see *10 Nov.) as the Latrocinium ('Gang of Bandits' or 'Robber Council'), were quashed by the Fourth Oecumenical Council, held at Chalcedon in 451, which laid down that Christ had two natures, divine and human.

Colman, sent by the Irish monks of Iona to be bishop of Lindisfarne, *c*.661, championed the Celtic form of tonsure and method of calculating Easter at the Synod of Whitby in 664; after his defeat he resigned his bishopric and retired to Iona. He subsequently set up a community of both Irish and English monks at Inishbofin (Inis Bó Finne, 'White Cow Island'), an island off the west of Ireland; but when the English monks complained that the Irish had made themselves scarce at harvest-time but come back in winter to demand their share, Colman set up a separate English house in Mayo. Bede speaks in glowing terms of his 'inborn wisdom'.

On this day in 1478 Edward IV's brother George, Duke of Clarence, having been condemned to death for high treason (of which he was manifestly guilty), was executed in the Tower of London; contemporaries reported that he was drowned at his own request in a butt of malmsey wine. Although his quarrel had been with the Queen and her family, the Wydvilles, the main beneficiary was another of their enemies, Edward's youngest brother, Richard, Duke of Gloucester, the future Richard III, who thus became next in line to the throne after Edward's sons, and who in Tudor times was blamed for Clarence's death; but blame should be attached entirely to Clarence himself, who from calling the King a bastard and a necromancer had progressed to actual rebellion.

19 FEBRUARY

a.d. XI Kalendas Martias   A

❦ HOLIDAYS AND ANNIVERSARIES   USA, Kentucky: Robert E. Lee Day

HRH the Duke of York born 1960; the Union flag is flown

❦ HOLY DAYS

Mesrop Maštots ' (d. 441), a missionary to the remoter parts of his native Armenia, who in order to provide his compatriots with books in their own language invented a 36-letter alphabet (still used today with the addition of a few extra letters); he is also credited with inventing the 38-letter Georgian alphabet and a 52-letter script for the 'Albanians' of the Caucasus, who preferred to write in Armenian. His life was written by his pupil Koriwn.

Boniface (d. 1260), bishop of Lausanne. Born in Brussels, he studied in Paris and continued as a lecturer until his students went on strike against the masters, whereupon he moved to Cologne. Two years later he was appointed bishop of Lausanne, a difficult post where he met continual opposition; wounded in 1239 in an attack apparently instigated by the emperor Frederick II, he resigned and lived out the rest of his life in a Cistercian nunnery.

February
I am lustration; and the sea is mine!
    I wash the sands and headlands with my tide;
My brow is crowned with branches of the pine;
    Before my chariot-wheels the fishes glide.
By me all things unclean are purified,
    By me the souls of men washed white again;
E'en the unlovely tombs of those who died
    Without a dirge, I cleanse from every stain.
                Henry Wadsworth Longfellow (1807–82), *The Poet's Calendar*

20 FEBRUARY

a.d. X Kalendas Martias   B

(HOLY DAYS

Wulfric (Ulric, Ulfrick) of Haselbury (*c.*1080–1154), priest and hermit. A nearly contemporary biography details his life as a rather worldly priest with a love of hunting who became an anchorite, walled up in a cell at the parish church at Haselbury Plucknett, near Exeter. Supported by Cluniac monks, in between mortifying himself with fasting, wearing chain mail, and immersing himself in cold water while reciting the psalter (a typical occupation of hermits), he copied and bound books. Many visitors, including kings, sought him out for his gift of prophecy and healing.

The Year's Awakening

How do you know that the pilgrim track
Along the belting zodiac
Swept by the sun in his seeming rounds
Is traced by now to the Fishes' bounds
And into the Ram, when weeks of cloud
Have wrapt the sky in a clammy shroud,
And never as yet a tinct of spring
Has shown in the Earth's apparelling;
  O vespering bird, how do you know,
    How do you know?

How do you know, deep underground,
Hid in your bed from sight and sound,
Without a turn in temperature,
With weather life can scarce endure,
That light has won a fraction's strength,
And day put on some moments' length,
Whereof in merest rote will come,
Weeks hence, mild airs that do not numb;
  O crocus root, how do you know,
    How do you know?

Thomas Hardy (1840–1928)

21 FEBRUARY

a.d. IX Kalendas Martias   C

(ANCIENT ROME Feralia, last day of Parentalia; unlike the preceding days (and the Caristia on the 22nd), this was recorded on the official calendar, though the nature of official involvement, if any, is unknown. An ugly old woman, seated amongst girls, performed magic rituals to appease the Silent Goddess, placing incense in the mouseholes, casting spells over threads and tying them to pieces of lead; with seven beans in her mouth she roasted a fish-head sealed with pitch, pierced with a pin, and sprinkled with wine, the rest of which she drank, having given a little to her companions. The object was to bind unfriendly tongues so that they could not utter curses. The Silent Goddess, according to Ovid, had been a chatterbox of a Naiad called Lala or Lara, who told tales on Jupiter when he was pursuing Juturna; in revenge he tore out her tongue and packed her off to the Infernal Lake in the charge of Mercury, who ravished her, the offspring being the Lares Compitales.

❦ HOLY DAYS Peter Damian (RC)

Peter Damian (Petrus Damiani, 1007–72), cardinal bishop of Ostia from 1057; learned canonist and supporter of the radical church reforms, both moral and institutional, undertaken in the eleventh century by strong popes in alliance with the Holy Roman Emperor; dying in 1072, he did not see the breakdown of this alliance in the papacy of Gregory VII. A fearsome moralist, he regarded all sexual intercourse, even in marriage, as sinful; his *Liber Gomorrhianus* or 'Book of Gomorrah' described the fleshly vices of the clergy in such explicit detail that Pope Alexander II tried unsuccessfully to keep it under lock and key. Even clerical marriage, which till then had been widely tolerated, in his eyes constituted heresy; but not content with denouncing sexual activity, he imposed a penance on a bishop of Florence for playing chess, which he classed with dicing. His day was formerly kept on 23 February, the day following the night of his death; he was moved when St Polycarp of Smyrna was transferred to that day from 26 January.

The Oxford Almanacks for 1674–7, which gave every day a saint, marked this day as 'Sixty-Nine Martyrs'. These would appear to be the seventy-nine martyrs of Sicily (also claimed by Zaragoza) said in early martyrologies to have suffered under Diocletian; ten have been cheated of their crown by the untimely mercy of a misprint. Indeed, this was a good day for collective martyrdoms: the *Acta Sanctorum* records 71 at Amasea, 26 at Hadrumetum, and 19 'elsewhere'.

22 FEBRUARY

a.d. VIII Kalendas Martias   D

❦ HOLIDAYS AND ANNIVERSARIES   St Lucia: Independence Day (from Great
        Britain, 1979)
    USA: Washington's Birthday (now commemorated on Presidents Day, third Monday
        in February)

❅ HOLY DAYS **The Chair of St Peter, apostle** (*Cathedra Petri*; RC)

In Roman times this day, called Caristia or Cara Cognatio, not an official institution but a cheerful day following on the solemnity of the Parentalia, was marked by a contributory feast for the extended family, presents of fowls and other foodstuffs, and even tips for schoolmasters. The Church redefined the day as the feast of Peter's Chair, celebrating Christ's injunction to Peter 'Feed my sheep', equated with the pastoral function of the church as teacher of the flock; but as late as 567, at the Second Council of Tours, the complaint was made that people were offering mashed food to the dead, 're-verting to the errors of the heathen and after the body of Our Lord receiving meats consecrated to the Devil'. The spread of the alternative celebration on *18 January caused 22 February to be reinterpreted as marking St Peter's consecration as bishop of Antioch.

Because of this feast, early flowers may be named after St Peter: in English the cowslip may be called 'Peterwort'; in Welsh daffodils are *cennin Pedr*, literally 'Peter's leeks'. A German weather-proverb states that if water is frozen on this day, the ice will not melt for a fortnight; a variant in Norway raises this to sixty days. In fact Norway has many local traditions concerning ice on St Peter's day; one tale is that (never being the most patient of saints) he threw hot stones into the water to melt the ice (and hence that anyone who after that date fell through the ice was not entitled to assistance), another that if there was no ice he made it, but this was more commonly said of St Matthias (*24 Feb.). It was further held that the weather on this day would last four weeks, or forty days, or even all spring; but there would be a good harvest if the sun shone long enough to saddle a horse, or there was enough moisture on the roof for a hen to slake her thirst.

Washington's Birthday. The Washington family Bible at Mount Vernon, Va., records:

George Washington, son to Augustine and Mary his wife, was born ye 11th day of February 1731/2 about 10 in the morning, and was baptized on the 30th of April following.

When Washington was born, Great Britain and her American colonies still used the Julian calendar, and England and the colonies still officially reckoned the year from 25 March; he therefore celebrated his 19th birthday on 11 February 1750/1, but his 20th (after 1 January had been made the first day of the year) on 11 February 1752; had no other reform been made, he would have come of age on 10 February 1753—not the 11th, for down to 1969 English law deemed one to have attained an age of *n* years at the first moment of the day before one's *n*th birthday. However, the Act of Parliament that introduced the New Style from 14 September 1752 prescribed that a 21st year of age current at the time of the change should be assigned the same number of days as if the reform had not been made; it followed that Washington came of age on 21 February 1752, and celebrated his 21st birthday on the next day. Nevertheless, when his birthday, as that of the national hero, became a matter of general concern, it was sometimes kept on the old date; in 1786 a young Scottish traveller in Virginia, Robert Hunter, recorded in his diary:

Saturday, February 11
This being General Washington's birthday, the guns were fired in honor of it. He is fifty-four
years of age. We dressed in the afternoon to go to a ball that was given on the occasion . . .

                                                                          Hunter, 225

In the early years of the Republic the holiday was appropriated by the Federalists and
therefore largely ignored by their Republican opponents. An Englishman reports in a
letter written from Philadelphia in February 1796:

On General Washington's birth day, which was a few days ago, this city was unusually gay; every
person of consequence in it, Quakers alone excepted, made it a point to visit the General on this
day. As early as eleven o'clock in the morning he was prepared to receive them, and the audience
lasted till three in the afternoon. The society of the Cincinnati, the clergy, the officers of the
militia, and several others, who formed a distinct body of citizens, came by themselves separately.
The foreign ministers attended in their richest dresses and most splendid equipages. . . . I never
observed so much cheerfulness before in the countenance of General Washington; but it was impossible for him to remain insensible to the attention and the compliments paid to him on this
occasion. . . . A public ball and supper terminated the rejoicings of the day.

   Not one town of any importance was there in the whole union, where some meeting did not
take place in honour of this day; yet singular as it may appear, there are people in the country,
Americans too, foremost in boasting to other nations of that constitution, which has been raised
for them by his valour and wisdom, who are either so insensible to his merit, or so totally devoid
of every generous sentiment, that they can refuse to join in commendations of those talents to
which they are so much indebted; indeed to such a length has this perverse spirit been carried,
that I have myself seen numbers of men, in all other points men of respectability, that have
peremptorily refused even to pay him the small compliment of drinking to his health after dinner; it is true indeed, that they qualify their conduct partly by asserting, that it is only as president of the United States, and not as General Washington, that they have a dislike to him; but
this is only a mean subterfuge, which they are forced to have recourse to, lest their conduct
should appear too strongly marked with ingratitude. During the war there were many, and not
loyalists either, who were doing all in their power to remove him from that command whereby
he so eminently distinguished himself. It is the spirit of dissatisfaction which forms a leading
trait in the character of the Americans as a people, which produces this malevolence at present,
just as it did formerly; and if their public affairs were regulated by a person sent from heaven, I
firmly believe his acts, instead of meeting with universal approbation, would by many be considered as deceitful and flagitious.   Weld, i. 104–9

In 1800, the year after Washington's death, the Republicans made an exception; but the
decline of the Federalists allowed the day to become a national celebration. By 1832
Washington was firmly regarded as the father of his country:

[New York], Tuesday [February] 21st [1832]. Tomorrow the centennial anniversary of Washing-
tons Birthday will be splendidly celebrated in this city. An Oration by General Lewis in the
morning, & a grand civic & military Ball at the City Hotel in the evening. . . . Our *proud* City Hall
is to be brilliantly illuminated, a spectacle from its situation very splendid indeed bewitching. We
must contrive to let our younkers see it, that they may learn to revere the memory of General
Washington, 'First in war, first in peace, & first in the hearts of his countrymen'. What a gracious compliment from a British nobleman, I do not recall his name & title.   Pintard, iv. 17–18

On 22 February 1997 the people of Fishguard in Wales commemorated the bicentenary
of the defeat by local people, together with the Pembrokeshire Yeomanry, of a French

invasion force very much the worse for looted drink; several were captured by the local cobbler Jemima Nicholas, who had led a party of women to carry out manoeuvres on the hilltops. It is popularly believed that the tall black hats and red capes worn by Welsh women at the time caused them to be mistaken for soldiers. Nevertheless, news of the invasion caused a panic, a run on the Bank of England, and the first issue of £1 and £2 notes.

23 FEBRUARY

a.d. VII Kalendas Martias E

❡ HOLIDAYS AND ANNIVERSARIES Brunei: National Day
Guyana: Republic Day (1970)
Russia: Defenders of the Fatherland Day (formerly Red Army Day)

❡ ANCIENT ROME Terminalia, in honour of the boundary god Terminus who had refused to make way on the Capitol for Jupiter himself; at every farm boundary he received honeycombs, wine, and sacrificial blood from the households on either side, followed by neighbourhood feasts. Under the pre-Caesarian calendar, the intercalary month of twenty-seven days was added sometimes after this day and sometimes after the next, the remainder of February being suppressed (see II: *Roman Calendar*).

❡ HOLY DAYS Polycarp (CY, RC, Orth.; formerly 26 Jan. in West); formerly Peter Damian (see *21 Feb.)

Polycarp, bishop of Smyrna (appointed, Tertullian says, by St John the Apostle), entrusted by St Ignatius on his way to martyrdom with tasks to be discharged on his behalf, and teacher of St Irenaeus; a champion of the faith against Gnostics, he recalled how St John, in the bathhouse at Ephesus, on catching sight of the heretic Cerinthus hastily departed for fear the roof should fall in on the enemy of truth. He was martyred at the age of 86 to appease the howling mob in the amphitheatre, despite the governor's attempts at persuading him to recant. According to the report of the church at Smyrna, the earliest martyr-acts preserved, the flames formed a vault around him and left him unscathed, so that he had to be finished off with a dagger; such stories recur in later martyrdoms. The report joins the local Jews to the pagan crowd crying out against 'the destroyer of our gods' and present at the Games on a 'great sabbath'; this would be problematic even without the dating of the martyrdom to 2 Xanthikos in the calendar of Asia Minor = 23 February when Statius Quadratus was proconsul of Asia. Modern scholars have proposed dates between 155 and 177, but none without sacrificing some of the evidence; Eusebius' chronicle gives 167, when the date in both calendars was a Sunday.

The Martyrdom of St Polycarp

He had known John
and others who had known the Lord
but he was betrayed by a servant,

arrested late in the evening
at a farm outside Smyrna,
hens scattering in panic,
geese retreating angrily,
children peeping from corners
to find out who are heroes,
who are villains.

This happens around the year 155,
the arrest of an old man
who had known those who had known
the Lord,
had known John.

In the city
a crowd assembles for the games,
officials, wives, magnates, courtesans,
labourers, idlers, children, artisans;
animals baying, trumpeting,
the stench not a clean farmyard stench
but a festering stink,
the reek of a blood circus.

The old man and the proconsul converse,
they see eye to eye,
they are the only philosophers
within five hundred miles,
and able to bear their differences,
the Roman reluctant
to condemn the venerable man
whose honour he can see.

The old man shrugs, smiles

'How can I curse Christ,
for in all my eighty-six years
I have never known him do me wrong ...'

And the crowd is yelling,
                              'Kill him,
he is the one who destroys our gods ...'

Even the cripples and lepers join in.

The circus gods need blood or ashes.

So because he is commanded
the proconsul orders the burning of Polycarp

'and the flames made a sort of arch,
like a ship's sail
filled with the wind,
and they were like a wall round the martyr's body;

and he looked, not like burning flesh,
but like bread in the oven,
or gold and silver being refined in the furnace.'

He was like bread in the oven!
Like gold or silver in the furnace!

He turned the torture circus
to a fiery circus of joy, flames of the spirit.

But the cruel spectators did not clap their hands,
or fall to their knees, or say to the children,
look, there is a miracle, a man alive in the flames.

Did the people say, have our gods done such things?

Did they warm themselves at those flames?

The old man stood
with the flames flowing round him
like a weir of fire,
sailing in his ship of fire,
safe in his tent of flames

as the outraged crowd damned him.

At a sign from the proconsul
(curious in private life
about the supernatural)
a bored boy-executioner
braves the miraculous ark of flame,
pierces the old man's heart,
freeing Polycarp,
who kicks his corpse aside
and becomes a soul
and the crowd go on cheering,
children laughing, the rubbish gods ungrieving.

                              Penelope Shuttle (1947–   )

In medieval English calendars St Mildburg, abbess of Wenlock (*c.*700); it is said that
after her tomb had been destroyed by Vikings her relics were found after boys playing
in the field had sunk into the earth.

24 FEBRUARY

a.d. VI Kalendas Martias   F

St. Matthie
sends sap into the tree.

Saint Matthee
shut up the bee.

❡ HOLIDAYS AND ANNIVERSARIES   Mexico: Flag Day (anniversary of Plan of
Iguala, advocating independence from Spain)
Estonia: Independence Day (from Russia, 1918)

❡ ANCIENT ROME This day was the Regifugium, 'Flight of the King', commonly interpreted as commemorating the expulsion of the Etruscan monarchy by the native aristocracy and the founding of the Republic. This explanation is rendered doubtful by the
existence of the equally mysterious Poplifugium, or 'Flight of the People', on 5 July;
there was much in Roman religious usage that Roman authors did not understand,
partly because it belonged to an unsophisticated rustic past, partly because the Latin
language had changed so much since the regal and early Republican periods that inherited names and prayers were no longer comprehensible. Before Caesar's reform of the
calendar, the Regifugium fell on the 23rd of the intercalary month when there was one
(*a.d. VI Kal. Mart. mense interkalari*).

❡ HOLY DAYS **Matthias, Apostle** (BCP; RC before 1969, now 14 May, also CY)

Matthias the Apostle was the apostle elected to fill the place of Judas after his suicide:

Beginning from the baptism of John, unto that same day that he was taken up from us, must one
be ordained to be a witness with us of his resurrection. And they appointed two, Joseph called
Barsabas, who was surnamed Justus, and Matthias. And they prayed, and said, Thou, Lord, which
knowest the hearts of all men, shew whether of these two thou has chosen, That he may take
part of this ministry and apostleship, from which Judas by transgression fell, that he might go
to his own place. And they gave forth their lots; and the lot fell upon Matthias; and he was numbered with the eleven apostles.   Acts 1: 22–6

He is said to have been martyred in Ethiopia. Another story has him miraculously rescued from cannibals by St Andrew; his relics are venerated in the Benedictine abbey of
Sankt Matthias at Trier, having reputedly been brought there in the early fourth century
by Bishop Agroecius.

St Matthias Day in leap year. In Julius Caesar's calendar this day was counted twice in leap
year (see II: **Leap Year*). At law the regular day, *a.d. VI Kal. Mart.*, was followed by leap day,
a.d. bis VI Kal. Mart. ('twice sixth day before the Kalends of March') or *bissextus* for short;
but two Roman writers reverse the dates, so that the *bissextus* immediately follows the

Terminalia, giving the sequence '7th, twice 6th, 6th, 5th'. This became the prevailing order in the Middle Ages; as a result, when Western Christians chose the 'sixth day before the Kalends of March' to honour St Matthias, his day was normally postponed in leap year to the 25th. Although some churches (notably in Iceland) kept the 24th in all years, and in 1172 Pope Alexander III ruled that either day was permissible in accordance with local custom, postponement was the rule at Rome, and is laid down in the Gregorian calendar; it remained in force until in 1969 the feast was shifted to 14 May.

In England postponement, explicitly attested by Byrhtferth of Ramsey c.1011 and thereafter in church calendars, remained the regular practice until the time of Charles II; it was by mere inadvertence that the Oxford Almanack gave the 24th for 1680 and 1684. On the second occasion the error was pointed out by John Wallis, Savilian Professor of Astronomy in the University of Oxford; but in that year William Sancroft, archbishop of Canterbury, ordered that St Matthias should always be honoured on the 24th. This appears to have been a hasty deduction from careless drafting in the 1662 Book of Common Prayer (see II: *Leap Year*); but although according to Wallis (who pestered successive archbishops about the matter) he privately acknowledged his mistake, his order was never revoked, so that non-postponement became the rule of the Church of England. The ASB adopted the new Roman Catholic date of 14 May, which since 1984 has been the judicial red-letter day; CY allows either. The Oxford Almanack, after displacing St Matthias to 14 May in 1993 and 1994, restored him to 24 February, where he has since remained, in the leap year 1996 as well as in common years.

Weather proverbs state that if there is sharp frost on St Matthias' feast it will last for several days, and conversely that after his day the fox is afraid to walk on ice; for 'Matthias breaks the ice, if he finds it; if he does not break it, he makes it all the harder.'

Francis Mortoft experiences St Matthias' Day in Rome in 1659:

February the 24. Being Sᵗ Mathewes [*sic*] day wee went to Saint Mary Majora, where wee saw a head exposed in a Christal Cupp wᶜʰ is affirmed to be yᵉ head of Sᵗ Mathew, but whether it was or noe I know not. but it was much adored by yᵉ People. Both Priests and people praying to it. and happy was he yᵗ could get but his heads [*sic* for 'hands'] to touch yᵉ outside of yᵉ Cupp where in this head was. The teeth of it are perfectly to bee seen, & it is affirmed to haue yᵉ same flesh. Beard & haire as it had when Sᵗ Mathew was aliue. Here was also very good Musicke by some 8 or 10 Voyces to stirr vp yᵉ people to be yᵉ more deuout; and yᵗ it might smell the sweeter yᵉ Preist came and cast yᵉ smoake of ffrankincense against yᵉ outside of yᵉ cupp. In yᵉ Chappel of Paul yᵉ 5ᵗʰ were exposed the Heads of yᵉ 12 Apostles in siluer, with some reliques of Saints. as Armes, fingers, and such like things, and the Picture of yᵉ Virgin Mary which is affirmed to be drawne by the hand of Sᵗ Luke. was open & euery one might haue a sight of it to which thousands I thinke this day made there prayers, and all yᵉ place was full of Candles upon siluer Candlestickes. so yᵗ yᵉ Chappell seemed like a little Paradise.   Mortoft, fos. 61ᵛ–62ʳ

The Venerable Bede records that Ethelbert of Kent, the first Christian king among the English, died on this day in 616; since he gives the date as 'die XXIIII mensis Februarii', not with reference to the Kalends of March or St Matthias, there can be no mistake about it. Nevertheless, he is commemorated on *25 February to avoid St Matthias.

25 FEBRUARY

a.d. V Kalendas Martias   G
(in leap year a.d. bis VI Kalendas Martias, F)

❦ HOLIDAYS AND ANNIVERSARIES   Kuwait: National Day

❦ HOLY DAYS

Ethelbert (Æthelberct, Edilbertus), king of Kent (560–616), whose power, though challenged by the rise of East Anglia, extended as far as the Humber; the first Christian
Anglo-Saxon king. Already married to the Christian Bertha, daughter of the Frankish
king Charibert of Paris, he welcomed Augustine and his fellow missionaries in 597,
giving them lodgement in his capital of Canterbury and according them freedom to
preach; they used the old Roman church of St Martin, where Queen Bertha prayed.
After a while Ethelbert himself was baptized (according to tradition on Whit Sunday
that year, 2 June), and gave strong support to his new religion and its teachers; he
assisted Augustine to build St Saviour's (now the cathedral of Christ Church, Canterbury) and encouraged him to found the monastery of SS Peter and Paul, subsequently
renamed St Augustine's; his lawcode, the first to be issued by an Anglo-Saxon king, included a clause protecting the clergy. He died on *24 February 616.

Walburg or Walpurga, daughter of Richard of England (see *7 Feb.), abbess of Heidenheim south of Nuremberg, died on this day in 779. On 1 May 870 her relics were translated to a monastic church newly built in her honour at Eichstätt, where she is patroness
of the diocese; for this reason the night of *30 April is known as Walpurgisnacht.

In Julius Caesar's reformed Roman calendar, this was leap day, the *bissextus*; however, unofficial and medieval usage made *24 February leap day and counted the 25th as the regular sixth before the Kalends of March. In particular St Matthias was culted on this day
in leap year down to 1680 in England, and down to 1968 by the RC Church, which likewise culted the saints of this and the remaining days of February one day later by the
forward count, that is to say on the same Roman date.

26 FEBRUARY

a.d. IV Kalendas Martias   A
(in leap year a.d. V Kalendas Martias, G)

❦ HOLY DAYS

Alexander, patriarch of Alexandria (d. 328). It fell to him to deal with Arius, the ori-
ginator of the Arian heresy (that the Son was created by the Father); when persuasion

failed, he excommunicated him. The heresy was condemned (though not suppressed) by the Council of Nicaea in 325, and Arius banished by the emperor. In the Orthodox Church his day is 29 May, in the Coptic Church 27 Pharmouthi = 22 April OS.

The rooks and New Style

The 26th of February, N.S., corresponds to the day which used to be assigned for the rooks beginning to search for materials for their nests, namely, the twelfth day after Candlemas, O.S.

The Rev. Dr Waugh used to relate that, on his return from the first year's session at the University of Edinburgh, his father's gardener undertook to give him a few lessons in natural history. Among other things, he told him that the 'craws' (rooks) always began building twelve days after Candlemas. Wishful to shew off his learning, young Waugh asked the old man if the craws counted by the old or by the new style, just then introduced by Act of Parliament. Turning upon the young student a look of contempt, the old gardener said—'Young man, craws care naething for acts of parliament.'

Chambers

27 FEBRUARY

a.d. III Kalendas Martias B

(in leap year a.d. IV Kalendas Martias, A)

☙ HOLIDAYS AND ANNIVERSARIES Dominican Republic: Independence Day (1844, when Haitians withdrew)

☙ ANCIENT ROME The Equirria, a horse-race in honour of Mars, were held on this day.

☙ HOLY DAYS George Herbert (CY); Leander (RC; see *13 Mar.)

George Herbert, priest, pastor, poet (1593–1633); public orator at the University of Cambridge 1620–8, MP for Montgomery in the parliaments of 1624 and 1625; in 1626 prebendary of Leighton Bromwold in Huntingdonshire, in 1630 rector of Bemerton near Salisbury; author of many fine religious poems, most of which were published in 1633 as *The Temple*.

The Pulley
When God at first made man,
Having a glasse of blessings standing by;
Let us (said he) pour on him all we can:
Let the worlds riches, which dispersed lie,
   Contract into a span.

So strength first made a way;
Then beautie flow'd, then wisdome, honour, pleasure:
When almost all was out, God made a stay,
Perceiving that alone of all his treasure
   Rest in the bottome lay.

For if I should (said he)
Bestow this jewell also on my creature,
He would adore my gifts in stead of me,
And rest in Nature, not the God of Nature:
    So both should losers be.

    Yet let him keep the rest,
But keep them with repining restlessnesse:
Let him be rich and wearie, that at least,
If goodnesse lead him not, yet wearinesse
    May tosse him to my breast.

28 FEBRUARY

pridie Kalendas Martias   C
(*in leap year* a.d. III Kalendas Martias, B)

❦ HOLIDAYS AND ANNIVERSARIES   Candlemas term day (Scotland since 1990)

❦ HOLY DAYS

Oswald of Worcester, consecrated bishop of Worcester in 961, a position he retained for life despite becoming archbishop of York in 972; a reforming bishop, he founded the monastic cathedral of St Mary's, Worcester, where he is buried. He died on *29 February 992; till 1968 this was his day in leap year.

A PRINCE so dear to the church as *Oswald*, and so attached to the professors of the monastic life, received every posthumous honor that they could bestow. He was raised to the rank of a saint; and his sanctity confirmed by numberless miracles. His reliques (which were removed the year following by *Oswy*) were efficacious in all disorders incident to man or beast. The very spot on which his pious corpse had laid, imparted its virtue by the mere contact: the horse of a traveller, wearied by excess of labor, stopt here, lay down, and, rolling about in agony, luckily tumbled on the place where *Oswald* fell. No sooner had he touched the ground, than he sprung up in full vigor. His master, a man of great sagacity! marked the spot; mounted his nag, and soon reached his inn. There he found a young woman ill of the palsy. He told the adventure of his horse; persuaded her friends to try the same remedy; caused her to be transported there; and she instantly found the same benefit.   Pennant, *Wales*, 248

29 FEBRUARY

pridie Kalendas Martias   C

Leap Day. In the modern form of the calendar, which dispenses with the Roman names of days, this is leap day, inserted every four years to make up the difference between the common year of 365 days and the solar year; by happy accident the sequence of leap years inherited from the Romans coincides with years AD divisible by 4. Since the true difference is some eleven minutes less than six hours, Pope Gregory XIII ordered in 1582 that leap day should be omitted when the year was divisible by 100 but not by 400; the years affected, in those countries that accepted the reform (which Great Britain did not till 1752), were 1700, 1800, and 1900 (see II: *Modern Calendar: Gregorian Reform*). There will again be a 29 February in 2000, but not in 2100.

Persons born on 29 February are humorously said to have a birthday only once in four years; on that basis Rossini, who was born on 29 February 1792, would have waited till 1804 for his second birthday, since 1800 was a common year. In practice, however, they have birthdays in common years on the 28th. By the legal rule noted under the 22nd, anyone born on either 29 February or 1 March 1948 in England (though not Scotland) came of age on 28 February 1969; but since the Act that abolished that rule also reduced the age of majority, persons born on 29 February 1952 came of age on 28 February 1970, but those born the next day not till 1 March.

Western saints such as Oswald of Worcester who died on 29 February used to be culted on that day in leap year and 28 February in common years; this was a last relic of the Roman reckoning, which made the last day of February *pridie Kalendas Martias* in either case. By contrast, the Orthodox Church, which uses the forward count, celebrates John Cassian (see *23 July) on 29 February in leap year and not at all in common years, reputedly as punishment for being last to arrive when the saints came to ask Christ for work. In Mytilene this is the shirkers' feast, and Cassian holds the keys of idleness.

An old Scotswoman in the nineteenth century, asked by a small boy why this day occurred only once in four years, consulted the 'funtin-heid', her Bible, which fell open at Job 3: 3, 'Let the day perish wherein I was born', and deduced that Job had been born on 29 February; the Lord had not altogether abolished that day, but done what he could for his servant by suppressing it three years out of four. That was mere fancy, but we read in a near-contemporary that in the second century AD the Athenians gratified the multimillionaire Herodes Atticus—or rather yielded to his unrestrained emotionalism and much-resented power—by removing from the calendar the day on which his daughter died (see II: *Greek Calendar*).

29th February
A day added to the year,
laconic or luminous.

The extra day can be seen
and touched, like any other.

Its hours are not difficult to count,
the weather varies but is weather,
no alien manifestation.

Lovers who marry on this day
have the usual eggshell hearts,
the lewdness of fish.

Children born on this day
are as fierce as any others.

Those who die on this day
must find new ways of being,
and on this day
singing still builds
the upstairs room of the sky.

This is the day
the year keeps for herself
but offers to you,
her breath for yours,
fair exchange.

Penelope Shuttle (1947–   )

On this day, in England and Denmark, a woman has the traditional right of asking a man to marry her; compare Sadie Hawkins Day (first Saturday in November) in the USA and Sainte-Catherine (*25 Nov.) in France:

IOCULO: Maister, be contented, this is leape yeare,
    Women weare breetches, petticoats are deare.

John Lyly, *The Maydes Metamorphosis* (1600), sig. F 1

On 29 February 1504 there was a lunar eclipse, predicted by the great astronomer Johann Müller of Königsberg ('Regiomontanus'); Columbus, who took an interest in eclipses as possible indicators of longitude, when stranded on Jamaica during his fourth voyage used that foreknowledge to secure food for his crew from the inhabitants by announcing before the eclipse that the moon would rise dark and bloody in sign of God's displeasure, and declaring after it that his prayers on their behalf had been answered. Mark Twain exploited this story in *A Connecticut Yankee at the Court of King Arthur*, H. Rider Haggard in *King Solomon's Mines*.

30 FEBRUARY

There is no truth in the assertion by some modern (but no ancient) writers that Julius Caesar gave all the odd months 31 days, February 29 days and 30 in leap year, and the other even months (including Oct.) 30, but that Augustus upset the logical arrangement in order to make his month of August as long as Caesar's July. Nevertheless, 30 February has existed three times in the calendars of particular countries: once in Sweden, twice in the Soviet Union.

In Sweden (which at the time included Finland), 1700 had been a common year under a plan to introduce the New Style gradually, by omitting all leap days between 1700 and 1740 inclusive (see II: *Modern Calendar: Gregorian Reform*: Sweden, and App. I); however, 1704 and 1708 had been kept as leap years, so that the Swedish calendar remained one day ahead of the Julian and ten behind the Gregorian. The calamitous defeat of

Charles XII by Peter the Great at Poltava on 28 June 1709 Swedish style (which British and Russian writers call 27 June and most Continental historians 8 July) was widely blamed on divine displeasure at the reform, which was undone by adding a second leap day in 1712; this day corresponded to 29 February OS = 11 March NS.

In the Soviet Union (see II: *Modern Calendar: Twentieth-Century Reforms*: Soviet Union), a new calendar was imposed from 1 October 1929 in which all months had 30 days, with five extra days kept as national holidays; the first of these, Lenin Day, corresponded to 31 January Gregorian. In consequence 30 February Soviet fell on 2 March Gregorian in the common years 1930 and 1931; in leap year it would have been 1 March Gregorian, but before the case could arise in 1932, the equalized months had been abandoned.

MARCH

I dout that Merche with his cauld blastis keyne
Hes slane this gentill herbe

William Dunbar

March winds and April showers
bring forth May flowers.

⁋ NAMES FOR THE MONTH Latin *Martius*, French *mars*, Spanish *marzo*, Portuguese *Março*, Italian *marzo*, German *März*, Welsh *Mawrth*, Scots Gaelic *am Màrt*, Irish *Márta*

Martius is named after Mars, the god of war (the campaigning season began in the spring) who was also an agricultural deity. It was originally the first month of the Roman year, a conception that remained available for poets who wished to use it.

An Old English name for March, *Hlўda* (probably related to 'loud', from the roaring March winds (see Pl. 4)), long survived as *Lide*. For Ælfric (see *18 Mar.) it was normal amongst the laity; John Aubrey says (*Remaines*, 13): 'The vulgar in the West of England doe call the month of March, Lide', citing a 'proverbiall rhythme' (i.e. rhyme):

> Eat Leekes in Lide, and Ramsins in May,
> And all the year after Physicians may play.

('play' = be idle, unemployed, a sense still found in northern England)

The name was still used in nineteenth-century Cornwall, where it was said: 'Ducks wan't lay till they've drink'd lide water.'

⁋ HOLIDAYS AND ANNIVERSARIES

First Monday Swaziland: Commonwealth Day
   USA, Illinois: Casimir Pulaski's Birthday (Polish patriot who went to America in 1777 to fight with Washington in the American Revolution; he died a hero in 1779)

Second Monday UK: Commonwealth Day (until 1958, Empire Day); the Union flag is flown

Fourth Monday Taiwan: Youth Day

Last Monday USA, Alaska: Seward's Day (Secretary of State under Lincoln and Andrew Johnson; negotiated the purchase of Alaska from Russia in 1867)
   USA, Virgin Islands: Transfer Day (purchase by USA from Denmark, 1917)

First Tuesday USA, Vermont: Town Meeting Day

Second Saturday Zambia: Youth Day

In the United Kingdom and much of Western Europe, Summer Time begins on the last Sunday in March.

> These [the seasons], marching softly, thus in order went,
>   And after them, the Monthes all riding came;
>   First, sturdy *March* with brows full sternly bent,
>   And armed strongly, rode vpon a Ram,
>   The same which ouer *Hellespontus* swam:
>   Yet in his hand a spade he also hent,
>   And in a bag all sorts of seeds ysame,
>   Which on the earth he strowed as he went,
> And fild her womb with fruitfull hope of nourishment.
>
> Spenser, *The Faerie Queene*, VII. vii. 32

A whole number of weather proverbs say that dry, windy weather in March will bode well for the spring. But March weather is very unpredictable:

February makes a bridge and March breaks it.

March hack ham comes in like a lion, goes out like a lamb.

('hack ham' = hackande, 'annoying')

> And now to mynde there is one olde prouerbe come:
> 'One bushell of March dust is worth a kynges raunsome.'
> John Heywood, *Play of the Weather* (1533), ll. 620–1

It is the destiny of proverbs to be endlessly repeated, rarely questioned. Thomas Fuller (1662) proves an exception:

Not so in Southern sandy Counties, where a dry *March* is as destructive, as here it is beneficial. How much a King's randsom amounteth unto, *England* knows by dear experience, when paying *one hundred thousand* pounds to redeem *Richard* the first, which was shared between the *German* Emperor and *Leopoldus* duke of *Austria*. Indeed a general good redounds to our Land by a dry *March*, for if our clay-grounds be over-drowned in that moneth, they recover not their distemper that year.

However, this *proverb* presumeth seasonable showers in *April* following, or otherwise *March-dust* will be turned into *May-ashes*, to the burning up of grass and grain; so easily can God blast the most probable fruitfulness.   Fuller, *Worthies*, 87

An Irish name for March is *mí na (bó) riaibhche*, 'the month of the brindled cow':

the legend is that the brindled cow complained at the dawn of April of the harshness of March, whereupon March borrowed a few days from April and these were so wet and stormy that the *bó riabhach* was drowned, hence March has a day more than April, and the borrowed days are called *laethanta na riaibhche*.   Dinneen, s.v. *riabhach*

Other versions of this legend assign the days to April but their weather to March: see *1 April.

The proverbial expression 'Mad as a March hare' has nothing to do with weather; March is the breeding season.

It is now March, and the Northerne wind dryeth vp the Southerne durt: The tender Lippes are now maskt for feare of chopping, and the faire hands must not be vngloued: now riseth the Sunne a pretty step to his faire height, and Saint Valentine calls the birds together, where Nature is pleased in the varietie of loue: the Fishes and the Frogs fall to their manner of generation, and the Adder dyes to bring forth her young: the Ayre is sharpe, but the Sunne is comfortable, and the day beginnes to lengthen: The forward Gardens giue the fine Sallets, and a Nosegay of Violets is a present for a Lady: Now beginneth Nature (as it were) to wake out of her sleepe, and sends the Traueller to suruey the walkes of the World: the sucking Rabbit is good for weake stomackes, and the dyet for the Rhume doth many a great Cure: The Farrier now is the horses Physitian, and the fat Dog feeds the Faulcon in the Mew: The Tree begins to bud, and the grasse to peepe abroad, while the Thrush with the Black-bird make a charme in the young Springs: the Milke-mayd with her best beloued, talke away wearinesse to the Market, and in an honest meaning, kind words doe no hurt: the Foot-ball now tryeth the legges of strength, and merry matches continue good fellowship: It is a time of much worke, and tedious to discourse of: but in all I find of it, I thus conclude in it: I hold it the Seruant of Nature, and the Schoole-master of Art: the hope of labour, and the Subiect of Reason. Farewell.   Breton (1626)

1 MARCH

Kalendae Martiae   D

> March, various, fierce, and wild, with wind-crack'd cheeks,
> By wilder Welchman led, and crown'd with leeks!
>   Churchill, 'Gotham', iii. 101

> *Upon Saint David's Day*
> *put oats and barley in the clay.*

❨ HOLIDAYS AND ANNIVERSARIES Bosnia-Hercegovina: National Day (anniversary of 1992 declaration of independence)
   USA, Nebraska: Admission Day (37th state, 1867)
   USA, Ohio: Admission Day (17th state, 1803)

❨ ANCIENT ROME This was originally the first day of the Roman year, still marked in classical times by tending of the sacred fire of the goddess Vesta, and the affixing of fresh laurels to the Regia (the home of the *pontifex maximus*, said to have been King Numa's), the houses of the *flamines* (priests of particular deities), and the Curiae Veteres (centre of the ancient *curiae*, see *17 Feb.). The Leaping Priests or Salii performed a procession in honour of Mars, chanting a hymn too archaic for Romans to understand, and carrying figure-of-eight shields called *ancilia* (see *14 Mar.). It was also the feast of Juno Lucina, the goddess of childbirth, the married women's festival, the Matronalia, on which they received presents and special attentions from their husbands, although Gaius Laelius came late to dinner because he had been busy writing a scene for his friend Terence; this Laelius was known as Sapiens, 'the Wise', after backing away from a controversial proposal for a secret ballot. Contrariwise, the bachelor Horace invites his friend and patron Maecenas to join him in celebrating it as the day on which he had narrowly escaped a falling tree.

❦ HOLY DAYS David (CofE, RC Wales and England)

David, patron saint of Wales; always Dewi in Welsh, whereas the biblical king is Dafydd. His day (Dydd Dewi) is the national day, and a red-letter day, but on the civil, not the ecclesiastical calendar. (In Wales the Union flag is flown.) Although there are references to him from the eighth century onwards, his life dates from *c*.1090, being written in order to show that the see of St David's was independent of Canterbury; it makes him the son of one Sanctus (Sant) prince of Cardigan (Ceredigion), who raped a woman called Nonna (Non: *3 Mar.); that these names mean respectively 'saint' and 'nun' does not assist belief. It also assigns him 147 years of life, which the Bollandists emended to 97, specifically from late 446 to early 544, citing evidence that St Teilo (see *9 Feb.), who consecrated his successor, was dead by 560; the tradition that he died in 601 is no more reliable than the tale that he bade his people wear leeks in battle to distinguish them from the Saxon enemy, thereby making it a national emblem. More probably the leek, an emblem of Wales, is associated with St David and his day because it is proverbially good to eat at this time (see the proverb quoted earlier).

On the eve of St David's Day 1997, bones discovered in the nineteenth century and popularly believed to be his relics were found to be too recent; the favoured candidate is now St Caradog (see *13 Apr.).

Pope Felix II (483–96), a rigid disciplinarian who in 484 excommunicated the emperor Zeno and patriarch Acacius of Constantinople for refusing to do his bidding in matters arising from the Christological arguments of the day (see *10 Mar.). Acacius responded to his excommunication by omitting the Pope's name from the 'diptychs', or list of persons publicly prayed for; in turn, even after the patriarch's death, Felix refused to make peace so long as Acacius' name was included in them; the schism was not ended till 519.

This day was the official beginning of the year in Venice, and in Russia down to the fourteenth century; it was also (reckoned in Old Style) the first month of the Ottoman financial year (see II: *Muslim Calendar: Turkey*). The Franks counted the year from it, so long as they kept their ancient annual muster then, but ceased to do so when the custom was abandoned in the eighth century.

The Greeks regard 1 March as the first day of fine weather. A 'March-thread' is left out overnight on a rosebush, then worn on the wrist or the great toe typically until Easter Day, after which it is returned to the bush; it is supposed to protect the wearer. St John Chrysostom complains of the red thread and other amulets (including bells) hung on children to protect them; woollen threads to ward off evil were worn by the initiates in the Eleusinian Mysteries at Athens. (A similar custom was observed in China in the fifth lunar month.) In the Dodecanese and elsewhere children go round with an effigy of a swallow, singing a song in honour of the bird and the fine weather it brings, and begging food at each house; this perpetuates a custom attested for ancient Rhodes. On the other hand the first three days of March are also known as 'sharp days': one should not wash clothes, for they will wear out, nor chop wood, for it will rot, nor bathe, for one's hair will fall out.

William Prynne, in his vehement invective against playgoing, *Histrio-Mastix: The Players Scourge, or, Actors Tragædie* (London, 1633), quotes the following from what he calls 'the sixteenth Play-condemning Councell . . . the sixth Councell of Constantinople, Anno Domini 680' (pp. 583–4):

Can. 62. Those things that are called Kalends, and those that are named winter wishes (*vota brumalia*), and that meeting which is made upon the first day of March, wee will shall bee wholly taken away out of the Citty of the faithfull: as also we wholly forbid and expell the publike dancing of women bringing much hurt and destruction: and likewise those dances and mysteries that are made in the name of those, who are falsly named Gods among the Graecians, or in the name of men and women, after the ancient manner, farre differing from the life of Christians: ordaining that no man shall henceforth bee clothed in womans apparell, nor no woman in mans aray. Neither may any one put on comicall, satyricall or tragicall vizards in Enterludes, neither may they invocate the name of execrable Bacchus, when as they presse their grapes in winepresses; neither pouring out wine in tubbes, may they provoke laughter, exercising those things through ignorance or vanity which proceed from the imposture of the Divel.

In Devon the first three days in March were called 'blind days'; so unlucky were they considered that no farmer would sow seed on any of the three.

St David's Day. Wearing of leeks on St David's Day:

FLUELLEN. Your grandfather of famous memory, an't please your majesty, and your great-uncle, Edward the Plack Prince of Wales, as I have read in the chronicles, fought a most prave pattle here in France.
KING HARRY. They did, Fluellen.
FLUELLEN. Your majesty says very true. If your majesties is remembered of it, the Welshmen did good service in a garden where leeks did grow, wearing leeks in their Monmouth caps, which your majesty know to this hour is an honourable badge of the service. And I do believe your majesty takes no scorn to wear the leek upon Saint Tavy's Day.
KING HARRY. I wear it for a memorable honour,
For I am Welsh, you know, good countryman.   *Henry V,* IV. vii. 90–103

William Schellinks, a visiting Dutchman, witnesses St David's Day in London in 1662:

On the first of March old style, being St. David's Day, the day of the patron saint of Wales, when according to ancient custom, all people born in that principality put a leek in the band of their hats. That is supposed to be in memory of a battle fought and won by them on St. David's Day, in which they wore them as a mark to distinguish themselves from their enemies. So His Majesty and many great Lords and gentlemen, common people, and even lackeys, coachmen, porters, and all kinds of riff-raff and layabouts wear one on their hats.

NB. The office to fix the leek to the King's hat on this day is worth 600 guilders.

We saw some countryfolk carry such large leeks on their hats that their heads hung almost sideways because of them. And so on this day the Welshmen are greatly teased by the English, not only by calling after them Taffey, Taffey, or David, David, but also by hanging out all kinds of dolls and scarecrows with leeks on their heads, and as they celebrate the day with heavy booz-ing, and both sides, from the ale, strong beer, sack and claret, become short-tempered, obstinate, and wild, so it is not often that this day goes by without mishaps, and without one or the other getting into an argument or a blood fight. Thus it happened this year that near Westminster a Welsh nobleman stabbed an Englishman. So too an English cook, who, for fun, stuck a leek on his hat and addressed, as a fellow countryman, a great lord, a Welshman, who passed by with his suite, who responded in Welsh, which is as different from English as French is from Dutch. When the cook replied sneeringly in English, the lord went for him, the cook fled into his shop and grabbed a spit from the fire and with this attacked the Welshman, who, supported by his ser-vants with their rapiers, all turned against the cook, who was immediately helped by all sorts of rabble, throwing dirt and other things, so that in the end he was compelled to retreat, and, the furore getting greater, he was forced to take to the water, and, although he had got help, the mob, fighting furiously, got into the boat, and if His Majesty had not sent help quickly by water, they could easily have been killed.   Schellinks, 75

2 MARCH

a.d. VI Nonas Martias   E

> On Saint Valentine's Day cast beans in clay
> But on Saint Chad sow good and bad.

❦ HOLIDAYS AND ANNIVERSARIES   USA, Texas: Texas Independence Day (from Mexico, 1836)

❦ HOLY DAYS   Chad (CofE)

Chad, in Old English Ceadda, pronounced Chad-da (d. 672), first bishop of Mercia and Lindsey at Lichfield; brother of St Cedd (see *26 Oct.). Irregularly consecrated bishop of York during St Wilfrid's absence (see *12 Oct.), he was deprived by Archbishop Theodore (*19 Sept.), but given the consolation prize of Lichfield, where he founded a monastery. Veneration as a saint began soon after his death; in Ireland St Egbert (see *24 Apr.) reported a vision of Chad's soul escorted to heaven by Cedd and a column of angels. He is patron saint of medicinal springs; St Chad's Well, in Lichfield, is so named from the stone in the bottom, 'on which, some say, St Chad was wont, naked, to stand in the water and pray'. Not inappropriately, Lichfield was the home of Sir John Floyer, author of *An Essay to Prove Cold Bathing both Safe and Useful* (1702); he describes St Chad (pp. 17–18) as:

one of the first Converters of our Nation, and used Immersion in the Baptism of the *Saxons*. And the Well near *Stow*, which may bear his Name, was probably his Baptistery, it being deep enough for Immersion, and conveniently seated near that Church; and that has the Reputation of curing Sore Eyes, Scabs, &c. as most Holy Wells in *England* do, which got that Name from the Baptizing the first Christians in them, and to the Memory of the Holy Bishops who baptized in them, they were commonly dedicated, and called by their Names.

Nicholas Owen (*c.*1550–1606), Jesuit lay brother and martyr. Born to a recusant family, and a carpenter by training, he specialized in building priest-holes, in one of which he himself had to hide without food for two weeks. Giving himself up to deflect attention from priests, he was tortured and eventually died on the rack, refusing to reveal any names.

3 MARCH

a.d. V Nonas Martias   F

❬ HOLIDAYS AND ANNIVERSARIES Bulgaria: Liberation Day (from Ottoman rule, 1878) (national day)
    Japan: Peach Festival (Momo no sekku) or Dolls' Festival (Hiramatsuri), solar equivalent of Chinese Pántáogōng on the third day of the third lunar month
    USA, Florida: Admission Day (27th state, 1845)

❬ HOLY DAYS

Kunigunde, widow of Holy Roman Emperor Henry II (1002–24), died as a nun 1033; canonized in 1200. Their childless union was converted by hagiographers, like that of Edward the Confessor and Edith Godwinsdaughter (see *13 Oct.), into a *mariage blanc*; in a further improvement, Kunigunde was said to have proved her virginity by walking over twelve red-hot ploughshares—a test that the Cunégonde of Voltaire's *Candide* would undoubtedly have failed. She is now generally culted together with her husband on 13 July. Clement XI named her as a patron of Lithuania in 1715; she was decreed patron of Luxembourg in 1914.

Non, mother of St David (see *1 Mar.); her well, on the Pembrokeshire coast, credited with healing powers and tidal flow, was found on being cleaned in 1825 to have been a receptacle for coins. It was restored by the RC Church in Wales and rededicated with a pilgrimage in July 1951. A nearby Bronze Age stone circle is said to bear the imprint of the fingers with which St Non gripped it during labour.

4 MARCH

a.d. IV Nonas Martias G

❧ HOLIDAYS AND ANNIVERSARIES USA: Constitution Day (1789)
USA, Vermont: Admission Day (14th state, 1791)

❧ HOLY DAYS Casimir of Poland (RC)

Casimir (Kazimierz) (1458–84), son of the Polish king Kazimierz IV, born 5 October 1458. Elected king of Hungary by a faction of the magnates, he was defeated by Matthias Corvinus and devoted himself to a life of celibacy and austerity; he died at Wilno (Vilnius in Lithuania) on 4 March 1484. Miracles occurred at his tomb; he was canonized in 1521. The Marian hymn 'Omni die dic Mariae' is wrongly ascribed to him. He was decreed patron of Lithuania in 1922, and one of the chief patrons of Russia in 1914.

The saying that March often comes in like a lion is common to England and North America:

In Earliest Spring

Tossing his mane of snows in wildest eddies and tangles,
    Lion-like, March cometh in, hoarse, with tempestuous breath,
Through all the moaning chimneys, and thwart all the hollows and angles
    Round the shuddering house, threating of winter and death.

But in my heart I feel the life of the wood and the meadow
    Thrilling the pulses that own kindred with fibres that lift
Bud and blade to the sunward, within the inscrutable shadow,
    Deep in the oak's chill core, under the gathering drift.

Nay, to earth's life in mine some prescience, or dream, or desire
    (How shall I name it aright?) comes for a moment and goes,—
Rapture of life ineffable, perfect,—as if in the brier,
    Leafless there by my door, trembled a sense of the rose.

William Dean Howells (1837–1920)

5 MARCH

a.d. III Nonas Martias A

❧ HOLY DAYS

Gerasimus (d. *c.*475), a monk who travelled from Lycia to Palestine, where he founded on the banks of the Jordan a lavra that became second in size to St Sabas' (see *5 Dec.). He is said to have drawn a thorn from the paw of a lion that thereafter became his companion; this tale, later told of St Jerome, recalls that of Androcles, recorded in the early first century AD by the self-publicizing man of letters Apion of Alexandria, who claimed to have personally witnessed the lion's recognition of his benefactor in the amphitheatre at Rome. But whereas Androcles was fed by the grateful beast on choice portions of his kill, Gerasimus made his pet eat bread and wet pulses.

Ciaran (5th–6th c.), Anglicized to Kieran, 'the first-born of the saints of Ireland', said to have been ordained bishop of Ossory by St Patrick; he founded the monastery of Saighir at which the kings of Ossory were buried. Legend has him assisted in the building by a wolf, a badger, and a fox; when the fox made off with his shoes, the wolf and the badger brought him back to be rebuked and shriven.

Piran or Perran (d. *c.*480), an Irish monk who went to north Cornwall; Perranporth is named after him. He was popular in the Middle Ages, when pilgrimages were made to the the site of his hermitage. He is patron saint of Cornish tinminers.

In Denmark, peasants were expected to plough the lord's land on this day.

Navigium Isidis, the voyage of Isis to Phoenicia, the start of the sailing season. Among the Greeks and Romans Isis acquired a considerable cult as a goddess of the sea and sailing; the Virgin Mary may owe the title *Stella Maris* to her, as she does much else.

Boston Massacre, 1770. There had been clashes between the people of Boston and British troops ever since the latter had been quartered there in 1768; but when Captain Preston of the 29th Regiment and seven of his men were pelted with stones and snowballs in King Street by a crowd of some fifty or sixty, they opened fire, killing three persons; one of them, Crispus Attucks, is commonly thought to have been black. In the face of angry protest the troops were withdrawn; although at the subsequent murder trial—in which the defending counsel were John Adams and Josiah Quincy—only two of the soldiers were convicted and they only of manslaughter, the feeling aroused by the incident greatly increased the colonists' resentment.

6 MARCH

pridie Nonas Martias   B

❦ HOLIDAYS AND ANNIVERSARIES Ghana: Independence Day (from Great Britain, 1957)

❦ HOLY DAYS Formerly SS Perpetua and Felicity (see *7 Mar.)

Colette (1381–1447), Franciscan nun and reformer. Daughter of a carpenter at the abbey of Corbie in Picardy, when orphaned at 17 she became a Franciscan tertiary and hermit close to the abbey, where she was renowned for her austerity. Visions directed her to reform the nuns of the Poor Clares to stricter observance; she encountered much resistance until she gained the support of the Avignon (anti)pope Benedict XIII, and went on to found seventeen new convents and reform others.

Cyniburg, daughter of the pagan Mercian king Penda and husband of Alcfrith, the son of King Oswiu of Northumbria, founder of the convent of Castor (Northants), d. *c.*680 and succeeded as abbess by her sister Cyneswith. Their relics were translated in 963 to Peterborough together with one of St Tibba, perhaps their kinswoman, an anchoress of Ryhall in Rutland much honoured before the Reformation by the fowlers and falconers of that county.

Rose of Viterbo honoured by the local church (see *4 Sept.).

Alamo Day. The Franciscan mission of the Alamo, garrisoned by the Texans, was stormed by Gen. Santa Ana, who shot the five surviving defenders (including Captain David Crockett) in cold blood; the infuriated Texans rallied and captured Santa Ana at the battle of San Jacinto on 21 April.

7 MARCH

Nonae Martiae   C

❦ HOLY DAYS Perpetua (BCP); Perpetua and Felicity (CY, RC); formerly Thomas Aquinas (see *28 Jan.)

Perpetua and companions (d. 203), martyrs of Carthage, were arrested under a decree of the emperor Septimius Severus forbidding new conversions to Christianity. The young mother Perpetua, her pregnant slave Felicity, and three male companions were imprisoned, then led to the Games, where the women were faced with a mad heifer, the men with leopards and bears. Perpetua was so ecstatic that she did not realize she had been thrown and injured. The martyrs were then killed by gladiators, Perpetua helping the shaking hand of her executioner by guiding the blade to her throat. Felicity had prayed successfully to give birth early so that she might suffer martyrdom with her companions. Perpetua's own affecting account of her imprisonment and visions survives, together with a contemporary and very full description of the martyrdom, which became widely known and was influential on later accounts of martyrs. This is the date of execution, and is the day assigned the feast in the *cisioianus* (see App. D); but the RC Church moved it to the 6th before restoring the 7th in 1969.

In Georgia, this day in common years, and the 6th in leap year, is the feast of the Nine Holy Children (22 Feb. OS), who insisted on being baptized against their heathen parents' wishes and paid the penalty of martyrdom.

Paul III granted the Feast of the Espousals of Our Lady to the Franciscans in 1537, setting the date as 7 March; some dioceses celebrated it on 23 January.

Her Spousals

Wife did she live, yet virgin did she die,
Untoucht of man yet mother of a sonne,
To save her selfe and child from fatall lie,
To end the web wherof the thred was sponne
In mariage knots to *Joseph* shee was tide,
Unwonted workes with wonted veiles to hide.

God lent his Paradise to *Josephs* care
Wherein he was to plant the tree of life,
His sonne of *Josephs* child the title bare:
Just cause to make the mother *Josephs* wife.
O blessed man betroth'd to such a spouse,
More bless'd to live with such a childe in house.

No carnall love this sacred league procurde,
All vaine delights were farre from their assent,
Though both in wedlocke bandes themselves assurde,
Yet streite by vow they seald their chast intent.
Thus had she Virgins, wives, and widowes crowne
And by chast child-birth dubled her renowne.

Robert Southwell (?1561–95)

8 MARCH

a.d. VIII Idus Martias   D

❦ HOLY DAYS Edward King (CY); John of God (RC)

Edward King (1829–1910), thought excessively pious as an undergraduate, became curate at Wheatley near Oxford in 1853, chaplain of the theological college at Cuddesdon in 1858, Regius Professor of Pastoral Theology at Oxford in 1873, and bishop of Lincoln in 1885; the last two appointments were made, despite political differences, by Gladstone, whose son Stephen had been King's student at Cuddesdon. In 1888 King was cited before the Archbishop of Canterbury for ritualistic practices at the communion service; when two years later the case came to trial, most of them (including the *Agnus Dei* after consecration, but not the sign of the Cross at absolution and blessing) were found to be lawful. This 'Lincoln Judgement' was upheld in 1892 by the Judicial Committee of the Privy Council. King was no extreme High Churchman, even sanctioning the remarriage in church of the innocent party to a divorce; but he was a staunch Conservative who shortly before his death voted in the House of Lords for the motion to amend the Budget in defiance of constitutional convention.

John of God (Juan de Dios; 1495–1550), founder of the Brothers Hospitallers. A native of Portugal, he was in succession a soldier for Spain, a shepherd, a pedlar of sacred books, and a merchant with a shop in Granada. At the age of 40 he went mad and gave away all his books. Upon his recovery, the preacher John of Ávila persuaded him to open a hospital for the poor and sick, a task he undertook with zeal and success. After his death his followers organized themselves into a religious order. He is patron of hospitals, nurses, heart patients, and the sick, and also of booksellers and printers.

International Women's Day, decreed in 1910 at the Second International Socialist Women's Conference in Copenhagen on the proposal of Clara Zetkin, later a Communist deputy to the Reichstag, and first kept in 1911 by comrades in Germany, Austria-Hungary, Switzerland, and Denmark, later joined by those elsewhere; at first the date varied, within March, from country to country, but from 1914 onwards observation was settled on the 8th. For many decades the day was chiefly honoured in the Soviet Union and its satellites; more recently, the collapse of its sponsor has permitted its spread, particularly in the United States. But it is also sacred to the misogynistic Irish saint Senan (d. 560), founder of the monastery on Slattery Island, who would allow no woman on shore; when the saintly Cannera, close to death, desired to receive the viaticum from him and be buried there, he would not let her land however pure her soul might be, and bade her depart. She replied she would die first, did so, and was duly buried on the island.

9 MARCH

❦ HOLIDAYS AND ANNIVERSARIES   Belize: Baron Bliss Day (in honour of benefactor, Sir Henry Edward Ernest Victor Bliss) (public holiday)

❦ HOLY DAYS   Frances of Rome (RC); Forty Martyrs of Sebaste (Orth.; 10th RC)

Frances of Rome (1384–1440), widow. She and her sister-in-law, from a well-to-do family in Trastevere, devoted themselves to helping the poor and nursing the sick, work that she continued even though her family and property suffered greatly in the invasion of Rome by Ladislaus of Naples. In 1425 she founded a society of like-minded women, modelled on the Rule of Benedict, but without vows, to work among the poor. Upon the death of her husband Frances became head of the Oblates of Mary, later known as the Oblates of Tor de' Specchi. For several years she had a continuous vision of her guardian angel (enabling her to see at night), which perhaps explains Pius XI's decision to declare her patron of Roman motorists; the decree was confirmed in 1951.

The Forty Martyrs of Sebaste (Sivas) were Christian soldiers of Legio XII Fulminata executed for their faith *c.*320 by the emperor Licinius, who having turned against his colleague Constantine suspected Christians of disloyalty; they were made to stand naked in the open air on a cold winter's night. They are celebrated by dishes in which the number 40 is involved: forty layers of pastry, forty different herbs or grains, forty pan-cakes, etc.

The martyrs' unit, whose base lay to the south-east at Melitene (now Malatya), is none other than the notorious 'Thundering Legion' of hagiographical fiction. In AD 172 a Roman army, encircled somewhere in what is now Slovakia, was suffering from heat and thirst when a sudden rainstorm saved it; as the men drank, the enemy attacked, only to be smitten by hail and thunder. Official credit was given to the Egyptian god Thoth, identified with the Greek Hermes and Roman Mercury; popular belief ascribed the miracle to the emperor's own virtues, but Christians asserted that the rain had come in response to the prayers of Christian soldiers, and claimed that the emperor had acknowledged so much in his report to Senate and People (a document to that effect was later forged). Some writers assign the Christian soldiers to the legion from Melitene, said to have earned the name 'Fulminata' as a result; in fact it had borne that name for over a century, nor is there independent evidence that it took part in this war. For another legion posted far from home by legend, see *22 September.

Catherine of Bologna (Caterina Vigri). Born in Bologna in 1413, she became a companion of Margareta d'Este in Ferrara, where she received a humanistic education. In 1432 she entered the newly founded convent of Poor Clares in Bologna, where she became abbess in 1456. Known for her mystic visions, she was also a painter, miniaturist, and poet, and author of a devotional treatise. She died in 1463. Her *violeta*, which she used in her devotions, has been preserved in its original state in her shrine, a rare example of an un-restored fifteenth-century string instrument. Her body was found to be incorrupt eight-een days after burial and was removed to her church, Corpus Domini in Bologna. In 1475, since her body was still flexible, the nuns decided to place her in a chair, where-upon she immediately grew stiff: the abbess then commanded her on her obedience to sit, at which she sat down in the position where she remains today. Since the fifteenth century she has drawn many visitors. Her body was one of the famed sights in seventeenth-century Bologna; the Englishman Francis Mortoft records his disappoint-ment at failing to view it on 7 April 1659:

In this Citty is to be seene the Body of A Nunn called Santa Catherina, who though dead about 400 yeares agoe; yet her Body, as is reported remaines in as perfect a shape as though she were Liuing; her eyes also looking as liuely and bright as any liuing persons; they report many strange storyes and miracles that she doth, she wants not persons dayly to visit her, & Most of those y^t visit her. forget not to performe their deuotions before this dead Body. Wee were to see this miracle, but it being a day whereon they vse to change her cloathes wee could not see it, unlesse wee came two howers after, which tyme not permitting vs. so that wee went out of ye Towne with-out seeing this Body, which is accounted one of ye wonderfullest things in Italy.

                                                                                    Mortoft, fo. 81^r

---

In Norway, as the weather is on this day, so (it is said) it will be for the next forty days.

10 MARCH

a.d. VI Idus Martias   F

HRH the Prince Edward born 1964; the Union flag is flown

❈ HOLY DAYS John Ogilvie (RC Scotland)

John Ogilvie (1580–1615), Jesuit priest and martyr. Born in Scotland and raised as a Calvinist, he turned Roman Catholic while studying in France and eventually became a Jesuit. After working in Austria and Paris he returned to Scotland in 1613, where he was arrested for propagating the Roman Catholic faith and tortured in a vain attempt to make him implicate others. Later he was tried for high treason; though he recognized James VI as king, he refused to acknowledge his spiritual jurisdiction and was hanged.

Pope Simplicius (468–83); resisted attempts by Acacius, Patriarch of Constantinople, to obtain recognition of his see's parity with Rome, as voted at the Council of Chalcedon, in 451, and to conciliate the many Eastern opponents of the Christological doctrine determined at the same council, that Christ was 'in two natures' (divine and human). The patriarch, secure in the emperor Zeno's support, dealt with his obstruction by ignoring it; in 482 Acacius produced, and Zeno promulgated, a compromise formula or *Hēnōtikon* ('Unifier') that satisfied the Eastern patriarchs—a prize in the short term well worth the alienation of Rome in an Italy ruled by heretical German warlords without allegiance to the empire; for in Simplicius' reign the last Western emperor *de facto*, Romulus Augustulus, was deposed in 476, and the last *de jure*, Julius Nepos, was murdered in 480.

11 MARCH

a.d. V Idus Martias   G

❈ HOLY DAYS

Óengus the Culdee (d. *c*.824), 'the Hagiographer', author of the earliest Irish martyrology, the *Félire Óengusso*. Born into the royal house of Ulster and educated at the monastery of Clonenagh, Co. Laois, he became a hermit, living a very austere life; upon entering the monastery at Tallaght he hid his identity and learning till recognized by abbot Maelruain (see *7 July). He collaborated with the abbot on the Martyrology of Tallaght, then completed his own verse martyrology.

The geese return from their southern migration in March in Wisconsin:

One swallow does not make a summer, but one skein of geese, cleaving the murk of a March thaw, is the spring.

A cardinal, whistling spring to a thaw but later finding himself mistaken, can retrieve his error by resuming his winter silence. A chipmunk, emerging for a sunbath but finding a blizzard, has only to go back to bed. But a migrating goose, staking two hundred miles of black night on the chance of finding a hole in the lake, has no easy chance for retreat. His arrival carries the conviction of a prophet who has burned his bridges. . . .

The geese that proclaim the seasons to our farm are aware of many things, including the Wisconsin statutes. The south-bound November flocks pass over us high and haughty, with scarcely a honk of recognition for their favorite sandbars and sloughs. 'As a crow flies' is crooked compared with their undeviating aim at the nearest big lake twenty miles to the south, where they loaf by day on broad waters and filch corn by night from the freshly cut stubbles. November geese are aware that every marsh and pond bristles from dawn till dark with hopeful guns.

March geese are a different story. Although they have been shot at most of the winter, as attested by their buckshot-battered pinions, they know that the spring truce is now in effect. They wind the oxbows of the river, cutting low over the now gunless points and islands, and gabbling to each sandbar as to a long-lost friend. They weave low over the marshes and meadows, greeting each newly melted puddle and pool. Finally, after a few *pro-forma* circlings of our marsh, they set wing and glide silently to the pond, black landing-gear lowered and rumps white against the far hill. Once touching water, our newly arrived guests set up a honking and splashing that shakes the last thought of winter out of the brittle cattails. Our geese are home again!

Leopold, 18–19

12 MARCH

a.d. IV Idus Martias   A

> *Sowe runcivals [large peas] timelie, and all that be gray,*
> *But sowe not the white till S. Gregories day.*
>
> Tusser

❡ HOLIDAYS AND ANNIVERSARIES   Mauritius: Independence Day (from Great Britain, 1968)

❡ HOLY DAYS   Gregory I (BCP, RC until 1969)

Pope Gregory I (c.540–604), fourth of the Latin Doctors of the Church; his title of Gregory the Great was recognized as well deserved even by Gibbon, no friend to popes:

The pontificate of Gregory the *Great*, which lasted thirteen years, six months, and ten days, is one of the most edifying periods of the history of the church. His virtues, and even his faults, a singular mixture of simplicity and cunning, of pride and humility, of sense and superstition, were happily suited to his station and to the temper of the times.   *Decline and Fall*, ch. 45

Yet Romans were slow to recognize his merits: in the collection of papal biographies known as the *Liber Pontificalis* his entry (probably written in 638) is briefer than those of far less significant popes. By contrast, in Ireland his writings made him Gregory of the Golden Mouth and 'chief of the pure fair Gaels' (*cenn na nGaidel nglanmass*), with an Irish ancestry to boot; but his permanent fame is due to the English. His first *vita* was written *c*.710 by a Northumbrian monk, the 'Anonymous of Whitby'; Bede devoted a chapter of his history to the topic. From England his virtues became known to the Franks.

Born into an eminent Roman family, Gregory served as prefect of the city *c*.572–4 before turning the family mansion into a monastery dedicated to St Andrew and entering it himself; it is now the church of San Gregorio Magno. However, his talents were too great to be left mouldering in personal holiness; successive popes made him deacon of Rome and *apocrisiarius* or papal representative in Byzantium, whence he returned with enhanced reputation in 586. Amidst his duties he had found the time to begin his *Moralia* on the book of Job, a classic of Latin theology. Elected pope in 590, he was faced with famine, floods, plague, and a Lombard invasion; he met them with the highest administrative and diplomatic skills, relieving the cares of office by writing the four books of *Dialogues* in which he lovingly relates such tales of miracles in the lives of saints and martyrs as an earlier age had sought to banish from the Church. His other works include the *Cura Pastoralis* or 'Pastoral Care' that King Alfred was to translate into English. It was Gregory who first styled himself *servus servorum Dei*, 'servant of the servants of God'.

Gregory's writings show a concern with liturgical matters, but forbid deacons to sing, lest they be chosen for beauty of voice. Nothing is said of any musical interests on his part till the late seventh century, when he is included in a list of popes who prescribed the cycle of chants for the year; but partly through conflation with Pope Gregory II (see *11 Feb.) and partly because his name had become authoritative, the chant melodies used in most Roman churches came in the ninth century to be known as Gregorian; he was said to have compiled the antiphoner and founded the Schola Cantorum. The dove (embodying the Holy Spirit) said by the Anonymous of Whitby to have dictated his commentary on Ezekiel was redeployed in medieval art to instruct him in the chant melodies; he is a patron saint of music, as well as of protection against the plague (see *29 Sept.).

The Anonymous relates that Gregory, by his tears, baptized the soul of the emperor Trajan; this was to be a favourite legend in the Middle Ages, as was his causing a Host to be transformed into a portion of a little finger when the woman who had baked it refused to believe it could be the Body of Christ. This is sometimes known as the Mass of St Gregory, a term also applied to the later legend of his receiving a vision, not seen by his attendants, of Christ standing in His tomb surrounded by the instruments of the Passion.

However, Gregory's fame amongst the English rests on the conversion of the Angles and Saxons through Augustine, prior of St Andrew's (see *26 May). Two years earlier the Pope had ordered a priest to buy English slave-boys to be trained in Roman monasteries. According to the Anonymous, while still a deacon he asked some fair-skinned and fair-haired youths, whom Bede specifies as slaves for sale, to what nation they belonged; on learning they were Angles, he called them angels of God, and by similar word-play turned the name of their homeland, the northern English kingdom of Deira, into *de ira* ('[saved] from the wrath [of God]') and of their king, Ælla, into *Alleluia*. He begged Pope Benedict I to send him as a missionary to England, for pity that so handsome a race should people hell, but was thwarted by public opinion, which would not let him leave Rome; since public opinion did not prevent departure for Byzantium, this must be mere fiction, explaining the lack of action in a manner that does honour to Gregory without any censure of Benedict. Bede omits the further embellishment that Gregory was disturbed in his journey by a locust, which he took for an omen, *locusta*, in late Latin pronunciation, sounding much like *loco sta*, 'stay where you are'; this, like Gregory's puns and his attraction to blond North Europeans, is quite in the Roman tradition, but depends on belief in the abortive mission. In any case, it was not to Deira that the mission was dispatched, but to Kent, where King Ethelbert (see *25 Feb.) had a Christian wife; but four years later Gregory sent reinforcements, one of whom, Paulinus (see *10 Oct.), converted the son of that King Ælla whose subjects Gregory is said to have admired.

St Gregory's Day. In 'runic' calendars—better called symbolic, since not all are runic— this day is marked with a dove, one of St Gregory's attributes, reinterpreted as a crow, whose inland migration is a sign of spring; but we also find a symbol often taken to represent strips of land to be manured on this day but perhaps originally intended for a book, from the same consideration that induced Olaus Worm to mark this day in his improved Danish calendar with a schoolmaster carrying cane and birch: as a contemporary translated his explanation:

> It is becaus at that time (as beeing about the beginning of the Spring) they use to send their children first to School. *Adeò superstitiosi sunt quidam, &c* and som are so superstitiously given as upon this night to have their children asked the question in their sleep, whether they have anie mind to Book, or no; and if they saie yes, they count it for a very good presage. *Sin tacuerint aut negent, stivæ eos adjudicant,* but if the children answer nothing, or nothing to that purpose, they put them over to the Plough.   Gregory (1650), 113

This custom is also attested for medieval England:

> we vseþ alonde ȝute
> To sette in is day children to lore · þe wile hi beoþ lute
> þat he mote is grace habbe · þulke lore to wite
> þat he vs sende bi seint Austin · & neuere forȝute

> (It is still our custom in this country to put children to learning on his day while they are little, that he may have his thanks in order to requite that learning [Christian doctrine] which he sent us through St Augustine, and never [to] forget [it].)   *South English Legendary,* i. 83

In his will of 1603 William Clapham left 4*s.* 4*d.*, the income to be applied

> towards a potation amongst the poor scholars of the Freeschool in Giggleswick (Yorkshire), on St. Gregory's day. The Commissioners [for Enquiring into Charities in England and Wales] report, that they found a custom formerly prevailed of giving figs, bread and ale, among the scholars on that day; and that at present there is a distribution amongst them on the same day

of bread and figs, to an amount considerably exceeding the sum of four shillings and four pence per annum. Edwards, 26–7

In Belgium, schoolchildren locked up their masters and demanded a holiday; students might demand other favours of professors. In Norway children, especially girls, were dressed up as 'bride(groom)s of Gregory' and went out begging.

13 MARCH

a.d. III Idus Martias   B

❦ HOLY DAYS

Euphrasia (Eupraxia) (*c.*420), virgin. A ward of the emperor Theodosius I, at age 5 she was betrothed to the son of a senator. She grew up in a convent, but did not wish to leave when the time came for marriage. The emperor acceded to her request to distribute her inheritance to the poor. Renowned for meekness and humility, she cheerfully carried out the task assigned to distract her from her worldly longings: carrying a pile of stones from one place to another, thirty times.

Leander (*c.*530–*c.*600), Bishop of Seville, brother of Isidore (see *4 Apr.); he championed Catholicism in Spain against the Arianism of her Visigothic rulers. In this he was aided by the five-year rebellion of the Catholic prince Hermenegild (see *13 Apr.) against his father, Leuvigild, which though ultimately unsuccessful had shown the strength of Catholic feeling amongst the native Spaniards; Hermenegild's brother Reccared (586–601) converted personally in 587 and two years later (after suppressing a few rebellions), at the Third Synod of Toledo, over which Leander presided, brought his nobility and clergy with him into the Roman Church. The Roman Martyrology sets him on 27 February, but the Bollandists preferred his Spanish date of 13 March.

14 MARCH

pridie Idus Martias   C

❦ ANCIENT ROME Equirria: horse-racing in Campus Martius. Mamuralia, in honour of Mamurius Veturius, manufacturer of the eleven replicas of the shield (*ancile*) that descended from heaven in the reign of King Numa, made so that no one could identify the original. Varro took him to originate in false understanding of *mamuri veturi* in a Saliar hymn, which he interpreted as *memoria vetus*; this may be a misplacement of the ceremony recorded in a late source as taking place on the 15th, in which a man dressed in goatskins was ceremonially beaten out of the city, presumably representing winter, but nothing is certain.

€ HOLY DAYS Benedict of Nursia (Orth.; see *21 Mar.)

> We like March – his Shoes are Purple.
> He is new and high –
> Makes he Mud for Dog and Peddler –
> Makes he Forests Dry –
> Knows the Adder's Tongue his coming
> And begets her spot –
> Stands the Sun so close and mighty –
> That our Minds are hot.
> News is he of all the others –
> Bold it were to die
> With the Blue Birds buccaneering
> On his British sky –
>
> Emily Dickinson (1830–86)

15 MARCH

Idus Martiae   D

€ HOLIDAYS AND ANNIVERSARIES Hungary: Anniversary of the Revolution of 1848
    (national day)
    USA, Maine: Admission Day (23rd state, 1820)

€ ANCIENT ROME

Ides of March. From 222 BC down to 154 BC inclusively, the day on which the new consuls
entered office, but chiefly notorious as the day on which Julius Caesar was murdered
in 44 BC, by a conspiracy of senators led by the praetor Marcus Junius Brutus and
Quintus Cassius Longinus, most of whom had received favours from him but, according to their republican ideology, resented receiving them from a master. Surrounding
him on the pretext of presenting a petition, they inflicted twenty-three blows on him,
in their frenzy and confusion wounding each other as well; two of Caesar's supporters
tried to intervene, the rest kept out of harm's way or even approved of the murder (one
reportedly said over the corpse, 'Enough currying favour with a tyrant'). It was alleged
(but our sources do not give credence to the story) that on seeing Brutus advancing to
the kill Caesar said in Greek *kai su teknon*, 'You too my son', the origin of Shakespeare's
Et tu Brute. The murderers then rushed out and ran through the Forum to the Capitol,
with naked swords, shouting that they had done their deed for the sake of general freedom, accompanied for protection by a great crowd of gladiators and slaves collected in
advance for the purpose. Our earliest account, that by Nicolaus of Damascus in his life
of Caesar's heir Augustus, tells us:

There was much rushing to and fro in the streets and about the Forum, for the report had already
spread among the masses that Caesar had been murdered, and the city looked as if it were falling

to the enemy. Having climbed up the Capitol they sent detachments to guard each portion, afraid that Caesar's army might fall upon them.

The corpse was still lying where it had fallen, abased and stained with blood—that of a man who had marched west to the British Isles and the Ocean, and intended to march east to the thrones of Parthia and India, so that they too might be made subject to a single empire and all land and sea be governed from one capital; but now he lay there, and no one dared to remain and recover his corpse. Those of his friends who were present had fled, those who were outside were hiding in their houses, or changed their clothes and departed for the countryside and the nearby towns.

It was soon clear that the Roman people was not so attached to constitutional principles as Brutus and his friends had supposed; within a few days the murderers found Rome too hot to hold them, though a political settlement allowed the chief conspirators provinces to govern. The collapse of this settlement resulted in a second civil war, and the final defeat of the republican cause at Philippi in 42 BC.

Ovid in his poem on the Roman calendar describes in detail the festivities of Anna Perenna, whose name suggests a goddess of annual return and hence of spring. The Roman *plebs* picnicked in a grove near the present Porta del Popolo and the Borghese gardens; amusements included drinking a cup of wine for each year of one's age, singing the latest hits, and dancing. The revellers were hailed as 'fortunati' as they staggered back home. Ovid offers various mythological explanations, in one equating Anna Perenna with Dido's sister Anna, cast ashore in Italy and sheltered by Aeneas, whose jealous wife, Lavinia, plotted against her; warned by Dido in a dream to escape, she was rescued by a river-god and turned into a nymph. In another, Anna, asked by Mars to help him seduce Minerva, took her place and mocked the god when he recognized her; this accounts for the bawdy songs that girls sang at her festival. It has been suggested that this day was chosen for Caesar's murder because the common people would be too far away and too drunk to intervene; but there is no mention of the festivities in our ancient accounts of the event.

❦ HOLY DAYS

Longinus. The soldier who pierced Christ's side on the Cross (John 19: 34) with a lance acquired in tradition the name Longinus; he was conflated with the centurion of Matt. 27: 54 who declared 'Truly this was the Son of God.' It was said that later in life he went blind, but regained his sight when Christ's blood dripped on his eyes from the lance, whereupon he left the army, took instruction from the Apostles, and lived for twenty-eight years as a monk at Caesarea in Cappadocia, making many converts. When he refused to offer pagan sacrifice, the governor ordered all his teeth to be knocked out and his tongue excised; nevertheless, he did not lose the power of speech, but took an axe to the idols with the words 'We shall see if they are gods.' The demons who had dwelt in the statues took possession of the governor and his companions, maddening them all and blinding the governor; Longinus undertook to pray for his recovery once he had been executed. The governor ordered him to be beheaded, did penance, recovered sight and sanity, and ended his days in good works. (His Eastern day is 16 Oct.)

In the sixth century a purported Holy Lance was kept at the basilica of Mount Sion in Jerusalem; it was captured by the Persian invaders in 614, minus the point, which was taken to Constantinople, sent to Paris by the Latin emperor Baldwin II in 1241, and lost when French revolutionaries looted the Sainte-Chapelle. The shaft, reportedly seen in Jerusalem *c.*670, reappeared at Constantinople in the tenth century. In 1489 Pope Innocent VIII agreed with Sultan Bayezit II to keep the latter's fugitive brother Cem Sultan in close confinement for a consideration of 40,000 ducats a year and the Holy Lance; it rests beneath the dome of St Peter's. This Holy Lance must be distinguished from the Holy Lance discovered at Antioch soon after its capture in 1098, which inspired the Crusaders to rout a Turkish army blockading the city, but was suspected from the start by the papal legate and discredited when its finder failed the ordeal of fire; and also from the Holy Lance of the Holy Roman Emperors, honoured by a feast on the Friday after Low Sunday.

Pope Zacharias (741–52), born in the Greek-speaking south of Italy, who translated Gregory's *Dialogues* into his mother tongue, the last pope to make a formal announcement of his election to Byzantium; he cooperated closely with St Boniface (see *1 Jan., *5 June) and with the Franks. Having at first kept the Lombards at bay by personal authority, on seeing that the new king, Aistulf, was not susceptible to such methods and would soon drive the Byzantines from their outpost at Ravenna, he encouraged the Frankish Mayor of the Palace Pippin III (son of Charles Martel and father of Charlemagne), already the holder of *de facto* power, to depose the Merovingian Childeric III and become king himself, anointed by Boniface; Zacharias died soon afterwards, but Pippin defeated Aistulf and conferred his conquests on the Church. The Merovingian kings, long sustained by the Church despite their violence (which did not distinguish them for their subjects) and their polygamy (which did), had ceased to be more than ceremonial figures; the deposition of Childeric established the principle that a king could be removed simply for being incapable of effective rule, a *rex inutilis*.

16 MARCH

a.d. XVII Kalendas Apriles   E

❨ ANCIENT ROME This day and the next were marked by a procession to the twenty-seven shrines known as Argei within the early 'Servian' boundaries (i.e. of King Servius Tullius, not including the Capitol or Aventine). See too *14 May.

❨ HOLY DAYS

Finnian Lobhar (6th c.), a pupil of St Columba, who made him abbot of Swords, north of Dublin. The Old Irish word *lobur*, modern *lobhar*, means 'weak' or 'sickly' in general, but acquired the specific meaning 'leper'; it was said that as a boy, having prayed that another boy might be cured of leprosy, Finnian received the revelation that his prayer would be answered only if the disease moved from the other boy to himself. He accepted the terms and became a leper.

Heribert, chancellor and counsellor of Emperor Otto III, archbishop of Cologne from 999, died on this day in 1021. His relics were subsequently translated to Deutz, an event celebrated in the diocese of Cologne on 30 August. The ivory comb, dating from the ninth century, with which he combed his hair before mass is preserved in a Cologne museum. For a legend in which he appears, see *24 December.

Cyriac, a Roman deacon who (according to the Roman Martyrology), after a long wasting away in prison, was covered in molten pitch, racked, stretched with cords, clubbed, and beheaded; he is also culted together with his companions on 8 August. As one of the Fourteen Auxiliary Saints he is invoked by persons possessed by the Devil.

St Urho's Day. In Minnesota, many of whose inhabitants are either of Scandinavian or of Irish origin, a Finnish-descended guest at a St Patrick's Day party in 1956 invented his own national saint, Urho, culted the previous day, who had banished frogs from Finland as St Patrick banished snakes from Ireland; Urho is Finnish for 'hero', and also a man's name, most notably borne by the statesman Urho Kekkonen, first elected President of Finland on the preceding 15 February. The tale was well received and grew with the retelling; St Urho was elevated into the patron saint of Finnish immigrants in the USA, and also of Finnish vineyard workers, who before the last Ice Age, when wild grapes grew in Finland, had banished grasshoppers from the country with the words *Heinäsirkka, heinäsirkka, mene täältä hiiteen*, 'Grasshopper, grasshopper, go away to hell.' This exploit was promptly commemorated with a statue at Menahga, Minn., showing a determined-looking Urho with a huge grasshopper on a pitchfork. An inscription on the pedestal records his achievement, and purports to relate how women and children, dressed in royal purple and Nile green, dance round the countless lakes of Finland every year chanting his spell; the listening menfolk depart with grasshopper-like movements to change costume from green to purple, after which everyone dances in the saint's honour and drinks to him in grape juice. Other cities have also adopted his cult; new St Urho ceremonies are devised every year and eagerly awaited during the long winters of northern Minnesota. His fame has spread to his homeland.

17 MARCH

a.d. XVI Kalendas Apriles   F

> *On Saint Patrick's day*
> *let all your horses play.*

❰ HOLIDAYS AND ANNIVERSARIES   Ireland: St Patrick's Day (national day)

UN member nations: World Maritime Day

USA, Massachusetts: Boston and Suffolk County: Evacuation Day (anniversary of evacuation of British troops, 1776)

❅ ANCIENT ROME Liberalia, in honour of Liber Pater, a fertility god equated with the Greek Dionysus, and his female counterpart, Libera. Old women wore ivy wreaths and offered sacrificial cakes (*libae*) on behalf of the purchaser; the disapproving Augustine mentions a phallic procession (at Lavinium the show lasted a whole month). At one time there were games in his honour: a character in an early play declares: 'With free tongue shall we speak at Liber's games' (*libera lingua loquemur ludis Liberalibus*); by Ovid's day these had been suppressed in favour of joint celebration with Ceres on 19 April, but fourth-century calendars attest a revival. This was the day on which boys came of age; they took off the purple-edged *toga praetexta* and the amulet or *bulla* of childhood, sacrificed to the Lares (the household gods), and put on the man's toga (*toga virilis*, also known as *toga pura* for lacking the purple edge) before being escorted to the Forum and enrolled as a full citizen.

This day was also the *agonium Martiale*, or sacrifice to Mars (see *9 Jan.).

❅ HOLY DAYS Patrick (CY, RC); Alexius (Orth., see *17 July)

Patrick son of Calpurnius (*Pádraig mac Calprainn, c.*390–461?, in the earliest Irish *Cothriche*), bishop of Armagh, apostle of Ireland. Of British origin, he was captured as a youth by Irish pirates and spent six years as a slave; he escaped, and after an adventurous journey home studied for the priesthood. One night (as he relates) he dreamt he received a letter in which 'the voice of the Irish' besought him to go among them; this was the beginning of his missionary work. There were already Christians in Ireland by 431, when Palladius (see *7 July) was sent to be their first bishop; but Patrick too was made bishop, as such pronouncing excommunication on a British warrior-prince Coroticus (the founder of Cardigan, *Ceredigion*) who had flouted his claims to authority and sold Christian prisoners into heathen captivity. Perhaps as a result, his British superiors censured him, even bringing up a youthful sin against him; like hierarchs throughout Christian history, they had little time for a prickly character who did not even express himself in the language of civilized education. The Latin of Patrick's two surviving works—a letter to Coroticus' soldiers and a *Confessio*—is an ungrammatical semi-vernacular in which phrases, images, and structures are biblical, not classical or even patristic; yet in this language he expresses himself with rhetorical skill and power.

Although the memory of St Patrick smothered that of Palladius, it was by no means strong in the two centuries after his death; not till nearly 700 did he surpass St Brigid as a focus for devotion (see *1 Feb.). Since then, however, he has been not only the patron saint but the apostle of Ireland, or, as the Martyrology of O'Gorman (*Félire hUí Gormáin*) calls him, 'Patraicc apstol Herend | cend creitme na nGóidhel' (Patrick the apostle of Ireland, the Gaels' head of faith'). Even now he is honoured by both traditions.

Numerous legends have grown up around him, the most famous being his expulsion of the snakes from Ireland and his explanation of the Trinity with the shamrock as its model; he is often depicted with a snake and a shamrock. The twelfth-century life by Jocelin of Furness relates an incident that befell the saint when, having turned monk, he was attempting to attain perfection by self-denial:

For a desire of eating meat came on him, until being ensnared and carried away by his desire, he obtained Swine's flesh and concealed it in a certain vessel; thinking rightly that he might thus satisfy his appetite privily, which should he openly do, he would become to his brethren a stone of offence, and a stumbling block of reproach. And he had not long quitted the place, when lo! one stood before him, having Eyes before, and Eyes behind; whom, when PATRICK beheld, having his Eyes so wonderfully, even so monstrously placed, he marvelled who he was, and what meaned his Eyes fixed before and fixed behind, did earnestly ask: and he answered, I am the Servant of God;—with the Eyes fixed in my forehead I behold the things that are open to view, and with the Eyes that are fixed in the hinder part of my head I behold a Monk hiding flesh-meat in a vessel, that he may satisfy his appetite privily. This he said, and immediately disappeared. But PATRICK striking his breast with many strokes, cast himself to the earth, and watered it with such a shower of tears, as if he had been guilty of all crimes;—and while he thus lay on the ground, mourning and weeping, the Angel *Victor*, so often before mentioned, appeared to him in his wonted form, saying, Arise, let thine heart be comforted, for the *Lord* hath put away thine offence, and henceforward avoid back-sliding. Then St. PATRICK rising from the earth, utterly renounced and abjured the eating of flesh-meat, even through the rest of his life; and he humbly besought the *Lord* that he would manifest unto him his Pardon by some evident Sign. Then the *Angel* bade PATRICK to bring forth the hidden meats and put them into Water; and he did as the *Angel* bade; and the flesh-meats being plunged into the Water and taken thereout, immediately became Fishes. This Miracle did St. PATRICK often relate to his Disciples, that they might restrain the desire of their Appetites. But many of the Irish, wrongfully understanding this miracle, are wont [original has *solebant*, 'were wont'] on St. Patrick's-day, which always falls in the time of Lent, to plunge Flesh-meats into Water, when plunged in to take out, when taken out to dress, when dressed to eat, and call them Fishes of St. PATRICK.   trans. E. L. Swift, 31–2

Gertrude of Nivelles (628–59), daughter of Pippin the Elder, founder of the Carolingian dynasty. Having as a child refused the husband chosen by King Dagobert I, with her mother Ida she founded a monastery at Nivelles, of which she eventually became abbess. She sheltered orphans, widows, prisoners of war, and pilgrims; her name was often given to hostels in the Middle Ages. She is also patron of gardeners, and protects against vermin:

> Saint Gartrude riddes the house of Mise, and killeth all the Rattes.
>
> Naogeorgus, 39

She was buried at Nivelles; in 1272 her remains were translated to a silver reliquary, destroyed in 1940.

Joseph of Arimathea (RC commem.; see *31 July).

St Patrick's Day. So well entrenched is this day that the Second Vatican Council did not displace it from Lent along with those of SS Thomas Aquinas, Gregory, and Benedict; nor does Lent dampen the revelries with which St Patrick is celebrated. Father

McGrath, annotating O'Sullivan (ii. 236), calls it a 'liquid banquet' (*cóisir leanna*); a party in the saint's honour is called 'Patrick's pot' (*pota Phádraig*):

St. Patrick's Day, a holiday . . . A jolly group of us drank our 'Patrick's Pot' at the parish priest's, Father James Henebry. We had for dinner fresh cod's head, salt ling softened by steeping, smoke-dried salmon and fresh trout, with fragrant cheese and green cabbage. We had sherry and port wine, whiskey and punch enough.   O'Sullivan, ii. 125 (1829)

St Patrick's Day is celebrated in New York with a parade first instituted by Irish troops in 1762, attended by US politicians even though not of Irish descent, and by Irish prime ministers in preference to the more recent imitation in Dublin—deemed a mere tourist trap by those who cross the Irish Sea to spend the week at the Cheltenham races in the hope, sometimes fulfilled, of backing and cheering Irish winners.

St Patrick's Day in Montreal in 1871, as seen by an Irish missionary priest:

St. Patrick's Day. A very great day in Montreal. A very great day in every city in America. A very great day anywhere but in Ireland. Before I go down stairs, I am presented with a magnificent shamrock, the present of some unknown friend. There is to be a great procession, with bands and banners, consisting of several Irish societies. They are to meet at Mass in St. Patrick's church, and form there when Mass is over. Accordingly at 10 o'clock there are great symptoms of preparations. The sound of music is heard, the well known anthem of 'Patrick's Day' floats on the breeze, and the bandsmen in a variety of costumes, halt before the church gate to finish the tune. Crowds are assembled without, and evidently enjoy the gathering pageant. . . . The Mass was beautifully sung, and the effect was greatly improved by a solo on the organ at the offertory of a pure Irish character—nothing less than the 'Minstrel Boy'. . . . At the end of the Mass the procession began to form. The weather had been wet, and the ground is covered with hard snow since last December. Hence under foot it is all wet and slushy, and walking without slipping is a matter of considerable difficulty. But I must walk; so I accompany Father Dowd and Father Singer, who march in their soutanes, and have bearskin caps on their heads. I slipped once or twice, and this puts me on my guard. I take Father Dowd's arm, and even so get on with great trouble. It was the most difficult three miles I ever walked, and the dirtiest. Such a state as my clothes were in! Oh, holy St. Patrick, what did I ever do, that you should treat me so? It was, nevertheless, a grand procession; the music was excellent, and in some places there were tri-umphal arches, with legends indicative of the blended feelings in the breast of religion and nationality. The spectators and gazers from windows enjoyed it as it passed along; but there was no shouting, no disorder. I asked if this procession gave offence to any party. No; on the con-trary, all classes of people like it, and would be greatly disappointed if it did not take place. I looked in vain for a drunken man. Strange to say, drunkenness is almost unknown in Montreal, and even in all Canada. This is very creditable to our people, and clearly proves that there is noth-ing in the national character incompatible with temperance.   Buckley, 231–3

The red diagonal cross upon a white background called 'St Patrick's Cross' has no hagiographical authority: St Patrick, not being a martyr, is not entitled to a cross. It is the ancient blazon (argent, a saltire gules) of the great Hiberno-Norman Fitzgerald or Geraldine family, which an eighteenth-century Duke of Leinster permitted the St Patrick's Society to use in its badge; in consequence, when, at the Union of Great Britain and Ireland in 1801, an Irish emblem was required on a par with St George's and St Andrew's crosses, this device, already associated with the national saint, matching the one in its colours and the other in its shape, seemed perfect for the purpose. It remains the flag of Northern Ireland, and is incorporated in the Union flag as four red strips within the white diagonals; these strips should be in the lower half of the diagonal in the hoist (the flagpole side), and the upper half in the fly.

Some calendars make this the day on which Woman was seduced by the Serpent, and Adam sinned.

In England in the Middle Ages 17 March was popularly thought to be the date on which Noah entered the Ark (cf. *29 Apr., *6 May). The mystery plays make much of his trials in getting the shrewish Mrs Noah on board. In the Towneley plays she refuses to step 'in such an oyster as this! In faith, I cannot find | Which is before, which is behind.' In the Chester plays her stubbornness causes Noah to exclaim: 'Lord, that women be crabbed aye! | And never are meke, that dare I saye.'

18 MARCH

a.d. XV Kalendas Apriles   G

❦ HOLY DAYS Edward, King of the West Saxons (BCP); Cyril of Jerusalem (RC, Orth., CY commem.)

Edward (*c*.962–78), king of England from 975, the second of that name before the Conquest, son of King Edgar by his first wife, or as others said a nun of Wilton; murdered at Corfe Castle in 978 by supporters of his half-brother Ethelred II, who unlike himself was born when his father was already king and whose mother, Ælfthryth, is said to have been party to the crime. Ethelred was consecrated king 'with much rejoicing', but the rejoicing did not last: his reign was blighted by Viking wars that he could not end either by fair means or by foul (see *13 Nov.), and neither by fighting nor by diplomacy. His attempt at the latter was the notorious 'Danegeld' stigmatized by the Anglo-Saxon Chronicle as *unræd*, 'bad counsel'; by mistranslation of this word he is known as 'the Unready'. These disasters caused Edward, slain unjustly though not for the Faith, and something of a brute, to be regarded as a martyr. His body, first buried at Wareham, was translated to Shaftesbury in 980 (feast 20 June in BCP). The supposed bones were exhumed in 1931; Anglican prelates having declined to reinter them, the Orthodox Church in England, after a legal dispute that caused them to be deposited in a bank vault, converted a chapel of rest into a basilica to house them.

Cyril of Jerusalem (*c*.315–86), Doctor of the Church. Having become bishop of Jerusalem *c*.349, he spent nearly half his reign in exile for his opposition to 'Arianism' (the traditional if inappropriate term for Eastern theologies that emphasized the hierarchy within the Persons of the Godhead); for a time he was also suspect to the staunch anti-Arians for his reluctance to say that the Son was consubstantial (*homoousios*) with the Father, this being a manmade term. Nevertheless, an official inquiry under Gregory of Nyssa (see *10 Jan.) concluded that heresy was not among the many abuses that had flourished in his see during his absence. His fame, however, rests on his twenty-four discourses for the instruction of catechumens, regarded as classics of their kind. See also *7 May.

Fra Angelico (Guido di Pietro, in religion Fra Giovanni da Fiesole) died on this date in 1455. Although commonly known as Beato Angelico, he was never formally beatified; nevertheless, in an Apostolic Letter of 21 February 1984 Pope John Paul II stated that he deserved to be the patron saint of painters because of the excellence of his art. He was a Dominican friar and in his early years a companion of St Antoninus (*10 May).

This was one of several days proposed by computists as the first day of Creation; it won the support of Bede, and soon became canonical. In a homily for 1 January written soon after 987, the learned abbot of Cerne Abbas in Dorset declared:

Se eahteteoða dæg þæs monðes þe we hata ð martius þone ge hata ð hlyda wæs se forma dæg þyssere worulde

The eighteenth day of the month that we [clergy] call March, which you [layfolk] call Lide, was the first day of this world.   *Ælfric*, 229

19 MARCH

a.d. XIV Kalendas Apriles   A

❦ ANCIENT ROME Quinquatrus, the fifth day inclusively from the Ides, sacred to Mars but understood as beginning a five-day festival (during which schools were closed) also honouring Minerva, goddess of all arts and crafts, probably because her temple on the Aventine had been dedicated on this day.

❦ HOLY DAYS **Joseph, husband of the Blessed Virgin Mary** (CY, RC; Sunday after Christmas Orth.)

Joseph (d. 1st c.). The Gospel of Matthew begins with a genealogy extending from Abraham to Joseph, who was espoused to Mary; 'before they came together, she was found with child of the Holy Ghost'. But Joseph, 'being a just man, and not willing to make her a publick example, was minded to put her away privily', but 'the angel of the Lord appeared unto him in a dream, saying, Joseph, thou son of David, fear not to take unto thee Mary thy wife: for that which is conceived in her is of the Holy Ghost'. He is often portrayed with the tools of his carpenter's trade (Matt. 13: 55). A Spanish joke that Pepe is the diminutive of José because Joseph was the *padre putativo* of Jesus shocks the pious Catholic less than the liberal agnostic; in many mystery plays he is the elderly cuckold, or the undomesticated husband who cannot prepare a decent dish of porridge for the Child. His cult expanded rapidly after Teresa of Ávila dedicated the mother-house of her order, the reformed Carmelites, to him. Pius IX declared him Patron of the Universal Church in 1870, and he has also been named patron of Austria (1675), Bohemia (1665), Canada (1624), Mexico (1555), Belgium (under Spanish rule, 1679), Peru (1957), Russia (1930), (South) Vietnam (1952), and Chinese missions (1678). He is a popular patron saint, of carpenters, working men, fathers of families, bursars, and those who seek a holy death (this last deriving from a late legend); a statue of St Joseph, buried in the garden, will ensure the quick sale of one's home. In 1962 he was added to the Canon of the mass.

This day is the occasion for enormous communal feasts in southern Italy, called 'St Joseph's table', with particular emphasis on ornamental loaves made to decorate an altar, St Joseph also being the patron saint of pastry-cooks. The largest loaf, the *pane grosso*, is shaped like Joseph's rod, which alone flowered among those of Mary's suitors. Bonfires mark St Joseph's Night in Valencia, said to have originated when carpenters annually swept out chips and trimmings from their shops, with a spectacular finale in the midnight burning of explosive-filled effigies, called *fallas*, earlier paraded through the streets.

Some say that this day was chosen to honour St Joseph because it began the Quinquatrus in honour of the craft goddess Minerva; however, it is not recorded as his feast before the Reichenau Martyrology of *c*.850. It is not to be confused with the feast of St Joseph the Worker on 1 May instituted in 1955.

20 MARCH

a.d. XIII Kalendas Apriles B

❰ HOLIDAYS AND ANNIVERSARIES Tunisia: Independence Day (from France, 1956)

❰ HOLY DAYS Cuthbert (CY, RC UK)

Cuthbert, bishop of Lindisfarne, one of the most popular saints in the Middle Ages, commemorated as far afield as Kirkcudbright in Galloway and Cubert in Cornwall. Having been monk of Melrose, guest-master of Ripon, and successively prior of Melrose and Lindisfarne, he lived as a hermit on the island of Farne (676–84); having long refused the bishopric of Hexham, he exchanged it for that of Lindisfarne in 685. After nearly two years of hectic activity (said to include the working of many miracles) he withdrew to Farne, where he died on 20 March 687, being buried in Lindisfarne. Upon the elevation of his body to a new shrine in 698, the report that it was incorrupt aroused great enthusiasm, manifested in the writing of two lives, one by Bede, which were read on the Continent as well as in England. After the Danish destruction of the abbey in 875, his shrine with its relics was transported around Northumbria, finally reaching Durham in 995; the relics were buried in a newly built church in 999, and translated into the Norman cathedral in 1104; it was said that not only were they incorrupt, but he was holding the head of St Oswald (see *5 Aug.). They were removed at the Reformation, but rediscovered in 1827. He is portrayed as a bishop, holding Oswald's crowned head, and sometimes surrounded by otters and swans; the Farne islands are now a National Trust wildlife sanctuary. In recent times this feast, which is in Lent, has been over-shadowed by that of his translation (see *4 Sept.). Cuthbert has been connected with two splendid manuscripts, the Lindisfarne Gospels and a Gospel of St John at Stony-hurst College. Having been a shepherd in his youth, he is patron of shepherds.

Battista Spagnoli (1448–1516), six times vicar-general of the Carmelite congregation in Mantua, general of the order from 1513. A friend of Erasmus and Pico della Mirandola, he wrote ten eclogues of classical style and Christian content much admired in the six-teenth century, being even thought to rival his fellow-townsman Vergil: in this capacity he was commonly known as *Mantuanus*. He is the 'good old Mantuan' whom Holofernes misquotes in *Love's Labour's Lost*, IV. ii. Beatified in 1885.

21 MARCH

a.d. XII Kalendas Apriles   C

> *Saint Benedick*
> *sow thy peas or keep them in thy rick.*

❊ HOLIDAYS AND ANNIVERSARIES   Namibia: Independence Day (from South
   Africa, 1990)
South Africa: Human Rights Day, commemorating Sharpeville Massacre in 1960,
   when a peaceful demonstration against apartheid was fired on
UN member nations: International Day for the Elimination of Racial Discrimina-
   tion
USA, Iowa: Bird Day

❊ HOLY DAYS   Benedict of Nursia (BCP, RC until 1969; CY and RC 11 July); Thomas
Cranmer (CY)

Benedict of Nursia (c.480–c.550), abbot and founder of Subiaco and Montecassino. Never achieving priesthood, he left his studies to live as a hermit in a cave at Subiaco, but was soon surrounded with disciples, whom he organized and for whom he wrote a rule, completed when he moved to Montecassino. This covered all aspects of monastic life, comprising prayer, sacred reading, and manual labour, but had enough latitude for the latter to be redirected to medicine and learning; versions of the Rule underlie those of several later orders. Its spirit is summed up in his motto, *Ora et labora*, 'Pray and work.' He was buried together with his sister, St Scholastica (see *10 Feb). His life, or rather a string of miracles related of him, occupies the second book of Pope Gregory's *Dialogues*; in ch. 35 Gregory bids his disciple take heed, 'quia animae videnti Creatorem angusta est omnis creatura', rendered in 1393 by the English anchoress Julian of Norwich: 'For a soul that seth the Maker of al thyng, all that is made semyth fulle lytylle.' This day is the traditional date of his death, said to have been Holy Saturday; that is impossible, for after 509 Holy Saturday did not fall on 21 March again till 604. His current RC date, and that in CY, is his translation-feast on 11 July; his Orthodox day is 14 March.

It was said in Denmark and Norway that a pig well enough fed to stand up on St Benedict's day even when struck could fend for itself thereafter.

Thomas Cranmer, Archbishop of Canterbury (1489–1556). The son of a lesser gentleman (some said a yeoman) of Aslockton (Notts.), he became a fellow of Jesus College, Cambridge, resigned in order to marry, but was reinstated after his wife's death. In the mid-1520s he was recruited by Cardinal Wolsey for diplomatic service on a mission to Spain; on his return he was drawn into Henry VIII's attempts to obtain the annulment of his marriage to Catherine of Aragon. Having proposed that papal obstruction should be outflanked by submitting the question to the divines of the European universities, he was appointed one of the agents charged with securing favourable opinions, being thus brought into contact with Continental reformers, with whom he had previously been out of sympathy; he secretly married a second wife. Having with great reluctance accepted the archbishopric of Canterbury, he pronounced the required annulment, and cooperated in the overthrow of papal power in England; doctrinally too he moved further in a Protestant direction, but in the reaction against the Reformers' teaching during the last years of Henry's reign was able to remain in office. Under the Protestant boy-king Edward VI (1547–53) he prepared an English Book of Common Prayer in 1549, with expedient concessions to conservative sentiment withdrawn in the staunchly Protestant revision of 1552. It is on this latter that the 1662 Prayer Book is based, owing to Cranmer's mastery of language its power to move even non-believers.

Progress towards further reform was intended; but by early 1553 it was obvious that King Edward would soon die. Under the terms of Henry VIII's will, overriding previous declaration of his daughters' illegitimacy, the succession would pass to Edward's half-sister Mary, a zealous Catholic; to prevent this, the king and his ministers arranged that the Crown should pass to Lady Jane Grey, the granddaughter of Henry's sister, who was duly proclaimed on Edward's death. But he had died too quickly for Mary to be arrested; when she marched to claim the crown the government lost its nerve. A few months later Cranmer was condemned to death for treason; however, Mary was more interested in proving him a heretic. Eventually, his will broken, he recanted in hope of clemency; when this was not forthcoming he rallied, and before the assembled congregation in the University Church at Oxford denounced not, as expected, his Protestant writings but his recent recantation, declaring: 'And as for the Pope, I refuse him, as Christ's enemy, and Antichrist, with all his false doctrine.' Dragged away to the stake in Broad Street, he stretched out his right hand, which had written the recantation, to be burnt first.

Protestants have been embarrassed by his recantation, Catholics by its repudiation, yet one excessively eager to avoid death if that seems possible may face it bravely when there is no escape. But more important than the subjective cause of his tergiversations is their objective effect: on his last day, Cranmer took over the stage management of his death and made the spectacle serve Protestant and not Catholic edification. To be sure, the effect would not have lasted had Mary lived long enough for her Catholic restoration to take hold; but had Edward lived, or Jane prevailed, England would under Cranmer's guidance have become a more decidedly Protestant (not merely non-papist) country than she did. It is because neither party succeeded that he is honoured as a martyr.

Those who regarded 18 March as the day of Creation supposed this to have been the day on which God made sun, moon, and stars, hence the beginning of measurable time.

Following the practice of the Church at Alexandria, this day is treated as the vernal equinox in calculating the date of Easter (see II: *Easter*); the erroneous belief that the rules had been laid down at the Council of Nicaea in AD 325 led to the notion that this had been the actual date of the equinox in that year (in fact it was the 20th).

22 MARCH

a.d. XI Kalendas Apriles   D

❦ ANCIENT ROME *Arbor intrat*: a pine-tree with drums and cymbals hanging from its branches and strips of wool and garlands of violets round its trunk was carried to the temple of Cybele, the Great Mother of the Gods from Ida (*Mater deum Magna Idaea*).

❦ HOLY DAYS

Paul of Narbonne, one of seven missionaries sent to Gaul *c.*250 with the rank of bishop by Pope Fabian (see *20 Jan.): the others were Martial of Limoges (*30 June), Dionysius of Paris (*9 Oct.), Austremonius of Clermont-Ferrand, Saturninus of Toulouse (*29 Nov.), Gatianus of Tours (*18 Dec.), and Trophimus of Arles (*29 Dec.). Several were moved back by later tradition to the apostolic age: Paul is a case in point, being identified with Lucius Sergius Paulus, proconsul of Cyprus, who on witnessing St Paul's blinding of a Jewish sorcerer (Acts 13: 6–12) 'was amazed' (so the Syriac text) or 'believed' (most others), and according to the legend was sent by Paul to preach the faith in Gaul.

Isnardo da Chiampo, Dominican, founder and first prior of the monastery of Santa Maria di Nazareth at Pavia; died on 19 March 1244. A much-admired spiritual director and fine preacher, he was credited with bringing many heretics back into the fold. Like his fellow Dominican Aquinas (whose portraits disguise the fact), he was a very large man, which conflicted with the popular stereotype of the emaciated saint; it is said that during a sermon a heckler declared: 'I can no more believe in the holiness of an old porpoise like Brother Isnardo than that this barrel over here will jump up by itself and break my leg.' Of course the impossible came to pass: the barrel jumped up and broke the sceptic's leg. We suggest that St Isnardo should be the patron of the fuller figure.

In Albania this day (9 Mar. OS) is the start of spring (Dit'e Verës). Children range fields and mountains to bring home sprays; round their throats and wrists mothers bind plaits of white and red threads, symbolizing perfect skin and therefore health and strength.

In medieval chronology this was the *sedes epactarum*, the day whose lunar date afforded the epact of the year (see II: **Computus*). It is also the first date on which Easter can occur, when the Paschal term is 21 March and this is a Saturday; in the Gregorian calendar the last case was in 1818, but Sweden and Finland observed the 29th, since the true full moon fell on the 22nd; the next case will not be till 2285, but in the Julian calendar the last was 1915, the next will be 2010 (both 4 Apr. NS).

23 MARCH

❦ HOLIDAYS AND ANNIVERSARIES   Japan: Spring Imperial Festival, or Shunki-Koreisan
New Zealand, Otago and Southland: Provincial Anniversary (public holiday)
Pakistan: Pakistan Day (1956) (national holiday)
UN member nations: World Metereological Day

❦ ANCIENT ROME   The last day of the Quinquatrus (see **19 Mar.), and also the Tubilustrium, when the ceremonial straight trumpets (*tubae*) were purified in the Atrium Sutorium ('Shoemakers' Hall').

❦ HOLY DAYS   Turibius of Mongrovejo (RC)

Turibius (Toribio) *of Mongrovejo* (1538–1606), archbishop of Lima. He had a most unusual career. He was a lay professor of law at Salamanca University when Philip II nominated him to the court of the Inquisition in Granada; having served there well, he was appointed archbishop of Lima, much to his surprise, and contrary to canon law, as he argued. Nevertheless, he was ordained and then consecrated bishop, arriving in Lima in 1581. The task that faced him was enormous, as was his diocese; it took him seven years to complete his first visitation. Baptized Indians were ignorant of the faith; Spanish conquerors placed gain above morality; clergy were lax if not corrupt. Turibius built churches and hospitals, and set up a seminary to train priests to serve throughout the New World. He himself learnt Indian dialects to further his missionary work. Long revered in the Americas, he was placed on the Universal Calendar as an example of pioneering missionaries and reforming bishops, representing South America.

If the world was created on the 18th, this was the day on which Adam was made, and fell; in Gaul and at Alexandria it was therefore considered the appropriate day for the

Crucifixion, whereby mankind was redeemed from the consequences. Others favoured *25 March.

24 MARCH

a.d. IX Kalendas Apriles   F

❦ ANCIENT ROME This day and 24 May were marked in the official calendar as QRCF, *quando rex comitiavit fas*, meaning that judicial business could not be transacted by the praetor until the *rex sacrificulus*, a priest who retained the name of king for rituals that only a king could perform, had dismissed the *comitia calata*, a special and largely obsolete assembly summoned to sanction wills.

❦ HOLY DAYS

Catherine (Karin) of Sweden (d. 1381). Daughter of St Bridget (Birgitta) of Sweden (see *23 July), whom she assisted in her work; after her mother's death, she pressed for her canonization and obtained papal approval of the Bridgettine Order.

Before 1969 the RC Church honoured the archangel Gabriel on this day, that preceding the Annunciation; he now shares 29 September with Michael and Raphael. A pink feather from his wing is said to have found its way to El Escorial.

March

I Martius am! Once first, and now the third!
    To lead the Year was my appointed place;
A mortal dispossessed me by a word,
    And set there Janus with the double face.
Hence I make war on all the human race;
    I shake the cities with my hurricanes;
I flood the rivers and their banks efface,
    And drown the farms and hamlets with my rains.

Henry Wadsworth Longfellow (1807–82),
The Poet's Calendar

25 MARCH

a.d. VIII Kalendas Apriles   G

❦ HOLIDAYS AND ANNIVERSARIES Greece: Independence Day (from Turkey, 1821), when Bishop Germanus (Yermanós) of Patras raised the standard of revolt at the Peloponnesian Ayia Lavra

UK (except Scotland): Lady Day (Quarter Day)
USA, Maryland: Maryland Day (arrival of first settlers, under Lord Baltimore, 1634)

The year was reckoned from this day in England up to 1751 (in Florence and Pisa up to 1749).

❧ HOLY DAYS **Annunciation of the Blessed Virgin Mary** (BCP, Orth.); **Annunciation of the Lord** (CY, RC). Traditional English name: Lady Day. Red-letter day

The Annunciation is nine months before the Nativity; the Armenian date is 7 April. Of the Gospels, only Matthew and Luke record the event, the latter in most detail:

And in the sixth month the angel Gabriel was sent from God unto a city of Galilee, named Nazareth, to a virgin espoused to a man whose name was Joseph, of the house of David; and the virgin's name was Mary. And the angel came in unto her, and said, Hail, thou that art highly favoured, the Lord is with thee: blessed art thou among women. And when she saw him, she was troubled at his saying, and cast in her mind what manner of salutation this should be. And the angel said unto her, Fear not, Mary: for thou hast found favour with God. And, behold, thou shalt conceive in thy womb, and bring forth a son, and shalt call his name JESUS. He shall be great, and shall be called the Son of the Highest: and the Lord God shall give unto him the throne of his father David: And he shall reign over the house of Jacob for ever; and of his kingdom there shall be no end. Then said Mary unto the angel, How shall this be, seeing I know not a man? And the angel answered and said unto her, The Holy Ghost shall come upon thee, and the power of the Highest shall overshadow thee: therefore also that holy thing which shall be born of thee shall be called the Son of God.   (Luke 1: 26–35)

Dismas. This day also commemorated the Penitent Thief, who together with his impenitent colleague acquired a remarkable variety of names in non-canonical sources: Zoatham and Camma, Joathas and Maggatras, Titus and Dumachus. Most familiar now are the names in the Golden Legend, Dismas for the Good Thief and Gesmas for the Bad, derived from the Dysmas and Gestas of the so-called *Acta Pilati*. Another text, purportedly written by Joseph of Arimathea (see *31 July), relates that Gestas used to strip and murder travellers, drinking babies' blood for refreshment, but Demas (as it calls the Good Thief) was a Galilean innkeeper who robbed the rich, helped the poor, and committed sacrilege in the Temple. Others said that in his youth he had captured, and released, the Holy Family on the flight to Egypt. He resided at Latrūn near Emmaus, evidently because, as the Gospels say, he was a *latro*; the Latin word, like the Greek *lēistēs*, is rather 'bandit' or 'highwayman' than 'thief'. A fragment of his cross is exhibited at the Roman church of Santa Croce in Gerusalemme.

A prophecy that the coincidence of the Annunciation with Good Friday in 970 would mark the end of the world was refuted by Abbo of Fleury; the coincidence was twice repeated before the millennium, in 981 and 992. More recently a similar prophecy, but relating to Easter Day, is reported from Ireland (Dinneen, s.v. *Muire*): near the end of the world 'Easter Sunday shall be on the day of Mary's Feast' (*beidh Domhnach Cásca ar lá Fhéile Muire*). From the early seventeenth century is attested the more specific variant:

> When Our Lord lights in Our Lady's Lap,
> Then let England look for a clap,

i.e. a misfortune. It is ascribed to disaffected Roman Catholics who hoped the Virgin would seize the chance to punish the kingdom for apostasy; but the last such Easter had been in 1554, during the first year of the Roman Catholic Mary I, whose brief and unhappy reign was rendered infamous by the persecution of Protestants and ignominious by the loss of Calais. Lady Day Easter proved calamitous for Charles I in 1627, when his favourite the Duke of Buckingham's expedition to relieve the Huguenots of La Rochelle ended in débâcle, and 1638, when Scotland began the rebellion that led at last to his execution some two months before the next coincidence in 1649. Since then it has occurred in 1722, 1733, 1744, 1883, 1894, and 1951, years marked sometimes by political excitement but never by national disaster; the same applies (supposing the Roman Catholics to have prophesied by the Pope's calendar) to the Gregorian instances in 1663, 1674, 1731, and 1742. When Easter is next on 25 March, in 2035 and 2046, both CofE and RC will transfer the Annunciation to another day.

Thomas Fuller (1662) doubted the prophecy:

I behold this proverbial prophecy, or this prophetical menace, to be not above six score yeares old, and of Popish extraction since the Reformation. It whispereth more then it dares speak out, and points at more then it dares whisper; and fain would intimate to credulous persons, as if the blessed Virgin offended with the English for abolishing her Adoration watcheth an opportunity of Revenge on this Nation. And when her day (being the *five and twentieth* of *March*, and first of the *Gregorian* year) chanceth to fall on the day of Christ's Resurrection, then (being as it were fortified by her *Sons* assistance) some signal judgment is intended to our State, and Church-men especially. . . . Sure I am so sinfull a Nation deserves that every year should be fatal unto it. But it matters not, *though our Lady falls in our Lords lap*, whilst *our Lord* sits at *his Fathers* right hand, if to him we make our addresses by serious repentance.   Fuller, *Worthies*, 83

Lady fast: the custom of fasting throughout the year on whatever day of the week Lady Day fell on; it was established by 1410, and not approved universally:

the mede of fastynge ne the vertu of fastynge is nought assyngnyd ne lymyt be the letterys of the kalender ne folwyn nout the cours of the kalender ne changyn nout from o day to another day, althey the letterys changyn from on day to onother.   *Dives and Pauper*, 1. 42 (i. 173)

The Tichborne Dole takes place on this day:

The *Winchester Observer*, a few years ago, gave an account of the 'Tichborne Dole', associated with one of the very oldest Hampshire families. The legend tells that, at some remote period, a Lady Mabella, on her death-bed, besought her lord, the Tichborne of those days, to supply her with the means for bequeathing a gift or *dole* of bread to any one who should apply for it annually on the Feast of the Annunciation of the Blessed Virgin. Sir Roger promised her the proceeds of as much land as she could go over while a brand or billet of a certain size was burning: she was nearly bedridden, and nearly dying; and her avaricious lord believed that he had imposed conditions which would place within very narrow limits the area of land to be alienated. But he was mistaken. A miraculous degree of strength was given to her. She was carried by her attendants into a field, where she crawled round many goodly acres. A field of twenty-three acres, at Tichborne, to this day, bears the name of the *Crawl*. The lady, just before her death, solemnly warned her family against any departure from the terms of the dole; she predicted that the family name would become extinct, and the fortunes impoverished, if the dole were ever withdrawn. The Tichborne dole, thus established, was regarded as the occasion of an annual festival during many generations. It was usual to bake fourteen hundred loaves for the dole, of twenty-six ounces each, and to give twopence to any applicant in excess of the number that could be then served. This custom was continued till about the middle of the last [18th] century; when, under the pretence of attending Tichborne Dole, vagabonds, gipsies, and idlers of every description, assembled from all quarters, pilfering throughout the neighbourhood; and at last, in 1796, on account of the complaints of the magistrates and gentry, it was discontinued. This gave great offence to many who had been accustomed to receive the dole. And now arose a revival of old traditions. The good Lady Mabella, as the legend told, had predicted that, if the dole should be withheld, the mansion would crumble to ruins; that the family name would become extinct through the failure of male heirs; and that this failure would be occasioned by a generation of seven sons being followed by a generation of seven daughters. Singularly enough, the old house partially fell down in 1803; the baronet of that day had seven sons; the eldest of these had seven daughters; and the owner of the family estates became a Doughty instead of a Tichborne.

Chambers

In 1865 one Arthur Orton, son of a Wapping butcher, turned up in Wagga Wagga, Australia, claiming to be Roger Charles Tichborne, the heir to the title who had disappeared in a ship bound for Jamaica in 1854. He was accepted by the real Roger's mother, but not by the family; brought to trial, he was exposed as an impostor and sentenced to fourteen years' penal servitude.

Although the title became extinct with the death of Sir Anthony Doughty-Tichborne in 1968, the Tichborne Dole still takes place in Tichborne Park, the family seat. Adult residents of Tichborne, Cheriton, and Lane End (near Winchester) each receive a gallon of self-raising flour, children half a gallon on Lady Day.

In the Roman calendar as reformed by Caesar this was counted the vernal equinox, being the normal date in the years following the reform; in the late Empire it was the day of the Hilaria, when the worshippers of Cybele, the Mother of the Gods, celebrated the resurrection of her castrated lover Attis. It was also the date of the equinox in the rules devised by the church at Rome for finding Easter, and in the somewhat different system used by Celtic Christians (see II: *App. J*). Some writers regarded the 25th, not the 18th, as the first day of Creation; Western tradition set the Crucifixion on this day in AD 29, though many in Gaul preferred to make 25 March the Resurrection (see II: *Christian Chronology*), as it was held to be in Alexandria; some Gaulish and Cappadocian churches kept Easter on it without regard to the day of the week.

26 MARCH

a.d. VII Kalendas Apriles   A

❦ HOLIDAYS AND ANNIVERSARIES Bangladesh: Independence Day (1971) (national day)

Spain: Fiesta del Árbol ('Feast of the Tree' or Arbour Day)

USA, Hawaii: Prince Jonah Kuhio Kalanianaole Day (birthday of Hawaii's second delegate to Congress)

❦ HOLY DAYS

William of Norwich. In 1144 a boy called William disappeared in Norwich on Monday of Holy Week, 20 March, and was found dead on Easter Eve; soon afterwards it was alleged that he had been killed by the local Jews. The story was at first disbelieved, but the coincidence that 20 March was 14 Nisan inspired the fantasy of a ritual crucifixion at Passover, such as had befallen Jesus Christ; in consequence, William acquired the status of a saint and martyr, culted on 26 March, the date of Easter in 1144. This assiduously propagated blood-libel was renewed by folk prejudice, or asserted as a cover, when other children were murdered, and sometimes given credence by authority: Simon of Trent (i.e. Trento), who disappeared on Maundy Thursday, 23 March 1475, and whose mutilated corpse was found on Easter Day, was from 1588 to 1963 officially honoured by the diocese. Indeed, the Passover connection, though present in this case (Simon disappeared on 15 Nisan), ceased to be essential; Anderl Oxner of Rinn in Tyrol, supposedly murdered by Jews, in fact by his uncle, in 1462, was culted on 12 July in a church erected to him in 1671 but now dedicated to the Visitation of the BVM (see *2 July), his bones having been removed from the high altar in 1985, and 'Little Sir Hugh' of Lincoln, for whose murder in 1255 eighteen Jews were hanged and whose memorial plaque remained in Lincoln Cathedral till 1959, on 18 August. Chaucer's Prioress mentions him at the end of her tale, in which a boy who constantly sings the Marian hymn *Alma redemptoris mater* is murdered somewhere in 'Asye' and miraculously permitted by the Virgin to continue singing after death; again Passover does not enter the fiction, but Marian devotion, on account of its emotionalism, was often accompanied by anti-Jewish feeling and worse than feeling. The lie was revived in the nineteenth century, and more than once printed in *franquista* Spain.

Although the blood-libel appears to be independent of classical precedent, similar tales of child murder in secret rituals, made more credible by the overt and notorious Phoenician and Carthaginian child-sacrifice or *molk*, were told against pagan deviants as well as Christians, redeployed by Christians against heretics and Jews, and still believed in Russia at the beginning of the nineteenth century: 'I have indeed heard of one sect, which is said to make it a point of duty to procure amongst themselves a first-born male child of a woman who has never been married, and to eat its flesh and drink its blood at the sacrament' (Wilmot, 265).

Synaxis of Archangel Gabriel (Orth.)

27 MARCH

a.d. VI Kalendas Apriles B

❦ HOLIDAYS AND ANNIVERSARIES Myanmar/Burma: Army Day (currently treated as Resistance Day by the opposition)

❦ HOLY DAYS

John of Egypt (d. 394), anchorite. Disciple of an anchorite, who taught him perfect obedience, he chose the same life, walling himself up, except for a small window, in a three-room cave. Many visitors were drawn by his gifts of prophecy and healing.

Rupert, bishop of Worms and Salzburg, apostle of Bavaria and Austria. Having come to Bavaria in 696, he founded the monastery of St Peter (the oldest in Austria) on the site of Roman Juvavum, now called Salzburg; he preached the Gospel and founded churches over a wide area (still further extended by legend). He died on Easter Sunday, 27 March 718, after celebrating mass. His translation-feast is 24 September, commemorating the solemn burial of his relics in 774 by St Virgilius in his newly built cathedral.

On 27 March 1672, while on the Isle of Thanet, John Evelyn remarked on a custom for which no explanation has been found:

> I came back through a Country the best cultivated of any that in my life I had any where seene . . . observing almost every tall tree, to have a Weather-cock on the top bough, & some trees halfe a dozen, I learned, that on a certain holy-day, the Farmers feast their Servants, at which solemnity they set up these Cocks in a kind of Triumph &c.   Evelyn, *Diary*, iii. 611

28 MARCH

a.d. V Kalendas Apriles C

❦ HOLY DAYS

Priscus, Malchus, and Alexander, youthful martyrs thrown to wild beasts *c.*260 at Caesarea Maritima, the seat of the governor of Judaea.

Pope Sixtus III (432–40), founder of the first known monastery in Rome (at S. Sebastiano on the Appian Way), builder of the octagonal baptistery at S. Giovanni in Laterano, and restorer of S. Maria Maggiore. Sometimes culted on 19 August, the date of his death.

A writer known as 'the Computist of 243' whose treatise *De computo paschali*, written in that year, has been handed down amongst the works of Cyprian dates Christ's birth to

Wednesday 28 March in the 1548th year after the Exodus, which in his chronology corresponds to 4 BC. Since he took the Creation to have taken place on 25 March, entailing that the sun and moon were made on Wednesday the 28th, this was the ideal day for the Sun of Righteousness to have been born.

29 MARCH

a.d. IV Kalendas Apriles   D

❦ HOLIDAYS AND ANNIVERSARIES   Taiwan: Youth Day (public holiday)
USA: Vietnam Veterans Day (withdrawal from Vietnam, 1973)
USA, Delaware: Swedish Colonial Day (first Swedish settlement, 1638)

❦ HOLY DAYS   In the Anglo-Saxon Church this day was celebrated as the Ordination of Gregory the Great to the priesthood; it was suppressed by Lanfranc, but replaced under Anselm by the feast of his consecration on 3 September.

30 MARCH

a.d. III Kalendas Apriles   E

❦ HOLY DAYS

John Climacus (d. 649), monk and abbot of Mount Sinai. He was first a monk, then for most of his life a hermit in Egypt, where he wrote his *Ladder to Paradise*, a treatise on the ideal state of monastic spirituality; the Greek for 'ladder' being *klîmax*, he is known as 'John of the Ladder', *Iōánnēs tês Klímakos*, of which his English name is a corruption. The concept of mounting by degrees was to influence countless later writers. He is culted on this day in both the RC and Orthodox Churches, but the latter also dedicates the fourth Sunday in Lent to him.

Zosimus, bishop of Syracuse, d. *c*.660. At the age of 7 he was given by his parents to the monastery of S. Lucia; it is said that, having been put in charge of the reliquary and shirked his duty, he had a vision of Lucy looking at him angrily, and the Virgin Mary defending him. In any case, he became abbot of the monastery before his nomination to the bishopric by Pope Theodore I (642–9).

31 MARCH

pridie Kalendas Apriles   F

❦ HOLIDAYS AND ANNIVERSARIES   Malta: National Day, or Freedom Day (independence from Great Britain, 1964)

❦ ANCIENT ROME   The Moon was worshipped in her temple on the Aventine Hill. The night of 31 March, preceding the three-day festival of Venus Verticordia (see *1 Apr.), is the occasion for the *Pervigilium Veneris*, a beautiful but problematic late Roman poem looking forward to the festival; it is best known for its refrain, bidding all who have never loved and all who have loved to love on the morrow:

> Cras amet qui numquam amavit, quique amavit cras amet.

The poem caught the imagination of Walter Pater, who in *Marius the Epicurean* invented a genesis for it in the second century AD; this is certainly too early, but scholars have not yet agreed how long before or after AD 400 it should be dated.

❦ HOLY DAYS
Guy of Pomposa, abbot (1046), who had a custom of withdrawing to a cell some three miles from his abbey, where he seemed to do nothing but fast and pray. His death at Parma as a result of sudden illness led to a dispute between Pomposa and Parma for the custody of his relics, which the emperor Henry III settled by sending them to the church of St John the Evangelist at Speyer.

In Brazil this was formerly the day for celebrating the overthrow in 1964 of President João Goulart in a military coup accompanied by well-organized demonstrations. The true date was 1 April, but the government did not care to call it the Glorious April Fool's Day Revolution.

APRIL

Sweete April showers,
Doo spring Maie flowers.

The April's in her eyes; it is love's spring,
And these the showers to bring it on.
                            Antony, in *Antony and Cleopatra*, III. ii. 43–4

Till April is dead
change not a thread.

(NAMES FOR THE MONTH Latin *Aprilis*, French *avril*, Spanish *abril*, Portuguese *Abril*, Italian *aprile*, German *April*, Welsh *Ebrill*, Scots Gaelic *an Giblean*, Irish *Aibreán*

Roman writers derived *Aprilis* from *aperire*, 'to open', or the Greek goddess Aphrodite; neither is linguistically credible. Modern scholars associate the name with an ancient root meaning 'other', i.e. the second month of a year beginning in March. The etymology of the Scots Gaelic name is obscure; the Irish appears to be a distortion of the Latin.

(HOLIDAYS AND ANNIVERSARIES

Third Monday USA, Maine and Massachusetts: Patriots' Day (Battle of Lexington and Concord, 1775; see *19 Apr.)

Fourth Monday USA, Alabama: Confederate Memorial Day
   USA, New Hampshire: Fast Day

Last Monday USA, Mississippi: Confederate Memorial Day

Second Friday Lesotho: Fast and Prayer Day

Arbor Day is observed in most US states on some day in April, often combined with Bird Day. First observed 10 April 1872 in Nebraska; special celebrations take place annually in Nebraska City. A National Arbor Day, to promote the recognition of the usefulness of trees, accompanied by tree-planting, has been proposed for the last Friday in April.

A recently invented celebration is Secretaries Day, on the Wednesday of the last full week in April.

In the USA, Daylight Saving Time begins on the first Sunday in April in those states that observe it (see II: *Days and Times*).

> Next came fresh *Aprill* full of lustyhed,
> And wanton as a Kid whose horne new buds:
> Vpon a Bull he rode, the same which led
> *Europa* floting through th'*Argolick* fluds:
> His hornes were gilden all with golden studs
> And garnished with garlonds goodly dight
> Of all the fairest flowres and freshest buds
> Which th'earth brings forth, and wet he seem'd in sight
> With waues, through which he waded for his loues delight.
>
> Spenser, *The Faerie Queene*, VII. vii. 33

> Faire is my loue for *Aprill* in her face,
> Hir louely brests *September* claimes his part,
> And lordly *Iuly* in her eyes takes place,
> But colde *December* dwelleth in her heart:
> Blest be the months, that sets my thoughts on fire,
> Accurst that Month that hindreth my desire.
>
> Robert Greene (1558–92), *Perymedes, the Blacksmith* (1588)

It is now April, and the Nightingale begins to tune her throat against May: the Sunny showers perfume the aire, and the Bees begin to goe abroad for honey: the Dewe, as in Pearles, hangs vpon the tops of the grasse, while the Turtles sit billing vpon the little greene boughes: the Trowt begins to play in the Brookes, and the Sammon leaues the Sea, to play in the fresh waters: The Garden bankes are full of gay flowers, and the Thorne and the Plumme send forth their faire Blossomes: the March Colt begins to play, and the Cosset Lamb is learned to butt. The Poets now make their studies in the woods, and the Youth of the Country make ready for the Morris-dance; the little Fishes lye nibling at a bait, and the Porpas playes in the pride of the tide: the shepheards pipe entertaines the Princesse of Arcadia, and the healthfull Souldier hath a pleasant march. The Larke and the Lambe looke vp at the Sun, and the labourer is abroad by the dawning of the day: Sheepes eyes in Lambs heads, tell kind hearts strange tales, while faith and troth make the true Louers knot: the aged haires find a fresh life, and the youthfull cheeks are as red as a cherry: It were a world to set downe the worth of this moneth: But in summe, I thus conclude, I hold it the Heauens blessing, and the Earths comfort. Farewell.   Breton (1626)

In this *Moneth* the *blood* increaseth, wherefore to eat pleasant meats, and River Fish, and Sallets often is commended, to Bleed and Bathe this Moneth very good, to purge the stomack by Potion or otherwise is good, but to eat any kind of *Roots* this Moneth is thought hurtful, all kind of Meat moderately taken, except Pigg, is counted good; Its safe to enter into Physick for any grief of the body, but drink moderately, because excessive drinking more contaminates the blood in this Moneth than in any other; to eat *Betony* and *Mints* prepared in *Honey*, and drink *first* in the morning before you *eat* any thing, and to *drink* sometimes the Herb of Grace [rue = *Gratia Dei*] in Wine is profitable; but beware of eating Salt Fish in this Moneth, for it fouls the blood, and breeds Itches and Scabs in the body.   Saunders (1665)

1 APRIL

Kalendae Apriles   G

If it thunders on All Fools' day
it brings good crops of corn and hay.

The first Day of April you may send a fool whither you will.

❦ HOLIDAYS AND ANNIVERSARIES Anguilla: Constitution Day

❦ ANCIENT ROME This was the day of Venus Verticordia ('Heart-turner'): statues of Venus were washed by female worshippers, who then bedecked her with fresh flowers. Also honoured was Fortuna Virilis, originally 'Men's Fortune' but by classical times interpreted as 'Luck with Men'; women of the lower orders prayed to her in the men's baths.

❦ HOLY DAYS Mary of Egypt (Orth.; see *2 Apr.)

Hugh (1052–1132), bishop of Grenoble. After initial reluctance, he served for fifty-two years altogether, and was renowned for his generosity. Attracted by the monastic life, and having joined the Benedictine Order at an early age, he gave St Bruno and his companions Chartreuse, whose monks, vowed to silence, later formed the Carthusian Order.

A tradition recorded by early calendars and again by the Bollandists made this the day on which Jesus Christ began preaching.

All Fool's Day. A pan-European observance of French origin, characterized by the *poisson d'avril*, literally 'April fish', a trick whereby credulous persons are hoaxed in some ingenious way, or made ridiculous by the attachment behind their backs of a cardboard fish to their clothing; in the oldest form of the trick, however, several persons conspired to send the victim on a fool's errand from one confederate to another, each alleging that it was the next with whom the business was to be done.

Some explanations of the custom, and the name, are such that only an April fool could believe. Some said that after Charles IX in 1564 had ordered the year to be reckoned from 1 January instead of Easter, bogus New Year presents were given on 1 April; this is to confuse the traditional New Year festivities with the change of date. Another tale is that the fruitless journeys recall those of Christ from the Sanhedrin to Pilate, from Pilate to Herod Antipas, and from Herod back to Pilate, April being the likely month of the Crucifixion (though Western tradition placed it on 25 March), and the fish standing for Christ as it did in early Christian times; this would be more convincing if the custom had originated amongst the clergy.

However, the April fish is the mackerel, abundant in that month, and known in French as *maquereau*, from the Dutch *makreel*; but since *maquereau* (this time from Dutch *makelaar*, 'broker') is also French for 'pimp', by the end of the fifteenth century *poisson d'avril* was in common use for a pander or go-between, especially a page sent to arrange a love affair. It is possible that the term was extended to the butt of the practical joke, though it is generally used to describe the joke itself, rather than the victim, and hence as an exclamation remains in the singular even when addressed to a group. Of Johann Clemens von Wittelsbach, Electoral Archbishop of Cologne and Bishop of Liège, who resided at Valenciennes during the War of the Spanish Succession we read:

Il s'avisa, un premier jour d'avril, de monter en chaire; il y avoit envoyé inviter tout ce qui était à Valenciennes, et l'église étoit toute remplie. L'Électeur parut en chaire, regarda la compagnie de tous côtés, puis tout à coup se mit à crier: «Poisson d'avril! poisson d'avril!» et sa musique, avec force trompettes et timbales, à lui répondre. Lui cependant fit le plongeon, et s'en alla. Voilà des plaisanteries allemandes, et de prince, dont l'assistance, qui en rit fort, ne laissa pas d'être bien étonnée.   Louis de Rouvroy, duc de Saint-Simon, *Mémoires*, under 1711

One April the first he decided to mount the pulpit; he had sent invitations to everyone at Valenciennes, and the church was packed full. The Elector appeared in the pulpit, looked the assembled company all over, then suddenly started to shout: 'April fool! April fool!', and his band, with all its trumpets and kettledrums, struck up in reply. For his part, he gave a low bow and departed. That is German humour for you, and princely at that; the audience, for all its loud laughter, was much astonished at it.

Newspapers and other media have not forborne to hoax the public. In 1846 the London *Evening Star* announced a grand donkey-show to be held at Islington on 1 April; those readers who made the journey found no donkeys on show but themselves. The British Broadcasting Corporation once enlivened its television schedules with a very plausible documentary on the Italian spaghetti harvest, and French radio caused spectacular traffic jams by announcing that traffic in Bordeaux would be directed by *une dolly-bird anglaise en minijupe*.

In 1969 the *Arkansas Law Review* published an account of a judgment said to have been delivered by the Supreme Court of Arkansas on 1 April 1968 in a case between J. R. Poisson and Étienne d'Avril that turned on an incautiously worded Arkansas statute of 1945 declaring all laws and parts of laws to be repealed. The case and the parties were fictitious; but the statute was not.

In 1994, while the recently announced proof of Fermat's Last Theorem was being refined to eliminate flaws detected in peer review, an e-mail hoaxer reported by way of April foolery that a counter-example had been found by the very mathematician who had recently disproved a similar conjecture.

In England the connection with 1 April seems not to have been made before the late seventeenth century (it appears in *Poor Robin* for the first time in 1692), but the practice of pinning something on an unsuspecting person's back is mentioned in the preface of Thomas Dekker's *Seven Deadlie Sinnes of London* (1606):

The Booke-seller ever after when you passe by, pinnes on your backes the badge of fooles to make you be laught to scorne, or of sillie Carpers to make you be pittied.

April Fool's Day in Scotland: hunting the gowk

What compound is to simple addition, so is Scotch to English April fooling. In the northern part of the island, they are not content to make a neighbour believe some single piece of absurdity. There, the object being, we shall say, to befool simple Andrew Thomson, Wag No. 1 sends him away with a letter to a friend two miles off, professedly asking for some useful information, or requesting a loan of some article, but in reality containing only the words:

> 'This is the first day of April,
> Hunt the gowk another mile.'

Wag No. 2, catching up the idea of his correspondent, tells Andrew with a grave face that it is not in his power, &c.; but if he will go with another note to such a person, he will get what is wanted. Off Andrew trudges with this second note to Wag No. 3, who treats him in the same manner; and so on he goes, till some one of the series, taking pity on him, hints the trick that has been practised upon him. A successful affair of this kind will keep rustic society in merriment for a week, during which honest Andrew Thomson hardly can shew his face. The Scotch employ the term gowk (which is properly a cuckoo) to express a fool in general, but more especially an April fool, and among them the practice above described is called *hunting the gowk*.

Chambers

The borrowing days. Since the beginning of April is often stormy, when March has gone out like a lion, the first three days are called the 'borrowing days', no longer April's but borrowed by March:

> March borrowed from Averil
> Three Days, and they were ill.

A Scottish account runs:

> March said to Aperill:
> I saw three hogs upon a hill;
> But lend your three first days to me,
> And I'll be bound to gar them die.
> The first, it sall be wind and weet;
> The next, it sall be snaw and sleet;
> The third, it sall be sic a freeze
> Sall gar the birds stick to the trees.—
> But when the borrowed days were gane,
> The three silly hogs came hirplin hame.   *poor; hobbling*

Jamieson, s.v. 'Borrowing Days'; other versions exist

there eftir i entrit in ane grene forrest, to contempil the tendir 3ong frutes of grene treis, be cause the borial blastis of the thre borouing dais of marche hed chaissit the fragrant flureise of euyrie frute tree far athourt the feildis.   *The Complaynt of Scotlande* (1549), 37–8

In Tiree these days are *trì latha na boin ruaidhe*, 'the three days of the red cow', cf. Irish *laethanta na riaibhche* (mod. *riabhaí*), 'the days of the brindled cow'; though another form of the tale assigns them to *March. Humphrey O'Sullivan applies *trí laethe na sean-riaibhiche*, 'the three days of the old brindled cow', to 1–3 April OS. March is called 'angry, windy, hard', April 'dripping, bleating, new'. But a Northern Ireland version extends the number to nine: three to fleece the blackbird, three to punish the stonechat, three days for the grey cow.

2 APRIL

a.d. IV Nonas Apriles   A

❨ HOLIDAYS AND ANNIVERSARIES USA, Florida: Pascua Florida Day (commemorating discovery of Florida by Ponce de León in 1513)

❨ HOLY DAYS Francis of Paola (RC)

Francis of Paola (1416–1507), founder of the Franciscan Minim Friars. A native of Calabria, he became a hermit at the age of 15 in a cave near Paola; others joined him, eventually forming the Hermits of St Francis of Assisi (founded 1452, sanctioned 1474), later known as the Friars Minim, who refused milk and eggs as well as meat. Famed for his prophecies and miracles during his lifetime, Francis was called to France by Louis XI, whom he consoled in his last illness; 'le saint homme' made a great impression not only on Louis but on the equally hard-headed chronicler of his reign Philippe de Commynes:

> He builded in the place where he liued two Churches, and neuer ate since the time he entred into this strait kinde of life, either fish, flesh, egs, any kinde of whitmeate, or of fat. I neuer saw in my time a man of so holy life, nor by whose mouth the holy Ghost seemed rather to speake; for he neuer had been scholler, but was vtterly vnlearned . . . His answers were so wise, that all men woondered at them; so far foorth that our holy Father gaue him leaue to erect a new order, called the heremites of Saint *Francis*. From thence he came to the King, who honored him as if he had been the Pope himselfe, falling downe before him, and desiring him to prolong his life: whereunto he answered as a wise man should. I haue often heard him talke with the King that now is, in presence of all the nobilitie of the realme, and that within these two moneths, and sure he seemed by his words, to be inspired with the holy Ghost, otherwise he could neuer haue communed of such matters as he did.   *Mémoires*, bk. 8, ch. 6 (trans. Danett, 226–7)

Louis's successor Charles VIII built him two monasteries. Many of his miracles are concerned with the sea (in one he sails across the Strait of Messina on his cloak); Pius XII named him patron saint of seafarers in 1943.

Mary of Egypt (Maria Aegyptiaca); having spent seventeen years in a life of pleasure, she went on a pilgrimage to the Holy Cross in Jerusalem, was converted, and lived another forty-seven years as a hermit east of the Jordan; in the sixth century her tomb was often visited by pilgrims. Many legends (some borrowed from Mary Magdalene) were told about her, as that she went clad only in her hair, and was buried by a lion; angels escorted her soul to heaven. She is a favourite subject for painters. This is her RC day; the Orthodox honour her on the 1st, and also on the fifth Sunday in Lent.

Day of the Unity of the Peoples proclaimed in Russia and Belarus' to celebrate the economic union between them signed on this day in 1996.

3 APRIL
—————

❨ HOLY DAYS Richard of Chichester (BCP; CY 16 June)

Richard of Chichester (Richard de Wyche) (1197–1253), bishop of Chichester (translation on 15 July). As a young man, he postponed studies to restore the family farm; he then attended Oxford University and later earned a degree in civil law at Bologna. Returning to Oxford, he was made Chancellor, but resigned to become chancellor of the Archbishop of Canterbury, after whose death he decided to enter holy orders, becoming first a parish priest, then again chancellor of the Archbishop of Canterbury. His election as bishop of Chichester (1244) led to a battle of wills between King Henry III, who had appointed his own candidate, and the Archbishop. Though confirmed and consecrated by the pope in 1245, it took Richard two years to secure the properties of the diocese. He proved a model diocesan bishop, severe towards sinners yet generous to those in need. He actively recruited for the Crusade, whose objective he saw less as military conquest than as opening the route for pilgrims to the Holy Land. He was canonized in 1262. The RC commemorates him on this date as well.

Nicetas (Orth.), banished for resisting the revival of Iconoclasm by the emperor Leo V (813–20). In Crete there is reported to be a hoofmark where his white winged horse landed after the rescue of a maiden in distress; he has a chapel on Mt Helicon, where the stamp of Pegasus' hoof opened the fountain Hippocrene.

⸻

The well-flowering at Droitwich:

This Custome is yearly observed at Droit-Wich in Worcester-shire, where on the day of St. Richard the Patron of yᵉ Well (i.e.) salt-well, they keepe Holyday, dresse the well with green Boughes and flowers. One yeare sc. Aᵒ 164.., in the Presbyterian times it was discontinued in the Civil-warres; and after that the spring shranke up or dried up for some time. So afterwards they kept their annuall custome (notwithstanding the power of yᵉ Parliament and soldiers), and the salt-water returned again and still continues. This St. Richard was a person of great estate in these parts, and a briske young fellow that would ride over hedge and ditch, and at length became a very devout man, and after his decease was canonized for a Saint.   Aubrey, 33

Before the calendar reform, this was the traditional day of the cuckoo's first appearance in England; see *14 April, but also *8 April.

4 APRIL

pridie Nonas Apriles   C

❦ HOLIDAYS AND ANNIVERSARIES   Senegal: Independence Day (sovereignty, 1960)

❦ ANCIENT ROME   Megalensia, in honour of the Great [in Greek *Megalē*] Mother of the Gods, who had been brought to Rome in 205/4 BC; the festivities eventually extended to the 10th. The celebration was an upper-class affair, marked by the exchanging of hospitality (*mutitatio*) by members of clubs (*sodalitates*) formed for the purpose; its counterpart amongst the common people was the Cerialia (see *19 Apr.).

The illustration in Pl. 5 is one of the two surviving copies of that in the Calendar of 354 (see II: *Roman Calendar*); it depicts a man, no longer in the flower of youth, in a short tunic with the typical late-antique shoulder-roundels called *orbiculi*, dancing with castanets in front of a male, or rather hermaphroditic, cult-image; this is usually taken for a Renaissance miscopying of a Venus, but the male worshipper and the castanets remain to be accounted for. It has been suggested that the deity is Attis, the Great Mother's sexually ambiguous consort, and the dancer the old man who, according to one explanation of the proverb *omnia secunda, saltat senex* ('All's well, the old man's dancing'), averted the goddess's wrath by dancing at her games. The castanets tell in favour of this interpretation.

❦ HOLY DAYS   Ambrose (BCP); Isidore of Seville (RC)

Ambrose, bishop of Milan, died on 4 April 397; he is commemorated on this day in the BCP, but the ASB and CY have joined with the Roman Catholic and Orthodox churches in observing *7 December, the date of his election in 374.

Isidore of Seville, 'Hispalensis', brother of Leander (see *13 Mar.), whom he succeeded as bishop of Seville *c*.600; d. 636. An excellent administrator who worked closely with the Visigothic kings of Spain, especially Sisebut (612–21), he is best known for his scholarly writings, above all the *Etymologiae* or *Origines*, an encyclopedic summary of late-antique learning.

Benedict the Moor (Benedetto Manasseri) (1526–89), a Franciscan friar, born in Sicily to African slaves; patiently supporting taunts because of his colour, he became a Franciscan lay brother, and eventually superior of his convent; he was known for healing and counselling. In 1998 he was reinstated as co-patron with Rosalia (see *15 July) of Palermo, where he died, as a symbol of racial and cultural tolerance.

According to Olaus Worm's Danish calendar, on this day 'they say that peas should not be cooked, but committed to the earth', i.e. sown.

5 APRIL

5 APRIL

Nonae Apriles   D

❲ ANCIENT ROME Dedication-day of temple of Fortuna Publica, one of three in the Quirinal (see too *25 May).

❲ HOLY DAYS Vincent Ferrer (RC)

Vincent Ferrer (1350–1419), Dominican friar and inspiring preacher. Born in Spain to an Englishman and a Spanish woman, he joined the Dominican Order in 1367, becoming famous as a preacher and securing many conversions. Unsuccessful in his attempts to persuade the schismatic Spanish pope Benedict XIII to be reconciled with the Roman Urban VI, he withdrew from the papal court at Avignon and returned to preaching, mainly in France and Brittany. In 1414 he attempted to persuade Benedict to abdicate; but this he refused to do even when the Council of Constance had set aside all three popes (himself, Gregory XII, and John XXIII).

Derfel (d. 6th century). Known as Derfel Gadarn ('the mighty'), he was a soldier in early life. Little is known of his life but much more of his afterlife in the form of his statue in Llandderfel (Gwynedd), a town founded by him. The great traveller Thomas Pennant records the following:

A little beyond the extremity of this romantic part [near Llandrillo], in an opening on the right, stand the church and village of *Llan-Dderfel*: the first was dedicated to *St. Derfel Gadarn*, and was remarkable for a vast wooden image of the saint, the subject of much superstition in antient times. The *Welsh* had a prophecy, that it should set a *whole forest on fire*. Whether to complete it, or whether to take away from the people the cause of idolatry, I cannot say; but it was brought to *London* in the year 1538, and was used as part of the fuel which consumed poor frier *Forest* to ashes, in *Smithfield*, for denying the king's supremacy. This unhappy man was hanged in chains round his middle to a gallows, over which was placed this inscription, allusive to our image:

> *David Darvel Gutheren*,
> As sayth the *Welshman*,
> Fetched outlawes out of Hell.
>
> Now is he come with spere and sheld,
> In harnes to burne in *Smithfeld*,
> For in *Wales* he may not dwel.
>
> And *Foreest* the freer,
> That obstinate lyer,
> That wylfully shalbe dead.
>
> In his contumacye,
> The gospel doeth deny,
> The kyng to be supreme heade.

[Source: *Hall's Chronicle*, ccxxxiii] Pennant, *Snowdon*, 64–6

According to some calendars, this was the day on which the Flood began.

6 APRIL

❦ HOLY DAYS

Notker Balbulus ('the Stammerer'), monk of Sankt Gallen, d. 6 April 912 (honoured at Sankt Gallen on 7 May); author of greatly admired hymns and sequences (texts in rhythmical prose), set to music by himself. It is related that when the emperor Charles the Fat visited Sankt Gallen, his delight in conversing with the Stammerer provoked his jealous chaplain into asking Notker the disdainful question: 'Tell me, you who are so learned, what is God doing now?' To which Notker sweetly replied: 'He is doing now what He has done in the past and will do so long as the world shall last: He is putting down the proud and exalting the humble.' Once when Satan infiltrated the monastery in the form of a dog Notker thwacked him so hard with St Columban's staff that he broke it; in consequence he is depicted with a broken stick above a cringing devil.

Founding of the Church of Jesus Christ of Latter-day Saints by Joseph Smith (1830).

This day is the beginning of the UK tax year. When in 1752 the official beginning of the English year was moved from 25 March to 1 January, it was nevertheless thought expedient to allow the financial year 1751 its full twelve months, and to reckon its successor from 25 March; the omission of eleven days from September that year caused the next financial year to be counted from Old Lady Day, 5 April 1753. In 1800, the suppression of the leap day caused the corresponding date to become 6 April; but in 1900, when the change of style was no longer a living memory, the further adjustment to 7 April was not made.

Birth (1483) and death (1520) of Raphael (Raffaello Sanzio). He is buried in the Pantheon in Rome, where his monument bears the inscription by Pietro Bembo:

Raphaeli Sanctio Ioannis F. Vrbinati Pictori eminentissimo veterumque aemulo cuius adspiranteis prope imagines si contemplere, naturae atque artis foedus facile inspexeris. Iulii II et Leonis X pontt. maxx. picturae et architecturae operibus gloriam auxit. V. A. XXXVII integer integros. Quo die natus est eo esse desiit. VIII. ID. APRIL. M.D.XX.

> Ille hic est Raphael timuit quo sospite uinci
> rerum magna parens et moriente mori.

To Raffaello di Giovanni Sanzio of Urbino, the most eminent painter and rival of the ancients, in whose almost breathing portraits you will by contemplating them easily discern the compact of nature and art. He increased the glory of Popes Julius II and Leo X by his works of painting and architecture. He lived an upright man for 37 whole years. On the same day on which he was born he ceased to be. 6 April 1520.

That Raphael is here, during whose life Nature, the great parent of the universe, feared she was being surpassed, and when he was dying that she was dying.

7 APRIL

❦ HOLIDAYS AND ANNIVERSARIES UN member nations: World Health Day
USA, New York: Verrazano Day (discovery of New York Harbor by Giovanni da
Verrazano, 1524)

❦ HOLY DAYS Jean-Baptiste de La Salle (RC)

Jean-Baptiste de La Salle (1651–1751), French educational reformer, founder of the Institute
of the Brothers of Christian Schools. He opened Sunday schools in 1699, established a
boarding-school in 1705, and pioneered whole-class teaching and the use of the vernacular. In 1950 he was declared the patron saint of schoolteachers.

In Armenia this is the Annunciation.

On this day in 1724 the first performance of Bach's *St John Passion* took place at the Nico-
laikirche in Leipzig; it was Good Friday in the Protestant states of Germany, though
not under either the Gregorian calendar used by Roman Catholic countries and the
Netherlands, or the Julian calendar still used by Great Britain; see II: *The Date of Easter:
Astronomical Easter.*

The Days of April
On the return of April some few days
Before it comes when every thing looks new
And woods where primroses burn in a blaze
of fire And sallows in the woods made new
Seen blazeing out in blossoms not a few
But bushes smothered over what a change
Is turned upon their brightness passing by
The very birds the pies and crows and Jays
Look downward on their bloom from dark trees high
And wood larks dropping from the rich blue sky
Winner and whistle to their very roots
Sitting beneath a canophy of gold
And wood anemonies the sharp air suits
Their sheltered blooms with beauties manifold
Daisies burn April grass with silver flies
And pilewort in the green lane blazes out
Enough to burn the fingers neath the briars
Where village Boys will scrat dead leaves about
To look for pootys—every eye admires   *landsnails*
The lovely pictures that the spring brings out
Meadows of bowing cowslips what mind tires
To see them dancing in the emerald grass
And trawling chrystal brook as clear as glass

Laughing groaning uggling on for miles   *gurgling*
That waves the silver blades of swimming grass
Upon the surface while the glad sun smiles
Such are the sights the showers and sunshine bring
To three or four bright days in the first of spring . . .

John Clare (1793–1864)

8 APRIL

a.d. VI Idus Apriles   G

❦ HOLIDAYS AND ANNIVERSARIES Japan: Hanamatsuri ('Flower Festival'; Buddha's
Birthday)
Korea: Buddha's Birthday

The Birthday of the Buddha was originally the eighth day of the fourth lunar month.

❦ HOLY DAYS

Gauthier of Pontoise, the first abbot of the abbey founded at Pontoise by Philip I of France;
he is said, on receiving his investiture, to have placed his hand on the staff not beneath
but above the king's, with the words: 'I take, not your hand from below, but this staff
from above; for it is not from you that I accept the charge of this church, but from God.'
However, finding the pressures too much for him, he begged Pope Gregory VII to release him from the charge; the Pope refused, and when Gauthier nonetheless sneaked
off to Cluny ordered him back to his duty.

The cuckoo makes its appearance about now (see also *14 Apr.):

About the 8th, 9th, or 10th Days the Cuckow comes, therefore you that keep Cows, provide
Curds and Cream against her coming.   *Poor Robin* (1682)

April
I open wide the portals of the Spring
    To welcome the procession of the flowers,
With their gay banners, and the birds that sing
    Their song of songs from their aerial towers.
I soften with my sunshine and my showers
    The heart of earth; with thoughts of love I glide
Into the hearts of men; and with the hours
    Upon the Bull with wreathèd horns I ride.

Henry Wadsworth Longfellow (1807–82), *The Poet's Calendar*

9 APRIL

a.d. V Idus Apriles   A

(HOLY DAYS

Maria Cl(e)ophae, the wife of Clopas and mother of St James the Less. She is one of the three Marys who stood under the Cross.

Gilbert White muses on the naked slug and the housed snail, which begin to appear about now:

The shell-less snails, called slugs, are in motion all the winter in mild weather, & commit great depredations on garden-plants, & much injure the green wheat, the loss of which is imputed to earth-worms; while the shelled snail, the φερέοικος ['house-bearer', a kenning used by the Greek poet Hesiod], does not come forth at all 'til about April the tenth; and not only lays itself up pretty early in the autumn, in places secure from frost; but also throws-out round the mouth of it's shell a thick operculum formed from it's own saliva; so that it is perfectly secured, & corked-up as it were, from all inclemencies. Why the naked slug should be so much more able to endure cold than it's housed congener, I cannot pretend to say.   White (31 Mar. 1775)

10 APRIL

a.d. IV Idus Apriles   B

(HOLIDAYS AND ANNIVERSARIES

Salvation Army Founder's Day (birth of William Booth, 1829)

(ANCIENT ROME Culmination of Megalensia, with games in the Circus Maximus preceded by a grand procession to the Great Mother's temple on the Palatium. (This was the ancient and medieval name for what is now called the Palatine Hill; it is the origin of our word 'palace', reflecting the fact that the emperor Augustus occupied its entirety with his own dwelling-place.)

(HOLY DAYS William Law (CY)

William Law (1686–1761). Having lost his Cambridge fellowship when he refused to take the Oath of Allegiance on the succession of George I, he found work as tutor to the father of the historian Edward Gibbon. A spiritual writer, his most influential work was *A Serious Call to a Devout and Holy Life*, by which he meant the everyday life. In Gibbon's autobiography he is remembered as 'a worthy and pious man, who believed all that he professed and practised all that he enjoined. The character of a nonjuror which he maintained to the last is a sufficient evidence of his principles in Church and State, and the sacrifice of interest to conscience will be always respectable.'

In the nineteenth century this day was remembered as that on which, in 1848, the Chartists had made their last and greatest demonstration in support of six political demands; five of these are now accepted principles of the constitution and the sixth, that a new Parliament should be elected every year, is dead even among reformers. The Monster Petition was reported to contain eleven signatures in the name of Queen Victoria and two in that of the Devil. Chambers recounts the occasion as follows:

The Parisian Revolution of February, 1848, had, as usual, stirred up and brought into violent action all the discontents of Europe. Even in happy England there was a discontent, one involving certain sections of the working classes, and referring rather to certain speculative political claims than to any practical grievance. The Chartists, as they were called, deemed this a good opportunity for pressing their claims, and they resolved to do so with a demonstration of their numbers, thus hinting at the physical force which they possessed, but probably without any serious designs against the peace of their fellow-citizens. It was arranged that a monster petition should be presented to parliament on the 10th of April, after being paraded through London by a procession. The Government, fearing that an outbreak of violence might take place, as had happened already at Manchester, Glasgow, and other large towns, assembled large bodies of troops, planted cannon in the neighbourhood of Westminster Bridge, and garrisoned the public offices; at the same time a vast number of the citizens were sworn in as special constables to patrol the streets. The Chartists met on Kennington Common, under the presidency of Mr Feargus O'Connor, M.P., but their sense of the preparations made for the preservation of the peace, and a hint that they would not be allowed to cross the bridges in force, took away all hope of their intended demonstration. Their petition was quietly taken 'in three cabs' along Vauxhall Bridge, and presented to the House of Commons; the multitude dispersed; by four o'clock in the afternoon London had resumed its ordinary appearances, and the *Tenth of April* remained only a memory of an apprehended danger judiciously met and averted.

In 1864 a Scottish publication could refer to the whole kingdom as 'England'; the English now do so, save amongst themselves, at their peril.

11 APRIL

a.d. III Idus Apriles   C

❆ HOLY DAYS Stanisław of Kraków (RC); formerly Leo I, Pope (now 10 Nov.)

Stanisław (Stanislaus) of Kraków (1030–79), bishop and martyr; patron of Poland (formerly 7 May). Born to a noble family in Szczepanów, after studies at Gniezno and perhaps Paris he became a canon at Kraków, and was consecrated bishop in 1072. He excommunicated the king, Bolesław II, for refusing to repent of his cruel and licentious behaviour, especially the kidnapping of the beautiful wife of a nobleman. In revenge, Bolesław ordered his soldiers to kill Stanisław as he was celebrating mass at a chapel outside the city; they were prevented from doing so by a great light, whereupon the king undertook the task himself. As a consequence, Pope Gregory VII laid Poland under interdict. Stanisław was canonized in 1253.

Guthlac (*c*.673–714). Born in the Midland kingdom of Mercia, which derived its name from the Marches or border with the Welsh, he did gallant service in war, then became successively a monk at Repton and a hermit at Crowland in the Fens. After his death on Wednesday of Easter Week, 11 April 714, an abbey (sometimes called 'Croyland') was built there in his honour by King Ethelbald, whose succession to the Mercian throne he is said to have posthumously predicted in a dream.

April in Town

Straight from the east the wind blows sharp with rain,
   That just now drove its wild ranks down the street,
   And westward rushed into the sunset sweet.
Spouts brawl, boughs drip and cease and drip again,
Bricks gleam; keen saffron glows each window-pane,
   And every pool beneath the passing feet.
   Innumerable odors fine and fleet
Are blown this way from blossoming lawn and lane.
Wet roofs show black against a tender sky;
   The almond bushes in the lean-fenced square,
     Beaten to the walks, show all their draggled white.
A troop of laborers comes slowly by;
   One bears a daffodil, and seems to bear
   A new-lit candle through the fading light.

Lizette Woodworth Reese (1856–1935)

12 APRIL

pridie Idus Apriles   D

❧ ANCIENT ROME This was the first day of the Ludi Ceriales, the Games of Ceres, goddess of corn, held in the Circus Maximus; they extended till the 19th.

❧ HOLY DAYS

Zeno (d. 371), patron saint of Verona. He came from Africa and was appointed Bishop of Verona in 362. He is usually represented with a fish dangling from his crosier; whether as fisher of souls or because he saved Verona from drought is not clear. A different explanation was offered to Thomas Coryat, who viewed the tomb and statue of St Zeno in Verona Cathedral in 1608:

Within the Church there is an extraordinary great front made of porphyrie. In a low crypta or vault of this Church I saw the monument of Saint Zeno, & againe above neare to the quire his statue made in stone with a miter upon his head. He is pourtrayed laughing and looking very pleasantly, in his left hand he held a reeden rod, the top whereof was pretily made with bone finely wrought, which indeed was nothing else but the top of his Crosier: at the ende hanged a counterfeited Trowte, in token that hee was much delighted in taking of Trowtes, as a Benedictine Monke tolde me. There I read this inscription, Anno Dom. trecentessimo [*sic*] primo Beatus Zeno moritur duodecima Aprilis.   Coryat, ii. 33

13 APRIL

❲ HOLIDAYS AND ANNIVERSARIES   Chad: National Day
   USA, Alabama and Oklahoma: Thomas Jefferson's Birthday

❲ ANCIENT ROME   Like all Ides, this was sacred to Jupiter; it was the dedication-day of a temple in honour of Jupiter Victor on the Palatium, vowed after a great league of Rome's Italian enemies had been defeated at Sentinum, near the modern Sassoferrato, in BC 295, and also of a temple of Jupiter Libertas on the Aventine.

❲ HOLY DAYS   Pope Martin I (RC)

Pope Martin I (649–54) (formerly 12 Nov.), a martyr persecuted not by pagans but by the Christian emperor Constans II, whose prohibition of theological discussion in respect to Monotheletism he had flouted by condemning the doctrine as heretical. He was imprisoned, banished to the Crimea, and deposed.

Hermenegild (d. 585), eldest son of the Arian Visigoth Leuvigild, king of Spain, married the Frankish princess Ingund, who refused to be rebaptized an Arian even when thrown bodily into the font by Queen Goiswinth, and instead converted her husband to Catholicism. A civil war, initiated by Hermenegild, ensued:

The rash youth, inflamed by zeal, and perhaps by ambition, was tempted to violate the duties of a son and a subject; and the catholics of Spain, although they could not complain of persecution, applauded his pious rebellion against an heretical father.   Gibbon, *Decline and Fall*, ch. 37

Eventually he was defeated, and executed; a thousand years later he was canonized by a Roman Catholic Church whose most zealous champion was the king of Spain and which claimed the right to depose heretical monarchs.

Caradog, harper to King Rhys of South Wales who became a monk at Llandaff and then a hermit; d. 1124. He is buried in St David's Cathedral, where his bones appear to have been found (see *1 Mar.).

Justin Martyr (*c*.100–*c*.165), who had not previously been honoured in the West (and whose works were not translated into Latin till 1554), was placed on this day by Florus, deacon of Lyon (9th c.), because it was already consecrated to two martyrs (Carpus and

Agathonice) whose martyrdom precedes Justin's in Eusebius' *Ecclesiastical History*. He was moved to the 14th by Leo XIII and to the Eastern date of *1 June in 1969.

Black Monday. On this day in 1360 an English force under the Earl of March, marshal of Edward III's army in France, was caught in a fearful storm of thunder, lightning, and hail; over 6,000 horses were killed, besides countless human losses. It has commonly been known as Black Monday, and even invoked (along with various other historical events) to explain the use of that term for the day after Easter; in fact it was Tuesday, and not in Easter week but the week after.

14 APRIL

a.d. XVIII Kalendas Maias   F

Pan American Day (first International Conference of American States, 1890)

(HOLY DAYS

Tiburtius and Valerian, third-century brothers of whom Valerian was married to St Cecilia (*22 Nov.); their steadfastness brought about the conversion and execution of the judge's secretary, one Maximus. Their day was reckoned the first day of summer in the Scandinavian two-season system.

Pedro González, d. 1246, confessor to Fernando III of Castile (*30 May), whom he accompanied on his campaigns against the Moors; he spent the last ten years of his life preaching in Galicia and Portugal, being also concerned with such practical assistance as the building of bridges. He died at Tuy on the River Miño, which became the centre of his cult. He was especially popular with sailors, who identified him with St Erasmus (see *2 June) under the name of San Telmo.

On this day (3 Apr. OS) the cuckoo was reputed to make its appearance. From that bird's habit of depositing its eggs in other birds' nests comes the name of *cuckold*, originally also the adulterer but now only the husband of the unfaithful wife, taunted with the cuckoo's call:

> Cuckoo, cuckoo—O word of fear,
> Unpleasing to a married ear.
>
> Spring, in Love's Labour's Lost, v. ii. 887–8

> In this same moneth on the third day
> The Cuckow doth come in, they say,
> Who much content to man doth bring,
> With pleasant note that he doth sing.

Since he doth Musick gratis give,
Make much of him, and let him live.
And do not bear to him a spight,
Though he upon thy tree doth light,
Nor think thy wife to be a whore
Although he sing just at thy dore,
For whatsoever he doth chat
Wife may be honest for all that:
But rather thank him for his labor,
And think he calleth to thy Neighbour.
Or let the worst that can befall,
He speaks to all in general;
Or, if that Cuckolds that street cumber,
That thou art not of that same number,
For none are Cuckolds, of truth know,
But such as think themselves are so.

Poor Robin (1668)

15 APRIL

a.d. XVII Kalendas Maias   G

❡ ANCIENT ROME The Fordicidia, on which, so Ovid relates, pregnant cows were sacrificed to Tellus (the Earth), one on the Capitol, one in each of the thirty ancient wards or *curiae* (*17 Feb.).

❡ HOLY DAYS
Ruadan (d. 584), founder and first abbot of Lothra. On his day, according to the Book of Leinster, the birds are released from the thrall of winter.

USA: income tax returns due. By an Act of Congress on 5 August 1861 a tax of 3% was imposed on all incomes, exempting $800, but no tax was assessed under the law. A new tax bill, signed on 1 July 1862, imposed a tax of 3% on incomes under $10,000 and 5% above that, with a $600 exemption; the tax was first levied in 1863. Raised to help pay the costs of the Civil War, it was abolished in 1872. A new income tax bill of 1894, imposing 2% on all incomes with an exemption of $4,000, was legally challenged by the states and declared unconstitutional by the Supreme Court in May 1895. It was therefore necessary to amend the Constitution, which allowed the levying of federal taxes, but only in proportion to population. The 16th Amendment was ratified in 1913, at which time the Tariff Act incorporated a federal income tax of 1% with exemptions of $3,000 for single persons and $4,000 for married persons, with surcharges on incomes above $20,000. (At that time the exemptions were very generous, and only the wealthy had to pay tax.)

16 APRIL

a.d. XVI Kalendas Maias   A

❨ HOLIDAYS AND ANNIVERSARIES   Denmark: Queen Margrethe's Birthday (national holiday)
  Puerto Rico: José de Diego's Birthday

❨ HOLY DAYS

Bernadette (Marie-Bernarde) *Soubirous* of Lourdes (1844–79), who in 1858, at the age of 14, reported eighteen visions of a lady, the first being on *11 February, the last on 16 July. On 25 February the lady, who bade her drink from and bathe in a spring that erupted on the spot, demanded the building of a chapel to which processions should be held, and called on mankind to repent and pray; when on the order of the sceptical parish priest Bernadette asked for her name she replied in Gascon: 'I am the Immaculate Conception.' Although Pius IX had proclaimed the Immaculate Conception as a dogma in 1854 (see *8 Dec.), and France was flooded with cheap reproductions of Murillo's painting of the subject in the Louvre, a peasant girl was supposed too ignorant to have heard of it; moreover, the spring had already been credited with miraculous cures. She died as Sister Marie-Bernarde of the Sœurs de la Charité et de l'Instruction Chrétienne on 16 April 1879; this is kept as her day outside France, where it is 18 February.

Benedict Joseph Labre (1748–83), patron saint of tramps and the homeless. The eldest of fifteen children, he was not inclined to follow his father's footsteps as a shopkeeper in Boulogne. Having been rejected by the Cistercians and the Carthusians as unsuited for monastic life, he undertook a pilgrimage to Rome, a journey that took four years on foot with detours to other places of pilgrimage, depending on charitable handouts along the way and sleeping rough. In Rome his 'accommodation' was the Colosseum, where he spent his nights quite probably in the company of other homeless people; but the days he passed in various Roman churches, praying. By the time of his death he had come to be regarded as a saint, and not as a verminous beggar; he was canonized in 1881.

Padarn or Paternus, *c.*500, founder of Llanbadarn Fawr in Dyfed and other monasteries along Roman roads; a great preacher. It was said that when King Arthur sought his tunic, the saint ordered the earth to swallow him up as far as his chin, and that his crosier, which like a warrior's sword had a name of its own (Cyrwen), had the power to quell armies engaged in battle.

Magnus of Scotland. Magnus Erlendsson, son of the Earl of Orkney, escaped from captivity in Norway to the protection of the Scottish king Malcolm III (Ceann Mòr, 'Bighead', 1058–93); at his father's death his succession was challenged by his cousin Håkon Pålsson, who murdered him on 16 April 1116; canonized 1135. He is the main saint of Orkney, Shetland, and northern Scotland; the cathedral at Kirkwall, where his relics were rediscovered in 1919, bears his name. (Some of the relics allegedly found their way to Aachen, whence the emperor Charles IV took part of a shoulder to St Vitus' Cathedral in Prague.) He is also one of the patron saints of Norway, where this day is known as *magnusmesse*; it is also called the third day of summer. In Norwegian primestaves it was marked with a half-cross, the bar extending to one side only, to indicate that it was a *halvhelg* or half-holy day; the other *halvhelger* were 1 August (Peter's chains), 1 September (St Giles), and 4 October (St Francis).

17 APRIL

a.d. XV Kalendas Maias   B

❦ HOLIDAYS AND ANNIVERSARIES Syria: Independence Day, or Evacuation Day (withdrawal of French troops, 1946)

❦ HOLY DAYS

Stephen Harding, abbot of Cîteaux, d. 1034, under whose rule the Cistercian Order was in danger of dying out until in 1112 St Bernard (see *20 Aug.) brought thirty followers to it, so augmenting the Order that further foundations were needed. Legend improved the story to make a mysterious disease deplete the monks' numbers, causing Stephen to wonder whether he was really doing the will of God; he asked a dying monk to bring back word from beyond the grave bearing witness to the divine will. Soon after his death the monk appeared to Stephen, saying that his way of life was pleasing to God; new monks would shortly come who, like bees swarming out of the hive, would fly away and spread over many parts of the world. Not long thereafter, at the monastery gates appeared a troop of thirty men, announcing to the porter that they had come to offer themselves to the religious life. All were of noble lineage, most were young; their leader was a youth of singular beauty whose name was Bernard. Harding was also a biblical scholar, who sought Jewish assistance in correcting the Cîteaux text of the Old Testament. This is his date in the Roman Martyrology, though in 1683 the Order transferred it to 16 July.

April and May
April cold with dropping rain
Willows and lilacs brings again,
The whistle of returning birds,
And the trumpet-lowing of the herds.
The scarlet maple-keys betray
What potent blood hath modest May,
What fiery force the earth renews,
The wealth of forms, the flush of hues;
What joy in rosy waves outpoured
Flows from the heart of Love, the Lord.
Ralph Waldo Emerson (1803–82)

18 APRIL

a.d. XIV Kalendas Maias   C

❨ HOLIDAYS AND ANNIVERSARIES   Zimbabwe: Independence Day (1980, from
British colonial rule resumed in 1979 after the failure of the white government that
had declared unilateral independence as 'Rhodesia' on 11 November 1965 to obtain
international recognition for its power-sharing settlement with some of its black
opponents)

❨ HOLY DAYS

Aye or *Aya*, venerated at Sainte-Waudru in Mons at least since 1314. She protects property and is invoked by victims of unjust lawsuits: when her relations contested her bequest to Sainte-Waudru she rebuked them from her tomb and ordered them to desist.
At her feast the statutes of the chapter required a reading from Prov. 31: 10 'mulierem
fortem quis inveniet? procul et de ultimis finibus pretium eius' ('Who shall find a valiant
woman? far and from the uttermost bounds is the price of her'), the Vulgate counterpart of AV 'Who can find a virtuous woman? for her price is far above rubies.'

19 APRIL

a.d. XIII Kalendas Maias   D

❨ ANCIENT ROME   Cerialia, the feast of Ceres, regarded with especial devotion by the
common people, who celebrated by exchanging hospitality; foxes with burning torches
tied to their tails were let loose. White robes were worn; spelt, salt, and incense were
offered.

❨ HOLY DAYS   Alphege (CofE)

Ælfheah (Alphege, Alphage), Archbishop of Canterbury (*c.*953–1012). First a monk, then
a hermit, he became abbot of Bath, and in 984 succeeded Ethelwold (see *1 Aug.) as
bishop of Winchester. Ten years later he was one of Ethelred II's emissaries to the invading Vikings under Olav Tryggvason and Svend Tyggeskæg ('Forkbeard') and secured
the agreement of the former not to raid England any more; confirmed by Ælfheah with
Ethelred as sponsor, he sailed home to set about imposing Christianity on Norway,
where he was king from 995 to 1000. In 1005 Ælfheah became archbishop of Canterbury;
six years later the Danes overran the city and held him hostage for seven months; when
he persisted in his refusal to let his own ransom of £3,000 be paid, drunken Danes attacked
him with oxen's bones and killed him, on the spot where the parish church of Greenwich was later built. After the Norman Conquest, Archbishop Lanfranc of Canterbury,

ill-disposed to native traditions, discarded him along with other Anglo-Saxon saints from the Canterbury calendar, as not having demonstrably died for the faith; St Anselm, then abbot of Bec, argued on a visit in 1079 that, since he had died resisting unjust exaction on his tenants, he had died for justice, and therefore for truth, which is simply a mode of justice. This last had been Lanfranc's own assertion in his commentary on Rom. 3: 4; he at once reversed himself, readmitted St Ælfheah to the calendar, included his day among the feasts 'celebrated magnificently' (on the same level as the Epiphany, Purification, Annunciation, and Ascension), and commissioned music for it (now lost) from the monk Osbern, said to have been the best musician of his day, along with a still extant life. Thomas Becket called Ælfheah 'the first martyr of Canterbury'.

Leo IX (1049–54), a reforming pope nominated by the emperor Henry III at a time when reforming popes were still the allies and not the enemies of Holy Roman Emperors. An Alsatian count's son baptized Bruno, he took the name Leo as recalling the supposedly still pure church of Leo the Great, and was the first name-changing pope to be canonized. For over 900 years the bishops of Rome, like other bishops, had retained their baptismal names with two exceptions: John II (533–5), baptized Mercurius, who (unlike Hormisdas, 514–23) exchanged the name of a pagan deity for that of the recent martyr-pope (see *18 May), and John III (561–74), who had changed his original name of Catelinus long before his election. In 955 the debauched teenage hooligan Octavianus, prince of the Romans, was elected pope and took the name of John XII after his uncle John XI; he was the last man to shy at a name of secular pomp, but some contemporaries make John his true name all along. When in 974 Benedict VI, elected with imperial support, was overthrown by the defeated faction, his rival in conclave, the cardinal deacon Franco, was consecrated as Boniface VII; an interesting choice, for the twice-unfrocked Boniface VI had been imposed on the Church in 896 by an anti-imperial mob. Boniface VII was soon deposed (but not before murdering Benedict); upon the next pope's death in 983, the imperial nominee Peter Canepanova, unwilling to invite comparison with the first pope and Prince of the Apostles, reigned as John XIV till Boniface came back in 984 and murdered him too. In 996 Bruno of Carinthia took the name Gregory V to recall Gregory the Great, in 999 Gerbert of Aurillac, appointed by the emperor Otto III, became Silvester II in honour of the Sylvester who had supposedly been spiritual guide to Constantine (see *31 Dec.); neither Bruno nor Gerbert was a name familiar to Romans. The next two retained their baptismal name of John (XVII and XVIII), but in 1009 another Peter, also unwilling to reign under that name, became Sergius IV. A few eleventh-century antipopes apart, all his successors have changed their baptismal names but for Hadrian VI (1522–3) and Marcellus II (1555); Julius II (1503–13), formerly Giuliano della Rovere, omitted a syllable in honour not of Julius I (337–52) but of Julius Caesar. Even popes baptized John have changed name, beginning with Silvester III (1045) and Gregory VI (1045–6). There has still been no Peter II (cf. *3 Nov., under Malachy O'More).

Expeditus, patron of merchants, navigators, and prompt solutions. His existence (as a fourth-century Armenian martyr) is extremely doubtful; in some sources his name is given as Elpidius. His cult appears very late, in seventeenth-century Germany; nevertheless Prince Charles d'Orléans, duc de Nemours, born on this day in 1905, was baptized Charles-Philippe-Emmanuel-Ferdinand-Louis-Gérard-Joseph-Marie-Ghislain-Baudouin-Chrétien-Raphaël-Antoine-Expédit-Henri. There is, alas, no truth in the story that he was invented when a packing-case containing a *corpo santo* was sent from the catacombs of Rome to a community of nuns in Paris, with the date of its dispatch next to the word *spedito*, 'sent'; the recipients, mistaking this for the name of the martyr whose relics were enclosed, translated it into Latin and *expeditiously* propagated his cult. Nevertheless, such things are not unknown. Pope Urban VIII once received a request from Spanish churchmen to enhance the liturgical rank of St Viar. His Holiness, never having heard of him, asked who he was and what proofs existed of his sanctity. In reply the Spaniards sent a fragment of ancient stonework, inscribed S. VIAR; but alas! The experts in Roman inscriptions reported that it came from a tombstone commemorating a commissioner of roads (*viarum*).

Patriots Day (Massachusetts, Maine), commemorating Paul Revere's arrival at Lexington in 1775 to announce that the Regulars were coming out against the Whigs (after Independence anachronistically misreported as 'The British are coming'); in Wayland, Mass., a great bell made by him is rung every year.

Hymn:
Sung at the Completion of the Concord Monument
April 19, 1836

By the rude bridge that arched the flood,
 Their flag to April's breeze unfurled,
Here once the embattled farmers stood,
 And fired the shot heard round the world.

The foe long since in silence slept;
 Alike the conqueror silent sleeps;
And Time the ruined bridge has swept
 Down the dark stream which seaward creeps.

On this green bank, by this soft stream,
 We set to-day a votive stone;
That memory may their deed redeem,
 When, like our sires, our sons are gone.

Spirit, that made those heroes dare
 To die, or leave their children free,
Bid Time and Nature gently spare
 The shaft we raise to them and thee.

Ralph Waldo Emerson (1803–82)

In the 1990s this day was adopted by extreme right-wingers in America to justify resistance to Federal authority, after a building in Waco, Tex., occupied by an armed religious sect had been stormed with considerable loss of life on 19 April 1993; two years later a government building in Oklahoma City was bombed.

Primrose Day, commemorating the death of Benjamin Disraeli, British Prime Minister in 1868 and 1874–80, in 1876 created 1st Earl of Beaconsfield, on 19 April 1881.

Yet there is no evidence that primroses played any important part in either the public or the private life of Lord Beaconsfield. Nor does he appear to have had any fondness for them. . . . The *Pall Mall Gazette* in the days when it was a liberal organ made public the following explanation of the anomaly: 'Apropos of Primrose Day and the very uncomplimentary allusions in Lord Beaconsfield's books to that flower, it may be worth while to recount the origin of the myth. When Lord Beaconsfield was buried, the queen sent a wreath of primroses, and wrote, on a card attached to the wreath, "*His* favorite flower." Her majesty referred, of course, to the late Prince Consort; but her words were misunderstood to mean that the primrose was Lord Beaconsfield's favorite flower. Hence the newspaper allusions to "the flower he loved so well", and the annual celebration of Primrose Day. The explanation of the myth has long been current among Lord Beaconsfield's colleagues, but for obvious reasons they did not care to make it public.'

W. S. Walsh, 823

20 APRIL

❡ HOLY DAYS Beuno (RC Wales)

Beuno (6th c.), abbot in North Wales. Numerous dedications attest to his popularity, which was long-lasting; as late as 1770 sick children were bathed in his well and left at night by his tomb. He was said to have raised seven persons from the dead, including his niece Gwenffrewi (Winifred; see *3 Nov.), and to have planted in his father's grave an acorn from which grew a mighty oak; any Englishman who passed between trunk and branch died, but Welshmen could do so unharmed. Thomas Pennant described the chapel of St Beuno, adjoining the church at Clynnog Fawr, in 1781:

The chapel was probably built after that traveller [John Leland] had visited the place, in the room of the old church, which might have fallen to ruin. In the midst is the tomb of the saint, plain, and altar-shaped. Votaries were wont to have great faith in him, and did not doubt but that by means of a night's lodging on his tomb, a cure would be found for all diseases. It was customary to cover it with rushes, and leave on it till morning sick children, after making them first undergo ablution in the neighboring holy well; and I myself once saw on it a feather bed, on which a poor paralytic from *Meirionyddshire* had lain the whole night, after undergoing the same ceremony. . . .

    At present there are, I believe, no sort of revenues to keep this venerable pile from falling to ruin. The offerings of calves and lambs, which happen to be born with the *Nôd Beuno*, or mark of St. *Beuno*, a certain natural mark in the ear, have not entirely ceased. They are brought to the church on *Trinity Sunday*, the anniversary of the Saint, and delivered to the churchwardens; who sell and account for them, and put it into a great chest, called *Cyff St. Beino*, made of one piece of oak, secured with three locks. From this the *Welsh* have a proverb for attempting any very difficult thing, 'You may as well try to break up St. *Beuno's* chest.' The little money resulting from the sacred beasts, or casual offerings, is either applied to the relief of the poor, or in aid of repairs.

Pennant, *Snowdon*, 209, 210–11

Agnes of Montepulciano (1268–1317), Dominican nun and prior of a convent built for her in Montepulciano. She had a precocious career: entering the convent as a 9-year-old, she was elected abbess of a convent in Procena at the age of 15, with papal dispensation. When her fame spread, the citizens of Montepulciano built a new convent for her, displacing some houses of ill repute.

A Tudor chronicle records the high point in the fortunes of Anne Boleyn:

Allso the same day (20 April 1534) all the craftes in London were called to their halls, and there were sworne on a booke to be true to Queene Anne and to beleeve and take her for lawfull wife of the Kinge and rightfull Queene of Englande, and utterlie to thincke the Ladie Marie, daughter to the Kinge by Queene Katherin, but as a bastarde, and thus to do without any scrupulositie of conscience; allso all the curates and priestes in London and thoroweout England were allso sworne before the Lord of Canterburie and other Bishopps; and allso all countries in Englande were sworne in lykewise, everie man in the shires and townes were they dwelled.

This yeare the Bishop of Rochester and Sir Thomas More, sometyme Chaunccellor of Englande, were put into the Tower of London for misprisonne, and there to remayne at the Kinges pleasure, but all the Bishopp of Rochesters goodes and bishopricke were taken into the Kings handes. Allso diverse priestes, religiouse men, and laymen, were sett in prison in the Tower of London becausse they would not be sworne.   Wriothesley, 24–5

The Thursday falling within the seven days from this day to the 26th, corresponding to 9–15 April OS before 1700, is kept in Iceland as the first day of summer; see II: *Other Calendars: Icelandic.*

21 APRIL

❡ HOLIDAYS AND ANNIVERSARIES Brazil: Tiradentes Day (Joaquim José de Silva Xavier, a dentist; conspirator in revolt against Portugal, 1789) (national holiday) USA, Texas: San Jacinto Day (commemorating Battle of San Jacinto; independence from Mexico, 1836)

HM Queen Elizabeth II born 1926; red-letter day; the Union flag is flown

❡ ANCIENT ROME Parilia: festival of Pales, the goddess (some said god) of shepherds, traditionally the day on which Rome was founded (but see *4 Oct.); the year was much disputed (see II: *Roman Calendar*). The festival, in Christian times discreetly renamed Urbs Aeterna, was celebrated with such enthusiasm that the Roman Church insisted on keeping Easter no later than this day, lest pagan merriment during Lent—culminating in attempts by well-refreshed revellers to leap over burning heaps of hay—should offend, or tempt, the fasting faithful; this rule, which had no point outside Rome, was of paramount importance to the popes until Leo the Great was compelled to give way before the intellectual and (it claimed) canonical authority of Alexandria (see II: *The Date of Easter*).

(HOLY DAYS Anselm (CY, RC); Januarius (Orth.; see *19 Sept.)

Anselm (1033–1109), Benedictine monk, prior and abbot of Bec in Normandy and archbishop of Canterbury. The pupil of Lanfranc (*28 May) and his successor both as prior and as archbishop, he was as much his inferior in administrative skill as his superior in power of thought; one of the most remarkable theologians in history, he propounded the ontological argument for the existence of God and overthrew the traditional view of the Redemption as the buying-out of the Devil's rights over man. He was long credited, although falsely, with giving respectability to the doctrine of the Immaculate Conception (see *8 Dec.). As archbishop he was in frequent conflict with Kings William II (1087–1100) and Henry III (1100–35); matters were made worse in 1099 when, attending a Vatican council, he learnt of the papal decrees against lay investiture, which thereafter he insisted on observing to the letter. His more constructive achievement was to relax the hostility of his predecessor towards the Anglo-Saxon Church (see *19 Apr., *8 Dec.).

22 APRIL

a.d. X Kalendas Maias G

(HOLIDAYS AND ANNIVERSARIES USA: Earth Day, instituted 1970
USA, Delaware and Nebraska: Arbor Day (first observance, in Nebraska, 10 Apr. 1872)
USA, Oklahoma: Oklahoma Day (opening of Oklahoma Territory for settlement, 1889)

(HOLY DAYS

Theodore of Sykeon (d. 613), monk and bishop of Anastasiopolis in Galati. Owing to a very full contemporary biography, Theodore's life emerges in colourful detail. He was the son of a circus acrobat and an innkeeper, who was also a prostitute; his mother, caring deeply about his future, was dissuaded from sending him to the emperor through an apparition of St George, who also intervened when the mother punished the boy for devoutness, which Theodore learnt from the inn's new cook. A teenage hermit, rescued on the point of collapse, he became a priest, making a pilgrimage to Jerusalem. Returning home to his now devout family, he sought ever more spectacular cells: first a wooden cage, in which he spent the time from Christmas to Palm Sunday, then an iron one suspended above his cave. He dressed in iron breastplate, collar, and belt, with rings around his feet and hands. Famed for his fasts, powers of healing, and clairvoyance, he eventually gathered enough disciples to found a monastery. When pressed to become bishop of Anastasiopolis, he reluctantly accepted, but found administration tedious and worried about the morals of his monks. After ten years he resigned, becoming a monk again. Invited to the emperor's court, he gained the right of monasteries to be sanctuaries, with abbots appointed by the patriarch. He cured the emperor's son and performed many other miracles. Among his other talents were those of physician and marriage-guidance counsellor. He is therefore the patron of unhappily married couples—at least those who wish to be reconciled.

23 APRIL

a.d. IX Kalendas Maias   A

❦ HOLIDAYS AND ANNIVERSARIES Bermuda: Peppercorn Day (commemorating the payment of one peppercorn to the Governor for the rental of the Old State House by the Masonic Lodge, 1816)
    England: St George's Day
    Germany: *Biertag* celebrated by beer-drinkers to commemorate the purity ordinance (*Reinheitsgebot*) issued by Duke Albrecht IV of Bavaria in 1516, regulating the ingredients permitted in brewing to malt, hops, yeast, and water

❦ ANCIENT ROME This was the Vinalia, which despite its name, indicating a wine festival, was dedicated not to Liber Pater (see *17 Mar.) but to Jupiter, to whom the first draught of the wine stored the previous autumn was poured as a libation. It was also the day, in 181 BC, on which a temple was dedicated outside the Colline Gate at Rome to Venus Erycina, the Venus (or rather the Phoenician goddess of love, Astarte) served by sacred prostitutes on Monte San Giuliano in Sicily; in consequence, prostitutes kept a festival in honour of Venus, whom they would present with myrtle (which was sacred to her) and mint, and chains of rushes covered with roses.

❦ HOLY DAYS **George** (CofE; RC)

George is the patron of England; very little is known of him, and his very existence is often doubted. Although the early life of the saint was condemned as the work of heretics (see *16 June), it is possible that he was martyred in the early fourth century; there is no evidence for the identification made famous (but not invented) by Gibbon with George 'of Cappadocia', a fuller's boy from Epiphaneia in Cilicia who rose to be a dishonest bacon-supplier to the Roman army before being appointed bishop of Alexandria by the emperor Constantius in 357, where he governed tyrannically with the help of imperial troops before being lynched on 24 December 361 when Constantius' death became known in the city.

    George was not widely venerated till the sixth century, but since then his cult has spread in both East and West, as a military saint and a martyr. When, during the First Crusade, the Christians defeated a Turkish attempt to recapture Antioch (cf. *15 Mar.), they were encouraged in the pursuit by a vision of SS George, Mercurius (see *25 Nov.), and Demetrius (see *26 Oct.); in the Third Crusade, Richard I placed his army under George's protection; Edward III, who instituted the Order of the Garter under his patronage (1348), may be thought to have made him patron saint of England in preference to Edward the Confessor; he was invoked in this capacity by Henry V after the victory at Agincourt in 1415. In that same year, his feast, made a lesser holiday by the Synod of Oxford in 1222, was raised to one of the principal feasts by Archbishop Chichele. A story that he visited England from the west has caused the sea between South Wales and Ireland to be called 'St George's Channel'.

St George is also patron of Catalonia, the Greek army, knights, archers, sufferers from syphilis, boy scouts, and (owing to a pun on his Greek name) husbandmen. Many cities and numerous churches are dedicated to him. He is best known, however, from the story, first attested in the twelfth century, of his encounter with the dragon. A king whose realm was plagued by a dragon with poisonous breath, having run out of the daily pair of sheep that kept it at bay, had to resort to human sacrifices. On the day on which the king's daughter drew the lot, St George rode forth and speared the dragon, collaring it with the maiden's girdle and leading it tamely back. He promised to kill it if the people agreed to convert; the dragon was dispatched and 15,000 men were baptized. The scene is normally set at Lydda, near where Perseus, in the Greek myth, had rescued Andromeda.

The first king of England to be called George was the Elector of Hanover, George I; the next three kings all bore the name, as did two much-loved kings in the twentieth century. In 1940 George VI instituted the George Cross, awarded for acts of the greatest heroism or the most conspicuous courage in circumstances of extreme danger; it is primarily a civilian award, Service personnel being eligible only for actions not normally rewarded with military honours. It is worn before all other decorations except the Victoria Cross. The central medallion of the cross bears a design depicting St George and the dragon. In 1942 the George Cross was awarded to the island of Malta for heroic resistance to the Axis siege; it is represented on the Maltese flag.

The English have often been regarded, particularly by their fellow Britons, as strangely lukewarm in their observation of their patron saint and his day; they cannot be trusted to remember his day (much less wear a rose on it), and at sporting fixtures they cause great offence in the other parts of the United Kingdom by waving not the flag of St George, the red cross on a white background, but the all-British Union flag, in which it is combined with the crosses of St Andrew and St Patrick. However, his emblem was much in evidence among English football supporters at the European Cup finals of 1996 (and again in the World Cup finals of 1998); a few weeks later the Church of England voted to include his day among the compulsory feasts. Yet it is still not a civil red-letter day, though in England the Union flag is flown.

St George was not neglected in the late Middle Ages: numerous guilds were dedicated to him and celebrated his feast-day as the great social event of the year, with banquets and elaborate processions featuring St George and the dragon. This caused embarrassment at the Reformation; moreover, the Order of the Garter, dedicated to St George, could not be abolished. In 1538 Henry VIII ruled that, while George could be honoured as a person, he must not be worshipped, and all images were to be taken down. But the celebration died slowly, even when the guilds were dissolved. John Bale, in his preface to *The Laboryeuse Journey and Serche of John Leylande for Englandes Antiquitees*, regrets the expense, which could more profitably be applied to public libraries:

O cyties of Englande, whose glory standeth more in bellye chere, than in the serche of wysdome godlye. How cometh it, that neyther you, nor yet your ydell masmongers, haue regarded thys most worthy commodyte of your contrey? I meane the conservacyon of your Antiquytees, and of the worthy labours of your lerned men: I thynke the renowne of suche a notable acte, wolde haue much longar endured, than of all your belly bankettes and table tryumphes, eyther yet of your newely purchased hawles to kepe S. Georges feast in.   Bale, sig. Cᵢᵛ–C2

In 1548 the statutes concerning the celebration of St George's Day by Knights of the Garter were reformed. The Protestant boy king Edward VI is said to have made fun of the ceremonies even then, demanding 'What saint is Saint George that we do here honour him?' To the marquess of Winchester's reply, 'St George mounted his charger, out with his sword and ran the dragon through with his spear', Edward returned, 'And pray you my lords, and what did he with his sword the while?' (*Acts of the Privy Council*, ii. 186, quoted in Hutton, *Stations*, 216). Under Queen Mary the feast was restored, but Queen Elizabeth abolished it again in 1567. From that time on, George and his dragon were transferred to May Day festivities. By Shakespeare's day, his image was more familiar as a tavern sign:

BASTARD: Saint George that swinged the dragon, and e'er since
   Sits on's horseback at mine hostess' door.   *King John*, II. i. 288–9

Charles II and James II both chose St George's Day for their coronation; but celebrations died out when William and Mary came to the throne.

Part of the campaign to dissuade England from venerating its patron saint involved casting doubt on his existence. In the eighteenth century a spoof version of his legend, highly embroidered, has St George terrorize the dragon with the contents of

a little Box, cover'd with Lace of *Hungary* made by St. *Epiphania*'s own Hands, the Mother of the three Kings, which Box contain'd his Relicks. He first drew out *Adam*'s usual String of Beads, the Cross whereof was made of Unicorn's Horn, and the Beads of the Teeth of the Fish that swallow'd up *Jonas*. At the Sight of this holy Object the Dragon shook his Ears, and froth'd at the Mouth most violently: He even gave back several Steps, but soon resuming Courage, advanc'd again: Then St. *George* putting up his String of Beads, took out of his Box the Abridgment of the Lives of the Saints, which the good *Abel* always carry'd about him in his Pocket, and the Pack of Cards which the wicked *Cain* carry'd in his. These he fasten'd to the End of his Lance, which was the same wherewith the Valiant *Don Quixot* had a thousand Years before exterminated so many Windmills; and these holy Relicks he shew'd to the Dragon: The Dragon, perceiving them, fell down, as if a Thunderbolt had struck him; his Belly swell'd, and contracting again made him fetch a double Sigh, one before and t'other behind, which really smelt not a little unsavoury.

Misson de Valbourg (1719), 112–14

Not surprisingly, St George also turns up in the English colonies. A Puritan views St George's Day in New England with high suspicion:

[Boston], Tuesday, Apr. 23 [1706].

Govr. comes to Town guarded by the Troops with their Swords drawn; dines at the Dragon, from thence proceeds to the Townhouse, Illuminations at night. Capt. Pelham tells me several wore crosses in their Hats; which makes me resolve to stay at home; (though Maxwell was at my House and spake to me to be at the Council-Chamber at 4. p.m.) Because to drinking Healths, now the Keeping of a Day to fictitious St. George, is plainly set on foot. It seems Capt. Dudley's Men wore Crosses. Somebody had fasten'd a cross to a Dog's head; Capt. Dudley's Boatswain seeing him, struck the Dog, and then went into the shop, next where the Dog was, and struck down a Carpenter, one Davis, as he was at work not thinking anything: Boatswain and the other with him were fined 10^s each for breach of the peace, by Jer. Drummer Esqr: pretty much blood was shed by means of this blody Cross, and the poor Dog a sufferer.   Sewall, 544–5

He was put to use as a political symbol by the partisans of another George; a Hessian mercenary soldier during the Revolutionary War, Captain Johann Ewald, noted in his diary in 1778:

[May] 4th. The day before yesterday the Americans, like ourselves, celebrated Saint George's Day, except for the difference that they painted a picture on a board showing the King of England kneeling on one knee with the latest compromise proposal in his hand. Next to him was the figure of General Washington, standing upright with his sword in his hand, uttering the following words to the King: 'My dear King, if you wish to beg for something, bend your knee, then let me speak.'

    It is astonishing that General Washington tolerates such disgraceful affairs in his army, because we assumed him to be of a very excellent character, and such things serve only to dishonor him personally.   Ewald, 128

In other countries and places under his patronage George has fared better. In Albania, it is the name-day of the national hero George Castriota, known as Scanderbeg, who resisted the Ottomans in the fifteenth century: people picnic by springs, and weigh themselves while holding sprigs. In Catalonia his cult, previously confined to the upper classes, has become more popular (see below). In Greece, he is especially honoured by shepherds: at Aráchova, of which he is patron, his image is led in procession round the town, after which there is a dance to pipes and tabors. It was formerly the custom to cut off the water-supply till the old men, who led the dance and sang the accompanying ballad, reached the line: 'Dragon, set free the water that the revellers may drink.'

On this day in 1616, by the Old Style used in England, William Shakespeare died, fifty-two years less three days after his christening; on the same nominal day by the New Style, but ten natural days earlier, Miguel de Cervantes y Saavedra, the author of *Don Quixote*, died. In Catalonia it became the custom for women to celebrate his memory by giving men books on this day in return for the red roses that men gave them in honour of St George; in recent years the demarcation has been challenged. UNESCO has designated this day World Book and Copyright Day.

This day is marked in Worm's calendar with a stallion, to be set to stud.

24 APRIL

❨ HOLY DAYS Mellitus (CY commem.); Fidelis of Sigmaringen (RC)

Mellitus, sent in 601 to reinforce the English mission, was consecrated bishop of the East Saxons by St Augustine of Canterbury; King Ethelbert of Kent built St Paul's in London for him, but an anti-Christian reaction sent him scurrying back to Gaul, whence he returned in 619 to become the third archbishop of Canterbury.

Fidelis of Sigmaringen (1577–1622), Franciscan friar and martyr, killed while preaching to unsympathetic Zwinglian peasants in Switzerland.

Conversion of St Augustine of Hippo (see *28 Aug.), who was baptized on this day in 387.

Translation of St Wilfrid (see *12 Oct.).

Egbert, called by Bede 'a most reverend and holy father and bishop' who 'lived his life in great perfection of humility, gentleness, continence, simplicity, and justice', while studying in Ireland fell ill of the plague in 664 and vowed, among other manifestations of penance, never to return to Britain; he strictly observed the Irish 'threefold Lent', fasting for forty days before Easter, after Whitsun, and before Christmas. He conceived the plan of evangelizing Germany, but learnt from a brother-monk's visions, confirmed by a storm when he attempted to set sail, that God wished him instead to reform St Columba's monasteries, which still kept their Celtic Easter and tonsure. In 716 he arrived in Iona (which did not count as part of Britain), and persuaded the monks to conform to Roman practice; he died at the age of 90 on Easter Day, 24 April 729, the first time it had ever been kept on this day, rejoicing, so Bede tells us, that he had lived to see the monks keeping Easter with him 'on that day which they had always previously avoided', for the Celtic Easter could fall no later than the 23rd.

Birthday of Joseph Smith (1805), founder of the Church of Jesus Christ of Latter-day Saints (see also *6 Apr.).

On this day, called *Vegadagen*, in Sweden, the Anthropological and Geographical Society (Sällskapet för antropologi och geografi) awards the Vega Medal for outstanding contributions to geography, instituted in 1880 to celebrate the return on 24 April in that year of the expedition led by Adolf Erik Nordenskiöld, on the ship *Vega*, from the first successful navigation of the North-East Passage.

St Mark's Eve. Fasting was observed on the days before major feasts; the twelfth-century Parisian theologian Johannes Beleth states that it replaced vigils, where 'girls and boys, singers and gamblers' spent the night in church, leading to drunkenness and other disorders. Perhaps related to the lightheadedness caused by fasting, many superstitions have become attached to the eves of feasts, particularly concerning divination of the future, whether the foreknowledge of one's future husband or of those who will die during the year. St Mark's Eve is particularly associated with the latter, and the day itself was considered an unlucky day (see *25 Apr.).

> On St. Mark's Eve, at Twelve o'Clock,
> The Fair Maid she will watch her Smock;
> To find her Husband in the Dark,
> By praying unto good St. Mark.
>
> *Poor Robin* (1770)

> 'Tis now', replied the village Belle,
>   'St. Mark's mysterious Eve;
> And all that old traditions tell
>   I tremblingly believe:—
>
> 'How, when the midnight signal tolls,
>   Along the churchyard green
> A mournful train of sentenced souls
>   In winding-sheets are seen.
>
> 'The ghosts of all whom DEATH shall doom
>   Within the coming year,
> In pale procession walk the gloom,
>   Amid the silence drear.
>
> James Montgomery (1771–1854), 'The Vigil of St Mark'

In some places it was said that if the watcher falls asleep during his vigil, he will die himself during the year.

25 APRIL

a.d. VII Kalendas Maias   C

❦ HOLIDAYS AND ANNIVERSARIES   Australia, New Zealand, Samoa, Tonga: ANZAC Day (see below)
Italy: Liberation Day (1945)
Portugal: Revolution Day (1974)

❦ ANCIENT ROME   On this day was held the ceremony for keeping rust off crops, the Robigalia; the participants, clad in white, went in procession to the grove of the god Robigus (according to others the goddess Robigo), where the entrails of a puppy and a sheep were burnt. It was also the festival day of boy prostitutes (*pueri lenonii*).

❦ HOLY DAYS   Mark the Evangelist (CofE, RC)

Mark the Evangelist. Companion of Peter and Paul, he preached at Cyprus and was with Paul in Rome, where his Gospel may have been written. Tradition places him as bishop of Alexandria; the Christians of Alexandria appropriated him to replace the Graeco-Egyptian divinity Serapis worshipped on 30 Pharmouthi (the corresponding day in the Egyptian calendar). His body was stolen thence in the ninth century and brought to Venice, whose patron saint he became (translation feast formerly 31 Jan.). The mosaics in St Mark's, dating from the twelfth and thirteenth centuries, record many aspects of his life. Patron of Egypt, Venice, notaries and secretaries, and Spanish cattle-breeders (declared by Pius XII in 1951, confirming a long-standing devotion of unexplained origin), his symbol, taken from Ezek. 1: 10, is the lion. Red-letter day.

> From dreadfull unprovided death, doth Marke deliver his,
> Who of more force than death himselfe, and more of value is.
>
> Naogeorgus, 39

Greater Litanies. The Church appropriated the day of Robigalia for litanies, which were given their classic form by Gregory the Great, a sevenfold procession converging on S. Maria Maggiore; these were known as the Greater Litanies, in contrast to the Lesser Litanies of Rogationtide (see *Western Church Year*). They were suppressed in 1969.

Since the Greater Litanies were penitential in nature, St Mark's Day was a fast-day, called 'Black Crosses' because men wore black and altars and crosses were draped in black. Legend has it that when Becket arrived in Rome on St Mark's Day, all the fish-shops were sold out; he therefore ate a roast capon, and gave his servants boiled meat. The cardinal sent to welcome Becket reported this fact to the Pope, who sent another cardinal to corroborate; the latter took the leg of the capon back with him, but when he produced the evidence it had turned into a carp. When Becket himself came for audience, the Pope asked him what he had eaten; he replied that he had eaten flesh because he could find no fish. Perceiving that a miracle had taken place, the Pope gave licence to everyone in the diocese of Canterbury to eat meat on St Mark's Day.

Although the proper day for baptism was the Sunday or major feast next after the child's birth, Shakespeare was baptized on Wednesday, 26 April 1564; presumably he was too sickly for his parents to risk awaiting the next Sunday, but Mark's day was avoided because of its ill luck. On the other hand, in times of danger the Greater Litanies could rally spirits. The 'bourgeois of Paris' describes the events in Paris on this day in 1429, at a time when the city's food supplies were constantly diverted to support the Anglo-Burgundian army besieging Orléans (the siege famously raised by Joan of Arc):

The grey friar mentioned earlier preached on St. Mark's day at Boulogne-la-Petite and there were great crowds there, as is said above. Indeed, when they came away from the sermon that day, the people of Paris were so moved and so stirred up to devotion that in less than three or four hours' time you would have seen over a hundred fires alight in which men were burning chess and backgammon boards, dice, cards, balls and sticks, *mirelis*, and every kind of covetous game that can give rise to anger and swearing. The women, too, this day and the next, burned in public all their fine headgear—the rolls and stuffing, the pieces of leather or whalebone that they used to stiffen their headdresses or make them fold forwards. Noblewomen left off their horns, their trains, and many of their vanities. Indeed, the ten sermons he preached in Paris and one at Boulogne did more to turn people towards piety than all the preachers who had preached in Paris for the past hundred years.   Bourgeois, 231

St Mark's Day in Venice in 1730 as observed by a German visitor:

The Festival of St. *Mark* is always celebrated with very great Solemnity. On the Day preceding, the Doge accompany'd by the Ambassadors repairs with a great Train to St. *Mark*'s Church, where he assists at the Vespers. Next Day the Confraternities, who are nine in number, meet in the Ducal Palace, accompany the Doge to Church in Procession, and are present at High Mass. After this the Doge returns to his Palace, and the Brotherhoods go round the Square. Each Society has magnificent Images, and two Canopies richly embroider'd with Gold and Silver; whose Poles or Supporters are of solid Silver. The Procession is clos'd by a Man dress'd in a Gown of red Damask, carrying a Pole with a moving Wheel at the end of it; which serves to support a gilt Lion surrounded with Laurel Branches, and little Standards of divers Colours. The Lion turns round incessantly, and the Man who carries it makes him leap, and play a hundred Gambols: He is surrounded with a Multitude of People, who cry out, God bless St. *Mark*. This Sight, how ridiculous soever, is nevertheless amusing, draws abundance of the Nobility to the Square, and on that Day every body is mask'd. After the Procession is over, the Maskers go to see the Doge's Table, who entertains the Ambassadors and the Senate at Dinner, on a Table in form of a Horse-shoe; which is extravagantly adorn'd with Kickshaws, and Machines made of Starch, which are here call'd *Triumphs*. Nothing of the kind can be better executed, or more magnificent. As there is a great Apprehension of a Croud, all the Maskers are turn'd away at Dinner-time. They keep on their Masks all day long; and after Dinner all the Nobility, or to speak more properly, the whole City of *Venice* appears mask'd upon the Square of St. *Mark*; and indeed, for one who never saw it before, 'tis a remarkable fine Shew. What surpriz'd me, and if I may say it, made me laugh, was to see all the Maskers fall on their Knees at the Sound of the *Angelus*; you wou'd swear every body was in Rapture, yet every thing that goes before and that follows the Stroke of the Bell is not the most devout.   Pollnitz, i. 401–2

Quite a different celebration took place on St Mark's Day in Alnwick:

The manner of making freemen of *Alnwick common* . . . is not less singular than ridiculous. The persons that are to be made free, or, as the phrase is, that are to *leap the well*, assemble in the market-place very early in the morning, on the 25th of *April*, being St *Mark*'s day. They are on horseback, with every man his sword by his side, dressed in white with white night-caps, and attended by the four chamberlains and the castle bailiffe, who are also mounted and armed in the same manner. From the market-place they proceed in great order, with music playing before them, to a large dirty pool, called the *Freemen's Well*, on the confines of the common. Here they draw up in a body at some distance from the water, and then all at once rush into it, like a herd of swine, and scramble thro' the mud as fast as they can. As the water is generally breast high and very foul, they come out in a condition not much better than the heroes of the *Dunciad*, after diving in *Fleet-ditch*; but dry cloathes being ready for them on the other side, they put them on with all possible expedition, and then taking a dram, remount their horses, and ride full gallop round the whole confines of the district, of which, by this atchievement, they are become free. And, after having completed this circuit, they again enter the town sword in hand, and are generally met by women dressed up with ribbons, bells, and garlands of gum-flowers, who welcome them with dancing and singing, and are called *timber-waits* (perhaps a corruption of *timbrel-waits*, players on timbrels, *waits* being an old word for those who play on musical Instruments in the streets). The heroes then proceed in a body till they come to the house of one of their company, where they leave him, having first drank another dram; the remaining number proceed to the house of the second, with the same ceremony, and so of the rest, till the last is left to go home by himself. The houses of the new freemen are on this day distinguished by a great holly-bush, which is planted in the street before them, as a signal for their friends to assemble and make merry with them at their return. This strange ceremony is said to have been instituted by King *John*, in memory of his having once bogged his horse in this pool, called *Freemen's well.*

Gentleman's Magazine, 26 (1756), 73–4

This is the latest possible date for Easter, often marked in calendars as *ultimum Pascha*, 'the last Easter'; the phrase was dramatically reinterpreted in a prophecy sometimes wrongly ascribed to Nostradamus as meaning the last Easter there would ever be: 'When George [23 Apr.] shall crucify God [on Good Friday], and Mark [25 Apr.] shall resurrect Him [on Easter Day], and St John [24 June] shall carry him [in the Corpus Christi procession], the end of the world shall come.' Another version replaces Good Friday with Whitsun on St Antony of Padua's day (13 June); in 1733 Jacobites revised this to foretell the restoration of 'King James III', but although the case arose by the Gregorian calendar of France in 1734 and by the Julian calendar of Great Britain in 1736, the Pretender still remained without a throne.

ANZAC Day (Australia and New Zealand), commemorating the landing by the Australian and New Zealand Army Corps at Gallipoli (now Gelibolu) in 1915; it was given liturgical recognition by local Roman Catholics, so that St Mark was shunted to the 26th. This was the two countries' first significant experience (despite a presence in the Boer War) of Imperial warfare; it is celebrated especially by ex-servicemen with much eating and drinking; the police overlook games of two-up or 'swy', in which two coins are tossed—the fairest gambling game in the world if played under laboratory conditions.

26 APRIL

a.d. VI Kalendas Maias

D

❬ HOLIDAYS AND ANNIVERSARIES Tanzania: Union Day (between Tanzania, Zanzibar, and Pemba, 1964) (national day)
USA, Florida and Georgia: Confederate Memorial Day

❬ HOLY DAYS

Marcellinus, bishop of Rome 296–304, was accused of complying with Diocletian's order to surrender copies of the Scriptures and worship pagan gods; as a result, for two centuries his name was omitted from the list of popes. He was rehabilitated through wholly unfounded legends of repentance and martyrdom, which caused him to be regarded as a saint.

Paschasius Radbertus (c.790–c.860), abbot of Corbie, said to have been brought up as a foundling by the nuns of Notre-Dame at Soissons. He became a learned and prolific writer; his works include scriptural commentaries, saints' lives, and a treatise on the body and blood of Christ that aroused criticism by its emphasis on the Real Presence.

The election of the Doge of the *Nicolotti*, the Venetian fishermen, described by a German visitor in 1730:

The Day after St. *Mark's* we had another publick Shew, and by consequence a fresh occasion for the *Venetians* to masquerade it. That was the Election which the Fishermen, who are here call'd the *Nicolotti*, made of a Chief, who bears the Title of the Doge of the *Nicolotti*. Their Choice fell this Bout upon a Gondolier belonging to the noble *Giustiniani*. After the Election he was conducted to an Audience of the Doge of *Venice*, dress'd in a Robe of red Sattin, and otherwise accoutred like a Jackpudding. He was preceded by a great Mob of Pipers, Hautboys, and Fishermen. Just before him was carry'd a red Flag, with the Effigies of St. *Mark*. The Doge receiv'd him sitting on his Throne, and attended by the Council. The Complement of the Doge of the Fishermen was made with great Gravity, and answer'd by the Doge of the Republick in few Words; which done, he return'd in the same Order that he came. This sham Doge has authority over all the Fishermen, is their Judge, gives them Licence to fish, and takes care that the City be well supplied with that sort of Provision. Pollnitz, i. 402–3

In 1829 Easter was kept on this day in Finland, even though it was outside the normal limit, because the 19th, the astronomical (and also Gregorian) date, coincided with the second day of Passover. See also *28 April.

This was the extra day added to April under Julius Caesar's reform, in order to avoid disrupting the Floralia (see *28 Apr.); in the other expanded months the addition day or days immediately preceded the Kalends (see II: *Roman Calendar).

27 APRIL

a.d. V Kalendas Maias E

❦ HOLIDAYS AND ANNIVERSARIES Sierra Leone: Independence Day (from Great Britain, 1961)
South Africa: Freedom Day (national day)
Yugoslavia: National Day (formation of Yugoslav federation in 1992, consisting of Serbia and Montenegro)

❦ HOLY DAYS Formerly Peter Canisius (see *21 Dec.)
Zita (Sitha, Citha) (1218–72), serving-maid of Lucca. A devout Christian, known for her charitable deeds, her popular cult spread as far as England. She was a servant of the Fatinelli family from the age of 12, maltreated till they recognized her sanctity; she had the exasperating habit of giving away her master's food, and even in one story his fur coat, to a shivering beggar one Christmas Eve in the church of San Frediano who returned it not (as promised) to her after mass, but to her master just before dinner,

immediately vanishing. (Was the story inspired by the similarity of *Frediano* to *freddo*, 'cold'?) During one of her ecstasies, angels baked her bread, whence she became the patron saint of bakers besides housewives and servants. She is also invoked by those who have lost their keys. She was not officially canonized until 1696, but public opinion had made her a saint ever since her death; Dante (*Inferno*, 21. 38) makes a devil call a Lucca city councillor 'one of St Zita's elders' (*un delli anzian di santa Zita*). Her body is kept at San Frediano and displayed on this day, guarded by two arquebusiers and presented with narcissi.

28 APRIL

a.d. IV Kalendas Maias   F

❅ ANCIENT ROME This day (but before 45 BC the 27th in a 29-day April) was the first day of Floralia, which lasted till 3 May, honouring the goddess Flora. It was marked by licentious festivities, in which naked prostitutes took the part of gladiators; the younger Cato is reported to have walked out, having gone there in order to be shocked. Hares and goats were let loose, since Venus was patroness of cultivated nature, not of wild; various small vegetables were scattered as fertility tokens amongst the crowds in their colourful clothes. The shows continued by night under generous torchlight.

❅ HOLY DAYS Pierre-Marie-Louis Chanel (RC; CY commem.); formerly St Paul of the Cross (see *19 Oct.)

Pierre-Marie-Louis Chanel (1803–41), priest and martyr. A missionary on the Fijian island of Futuna, he was executed by command of a chieftain whose son he had converted; soon afterwards the entire island became a bastion of the Roman Church.

In 1867 the Finns abandoned their astronomical Easter with Passover postponement, which would have taken Easter to this day because the 21st coincided with the second day of Passover (see II: *The Date of Easter: Astronomical Easter*).

29 APRIL

a.d. III Kalendas Maias   G

❅ HOLIDAYS AND ANNIVERSARIES Japan: Greenery Day

❅ HOLY DAYS Catherine of Siena (CY, RC)

Catherine of Siena (*c.*1347–80), virgin. The twenty-fifth child of a wool-dyer, Caterina Ben-incasa practised prayer and penance from an early age, later becoming a Dominican ter-tiary; her reputation for holiness attracted clerical and lay followers called *caterinati*. She persuaded Pope Gregory XI in 1376 to leave Avignon for Rome (he soon regretted it), and rallied Italian support for his successor, Urban VI, against whom the French cardi-nals, disgusted at his despotic insolence, had set up a rival pope at Avignon, Clement VII. Her writings, including nearly 400 letters, were exalted by a fellow Sienese in the eighteenth century as models of pure Tuscan. She died on 29 April 1380, and was buried at Rome in Santa Maria sopra Minerva (though San Domenico at Siena has her head). Pius II canonized her in 1461, assigning her feast, since she had died on St Peter Mar-tyr's day (see below), to the first Sunday in May; in 1630 Urban VIII transferred it to 30 April, but the current RC calendar puts her on the 29th. She is patron saint of Siena and Italy, and also of Italian nurses; in 1970 she was declared a Doctor of the Church. In art, as the mystic bride of Christ, she is distinguished from Catherine of Alexandria by her hood and veil. Dominicans represented her with the stigmata until in 1475 the Franciscan pope Sixtus IV forbade their portrayal on any saint but Francis, a restriction lifted by Urban VIII provided that they took the form of light and not blood.

Peter Martyr (*c.*1205–52), the first martyr of the Dominican Order, into which, while a student in Bologna, he had been received by St Dominic. Highly successful in preach-ing, he was made Dominican inquisitor into the Cathar heretics of Lombardy, against whom he had considerable success until in 1252 they waylaid and murdered him on the road between Como and Milan; he was canonized the following year. He is commonly depicted with a knife slicing through his head.

In medieval English calendars, the date of Noah's departure from the Ark; see also *6 May.

30 APRIL

pridie Kalendas Maias   A

❦ HOLIDAYS AND ANNIVERSARIES Finland: May Day Eve
  Germany and Scandinavian countries: Walpurgis Night
  Mexico: Children's Day
  Netherlands: Queen's Day (Koninginnedag), marking accession of Queen Beatrix,
    1980
  USA, Louisiana: Admission Day (18th state, 1812)

❦ HOLY DAYS Pius V (RC); James brother of St John the Divine (Orth.; see *25 July); formerly Catherine of Siena (see *29 Apr.)

Pius V (1504–72), Dominican friar, appointed inquisitor-general in 1558, bishop successively of Nepi and Sutri (1556) and Mondovi (1560). Elected pope in 1565, he devoted himself to putting into effect the decrees of the Council of Trent, publishing the Roman catechism and the revised breviary and missal. Stern and devout, he imposed moral reform on the city of Rome (outlawing prostitution and bullfighting), purged the curia, and through the Inquisition strove to stamp out heresy in Italy and Spain. His excommunication of Queen Elizabeth I in 1570, far from recovering England for the papacy, led to official persecution of Catholics and alienated even Catholic sovereigns already offended by his resistance to state control of the Church. His greatest achievement was the formation of the Holy League, whose combined papal, Spanish, and Venetian fleet decisively defeated the Turkish navy at Lepanto in 1571 (see *7 Oct.). Feast-day formerly 5 May.

May Eve or Walpurgisnacht. The night of 30 April–1 May is called *Walpurgisnacht* in Germanic lands as being the eve of the translation of St Walburg (see *25 Feb.); but it owes its fame not to her, but to the folk belief that on this night witches flew from all quarters on broomsticks and billygoats to hold their sabbat, eat, drink, dance, etc., the Devil being their lord and leader, until the Queen of the May appeared at midnight to mark the driving away of winter. Although several places laid claim to the honour of hosting the *Hexensabbat*, the North German account, making the venue the Blocksberg or Brocken in the Harzgebirge, has become canonical; this range is as rich in supernatural stories as it is in minerals. A seventeenth-century source added to the company 'exalted persons, emperors, princes, barons, nobles, and the like . . . also learned and famous doctors [i.e. scholars]'; such folk duly appear alongside the witches in Part I of Goethe's *Faust*, in which Faust and Mephistopheles, guided by a will-o'-the-wisp, visit the Harzgebirge on this night and watch a playlet called *Walpurgisnachtstraum, oder Oberons und Titanias goldene Hochzeit* ('A Walpurgis Night's Dream, or the Golden Wedding of Oberon and Titania'); when they return in Part II, Act II to a *Klassische Walpurgisnacht*, Mephistopheles, amidst several adventures that perplex him, finds classical nudity 'too lively'.

Fancy-dress festivals on the witch theme are held in several places, but the night was also marked with other revelries, not always approved of by authority: the *Deutsches Wörterbuch* begun by the Brothers Grimm quotes an Altenburg city ordinance of 16 February 1837:

Es ist wahrzunehmen gewesen, daß gewöhnlich in der Walpurgisnacht vom 30. April zum 1. Mai ein polizeiwidriger und feuergefährlicher Unfug getrieben werde, indem auf dem Lande . . . vorzüglich durch das Gesinde . . . Feuer angezündet und mit brennenden Besen herumgelaufen werde, dabei unnützer Lärmen zur Beunruhigung des Publicums gemacht und von Erwachsenen und Kindern aus Muthwillen Excesse aller Art begangen werden.

It has come to our attention that commonly on Walpurgis Night, from 30 April to 1 May, mischief is practised contrary to police regulation and constituting a fire-hazard, inasmuch as in the countryside . . . farmhands in particular light fires and run around with burning brooms, creating unnecessary din to the disturbance of the public, and adults and children wantonly commit excesses of every kind.

In Sweden this night is *valborgsmässoafton*; songs are sung round bonfires (often amid falling snow) to celebrate the arrival of spring, with such texts as *Sköna maj, välkommen hit till oss igen* ('Lovely May, welcome hither to us again') and *Vintern rasat ut* ('Winter has lost its force'). But even in countries where Walpurgis' name is unknown, the association with witches is strong.

Superstitions to keep away fairies and witches
The common people formerly gathered the Leaves of *Elder* upon the last day of *Aprill*, which to disappoint the Charmes of Witches, they had affixed to their Doores and Windowes.

Coles (1656), 66–7

May Eve, Saturday [1870]
This evening being May Eve I ought to have put some birch and wittan (mountain ash) over the door to keep out the 'old witch'. But I was too lazy to go out and get it. Let us hope the old witch will not come in during the night. The young witches are welcome.   Kilvert, i. 119–20

Divinations on May Eve in Ireland
If a young woman wishes to know who is to be her future spouse, she goes, late on May Eve, to a black sally-tree, and plucks therefrom nine sprigs, the last of which she throws over her right shoulder, and puts the remaining eight into the foot of her right stocking. She then, on her knees, reads the third verse of the 17th chapter of Job; and on going to bed she places the stocking, with its contents, under her head. These rites duly performed, and her faith being strong, she will, in a dream during the night, be treated to a sight of her future husband.   W. R. Wilde, 53 (1852)

In the Authorized Version Job 17: 3 reads 'Lay down now, put me in a surety with thee; who is he that will strike hands with me?', which might out of context be understood of the wedding handfast; the Vulgate has 'Libera me Domine et pone me iuxta te, et cuiusvis manus pugnet contra me' ('Deliver me, O Lord, and set me beside thee, and let any man's hand fight against me'), which seems more appropriate for a boxing challenge.

May Eve in Callan, Ireland, 1828
May Eve . . . I hear the cuckoo on my right. Of course it does not matter on which side it is heard. I see the first butterfly to-day. I hear that young lads had along with them to-day two golden May balls which they had got from two couples married last Shrovetide. They are wont to have a May bush on top of a short stick or long cudgel, the golden ball in the middle of it, and themselves and young women dancing round it. A wisp is lighted on each side of a gap, and cattle are driven through the fires. This is an old custom, from the time of the [false] gods, which was likewise practised by the druids: every fire in Ireland was extinguished on Hallow E'en, and to light fire of earth by fire from heaven (as they used to say), and to give this sacred fire to the people. But St. Patrick ordered [his followers] to light the fire on Hallow E'en; that is the day on which the druids put it out, to show the people that there was no danger from a false god in their not having his sacred fire, but only natural fire.   O'Sullivan, i. 257, 259

MAY

As welcome as flowers in May.

Cold Maie and windie,
Barne filleth up finelie.

A hot May makes a fat churchyard.

He that would live for aye must eat sage in May.

If you would the doctor pay
leave your flannels off in May.

❰ NAMES FOR THE MONTH   Latin *Maius*, French *mai*, Spanish *mayo*, Portuguese *Maio*, Italian *maggio*, German *Mai*, Welsh *Mai*, Scots Gaelic *an Cèitean*, Irish *Bealtaine*

Maius is named after Maia, a goddess of growth (cf. *maior*, 'bigger', from *magnus*; see *1 May); she is not the same deity as Maia, the mother of Hermes and one of the Pleiades, though Romans, by spelling the latter *Maiia* or *Maia* instead of *Maea*, appear to have equated them. The Scots Gaelic name is related to Old Irish *céitemain*, 'beginning (of summer)', though one also finds *a' Mhàigh*; for the modern Irish name, see *1 May.

❰ HOLIDAYS AND ANNIVERSARIES

Second Sunday
   USA (and many other countries): Mother's Day (proposed by Anna Jarvis of Philadelphia, 1907)

Last Sunday
   France: La Fête des Mères

First Monday
   Japan: Constitution Day
   Lesotho: King's Birthday
   UK: Bank Holiday

Third Monday
   Cayman Islands: Discovery Day
   Uruguay: Battle of Las Piedras (independence from Brazil, 1828)

Fourth Monday
    Belize: Commonwealth Day

Monday before 25 May
    Canada: Victoria Day

Last Monday
    UK: Bank Holiday
    USA: Memorial Day (with the exception of New Mexico, 25 May; Puerto Rico, 28
        May; Delaware, Illinois, Maryland, New Hampshire, South Dakota, Vermont,
        and some localities, 30 May)
    USA, Virginia: Confederate Memorial Day

Last Tuesday
    Zambia: Africa Freedom Day

First Saturday
    USA: Kentucky Derby, Churchill Downs, Louisville, Ky. (since 1875; first race of the
        'Triple Crown'; the Preakness follows two Saturdays later, the Belmont Stakes five
        Saturdays later)
    Naples: phials said to contain the blood of St Januarius are borne in procession from
        the cathedral to the church of Santa Chiara (see *19 Sept.)

First or second Saturday
    Denmark: Prayer Day

Second Saturday
    Netherlands: Windmill Day

Third Saturday
    USA: Armed Forces Day

Last Saturday
    Central Africa Republic: Mother's Day

> Then came faire *May*, the fayrest mayd on ground,
>   Deckt all with dainties of her seasons pryde,
>   And throwing flowres out of her lap around:
>   Vpon two brethrens shoulders she did ride,
>   The twinnes of *Leda*; which on eyther side
>   Supported her like to their soueraine Queene.
>   Lord! how all creatures laught, when her they spide,
>   And leapt and daunc't as they had rauisht beene!
> And *Cupid* selfe about her fluttred all in greene.
>
>   Spenser, *The Faerie Queene*, VII. vii. 34

It is now May, and the sweetnesse of the Aire refresheth euery spirit: the sunny beames bring
forth faire Blossomes, and the dripping Clouds water Floraes great garden: the male Deere puts

out the Veluet head, and the pagged Doe is neere her fawning: The Sparhawke now is drawne out of the mew, and the Fowler makes ready his whistle for the Quaile: the Larke sets the morning watch, and the euening, the Nightingale: the Barges like Bowers keep the streams of the sweet Riuers, and the Mackrell with the Shad are taken prisoners in the Sea: the tall young Oke is cut downe for the Maypole: the Sithe and the Sickle are the Mowers furniture, and fayre weather makes the Labourer merry: the Physitian now prescribes the cold Whey, and the Apothecary gathers the dw for a medicine: Butter and Sage make the wholsome breakfast, but fresh cheese and creame are meat for a dainty mouth: and the Strawbery and the Pescod want no price in the market: the Chicken and the Ducke are fatned for the market, and many a Goslin neuer liues to be a Goose. It is the moneth wherein Nature hath her full of mirth, and the Senses are filled with delights. I conclude, It is from the Heauens a Grace, and to the Earth a Gladnesse. Farewell.

Breton (1626)

Charlemagne is said to have called May *wunnimanoth*, 'joy-month', which has remained the normal Western conception, celebrated in countless poems and songs (*Kalenda Maya, Ben venga maggio, Now is the month of Maying, Im wunderschönen Monat Mai*); but we shall see that there is also sorrow. The Romans thought it an unlucky month to marry in; but according to Ovid (*Fasti* 5. 489–90) it was because the Lemuria were observed in that month, in honour of the ghosts:

> Hac quoque de causa, si te proverbia tangunt,
>   mense malas Maio nubere vulgus ait.

> And for this cause, if you for proverbs stay,
>   The people have it, *Bad girls wed in May.*

However, the superstition is not confined to ancient Rome:

> Marry in May
> And you'll rue the day.

> Who weds in May
> throws all away.

German proverbs tell the same story, and May is also considered an unlucky month in Greece, especially if it begins on Saturday; marriage will lead to early death. The similarity of *Máis* to *mayá*, 'magic' no doubt helped confirm the opinion; but the importance of this month's weather to the farmer must also play a part. The first three days are 'sharp days' (cf. *1 Mar.): no work should be begun, women should not do laundry, men should not dig gardens.

A Spanish proverb recorded in the seventeenth century runs *Hasta Mayo no te quites el sayo*, 'do not take off your cloak before May'; but a variant begins *Hasta pasado Mayo*, 'till May is over'. To this corresponds the English saying 'Cast ne'er a clout till May be out', sometimes over-ingeniously expounded as meaning till the may, i.e. the hawthorn, is in bloom; the hawthorn is known as the may or may-tree because it normally blossoms about Old Style May Day (now the 14th). Like much else about this month, the tree cuts a poor figure in folklore; within the house, its blossoms are said to bring bad luck:

To sleep in a room with the whitethorn bloom in it during the month of May, will surely be followed by some great misfortune.   *N & Q*, 1st ser., ii (1850), 5 (Suffolk)

May advice:

In this Moneth *wash* often thy face with fair running Water, but eat not of such meats as be hot in quality; good to bleed especially in the Feet upon occasion; beware of eating stale Fish, or tainted Flesh, but eat your meals in due season, and drink but little Wine this Moneth; to drink clarified Whey simple, or drawn with cool Herbs is very healthful unto hot stomacks: *Sharp* drinks are good, pure Wine mixed with Goats Milk to annoint both the head and brest is greatly commended, good to take Physick, not good to eat the Head or Foot of any Beast this Moneth; to drink *Wormwood Wine* is very good, used moderately, but otherwise it attracteth the lightest parts of the Humors, and leaves the mass of Humors more obstinate, eat *Fennell Roots* tenderly sodden, take gentle Physick, to purge the Blood and Body very good, and to sleep after Dinner in this Moneth is not discommended.   Saunders (1665)

Pilgrimage to St Mary's Well in Culloden on the first Sunday in May:

This year I joined in the pilgrimage, and indeed all roads on that Sunday afternoon led to Culloden . . . The ritual . . . has survived the centuries: first a coin must be thrown into the well, a tribute to the spirit dwelling there; then a sip taken of the water, a charm against evil, and then, after the wish, a 'clootie', or small rag, must be tied to the branch of an over-hanging tree. This is considered so important that this wishing-well of Culloden is now known far and wide as the Clootie Well. . . . Rags there were of all colours . . . they must hang until an-other winter has rotted them away; to remove them would bring bad luck, if not a transfer of the very afflictions of which the first owners had been trying to rid themselves!

                                                                    The Times, 25 May 1957

1 MAY

Kalendae Maiae   B

At Philip and Jacob, away with the lams
that thinkest to have any milke of their dams.

You must not count your yearlings till May Day.

❦ HOLIDAYS AND ANNIVERSARIES May Day (Scotland: Beltane Day)
USA, Oklahoma: Bird Day

❦ ANCIENT ROME A pregnant sow was sacrificed by the priest of Vulcan (*flamen Volcanalis*) to Maia; the list of deities to whom official prayers were made included *Maia Volcani*, but the connection is debated. Since the victim was appropriate to an earth goddess, she was equated by some Roman writers with the Earth, as was the Good God-dess, Bona Dea, whose temple on the Aventine had its dedication feast on this day. Little is known of proceedings; there is rather more information about the December ritual (see *1 Dec.). Mythology made her cult even older than that of Hercules at the Ara Maxima (see *12 Aug.), itself pre-Roman.

The Lares of the city were worshipped as Lares Praestites (Guarantors or Guardians) on this day; their fellow-guardian, the dog, was associated with them in visual representations and (we are told) in the dogskin garments draped over their legs.

❦ HOLY DAYS Philip and James (CofE; RC now 3 May); Joseph the Worker (RC); red-letter day

Philip and *James the Less* are both listed among the Twelve Apostles; St John makes Philip a sober and literal soul, who declares that 'two hundred pennyworth of bread' is not enough to feed the 5,000 (John 6: 7), and at the Last Supper bids Jesus 'Lord, shew us the Father and it sufficeth us', to which Jesus replies: 'he that hath seen me hath seen the Father'. Nothing is related of James the Less, son of Alphaeus, but several places claim his relics (including Compostela, not content with those of James the Greater); he was formerly identified with James the brother of the Lord (see *11 May). Among the Orthodox, James is culted on 9 October, Philip on 14 November. In the RC Church this traditional feast-day was changed to 11 May in 1955 when the feast of Joseph the Worker was introduced, and subsequently to the 3rd.

Joseph the Worker, a feast proclaimed by Pius XII in 1955; see below under 'Labour holiday'.

May Day. May Day is rich in customs, perhaps more so than any other day of the year. Records of bringing in the May are found as early as the thirteenth century in England. In the mid-fourteenth century the Welsh poet Gruffydd ab Addaf ap Dafydd laments the removal of a beautiful birch to serve as a maypole in the market-place at Llanidloes; soon afterwards we read of a permanent maypole at Cornhill in London. 'Garlanding', carrying around garlands of flowers and singing May songs, offered children yet another opportunity to collect money; in the days before they were normally given pocket money, such practices were accepted. By the seventeenth century milkmaids took to parading, first with their milk-pails, then with elaborate constructions of silver objects decked with ribbons and greenery, often accompanied by blind musicians. This too was the chimney sweeps' day; dressed in their best and beribboned, they paraded with a collection box and a chimney brush. Then silver went out of fashion—no doubt it was a worry to protect from prying hands—and the Jack in the Green, a man concealed in a green bush, came into favour.

Going a-maying
Against May, Whitsonday or other time, all the yung men and maides, olde men and wives run gadding over night to the woods, groves, hils & Mountains, where they spend all the night in plesant pastimes, & in the morning they return bringing with them birch & branches of trees, to deck their assemblies withall, and no mervaile, for there is a great Lord present amongst them, as Superintendent and Lord over their pastimes and sportes, namely, Sathan prince of hel: But the cheifest iewel they bring from thence is their May-pole, which they bring home with great veneration, as thus. They have twentie or fortie yoke of Oxen, every Oxe having a sweet nose-gay of flours placed on the tip of his hornes, and these Oxen drawe home this May-pole (this stinking Idol rather) which is covered all over with floures, and hearbs bound round about with

strings from the top to the bottome, and sometimes painted with variable colours, with two or three hundred men, women and children following it with great devotion. And thus beeing reared up, with handkercheefs and flags hovering on the top, they straw the ground rounde about, binde green boughes about it, set up sommer haules, bowers and arbors hard by it. And then fall they to daunce about it like as the heathen people did at the dedication of the Idols, wherof this is a perfect pattern, or rather the thing it self. I have heard it credibly reported (and that, viva voce) by men of great gravitie and reputation, that of fortie, threescore, or a hundred maides going to the wood over night, there have scarcely the third part of them returned home againe undefiled.

Stubbes, sig. M3ᵛ–4 (1583)

Those riotous assemblies of idle people who under pretence of going a maying (as they term it) do oftentimes cut down, and carry away fine straight trees, to set up before some alehouse, or revelling place, where they keep their drunken Bacchanalias . . . I think it were better to be quite abolished amongst us, for many reasons, besides that of occasioning so much waste and spoil . . . to adorn their wooden idols.

Evelyn, *Sylva*, 206–7 (1670)

Henry VIII and Catherine of Aragon celebrate May Day with Robin Hood in 1515:

Edward Hall hath noted, that King Henry VIII., as in the 3rd of his reign, and divers other years, so namely, in the 7th of his reign, on May-day in the morning, with Queen Katherine his wife, accompanied with many lords and ladies, rode a-maying from Greenwich to the high ground of Shooter's Hill, where, as they passed by the way, they espied a company of tall yeomen, clothed all in green, with green hoods, and bows and arrows, to the number of two hundred; one being their chieftain, was called Robin Hood, who required the king and his company to stay and see his men shoot; whereunto the king granting, Robin Hood whistled, and all the two hundred archers shot off, loosing all at once; and when he whistled again they likewise shot again; their arrows whistled by craft of the head, so that the noise was strange and loud, which greatly de-lighted the king, queen, and their company. Moreover, this Robin Hood desired the king and queen, with their retinue, to enter the greenwood, where, in harbours made of boughs, and decked with flowers, they were set and served plentifully with venison and wine by Robin Hood and his men, to their great contentment, and had other pageants and pastimes, as ye may read in my said author.

Stow, 123–4

Parade of the milkmaids and chimney sweeps in London

Thursday, 2 May [1776]
Yesterday being May day the Milk maids appear in fine and fantastic attire and carrying on their heads pyramids of 3 or 4 feet in heigth finely decorated. The young chimney sweepers with their sooty and chalk's faces, dressed out with ribbons and gilt paper, a grotesque and merry andrew appearance, coal and brushes making a kind of musical sound, raising contributions on their em-ployers and others.

[4 May] . . . in Ave Mary Lane [I] saw a garland so called, being a pyramid consisting of 7 or 8 stories in the 4 angles of which stood a silver tankard; and in the sides, between each, lessen-ing in heigth, as the stories rose, stood a silver salver the top crowned with a chased silver tea kettle round which were placed sundry small pieces of plate the whole adorned with wreaths and festoons of flowers, gilt paper &c., carried on a bier and handbarrow, being a custom amongst the milk men and maids, to collect of the customers a yearly contribution. The worth of the sil-ver appeared to be many £100, and is borrowed of the silver smiths for the occasion.

Curwen, i. 153–4

I arrived in London on May Day, which is a holiday for the chimney sweepers. All the chimney sweepers, little and great, on that day are dressed as fine as they can make themselves, with ribbons of all colours, and a great deal of gilding about them, and feathers in their caps; and they go about the streets with a wooden thing in one hand (such as the churchwardens carry about in the church to collect money for a brief), and their brush in the other; and with these they make a clatter, and beg money from those who stop to look at them. They have generally a green man in company who is also called 'Jack in the Bush', because he is in the middle of a green bush, which covers him all over, head and all, so that you can see nothing but his feet, and he goes dancing with the rest. This bush is ornamented with ribbons, and I have seen them in former times half covered with bright pewter pots and dishes, which it must have been a great fatigue to carry about and dance under their weight, especially in a hot day, and being so shut up from the air. This Jack in the Bush is a comical sight, but I am sorry to say that it does harm by frightening horses . . . I must not forget to observe that the chimney sweepers make a feast with the money which is given them; and they are so fond of their holiday that they make the first of May last the whole of the week . . .

> Robert Southey to his daughter Katharine, 4 May 1820; Southey, *Letters*, 314–15

Mayday in London has long been the chimneysweepers' holiday: they decorate themselves with flowers, ribands, and tinsel, and dance in the streets. This practice is likely to become obsolete, as infant chimneysweepers are going out of fashion, from the excessive cruelty necessary to be used in training them to climb the flues, and from the adoption of a machine invented by Mr. Smart for cleansing chimneys, in order to supersede the use of climbing children. There exists in London a society for this purpose, which was established on the 4th of February, 1803.

> Forster, 211 (1824)

Seeing and being seen in coaches in Hyde Park

1 [May 1667]. . . . Thence Sir W. Penn and I in his coach, Tiburne way, into the park; where a horrid dust and number of coaches, without pleasure or order. That which we and almost all went for was to see my Lady Newcastle; which we could not, she being fallowed and crowded upon by coaches all the way she went, that nobody could come near her; only, I could see she was in a large black coach, adorned with silver instead of gold, and so with the curtains and everything black and white, and herself in her cap; but other parts I could not make. But that which I did see and wonder at, with reason, was to find Pegg Penn in a new coach, with only her husband's pretty sister with her, both patched and very fine, and in much the finest coach in the park and I think that ever I did see, one or other, for neatness and richness in gold and everything that is noble. . . . When we had spent half an hour in the park, we went out again, weary of the dust and despairing of seeing my Lady Newcastle . . .

> Pepys, viii. 196–7

Setting up maypoles

[At] St. Andrew the Apostle . . . so called St. Andrew Undershaft, because that of old time every year on May-day in the morning, it was used, that an high or long shaft, or May-pole, was set up there, in the midst of the street, before the south side of the said church: which shaft, when it was set on end and fixed in the ground, was higher than the church steeple. . . . This shaft was not raised at any time since evil May-day (so called of an insurrection made by apprentices and other young persons against aliens in the year 1517); but the said shaft was laid along over the doors, and under the pentises of one row of houses and alley gate, called of the shaft Shaft Alley.

> Stow, 163–4

Maypoles were banned by Parliament on 8 April 1644:

And because the profanation of the Lord's-day hath been heretofore greatly occasioned by Maypoles (a heathenish vanity, generally abused to superstition and wickedness), the Lords and Commons do further order and ordain That all and singular May-poles that are, or shall be erected, shall be taken down and removed.

> quoted in Whitaker, 149

Robin Hood's Day. Robin Hood was thought to be a yeoman (later a dispossessed nobleman) who haunted Sherwood Forest (or any of the competing greenwoods from Devon to Scotland) with a band of outlaws (including Friar Tuck, so called from his tucked-up gown, at first an unsympathetic personage, latterly a cheerful glutton); he is said to have robbed the rich to subsidize the poor and held up the Sheriff of Nottingham. Ballads about him from the fourteenth century pre-date the plays and games involving him and his company, which were also used to raise money.

Bishop Latimer was shocked to discover the reason that no one turned up to hear his sermon on the first of May:

I came once my selfe to a place, ridyng on a iornay home warde from London, and I sente worde ouer nyghte into the toune that I would preach there in ye morninge because it was holy day, and me thought it was an holye dayes worcke, The church stode in my waye, and I toke my horsse, and my companye, and went thither, I thoughte I shoulde haue founde a greate companye in the churche, and when I came there, the churche dore was faste locked.

I tarried there halfe an houer and more, at last the keye was founde, and one of the parishe commes to me and sayes. Syr thys is a busye daye wyth vs, we can not heare you, it is Robyn hoodes daye. The parishe are gone a brode to gather for Robyn hoode, I praye you let them not. I was fayne there to geue place to Robyn hoode, I thought my rochet shoulde haue bene regarded, thoughe I were not, but it woulde not serue, it was fayn to geue place to Robyn hoodes men.

It is no laughynge matter my friendes, it is a wepyng matter, a heauy matter, a heauy matter, vnder the pretence for gatherynge for Robyn hoode, a traytoure, and a thefe, to put out a preacher, to haue hys office lesse estemed, to prefer Robyn hod before the ministration of Gods word, and al thys hath come of vnpreachynge prelates.

Sixth Sermon preached before the king at Westminster, 12 April 1549

Morris dancing is recorded as early as the mid-fifteenth century in England and seems to have arisen as a court entertainment, not particularly connected with May Day; as such it was also known in other European countries. By the sixteenth century it had spread out to towns and then villages as popular entertainment. Both the meaning of the term and the origins of the custom have greatly exercised folklorists. Morris dancing still takes place in many parts of the country; the participation of women is sharply contested. The name is probably a corruption of 'Moorish' (the Italian is *moresca*).

> Ho! who comes here all along with bagpiping and drumming?
> O 'tis the morris dance I see a-coming.
>   Come ladies out, come quickly!
>   And see about how trim they dance and trickly.
>   Hey! there again! how the bells they shake it!
>   Hey ho! now for our town! and take it!
> Soft awhile, not away so fast! They melt them.
> Piper, be hanged, knave! see'st thou not the dancers how they swelt them?
>   Stand out awhile! you come too far, I say, in.
>   There give hobby-horse more room to play in!

Thomas Morley, *Madrigals to Four Voyces* (1594)

Queen of the May. A young girl or woman was often chosen to lead processions on May Day. Tennyson, who understood the month's dark side, portrays in 'The May Queen'

first the girl's excitement at being chosen, but then her realization that she will never see
another May:

> You must wake and call me early, call me early, mother dear;
> To-morrow 'ill be the happiest time of all the glad New-year;
> Of all the glad New-year, mother, the maddest merriest day;
> For I'm to be Queen o' the May, mother, I'm to be Queen o' the May.

> To-night I saw the sun set: he set and left behind
> The good old year, the dear old time, and all my peace of mind;
> And the New-year's coming up, mother, but I shall never see
> The blossom on the blackthorn, the leaf upon the tree.

> Last May we made a crown of flowers: we had a merry day;
> Beneath the hawthorn on the green they made me Queen of May;
> And we danced about the may-pole and in the hazel copse,
> Till Charles's Wain came out above the tall white chimney-tops.

> All in the wild March-morning I heard the angels call;
> It was when the moon was setting, and the dark was over all;
> The trees began to whisper, and the wind began to roll,
> And in the wild March-morning I heard them call my soul. . . .

Padstow hobby-horse day. At Padstow in Cornwall May Day is celebrated with particular
enthusiasm. Drums are beaten, a song is sung; two hobby-horses with fearsome masks
dance through the greenery-bedecked streets in different parts of the town, from time
to time sinking to the ground and getting up again. These horses are in fact men dancing inside capes, under which they will sometimes snatch a woman for a moment,
thereby (it is said) bringing her good luck; this practice is apparently a local addition to
the amalgam of English May rituals constituting the ceremony, first attested in 1803.

On the first of May, another species of festivity is pursued in Padstow. This is called *The Hobby
Horse*; from canvas being extended with hoops, and painted to resemble a horse. Being carried
through the street, men, women, and children, flock round it, when they proceed to a place called
Traitor Pool, about a quarter of a mile distant, in which the hobby-horse is always supposed to
drink; when the head being dipped into the water, is instantly taken up, and the mud and water
are sprinkled on the spectators, to the no small diversion of all. On returning home, a particular song is sung, that is supposed to commemorate the event that gave the hobby-horse birth.
According to tradition, the French on a former occasion effected a landing at a small cove in the
vicinity; but seeing at a distance a number of women dressed in red cloaks, which they mistook
for soldiers, they fled to their ships, and put to sea. The day generally ends in riot and dissipa-
tion.   Hitchins, i. 720 (1824)

A similar hobby-horse, the Sailors' Horse, makes its appearance in Minehead (Somerset), starting out from the pub The Old Ship Aground, and ending at Dunster Castle,
where nowadays the host is the National Trust administrator. Festivities continue for
two more days.

Moving day in New York. In several societies there has been a traditional day for moving
house; in Scotland it was 15 May (OS), in ancient Rome 1 July. In New York it was
1 May; a native New Yorker noted in 1832:

Tuesday 1st May. Hazy, raw. Yesterday was very unfavourable for the general moving of our great city. High rents, incommodious dwellings, & necessity combine to crowd our streets with carts overloaded with furniture & hand barrows with sofas, chairs, sideboards, looking glasses & pictures, so as to render the sidewalks almost impassable. The practice of all moving on one day, & give up & hiring Houses in February is of antient custom & when the city was small & inhabitants few in number, almost every body owned or continued for years tenants in the same houses. Few instances of removals were seen, but now N York is literally in an uproar for several days before & after the 1st of May. This practice of move all, to strangers appears absurd, but it is attended with the advantage of affording a greater choice of abodes in the February quarter.

Pintard, iv. 44

Lydia Maria Child commented in 1843:

That people should move so *often* in this city, is generally a matter of their own volition. Aspirations after the infinite, lead them to perpetual change, in the restless hope of finding something better and better still. . . . A lady in the neighbourhood closed all her blinds and shutters, on May-day; being asked by her acquaintance whether she had been in the country, she answered, 'I was *ashamed* not to be moving on the first of May; and so I shut up the house that the neighbours might not know it.' One could not well imagine a fact more characteristic of the despotic sway of custom and public opinion, in the United States, and the nineteenth century. Elias Hick's remark, that it takes '*live* fish to swim *up* stream', is emphatically true of this age and country, in which liberty-caps abound, but no one is allowed to wear them.   Child, 273–4

May Day celebrations in colonial Massachusetts. Governor Bradford rails against May Day celebrations at Ma-re Mount in 1628:

They allso set up a May-pole, drinking and dancing aboute it many days togeather, inviting the Indean women, for their consorts, dancing and frisking togither, (like so many fairies, or furies rather,) and worse practises. As if they had anew revived and celebrated the feasts of the Roman Goddes Flora, or the beasly practieses of the madd Bacchinalians. Morton likwise (to shew his poetrie) composed sundry rimes and verses, some tending to lasciviousnes, and others to the detraction and scandall of some persons, which he affixed to this idle or idoll May-polle. They chainged allso the name of their place, and in stead of calling it Mounte Wollaston, they call it Meriemounte, as if this joylity would have lasted ever. But this continued not long, for after Morton was sent for England . . . shortly after came over that worthy gentlman, Mr. John Indecott, who brought over a patent under the broad seall, for the govermente of the Massachusets, who visiting those parts caused that May-polle to be cutt downe, and rebuked them for their profannes, and admonished them to looke ther should be better walking; so they now, or others, changed the name of their place againe, and called it Mounte-Dagon.   Bradford, 238

May morning in Oxford. At 6 a.m. on this day the choir of Magdalen College, Oxford, sings a Latin hymn on the college tower, watched (and given favourable conditions heard) by revellers and tourists. The explanations relating the ceremony to the obit of Henry VII, also kept on this day by the college, may be discounted; in fact the earliest account, from the seventeenth century, suggests a secular occasion:

The choral Ministers of this House do, according to an ancient custom, salute Flora every year on the first of May at four in the morning with vocal music of several parts. Which having been sometimes well performed hath given great content to the neighbourhood and auditors underneath.   Wood, 350

By the mid-eighteenth century it had become a regular concert, vocal and instrumental, lasting nearly two hours, until one year, when this proved impossible, it was replaced by the singing, at 5 a.m., of a short hymn well known to the choir. This has remained the practice ever since, though the hour has been adjusted to 6 a.m. to take account of British Summer Time; from 1844 onwards the singers have worn surplices to mark the religious nature of the proceedings—a nature lost on the boisterous spectators. After leaving Magdalen Bridge, one eats a hearty breakfast, and watches or takes part in morris dances.

Beltane. Irish *Lá Bealtaine*, 'Beltane Day', Scots Gaelic *Là Bealltuinn*, the day of the ancient festival celebrating the beginning of summer. Beltane, as it is Anglicized, is one of the rare survivals of pagan ritual. According to a saying recorded by O'Sullivan, the best time to plant potatoes is between the two May Days (*idis an dá Bhealtaine*), i.e. between New and Old May Day. In general the emphasis in Ireland and the Highlands was more on bonfires, that in England, Wales, Cornwall, and the Lowlands on maypoles.

Thomas Pennant reports the custom in the Scottish Highlands in 1769:

On the 1st of May, the herdsmen of every village hold their *Bel-tein*, a rural sacrifice: they cut a square trench on the ground, leaving the turf in the middle; on that they make a fire of wood, on which they dress a large caudle of eggs, butter, oatmeal and milk; and bring, besides the ingredients of the caudle, plenty of beer and whisky; for each of the company must contribute something. The rites begin with spilling some of the caudle on the ground, by way of libation: on that every one takes a cake of oatmeal, upon which are raised nine square knobs, each dedicated to some particular being, the supposed preserver of their flocks and herds, or to some particular animal, the real destroyer of them: each person then turns his face to the fire, breaks off a knob, and flinging it over his shoulders, says: *This I give to thee, preserve thou my horses; this to thee, preserve thou my sheep*; and so on. After that, they use the same ceremony to the noxious animals: *This I give to thee, O fox! spare thou my lambs; this to thee, O hooded Crow! this to thee, O Eagle!*.

When the ceremony is over, they dine on the caudle; and after the feast is finished, what is left is hid by two persons deputed for that purpose; but on the next *Sunday* they re-assemble and finish the reliques of the first entertainment.   Pennant, *Scotland 1769*, 90–1

Beltane bannocks are baked and rolled down a hill:

[At Beltane Eve] the matron or housekeeper is employed in . . . baking the Belton bannocks. Next morning the children are presented each with a bannock, with as much joy as an heir to an estate his title-deeds; and having their pockets well lined with cheese and eggs, to render the entertainment still more sumptuous, they hasten to the place of assignation, to meet the little band assembled on the brow of some sloping hill, to reel their bannocks, and learn their future fate. With hearty greetings they meet, and with their knives make the signs of life and death on their bannocks. These signs are a cross, or the sign of life, on the one side; and a cypher, or the sign of death, on the other. This being done, the bannocks are all arranged in a line, and on their edges let down the hill. This process is repeated three times, and if the cross most frequently present itself, the owner will live to celebrate another Belton day; but if the cypher is oftenest uppermost, he is doomed to die of course. This sure prophecy of short life, however, seldom spoils the appetites of the unfortunate short-livers . . . Assembling around a rousing fire of collected heath and brushwood, the ill-fated bannocks are soon demolished.

Grant Stewart, 260–1 (1823)

Sunday after May Day in Callan, Ireland, 1829
Sunday . . . Two May balls were taken up, (that is a May bush covered with silk, ribbons, flowers, &c., with the ball in the middle of it hanging down and covered likewise with adornments), the one from the Grants of Coolalong, and the other from the Walshes of [lit.] on the Fair Green. The young men played for one of them [in a hurling match] afterwards. The golden apple that Paris raised aloft among the goddesses did not do as much mischief as some of these May balls do. Up to this day, no May ball has been taken for the past fifty years, since a man was killed on the crossroads of Callan taking a May bail from a newly married minister, Dr. Lambart.

O'Sullivan, ii. 149

May Day superstitions
They take any one for a witch that comes to fetch fire on May-day, and therefore refuse to give any, unless the party asking it be sick, and then it is with a curse, believing that all their butter will be stole away next summer by this woman. . . . But they think it foretells them a plentiful dairy, if they set boughs of trees before their doors on a May-day.   Camden, 1046 (1586)

[In Cornwall] it is unlucky to buy a broom in May.   Couch, 163 (1871)

The Natives in the Village *Barvas* [Isle of Lewis] retain an antient Custom of sending a Man very early to cross *Barvas* river, every first Day of *May*, to prevent any Females crossing it first; for that they say would hinder the Salmon from coming into the River all the year round: they pretend to have learn'd this from a foreign Sailor, who was shipwreck'd upon that Coast a long time ago. This Observation they maintain to be true from Experience.   M. Martin, 7 (1716)

> Last *May-day* fair I search'd to find a Snail
> That might my secret Lover's Name reveal;
> Upon a Gooseberry Bush a Snail I found,
> For always Snails near sweetest Fruit abound.
> I seiz'd the Vermine, home I quickly sped,
> And on the Hearth the milk-white Embers spread.
> Slow crawl'd the Snail, and if I right can spell,
> In the soft Ashes mark'd a curious *L*:
> Oh, may this wondrous Omen lucky prove!
> For *L* is found in *Lubberkin* and *Love*.

John Gay (1685–1732), *The Shepherd's Week*, Thursday, 49–58

In Greece, instead of a May Queen, there is a May boy; in some places he lies down as if dead, is mourned by the local girls, and then jumps up. In Italy one eats *pecorino* and *fave*, in France one gathers *muguet*, lily of the valley, and distributes it to friends and family as a *porte-bonheur*. In Norway *gauksmesse*, 'Cuckoomass', because one awaited that bird's arrival; but also another Fools' Day, the victim being called *maikatt* (May cat) or *maigås* (May goose) (cf. *1 Apr.).

Labour holiday. The eight-hour movement, to reduce the working day from ten to eight hours, began after the Civil War. It was a major aim of the National Labor Union, whose first congress met in 1866. By 1868 Congress and six states had passed eight-hour legislation. The Illinois legislature passed an eight-hour law in 1867, to take effect on 1 May. On that day forty-four Chicago unions celebrated the death of the ten-hour day with a procession and mass meeting. But the battle was not over: businessmen had won the concession from the legislature that the eight-hour day applied only where no written contract existed with the workers, and many employers were intransigent. Many workers who did not participate in the parade joined in a general strike, which the *Tribune*, turning against the movement, reported as a riot.

In 1884 the National Federation of Organized Trades and Labor Assemblies decided to call for a general strike on 1 May 1886 to enforce demands for observance of the eight-hour day. The socialists were in the forefront of the organization, and issued circulars to encourage more workers to join:

Arouse, ye toilers of America! Lay down your tools on May 1, 1886, cease your labor, close the factories, mills and mines—for one day in the year. One day of revolt—not of rest! A day not ordained by the bragging spokesmen of institutions holding the world of labor in bondage! A day on which labor makes its own laws and has the power to execute them! All without the consent or approval of those who oppress and rule. A day on which in tremendous force the unity of the army of toilers is arrayed against the powers that today hold sway over the destinies of the people of all nations.

                                                                          quoted in Foner, 19

The May Day processions and strike were held peacefully, but in Chicago the strikes continued, exacerbated by a split within the labour movement that pitted trade unionists (viewed as native, honest Americans) against socialists (ignorant and subversive immigrants). The strikes led to violence outside the McCormick Reaper factory on 3 May and at Haymarket Square on 4 May, with police and workers killed and injured. The leaders of the radical branch of the labour movement were arrested, in an attempt to stamp out the anarchists.

These facts, long forgotten in the USA, are the origin of the May Day holiday demanded, and in many cases obtained, by socialist and trade union movements throughout the world, its most spectacular manifestation being the military and political parade in Moscow during the Soviet period. In many countries the holiday was obtained by trade union agitation, supported by socialist parties; but in Germany, where such agitation had proved fruitless, it was instituted in 1933 as a gift from Hitler, being promptly followed by the abolition of trade unions. This did no damage to its left-wing credentials, which in 1955 caused the rigorously anti-communist Pope Pius XII, following the ancient tradition of Christianizing heathen festivals, to proclaim 1 May the feast of Joseph the Worker. This was done without prejudice to St Joseph's proper feast-day on 19 March, but entailed the displacement of SS Philip and James.

In the UK, a so-called May Day Bank Holiday was instituted in 1978 for trade unionists to celebrate, but on the first Monday in May (which in that year happened to be 1 May) so as to minimize the damage to business; such celebration as there was took place in pouring rain. Although Conservatives objected to it as politically partisan, and many others would rather have had an additional free day in the four months between the Late Summer Bank Holiday and Christmas than in the few weeks between Easter Monday and the Spring Bank Holiday, the Conservative governments in office between 1979 and 1997 neither abolished the holiday nor moved it. So feeble, indeed, was the association between even the genuine May Day and political radicalism that in the latter year neither the Conservatives nor their opponents recognized an omen in the choice of 1 May for a general election even when the Labour Party gained an overwhelming victory. By contrast, in many European countries it was the occasion for political demonstrations not only by the left, but by the extreme right.

St Tammany's Day. In colonial Philadelphia this was Spring Day, the opening of the fishing season; it was also the day on which the Sons of Liberty forgathered in a tavern whose host bore the appropriate name of Pole. The festivities were improved by the observation of the day as St Tammany's Day; the original Tammany was a Delaware Indian chief from whom William Penn had secured land in the late seventeenth century, but during the struggle over the Stamp Acts he was invoked by the patriots, first as a mock king in opposition to George III, then as a mock saint in opposition to the four British patron saints. On 1 May 1783 the new-won independence was celebrated in triumphant song:

> Of Andrew, of Patrick, of David, and George,
> What mighty achievements we hear!
> Whilst no one relates great Tammany's feats,
> Although more heroic by far.

Two years later the flag of the United States was first displayed at a Tammany gathering, complete with a drawing of the saint. In the nineteenth century, however, Tammany Hall in New York City became notorious for political corruption and criminality funded with public money.

2 MAY

a.d. VI Nonas Maias   C

❡ HOLY DAYS Athanasius (CY, RC)

Athanasius (*c.*296–373), bishop of Alexandria. As secretary to the bishop of Alexandria he attended the Council of Nicaea in 325, which condemned Arianism (see *26 Feb.) and declared the Son consubstantial (*homoousios*) with the Father, a term that to many Easterners itself had heretical implications. In the following years, doctrines that refused the Nicene formula were favoured by leading churchmen in the East and even emperors; Athanasius, who became bishop in 328, devoted himself to attacking them. His use of strong-arm methods enabled his enemies to depose him at the Council of Tyre in 335; in all he was exiled five times, but he continued the struggle even after the 'Homoian' doctrine (that the Son was 'like', *homoios*, the Father) had been officially adopted in 359. It was this form of Christianity, called 'Arian' by pro-Nicenes and by church historians though not by its own exponents, that was accepted by the Goths, who remained faithful to it even after its repudiation by the empire. The accession of Julian the Apostate, who having rejected Christianity withdrew the persecuting power from the Homoians, permitted their opponents to fight back and develop a coherent theology to challenge them; in this Athanasius (despite further periods of exile) played a crucial part, especially after accepting the orthodox intentions of the so-called Semi-Arians who favoured the term *homoiousios*, 'of like substance'. Eight years after his death, the Homoousian faith was upheld at the First Council of Constantinople.

On the first Monday after this day the Procession of the Holy Blood takes place in Bruges, in which the purported drop of Christ's blood brought back from the Holy Land in 1147 by Count Thierry of Alsace is carried from the Chapel of the Holy Blood to the cathedral.

On this day in 1808 the commander of French forces in Spain, Joachim Murat, following the forced abdications of King Carlos IV and his disloyal son Fernando VII, attempted to remove the rest of the royal family to France; the people of Madrid rose in revolt. Although they were suppressed, and savage reprisals taken, the rest of the country rallied to the cause, beginning the Peninsular War in which Spain and Portugal, in alliance with Great Britain, were freed of the French invader. For this reason *el Dos de Mayo* is remembered as one of the most glorious days in Spanish history.

3 MAY

a.d. V Nonas Maias   D

❦ HOLIDAYS AND ANNIVERSARIES   Japan: Constitution Memorial Day
    Mexico: Day of the Holy Cross (celebration for construction workers and miners)
    Poland: Constitution Day, celebrating the Constitution of 1791, a monument of Enlightenment principles that was overthrown by a faction of nobles in alliance with Catherine the Great (national day)

❦ ANCIENT ROME   Last day of Floralia (see *28 Apr.).

❦ HOLY DAYS   Invention of the Cross (BCP); Philip and James (RC; *1 May CofE)

Invention of the Cross (Rood-Day). This is the Western date (first attested in 7th-c. Gaul) for celebrating the empress Helena's supposed discovery (*inventio*) of the True Cross (see *14 Sept.), which related to a tale already told in the fifth century, of a Jew called Judas, whom she tortured into revealing it; he became a Christian, and was made bishop of Jerusalem under the name of Cyriac, 'the Lord's Man'. (Jewish legend makes the wise Rabbi Judah arrange a bogus discovery to take the pressure off his people.) The feast was suppressed in the RC Church in 1960, as had been proposed in 1741.

Timothy and Maura (RC, Orth.). A newly wedded couple reportedly martyred under Diocletian by being nailed to a wall for nine days after Timothy had refused to surrender his Bible. In Greece, since *mavra* = black, one abstains from cutting, sewing, or any other handiwork, lest black spots appear on one's hands, nor is cloth bleached on this day for fear it should turn black; indeed, 'all activities which are not absolutely safe are generally avoided' (Megas, 121).

This is one of the 'Egyptian' or 'dismal' days; in the Scottish Highlands it was the worst of them, imparting its bad luck to the day of the week on which it fell the whole year through (cf. *14 May, *28 Dec.; *Days: Unlucky, 'Egyptian', or Dismal Days):

A Highlander never begins any thing of consequence on the day of the week on which the third of May falls, which he styles *Lagh Sheachanna na bleanagh*, or the dismal day.

> Pennant, *Scotland* 1769, 90

On the third of May they take the Urine and Dung of the Catle together with mans urine and therwith they sprinkle their Catle; thinking this an Antidose against all Charms and Divelrie.

> Kirkwood, 67

It was also 'on Mayes day the thrydde' that Chaucer's Pandarus tells Criseyde of Troilus' love; on the same day (all the unluckier for being a Friday) Chantecleer was devoured by the fox. (On the third night of May, Palamon breaks prison in *The Knight's Tale*; but ultimately all ends well.)

The zealous pilgrim of the Middle Ages sought out every relic he could clap eyes or lay hands on. Some must have taxed the credulity of even the most ardent believer: what was he to think when faced with two heads of John the Baptist? One ingenious explanation was that one head was of the saint in his youth, the other in maturity. Fragments of the True Cross, on the other hand, were more easily accepted. The reformer John Calvin calculated, in his treatise 'Declarynge what great profit might come to al Christendome, yf there were a regester made of all Sainctes' Bodies, and other Reliques' (English edn., 1561), that the claimed fragments would fill more than one ship—indeed, it would take not one man but 300 to carry the fragments reunited.

Every pilgrim to the Holy Land was drawn to the site of the Crucifixion, and 3 May was an especially important time to be present at the place where Helena had supposedly discovered the Cross. One traveller, visiting Mount Calvary in 1818, wrote:

On Calvary we were shown the place where Christ was nailed to the cross, where the cross was erected, and the hole into which the end of it was fixed, and the rent in the rock; all of which are covered with marble, perforated in the proper places, so that the ancient recipient of the cross and the rent in the rock may be seen and touched. Close by a cross is erected on an elevated part of the floor, and a wooden body stretched upon it in an attitude of suffering.

Descending from Mount Calvary we entered into the chapel of St. Helena, and descended to the low rocky vault in which the cross was found; in this murky den the discovery of the cross is celebrated in an appropriate mass every year on the 3d of May; it is large enough to contain about thirty or forty persons wedged in close array, and on that occasion it is generally crowded to the door. This year it happened that the day on which the festival was to be celebrated by the Romans, interfered with that on which it was to be celebrated by the Greeks, and we witnessed all the tug of war, the biting and the scratching, the pommeling and the pelting, the brickbats and clubs, the whimpering and the mewling, of exstatic, spawling, palpitating monks fighting for their chapel like kites and crows for their nests. When rogues come to reckoning, and thieves fight about their den, let the thickest skin best 'bide the blows. All are lost that miss. The Romans are routed: 'The Devil aids the Greeks, and they are schismatics', said the panting superior, swooning from a blow that might have cleft him in twain; 'and you Englishmen, you live in our convent, and you see us beat, back and side, and you don't assist us.' 'How can you expect it?' rejoined a gallant Briton, 'when, if we fell in your cause, you would not allow us a Christian burial.' 'Humph!' said the Roman, and called for the apothecary to rub his back with the balsam of Jerusalem, that had been well basted with the blows of the cudgel, and undulated with bumps that rose like tubercles on the sides of a burning mountain; coffee, and Rosoglio consoled him for his defeat, and he whined himself asleep on that night as he had done on other nights before. The Greeks spent the night in firing pistols, and rejoicing, and were fined by the Cadi next morning for disturbing his repose. Letters were instantly sent to Rome and Constantinople, complaining of the outrage, and calling for redress.   R. Richardson, ii. 325–6

(The Greek celebration in question was in fact Thomas Sunday, the Sunday after Easter, on 21 Apr. OS 1818.)

4 MAY

a.d. IV Nonas Maias   E

❦ HOLIDAYS AND ANNIVERSARIES   China: Youth Day (public holiday, commemorating 1919 demonstration by students in Tiananmen Square, against imperialist aggression)
    USA, Rhode Island: Independence Day (from Great Britain, 1776)

❦ HOLY DAYS   English Saints and Martyrs of the Reformation Era (CY); Beatified Martyrs of England and Wales (RC England and Wales); formerly Monica (see *27 Aug.)

Pelagia (d. *c.*300), supposed to have been burnt in a brazen bull at Tarsus for resisting the advances of Diocletian's son. We know of no such son, but recall the rape of Lucretia by the son of Tarquin the Proud and in the previous generation the brazen bull in which the tyrant Phalaris burnt his political opponents (see *20 Sept.).

Florianus, martyr from Lauriacum (Lorch), said to have been thrown into the Enns in 304. The monastery of Sankt Florian developed from a chapel supposedly standing where the Christian matron Valeria, having found his body, buried it on her estate. He was an extremely popular saint in southern Germany and Austria; qualified by his drowning as a water saint, he is above all revered as the saint who prevents, or starts, house-fires, being invoked in the famous rhyme 'O heiliger Sankt Florian, verschon dies Haus, zünd andre an!' ('O holy St Florian, spare our house, set light to others'). He is patron of Upper Austria, Kraków, and Bologna.

5 MAY

a.d. III Nonas Maias F

❨ HOLIDAYS AND ANNIVERSARIES Japanese Boys' Festival (*Tango no sekku*) or Banner
Festival (*Nobori no sekku*), being the solar counterpart of the Chinese Dragon-Boat
festival
Japan: Children's Day, or *Kodomo no hi* (national holiday, since 1975)
Mexico: Cinco de Mayo
Netherlands: Liberation Day (from Nazi Germany, 1945)
South Korea: Children's Day

❨ HOLY DAYS Asaph (RC Wales); formerly Pius V (see *30 Apr.)

Asaph (6th c.) was named after the musician at King David's court to whom several
psalms are ascribed (Old Testament names were popular in early Wales). The life by
Jocelin of Furness (12th c.) makes him a protégé of St Kentigern (see *13 Jan.), who
while in exile from Strathclyde *c.*560 had at the confluence of Clwyd and Elwy established the monastery of Llanelwy; on his recall some ten years later he left Asaph as
abbot, whence the two aisles of the parish church were called *Eglwys Cyndeyrn* ('Kentigern's Church') and *Eglwys Asaff*. In the twelfth century St Asaph became a territorial
diocese. A fair in the saint's honour used to be held on 1 May, his reputed date of death.
His great well in Cwm parish, Ffynnon Asa, held till the nineteenth century to cure nervous disorder and rheumatism, was thereafter celebrated for its trout. Also exhibited was
the print of his horse's hoof, made on landing from a two-mile leap.

Godehard or Gotthard (960–1038), abbot of Niederaltaich, Hersfeld, and Tegernsee,
bishop of Hildesheim, a champion of Cluniac reform who founded some thirty
churches. He is portrayed trampling on a dragon and holding a model church, waking
the dead in order to hear their confessions, driving out devils, and carrying hot coals in
his surplice. The Sankt-Gotthard-Pass is named after him.

Angelo of Sicily, a Carmelite martyr whose life was purportedly written by 'Enoc,
Carmelite patriarch of Jerusalem' in the early fourteenth century, but in fact by an
unknown Sicilian some 100 years later; it is not to be believed except when confirmed
from other sources. He was among the first Carmelites to come to Sicily from Mount
Carmel *c.*1235, and was killed in Licata by an impious infidel as supposedly prophesied
by St Francis during an encounter in the basilica of St John Lateran much represented in Carmelite iconography; Angelo had replied that Francis would receive the
stigmata.

The Western tradition setting the Crucifixion on 25 March AD 29 requires this day to
be the date of Christ's Ascension.

The Mexican national holiday of Cinco de Mayo celebrates the defeat of 6,000 French by 2,000 Mexicans at Guadalupe in 1862. Mexico having defaulted on her bonds, Britain, France, and Spain made a joint naval demonstration to compel payment. When negotiations were opened, the British and Spanish departed; but France was bent upon conquest. The battle did not prevent France from overrunning the country and imposing Napoleon III's brother-in-law Maximilian on it as emperor; but after the Federal victory in the US Civil War had induced the French to depart (abandoning Maximilian to be overthrown and shot), the previous victory was chosen for commemoration.

6 MAY

❦ HOLIDAYS AND ANNIVERSARIES Vatican City: Swearing-in of new recruits to Swiss Guards, commemorating their heroic resistance during the Sack of Rome in 1527

❦ HOLY DAYS John the Evangelist, ante Portam Latinam (BCP; RC before 1969)

John the Evangelist's main feast-day is *27 December. 6 May is the feast of the dedication of the church of St John before the Latin Gate (founded *c.*550) and commemorates the late tradition that John, when in Rome, was cast into a cauldron of boiling oil at the order of Domitian, but emerged in better physical condition than before. The nearby chapel that bears the name San Giovanni in Oleo is thought to mark the spot.

According to some calendars, it was on this day that Noah left the Ark and St Matthew was called.

> May is a pious fraud of the almanac,
> A ghastly parody of real Spring
> Shaped out of snow and breathed with eastern wind;
> Or if, o'er-confident, she trust the date,
> And, with her handful of anemones,
> Herself as shivery, steal into the sun,
> The season need but turn his hourglass round,
> And Winter suddenly, like crazy Lear,
> Reels back, and brings the dead May in his arms,
> Her budding breasts and wan dislustred front
> With frosty streaks and drifts of his white beard
> All overblown. Then, warmly walled with books,
> While my wood-fire supplies the sun's defect,
> Whispering old forest-sagas in its dreams,
> I take my May down from the happy shelf
> Where perch the world's rare song-birds in a row,

Waiting my choice to open with full breast,
And beg an alms of spring-time, ne'er denied
Indoors by vernal Chaucer, whose fresh woods
Throb thick with merle and mavis all the year.

James Russell Lowell (1819–91), 'Under the Willows'

7 MAY

Nonae Maiae   A

(HOLY DAYS Formerly St Stanislaus (see *11 Apr.)

John of Beverley (d. 721), a monk of Whitby famous as a scholar and teacher, successively bishop of Hexham (*c*.687) and of York (705), the latter claimed by St Wilfrid (see *12 Oct.), who accepted defeat and took over at Hexham. In 1416 Henry V, who attributed his victory at Agincourt to John, ordered his feast to be kept throughout England. Beverley Minster, on the site of a church that he founded, is one of the finest early Gothic buildings in Great Britain.

Appearance of the Sign of the Honoured Cross in the Heavens (Orth.). On this day in 351, at the third hour of daylight, Archbishop Cyril of Jerusalem (*18 Mar.) had a vision of the Holy Cross, very large and made of light, extending from Golgotha to the Mount of Olives; he reported the event in a letter to the emperor Constantius. The feast was in existence by the seventh century.

Now is the month of maying,
When merry lads are playing, fa la,
Each with his bonny lass,
Upon the greeny grass. Fa la.

The Spring clad all in gladness,
Doth laugh at winter's sadness, fa la,
And to the bagpipe's sound
The nymphes tread out their ground. Fa la.

Fie then! why sit we musing,
Youth's sweet delight refusing? Fa la.
Say, dainty nymphes, and speak,
Shall we play barley-break? Fa la.

Thomas Morley, *The First Booke of Ballets to Five Voyces* (1595)

8 MAY

❦ HOLIDAYS AND ANNIVERSARIES VE Day: end of the Second World War in Europe (Western allies), celebrated with great pomp on the fiftieth anniversary in 1995
France: Liberation Day
Norway: Liberation Day
USA, Missouri: Truman Day

❦ HOLY DAYS Julian of Norwich (CY)

Julian of Norwich (*c*.1342–after 1416). Never formally beatified, Julian takes her name from the church of St Julian in Norwich, where she was an anchoress. Having experienced a series of fifteen 'showings' in May 1373, she wrote a short treatise soon thereafter, and later a longer version, known as the *Showings* or *Revelations of Divine Love*, in which she expounded theological doctrine in a remarkably original and sophisticated way.

John the Divine, Apostle and Evangelist (Orth.); see *27 December. Popularly called *Yánnis Chalazás* ('Hailman') or *Vrocháris* ('Rainman'). Some calendars record against this day 'the Vision of St John the Evangelist and the holy angel'.

Apparition of St Michael, Archangel. The popularity of Michael's cult in the West dates from his apparition at Monte Gargano in south-east Italy in the late fifth century (for his main date, see *29 Sept.). It was a favourite with Norman pilgrims, some of whom were recruited in 1020 for a rebellion against Byzantine rule; despite its failure they remained in Apulia and summoned reinforcements, thus preparing the way for the Norman conquest of Sicily and southern Italy.

Despite the ill luck of May marriage and the day after the Nones (see *16 July), we read in Lodowick Lloyd (see *7 Sept.):

> The Virgins of Rome as vpon this daye, in the temple of S. Michael, vsed in old time to be married, for that the Romans suppose that Michaell the Archangell appeared in that place where they then builded and dedicated a temple in memory therof in the suburbes of Rome, and therefore all the maides of Rome made choise of this day to marrie.   Lloyd, *Diall of Daies*, 147 (1590)

The *Helston* (Cornwall) *Furry Dance* takes place on this day (on 7 May when the 8th falls on Sunday or Monday). Like the Padstow hobby-horse festival (see *1 May), this one is still going strong. The mysterious word *furry* probably derives from the Cornish *feur*, possibly related to the Latin *feria*, although the original meaning of 'festival' had acquired its modern meaning 'weekday' as early as Tertullian.

At Helstone, a genteel and populous borough-town in Cornwall, it is customary to dedicate the 8th of May to revelry (festive mirth, not loose jollity). It is called the *Furry-day*, supposed Flora's Day; not, I imagine, as many have thought, in remembrance of some festival instituted in honour of that goddess, but rather from the garlands commonly worn on that day. In the morning, very early, some trublesome rogues go round the streets with drums, or other noisy instruments, disturbing their sober neighbours, and singing parts of a song, the whole of which nobody now recollects, and of which I know no more than that there is mention in it of 'the grey goose quill', and of going to the 'green wood to bring home the Summer and the May-o'; and, accordingly, hawthorn flowering branches are worn in hats. The commonalty make it a general holiday; and if they find any person at work, make him ride on a pole, carried on men's shoulders, to the river, over which he is to leap in a wide place, if he can; if he cannot, he must leap in, for leap he must, or pay money. About 9 o'clock they appear before the school, and demand holiday for the Latin boys, which is invariably granted; after which they collect money from house to house. About the middle of the day they collect together to dance hand-in-hand round the streets, to the sound of the fiddle playing a particular tune, which they continue to do till it is dark. This they call a 'Faddy'. In the afternoon the *gentility* go to some farm-house in the neighbourhood to drink tea, syllabub, &c., and return in a morrice-dance to the town, where they form a Faddy, and dance through the streets till it is dark, claiming a right of going through any person's house, in at one door, and out at the other. And here it formerly used to end, and the company of all kinds to disperse quietly to their several habitations; but latterly corruptions have in this, as in other matters, crept in by degrees. The ladies of this town . . . all elegantly dressed in white muslins . . . [are now conducted by their partners] to the ball-room, where they continue their dance till supper-time, after which they all Faddy it out of the house, breaking off by degrees to their respective houses. The mobility imitate their superiors, and also adjourn to the several public-houses, where they continue their dance till midnight.   *Gentleman's Magazine*, 60 (June 1790), 520

9 MAY

❧ HOLIDAYS AND ANNIVERSARIES Russia, Poland: Victory Day (defeat of Nazi Germany, 1945)
UK, Channel Islands: Liberation Day

❧ ANCIENT ROME This was the first day, or rather night, of the Lemuria, during which the *lemures*, ghosts of one's ancestors, were appeased: at dead of night the worshipper went barefoot to wash his hands in spring water, threw black beans behind him, washed his hands again, and clashed bronze cymbals to summon the ghosts from the grave. The same ritual was observed on the 11th and the 13th.

❧ HOLY DAYS Formerly Gregory of Nazianzus (see *25 Jan.); Christopher (Orth.; see *25 July)

Translation of St Nicholas from Myra to Bari, 1087, essentially an act of Norman piracy but colourable as the rescue of the saint's relics from the advancing Selçuk Turks; that indeed is how it was represented in the earliest Byzantine account, but the Greek Church does not celebrate it. On the other hand, the Russian Church admitted the translation to its calendar in 1091 and celebrates it to this day on 22 May NS. In the cathedral at Santiago de Compostela the first chapel the pilgrims met was devoted to St Nicholas

of Bari, perhaps because the pilgrim should thank St Nicholas for his protection during the long—and dangerous—journey.

At the European Summit of 1985, in Milan, this day was proclaimed the Day of Europe,
commemorating the announcement on 9 May 1950 of the project for a European Coal
and Steel Union.

10 MAY

a.d. VI Idus Maias   D

❦ HOLIDAYS AND ANNIVERSARIES Guatemala, Mexico: Mother's Day
  USA, North Carolina and South Carolina: Confederate Memorial Day

❦ ANCIENT ROME Ludi Martiales: temple of Mars Ultor (the Avenger) dedicated in
  2 BC, to commemorate Augustus' avenging his adoptive father's murder.

❦ HOLY DAYS Simon the Zealot (Orth.; see *28 Oct.)

Job, a righteous figure of antiquity along with Noah and Daniel (Ezek. 14: 14, 20), whose
undeserved suffering is the theme of a famous book in the Bible. For his curse on his
birthday, see *29 February; for the list of lucky and unlucky days allegedly dictated to
him by an angel, see *Days: Unlucky (and cf. Pachomius, *14 May).

Gordian and Epimachus. The existence alongside the Via Latina at Rome of an early Christian cemetery named after Gordian and Epimachus, in which stood a church dedicated
to the latter, gave rise to the legend that the high imperial official Gordian was tortured
and executed under Julian the Apostate and buried in the grave of Epimachus, already
martyred in Alexandria. In fact Gordian was a small boy, whose remains were kept under
the high altar of St Epimachus' Church.

Antoninus of Florence (1389–1459), archbishop. In early life he was a friar of the Observant
branch of the Dominicans, rising rapidly to become prior at Santa Maria sopra Minerva
in Rome, where he was appointed auditor-general of the Rota and vicar-general of the
Observant Dominicans. Upon his return to Florence he founded the convent of San
Marco, whose famous frescos were painted by his fellow-novice in Cortona, Fra Angelico, himself buried in the Minerva (see *18 Mar.). Although undertaking increasingly
onerous obligations, first as delegate to the Council of Florence (1439), then as archbishop of Florence (1446), and finally as Florentine ambassador to Rome, he found
time to write his magisterial and influential *Summa* of moral theology. He remained true
to the austere regime of the reformed branch of his order and was renowned for his
charity.

This is the first possible date for Whit Sunday.

11 MAY

a.d. V Idus Maias   E

❦ HOLIDAYS AND ANNIVERSARIES   Jamaica: Bob Marley Day
USA, Minnesota: Admission Day (32nd state, 1858)

❦ ANCIENT ROME A fragmentary inscription records a sacrifice to a deity whose
name begins 'MA', probably Mania the mother of the Lares, whose name, from an ancient word for 'good', suggests a death goddess appropriately worshipped during the
Lemuria. The word was also used for ugly effigies made from flour, and as a bogey to
scare children.

❦ HOLY DAYS Cyril and Methodius (Orth.; 14 Feb. RC)

Cyril and Methodius, Apostles of the Slavs. Constantine 'the Philosopher' and his elder
brother Methodius, who abandoned provincial administration for the monastery, were
the sons of a middle-ranking Byzantine officer from Thessalonica, a bilingual city (in
Slavonic called Solun) with a largely Slavonic-speaking countryside; after completing a
diplomatic mission to the Khazars in 860/1, where they found a body believed to be
St Clement's (see *23 Nov.), they were chosen in 862 to fulfil a request by Rastislav, prince
of Moravia, for Slavonic-speaking missionaries to train a native clergy independent of
the Frankish clerics currently in place. Using their new Slavonic alphabet, known nowadays as Glagolitic from *glagolŭ* 'the Word', they translated Gospel texts and the Byzantine service-books into the West Bulgarian or Macedonian dialect of Thessalonica, now
known as Old Church Slavonic. For the next few years, amidst severe tensions between
Rome and both Franks and Byzantines, their mission prospered; against precedent,
Pope Nicholas I permitted the use of Slavonic in the liturgy, and in 867 invited them
to Rome, though he died before their arrival with the supposed relics of St Clement.
Constantine became a monk under the name of Cyril, by which he is now generally
known; the Greek-based alphabet that outside Dalmatia replaced Glagolitic as the
medium of Slavonic writing is known as 'Cyrillic' from the false belief that he invented
it. He died on 14 February 869; when Methodius' request to take his body back to
Greece produced an outcry, he asked instead that it should be buried in San Clemente,
which was granted.

Methodius, appointed archbishop of Pannonia by Pope Hadrian II, fell out with the
Frankish bishops and was imprisoned for two and a half years before returning to
Moravia, where he lived from 873 till his death in 885, translating more texts and defending his position, and Orthodox doctrine, against the Franks and the *Filioque*. After
his death his pupils, expelled from Moravia, were made welcome in the newly converted
kingdom of Bulgaria (see *27 July), where they established a vernacular Church owing
allegiance to the Patriarch of Constantinople; this was the true beginning of Orthodoxy among the Slavs. Both RC and Orthodox Slavs from the mission-lands of SS Cyril

and Methodius have dedicated monuments to them in San Clemente. John Paul II, in 1980, made them joint patrons of Europe together with St Benedict, symbolizing the union of East and West.

James the brother of the Lord seems not to have believed in Jesus' claims until the Resurrection, but thereafter took a leading role in the Church at Jerusalem; he is the St James of the New Testament 'Epistle General'. He was also called James the Just for his adherence to Jewish law, which he demanded of Jewish Christians but not of Gentile converts. Since Jerome, Catholic tradition has understood the Lord's 'brothers' to have been His cousins, the sons of Clopas or Cleophas and Mary sister of the Virgin; the Orthodox make them His half-brothers, Joseph's sons by a previous wife. Protestants have reverted to the literal meaning accepted in the early Church. He was martyred in 62; his head is claimed by Ancona.

Mamertus, bishop of Vienne, who in 463 consecrated his brother Claudius Mamertus bishop of Die; seven years later, after censure by Pope Hilarus and a series of earthquakes and fires, he introduced three penitential processions before Ascension Day (which in that year fell on 14 May). In North Germany and the Netherlands he is the first of the Ice Saints, whose days often coincide with a cold spell; in the rest of the German world that honour falls to St Pancratius (see *12 May).

Official foundation-date of Constantinople in 330.

12 MAY

> 'Tis said that from the twelfth of May
> to the twelfth of July all is day.

> From the twelfth day of May
> To the twelfth of July
> Adieu to starlight,
> For all is twilight.

❦ HOLY DAYS Nereus and Achilleus (RC); Pancratius (RC)

Nereus and Achilleus. According to unreliable acts, they were soldiers who upon conversion deserted their posts and were put to death; alternatively they were eunuchs in the service of Flavia Domitilla (see *22 June), baptized in person by St Peter, exiled with their mistress, and beheaded for obstinate adherence to their faith. Their relics lie under the high altar of their church in Rome by the Baths of Caracalla; it is much in demand for weddings despite its gruesome frescos of saintly martyrdoms.

Pancratius (Pancras), probably martyred under Diocletian *c.*304, allegedly at the age of 14. Over his tomb in the Via Aurelia a church was built in the early sixth century by Pope

Symmachus and embellished in the seventh by Pope Honorius I; since 1517 it has been the title-church of San Pancrazio fuori le Mura. He became popular in England because Augustine dedicated a church to him in Canterbury, and Pope Vitalianus sent some of his relics to King Oswiu of Northumbria *c*.664. The name of his church in north London is now better known from a railway terminus, and more recently from the site of the new British Library. He is one of the Fourteen Auxiliary Saints, and an Ice Saint in the Netherlands and German-speaking countries. He is invoked against cramps, a patronage that stems from a story that he punished a perjurer who swore on his tomb by freezing his arm. It is fervently to be hoped that he will protect the British Library conveyor system from cramps; the monumental brass at Cowfield (W. Sussex) shows him holding a book.

Beltane, Old Style, in Banffshire:

Even at present, witches are supposed, as of old, to ride on broomsticks through the air. In this country, the 12th of May is one of their festivals. On the morning of that day, they are frequently seen dancing on the surface of the water of Avon, brushing the dews of the lawn, and milking cows in their fold. Any uncommon sickness is generally attributed to their demoniacal practices. They make fields barren or fertile, raise or still whirlwinds, give or take away milk at pleasure. The force of their incantations is not to be resisted, and extends even to the moon in the midst of her aerial career. It is the good fortune, however, of this country to be provided with an anti-conjuror that defeats both them and their sable patron in their combined efforts. His fame is widely diffused, and wherever he goes, *crescit eundo.* If the spouse is jealous of her husband, the anti-conjuror is consulted to restore the affections of his bewitched heart. If a near connexion lies confined to the bed of sickness, it is in vain to expect relief without the balsamick medicine of the anti-conjuror. If a person happens to be deprived of his senses, the deranged cells of the brain must be adjusted by the magic charms of the anti-conjuror. If a farmer loses his cattle, the houses must be purified with water sprinkled by him. In searching for the latent mischief, this gentleman never fails to find little parcels of hetrogeneous ingredients lurking in the walls, consisting of the legs of mice, and the wings of bats; all the work of the witches. Few things seem too arduous for his abilities; and though, like Paracelsus, he has not as yet boasted of having discovered the Philosopher's stone; yet, by the power of his occult science, he still attracts a little of their gold from the pockets where it lodges; and in this way makes a shift to acquire subsistence for himself and family.   Sinclair, xii. 465 (1794)

13 MAY

a.d. III Idus Maias   G

❧ HOLIDAYS AND ANNIVERSARIES   Sweden: Linnédagen (Birthday of Linnaeus)

❧ HOLY DAYS   Formerly St Robert Bellarmine (see *17 Sept.)

Servatius (Servais), bishop of Tongeren, d. 384, though later legends connect him with both St Peter (d. *c*.64) and Attila the Hun (d. 454); an Ice Saint. On his day, till the end of the nineteenth century, an annual battle for his statue was fought on the mountains of Aré in Brittany, between teams representing Cornouaille and Vannetais; the winner was assured a good harvest. The suppression of this festival was blamed for an agricultural depression.

Our Lady of Fátima, commemorating the six appearances of a vision of 'Our Lady of the Rosary' to three children in Fátima (Estremadura, Portugal) on this day in 1917. It has since become a place of pilgrimage. The surviving child, Lucia Santos, who became a Carmelite nun, revealed that she had received a threefold message, known as the 'three secrets', which she transmitted to Pope Pius XII (1939–58), saying that their meaning would not become clear until 1960. Two have since been made public: bodies charred by fire (as in representations of hell, but applied by believers to the Second World War) and the spread of Marxist error from Russia, which might however be reconverted (this latter was announced in 1942 by the cardinal archbishop of Milan, while Italy was at war with the Soviet Union, but has proved accurate none the less). The third has not been disclosed, though the sequence of earthquakes in central Italy during October 1997 prompted the Vatican to deny that it assigned the end of the world to that of the millennium.

On this day in 609 or 610 Pope Boniface IV converted the Pantheon in Rome, built by Augustus' lieutenant Agrippa in 27 BC, into a church dedicated to the Virgin Mary and all martyrs; it was thereafter known as *Sancta Maria ad martyres*. The feast of All Martyrs, till then kept on the first Sunday after Pentecost, was transferred to this day in the West; in both the East, where it remained on the original date, and in the West it was reinterpreted as a feast of all saints, whether or not martyred. The feast was transferred anew to *1 November.

On this day, according to the Swedish calendar (see II: *Modern Calendar: Gregorian Reform: Sweden*), was born in 1707 the great botanist Carl von Linné, known outside his homeland as Carolus Linnaeus; the Old and New Style equivalents were respectively the 12th and the 23rd.

Abbotsbury (Dorset) Garland Day (Old May Day in the 19th c.): children carry garlands on poles and lay them on the war memorial (a pious alteration of the original begging for money).

14 MAY

❦ ANCIENT ROME Sacrifice to Mars Invictus at his great temple in the Circus Flaminius, dedicated in 135 BC; it was inscribed with verses by the leading Roman poet of the age, Lucius Accius, and housed a huge statue of the god.

On this day human effigies made of rushes and called *Argei* were thrown into the Tiber from the Pons Sublicius; the procession included the *pontifices*, the Vestal Virgins, the praetors, and the *flaminica* or wife of the priest of Jupiter (*flamen Dialis*), who was required to attend with unkempt hair to symbolize mourning. A considerable amount of detail is preserved concerning the ritual; accounts conflict (were there thirty *Argei* or twenty-seven, i.e. in magic thrice nine, like the shrines of the same name?), and the meaning had become lost to the Romans themselves, though Plutarch calls it the greatest of purifications.

❆ HOLY DAYS **Matthias** (CY; RC since 1969; BCP *24 Feb.); red-letter day since 1984

Pachomius (b. *c*.287, d. 14 May 347), an Egyptian hermit, founded *c*.320–5 the first monastery, which by his death had expanded into an association of nine houses for men and two for women; his Rule for monastic life influenced those of St Basil and St Benedict. He is sometimes called 'the Elder' to distinguish him from a fictitious namesake. Computistic tradition alleged that a set of doggerel Latin verses stating the number of weekdays between 24 March and the Paschal term (see II: *Computus*) had been dictated to him by an angel (cf. Job, *10 May).

Boniface of Tarsus, allegedly martyred at Tarsus *c*.307 and buried in Rome in the church of SS Alexius and Boniface on the Aventine; an Ice Saint in Central and South Germany, Austria, and Switzerland.

The Restoration of Charles II was proclaimed at Edinburgh in 1660:

Charles the Secund proclamed King of all his Fatheris dominiones. This Proclamatione being solempnie actit at Lundon the 8 of Maij 1660, was thaireftir proclamed at the Mercat Croce of Edinburgh, upone Monday thaireftir, being the 14 of the same moneth, with all solempniteis requisite, by ringing of bellis, setting out of bailfyres, sounding of trumpetis, roring of cannounes, touking of drumes, dancing about the fyres, and using all uther takins of joy for the advancement and preference of thair native king to his croun and native inheritance. Quhairat also, thair wes much wyne spent, the spoutes of the croce ryning and venting out abundance of wyne, placed thair for that end; and the magistrates and counsell of the toun being present, drinking the Kinges helth, and breking numberis of glasses.   Nicoll, 283 (May 1660)

After the reform of the calendar, Old Rood Day [i.e. the Old Style Invention of the Cross] was still considered an unlucky day in the Scottish Highlands; Thomas Pennant reports in 1772:

They pay great attention to their lucky and unlucky days. The *Romans* could not be more attentive on similar occasions; and surely the highlander may be excused the superstition, since *Augustus* could say, that he never went abroad on the day following the *Nundinæ*, nor began any serious undertaking on the *Nonæ*, and that, merely to avoid the *unlucky* omen. The *Scottish* mountaineers esteem the 14th of *May* unfortunate, and the day of the week that it has happened to fall on. Thus *Thursday* is a black day for the present year.   Pennant, *Scotland* 1772, 46–7

15 MAY

Idus Maiae   B

❨ HOLIDAYS AND ANNIVERSARIES Paraguay: Independence Day (from Spain, 1811)

❨ ANCIENT ROME This day was sacred to Mercury, being the foundation-day of his temple on the south-western slope of the Aventine in 495 BC, near his sacred spring at the Porta Capena. According to Ovid, merchants would sprinkle their wares with its water and pray to this god of persuasiveness, trade, and deceit that their perjuries might be forgiven: Mercury would smile down from heaven, remembering his theft of the cattle belonging to his brother Apollo. The spot is now marked by a rectangular building railed off to prevent any modern traders from digging for the spring in case it should still prove efficacious.

❨ HOLY DAYS Formerly St John Baptist de La Salle (see *7 Apr.)

Dymphna, legendary daughter of a seventh-century Celtic king, who fled abroad with her confessor, St Gerebernus, to escape her father's incestuous desires. They were tracked down to Geel, near Antwerp, by her father, who killed her while his soldiers killed the priest. Upon translation of the bodies in the thirteenth century numerous miracles were attested, especially the cure of epileptics and the insane. A hospital was established and Dymphna became known as the patron of the insane, who came to Geel for treatment. The enterprise was taken over by the state in 1852; the patients are boarded out with villagers, who willingly and successfully practise that care in the community which elsewhere has been an empty phrase for relieving doctors and taxpayers of a burden. On her day a relic from her tomb, formerly applied to the patients as a curative, is borne in procession.

Isidore the Peasant (Isidro el Labrador), d. 1130. When his lord, moved by envious tittle-tattle from other peasants, caught him arriving late for work because he had been at church, an angel clad in white ploughed his furrow for him. He is greatly honoured in Madrid, where he is reputed to cure the sick (notably King Philip III) and bring rain in time of drought. He was kind to animals and the poor. In 1960 John XXIII declared him patron saint of farm labourers.

Sophia, alleged Diocletianic martyr; known in southern Germany and Austria as *die kalte Sophie*, 'Cold Sophia', or *die Eisfrau*, 'the Icewoman', which in Swiss German is *s Yswybli*. She is the female counterpart of the male Ice Saints (see *11–14 May).

Hallvard Vebjørnsson of Lier, the patron saint of Oslo (11th c.), drowned with a millstone round his neck, which became his emblem.

From the Western tradition for the date of the Crucifixion, 25 March, and Resurrection, 27 March, it follows that this was the day of the first Whit Sunday; in some calendars we find the note *primum Pentecoste*, evidently meaning that and not 'first possible date' like *primum Pascha*. Before 1990 it was a Scottish term day, known as Whitsunday (so spelt) irrespective of either the day of the week or the date of Whit Sunday.

16 MAY

a.d. XVII Kalendas Iunias   C

❦ HOLY DAYS

Ubaldus (Ubaldo Baldassini, *c*.1100–60), bishop of Gubbio. Several counts of Urbino incorporated his name in the name 'Guidobaldo'. Exceptionally, a contemporary life has survived with reliable details. Having had some success at an early age in reforming his cathedral at Gubbio, despite recalcitrant canons, Ubaldus wished to retire to solitude, which his adviser regarded as a dangerous temptation. Nor did he care to become bishop of Perugia, first hiding, then travelling to Rome and pleading with the pope to be spared that employment. But he was not allowed to refuse the bishopric of Gubbio two years later, in 1128. Extraordinarily mild, he declined to rebuke a labourer who had angrily pushed him into a pool of mortar when he gently pointed out that his vines were being disturbed. Greatly beloved by his people, he prevented the emperor Frederick Barbarossa from sacking Gubbio as he had Spoleto nearby. Owing to cures and miracles at his tomb, Ubaldus is invoked by those suffering from dog-bites and rabies.

Every year in spring, on or about this day, St Ubaldus is honoured in Gubbio with a race known as the *Corso dei Ceri*, up from the hillside town to the Sanctuary of Sant'Ubaldo (where his remains lie) on the summit. There are three teams: Sant'Ubaldo (in yellow), San Giorgio (in blue), and Sant'Antonio (in black). Each team carries an enormous *cero* ('candle'), made of solid wood and surmounted by a figure of its saint; townsfolk and tourists follow. Sant'Ubaldo, having the privilege of starting first, always wins; San Giorgio usually comes second. Support for the teams is determined by geography and profession; students usually cheer on Sant'Antonio, the traditional loser. The previous night is marked by a celebration with much food, wine, and dancing.

Simon Stock, Carmelite friar (d. 1265). As a young man on pilgrimage to the Holy Land, he was attracted by the hermits of Carmel and joined them. Having returned to Europe, he went to Aylesford in Kent, and then to London, where he was prior general of the Carmelites some time between 1254 and 1265, when the Order was changing into one of mendicant friars. By the fifteenth century a legend had developed that he was the 'holy Simon' to whom the Virgin, in a vision, had given a scapular, promising that whoever wore it would not go to hell. The devotion, promoted by the Carmelites, became widespread in Europe and continues to this day. Simon was never canonized but his feast was approved for the Carmelite Order in 1564; he died in the Carmelite province of Gascony, whence his relics were translated to Aylesford in 1951.

John of Nepomuk (Nepomucene), vicar-general of the archdiocese of Prague. Drowned in the Vltava on 20 March 1393 for resisting the Bohemian king Václav IV's interference in church affairs, he is invoked against floods, but also against slander, for a fifteenth-century legend has the king, doubting his wife's chastity since she went so often to confession, order John to tell him what sins she had committed, which the saint refused to do. (In fact he was not her confessor.) His body was recovered during the Counter-Reformation and buried in St Vitus' Cathedral; he is patron of the Czech Republic.

Brendan, sixth-century founder of Irish monasteries, notably Cluain Fearta (Clonfert), Co. Galway, reputed to have put out to sea in a coracle and reached 'the northern and western islands', after celebrating mass on a whale's back. The story of his adventures was constantly retold, progressing to a seven-year voyage on the whale; but one such poem in the twelfth century provoked a protest (preserved in a manuscript belonging to Lincoln College, Oxford) at the notion that a man with the cure of 3,000 souls should abandon his duties to gallivant across the ocean, adding for good measure that the salvation of devils, which formed part of the tale, was contrary to the Catholic faith.

Honoratus of Amiens (d. *c.*600), particularly honoured in France since the elevation of his body in 1060, to which many cures were attributed; at Amiens his feast had an octave. In 1204 a church was built in his honour in Paris, which gave its name to a street and a suburb. He is now best known as the eponym of the gâteau Saint-Honoré, though his connection with millers, bakers, and confectioners (confirmed for Argentina by John Paul II in 1980) goes back to a legend that during mass he had a vision of God's hand taking the bread and giving him communion.

17 MAY

a.d. XVI Kalendas Iunias   D

❦ HOLIDAYS AND ANNIVERSARIES Norway: Independence Day. Subject to the Danish crown since the late fourteenth century, Norway had been transferred to Sweden by treaty of 14 January 1814; the Norwegians declared their independence, chose a Danish prince as king, and adopted the constitution of 17 May. The Powers refused to accept their choice of king, but agreed that Norway should be an independent kingdom under the Swedish king. This union of crowns was dissolved on 26 October 1905.

A legend among farmers in south-east Devonshire:

St. Dunstan bought up a quantity of barley, and therewith made beer. The Devil, knowing that the saint would naturally desire to get a good sale for the article which he had just brewed, went to him and said—That if he (the saint) would sell himself to him (the Devil), the latter would go and blight all the apple trees; so that there should be no cider, and consequently there would be a greater demand for beer. St. Dunstan, wishing to drive a brisk trade in the article in which he had just become interested, accepted the offer; but stipulated that the trees should be blighted in three days, which days fell on the 17th, 18th, and 19th of May. In the Almanacs we see that the 19th is marked as St. Dunstan's Day.   *N & Q*, 2nd ser., xii (1861), 303

On this day in 1649 three ringleaders of the Leveller mutiny were shot by Cromwell's men at Burford church in Oxfordshire; the event is now commemorated by an annual gathering of radicals.

In Germany, *am 17. Mai geboren* is a euphemism for 'homosexual', because the relevant provisions of the Strafgesetzbuch or Penal Code were contained in Art. 175. The story is told (in one of Upton Sinclair's novels) of an art exhibition during the Nazi years at which the number was allocated to a painting of young men on the march entitled 'Spirit of National Socialism'; unfortunately, the fact was pointed out at a preview by an American journalist, the director shot, and the number reallocated to a still-life depicting a vase of flowers.

18 MAY

a.d. XV Kalendas Iunias   E

❦ HOLY DAYS John I (RC)

Pope John I (523–6). Angered by the emperor Justin's measures against Arians (see *2 May), the great Ostrogothic king of Italy, Theoderic, himself an Arian but a model of toleration, sent Pope John to protest, with the threat of reprisals against Catholics in Italy if the measures were not rescinded; after personally crowning the emperor, John obtained everything demanded except restitution of converted Arians to their own community. An enraged Theoderic declared that John was in his displeasure and clapped him in prison; the pope, already exhausted from the journey, died, and was promptly hailed as a miracle-working martyr. It was in his papacy that Dionysius Exiguus produced his Easter tables (see II: *Easter). Feast-day formerly 27 May.

Erik IX Jedvardsson, king of Sweden, called the 'Lawgiver', murdered on this day in 1160 by agents of the Danish king's son Magnus during a church service at Old Uppsala; in 1273 his relics were translated to Uppsala, where they are kept in a golden shrine behind the high altar. He was decreed patron saint of Sweden in 1926, together with St Birgitta.

May

Hark! The sea-faring wild-fowl loud proclaim
My coming, and the swarming of the bees.
These are my heralds, and behold! my name
Is written in blossoms on the hawthorn-trees.

I tell the mariner when to sail the seas;
  I waft o'er all the land from far away
The breath and bloom of the Hesperides,
  My birthplace. I am Maia. I am May.

Henry Wadsworth Longfellow (1807–82), *The Poet's Calendar*

19 MAY

a.d. XIV Kalendas Iunias   F

❦ HOLY DAYS Dunstan (CofE)

Dunstan (*c.*910–88); he became abbot of Glastonbury *c.*940, and imposed strict observance of the Benedictine Rule. A monk of noble birth, Dunstan devoted his life to moral reform in church and state, thereby making many enemies. Having been treasurer to King Edred (946–55), he was exiled in 956 by his nephew Edwy (Eadwig) and fled to Ghent; but next year England north of the Thames rebelled against Edwy, choosing as king his brother Edgar, who promptly recalled Dunstan from Flanders to be bishop of both Worcester and London. Upon Edwy's death in 959, Edgar became king of all England; in 960 Dunstan was consecrated archbishop of Canterbury. With the firm support of the king, he carried through notable and often unpopular reforms, in particular the revival of English monasticism; in many cathedrals secular canons, often of noble birth, were compelled to put away their wives and when they disobeyed to make way for monks. In this policy he was ably and vigorously assisted by Bishop Ethelwold of Winchester (see *1 Aug.). After Edgar's death, Dunstan helped secure the election of Edward the Martyr (see *18 Mar.), but could not prevent either an anti-monastic reaction in the country or Edward's downfall. At a meeting of King Edward's council, so the *Anglo-Saxon Chronicle* reports, the entire floor gave way except for the beam on which St Dunstan's chair was placed; later writers transfer the incident to King Edgar's time, representing it as a miracle that gave victory to the monks over the secular clergy, and prompting a sceptical author to observe that 'whether the floor had been previously prepared for the working of the wonder, is worthy of consideration' (Brady, i. 390). Himself skilled alike in music and in metalwork, Dunstan held that the clergy should acquire an art or craft in which to instruct the people; his encouragement of plainchant caused legend to ascribe to him a vision of singing angels, and his practical skills not only made him the patron saint of goldsmiths but caused him to be depicted holding a metalworker's tongs, which later writers made him take to the nose of the beautiful woman in whose disguise he recognized the devil. (For another legend, see *17 May.) The RC Church commemorates him on this day as well.

Peter Celestine, Pope (*c.*1215–96). A former abbot turned hermit, in 1294, after a two-year delay in choosing a new pope caused by rivalry between the Orsini and Colonna families, he was elected as a simple holy man, the 'angel pope' prophesied by religious radicals. Having protested in vain against his elevation at such an age, he took the name Celestine V; he proved a complete disaster, ignorant of Latin, administratively incompetent, and in political matters a tool of the Angevin king of Naples, Charles II. On 13 December he abdicated, having been incorrectly advised by the canonist Benedetto Caetani that there were precedents; eleven days later Caetani was elected to succeed him, becoming Pope Boniface VIII. Among the many enemies this latter pope made was Dante, who in his bitterness blamed his election on Celestine, if commentators since the fourteenth century have rightly seen in him the man 'who made through cowardice the great refusal' (*che fece per viltade il gran rifiuto*). Nevertheless, he was canonized in 1319, the further to blacken Boniface. In Catalonia he is, in splendid defiance of chronology, supposed to have invented the organ and the harp. One day, having been entrusted with a fine leather-bound book of music, he left it by an open window; a raven came in, carried it off, and set about eating the cover. The saint succeeded in extracting the book, but the cover was all gone; unable to pay for rebinding, he performed the task himself, with a result of rare beauty. He thus became the patron saint of bookbinders as well as of organists and harpists.

Yves, patron saint of lawyers and of Brittany. Yves Hélory (1253–1303, canonized 1347), a Breton lawyer from Kermartin who, having distinguished himself as a fair-minded and incorruptible judge always keeping in view the interests of the poor, was ordained priest in 1284, and put his legal knowledge as well as his time and his goods at his parishioners' disposal. He is especially loved in Brittany. Known as the Advocate of the Poor, he is also the patron saint of lawyers, a profession said to be very thinly represented in heaven. The paradox gave rise to popular tales. In one, Our Lord, having given strict orders that no lawyers should be admitted to heaven, relented only to the extent of allowing him to serve outside the gates as assistant to St Peter; however, Yves persuaded the celestial doorkeeper that he was a grievously exploited proletarian with no security of employment. Jesus thereupon ordered Yves to come in and stay at His side where He could keep an eye on him. Another is related by William Carr in 1688:

And now because I am Speakeing of *Pettyfogers*, give me leave to tell you a story I mett with when I lived in *Rome*, goeing with a Romane to see some *Antiquityes*, he shewed me a Chapell dedicated to one St *Evona* a Lawyer of *Brittanie* who he said came to *Rome* to Entreat the *Pope* to give the *Lawyers* of *Brittanie* a *Patron*, to which the Pope replyed that he knew of no *Saint* but what was disposed of to other Professions, at which *Evona* was very sad and earnestly begd of the *Pope* to think of one for them: At the last the *Pope* proposed to St *Evona* that he should goe round the Church of St. *John de Latera* blind fould, and after he had said so many Ave *Marias*, that the first *Saint* he layd hold of, should be his *Patron*, which the good old *Lawyer* willingly undertook, and at the end of his Ave Maryes, he stopt at St. *Michels Altar*, where he layd hold of the *Divell*, under St. Michels feet, and cryd out, this is our Saint, let him be our *Patron*, so beeing unblindfolded and seeing what a *Patron* he had chosen, he went to his Lodgings so dejected, that in a few moneths after he die'd and coming to *heavens Gates* knockt hard, whereupon St *Peoter* [*sic*] asked who it was that knockt so bouldly, he replyed, that he was St. *Evona* the *Advocate*, Away, away said St. *Peter* here is but one *Advocate* in heaven, here is no roome for you *Lawyers*, O but said St. *Evona*, I am that honest lawyer who never tooke fees on both sides, or ever pleaded in a bad Cause, nor did I ever set my Naibours together by the Eares, or lived by the sins of the people; well then said St. *Peter*,

come in; This newes coming downe to *Rome* a witty Poet writ upon St. *Evonas* Tomb these words:
St. *Evona* un *Briton, Advocat non Larron, Haleluiah.*   Carr, 80–2

The Breton advocate who was no thief is buried at Tréguier, not at Rome; but he is honoured there by two churches: Sant'Ivo dei Bretoni by the Campana restaurant and Sant'Ivo alla Sapienza, built by Borromini behind an exedra by Giacomo della Porta for the papal university; his design is at once a spirited revival of ancient *tempietti* and an impassioned defence of the (largely legal) learning offered by the Sapienza. There is now no altar of St Michael in St John Lateran.

When St George goes on horseback, St Yves goes on foot [i.e. in wartime the lawyers have no business].

20 MAY

a.d. XIII Kalendas Iunias   G

❨ HOLIDAYS AND ANNIVERSARIES Cameroon: National Holiday (declaration of republic, 1972)
Indonesia: National Day of Awakening (beginning of anti-colonial movement, 1908)
USA, Massachusetts: Lafayette Day
USA, North Carolina: Anniversary of Mecklenburg Declaration of Independence, 1775

❨ HOLY DAYS Alcuin of York (CY); Bernardino of Siena (RC)

Alcuin (c.740–804), the great scholar and teacher, who having helped create the cathedral library at York was invited by Charlemagne, whom he met in 781 at Parma, to join his court; thereafter he spent most of his life in France, becoming abbot of Saint-Martin at Tours in 796. With Charlemagne's support, he imposed reforms of Latin orthography and perhaps pronunciation that appear (though the topic is a subject of lively dispute) to have effected the final separation in France, even at the conceptual level, between the learned language and the vernacular.

Bernardino of Siena (1380–1444), Franciscan friar of the Observant branch. He was famed throughout Italy as a preacher, attracting such huge crowds that he frequently delivered his sermons in the open air; his theme was penitence and moral reform, and he railed against superstition and gambling. He is particularly remembered for his devotion to the Holy Name; in paintings he is portrayed holding a plaque with the initials IHS displayed in golden rays. Numerous miracles were attributed to him, and he was canonized only six years after his death. In 1956 Pius XII named him patron saint of advertisers and advertising (attesting to the power of persuasion of his sermons, which he enlivened with anecdotes and mimicry). He is also invoked by those suffering hoarseness, since he had a weak voice and easily became hoarse when he started preaching; he attributed his cure to the Virgin.

Ethelbert, king of the East Angles, beheaded by order of Offa, king of Mercia, in 794. The reasons and circumstances are unknown, though a later report of a treacherous murder on the conclusion of a peace treaty seems more credible than romantic tales that blame Offa's consort, for no subsequent king of the East Angles is known before St Edmund (see *20 Nov.), when Mercia's greatness was over; Ethelbert's relics were translated to Hereford.

21 MAY

a.d. XII Kalendas Iunias   A

❡ HOLIDAYS AND ANNIVERSARIES   Chile: Iquique's Naval Combat Day (1879)

❡ ANCIENT ROME   Agonia (see *9 Jan.), probably in honour of the ancient god Vediovis, who was in any case worshipped on this day, and also on 1 January and 7 March; he had a temple on the Insula Tiberina and another on the Capitol, but the Romans did not know who he was, and modern scholars can but guess. We are told that his sacrificial animal was a nanny-goat sacrificed *humano ritu*, by human ritual; what that means is equally obscure.

❡ HOLY DAYS   Emperor Constantine and his mother Helena (Orth.); Helena (CY commem.; see *18 Aug.)

Constantine was born at Naissus (now Niš in Serbia) *c*.285 to the Roman general Flavius Valerius Constantius, in later writers called Chlorus, who rose to become emperor himself in 305 with two colleagues, both hostile to him. When in the following year he died at Eboracum (now York), his army immediately proclaimed Constantine emperor; the other emperors did not allow his claim, but in a complex power struggle he established his position first as joint, and from 324 as sole emperor. He had successively attributed his victories to Apollo, to the Unconquerable Sun, and to the God of the Christians, claiming to have had a vision of the Cross with a Greek inscription stating 'Conquer by this'; scholars dispute when, and even whether, he became aware of the difference between Christianity and sun-worship, but under him Christianity progressed from a tolerated cult to the official, though not yet exclusive, religion of the Empire. In 325 he presided over a council at Nicaea intended, by settling all disputes of doctrine and discipline, to unify the Empire; although it failed in this purpose, it is recognized as one of the chief events in church history. Having observed at first hand the advantages of the site where the old Megarian colony of Byzantion had stood, he built a new capital there, called Constantinople.

His personal conduct has embarrassed his Christian admirers and grimly amused his pagan foes (who found his god over-ready to forgive sin): among the many persons whom he put to death were, in brief succession, his eldest son, Crispus, for an unspecified crime, and his second wife, Fausta, perhaps for denouncing Crispus. He died on Whit Sunday, 22 May 337, after baptism by Eusebius, bishop of Nicomedia; since the sins of baptized persons were then considered unforgivable, persons whose worldly duties included such un-Christian conduct as bloodshed commonly deferred baptism till their deathbeds. Later, when Eusebius' theology had been condemned as heretical, Constantine was said to have been baptized by Pope Silvester, dead two years earlier, a falsehood still proclaimed on the obelisk outside St John Lateran in Rome; for a more audacious fiction concerning pope and emperor, see *31 December. For the Eastern Church Constantine is a saint; Westerners are less willing to let the good obliterate the bad.

Constantine's mother was Constantius' concubine Helena, daughter of an innkeeper—a profession regarded in Roman law and society as little different from brothel-keeping. Constantius dismissed her in order to marry the daughter of the co-emperor Maximian; but in her son's reign, especially during his sole rule, she was a powerful figure at Court, commonly said to have persuaded him that he ought not to have believed Fausta's charges against Crispus. In 326 or 327 she undertook a journey to the East, apparently in furtherance of Constantine's religious policy and also in order to reconcile the former adherents of the defeated co-emperor Licinius; it was later represented as a model pilgrimage and as the occasion for the discovery of the True Cross. In CY she is commemorated on this day as 'Protector of the Holy Places, 300'; her former Western day was 18 August.

In northern and western Thrace this day is celebrated with firewalking and other rituals designed to ward off evil; they are opposed by the Church as survivals from the ancient worship of Dionysos, the god of wild nature in such manifestations as plant growth, wine, and ecstasy, but are stoutly defended by their practitioners as Christian defences against the devil.

Godric, pilgrim and hermit (1170), born at Walpole in Norfolk of a poor family, a pedlar and pilgrim (some also say pirate) who visited Jerusalem, Compostela, Rome, and Saint-Gilles before becoming a hermit with St Jerome's psalter for company. After some further travels within and without the kingdom he settled down at Finchale, on land belonging to the bishop of Durham, to live a life of great austerity and great serenity. He received visitors with sympathy, and in cold weather brought rabbits and fieldmice to be warmed by his fire and released; once, when a stag took refuge in his hermitage, he told the bishop's huntsmen, 'God knows where it is', at which they apologized for disturbing him and rode off. Some of his hymns survive together with the music to which he set them; one, in honour of the Virgin, was reportedly dictated by her in a dream.

22 MAY

a.d. XI Kalendas Iunias   B

❦ HOLIDAYS AND ANNIVERSARIES   Republic of Yemen: National Day (unification of North and South Yemen, 1990)

❦ HOLY DAYS

Rita of Cascia (*c.*1381–*c.*1457), Augustinian nun; patron of desperate cases. Patiently enduring a vicious husband until he was killed in a vendetta, she then had to cope with her two sons, who had inherited their father's propensities; to her relief, they died before they could avenge his murder. She then became a nun, ministering to the sick, and suffering from a chronic wound on her forehead, connected with her visions of the Passion. An early life and record of miracles survives, and her cult has become enormously popular, especially with the unhappily married.

In Norway *bjørnevåk*, 'bear-waking', the day when the bear awakes from hibernation and leaves his den.

National Maritime Day was proclaimed by President Franklin Delano Roosevelt in 1933 to commemorate the departure of the *Savannah* in 1819 on the first transoceanic voyage by a steamer. Off the coast of Cork she was pursued by the British revenue cruiser *Kite*, which mistook her for a vessel on fire.

23 MAY

a.d. X Kalendas Iunias   C

The sun shines on both sides of the hedge.

❦ ANCIENT ROME   This day, like **23 March, was marked by a Tubilustrium, or cleansing of the ceremonial straight trumpets; it was sacred to the craftsman-god Vulcan.

❦ HOLY DAYS

Ivo (*c.*1040–1115), a former student of Lanfranc, bishop of Chartres from 1090; a great canon lawyer, his separation between spiritualities and temporalities led to the solution of the investiture problem. His writings on canon law were compiled during his conflict with Philip I of France, whom he had denounced as an adulterer for repudiating his own wife (Bertha of Holland) in order to marry someone else's (Bertrade de Montfort, married to Count Fulk IV of Anjou); Philip imprisoned him in 1092 and put him on trial for high treason in 1094, but eventually released him.

On this day, as a plaque in the Piazza della Signoria at Florence still records, Girolamo Savonarola was *impiccato e poi arso*, 'hanged and then burnt', after the failure of his attempt to institute the reign of King Jesus. Notorious for the bonfire of vanities in which the citizens were persuaded to destroy works of art and musical instruments, he was yet widely revered; attempts were made to have him canonized. Pius IV, however, called him an Italian Luther, which was not meant as a compliment. In Machiavelli's carefully expressed judgement, Savonarola, inspired by God's virtue, held the Florentines in thrall, but since many feared they were witnessing the gradual ruin of their country under his prophetic teachings, unity could not be restored unless his divine light either grew or was quenched by greater fire:

> non si trovava a riunirvi loco,
> se non cresceva o se non era spento
> el suo lume divin con maggior foco.
>
> *Decennale primo*, ll. 163–5

Although the Derby is now run in June, this was not always so; the race still regarded as the finest Derby of all times was run on this day in 1867:

The Derby day in 1867 will long be remembered by all turfmen, not only by reason of the astounding vicissitudes in the betting, but for the triumph of 'poor Hermit', as he was derisively called only a few days since, when his chance seemed forlorn indeed. The air on the Downs from noon was at times piercingly raw and cold, and the holyday makers were suggestively silent by the time they reached Epsom. . . . When the lot got to the post three-quarters of an hour elapsed before they were despatched on their eventful journey, but the interest attaching to the actual start was considerably marred by the delay and the biting wind, sleet, and snow which swept over the downs. There were at least half a score of false starts, and these were in some degree caused by the fractiousness of D'Estournel, who exhibited some of the wild freaks of Tambour Major a few years ago, despite the reports of his improved temper. In the mean time, the spectators were becoming so accustomed to the false starts that they were scarcely prepared for the tremendous shout of 'They're off', and the familiar clanking of the starting bell. From the second tremendous shout which followed it was evident that some favourite had been left at the post, and in an instant the animal was recognized in the now notorious D'Estournel, who reared up on his hind legs, and the moment the flag was lowered darted off in an entirely opposite direction, and actually attacked the people who were on the rails next the post. . . . From the distance only Vauban, Marksman, Hermit, and Van Amburgh appeared in the struggle, and loud cheers were raised when Marksman was seen on the 'Thormanby side' of the course. On breasting the hill Vauban was beaten, and Hermit won after a game and determined race. . . . Thus ended one of the most sensational Derbys on record.   *The Times*, 23 May, p. 9

24 MAY

a.d. IX Kalendas Iunias   D

❦ HOLIDAYS AND ANNIVERSARIES Eritrea: Independence Day (from Ethiopia, 1993)

❦ ANCIENT ROME See *24 March.

❦ HOLY DAYS John and Charles Wesley (CY)

John (1703–91) *and Charles* (1707–88) *Wesley.* This was the day in 1783 that John Wesley was converted, while reading Martin Luther's preface to St Paul's Epistle to the Romans. It is called the Aldersgate Experience, after the street in London where it happened. Methodists commemorate this event on the Sunday nearest 24 May.

Vincent of Lérins (first half of 5th c.), who declared that the canon for determining Catholic doctrine is *quod ubique, quod semper, quod ab omnibus creditum est,* 'that which has been believed everywhere, always, by all'; it appears that in Vincent's eyes this test disqualified (amongst other things) Augustine's newfangled teaching on predestination. It is often misquoted with *quod semper* first.

Queen Victoria born, 1819, a Monday: Victoria Day is celebrated in Canada on the Monday before the 25th; Empire, later Commonwealth Day in Britain till 1965.

On this day in 1915 Italy declared war on Austria, which still incorporated the 'unredeemed' territories claimed by patriots (*Italia irredenta*): many streets in Italy are named Via 24 Maggio.

May

Shyly the silver-hatted mushrooms make
   Soft entrance through,
And undelivered lovers, half awake,
   Hear noises in the dew.

Yellow in all the earth and in the skies,
   The world would seem
Faint as a widow mourning with soft eyes
   And falling into dream.

Up the long hill I see the slow plough leave
   Furrows of brown;
Dim is the day and beautiful; I grieve
   To see the sun go down.

But there are suns a many for mine eyes
   Day after day:
Delightsome in grave greenery they rise,
   Red oranges in May.

John Shaw Neilson (1872–1942)

25 MAY

a.d. VIII Kalendas Iunias   E

> *If it rain on the 25th, wind shall do much hurt that year;*
> *if the sun shine, the contrary.*

❦ HOLIDAYS AND ANNIVERSARIES African Freedom Day (Chad, Zambia), Africa
Day (Zimbabwe); Organization of African Unity formed 1963
Argentina: Veintecinco de Mayo, Independence Day (from Spain, 1810) (national
day)
Jordan: Independence Day (1946 proclamation of autonomy; full independence,
1949)
USA, New Mexico: Memorial Day

❦ ANCIENT ROME On this day in 194 BC a temple was dedicated on the Collis
Quirinalis to Fortuna Populi Romani Quiritium Primigenia, ten years after it had been
vowed by Lucius Sempronius Tuditanus if he should defeat Hannibal in a battle near
Crotone.

❦ HOLY DAYS Venerable Bede (CY, RC; RC formerly and BCP on *27 May); Gregory
VII (RC); Mary Magdalene de' Pazzi (RC)

Gregory VII (1073–85), the reforming pope often known by his previous name of Hildebrand, a monk of Cluny who had played a considerable part in Roman affairs even before his election as pope; in particular, he had helped draft Nicholas II's decree of 1059
restricting to the cardinals the right of electing the pope. As pope, he issued decrees
against simony (the sale of church offices) and clerical unchastity, but came into conflict
with secular rulers, above all the German king Henry IV, who in 1076 called synods to
depose him; the Pope replied in kind. For the moment the political advantage lay with
the Pope; in January 1077 Henry spent three days in the snow outside the Tuscan castle
of Canossa, where Gregory was a guest, before being admitted for penance and absolution on the 28th; this humiliation has passed into German folklore, being recalled by
Bismarck in his anti-Catholic *Kulturkampf* with the words 'Nach Canossa gehen wir
nicht' ('We are not going to Canossa'). However, as the *Kulturkampf* was far from a triumph for Bismarck, so was Canossa for the Pope: Henry broke his promises, saw off an
antiking put up by his opponents, and in 1084 marched on Rome to set up an antipope.
Gregory was obliged to call in Robert Guiscard's Normans, who liberated the city and
pillaged it. The exasperated people turned against the Pope and drove him into exile; he
died at Salerno, allegedly declaring that this was the result of his loving righteousness
and hating iniquity. His relations with other Western rulers were less strained, though
he did not always succeed in binding them feudally to the Holy See; in particular
William I enjoyed good relations with him, yet resisted more extreme demands.

Mary Magdalene de' Pazzi (1566–1607), Carmelite mystic. Choosing a religious vocation against the wishes of her wealthy family, she became a Carmelite nun and devoted herself to mystical prayer and underwent great suffering; her visions and spiritual counsels were recorded by the nuns and later published. Feast-day formerly 29 May.

Aldhelm (d. 709), a kinsman to Ine, king of Wessex; abbot of Malmesbury *c*.675, first bishop of Sherborne 705. He was the first known Latin writer among the English or any other Germanic people; his style displays the flamboyant ingenuity of the Irish Latin in which he was trained under Maeldubh, the founder of Malmesbury; but having later studied at Canterbury under Archbishop Theodore (*19 Sept.) and Abbot Hadrian (*9 Jan.), whose syllabus included classical metre, he championed the superiority of that school to anything available in Ireland.

Pope Urban I (d. 230), allegedly martyred with a nail through his head, therefore invoked against migraine. In Germany he is the patron saint of wine-growers; if his day is fine, plentiful good wine is expected (*Hat Urbanstag schön Sommerschein, verspricht es viel und guten Wein*); in former times his statue was sprinkled with wine, but on a rainy day water or worse:

> But if the day be clowdie nowe, or given unto raine,
> On him they list not to bestow such honour, nor such paine,
> Poore knave into some ryver than, they cast him cruellie,
> And all to souse him in the streame, or durtie let him lie.
>
> Naogeorgus, fo. 54^v

Hence a Protestant almanac represents the peasants as complaining against the Gregorian reform, for moving St Urban ten days earlier:

> Hettest doch nur in seiner massen,
> S. Urbans tag vns bleiben lassen,
> Da wir Bawren vns trancken voll,
> So gefiel vns dein Kolender wol.
> Aber du hast den auch entzogen,
> Und mit dem Weinwachß vns betrogen.
>
> 'Bawrenklag Vber des Röm. Bapsts Gregorii XIII newen Calender', cited in Uhl, 101

That is to say, if the Pope had only left the peasants St Urban's day in its proper place, when they were used to drinking their fill, they would be well content with his calendar; but he has taken that away too, and cheated them of their predictor for the wine-harvest.

Flitting [i.e. house-moving] Day in Scotland in the nineteenth century, being the Old Style equivalent of *15 May (and see *Days: Quarter Days, Term Days, Removal Days*).

26 MAY

a.d. VII Kalendas Iunias   F

(HOLIDAYS AND ANNIVERSARIES   Georgia: Independence Day (from the
USSR, 1991)
Guyana: Independence Day

(HOLY DAYS Augustine of Canterbury (CofE; RC 27th); Philip Neri (RC; CY
commem.)

Augustine of Canterbury. The prior of Gregory the Great's abbey of St Andrew on the
Clivus Scauri (now the church of San Gregorio Magno; see *12 Mar.), he was dispatched
to convert the English in 596, but owing to various difficulties (including his own reluctance) he did not reach his destination till 597. Within a few months he had converted King Ethelbert of Kent (see *25 Feb.); further progress was slower, and the
attempt to associate the British churches with his mission broke down (see *11 Sept.),
owing, as even the anti-British Bede cannot conceal, to his inflexible Roman haughti-
ness. Having received reinforcements from Rome and set them to work in neighbouring parts of south-eastern England, he died in the first decade of the seventh century;
in 978 the abbey of SS Peter and Paul at Canterbury was formally dedicated to him.

Philip Neri (1515–95), founder of the Congregation of the Oratory. Although educated
in the Dominican convent of San Marco in Florence, it took many years till he discovered his vocation. In Rome in 1544 he had a vision of a globe of fire entering his
heart, and four years later he founded a confraternity to care for pilgrims; only in 1551
did he become a priest. The Congregation of the Oratory was approved in 1575 and the
Chiesa Nuova was built to replace S. Maria in Vallicella. The Oratorio dei Filippini, rebuilt by Borromini in the seventeenth century, still remains. Regarded as a saint in his
own lifetime, and consulted by popes and kings, he was anything but a recluse and loved
practical jokes. The services in his Oratory were enhanced by the use of *laudi* and spiritual madrigals; out of these grew the oratorio.

After eight months in Italy, Goethe decides it is time to choose his own saint:

Naples, Saturday, May 26, 1787.
Looking at the matter closely, one might approve of the fact that there are so many saints; for
every believer can select his own and with complete trust turn straight to the one that really ap-
peals to him. Today was my saint's day, and I celebrated it in his honor with cheerful piety, after
his own manner and teachings.
   Filippo Neri is highly esteemed and at the same time remembered happily; it is edifying and
pleasing to learn about him and his great piety, and at the same time to hear many stories about
his good humor. From his childhood years onward he felt the most fervent religious impulses,
and in the course of his life he developed the greatest talents for religious enthusiasm: the gift
of involuntary prayer, of profound unspoken worship, the gift of tears, of ecstasy, and at last

even of rising from the ground and hovering over it, which is considered greatest of all. . . . Even if we are justly doubtful about his miraculous levitation, in spirit he was certainly raised high above this world; and therefore nothing repelled him as much as vanity, pretence, and arrogance, which he always vigorously combated as the greatest hindrances to a truly God-pleasing life. But he always did this in a good-humored fashion, as many a story tells us. . . .

When he had founded the Congregation of Padri dell'Oratorio, which quickly acquired great prestige and a good many people wanted to become members of it, a young Roman prince came asking admission and was granted the novitiate, along with the requisite clothing. However, when after some time he applied for actual entrance, he was told that first there were a few tests to be passed; and he declared himself ready for them. Then Neri produced a long foxtail and demanded that the prince have this attached to the back of his long frock and then walk quite gravely through all the streets of Rome. The young man . . . was horrified, and said that he had come forward to reap honor, not shame. Then Father Neri said that this could not be expected of their circle, where self-denial remained the supreme law. Whereupon the youth took his leave.

Goethe, 258–60

Euthymius, properly Ekvtime Atoneli (963–1028), celebrated in Georgia (13 May OS); a monk on Mount Athos, he was a great cultural intermediary who translated 160 texts from Greek into Georgian, and the tale of Barlaam and Josaphat from Georgian into Greek (see *27 Nov.).

27 MAY

❡ HOLY DAYS Venerable Bede (BCP; RC and CY on the 25th); Augustine of Canterbury (RC; CofE on *26 May)

Venerable Bede (*c.*673–735), the greatest scholar of his age, and of the English Church. He was given at 7 years old as an oblate to Benedict Biscop's abbey at Wearmouth (see *12 Jan.) and then to the newly founded Jarrow in 682, where he remained for most of his life. He wrote pedagogical treatises whose utility is proved by the large number of manuscripts containing them, and highly regarded biblical exegeses; as a hagiographer he made St Cuthbert (see *20 Mar.) a favourite saint; his writings on the calendar, the brief *De temporibus* of 701 followed by the definitive *De ratione temporum* of 725, earned him the name of *Beda computista* and were fundamental to medieval understanding of the subject. In modern times, however, he is best known for his indispensable history of the English church, the *Historia ecclesiastica gentis Anglorum* of 731, which amongst its many other merits gave AD dating general currency in the Western world. An account of his last days shows him still expounding Scripture, and implicitly dates his death to 26 May 735. The title of *Beda venerabilis* given him soon afterwards has never been disputed; his tomb is still conspicuous in Durham cathedral, to which his remains were translated in the eleventh century.

28 MAY

a.d. V Kalendas Iunias   A

❦ HOLIDAYS AND ANNIVERSARIES   Azerbaijan: Independence Day (national day)
Ethiopia: National Day
Scotland: Whitsunday Term Day since 1990

❦ HOLY DAYS   Lanfranc (CY commem.)

Lanfranc (*c.*1010–89). Born at Pavia, after a North Italian education he came to northern
France; in 1042 he entered the abbey of Bec, becoming prior in 1045. A sound scholar
and a brilliant administrator, he not only made Bec a great monastery but won the confidence of Duke William, who made him in 1063 abbot of Saint-Étienne at Caen and in
1070 archbishop of Canterbury. For eighteen years the see had suffered from the irregular status and second-rate talents of his predecessor, Stigand, intruded by rebellion in
1052, who had used first the pallium left behind by the lawful Norman archbishop
Robert of Jumièges and then one conferred by the schismatic Benedict X; but Lanfranc
regarded not merely Stigand but the entire English Church with disdain, and set about
its reform, suppressing its cults (see *29 Mar.), slighting its saints (see *19 Apr.), and deposing all the Saxon bishops except Wulfstan of Worcester (see *19 Jan.). His hostility
to its ways was somewhat mitigated by his pupil and successor Anselm (*21 Apr.); in
commemorating him the Church of England admits the value of his work.

Bernard of Aosta (Bernard of Menthon) (*c.*996–1081). For forty-two years he was vicar-
general of the Alpine diocese of Aosta, an assignment that required great stamina and
skill as a mountaineer. Bernard built hospices for pilgrims and travellers at the Great
and Little St Bernard Passes, later named after him, as is the breed of dog developed
especially to cope with alpine conditions. Pius XI, himself a keen climber, named him
patron of mountaineers in 1923.

Germanus, bishop of Paris (*c.*496–576). He tried in vain to bridle the lifestyle of the
adulterous, incestuous, and sacrilegious King Charibert (Herbert), father-in-law to
King Ethelbert of Kent; it is he who is buried at Saint-Germain-des-Prés.

William of Aquitaine (755–812). As Duke of Aquitaine he fought with success and distinction for Charlemagne against the Saracens; he is celebrated in Old French epic as
William of Orange and is the hero of Wolfram von Eschenbach's Middle High German epic *Willehalm*. He founded the monastery of Gellone in 804, took the cloth of the
Benedictine Order on 29 June 806, and served the community as cook and baker.

29 MAY

a.d. IV Kalendas Iunias   B

❦ HOLIDAYS AND ANNIVERSARIES USA, Rhode Island: Admission Day (13th state, 1790)
USA, Wisconsin: Admission Day (30th state, 1848)

❦ HOLY DAYS Formerly St Mary Magdalene de' Pazzi (see *25 May)

Oak-apple Day. The restoration of Charles II in 1660, his 30th birthday. He was proclaimed king in London on 8 May; he embarked from the Low Countries on 23 May, arriving in Dover two days later. The oak had become his badge after he had hidden in one at Boscobel following the defeat at Worcester (1651); for many years it was unwise not to wear oak-leaves on this day. Also called 'Shick-shack Day'.

29 May 1661. This was the first *Anniversary* appointed by *Act* of *Parliament* to be observ'd as a day of gen: Thanksgiving for the miraculous Restauration of his *Majestie*.   Evelyn, *Diary*, iii. 289

[Bristol, 1780]: This being Restoration Day, some houses are distinguished by oak branches in front. 'Tis a mark of attachment to Monarchy, and by many of regard to the excluded family at least in some places as Manchester, Exeter &c. &c.   Curwen, ii. 616

Monday, 29 May [1876]. Oak-apple day and the children all came to school with breast-knots of oak leaves.   Kilvert, iii. 323

By an Act of Parliament in 1859 the commemoration was dropped from the Book of Common Prayer, together with the Martyrdom of Charles I on *30 January and the Gunpowder Plot Day on *5 November. Chambers comments on the decision in 1864:

It is a curious proof of that tendency to *continuity* which marks all public institutions in England, that the services appointed for national thanksgiving on account of the Gunpowder Plot, for national humiliation regarding the execution of Charles I., and for thanksgiving with respect to the Restoration of Charles II., should have maintained their ground as holidays till after the middle of the nineteenth century. National good sense had long ceased to believe that the Deity had inspired James I. with 'a divine spirit to interpret some dark phrases of a letter', in order to save the kingdom from the 'utter ruin' threatened by Guy Fawkes and his associates. National good feeling had equally ceased to justify the keeping up of the remembrance of the act of a set of infuriated men, to the offence of a large class of our fellow-Christians. We had most of us become very doubtful that the blood of Charles I. was 'innocent blood', or that he was strictly a 'martyred sovereign', though few would now-a-days be disposed to see him punished exactly as he was for his political shortcomings and errors. Still more doubt had fallen on the blessing supposed to be involved in the 'miraculous providence' by which Charles II. was restored to his kingdom. Indeed, to say the very least, the feeling, more or less partial from the first, under which the services on these holidays had been appointed, had for generations been dead in the national heart, and their being still maintained was a pure solecism and a farce.   Chambers, 17 Jan.

The Restoration is still commemorated in Castleton (Derbyshire), with a procession headed by Charles II on horseback. In Aston-on-Clun (Shropshire) the village's large black poplar tree is decorated with flags, which remain up for a year. In Wishford Magna (Wiltshire) villagers carry oak branches in procession.

30 MAY

a.d. III Kalendas Iunias   C

❅ HOLIDAYS AND ANNIVERSARIES   Croatia: Statehood Day (independence from
   Yugoslavia, 1991)
   USA: Memorial Day (celebrated on various days; the federal holiday is the last Mon-
   day in May)
   USA, Virginia: Confederate Memorial Day

❅ ANCIENT ROME On this or a nearby day the Ambarvalia were held, both by individuals and the state. The name means 'Round the Fields'; the farmer commanded a pig,
sheep, and bull (*suovetaurilia*) to be led around his land, with a prayer and libation to
Janus and Jupiter, and a long invocation of Father Mars, a god of agriculture as well as
war. Ceres and Bacchus were also addressed, and no work was to be done; the household sang and danced.

   The public ritual is less well known, unless it was that conducted by the Fratres
Arvales or Arval Brethren in their grove outside Rome in honour of the Dea Dia; they
also sang a hymn invoking the Lares, the Sowing Gods (Semones), and Mars, in highly
archaic Latin that the stonecutter who inscribed it in AD 218 evidently did not understand.

❅ HOLY DAYS Josephine Butler (CY)

Josephine Butler (1828–1906). As the wife of a canon of Winchester, she was energetic in
reclaiming prostitutes and suppressing the white-slave trade, forming in 1869 the Ladies'
National Association for the Repeal of the Contagious Diseases Acts.

Joan of Arc, or rather *Jeanne Darc*, 'la Pucelle' or the Maid of Orléans (on second Sunday
in May in France); a peasant's daughter from Domrémy in Champagne who from 1425
onwards described visions of blazes of light accompanying voices, in time identified as
particular saints conferring on her a mission to save France from English rule. In 1420
King Charles VI, unable to withstand the combined forces of England and Burgundy,
had been compelled to recognize Henry V of England as his heir; after Henry's death
on 31 August 1422, his rights devolved on his infant son Henry VI, who after Charles's
death on 22 October in the same year was crowned on 17 December as king of France,
the duke of Bedford being regent; the opposing 'Armagnac' faction championed Charles
VI's disinherited son and namesake, who had not been crowned.

   Having failed in 1428 to persuade the Armagnac leaders, Joan convinced them the
next year that her visions were genuine, allegedly by recognizing Charles through his

disguise. Nevertheless, she was subjected to theological examination before being permitted to lead an expedition to Orléans, then under siege; wearing white armour, she inspired the troops to the city's relief and brought Charles to Reims for coronation on 17 July. She had said that this would be the term of her mission; but in the excitement of success she was persuaded that other tasks lay ahead for her, beginning with the capture of Paris. Christine de Pisan, in her *Ditié de Jehanne d'Arc*, written a fortnight after the coronation, predicted ever greater triumphs for the female champion who surpassed Esther, Judith, and Deborah, and was foretold by Merlin, the Sibyl, and Bede: once she had taken Paris and overthrown the English, she would restore concord in the Church, destroy the heretics (meaning the Hussites of Bohemia), sweep away the Saracens, and together with Charles conquer the Holy Land, where she would die. In fact the march on Paris failed, and on taking the field again in the following year Joan was captured by Burgundian forces at Compiègne, sold to the English, and brought to trial at Rouen for witchcraft and heresy before Pierre Cauchon, bishop of Beauvais. When her visions were found to be false and diabolical (the University of Paris joined in the condemnation), she recanted on 23 May 1431, but having resumed male attire she was condemned as a relapsed heretic and burnt at the stake on the 30th.

Nevertheless, the tide of war soon turned against the English, particularly after Duke Philip the Good of Burgundy switched sides in 1435; in 1449 Charles VII, who had lost all interest in Joan after his coronation, decided that since he would soon win the war it was time to do something for her, and ordered a re-examination of her trial (in technical language, a revision of the process). This finally got under way in 1452, but made little progress until Joan's supporters laid the matter before Pope Callistus III; her definitive acquittal was pronounced on 7 July. Her reputation was not thereby repaired: in England, Shakespeare could still present her in the First Part of *Henry VI* as a witch and a whore; even in France, Voltaire could write an ironic and racy poem on *La Pucelle* that is now little remembered. A more favourable view was taken by Schiller (*Die Jungfrau von Orleans*), but the decisive change was effected by the publication, from 1841 onwards, of the full proceedings in her trial and the subsequent revision, which established her as a historical figure and not merely the stuff of pious or patriotic legend; ever more admired, not only in France, she was beatified in 1909 and canonized in 1920, and declared patron of France in 1922. Her cult has even survived her exploitation by the Vichy regime as the implacable foe of the *godams* (as she called the English, from 'God damn'); in 1952 she was declared patron of the French army.

The Bourgeois of Paris mentions her in his journal in 1429, but in a distinctly cool fashion since Paris was on the Anglo-Burgundian side:

There was at this time a Maid, as they called her, in the Loire country who claimed to be able to foretell the future and who used to say 'Such a thing will certainly happen'. She was altogether opposed to the Regent of France and his supporters. And it was said that in spite of all the forces in front of Orleans she made her way into the city, bringing in large numbers of Armagnacs and a good supply of provisions, and that none of the army made any move to stop her, although they could see them going by about one or two bowshots away from them and although they needed food so desperately that one man could well have eaten three *blancs*' worth of bread at one meal. Other things were said of her too, by those who loved the Armagnacs better than the

Burgundians or the Regent of France, such as that, when she was very small and looked after the sheep, birds would come from the woods and fields when she called them and eat bread in her lap as if they were tame. . . . This Maid went everywhere with the Armagnacs, wearing armour and carrying her banner, which bore the one word, 'Jesus'. It was said that she told an English commander to leave the siege with all his men or they would all come to grief and shame. He answered her abusively, calling her bitch and tart; she told him that in spite of them all they would very soon all be gone but that he would not see it and that many of his men would be killed. And so it happened, for he was drowned the day before the slaughter. Afterwards he was fished up, cut in quarters, boiled and embalmed, and taken to St. Merry, where he remained for a week or ten days in the chapel in front of the crypt. Four candles or torches burned before his body night and day; then it was taken to his own country for burial.   Bourgeois, 233–4

Fernando III (1198–1252), king of Castile from 1217, of León from 1230, who reconquered much of southern Spain from the Moors. He founded the cathedral of Burgos and gave the University of Salamanca its charter. A man who knew how to delegate responsibility, he is patron of state officials, but also was named patron of engineers of the Spanish army in 1961, on account of his military prowess.

Bona of Pisa (1156–1207), patron saint of air hostesses and flight attendants, so named by John XXIII in 1962 for her pilgrimages to Jerusalem, Santiago de Compostela, and Rome.

Memorial Day. Formerly known as Decoration Day. It originated as a day set aside to decorate the graves of Federal soldiers who died during the American Civil War; General John Alexander Logan ordered its observance, beginning on 30 May 1868. Since 1971 it has been observed as a legal holiday on the last Monday in May, and honours all the nation's war dead. Many communities mark the day with parades and speeches. Some southern states observe Confederate Memorial Day (see *26 Apr., *April: Fourth Monday, and *April: Last Monday).

Decoration Day

Sleep, comrades, sleep and rest
   On this Field of the Grounded Arms,
Where foes no more molest,
   Nor sentry's shot alarms!

Ye have slept on the ground before,
   And started to your feet
At the cannon's sudden roar,
   Or the drum's redoubling beat.

But in this Camp of Death
   No sound your slumber breaks;
Here is no fevered breath,
   No wound that bleeds and aches.

All is repose and peace,
   Untrampled lies the sod;
The shouts of battle cease,
   It is the truce of God!

Rest, comrades, rest and sleep!
  the thoughts of men shall be
As sentinels to keep
  Your rest from danger free.

Your silent tents of green
  We deck with fragrant flowers;
Yours has the suffering been,
  The memory shall be ours.

Henry Wadsworth Longfellow (1807–82)

31 MAY

pridie Kalendas Iunias   D

If on the last day of this month oak trees begin to bear blossoms, it will be a good year for tallow, and plenty of fruit. (Lilly)

❦ HOLY DAYS **The Visitation of the Blessed Virgin Mary** (CY, RC since 1969; BCP on *2 July); formerly Queenship of Mary (RC; see *22 Aug.)

Cantius, Cantianus, and *Cantianilla,* martyred at Aquileia with their tutor Protus *c.*304, praised in a fifth-century sermon. Tradition associated them with the Anicii, the leaders of the Christian minority among the great families of Rome.

Petronilla or Petronella, an early martyr buried next to SS Nereus and Achilleus (see *12 May). Association of names made her St Peter's daughter, so beautiful that Peter afflicted her with fever 'for her own good' before bidding her arise; 'she at once arose cured and ministered unto them'—like St Peter's mother-in-law when Jesus cured her (Mark 1: 31). The Frankish king Pippin, who owed his throne to Pope Zacharias (see *15 Mar.) and fought the Lombards as his successors' ally, took her for patron; in 757 her relics were translated from the catacomb of Domitilla to St Peter's. Her mausoleum became a French royal chapel, for which Michelangelo's *Pietà* was commissioned by a French cardinal; in Bramante's rebuilding her altar was moved to the end of the right aisle. On this day mass is offered there for France, 'the eldest daughter of the Church'. Her cult spread to late medieval England, where she appears on stained glass and painted screens with her father's keys.

Petronilla, virgyn of great vertu,
  Clad in all floures of spirituall freshnesse,
Petyrs doughter, for love of Crist Ihesu
  Ladest thy lyf in prayer and clennesse,
  Of herte ay founde moost meke in thy sekenesse,
To do seruise with humble diligence
  Unto thy fader, thy story bereth witnesse,
Callyd for thy merytes myrrour of pacience;

God and nature gaue the greate fayrenesse
   To excelle all other of port and of beutye,
Trauaylyd with feuerys and many stronge accesse,
   Gaue thanke to God, thy legend who list se,
   Vertu was preuyd in thyn infirmyte,
Wherfore we pray with humble reuerence
   Do mytigacion of all that seke the,
And with their accesse vertuous pacience.

        John Lydgate (?1370–1449), *The Legend of St Petronilla*

JUNE

In Iune, Iuly and August,
Touch neither women nor sweete must.

A dry May and a dripping June
brings all things in tune.

❦ NAMES FOR THE MONTH Latin *Iunius*, French *juin*, Spanish *junio*, Portuguese *Junho*, Italian *giugno*, German *Juni*, Welsh *Mehefin*, Scots Gaelic *an t-Òg-mhìos* ('the young month'), Irish *Meitheamh*

Iunius, as the name of a month no less than of a noble house, is taken to derive from the goddess Juno, *Iuno*, whose name in turn denotes the young woman (cf. *iuvenis*, 'young', *iunior*, 'younger') ready for a man; since the month name is older than the cult recorded on the 1st, and in any case all Kalends were sacred to her, the link must be the ripening of the crops rather than the rituals of the month. But, as often, the Romans themselves did not know the origin: a rival explanation, propounded by Marcus Fulvius Nobilior (see *30 June), associated May and June with the *maiores* (ancestors) and *iuniores* (men under 45). The Scots Gaelic name also means 'the young month', but another name on record is *Meadhan-Samhraidh*, 'midsummer'; the Welsh name has the same sense, and the Irish name means 'middle'.

❦ HOLIDAYS AND ANNIVERSARIES
First Sunday Bulgaria: Rose Harvest Festival

Second Sunday USA: Children's Day (begun in 1856 at the Universalist Church in Chelsea, Mass.; the Methodist Church adopted it in 1868)

Third Sunday USA: Father's Day (first celebrated 1910; not proclaimed by President until 1966)

First Monday Ireland: Bank Holiday
  New Zealand: Queen's Birthday Holiday
  Tuvalu: Queen's Official Birthday
  USA, Alabama, Mississippi: Jefferson Davis's Birthday, commemorating the President of the Confederate States (1861–5)

Second Monday Australia, Belize, Bermuda, Cayman Islands, Fiji, and Papua New Guinea: Queen's Official Birthday

Third Tuesday to Friday (formerly last three days in May) UK: Royal Ascot

Last Wednesday UK: Henley Royal Regatta, Henley-on-Thames

First Friday Bahamas: Labor Day

Saturday after the first Wednesday UK: the Derby (since 1995; previously on first Wednesday; see also *23 May)

Second or third Saturday Official Birthday of HM the Queen; the date is appointed annually. The Union flag is flown.

Third Saturday Trinidad and Tobago: Labour Day
  Sweden: Midsummer Day celebrated in Sweden by consumption of pickled herring with schnapps and by dancing; girls pick seven flowers to put under their pillows, that they may dream of their future husbands.

> And after her, came iolly *Iune*, arrayd
>   All in greene leaues, as he a Player were;
>   Yet in his time, he wrought as well as playd,
>   That by his plough-yrons mote right well appeare:
>   Vpon a Crab he rode, that him did beare
>   With crooked crawling steps an vncouth pase,
>   And backward yode, as Bargemen wont to fare
>   Bending their force contrary to their face,
> Like that vngracious crew which faines demurest grace.
>
> Spenser, *The Faerie Queene*, VII. vii. 35

It is now Iune and the Hay-makers are mustered to make an army for the field, where not alwayes in order, they march vnder the Bagge and the Bottle, when betwixt the Forke and the Rake, there is seene great force of armes: Now doth the broad Oke comfort the weary Laborer, while vnder his shady Boughes he sits singing to his bread and cheese: the Hay-cocke is the Poore mans Lodging, and the fresh Riuer is his gracious Neighbour: Now the Faulcon and the Tassell try their wings at the Partridge, and the fat Bucke fils the great pasty: the trees are all in their rich aray: but the seely Sheep is turned out of his coat: the Roses and sweet Herbes put the Distiller to his cunning, while the greene apples on the tree are ready for the great bellied wiues: Now begins the Hare to gather vp her heeles, and the Foxe lookes about him, for feare of the Hound: the Hooke and the Sickle are making ready for haruest: the Medow grounds gape for raine, and the Corne in the eare begins to harden: the little Lads make Pipes of the straw, and they that cannot dance, will yet bee hopping: the Ayre now groweth somewhat warme, and the coole winds are very comfortable: the Sayler now makes merry passage, and the nimble Foot-man runnes with pleasure: In briefe, I thus conclude, I hold it a sweet season, the senses perfume, and the spirits comfort. Farewell.   Breton (1626)

In this Moneth *abstain* from such meats as do ingender *flegm*, and *drink* then of the pleasantest Wine, and drink sometimes fasting a cup of *white Wine*, for it purgeth Choler, and noxious humors from the stomack, good to eat Sallets of Lettice prepared with Vinegar, eat such meats as be light of digestion, and all this Moneth glut not the *stomack*, but *arise* from the Table with an *appetite*; arise betimes in the morning, and exercise your body with some long *walk*; you may bleed, beware of eating *Milk* unless the same be well sodden, take heed of eating *Cheese* and *Apples* this moneth, not good to stay long in the Bath, to wash the *Feet* this moneth often in cold water is commended.   Saunders (1665)

I JUNE

Kalendae Iuniae   E

❴ HOLIDAYS AND ANNIVERSARIES Samoa: Independence Day (1962)
Tunisia: Constitution Day, or Victory Day (promulgation of constitution, 1959)
USA, Kentucky: Admission Day (15th state, 1792)
USA, Tennessee: Admission Day (16th state, 1796)

❴ ANCIENT ROME On this day in 344 BC was dedicated the temple of Juno Moneta on the Capitol, on the site now occupied by the church of Santa Maria in Araceli. Her epithet, from *monere*, 'to warn', was explained either by the warning that her geese had given some forty years earlier when the Gauls climbed up the Capitol, or because a voice was heard from her temple during an earthquake admonishing the people to perform an expiation. When in the third century BC the Romans began to strike coins, it was in her temple that they did so; from Moneta, accordingly, come the words 'mint' and 'money', and their cognates in other languages. There were also ceremonies in honour of Mars, the Storms, and Carna, possibly a goddess of flesh, though equated by Ovid with Cardea, goddess of hinges; hot bacon was eaten on her day, and beans mixed with emmer-wheat, causing the festival to be known as the Bean Kalends, *Kalendae Fabariae*.

❴ HOLY DAYS Nicomedes (BCP; RC 15 Sept.); Justin Martyr (CY, RC since 1969, Orth.); formerly St Angela Merici (see *27 Jan.)

Nicomedes, early Christian martyr, said to have been beaten to death with leaded whips; buried in Via Nomentana. This is the dedication-feast of the seventh-century church in Rome.

Justin Martyr (*c*.100–*c*.165), from a leading family at Flavia Neapolis (now Nablus), was the first Christian Apologist to set up a system of thought (based on the Logos) to challenge classical philosophy; he was executed at Rome *c*.165 by the city prefect Quintus Junius Rusticus, who had made a Stoic philosopher out of the emperor Marcus Aurelius. Honoured from antiquity in the East, but in the West not till the ninth century (see *13 Apr.), he is patron saint of philosophers.

Íñigo (Enneco), abbot of San Salvador at Oña north-east of Burgos, d. 1 June 1057, said to have been mourned even by Jews and Saracens. Loyola was baptized with his name (see *31 July); the architect Inigo Jones was himself the son of an Inigo.

Birthday of Brigham Young (1801), second President of the Church of Jesus Christ of Latter-day Saints; it was he who brought the Mormons to Utah.

The Glorious First of June. On 1 June 1794 during the French Revolutionary Wars a British fleet of 25 sail under Lord Howe defeated 26 French ships under Admiral Villaret de Joyeuse at Ushant. The French lost some 3,000 men, besides prisoners (English killed and wounded being 922); six ships were taken and the *Vengeur* sunk. The French propa-gandist variously spelt Barère and Barrère asserted that she had refused to surrender and gone down heroically with all hands; the story inspired Jules Verne's Captain Nemo, but:

Alas, alas! The *Vengeur*, after fighting bravely, did sink altogether as other ships do, her captain and above two-hundred of her crew escaping gladly in British boats; and this same enormous in-spiring Feat, and rumour 'of sound most piercing,' turns out to be an enormous inspiring Non-entity, extant nowhere save, as falsehood, in the brain of Barrère! Actually so! Founded, like the World itself, on *Nothing*; proved by Convention Report, by solemn Convention Decree and De-crees, and wooden '*Model of the Vengeur*,' believed, bewept, besung by the whole French People to this hour, it may be regarded as Barrère's masterpiece; the largest, most inspiring piece of *blague* manufactured, for some centuries, by any man or nation. As such, and not otherwise, be it hence-forth memorable.   Carlyle, iii, bk. v, ch. 6

At New College, Oxford, a mint julep is drunk from a silver loving-cup on an endow-ment instituted in 1873 by a distinguished American visitor who asked for such a drink on a hot day, to the utter bewilderment of the butler. A decision to discontinue it after its unexpected potency had caused the undergraduates to misbehave was set aside when the visitor's son himself paid a visit and asked whether the mint julep was still served. On being told, by way of a white lie, that the money had run out, he renewed the en-dowment.

2 JUNE

❦ HOLIDAYS AND ANNIVERSARIES Italy: Republic Day (commemorating the refer-endum of 1946 that established the republic) (national day)
   UK: Coronation of HM Queen Elizabeth II 1953; red-letter day; the Union flag is flown

❦ HOLY DAYS Marcellinus and Peter (RC)

Marcellinus and Peter (d. *c.*305) are said to have been respectively a priest and an exorcist, beheaded under Diocletian and buried 'by the Two Bay Trees' in the Via Labicana; Constantine the Great erected on the site a basilica (demolished in 1956) with the mausoleum of his mother, St Helena. A grave was discovered there in 1896, but Einhard had conveyed their relics to Seligenstadt in 827.

Erasmus (d. *c.*305), one of the Fourteen Auxiliary Saints. In the Mediterranean he is venerated as 'St Elmo', and often conflated with St Pedro González (see *14 Apr.); the blue lightning that plays around ships' masts is called 'St Elmo's fire'. He is attested in early martyrologies, but knowledge of his life is scant: he was bishop of Formiae in the Campagna and became the patron saint of Gaeta when his relics were translated there. Legend makes him bishop 'in Syria', fleeing to Mount Lebanon from Diocletian's agents, who captured him, beat him, covered him in pitch, set it alight, and only then threw him into prison. An angel conveyed him halfway across the Empire to Sirmium (Sremska Mitrovica), when torture resumed; he was again angelically transported to Formiae, where he died. More famous, however, is the later and even more gruesome tale in which he is martyred by the extraction of his intestines, efficiently reeled in by a windlass; this seems to be a landlubberly misinterpretation of the capstan on board the vessel on which Erasmus preached during a thunderstorm, an appropriate emblem for a patron saint of sailors. In consequence of this torture he became the patron of turners and of persons suffering from stomach pains, including children with colic and women in labour.

Erasmus heales the Collicke and the griping of the guttes.   Naogeorgus, fo. 38ᵛ

In England this was an unlucky day for marriage.

3 JUNE

a.d. III Nonas Iunias   G

(HOLIDAYS AND ANNIVERSARIES USA, Florida, Georgia, South Carolina: Jefferson Davis's Birthday
    USA, Kentucky, Louisiana: Confederate Memorial Day

(HOLY DAYS Charles Lwanga and Companions (RC); Martyrs of Uganda, 1886 and 1978 (CY commem.)

Charles Lwanga, martyr (d. 1886) and companions, servants of King Mwanga of Uganda, converted and martyred between 1885 and 1887, and canonized in 1964. Pius XI proclaimed him patron of African youth in 1934, even before he had been canonized.

Clothilda, daughter of the Burgundian king Chilperic and therefore brought up as a Catholic Christian, persuaded her husband, Clovis, to convert (see *22 Sept.); after the murder of her grandson by her sons (see *7 Sept., Clodoald) she devoted herself to prayer and good works.

Coemgen (Caoimhín, Kevin), d. 618; founder of Glendalough monastery, Co. Wicklow; in Irish *Gleann dá Locha* means 'Valley of Two Lakes'. Several legends ascribe to him the affinity with nature typical of Irish monks, as that when a blackbird laid an egg in his hand, which he had stretched out in a six-week 'cross-vigil', he kept it in that position till the egg was hatched. When bidden leave off his austerities by an angel he refused (since the pain he suffered for God was nothing to that which God had suffered for man) until God should confirm the privileges of his monks. Like some other friends to animals he was less considerate to human beings, if it be true that he flung a woman who attempted to seduce him into a bed of nettles; but he fed his monks on salmon caught for him by an otter.

In 1997 this day was commemorated as Enoch Soames Day, after the title-hero of Max Beerbohm's short story, written in 1912 but set in the 1890s. Soames is a would-be decadent, the author of *Negations*, which the narrator (Beerbohm himself) begins to read:

> Lean near to life. Lean very near—nearer.
> Life is web, and therein nor warp nor woof is, but web only.
> It is for this I am Catholick in church and in thought, yet do let swift Mood weave there what the shuttle of Mood wills.

These were the opening phrases of the preface, but those which followed were less easy to understand.

His second volume is a book of poems called *Fungoids*; Beerbohm forgets the name of the third. Depressed by his lack of renown, Soames consoles himself with the expectation that his merits will be discovered by posterity; he enters into a pact with the Devil, that he shall travel 100 years ahead in time to visit the Reading Room of the British Museum 'just as it will be upon the afternoon of June 3rd, 1997' and look up the materials on him there, in return for immediate delivery of his soul thereafter. On visiting the Museum, however, he finds nothing except a reference in a literary history, written by one T. K. Nupton in a reformed spelling, to a story in which Max Beerbohm 'pautraid an immajnary karrakter kauld "Enoch Soames" ', with the comment that now the literary profession has been organized as a branch of the public service, writers do their duty without thought of the morrow: 'Thank hevvn we hav no Enoch Soameses amung us to-dai!' He surrenders to the Devil, with a last despairing cry to Beerbohm: 'Try, *try* to make them know that I did exist!'

Predictions of the future are rarely accurate: English spelling has not been reformed, the books and manuscripts of the British Museum have been transferred to the British Library, which in 1997 was in the process of abandoning the Reading Room. A search of the catalogue failed to reveal Enoch Soames as author, title, or subject; but it came to light that into the 1954 edition of *Grove's Dictionary of Music and Musicians* a bogus entry was smuggled concerning a composer who had set a poem from *Fungoids*, 'To a Young Woman'. In case any reader may be inspired to emulate him, we subjoin the text:

> Thou art, who hast not been!
> Pale tunes irresolute
> And traceries of old sounds
> Blown from a rotted flute

Mingle with noise of cymbals rouged with rust,
Nor not strange forms and epicene
Lie bleeding in the dust,
Being wounded with wounds.
For this it is
That in thy counterpart
Of age-long mockeries
Thou hast not been nor art!

The arrival of the day provoked renewed interest; Beerbohm's story was dramatized by the BBC, Soames's haunts were revisited, and an actor personating him was sent to the British Library. There is even an Enoch Soames Society, which threatens to republish his complete works.

4 JUNE

pridie Nonas Iunias   A

❨ HOLIDAYS AND ANNIVERSARIES Finland: Flag Day (birthday of Carl Gustaf Mannerheim, 1867; military leader in campaign against Russia in the Second World War)
Tonga: Emancipation Day, or Independence Day (from Great Britain, 1970)

❨ HOLY DAYS Mary of Bethany (Orth.; see also *22 July)

Mary of Bethany, the sister of Martha and Lazarus (see *29 July), who sat at Jesus' feet while Martha did the housework.

Speech Day at Eton (birthday of George III, a patron of the school). Parents picnic on Agar's Plough, and embarrass their offspring by displaying their poverty or their wealth.

5 JUNE

Nonae Iuniae   B

❨ HOLIDAYS AND ANNIVERSARIES Denmark: Constitution Day (1849, 1953) (national day)
United Nations: World Environment Day

❨ HOLY DAYS Boniface, archbishop of Mainz (CofE, RC)

Boniface (*c.*675–754), baptized Wynfrith, was a Wessex man of scholarly tastes who in 716 made an unsuccessful missionary journey to Frisia; resolved to try again with papal support, he travelled to Rome, where Gregory II commissioned him to evangelize the heathen under the new name of Bonifatius. After returning to Frisia, where he assisted St Willibrord (see *7 Nov.), he transferred his attention to Hessen, where he enjoyed considerable success, especially after felling an oak sacred to the thunder-god Donar (English Thunor, Norse Thor). His efforts were directed not only against heathens but against Frankish Christians who, not owing their faith to papal initiative, lacked the English attachment to Rome and Roman church discipline. Through his pupil Sturmius he founded the great monastery at Fulda, a centre of Christian and classical learning until the Thirty Years War. Having in 722 been made bishop without a see, in 748 he was elevated to the archbishopric of Mainz while remaining the papal legate for all Frankland; in 753 he resumed his missionary work in Frisia, where he was murdered on 5 June 754. His body was borne home in ceremony to Fulda, where his remains still lie in the cathedral crypt. He is revered as the Apostle of Germany.

According to some early medieval calendars, on this day the birds cease to sing. Gilbert White noted in his journal for 10 June 1768: 'The nightingale, having young, leaves off singing, & makes a plaintive & a jarring noise.'

6 JUNE

a.d. VIII Idus Iunias   C

 HOLIDAYS AND ANNIVERSARIES Sweden: National Day, commemorating Gustav Vasa's election to the throne in 1523, after the national rebellion against Denmark, and the signature of the 1809 constitution (superseded in 1973); nevertheless it is a normal working day
  D-Day, commemorating the Allied landing on the beaches of Normandy in 1944

 HOLY DAYS Norbert (RC); Philip the Deacon (RC; see *11 Oct.)

Norbert (*c.*1080–1134), founder of the Premonstratensians. Of noble birth, he was a canon at Xanten on the lower Rhine until a narrow escape from death in a thunderstorm in 1115; he changed his secular way of life, sold his goods, became a priest, and lived as an itinerant preacher in northern France. He founded a community under the reformed Augustinian Rule at Prémontré in 1121, approved in 1126, the year he became bishop of Magdeburg. His zeal in protecting church property and promoting celibacy of the clergy earned him many enemies. He was canonized in 1582; his relics were translated to Strahov, near Prague, in 1627.

A 1699 almanac commemorates this day as follows:

June the 6. I cannot call this a Saints day, but some may think it as good, for on this day the Tax of the Apostolick Chamber was licensed by the Parliament of *Paris*, and because 'tis fit that every one should know at what rate he may safely sin, I will give you some particulars; a Monk that do's not keep to his proper garb 7 groats, a Priest that marries Persons within the prohibited degrees 7 groats, he that lies with a woman in the Church, and doth other evil things 6 groats, he that lies with his Mother, his Sister, his Gossip, or any near of kin 5 groats, he that deflowers a Virgin 6 groats, perjury 6 groats, for a Lay-man that kills an Abbot, Monk, or Priest 8 or 9 groats, but if he be a Priest, he must also visit See Apostolick. For a man that beats his wife till she miscarry 6 groats, for the woman that eats or drinks any thing to make her miscarry 5 groats, and is not this dog cheap? To give them their due, they afford good penyworths, if they keep to their old Rates, but there is no reason they should, considering what alteration hath been in the value of money, but some get more by quick returns, then by larger gains in slow returns.

Dove (1699)

On this day in 1996, peasants in Colombia hammered on church doors to have their babies baptized against the coming of Antichrist, because his number is 666 and the day, so close to the millennium, was 6.6.96.

7 JUNE

a.d. VII Idus Iunias   D

❦ HOLIDAYS AND ANNIVERSARIES   Malta: National Day

❦ ANCIENT ROME On this day the *penus* or storehouse in the temple of Vesta (to which only women were allowed) was opened. The shape of the temple recalled the huts of early Rome; in Latin it is always the *aedes Vestae*, not being a *templum* according to augural law.

❦ HOLY DAYS
Robert, Cistercian monk, founder and first abbot of Newminster, d. 7 June 1159; in consequence this day is celebrated as the name-day of the Bernese Overland Railway (Berner Oberland Bahn, BOB). He is represented as a soul in the form of a fiery ball rescued by angels from the pursuing hounds of hell.

Death of Robert the Bruce at Cardross in 1379. He gave the following instructions:

I woll, that as soone as I am trespassed out of this worlde, that ye take my harte owte of my body, and enbawme it, and take my treasoure, as yet shall thynke sufficient for that entreprise, both for yourselfe, and suche company as ye wyll take with you, and present my hart to the holy Sepulchre, where as our Lorde laye, seying, my body can nat come there . . . And where so ever ye come, let it be knowen, howe ye cary with you the harte of kyng Robert of Scotland, at his instance and desire, to be presented to the holy Sepulchre.   Froissart, i. 68

However, the knight charged with carrying the heart was killed while fighting in Spain; it was taken back to Scotland and buried in Melrose Abbey, where the casket thought to contain it was uncovered during the excavation of the chapter house in 1996. It was reburied in 1998 on the 684th anniversary of Bannockburn (see *24 June).

8 JUNE

❦ ANCIENT ROME The goddess Mens ('Mind') was honoured on the Capitol in consequence of a vow undertaken after defeat by Hannibal at Lake Trasimene in 217 BC, perhaps to atone for the mindlessness of the consul Gaius Flaminius, on which the defeat was blamed.

❦ HOLY DAYS Thomas Ken (CY)

Thomas Ken (1637–1711). Having as chaplain to Charles II refused the use of his house to Nell Gwynn, he was made bishop of Bath and Wells, reputedly as a sign of the king's regard. A staunch opponent of 'Popish and Puritan innovations', he preached against James II's attempts to co-opt the Protestant Dissenters in his struggle against the Church of England; in 1688 he was one of the Seven Bishops who declined to read the king's Declaration of Indulgence granting liberty of worship and suspending the laws against recusants and nonconformists. However, though opposed to rule by a popish king and eager that William of Orange should administer the country, he could not find it in his conscience to swear allegiance to him as king, having already sworn it to James; in 1691 he was deprived of his see by Act of Parliament. In the subsequent divisions amongst the nonjurors (who included five of the Seven Bishops), Ken took a moderate line, and would have nothing to do with the perpetuation of the schism by fresh ordinations.

William Fitzherbert (d. 1154) was in 1141 elected archbishop of York by a majority in the cathedral chapter, defeating the Cistercian Henry Murdac of Fountains Abbey; the minority, supported by the local Cistercians and by St Bernard of Clairvaux himself, appealed to Rome on the grounds that he was a dissolute simoniac, thrust into the see by King Stephen. Pope Innocent II permitted the consecration if the charges of political pressure and financial inducement were denied on oath; the next pope but one, Lucius II, sent him the pallium, which he did not bother to collect. This failure played into his enemies' hands under Lucius' successor, the Cistercian Eugenius III, who under pressure from Bernard and the rival candidate, Henry Murdac, by now abbot of Fountains Abbey, overruled the majority of his cardinals and suspended William on a technicality. The archbishop's kinsmen and supporters, outraged by these manoeuvres and sharing the general ill-will towards the Cistercian Order detectable in contemporary sources, ransacked the Abbey; the Pope now deposed him, and when the chapter failed to elect a successor consecrated Henry Murdac. William, still supported by king and people, betook himself to Winchester and a saintly mode of life. This was rewarded in 1153 by the deaths of his three arch-enemies, Eugenius, Bernard, and Murdac; the new pope, Anastasius IV, reinstated William and gave him the pallium, but the defeated party (it is said) avenged itself with poison. Miracles were reported: when the Old Minster caught fire, William's incorrupt body was preserved in its silken robe; some years later holy oil exuded from the tomb. York, which lacked a notable saint, pressed for his canonization; when the Cistercian abbots of Fountains and Rievaulx, appointed to investigate as being predisposed to reject the claims, nevertheless reported in his favour, Pope Honorius III canonized him in 1227. His life and miracles are depicted in stained glass at York Minster.

Médard (*c.*479–*c.*560), bishop of Noyon, who combated the remnants of paganism and consecrated the Frankish queen Radegunde (see *13 Aug.) a deaconess when she fled from her bloodthirsty husband, Clothar I. Nevertheless, at his death Clothar had him buried at Soissons, where an abbey was later dedicated to him; and Clothar's son Chilperic I wrote a dreadful Latin poem in his honour. He is said to have instituted the award of a rose on this day to the worthiest maiden in his birthplace, Salency.

St Médard's Day is a French equivalent of St Swithun for weather predictions (the other is *19 June), since an eagle is supposed to have sheltered the saint from a storm. Similarly in Norway, rain will last for forty days; others say this day's weather will remain for four or five weeks, or recur at haying time.

St Médard is the hero of one of Barham's *Ingoldsby Legends*, 'A Legend of Afric'. It has nothing to do with weather proverbs but describes how St Médard foils the Devil's prospective gourmet dinner by cutting open his sack, which Old Nick had stuffed so full that he could not lift it off the ground. 'Saints were so many and sins so few', but nevertheless he had managed to collect 'a decentish lot':

> He had pick'd up in France a *Maître de Danse*,—
>   A *Maîtresse en titre*,—two smart *Grisettes*,
>   A Courtier at play,— And an English *Roué*—
>   Who had bolted from home without paying his debts.—
>
> —He had caught in Great Britain a Scrivener's clerk,
>   A Quaker,—a Baker,—a Doctor of Laws,—
>   And a Jockey of York— But Paddy from Cork
>   'Desaved the ould divil', and slipp'd through his claws!
>
> In Moscow, a Boyar knouting his wife—
>   A Corsair's crew, in the Isles of Greece—
>   And, under the dome Of St. Peter's, at Rome,
>   He had snapp'd up a nice little Cardinal's Niece.—
>
> He had bagg'd an Inquisitor fresh from Spain—
>   A mendicant Friar—of Monks a score;
>   A grave Don or two, And a Portuguese Jew,
>   Whom he nabb'd while clipping a new Moidore.

And he said to himself, as he lick'd his lips,
'Those nice little Dears! what a delicate roast!—
Then, that fine fat Friar, At a very quick fire,
Dress'd like a Woodcock, and serv'd on toast!'

Richard Harris Barham ('Thomas Ingoldsby') (1788–1845)

9 JUNE

a.d. V Idus Iunias   F

❦ HOLIDAYS AND ANNIVERSARIES   USA, Oklahoma: Senior Citizens Day

❦ ANCIENT ROME   Vestalia, the main public festival of the hearth goddess Vesta, on
which the Vestal Virgins offered the *mola salsa* or salt-cake, made from water carried in
vessels that could not be set down without spilling and from salt pounded in a mortar,
baked, and sawn. The day became a holiday for millers and bakers.

❦ HOLY DAYS   Ephraem the Syrian (RC; CY commem.); Columba (CY, RC Ireland
and Scotland); Cyril of Alexandria (Orth.; see *27 June)

Ephraem the Syrian (*c.*306–73), also called 'the Deacon' and 'the Harp of the Holy Ghost'.
He was famed for his biblical commentaries and hymns, written in Syriac, and for
organizing relief during a plague. Benedict XV named him a Doctor of the Church in
1920. His feast-day was formerly 18 June.

Columba (Colm Cille, 'Dove of the Church'), born *c.*520 and named *Crimthann*, 'fox', died
on this day in 597, the second Sunday after Pentecost by the Celtic reckoning (the first
by the Roman) and not, as tradition asserts, Pentecost itself. It is related that as abbot
of Derry he quarrelled like other monks with Diormit mac Cerbaill, also known as Di-
armaid the Good, High King of Ireland, who gave judgment against him for making a
pirate copy of a Gospel-book brought back from Rome by Finnian of Moville: 'As a
calf is to the cow, so is the copy to the book.' When the king of Connacht's son, having murdered a man during the feast at Tara in 560, sought sanctuary with Columba,
Diormit overrode him and did justice; the infuriated abbot raised a coalition of kings
that routed Diormit at *Cúl Drebene* (thought to be a few miles north of Sligo) despite
the prayers of Finnian, destroying the power of the high kingship and condemning Ireland to the constant wars of petty kinglets. In 563, condemned to excommunication by
a synod of monks but granted a stay of sentence, Columba left Ireland for ever, and
founded a monastery off the Scottish coast on the island of Iona.
    Columba's first biographer, Adomnán, says very little about his Irish years, preferring
to recount his miracles, such as the running commentary he gave soon after his arrival
on a battle being fought in Ireland; even so had the augur Gaius Cornelius at Padua,

according to his acquaintance and fellow-townsman Livy, described Caesar's defeat of Pompey at Pharsalus in 48 BC. He also relates that Columba, on witnessing the burial of a man bitten by an *aquatilis bestia* in the River Ness, bade a companion swim across to fetch a boat; lured by this bait, the monster rose to the surface, whereupon the saint made the sign of the Cross and ordered it back. The creature fled; the astonished Picts were converted. This tale was probably not known to the twentieth-century journalists who invented the Loch Ness monster, which scientists drilling in the loch bed for palaeoclimatic and other data have failed to find. Belief in evil creatures inhabiting lakes is widespread; one of us has been told by a correspondent in Ireland that in the mid-1980s she was warned to keep a tight hold on her little daughter lest she fall prey to the kelpie, which had seized its last known victim some forty years earlier.

It is said that in his haste to leave Derry Columba put on one shoe before his other stocking was on, and limped in consequence; children in Ireland are told to take warning by him and always put both socks or stockings on before they put on the first shoe.

That man is little to be envied, whose patriotism would not gain force upon the plain of Marathon, or whose piety would not grow warmer among the ruins of Iona.

Johnson, *Journey*, 148

It is this passage that ensured the triumph of 'Iona' (a distortion of Adomnán's *Ioua*) over the previous English name (which Johnson also used), 'Icolmkill', Gaelic *Í Choluim Chille*.

In Norway Columba's name was naturalized as Kolbjørn, and the day called *Kolbjørn med laksen*, 'with the salmon', since the fish was said to leap up on it.

10 JUNE

a.d. IV Idus Iunias   G

❡ HOLIDAYS AND ANNIVERSARIES Macao: Camões and Portuguese Communities Day (commemorating death of Portugal's national poet, Luís Vaz de Camões, 1580)

Portugal: Portugal Day (death of Luís Vaz de Camões, 1580) (national day)

HRH the Duke of Edinburgh born 1921; red-letter day; the Union flag is flown

❡ HOLY DAYS Formerly Margaret, Queen of Scotland (see *16 Nov.)

White Rose Day, celebrated by Jacobites as the birthday of Prince James Francis Stewart, 'the Old Pretender', son of James II, in 1688 (see *10 Dec.).

June (in Australia)
Not like that month when, in imperial space,
The high, strong sun stares at the white world's face;

Not like that haughty daughter of the year
Who moves, a splendour, in a splendid sphere;
But rather like a nymph of afternoon,
With cool, soft sunshine, comes Australian June:
She is the calm, sweet lady, from whose lips
No breath of living passion ever slips;
The wind that on her virgin forehead blows
Was born too late to speak of last year's rose;
She never saw a blossom, but her eyes
Of tender beauty see blue, gracious skies;
She loves the mosses, and her feet have been
In woodlands where the leaves are always green;
Her days pass on with sea-songs, and her nights
Shine, full of stars, on lands of frosty lights.

                                      Henry Kendall (1841–82)

11 JUNE

a.d. III Idus Iunias   A

At Saint Barnabas the scythe in the meadow.

Barnaby bright,
The longest day and shortest night.

❦ HOLIDAYS AND ANNIVERSARIES USA, Hawaii: King Kamehameha I Day (1737–1819) (state holiday)

❦ ANCIENT ROME Matralia in honour of Mater Matuta, to whom women commended their own or their sisters' children; slaves were excluded, apart from one who was ritually expelled. Her temple was in the Forum Boarium, alongside one of Fortuna, who was also worshipped on this day; they were said to have been built in the sixth century BC by King Servius Tullius, to whom many good institutions were attributed. The temple of Fortuna contained a statue said to be of Servius, but wrapped in togas; Ovid offers three explanations: that the goddess wished to conceal the fact that the king had been her lover, or that his grieving people had covered his corpse with their togas, or that he had not wished to see his wicked daughter Tullia, who had murdered him. This statue survived the fire that swept through both temples in 213 BC; they were rebuilt the next year. Remains of very ancient temples have been found under the church of St Homobonus (see *13 Nov.).

❦ HOLY DAYS **Barnabas** (CofE); Barnabas (RC, Orth.); red-letter day; Bartholomew (Orth.; see *24 Aug.)

Barnabas, cousin of St Mark, a Levite from Cyprus properly called Joseph but nick-named Barnabas ('Son of Encouragement'), who sold his estate and donated the proceeds to the apostles. When the persecutor Saul became the convert Paul, it was Barnabas who persuaded the community of his sincerity; thereafter he accompanied him on his early missions until they quarrelled over Barnabas' insistence on taking Mark with him despite what Paul regarded as his desertion on a previous enterprise. Accom-panied by Mark, Barnabas returned to Cyprus, where tradition has him stoned to death by the Jews of Famagusta; however, Paul's first Epistle to the Corinthians shows Barnabas once more working with him. The Epistle to the Hebrews, which the West-ern Church (rightly, as modern critics have found) did not regard as Pauline before St Jerome, was sometimes ascribed to him. In England his was the day for the hay harvest.

In Denmark this was the traditional end of the contract-year, when rents fell due and masters and servants were free to renegotiate or part. The Norwegian-born playwright Ludvig Holberg wrote a comedy on this topic, *Den 11. juni,* first performed at Copen-hagen on 11 June 1723; in the first scene a landlord voices the eternal complaint that the world is going downhill because of fashionable frippery:

> In the old days the best merchants were called Hans Jensen [i.e. Jens's son] or Per Persen and the wife was Anne Pers [i.e. Per's wife] or Else Christensens, but one got one's rent all right on the 12th or 13th of June; but now they've become gentry, and maybe have a surname with *von* in front of it, and a crowd of caterpillars—lackeys in stripes—at their heels and pouches on the back of their wigs, the 24th of June counts as prompt payment; at this rate in ten years' time the 24th of July will be prompt payment, then the 24th of August, and in the end we shall find ourselves rid-ing home empty-handed and counting it as prompt payment if they promise to settle with us on the 11th of June after that. If there were as many pence as pouches here, this city would be richer than Amsterdam or London, but unfortunately they just hang down the neck with absolutely nothing in them.

12 JUNE

❦ HOLIDAYS AND ANNIVERSARIES Brazil: Dia dos Namorados (Sweethearts' Day); the local (and no less commercial) counterpart of St Valentine's Day
Paraguay: Peace with Bolivia Day, or Peace of Chaco Day (end of war with Bolivia, 1935)
Philippines: Independence Day (from Spain, 1898)
Russia: Independence Day (from the USSR; declared 1990)

❦ HOLY DAYS

Basilides, Cyrinus, Nabor, and Nazarius, recorded in the Roman Martyrology. The former two appear to be Basilides, martyred at Rome *c.*274, and Quirinus of Siscia, drowned with a millstone round his neck in 308 or 309, whose proper days are respectively 10 and 4 June; the latter two Milanese martyrs of whom nothing is known, though Catalan legend made of Nazarius a handsome and inordinately vain man whom God punished by lengthening his nose (Cat. *nas*), which drove him mad; his nose having shrunk to its due proportions, he recovered his wits and spent the rest of his days in penitent devotion.

Onuphrios (*c.*400?), hermit. Greeks will not reap on this day because 'Rúfnis' devours (*rufá*) the fruits, but according to Abbot Paphnutius, who discovered him in the desert clothed in a loincloth of leaves, he subsisted solely on the dates from a palm tree outside his cave; when bread and water miraculously appeared on the table after their day-long discussion, Onuphrios gratefully ate it, and died the next day. A Catalan folk belief made him a husband-finder:

> Gloriós sant Onofre,   Glorious St Onuphrios,
> deu-me un casador   Give me a husband
> amb un bon cofre.   With a chest full of money.

The Viale XII Giugno in Bologna celebrates the flight of the papal legate before the Italian advance in 1860.

Readers who recoil from too much sanctity may choose this day to commemorate the greatest and most successful timeserver in English history, Richard Rich, who died on 12 June 1567. A man of loose life, but a sound lawyer, he had risen to be solicitor-general in 1532; the next year he betrayed Fisher by revealing a conversation he had promised to keep secret, and sent More to his death with perjured evidence (see *22 June, *6 July). He was duly rewarded with further offices; in 1536 he was elected Speaker of the House of Commons, in which capacity he delivered a speech likening Henry VIII to Solomon, Samson, Absalom, and the sun. Having played his part in the dissolution of the monasteries (notably by administering, and diverting, their revenues), when the architect of the policy, and his own benefactor, Thomas Cromwell, fell from power, Rich not only provided evidence against him but joined in the persecution of reformers, even joining in the racking of one victim with his own hands. Nevertheless, another timely switch, and another smooth betrayal, this time of his fellow-torturer, brought him the Lord Chancellorship under the Protestant Edward VI; having served Lord Protector Somerset, he served his enemies instead when that course of action seemed more expedient. Illness compelled him to resign the Lord Chancellorship, though his own great-grandson explained that he had been caught telling tales on the new Lord Protector to the old in the mistaken belief that Somerset would return to power. On Edward's death he supported Queen Jane, but then deserted to Queen Mary; he was vigorous in persecuting the Protestants of Essex, but remained in service under Elizabeth. His religious inclinations were Catholic, but never stood in the way of business: he would persecute Catholics as readily as Protestants if his interests were thereby advanced, and then betray those who had advanced them. Yet so valuable were his services that neither scruple nor caution held back his employers; in consequence, he died a wealthy man and a peer of the realm. But for all his faults he was a patron of learning; at Felsted in Essex, where he is buried (his effigy shows his sharp features), he founded a grammar school whose pupils would include Oliver Cromwell and the mathematicians Isaac Barrow and John Wallis.

13 JUNE

Idus Iuniae   C

❦ HOLIDAYS AND ANNIVERSARIES Lisbon: St Antony of Padua Feast-Day (public holiday)

❦ ANCIENT ROME Quinquatrus minusculae ('lesser'); the guild of *tibicines* or pipers, who attended sacrifices, funerals, and feasts, began a three-day festival in which they roamed the streets in masks and women's clothes, singing drunkenly. To account for this, the story was told (with the usual variations in detail) that in protest at the suppression in 312 BC of their traditional banquet in the temple of Jupiter they had quit Rome for Tivoli; the townsmen, caught between the Senate's demand for their return and the pipers' own refusal to go home, arranged that at the next local festival they should be invited to perform and plied with so much wine, 'of which such folk are generally fond', that they fell asleep, whereupon they were bundled onto carts and packed off back to Rome. When the pipers woke up they were in the Forum; the strike was promptly settled on their terms, and the festival instituted. It was known as the Lesser Quinquatrus because they forgathered at the temple of Minerva, who in her Greek guise as Athena had invented their instrument. Plutarch explains that most of them had been wearing women's clothes at the party; but Ovid has only some of the pipers brought home, under instructions to don masks and gowns so that their numbers could be made up with other pipers of both sexes without the knowledge either of the Senate, which wanted the whole guild back, or of their comrades, who would have accounted them blacklegs.

❦ HOLY DAYS Antony of Padua (RC)

Antony of Padua (1195–1231), Franciscan, patron saint of Portugal and Brazil. Born to a noble Portuguese family, he joined the Order of Austin Canons and studied at Coimbra, but was so affected by the martyrdom of a group of Franciscans in Africa that he joined the newly founded Franciscan Order and himself went to Africa. His health, however, discouraged such a strenuous calling, and his intellectual talents began to impress; he became the first Franciscan lecturer in theology and taught at Bologna, Montpellier, and Toulouse. He soon became famed as a preacher; churches were not large enough to accommodate the crowds who came to hear him, and he often preached outdoors; hence the legend of his sermon to the fishes. Antony is the patron saint of Padua, where he died, and his relics remain in the great church known affectionately as 'Il Santo'. He was canonized in the year following his death. He is represented as holding the Christ child in accordance with his vision.

Many miracles have been attributed to him and legends have proliferated. His help has been invoked to find lost objects since the seventeenth century; the story is told that he made a frightful apparition to a novice who had borrowed his psalter without permission. Antony is also patron saint of barren women, and became the saint of choice for related requests, finding rich husbands for women who burn a candle on his day:

Sant Antoni beneït,	Blessed St Antony,
feu-me trobar un marit	Make me find a husband
que sigui bon home i ric,	Who is a good man and rich,
i, si pot ser, de seguit.	And if possible right away.

(Evidently if St Onuphrios had been invoked without immediate success; cf. *12 June.) Reginald Scot reports in his chapter on 'Certeine popish and magicall cures, for them that are bewitched in their privities':

One *Katharine Loe* (having a husband not so readilie disposed that waie as she wished him to be) made a waxen image to the liknes of hir husbands bewitched member, and offered it up at S. *Anthonies* altar; so as, through holiness of the masse it might be sanctified, to be more couragious, and of better disposition and abilitie, &c.   Scot, v. viii (1584)

The last possible date of Whit Sunday.

14 JUNE

❦ HOLIDAYS AND ANNIVERSARIES   USA: Flag Day (commemoration of John Adams's introduction of resolution concerning the national flag) (legal holiday in Pennsylvania)

❦ HOLY DAYS   Richard Baxter (CY commem.); formerly Basil the Great (RC; see *1 Jan.)

Richard Baxter (1615–91), a largely self-taught Shropshire man who came to London in 1633 but left in disgust at the frivolity of court life to study divinity; in 1641 he became curate at Kidderminster. He did his best to ignore sectarian differences in pastoral cooperation with other local ministers; a moderate Puritan, he rejected episcopacy, but also opposed both the Solemn League and Covenant with the Scots Presbyterians and the Independency of Cromwell, nor was he sympathetic to republicans and sectaries. In 1650 he wrote a classic of devotional literature, *The Saints' Everlasting Rest*, in 1656 *Gildas Salvianus: The Reformed Pastor*; these are only two works among nearly 200. Having played no small part in the recall of Charles II, he was offered the bishopric of Hereford, but on declining it from dislike of episcopacy was deprived of his living and debarred from ecclesiastical office. At the Savoy Conference of 1661 he presented the Puritan 'Exceptions' or objections to the 1604 Prayer Book, together with a 'Reformed Liturgy', but could wring few concessions from the High Churchmen; even a man of his moderation thereafter suffered persecution, intensified in the early years of James II, but the Toleration Act that followed the Glorious Revolution put him at peace with authority.

In middis of Iune, that ioly sweit seasoun,
Quhen that fair Phebus with his bemis bricht
Had dryit up the dew fra daill and doun,
And all the land maid with his lemis licht,
In ane mornyng betuix mid day and nicht
I rais and put all sleuth and skip asyde,
And to ane wod I went allone but gyde.

Sweit wes the smell off flouris quhyte and reid,
The noyes off birdis richt delitious,
The bewis braid blomit abone my heid,
The ground growand with gresis gratious;
Off all plesance that place wes plenteous,
With sweit odouris and birdis harmony;
The morning myld; my mirth wes mair for thy.

The rosis reid arrayit rone and ryce,
The prymeros and the purpour viola;
To heir it wes ane poynt off paradice,
Sic mirth the mauis and the merle couth ma;
The blossummis blythe brak vp on bank and bra;
The smell off herbis and the fowlis cry,
Contending quha suld have the victory.

Robert Henryson (*c*.1424–*c*.1506), *The Taill of the Lyoun and the Mous*, Prologue

15 JUNE

a.d. XVII Kalendas Iulias   E

If Saint Vitus' day be rainy weather
it will rain for thirty days together.

❦ HOLIDAYS AND ANNIVERSARIES USA: Arkansas: Admission Day (25th State, 1836)
USA, Delaware: Separation Day
USA, Idaho: Pioneer Day (first white settlement at Franklin, 1860)

❦ ANCIENT ROME This was the day for cleansing the round temple of Vesta in the Forum; the filth was removed to the Tiber, after which the *penus* was closed, the Vestals returned to their normal duties, and the day became available for judicial business. It is therefore marked in Roman calendars Q.ST.D.F., *quando stercus delatum fas*, 'once the dirt has been removed, a lawful day'. Only from this day on was marriage advisable, if one had not wedded before May.

❦ HOLY DAYS

Vitus (Ger. Veit, Fr. Gui), patron saint of Bohemia (d. *c*.303?). One of the Fourteen Aux-iliary Saints. He is believed to have been a child martyr, from Lucania or Sicily; later legend has him, together with his tutor Modestus and his nurse Crescentia, successively boiled in oil, thrown to the lions, and stretched on the rack, yet emerging unscathed to die peacefully at home in Lucania. He was said to cause, or cure, the *Tanzwut* or dan-cing mania in which wild leaps and gyrations, often to music specially requested for the purpose, led to mass fainting especially among girls and young women; the phenome-non has been compared with proceedings at modern rock concerts. Its Italian counter-part was the *tarantella*, which particularly affected the garishly clad young; it is recalled by the 'tarantellas' of nineteenth- and twentieth-century music. This was unjustly blamed on the bite of the tarantula; no doubt the saint was as innocent as the spider, but the name 'St Vitus' dance' has not only remained in use but annexed the nervous disease technically known as 'Sydenham's chorea'. He is patron saint of dancers and by extension actors and comedians. His emblems include the fighting cock. See also *28 June.

> The raging minde of furious folkes doth Vitus pacifie
> And doth restore them to their witte, being calde on speedilie.
>
> Naogeorgus, fo. 38

On this day in 1215, at Runnymede, King John and rebel barons reached formal agree-ment, subsequently recorded in a charter, designed to end the rebellion against his strong but arbitary rule. In this it failed, for neither the king nor the extremists among the rebels intended to abide by it; the so-called 'Army of God' continued to hold Lon-don against their sovereign, who for his part obtained the nullification of the charter from Pope Innocent III—formerly his bitter enemy, but his firm supporter since 1213, when John had recognized him as feudal overlord. The diehards invited the French king's son to conquer England; but their cause had already passed its peak when John's death removed the object of their hatred. The King's Men governing on behalf of his infant son, Henry III, conciliated waverers by issuing a modified charter themselves; the next year saw the decisive defeat of rebels and invaders.

Over the next century there were periodic reissues both of the 'little charter' con-taining the clauses on forests and the 'great charter' (*magna carta*) comprising the others; by the death of Edward I the document had lost its relevance. When in the sixteenth century King John was rehabilitated as a valiant reformer of abuses, particularly in the Church, a charter extorted by bad subjects but denounced by the pope did not fit into the story told in John Bale's play *King Johan* of a great and virtuous prince betrayed by Nobility, Clergy, and Civil Order in league with Rome; nor is it mentioned by

Shakespeare, whose John is both a wicked king and a staunch champion of his country against the Pope and the Frenchman. In the seventeenth century, however, when King John was no longer needed as a Protestant hero, the Charter was invoked against the autocratic rule of the Stuarts, thus becoming the foundation-text of English liberties—those same English liberties that in the eighteenth century the American colonies invoked against the government of George III.

For all the services that the enemies of Charles I had wrung out of the Charter, one man among them was not to be constrained by it. In 1658 Oliver Cromwell committed a former intimate for refusing, and encouraging others to refuse, the payment of a new tax; the undaunted 'Fanatick' made an application for habeas corpus:

Maynard, who was of Council with the Prisoner, demanded his Liberty with great confidence, both upon the illegality of the Commitment, and the illegality of the imposition, as being laid without any lawful Authority. The Judges could not maintain or defend either, and enough declared what their Sentence would be; and therefore the Protector's Atturney required a farther day, to answer what had been urged. Before that day, *Maynard* was committed to the Tower, for presuming to question or make doubt of his Authority; and the Judges were sent for, and severely reprehended for suffering that Licence; when they, with all humility, mention'd the Law and *Magna Charta*, *Cromwell* told them, with terms of contempt, and derision, 'their *Magna Farta* should not controle his Actions; which he knew were for the safety of the Common-wealth.'

Clarendon, bk. xv, §150 (iii. 650)

Little as Clarendon loved Cromwell, he shows a grudging respect for his rough treatment of the party talisman; under Charles II Lord Chief Justice Kelyng used a similar phrase.

16 JUNE

a.d. XVI Kalendas Iulias   F

⁋ HOLIDAYS AND ANNIVERSARIES South Africa: Youth Day, commemorating the uprising in Soweto township by black schoolchildren against the ordinance that they should be taught in Afrikaans; this is celebrated as a major event in the struggle against apartheid

⁋ HOLY DAYS Richard of Chichester (CY; BCP on *3 Apr.)

Julitta of Iconium (Konya in Turkey) is honoured on this day (but on 15 July in the East), together with her 3-year-old son Cyriac, supposedly flung on the ground by a magistrate whose face he had scratched. His name, properly Cyriacus, is variously corrupted to Quiricus, Cyricus, Cyres (as in Newton St Cyres in Devon), and Cyr, as in the name of the great French military academy founded by Napoleon in 1808 at Saint-Cyr-l'École (Yvelines), on the site of a girls' school founded in 1686 by Mme de Maintenon. The so-called *Decretum Gelasianum*, however (see *21 Nov.), in upholding the traditional prohibition on reading saints' lives in church, singles out 'the passions of one Quiricus and Julitta, of George and others, which are thought to have been composed by heretics'.

Bloomsday, the day in the life of Leopold Bloom, 16 June 1904, described by James Joyce in *Ulysses*; celebrated annually in Dublin by a tour of the public houses, hotels, and shops in Dublin where Bloom stopped, beginning with the South Bank Restaurant in Sandycove.

David Norris, a senior lecturer in English at Trinity College Dublin, was responsible for rekindling interest in Bloom's journey in the late 1960s. 'I dressed up in a straw hat and, with a silver cane, walked through Dublin and read from the book. Everyone thought I was mad, but it seems to have caught on.'   *The Times*, 17 June 1994

17 JUNE

a.d. XV Kalendas Iulias   G

❨ HOLIDAYS AND ANNIVERSARIES   Iceland: Independence Day (from Denmark, 1944)
   USA, Boston, Massachusetts: Bunker Hill Day (Suffolk County, Massachusetts): commemorates Battle of Bunker Hill, 1775

❨ HOLY DAYS   Alban (BCP; CY on *22 June)

Nectan, sixth-century Welsh hermit killed by thieves whom he was endeavouring to convert; he then carried his head half a mile to the spring by his hut. Similar tales are told of several saints, having become a commonplace among hagiographers determined to show that their subject was as mighty a saint as any other; the motif is due to literal-minded misinterpretation of instructional pictures in which the holding of the severed head symbolizes martyrdom, as when St Agatha holds her breasts or St Lucy her eyes.

Moling, d. 697, abbot at Timolin (*Tigh Moling*, St Mullin's), Co. Carlow. He is said to have initiated the ferry across the River Barrow (Bearbha), won a debate with the Devil, and owned a pet fox. One night, when fishing, he reputedly caught a huge salmon in his net and opening it found a bar of gold, which he split into three parts, giving one to the poor, using another to make reliquaries, and spending the third on good works.

Botulph, founder in 654 of the Benedictine monastery of Icanhoe in Boston (Botulphston) in Lincolnshire, of which only the 'Boston Stump' remains; after Lincolnshire had been conquered by the Vikings, his cult extended to Scandinavia. In 1276 the opening of the Norwegian *lagting* was assigned to this day; however, 'Botolv' was taken for a woman's name, so that he was represented in primestaves by a female head or figure.

On this day in 1953 East Berlin workers rebelled against the Soviet-imposed government of the 'German Democratic Republic'; the event was commemorated in the Federal Republic as the Day of German Unity until the reunification of 1990 (see *3 Oct.).

18 JUNE

a.d. XIV Kalendas Iulias A

❲ HOLIDAYS AND ANNIVERSARIES Seychelles: National Day

❲ HOLY DAYS Formerly Ephraem the Syrian, Deacon (now *9 June)

Copts celebrate on 11 Ba'ūna (5 June OS) the fall of a miraculous drop of water into the Nile; their ancestors had believed that the inundation was caused by the tears of Isis.

On this day in 1815 the British army and its allies from the Low Countries, led by the Duke of Wellington, faced Napoleon, Emperor of the French, who had escaped from exile in Elba to resume power. The battle was keenly fought; but at last Wellington, joined late in the day by Field Marshal Blücher's Prussians, was able to order a general advance and drive the French from the field. This was the end of Napoleon's Hundred Days.

> There sunk the greatest, not the worst of men,
> Whose spirit, antithetically mixt,
> One moment of the mightiest, and again
> On little objects with like firmness fixt;
> Extreme in all things! hadst thou been betwixt,
> Thy throne had still been thine, or never been;
> For daring made thy rise as fall: thou seek'st
> Even now to re-assume the imperial mien,
> And shake again the world, the Thunderer of the scene!
>
> Byron, *Childe Harold's Pilgrimage*, III. xxxvi

In Germany (but naturally not in France) the battle is sometimes known, as Blücher had wished, as 'La Belle Alliance', politically auspicious but in fact the name of a nearby farm; Wellington preferred to style it after his own headquarters at Waterloo. From that day to this, Britons have tended to think of the victory as their own, forgetting the co-operation that the other name might have symbolized; in *The Wellingtoniad*, an epic poem satirically imagined by Macaulay as composed in the year 2824, 'The arrival of the Prussians, from a motive of patriotism, the poet completely passes over.' For compensation, Prussians, and then Germans, preferred to see the battle as Blücher's rescue of the beaten British; this too is an oversimplification, although Wellington himself admitted he had never before been so close to defeat. The French are more even-handed as between their enemies upon that dismal plain, preferring to blame higher forces: in the bloody clash between Europe and France, says Victor Hugo in his noble lament for the French dead, God betrayed the heroes' hopes, Victory deserted, and Fate was weary:

> Waterloo! Waterloo! Waterloo! morne plaine!
>
> .   .   .   .
>
> D'un côté c'est l'Europe et de l'autre la France.
> Choc sanglant! des héros Dieu trompait l'espérance;
> Tu désertais, Victoire, et le sort était las.
>
> 'L'Expiation', *Les Châtiments*, v. xiii

19 JUNE

a.d. XIII Kalendas Iulias   B

❦ HOLIDAYS AND ANNIVERSARIES   USA, Texas: Emancipation Day

❦ ANCIENT ROME   There was a sacrifice to Minerva in her temple on the Aventine (cf. *19 Mar.).

❦ HOLY DAYS   Romuald, Abbot of Camaldoli (RC); Jude, brother of James brother of the Lord, author of the Epistle (Orth.; see *28 Oct.)

Romuald, born *c*.952 at Ravenna, led a worldly life before becoming a Benedictine monk of Sant'Apollinare in Classe; having left to become a hermit, he was appointed abbot by the emperor Otto III in 998, but resigned the next year and set about founding hermitages. Amongst these was Camaldoli, north of Arezzo, the home of the Camaldolese Order. He died on this day in 1027.

Gervase and Protase, protomartyrs of Milan. Their dates are unknown; Ambrose discovered their bodies in 386, and miracles were recorded during the removal of their relics from the church of Nabor and Felix to the cathedral. Ambrose himself wished to be buried with them; the porphyry sarcophagus can be seen today. Weather proverbs similar to St Swithun's forty days attach to their day:

> S'il pleut le jour de Saint Gervais
> Et de Saint Protais,
> Il pleut quarante jours après.

Juneteenth, the anniversary of emancipation day in Texas, declared 19 June 1865, when Major-General Gordon Granger arrived in Galveston as commander of the District of Texas after the Civil War. It was regularly celebrated by the Black population until the 1940s, and has been sporadically revived since then.

20 JUNE

a.d. XII Kalendas Iulias   C

❦ HOLIDAYS AND ANNIVERSARIES USA, West Virginia: Admission Day (35th state, 1863)

❦ ANCIENT ROME This was the dedication-day of the temple near the Circus Maximus in the name of Summanus, 'whoever he is', says Ovid; he was generally held responsible for lightning by night, and Jupiter by day (*7 Oct.), but it is not clear whether he was an ancient Latin deity in his own right or an epithet of Jupiter that took on a life of its own when his statue on top of Jupiter Best and Greatest's temple on the Capitol was struck by lightning c.278 BC. Summanus' own temple was struck in 197 BC; the bad marksmanship of the thunder-god who hit his own temple was a commonplace of irreligious humour.

❦ HOLY DAYS Translation of Edward, king of the West Saxons (BCP) (see *18 Mar.); Alban (RC England and Wales; see *22 June)

Silverius (d. 537), pope, son of Pope Hormisdas, and like him on good terms with the Gothic rulers of Italy, but in changed political circumstances, when the loyalty of the Roman Church against Byzantium was no longer to be relied on; he was a subdeacon when in 536 King Theodahad forced the clergy to elect him pope. Nevertheless, a few months later, Silverius joined the senators in persuading the Romans to surrender their city without a fight to the Byzantine general Belisarius; this did him no good, for the empress Theodora had her own candidate for the papacy, the deacon Vigilius, who had undertaken to restore the Monophysite patriarch of Constantinople, deposed by the late pope Agapitus. When Silverius refused to stand down in Vigilius' favour, he was accused, on the basis of forged letters, of plotting to open the city's gates to the Goths, who were then besieging it. Belisarius deposed him, and deported him to an island off Asia Minor; the local bishop protested to the emperor Justinian, who returned him to Italy for fair trial, with reinstatement if acquitted or redeployment to another see if convicted. Vigilius, now pope, was having none of it: he arranged that Silverius should be delivered into his own custody, dispatched him to an island off the coast of Italy, and forced him to make a formal abdication. Soon afterwards Silverius died, and began, so it was said, to work miracles from his tomb; Vigilius remained pope for eighteen years, came in his turn into conflict with Justinian, and after a period of resistance surrendered the faith of the West to the political compromises of the East.

On this day in 1837 Queen Victoria, having come of age a month before, succeeded her uncle William IV, beginning a reign of nearly sixty-four years that was to revive the prestige of the monarchy and coincide with the greatest increase in national wealth and power ever achieved by Great Britain in such a period.

21 JUNE

a.d. XI Kalendas Iulias   D

❰ HOLIDAYS AND ANNIVERSARIES
HRH Prince William born 1982

❰ HOLY DAYS Aloysius Gonzaga (RC)

Aloysius Gonzaga (1568–91), Jesuit. As the son of a marquis, he had been destined to join
the military, but a childhood kidney disease left him time for pious reading and contemplation, and he decided to become a Jesuit rather than a courtier (his mother was
lady-in-waiting to the queen of Spain). Never in good health, he caught the plague
while nursing victims, and died at the age of 23. Benedict XIII declared him patron of
students in Jesuit colleges in 1729, and in 1926 Pius XI proclaimed him patron of Christian youth.

Alban of Mainz, martyred during the Vandal sack of Mainz in 406. Not to be confused
with the British St Alban.

Translation of St Werburg's relics to Chester (feast-day *3 Feb.), formerly marked with
a fair that extended until Midsummer's Day. In 1770 Thomas Pennant visited Chester
Cathedral, the site of the former abbey of St Werburg:

This abby afforded only a temporary sanctuary to the profligate. The privilege which *Hugh Lupus*
[the first earl] granted is particular: he ordered, that no thief or other malefactor, that attended
the fair held at the feast of St. *Werburgh*, should be attached, unless he committed some new
offence there. This, says [the antiquarian Daniel] *King*, drew a vast concourse of loose people together at that season, and proved of singular advantage to *Randle the third*, earl of *Chester*; who, in
being surrounded in the castle of *Rudland* [Rhuddlan] by a numerous army of *Welsh*, and in great
danger, sent for relief to his general, *Roger Lacy*, at that time attending the midsummer-fair. *Lacy*
instantly collected a body of minstrels, fiddlers, and idle people, who were assembled here on
account of this privilege; marched with them into *Wales*, and relieved the earl from his distress.
Randle, on his return, immediately rewarded *Lacy* with a full power over all the instruments of his
preservation, *magisterium omnium lecatorum et meretricum totius* CESTRESHIRE. By this grant he was
empowered to require the attendance of all the minstrels and musicians of the county on the
anniversary of the exploit. They were to play before him and his heirs for ever, in a procession
to the church of St. *John*; and, after divine service, to the place where he kept his court.

                                                          Pennant, *Wales*, 184–5

Longest Day, the normal date of the summer solstice.

22 JUNE

❰ HOLY DAYS Alban (CY; RC until 1969, now locally 20 June; BCP on 17 June); Paulinus of Nola (RC); John Fisher (RC; CY on 6 July); Thomas More (RC; CY on *6 July)

Alban, first martyr of Britain, *c.*209. Alban, burgher of Verulamium, now called St Albans, was converted by a fugitive priest; when the authorities got wind of his presence, Alban abetted his escape by changing clothes with him. The first account of his martyrdom ascribes it to the reign of Septimius Severus (193–211), not as in later authors Diocletian. The BCP date of the 17th is commonly supposed to be a misreading of xxii as xvii, but a Veronese calendar of *c.*900 puts 'in Brittania sancti Albini [*sic*] martyris' on both the 17th (XV Kal. Iul.) and the 22nd (X Kal. Iul.).

His legend, recorded from the fifth century onwards, abounded in miracles: in his haste to be martyred he parted the River Ver, thereby converting the executioner, who cast away his sword; having reached the place of execution, he asked for water, whereupon a spring appeared at his feet; he was then beheaded together with the intended executioner by a soldier whose eyes fell out and struck the ground at the same time as the saint's head. In the twelfth century the fugitive priest acquired a legend of his own; see *25 June.

Paulinus of Nola, from a noble Aquitanian family, educated at Bordeaux, *c.*390 underwent a spiritual crisis that caused him to abandon secular poetry; this dismayed his former teacher, the poet Ausonius, himself a Christian of a more relaxed persuasion. He became a priest and took up a monastic life near the tomb of St Felix (*14 Jan.) at Nola in Campania, to whom he built a new church; the assertion that this gave rise to the late Latin terms for 'bell', *campana* and *nola,* is without foundation. He continued to write poetry, but on Christian themes, most notably the praise of St Felix.

John Fisher, bishop of Rochester, anti-Lutheran polemicist and foremost defender of Queen Catherine, was executed on this day in 1535 for refusing the oath of allegiance to the children of Henry VIII and Anne Boleyn; he is celebrated as a saint by Roman Catholics together with Sir Thomas More, the former chancellor, who was executed on *6 July for the same cause.

> *An English Martyr*
> *Tower of London, 1535*
>
> Now winter and all death are past.
> Returning birds, returning leaves
> And sun returning: can it be
> That any heart this morning grieves?
>
> And surely none grieves less than mine
> Which in an hour shall beat no more.

O men unborn who, looking back,
Count me dishonoured and most poor,

I need no tears: I leave behind
All change of seasons and of men,
The pomp and treachery of kings,
Corruption, agony and sin.

The fine and running sand that marks
The hour sifts down within the glass.
A little longer and it's spent:
So lightly may this spirit pass.

And warmth of sunlight falling still
Upon this hewn, this bitter stone,
I take as greeting from my Lord
And rise up joyful to be gone.

            Philip Martin (1931–   )

It is right and proper for Roman Catholics to celebrate these martyrs; but Anglicans should remember that had they prevailed there would be no such thing as Anglicanism.

Martyrdom of Titus Flavius Clemens, consul AD 95, cousin of the emperor Domitian, whose niece Flavia Domitilla he had married; in 96 he was put to death and Domitilla banished for Jewish sympathies that appear to have had a Christian tinge. The murder hardened determination to be rid of Domitian; the ever more suspicious tyrant, who famously complained that no one believed reports of plots unless the emperor was assassinated, fell victim to one before the year was out. The first blow was struck by Domitilla's steward, who had been charged with embezzlement.

Acacius the Soldier, said to have been martyred with 10,000 companions on Mount Ararat in Armenia, one of the Fourteen Auxiliary Saints. Acacius and his men were popular at the time of the Crusades, along with other warrior saints such as Maurice (see *22 Sept.), but were removed from the calendar in 1969 as purely legendary. Their cult was especially widespread in Germany and Switzerland. The name is often spelt 'Achatius'.

Among the Copts, this is 15 Ba'ūna (9 June OS), known as *Laylat al-saraṭān,* the Night of the Crab, when the Sun enters Cancer; charms are hung on walls to drive away insects.

23 JUNE

a.d. IX Kalendas Iulias   F

❦ HOLIDAYS AND ANNIVERSARIES   Latvia: Midsummer Eve
  Luxembourg: National Day (also official birthday of Grand Duke Jean)

❦ HOLY DAYS   Etheldreda, Abbess of Ely (CY; BCP 17 Oct.)

Etheldreda (Audrey, Æthelthryth; d. 679), daughter of Anna king of the East Angles, retired between two unconsummated marriages to the life of prayer on a marshy island
known from its abundance of eels as Ely; eventually permitted by her second husband
to become a nun, she founded a double monastery there, remaining abbess till her death.
The RC Church commemorates her on this day as well. For the fair formerly held on
the feast of her translation, which gave rise to the word 'tawdry', see *17 October.

Midsummer Eve. Midsummer Eve and Day were traditionally a time of great revelry. On
the Eve it was customary throughout Europe to make bonfires (to chase away dragons,
some said) and often to roll a wheel (sometimes aflame) down a hill; this has been explained as representing the sun, which reaches its highest point and then falls back along
the same points of the horizon as it touched when rising. Fires were lit in fields, and
cattle sometimes driven through them.

The monk of Winchcomb (Gloucestershire) records all three activities as early as the
thirteenth century:

> Let us speak of the revels which are accustomed to be made on St. John's Eve, of which there are
> three kinds. On St. John's Eve in certain regions the boys collect bones and certain other rub-
> bish, and burn them, and therefore a smoke is produced on the air. They also make brands and
> go about the fields with the brands. Thirdly, the wheel which they roll, which, with the rubbish
> they burn, they have from the pagans . . . The wheel is turned to signify that the sun then ascends
> to the highest point of its circle and immediately goes back.   Kemble, i. 361–2

John Aubrey thought that fires in the fields were intended to bless the apples; as usual,
he traced the origin to the source that he knew best, the myths and usages of classical
antiquity:

> Memorandum in Herefordshire, and also in Somersetshire, on Midsommer-eve, they make fires
> in the fields in the waies: sc. to Blesse the Apples. I have seen the same custome in Somerset, 1685,
> but there they doe it only for custome-sake; but I doe guesse that this custome is derived from
> the Gentiles, who did it in remembrance of Ceres her running up and downe with Flambeaux in
> search of her daughter Proserpina, ravist away by Pluto; and the people might thinke, that by
> this honour donne to yᵉ Goddesse of husbandry, that their Corne, &c. might prosper the better.
>   Aubrey, 96–7

More recent writers, often with little better judgement, have invoked Celtic—usually
Irish—precedent as a reach-me-down explanation; in fact, there is no evidence that
Midsummer was a Celtic festival before the Middle Ages, though it certainly became
one thereafter. Rituals of lighting bonfires and dancing round or leaping through them
are extremely widespread in Europe; in Vestlandet, Norway, wooden contrivances
known as 'old man' (*kall*) or 'old woman' (*kjerring*) were burnt, and a make-believe wedding (*jonsokbryllaup*) was celebrated between adults or children. These fires are still burnt
in Brazil, and hot-air balloons carried, although it is the winter, not the summer, solstice.

Midsummer Watch. Originally instituted to damp down rowdiness on Midsummer Eve,
it developed into an occasion for grand parades, especially by the guilds, often with

elaborate pageants. The London parade was abolished by Henry VIII in 1539, but survived in the Lord Mayor's Show, originally on the feast-day of SS Simon and Jude, then moved to *9 November (see also *Other Holidays). Stow describes its celebration in the sixteenth century:

On the vigil of St. John the Baptist, and on St. Peter and Paul the Apostles, every man's door being shadowed with green birch, long fennel, St. John's wort, orpin, white lilies, and such like, garnished upon with garlands of beautiful flowers, had also lamps of glass, with oil burning in them all the night; some hung out branches of iron curiously wrought, containing hundreds of lamps alight at once, which made a goodly show, namely, in New Fish Street, Thames Street, &c. Then had ye besides the standing watches all in bright harness, in every ward and street of this city and suburbs, a marching watch, that passed through the principal streets thereof . . . The marching watch contained in number about two thousand men, part of them being old soldiers of skill, to be captains, lieutenants, sergeants, corporals, &c., whifflers, drummers, and fifes, standard and ensign bearers, sword players, trumpeters on horseback, demilances on great horses, gunners with hand guns, or half hakes, archers in coats of white fustian, signed on the breast and back with the arms of the city, their bows bent in their hands, with sheaves of arrows by their sides, pikemen in bright corslets, burganets, &c., halberds, the like billmen in almaine rivets, and aprons of mail in great number; there were also divers pageants, morris dancers, constables . . .

Stow, 126–8 (1598)

Fern seed gathered on Midsummer night was reputed to make one invisible:

GADSHILL. We have the recipe of fern-seed, we walk invisible.
CHAMBERLAIN. Nay, by my faith, I think you are more beholden to the night than to
    fern-seed for your walking invisible.   *1 Henry IV*, II. i. 86–90

As with all fast-days, many superstitions were prevalent on Midsummer Eve, especially concerning divination of the future. We quote only some early ones and those having to do with the plant orpine, called 'Midsummer-men'; others, involving apple seeds, hemp seeds, ashes, shoes, dumb-cake, smocks, etc. are similar to those recorded under *31 October.

'Tis *Midsommer-night*, or Midsommer-eve (S^t Jo: Baptist) is counted or called the *Witches night*. q. M^{ris} Fincher, &c., of the breaking of Hen-egges this night, in which they may see what their fortune will be.   Aubrey, 133

I remember, the mayds (especially the Cooke mayds & Dayrymayds) would stick-up in some chinkes of the joists or &c.: Midsommer-men, wch are slips of Orpins. they placed them by Paires, sc.: one for such a man, the other for such a mayd his sweet-heart, and accordingly as the Orpin did incline to, or recline from ye other, that there would be love, or aversion; if either did wither, death.   Aubrey, 25–6

Midsummer Eve was also suited to cures:

Yf ony woman wyll that her husbande, or her paramoure loue her well, she ought to put in his shoo a lefe of brekens that had ben gadred on saynt Johans euen whyles that they rynge none, so that it be in the lefte shoo, and without faute he shall loue her meruaylously.

Gospelles of Dystaues (1520), sig. Di^r

Take on Midsummer-night, at xii., when all the planets are above the earth, a Serpent and kill him; and skinne him; and dry it in the shade and bring it to a powder. Hold it in your hand and you will be invisible. This Receit is in Johannes de Florentià (a Rosycrusian) a booke in 8° in high Dutch. Dr. Ridgeley the Physitian hath it, who told me of this.   Aubrey, 53–4

How to get around a stingy husband:

Yf ye haue a husbande rebell the which wyll gyue you no money at your nede, take the fyrste knotte of a whete strawe, but it must be gadered nere the erthe upon saynt Johannes euen whyles that they rynge none, and put y^t in the keye hole of the coffre, and withouten faute it shall ones open.   *Gospelles of Dystaues*, sig. E_3^r

Like St Mark's Eve (see *24 Apr.), Midsummer Eve was the time to watch for apparitions:

Memorandum y^e sitting-up on Midsommer-eve in y^e churche porch to see the Apparitions of those that should dye or be buried there, that yeare: mostly used by women: I have heard 'em tell strange stories of it. Now, was not Ceres mother-in-law to Pluto, King of the infernal Ghosts? and Virgil makes Æneas to sacrifice a barren cowe to Proserpine for his trumpeter Misenus, 'sterilemq. tibi Proserpina, vaccam.'   Aubrey, 97

The first Henley Regatta took place on 23 June 1775:

Lady Montague's description of a regatta, or *fête* held on the water, which she witnessed at Venice, stimulated the English people of fashion to have something of a similar kind on the Thames, and after much preparation and several disappointments, caused by unfavourable weather, the long expected show took place on the 23rd of June 1775. The programme, which was submitted to the public a month before, requested ladies and gentlemen to arrange their own parties, except those who should apply to the managers of the Regatta for seats in the barges lent by the several City Companies for the occasion. The rowers were to be uniformly dressed in accordance with the three marine colours—white, red, and blue. . . .

Early in the afternoon, the river, from London Bridge to Millbank, was crowded with pleasure boats, and scaffolds, gaily decorated with flags, were erected wherever a view of the Thames could be obtained. Half-a-guinea was asked for a seat in a coal-barge; and vessels fitted for the purpose drove a brisk trade in refreshments of various kinds. The avenues to Westminster Bridge were covered with gaming-tables, and constables guarded every passage to the water, taking from half-a-crown to one penny for liberty to pass. Soon after six o'clock, concerts were held under the arches of Westminster Bridge; and a salute of twenty-one cannons announced the arrival of the Lord Mayor. A race of wager-boats followed, and then the procession moved in a picturesque irregularity to Ranelagh. The ladies were dressed in white, the gentlemen in undress frocks of all colours; about 200,000 persons were supposed to be on the river at one time.

The company arrived at Ranelagh at nine o'clock, where they joined those who came by land in a new building, called the Temple of Neptune. This was a temporary octagon, lined with stripes of white, red, and blue cloth, and having lustres hanging between each pillar. Supper and dancing followed, and the entertainment did not conclude till the next morning. Many accidents occurred when the boats were returning after the *fête*, and seven persons were unfortunately drowned.   Chambers

Farthing Loaf Day at Kidderminster, 1831:

A *farthing loaf* is given, on Midsummer-eve, to every person *born* in *Church-street*, Kidderminster, who chooses to claim it, whether they be rich or poor, child or adult. And let not the reader contemn the smallness of the boon. The bequest is of very ancient standing; and the farthing loaf, at the time of its date, was of jolly proportions, far different to the minims which are prepared expressly for this occasion at the present time. The donor was a benevolent old maid, who, no doubt, intended to confer a benefit on the denizens of Church-street, Kiddermister, and had she lived in these days, and had understood the subtleties of the currency question, would doubtless have bestowed it in a less ludicrous shape. The day is called Farthing Loaf Day, and the bakers' shops are amply furnished with these diminutives, as it is the practice of the inhabitants through-out the town to purchase them.   Hone, *Year*, 373

St John's Eve. Washington Irving relates a legend concerning the last army of Muslim Granada:

'This', said the trooper, 'is a great and fearful mystery. Know, O Christian, that you see before you the court and army of Boabdil the last king of Granada.'

'What is this you tell me?' cried I, 'Boabdil and his court were exiled from the land hundreds of years agone, and all died in Africa.'

'So it is recorded in your lying chronicles,' replied the Moor, 'but know that Boabdil and the warriors who made the last struggle for Granada were all shut up in the mountain by powerful enchantment. As for the king and army that marched forth from Granada at the time of the sur-render, they were a mere phantom train of spirits and demons, permitted to assume those shapes to deceive the Christian sovereigns. And furthermore let me tell you, friend, that all Spain is a country under the power of enchantment. There is not a mountain cave, not a lonely watchtower in the plains, nor ruined castle on the hills, but has some spell-bound warriors sleeping from age to age within its vaults, until the sins are expiated for which Allah permitted the dominion to pass for a time out of the hands of the faithful. Once every year, on the eve of St. John, they are released from enchantment, from sunset to sunrise, and permitted to repair here to pay homage to their sovereign! . . . It is written in the book of fate, that when the enchantment is broken, Boabdil will descend from the mountain at the head of this army, resume his throne in the Alhambra and his sway of Granada, and gathering together the enchanted warriors, from all parts of Spain, will reconquer the Peninsula and restore it to Moslem rule.'   Irving, 654–5

Sir Walter Scott's ballad tells of a lady who invited to visit her at midnight on St John's Eve her lover, as she thought, but in fact his ghost, whom three days earlier her husband had killed instead of taking part in the battle of Ancram Moor (in fact fought on 17 Feb. 1545) against English invaders:

> The Baron return'd in three days space,
>   And his looks were sad and sour;
> And weary was his courser's pace,
>   As he reach'd his rocky tower.
>
> He came not from where Ancram Moor
>   Ran red with English blood;
> Where the Douglas true and the bold Buccleuch
>   'Gainst keen Lord Evers stood.
>
> Yet was his helmet hack'd and hew'd,
>   His acton pierced and tore,
> His axe and his dagger with blood imbrued,—
>   But it was not English gore.
>
>   .   .   .   .
>
> 'By the Baron's brand, near Tweed's fair strand,
>   Most foully slain I fell;
> And my restless sprite on the beacon's height
>   For a space is doom'd to dwell. . . .'

On this evening, in old Belorussia, girls washed in dew, then went to bed silently to receive prophetic dreams; the festival was particularly popular in the Baltic region.

24 JUNE

a.d. VIII Kalendas Iulias   G

> Why, this is very midsummer madness.
>
> Olivia, in *Twelfth Night*, III. iv. 54

> *At Midsommer, downe with the brembles and brakes,*
> *and after, abrode with thy forks and thy rakes:*
> *Set mowers a mowing, where meadow is growne,*
> *the longer now standing the worse to be mowne.*
>
> Tusser

❦ HOLIDAYS AND ANNIVERSARIES In many countries this is kept as St John's Day or Midsummer's Day.

Macao: Macao Day (defeat of Dutch invasion, 1622; St John is the patron saint of Macao)

Spain: King Juan Carlos's Saint's Day

UK (except Scotland): Midsummer Quarter Day

❦ ANCIENT ROME Fors Fortuna, a goddess of good luck much beloved of the common people, was worshipped at temples in Trastevere, where many of them lived then as now.

❦ HOLY DAYS **Nativity of St John the Baptist** (BCP); **Birth of St John the Baptist** (CY, RC); red-letter day

John the Baptist is patron saint of Jordan, Florence, Genoa, and Turin. He is also patron saint of spas, and has been mooted as potential patron of motorways, recalling his words 'Make straight the ways of the Lord'. See also *29 August.

Midsummer's Day. The term 'midsummer' is first found in the Old English translation of Bede's *Ecclesiastical History*, where mention is made of the quarter in which the sun rises at the solstice; Bede's *solstitialem* becomes 'æt middum sumere'. It was applied to the great Christian celebration of the Baptist's birth, just as the feast kept six months later became Midwinter or Midwinter's Mass (rarely Christmas till after the Norman Conquest). Those who consider the seasons to begin with the cardinal days find it hard to understand how Midsummer's Day can fall only three days after the solstice; the story is told of a frustrated American tourist who reported on a postcard home his experience of an English summer: 'Had no luck—it rained *both* days.'

St John's Day. Legend had it that St John the Evangelist died on this day, but was not culted on it because it was already dedicated to the Baptist. This did not mean the Baptist was the greater saint; when two doctors of theology, one devoted to the Baptist and the other to the Evangelist, announced a formal disputation to determine which John was the greater, each saint appeared to his supporter with the message: 'We are good friends in heaven, do not dispute about us on earth.'

In Lazio St John was believed to be the protector of witches, who broomsticked into Rome in his honour; men wore sorghum in their buttonholes, or carried cloves of garlic in their pockets, and rang a cowbell to ward them off. At first light they returned to the walnut tree at Benevento that served all the witches of Italy as their meeting-point. As in other Christian countries, faith in the Devil and his disciples has dwindled; but more wholesome customs remain, such as forgathering in *osterie* near S. Giovanni in Laterano to eat *lumache alla romana.* (The poor used to take their snails home in big earthenware pots under a cloth to eat in the surrounding to the basilica; they were therefore called *fagottari* or 'brown-baggers'.)

Not surprisingly, rain is unwelcome:

> Baptistae fuerit cum lux pluviosa Ioannis
> Ingrati messis plena laboris erit.
>
> Buchler 308 (1602)

> When rain the holy Baptist's day doth spoil,
> The harvest will be full of hateful toil.

Naogeorgus records German customs on this day in the sixteenth century:

> Then doth the ioyfull feast of John the Baptist take his turne,
> When bonfiers great with loftie flame, in every towne doe burne:
> And yong men round about with maides, doe daunce in every streete,
> With garlands wrought of Motherwort, or else with Vervain sweete,
> And many other flowres faire, with Violets in their handes,
> Whereas they all do fondly thinke, that whosoever standes,
> And thorow the flowres beholds the flame, his eyes shall feele no paine.
> When thus till night they daunced have, they through the fire amaine
> With striving mindes doe runne, and all their hearbes they cast therin,
> And then with wordes devout and prayers, they solemnely begin,
> Desiring God that all their illes may there consumed bee,
> Whereby they thinke through all that yeare, from Agues to be free.
> Some others get a rotten wheele, all worne and cast aside,
> Which covered round about with strawe, and tow, they closely hide:
> And caryed to some mountaines top, being all with fire light,
> They hurle it downe with violence, when darke appeares the night:
> Resembling much the Sunne, that from the heavens downe should fal,
> A straunge and monstrous sight it seemes, and fearefull to them all:
> But they suppose their mischiefes all are likewise throwne to hell,
> And that from harmes and daungers now, in safetie here they dwell.

Among the classics of Russian poetry is a translation of Scott's ballad 'The Eve of Saint John' (see *23 June) by Vasilii Zhukovsky; its publication in 1824 was held up by the censors, who objected to the portrayal of adulterous love at so holy a time, until 'St John's Day' (*Ivánov den'*) had been changed for a 'Duncan's Day' (*Dunkánov den'*) unknown to any calendar, but recalling Scotland through Shakespeare. In fact it was another king of Scots who made this day illustrious: on 24 June 1314 at Bannockburn the Scottish army under Robert I (the Bruce) routed Edward II's much larger English force.

25 JUNE

a.d. VII Kalendas Iulias   A

❲ HOLIDAYS AND ANNIVERSARIES Mozambique: Independence Day (from Portugal, 1975)
Slovenia: Independence Day (from Yugoslavia, 1991)

❲ ANCIENT ROME Every four years the Ludi Taurei were held in the Circus Flaminius; they appear to have been of Etruscan origin, and involved horse races round a turning-post. They were allegedly instituted under Tarquin the Proud in the late sixth century BC after beef sold to the public (perhaps after sacrifice) had caused an epidemic among pregnant women.

❲ HOLY DAYS

Amphibalus, the fugitive priest who took refuge with St Alban (see *22 June); the name, which means 'cloak' and alludes to the priestly vestment that Alban donned in his stead, was invented in 1136 by Geoffrey of Monmouth, who found the word in an account of a dynast in Devon who according to Gildas (*c.*540) had just committed an atrocity in church 'under a holy abbot's cloak' (*sub sancti abbatis amphibalo*). Notwithstanding this un-prepossessing origin, within half a century Amphibalus had become a substantial figure: his bones were discovered at St Albans on the Friday before the patron's day and solemnly translated to the church, so Matthew Paris relates, 'in the 886th year from his passion', on Saturday, 25 June 1177 (though since the entire tale is registered under the year 1178 one might have expected 24 June 1178); a monk named William, commissioned by Abbot Simon to write the new saint's life, responded with a stirring tale that he claimed to have translated from a book in English itself transcribed (according to its author) in the nick of time from a collapsing wall. We are informed that Amphibalus, having fled to Wales, reconstituted the bodies of 999 martyrs before being stoned to death; the pagans fell out amongst themselves, which allowed a Christian to steal his corpse in frustration of the magistrate's vow to take him dead or alive. Later writers made him a citizen of Caerleon, on the Roman road to Wales, where the martyrs Aaron and Julius had suffered, or the burgomaster of Cambridge; a priory was dedicated to him at Redbourn near St Albans. The similarity of his name to *amphibolus*, 'ambiguous', will not have escaped the sophisticated William, whose learning and piety were not incompatible with humour; Matthew Paris, in writing his own life of St Alban, trumped his dilapidated wall with an ancient book, in beautiful roman script but written in 'British' (i.e. Welsh), or as he later says in 'English', which only an aged priest called Unwona (meaning 'Unusual') could decipher—and translate with total accuracy—before it crumbled into dust.

Lugaidh or Moluag, Pict who set up a monastery on Lismore Island *c.*562 and brought Christianity to Inverness and the Hebrides; died at Rossmarkie. Legend makes him contend for the island with St Columba and prevail by cutting off his thumb and casting it ashore; Columba countered with a curse, evidently to less effect than the norm for Irish saintly curses. A blackthorn staff said to be his (*an Bhachall Mhòr*) is preserved by the Livingstone clan.

Old Style date for the Coptic feast of the martyr Pontius Pilate (see *8 July).

On this day in 1530 the Lutheran confession of faith was presented at Augsburg to the emperor Charles V; it was first published in a slightly amended form in 1531, and thereafter revised in various reissues until 1580, when the so-called *Invariata* edition, more faithful to the text of 1530, was adopted.

26 JUNE

❦ HOLIDAYS AND ANNIVERSARIES   Madagascar: Independence Day (from France, 1960)
United Nations: Charter Day

❦ HOLY DAYS

John and Paul, supposed Roman martyrs, commemorated since the sixth century on the Mons Caelius at Rome, but most notably in the great Dominican church of SS. Giovanni e Paolo at Venice, where doges were traditionally buried. In 1978 the patriarch of Venice, Luciano Albini, on being elected pope, took the name John Paul, which he explained as a tribute to his immediate predecessors, John XXIII and Paul VI; on his unexpected death after only thirty-three days in office, his successor, Karol Wojtyła, took the name John Paul II.

SS John and Paul, however, are most famous as the saints on whose day in 1284 the Pied Piper led 130 children out of the north German town of Hameln into a hill called the Köppe or Koppelberg.

Pied Piper Day. A poem said to have been entered in 1384, exactly 100 years after the event, on the title-page of a now-vanished missal, in Latin so atrocious as to vindicate its authenticity against the suspicion of Renaissance forgery, reports the affliction of men and women in 1284 at the loss of 130 Hameln children on John and Paul's Day: 'It is said that Calvary swallowed them alive; Christ, guard thine own lest so bad an affair do harm to any persons.' *Calvaria*, 'the Place of the Skull', translates *Koppen* or *Koppelberg*, but recalls the scene of the Crucifixion, and is so understood in the first surviving narrative, found in a manuscript note from the 1430s:

A very strange wonder must be related that happened in the town of Hameln, in the diocese of Minden, in the year of our Lord 1284, on John and Paul's Day. A handsome youth of thirty, very well dressed, so that all who saw him wondered at his person and clothing, entered by the bridge and the Weser gate with a silver pipe of strange shape. He began to play his pipe throughout the town, and all the children who heard that pipe, some 130 in number, followed him out of the East Gate as if to the place of Calvary or execution and vanished and departed, so that no one could trace where any one of them might be. The children's mothers ran from town to town, and found absolutely nothing. Hence 'a voice was heard in Rama', and every mother bewailed her own child. And just as one reckons by years of Our Lord or the first, second, or third year after the Jubilee, so in Hameln they reckoned by the first, second, or third year after the exit and departure of the children. I found this in an old book, and the mother of Dean Johann von Lüde watched the children departing.

This last clause no doubt means 'Dean Lüde told me that his mother saw the children leave'; Lüde was dean of the local collegiate church by 1353, and died in 1378. The same hand appends a brief account of a fatal accident, also in Hameln, that took place in 1347, blamed by some on a basilisk, but explained by the author as due to foul air; it is likely that both notes were originally written in the mid-fourteenth century. If so, our text well antedates the poem of 1384; the account in the 'old book' will have been entered while the event, whatever it was, remained in living memory, and perhaps with a date in the form *anno Domini . . . post exitum puerorum*. Such reckoning, though often alleged, was never official practice, though in a city ordinance of 1351 a reference to the departure of the children in 1283 (*sic*) has been added to the date.

In the sixteenth century a number of public and private inscriptions commemorate the event; with minor variations they state that in 1284, on John and Paul's Day, 26 June, 130 Hameln-born children were abducted by a piper clad in all manner of colours and lost at Calvary by the Köppe. The report spread to other parts of Germany, where it was combined with a widespread motif of folktales, not unknown in history, the plague of mice, to produce the familiar story that the Pied Piper, having agreed to rid the town of its rats in consideration of a handsome fee, on being cheated of his money took the children with him in revenge; we first find this expanded narrative in the 1560s, as far away as Bavaria, in the Chronicle of Zimmern. The good burghers of Hameln were not at first pleased with this unauthorized and unflattering addition to their legend; nevertheless, it prevailed, and has long since brought them fame and fortune. There is a ratcatcher collection in the local history museum, and since the 1870s the name *Rattenfängerhaus* has been bestowed on a three-storey half-timbered house, which indeed contains a Pied Piper inscription (with no word of rats), but is some three centuries too late and the least suitable dwelling one could imagine for a strolling player.

In the seventeenth century the story was transmitted to England (where it swiftly became as familiar as in Germany) by the recusant 'Richard Verstegan' (Richard

Rowlands), who adopted from the chronicler Johann Pomarius in 1588 the erroneous date of 22 July 1376, and added the lame boy who escaped to tell the tale and the other children's reappearance in Transylvania; but although a large German population survived there till the 1980s, the colonization had taken place much earlier, in the twelfth century. Careful study of surnames and place-names has suggested the young persons were recruited for the colonization of Brandenburg and Pomerania; but while learned writers have sought a kernel of truth in the legend, creative writers have reinterpreted it. The promised reward has sometimes been not money but the burgomaster's daughter; the Pied Piper has been variously represented as the Devil, a demagogue, an artist who can find no place in society, and a free spirit who does not want one.

Browning's famous poem, which is closest to Verstegan's account, was originally written to amuse a friend's sick son; his own father had enjoyed telling the story, which he versified at least twice.

> Rats!
> They fought the dogs and killed the cats,
>   And bit the babies in the cradles,
> And ate the cheeses out of the vats,
>   And licked the soup from the cooks' own ladles,
> Split open the kegs of salted sprats,
> Made nests inside men's Sunday hats,
> And even spoiled the women's chats
>   By drowning their speaking
>   With shrieking and squeaking
> In fifty different sharps and flats.
>
> *The Pied Piper of Hamelin*, 10–20

27 JUNE

❨ HOLIDAYS AND ANNIVERSARIES   Djibouti: Independence Day (from France, 1977)

❨ ANCIENT ROME   This day was marked by a sacrifice to Lares, whether those of the Roads (Viales) is disputed, and by the dedication-feast of the temple of Jupiter Stator, 'Stopper of the Rout', allegedly vowed by King Romulus but not built till 294 BC. It was in this temple (near where the Arch of Titus was later built) that, at the meeting of the Senate on 8 November 63 BC, Cicero attacked the subversive conspirator Catiline: 'Quousque tandem abutere Catilina patientia nostra?' ('How long, Catiline, will you continue to exploit our tolerance?')

❨ HOLY DAYS   Cyril (RC; CY commem.; Orth. on 9 June)

Cyril, patriarch of Alexandria (412–44), a great theologian, but a man of strife. Three years into his reign, his followers murdered the scholarly philosopher Hypatia, a pagan but no enemy of Christians; amongst her Christian friends, however, was the city prefect Orestes, who was resisting the patriarch's encroachment on his authority until the murder frightened him into flight. As the beneficiary of the crime Cyril was suspected of being its instigator; the imperial government forbore to investigate. He remained a bitter enemy of all who disagreed with him, whether on theological grounds or touching the dignity of his see. Both causes united to spur him into conflict with Nestorius, holder of the upstart bishopric of Constantinople, who denied that the Virgin Mary could be called *Theotókos* ('She who bore God'), since God was not a baby three hours old; the ensuing controversy (in which each used the same terms in different senses, and each read them in the other with the sense he himself would have given them) pitted Nestorius, brought up at Antioch in a tradition that emphasized the humanity of Christ, against both Cyril, whose Alexandrian tradition paid more attention to His divinity, and the popular devotion represented by the title in dispute. A council called to settle the question broke into two, each of which deposed the other party's leader; the emperor ratified both depositions, but Cyril was reinstated after making concessions that some of his followers regretted.

Many German calendars, and the *cisioianus* (see App. D), put the Seven Sleepers on this day instead of *27 July.

28 JUNE

❦ HOLY DAYS Irenaeus (CY, RC); Leo the Great in the Sarum calendar, the Golden Legend, the *cisioianus*, and many monastic calendars (see *10 Nov.)

Irenaeus, bishop of Lyons (*c.*130–200). He came from Asia Minor and became bishop of Lyons *c.*177 in succession to the martyred Pothinus, like whom he was a pupil of Polycarp; as such he was able, *c.*190, to talk Pope Victor I out of excommunicating the Christians of Asia Minor for keeping Easter on the Jewish 14 Nisan (see II: *The Date of Easter: Early Church*) whichever day of the week it fell on. He is chiefly remembered, however, for his treatise attacking the heresies of his day, in particular the various forms of Gnosticism; it was written in Greek, but survives for the most part in Latin translation.

St Peter's Eve. Many towns in earlier times re-enacted midsummer festivities on this day.

Vidovdan, St Vitus' day (15 June Old Style), kept in Serbia as the anniversary of defeat and conquest by the Ottoman Turks at Kosovo Polje ('Blackbird Field') on 15 June 1389, a hard-fought battle in which the supreme commanders on both sides died, commemorated by countless ballads. It was on this day in 1914 that the Bosnian Serb Gavrilo Princip murdered Archduke Franz Ferdinand of Austria at Sarajevo, leading to the First World War. The 600th anniversary of the battle, on 28 June 1989, was marked by a great patriotic rally, at which President Slobodan Milošević of Serbia declared that national integrity was restored; the immediate context was the bitter ethnic conflict in the autonomous region of Kosovo, the heartland of Serbian history but overwhelmingly inhabited by Albanians. Earlier in the decade Serbs had complained of oppression by the Albanian majority, which dominated the regional government; but Milošević abolished Kosovar autonomy, subjecting the Albanians to Serbian rule.

On this day in 1497, as is still remembered in Cornwall, was hanged Michael Joseph, known as *An Gôf* ('the Smith'), ringleader of a rebellion against Henry VII's high taxes.

This Mighell Joseph, surnamed the black smyth one of the capteins of this donge hill and draffe sacked ruffians, was of such stowte stomack and haute courage, that at thesame time that he was drawen on the herdle toward his death, he sayd (as men do reporte) that for this myscheuous and facinorous acte, he should haue a name perpetual and a fame permanent and immortal. So (you may perceaue) that desire and ambicious cupidite of vaine glorie and fame, enflameth, and encourageth aswel poore and meane persones, as the hartes of great lords and puyssant princes to trauayle and aspire to thesame.   *Hall's Chronicle*, 479–80

The event was commemorated in 1997.

29 JUNE

a.d. III Kalendas Iulias   E

❦ HOLY DAYS **Peter, Apostle** (BCP); **Peter and Paul, Apostles** (CY, RC); red-letter day

The day was originally an eastern feast of the Apostles in general, but in Rome was restricted to Peter, the Prince of the Apostles, and Paul, the Apostle *par excellence*; from the year 258 onwards there was an annual commemoration of the two *ad Catacumbas*, at the place on the Via Appia where the church of San Sebastiano now stands, and which has given its name, as 'catacombs', to underground burial-places, especially those of early Christians. The East accepted the new significance of the day; the Apostles as a group were commemorated on Thomas Sunday (the Sunday after Easter), and subsequently on 30 June.

Peter, a fisherman of Bethsaida on the Sea of Galilee, was the dominant personality amongst the Apostles. His true name was 'Simon son of Jonah', with the nickname *qēphā* ('Cephas' in the Bible), Aramaic for 'rock', to which Jesus alluded when he called Peter the rock on whom he would build his church (Matt. 16: 18); the Greek for 'rock' is *petra*, whence the name *Petros*. He was a man of action who in St John's Gospel (18: 10), when

Jesus was arrested, cut off the right ear of the high priest's servant Malchus, but who for all his brave words denied his master thrice before cockcrow. After the Resurrection he was the leader of the community, which he persuaded to admit Gentiles without requiring obedience to the Mosaic laws; on a visit to Antioch, however, he appeared to backtrack, for which he was rebuked by St Paul. He was later said to have been bishop there (see *22 Feb.).

His last years were spent in Rome, where he and St Paul are said to have founded the church of which he is later, and anachronistically, called the first bishop; it is certain that he was martyred there under Nero, though the story that he was crucified upside down comes from an unreliable source; on the other hand, the tradition that he was buried in the Ager Vaticanus has been strengthened by excavations underneath the Confessio at St Peter's. He is commonly portrayed with the keys of the Kingdom of Heaven bestowed on him by Jesus (Matt. 16: 19); in popular belief he keeps the heavenly gate, deciding whom to admit and whom to send elsewhere. He is the patron saint of fishermen and allied trades, but also of bridge-builders, from the papal title of Pontifex Maximus (the Roman high priesthood renounced by the emperor Gratian in 378 and assumed in its new sense by Leo the Great), and of workers in clay, stone, and metal (from the Rock and the keys).

Paul, a Jew of Tarsus whose Hebrew name was *Shā'ūl*, but also a Roman citizen with the Latin cognomen *Paulus*. He was by trade a tent-maker, brought up by his father on strict Pharisaic principles, but also given the good Greek education offered by his native city, and a fanatically anti-Christian religious student who stood by as an approving witness at the martyrdom of St Stephen (*26 Dec.). But while travelling to Damascus with letters calling on local Jews to send any Christians they caught to Jerusalem, 'suddenly there shined round about him a light from heaven: And he fell to the earth, and heard a voice saying unto him, Saul, Saul, why persecutest thou me? And he said, Who art thou, Lord? And the Lord said, I am Jesus whom thou persecutest' (Acts 9: 3–5; see *25 Jan. for the Western feast of his conversion). From then on, he became a devoted Christian, a tireless missionary, and the most original thinker of the community (which is why revisionist Christians blame him for any doctrine they dislike, as self-applauding Marxists do Engels). Having been imprisoned in Jerusalem on charges brought by the Jews, Paul appealed to Caesar and was sent to Rome; during the voyage he was shipwrecked on Malta (see *10 Feb.), where according to Acts 28: 3–6 a viper bit him on the hand, but he shook it off without ill effects (for which reason he is invoked against snakebite). In Rome, he was beheaded in Nero's persecution; over his grave stands the great church of San Paolo fuori le Mura. According to legend his head bounced three times, and at each place a spring burst through the soil; this story is commemorated by the church of Tre Fontane.

On this day a buck used to be offered at the high altar of St Paul's, and a doe on the feast of St Paul's Conversion (see *25 Jan.). In some parts of Belgium the day is observed with bonfires. It is also a day for weather proverbs:

> Saint Pierre et saint Paul pluvieux,
> Pour trente jours dangereux.

If the 19th [*sic*] of this month (which is St. Peter and Paul's day) be fair, fruit will be plenty; but the tender lambs and other weak cattle will die that year.   *Lilly's New Erra Pater*, 7

According to a famous folklorist whose vagueness as to his sources has frustrated subsequent researches, Scottish fishermen predicted the weather from the winds on this day:

> Wind from the west, fish and bread;
> Wind from the north, cold and flaying;
> Wind from the east, snow on the hills,
> Wind from the south, fruit on trees.
>
> trans. Carmichael, *Carmina Gadelica*

30 JUNE

pridie Kalendas Iulias   F

❦ ANCIENT ROME Dedication-day of the temple of Hercules and the Muses, built by Marcus Fulvius Nobilior out of the fines he had collected as censor in 179 BC; Fulvius, a man of literary tastes and a friend of the poet Ennius, had apparently heard in Greece, during his victorious campaign against the Ambraciots, of a *Hēraklēs Mousagétēs* or Herakles Leader of the Muses (normally Apollo's function). In fact the hero's connections with the higher culture were somewhat ambivalent: he had been taught to play the lyre by the centaur Chiron, but then brained him with it. In the temple, on the south-west side of the Circus Flaminius and north-west of the Porticus Octaviae, Fulvius set up a calendar inscription (*fasti*), statues of the nine Muses (portrayed on a coin of 66 BC) and of Heracles playing the lyre, together with an old bronze shrine of the Muses taken from another temple. It was restored in 29 BC, and a portico put round it, by Lucius Marcius Philippus, formerly married to Augustus' maternal aunt.

❦ HOLY DAYS First Martyrs of the Church of Rome (RC); formerly Commemoration of St Paul (see *29 June); Synaxis of the Twelve Apostles (Orth.)

Martial of Limoges, missionary bishop *c.*250 (see *22 Mar.). After his death, miracles were reported; according to Gregory of Tours, when one Leo of Poitiers, retainer to a Merovingian prince, observed that the much-lauded SS Martin and Martial had left nothing to the royal treasury, the two saints struck him deaf, dumb, and mad. In 848 the Benedictine abbey of Saint-Martial was dedicated; from it comes some of the earliest polyphonic music still extant. In 994 his relics were raised for a peace council in Limoges, whereupon a deadly plague ceased; in the turmoils of the time, on the eve of the millennium, pilgrims flocked to the saint's tomb, and began to spread the story that he had been a companion of Jesus and a disciple of St Peter. In accordance with the new interest in St Martial, on 18 November 1028 a new basilica was dedicated in his honour; soon afterwards the monk Adémar of Chabannes, who like all educated men knew that the popular legend was twaddle, nevertheless set about having this first-century St Martial recognized as the apostle of Aquitaine, and even of all Gaul. The bishop was prevailed upon to support the fraud by threatening to excommunicate anyone who should doubt the apostle's *vita*; Adémar composed an apostolic liturgy, to be performed at a great ceremony on 3 August 1029, the 966th anniversary, it was asserted, of Martial's dedication of St Stephen's Cathedral. Although anyone who preached the Gospel where it was not known might be called an apostle, an apostolic liturgy was appropriate only for the Twelve (with St Matthias in place of Judas) and St Paul. But on that very morning a Lombard prior named Benedict of Chiusa, not being subject to the bishop and claiming personal acquaintance with Pope John XIX, denounced the cult and the tale on which it was based; the bubble burst, and Adémar left Limoges in disgrace. However, he devoted his few remaining years to a campaign of wholesale forgery that within a few decades carried the cause to triumph. His master-stroke was to compose an Easter table for the cycle 1064–1595, which no one would look at till the next generation, and append to it an alleged letter from the pope himself declaring that Martial was indeed an apostle; he then concocted a mass of documents that purported to show the claim upheld at councils in 1031. The imposition was successful; it found especially willing believers in the Limousin popes at Avignon, beginning with Clement VI. In the Saint-Martial chapel of the Palais des Papes at Avignon, Jesus is depicted instructing the Twelve at Capernaum, using young Martial as a living example of humility: 'Unless ye become as this little one . . .'. The fraud was not discovered till the twentieth century.

JULY

A swarm of bees in May is worth a load of hay
A swarm of bees in June is worth a silver spoon
But a swarm in July is not worth a fly.

No tempest, good Julie [July],
Least corn lookes rulie.

❦ NAMES FOR THE MONTH   Latin *Iulius*, French *juillet*, Spanish *julio*, Portuguese *Julho*, Italian *luglio*, German *Juli*, Welsh *Gorffennaf*, Scots Gaelic *an t-Iuchar*, Irish *Iúil*. Up to the mid-eighteenth century English *July* rhymed with *truly*; conversely, Germans may on the telephone call the month *Julei* with final stress to avoid confusion with *Juni*.

Until 44 BC this month was called *Quinctilis* or *Quintilis* (from *quintus*, originally *quinctus*, 'fifth'); it was renamed in honour of the murdered Julius Caesar, who had been born on the 12th. The Scots Gaelic name originally denoted the warmest part of the year, defined in one source as comprising the last three weeks of July, beginning on a Friday, and the first three weeks of August, ending on a Tuesday. Other names attested are *Deireadh-Samhraidh*, 'end of summer', which seems also to be the sense of the Welsh term; *am mìos buidhe*, 'the golden month'; and *a' Mhadhrail*, 'canine', presumably an allusion to the dog days (see *19 July) (Dinneen similarly notes *mí madramhail* in Irish).

❦ HOLIDAYS AND ANNIVERSARIES

Third Sunday   Venice: Feast of the Redeemer, first celebrated in 1575 in memory of an averted plague. A wooden pontoon bridge is put up so that people can walk from Dorsoduro over the Giudecca canal to the church of San Redentore, where low mass is said. The evening is spent preferably banqueting on the water and watching spectacular fireworks (see *20 July); hardy souls watch the sun rise the next morning on the Lido.

Last Sunday   In Ireland pilgrims climb mountains and high places, above all Croagh-patrick (Cruach Phádraig), Co. Mayo, the mountain on which St Patrick fasted for forty days in 441, doing battle (it is said) with evil spirits and the Devil's dam; up till then it had been sacred to a heathen deity, *Crom Cruach* ('Crom of the Reek'), still commemorated in the Irish name for this day, *Domhnach Chrom Dubh* (Black Crom's Sunday). Evidence that the mountain, which is 2,510 ft high (765 m), possessed importance long before appropriation by the saint has recently been provided by the discovery of a hill-fort and late Bronze Age hut-sites; art of that period has been discovered on a natural rock outcrop, known as St Patrick's Chair, along the pilgrim route. The pilgrimage is penitential (some participants go barefoot); the ascent, over rocks and muddy streams, takes an hour and a half. On the slope there are stations at which prayers should be said to earn a plenary indulgence, and a cairn round which pilgrims walk seven times, reciting seven Our Fathers, seven Hail Marys, and one Creed before making the steep climb to the summit, where mass is held in a small church built in 1905, and where St Patrick is reported, by ringing his bell, to have banished all snakes from Ireland.

First Monday Caribbean or Caricom Day: public holiday in Barbados, Guyana, Jamaica, and Trinidad and Tobago (treaty establishing Caribbean Community, 1973)
   Cayman Islands: Constitution Day
   Zambia: Heroes Day (national holiday)

Second or third Monday Botswana: President's Day

Fourth Monday Virgin Islands: Hurricane Supplication Day (legal holiday)

> Then came hot *Iuly* boyling like to fire,
>   That all his garment he had cast away:
>   Vpon a Lyon raging yet with ire
>   He boldly rode and made him to obay:
>   It was the beast that whylome did forray
>   The Nemæan forrest, till th'*Amphytrionide*
>   Him slew, and with his hide did him array;
>   Behinde his back a sithe, and by his side
> Vnder his belt he bore a sickle circling wide.
>
> Spenser, *The Faerie Queene*, VII. vii. 36

It is now Iuly and the Sunne is gotten vp to his height, whose heat parcheth the earth, and burnes vp the grasse on the mountaines. Now begins the Canon of heauen to rattle, and when the fire is put to the charge, it breaketh out among the Cloudes: the stones of congealed water cut off the eares of the Corne: and the blacke stormes affright the faint-hearted: the Stag and the Bucke are now in pride of their time, and the hardnesse of their heads makes them fit for the Horner: Now hath the Sparhawke the Partridge in the foot, and the Ferret doth tickle the Cony in the borough. Now doeth the Farmer make ready his teame, and the Carter with his whip, hath no small pride in his Whistle: Now doe the Reapers try their backs and their Armes, and the lusty Youthes pitch the sheafes into the Cart. The old Partridge calles her Couey in the morning, and in the euening, the Shepheard fals to folding of his flocke: the Sparrowes make a charme upon the greene Bushes, till the Fowler come and take them by the dozens: the Smelt now begins to be in season, and the Lamprey out of the Riuer leapes into a Pye: the Souldier now hath a hot March, and the Lawyer sweats in his lyned Gowne: The Pedler now makes a long walke, and the Aqua vitæ Bottle sets his face on a fiery heat: In summe, I thus conclude of it, I hold it a profitable season, the Labourers gaine, and the rich mans wealth. Farewell.   Breton (1626)

In this Moneth it is not good to eat *strong* meats, nor those which do greatly *nourish*, nor pleasant *spiced* meats, hotness of the season; beware of *bleeding* and *purging*, yet both may safely be done, being guided by discretion; drink but little *Wine* in this and the Month following, for that it dryes the stomack and liver, and too much increaseth *choler*, the smallest and weakest drinks are best, to be used fasting against choler, abstain from Venery, and use to eat every morning a little *Sage*, and *Herbagrace*, with a bit of *bread*, beware of eating any muddy Fish taken with net this Moneth; use to eat *oft* Verjuyce with your Sallets and Meat, for the same doth cool and refresh the body, refrain eating of green Fruits this Month, its wholsome to annoint the neck and brest with the juyce of *Herbagrace*, *Hysope*, and *Smallage* mixt with Honey, if you bath do it fasting, and very moderately, for to do otherwise is dangerous this Moneth, and beware of eating either *Beets*, or *Lettice* this Moneth, for that they have in them a *venenous* poysonous quality, very noxious to nature, *Garlick*, *Onions*, *Sage*, and fat Bacon is good for the Husbandman, and laborious bodies.

Saunders (1665)

Fruit is certainly most salubrious in hot weather; but, if the opinion be well founded that it does most good when taken before dinner, the dessert ought to take place of that spurious meal called the lunch, which, being usually made of animal food, too often banishes the appetite irrecoverably for the day. In reality, to lunch is to dine.   Hone, *Year* (1832), 388

July is called the THUNDER MONETH. It was a Custom at *Malmsbury-Abbey*, to Ring the great Bell, call'd St. *Adam's Bell*, to drive away THUNDER AND LIGHTNING. The like Custom is still in Use at St. *Germains*, and in sundry other parts of *France*.   Gadbury (1696)

1 JULY

Kalendae Iuliae   G

If the first of July it be rainy weather,
'twill rain more or less for four weeks together.

❨ HOLIDAYS AND ANNIVERSARIES Burundi: Independence Day (from Belgian trust
    territory of Rwanda-Urundi, 1962)
  Canada: Canada Day, or Dominion Day (commemorating confederation of 1867)
    (national day) (on 2 July when 1st is a Sunday)
  Rwanda: Independence Day (from Belgian trust territory of Rwanda-Urundi, 1962)

❨ HOLY DAYS Oliver Plunkett (RC Ireland); Cosmas and Damian, martyrs (Orth.,
main feast; see *27 Sept.)

Oliver Plunkett (1625–81), RC archbishop of Armagh and primate of all Ireland, highly regarded by Protestant landowners but denounced on trumped-up charges at the height of the Exclusion crisis as plotting rebellion in league with France; executed for high treason 11 July 1681 (1 July OS); canonized 1975.

Samuel Curwen observes the annual festival of the lacemakers of Honiton (near Exeter) in 1778:

With my 2 fellow boarders rode to Honiton to see annual performance of Lacemakers . . . They are comprised of Churchmen and Dissenters, have an P.M. sermon, alternating in the Church and Meeting House. After service they walk in following order—first the head walks the President alone, holding in her hand a rod or wand adorned with flowers of all kinds in the season preceded by 4 little maidens of 8 or 9 years old carrying large bouquets, which, once for all, everyone in the procession has, and each carries a basket of flowers, walking between 2 arches adorned with great variety of flowers. Then follow The honorary members or Patronesses of the Society, each having a white rod, the top made up of flowers, then follows the Standard bearer, behind whom goes a dozen Couples having a standard bearer attending them which closes the [procession?]. On one is depicted a ship with a motto or inscription in a scrawl forgotten, the device and motto on the other was never within my knowledge. In this order they paraded the different streets and then adjourn to the Golden Lion Inn to take their tea and pass the evening in dancing and festivity. To this we were invited by a ticket for which paid 1/ each but my occasions calling me to Exeter and want of relish for such promiscuous confused noisy mirth concurred to send me off the ground before the street parade was over, leaving my Companions to return home by Moonlight which it not my choice to do.   Curwen, i. 457–8

2 JULY

a.d. VI Nonas Iulias   A

❦ HOLIDAYS AND ANNIVERSARIES Siena: Il Palio. The second of two horse races run in Siena, this one for the banner (*palio*) bearing the image of the Madonna di Provenzano. See *16 August.

❦ HOLY DAYS Visitation of Our Lady (BCP, RC till 1969, and still in German-speaking countries; RC, CY on 31 May)

Visitation. Luke (1: 39–56) records the visit of Mary, soon after the Annunciation, to her cousin Elizabeth, then pregnant with John the Baptist. This passage is the source for both the last words of the Hail Mary, 'blessed is the fruit of thy womb', spoken by Elizabeth, and the Magnificat, Mary's song of thanksgiving.

The Visitation

Proclaimed Queene and mother of a God,
The light of earth, the soveraigne of Saints,
With Pilgrim foote, up tyring hils she trod,
And heavenly stile with handmaids toile acquaints,
Her youth to age, her health to sicke she lends,
Her heart to God, to neighbour hand she bends.

A prince she is, and mightier prince doth beare,
Yet pompe of princely traine she would not have,
But doubtles heavenly Quires attendant were,
Her child from harme her selfe from fall to save,
Word to the voice, song to the tune she brings,
The voice her word, the tune her dittie sings.

> Eternal lights inclosed in her breast,
> Shot out such piercing beames of burning love,
> That when her voice her cosens eares possest,
> The force thereof did force her babe to move,
> With secret signes the children greet each other,
> But open praise each leaveth to his mother.
>
> Robert Southwell (?1561–95)

Processus and Martinian, early Roman martyrs, buried in the Via Aurelia, translated to St Peter's by Paschal I; legend made them Roman officers converted by their prisoners SS Peter and Paul. A weather proverb states that if it rains on this day, there will be excessive rain all summer that smothers the corn:

> Si pluat in festo Processi et Martiniani
> imber erit nimius et suffocacio grani.

Swithun, bishop of Winchester, chancellor of Egbert, king of Wessex, and tutor to his son Ethelwulf, was buried on this day in 862; it was still his feast in a St Albans calendar of 1149 now in the Bodleian Library (see Pl. 6), and has remained his day in Continental countries, for instance in Norway, where Stavanger cathedral was dedicated to him, and a weather proverb of similar import to that just cited runs:

> Syftesokdag   On St Swithun's day
> setter skyen i lag,   if the clouds are stacked
> det varer til olsokdag.   it lasts to St Olaf's day [29 July].

In England, however, this day, both as his feast and as a weather-mark, was supplanted by his translation on *15 July.

For the Orthodox, this is the Deposition of the Honourable Mantle of the Theotokos, a much-honoured relic in the church of Blachernae at Constantinople. One tale had it found in Jerusalem by a pious Jewess in the reign of the emperor Leo I (457–74); another made two patrician brothers called Galbius and Candidus, on a pilgrimage to Jerusalem, stay overnight at a house at Capernaum in Galilee, where they saw a room full of lights and incense. On being told that Mary's robe was kept there (cf. *31 Aug.), they obtained the landlady's permission to spend the night in it, took the measurements of the casket, and went on their way to Jerusalem, where they had a replica made; on their return journey they lodged at the same house and effected the substitution. They brought the relic back to their estate at Blachernae, where Leo built a reliquary shrine (*sorós*) for it. During an Avar raid the Mantle was removed for safe keeping; the feast celebrates its return in 620. We are informed that the first Russian raid on Constantinople (in 860) was repelled when the Patriarch Photius plunged the relic into the Bosporus, causing the waters to boil up and wreck the ships, a miracle the patriarch unaccountably neglected to record in his many writings.

John Taylor, the Water Poet, spends a disastrous day on his travels:

Monday the second of *Iuly*, I went to *Bridgewater* ten miles, where all that was worthy of note was, that neare the Towne, at a stile I had a great disaster; for a shagge or splinter of the stile tooke hold of my one and onely breeches, and tore them in that extreme unmercifull, unmannerly manner, that for shame and modesties sake I was faine to put them off, and goe breechlesse into the Towne, where I found a botching threepenny Taylor, who did patch me up with such reparations as made me not ashamed to put my breeches on againe, and trot five miles further to a ragged Market Towne called *Neather-Stoy*, where extreame weary, I tooke up my lodging, at a signe and no signe, which formerly was the Rose and Crowne; but Roses are withered, and Crownes are obscured, as the signe was.

Surely that day was a mad, sad, glad, auspicious, unlucky day to me, worse then an Ominous, Childermas, or a dogged byting dog-day; for the Hostesse was out of Towne, mine Host was very sufficiently drunke, the house most delicately deckt with exquisite artificiall, and naturall sluttery, the roome besprinckled and strewed with the excrements of Pigs and Children; the wall and sielings were adorned and hanged with rare Spiders Tapistry, or cobweb Lawne; the smoake was so palpable and perspicuous, that I could scarce see any thing else, and yet I could scarce see that, it so blinded me with Rheum a signe of weeping; besides all this, the odorifferous and contagious perfume of that house was able to outvie all the Millainers in Christendome or Somersetshire.   Taylor, *Wandering* (1649)

Lastly, a prediction that was correct in everything but one crucial detail:

The second day of July, 1776, will be the most memorable epocha in the history of America. I am apt to believe that it will be celebrated by succeeding generations as the great anniversary festival. It ought to be commemorated as the day of deliverance, by solemn acts of devotion to God Almighty. It ought to be solemnized with pomp and parade, with shows, games, sports, guns, bells, bonfires, and illuminations, from one end of this continent to the other, from this time forward forevermore.   John Adams to Abigail Adams, 3 July 1776 (J. Adams, 193–4)

The occasion was the approval by the Continental Congress of Richard Henry Lee's resolution, moved on 7 June, 'that these United Colonies are, and of right ought to be, free and independent States'; there were no adverse votes, though the New York delegation abstained in accordance with its instructions. History, however, preferred to remember the more detailed declaration of 4 July.

3 JULY

a.d. V Nonas Iulias   B

❰ HOLIDAYS AND ANNIVERSARIES Belarus': Independence Day (national day)
   USA, Idaho: Admission Day (43rd state, 1890)

❰ HOLY DAYS **Thomas, Apostle** (CY, RC since 1969), properly his translation, but made the main feast in lieu of *21 December; the judicial red-letter day since 1984; formerly St Irenaeus (see *28 June)

Thomas the apostle was said to have been translated on this day from 'Calamina' in India (location unknown; perhaps Mailapur), where he had been martyred, to Edessa in Syria (now Urfa in Turkey) in 394; in 1258 he was translated again to Chios, finally reaching Ortona in the Abruzzi.

Pope Leo II (682–3), who ratified the proceedings of the Sixth Oecumenical Council, including the anathema on his predecessor Honorius (625–38) for countenancing the Monothelete heresy (see *10 Jan.), in a letter that according as one reads the Greek or the Latin version makes that Pope, by a profane treason, permit the pure faith to be defiled, or attempt to overthrow it. He restored the Roman church of Santa Sabina and for the Greeks in Rome built the church of San Giorgio in Velabro, now restored after being blown up by a Mafia bomb in 1993.

Hyakinthos (Orth.), reputedly a pure and innocent youth of 20 from Caesarea in Cappadocia (modern Kayseri) who starved to death rather than eat meat sacrificed to pagan gods; in 1994 he was declared by the Holy Synod of the Greek Orthodox Church to be the true patron of love and passion in contrast to the Latin Valentine (see *14 Feb.). He was named after the beautiful youth from Amyclae near Sparta with whom Apollo fell in love; the god, always unlucky in love, accidentally struck him with an unlucky ricochet from a discus-throw. In grief and remorse, Apollo turned his blood into a red flower inscribed with the cry of grief *AI AI*; this was not our hyacinth, *Hyacinthus orientalis*, but perhaps the field gladiolus, *Gladiolus italicus*. He was commemorated at Sparta in the Huakinthia on the first three days of the month Huakinthios, which may, as in some other Dorian cities, have been the June–July lunation.

In some almanacs this day is given as the first of the dog days, the last being 11 August; they are thus the forty days before the cosmical rising of Sirius; see *Days: Dog Days*.

4 JULY

❡ HOLIDAYS AND ANNIVERSARIES USA: Independence Day (signing of the Declaration of Independence, 1776)
   USA, Wisconsin: Indian Rights Day

❡ HOLY DAYS Translation of Martin, Bishop (BCP) (see also *11 Nov.); Elizabeth of Portugal (RC)

Martin. In the Roman Martyrology this is the combined feast of St Martin's ordination as bishop, the translation of his corpse, and the dedication of the basilica in Tours. In Scotland it was known as Bullion's day; this is derived from a French term *Saint Martin le bouillant*, variously explained from a portrayal of the saint with a globe of fire above his head and the summer heat of this festival as opposed to that on 11 November.

Weather proverbs in medieval Latin and Scots English combine to relate of this day what is said in England of St Swithun's translation on the 15th:

> Martini magni translatio si pluuiam det
> Quadragintă dies continuare solet
>
> Bullion's day gif ye be fair
> for forty days there'll be na mair.

In Scotland . . . it was a proverb, that if the deer rise dry and lie down dry on Bullion's Day, it was a sign there would be a good gose-harvest—gose being a term for the latter end of summer; hence gose-harvest was an early harvest. It was believed generally over Europe that rain on this day betokened wet weather for the twenty ensuing days.   Chambers

Elizabeth (Isabel) of Portugal (1271–1336), great-niece of St Elizabeth of Hungary, daughter of King Pedro III of Aragon, and wife of Dinis, King of Portugal. She managed to lead a very devout life while attending to her royal duties, founding monasteries, churches, and hospitals. Famed as a peacemaker (not least between her son and his father), she is credited with having stopped war several times between rulers of Castile and Aragon. After her husband's death she became a Franciscan tertiary in a convent of Poor Clares she had founded at Coimbra. She is patron saint of Portugal and Coimbra.

Ulrich or Udalricus (*c*.890–973), bishop of Augsburg. Educated at Sankt Gallen, to which he retired, and a supporter of the emperor Otto I, he was the first saint formally canonized by a pope, John XV, in 993. His tomb in the church of SS Ulrich and Afra in Augsburg is still a place of pilgrimage. Ulrich is connected with fish through a legend that he humbled a slanderer by turning a piece of meat into fish:

> Wheresoever Huldryche hath his place, the people there brings in,
> Both Carpes, and Pykes, and Mullets fat, his favour here to win.
>
> Naogeorgus, fo. 55

Independence Day. On this day in 1776 the Continental Congress, having already voted the American colonies to be independent states (see *2 July), passed with no dissent (though New York abstained) the Declaration of Independence, which from 'a decent Respect to the Opinion of Mankind' stated its reasons for so acting:

We hold these Truths to be self-evident, that all Men are created equal, that they are endowed by their Creator with certain unalienable Rights, that among these are Life, Liberty, and the Pursuit of Happiness—That to secure these Rights, Governments are instituted among Men, deriving their Just Powers from the Consent of the Governed, that whenever any Form of Government becomes destructive of these Ends, it is the Right of the People to alter or abolish it, and to institute new Government, laying its Foundations on such Principles, and organizing its Powers in such Form, as to them shall seem most likely to effect their Safety and Happiness.

George Washington observes Independence Day in 1790:

Monday, 5th [celebration postponed from the 4th, a Sunday]:
The members of the Senate, House of Representatives, Public Officers, Foreign Characters etc., The Members of the Cincinnati, Officers of the Militia etc., came with the compliments of the

day to me—about one o'clock a sensible Oration was delivered in St. Pauls Chapel by Mr. Brock-holst Livingston, on the occasion of the day—the tendency of which was to show the different situation we are now in, under an excellent government of our own choice, to what it would have been if we had not succeeded in our opposition to the attempts of Great Britain to enslave us; and how much we ought to cherish the blessings which are within our reach, and to cultivate the seeds of harmony and unanimity in all our public Councils.   Washington, iv. 136

An Englishman's view of Independence Day in New York in 1837:

Pop—pop—bang—pop—pop—bang—bang—bang! Mercy on us! how fortunate it is that anniversaries come only once a year. Well, the Americans may have great reason to be proud of this day, and of the deeds of their forefathers, but why do they get so confoundedly drunk? why, on this day of independence, should they become so *dependent* upon posts and rails for sup-port?—The day is at last over; my head aches, but there will be many more aching heads to-morrow morning!

What a combination of vowels and consonants have been put together! what strings of tropes, metaphors, and allegories, have been used on this day! what varieties and gradations of elo-quence! There are at least fifty thousand cities, towns, villages, and hamlets, spread over the sur-face of America—in each the Declaration of Independence has been read; in all one, and in some two or three, orations have been delivered, with as much gunpowder in them as in the squibs and crackers.   Marryat, 83

Another view of Independence Day by Frederick Douglass (1817–95), the freed slave who became a famous orator, in his Fourth of July address to the Rochester Ladies' Anti-Slavery Society in 1852:

I am not included within the pale of this glorious anniversary! Your high independence only re-veals the immeasurable distance between us. The blessings in which you this day rejoice are not enjoyed in common . . . This Fourth of July is *yours*, not *mine*. *You* may rejoice, *I* must mourn. To drag a man in fetters into the grand illuminated temple of liberty, and call upon him to join you in joyous anthems, were inhuman mockery and sacrilegious irony.

'What to the Slave is the Fourth of July?'

Independence Day as seen by a Scots visitor in the late 1860s:

it is unfair to judge of American feeling by Fourth of July speeches. The patriots who shriek on that day about 'British tyranny,' 'shaking thrones,' 'effete monarchies,' 'American Eagle striking his talons into the prostrate Lion,' etc. etc., are often exceedingly good friends of this country, and would laugh at being supposed to mean hostility. It is a day sacred to the Spread Eagle—a day on which the national enthusiasm boils over, and the American's pride in his country bursts into wild and exulting expression. But many of them are coming to see that the Spread-eagleism of the Fourth of July is, as applied to us, meaningless. They are coming to know that the mass of people in this country are entirely at one with them in regard to the stand made by the Revolutionary fathers against the tyranny of the King; and that British children are taught from infancy to name Washington amongst the patriots whom they are to imitate and revere.

Macrae, i, p. xxiii

By the 1890s sporting events had become indispensable fixtures of Fourth of July celebrations, particularly baseball and bicycle races, and, in the West, rodeos.

In one of those coincidences that in ancient history would be dismissed as obvious fictions, the second and third presidents, John Adams and Thomas Jefferson, died on this day in 1826, fifty years after the Declaration; and in 1863 the Union won two signal victories against the Confederacy when Lee retreated from Gettysburg and Vicksburg surrendered.

5 JULY

a.d. III Nonas Iulias D

❦ HOLIDAYS AND ANNIVERSARIES Cape Verde: Independence Day (from Portugal, 1975)
    Isle of Man: Tynwald ceremony (see below)
    Slovakia: Day of the Slav Missionaries (national holiday)
    Venezuela: Independence Day (from Spain, 1811) (national holiday)

❦ ANCIENT ROME Poplifugia, 'Flights of the People'; as the only festival before the Nones of any month to be inscribed in large letters on the official calendars, it must at one time have been important, but no one knew what flights it commemorated. One story, told by Plutarch, relates it to the confusion caused by Romulus' assumption into heaven (see *17 Feb.), in commemoration of which men rushed out of the city shouting the standard personal names such as Marcus, Lucius, and Gaius. However, he identifies this day with the *Nonae Caprotinae* (see *7 July), since Romulus was said to have disappeared at the *Lacus Caprae*; there is no agreed solution to the problem.

❦ HOLY DAYS Antony Maria Zaccaria (RC)

Antony Maria Zaccaria (1502–39), founder of a congregation known as the Barnabites. He was canonized in 1897.

Tynwald ceremony in Isle of Man, called Feaill Eoin (Feast of John), until 1752 held on 24 June. After a short service in St John's Chapel (*Skeeill Eoin*), the Sword of State, emblazoned with the badge of three greaved legs conjoined at 120° and the motto *Quocunque ieceris stabit* ('Wherever you throw it, it will stand', in Manx *Raad erbee cheauys oo eh, hassys eh*), is borne before the Lieutenant-Governor at the head of a solemn procession along a rush-strewn path to Tynwald Hill (*y Cronk Tinvaal*, from Old Norse *þingvǫllr*, 'Assembly Field'), where the Chief Coroner, having 'fenced' the assembly by forbidding those present to 'quarrel, brawl, or make disturbance', reads summaries, in English and Manx, of statutes passed by the island legislature, the House of Keys (*yn Chiare as Feed*, 'the Four and Twenty'), in the last twelve months; after those present have cheered the Queen, the Lieutenant-Governor signs the new laws. Both the fencing and the cheers of assent are survivals of Norse direct democracy, when all the Manx freemen gathered annually on St John's Day for an assembly or Thing at which the island's laws were read thrice, and all lawsuits and blood feuds settled by the two lawmen (called 'deemsters' in

English and *briwnyn* in Manx); the Four and Twenty—sixteen great landowners from Man and eight from the Hebrides—met wearing mugwort (*yn vollan vane*, 'the white herb') on their heads.

6 JULY

pridie Nonas Iulias   E

❅ HOLIDAYS AND ANNIVERSARIES The Comoros: Independence Day (from France, 1975)
  Malawi: Independence Day (from Britain, 1964; Republic, 1966) (national day)

❅ ANCIENT ROME From the end of the Roman Republic, this was the first day of the *Ludi Apollinares* (see *13 July).

❅ HOLY DAYS Thomas More (CY; RC on 22 June); John Fisher (CY; RC on *22 June); Maria Goretti (RC)

Sir Thomas More (1478–1535), humanist and jurist, the close friend of such leading men of culture and intellect as Colet, Holbein, and above all Erasmus, who called him *omnium horarum homo*, 'a man for all seasons', whether serious or relaxed, and played on his name in his *Moriae encomium*, 'Praise of Folly'; his many writings include *Utopia* (1516), which combined an ideal community free from current abuses, or what he saw as such—most famously the rise of sheep-farming on enclosed commons—and his life of Richard III, much reviled by the modern admirers of that monarch. After brief service as an MP in 1504, when he persuaded the House of Commons to refuse Henry VII an aid of £113,000, he returned to public life when Henry VIII, who greatly admired his wisdom and learning, made him a privy councillor in 1517; he became successively Master of Requests, Speaker of the House of Commons, Chancellor of the Duchy of Lancaster, and upon Wolsey's fall Lord Chancellor, dispatching suits with exemplary swiftness and incorruptibility. However, despite his awareness of abuses he remained in many respects a social and religious conservative, opposing enclosures and burning Lutherans; tolerance was strictly for Utopia. Distressed by Henry's determination to put aside Catherine of Aragon and take command of the English Church, he resigned the chancellorship immediately upon the Submission of the Clergy in 1532, and took no further part in political life; but on refusing to take the oath required by the Act of Succession in 1534, bastardizing Henry's daughter Mary and conferring the succession on his future children by Anne Boleyn, he was imprisoned in the Tower of London. There the Solicitor-General, Richard Rich—perhaps the most successful and least scrupulous timeserver in English history (see *12 June)—claimed to have heard him deny the Royal Supremacy, which was high treason; More declared that this was perjury, and Rich's own witnesses failed to support the charge, but the prisoner was convicted anyway and beheaded, after removing his beard from the path of the axe with the words: 'Pity that should suffer: *that* hath not committed treason!' Despite Protestant antipathy to a persecutor, his virtues continued to be recognized; in the 1590s a play was written on his career by Anthony Munday and others, among the revisions being a scene thought to be in Shakespeare's hand, in which More tries to quell the xenophobic passions that would lead to the riots of Evil May Day (1 May 1517), and a soliloquy also ascribed to him, in which the newly appointed Lord Chancellor warns himself against pride:

> But, More, the more thou hast
> Either of honour, office, wealth and calling,
> Which might accite thee to embrace and hug them,
> The more do thou e'en serpents' natures think them:
> Fear their gay skins, with thought of their sharp stings,
> And let this be thy maxim: to be great
> Is, when the thread of hazard is once spun,
> A bottom great wound up, greatly undone.   *bobbin*

Maria Goretti (1890–1902), killed by the landlord's son, Alessandro Serenelli, for resisting his attempted rape; on her deathbed she took her first communion and forgave her murderer. He was sentenced to thirty years' hard labour; he remained unrepentant until he dreamt that she was picking flowers and offering them to him. This brought about a change of heart that led, after release at Christmas 1928, to his joining the Capuchin Order as a lay brother. She was canonized in 1950 at a ceremony in St Peter's Square, her mother being among the half-million people present.

7 JULY

Nonae Iuliae   F

❰ HOLIDAYS AND ANNIVERSARIES   Solomon Islands: Independence Day (from Great Britain, 1978)

❰ ANCIENT ROME   This day was known as the Nonae Caprotinae: women sacrificed to Juno Caprotina under a wild fig-tree, *caprificus*, outside the city. In classical times it was also a holiday for female slaves (*ancillarum feriae*), who dressed up in fine clothes, demanded gifts, mocked all comers, and fought a sham battle; the tale was told that when the Latins exploited the Gaulish sack of Rome by demanding to be supplied with wives to renew their kinship, the slave-girls had put on free women's dress and gone out to the Latins, but at night their leader signalled to the army to attack by setting light to a *caprificus*. On this day there was also a sacrifice by the *sacerdotes publici* or state priests to Consus, probably the god of the grain-store, though later associated with counsel (see *21 Aug., *15 Dec.).

❦ HOLY DAYS Formerly the translation of St Thomas Becket; formerly SS Cyril and Methodius (see *11 May)

Thomas Becket. In 1220 the relics of Thomas Becket (see *29 Dec.) were translated to a new shrine at Canterbury; it is to this shrine that Chaucer's pilgrims made their way. It was destroyed on the orders of Henry VIII in September 1538; yet so important was this feast even for the secular purpose of summer fairs that Edward VI's primer of 1553 could not suppress it in its calendar, but recorded the day as 'Becket Traitor'. (It is also noted in Robert Plot's clog calendar, Pl. 14.) The English priest Gregory Martin, in 1581, described other relics in the Roman basilica of Santa Maria Maggiore, chagrined that they were more honoured in Rome than in his own country:

the Dalmatica that S. Thomas of Canterburie ware, when he was martyred of his arme, his bloud, his brayne, his hearecloth, and other Relikes; that our countrie men may be ashamed to their condemnation, if Rome honour and esteme this English Sainte and glorious Martyr more then they.   G. Martin, 41

On the Monday following Thomas's feast-day the Bodmin Riding used to take place:

At Bodmin there is still celebrated a festival, which is called Bodmin Riding; which, from the manner of the procession is probably deducible from the pagan worship of the goddess of flowers. But it has degenerated from the design of its primitive institution, being now strongly tinctured with papal superstition. It always takes place in July, on the Monday following the day of Thomas a Becket, in whose honour it seems to be ignorantly continued. The people mounted on horses and asses, ride into the country; and after collecting garlands of flowers, they return, and proceed to the priory, where they present them, according to ancient custom. There can be no doubt that this offering of flowers was at the shrine of Thomas a Becket, which saint has had the honour of superseding the pagan deity.   Hitchins, i. 722 (1824)

Palladius, a deacon from the leading family in Auxerre who in 429 prompted Pope Celestine I to send St Germanus (see *31 July) to combat British Pelagianism, and in 431 was himself sent to the Christians of Ireland as their first bishop; the facts are recorded by the contemporary chronicler and theologian Prosper of Aquitaine, who is himself culted on this day. Prosper elsewhere praises Celestine for making the Roman island Catholic and the barbarian island Christian, in other words stamping out heresy in Britain and bringing Ireland into the fold of the Church; in 441 Pope Leo proclaimed the spread of Christianity where Roman arms had never gone. Later writers either equated Palladius with St Patrick or had him martyred soon after arrival; he is sometimes identified with an 'Elder Patrick' (see *24 Aug.). Place-names in south-eastern Ireland said to commemorate companions of St Patrick seem geographically more appropriate to the Palladian mission than to Patrick's work in the north.

Maelruain (d. 792), abbot of Tallaght, founder of the Culdees (from Irish *céile Dé*, 'servant of God'), extreme ascetics who called women 'men's guardian devils', prohibited alcohol, and observed Sunday in Sabbatarian manner; yet the founder of these enclosed puritans was commemorated in after times with a house-to-house procession, and with dancing by day and drinking by night, till the Dominicans suppressed his feast in 1856.

The Culdees were distinguished for study; they produced two martyrologies (see *11 Mar.) and the unique record of early Irish liturgy called the Stowe Missal.

Willibald (700–87), son of Richard of England (see *7 Feb.), first bishop of Eichstätt, where he built the cathedral; an active missionary in Bavaria, Franconia, and Swabia, he founded the abbey of Heidenheim, making his brother and co-founder Wunibald (see *15 Dec.) its first abbot and his sister Walburg its abbess (see *25 Feb.).

In Japan, the Seventh Night festival (*Tanabata, Shichiseki*), corresponding to the Chinese festival of the Cowherd and the Weaving Maiden, was transferred to this day, the seventh of the seventh month, from its nominal counterpart in the lunar calendar; prayers are offered for children's artistic development.

8 JULY

a.d. VIII Idus Iulias   G

❡ HOLY DAYS

Kilian (d. *c*.689), an Irishman who became bishop (and a patron saint) of Würzburg and is known as the 'Apostle of Franconia' for his missionary work; his relics were translated on this day in 752 to Würzburg cathedral. In Norway *Kjell* or *Kjell fut*, 'bailiff', is coupled with *Knut* (Knud, *10 July) as sending the peasant out with his scythe to mow hay.

Grimbald (*c*.825–901), a scholarly monk of Saint-Bertin who went to Reims in 886 and a year later was invited to England by King Alfred to help him with his translations from the Latin, in particular of Gregory the Great's *Cura pastoralis*. Having refused the archbishopric of Canterbury, he became dean of the secular canons of the New Minster in Winchester (a town church distinct from the cathedral), in which he was buried; his relics were translated more than once, finally moving with the entire establishment of the New Minster to Hyde. It is an interpolated life from Hyde that first attests the legend of King Alfred as founder of University College at Oxford; this legend was long believed, not merely because it gave the college a head start over Balliol and Merton, but because it suited the national myth that everything good in church and state was due to the Saxons, or to the Britons before them, and everything bad to the Normans or the pope.

Pontius Pilate. In Ethiopia this day (25 June OS, in the local calendar 1 Ḥämle) is dedicated to the prefect of Judaea in whose term Jesus Christ was crucified (that, as the Greek original shows, is all that 'suffered under Pontius Pilate' means in the Creed) and who, according to a second-century legend, was converted by the Resurrection and submitted an official report to the emperor Tiberius. In the Gospel narratives, finding no grounds to condemn Jesus, he repeatedly fastens responsibility on the Jewish faction led by the high priest Caiaphas, which forces his hand by questioning his loyalty to the emperor (not an insult but a threat; see II: *Christian Chronology: Nativity and Crucifixion*); his final gesture of hand-washing has become proverbial, often in a bad sense not intended by authors who recalled Deut. 21: 6, Ps. 73: 13. The reliability of these accounts is much disputed, since Christians, on ever worse terms with Jews and anxious to defend themselves against the charge of following a common criminal, had every reason to present the matter in this light; but Pilate might well have sought to cover himself against the wrath of Jesus' followers, should Caiaphas' party fall from power. The scornful Roman Tacitus states that Christ was executed by Pilate—anachronistically styled 'procurator'—without mention of the Jews; conversely, certain Jewish texts eliminated Rome by moving the execution of the blasphemer Yeshu into the time of Judaean independence.

Jesus being a Galilaean, St Luke has Pilate remit the interrogation to Herod Antipas, tetrarch of Galilee, who was in Jerusalem for the festival; after putting some questions to him without receiving an answer, Herod sent him back. A confused recollection of this passage has given rise to the German expression *von Pontius zu Pilatus schicken*, corresponding to the English idiom 'to send from pillar to post'.

Pilate was arrogant, insensitive, and not above corruption; he was sent back to Rome by the proconsul of Syria after a massacre of Samaritans. Nevertheless, printers and publishers tormented by authors who continually revise their work may legitimately have a soft spot for the man who declared, 'What I have written I have written.'

9 JULY

July

My emblem is the Lion, and I breathe
    The breath of Libyan deserts o'er the land;
My sickle as a sabre I unsheathe,
    And bent before me the pale harvests stand.
The lakes and rivers shrink at my command,
    And there is thirst and fever in the air;
The sky is changed to brass, the earth to sand;
    I am the Emperor whose name I bear.

Henry Wadsworth Longfellow (1807–82), *The Poet's Calendar*

10 JULY

a.d. VI Idus Iulias B

❦ HOLY DAYS AND ANNIVERSARIES The Bahamas: Independence Day (from Great
Britain, 1973)
Japan: Bon or O-Bon or Feast of Fortune
USA, Wyoming: Admission Day (44th state, 1890)

❦ HOLY DAYS

The Seven Brothers, sons of St Felicity (commemorated with them on this day and by herself on 23 Nov.), supposedly martyred under Marcus Aurelius; a Christian appropriation of the story in 2 Maccabees 7 of the seven Jewish brothers and their mother who
suffered martyrdom under Antiochus IV rather than violate the Mosaic law.

King Knud IV Svendsen of Denmark (r. 1081–6), called *Le-Knud* (Scythe-Knud) or *Bonde
Knud* (Peasant Knud), because on his day it was time to mow hay, was the grand-nephew
of Knud the Great, and in his own estimation the rightful king of England as well as
of Denmark. Having in 1075, before ascending the Danish throne, raided York in support of northern rebels against William the Conqueror, ten years later he mustered a
great fleet with his Norwegian and Flemish allies for another attempt. William hastened
back from Normandy with a formidable army and harried the coastal lands to deny the
enemy supply; the danger was increased by the disaffection of the native English, who
might be expected to provide a fifth column. However, Knud had stirred up opposition
at home by reforms that strengthened the king and the Church against the nobles, who,
led by his own brother Olaf, rebelled against him and murdered him on this day in 1086
before the altar of St Alban's church at Odense. In some places his day was kept on
19 January.

Old Little St John's Day in Ireland (octave of the Nativity of St John the Baptist, OS):

The fair day of the Feast of St. John; that is, the Feast of St. John of the Fair, that is Old Little St. John's Day. It is on New Little St. John's Feast the Thomastown (Ireland) fair was. From
this it is probable that it was at some time before Pope Gregory changed the computation of the
time that the St. John's fair was fixed in Thomastown. . . . A number of innocent people were
beaten by the devilish police. They beat two merchants in their own houses. It was impossible to
put up with them.   O'Sullivan, i. 299 (10 July 1828)

11 JULY

11 JULY

a.d. V Idus Iulias   C

❨ HOLIDAYS AND ANNIVERSARIES Mongolia: National Day (independence from China, 1921)

❨ HOLY DAYS Benedict of Nursia (RC since 1969, CY; BCP on 21 Mar.)

Benedict of Nursia. This day commemorates the translation of Benedict's remains in 673 to the abbey church at Fleury, Saint-Benoît-sur-Loire, which in the tenth century played a great part in the monastic reform of the English Church. Under Pope Zacharias some relics were returned to Montecassino; after the abbey's destruction by Allied forces in 1944, a grave was discovered during reconstruction. At the reconsecration of Montecassino in 1964 Paul VI named St Benedict patron of Europe. This ended a remarkable decade of new patronages for him: in 1954 Pius XII had declared him patron of Italian cavers for his three years spent in an inaccessible cave, and in 1957 of Italian engineers and architects, for his building of monasteries; John XXIII declared him patron saint of farm workers in 1961 and of the Italian Knights of Labour in 1962. See also *21 March.

Euphemia (Orth.), martyred at Chalcedon on 16 September 303 (a wide range of tortures is recounted in her lives) and honoured there by a splendid basilica in which the Fourth Oecumenical Council was held in 451. Whereas the RC Church keeps her martyrdom (16 Sept.), the Orthodox commemorate a miracle said to have befallen after the Council had adopted the definition of Christ as being in two natures. The defeated Monophysites, as a last resort, asked that her shrine be opened and the text of the definition submitted for her approval; no sooner had the shrine been opened than she reached out, took the text, reverently kissed it, and handed it to the representatives of the majority.

12 JULY

a.d. IV Idus Iulias   D

❨ HOLIDAYS AND ANNIVERSARIES Kiribati: Independence Day (from Great Britain, 1979)
   Northern Ireland: Orangeman's Day (on Monday if the 12th is a Saturday or Sunday)
   São Tomé and Príncipe: National Independence Day (from Portugal, 1975)

❧ ANCIENT ROME Birth of Julius Caesar (100 BC), *a.d. IIII Eidus Quinctileis C. Mario VI L. Valerio Flacco coss.* ('on the fourth day before the Ides of Quintilis, Gaius Marius for the sixth time and Lucius Valerius Flaccus being consuls').

❧ HOLY DAYS John Jones (RC Wales)

John Jones (d. 1598), a native of Clynnog Fawr, Gwynedd, became a Franciscan in Rome, returning to work in London from 1592 to 1597; he was martyred at Southwark for being a priest and is one of the Forty Martyrs of England and Wales.

Berenice (in the West Veronica), the woman with an issue of blood (in Greek, *haimor-rhooûsa*) cured by Jesus at Capernaum (Matt. 9: 20–2); she was said to have come from Caesarea Philippi (also called Paneas, now Bāniyās on the Golan Heights), and to have erected there a statue of Christ in front of her house. The origin of this story appears to have been a statuary group, probably representing the emperor Hadrian and the province of Judaea, but reinterpreted by Christians as a depiction of Christ and the Haimorrhoousa; even the local pagans were deceived, and smashed the statues under Julian the Apostate. See also *4 February.

Orangeman's Day in Northern Ireland, celebrating the victory of William III ('William of Orange') against James II on 1 July (OS) 1690 in the Battle of the Boyne; the defeated monarch deserted the field so soon and so fast that a Dublin lady congratulated him on winning the retreat. The date of the commemoration, like that on *12 August, was corrected for the change of style in the eighteenth century but not thereafter. It is celebrated by Protestants with great marches; an anecdote tells of an English visitor who asked the significance of the parade and was told: 'Ut's the twaalfth.' A further enquiry elicited the clarification, 'The twaalfth of Ju-läy'; but when he still did not understand he was bidden, 'Aw, gaw hawme and read yer Bible.' The staunch Ulster Protestant found the deliverance of 1690 prefigured in sacred history; the Englishman, no less typically, had forgotten an event no less important for English history than for Irish.

13 JULY

a.d. III Idus Iulias   E

❧ ANCIENT ROME In 208 BC this day was appointed, during a plague, for annual games in honour of Apollo, *Ludi Apollinares*; they had already been held four years earlier in an attempt to win the god's support against Hannibal. They were steadily extended backwards through the month, beginning on the 11th in 190 BC and on the 6th in 44 BC; two days were given to circus games, the other six to the stage.

❧ HOLY DAYS Henry (RC); Marina of Antioch (Orth.; see *20 July)

Henry II, Holy Roman Emperor, died on this day in 1024; his empress, Kunigunde (see *3 Mar.), is now culted with him, their marriage having been represented as chaste. Henry, born in 973, was elected and crowned German king in 1002; his imperial coronation took place in 1014. A vigorous and effective ruler, he was a supporter of monastic reform (in its German form, somewhat different from that propagated from Cluny) and a skilful diplomat, ready to annoy the Church by allying himself with the heathen Slavs known as Ljutici; by his alliance with Vladimir of Kiev (see *15 July) against Bolesław the Brave of Poland he inaugurated a policy that bore its evil fruit in the eighteenth-century Partitions and the Nazi–Soviet pact. Pius X named him patron of Benedictine oblates.

Mildred (Mildthryth), abbess of Minster-in-Thanet; much venerated for her gentleness in England and abroad. Her relics were translated from St Augustine's, Canterbury, to Deventer, in the diocese of Utrecht, though Lanfranc found another set to give St Gregory's hospital.

Jacobus de Voragine (Jacopo da Varazze), a Genoese Dominican born *c.*1230; from 1292 till his death six years later he was archbishop of Genoa. He wrote a chronicle of the city as well as sermons, but is chiefly renowned as the author of the Golden Legend.

On this day in 1647, being the second Tuesday of the month, was observed the first of the monthly days of recreation created by Parliament in lieu of Christmas, Easter, Whitsun, and other suppressed church festivals.

14 JULY

pridie Idus Iulias   F

(HOLIDAYS AND ANNIVERSARIES France: Bastille Day (Fall of the Bastille, 1789) (national day)

(HOLY DAYS John Keble (CY); Camillus de Lellis (RC; formerly 18 July); formerly St Bonaventura (see *15 July)

John Keble (1792–1866), Tractarian. After a brilliant career at Oxford, he became a country curate; his collection of poems, *The Christian Year*, published in 1827, earned him election as Professor of Poetry at Oxford in 1831. Increasingly concerned about the liberal and reformist direction of the Church of England, he delivered the Assize sermon on 'national apostasy' (14 July 1833) that initiated the Oxford Movement, committed to High Churchmanship and the doctrine of Apostolic Succession. He collaborated with John Henry Newman on the *Tracts for the Times*, directed 'against Popery and Dissent'; unlike Newman, he did not abandon this position for the Church of Rome. From 1836 till his death on 29 March 1866 he was vicar of Hursley near Winchester. Keble College, Oxford, was founded in his memory (1870).

Camillus de Lellis (1550–1614), an unlikeable braggart soldier and gambler until his conversion at the age of 25. An incurable leg disease prevented him from joining the Franciscans, but he realized his vocation as a hospital attendant in Rome, founding the Ministers of the Sick as well as a number of hospitals and religious houses. In 1930 he was declared patron saint of nurses.

Le Quatorze Juillet commemorates the ransacking and demolition of the Bastille in 1789. This fortress, no. 232 rue Saint-Antoine, built as a defence against the English in the Hundred Years War and soon converted into a state prison, had since the seventeenth century been notorious as the place in which political prisoners were detained without trial; not all its inmates were of this description, for among those held there, till a week before the destruction, was the marquis de Sade. It was also the main store of gunpowder, which the people of Paris were determined to seize for use against the royal troops they expected to attack them. Amidst much confusion the building was stormed, the seven prisoners released, and the governor captured, abused, and finally killed. Louis XVI noted in his diary: 'Rien', meaning that he had killed nothing in the hunting-field; a later anecdote makes him ask the duc de La Rochefoucauld-Liancourt, 'Est-ce une révolte?' and the duke reply, 'Non, Sire, c'est une révolution.' If this interchange did not take place it ought to have done, for the king was compelled to recognize the new political reality (though not without the option of reversing it), and the revolutionaries at once represented it as the day of liberation. As such it was celebrated annually from 1790 onwards; on 21 messidor year IX, corresponding to 10 July 1801, the Consuls of the Republic issued a proclamation under the heading 'Quatorze Juillet', which the First Consul Bonaparte ordered to be printed and displayed in all départements of the Republic; it begins:

Français, Ce jour est destiné à célébrer cette époque d'espérance et de gloire où tombèrent des institutions barbares, où vous cessâtes d'être divisés en deux peuples, l'un condamné aux humiliations, l'autre marqué pour les distinctions et pour les grandeurs; où vos propriétés furent libres comme vos personnes, où la féodalité fut détruite et avec elle ces nombreux abus que des siècles avaient accumulés sur vos têtes.

Frenchmen, This day is appointed to celebrate that hopeful and glorious time when barbarous institutions were overthrown, when you ceased to be divided into two peoples, the one condemned to be humiliated, the other marked out for honours and greatness; when your properties became free like your persons, when feudalism was destroyed and with it those many abuses that centuries had piled up on your heads.

It is now commemorated with a military parade along the Champs-Élysées, and such other spectacles as a firework display at the Palais Maillot.

15 JULY

Idus Iuliae　　　　　　　　　　　　　　　　　　　　　　　　　　　　　　　　G

> *St Swithin's day, if thou dost rain,*
> *for forty days it will remain;*
> *St Swithin's day, if you be fair,*
> *for forty days 'twill rain nae mair.*

❦ ANCIENT ROME　This was the Travectio equitum, a parade of cavalry in front of the temple of Castor and Pollux, the great Twin Horsemen, to thank them for their part in the victory of Lake Regillus in 496 BC. It was first instituted in 304 BC, but lapsed until it was revived with great spectacle by Augustus; the riders, up to 5,000 in number, wore olive garlands and *trabeae* (purple togas with red stripes), besides any military decorations. It remains unclear what relation, if any, this parade bore to the quinquennial review in which the cavalry filed one by one past the censors, those they deemed unsuitable being discharged, such as the plump and well-groomed knight with a scrawny and neglected horse, who when asked why he was in better condition than his mount explained: 'Because I look after myself, but leave the horse to my worthless slave Statius.'

❦ HOLY DAYS　Translation of St Swithun (CofE; see also *2 July); Bonaventure (RC, formerly 14 July; CY commem.)

St Swithun was translated in 971 from his grave outside the Old Minster at Winchester to a shrine within it. According to legend, this was at his own demand; yet he was also said, with some exaggeration, to have deliberately chosen a humble burial-place, 'equally open to the lower among the common people', as the eleventh-century *Vita S. Swithuni* puts it; or to quote William of Malmesbury, *c.*1125:

> On the point of bidding farewell to earthly life, on his authority as bishop he ordered those present to inter his corpse outside the cathedral, where it should be exposed both to the feet of passers-by and to the dripping of water from the eaves.　　　　　　　　　Malmesbury, 162

This last phrase is an early allusion to the saint's interest in rain; of all the marker-days for prognosticating the weather, the translation of St Swithun became the most famous, even after other such lore had been forgotten. If it is fair, then fair weather will prevail for forty days; but if it rains, the next forty days will be wet, as if the saint were complaining that his wish had been ignored:

> In the daye of seynte Svithone rane ginneth rinigge Forti dawes mid ywone. [On St Swithin's day it usually begins to rain for forty days.]
> 　　　　early 14th-c. MS in Emmanuel College, Cambridge, MS 27, fo. 163 (quoted in Opie, 337)

Naturally the prediction sometimes fails, to the puzzlement of Ben Jonson's farmer, who is reading his almanac:

SORDIDO. O here, *St. Swithuns*, the xv day, variable weather, for the most part raine, good; for the most part raine: Why, it should raine fortie daies after, now, more or lesse, it was a rule held, afore I was able to hold a plough, and yet here are two daies, no raine; ha? it makes me muse.   *Every Man out of his Humour*, I. iii

St Swithun has sometimes been termed 'the drunken saint', probably a jocular reference to heavy rainfall, but the charge was taken seriously by Chambers:

It is only to be remarked, in conclusion, that the epithet of the 'drunken saint', sometimes applied to St Swithun, is a base slander on the worthy bishop's memory. True, the Saxons were rather noted for their convivial habits, and St Swithun, doubtless, had no objection to a cheerful glass in moderation. But no aberrations whatever, on the score of temperance, are recorded of him. The charge belongs clearly to the same category as that veracious statement in the popular ditty, by which St Patrick, the apostle of Ireland, is represented as a lover of potheen, and initiating his converts in the art of manufacturing that liquor.   Chambers

Bonaventure (*c.*1217–74), in the world Giovanni di Fidanza, Franciscan theologian, known as the *Doctor seraphicus*; from 1257 Minister-General of his Order, he codified its statutes and wrote the official life of its founder. Less sympathetic to Aristotelian philosophy than his Dominican contemporary Aquinas, he concurred with him in rejecting a doctrine that later Franciscans made their own, the Immaculate Conception of the BVM.

Rosalia, an obscure twelfth-century Sicilian anchoress (see *4 Sept.) who underwent a remarkable surge in popularity upon discovery of her relics in Palermo in 1624, when she became patron saint of the city. It continued unabated in the eighteenth century. Her feast-day, still celebrated as *u'fistinu* ('il festino'), was a four-day affair in 1770, when viewed by an English traveller. It began on 12 July:

The triumphal car was preceded by a troop of horse, with trumpets and kettle-drums; and all the city officers in their gala uniforms. It is indeed a most enormous machine: it measures seventy feet long, thirty wide, and upwards of eighty high; and, as it passed along, greatly over-topped the loftiest houses of Palermo. The form of its under part is like that of the Roman gallies, but it swells as it advances in height; and the front assumes an oval form like an amphitheatre, with seats placed in the theatrical manner. This is the great orchestra, and was filled with a very numerous band of musicians placed in rows, one above the other: Over this orchestra, and a little behind it, there is a large dome supported by six fine Corinthian columns, and adorned with a number of figures of saints and angels; and on the summit of the dome there is a gigantic silver statue of St. Rosolia [*sic*].—The whole machine is dressed out with orange trees, flower-pots, and large trees of artificial coral. The car stopped every fifty or sixty yards, when the orchestra performed a piece of music, with songs in honour of the saint. It appeared a great moving castle, and completely filled up the street from side to side.   Brydone, ii. 156

It culminated with a procession and mass on the 15th, for which the church had been specially decorated and illuminated.

Vladimir, Grand Prince of Kiev, a mighty warrior who achieved sole rule over Rus' from the Black Sea to the Baltic, and in 988 was baptized a Christian according to the Byzantine rite in order to marry the joint emperors' sister Anna; thereupon he converted his subjects by force. He is particularly honoured in Ukraine as Volodymyr the Great.

On this day in 1099 the First Crusade captured Jerusalem; the ensuing massacre of Jews and Muslims is complacently described by Crusading authors, dispensing modern historians from reliance on hostile sources.

This day was formerly the feast of *Divisio Apostolorum*, on which the Apostles were split up and sent to preach.

16 JULY

a.d. XVII Kalendas Augustas   A

❦ HOLIDAYS AND ANNIVERSARIES Ukraine: Independence Day

❦ ANCIENT ROME On this day, immediately following the Ides, sacrifice was offered before the disastrous battle of the Allia (see *18 July); sacrifices on the day after Kalends, Nones, or Ides were afterwards prohibited, as leading to lost battles, and travel on them was deemed unlucky.

❦ HOLY DAYS Our Lady of Mount Carmel (RC); Osmund (CY commem.)

Mount Carmel, in Palestine, was the site of a community of hermits that eventually became the Carmelite Order; St Simon Stock (see *16 May) is said to have received a vision of the Virgin there on 16 July 1251. Bernardo O'Higgins, the liberator of Chile, was particularly devoted to Our Lady of Mount Carmel, and placed his army under her protection in January 1817, subsequently winning victory over the Spaniards; a sanctuary was then built in her honour. In 1926 she was crowned Queen of Chile. She is also patron saint of Bolivia (since 1914) and the Spanish navy.

Osmund (d. 1099), bishop of Salisbury from 1078. The cathedral at Old Sarum was completed during his time, but his body was translated to Salisbury Cathedral in 1226. Despite energetic attempts and a good deal of money from Salisbury's coffers, efforts to get him canonized succeeded only in 1456. A new shrine was built in 1457, at which a paralytic was healed; hence he is patron of those suffering from paralysis.

July
The air without has taken fever;
Fast I feel the beating of its pulse.
The leaves are twisted on the maple,
In the corn the autumn's premature;
The weary butterfly hangs waiting
For a breath to waft him thither at
The touch, but falls, like truth unheeded,
Into dust-blown grass and hollyhocks.

The air without is blinding dusty;
Cool I feel the breezes blow; I see
The sunlight, crowded on the porch, grow
Smaller till absorbed in shadow; and
The far blue hills are changed to gray, and
Twilight lingers in the woods between;
And now I hear the shower dancing
In the cornfield and the thirsty grass.

Alexander L. Posey (1873–1908)

17 JULY

a.d. XVI Kalendas Augustas B

❦ HOLIDAYS AND ANNIVERSARIES Iraq: 17 July Revolution or Baath Revolution Day (commemorating overthrow of government by Revolutionary Command Council, 1968) (national day)

❦ HOLY DAYS

Alexius of Edessa, the Man of God, ascetic (*fl. c.*400) especially beloved of the Orthodox (among whom his day is 17 Mar.), but also celebrated in the West from the tenth century onwards. Having sworn his fiancée to chastity he fled to Edessa, where he remained as a beggar outside the church of the Virgin for seventeen years until her statue spoke and gave him away; shunning publicity, he returned home and remained hidden for another seventeen years, fed by his father but insulted by the slaves; for this reason he is often portrayed lying underneath a staircase. As death approached he recorded his life-story.

Kenelm (Cynehelm), son of the Mercian king Cœnwulf (796–821), supposed to have succeeded at the age of 7 and been promptly murdered at the instigation of his sister, Abbess Cwœnthryth, by his tutor, Æscberht; a milk-white dove flew from his head.

Jadwiga, queen of Poland, b. 1374, was betrothed at the age of 4 to Wilhelm of Habsburg, but on succeeding in 1384 was obliged to break off her engagement and instead, the next year, to marry Grand Duke Jogaila (in Polish known as Jagiełło) of Lithuania, an expansionist power that included much of modern Belarus', Ukraine, and western Russia. Lithuania was the last pagan state in Europe; although in the ethnic heartland allegiance to the national religion remained strong, her rulers had been more concerned to preserve their diplomatic freedom by evading the choice between the confession, and with it the alliance, of Catholic Poland and Orthodox Muscovy. Upon marrying Jadwiga, the Grand Duke was baptized a Catholic (with the font-name of Władysław) and undertook to impose his new religion on his subjects; despite some resistance, the new political reality proved more successful in Christianizing the Lithuanians than the aggression of the Teutonic Order and their allies such as Chaucer's 'verray, parfit gentil knyght'. She died on 17 July 1399; at an open-air ceremony in Kraków on 8 June 1997 she was canonized by her compatriot Pope John Paul II.

Marina (Orth.); see Margaret of Antioch (*20 July).

18 JULY

a.d. XV Kalendas Augustas   C

❦ ANCIENT ROME Dies Alliensis 387 BC (not, as in standard reckoning, 390; the year is determined by firm synchronisms): the Roman army was routed by Gauls, who went on to capture most of Rome, but were thwarted in their assault on the Capitol by the cackling of some geese. There are many inspiring legends concerning these events: the grave senators sitting motionless like gods, the Gaulish leader Brennus (named after the leader of the Gaulish army that in 279 BC attacked Delphi and overran Galatia) casting his sword into the scales with the comment *Vae victis*, commonly translated 'Woe to the conquered', but closer in tone to 'Hard luck, you lost.' The day was afterwards confused with the date of a legendary disaster in 477 BC, when the Fabii, having taken it upon themselves to repulse an Etruscan invasion, were massacred at the Cremera (see *13 Feb.).

❦ HOLY DAYS Formerly Camillus de Lellis (see *14 July)

Arnulf of Metz, a Frankish noble who after serving King Clothar II took holy orders, was bishop of Metz 614–29, then resigned to be a hermit; d. *c.*640; ancestor of Carolingians. As a layman he had cast his ring into the sea, declaring that he would not believe his sins forgiven unless God should return it to him; it was found inside a fish. For a variation on this theme, see *13 January. The same miracle is said to have befallen Polycrates, tyrant of Samos, but as a sign of impending doom, for he had been advised to avert the gods' envy of his wealth and power by throwing away his favourite possession; he was treacherously murdered by a Persian satrap in 522 BC.

19 JULY

a.d. XIV Kalendas Augustas   D

❦ ANCIENT ROME On this day and the 21st the Lucaria were celebrated in a large grove (*lucus*), where the survivors of the Allia disaster (see *18 July) were said to have taken refuge. Presumably the ceremony had been intended to propitiate the spirits of the woodland before the felling of trees; even in the second century BC the Elder Cato records a prayer to be said by the farmer, over the sacrifice of a pig, before clearance, but by the late Republic intellectual city-dwellers sought rational explanations even if they had to make them up.

❦ HOLY DAYS Gregory of Nyssa and Macrina (CY; RC 9 Mar., Orth. *10 Jan.); formerly Vincent de Paul (now *27 Sept.)

Dog days. In Oxford almanacks, this was long given as the beginning of the dog days, which were said to end on 27 August up to 1721, on 28 August from 1722; the information was suppressed in 1753, when a decision would have been needed whether or not to correct the dates for New Style. See *Days: Dog Days.*

20 JULY

a.d. XIII Kalendas Augustas   E

❦ HOLIDAYS AND ANNIVERSARIES Colombia: Independence Day (from Spain, 1819)
Japan: Marine Day

❦ ANCIENT ROME First day of Ludi Victoriae Caesaris, which lasted until the 30th, commemorating the battle of Pharsalus (see also *26 Sept.).

❦ HOLY DAYS Margaret of Antioch (CofE, RC); formerly Jerome Emiliani (now *8 Feb.)

Margaret, from Antioch-in-Pisidia (near Yalvaç in Turkey), is one of the Fourteen Auxiliary Saints (see *8 Aug.), called Marina in the East and culted on 17 July. Fictitious acts, denounced as such in the *Decretum Gelasianum*, were too appealing to be ignored: maidens and dragons made wonderful stories (cf. St George, *23 Apr.). According to the legend, Margaret was swallowed by Satan in the form of a dragon, but since she was holding a cross or made the sign of a cross, the dragon split open and she stepped out unharmed, for which she was beheaded. Margaret's cult became very popular in the Middle Ages through her reputed promise that pregnant women invoking her would escape the dangers of childbirth and those praying to her on their deathbed would escape the Devil. Her chief emblem is the dragon.

Wilgefortis (presumably from Virgo Fortis, 'Mighty Maiden'), alias Uncumber (from Dutch *ontkomen*, 'escaped'), alias Liberata (Livrade, Librada), alias Kümmernis ('Woe'), alias Hülpe ('Help'), alias Regenfledis, alias Caritas, septuplet daughter of a pagan king of Portugal who after taking a vow of virginity evaded her projected marriage to the king of Sicily by growing a beard and moustache (cf. Galla, *5 Oct.); her enraged father

had her crucified. This is evidently derived from misinterpretation of Byzantine Crucifixions in which Christ is portrayed not as the Man of Sorrows but as the Pantocrator
or Lord of All, in a long robe with crown and beard. Her cult was extremely popular
from the late Middle Ages onwards, not least amongst unhappily married women; Sir
Thomas More's interlocutor sneers at their custom of offering her oats:

Whereof I can not perceyue the reason / but yf it be bycause she shold prouyde an horse for an
euyll housbonde to ryde to the deuyll vpon. For that is the thynge that she is so sought for as
they say. In so moch that women hath therfore chaunged her name and in stede of saint wylge-
forte call her saynt Vncumber / bycause they reken that for a pecke of otys she wyll not fayle to
vncomber theym of theyr housbondys.   T. More, i. 227

In 1608 the Venetian Feast of the Redeemer took place on 20 July, the third Sunday of
the month, during Thomas Coryat's visit to Venice:

In the yeare of our Lord M.D.Lxxvi. there hapned a most grievous pestilence in Venice which
destroyed at least a hundred thousand persons, but at last God looked downe from heaven with
the eyes of mercy, and sodainly stayed the infection. Whereupon the Senate to the end they
might be thankfull unto God for their sodaine deliverance from so great a contagion, vowed to
build a faire Church, and to dedicate it to Christ the Redeemer, to the end they might yearly
honour him upon the same day wherein the plague ceased, with certayne speciall and extraordinary solemnities. . . . At that time there was made a faire broade bridge over the water consisting of boates very artificially joyned together, over the which were fastened boords for the
people to walke on to and fro to the Redeemers Church . . . This Venetian bridge which was prepared against this religious solemnity, reached from one shore to the other, and was almost a mile
long. There was I also, where I observed an exceeding multitude of people flocking together to
that Church, and passing forth and backe over the bridge. . . . That day I saw a marvailous
solemne Procession. For every Order and Fraternity of religious men in the whole city met together, and carried their Crosses and candlesticks of silver in procession to the Redeemers
Church, and so backe againe to their severall Convents. Besides there was much good fellowship
in many places of Venice upon that day. For there were many places, whereof each yeelded
allowance of variety of wine and cakes and some other prety junkats to a hundred good fellowes
to be merry that day, but to no more: this I know by experience. For a certaine Stationer of the
city, with whom I had some acquaintance, one Joannes Guerilius met me by chance at the
Redeemers Church, and after he had shewed me the particular places of the Capucins
Monastery, brought me to a place where we had very good wine, cakes, and other delicates gratis,
where a Priest served us all.   Coryat, i. 365–7

For the ancient Egyptians the heliacal rising of Sirius ('Sothis') on this or the previous
day was theoretically the beginning of the Nile flood on which all life depended, and
(even more theoretically) the beginning of the year; when they coincided, a new 'Sothic'
period of 1461 Egyptian years was said to begin (see II: *Egyptian Calendar). Local Christians adopted the day as the death of St Joseph. A mnemonic makes this day the start
of the dog days:

> Margaris os canis est, caudam Laurentius adfert.
> Margaret is the dog's mouth, Laurence brings his tail.

That is, the dog days last from 20 July to 10 August; for a more generous estimate, see
*Days: Dog Days.

On this day in 1944 officers of the Wehrmacht attempted to overthrow the Nazi regime and assassinate Adolf Hitler; but the briefcase containing Claus von Stauffenberg's bomb was moved before detonation, so that Hitler survived. The officers' attempted coup was soon reversed; the most brutal reprisals were taken against the plotters, who are held to have belatedly redeemed the honour of the Prussian aristocracy.

21 JULY

a.d. XII Kalendas Augustas   F

❪ HOLIDAYS AND ANNIVERSARIES Belgium: Accession of King Leopold I, 1831 (national day)

❪ ANCIENT ROME Lucaria (see *19 July).

❪ HOLY DAYS Laurence of Brindisi (RC)

Laurence of Brindisi (1559–1619), Capucin friar and famous preacher who combated Lutheranism in Bohemia, Austria, and Germany. As their chaplain, armed with a crucifix he led the Imperial troops against the Turks in Hungary in 1601. Pope John XXIII declared him a Doctor of the Church in 1959.

Praxedis, virgin, perhaps founder of the church of Santa Prassede in Rome; legend made her a member of a family that gave hospitality to St Peter. Readers of Browning's poem 'The Bishop Orders His Tomb at Saint Praxed's Church' will remember the cultured but worldly Renaissance bishop who on his deathbed enjoins his 'nephews' in vain to build him an elaborate tomb, and speaks in his rambling of 'St Praxed at his sermon on the mount' (l. 95).

Rush-bearing, bringing greens in procession to strew on the unpaved floors of parish churches, was a harvest custom in north-west England probably dating back to medieval times, though recorded only since the sixteenth century. A rush-bearing in Grasmere on 21 July 1827 is described by T.Q.M.:

The church door was open, and I discovered that the villagers were strewing the floors with fresh rushes. I learnt from the old clerk, that, according to annual custom, the rush-bearing procession would be in the evening. I asked the clerk if there were any dissenters in the neighbourhood; he said, no, not nearer than Keswick, where there were some that called themselves Presbyterians; but he did not know what they were, he believed them to be a kind of *papishes*. During the whole of this day I observed the children busily employed in preparing garlands of such wild flowers as the beautiful valley produces, for the evening procession, which commenced at nine, in the following order:—The children (chiefly girls) holding these garlands, paraded through the village, preceded by the *Union* [i.e. workhouse] band, (thanks to the great drum for this information;)

they then entered the church, where the three largest garlands were placed on the altar, and the remaining ones in various other parts of the place. (By the by, the beautifiers have placed an ugly window above the altar, of the nondescript order of architecture.) In the procession I observed the 'Opium Eater' [Thomas De Quincey], Mr. Barber, an opulent gentleman residing in the neighbourhood, Mr. and Mrs. Wordsworth, Miss Wordsworth, and Miss Dora Wordsworth. Wordsworth is the chief supporter of these rustic ceremonies. The procession over, the party adjourned to the ball-room, a hayloft, at my worthy friend, Mr. Bell's, where the country lads and lasses tripped it merrily and *heavily*. . . . Billy Dawson, the fiddler, boasted to me of having been the officiating minstrel at this ceremony for the last six and forty years. He made grievous complaints of the outlandish tunes which the 'Union band chaps' introduce: in the procession of this evening they annoyed Billy by playing the 'Hunters' Chorus in Friskits' [*Der Freischütz*]. 'Who', said Billy, 'can keep time with such a queer thing?'

T.Q.M., 'Notes on a tour, chiefly pedestrian, from Skipton in Craven, Yorkshire, to Keswick, in Cumberland', in Hone, *Table*, 553–4

22 JULY

a.d. XI Kalendas Augustas   G

❦ ANCIENT ROME Dedication of the temple of Concordia in the Forum, reputedly built by Camillus in 367 BC after the plebeians had won the right to the consulate, but more probably in 121 BC by the consul Lucius Opimius after his ruthless suppression of Gaius Gracchus' supporters, into whose wounds he was not unhappy to rub salt. His temple was restored in 7 BC by Tiberius Claudius Nero (the future emperor Tiberius) to signify unity in the imperial household; the next year he left it and settled in Rhodes.

❦ HOLY DAYS Mary Magdalen (BCP), **Mary Magdalene** (CY; RC commem.)

Mary Magdalene, the witness to the Resurrection out of whom (according to Luke and the long ending of Mark) Jesus had cast seven devils; in some Gnostic texts she becomes a great apostle. In the Orthodox Church she is honoured on this day as 'the Holy Myrrh-Bearer and Equal of the Apostles Mary Magdalene'; she is also feasted with the other Myrrh-Bearers on the second Sunday after Easter. However, she is kept apart from Mary of Bethany (sister of Martha and Lazarus; see *4 June, *29 July), and most emphatically from the harlot ('sinner in the city') who in Luke wiped Jesus' feet with her hair (in John a similar office is performed by Mary of Bethany, in Mark and Matthew by an anonymous 'woman'); in the West all three had become conflated by the time of Gregory the Great, and it is the harlot, albeit reformed, who predominates. Her association with music in the Middle Ages stems from the elaborate story in the Golden Legend: having reached Provence with her sister Martha and brother Lazarus, and after preaching to the pagans of Marseille, she became a hermit on a mountain-top near Sainte-Baume, where for thirty years she was lifted up to heaven by angels at each of the canonical hours, accompanied by 'the joyful jubilation of the heavenly hosts'. However, her frequent portrayal as a lutenist or dancer reflects the worldliness of her earlier life, before her conversion. In the Digby cycle of the late fifteenth century the Devil, disguised as a handsome young man, tempts her: 'But wol you dawns, my own dere?' To which she replies: 'Ser, I asent in good maner.' Devil or no, thirteenth-century nuns in Normandy danced on her feast-day.

Her emblem is a jar of ointment; she is patroness of apothecaries, of fallen women, and of hairdressers (from her long hair), and is invoked against the plague (Marseille having been spared through her intervention during the reign of Louis XV).

The epithet *Magdalēnē* ('the woman from Magdala'), which in Greek has four syllables, was shortened in English speech to 'maudlin', as still in the names of our saint's colleges at Oxford (spelt Magdalen) and Cambridge (spelt Magdalene); otherwise the written form (usually without the final -*e*) gave rise to a spelling-pronunciation with three syllables, used even for the Oxford church of St Mary Magdalen, leaving *maudlin* to become an adjective meaning 'cheaply sentimental'.

23 JULY

a.d. X Kalendas Augustas   A

❦ HOLIDAYS AND ANNIVERSARIES Egypt: National Day (Anniversary of the Revolution of 1952)

❦ ANCIENT ROME This day marked the Neptunalia, a popular holiday celebrated by alfresco revelries; but Horace (*Odes* 3. 28) prefers to keep it (and the night) at home with an invited girlfriend and superior wine.

❦ HOLY DAYS Bridget of Sweden (RC, formerly 7 Oct.; CY commem.); Philip Evans and John Lloyd (RC Wales)

Bridget (Birgitta) *of Sweden* (1303–73), founder of the Bridgettine Order. Married at the age of 13, she had borne eight children when she became principal lady-in-waiting to the queen of Sweden, Blanche of Namur. It was then that she began to experience revelations, distinctly at odds with court life. She and her husband made pilgrimages as far as Santiago de Compostela; after his death she founded a monastery for both sexes at Vadstena, where poverty was the rule but books were allowed for study. In 1349 she went to Rome, remaining in Italy for the rest of her life save for a pilgrimage to Jerusalem. Her revelations were widely disseminated; opposition was aroused by those concerning contemporary affairs, in particular the Great Schism. Five hundred years after her daughter St Catherine (*24 Mar.) had secured her canonization, she was named patron saint of Sweden by Leo XIII in 1891, confirmed in 1926.

Philip Evans and John Lloyd, Popish Plot martyrs, 1679; so pampered in prison that Evans refused to hear the sheriff's announcement concerning his execution till he had finished his game of tennis; then played the harp while waiting to be hanged.

Apollinaris, reputedly a disciple of St Peter, certainly the first bishop of Ravenna, where two beautiful churches are dedicated to him, Sant'Apollinare in Classe, dating from 549 and Catholic from the outset, and the former Arian royal church rededicated for Catholic worship as Sant'Apollinare Nuovo.

John Cassian (*c*.360–after 430). His dialogues of Egyptian ascetics, called *Collationes* ('Conferences'), were ordered in the Rule of St Benedict to be read to the brethren before compline; in course of time, to this spiritual sustenance was added physical, whence the English use of 'collation' for a light meal and the Italian *colazione*, 'breakfast' or 'lunch' according to region. He is not in the Roman Martyrology, but is honoured on this day in Marseille, where he founded two monasteries and is buried. The Orthodox Church keeps his feast in leap year only, on *29 February.

Apparition of 'Nossa Senhora da Barraca' near Lisbon, 1822:

Every creature in Lisbon and its environs is hastening to pay due adoration at the shrine of the newly discovered virgin, who is about four inches long, and, being found . . . in a cave near this place, is consequently denominated 'Nossa Senhora da Barracca', (our lady of the cave). Here, every evening, a friar descants upon the miracles said to have been performed by her; and a small book, descriptive of them, has been published by *authority*. The image is already covered with costly ornaments, among which are, a crown set with brilliants, and numerous gold chains; the gifts of those votaries who are able to afford such demonstration of their faith. An aged fidalga [gentlewoman], and somewhat fanciful withal, living in this neighbourhood, and who has been bed-ridden for years past, has caused herself to be carried to the cave, and has in consequence, (as she declares,) recovered the use of her limbs; the circumstance being well authenticated, affords additional proof of the extraordinary power of the imagination in nervous and hypochondriac complaints. The Queen goes in grand state this evening, and makes an offering of a silver lamp. The field resembles an immense fair, and restaurateurs regularly attend in their booths, to provide for the refreshment of the company. Last night, there were no less than thirty carriages upon the ground, and it is common to see more than a thousand of the peasantry and townspeople upon their knees, at one time, surrounding the mouth of the cave. The friars have thought proper to declare, that a balsamic fragrance flows constantly from the image; and though there is always a strong smell of garlic and oil in the grotto, it is the fashion, upon entering, to exclaim, 'What a delicious odour!'   Baillie, ii. 128–9

24 JULY

a.d. IX Kalendas Augustas   B

❦ HOLIDAYS AND ANNIVERSARIES Ecuador: Bolívar's Birthday (1783)
   USA, Utah: Pioneer Day, commemorating the arrival of Mormon settlers in the
      valley of the Great Salt Lake, Utah, 1847
   Venezuela: Bolívar's Birthday (1783)

(HOLY DAYS

Christina. Two saints Christina were honoured on this day, Christina of Bolsena, martyred *c.*304 near Bolsena (also confused with Christina of Tyre, of doubtful existence), and Christina the Astonishing (1150–1224), who startled mourners by waking up at her own funeral and announcing that she was to complete her time in purgatory on earth, proceeding to do so in a spectacular fashion.

Declan, an early fifth-century Irish bishop who founded the church of Ardmore, the site of a holy well; a stone on the beach is known as 'St Declan's stone'. Pilgrims still come to Ardmore during the week that includes his feast-day, 'Pattern week'. In 1826 the celebration took the following form:

The 24th of July being the day appointed by the Roman Catholic Church on which honour is publicly paid to the memory of St. Declan, the tutelar saint of that district, several thousand persons of all ages and sexes assembled upon this occasion. . . . At an early hour in the day, those whom a religious feeling had drawn to the spot commenced their devotional exercises (in a state of half nudity) by passing under the holy rock of St. Declan. . . . This was not effected without considerable pain and difficulty, owing to the narrowness of the passage, and the sharpness of the rocks within. Stretched at full length on the ground, on the face and stomach, each devotee moved forward, as if in the act of swimming, and thus squeezed or dragged themselves through. Both sexes were obliged to submit to this humiliating mode of proceeding; and upwards of eleven hundred persons were observed to go through this ceremony in the course of the day. . . .

This object of so great veneration is believed to be holy, and to be endued with miraculous powers. It is said to have been wafted from Rome upon the surface of the ocean, at the period of St. Declan's founding his church at Ardmore, and to have borne on its top a large bell for the church tower, and also vestments for the saint himself.

At a short distance from this sacred memorial, on a cliff overhanging the sea, is the well of the saint: thither the crowds repair, the devotions at the rock being ended. Having drunk plentifully of its water, they wash their legs and feet in the stream that issues from it, and telling their beads, sprinkle themselves and their neighbours with the sanctified liquid.—These performances over, the grave of the patron saint is then resorted to. Hundreds at a time crowded around it, and crushed and trampled one another in their eagerness to obtain a handful of the earth which is believed to cover the mortal remains of Declan. . . . In the course of time the abode of the saint has sunk to the depth of nearly four feet, its clay having been scooped away by the finger nails of the pious Catholics. A human skull of large dimensions was placed at the head of the tomb, before which the people bowed, believing it to be the identical skull of their tutelar saint, who that day was present to look upon their devotions, and who would, upon his return to the mansions of bliss, intercede at the throne of grace for all such as did him honour. This visit to St. Declan's grave completed the devotional exercises of a day, held in greater honour than the Sabbath by all those who venerate the saint's name, and worship at his shrine. Nevertheless, the sanctity of a day, marked even by the most humiliating exercises of devotion, did not prevent its night being passed in riot and debauchery.   *Time's Telescope* (1827), 241–2

25 JULY

a.d. VIII Kalendas Augustas   C

> *Till Saint James's Day be come and gone*
> *You may have hops or you may have none.*

❦ HOLIDAYS AND ANNIVERSARIES Spain: St James Day

❦ ANCIENT ROME Furrinalia, honouring an ancient Italic goddess who had a priest of her own (the *flamen Furrinalis*) and a sacred grove on the Janiculum, the *lucus Furrinae*, where Gaius Gracchus perished; the site is now occupied by the Villa Sciarra. Classical authors, including Cicero, near whose home town of Arpinum she was also worshipped, associate her with the Furies; many modern scholars dismiss this as a mere assimilation of names, and suspect she was the nymph of a spring that had lost its importance.

❦ HOLY DAYS **James the Greater, Apostle** (CofE, RC; 30 Apr. Orth.); red-letter day; Dormition of Anne, mother of Theotokos (Orth.; see *26 July)

James the Greater, brother of St John (*27 Dec.), patron saint of Spain from at least the ninth century, and of Guatemala and Nicaragua. He was executed by King 'Herod' (Acts 12: 2), in fact Marcus Julius Agrippa, king of Judaea 41–4. In the seventh century some Spaniards had launched the legend that St James preached, died, and was buried in their country; this later became an abortive mission from which he returned to greater success in Judaea. After making a Christian of a sorcerer who strove to undermine his work, on his way to execution he cured a paralytic and converted the executioner; his body was then conveyed to Spain and buried there. Others say that his remains were translated upon the fall of Jerusalem in 70 to Sinai and later removed ahead of Saracen attacks to Spain, his monastery being rededicated to St Catherine (*25 Nov.); frescoes of James have indeed been found underneath those depicting Catherine. In any case, the relics were solemnly buried on 25 July 816 in the great church at Santiago de Compostela, erected over a Roman mansion, one of the chief pilgrimage centres of the Middle Ages. Those who had visited his shrine put a cockleshell in their hats; on primestaves the hat was portrayed with rain dripping from it, earning him the name *Jakob våthatt*, 'James Wethat'.

During the siege of Malta in 1565 the besieged expected (in vain) to be relieved on this day by Don García de Toledo, viceroy of Sicily, because he belonged to the Order of Spain's patron saint; in Marlowe's play *The Jew of Malta*, which is loosely based on the siege, gifts are made to nuns on the eve.

Christopher. One of the Fourteen Auxiliary Saints. He was formerly thought to be a martyr under Decius, but that identification is now discounted. According to legend, he was a gigantic man (the Golden Legend makes him 18 ft high) who, upon conversion to Christianity, was assigned the task of conveying travellers across a river. One day, a child he was carrying on his shoulders became progressively heavier, and Christopher barely made it to the other bank; once there the child revealed himself as Christ, carrying the weight of the world. Hence the name, which means Christ-bearer. He is patron saint of travellers and invoked against water. Many people carry St Christopher medals (especially in cars) in the belief that seeing his image will protect them from death on that day. The Orthodox day is 9 May.

At Guadalajara in Mexico a huge stone statue known as *San Cristobalazo* ('Hulking St Christopher') inspired the porters' prayer:

Dichoso Cristobalazo,	Fortunate Great Christopher,
santazo de cuerpo entero	mighty saint with sturdy body,
y no como otros santitos	and not like other saintlings
que ni se ven en el cielo,	who aren't even noticed in heaven.
Hercúleo Cristobalazo,	Herculean Great Christopher,
forzudo como un Sansón,	brawny as a Samson,
con tu enorme cabezón	with your huge great head
y tu nervoso pescuezo,	and your sinewy neck,
Hazme grueso y vigoroso,	make me stout and strong,
hombrazo de cuerpo entero	a real man with sturdy body,
y no come estos tipitos	and not like these feeble fellows
que casi besan el suelo.	who all but kiss the ground.

St James's Day was traditionally the opening of the oyster season, subsequently transferred to *5 August, Old St James's Day, but some continued to observe the original date:

'Whoever eats oysters on St James's day will never want money.' In point of fact, it is customary in London to begin eating oysters on St James's Day, when they are necessarily somewhat dearer than afterwards; so we may presume that the saying is only meant as a jocular encouragement to a little piece of extravagance and self-indulgence. In this connection of oysters with St James's Day, we trace the ancient association of the apostle with pilgrims' shells. There is a custom in London which makes this relation more evident. In the course of the few days following upon the introduction of oysters for the season, the children of the humbler class employ themselves diligently in collecting the shells which have been cast out from taverns and fish-shops, and of these they make piles in various rude forms. By the time that old St James's Day (the 5th of August) has come about, they have these little fabrics in nice order, with a candle stuck in the top, to be lighted at night. As you thread your way through some of the denser parts of the metropolis, you are apt to find a cone of shells, with its votive light, in the nook of some retired court, with a group of youngsters around it, some of whom will be sure to assail the stranger with a whining claim—*Mind the grotto!* by which is meant a demand for a penny wherewith professedly to keep up the candle. It cannot be doubted that we have here, at the distance of upwards of three hundred years from the Reformation, a relic of the habits of our Catholic ancestors.

Chambers

26 JULY

26 JULY

a.d. VII Kalendas Augustas   D

❦ HOLIDAYS AND ANNIVERSARIES Liberia: Independence Day (republic, 1847)
(national holiday)
The Maldives: Independence Day (from Great Britain, 1965)

❦ HOLY DAYS Anne, mother of the BVM (BCP; Orth. 25 July); Joachim and Anne
(RC, with Joachim since 1969); Anne and Joachim (CY)

Anne. The name of the Virgin's mother does not occur in the Bible but in the second-
century Protevangelium of James, where Mary's ancestry is traced. In a story that seems
modelled on the Old Testament figure of Hannah (Latin 'Anna'), who conceived
Samuel after years of barrenness (1 Sam. 1–2: 11), Anne found her prayers answered by
an angelic annunciation that she would conceive 'and thy seed will be spoken of in all
the world'; her husband, Joachim, also received an angelic prophecy while in the wilderness, and their chaste kiss upon meeting at the Golden Gate was deemed the moment
at which Mary was conceived (see *8 Dec.). The cult of St Anne developed during the
Middle Ages as a result of increasing devotion to the Conception (especially strong
in England); in the fully developed form of the legend she becomes the matriarch of
the Holy Family, by her successive husbands Joachim, Cleophas, and Salome (*sic*)
mother of three Marys, and by them respectively grandmother of Jesus Christ, of James
the Less and Philip, and of James the Greater and John the Evangelist. By the sixteenth
century her legend was so popular as to draw a powerful attack from Martin Luther
(who had made his monk's vow to St Anne); the Council of Trent took steps to down-
play what it deemed a 'misplaced devotion'. Little attention was paid to St Joachim until
the later Middle Ages; his feast was authorized only in the early sixteenth century, by
Pope Julius II.

St Anne's Day was long venerated in Florence as the day on which in 1343 the revolt
against the titular Duke of Athens, Walter VI of Brienne, led to his expulsion and the
restoration of republican government. Walter had inherited the title from his father,
who had lost Athens to the Catalan Company in 1311; he was initially hired by the Florentines to fight Pisa, then proclaimed their *signore* for life on 8 September 1342, a decision of which they soon repented: having relinquished political control, his original
supporters in the mercantile patriciate saw themselves liable for heavy taxes, and their
noble and lower-class enemies, whom he tried to cultivate, joined forces with them instead to expel the foreign tyrant before resuming the internal struggle. The Florentines
credited St Anne with the victory and made her protectress of their city; she remained
the symbol of republican freedom until the sixteenth century, when the Medici dukes
appropriated her blessing for themselves.

Whereas the month of June is subject to cold spells, July is hot (especially in North America):

> July breathes hot, sallows the crispy fields,
> Curls up the wan leaves of the lilac-hedge,
> And every eve cheats us with a show of clouds
> That braze the horizon's western rim, or hang
> Motionless, with heaped canvas drooping idly,
> Like a dim fleet by starving men besieged,
> Conjectured half, and half descried afar,
> Helpless of wind, and seeming to slip back
> Adown the smooth curve of the oily sea.
>
> James Russell Lowell (1819–91), 'Under the Willows'

27 JULY

a.d. VI Kalendas Augustas   E

❦ HOLY DAYS

Pantaleon (RC), said to have been personal physician to the emperor Maximian; converted and baptized by the priest Hermolaus, he was betrayed by his colleagues and tied to an olive tree (*c.*305); when he prayed for his executioners to be forgiven, Christ's voice was heard renaming him *Panteleēmōn* ('all-compassionate'). It is by this name that he is known to the Orthodox, who venerate him as a wonder-worker and one of the 'unmercenary' physicians who refuse payment. In the West, he is one of the Fourteen Auxiliary Saints. A relic of his blood at Ravello is said to liquefy in the same manner as that of St Januarius at Naples, though according to his legend milk instead of blood flowed from his veins when he was beheaded. He is patron of doctors and midwives.

Seven Sleepers of Ephesus, supposedly Christian youths (originally eight in number) who hid in a cave to avoid the Decian persecution (250), were walled up by the emperor, fell asleep, woke up nearly 200 years later, testified to the resurrection of the dead, and then went back to sleep; when they turn over, ill is boded. The tale was so widespread in the East that a version of it, with Muslim sleepers, is told in the eighteenth *sūra* of the Koran; in the sixth century it reached the West. Edward the Confessor was said to have seen them turn onto their left sides in a vision on Easter Day, 26 March 1060, and foretold seventy-four years of turmoil before they should turn again; the tale is first recorded when nine years still remained of the seventy-four, a number that neither reason nor mystery has yet accounted for. In many German calendars they are set down on 27 June; their Orthodox days, as the Seven Holy Children, are 4 August and 22 October.

Clement of Ohrid (d. 916), missionary in Macedonia; this day is kept by the Orthodox, the 17th by RCs. A Slav companion of Cyril and Methodius who played a part in devising the Glagolitic alphabet, he was probably named by them at ordination after St Clement of Rome (see *11 May, *23 Nov.). Expelled from Moravia in 885 for opposing the Western doctrine, zealously promoted by the Franks, that the Holy Spirit proceeds from the Father and the Son (*Filioque*), he was sent by Boris I of Bulgaria as a missionary to the outlying province of Macedonia, where he founded the monastery of St Panteleimon at Ohrid; in 893 he was appointed to a bishopric. An effective preacher and evangelist, he was also a notable writer in Old Slavonic.

28 JULY

a.d. V Kalendas Augustas   F

❦ HOLIDAYS AND ANNIVERSARIES Peru: Anniversary of Independence (from Spain, 1821) (national day)

❦ HOLY DAYS

Samson, bishop of Dol (d. 565). Born and educated in Wales, he was famed as a missionary, both in Cornwall (one of the Isles of Scilly is named after him) and in Brittany. After Athelstan, king of Wessex (924–39), acquired some of his relics for a monastery at Milton Abbas, Samson's cult spread from Wales and Brittany to England.

A gardening tip from John Evelyn:

Now begin to streighten the entrance of your *Bees* a little; and help them to kill their *Drones*, if you observe too many; setting the new-invented *Cucurbit-Glasses* of *Beer* mingled with *Honey*, to entice the *Wasps, Flies*, &c. which waste your *Store*. Also hang *Bottles* of the same *Mixture* near your *Red Roman Nectarines*, and other tempting *Fruits* and *Flowers*, for their destruction, else they many times invade your best *Fruit*. Set therefore up *Hoofs* of *Neats-feet* for the *Earwigs*, and remember to cleanse and shake them out at *Noon*, when they constantly repair for the Shade: They are cursed *Devourers*; nor ought you to be less diligent to prevent the *Ants*, which above all invade the *Orange-Flower*, by casting scalding Brine on their *Hills*, and other Receptacles.

Evelyn, *Kalendarium*, 75–6

29 JULY

a.d. IV Kalendas Augustas   G

❦ HOLIDAYS AND ANNIVERSARIES Faeroes: Ólavsøka (Olav's Wake)

❦ HOLY DAYS Martha of Bethany (RC); Mary, Martha, and Lazarus (CY; for Lazarus, see also *17 Dec.)

Martha, sister of Lazarus and Mary of Bethany (see *4 June, *22 July), the single-minded housewife of the Gospel, who busied herself with serving Jesus while her sister Mary sat at his feet. Upon her question 'Lord, dost thou not care that my sister hath left me to serve alone?' Jesus answered 'Martha, Martha, thou art careful and troubled about many things: But one thing is needful: and Mary hath chosen that good part, which shall not be taken away from her' (Luke 10: 40–2). According to later legend, she, Lazarus, and Mary were baptized and put on rafts, eventually arriving in Marseille; Martha evangelized Tarascon, where her relics were discovered in 1187. Tarascon being the home of that genial boaster Tartarin, we may record that she is also said to have stunned a ravaging dragon that lurked in the Rhône with a sprinkling of holy water, tied it up with her girdle, and killed it. Her tomb became a place of pilgrimage; Clovis, King of the Franks, was reportedly cured there of a kidney ailment. Louis XI was also devoted to her. Martha is patron saint of housewives, and since 1963 of Italian hoteliers and their staff, waiters and waitresses; she is often portrayed with keys or a broom.

Olav II (995–1030), king of Norway 1016–29, and national patron together with Magnus (*16 Apr.). After an early career as a pirate, he was baptized at Rouen, then fought in England with Ethelred II against the Danes. On returning to Norway he took power as king, enforcing conversion with more zeal than discretion; he was exiled in 1029 and killed the next year in his attempt to regain the throne. A healing well, miracles, and enshrinement of his incorrupt body helped to spread his cult, which was also strong in England, especially in the north. This is the chief holiday in the Faeroes, celebrated with boat-races and all-night festivities.

30 JULY

a.d. III Kalendas Augustas					A

❧ ANCIENT ROME On this day (or rather date) in 101 BC the Roman consul Marius and the previous year's consul Quintus Catulus crushed the Cimbri at Vercellae; Catulus vowed a temple to Fortuna Huiusce Diei, the Fortune of This Day, in the Campus Martius, which has been speculatively identified with one of the temples unearthed in the Largo Argentina, and now inhabited by cats.

❧ HOLY DAYS Peter Chrysologus (RC); William Wilberforce (CY)

Peter Chrysologus (*c.*400–50), bishop of Ravenna, earned his epithet ('Goldenword') from his sermons as a Western counterpart to John Chrysostom, 'Goldenmouth' (*13 Sept.); for such names, see too Gregory the Great (*12 Mar.) and John Damascene (*4 Dec.), whose day used also to be Peter's. He was declared a Doctor of the Church in 1729.

William Wilberforce (1759–1833). Member of Parliament for Hull and friend and supporter of the younger Pitt: 'a young man of his [Pitt's] own age, who had already distinguished himself in Parliament by an engaging natural eloquence, set off by the sweetest and most exquisitely modulated of human voices, and whose affectionate heart, caressing manners, and brilliant wit, made him the most delightful of companions' (Macaulay, *William Pitt*). Having converted to Evangelicalism, he founded the Proclamation Society in 1787 'for the reformation of manners'. He campaigned vigorously first for the abolition of the slave trade (enacted in 1807), then for the abolition of slavery (achieved with the Emancipation Act of 1833).

Abdon and Sennen, martyrs of Oriental origin in Rome, buried since 826 in San Marco; they are patrons of coopers.

31 JULY

❆ HOLY DAYS Ignatius of Loyola (RC; CY commem.)

Ignatius of Loyola, properly Íñigo López de Loyola (1491–1556), founder of the Society of Jesus; named Íñigo after the abbot of Oña (see *1 June), he called himself Ignatius after the bishop of Antioch (see *17 Oct.). Born to a noble Basque family, he became an officer under the Spanish viceroy of Navarra till on 20 May 1521 a cannonball struck his leg during the French siege of Pamplona; on his sickbed he read and reflected on the life of Christ and the saints. He gave up military life, changed clothes with a beggar, and underwent spiritual despair and consolation, eventually travelling to Jerusalem on pilgrimage. On his return he gave himself to study; in 1537, with five companions, he became a priest, and set out again for Jerusalem. The voyage being prevented by Turkish hostility, they went instead to Rome, where Ignatius had a vision of the Father bidding the crucified Christ take him for his servant. The outcome was the Society of Jesus, approved by Paul III in 1540. He died on 31 July 1556, and was canonized in 1622. Owing to the success of his *Spiritual Exercises*, Pius XI proclaimed him patron of retreats in 1922. Many RC universities are named after him.

Germanus of Auxerre, bishop. Sent to Britain in 429 as the Pope's representative to combat the Pelagian heresy (see *28 Aug.), he reportedly took command against a raiding-party of Picts and Saxons, whom he ambushed in a valley on Easter Day (7 Apr.); the Britons' well-timed war-cry of *Alleluia! Alleluia! Alleluia!*, re-echoing off the hills, panicked the invaders into headlong flight. Apart from this detail (often doubted in the mistaken belief that it is miraculous), all else is uncertain, including the site of the valley. The traditional location at Maes Garmon ('Germanus' Field') near Yr Wyddgrug (Mold) in Clwyd rests on nothing more than Germanus' posthumous appropriation by the kingdom of Powys through confusion with a fifth-century bishop Germanus of Man; the pirates had better places to plunder than North Wales.

Joseph of Arimathea (American BCP, Orth.; RC commem. 17 Mar.); after the Crucifixion he obtained Pilate's permission to recover Jesus' body and (together with Nicodemus, according to St John) gave it an opulent funeral in a newly cut rock tomb. For this apocryphal tales have him punished, but miraculously set free to found the church in Lydda (now Lod), preach in Gaul and Britain, and be buried in Jerusalem, whence his remains were translated to Moyenmoutier in the Vosges. Yet another legend has him come to England with the Holy Grail (the chalice used by Christ at the Last Supper) and found a church at Glastonbury. He is patron saint of gravediggers and undertakers.

Neot (9th c.), a Cornish saint said to have been a monk of Glastonbury who became a hermit in what is now St Neot in Cornwall. His advice was greatly valued by King Alfred (it is the *Chronicle of the Sanctuary of St Neot* that launched the legend of burnt cakes). St Neots in Cambridgeshire is also named after him, owing to a transfer or theft of relics by monks from Thorney; Anselm declared them genuine, and extracted a cheekbone to give to the Abbey of Bec.

AUGUST

Dry August and warme,
Doth harvest no harme.
It is good to eat the briars [berries] in the sear month.

❨ NAMES OF THE MONTH Latin *Augustus*, French *août*, Spanish *agosto*, Portuguese *Agosto*, Italian *agosto*, German *August*, Welsh *Awst*, Scots Gaelic *an Lùnasdal*, Irish *Lughnasadh* (now spelt *Lúnasa*)

Until 8 BC the month was called *Sextilis* (from *sextus*, 'sixth'); it was renamed in honour of the First Citizen, who in it had obtained his first consulate (i.e. extorted it by force of arms) in 43 BC and made Egypt a Roman province in 30 BC. The Scots Gaelic and Irish names commemorate the harvest games in honour of Lugh, god of light and genius (see *1 Aug.).

❨ HOLIDAYS AND ANNIVERSARIES
First Monday Colorado: Colorado Day (admission day as 38th state, 1876)
 Jamaica: Independence Day (from Great Britain, 6 Aug. 1962)
 Northern Territory, Australia: Picnic Day
 Zambia: Youth Day (national holiday)

Last Monday UK: Summer Bank Holiday

Second Thursday Sweden: Kräftpremiär, first day of crayfish season

Third Thursday Sweden: Surströmmingspremiär, first day for selling *surströmming* (fermented Baltic herring, produced on Ulvön and sold in tins) eaten with *mandelpotatis* ('almond potatoes', a north Swedish variety), chopped onion, sour cream, and flatbread

Third Friday Hawaii: Admission Day (50th state, 1959) (state holiday)

> The sixt was *August*, being rich arrayd
> In garment all of gold downe to the ground:
> Yet rode he not, but led a louely Mayd
> Forth by the lilly hand, the which was cround
> With eares of corne, and full her hand was found;
> That was the righteous Virgin, which of old
> Liv'd here on earth, and plenty made abound;

But, after Wrong was lov'd and Iustice solde,
She left th'vnrighteous world and was to heauen extold.

Spenser, *The Faerie Queene*, VII. vii. 37

It is now August, and the Sunne is some what towards his declination, yet such is his heat as
hardeneth the soft clay, dries vp the standing ponds, wythereth the sappy leaues and scorcheth
the skin of the naked: now beginne the Gleaners to follow the Corne Cart, and a little bread to
a great deale of drinke makes the Trauailers dinner: the Melowne and the Cucumber is now in
request: and Oyle and vineger giue attendance on the Sallet hearbes: the Alehouse is more frequented then the Tauerne, and a fresh Riuer is more comfortable than a fiery Furnace: the Bathe
is now much visited by diseased bodies, and in the fayre Riuers, swimming is a sweet exercise: the
Bow and the Bowle picke many a purse, and the Cockes with their heeles spurne away many a
mans wealth: The Pipe and the Taber is now lustily set on worke, and the Lad and the Lasse will
haue no lead on their heeles: the new Wheat makes the Gossips Cake, and the Bride Cup is caried
aboue the heads of the whole Parish: the Furmenty pot welcomes home the Haruest cart, and
the Garland of flowers crownes the Captaine of the Reapers. Oh, 'tis the mery time, wherein
honest Neighbours make good cheere, and God is glorified in his blessings on the earth. In
summe, for that I find, I thus conclude, I hold it the worlds welfare, and the earths Warming-
pan. Farewell.   Breton (1626)

In *August* Choler and Melancholy much increase, from whence proceeds long lasting Fevers and
Agues not easily cured. Avoid immoderate exercise this month, especially the recreations of *Venus*.
Sleep but little in the day time, and beware of taking cold: be cautious of vomit, purge, or bleeding this month: to eat *Sage* is wholsom now, and to drink moderately a glass of good and pleasant Wine, is good and profitable for the body; and all meats or herbs that be cold of quality this
month, are accounted good and wholsom.   Saunders (1679)

I AUGUST

Kalendae Augustae   C

After Lammas corn ripens as much by night as by day.

❦ HOLIDAYS AND ANNIVERSARIES Switzerland: National Day (founding of Swiss
    Confederation, 1291)

❦ HOLY DAYS Lammas Day (BCP); Alphonsus Mary de Liguori (RC); Procession of
the Cross (Orth.)

Lammas Day owes its name to the Old English words for 'loaf' or 'bread' and 'mass',
Loafmass being the festival at the beginning of the harvest at which loaves of bread
from the new season's corn were blessed; in the translation of Orosius' anti-pagan
history formerly attributed to King Alfred, the date of Antony's attempt in 30 BC to
assemble a fleet against Octavian, 'Kalendis Sextilibus', becomes 'on the Kalends of
August, and [= namely] on the day that we call *Hlafmæsse*'. In the Middle Ages, when
phonetic change had obscured the etymology, the word was often assumed to come

from 'lamb'; as the illustration in Pl. 7 shows, this error lasted as late as the eighteenth century.

On this day, the fences put up on 'Lammas meadows' at Candlemas were taken down to permit common pasture on the aftermath, after individuals had taken their share of grass for hay; this practice continued wherever the common lands had not been enclosed, and the attendant festivities lasted in some parts of the country even into the 1960s.

'At latter Lammas' became proverbial for 'never'; similar expressions exist in many languages, ranging from Irish *lá Thaidhg na dTadhgann*, 'Taig of the Taigs' Day', to Chinese *lúzinián*, 'Year of the Donkey', but the most famous is the emperor Augustus' catch-phrase *ad Kalendas Graecas*, 'at the Greek calends', now an English idiom. In Fuller's *Holy State* 4. 15, the demands presented by the Spanish Ambassador to Elizabeth I before the Armada are versified as follows:

> These to you are our commands,
> Send no help to th' Netherlands:
> Of the treasure took by Drake,
> Restitution you must make:
> And those Abbies build anew,
> Which your Father overthrew:
> If for any peace you hope,
> In all points restore the Pope.

Her extempore reply was:

> Ad Graecas, bone Rex, fient mandata calendas.

which Fuller versified as:

> Worthy King, know this your will
> At latter lammas wee'l fulfill.

The day was sometimes called the Gule of August, in Latin *Gula Augusti*, 'the Gullet of August'; this may mean no more than 'entrance' or 'beginning', but no agreed explanation has been found. Fanciful etymologies range from '(Festum Sancti Petri) ad vincula' to Welsh *gŵyl Awst*, the Feast of August; some have even invoked the legend of Balbina, daughter of the tribune Quirinus, cured of her throat disease by kissing the chains of St Peter. 'Gule' was occasionally corrupted to 'Yule'.

In Ireland this was the day of Lughnasadh, the harvest games in honour of Lugh, god of light and genius, in Gaulish *Lugos*, in Welsh *Lleu*. The Irish diarist Humphrey O'Sullivan (i. 102) notes that this day is 'Lá Lughnasa', Christianized in Father Mc-Grath's translation to 'Lammas Day'. Before 1990 it was also Lammas term day in Scotland; it has now been moved to the 28th.

Alphonsus Mary de Liguori (1696–1787), founder of the Congregation of the Most Holy Redeemer. Pius XII declared him patron of confessors and moral theologians in 1950. He is patron saint of Agrigento, along with St Gerland. Feast-day formerly 2 August.

The Procession of the Cross commemorates the Byzantine custom of bearing the True Cross in procession round Constantinople on the first fifteen days of August as a preservative against plague.

St Peter's Chains (festum Sancti Petri ad vincula). According to Acts 12: 3–11 'Herod the king' (in fact Marcus Julius Agrippa, the Roman client-king of Judaea), having executed St James the Greater (see *25 July), imprisoned St Peter and had him bound with two chains, intending to do the same to him after the Passover week should be over; but on the night before execution he was released by an angel. In the fifth century, a church in Rome dedicated to SS Peter and Paul became known as the repository of these chains; they can still be seen at San Pietro in Vincoli, under the high altar. The feast probably commemorates the rededication of this church to St Peter; it was dropped from the RC calendar in 1960. There is a chapel of St Peter ad Vincula in the Tower of London.

Holy Maccabees, a Jewish mother and her seven sons put to death *c*.168 BC under Antiochus IV Epiphanes for refusing to eat pork; they were viewed by Christians as forerunners of the martyrs. Their relics were thought to have been preserved in San Pietro in Vincoli, but have been determined to be canine and removed, as has the feast from the calendar. As is often the case, more than one church claimed the relics. On a visit to Cologne in 1608, Thomas Coryat

> went to the Church of the Maccabees, in which they report the Bones of that holy mother of the Maccabees and her seven sonnes doe lye, that were with such most horrible and exquisite tortures punished by King Antiochus before the incarnation of Christ, as it appeareth at large in the seventh chapter of the second booke of the Maccabees, where it is mentioned that the seven sonnes together with their mother had their tongues and the utmost parts of their bodies cut off by the commandement of King Antiochus, their skinne pulled over their heads with their haire; and lastly were fryed in a frying pan, only because they would eate no swines flesh. Certainly this monument is very memorable, and worthy to be seene by a curious traveller, if a man were sure that these were the true bones of them. For truly for my owne part I will confesse, I love to see these kind of things as much as any man living, especially when I am perswaded that there is no delusion. But indeed there is so great uncertainty in these Papisticall reliques, that a man cannot certainly tell which are true, and which are false.   Coryat, ii. 340

The taste for horror is not confined to degenerate moderns, among whom few educated writers would admit it as candidly as Coryat.

Ethelwold, tutor of King Edgar, bishop of Winchester 963–84. A zealous reformer, he expelled the secular canons at Winchester, allegedly too idle even to say mass, and replaced them with monks from Abingdon. He prepared the way for his own canonization by informing his loyal disciple and biographer, Wulfstan, of miracles that had befallen him (and one that had befallen his mother before his birth); his cult survives at Winchester, but made little headway outside those (mainly monastic) churches that had links with him.

On this day in 1714 Queen Anne died before she could sign the Schism Bill requiring all schoolmasters to conform to the Church of England. At Abingdon Baptist Church the minister was paid 20s. to preach a 'Schism Sermon' on the Sunday evening nearest this date; the tradition is still maintained. Anne was succeeded by the elector of Hanover, George I; two years later the actor Thomas Doggett (d. 1721) celebrated the anniversary by advertising:

This being the day of His Majesty's happy accession to the throne, there will be given by Mr. Doggett an orange colour livery with a badge representing liberty, to be rowed for by six watermen that are out of their time [have finished their apprenticeship] within the year past. It will be continued annually on the same day for ever.   *DNB* s.n. 'Doggett'

The organization of the race was subsequently vested in the Fishmongers' Company; it still takes place, but usually in late July, depending on the tide of the Thames. It is the oldest event in the English sporting calendar.

This day was believed to see the annual reappearance of the fairy from Llyn y Fan Fach (near Llanddeusant in Dyfed), who married a mortal on the condition that if he struck her three times she would leave him. He struck her once for laughing at a funeral, again for weeping at a wedding, and a third time by accident; but before departing she gave books of medical lore to her sons, the ancestors of the renowned physicians of Myddfai; the legend of their skill, and its supernatural origin, is the basis for Peter Maxwell Davies's opera *The Doctor of Myddfai* (libretto by David Pountney), first performed in 1996. Pilgrimages were made to the lake on the first Sunday in August.

In Greece, the first three days of August are 'sharp days': apart from the prohibitions on washing clothes and chopping wood, one must not bathe in the sea. If it is absolutely necessary to wash clothes, one must put a nail into the laundry in order to nail the sharp days, *i dhrímes*, conceived as a kind of evil fairies.

On this day in 1834, slaves in the British colonies were emancipated.

2 AUGUST

a.d. IV Nonas Augustas   D

❦ HOLIDAYS AND ANNIVERSARIES Costa Rica: Our Lady of the Angels (patron saint)

❦ ANCIENT ROME Battle of Cannae, 216 BC, in which the Romans were crushingly defeated by Hannibal; in the Roman calendar the fourth (inclusively) before the Nones of Sextilis (as the month was then called), whence it was said that ill-fortune was attached to all fourth days before a named day; however, it was already ill-omened as being the day after such a named day (cf. *16 July). None of this availed Pharnaces, son of Mithridates and Bosporus, whose army collapsed so completely in the battle of Zela on this day in 47 BC that Caesar could boast *veni vidi vici*. For a similar change in a day's fortunes, see *6 October.

❦ HOLY DAYS Eusebius of Vercelli (RC); formerly Alphonsus Mary de Liguori (see *1 Aug.)

Eusebius of Vercelli (d. 371), bishop of Vercelli, a victim of persecution by the Arians when they were dominant in the Eastern Church; legend had him stoned to death by them. Feast-day formerly 16 December.

Stephen I, pope 254–7, apparently the first to base Roman primacy on Jesus' commission to Peter (see *29 June); he took a hard line against those who like Cyprian (see *15 Sept.) challenged his teaching that persons baptized by heretics were not to be rebaptized. Having died on the eve of persecution, he was often taken for a martyr, an error assisted by the Invention of St Stephen on the 3rd.

Thomas of Hales, a Benedictine monk of St Martin's priory, Dover, was killed in 1295 by French raiders for refusing to disclose the hiding-place of the monastery's riches; he was buried in the priory church before the altar of Our Lady and St Katherine. Within a few years he was hailed as a saint and martyr even on a par with the other Thomas, the great Becket: the two are explicitly paired in a remarkably jaunty motet, dating from the early fourteenth century, in which one voice praises 'Thomas the jewel of Canterbury' (*Thomas gemma Cantuariae*), the other 'Thomas slain in Dover' (*Thomas caesus in Doveria*); the notion of twinship, inherent in the name Thomas (see *21 Dec.), is exploited in both the text and the music. However, Thomas of Hales was never formally canonized, not even to reward England for supporting the Roman Pope against his French-backed rival in Avignon.

In Russia this is the feast (OS; 15th NS) of Basil the Blessed (d. 1552), a *yuródivyĭ* or Holy Fool greatly honoured and even feared by Ivan the Terrible for his ability to see into men's hearts and thoughts; his remains are buried in the *Pokróvskiĭ sobór* or Cathedral of the Protection (see *14 Oct.), which is popularly named after him.

3 AUGUST

a.d. III Nonas Augustas   E

❦ HOLIDAYS AND ANNIVERSARIES Guinea-Bissau: Colonization Martyrs Day (national holiday)

❦ ANCIENT ROME Dogs were crucified on this day, allegedly for having slept on guard at the Capitol during the Gaulish invasion; it was the geese that gave the alarm.

❦ HOLY DAYS

Invention of St Stephen, the Protomartyr (see *26 Dec.), whose remains are said to have been flung into a filthy pit later revealed at Kafar Gamala in Palestine to a priest of Jerusalem called Lucian; a church was built outside the Damascus Gate to house them and dedicated in 439. They were successively translated to the church on Mount Zion and to Constantinople, being afterwards split up: some went to San Lorenzo fuori le Mura at Rome, but the left hand was sent in 1141 to Zwiefalten, south-west of Ulm. The feast (known in Germany as *Sankt Stephan im Schnitt* [harvest]) was suppressed in 1960.

Day-Dreams

Broad August burns in milky skies,
    The world is blanched with hazy heat;
The vast green pasture, even, lies
    Too hot and bright for eyes and feet.

Amid the grassy levels rears
    The sycamore against the sun
The dark boughs of a hundred years,
    The emerald foliage of one.

Lulled in a dream of shade and sheen,
    Within the clement twilight thrown
By that great cloud of floating green,
    A horse is standing, still as stone.

He stirs nor head nor hoof, although
    The grass is fresh beneath the branch;
His tail alone swings to and fro
    In graceful curves from haunch to haunch.

He stands quite lost, indifferent
    To rack or pasture, trace or rein;
He feels the vaguely sweet content
    Of perfect sloth in limb and brain.

              William Canton (1845–1926)

4 AUGUST

pridie Nonas Augustas   F

❲ HOLIDAYS AND ANNIVERSARIES UK: HM Queen Elizabeth the Queen Mother born 1900; red-letter day; the Union flag is flown

❲ HOLY DAYS John Mary Vianney (RC; CY commem.); Seven Sleepers (Orth.; see *27 July); formerly Dominic (RC; see *8 Aug.)

John Mary Vianney (1786–1859), the *curé d'Ars*. Despite interruption to his priestly training by military conscription (he deserted), and difficulty in learning Latin, he was ordained in 1815 and appointed parish priest at Ars in February 1818; his wisdom as a confessor attracted penitents from all over France and even beyond. By 1855 he was receiving 20,000 visitors a year, and spending a heroic sixteen to eighteen hours a day in the confessional; he was canonized in 1925 and four years later created the patron saint of parish priests. Feast-day formerly 8 August.

In Britain, this day is regarded as the beginning of the First World War, since it was on 4 August 1914 that the United Kingdom declared war on Germany; the declaration was received with an outpouring of joy at both élite and popular levels, as if all the questions confronting the nation, from women's suffrage to Ireland, had been transcended, and all moral ambiguity cleansed away.

The Fourth of August

Now in thy splendour go before us,
Spirit of England, ardent-eyed,
Enkindle this dear earth that bore us,
In the hour of peril purified.

The cares we hugged drop out of vision,
Our hearts with deeper thoughts dilate.
We step from days of sour division
Into the grandeur of our fate.

For us the glorious dead have striven,
They battled that we might be free.
We to their living cause are given;
We arm for men that are to be.

Among the nations nobliest chartered,
England recalls her heritage.
In her is that which is not bartered,
Which force can neither quell nor cage.

For her immortal stars are burning
With her the hope that's never done,
The seed that's in the Spring's returning,
The very flower that seeks the sun.

She fights the force that feeds desire on
Dreams of a prey to seize and kill,
The barren creed of blood and iron,
Vampire of Europe's wasted will . . .

Endure, O Earth! and thou, awaken,
Purged by this dreadful winnowing-fan,
O wronged, untameable, unshaken
Soul of divinely suffering man.

Laurence Binyon (1869–1943)

Such sentiments were not confined to Britain; nor (as in some other wars) were they expressed only from the safety of home. The disgust and disillusion that replaced them during the military impasse and wholesale slaughter of trench warfare have made them hard to revive, at least in democratic countries; but when in the winter of 1916/17 Britain, France, and Germany faced the choice between a negotiated peace and a more vigorous prosecution of the war, all three chose the latter.

5 AUGUST

Nonae Augustae   G

> *Greengrocers rise at dawn of sun*
> *August the fifth—come haste away*
> *To Billingsgate the thousands run*
> *Tis Oyster Day! Tis Oyster Day!*

❡ ANCIENT ROME Salus Publica Populi Romani on the Quirinal; the temple was vowed in 311 BC by the consul Gaius Iunius Bubulcus during the Samnite war and dedicated by him as dictator at his triumph in 302 BC; the goddess is also called Semonia.

❡ HOLY DAYS Oswald, King of Northumbria, 642 (CY); Dedication of the Basilica of Santa Maria Maggiore (RC); Dominic (RC Australia; see *8 Aug.)

Oswald, king of Northumbria, slain at the battle of 'Maserfelth' in 642 against Penda, the heathen king of Mercia; if as commonly supposed the place was Oswestry, it is probable that Oswald was attempting to cut Penda off from his Welsh ally Cadwaladr, son of the Cadwallon who had attacked his predecessor Edwin (*12 Oct.). His relics were translated to Bardney in Lincolnshire, where many healing miracles are reported by Bede. His cult quickly spread to Ireland and the Continent, above all the German-speaking lands and northern Italy. His head was discovered in St Cuthbert's tomb in Durham in 1827. His traditional day is the 5th, the date of the battle, but English Roman Catholics keep the 9th.

Oswald is invoked by shepherds:

At Sᵗ Oswald's-Downe and Forde-downe, &c. thereabout the Shepherds prayd at night & at morning to Sᵗ Oswald (that was martyred there) to preserve their Sheepe safe in the fold. Sᵗ Oswald was slayne by Penda on the great downe east of Marsfield in Glocestershire as you ride to Castlecombe from whence it is called Sᵗ Oswald's-downe: in these parts, nay as far as Auburne-chase (and perhaps a great deale further) when they pent their sheep in yᵉ Fold, they did pray to God & Sᵗ Oswald to bring the sheep safe to yᵉ Fold: and in the morning, they did pray to God & Saint Oswald, to bring their sheep safe from yᵉ Fold. The countrey folk call St. Oswald St. Twosole.   Aubrey, 29

Dedication of the Roman basilica of Santa Maria Maggiore, also known as Sancta Maria ad Nives or Our Lady of the Snows. A legend of the thirteenth century recounts that the Virgin appeared to Pope Liberius on the night of 4 August 352 and told him to build a church on the area of the Esquiline hill that would be covered with snow the following morning. The event is still commemorated on this day; at the end of the ceremony a coffer in the ceiling opens up and thousands of white flower petals drift down, simulating snow.

Emygdius (Emidio), honoured in Italy as patron of Ascoli, which claims his relics. His legendary acts make him a late second-century German from Trier who came to Rome,

was ordained by Pope Marcellus I, and enraged pagans by destroying a statue of Aesculapius in his temple. His later fame comes as intercessor against earthquakes, ever since
Ascoli escaped damage in the earthquake of 1703. Not surprisingly, his cult has flourished in earthquake zones (Italy, San Francisco, and Los Angeles).

Oyster Day (Old St James's Day). The legal close season for oysters is 15 June to 4 August.
5 August is Old St James's Day; 25 July was formerly the beginning of the oyster season.

Common people are indifferent about *the manner of opening Oysters*, and the time of eating them
after they are opened; nothing, however, is more important, in the enlightened eyes of the experienced Oyster eater. Those who wish to enjoy this delicious restorative in its utmost perfection,
must *eat it the moment it is opened*, with its own gravy in the under shell:—if not *Eaten while Absolutely
Alive*, its flavour and spirit are lost.

   The true lover of an Oyster, will have some regard for the feelings of his little favourite, and
will never abandon it to the mercy of a bungling operator,—but will open it himself, and contrive to detach the Fish from the shell so dexterously, that the Oyster is hardly conscious he has
been ejected from his Lodging, till he feels the teeth of the piscivorous *Gourmand* tickling him to
Death.   Kitchiner, 211

Some were so fond of oysters that they ate them both in and out of season. One such
was Henry Hastings (1551–1650), a true 'originall in our age', as Anthony Ashley Cooper,
the first Earl of Shaftesbury, called him. A great hunter of game and his neighbours'
wives and daughters, Hastings's appetite was both exacting and voracious:

. . . an oyster table att the lower end, which was of constant use twice a day all the year round,
for he never fayld to eat oysters before dinner and supper through all seasons, the neighbouring
town of Pool[e] supplyed him with them: the upper part of this roome had two small tables and
a deske on the one side of which was a church Bible on the other the booke of Martyrs; on the
tables were hawkes hoods bells and such like, two or three old green hatts with their crownes
thrust in soe as to hold ten or a dosen eggs, which were of a phesant kind of poultry he tooke
much care of and fed himself; tables dice cards and boxes were not wanting, in the hole of the
desk were store of tobaccoe pipes that had been used. On one side of this end of the roome was
the doore of a closett where in stood the strong beer and the wine, which never came thence but
in single glasses that being the rule of the house exactly observed for he never exceeded in drinke
or permitted itt, on the other side was a doore in to an old chappel not used, for devotion, the
pulpit as the safest place, was never wanting of a cold chine of bief pasty of venison gammon
of Bacon or great apple pye with thicke crust extreamly baked. His table cost him not much
though it was very good to eat att, his sports supplying all but beef or mutton, except Fridayes
when he had the best sea fish as well as other fish he could gett; and was the day that his neighbors of best quality most visited him. He never wanted a london pudding and alwais sung it in;
with my part lyes therein a; he drunke a glass or two of wine at meales very often sirrup of
gillyflower in his sack and had alwais a tunn glass without feet stood by him holding a pint of
small beer which he often stired with a great sprig of Rosemary.   A. Cooper, 384–5

Others believed that oysters should not be eaten in months without an 'r':

It is unseasonable and unholesome in all monethes, that haue not the letter *R.* in their name,
because it is then venerious.   Buttes, sig. N1 (1599)

6 AUGUST

❮ HOLIDAYS AND ANNIVERSARIES Bolivia: Independence Day (from Spain, 1825) (national holiday)

❮ HOLY DAYS **Transfiguration of the Lord** (CofE, RC, Orth.)

Transfiguration. This feast commemorates the event thus described by St Matthew (17: 1–3): 'And after six days Jesus taketh Peter, James, and John his brother, and bringeth them up into an high mountain apart, And was transfigured before them: and his face did shine as the sun, and his raiment was white as the light. And, behold, there appeared unto them Moses and Elias talking with him.' Tradition identified the mountain with Mount Tabor. The feast has been kept in the East since the fourth or fifth century; Orthodox teaching, established after controversy in the fourteenth century, identifies the Divine Light of Mount Tabor with the uncreated energies of the Godhead, maintains that this (not God's essence as in the West) is the object of the Beatific Vision, and asserts that a few individuals may behold it in their lifetime. In the West the feast, though increasingly known in the later Middle Ages, was not universal till Pope Callistus III, without adopting the Orthodox doctrines, imposed it in 1457 (displacing Pope Sixtus to *7 Aug.) to commemorate the announcement in Rome on 6 August 1456 of the Christian victory over the Turks outside Belgrade on 22 July; he died on Transfiguration Day in 1458.

Izaak Walton, who never failed to recognize an illustrious fisherman, observed:

when our blessed Saviour went up into the Mount, when he left the rest of his Disciples and chose only three to beare him company at his Transfiguration, . . . those three were all Fishermen. And it is believed, that all the other Apostles after they betook themselves to follow Christ, betook themselves to be Fisher-men; but it is certain that the greater number of them were found together a fishing by Jesus after his Resurrection, as is recorded in the 21. Chapter of St. *Johns* Gospel.   Walton, 52 (1655)

In Armenia the Transfiguration is celebrated seven weeks after Pentecost; the following Monday and Tuesday as Vardavaṙ, Rose Day, originally in honour of Anahid, goddess of love and chastity, who was offered a rose and a dove; roses and doves still form part of Vardavaṙ rituals. Worshippers sprinkled water on one another, commemorating baptism.

Boris and Gleb (Russ. Orth.; 24 July OS), sons of St Vladimir (see *15 July), murdered in the act of prayer by their uncle Svyatopolk.

7 AUGUST

❆ HOLY DAYS Name of Jesus (BCP); Sixtus II and companions (RC); Gaetano of Tiene (RC)

Name of Jesus. At Mark 9: 39 and at several places in Acts miracles are performed in the name of Jesus; in Phil. 2: 9–11 St Paul says: 'Wherefore God also hath highly exalted him, and given him a name which is above every name: That at the name of Jesus every knee should bow, of things in heaven, and things in earth, and things under the earth; And that every tongue should confess that Jesus Christ is Lord, to the glory of God the Father.' The feast of the Name of Jesus has been kept on various days; 7 August was the date in the Sarum rite and remains so in the BCP, but some Anglican communities observe it on 1 January in place of the Circumcision. In 1530 it was confirmed for the Franciscans, who had done much to advance this devotion, on 14 January; in 1721 Pope Innocent XIII prescribed it for the entire RC Church, but on the second Sunday after Epiphany. Pius X moved it to the Sunday between the Circumcision and Epiphany (or 2 January if there was no such Sunday); it was suppressed in 1969.

Sixtus II (257–8), and his deacons *Felicissimus and Agapitus*, martyred with him in Rome on 6 August 258; the feast was transferred to the 7th after the Transfiguration had been added to the calendar.

Gaetano, in English sometimes Cajetan (1480–1547), son of Gasparo, lord of Tiene, became Julius II's secretary and papal protonotary, co-founder with Gianpietro Carafa (later Paul IV) of the Theatines, named after Theate (Chieti), where Carafa was bishop, and devoted to pastoral work; the Order played an important part in the Counter-Reformation. He was canonized in 1671. Among his devotees was Pompilia Comparini, whose murder by her husband in January 1698 is the subject of Browning's *The Ring and the Book*, and who called her son after him; as the poet conceives the matter, she reflects that the boy will never know his father and that she herself is not her supposed parents' daughter:

> That is why something put it in my head
> To call the boy 'Gaetano'—no old name
> For sorrow's sake; I looked up to the sky
> And took a new saint to begin anew.
> One who has only been made saint—how long?
> Twenty-five years: so, carefuller, perhaps,
> To guard a namesake than those old saints grow,
> Tired out by this time,—see my own five saints!
>
> *The Ring and the Book*, vii. 100–7

This Gaetano is to be distinguished from the Cardinal Cajetan or Gaetano (1469–1534), Thomist theologian and general of the Dominicans, who was sent to debate with

Luther at the Augsburg Diet of 1518, and who was said to have threatened the sun with excommunication if it did not bring more warmth to Germany while he was there.

Afra, said to have been a reformed prostitute martyred under Diocletian by burning at the stake in Augusta Vindelicorum, now Augsburg, of which she is the very popular patron together with Ulrich (see *4 July); her relics lie in the Ulrichsmünster. Hermannus Contractus (see *24 Sept.) wrote an office in her honour; her story is told in a very accomplished Latin poem written by an English author *c*.1200.

8 AUGUST

❲ HOLY DAYS Dominic (CY, RC); formerly John Mary Vianney (see *4 Aug.)

Dominic (*c*.1172–1221), founder of the Order of Friars Preachers (Dominican Order). Born in Calaruega in Old Castile, he became an Augustinian. Upon a mission to southern France, he began preaching against the Albigensians, seeking converts with notable success. His Order, centred in Toulouse, was founded in imitation of the Apostles as itinerant preachers, and was officially recognized in 1216. Dominic also founded nunneries, including one in Rome, where too many nuns were living at large. His followers' habit of travelling in groups to convert the heretics earned them the punning nickname *Domini canes*, 'the hounds of the Lord'; this was later reinterpreted by their enemies as meaning that they attended the deathbeds of the great in order to seize their wealth, and converted by their friends into the story that his mother Juana de Aza had dreamt while pregnant of a dog in her womb that broke away from her with a torch that set fire to the world, taken to portend the birth of a great enlightener (but Hecuba's dream of bearing a firebrand had foretold the destruction of Troy that came through her son Paris, after which she was turned into a dog). Feast-day formerly 4 August; in Australia it has been moved to the 5th to accommodate the Blessed Mary McKillop (1842–1909), who founded the Sisters of St Joseph of the Sacred Heart.

Cyriac of Rome, martyred *c*.305 with five companions (so the Calendar of 354); later writers gave different numbers, and the names Largus and Smaragdus; but he was also culted by himself on *16 March.

The Fourteen Holy Helpers or Auxiliary Saints, invoked by particular groups or against particular evils: Acacius (22 June: by soldiers), Barbara (4 Dec.: against lightning, fire, explosion, and sudden death); Blaise (3 Feb.: against throat disease); Catherine (25 Nov.: by philosophers, students, and wheelwrights); Christopher (25 July: by travellers in difficulty), Cyriac (16 Mar., 8 Aug., against demonic possession); Denys (9 Oct.: against headache and rabies); Erasmus (2 June: against colic and cramps); Eustace (20 Sept.: by huntsmen); George (23 Apr.: by soldiers), Giles (1 Sept.: against epilepsy, insanity, and sterility); Margaret (20 July: against possession and by pregnant women); Pantaleon (27 July: against phthisis); and Vitus (15 June: against epilepsy and his 'dance'). The cult became widely diffused during the fifteenth century and spread from Germany to Hungary, Italy, and France. At Bamberg they had a liturgy on the fourth Saturday after Easter. In France the Helpers are fifteen, including the BVM; other lists may include Antony, Leonard, Nicholas, Roch, Sebastian.

9 AUGUST

a.d. V Idus Augustas D

(HOLIDAYS AND ANNIVERSARIES Singapore: Independence Day (from Malaysia, 1965)
South Africa: National Women's Day

(ANCIENT ROME Public sacrifice on the Quirinal to Sol Indiges, an ancient sun god; *indiges* is variously explained as a lesser, single-function deity, or a native god as opposed to an import. The Quirinal is now most notable for the sixteenth-century palazzo successively occupied by popes, kings, and presidents of the Italian Republic.

(HOLY DAYS Matthias (Orth.; see *24 Feb.); Mary Sumner (CY)

Mary Sumner (1828–1921), founder of the Mothers' Union. The wife of a parish rector, she presented the idea of a union of mothers, to foster moral education in the family, at a church congress in 1885, and saw her dream develop from a diocesan to an international organization, in which she took an active part into her 90s.

In Norway, this or the next night was said to begin a sequence of 'frost-nights' (*frost-netter*), which warned the farmer that winter was on its way; in Solør 10–12 August were called *laurentiusnetter*, Klara (12th) being the worst.

IO AUGUST

a.d. IV Idus Augustas E

(HOLIDAYS AND ANNIVERSARIES Ecuador: Independence Day (from Spain, 1822)
USA, Missouri: Admission Day (24th state, 1821)

(HOLY DAYS Laurence (CofE); **Laurence** (RC); Matthew (Orth.; see *21 Sept.)

Laurence, also spelt 'Lawrence', in Latin 'Laurentius' (d. 258), one of the seven deacons of Rome, instructed by the city prefect to surrender the church treasures, is said to have assembled the beggars who fed off its charity instead; for this insolence he was sentenced to death by grilling over a slow fire, though later accounts, finding this torture inadequate, have him first whipped with scorpions, beaten with clubs, and scourged with lead-filled whips. His face appeared to be surrounded with a beautiful light, and his body gave off a sweet smell; after suffering a long time, he said with a cheerful smile: 'Turn me over, one side is done.' The prefect gave command, whereupon Laurence invited him to test whether he tasted better cooked or raw. He was buried in Rome at the place where the basilica of San Lorenzo fuori le Mura, on the Via Tiburtina, stands; but his grill is exhibited in San Lorenzo in Lucina, off the Corso. St Laurence is patron saint of cooks.

Gregory Martin, in *Roma sancta* (1581), testifies to his veneration:

If the martyrdome of this Sainte was so glorious (being softely and leasurely broyled on a gridyron, as SS. Ambrose, Austen, Leo, Prudentius, al antiquitie maketh mention) so glorious I say, that Rome in the memorie and honour therof hath diverse Churches, one where he suffred, an other where he was imprisoned, an other where part of the verie gridyron is yet to be seen under the high aultar, and others byside: what shal we thinke of the holenesse of this Churche the principal of al the rest, where the bodie it self lieth that indured those tormentes?

G. Martin, 38

The Perseids, an annual meteor-shower observed at this time (peaking about the 12th), are sometimes called 'fiery tears of St Lawrence':

Thursday, 10 August [1871]. St. Lawrence's Day. Meteor Day
   Tonight was the great August meteor shower and Uncle Will and I went up to the gate to watch for the meteors which the Irish call 'St. Lawrence's tears'.   Kilvert, i. 393

Erik Plovpenning (Ploughpenny), king of Denmark 1241–50, who gained his nickname by imposing a tax of one silver penny per plough to finance a crusade against Estonia, where thirteenth-century Denmark had aspirations of conquest (the name of the capital, Tallinn, means 'Daneburg'), but was murdered at the behest of his brother Abel.

Danish farmers used to predict the forthcoming winter by the weather on this day: if the sun shone brightly on rising, and glowed when setting, there would be prolonged frost. Cf. the Venetian saying quoted under *17 January.

11 AUGUST

❨ HOLIDAYS AND ANNIVERSARIES   Chad: Independence Day (national holiday)
Zimbabwe: Heroes' Day

☾ HOLY DAYS Clare of Assisi (CY, RC)

Clare of Assisi (1193/4–1253), foundress of the Poor Clares. Having been inspired by the preaching of St Francis, she desired to become a Franciscan herself; an order for women was founded between 1212 and 1214. Not all members wished to live in extreme poverty, so different rules were authorized; the milder 'Urbanist' one prevailed until St Colette (*6 Mar.) reformed the order in the fifteenth century. In 1958 Pius XII named Clare patron saint of television writers, owing to a vision she had of a matins service, complete with singers and organ, which she was too ill to attend (those addicted to soap operas often claim that they became hooked while off sick). Since she is said to have spent her time while ill in embroidering liturgical vestments, she is also patron saint of embroiderers. Feast-day formerly 12 August.

August in New Zealand:

Late Winter Snow

The child has never been older
than in August
snow blanketing the countryside
and we never to be younger
greet the misty morning
sunlight spraying iridescent mountains
across the lake . . .
               the birch trees sway
like frail dancers,
strings of light merge
and the violas of night put down their bows
as feet move in search of hands to clasp
and I say
             Lead me not into harsh ministrations
of cruellest spring
or the wells of inconsolable days
but down pathways leaf-lined to summer
in the absence of fog,
ladders of rain.

Brian Turner (1944–   )

12 AUGUST

pridie Idus Augustas   G

☾ HOLIDAYS AND ANNIVERSARIES Thailand: Queen's Birthday

☾ ANCIENT ROME There was a sacrifice on this day to Hercules Invictus ('the Invincible') at the Ara Maxima, the great altar near the Circus Maximus; in myth it was far older than Rome itself, having been instituted after Hercules had slain the brigand Cacus, who was ravaging Evander's kingdom on the banks of the Tiber. Women were excluded, either because Evander's mother Carmentis had declined her invitation, or because, ravaged with thirst after his battle with the fire-breathing Cacus, he was refused a drink of water by the worshippers of the Bona Dea, who admitted no man to her presence. Hercules was a man's god, famous for his hearty appetites, and all the more popular for having been a man himself and therefore knowing what real life was like. Merchants offered tithes of their profits, generals of their booty; the proceeds may have been spent on a public feast, for no part of any beast sacrificed to Hercules was allowed to be removed uneaten, and in contrast to other deities he imposed no restriction on the kinds of food and drink that might be offered him.

☙ HOLY DAYS Formerly Clare (now *11 Aug.)

Glorious Twelfth. Opening of the grouse season (to 10 December). An American visitor reported on his experience in 1873:

Do any of my readers know why the British Parliament invariably adjourns just before the 12th of August? Because, if the session continued beyond that date, both Houses would be left without a quorum. . . . On the 12th of August the shooting season is inaugurated, and for days, if not weeks, previous the minds of a large mass of the titled and wealthy classes are occupied, to the exclusion of almost everything else, in preparation for the moors. [My host wrote:] 'This game-killing is a sort of solemn duty with us squires; we go through it in the usual sad manner of Englishmen enjoying themselves; indeed, a real game-keeping squire, who lives for nothing else (and there are many of this class), is one of the curious creations of modern civilization.' . . .

After a capital afternoon's shooting we again assemble at half past six at a farm-yard, where the carriage is waiting for us. As each party came in the bags were emptied, and the result of the day's sport was spread out before us, the grouse being placed in lines of twenty, with the hares and snipe in the rear, and summing up as follows: 264 grouse, seven hares, and eight snipe.

J. G. Wilson, 567, 570

Apprentice Boys of Derry march (Northern Ireland). Late in 1688, when rumours abounded that all Protestants in Ireland would be murdered on 9 December, James II, on the point of losing his English and Scottish thrones, sent a Roman Catholic army to occupy the Protestant city of Londonderry; thirteen apprentice boys closed the gates against it. In the spring and summer of 1689 the city was besieged by French and Irish troops; the defeatist governor Lundy, who had attempted to surrender, is still reviled among Unionists as the incarnation of cowardice and treason. The siege was raised on 1 August OS, which in New Style was 11 August in 1689, but the 12th at the change of calendar; the anniversary has remained on this date. However, the greater part of the city's population now consists of Roman Catholics (who call it simply Derry), although the corporation long remained in Protestant hands; resentment at these conditions brought disorders to the city in 1968 and 1969 that induced the government to send British troops as protectors of the Roman Catholic and Nationalist population, a role too paradoxical to be long sustained.

13 AUGUST

Idus Augustae   A

❦ ANCIENT ROME This was a notable day for religious observances. The chief festivity was that of Diana on the Aventine; this was traditionally the plebeians' hill, facing the upper-class Palatium across the Circus Maximus, though once the emperors had taken over the Palatium for themselves (see *10 Apr.) the Aventine became gentrified. The goddess's temple was said to have been founded in the sixth century BC by that great friend of the people King Servius Tullius, whose mother had reputedly been a slave; the temple became an asylum for runaway slaves and this day a holiday for all slaves of both sexes. Women, both slave and free, made a point of washing their hair. Other sacrifices were made to Vertumnus (an ancient Etruscan god associated by the Romans with change, especially of seasons), Fortuna Equestris (in honour of a victory won in 180 BC by a cavalry charge, unusual in Roman warfare), Hercules, Castor and Pollux, the Camenae (goddesses of springs later identified with the Muses), and Flora.

❦ HOLY DAYS Jeremy Taylor (CY); Pontianus and Hippolytus (RC)

Jeremy Taylor (1613–67), Anglican chaplain, in 1660 made bishop of Down and Connor, later also of Dromore. His devotional treatises are still admired; he also wrote an Anglican liturgy.

Pope Pontianus, of whom little is known, and *Hippolytus*, the most learned churchman in the West before Augustine, were exiled in 235 to the Sardinian mines, whose rigours, as intended, were to kill them. Pontianus was for a time culted on 19 November; Hippolytus' Orthodox day is 30 January. Hippolytus, a pupil of Irenaeus (see *28 June), is most renowned for his *Refutation of All Heresies*, and for an Easter table purporting to give the date of Easter from 222 till 333. At the foot of the stairs to the Vatican Library is a seated statue, discovered in 1551 and identified as Hippolytus; a partial list of his works is inscribed on the back of the chair, the Easter table on the sides. His attacks on contemporary popes have caused some modern writers to make him the first antipope.

Cassian of Imola (?250), martyr. At their congress in 1951, Italian shorthand-writers requested that he be named their patron saint; Pius XII obliged in an Apostolic Letter of 23 December 1952. According to his legend Cassian was a schoolmaster martyred when a judge ordered his pupils to stab him to death with their iron pens. Two hundred of them happily joined in, some carving letters in his skin; evidently he was not a popular teacher.

Radegunde (587), wife of Clothar I, son of Clovis; she fled the court and became a deaconess, then founded a nunnery in Poitiers, to which in 569 the emperor Justin II gave a relic of the Cross; this inspired Venantius Fortunatus, who had the cure of souls in her community, to compose his two famous hymns (see *14 Dec.).

Radegunde, whose husband was notoriously unfaithful, was the saint of choice for those afflicted with the pox; one English remedy for a woman so stricken, after application of the skin of a black lamb, was that her *husband* make a pilgrimage to St Radegunde:

Yf a woman haue the final pockes, it behoueth that her husbande bye her a blacke lambe of the same yere, and after bynde her in the skynne, and then let hym make hys pylgrymage and offrynge to saynt Arragonde, and for a trouthe she shall hele.   *Gospelles of Dystaues* (1520), sig. E3ᵛ

In Brazil this day, should it fall on a Friday, is even more unlucky than any other Friday the thirteenth, since *agosto* (so spelt) rhymes with *desgosto* ('sorrow').

14 AUGUST

a.d. XIX Kalendas Septembres   B

❦ HOLIDAYS AND ANNIVERSARIES Pakistan: Independence Day (1947)

❦ HOLY DAYS

Maximilian Kolbe (1894–1941), Franciscan priest. Born near Łódź, he became a Franciscan in 1910, later studying in Rome. Having contracted tuberculosis soon after his ordination, he returned to Poland, where he taught in a seminary. Upon recovering from another serious attack of tuberculosis, he brought out a Christian magazine that became highly successful and expanded to daily and weekly newspapers. In the mean time a Franciscan community had been created around these publishing activities, at Niepokalanów near Warsaw. He founded a similar community in Japan, but returned to head the Polish community in 1936. Upon the German invasion in 1939, Maximilian and his followers were first arrested and interned, but then released; their community became a place of refuge for both Poles and Jews. But the publishing activities became too dangerous for the Nazis to ignore, and Maximilian and four others were rearrested and sent to Auschwitz in May 1941. When, because of an escape attempt, one member of his barracks was selected to be starved as punishment, Maximilian offered himself in his place; he survived for two weeks in a cell of the death chamber, when he was killed by injection. At his canonization by John Paul II in 1982, the man whose life he had saved was present. CY has added a commemoration on this day.

Eusebius of Rome, a fierce opponent of Arianism (championed by his namesakes of Caesarea and Nicomedia), put under house arrest by the emperor Constantius II (legend improved this to martyrdom). He founded a church known as the *Dominicum Eusebii*, 'Property of Eusebius'; the term, and institution, of *dominicum* belongs only to the earliest centuries of Continental Christianity, but survived longer in Ireland as *domhnach*.

The Guild of the Assumption in Dieppe instituted a ceremony on this day in 1443 to commemorate the final expulsion of the English. A girl 'of the most exemplary character' was elected to represent the Virgin Mary, a member of the clergy to be St Peter, and eleven of the laity to be the other apostles. On the morning of the 14th the Virgin was carried to the church of St Jacques, to which a great procession was made, 'further augmented by numbers of the youth of either sex, who assumed the garb and attributes of their patron saints',

where *Te Deum* was sung by the full choir, in commemoration of the victory over the English, and high mass was performed, and the Sacrament administered to the whole party. During the service, a scenic representation was given of the Assumption of the Virgin. A scaffolding was raised, reaching nearly to the top of the dome, and supporting an azure canopy intended to emulate the 'spangled vault of heaven'; and about two feet below the summit of it appeared, seated on a splendid throne, an old man as the image of the Father Almighty, a representation equally absurd and impious, and which could be tolerated only by the votaries of the blasted superstitions of popery. On either side four pasteboard angels of the size of men floated in the air, and flapped their wings in cadence to the sounds of the organ; while above was suspended a large triangle, at whose corners were placed three smaller angels, who, at the intermission of each office, performed upon a set of little bells the hymn of '*Ave Maria gratia Dei plena per secula*', &c. accompanied by a larger angel on each side with a trumpet. . . . At the commencement of the mass, two of the angels by the side of the Almighty descended to the foot of the altar, and, placing themselves by the tomb, in which a pasteboard figure of the Virgin had been substituted for her living representative, gently raised it to the feet of the Father. The image, as it mounted, from time to time lifted its head and extended its arms, as if conscious of the approaching beatitude, then, after having received the benediction and been encircled by another angel with a crown of glory, it gradually disappeared behind the clouds. At this instant a buffoon, who all the time had been playing his antics below, burst into an extravagant fit of joy; at one moment clapping his hands most violently, at the next stretching himself out as if dead. Finally, he ran up to the feet of the old man, and hid himself under his legs, so as to shew only his head. The people called him *Grimaldi*, an appellation that appears to have belonged to him by usage.

D. Turner, 24–6 (1820)

15 AUGUST

a.d. XVIII Kalendas Septembres   C

If the sun shine on the 15th, it is a good token of a mild winter.

❦ HOLIDAYS AND ANNIVERSARIES Congo: National Day
  India: Independence Day (1947)
  Liechtenstein: National Day
  South Korea: Liberation Day (from Japan, 1945) (national day)
  USA, Hawaii: Floating Lantern Ceremony (Toro Nagashi) (Buddhist ceremony in Honolulu, commemorating the end of the Second World War; lanterns bearing the name of the dead are lit and set afloat)
  Vatican City: Assumption Day

HRH the Princess Royal born 1950; the Union flag is flown

❆ HOLY DAYS **Assumption of the Blessed Virgin Mary** (RC); **The Blessed Virgin Mary** (CY); **Dormition of the Theotokos** (Orth.)

Assumption of BVM (West)/Dormition of Theotokos (Orth.), in Irish 'the Feast of Mary in Harvest', *Lá Fhéile Muire san bhFóghmhar*. The RC belief that Mary was bodily assumed into heaven, though long an article of faith, did not become dogma until 1950, when Pius XII issued the bull *Munificentissimus Deus*. This is the major feast of Mary, and the titular feast of all churches that bear her name unless another feast is designated. As the Assumption is commonly depicted with Mary ascending through the clouds, she is the appropriate patron of aircraft pilots and crew; she was so designated for France in 1952. The Orthodox, while not denying the doctrine, have not made it a dogma, and retain the older name of 'Falling Asleep', in Latin *Dormitio*, in Greek *Koímēsis*; from the Russian equivalent, *Uspénie*, comes the name of the great Kremlin cathedral, the *Uspénskiĭ sobór*.

Formerly on this day, women were admitted to the Sistine Chapel between first and second vespers, being excluded for the rest of the year lest they should disturb devotions with their noise. The singers remained in the chapel wherever the Pope might be; if no one else was present to celebrate mass, one of their number did so.

In Armenia the feast is celebrated on the nearest Sunday, till when no one may eat grapes; on that day a tray filled with them is blessed in church and distributed after the service. Women called Mary entertain their friends. Parties are held in vineyards.

Naogeorgus on the Assumption, with some disapproving words on rush-bearing:

> The blessed virgin Maries feast, hath here his place and time,
> Wherein departing from the earth, she did the heavens clime:
> Great bundels then of hearbes to Church, the people fast doe beare,
> The which against all hurtfull things, the Priest doth hallow theare.
> Thus kindle they and nourish still, the peoples wickednesse,
> And vainely make them to beleeve, whatsoever they expresse:
> For sundrie witchcrafts, by these hearbes are wrought, and divers charmes,
> And cast into the fire, are thought to drive away all harmes,
> And ever painefull griefe from man, or beast for to expell,
> Farre otherwise than nature, or the worde of God doth tell.

> > Naogeorgus, fo. 55

A minstrels' court took place in Tutbury, Staffs. The king of the minstrels was appointed by minstrels' juries from Staffordshire, Derbyshire, Nottinghamshire, Leicestershire, and Warwickshire. Proceedings began with a speech on the civilizing power of music and ended with the minstrels attempting to cut a piece of skin of a bull shorn of his horn-tips, ears, and tail, smeared with soap, and roused with powder blown into its nose; if the skin was cut the bull belonged to the king of the minstrels, but if it escaped over the River Dove into Derbyshire it reverted to the Lord Prior. The Tutbury revels 'were entirely abolished by the Duke of Devonshire in the year 1778, at the request of the inhabitants of that village, owing to the outrages usually committed on these occasions' (not those against the bull).

16 AUGUST

a.d. XVII Kalendas Septembres   D

❴ HOLIDAYS AND ANNIVERSARIES Siena: Il Palio. Starting with the blessing of the Palio (a standard bearing the image of the Madonna del Voto), the day continues with a colourful medieval procession featuring standard-bearers twirling banners and culminates in a swift and dangerous horse-race in the Campo in which ten of Siena's seventeen *contrade*, drawn by lots, take part, the winner claiming the Palio for his *contrada* for the coming year. A second race, for the Palio of the Madonna di Provenzano, takes place on 2 July.

USA, Vermont: Bennington Battle Day (1777) (legal holiday)

❴ HOLY DAYS Stephen of Hungary (RC); formerly Joachim (RC 1913–69, now with St Anne on *26 July); Translation of Acheiropoiētos Icon of Christ from Edessa to Constantinople in 944 (Orth.)

Stephen of Hungary. Died 15 August 1038, but the 15th was otherwise spoken for. See *20 August, the date of his burial.

Translation of Acheiropoiētos Icon. The letter that Jesus had supposedly sent to Abgar V at Edessa (see *21 Aug.) acquired as a companion-piece a portrait painted by the king's messenger Ananias (Hannan); but in the late sixth century the local bishop Euagrius, describing the Persian siege of 544, declared that the fire with which the siege-tower had been destroyed would not take until the defenders introduced into their mine the image 'not made by hands' (*acheiropoiētos*) that Christ had produced for Abgar by impressing on his face the linen garment of a painter who could not look upon the radiance of his glory. Contemporary reports of the siege know nothing of this image or this miracle; it is suggestive that in 574 an 'unmanufactured' image, reputedly vouchsafed to a Cappadocian pagan called Hypatia willing to believe only what she could see, had been taken to Constantinople and become a talisman for the imperial army. Within a few years, Edessa had not only its own miracle-story but an actual image, on a cloth known as the *mandēlion* (often misspelt *mandylion*), exhibited on major festivals and above all Easter Day, when the eye of faith could discern Christ appearing to grow from childhood to maturity. The city, captured by Persian forces in 609, was retaken by the Emperor Heraclius but fell to the Muslims in 639. In 944 the emperor Romanus Lecapenus, having recovered the icon for 20,000 lb. of silver, translated it to Constantinople; the enterprise failed to save him from overthrow a few months later by Constantine VII, whose throne he had usurped.

From this time onwards (and not before) the *mandēlion* becomes a stock image of Byzantine art; the translation has been an important festival since its first anniversary in 945, when Constantine read a newly composed *Narrative of the Sacred Icon of Jesus Sent to Abgar*. In this the image is said to have been long forgotten until, during the siege of 544, its existence was revealed in a vision by a stately woman to 'Bishop Eulalius' (a politically correct substitution for the Monophysite Jacob Baradaeus); the female element was new in this legend, though prominent with other such images (see *4 Feb.). The Edessene icon appears to have been sold by the Latin emperor of Constantinople Baldwin II to Louis IX of France in the 1240s and been lost in the dispersal of the Sainte-Chapelle relics at the Revolution; we are therefore unable to date the portrait according to its artistic style, for its purported copies exhibit no one consistent style, but rather that current when they were made.

Roch or Rock (Rocco in Italian) (*c*.1295–1327?), hermit. Of French origin, he contracted the plague at Piacenza on his return from a pilgrimage to Rome; a dog is supposed to have brought him food in the forest, and he recovered—hence the expression 'St Roch and his dog', said of inseparable companions. He then became renowned for curing victims of the plague, displacing Sebastian as the favoured intercessor. But in non-plague years sufferers from all kinds of skin diseases invoked him:

> Rooke healeth skabbes and maungines, with pockes and skurfe and skall,
> And cooleth raging Carbuncles, and byles and botches all.
>
> Naogeorgus, fo. 38

Roch's popularity dates only from the second half of the fifteenth century, perhaps in relation to the plague epidemics of 1477–9; Francesco Diedo, the Venetian governor of Brescia, wrote a biography of him in 1478. Roch seems to have had particular appeal to confraternities in northern Italy. His supposed relics were transferred to Venice in 1485, and the story of his life told in the spectacular cycle of paintings by Tintoretto in the Scuola Grande di San Rocco.

17 AUGUST

a.d. XVI Kalendas Septembres　　　　　　　　　　　　　　　　　　　　　　　　　E

❡ HOLIDAYS AND ANNIVERSARIES Gabon Republic: National Day (independence from France, 1960)
Indonesia: Independence Day (from the Netherlands, 1945)

❡ ANCIENT ROME This was the day of the Portunalia, in honour of the harbour god Portunus; he seems to have originally been a door god, and is portrayed with a key. His temple near the Pons Aemilius still survives; in ancient times fish and flowers were sold nearby. Until AD 17 this was also kept as the dedication day of Janus' temple by the theatre of Marcellus (see *18 Oct.).

❦ HOLY DAYS

Hyacinth (1185–1257), 'the Apostle of Poland'. Born in Silesia, he was one of the earliest Dominicans, confirmed by St Dominic himself. Innocent XI named him one of the patrons of Lithuania in 1686.

A band of gypsies arrives in Paris on this day in 1427:

On the Sunday after mid-August day, August 17th 1427, twelve penitents as they called themselves came to Paris—one duke, one count, and ten other men, all on horseback. They said that they were good Christians; they came from Lower Egypt. Also they said that they had been Christians formerly; it was not long since the Christians had conquered them and their whole country and compelled them all to become Christians or be killed. . . . And, they said, some time after they had received the Christian faith, the Saracens made war upon them. As they were but weak in our faith, they . . . became Saracens again, and denied Our Lord. What happened next was that certain Christian lords—the Emperor of Germany, the King of Poland, and others— heard that they had thus falsely and easily abandoned our faith, so soon turning Saracens and idolaters again, and made war upon them. They yielded very soon, as if they supposed that they would again be left in their own country as long as they became Christians. But the Emperor and the other lords, after much deliberation, said that they should never hold land in their country without the Pope's consent and that they must go to Rome, to the Holy Father. There they all went, old and young, and a hard journey it was for the children. When they got there they made general confession of their sins. The Pope, having heard their confession, after much thought and consultation imposed on them this penance: that for seven years they should go to and fro about the world without ever sleeping in a bed. He also ordered, it was said, that so as to provide some means for them every bishop and every abbot who bore a crosier should give them, once, ten pounds *tournois*. He gave them letters about this addressed to the prelates of the church, blessed them, and so they departed. They had been wandering for five years before they came to Paris . . .

There were not more than a hundred of them altogether, or six score or so, men, women, and children. When they left their own land there had been ten or twelve hundred of them, but the others had died on the way, also their king and their queen. The survivors still hoped for worldly possessions, since the Holy Father had promised them that he would give them a good and fertile land to live in when once they should sincerely have completed their penance. You never saw greater crowds going to the Lendit benediction than went flocking to La Chappelle to see them while they were there. People went from Paris, from St. Denis, and from all around the city. And, indeed, their children were very, very clever, both the girls and the boys. Most of them—almost all of them—had their ears pierced and wore a silver ring in each ear, or two rings in each. This, they said, was mark of good birth in their country. The men were very dark, with curly hair; the women were the ugliest you ever saw and the darkest, all with scarred faces and hair as black as a horse's tail. They had no dresses but an old coarse piece of blanket tied on the shoulder with a bit of cloth or string; under this all their covering was a wretched smock or shift. In short, they were the poorest creatures that anyone had ever seen come into France. But in spite of their poverty they had sorceresses among them who looked at people's hands and told them what had happened to them or what would happen. They brought trouble into many marriages, for they would say to the husband, 'Your wife has cuckolded you', or to the wife, 'Your husband has deceived you'. What was worse, it was said that when they talked to people they contrived—either by magic arts or by other means, or by the devil's help or by their own skill and cunning—to make money flow out of other people's purses into their own. I must say I went there three or four times to talk to them and could never see that I lost a penny, nor did I see them looking into anyone's hands, but everyone said they did. Word of this came to the Bishop of Paris, and he went to see them, taking with him a Minorite called the little Jacobin who, at the bishop's order, preached an excellent sermon, excommunicating all the men and women who had done this and who had believed their claims and had had their hands looked at. They had to go, and so on Lady Day in September they departed and set off for Pontoise.   Bourgeois, 216–19

18 AUGUST

a.d. XV Kalendas Septembres   F

❦ HOLY DAYS

Agapitus, third-century martyr at Praeneste (Palestrina), over whose tomb at Le Quadrelle a basilica was built; it was restored by Pope Leo III (795–816) and excavated in 1864.

Helena, mother of Constantine (*c.*255–*c.*330). At the age of about 70 she made a pilgrimage to the Holy Land, founding basilicas on the Mount of Olives and at Bethlehem. From the late fourth century she is credited with discovering the crosses on which Jesus and the Good and Bad Thieves were crucified (see *3 May, *14 Sept.). Because of this, St Helena was thought efficacious in discovering thieves.

19 AUGUST

a.d. XIV Kalendas Septembres   G

❦ HOLIDAYS AND ANNIVERSARIES Afghanistan: Independence Day (Treaty of Rawalpindi, 1910)

❦ ANCIENT ROME At Rome this was the second or rustic Vinalia, intended to secure Jupiter's protection for the growing vines; houses and gardens were dedicated to Venus, and kitchen gardeners had the day off. It was also the dedication-day of the temple of Venus Libitina, the headquarters of the Roman undertakers, on the Esquiline, which was the poor people's burial-ground, and haunt of undesirables, until it was cleansed by Maecenas.

❦ HOLY DAYS John Eudes (RC)

John Eudes (1601–80), French missioner and founder of two orders: the Order of our Lady of Charity (1641) to care for fallen women, and the Congregation of Jesus and

Mary (1643), now mainly concerned with secondary education. He was particularly devoted to the Sacred Heart of Jesus.

Sebald (?11th c.), patron saint of Nuremberg. His life is quite obscure, but his afterlife magnificent: the Sebalduskirche in Nuremberg, built between 1330 and 1377, houses his relics in a famous shrine by Peter Vischer; he was canonized by Martin V in 1425 at the city's request. Legends abound; the most charming has him counselling a peasant woman to throw icicles in the fire because there was no fuel. One may thus invoke him during cold spells.

Louis of Toulouse (1274–97), grand-nephew of St Louis (*25 Aug.) and son of Charles II of Anjou, who inherited the throne of Naples as a prisoner in Aragon and for whom he served as a hostage from 1288 to 1295. In 1296 he renounced his right of succession, became a priest, joined the Franciscan order, and was consecrated archbishop of Toulouse, but died only eight months later; in 1319 he was canonized in his mother's presence. He appears frequently in Renaissance paintings, as a young bishop.

Foundation of St Isaac's Cathedral, St Petersburg, in 1768 (OS):

I am just returned from witnessing the ceremony of the Empress's laying the foundation-stone of a church dedicated to St. Isaac; and which is intended to be the largest in St. Petersburgh. St. Isaac is held in esteem by the Russians, not so much for any distinguished character of his own, as that the day consecrated to him [30 May] was the birth-day of Peter the Great. As the Russians apprehend that every day of the year is consecrated to some particular Saint, they are convinced that every individual is under the peculiar protection of that holy person, on whose day he happened to have been born; and all of them carry about them a small metal image of their tutelary Saint. Heredotus, if I rightly recollect, gives a similar account of the Egyptians. He tells us, that they believed every day sacred to some particular God; that they were under the peculiar protection of that divinity on whose day they were born; and that they rendered him particular homage. So much alike are all superstitions.   W. Richardson, 15–16

St Isaac foretold the downfall of the Arian emperor Valens, killed in the great Gothic victory of Adrianople (9 Aug. 378).

20 AUGUST

(HOLIDAYS AND ANNIVERSARIES   Hungary: St Stephen's Day (national day; see also *15 Mar., *23 Oct.)

(HOLY DAYS   Bernard of Clairvaux (CY, RC)

Bernard (1090–1153), abbot of Clairvaux. Having in 1112 revived the Cistercian order by bringing thirty followers to Cîteaux (see *17 Apr.), three years later he founded a new monastery at Clairvaux, which under his leadership played a major part in the order as a whole. St Bernard was highly influential in public affairs, obtaining recognition for the

Knights Templar (whose rules he was said to have drafted), helping Pope Innocent II to triumph over the antipope Anacletus, and preaching the Second Crusade; when this ended in disaster, he blamed the crusaders for their little faith. His many writings include sermons on the Song of Songs; he was a zealous opponent of heretics (including Abelard), but unlike most contemporaries he opposed persecution of Jews. He was canonized in 1174; in 1830 Pius VIII created him a Doctor of the Church. He is patron saint of Seborga (Liguria), which on 20 August 1996 solemnly proclaimed itself an independent state; the anniversary was celebrated in 1997. The Italian Republic continues to take a relaxed view of the matter, since its taxes are still paid.

Philibert, OSB, d. *c*.684, son of Philibald, bishop of Aire. He founded the monastery of Jumièges *c*.654 on a royal estate given him by St Baldhild (see *30 Jan.), which became a great centre of learning; the monks liked to derive its Latin name, *Gemmeticus*, either from *gemma*, because in its fruitfulness it glowed like a jewel on a ring, or from *gemere*, 'to groan', because those who there groaned for their sins would not groan in the flames of hell. Philibert himself, having been expelled by Ebroin, founded the monastery of Noirmoutier in 676. He is venerated as apostle and patron of the Vendée, which rose up against the French Revolution and was brutally suppressed, and is portrayed as an abbot with a donkey, allaying a storm. Hazelnuts are often known as 'filbert nuts' because they flourish about his day.

Stephen. Formerly the saint's day of St Stephen (King István I), commemorating his burial in 1038 in the basilica of Székesfehérvár. Born *c*.969 as Vajk, son of Géza, a prince of Árpád's line, he was baptized in his fifth year; in 995 he married Gisela, sister of the emperor Henry II, and in 997 succeeded his father as prince and set about consolidating his power and imposing Christianity in the Roman obedience on his country, by defeating his rival princes, whether heathen or baptized in Byzantium. The crown said to have been sent him by Pope Silvester II was carried off to Bohemia in 1270 and disappeared soon afterwards; a substitute crown was made, with a skewed cross. This crown, misleadingly known as 'St Stephen's crown', was taken to the United States in 1945 but returned to Hungary in 1978. The RC Church now celebrates him on 16 August.

21 AUGUST

a.d. XII Kalendas Septembres   B

HRH the Princess Margaret born 1930; the Union flag is flown

❡ ANCIENT ROME On this day Consualia were held in honour of Consus (see *7 July); there were races for horses and chariots.

❡ HOLY DAYS Pius X (RC, formerly 3 Sept.); formerly Jane Frances de Chantal (now *12 Dec.)

Pius X (1835–1914) was elected in 1903 after the Emperor of Austria had purported to debar his rival, Cardinal Rampolla, secretary of state to his predecessor, Leo XIII; although the veto had not in fact terminated Rampolla's candidacy, there was a wish for a less diplomatic pope than Leo had been. This wish was amply fulfilled when Pius' intransigence left the French Church helpless in the face of an anti-clerical government. Bitterly hostile to current trends in political thought and biblical scholarship, he invented an all-embracing ideology of modernism for the Church to fight; every cleric had repeatedly to take an oath against it, and a rigorous system of denunciation and thought-control was imposed. Where the critical intellect was not engaged, Pius was no less energetic as a reformer in everything from canon law to church music. He was the last pope to be made a saint, being canonized in 1950 by the anti-modernist Pius XII.

Thaddaeus (Orth.). According to a tradition first recorded in the early fourth century by Eusebius, who claims to translate it from Syriac documents found in the archives at Edessa, the local ruler or 'toparch', Abgar V (a historical personage, who reigned 4 BC–AD 7 and again AD 13–50), sent a request to Jesus that He should come and heal him of his sickness, promising him sanctuary from the Jews; Jesus replied that He could not come, but after His ascension would send a disciple to cure him; after Jesus' death, St Thomas dispatched one of the Seventy (see *4 Jan.), called Thaddaeus, to Edessa, where he performed miraculous cures. As soon as he entered Abgar's chamber, the king beheld 'a great vision' on Thaddaeus' face, and did him reverence, to the astonishment of his courtiers, who had not seen the miracle; he declared his faith in Jesus and was cured. (This vision was later converted into a portrait painted by the king's messenger; see *16 Aug.) The next day, Thaddaeus preached the Word at a citizens' assembly summoned by the king; he is thus regarded as the founder of the Edessene Church, and greatly venerated under his Syriac name of Addai. In the West, where the whole story of Abgar's letter was long denied, Thaddaeus is identified with St Jude (see *28 Oct.).

Thaddaeus is not a familiar name in the English-speaking world, though it is used to represent the Irish name Tadhg (Anglicized as Teague or Taig), properly a word for poet; it recurs in Russian as Faddey and in Polish as Tadeusz. Adam Mickiewicz wrote an epic poem entitled *Pan Tadeusz*; the Polish boy with whom the narrator of *Death in Venice* is obsessed is called by the diminutive form Tadzio.

In the United States, Lawyers' Day, celebrating the organization of the American Bar Association in 1878.

22 AUGUST

❦ HOLY DAYS Queenship of Mary (RC, formerly 31 May); formerly Immaculate Heart of Mary

The *Queenship of Mary* is a late feast; Spanish and Latin American dioceses were given permission to celebrate it on 31 May. In 1954 Pius XII extended it to the whole Church, to mark the 100th anniversary of the dogma of the Immaculate Conception. The commemoration now takes place on the Octave of the Assumption.

Timotheus, Roman martyr under Diocletian, posthumously promoted bishop of Antioch.

August

The Emperor Octavian, called the August,
    I being his favorite, bestowed his name
Upon me, and I hold it still in trust,
    In memory of him and of his fame.
I am the Virgin, and my vestal flame
    Burns less intensely than the Lion's rage;
Sheaves are my only garlands, and I claim
    The golden Harvests as my heritage.

Henry Wadsworth Longfellow (1807–82), *The Poet's Calendar*

23 AUGUST

a.d. X Kalendas Septembres   D

❦ ANCIENT ROME This was the day of the Volcanalia, of which we know virtually nothing except that people drove animals into a fire as substitutes for themselves; Vulcan was less important in the city than at Ostia, of which he was practically patron.

❦ HOLY DAYS Rose of Lima (RC)

Rose of Lima (1586–1617), the first saint of the Americas to be canonized. She was called Rose because she grew flowers in her youth; after vowing virginity and joining the Third Order of St Dominic, she lived in a hut in her parents' garden. An extreme penitent, she disfigured her face and hands to hide her beauty, and wore a crown of thorns, becoming a symbol of her name. She was canonized in 1671, and is patron saint of South America and the Philippine Islands, as well as of florists. Feast-day formerly 30 August.

Philip Benizi (1233–85). An early member of the Order of Servites, he was responsible for sending Servite missionaries as far as India, and is known as the 'Second Founder of the Servite Order'.

24 AUGUST

E

Saint Bartholomew
brings the cold dew.

If St Bartholomew's Day be fair and clear,
Then a prosperous autumn comes that year.

St Bartlemy's mantle wipes dry
All the tears that St Swithin can cry.

❨ HOLIDAYS AND ANNIVERSARIES Ukraine: Independence Day (from the USSR, 1991)

❨ ANCIENT ROME This was one of the three days (the others being 5 Oct. and 8 Nov.) on which the Mundus, an underground building like an inverted sky, was opened; marked in the calendar as *Mundus patet*. We also read of a sacrifice to the Moon.

❨ HOLY DAYS **Bartholomew, Apostle** (CofE, RC; Orth. 11 June)

Bartholomew is mentioned in three of the Gospels as an apostle, and may be the Nathanael of John 1: 45–51, 21: 2. According to tradition he was flayed alive and then beheaded in Armenia, and hence is portrayed with a knife; this is also his symbol on primestaves, where it serves as a reminder to slaughter goats. He is patron saint of tanners, but also of plasterers. His relics are claimed by the church that bears his name in Rome, San Bartolomeo on the Isola Tiberina, where the Fatebenefratelli hospital perpetuates the good work of Aesculapius. Crowland Abbey (see *11 Apr.) was dedicated to him; his English cult was also furthered by an arm given to Canterbury Cathedral in the eleventh century by Queen Emma, wife of Cnut, and by the great London hospital founded in 1123. Other relics are at Benevento and Frankfurt am Main. In Carolingian calendars, and Baronius' Roman Martyrology, his day is the 25th.

The Elder Patrick, a mysterious Irish saint in early martyrologies, predecessor of the more familiar Apostle of Ireland and sometimes identified with Palladius (*7 July). This is also the day of St Patrick of Nevers, whose relics at Glastonbury were later passed off as the great St Patrick's; the resulting complex of legends has resisted disentangling.

Ouen or Audoenus (*c.*610–84). He became acquainted with his lifelong friend St Eligius (*1 Dec.) at the court of Clothar II and later of Dagobert I, where he was chancellor; like Eligius, he gave up secular life, and was consecrated bishop of Rouen in the same year, 641, as Eligius was made bishop of Noyon. His cult spread to Canterbury, which claimed relics whose authenticity was doubted until miracles happened.

St Bartholomew's Fair, Smithfield, London (St Bartholomew's hospital was located in Smithfield). From 1133 to 1752 it began on St Bartholomew's Day; after the calendar reform it was changed to 3 September. In 1840 it was moved to Islington, and ceased after 1855. It has given its name to a 'Bartholomew doll' (an overdressed woman, after the dolls sold at the fair) and a 'Bartholomew pig', a very fat person (after the roast pig that was a staple of the fair).

No season through all the yeere accounts hee more subject to *abhomination* than *Bartholomew* faire: Their *Drums, Hobbihorses, Rattles, Babies, Iewtrumps*, nay *Pigs* and all, are wholly *Iudaicall*. The very *Booths* are *Brothells* of iniquity, and distinguished by the stamp of the *Beast*.

Brathwait, *Whimzies*, 117 (1631)

Bartleme Fair

While gentlefolks strut in their silver and satins,
We poor folks are tramping in straw hats and pattens,
As merrily Old English ballads can sing-o,
As they at their opperores outlandish ling-o
Calling out bravo, encoro, and caro,
Tho'f I will sing nothing but Bartleme Fair-o.

Here first of all, crowds against other crowds driving,
Like wind and tide meeting, each contrary striving;
Here's fiddling and fluting, and shouting and shrieking,
Fifes, trumpets, drums, bagpipes, and barrow-girls squeaking.
My ware round and sound, here's choice of fine ware-o,
Though all is not sound sold at Bartleme Fair-o.

Here are drolls, hornpipe dancing, and showing of postures;
Plum-porridge, black-puddings, and op'ning of oysters;
The taphouse guests swearing, and gall'ry folks squalling,
With salt-boxes, solos, and mouth-pieces bawling;
Pimps, pick-pockets, strollers, fat landladies, sailors,
Bawds, baileys, jilts, jockeys, thieves, tumblers and tailors.

Here's Punch's whole play of the gunpowder-plot, sir,
Wild beasts all alive, and pease-porridge hot, sir:
Fine sausages fried, and the Black on the wire;
The whole court of France, and nice pig at the fire.
The ups-and-downs, who'll take a seat in the chair-o?
There are more ups and downs than at Bartleme Fair-o.

Here's Whittington's cat, and the tall dromedary,
The chaise without horses, and Queen of Hungary;
The merry-go-rounds, come who rides? come who rides?
Wine, beer, ale and cakes, fire-eating besides;
The famed learned dog that can tell all his letters,
And some men, as scholars, are not much his betters.

This world's a wide fair, where we ramble 'mong gay things;
Our passions, like children, are tempted by play-things;
By sound and by show, by trash and by trumpery,
The fal-lals of fashion, and Frenchified frumpery.

Life is but a droll, rather wretched than rare-o,
And thus ends the ballad of Bartleme Fair-o.

George Alexander Stevens (1710–84)

St Bartholomew's Day Massacre (*la Saint-Barthélemy*): murder of over 3,000 Protestants in Paris during the night of 23–4 August 1572 at the hands of a Catholic mob summoned as if ritually by the tocsin of Saint-Germain-l'Auxerrois; the queen mother, Catherine de Médicis, sharing the Catholic discontent at current policy, chiefly directed by the Protestant Coligny, had extorted approval for the slaughter from Charles IX. The victims included Coligny himself; many of them had come to Paris for the marriage to Catherine's daughter Marguerite de Valois of the Protestant Henri of Navarre, the future Henri IV, one of the Catholic party's grievances.

Black Bartholomew (1662). The date by which clergymen had to accept the Book of Common Prayer or lose their livings.

25 AUGUST

a.d. VIII Kalendas Septembres   F

❡ HOLIDAYS AND ANNIVERSARIES Uruguay: Independence Day (from Brazil, 1825)

❡ ANCIENT ROME This day was called 'Opeconsiva', being marked by sacrifices to Ops Consiva, 'Wealth from Planting'; the officiating priest at her small shrine in the Regia wore a white veil. Her other festival, the Opalia, was held on 19 December; like this, it fell four days after Consualia.

❡ HOLY DAYS Louis IX (RC); Joseph Calasanz (RC)

Louis IX, king of France, b. 1214, succeeded his father, Louis VIII, in 1226. He was a man of deeply religious private life, who reformed French administration, frequently did justice in person, and was invited more than once to arbitrate in foreign disputes. Having led an unsuccessful Crusade in 1248–54, he embarked on another in 1267, but died at Tunis; his body was brought home to Paris, but his heart was taken to Monreale in Sicily. He was revered both in his own day and afterwards as the model of a just and Christian king. In 1952 St Louis was declared patron of French troops. He is also, for an unknown reason, patron of button-makers.

Joseph Calasanz (1557–1648), founder of the Clerks Regular of the Religious Schools. Born to a noble Aragonese family, he first studied law and theology. After a period as Vicar-General of the bishop of Urgell in the Pyrenees he gave everything up and went to Rome to tend victims of the plague, but then decided that his vocation lay in education, and many schools were opened under his direction. Pius XII declared him patron of Christian schools in 1948. Feast-day formerly 27 August.

Genesius of Arles (d. *c.*303), a notary under Diocletian who gave up his office in disgust at the edict of persecution. Later he was confused with another Genesius, a Roman, and by the sixth century he was known as 'Genesius the comedian', who was converted to Christianity on stage; this was thought to be an act until the very end, when he declared that he had been truly converted; he was then tortured on the rack and beheaded. The latter, legendary Genesius is patron of actors and comedians.

Detectives' Day, celebrating the birth of Allan Pinkerton in 1819.

26 AUGUST

❮ HOLY DAYS Ninian (RC Scotland; CY 16 Sept.); David Lewis (RC Wales)

Ninian (5th c.), founder of Candida Casa or Whithorn (Wigtownshire), from which he and his monks were said to have evangelized the northern Britons and the Picts.

David Lewis (1616–79), Jesuit in South Wales, martyred at Usk; he is one of the Forty Martyrs of England and Wales.

Teresa of Jesus Jonet e Ibars (1843–97), co-foundress of the Little Sisters of the Aged Poor. Whereas the young have many patron saints, they have been lacking for the old until recently; in 1980 John Paul II confirmed Teresa as patron of the old in Colombia and in 1984 in Brazil and Ecuador.

The end of harvest in England was often celebrated with church wakes. An American visitor describes one in 1776:

Here [Birmingham] and hereabouts are many wakes as they are called, being neither more nor less than people of the lower classes encouraged to assemble together on various occasions to direct and amuse them in sports in the streets, lanes and Fields, and in ale houses mughouses and Inns which they do to the emolument only of the Keepers, but to the great injuries, damage and hurt of themselves and families, who suffer by 'em. Yesterday was one collected in that part of the town near St. Georges Chappell called St. Georges wake, kept in remembrance of some circumstance relative to that chappell; but what I have not curiosity to inquire though I had to march through the crowds who were collected in great numbers and reminded me of my own Country; the appearance of them in dress and behaviour very nearly resembling ours.

Curwen, i. 213 (27 Aug. 1776)

Charles Burney witnesses the 'Little Pig' festival in Bologna in 1770, which ends with scenes from Tasso's *Gerusalemme liberata*:

This is a day of Jubilee here, equal to that of our Lord Mayor, in London. After dinner, upon the great Piazza or Square in the Theatre constructed for the Fair, by the Majistrates, which began at the Assumption, the 15th inst. and which is continued during the whole month. The usual popular festival called The *Porchetta*, or little Pig, is kept in memory of the extinction of the civil war, about the year 1278; in which by the accident of a Pig running across the street, the stout Antonio Lambertazzi, head of the Ghibeline Faction, was killed. In this occasional Amphitheatre, after a popular spectacle, diversified every year, peacocks, cocks and Hens, and money are thrown to the people, and, lastly, a Pig, ready dressed. The Cardinal Legate attended in a Balcony, and threw money to the mob. The crowd was prodigious—stages built all around, and the windows, and even tops of houses were crowded with people. We now had a pageant, or mock Triumphal Car, with ordinary girls dressed very fine, in it; these were followed by others in procession. There was next represented the palace of Armida, into which she conducted Rinaldo. Then appear two of his followers in quest of him, armed *Cap à piè*, upon which a huge Dragon comes out of a cave under the palace to attack them, together with two Griffins spitting fire, and made hideously frightful. These are vanquished; and then the two Champions enter the Palace, and carry off Rinaldo, in spite of the threats and entreaties of Armida. The Hero is put on board a vessel which sails out of sight. Upon which more monsters appear all in flames, and set fire to the Palace, while Armida flies away on a fiery dragon. The whole of this was rendered comic by the burlesque air that was given to it: sometimes the machinery of the monsters took fire, and threatened to burn the men underneath; upon which they threw off the whole apparatus, and appear half naked to the spectators. The scrambling for the money, the poultry etc, likewise afforded great diversion.   Burney, 157–8

27 AUGUST

❦ HOLIDAYS AND ANNIVERSARIES Moldova: Independence Day (from the USSR, 1991) (national day)

  USA, Texas: Lyndon B. Johnson's Birthday (1908)

❦ ANCIENT ROME This was the Volturnalia, in honour or appeasement of a god variously identified as the Sirocco and as a river in Campania.

❦ HOLY DAYS Monica (CY, RC); formerly Joseph Calasanz (now *25 Aug.)

Monica (*c.*331–87), mother of St Augustine. She was born in North Africa, probably at Thagaste. Her husband was a determined pagan, but was eventually converted by her. She had more difficulty with her son, who fled to Rome, where she pursued him, and then to Milan, where he eventually converted in 386 (see *28 Aug.). She died the following year in Ostia, on the way back to Africa, all her hopes, as she said, having been fulfilled. Some of her relics were translated by Austin canons to Arrouaise in France, whence her cult spread; the remaining relics were translated to Rome in 1430 and are now in the church of S. Agostino. Monica is patron of mothers (and especially, it seems, of those with undisciplined sons). She might also appropriately be invoked by recovering alcoholics, having overcome addiction brought on by a hostile mother-in-law and recalcitrant husband. We know this from her son's Confessions; as Thomas Fuller, in his seventeenth-century description of her life, puts it:

[Her mother] instructed her with holy severity, never allowing her to drink wine, or between meals. Having out-grown her tuition, she began by degrees to sip, and drink wine, lesser draughts like wedges widening her throat for greater, till at last (ill customes being not knockt, but insensibly scru'd into our souls) she could fetch off her whole ones. Now it happened that a young maid (formerly her partner in potting) fell at variance with her, and (as malice when she shoots draws her arrow to the head) called her Tos-pot, and drunkard; whereupon Monica reformed her self, and turned temperate.   Fuller, *Holy State*, 4–5

'*Little Sir Hugh*' of Lincoln was formerly celebrated on this day, the boy whose murder in 1255 was superstitiously blamed on the Jews (cf. *26 Mar.); he is invoked at the end of 'The Prioress's Tale'.

28 AUGUST

a.d. V Kalendas Septembres   B

❮ HOLIDAYS AND ANNIVERSARIES Scotland: Lammas Term

❮ ANCIENT ROME This was the dedication-day of the temple of the Sun and Moon near the Circus Maximus; in the late empire, games were held in their honour.

❮ HOLY DAYS Augustine (CofE, RC)

Augustine (354–430), born at Thagaste in Numidia (now Souk Ahras in Algeria), son of a pagan father and the Christian St Monica (see *27 Aug.); brought up (though not baptized) as a Christian, but diverted from the faith first by Platonic philosophy and then by Manichaeism. After teaching rhetoric in Rome, he moved to Milan, where the emperor resided; he was finally converted, and baptized by St Ambrose on Holy Saturday, 24 April 387. Next year he returned to Thagaste, where a religious community developed around him (its precise nature is disputed); in 391 he was ordained priest at Hippo Regius (near the modern Annaba, previously called Bône), where he established another community and made himself indispensable to Bishop Valerius, a Greek who found it hard to preach in Latin; *c.*396 he succeded him in the episcopate, which he retained for the rest of his life. He died in Hippo on 28 August 430 during the Vandal siege; his relics lie in the Augustinian church of San Pietro in Ciel d'Oro at Pavia.

As bishop, Augustine had to combat the Donatists, whose religious rigorism was all too often expressed in terroristic violence against the Catholics; he ultimately accepted that government coercion was needed, in words twisted in later ages to justify persecution in general.

It were small praise to call him the greatest thinker of the Western Church in Roman times, for Latin culture was in those days even further behind Greek in theology than in philosophy; rather must he be called one of the greatest Christian thinkers of all times. So great was his pre-eminence in the West that popes were sometimes dismayed to find his opinions treated as final: in 1690 Alexander VIII accused the Jansenists of holding that a doctrine clearly made out in Augustine could be held without regard to papal bulls; in 1930 Pius XI warned against preferring Augustine speaking to the Church teaching. Catholic reservations particularly apply to his writings on grace and free will. Augustine conducted a polemic against the Briton Pelagius, who maintained that man could choose good over evil of his own free will, without the grace of God. He has often been read as implying double predestination, that is to say that God has determined in advance who is to be saved and who damned; this doctrine was aired and condemned more than once before its revival by the sixteenth-century Reformers. Nevertheless, Augustine was largely quoted in the Council of Trent's decree on the subject. The pessimistic view of human freedom, wholeheartedly upheld by Protestants, has never been accepted by the Orthodox, most of whom also deny the contention, of which he is the chief though not the only propounder, that the Holy Spirit proceeds from the Son as well as the Father; this doctrine is the unchallenged faith of the West, asserted through the interpolation of *Filioque* ('and the Son') in the Creed. This was instigated by Frankish kings as an anti-Greek measure and resisted by successive popes on diplomatic grounds till 1014; it outrages even those Orthodox who accept the doctrine.

The originality and depth of Augustine's thought are most familiar to the general reader from his *Confessions*, an account of his spiritual development, and his *City of God*, his reaction to Alaric's sack of Rome in 410, distancing the Christian from the political order of this world; these works are as easily available in translation as the Greek and Roman classics. No other ancient Christian writer is so widely read today.

29 AUGUST

a.d. IV Kalendas Septembres   C

❦ HOLIDAYS AND ANNIVERSARIES Slovakia: National Day (National Uprising, 1848)

❦ HOLY DAYS Beheading of St John the Baptist (CofE, RC)

Beheading (Decollation) *of John the Baptist.* When John's preaching attracted a mass following, Herod Antipas, tetrarch of Galilee and Peraea, 'who feared lest the great influence John had over the people might put it into his power and inclination to raise a rebellion (for they seemed ready to do anything he should advise), thought it best, by putting him to death, to prevent any mischief he might cause, and not bring himself into difficulties, by sparing a man who might make him repent of it when it should be too late' (Josephus, tr. Whiston, 382). St Luke confirms (3: 19) that John was denouncing Herod's misdeeds, among them his marriage to his niece Herodias, who had previously been married to his half-brother and fellow tetrarch Philip; indeed, John told him to his face: 'It is not lawful for thee to have thy brother's wife' (Mark 6: 18). However, although

Herod clapped him in prison, St Matthew states (14: 5) that he at first refrained from putting him to death for fear of public opinion; according to St Mark (6: 20), Herodias wanted him dead, but Herod was afraid of him, 'knowing that he was a just man and an holy', and indeed 'heard him gladly'. The impasse was resolved when Salome, Herodias' daughter by Philip, so pleased Herod with her dancing at his birthday party that he swore to give her anything she wished, 'And she, being before instructed of her mother, said, Give me here John Baptist's head in a charger' (Matt. 14: 8). Compelled to keep an oath sworn in company, Herod had John beheaded; his head is claimed as a relic by a number of churches, some allegedly asserting that a rival has only his head as a young man, but his burial-church was at Sebaste (now Sabasṭiyya) in Samaria, whose dedication-feast was 29 August. In Rome the Decollation was long celebrated on the 30th, since the 29th belonged to the very popular but probably fictitious St Sabina, whose church on the Aventine had originally belonged to a lady of that name.

30 AUGUST

a.d. III Kalendas Septembres   D

❰ HOLIDAYS AND ANNIVERSARIES USA, Louisiana: Huey P. Long Day (see below)

❰ HOLY DAYS John Bunyan (CY); formerly Rose of Lima (see *23 Aug.)

John Bunyan (1628–88). Among the radical writers of the mid-seventeenth century, two stand head and shoulders above the rest, each supreme in his own class: amongst the élite John Milton, amongst the popular authors John Bunyan. The author of *Paradise Lost* is debarred from commemoration by the Church of England for justifying the execution of King Charles the Martyr; but the author of *The Pilgrim's Progress* has no less just a claim on the admiration of even the literary public:

In general, when the educated minority and the common people differ about the merits of a book, the opinion of the educated minority finally prevails. The 'Pilgrim's Progress' is perhaps the only book about which, after the lapse of a hundred years, the educated minority has come over to the opinion of the common people.   Macaulay, 'John Bunyan' (1854)

Bunyan was born at Elstow in Bedfordshire, of a poor but not destitute family; in 1644 he joined the parliamentary army, where he encountered religious and political radicalism, together with sharp polemics amongst their exponents. During the Interregnum he moved to Bedford, was accepted into its Independent congregation, and became a well-known preacher, who gave no little offence to the local gentry; at the Restoration he was arrested, and remained in prison for twelve years, during which he wrote his spiritual autobiography, *Grace Abounding to the Chief of Sinners*. Released in 1672, he was again imprisoned in 1676–7; in February 1678 he published the First Part of the *Pilgrim's Progress*, recounting Christian's journey from the City of Destruction to the Celestial City; the

Second Part, in which Christian's wife Christiana follows him with their four sons and the girl Mercy, appeared in 1684. His other works include *The Life and Death of Mr Badman* and *The Holy War*. He died in 1688 on 31 August, under which day the ASB recorded him as 'John Bunyan, Author, 1688'; CY promotes him to 'Spiritual Writer', but moves him to the 30th to avoid Aidan. We are left to wonder what he would have made of such a commemoration.

Fiacre (d. *c.*670), hermit (1 Sept. in France and Ireland). One of a number of Irish hermits who went to France, he was given land for a hermitage by the Bishop of Meaux. Known for his misogyny—he is patron of sufferers from venereal diseases—he devoted himself to gardening, tilling the land with his staff, and hence also patron saint of gardeners. His patronage of taxi drivers came about quite accidentally, from the location of a stand of hired carriages in Paris near the Hôtel Saint-Fiacre, which occasioned the French term *fiacre*. His cult was particularly important in the seventeenth and eighteenth centuries, and received royal patronage. He is also invoked by those suffering from haemorrhoids; there is a stone in Brittany with the purported imprint of his buttocks, on which sufferers sit to be cured. Tobias Smollett, claiming Fiacre for a fellow-Scot, reports his vengeance on an English king:

> those who are afflicted with the piles, who make their joint invocations to her [Veronica] and St. Fiacre, the son of a Scotch king, who lived and died a hermit in France. The troops of Henry V. of England are said to have pillaged the chapel of this Highland saint; who, in revenge, assisted his countrymen, in the French service, to defeat the English at Baugé, and afterwards afflicted Henry with the piles, of which he died. This prince complained, that he was not only plagued by the living Scots, but even persecuted by those who were dead.

> Smollett, 28 (letter of 1 Sept. 1763 at Boulogne)

Huey Pierce Long (1893–1935), nicknamed 'the Kingfish', governor of Louisiana from 1928 and US Senator from 1932; corrupt and autocratic, he was also populist and popular, the sworn enemy of Standard Oil and champion of economic redistribution. He is credited with saying 'It would be very easy to bring fascism to America—just call it anti-fascism' and 'In every State of the Union there's graft; in Louisiana there's graft and railroads.' Having made himself legal dictator of his state, he was assassinated in 1935.

31 AUGUST

❦ HOLIDAYS AND ANNIVERSARIES Kyrgyzstan: Independence Day (from the USSR, 1991)

  Malaysia: Hari Kebangsaan (national day; independent status within the Commonwealth, 1957)

  Trinidad and Tobago: Independence Day (from Great Britain, 1962)

❡ HOLY DAYS Aidan (CY)

Aidan (d. 651), Irish monk at Iona, whence he was sent at King Oswald's request to Northumbria in order to teach his subjects; Bede calls him 'a man of the greatest gentleness, and piety, and moderation, and having the zeal of the Lord, though not entirely according to knowledge', this last referring to his adherence to the Celtic mode of reckoning Easter. The Old English translation, made when all passion on that question had been spent, substitutes for the last phrase 'and great love of Him'. Oswald gave him land on the island of Lindisfarne, where he established a monastery under the Rule of St Columba; Bede depicts the conduct of Aidan and his monks in glowing colours. When Aidan preached, Oswald himself served as his interpreter, for the king's Irish was better than the bishop's English. Bede reports a tradition that on receiving Oswald's request for a missionary, the community of Iona had first sent a man of harsh temper who had made no converts and reported adversely on the unteachable English; but Aidan suggested that he ought to have offered them 'the milk of milder doctrine, until, gradually nurtured on the word of God, they should be able to receive more complete instruction, and perform God's higher commandments'. This evidence of discretion, 'which is the mother of the virtues', induced the brethren to send him in the other's stead. The RC Church commemorates him on this day as well.

Raymund Nonnatus (*c.*1204–40), Mercedarian missioner. His name, Latin for 'not born', is taken to mean that his mother died in labour; hence he is patron of midwives. He is also patron of the falsely accused. The mission of the Mercedarians was to ransom slaves; Raymund, who proselytized among Muslims when his funds ran out, had himself to be ransomed. He was named cardinal in 1239, but died at Cardona (near Barcelona) on the way to Rome.

On this day, the Orthodox Church celebrates the Deposition of the Honourable Girdle of the Theotokos. Legend relates that when Mary was about to depart this life, she gave her two items of clothing, a mantle and a girdle, to two poor virgins, from whom they descended to other virgins through the generations. The mantle was filched, or translated, from Capernaum in the fifth century (see *2 July); the girdle was found at Zela in the reign of Justinian and brought to Constantinople, where it was kept in a reliquary at the church in the Chalcoprateia ('Copper Market'). Another account has it deposited by the emperor Arcadius (395–408) and brought out 410 (*sic*) years later by Leo VI (886–912) to cure his fourth wife, Zoe Carbonopsina ('of the coal-black eyes')—whom he had married in defiance of the Byzantine Church by appealing to the Pope—of the evil spirit afflicting her. Since the fourteenth century the relic has been preserved at the Vatopedi monastery on Mount Athos.

Lady Morgan experiences the feast-day of San Abbondio, patron saint of Como, celebrated in an unusual manner in 1819:

In the summer of 1819, the Emperor had announced his *'beneficent intention'* (*la sua benefica intenzione*) of visiting his Italian dominions, of passing some weeks at Milan, and of sailing down the lake of Como, with the whole imperial court, in a splendour, to which nothing comparable had occurred, in the *fasti* of imperial journeys, since the memorable sail of Cleopatra down the Cydnus. . . . The Opera-house and Cathedral were put into requisition, and every old woman in the diocese was employed in making paper lanterns to illuminate the town. The Austrian garrison was *caned* and paraded oftener than usual, and fireworks to an immense amount were prepared. Joy was commanded by imperial authority, and '*vivats*' rehearsed, till the police were as hoarse as the cranes they had frightened from their ancient stations. When, lo! just as the lanterns, the barge, and the fireworks were ready, the news arrived, that the Emperor and Empress, within fifty miles of Milan, had resolved to proceed no further:—the reception they had received at Venice and Padua, and that which they were taught to expect at Milan, having suddenly cooled their '*benefica intenzione*', they omitted their '*sail of greatness*' down the lake, and returned post to Vienna.

This disappointment plunged the constituted authorities of Como into despair; when it was suggested by the heads of the church to the heads of the state, that what was intended to do honour to the Emperor Francis, might serve the turn of Saint Abbondio, whose festival was approaching; and that the mundane splendours which were expected to bring such multitudes of strangers to Como, and stimulate trade and loyalty together, would still bring grist to the mill, by being converted to holy purposes. Accordingly, the following '*Avviso Sacro*' was printed and circulated through the country, and hung over the gates of the cathedral.

HOLY ADVERTISEMENT

The artificial fireworks which the public (the Municipality) of Como had prepared, to evince its joy on the occasion of the desired arrival of their Royal and Imperial Majesties in this royal city, offer, this year, the means of celebrating in a singular manner, the Festival of Saint Abbondio, patron of the city and diocese of Como. To this effect will contribute the aforementioned fireworks, ceded by the municipal congregation to the pious, who propose, in concert with the authorities, to *set fire* (*incendiare*) to the *grandiosa macchina*, which represents a Temple, on the evening of the thirty-first of August, the festival of our holy protector; and thus in an extraordinary manner, and to the usual pomp of the cathedral, where with due veneration the service will be solemnized by our Lord the Bishop. Under these fortunate circumstances, all the faithful may partake of the treasure of the Papal *Benediction*, of a plenary indulgence, and at the same time profit by the spectacle of the artificial fireworks.—Como, 14th of August, 1819.

Printed by Carlantonio Ostinelli, Episcopal Printer

. . . The Saint's day was ushered in by all the splendour of Italian skies; the waters were blue and brilliant as the heavens: every steeple sparkled in the sunshine; and every bell tolled, from the shores of the *Chiavenna*, to the Duomo of Como. Not a mountain, not a *paese* in the district, but had yielded up its inhabitants to the festivity of the season . . . all bending their steps to that venerable dome, where glittered in large golden characters—'*Indulgenza Plenaria*'. The day began with a musical mass, at which the Bishop of Como officiated *in pontificalibus*; the whole sumptuous parade of the most sumptuous and most attractive of all religions was exhibited; and the same orchestra which performed the *Cenerentola*, at the Opera, the night before, and symphonized the triumphs of the Glass Slipper, now with the exact same strains (the brilliant harmonies of Rossini) accompanied the most solemn and imposing ceremonies of the most holy of mysteries. The rest of the day was filled up with sauntering and feasting, *Pulcinello* and prayers; till, at last, the *benediction-bell* announced the arrival of evening, and the commencement of the long-expected fireworks. Then the crowded boats put out again to the lake, to catch the effect in all its splendour; the shores were covered with eager multitudes, and joyous expectation sat on every face— but, suddenly, the air exhibited those meteoric phenomena portentous of the dreaded *Burasca!*—the forked lightning darted through the atmosphere—the thunder crashed among the mountains—the lake swelled—and the rain fell, as it only falls in Italy, in broad sheets of continuous water. It was in vain that the moment assigned to '*incendiare la grandiosa macchina*' was anticipated, the rain already prevailed; and a few abortive and smoky spirts of fire were all that could be obtained from the cumbrous and complicated machine ... The timid boatmen, invoking every saint in the calendar, laboured to gain any port or creek; the drenched crowds on the shore fled to shelter. It was evident that the offerings were not propitiated, and that St. Abbondio did not choose to be the *pis-aller* of unappropriated loyalties. ... It was in vain that the peasantry returned to their homes, blessed by the Pope, and absolved by the Church: the tempest, and the spoiled fireworks, were the sole themes of conversation. Even the saint lost much of his popularity, and received but few invocations as long as the regrets lasted, for pleasures not to be compensated by a plenary indulgence for thirty years.   Morgan, i. 279–83

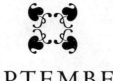

SEPTEMBER

September blowe soft,
Till fruite be in loft.
Forgotten, month past,
Doe now at the last. (Tusser)

❆ NAMES FOR THE MONTH Latin *September*, French *septembre*, Spanish *setiembre*, Portuguese *Setembro*, Italian *settembre*, German *September*, Welsh *Medi*, Scots Gaelic *an t-Sultuine* (and variant spellings), Irish *Meán Fómhair*

The Latin name indicates that this was originally the seventh month of the year. The Welsh name is the word for 'reaping'; the Scots Gaelic refers to the abundance and cheerfulness of harvest; the Irish means 'mid-autumn'.

❆ HOLIDAYS AND ANNIVERSARIES

First Sunday Venice: The *regata storica*, a parade of fully decked boats with rowers and passengers in historic costumes down the Grand Canal, precedes the rowing events, which culminate in the *regata* proper, the race of *gondolini* rowing *alla veneta* for the title of best pair.

First Sunday after first Monday USA: National Grandparents Day, instituted 1979

Last Sunday KwaZulu/Natal (South Africa): Shaka Day, commemorating the great Zulu king

First Monday USA: Labor Day. The first Labor Day parade took place in New York City on 5 September 1882, sponsored by the Central Labor Union, which was dominated by the Knights of Labor. Oregon instituted the first official Labor Day in 1887, the federal government not until 1894 (by this time it was an official holiday in 31 states). The success of the holiday was ensured by the determination to make it a joint partnership of capital and labour.
USA, New York: since 1968 West Indian–American Day Parade
South Africa: Settlers' Day

Fourth Friday American Indian Day

First Saturday after Full Moon in September Oklahoma: Indian Day

Next him, *September* marched eeke on foote;
Yet was he heauy laden with the spoyle

> Of haruests riches, which he made his boot,
> And him enricht with bounty of the soyle:
> In his one hand, as fit for haruests toyle,
> He held a knife-hook; and in th'other hand
> A paire of waights, with which he did assoyle
> Both more and lesse, where it in doubt did stand,
> And equall gaue to each as Iustice duly scann'd.
>
> Spenser, *The Faerie Queene*, VII. vii. 38

It is now September, and the Sunne begins to fall much from his height, the medowes are left bare, by the mouthes of hungry Cattell, and the Hogges are turned into the Corne fields: the windes begin to knocke the Apples heads together on the trees, and the fallings are gathered to fill the Pyes for the Houshold: the Saylers fall to worke to get afore the winde, and if they spy a storme, it puts them to prayer: the Souldier now begins to shrug at the weather, and the Campe dissolued, the Companies are put to Garison: the Lawyer now begins his Haruest, and the Client payes for words by waight: the Innes now begin to prouide for ghests, and the night-eaters in the stable, pinch the Trauailer in his bed: Paper, pen, and inke are much in request, and the quarter Sessions take order with the way-layers: Coales and wood make toward the Chimney, and Ale and Sacke are in account with good fellowes: the Butcher now knocks downe the great Beeues, and the Poulters feathers make toward the Upholster: Walflet Oysters are the Fishwiues wealth, and Pippins fine are the Costermongers rich merchandise: the flayle and the fan fall to work in the Barne, and the Corne market is full of the Bakers: the Porkets now are driuen to the Woods, and the home-fed Pigges make porke for the market. In briefe, I thus conclude of it, I hold it the Winters forewarning, and the Summers farewell. Adieu.   Breton (1626)

Now *Libra* weighs the days and nights in an equal balance, so that there is not an hairs breadth difference betwixt them in length: this moneth having an R in it, Oysters come again in season, which will cause as great a bawling at *Billingsgate*, as is at *Westminster-Hall* amongst the Lawyers in Term time.   *Poor Robin* (1666)

A seventeenth-century dietary counsel for September:

In this Moneth *eat* all manner of *meats* and *fruits* that your stomack desires, for all things are now in their proper vigor and perfection, good to purge, and to this end is highly commendable the flour of *Cassia* new drawn, that gently purgeth and comforts nature, and use cordial powders in your broths, these preserve the body sound till the next Spring; all Simples [plants used for medicinal purposes], Roots, Fruits and Seeds, may be well applied this Moneth, and used on all occasions, as being in their full perfection; *Goats milk* and *Pomegranats* eaten this Moneth are commendable, for that they both increase *blood*, and cause a good *colour*.   Saunders (1665)

1 SEPTEMBER

Kalendae Septembres   F

⟨ HOLIDAYS AND ANNIVERSARIES Cameroon: Union Nationale Camerounaise Day
Japan: Disaster Prevention Day, commemorating Kantō earthquake (1923)

Libya: Revolution Day (1969) (national day)
Mexico: Public Holiday
Slovakia: Constitution Day
Tanzania: Heroes' Day
Uzbekistan: Independence Day (from the USSR, 1991)

❦ HOLY DAYS Giles (CofE)

Giles or Aegidius (7th c.), a hermit for whom the Visigothic King Wamba (672–80) reportedly founded an abbey at Saint-Gilles in Provence, given a charter by Pope Benedict II (684–5). According to legend, while sheltering a hind that King Wamba was hunting, he was crippled by an arrow from the king's bow. In splendid defiance of chronology, another legend makes him an Athenian drawn by the preaching of St Caesarius, archbishop of Arles, who died in 542, and a third has him absolve Charlemagne, who was born some 200 years later, for a sin so heinous that the emperor durst not confess it: an angel displayed it to the saint in writing that disappeared as he prayed. He was further said to have visited Rome late in life to obtain privileges for his monastery by offering it to the pope; the Holy Father gave him two doors of cypresswood that, thrown into the sea, were transported to a beach near the present Saint-Gilles.

Be that as it may, his cult spread over Europe; he became the patron of nursing mothers (from the hind that nourished him), lepers, and above all cripples; the legend concerning Charlemagne increased his popularity by implying that he could obtain forgiveness for sins not fully confessed by the penitent. Since he was also patron of blacksmiths, his churches were often built at crossroads, where the rider could worship while his horse was shod at the nearby smithy. In England alone some 160 churches were dedicated to him, most famous being that at Cripplegate in London; in Scotland, it was at St Giles' Cathedral in Edinburgh that the revolt against Charles I's Scottish prayer book was said to have been launched when Jenny Geddes hurled her stool at the head of Bishop Lindsay on Sunday, 23 July 1637 OS. Giles was counted one of the Fourteen Auxiliary Saints. His emblem is an arrow. The RC Church commemorates him on this day as well.

A fair is held in Oxford in the street that bears his name, running south from his church, on Monday and Tuesday following the first Sunday after 1 September; first celebrated in 1634, it was formerly a market-fair, but, having been suspended during the Second World War, on resumption turned into a funfair.

Among the leaders of the First Crusade was Raymond of Saint-Gilles, count of Toulouse; his name was adapted by the Byzantine Greeks to *Isangelēs*, 'Equal of the Angels'.

Lupus (Loup, Leu) (d. 623), archbishop of Sens, where he founded the monastery of Sainte-Colombe. He was exiled for a time after the Frankish king Clothar II's seizure of Burgundy. According to legend he delayed Clothar's enterprise by ringing the great bell in his cathedral of Saint-Étienne so loudly as to scare away the royal troops. One Sunday, while he was saying mass, a precious stone fell from heaven into his chalice;

when his prayers were interrupted one night by a powerful thirst, he called for cold water, then recognizing the origin of his craving, placed his couch on the vessel and thus imprisoned the Devil, 'who began to howl and scream all night long'. Accused of loving his predecessor's daughter, who was a nun, he kissed her in front of his enemies, declaring: 'Other men's words harm him nothing whose own conscience stains him not.'

On St. Lupus and St. Giles's day, which was Saturday, 1st September 1425, some members of the parish suggested putting on another entertainment, which they did, and this was it: they got a good long pole about six *toises* [*c*.36 ft] long, stuck it into the ground, and at the very top they put a basket in which were a fat goose and six *blancs*. Then they greased the pole very thoroughly and announced that whoever could scramble up it unassisted and get the goose should have it, together with the pole, the basket, and the six *blancs*. But no one, however well he climbed, could reach it. In the evening, however, a boy who had got higher than anyone else was given the goose, but not the six *blancs* or the basket or the pole.   Bourgeois of Paris, 206

Priscus of Capua, of whom nothing is known (his fine ancient church has been destroyed), but who is commemorated in the Roman Martyrology and in thirteen English monastic calendars; his feast is sometimes used for dating.

St Fiacre's feast is on this date in France and Ireland; see *30 August.

From the mid-fifth century (perhaps from 462) 1 September was the first day of both the calendar year and the 'Greek' indiction year at Constantinople; it is still the beginning of the Orthodox ecclesiastical year. (See *23 Sept.)

This day is traditionally thought to be the beginning of the oyster season, the eight months containing the letter R in which it was considered safe to eat oysters. However, the official opening for oyster-fishing was Old St James Day (see *5 Aug.).

Wednesday 1st September [1830]. This morning I treated mother to some fine oysters, the prohibition against offering them for sale having ceased to the great joy of our gourmands whose appetite for oysters is insatiable.   Pintard, iii. 172

The partridge-shooting season also begins. Hence 'St Partridge Day', the opening of the partridge season (to 1 Feb.):

'Well, this *is* friendship! What on earth brings you here, old fellow? Why aren't you in the stubbles celebrating St. Partridge?'   Mrs Humphry Ward, *Robert Elsmere*, ch. 48 (1888)

2 SEPTEMBER

a.d. IV Nonas Septembres   G

℃ HOLIDAYS AND ANNIVERSARIES Vietnam: Independence Day (1945)

℃ HOLY DAYS Formerly Stephen, king of Hungary (see *16 Aug., *20 Aug.)

William, bishop of Roskilde (d. 1067), chaplain to St Knud, king of Denmark (see *10 July). While accompanying the king on his voyages, he saw the great spiritual need of the Danes and stayed in Denmark, being named bishop of Roskilde in Sjælland. His principal efforts were directed at Knud's nephew, King Svend Estridsen, guilty of incest, arbitrary death-sentences, and violation of church sanctuary; Svend eventually confessed, and after death both king and bishop were buried in the cathedral of Roskilde.

Mammas (Orth.), martyred under Aurelian (270–5); reported by the Roman Martyrology to have undergone a prolonged persecution from youth to old age. His head, and one arm, are said to be preserved at Langres. The East, however, which celebrates him on 2 September, makes him a 15-year-old herdboy stoned to death at Kayseri; for that reason he is the patron of cattle. The Western date is 17 August.

On this day in 1666 a fire at the King's baker's shop was fanned by an east wind into the Great Fire of London, which as folk memory delights to recall began in Pudding Lane and extended to Pie Corner. Despite the best efforts of workmen under the direct supervision of Charles II and the Duke of York, it burned for four days, destroying more than 13,000 houses and gutting St Paul's, Guildhall, and the Royal Exchange.

3 SEPTEMBER

a.d. III Nonas Septembres   A

❡ HOLIDAYS AND ANNIVERSARIES France, Monaco: Liberation of Monaco
    Qatar: Independence Day (from Great Britain, 1971)
    San Marino: St Marinus' Day or Republic Day
    Tunisia: Commemoration of 3 September 1934 (beginning of independence movement)

❡ HOLY DAYS Gregory the Great (CY, RC; BCP *12 Mar.); formerly Pius X (see *21 Aug.)

Gregory the Great, celebrating his consecration in 590; kept in the pre-Reformation English church from the early twelfth century (see *29 Mar.), and now replacing his traditional feast on *12 March.

Marinus (4th c.), said to have been a stonemason born on an island off Dalmatia who came to Rimini, whose walls he was ordered to help rebuild in 305. Having constructed a cell in Monte Titano he lived there as a hermit; his hermitage became the nucleus of a city that now constitutes the Republic of San Marino. His merits were recognized in 359, when Bishop Gaudentius of Rimini ordained him deacon; his body was discovered in the basilica of San Marino in 1586. In San Marino this has always been his day, but the 4th at Pavia, where there are purported relics, and in the Roman Martyrology.

Basilissa (d. *c*.303). She was listed in the Roman Martyrology as a 9-year-old virgin from Nicomedia (now İzmit) who during Diocletian's persecution withstood scourges, fire, and wild beasts with such steadfastness as to convert the governor; her cult existed as late as the fourteenth century at Constantinople. She is invoked as patron saint by nursing mothers and for warding off chilblains; nothing in her legend suggests a reason, but perhaps nursing mothers preferred to pray to a woman than to St Giles.

In the Middle Ages the third of September was commonly reckoned an 'Egyptian' or ill-omened day (see **Days: Unlucky*), a fact recorded by contemporary sources in connection with Richard I's coronation in 1189; one writer notes that it was an Egyptian day for the Jews, against whom the populace unleashed a pogrom. This was also the day on which Oliver Cromwell won two battles in successive years, in 1650 at Dunbar against the Scottish Covenanters, in 1651 at Worcester against the English and Scottish royalists; on the same day in 1658 he died amidst a fearful thunderstorm:

> . . . about the middle of *August*, he was seised on by a common tertian Ague, from which, he believ'd, a little ease and divertisement at *Hampton* Court would have freed him. But the fits grew stronger, and his Spirits much abated: so that he return'd again to *White-hall*, when his Physicians began to think him in danger, though the Preachers, who pray'd always about him, and told God Almighty what great things he had done for him, and how much more need he had still of his Service, declared as from God, that he should recover: and he himself was of the same mind, did not think he should die, till even the time that his Spirits fail'd him. Then he declared to them, 'that he did appoint his Son to succeed him, his eldest Son *Richard*'; and so expired upon the third day of *September* 1658, a day he thought always very propitious to him, and on which he had triumphed for two of his greatest victories. And this now was a day very memorable for the greatest storm of Wind that had been ever known, for some hours before and after his death, which overthrew Trees, Houses, and made great Wrecks at Sea; and the tempest was so universal, that the effects of it were terrible, both in *France* and *Flanders*, where all People trembled at it; for besides the Wrecks all along the Sea-Coast, many Boates were cast away in the very Rivers; and within few days after, circumstance of his death, that accompanied that Storm, was universally known.   Clarendon, bk. xv, §146 (iii. 648)

In the United Kingdom, and in France, this day is also regarded as the beginning of the Second World War, since on the expiry of their ultimata to Germany to withdraw from Poland they declared war.

4 SEPTEMBER

pridie Nonas Septembres   B

❡ HOLIDAYS AND ANNIVERSARIES Venezuela: Civil Servants' Day

❡ ANCIENT ROME Ludi Magni or Romani, in honour of Jupiter Best and Greatest, whose temple was dedicated on 13 September 509 BC; they were made annual in 366 BC if not before, and gradually extended from one day to fifteen (5–19 September), this day being added in honour of the murdered Caesar.

(HOLY DAYS Birinus (CY commem.; see *3 Dec.)

This day is properly St Cuthbert's translation, but is often kept as his main feast in preference to his traditional day of *20 March, which is in Lent.

Rose of Viterbo, virgin (1234–52). At 8 years old she had a vision in which the Virgin instructed her to take the Franciscan habit, but to live at home. By the age of 12 she was preaching in the streets of Viterbo against the emperor Frederick II and in favour of the pope. The emperor tolerated this for a few years, then had Rose and her family exiled. They returned after his death, which Rose had predicted. Refused admission to the Poor Clares' convent of St Mary of the Roses for lack of a dowry, she was set up in a nearby house with a few religious companions, but the nuns succeeding in closing it, and she returned to her family. She is said to have died on 6 March 1252; in Viterbo the Church honours her on that day, but the great public celebration, in which her incorrupt body is borne in procession through the city streets, is on 4 September, commemorating her burial in the Poor Clares' convent by order of Pope Alexander IV in 1258. She was canonized in 1457; because of her name, and that of the convent, she is patron of florists and flower-growers in central Italy.

Rosalia, virgin (d. 1160?). According to Sicilian tradition she was an anchoress in a cave near Palermo; her cult was popular in Sicily in the later Middle Ages. She became patron of Palermo in 1624, after her relics were found (see *15 July), and she was credited with ridding the city of the plague.

5 SEPTEMBER

Nonae Septembres   C

(ANCIENT ROME Jupiter Stator, so called because he stopped the enemy, or gave the city of Rome stability; the military explanation is probably the older, though no one is required to believe the legend that King Romulus vowed him a temple on the Palatium before making a stand against the invading Sabine army of Titus Tatius.

(HOLY DAYS

Laurence Giustiniani (Lorenzo Giustinian), patriarch of Venice (1381–1455). Born into a patrician Venetian family (a namesake was a noted poet), he joined the order of San Giorgio in Alga, becoming their general. Reluctantly he accepted the bishopric of Castello; when Pope Nicholas V transferred the see of Grado to Venice in 1451, he named Laurence patriarch, a post often subject to friction with the civic authorities, but left him and his successors in the church of San Pietro di Castello, on a small island well away from doge and Signoria (St Mark's was the doge's church, not the patriarch's). Widely renowned for his holiness, he wrote several ascetic treatises; he was canonized in 1690.

From this day in 3114 BC was reckoned the Mayan Long Count current at the time of the Spanish conquest (see II: *Other Calendars: Mesoamerican*), designed to end (had it not been discontinued in 1752) on 21 December 2012.

6 SEPTEMBER

a.d. VIII Idus Septembres   D

❦ HOLIDAYS AND ANNIVERSARIES Pakistan: Defence of Pakistan Day
São Tomé and Príncipe: National Heroes' Day
Swaziland: Independence Day (1968)

❦ HOLY DAYS

Bega or Bee, virgin (7th c.), reputedly an Irish king's daughter who narrowly escaped marriage by wearing a bracelet marked with a cross given her by an angel. Using a clod of earth as boat, she crossed the Celtic Sea and lived as an anchoress, fed by seagulls, on a promontory in Cumbria, known as St Bees Head, where she founded a convent. Her name recalls the feminine form of the Irish word for 'little' (*beag*, Old Irish *beg*); but her bracelet recalls the Old English word for that ornament, *bēag*. Her life is the subject of a recent novel (Melvyn Bragg, *Credo*). Her day is sometimes given as 31 October, the date (in one source) of her death. She is not to be identified with Begu, the English nun of Hackness near Whitby who according to Bede was vouchsafed a vision of Abbess Hilda's soul received into heaven (see *19 Nov.).

Mang or Magnus (*c.*699–*c.*772), a Benedictine from Sankt Gallen, became a missionary first in the Allgäu, then on the upper Lech, and built a hermitage in Füssen, which was enriched by benefactions (especially from Pippin the Younger) and became a monastery. He was buried there; his remains, translated *c.*840 to a new chapel there, disappeared in the eleventh century. His cult is strong in Swabia, Bavaria, Tyrol, and Switzerland. He is portrayed holding up the Cross to a dragon or casting a torch in its maw, surrounded by wild beasts and snakes, or reproving a bear under an apple tree. He is invoked for protection of crops from vermin and against lightning.

A menu for September suggested by Robert May (1665):

A Bill of Fare for September

Oysters
1   An Olio
2   Breast of Veal in stoffado
3   Twelve Partridge hashed
4   Grand Sallet
5   Chaldron Pie
6   Custard

A second Course
1   Rabits
2   Two Hearns, one larded
3   Florentine of tongues
4   8 Pidgeons roast, 4 larded
5   Pheasant pouts, 2 larded
6   A cold hare pie
Selsey cockles broild after

7 SEPTEMBER

a.d. VII Idus Septembres   E

☾ HOLIDAYS AND ANNIVERSARIES Brazil: Independence Day (from Portugal, 1822)
Mozambique: Victory Day

☾ HOLY DAYS Evurtius (BCP)

Heortius, whose name is commonly corrupted to 'Enurchus' or 'Evurtius', a fourth-century bishop of Orléans of whom very little is known, despite an account printed by the Bollandists under the heading *Vita fabulis foedata*, 'a life defiled by fables', which tells us that he put out a fire and found a treasure. But it was not for such achievements, not even for his election by the Holy Ghost, signified (as in many other cases) by a dove's perching on his head, that since 1604 he has been commemorated in the Book of Common Prayer: his inclusion was a subterfuge to enable the birthday of Queen Elizabeth I in 1533 to be celebrated under her successor James I.

The devotion that Elizabeth inspired towards the end of her reign is expressed in language too strong for the most loyal monarchist to use in our tongue-tied age:

What shall we write further of triumphes and of natiuities: But our day began the seuenth of September, the most happy and blessed day of Queene Elizas natiuitie, of whome wee haue triumphed 20295 daies, euery day being a triumphant day, sithence her Maiesties byrth vnto this present time.

This flourish was composed (if the days are reckoned inclusively) on 31 March 1589, soon after the defeat of the Spanish Armada, by Lodowick Lloyd, the Queen's serjeant-at-arms; it was published in *The Triplicitie of Triumphes* (1591), an anniversary celebration of

Elizabeth's birth (7 Sept. 1533), her accession (17 Nov. 1558), and coronation (15 Jan. 1559), cast as a study of the honours paid on such occasions to foreign princes (but also on their funerals, a topic not dear to the Queen). Lloyd, ever the loyalist, honoured James I no less effusively in atrocious verse; but Good Queen Bess's memory was preserved, not only in public. The Bodleian Library copy is bound together with one of Lloyd's *Diall of Daies* (see *8 May) containing copious manuscript notes by one Robert Nicholson, those for September being dated 1608; under this day we read:

7. The rare, faire and farre renowmed and admirable, ELIZABETH, Queene of England, France, Ireland, & Virginia: daughter of King Henry the viij^th and Queen Anne Bulleine his wife: was borne at Greenwich in Kent, on Sonday the vijth day of September A° D° 1533; 24° Hen: 8; betwene .3. & .4. of the clock in the afternoone: to the great ioy, & perpetuall honour of England.

These were private notes, written under King James, who would not have been pleased to see them, knowing that praise of Elizabeth was all too often dispraise of himself; indeed, popular as she had been in her lifetime, she became even more popular under the Stuarts (and a far less ambiguous champion of Protestantism than she had been in her lifetime).

Clodoald or Cloud (d. *c.*560), Frankish prince. Orphaned at an early age, when his father King Clodomar fell victim in 524 to a Burgundian ruse in battle, he was brought up with his brothers, Theudowald and Gunthar, by his grandmother, St Clothilda (*3 June). The affection she bestowed on them rankled with her own sons, Lothar and Childebert, who compelled her to choose whether the elder brothers (who were respectively 10 and 7) should have their hair cut, which would disqualify them from the throne, or be killed; she chose the latter, and the thing was done. Clodoald, whose life had been saved by courageous guards, did not choose to fight his uncles for power, but cut his own hair and became a priest at Nogent, near Versailles, where in 555 he founded a monastery renamed Saint-Cloud in 811. The similarity of his name to the French for 'nail' (*clou*) has led to his veneration in France as patron of nail-makers.

8 SEPTEMBER

a.d. VI Idus Septembres   F

> *Pare saffron betweene the two S. Maries daies* [15 Aug. and 8 Sept.],
> *Or set or go shift it, that knowest the waies.* (Tusser)

❰ HOLIDAYS AND ANNIVERSARIES Andorra: National Day (Our Lady of Meritxell) Malta: National Day (Our Lady of Victories) North Korea: National Day, commemorating foundation of state in 1948

❰ HOLY DAYS Nativity of the Blessed Virgin Mary (CofE); **Birthday of the Blessed Virgin Mary** (RC); **Nativity of the Theotokos** (Orth.)

Nativity of the BVM. This feast is probably derived from the dedication-feast for the fifth-century church of St Mary in Jerusalem, built on her supposed birthplace but rededicated by the Crusaders to St Anne; by the sixth century it was established in Constantinople, where Romanos the Melode (*1 Oct.) wrote hymns for it. First mentioned in the West *c.*600, it became part of the Roman calendar under Pope Sergius I (see below).

> Joy in the rising of our Orient starre,
> That shal bring forth the Sunne that lent her light,
> Joy in the peace that shall conclude our warre,
> And soone rebate the edge of Sathans spight,
> Load-starre of all engolfd in worldly waves,
> The card and compasse that from ship-wracke saves.
>
> The Patriarchs and Prophets were the flowers,
> Which Time by course of ages did distill,
> And cul'd into this little cloud the showers,
> Whose gratious drops the world with joy shall fil,
> Whose moisture suppleth every soule with grace,
> And bringeth life to *Adams* dying race.
>
> For God on earth she is the royall throne,
> The chosen cloth to make his mortall weede,
> The quarry to cut out our corner stone,
> Soile ful of fruit, yet free from mortall seede,
> For heavenly flowre shee is the *Jesse* rod,
> The child of man, the parent of a god.
>
>   Robert Southwell (?1561–95), 'Her Nativity'

In 1917 Mary of the Nativity was declared the patron saint of Cuba; the devotion centred around a particular statue, said to have been left by one of the *conquistadores* in 1508 as a thank-offering in an Indian village near Santiago de Cuba.

Pope Sergius I (d. 701). Born into a Syrian family at Palermo and elected in 687 despite challenges from two rivals, he enriched the Roman church year with litanies and processions on the Eastern festivals of Hypapante (2 Feb.: the Presentation in the Temple, or Purification), Annunciation (25 Mar.), Dormition or Assumption (15 Aug.), and the Nativity of the Virgin, as well as Holy Cross Day (14 Sept.). He also introduced the Agnus Dei into the Mass; this was a response to the prohibition on representing Jesus as a lamb passed by the so-called Quinisext Council or Council *in Trullo* (692), whose canons, forbidding standard Western practices such as clerical celibacy and Saturday fasting in Lent and reviving Constantinople's claim to a patriarchal status second only to Rome, Sergius steadfastly refused to ratify. The emperor Justinian II ordered Byzantine troops in Italy to arrest him and bring him to Constantinople, but they refused. He also restored and embellished Roman churches, baptized the West Saxon king Ceadwalla (689), authorized St Willibrord's mission to the Frisians (see *7 Nov.), ordered St Wilfrid (*12 Oct.) to be restored to his see, and in 700 received Aquileia back into communion with Rome after a schism caused by Pope Vigilius' capitulation to Justinian I in 553. This great pope died on 8 September 701 and is commemorated on this day.

9 SEPTEMBER

a.d. V Idus Septembres   G

❦ HOLIDAYS AND ANNIVERSARIES Japan: Chrysanthemum Day, *Kiku no Sekku*, the
adaptation to the Gregorian calendar of the traditional chrysanthemum festival
on the ninth day of the ninth lunar month
Tajikistan: Independence Day (from the USSR, 1991)
USA, California: Admission Day (31st state, 1850)

❦ HOLY DAYS Synaxis of the Theopatores Joachim and Anna (Orth.)

Joachim and Anna, Ancestors of God (*theopátores*) as parents of the Theotokos, the Virgin
Mary, are celebrated in the Orthodox Church on the day after her Nativity, in the RC
and CY on *26 July.

Gorgonius and Dorotheus, martyred 304, allegedly for protesting against the torments
inflicted on a Christian named Peter; Gorgonius was buried in the Via Labicana in Rome;
Pope Damasus inscribed his tomb with an epitaph that survived till the eighteenth
century.
    William Patten puzzles over the identity of St Gorgonius on his feast-day in 1547:

Fryday yᵉ ix. of september.
This dai is markt in yᵉ kallender with the name of saincte Gorgon, no famous saint sure, but
eyther so obscure that no man knowes him, or els so aunciente as euery man forgettes him. Yet
wear it both pitee and blame that he shoulde lose hys estimacion amonge us. And me thinkes
oute of that litle that I haue red, I coulde somewhat saye to bryng hym to lighte agayne, but then
am in doubte, what to make of hym, a he saint a she sainte or a neuter (for we haue all in oure
Kallendar.) Of the male and female sayntes, euery leafe thear showthe samples inowe. And as for
the neuter, they or [*sic*: read 'are'] rather I wot unmarked then unknowen, as sainct Christmas,
s. Candelmas, sainct Easter, Sainct Whitsontide & swete sainct Sunday yᵗ cums ones a weke.
Touchynge my doubte nowe: If the day beare name in yᵉ woorship & memorie of hym whome
the preacher Horace doth mencion in his first booke of sermons by these wordes *Pastillos Rufillus
olet, Gorgonius hircum.* then may we be bold to beleue it was a he sainct, but yet a very sloouen
[= slovenly] saynt & belyke a nesty [= nasty, smelly]. If this name were Kallendred of Medusa
Gorgon that had the heare of her hed tourned into adders, whome Perseus ouercame and kylde,
as doctour Ouide declares in his .iiii. booke of chaunges *Gorgonis anguicomæ Perseus superator*, then
maye we be sure it was a she saynte. But yf it wear in yᵉ honour of Pallas shelde whearin thys
Medusa Gorgons hed was grauen as Titus Stroza (a deuout doctour to, but of later daies) doth
say, *Gorgonis anguicomæ cælatos ægide vultus, Pallas habet.* Then was it neyther a he nor a she but a playne
neuter saynte. And thus with yᵉ aunciente authoritie of mere poeticall scriptures, my conscience
is so confounded, as I wot not in the worlde what saynte to make of hym. James of the synkhole
(sauyng your reuerence) a frier forsooth that wrote the Legendaurie, telleth me a very prepos-
terous order in good cookerie, of one Gorgon & his fellow Dorotheus, that wear first sauced with
vineger and salt, and after yᵗ then broiled on a girdyron. But to be playn (as it is best for a man
to be wᵗ his frendes) he hath farced hys boke so full of lyes, yᵗ it is quite out of credite in al honest company. And for my part, I am half a shamed to say yᵗ I saw it, but synce it is sayd,

& sumwhat to tell you what that I sawe, he makes me Thomas the traytour, *Lupus* y*ᵉ* Lechour Peter the knaue (yf I may call a coniurer so) & *Thais* the hoor all to be hye & holye sainctes in heauen, & y*ᵗ* w*ᵗ* such prodigal impudencie & so shameles liyng as I may safely thinke he had eyther a Bul to make sainctes of diuels, or els a placarde to play the knaue as he list. But as for Gorgon, be he as he be may, yt makes no great matter, for he shal haue my hart while he stondes in y*ᵉ* kallen-der, he hath bene euer so lucky. But what saynte so euer he bee, he is sure no Scottes mans frend, but a very angry sainte to warde them, for vpon hys daye .xxxiiii. yere paste, they had a greate ouerthrowe by us at Floddom feld, and their kyng Jamy y*ᵉ* fourth slayn, and thearfore is this day not smally markt among them. Patten, sig. D6ᵛ–8ᵛ

Horace: see *Sermones* [meaning of course 'chatty poems', not 'sermons'], I. 2. 27: 'Rufillus smells of breath-fresheners, Gargonius [the correct reading, but Gorgonius is an early variant] of billy-goat'.

Ovid: see *Metamorphoses*, 4. 699: 'Perseus who overcame the snake-haired Gorgon'.

Tito Strozza: Tito Vespasiano Strozzi, 'Ad Herculem Ferrariae ducem, de nuptiis Alfonsi, et Annae', *Aeolostichon liber quartus*, in *Strozzii poetae pater et filius* (Venice, 1513): 'Pallas has the snake-haired Gorgon's countenance graven on her shield', fo. 129ᵛ.

James of the Synkhole: Jacobus de Voragine, author of the Golden Legend: see 29 December (Thomas), 1 September (Lupus of Sens), 2 June (Peter the Exorcist), 8 October (Thais).

The 'great overthrow' of Flodden Field took place, as Patten records, on 9 September 1513, when the Earl of Surrey led the English army against James IV of Scots, who had invaded England while Henry VIII was fighting in France. The disaster (initially reported in France as a great victory) is commemorated in a famous lament, 'The Flowers of the Forest', given classic form by Jane Elliot in 1756; the last two stanzas run:

> Dool and wae for the order, sent our lads to the Border!   *Sorrow and woe*
> The English, for ance, by guile wan the day;
> The Flowers of the Forest, that fought ay the foremost,
> The prime of our land, are cauld in the clay.

> We'll hear nae mair lilting at the ewe-milking;   *blithe singing*
> Women and bairns are heartless and wae;   *disheartened and woebegone*
> Sighing and moaning on ilka green loaning—   *every green broad lane*
> The Flowers of the Forest are a' wede away.   *gone*

The English victory was not in fact due to guile, but such explanations comfort the defeated; Spenser claims in the *Faerie Queene* that Queen 'Bunduca' (Boudicca) was defeated 'By reason that the Captaines on her side, | Corrupted by *Paulinus*, from her sweru'd', which is contradicted by the ancient accounts.

10 SEPTEMBER

a.d. IV Idus Septembres   A

❦ HOLIDAYS AND ANNIVERSARIES Belize: St George's Cave Day (public holiday)
Bulgaria: Liberation Day
China: Teachers' Day

❦ HOLY DAYS

Nicholas of Tolentino (1245–1305). Named after St Nicholas of Bari, invoked by his long-
childless mother, he became an Augustinian hermit in 1263; by the time of his ordination he had become famous for healing, which he performed by giving his supplicants
pieces of bread over which he had invoked the blessing of the Virgin, known as 'St
Nicholas' bread'. According to legend the miraculous bread extinguished fires, including one at the Doge's palace in Venice. Hence he is one of the saints invoked against fire;
he is also protector of babies and mothers, and patron saint of the dying, souls in purgatory (having had visions of freeing souls, and even rescuing one in a state of damnation), and sickness in animals.

An eighteenth-century Englishman in Russia experiences the feast-day of a saint new
to him on 30 August OS:

This day being sacred to Alexander Nevski, a saint highly revered by the Russians, and in whose
honour an order of knighthood is instituted, was kept with great solemnity and magnificence.
Service was performed in the principal churches of Moscow with all the pageantry peculiar to
the Greek religion; and the governor of the province gave a splendid entertainment, to which the
principal nobility and clergy of this city were invited. . . .
   Alexander Nevski, a name more respectable than most of the saints who fill the Russian calendar, was son of the great-duke Yaroslaf, and flourished in the beginning of the 13th century, at
a period when his country had been reduced to the utmost extremity by a combination of formidable enemies. He repulsed an army of Swedes and Teutonic knights and wounded the king
of Sweden with his own hand on the bank of the Neva, from whence he obtained the appellation of Nevski. He defeated the Tartars in several engagements, and delivered his country from
a disgraceful tribute imposed by the successors of Zinghis Khan. His life seems to have been almost one continued scene of action; and he shewed such prowess, and performed such almost
incredible acts of valour, that it is no wonder ignorant and superstitious people should consider
him as a superior being, and should consecrate his memory: indeed, of all idolatry, that which is
paid to real merit, and in gratitude for real services, is the most natural, and the most excusable.
He died about the year 1262 at Gorodetz near Nishnei Novgorod. The great superiority of his
character was evinced, as well by victories which distinguished the Russian arms during his life,
as by the numerous defeats which immediately took place on his decease.   Coxe, i. 408

This was in fact his translation-feast; that of his death is on 23 November OS = 6 December NS.

11 SEPTEMBER

a.d. III Idus Septembres B

❮ HOLIDAYS AND ANNIVERSARIES Chile: National Liberation Day
Ethiopia: Ethiopian New Year (12th in year before western leap year)
Pakistan: Founder's Death Anniversary (Qaid-i-Azam Mohammed Ali Jinnah, 1948)
(public holiday)
Philippines: Barangay Day

❮ HOLY DAYS Deiniol (RC Wales)

Deiniol (d. *c*.584), reputedly the first bishop of Bangor Fawr and founder of monasteries both there and at Bangor Iscoed; Bede reports that the latter numbered over 2,100 monks, more than half of whom were killed by the heathen king Æthelfrith of Northumbria at the battle of Chester (616?). For Bede, this was just punishment, predicted by St Augustine of Canterbury, for the British refusal to preach the Gospel to the English; the Britons had found him too arrogant in his assertion of Roman usage, but some may have been happier to make sure the Saxons went to hell. Welsh saints do not save English souls; see David (*1 Mar.) and Beuno (*20 Apr.); or if these tales be later figments, in the seventh century Welsh princes sided with the heathen Penda of Mercia against the Christian kings of Northumbria.

Protus and Hyacinthus, third-century martyrs of whom Protus' remains are preserved in San Giovanni dei Fiorentini in Rome, and Hyacinthus' were discovered in 1848 in a catacomb off the old Via Salaria and are now in the new Propaganda on the Gianicolo.

Our Lady of Coromoto was declared patron of Venezuela by Pius XII in 1944. The name comes from a village settled by a tribe of Indians who had converted to Christianity in 1651–2. The Virgin appeared to their chieftain, who had postponed baptism and returned to old ways, and rebuked him so forcefully that he attacked her; when the vision vanished, he was left holding a statue of the Virgin, which subsequently became the object of pilgrimage.

12 SEPTEMBER

pridie Idus Septembres C

❮ HOLIDAYS AND ANNIVERSARIES Ethiopia: National Revolution Day (coup of 1974, removing Emperor Haile Selassie from power) (national holiday)
USA, Maryland: Defenders Day

❦ HOLY DAYS

Holy Name of Mary. The devotion to Mary's name is first recorded in Spain in the early sixteenth century, and was modelled on Bernardino of Siena's preaching on the name of Jesus (see *7 Aug.). Innocent XI extended the feast to the whole Church when Vienna was freed from the threat of the Turks in 1683.

Guy of Anderlecht (d. *c*.1012). Known as 'the Poor Man of Anderlecht', he was the model of a pious layman, using his modest salary as sacristan at Laken, near Brussels, to support the poor. Unwisely investing his small savings in order to increase his aid, he lost everything. He made a pilgrimage to Rome on foot, then to the Holy Land, returning to die in Anderlecht after seven years; his grave was almost forgotten, till miraculous cures were reported.

One of Dove's 'observations to foreknow the state of the year' (1664):

Ptolemy (to whom *Stadius* assenteth) saith, that as the swallows begin not at all to appear before the tenth day of *March*, so after the twelfth of *September*, they be seen that year no more.

13 SEPTEMBER

Idus Septembres   D

❦ ANCIENT ROME In the late Roman Republic or the early Empire, this day became an *epulum Iouis* or banquet of Jupiter, as 13 November already was; the Ides were Jupiter's especial day in any month, but the Ides of September fell during the Ludi Romani (see *4 Sept.) as the Ides of November during the Ludi Plebeii.

❦ HOLY DAYS John Chrysostom (CY, RC; Orth. 13 Nov., translation 27 Jan.)

John Chrysostom (*c*.347–407). The star pupil of the pagan orator Libanius, he deployed the skills of classical rhetoric to such effect as to earn the name 'Goldenmouth' (*Chryso-stomos*; cf. Peter Chrysologus, *30 July) already given to the Greek orator Dio of Prusa (1st–2nd cc. AD). His eloquence was matched by his integrity but not by his tact; as bishop of Constantinople from 397, be became increasingly embroiled in disputes, and having successively likened the empress Eudoxia, not without justification, to Jezebel and Herodias, he died an exile in 407. The ascription to him of the Constantinopolitan liturgy, like that of Gregorian chant to Pope Gregory I, is a tribute to his greatness, not a statement of breveted fact. He is patron saint of preaching, sacred oratory, and eloquence, and of Constantinople (from 1914), together with St George.

Venerius, a hermit of the sixth or seventh century who lived on the island of Tino in the Gulf of La Spezia. His life is as obscure as his cult was long-lived: in 1960 a relic was rediscovered and solemnly returned to Tino. At local urging Pope John XXIII declared him patron saint of lighthouse-keepers, owing to the radiance of his life; he is also patron saint of La Spezia.

In Mexico, this day commemorates the battle of Chapultepec in 1847, the last action of the war with the United States: Gen. Winfield Scott captured a fort overlooking Mexico City, which he went on to storm. Tradition tells of six heroic cadets, the Niños Héroes, who fought to the death.

14 SEPTEMBER

a.d. XVIII Kalendas Octobres   E

❦ HOLIDAYS AND ANNIVERSARIES Bolivia (Cochabamba): public holiday
Nicaragua: Battle of San Jacinto

❦ HOLY DAYS **Holy Cross Day** (CofE); **Triumph of the Cross** (RC); **Exaltation of the Honoured and Life-Giving Cross** (Orth.)

Holy Cross Day (Crouchmas, Holy Rood Day, Roodmas Day). This day originally commemorated the dedication in 335 of the emperor Constantine's basilica on the site of the Holy Sepulchre in Jerusalem. During its construction the supposed True Cross was discovered; within a few decades the discovery was credited to Constantine's mother, the empress Helena (see *18 Aug.), who had made a visit to the eastern provinces, including a pilgrimage to Jerusalem, in 326 or 327. (The tale is sufficiently disproved by the silence of Constantine's effusive biographer, Eusebius of Caesarea, our sole contemporary witness to her travels. See also *3 May.) At once portions of it began to be distributed as relics; in 386 St John Chrysostom was moved to protest:

And that very piece of wood on which the sacred body was stretched and crucified, how comes it that all contend for it, and many take a small portion of it and enclose it in gold and hang it, both men and women, from their necks for an ornament? Yet it is the mark of condemnation, of punishment. But He that formeth all things and changeth them, that removed the world from such great evil, and made a heaven of the earth, He took this thing of shame, this most dishonourable of all deaths, up into the heavens.   *Patrologia Graeca*, xlviii, cols. 826–7

The Roman church of Santa Croce in Gerusalemme proudly displays a cross-piece, authenticated for Pope Alexander VI, with inscriptions in Latin, Greek, and Hebrew highly impressive to visitors who do not know those languages; nearby is a relic of the Good Thief's cross (see *25 Mar.), which Helena was also said to have found along with that of his unrepentant comrade. The remainder was kept in Jerusalem till May 614, when the Persian king Khosraw II, having captured the city, sent it and the supposed Instruments of the Passion as a gift to his Nestorian Christian queen Maryam

(= Mary); it was recovered by the emperor Heraclius in the spring of 629, which event the feast is commonly taken to commemorate. The relic was solemnly restored on 21 March 630, but irrecoverably lost after Saladin's victory at Ḥaṭṭīn on 4 July 1187 over King Guy of Jerusalem, whose forces had borne it into battle.

From 1584, in the pontificate of Gregory XIII, until 1847, in that of Pius IX, Jews in Rome were compelled to attend an annual Christian sermon in the church of S. Angelo in Pescheria, on the edge of the Ghetto. The imposition is now principally remembered in Browning's poem 'Holy-Cross Day', written in 1854, imagining what the 'Jews really said, on thus being driven to church'. It ends, in words presented as 'Ben Ezra's Song of Death':

> 'By the torture, prolonged from age to age,
> 'By the infamy, Israel's heritage,
> 'By the Ghetto's plague, by the garb's disgrace,
> 'By the badge of shame, by the felon's place,
> 'By the branding-tool, the bloody whip,
> 'And the summons to Christian fellowship,—
>
> 'We boast our proof that at least the Jew
> 'Would wrest Christ's name from the Devil's crew.
> 'Thy face took never so deep a shade
> 'But we fought them in it, God our aid!
> 'A trophy to bear, as we march, thy band,
> 'South, East, and on to the Pleasant Land!'

Browning added a note, 'The present Pope [Pius IX] abolished this bad business of the Sermon', but later changed it to 'Pope Gregory XVI', thus crediting the reform to the acknowledged reactionary, rather than the man who had first aroused and then dashed liberal hopes.

In 1752, 14 September followed immediately after the 2nd in Great Britain, Ireland, and the American colonies (see Pl. 8):

14. This day the use of the new Stile in numbring the days of the month commenceth and according to that computation, the last day of October will be my Birthday.   Clegg, 807–8

Popular discontent with the reform was aired during the notorious Oxfordshire election of 1754. In accordance with the normal eighteenth-century avoidance of contested elections, Whigs (supporters of the Hanoverian monarchy) had left the shire to the Tories (led by theoretical Jacobites who drank the Pretender's health but did not care to fight for him) in return for going unchallenged in the boroughs; but in 1752 the Duke of Marlborough determined to force a contest (the first since 1710) by putting up Whig (or 'New Interest') candidates for both county seats at the forthcoming general election against the sitting Tory (or 'Old Interest') members, Lord Wenman and Sir James Dashwood; after Sir Edward Turner (a man with a chequered political history) had first come forth, then withdrawn until a second candidate should offer, Lord Parker, son of Lord Macclesfield, was put up. A Tory balladeer commented:

And as for his long-look't-for Friend, on my Troth,
His fine moving Speeches are nothing but Froth;
Our time he has alter'd and turn'd it about,
So he like *Old Christmas* shall too be turned out.

Tho' Lords and great Placemen do with him combine,
'Twill signify nothing, when honest Men join;
Drink *Wenman* and *Dashwood*, and stand to the Tack,
We want no *old Turner* nor *new Almanack.*

The Oxfordshire Contest, 56

Whereas the Tories were happy to include calendar reform in their complaints against the Whigs, along with corruption, high taxation, and Roundhead sympathies, Whigs generally left it alone, preferring to call the Tories a narrow clique of Jacobites and Papists in all too thin disguise; however, one song combined this charge with a defence of the calendar:

Say they the New Stile is a damnable Thing,
'Twas first made by a Pope so must Popery bring,
They strain at a Gnat yet a Camel gulp down,
Who have kiss'd the Pope's Toe it is very well known.

The Old and New Interest, 42

Parker had to endure the cry of 'Give us back the eleven days we were robbed of.' The election was marked by scandal before, during, and after the poll; the Tories had more votes, but the House of Commons seated the Whigs. The excesses of the campaign inspired Hogarth's painting 'An Election Entertainment' (now in Sir John Soane's Museum), in which the Whigs are portrayed at their potations (Whig entertainments in Oxfordshire had been more lavish than Tory); a rough whose head was broken in a battle with the Tory mob outside sits with his foot on a captured placard with the words 'Give us our eleven days' lying on the floor. In the engraved version the placard lies next to a no less futile copy of 'An Act against Bribery and Corruption'.

Hogarth's picture has given rise to the notion that riots broke out against the new calendar; in fact, the riots of the time were directed at the recently enacted naturalization of Jews, which public opinion compelled the government to undo. Dashwood helped whip up the protest, in which Hogarth's Tories are taking part. As in their Jacobitism, the masses were to be feared not as revolutionary radicals but as reactionary bigots.

It is best not to gather nuts on this day:

The Devil, as some People say,
A Nutting goes *Holy-Rood* day.
Let Women then their Children keep
At home that day, better asleep
They were, or Cattle for to tend
Than Nutting go, and meet the Fiend;
But if they'll not be ruled by this,
Blame me not if they do amiss.

Poor Robin (1693)

15 SEPTEMBER

a.d. XVII Kalendas Octobres F

❦ HOLIDAYS AND ANNIVERSARIES Costa Rica: Independence Day (from Spain, 1821) (national holiday)
El Salvador: Independence Day (from Spain, 1821) (national holiday)
England: Battle of Britain Day (last daylight bombing raid by German Luftwaffe)
Guatemala: Independence Day (from Spain, 1821) (national holiday)
Honduras: Independence Day (from Spain, 1821) (national holiday)
Japan: Respect for the Aged Day (national holiday)
Nicaragua: Independence Day (from Spain, 1821) (national holiday)

HRH Prince Harry born 1984

❦ HOLY DAYS Cyprian of Carthage (CY; RC on the 16th); Our Lady of Sorrows (RC)

Cyprian of Carthage (d. 258), having objected to the leniency with which Christians were treated who had lapsed during the persecution of 249, found himself at odds with extremists who took their objections so far as to set up their own pope, Novatian: holding that sacraments could not be validly administered outside the Church, Cyprian insisted, against Roman policy, on rebaptizing persons christened by Novatianists. Before the dispute had been settled he was executed in a new persecution; but his view remained predominant in Africa, and underlay the Donatist schism in the fourth century. He is patron of North Africa, and of Algeria in particular. He was martyred on 14 September 258, but is not culted on that date since it is Holy Cross Day. The Church of England, having recognized that his BCP date of 26 September was due to confusion with Cyprian of Antioch, placed him on the 13th in the abortive Prayer Book of 1928 and the ASB, but in its CY calendar on the 15th. The RC Church combines his feast with that of Pope Cornelius on the 16th.

Our Lady of Sorrows, Mater dolorosa. The first altar to Mary under this title was set up in 1221 at the monastery of Schönau; her special hymn, *Stabat mater dolorosa*, is of Franciscan origin, but it was the order of Servites, established *c.*1240 to honour her, that instituted the feast on this date, which was extended to the whole RC Church by Pope Pius VII in 1814 to give thanks for his release from French captivity. Her other feast, on Passion Friday, made universal in 1727, is no longer in the General Calendar.

Nicomedes (RC): see *1 June.

In Great Britain this day is remembered as Battle of Britain day, from the RAF's thwarting of a massive Luftwaffe attack on 15 September 1940 intended to clear the way for an invasion six days later. Sixty German planes were shot down, though multiple sightings of the same kill raised the announced figure to 175 and also exaggerated British losses. The Battle of Britain—the conflict between German bomber squadrons and Fighter Command—began on 10 July; its end is taken to be 12 October, when Hitler cancelled his invasion plans (Operation Sealion), although air raids continued afterwards.

The conjunction of Sun, Jupiter, and Saturn in 7 BC has been invoked by persons wishing to rationalize the Star of Bethlehem in Matt. 2 and set the Nativity before Herod's death in 4 BC. It does not resolve the other difficulties in this narrative (see *28 Dec.); nevertheless, much journalistic attention was paid to this conjunction on its 1,999th anniversary in 1993.

How to gather apples:

Apples must be gathered when the moone is at the full, in faire wheather and about the fifteenth of September, and that by hand without any pole or pealing downe: because otherwise the fruite would be much martred & the yong sciences broken or brused, and so the apple tree by that means should be spoild of his yong wood which would cause the losse of the tree....
Infinite are the sorts and so the names of apples comming as well of natures owne accord without the helpe of man, as of the skill of man ... in everie one of which there is found some speciall qualitie, which others have not: but the best of all the rest, is the short shanked apple, which is marked with spottings, as tasting and smelling more excellently then any of all the other sorts. And the smell of it is so excellent, as that in the time of the plague there is nothing better to cast upon the coales & to make sweete perfumes of then the rinde thereof.... Sweet apples do much good against melancholick affects and diseases, but especially against the pleurisie.

Estienne and Liebault, 485–6 (1600)

16 SEPTEMBER

a.d. XVI Kalendas Octobres   G

❦ HOLIDAYS AND ANNIVERSARIES Mexico: Independence Day (national holiday)
Papua New Guinea: Independence Day (national holiday)
USA, Oklahoma: Cherokee Strip Day (commemorating run for Oklahoma land, 1893)

❦ HOLY DAYS Cornelius and Cyprian (RC; CY *15 Sept.); Ninian (CY; RC *26 Aug.)

Cornelius, pope and martyr (d. 253). When appointed bishop of Rome after the persecutions of Decius, he forgave those Christians who had lapsed; a rigorist minority elected Novatian as an antipope, and departed into schism. Renewal of persecution forced Cornelius to flee; he died in exile at Centumcellae (Civitavecchia), traditionally as a martyr.

Edith (Eadgyth, 961–84), daughter of King Edgar and his concubine Wulfthryth, a novice of Wilton, though given an excellent education to prepare her for her station in society, insisted on remaining at Wilton with her mother, now the abbess; on the murder of her half-brother Edward (see *18 Mar.) she refused the throne, preferring to build an oratory in honour of St Denys (*9 Oct.), at whose dedication St Dunstan supposedly prophesied that she would soon die, and that her thumb would remain incorrupt. She was renowned for charity to the poor and friendship with wild animals. Her relics were translated in 997; she was much revered in medieval England.

Ludmilla or Lidmila (*c.*860–921), daughter of a Slav prince, married the Christian convert Bořivoj, duke of Bohemia; she brought up her grandson Václav (Wenceslaus; see *28 Sept.) but was strangled to end her influence over him, perhaps by her daughter-in-law. She was declared one of the patron saints of the then Czechoslovakia in 1935.

Louis Allemand or Aleman (d. 1450), created archbishop of Arles in 1423 and cardinal three years later; he was appointed papal legate and governor of Bologna in 1424 to replace the much-loathed Gabriele Condulmer, but in 1428 was expelled by the anti-papal faction. In 1431 Condulmer became Pope, under the name of Eugenius IV; having been obliged to summon the Council of Basle, he was drawn into an increasingly bitter conflict for control of the Church that culminated in 1439, when the Council, under Allemand's presidency, declared him deposed from the papacy and nominated Count Amadeus VIII of Savoy in his stead, the antipope Felix V; Eugenius not only stripped Allemand of his cardinalate but excommunicated him. The revolt was a failure: Eugenius' apparent achievement of union with the Greek Church impressed opinion far more than the outdated agenda of the Conciliarists. Under the next pope, Nicholas V, Allemand was reinstated in 1449, a year before his death; in 1527 he was beatified by Clement VII, to the obvious embarrassment of the Bollandist charged with writing his life in the *Acta Sanctorum*: he dare not deny a beatitude revealed by God in miracles and approved by judgement of the Holy See, but must no less avoid the opposite extreme of praising all his actions.

Euphemia (RC): see *11 July.

17 SEPTEMBER

a.d. XV Kalendas Octobres   A

❦ HOLIDAYS AND ANNIVERSARIES Angola: Day of the National Hero
   US Constitution signed in 1787; Constitution Day was renamed Citizenship Day in
      1952, subsuming former I Am An American Day (third Sunday in May).

❦ HOLY DAYS Lambert, bishop of Maastricht (BCP); Hildegard of Bingen (CY); Robert Bellarmine (RC)

Lambert was designated bishop in 672, but expelled by Ebroin in the civil wars that followed the murder of the Frankish king Childeric II. After living as a monk for seven years, he returned during a period of uneasy peace to his see, where he restored order in church affairs and furthered the mission of St Willibrord (see *7 Nov.), but in asserting the rights of his church fell foul of a Count Dodo, who had him murdered in Liège after two of his own men had been killed. He is portrayed as a bishop, on his knees, being pierced by a lance or a javelin, or else carrying fiery coals in his rochet to the altar; he is patron of bandagers, surgeons, dentists, and peasants. In some places he is culted on the 18th.

Hildegard of Bingen, abbess of Rupertsberg (1098–1179), known as 'the Sibyl of the Rhine'. The tenth child of noble parents, who promised her to the Church, she became a novice at the age of 8 and seven years later took the veil; in or shortly before 1150 she founded a convent on the Rupertsberg near Bingen, and *c.*1165 a daughter house at Eibingen across the Rhine. During the 1160s she undertook four missions in Germany; her correspondents included the emperor Frederick Barbarossa and more than one pope, as well as kings and bishops. A visionary from childhood, she wrote three mystical works, together with saints' lives and works on natural history and medicine, but is more famous now for her poetical and musical achievement: her morality play *Ordo virtutum* is the oldest known by over a century, and her lyrical collection *Symphonia armonie celestium revelationum*, seventy-seven songs full of brilliant imagery and apocalyptic language, is preserved with musical notation, in which from a few underlying patterns, treated with great freedom, remarkably varied and often highly elaborate melodies result; in recent years several recordings have been published. Miracles were reported from her tomb, and anti-papal prophesies put posthumously in her mouth; she has not been canonized even though several popes ordered a process of information, but is included on this day as a saint in the Roman Martyrology, and is honoured in many German churches. She is portrayed sending a letter to the Pope, or with St Bernard examining her works (it was he who persuaded Eugenius III to approve her mystical *Scivias*). Hildegard is patron of Esperantists and students of linguistics.

Robert Bellarmine, cardinal and Doctor of the Church (1542–1621). Born at Montepulciano, he joined the Jesuits in 1560. Professor of Greek, Hebrew, and theology at a young age—the first Jesuit to hold a professorship at the University of Louvain—he became a prominent figure of the Counter-Reformation. He was created cardinal in 1598 and in 1605 became prefect of the Vatican Library. In 1931 he was declared a Doctor of the Church. Author of two catechisms, and having taught catechism to children, he was named patron saint of catechists by Pius XI in 1932, together with St Charles Borromeo. Feast-day formerly 13 May.

Impression of the Stigmata upon St Francis on Mount La Verna (1224).

This was the day on which in 1398 Henry duke of Hereford and Thomas Mowbray duke of Norfolk were to settle their differences in combat:

> Be ready, as your lives shall answer it,
> At Coventry upon Saint Lambert's day.

> There shall your swords and lances arbitrate
> The swelling difference of your settled hate.
> Since we can not atone you, we shall see
> Justice design the victor's chivalry.
>
> King Richard, in *Richard II*, 1. i. 198–203

Richard's unwise interruption of the duel, and arbitrary punishments of both participants, set in train the events that caused his overthrow.

18 SEPTEMBER

a.d. XIV Kalendas Octobres   B

(HOLIDAYS AND ANNIVERSARIES Chile: Aniversario Nacional (independence
from Spain, 1818)

(HOLY DAYS
Joseph of Cupertino (1602–63). He was born to a poor family at Cupertino, near Brindisi.
He exasperated his widowed mother by forgetting to eat and wandering around with his
mouth open, earning him the nickname *Boccaperta*, 'gaper'. Unpopular also because of his
hot temper, he was nevertheless exemplary in his religious devotion. His gifts were not
recognized by the Franciscans or Capuchins, who refused to admit him, but he finally
found success working in the stables as a tertiary Franciscan. Though a failure in his
studies, he managed to be ordained. Much given to fasting and ecstasies and other
disturbing phenomena, he was largely kept out of public sight, being moved from one
religious house to another when pilgrims discovered him. He is chiefly known for his
ability to levitate; over seventy occasions were remembered posthumously. He is patron
saint of students (diligence will win out in the end) and examination or degree candidates. Popularly, he is the patron saint of flying, including astronauts.

September

I bear the Scales, where hang in equipoise
    The night and day; and when unto my lips
I put my trumpet, with its stress and noise
    Fly the white clouds like tattered sails of ships;
The tree-tops lash the air with sounding whips;
    Southward the clamorous sea-fowl wing their flight;
The hedges are all red with haws and hips,
    The Hunter's Moon reigns empress of the night.

Henry Wadsworth Longfellow (1807–82), *The Poet's Calendar*

19 SEPTEMBER

a.d. XIII Kalendas Octobres C

❦ HOLIDAYS AND ANNIVERSARIES St Christopher and Nevis: Independence Day (from Great Britain, 1983); sometimes called 'St Christopher's Day'

❦ HOLY DAYS Januarius (RC); Theodore of Tarsus (CY commem.)

Januarius (San Gennaro) is said to have been bishop of Benevento and martyred under Domitian; his relics were translated to Naples in the fifth century. He is chiefly renowned for the miraculous liquefaction of his blood, first reported in 1389. The substance is contained in two phials normally kept in the cathedral, but borne in procession to the church of Santa Chiara on the first Saturday in May; liquefaction usually takes place on the return of the phials to the cathedral (but sometimes in Santa Chiara), on 19 September, and on 16 December (commemorating a threatened eruption of Vesuvius in 1631 said to have been prevented by his intercession). The true explanation has not yet been found, but it is certain that the phenomenon has been neither confined to those days nor entirely regular in its occurrence. When it fails on a due day, great is the popular consternation; it is suspected that the saint's apparent displeasure is wrought for political reasons by the priests, as when a Communist was first elected mayor. Nevertheless, no such suppression took place under the French-sponsored Parthenopaean Republic (Jan.–June 1799); indeed, the first liquefaction, for the newly triumphant General Championnet, took less time than usual, for fear (it is said) that substitute blood might be drawn by a French soldier's sword. After the republic had been overthrown, the saint was under a temporary cloud with the authorities for his want of counter-revolutionary zeal. Januarius is patron saint of blood banks.

The liquefaction was and still is a great tourist attraction; when in 1996 the ex-communist mayor of Naples, in expansive mood, made the delightful remark 'San Gennaro is the mayor of saints', a journalist was heard to mutter, 'More likely the saint of mayors'. It was viewed with extreme scepticism by Protestant visitors, for example Mark Twain in 1867:

In this city of Naples, they believe in and support one of the wretchedest of all the religious impostures one can find in Italy—the miraculous liquefaction of the blood of St. Januarius. Twice a year the priests assemble all the people at the Cathedral, and get out this vial of clotted blood and let them see it slowly dissolve and become liquid—and every day for eight days, this dismal farce is repeated, while the priests go among the crowd and collect money for the exhibition. The first day, the blood liquefies in forty-seven minutes—the church is crammed, then, and time must be allowed the collectors to get around: after that it liquefies a little quicker and a little quicker, every day, as the houses grow smaller, till on the eighth day, with only a few dozens present to see the miracle, it liquefies in four minutes. *The Innocents Abroad*, ch. 29

An Englishman witnesses the miracle of San Gennaro in 1860, shortly after Garibaldi entered Naples:

I have just returned from San Gennaro, where I have witnessed the far-famed miracle. I went about half-past eight and found the Cathedral partially filled, and a dense crowd in and about the chapel of San Gennaro—a spacious octagon on the south side of the nave. National guards were keeping the door. At a quarter before nine, a loud shout rose from the crowd within. It was a greeting to the saint, whose image in silver gilt had just been placed on the altar. The shout was renewed as the priest adjusted the mitre and cope with which the image was clothed, and again, as an attendant lighted candle after candle beside it. An aged priest, standing within the altar rails, then raised aloft the vessel containing the sacred blood, and at once a forest of waving arms rose above the crowd, and the building rang with frenzied exclamations. Some other priests and assistants now appeared in the organ loft ready to lead the *Te Deum* whenever the miracle should be achieved; meanwhile, the old man continued to hand round the vessel to let all the bystanders see that there was no deception, that the blood was really solid. . . . In order to show that it was solid, the priest turned the monstrance upside down, holding a lighted candle behind it, and showed it, round to the spectators just as a conjuror does before commencing his performance. All this time the crowd kept shrieking and screaming . . .

The priest then turned his back on the audience, and the agitation of the crowd reached a point where it could no longer be expressed in articulate cries, for nothing was heard but sobs and groans. A very few minutes had elapsed, when the priest suddenly turned round and exhibited the blood LIQUID! A wild howl of exultation rose up; flowers were thrown towards the saint, and, strange to say, a number of birds let loose, which the spectators had brought with them for the purpose. Never had the miracle been performed so soon. . . . It was clear that San Gennaro was in the best of tempers towards his dear clients, and not at all displeased with them for turning out their king. Two of Garibaldi's red-shirted soldiers, who were making their way out of the chapel, were the objects of tenderly affectionate demonstrations; old women held up their hands to bless them, others patted them on the back and smiled approvingly.   Clark, 53–5

Theodore of Tarsus (d. 690), appointed archbishop of Canterbury in 669 when Pope Vitalian's original choice, Hadrian (*9 Jan.), refused; the first archbishop to be obeyed by the entire English Church, he proved a highly effective ruler of it, summoning its first synods and reforming the diocesan structure. Together with Hadrian he established the admirable school at Canterbury whose pupils, says Bede, knew Latin and Greek as thoroughly as their native language; 'Never at all since the Angles made for Brittany were there happier times: for, having very valiant and Christian kings, they were a terror to all the barbarian peoples, and the desires of all were inclined towards the joys of the heavenly kingdom about which they had recently heard, and all those who wished to be educated in Holy Scripture had masters at hand to teach them' (*Ecclesiastical History*, iv. 2). The RC Church commemorates him on this day as well.

20 SEPTEMBER

a.d. XII Kalendas Octobres   D

❦ HOLY DAYS John Coleridge Patteson and Companions (CY)

John Coleridge Patteson (1827–71), first missionary bishop in Melanesia. After an undistinguished career at Oxford, he developed an interest in languages while travelling in

Europe. A year after his ordination in 1853 he met George Augustus Selwyn, bishop of New Zealand, and decided upon a missionary career, devoting himself to the schooling of Melanesian boys. He became bishop in 1861, and deepened his study of Melanesian dialects, of which he spoke twenty-three. At first supporting labour traffic as beneficial to the Melanesians, he came to oppose it as slavery, and the trade was eventually regulated by parliament. He died at the hands of natives as an act of revenge for an injustice they had suffered from some Englishmen.

Eustace (d. 118), a Roman general named Placidus said to have been converted while hunting by the vision of a stag with a crucifix between his antlers (Eastern date 2 Nov.). He was martyred under Hadrian with his wife Theopiste and his sons Agapetos and Theopistos. One of the Fourteen Holy Helpers (see *8 Aug.), his widespread cult is undoubtedly a result of the Golden Legend's account of his travails: he lost his wife to a ship's captain, one son to a wolf, and the other to a lion. Eventually they were all reunited. Returning in triumph to Rome, he refused to sacrifice to the pagan gods, and he and his family were placed in an arena with a lion, which proved friendly. They were then dispatched by roasting in a brazen bull, like the opponents of Phalaris, tyrant of Akragas (Agrigento) in the sixth century BC (see *4 May). Eustace is patron saint of hunters, together with Hubert (*3 Nov.), and of those in difficult situations.

On this day in 1870 Italian forces entered Rome after token resistance by the papal army; the memory of the event is preserved in the street name Via XX Settembre.

21 SEPTEMBER

a.d. XI Kalendas Octobres   E

S. Matthee shut up the Bee.

Saint Matthew
get candlesticks new.

(HOLIDAYS AND ANNIVERSARIES Armenia: Independence Day (from USSR, 1991)
Belize: Independence Day (from UK, 1981)
Malta: Independence Day (national holiday)
Philippines: Thanksgiving Day

(HOLY DAYS **Matthew, Apostle and Evangelist** (CofE, RC)

Matthew (first century), apostle and evangelist. He was a publican, or tax-collector, for the Romans, a difficult and much-hated profession, when Jesus called him, saying 'Follow me' (Matt. 9: 9). Notable amongst the depictions of the event is the painting by Carpaccio at San Giorgio degli Schiavoni in Venice, where behind him, utterly disdainful of such *naïveté*, stands a colleague with the features of Sebastiano Michiel (d. 1534), the Grand Prior in Venice of the Knights of St John, a man single-minded in pursuing the sweets of office. Although St Matthew is said to have preached in the East and been martyred, no evidence remains. He is the author of the first Gospel, and his symbol is the angel, read by Christian tradition into the man's face of Ezek. 1: 10; this same verse gave the other three evangelists their emblems, the lion, the ox, and the eagle. He is patron saint of accountants, tax-collectors, customs officers, and security guards, and is often portrayed with a bag of coins or a money-box. His day was marked in primestaves with an axe to signify that it is time to gather leaves for fodder.

The Sarum calendar includes a remembrance, sometimes used as a datemark in medieval English documents, of Laudus, or Lauto, bishop of Coutances (528–68), whose family estate became the Norman town of Saint-Lô. In other sources he is assigned to the 22nd.

22 SEPTEMBER

a.d. X Kalendas Octobres   F

❨ HOLIDAYS AND ANNIVERSARIES Mali: Proclamation of the Republic Anniversary (independence from France, 1960)

❨ HOLY DAYS

Maurice (d. *c.*302). He and his companions supposedly belonged to a Theban legion of 6,000 Christians from the Thebais in Upper Egypt martyred at Agaunum (Saint-Maurice-en-Valais in Switzerland) on the orders of the emperor Maximian when they refused to fight against fellow-Christians. The story has become proverbial, coupled with the demonstrable falsehood of the 'Thundering Legion', for hagiographical absurdity (see *9 Mar.): 'two obsolete legends,' wrote Gibbon, 'the least absurd of which staggered the well-disciplined credulity of a Franciscan Friar' (*Vindication*, 107). Although Christians were purged from the army at that time, and two legions had been raised in the Thebais for the defence of Upper Egypt, there is no evidence that either of them was posted to Gaul. Nevertheless, the story goes back to the fifth century, the martyrs' supposed remains having been discovered *c.*380; several German and Swiss cities, and also Turin, claim to have relics of the legionaries, perhaps by posthumous enrolment of their local martyrs. His lance found its way to Vienna, where it was retrospectively bestowed on St Longinus (see *15 Mar.). Maurice is patron saint of soldiers, armies, and Alpine troops, and is honoured especially in Austria, Piedmont, Savoy, and Sardinia. He is often portrayed as black, either from his place of origin or from his name, which is conjecturally derived in the Golden Legend from the late Greek *mauros*, 'black'. Perhaps because of this he is also patron of dyers and weavers.

On 22 September 1996, not as originally planned in Reims Cathedral but at an airbase, Pope John Paul II celebrated a mass to commemorate the 1,500th anniversary of the baptism of Clovis, king of the Franks, by St Remigius (see *1 Oct.). The Franks' historian, Gregory of Tours, writing not quite a century after the event, makes Remigius address the king as 'fierce Sygambrian' (an impressively obsolete term for a German, being the name of a tribe long since dissolved) and bid him meekly bow the neck: 'Worship what thou hast burnt, burn what thou hast worshipped.' Remigius' biographer, Hincmar of Reims, not only improved this scene by introducing a dove, whiter than snow, that carried in its beak an ampulla filled with holy chrism, but claimed to use the same ampulla with its miraculous contents at the coronation of Charles the Bald in 869. No more is heard of it till 1131, when Pope Innocent II crowned Louis VII of France; from then on the *Sainte Ampoule* was a regular component of the French coronation ceremony. The *depositio* of Clovis, an effective but murderous ruler, was celebrated at Sainte-Geneviève on 29 (later 27) November; at Saint-Denis he was commemorated along with Genevieve on *3 January. The year of his baptism is disputed, but the date is recorded by his contemporary Bishop Avitus of Vienne as Christmas Day; instead, by a choice neither accidental nor uncontroversial, the founder of the French monarchy was honoured on the 204th anniversary of the proclamation of the First Republic.

23 SEPTEMBER

a.d. IX Kalendas Octobres   G

❦ HOLIDAYS AND ANNIVERSARIES Japan: Autumnal Equinox
   Puerto Rico: Grito de Lares
   Saudi Arabia: Kingdom Unification (1932) (national holiday)

❦ ANCIENT ROME Birthday of the emperor Augustus, celebrated by Ludi Natalicii from 8 BC. The Gaius Octavius whom Caesar made his heir was born, so Suetonius tells us, *M. Tullio Cicerone C. Antonio conss. VIIII Kal. Octob., paulo ante solis exortum*, i.e. in 63 BC, on the ninth before the Kalends of October, a little before sunrise. At his birth, the ninth day (reckoned inclusively) before the Kalends of October was the 22nd of a 29-day September, but after Caesar's reform of the calendar he continued to celebrate his birthday on the same nominal day, though now by forward reckoning (which Romans did not use) the 23rd. As such, it was made New Year's day in the calendar decreed by the Roman province of Asia in 9 BC; it remained the first day of the year at Constantinople until the mid-fifth century, and long afterwards in ecclesiastical usage, being marked 'new year' in various Greek and Slavonic liturgical texts. Being only a day before the autumn equinox, it was adopted as the Eastern date for the conception of John the Baptist (six months before that of Jesus, Luke 1: 26), whose birth was celebrated on the summer solstice (24 June).

Adomnán (*c*.628–704), who became the ninth abbot of Iona in 679, wrote a life of its founder, St Columba (his own cousin thrice removed), and also a work on the Holy Places. On a visit to Northumbria in the 680s he was persuaded that the Roman mode of calculating Easter was superior to that of the Celtic tradition; he was unable to persuade his own monks to adopt it, but had greater success in the northern provinces of Ireland except among dependencies of Iona, though Irish sources speak of battles and bloodshed. (The southern provinces had adopted it over half a century before.) In 697, at a synod in Birr, Co. Offaly, Adomnán secured acceptance of the so-called Law of the Innocents or Code of Adomnán, which punished acts of violence against women, children, and churchmen, whether in war or in peace, with fines to be paid in part to the Columban monasteries of which, as abbot of Iona, he was the head. The correct spelling of his name is as given; but perhaps even in his lifetime it was corrupted to 'Adamnán', and in Scottish place-names we find 'Eodhnan' or 'Eunan'. He may be the Adamnanus who reports in a commentary on Vergil that he could find no information about the bad poet Maevius mocked in the third eclogue of the *Bucolics*.

Thecla of Iconium (now Konya). According to the apocryphal *Acts of Paul* she was so overcome by the Apostle's preaching on chastity that she sat by the window and paid no attention to her mother or her fiancé. The latter, with other men similarly cheated of their womenfolk, brought Paul before the proconsul, who remanded him in custody; Thecla visited him. The proconsul let Paul off with a caution in the form of a flogging, but Thecla he condemned to the flames; however, God sent a storm to quench the fire. She sought out Paul, and accompanied him to Antioch, but after resisting the advances of a wealthy citizen was condemned to fight wild beasts. The female citizens were outraged; the widow of a client chieftain, Queen Tryphaena—who is a historical figure—took her home in lieu of her deceased daughter Falconilla. The author reports at length, with much dramatic detail, how Thecla remained unscathed in the arena, and took the opportunity to baptize herself in a seal-pit, till as enraged bulls were about to be sent against her Queen Tryphaena fainted, seemingly dead; since she was great-niece to the emperor Claudius, proceedings were hurriedly terminated and Thecla released. She again sought out Paul, who sent her back to Iconium to preach the Word; she afterwards settled in a cave at Seleuceia (north of Baghdad), curing the sick till the local physicians, seeing their trade ruined, set some young men to ravish her (she was 90 at the time); the rock opened up to swallow her. Her cult is attested from the mid-fourth century. According to Tertullian this narrative (or possibly one similar) was composed by a presbyter to provide a precedent for women's preaching and baptizing; he was put out of office for his pains.

    In his *Tour of Wales* of 1773 Thomas Pennant describes the cures effected by the well near the church at Llandegla in Denbighshire, reputed to be very beneficial to those suffering from the falling sickness, epilepsy:

About two hundred yards from the church, in a quillet [strip of land] called *Gwern Degla* [Thecla's Marsh], rises a small spring, with these letters cut on free-stone: A. G θ C: G. The water is under the tutelage of the saint; and to this day held to be extremely beneficial in the *Clwyf Tegla*,

St. *Tecla's* disease, or the falling-sickness. The patient washes his limbs in the well; makes an offering into it of four pence; walks round it three times; and thrice repeats the Lord's prayer. These ceremonies are never begun till after sun-set, in order to inspire the votaries with greater awe. If the afflicted be of the male-sex, like *Socrates*, he makes an offering of a cock to his *Æsculapius*, or rather to *Tecla Hygeia*; if of the fair-sex, a hen. The fowl is carried in a basket, first round the well; after that into the church-yard; when the same orisons, and the same circum-ambulations are performed round the church. The votary then enters the church; gets under the communion-table; lies down with the Bible under his or her head; is covered with the carpet or cloth, and rests there till break of day; departing after offering six pence, and leaving the fowl in the church. If the bird dies, the cure is supposed to have been effected, and the disease transferred to the devoted victim.   Pennant, *Wales*, 379

Conception of St John the Baptist (Orth.); see above, and *24 September.

24 SEPTEMBER

a.d. VIII Kalendas Octobres   A

❧ HOLIDAYS AND ANNIVERSARIES Bolivia (Santa Cruz and Cobija): public holiday
Dominican Republic: Feast of Our Lady Mary
Ghana: Third Republic Day (1981 assumption of power by Flight Lieutenant Jerry Rawlings)
Guinea-Bissau: Independence Day (from Portugal, 1974)
New Caledonia: Territorial Day
Peru: Feast of Our Lady Mary
South Africa: National Heritage Day
Trinidad and Tobago: Republic Day (1976) (national day)
Venezuela: Day of the Public Functionary

As a common Roman date for the autumnal equinox, this day was assigned in the West to the conception of John the Baptist; used by Bede as the beginning of the indiction-year, a reckoning found in much of Western Europe in the ensuing centuries and called 'Caesarean' or 'Imperial' from its use by Holy Roman Emperors (see II: *Chronology: Cycles: Indiction*).

❧ HOLY DAYS

Our Lady of Mercy, or Ransom, patron of the Mercedarians, a lay confraternity founded *c.*1218 to ransom captives from the Moors. The order has its origin in a vision of Peter Nolasco, in which he was requested by the BVM to establish a religious order especially devoted to the ransom of captives. The devotion to Our Lady of Mercy became popular in Savona in Italy in 1536, when the Virgin appeared in a vision to announce that the inhabitants would obtain mercy rather than justice if they repented of their sins; she has also been adopted by English Roman Catholics as the patron of their aim to recapture England for the Roman obedience. But the image of the Madonna sheltering sinners under her outspread cloak is much older. Our Lady of Mercy is patron saint of the Dominican Republic and the Argentinian and Ecuadorian armies.

Hermannus Contractus (Hermann the Cripple, *Hermann der Lahme*), monk of Reichenau, died on this day in 1054; although the crown of his head, and other relics, were claimed by the great Benedictine abbey of Weingarten, he was never canonized, yet may be found a more inspiring figure than many who were. Born in Swabia of the house of Altshausen, he suffered from a cerebral palsy that left him barely able to speak or use his limbs, yet overcame these handicaps to become an inspiring teacher, an influential monk, and one of the most learned men of his age, being the author of a long unfinished poem on the deadly sins, astronomical treatises, a book of music theory in which an error of Boethius' is corrected, and several pieces of music (some in a unique notation), to which tradition has added the antiphons *Salve Regina* (of whose origin many other tales are told) and *Alma redemptoris mater* (inspired according to legend by the sound of waterwheels along the Rhine). He also compiled a world chronicle from the birth of Jesus Christ to the year of his own death, in which he records the date of his birth (18 July 1013) and first studies (15 Sept. 1020); but our main source of his life is the first entry in the continuation of that chronicle by his pupil Berthold. By 1140 another account of his life was current in England, in which as a child, having been mauled by a bear, he is offered in a vision the choice between physical health and intellectual distinction; he chooses the latter, and is sent to school at Augsburg. (This last is reported elsewhere; it is a fact that he composed an office for the city's patron St Afra; see *7 Aug.) The same source has him play the *Salve Regina* on a monochord because his voice was too bad to sing it; this (as the detail of the description shows) is a confused allusion to his musical treatise. Other accounts have him choose between growing up to be a bishop, as his merciless schoolmaster intends, and becoming a fine cleric, or born to the king and queen of Thrace, his mother choosing deformity and wisdom for him in advance. Far more moving than these stock tales of wonder is the report of the pupil who had known and loved him, that without any admixture of the fabulous describes the many saintly virtues and erudite accomplishments with which he triumphed over his disability. Shortly before his death Hermann dreamt he was reading Cicero's *Hortensius*—the exhortation to philosophy, lost in his day as in ours, that had profoundly impressed the young Augustine—and awoke desiring to leave the present world for the next; having bidden his fellow monks not to mourn for him, 'in a happy consummation—the one thing that he ever wished for above all things—that happy and incomparable man of God died, in complete happiness, on the eighth before the Kalends of October'.

25 SEPTEMBER

a.d. VII Kalendas Octobres   B

❦ HOLIDAYS AND ANNIVERSARIES Mozambique: Day of the Armed Forces
Rwanda: Kamarampaka Day (commemorating 1961 referendum)

❦ HOLY DAYS Lancelot Andrewes (CY)

Lancelot Andrewes (1555–1626), Fellow of Pembroke Hall, Cambridge, polyglot scholar
and outstanding preacher; having refused two bishoprics from Elizabeth I rather
than alienate revenues to her, he rose under James I to become bishop successively of
Chichester, Ely, and Winchester. He was the chief translator of the Pentateuch and the
historical books in the Authorized Version; he defended James I against attacks by
Cardinal Bellarmine, but also played a leading part in the reaction against Calvinism.

Finbarr (Barr), hermit of Gougane Barra (*Guagán Barra*), founder of the monastery
around which the city of Cork arose; consecrated bishop in the early seventh century.
It is said that when he went to Rome for ordination as bishop, the Pope said, 'In no way
are We worthy to ordain you. But it has been revealed to Us that you must return to
Cork, and there God has prepared worthier ministers for your ordination.' So home he
came, and passed on the message to the assembled brethren in the church, on the site of
what is now St Fin Barre's Church of Ireland Cathedral. Even as he spoke, he was lifted
up in the sight of the onlookers into the rafters by the holy angels, who there ordained
him bishop. Some of his disciples settled on a Hebridean island, named Barra after him;
in 1716 Martin Martin (who calls it Kismul; there is a Kiessimul Castle on its south-
eastern shore) reported that:

The Church in this Island is call'd *Kilbarr*, i.e. St. *Barr's* Church. There is a little Chappel by it, in
which *Mackneil*, and those descended of his Family, are usually interred. The Natives have St.
Barr's wooden Image standing on the Altar, cover'd with Linen in form of a Shirt: all their greatest Asseverations are by this Saint. I came very early in the Morning with an intention to see this
Image, but was disappointed; for the Natives prevented me, by carrying it away, lest I might take
occasion to ridicule their Superstition, as some Protestants have done formerly: and when I was
gone, it was again expos'd on the altar. . . .
    All the Inhabitants observe the Anniversary of St. *Barr*, being the 27th [*sic*] of *September*; it is
perform'd riding on Horseback, and the Solemnity is concluded by three Turns round St. *Barr's*
Church. This brings into my Mind a Story which was told me concerning a foreign Priest, and
the Entertainment he met with after his Arrival there some Years ago, as follows: this Priest happen'd to land here upon the very Day, and at the particular Hour of this Solemnity, which was
the more acceptable to the Inhabitants, who then desir'd him to preach a Commemoration Sermon to the Honour of their patron St. *Barr*, according to the antient Custom of the Place. At
this the Priest was surpriz'd, he never having heard of St. *Barr* before that Day; and therefore
knowing nothing of his Virtues, could say nothing concerning him: but told them, that if a Sermon to the Honour of St. *Paul* or St. *Peter* could please them, they might have it instantly. This
Answer of his was so disagreeable to them, that they plainly told him he could be no true Priest,

if he had not heard of St. *Barr*, for the Pope himself had heard of him; but this would not persuade the Priest, so that they parted much dissatisfy'd with one another.

M. Martin, 92, 99–100

Battle of Stamford Bridge in Yorkshire (1066). Harold Godwinson, king of England, defeated Haráldr Hárðráði (Harold Hardcounsel), king of Norway, who with the support of Harold's brother Tostig had laid claim to England; on hearing of this demand, the English king is said to have replied that he would allow the invader only six feet of English soil to be buried in—'or seeing he is tall, seven'. The invaders were driven back, and King Harold made good his boast; within three weeks he was dead, having marched back to face another invader at Hastings (see *14 Oct.).

26 SEPTEMBER

a.d. VI Kalendas Octobres   C

❧ ANCIENT ROME In 46 BC Julius Caesar dedicated a temple of solid marble in his new forum to Venus Genetrix, from whose grandson Iulus (Aeneas' son, also called Ascanius) the Julii were supposedly descended, in fulfilment of a vow at the battle of Pharsalus. The sacrifice remained on this day, but the celebratory games were transferred the next year to 20 July.

❧ HOLY DAYS Cyprian (BCP; CY *15 Sept.); Cosmas and Damian (RC, formerly *27 Sept.); Death of St John the Divine, Apostle and Evangelist (Orth.)

Cyprian, bishop of Carthage, 258. As noted under 15 September, Cyprian of Carthage is recorded on this day in the BCP by confusion with Cyprian of Antioch, whose conversion to Christianity by his intended victim, the virgin Justina (which caused him to abandon his arts and break off his league with the Devil), was celebrated by the RC Church till 1969 and in some parts thereafter; it was said that she was scourged, he was torn with iron hooks, and they both were boiled in a cauldron of pitch before being beheaded. Justina's defeat of the Devil and conversion of Cyprian, combined with the Faust theme, is the basis of Calderón's play *El mágico prodigioso* (1637).

> Grey Winter hath gone, like a wearisome guest,
>   And, behold, for repayment,
> September comes in with the wind of the West
>   And the Spring in her raiment!
> The ways of the frost have been filled of the flowers,
>   While the forest discovers
> Wild wings, with the halo of hyaline hours,
>   And a music of lovers.
>   Henry Kendall (1841–82), 'September in Australia'

27 SEPTEMBER

a.d. V Kalendas Octobres D

❦ HOLIDAYS AND ANNIVERSARIES Ethiopia: Feast of the Finding of the True Cross (corresponding to the 14th OS; the 28th in the year before a Julian leap year)

❦ HOLY DAYS Vincent de Paul (CY, RC)

Vincent de Paul (1581–1660). He grew up in Gascony, the son of farmers who sent him to study with the Franciscan Recollects. Having studied at the University of Toulouse and been ordained priest at the age of 20, he settled into a comfortable life as chaplain to Queen Margaret of Valois. His life changed when, on a visit to Paris, he was accused by a friend of stealing 400 crowns from him. Cleared after six months, he became tutor to the children of the Count of Joigny. At their country seat, he perceived the spiritual needs of the peasantry; supported by his patron, he undertook a mission to the common people, which eventually became the Congregation of the Mission and the Sisters of Charity. Pope Leo XIII named him patron of all charitable societies. The Society of St Vincent de Paul was founded in Paris in 1833. He is patron saint of hospitals and prisoners, and also of Madagascar, one of the first places he sent his missionaries. Feast-day formerly 19 July.

Cosmas and Damian. This was the traditional Western feast-day (now moved to the 26th) of SS Cosmas and Damian, martyrs (d. *c.*303), twin brothers who studied sciences in Syria; their main Orthodox feast is on 1 July, but they are also remembered on 1 November. They were renowned not only for their skill in medicine but also for their humanity: they were called Anargyroi, 'moneyless ones', as they accepted no fees. Equally zealous in preaching, they were persecuted and martyred in Syria. Their relics were brought to Rome, where the basilica named after them on the edge of the Forum was dedicated by Pope Felix IV *c.*530. Many legends grew up around them, notably of miraculous healings. Their cult spread widely, but was especially important in Florence from the time of Cosimo de' Medici (1389–1464), whose name may be translated 'Cosmas of the physicians'. His grandson Giovanni, who became Pope Leo X, treated the feast-day of SS Cosmas and Damian as if it were his birthday, sometimes staging elaborate entertainments on a medical theme. In 1520 a Venetian visitor reported:

The pope had a solemn Mass celebrated in the Sistine Chapel, as usual, and invited all the cardinals, for thirty of whom (because the elderly ones did not wish to stay) he had prepared an impressive banquet, also for many other prelates and gentlemen . . . and after dinner he presented singing and playing, and the music was done in this manner: some fifty singers and players of various instruments, dressed as physicians, that is with a long gown, partly pink and partly violet, and red stoles, came out two by two, led by Maestro Andrea and another buffoon, dressed up like Spirone and Maestro Archangelo, the pope's physicians. They imitated them, cracking many jokes, and made everyone laugh. And there before the pope alternately they sang and played a number of pieces, and at the end all, including the first, sang some songs about physicians, and for the finale everyone sang a motet for six voices.

Marcantonio Michiel, quoted in Blackburn, 25

Cosmas and Damian are the patron saints of physicians and surgeons, chemists and pharmacists, barbers and hairdressers (barbers having been surgeons in the Middle Ages). They ought also to be the patron saints of amputees. Fra Angelico's cycle of paintings devoted to the saints' lives at San Marco in Florence includes a miracle reported in the Golden Legend, set in the Roman church of Santi Cosma e Damiano:

In this church a certain man served the holy martyrs, one of his legs completely eaten away by a cancer. Behold, while he slept, SS Cosmas and Damian appeared to their devotee, carrying salves and surgical instruments; one said to the other: 'Where shall we get flesh to fill the gap after cutting away the rotted flesh?' The other said: 'Just today a black man was buried in the cemetery of San Pietro in Vincoli. Fetch from him wherewith to mend our patient.' Off the saint sped to the cemetery and fetched the Moor's thigh; they amputated the sick man's thigh, inserted the Moor's in its stead, carefully anointed the wound, and took the sick man's thigh to the dead Moor's body. When he awoke, the patient discovered he was free of pain, put his hand to his thigh, and found no injury. On examining his leg by candlelight he saw no sign of disease, and started wondering whether he was not himself but somebody else. Coming back to his senses, he leapt out of bed for joy and told everyone what he had seen in his dream and how he had been healed. His hearers excitedly sent to the Moor's tomb, and found that his thigh had indeed been cut off and the other's substituted for it in the tomb.   Jacobus de Voragine, 639

We write 'thigh' for *coxa* because that is the medieval sense (in classical Latin it is the hip); but no doubt it was meant as mere variety for *crus*, 'leg'. In Fra Angelico's painting the whole leg is black.

For many years the inhabitants of Isernia held a three-day festival in honour of SS Cosmas and Damian, at which the devotees brought wax figures 'consisting of feet, legs, arms, eyes, heads, hands, *membri genitali*, and even whole figures; according as a part, or the whole body, is affected by disease', to be blessed by the priest, as reported by Richard Colt Hoare in 1790; the body part so delicately named in Italian put him in mind of the ancient Roman festival in honour of Priapus. However, when a new road built through Isernia made the festival more widely known, 'a certain degree of scandal was attached to a part of the ceremony, [and] a royal order was accordingly issued, to prohibit the offering of a certain class of *ex voto*, and it is still strictly and properly enforced'. Hoare, however, 'procured a specimen of these votive memorials, which, though indelicate in themselves, are yet curious to an antiquary, as proofs of the deep hold which this ceremony, originally heathen, had taken on the public mind' (*Classical Tour*, 171–2).

28 SEPTEMBER

a.d. IV Kalendas Octobres   E

❦ HOLIDAYS AND ANNIVERSARIES Guinea: Referendum Day
Taiwan: Confucius' Birthday and Teachers' Day (national holiday)
USA: Grandparents' Day
USA, Minnesota: Frances Willard Day

❦ HOLY DAYS Wenceslaus (RC)

Wenceslaus (Václav) of Bohemia, martyr (907–29). Eldest grandson of Bořivoj, ruler of Bohemia, and St Ludmilla (see *16 Sept.), he was brought up by the latter, who encouraged him to take over the reins of government from his widowed mother. He was resented by the nobles for his friendly relations with Germany, by the populace for the influence of the clergy, and by his brother Boleslav for having had a male heir. Having invited him to celebrate the feast of Cosmas and Damian, Boleslav attacked him and left his men to finish him off. He is patron saint of the Czech Republic and therefore of brewers (though he himself produced wine for mass from his own vineyards).

In the northern Hebrides, where St Michael was regarded as the patron saint of the sea, this day, Michaelmas Eve, was marked by the baking of a huge bannock or *struan* incorporating all the varieties of grain grown on the farm; it would be eaten after the morning service together with lamb, the remains being given to the poor, after which a mounted procession rode clockwise round the island, led as the case might be by the local Protestant minister or Roman Catholic priest; the Catholics also sang a hymn to St Michael both before the meal and during the procession. Horse races and other sports followed, and in the evening an exchange of gifts and dancing to hired musicians at the largest house in the townland.

Goethe first sets eyes on Venice on this day:

So it was written on my page in the Book of Fate that in 1786, on the twenty-eighth of September, at five o'clock in the evening by our reckoning, I should for the first time lay eyes on Venice, sailing out of the Brenta into the lagoons, and soon thereafter enter and visit this wonderful island city, this beaver republic. And so, God be thanked, Venice too is no longer a mere word to me, a hollow name which has often made me uneasy, me, the mortal enemy of verbal sounds.

Goethe, 56

29 SEPTEMBER

a.d. III Kalendas Octobres   F

> *So many days old the moon is on Michaelmas Day, so many floods.*
>   (Stevenson)

> *San Michiel*
> *Le marende va in ciel.*
> (a Venetian saying: the end of Lido picnics)

> *Eat less and drink less*
> *and buy a knife at Michaelmas.*

❪ HOLIDAYS AND ANNIVERSARIES Brunei: Constitution Day (1959)
Paraguay: Battle of Boquerón Day

❪ HOLY DAYS **Michael and All Angels** (CofE); **Michael, Gabriel, and Raphael** (RC)

Michael and All Angels. 29 September marks the dedication of the Basilica of St Michael on the Via Salaria outside Rome, before the seventh century. Michael, whose name means 'Who is like unto God?', is chief amongst the seven archangels. He is the warrior angel, the head of the celestial army. Gabriel is the messenger angel, Raphael ('God heals') the angel who led Tobias. The other archangels are Uriel, Chamuel, Jophiel, and Zadkiel. These are the only named angels; seraphim and cherubim are mentioned in the Old Testament, and thrones, dominions, principalities, and powers by St Paul (Eph. 1: 21 and Col. 1: 16). The heavenly host was imagined by Pseudo-Dionysius in the sixth century to be arranged in a hierarchy of ninefold division: Seraphim, Cherubim, and Thrones; Dominions, Virtues, and Powers; and Principalities, Archangels, and Angels.

And at that time shall Michael stand up, the great prince which standeth for the children of thy people: and there shall be a time of trouble, such as never was since there was a nation even to that same time: and at that time thy people shall be delivered, every one that shall be found written in the book. (Dan. 12: 1)

And there was war in heaven: Michael and his angels fought against the dragon; and the dragon fought and his angels, And prevailed not; neither was their place found any more in heaven. (Rev. 12: 7–8)

> Goe *Michael* of Celestial Armies Prince,
> And thou in Military prowess next
> *Gabriel,* lead forth to Battel these my Sons
> Invincible, lead forth my armed Saints
> By Thousands and by Millions rang'd for fight.
>   Milton, *Paradise Lost,* vi. 44–8

Two apparitions were prominent in establishing the cult of St Michael in the West. That on Monte Gargano, in southern Italy, took place in the 490s; its commemoration was celebrated on 8 May by the RC Church until 1960. The other was reported from the first year of Gregory the Great's pontificate (590–604), during a devastating plague. Gregory ordered city-wide processions to beg for divine mercy; passing over the bridge near Hadrian's Tomb, he had a vision of St Michael sheathing his sword on the summit of the tomb, and the plague ceased forthwith. The Castel Sant'Angelo takes its name from a chapel built on top of the tomb to commemorate the apparition. (Although the legend assumes that the angel was Michael, the 'persecuting angel' in 1 Chron. 21: 15 is unnamed: 'And God sent an angel unto Jerusalem to destroy it [through pestilence]: and as he was destroying, the Lord beheld, and he repented him of the evil, and said to the angel that destroyed, It is enough, stay now thine hand.') Many other shrines dedicated to Michael were built in high places, the most famous being the tenth-century Benedictine abbey of Mont-Saint-Michel in Normandy, which in the later Middle Ages inspired spontaneous mass pilgrimages in northern Europe as Rome did in the south. His cult was firmly rooted in England and Wales by the early Middle Ages. St Michael's Mount in Cornwall is supposed to commemorate an apparition of St Michael in the eighth century.

Michael is patron saint of Christians in general and Christian soldiers in particular. By extension, he is invoked as patron saint by policemen, fencers, and fencing-masters. Often portrayed as a weigher of souls at the Last Judgement ('the Lord of the Souls'), he is also patron saint of all professions using scales, among them grocers, pastry-cooks, and chemists. Pius XII declared him patron saint of radiologists. In 1921 Benedict XV named Gabriel the celestial patron of telecommunications. He is also patron saint of the signals regiments of Italy, France, and Colombia, the diplomatic services of Spain and Argentina, and postal workers. Stamp-collectors too enjoy his patronage. Raphael, who helped Tobias cure his father's blindness, is patron saint of pharmacists, of voyagers on land and sea, and is protector of adolescents.

Michaelmas Day. One of the four quarter days of the English business year (see *25 Mar.). The autumn term at Oxford and Cambridge, and some other universities, is designated Michaelmas, as was one of the four legal terms formerly observed by the High Court of Justice. Michaelmas daisies (asters) and crocuses bloom at this time of year.

On Michaelmas in 1661 (a Sunday) a chagrined Samuel Pepys made the following entry in his diary:

when at dinner and supper, I drank, I know not how, of my owne accord, so much wine, that I was even almost foxed and my head aked all night. So home, and to bed without prayers, which I never did yet since I came to the house of a Sunday night: I being now so out of order that I durst not read prayers, for fear of being perceived by my servants in what case I was.

Pepys, ii. 186

Distrustful of plain water, which he found too 'heavy' (nor was it the custom at the time to drink water), Pepys took much delight in French wine. However, he found that his work suffered, and on the last day of 1661 he vowed to abstain from wine and from another pleasure, the theatre. Like many of his vows, this one was broken from time to time, but overall he was very satisfied to observe the improvement in his conduct of business. By Michaelmas 1662, the term of his vow having expired, he noted in his diary:

29 [Sept. 1662] *Michaelmas Day*. This day my oaths for drinking of wine and going to plays are out, and so I do resolve to take a liberty today and then to fall to them again . . . I sent for some dinner and there dined . . . and then to the King's Theatre, where we saw *Midsummers nights dreame*, which I have never seen before, nor shall ever again, for it is the most insipid ridiculous play that ever I saw in my life.   Pepys, iii. 207–8

The custom of serving goose on Michaelmas Day, which is now being revived (in the authors' household, for one), goes back centuries. While in other countries that custom is connected with St Martin's Day (11 Nov.), in England it was associated with paying the rents on quarter day, geese being 'in their perfection' in that season:

> And when the tenauntes come to paye their quarters rent,
> They bring some fowle at Midsommer, & a dish of Fish in Lent,
> At Christmasse a capon, at Mighelmasse a goose:
> And somwhat else at Newyeres tide, for feare their lease flie loose.

> George Gascoigne, from *A Hundreth Sundry Flowres* (1573), a satirical gloss
> on 'the Lord hath need', ensuring the landlord's well-being

One legend has it that eating goose on Michaelmas will ensure financial prosperity in the coming year:

I dined upon Goose yesterday [Old Michaelmas Day]—which I hope will secure a good Sale of my 2ᵈ Edition.   Jane Austen (1813), 235

> Provide against Mihelmas, bargaine to make,
>   for ferme to give over, to keepe or to take:
> In dooing of either, let wit beare a stroke,
>   for buieng or selling of pig in a poke.

> Tusser

Michaelmas marks the change in agricultural seasons:

About Michaelmas take oak apples and cut them, and by them you may know how it shall go that year; spiders shew a naughty year, flies a mery year, maggots a good year, nothing in them portends great death.   *Lilly's New Erra Pater*, 7–8

In southern Norway as many days as there is hoarfrost in the field before Michaelmas, so many days it will remain after *gauksmesse* ('Cuckoomass') on *1 May.

A particular superstition associated with Michaelmas attaches to eating blackberries from that day on (one source says that flies deposit their eggs on the fruit then):

At that season of the year called Michaelmas, [the devil] is said to touch with it [his club] the black-berries, or to 'throw his club over them', none daring after that period to eat one of them, or the 'worms will eat their ingangs'.   Mactaggart, 167 (1824)

It is a popular belief . . . that the *pooca*, as he rides over the country, defiles the blackberries at Michaelmas and Holly-eve.   W. R. Wilde, 14 n. (1852)

30 SEPTEMBER

pridie Kalendas Octobres   G

❦ HOLIDAYS AND ANNIVERSARIES Botswana: Independence Day (1966; formerly British Protectorate of Bechuanaland) (national holiday)
São Tomé and Príncipe: Nationalization Day

❦ HOLY DAYS Jerome (CofE, RC)

Jerome, Doctor of the Church (*c.*331–420), translator of the Scriptures into Latin. He was a great scholar and even greater controversialist, with a lifelong capacity for making enemies of friends, but also of inspiring the devotion of high-born ladies. Born of Christian parents at Stridon (perhaps near Aquileia), he studied in Rome under the great grammarian Aelius Donatus, from whom he quoted the catchphrase *Pereant qui ante nos nostra dixerunt* (roughly, 'To hell with those who said it before me'). Having travelled to Trier, the seat of the imperial court but also a centre of monasticism, instead of entering the public service he devoted himself to God. He returned to northern Italy and Dalmatia, but having given mortal but unspecified offence to zealous Christians, he departed for Antioch. While there, improving his Greek but still reading his beloved Latin classics in preference to the Scriptures with their uncouth style, he fell at mid-Lent—as he related in his finest prose—into a feverish delirium in which he was arraigned before Christ. When asked what he was, he replied that he was a Christian. 'Thou liest,' came the stern response: 'Thou art a Ciceronian: for where thy treasure is, there is thy heart also.' Mortified, he swore never to read pagan literature again; on coming to himself, he says not that he disposed of his classical library, but that he read the sacred writings more eagerly than ever he had read the others. For some years he appears to have relied on his memory of the classical authors; later in life his practice and precept became more liberal.

He left Antioch for the Syrian desert, where he indulged in penances lovingly depicted in his own letters and in later paintings; in these he is often portrayed as an old man in the wilderness, his cardinal's robes (an anachronism) cast aside, beating his naked breast with a stone as he prays before a crucifix, beside him the lion from whose paw, like Androcles before and St Gerasimus (see *5 Mar.) after him, he had withdrawn a thorn. However, having set his fellow-monks against him, he abandoned the desert, returned to Antioch, and moved on to Constantinople and thence to Rome, where he served Pope Damasus as secretary and aroused ill will by polemics in favour of virginity, in which he declared that the 'brothers' of Jesus were in fact his cousins. His enemies drove him from Rome, alleging unchastity with his admirer Paula (*26 Jan.); taking her with him, he set up a monastery in Bethlehem (386). His most important writings are the 'Vulgate' Latin Bible, in which the Old Testament is translated directly from the Hebrew, and his translation and continuation of Eusebius' chronicle, for long the basis of sacred and profane chronology in the Christian West. In 1920, on the 1,500th anniversary of his death, Pope Benedict XV declared him patron of all those who study Scripture.

> Pluck fruite to last,
> When Mihell is past.
> Forget it not,
> fruit bruised will rot:
> Light ladder and long,
> doth tree least wrong.
>
> Tusser

Pl. 1. Janus feasting and a representation of the zodiac sign Aquarius. Illustration heading the month of January from the Fastolf Hours, illuminated by the Master of Sir John Fastolf, England, *c*.1440–50. Bodleian Library, University of Oxford, MS Auct. D. inf. 2. 11, fo. 1ʳ.

Pl. 2. Engraving by Paulus Pontius after Jacob Jordaens, *Le roi boit*. Photo: AKG London. The inscription on the wall is 'There is nothing more like a madman than a drunkard'; beneath the image is a quotation from Ecclesiasticus 31: 30 (Vulgate): 'Challenge not them that love wine: for wine hath destroyed very many.'

Pl. 3. Pruning trees, a typical labour for the month of February, from an eleventh-century English MS. British Library, Cotton Julius A. VI, fo. 3ᵛ.

Pl. 4. A windy day in March. Etching by George Cruikshank to illustrate *The Comic Almanack for 1835*, published by Charles Tilt, Bibliopolist, in Fleet Street. British Museum, BL C 58 C 7.

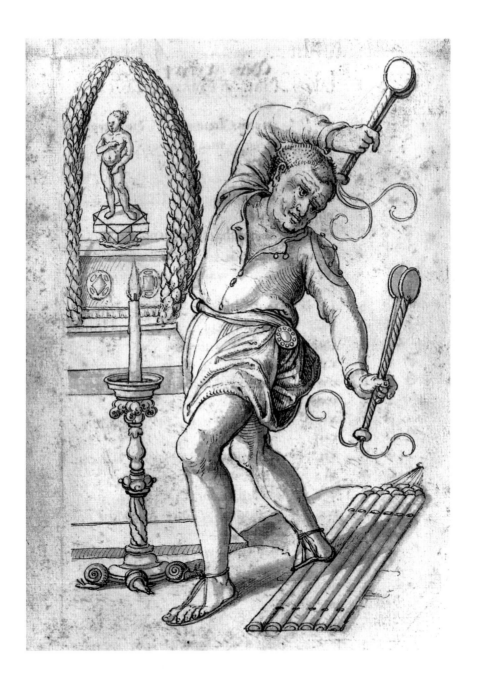

Pl. 5. An old man with castanets dancing before an ambiguous cult-image. Illustration for the month of April from a Roman calendar of 354, preserved in a sixteenth-century MS copy. Österreichische Nationalbibliothek, Vienna, MS 3416, fo. 5ᵛ.

Pl. 6. Beginning of a liturgical calendar for the month of July, showing a mower resting from his labours in the initial K, from a twelfth-century English MS. Bodleian Library, University of Oxford Auct. D. 2. 6, fo. 4^v.

AUGUST.

1 Lammas Day,
2 ſo call'd from
3 Maſs ſaid
4 for Preſer-
5 vation of
6 Lambs.
7
8
9
10 St Lawrance
11 a Deacon, who
12 ſuffer'd Mar-
13 terdom with
14 great Courage
15 was broil'd on
16 a Gridiron.
17 Winter's Thun
18 der, Summer's
19 Flood, never
20 boaded Eng-
21 land Good.
22
23
24 S Bartholomew
25 preach'd in
26 Judea.
27 Dog days E.
28
29
30
31

NOW with Thank-
fullneſs reap
your deſired
Harveſt: Sow
Winter Herbs
in the New
of the Moon,
eſteem fair
Weather as
precious, and
miſpend it
not. Gather
Garden Seeds
near the full,
forbear to
ſleep preſen-
tly after Meat:
Take heed of
ſudden cold
after heat.
Beware of
Phyſick and
Blood letting
in the Dog
Days, if the
Air be hot.
otherwiſe Uſe
thereof.

I AM call'd, Spectator, the Month of Auguſt: The Antient Painters
dreſt me in a flame colourd, or Scarlet Robe, and adorn'd my Head with
a Wreath or Garland, compoſd of Ieſſemin, damaſk Roſes, and a thouſand
other particolour'd Flowers. One Hand was fill'd with divers kinds of
Nuts; In the Other I bore the Sign Virgo, or the Virgin, and my face
was repreſented as red as ſcarlet. In regard to the Sign which they
conferr'd upon me, the Reaſon of it, in fact, was this: As a Virgin is barren & y productreſs of Nothing; ſo y Sun, during my Courſe, has no
generating Faculty, & only brings to Maturity thoſe Fruits which were
y product of y preceeding Months. My ruddy Countenance denotes
the Sultry Heat of y Dog Days, at which time y Blood of all living Creatures are in a ferment. I was call'd by y Antients Sextilis, or y Sixth Month:
But as Auguſtus Cæſar made 3 triumphant Entries into Rome, in my Circuit
I was dignified with y Title of Auguſt, and have retaind it ever ſince.

Pl. 7. Calendar for the month of August from *The New Years Gift or Times Progress for the Year of Our Lord
1743*, perpetuating the medieval misunderstanding of Lammas as coming from 'lamb', here interpreted as 'Mass said for Preservation of Lambs'. Bodleian Library, University of Oxford, Alm. e. 1743.1.

September hath xix Days this Year. 1752

First Quarter, *Saturday* the 15th, at 1 aftern.
Full Moon, *Saturday* the 23d, at 1 aftern.
Last Quarter, *Saturday* the 30th, at 2 aftern.

| 1 | f | Giles Abbot | 5 | 38 | 6 | 22 | secret | □ ♃ ☿ | 5 |
| 2 | g | London Burnt | 5 | 40 | 6 | 20 | memb. | Wind, | | 6 |

ACcording to an Act of Parliament passed in the 24th
Year of his Majesty's Reign, and in the Year of our
Lord 1751, the Old Style ceases here, and the New takes
place; and consequently the next Day, which in the Old
Account would have been the 3d, is now to be called the
14th; so that all the intermediate nominal Days from the
2d to the 14th are omitted, or rather annihilated this Year;
and the Month contains no more than 19 Days, as the
Title at the Head expresses.

14	e	Holy Cross	5	42	6	2?	thighs	and stor-	7
15	f	Day decreas'd		45		2c	hips	my Wea-	8
16	g	4 hours		46		18	knees	ther.	☽
17	A	15 S. aft. Tri.		48		1?	and	Fair and	10
18	b	Day br. 3. 45		50		14	hams	seasonab.	11
19	c	Clo. slow 6 m.		52		12	legs	☌ ☉ ☽	12
20	d	Ember Week		54		1c	ancles	☌ ♀ ☿	13
21	e	St. Matthew,		56		8	feet	Rain and	14
22	f			56		6	toes	Windy.	15
23	g	Eq. D. & N.	5	58		4	head	☌ ☉ ☍	●
24	A	16 S. aft. Tri.	6	0		2	and		17
25	b	Day dec. 4, 34		2	6	c	face	□ ♃ ♀	18
26	c	S. Cyprian		4	5	5?	neck	☌ ☉ ☿	19
27	d	Holy Rood		6		54	throat	Inclin. to	20
28	e	Clo. slow 9 m.		8		5?	arms	☌ ☍ ☿	21
29	f	St. Michael		10		5c	should.	wet, with	22
30	g	St. Jerom		12		4?	breast	Thunder.	☾

Pl. 8. Calendar for the month of September from *Fly. An Almanack, For the Year of Our Lord God, 1752*,
showing the nineteen-day September in 1752, when the Gregorian calendar replaced the Julian.
Bodleian Library, University of Oxford, Douce A. 618 (16).

Pl. 9. 'A penny for the Guy': Guy Fawkes Day, commemorating the failure of the Gunpowder Plot on 5 November 1605, as illustrated by George Cruikshank in *The Comic Almanack for 1835*. British Museum, BL C 58 C 7.

KL	October		ı	A	Antiochi epi.
	habet dies			b	Galli confes.
xxxı. Luna. xxx.			ıx	c	Florentii epi
xvı	A	Remigii epi		d	Luce euange
v	b	Leodegarii	xvıı	e	Pelagie virgi.
xııı	c	Candidi mr.	vı	f	Maximi mris.
ıı	d	Francisci cō		g	Vrsule virgis
	e	Placidi mr.	xıııı	A	Macharii epi.
x	f	Magni epi	ııı.	b	Theodori mr.
	g	Iustine vir.		c	Fortunati mr.
xvııı	A	Vgi Archiepi.	xı	d	Chrysanti mr.
vıı.	b	Dyonisii.		e	Euaristi ppe.
	c	Cerbonii epi	xıx	f	Vigilia.
xv	d	Firmini epi	vııı	g	Symo. & iude.
ıııı.	e	Eustachii p.		A	Zenobii presb.
	f	Venātii abb.	xvı	b	Bernardi epi.
xıı.	g	Calixti ppe.	v	c	Vigilia.

Pl. 10. Liturgical calendar for the month of October from a sixteenth-century French book of hours. This month's occupation is making wine: trampling grapes at the top, making barrels at the bottom. The scorpion in the top right compartment stands for the zodiac sign Scorpio. On the left side a man knocks acorns(?) from a tree to feed his sheep. Bodleian Library, University of Oxford, MS Douce 135, fo. 6ᵛ.

PI. 11. Calendar in a tenth-century manuscript (perhaps from Sankt Gallen) containing Bede's computistic works, Biblioteca Apostolica Vaticana, MS Vat. lat. 644, fo. 25ʳ, showing 12 Feb.–24 Mar.; for the computistic information to the left of the Roman dates see p. 758. Entries include: 13 Feb., 'Here the birds begin to sing, and Hell was made'; 15 Feb., 'The Devil left the Lord'; 21 Feb. is noted as 'finis lxxᵉ', i.e. the last possible date of Septuagesima; the 24th as the 'locus bissexti' or place of leap day; the beginnings of the seventh and third embolisms are recorded on 5 and 6 Mar. respectively, and the earliest date of the Paschal new moon ('first kindling of the moon') on the 8th; 18 Mar. is the first day of the world, the 22nd the seat of the epact and the earliest Easter, the 24th the place of the concurrent. On the right, a 14th-c. hand has added Roman notations, not always accurately: thus the Caristia, Terminalia, and Regifugium appear against 19, 20, and 23 Feb. instead of the 22nd, 23rd, and 24th. Photograph: Biblioteca Apostolica Vaticana.

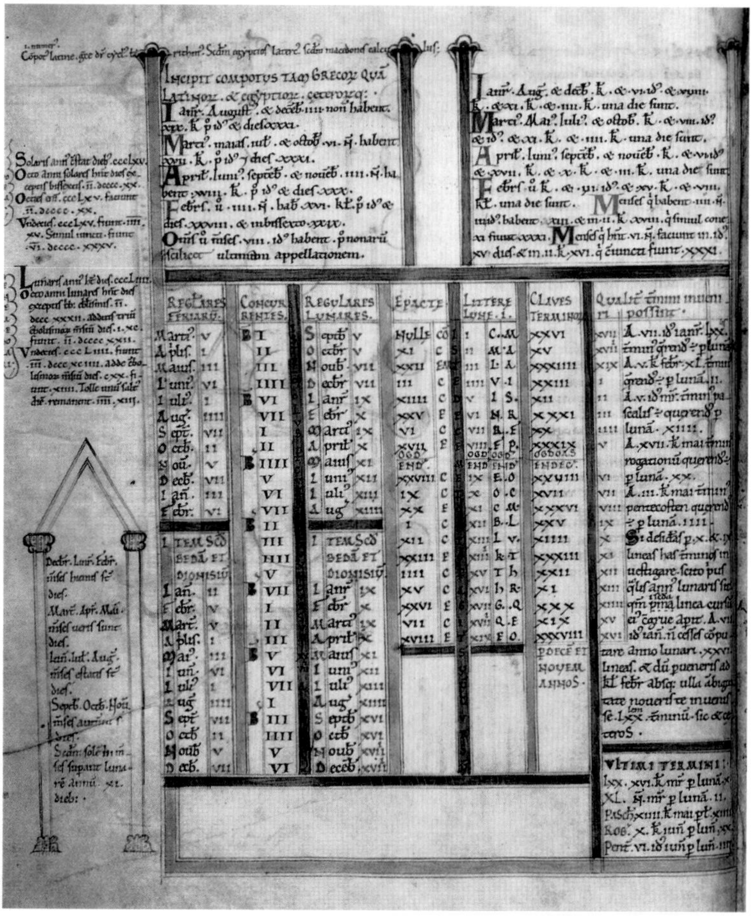

Pl. 12. A table giving basic information about months, cycles, and seasons, together with computistic tables, from an English computistic manuscript (Thorney Abbey, 1110–11), Oxford, St John's College, MS 17, fo. 13ᵛ. From left to right it exhibits: ferial (i.e. solar) regulars reckoned from March (Abbo of Fleury's system) and from January 'according to Bede'; concurrents for the solar cycle, leap years being marked B for *bissextilis*; lunar regulars reckoned from September (the original Byzantine system) and from January 'according to Dionysius and Bede' (in fact Dionysius had not given either sequence, but his rule for the Easter lune counted months from September); epacts, each year of the decemnovenal cycle being marked as common or embolismic; the correlation of new moons with a sequence of lunar letters (see p. 759); the *clavis terminorum* with an explanation of its use related to the age of the moon; between table and explanation the lunar cycle is set out without a heading.

At the bottom right are given the last dates of Septuagesima, Quadragesima, Easter, Rogation Sunday, and Pentecost. The texts are printed in an appendix to Baker and Lapidge's edition of Byrhtferth, pp. 380–4.

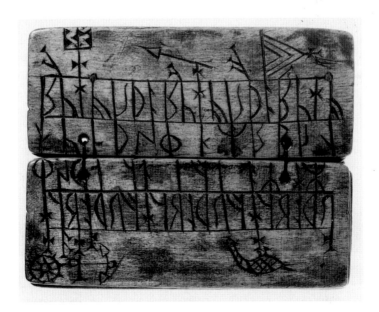

Pl. 13. Facing pages of runic calendar on wooden leaves in book form, probably made in 1535. Ashmolean Museum, Oxford, 1685 A no. 452 = 1836 p. 133 no. 344 = MacGregor no. 194 (pp. 253–62). The pages illustrated are 7 (19 Oct.–5 Nov.) and 8 (6–25 Nov.). On each page the middle row consists of the first seven letters of the runic alphabet, *Frey Ur Thor Os Reid Kan Hagl*, in continuous cycle, beginning with *Reid* on p. 7 and *Ur* on p. 8; these correspond in function to the Sunday Letters, 19 October being E and 6 November B. Along the inner row, a character from an extended runic alphabet against a day indicates the Golden Number of the new moon assigned to that day in the Julian calendar. In both rows some of the characters are inverted and reversed. In the outer row the saints' days or eves are marked.

Day	GN	Day	GN
19 Oct.	17	7 Nov.	18
20 Oct.	6	8 Nov.	7
22 Oct.	14	10 Nov.	15
23 Oct.	3	11 Nov.	4
25 Oct.	11	13 Nov.	12
26 Oct.	19	14 Nov.	1
28 Oct.	8	16 Nov.	9
30 Oct.	16	18 Nov.	17
31 Oct.	5	19 Nov.	6
2 Nov.	13	21 Nov.	14
3 Nov.	2	22 Nov.	3
5 Nov.	10	24 Nov.	11
		25 Nov.	19

20 Oct.	branch	eve
21 Oct.	cross with un-identified symbol	Ursula and 11,000 virgins
27 Oct.	branch	eve
28 Oct.	cross and spear	Simon and Jude
31 Oct.	double branch	eve and fast
1 Nov.	church spire sideways?	All Saints
2 Nov.	half-cross	All Souls
6 Nov.	half-cross	Leonard
11 Nov.	cross and goose	Martin
22 Nov.	half-cross	Cecilia
23 Nov.	cross and anchor	Clement
24 Nov.	double branch	eve
25 Nov.	cross and wheel	Catherine

Unlucky days are indicated by metal plugs; these appear on 22 Oct and 5 Nov, both of which were Egyptian days in the common list.

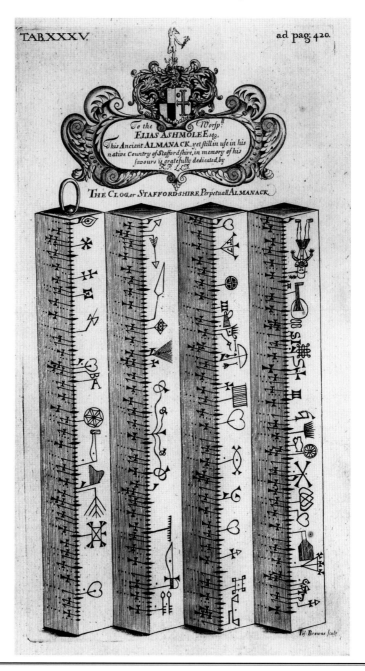

Pl. 14. Seventeenth-century clog calendar illustrated in Robert Plot, *The Natural History of Staffordshire* (Oxford, 1686), facing p. 421, an exploded drawing of the smaller of two similar clogs in the Ashmolean Museum, Oxford (1836, p. 133, no. 343), of which the larger is dated 1644. Bodleian Library, University of Oxford, Gough Staffs. 14, opposite p. 420.

1 Jan.	**Circumcision** symbol 'somewhat resembling the cutting off of the *prepuce*'	7 Aug	**Name of Jesus** a cross
6 Jan.	**Epiphany** a star (for the Wise Men)	10 Aug.	**Laurence** a grid iron
13 Jan.	**Hilary** a bishop's cross	15 Aug.	**Assumption** a heart
17 Jan.	**Anthony Abbot** an inverted M (from AA?)	24 Aug.	**Bartholomew** an elaborated knife?
25 Jan.	**Conversion of St Paul** an axe (for his martyrdom)	1 Sept.	**Giles** G
		8 Sept.	**Nativity of BVM** a heart
2 Feb.	**Purification** a heart	14 Sept.	**Holy Cross Day** cross and mitre
3 Feb.	**Blaise** B	21 Sept.	**Matthew** abstract
5 Feb.	**Agatha** A	29 Sept.	**Michaelmas** scales for weighing souls
14 Feb.	**Valentine** 'a true *Lovers knot* . . . importing the time of *marriage* or *coupling* of birds'	13 Oct.	**Translation of Edward the Confessor** a man
22 Feb.	**Matthias** a mallet	16 Oct.	**St Michael at Mont-St-Michel** M
1 Mar.	**David** a harp (by confusion of king and saint)	18 Oct.	**Luke** a lute
		25 Oct.	**Crispin** shoes
2 Mar.	**Chad** a bough 'for Sᵗ *Ceadda*, who lived a *Hermits* life in the woods near *Lichfield*'	28 Oct.	**Simon and Jude** SI
		1 Nov.	**All Saints** abstract
12 Mar.	**Gregory** square with elaborations	2 Nov.	**All Souls** S
25 Mar.	**Annunciation** a heart	5 Nov.	**Gunpowder** flag (smaller clog only)
3 Apr.	**Richard of Chichester** a mitre	6 Nov.	**Leonard** L
4 Apr.	**Ambrose** an arrow	11 Nov.	**Martinmas** M
23 Apr.	**George** a spear	17 Nov.	**Hugh** H
25 Apr.	**Mark** abstract (a mark?)	20 Nov.	**Edmund** flesh bristling with Danish arrows?
1 May	**May Day** a bough 'such as they usually set up about that time with great solemnity'	23 Nov.	**Clement** a pot, 'from the ancient custom of going about that night, to begg drink to make merry with'
3 May	**Invention of the Cross** a cross		
19 May	**Dunstan** florid design based on D	25 Nov.	**Catherine** a wheel
11 June	**Barnabas** a rake (for the hay harvest)	30 Nov.	**Andrew** a decussated cross
24 June	**Nativity of St John the Baptist** a sword?	6 Dec.	**Nicholas** three balls made into a mitre?
		8 Dec.	**Conception of BVM** a heart
29 June	**Peter** the keys of heaven	13 Dec.	**Lucy** a leister? a creel?
2 July	**Visitation** a heart	21 Dec.	**Thomas** abstract
7 July	**Translation of Becket** T7	25 Dec.	**Christmas** a wassail horn (Plot); or C
15 July	**Swithun** ??	26 Dec.	**Stephen** S
20 July	**Margaret** M	27 Dec.	**St John the Evangelist** I
22 July	**Mary Magdalene** an ointment-jar debased to a tankard?	28 Dec.	**Childermas** mirror image of Christmas symbol
25 July	**James the Greater** a head wearing a hat?	29 Dec.	**Becket** cross and mitre
26 July	**Anne** ??		
1 Aug	**Peter's Chains** keys on a ring? (arrows under parasol)		

A dot in the middle of a symbol indicates a major feast, one before it a fast on the eve.

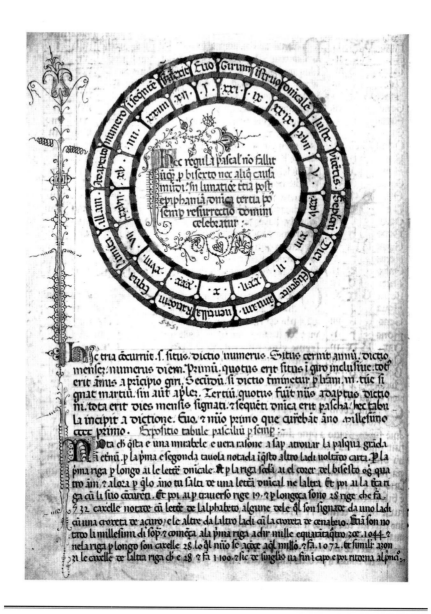

Pl. 15. A table for finding Easter with an explanation in Latin beneath it, from a Trieste martyrology of 1476. Bodleian Library, University of Oxford, MS Canon. Liturg. 333, fo. 3ᵛ. In the outer ring, which contains nineteen words, count (inclusively) as many words from *Euo* as there are years from 1401; if the word ends in *m*, Easter will be in March, otherwise in April, but in either case on the Sunday following the *quantième* indicated in the inner ring. (That is to say, *Euo* corresponds to Golden Number 15, with Paschal term 1 Apr.) In the centre we read: 'This Paschal Rule never misleads for leap year or any other reason in the world. The Lord's Resurrection is always celebrated in the third lunation after Epiphany, specifically on the third Sunday.' Underneath the Latin text is an explanation in Venetian dialect of a 532-year table on the recto.

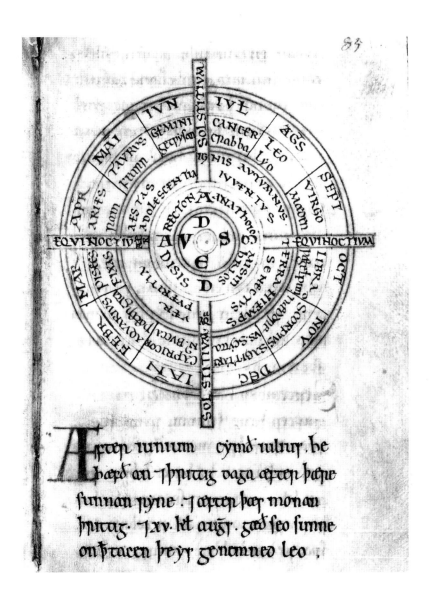

Pl. 16. A circular table from Byrhtferth's *Enchiridion* (p. 76 in the edition by Baker and Lapidge). Bodleian Library, University of Oxford, MS Ashmole 328, p. 85 (mid-11th c.). In the outermost ring of the table are the months, related in the adjoining ring to a sign of the zodiac named in Latin and Old English, and grouped into threes by the axes of the equinoxes and solstices, corresponding in the third ring to the seasons and the ages of man, and in a fourth ring to the cardinal points (named in transliterated Greek); thus January to March are equated with spring (*ver*), boyhood (*pueritia*), and the west (*disis*). In the middle is the name DEVS, 'God'. The text below is in Old English: 'After June comes July; it has thirty-one days according to the sun's course and according to the moon's thirty; and on *XV Kal. Aug.* (18 July) the sun enters the sign that is called Leo.'

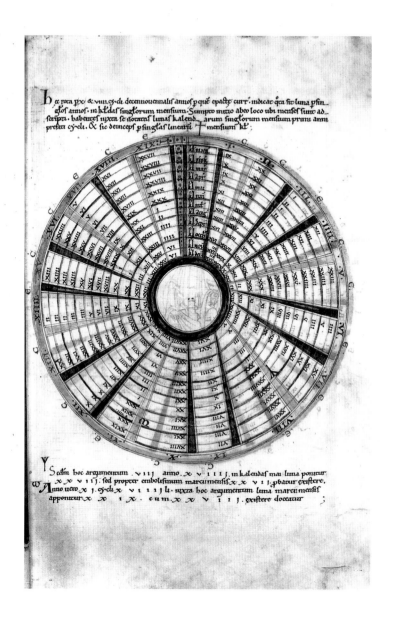

PI. 17. A *rota computistica* from an English computistic manuscript (Thorney Abbey, 1110–11), St John's College, Oxford, MS 17, fo. 27ʳ, showing the decemnovenal cycle with the lune of the first day of each month; the note at the foot corrects the results given by mechanical application of the lunar regulars (see p. 814).

OCTOBER

Dry your barley-land in October
or you'll always be sober.

Often drunk and seldom sober
falls like the leaves in October.

In October dung your field
and your land its wealth shall yield.

❦ NAMES OF THE MONTH Latin *October*, French *octobre*, Spanish *octubre*, Portuguese *Outubro*, Italian *ottobre*, German *Oktober*, Welsh *Hydref*, Scots Gaelic *an Damhar*, Irish *Deireadh Fómhair*

The Latin name indicates that this was originally the eighth month of the year. The Welsh name, originally *hyddfref*, denotes the lowing of cattle; the Scots Gaelic, derived from *damh*, 'ox', 'stag', means 'rutting time'; the Irish is literally 'end of autumn'.

❦ HOLIDAYS AND ANNIVERSARIES

Last Sunday The end on this day of British Summer Time has been marked at Merton College, Oxford, since 1972 with a backward procession round Fellows' Quad between 2 a.m. BST (the moment at which Greenwich Mean Time is restored) and 2 a.m. GMT. The USA returns to standard time on this day as well.

Second Monday Canada: Thanksgiving Day
  USA: Columbus Day (still 12 Oct. in Maryland, Puerto Rico)
  Alabama: Fraternal Day
  Florida: Farmers Day
  Hawaii: Discoverers Day
  South Dakota: Native Americans Day
  Virgin Islands–Puerto Rico Friendship Day

Third Monday Jamaica: National Heroes' Day
  Virgin Islands: Hurricane Thanksgiving Day (end of hurricane season) (legal holiday)

Fourth Monday New Zealand: Labour Holiday
  USA: Veterans Day
  Zambia: Independence Day

Last Monday Ireland: Bank Holiday

Third Wednesday USA, Missouri: Missouri Day

Fourth Wednesday Nauru: Angam Day

First Thursday, Friday, and Saturday Nottingham Goose Fair (since 1284)

Last Thursday evening Punky Night at Hinton St George in Somerset: children carry can-
    dles in 'punkies', hollowed-out mangel-wurzels with faces or other designs carved
    into the shell; the candles represent the lanterns formerly lit to guide the menfolk
    home from a fair in a neighbouring village to a festive welcome that seemed far
    too good to abandon when the fair lapsed.

> Then came *October* full of merry glee:
>   For, yet his noule was totty of the must,
>   Which he was treading in the wine-fats see,
>   And of the ioyous oyle, whose gentle gust
>   Made him so frollick and so full of lust:
>   Vpon a dreadful Scorpion he did ride,
>   The same which by *Dianaes* doom vniust
>   Slew great *Orion*: and eeke by his side
> He had his ploughing share, and coulter ready tyde.
>
>   Spenser, *The Faerie Queene*, VII. vii. 39

It is now October, and the lofty windes make bare the trees of their leaues, while the hogs in the
Woods grow fat with the falne Acorns: the forward Deere begin to goe to rut, and the barren
Doe groweth good meat: the Basket-makers now gather their rods, and the fishers lay their leapes
in the deepe: the loade horses goe apace to the Mill, and the Meal-market is seldome without
people: the Hare on the hill makes the Greyhound a faire course, and the Foxe in the woods cals
the Hounds to a full cry: the multitude of people raiseth the price of wares, and the smoothe
tongue will sell much: the Saylor now bestirreth his stumps, while the Merchant liueth in feare
of the weather: the great feasts are now at hand for the City, but the poore must not beg for feare
of the stockes: a fire and a paire of Cards keepe the ghests in the Ordinary, and Tobacco is held
very precious for the Rhewme: The Coaches now begin to rattle in the Street: but the cry of the
poore is vnpleasing to the rich: Muffes and Cuffes are now in request, and the shuttel-Cocke with
the Battel-doore is a pretty house-exercise: Tennis and Baloune are sports of some charge, and a
quicke bandy is the Court-keepers commodity: dancing and fencing are now in some vse, and
kind hearts and true Louers lye close, to keepe off cold: the Titmouse now keepes in the hollow
tree, and the black bird sits close in the bottome of a hedge: In briefe, for the little pleasure I find
in it, I thus conclude of it: I hold it a Messenger of ill newes, and a second seruice to a cold
dinner. Farewell.   Breton (1626)

In this *Moneth* doth the Body wax *dry*, and the Brain *moist*; therefore it behoveth to eat roasted
meats often in this Moneth, and drink *pleasant Wine*, also drink *new Wine*, and eat pleasant meat
often; *Goats* milk is held to be excellent good for this Moneth, because it *purifieth* the blood, and
cleanseth the Lungs; its good to eat often *Appletarts* prepared with comfortable Spices and Sugar,
for they comfort greatly the stomack, but wash not the *head* this Moneth, let Blood and Purge
as occasion requires, beware of eating too liberally of new Fruits, to eat the *Rhadish* root is
wholesome, and to eat *Mustard* with your meats is very commendable; all *wild* Fowls this Moneth

are wholsome and good, and *Cloves* with *Cinnamon* in meats, sauce, drinks or champed in the mouth are very good.   Saunders (1665)

The Garments you put on last Month in jest, now button them close in good earnest, to prevent insensibly taking cold; many times one Fog begets a whole Winters Cold.

Kalendarium Ecclesiasticum (1699)

I OCTOBER

Kalendae Octobres   A

(HOLIDAYS AND ANNIVERSARIES China: Founding of People's Republic (national day)
Cyprus: Independence Day (1960, from Britain; national holiday)
Nigeria: Independence Day (1960, from Britain; national holiday)
Republic of Palau: Independence Day (1994, from UN Trust Territory)
Tuvalu: Independence Day (commemorating separation from Gilbert Islands, now Kiribati, 1975)

(HOLY DAYS Remigius (CofE); Thérèse of Lisieux (RC); Protecting Veil of the Theotokos (Orth.)

Remigius (Remi), Bishop of Reims, d. *c.*533, 'Apostle of the Franks' and founder of bishoprics in northern France. He baptized the Frankish king Clovis, supposedly in 496 (see *22 Sept.). This feast (no longer in the Universal Calendar) commemorates the date of the translation of his relics in 1049, when Pope Leo IX, preaching the reform of the Church, took them not as expected to a new crypt in the abbey but to the high altar, where (he informed the assembled French clergy) they would reveal which clerics were guilty of the offences, such as simony and unchastity, against which the reform was directed. Some hastened to repent at Leo's feet, others slunk away; those who attempted to lie their way out were (we are told) struck dumb. At Reims his day is 13 January.

Thérèse of Lisieux (Teresa of the Child Jesus) (1873–97), Carmelite. She died at a very young age, having profoundly affected her contemporaries. She left behind an autobiography, *The Story of a Soul*; a number of miracles are attributed to her. She was canonized in 1925 and declared patron of missions in 1927, having been prevented by her last illness from her desire to become a missionary in Hanoi; it was she who inspired Mother Teresa of Calcutta. Her other patronage, of florists and flower-growers, stems from a remark she made, 'I will let fall a shower of roses' (a promise of favours for those who sought her intercession); from this she is also known as 'the Little Flower of Jesus'. In 1947 she was named a patron saint of France. On 19 October 1997 Pope John Paul II declared her a Doctor of the Church, only the third woman to be so honoured, after Catherine of Siena and Teresa of Ávila. Feast-day formerly 3 October.

The Protecting Veil of the Theotokos was reportedly seen in a vision by Andrew the Holy Fool (early 10th c.), spread out over the congregation at Blachernae. It is especially celebrated in Russia (see *14 Oct.).

Romanos the Melode (*fl. c.*540), the Christian Pindar, author of classic *kontakia* still used in the Orthodox Church, in whose complex accentual strophes fundamental doctrines are expounded in powerful language.

2 OCTOBER

a.d. VI Nonas Octobres   B

❨ HOLIDAYS AND ANNIVERSARIES Guinea: Independence Day (from France, 1958) India: Birthday of Mahatma Gandhi

❨ ANCIENT ROME First day of the Ludi Augustales, celebrating Augustus' return from the East in 19 BC, having recovered by diplomatic means the standards lost at Carrhae.

❨ HOLY DAYS The Guardian Angels (RC)

Guardian Angels. The devotion to a personal guardian (of body and soul) is pre-Christian: at Rome every man had his *genius*, every woman her *Iuno*. Among Church writers, it was disputed which persons had guardian angels, and which angels they were. Formerly commemorated together with St Michael (*29 Sept.), they have had their own official feast since 1670. The Guardian Angels were decreed patron saints of the Spanish armed police in 1961.

Leudegar or *Leger*, made bishop of Autun in 663 by Baldhild (see *30 Jan.), who after her forced retirement led other of her protégés in opposition to Ebroin, mayor of the palace to King Clothar III of Neustria and Burgundy. When in 673 Clothar died, Ebroin made his younger brother King Theuderic III, but an aristocratic revolt gave the throne to the middle brother, Childeric II of Austrasia; Theuderic and Ebroin were compelled to become monks at Saint-Denis and Luxeuil respectively. The latter was soon joined by Leudegar, who had fallen out with Childeric; soon afterwards the king was assassinated, in 675, for attempting to make an Austrasian mayor of the palace for all three kingdoms. If, as has been suggested, this was a joint enterprise by Ebroin and Leudegar, their cooperation did not last: Leudegar restored Theuderic, and made a new Mayor of the Palace, the son of Ebroin's predecessor; Ebroin promoted a supposed son of Clothar's as Clovis III, had both Leudegar and his mayor put to death, and governed Neustria and Burgundy till his murder in 680. Improving tales are told of Leudegar's repeated tortures and his final execution: three of the four executioners begged for mercy, the fourth cut off his head and was promptly carried off by the Devil.

On St Catherine's Hill, near Guildford, a fair used to be held on the Sunday preceding this day at which any person, with or without a licence, was permitted to sell beer on the hill, or, as the phrase went, 'to open a tap'. It was therefore called 'Tap-up Sunday'.

3 OCTOBER

a.d. V Nonas Octobres   C

❡ HOLIDAYS AND ANNIVERSARIES Germany: Tag der Deutschen Einheit (Day of German Unity) (national day), celebrating incorporation in 1990 of the five Länder that had comprised the German Democratic Republic into the Federal Republic of Germany. Previously this holiday had been kept on 17 June, in honour of the East Berlin workers' revolt in 1953

    South Korea: National Foundation Day (Tangun Day; established kingdom of Chosun in 2333 BC) (national holiday)

❡ ANCIENT ROME On 3 October 78 BC, at Pompeii, an ancient Kilroy wrote *C. Pumidius Dipilus heic fuit a.d. V Nonas Octobreis M. Lepid(o) Q. Catul(o) co(n)s(ulibus)*, 'Gaius Pumidius Diphilus was here on the fifth day before the Nones of October when Marcus Lepidus and Quintus Catulus were consuls.'

❡ HOLY DAYS Formerly St Thérèse of Lisieux (see *1 Oct.)

Thomas de Cantilupe (c.1218–82), bishop of Hereford. He studied at Oxford, Paris, and Orléans before being named Chancellor of Oxford in 1261. A strict disciplinarian, Thomas acquired a significant armoury by confiscating from the students weapons they had misused. Siding with the barons against King Henry III, he was briefly Chancellor of England when the king was defeated. Dismissed after Simon de Montfort's death at Evesham, he returned to Paris. In 1275 he became bishop of Hereford, but following a jurisdictional dispute with the Archbishop of Canterbury, John Pecham, Thomas was excommunicated; having appealed to the Pope, he died on the journey to Rome. After receiving the certificate of absolution from Martin IV, Pecham allowed Thomas's body to be buried in Hereford cathedral, which became the most frequented shrine in the west of England: after a process in which 429 miracles were attested, he was canonized in 1320 despite having died excommunicate. At the Reformation his bones were dispersed; their loss was confirmed during restoration in 1997, though in compensation there was found a piece of slate inscribed 'gone to the dogs by the time you read this' and dated 1861. Feast-day formerly 2 October.

4 OCTOBER

a.d. IV Nonas Octobres   D

❡ HOLIDAYS AND ANNIVERSARIES Lesotho: Independence Day (from Great Brit-
    ain, 1966)

❡ ANCIENT ROME

Ieiunium Cereris or Fast of Ceres, instituted in 191 BC after a sequence of alarming prod-
igies: two tame oxen climbed the steps of a public building and reached the roof; from
other towns there were reports that stones had rained down on several occasions, that a
temple of Jupiter and some shops had been struck by lightning, and that two ships, also
struck by lightning, had caught fire. It was to be held *quinto quoque anno*, which usually
means, according to English idiom, not every fifth but every fourth year; by Augustus'
reign it had become annual. The celebrants were instructed to wear garlands, in the
Greek fashion; there was also Greek precedent for honouring the goddess of grain with
a fast, for the second day of the Athenian Thesmophoria held in honour of Demeter
on 11–13 Pyanopsion, just before the full moon of September–October—what in English is called the Harvest Moon—was kept as a fast. However, since in 191 BC the Roman
calendar was some four months ahead of true (see p. 670), nominal 4 October must
have fallen in late spring; this suits the circumstances, for one consul had marched off
to war and the other did so later.

The astrologer L. Tarutius of Firmum (Fermo), in the first century BC, determined to
his own satisfaction that Rome had been founded at a date and time equivalent in modern reckoning to about 8 a.m. (Roman time) on 4 October 754 BC; this conflicted with
the normal foundation-day of *21 April.

❡ HOLY DAYS Francis of Assisi (CY, RC)

Francis of Assisi (1181–1226), founder in 1209 of the Order of Friars Minor (Franciscans),
and one of the most beloved medieval saints. His calling came late, after he had been
deeply affected having exchanged clothes with a beggar for one day on a pilgrimage to
Rome. Like-minded men (and soon women) joined the Order, which remained without a formal rule for many years; the ecclesiastical hierarchy balked at the all too obvious reminder that Christ had enjoined poverty on his followers; nevertheless Honorius
III approved the rule in 1223. In the following year Francis, on a retreat at Monte La
Verna, received the stigmata (commemorated on 17 Sept.). He requested to be buried
in the criminals' cemetery on the Colle d'Inferno, but his body was brought to the
church of St George in Assisi, where it remained until in 1230 it was secretly removed to
the great basilica; there it remained hidden until 1818, after a 52-day search found it deep
beneath the high altar of the lower church. Pius XII declared him patron saint of Italy
in 1939, and parliament gave its formal approval on 25 February 1958. Pius XII also

named him patron of Italian merchants in 1952 (an interesting choice; Francis's father had been a rich merchant). When ecology became a major field of study John Paul II proclaimed him patron of ecologists and ecology (1979).

The thirteenth-century chronicler Roger of Wendover tells the following story of Francis's attempt to get Pope Innocent III to approve his Order in 1209:

The pope gazed fixedly on the ill-favoured mien of the aforesaid brother, his mournful counten-ance, lengthened beard, his untrimmed hair, and his dirty, overhanging brow, and when he heard his petition read which it was so difficult and impracticable to carry out, despised him, and said, 'Go, brother, go to the pigs, to whom you are are more fit to be compared than to men, and roll with them, and to them preach the rules you have so ably set forth.' Francis, on hearing this, bowed his head and went away, and having found some pigs he rolled with them in the mud till he had covered his body and clothes with dirt from head to foot; he then, returning to the con-sistory, showed himself to the pope, and said, 'My lord, I have done as you ordered me; grant me now, I beseech you, my petition.' The pope was astonished when he saw what he had done, and felt sorry for having treated him with contempt, at the same time giving orders that he should wash himself and come back to him again; he therefore cleansed himself from his dirt, and re-turned directly to the pope. The pope, being much moved, then granted his petition, and, after confirming his office of preaching as well as the order he applied for, by a privilege from the church of Rome, he dismissed him with a blessing.   Wendover, ii. 494 (under 1227)

Petronius (early 5th c.), bishop of Bologna, popular in the Middle Ages through a ficti-tious life written soon after his relics were discovered in 1141. He is patron saint of Bologna, whose imposing cathedral is named after him. Begun in 1390, it was never finished; the façade remains half brick. The original plan was even grander, but con-struction was curtailed when the edifice threatened to exceed the length of St Peter's.

In 1582, by the Bull *Inter gravissimas* of Pope Gregory XIII, this day was immediately fol-lowed by the 14th. The intervening feasts were moved, for that year only, to the 15th and 16th. But for the reform, the 7th would have been the eighteenth Sunday after Pente-cost; the day retained that quality under its new designation of 17 October (or rather the sixteenth before the Kalends of November), the Sunday letter for the remnant of the year being changed from G to C. From St Luke on the 18th onwards, every feast was kept on the same date as before the reform.

According to Olaus Worm, this is the time for making cider and perry.

On this day in 1779 the 7-year-old Samuel Taylor Coleridge pulled a knife on his brother Frank, ran away, and spent the night in the stormy open; two years later, his father dreamt he was dying. Ever afterwards, Coleridge preferred to publish on 4 Octo-ber, and chose that day for both his marriages.

5 OCTOBER

a.d. III Nonas Octobres   E

❰ ANCIENT ROME Mundus patet (cf. *24 Aug.).

❰ HOLY DAYS

Galla, sister-in-law of Boethius; Gregory the Great (*Dial.* 4. 13) invites us to believe that, rather than remarry after being widowed, she allowed her natural body-heat to give her a beard. She became a nun at St Stephen's monastery near St Peter's (known in eighth-century dog Latin as *cata Galla patricia*), where she died of breast cancer, reportedly after a vision in which St Peter told her that another nun would die together with her; she asked that her especial friend Sister Benedicta should accompany her instead, but St Peter replied that Benedicta would die thirty days later.

October

Aye, thou art welcome, heaven's delicious breath!
  When woods begin to wear the crimson leaf,
  And suns grow meek, and the meek suns grow brief,
And the year smiles as it draws near its death.
Wind of the sunny south! oh, still delay
  In the gay woods and in the golden air,
  Like to a good old age released from care,
Journeying, in long serenity, away.
In such a bright, late quiet, would that I
  Might wear out life like thee, 'mid bowers and brooks,
  And dearer yet, the sunshine of kind looks,
And music of kind voices ever nigh;
And when my last sand twinkled in the glass,
Pass silently from men, as thou dost pass.

William Cullen Bryant (1794–1878)

6 OCTOBER

pridie Nonas Octobres   F

❰ HOLIDAYS AND ANNIVERSARIES Egypt: Armed Forces Day (commemorating
    crossing into Sinai, 1973)
  Ireland: Ivy Day (anniversary of death of Charles Stewart Parnell, champion of
    Home Rule for Ireland) (cf. Joyce's short story, 'Ivy Day in the Committee Room')
  United Nations: Children's Day

❡ ANCIENT ROME On this day in 105 BC a disagreement over protocol between commanders caused a disastrous Roman defeat at Arausio (Orange); when in 69 BC Lucullus, about to fight Tigran the Great of Armenia, was warned that the day was ill-omened, he promised to change its luck, and did so.

❡ HOLY DAYS Faith (BCP); William Tyndale (CY); Bruno (RC); Thomas the Apostle (Orth.; see *3 July, *21 Dec.)

Faith (3rd c.), a virgin martyr, attested in the Martyrology of Jerome, but her acts portraying her martyrdom, by being roasted on a bed of coals and then beheaded, are fictitious. Her relics in Conques, along the pilgrimage route to Compostela, ensured her later fame, which spread as far as England; chapels were dedicated to her in Westminster Abbey and St Paul's Cathedral. She is invoked by soldiers, prisoners, and pilgrims. The RC Church celebrates her on this day as well.

> O good St. Faith, be kind to-night,
> And bring to me my heart's delight;
> Let me my future husband view,
> And be my visions chaste and true.
>
> Halliwell, 216 (1849)

William Tyndale (*c.*1494–1536), biblical translator. Having failed to win ecclesiastical support at home for his project, he moved to Hamburg and later settled in Antwerp, never returning to England. His New Testament, first published in 1525 and several times revised, is a masterpiece of vigorous English, justly becoming the basis for several subsequent translations, including the Authorized Version; it was followed in 1530 by the Pentateuch and in 1531 by Jonah. It is to Tyndale that we owe the name 'Passover', both translating *pesah/pascha* and suggesting the sound; he is also among the first writers to use the adjective 'beautiful'. Besides his translations, he published theological works. He aroused fierce opposition among religious conservatives, Sir Thomas More being particularly implacable; his New Testament was officially burnt, but still found its readers. This was not to the liking of Henry VIII, even after his break with Rome; Tyndale was arrested by underhand means, and burnt at the stake in 1536, probably on this day. At his death he left manuscript versions of the historical books from Joshua to 2 Chronicles.

Bruno (*c.*1032–1101), founder of the Carthusian Order. Educated at Cologne, he then taught grammar and theology at the cathedral school of Reims, before being named chancellor of the diocese. Conflict with his archbishop led him to resign and become a hermit under Robert of Molesmes (who was to become founder of Cîteaux). With the assistance of St Hugh, bishop of Grenoble, he and his companions were granted land high in the mountains nearby, named Chartreuse, from which his order takes its name. Requested to come to Italy by his former pupil Pope Urban II, he subsequently declined an archbishopric in Calabria and instead founded a monastery there, where he died. He was perhaps the last great saint not to be canonized formally. His first foundation has given its name to a fine liqueur.

7 OCTOBER

Nonae Octobres G

❦ ANCIENT ROME An open shrine on the Capitol was dedicated to Iuppiter Fulgur (Jupiter Thunderbolt), responsible for lightning by day (see *20 June).

❦ HOLY DAYS Our Lady of the Rosary (RC); formerly Bridget of Sweden (see *23 July)

Our Lady of the Rosary. Although the habit of repeating prayers, counted off on a string of beads, goes back to early Christianity, the rosary itself did not become a popular devotion until the early fifteenth century, first promoted by the Carthusians and then by the Dominicans, who sponsored Confraternities of the Rosary and until 1984 had the exclusive right to bless rosaries. Originally it consisted only of repetitions of the Lord's Prayer (hence the chains of beads were known as 'paternosters'); the Hail Mary began to be added in the twelfth century. The rosary now consists of the Lord's Prayer, ten Hail Marys, and a Gloria Patri said fifteen times, making up the so-called Marian Psalter, an analogue of the 150 Psalms for those who could not read. This is a relatively new feast, introduced by Pius V in 1572; the day was chosen to commemorate the victory over the Turks at the Battle of Lepanto on this day in 1571, and was then known as the feast of Our Lady of Victory (the Venetians preferred to credit Justina, however; see below). His successor, Gregory XIII, having permitted churches with an altar of the Rosary to hold a Feast of the Sacred Rosary on the first Sunday in October, this was extended to the whole Church by Clement XI after the defeat of the Turks at Petrovaradin on 5 August 1716. Pius X combined the two into a feast of Our Lady of the Rosary on 7 October.

Justina, supposedly a Paduan virgin martyr under Diocletian, honoured in the Veneto; after the discovery of her alleged relics in 1117 at Padua, a forged account of her passion was published. Her cult flourished all the more after the great victory of the Holy League (the papacy, Spain, and Venice) against the Ottoman fleet at Lepanto on this day in 1571; an *andata* or solemn state procession to her church in Venice was added to the many already prescribed by the Venetian calendar, and the *pala d'oro* was revealed at second vespers in S. Marco. In Rome, however, Pius V proclaimed a feast of Our Lady of Victory (see above).

Osyth. Formerly in the English calendar the feast-day of St Osyth (d. *c.*700), a princess of the Hwicca tribe, mother of Offa, king of the East Saxons. Founder of a convent in Essex, she was thought to have carried her head, cut off by pirates, to a church three miles away. Thomas Fuller, in his *Worthies* (145), comments on this fanciful tale: 'The same *mutatis mutandis* is said of St Denys in France, St Winifrith in Wales and others, such being the barrenness of monkish invention, that, unable to furnish their several saints with a variety of fictions, their tired fancy is fain to make the same miracle serve several saints.' The place in Essex named after her, St Osyth, is locally pronounced as if 'Toozey'.

Sergius and Bacchus, said to have been Roman officers and close friends on the classical Greek model, put to death in northern Syria *c.*305 as Christians. When they refused to enter the temple of Jupiter with the emperor Maximian, he stripped these soldiers of their uniforms and made them walk the streets in women's clothes; later they were martyred separately, Sergius being beheaded, Bacchus whipped to death. Their cult spread in the East, especially that of Sergius; hence the popularity of Sergey as a man's name in Russia.

8 OCTOBER

a.d. VIII Idus Octobres   A

❴ HOLY DAYS

Keyne, virgin (?6th c.), who refused marriage and chose a solitary life in Cornwall, then in Wales. She is patron of St Keyne (Cornwall), where a well, near Liskeard, is named after her.

> 'St. Keyne,' quoth the Cornish-man, 'many a time
>   Drank of this crystal well,
> And before the Angel summon'd her,
>   She laid on the water a spell.
>
> 'If the Husband of this gifted Well
>   Shall drink before his Wife,
> A happy man thenceforth is he,
>   For he shall be Master for life.
>
> 'But if the Wife should drink of it first,
>   God help the Husband then!'
> The Stranger stoopt to the Well of St. Keyne,
>   And drank of the water again.
>
> 'You drank of the Well I warrant betimes?'
>   He to the Cornish-man said:
> But the Cornish-man smiled as the stranger spake,
>   And sheepishly shook his head.
>
> 'I hasten'd as soon as the wedding was done,
>   And left my wife in the porch;
> But i' faith she had been wiser than me,
>   For she took a bottle to Church!'
>
>   Robert Southey (1774–1843)

Otherwise this day commemorates two women of shady pasts, Pelagia the Penitent, an Antiochene actress (which in the ancient world automatically meant 'prostitute' as well), converted and baptized by St Nonnus, after which she put on men's clothes and went to live as a hermit (her legend became attached to the name of a genuine Pelagia; see *4 May); and Thais, supposedly an Egyptian courtesan converted by St Paphnutius; she made a bonfire of her vanities, then allowed Paphnutius to lock her in a cell for three years, mercilessly with no provision for waste. '*Thais* the hoor' is one of the saints about whom William Patten waxed so indignant (see *9 Sept.) and the subject of Massenet's opera *Thais*.

Sergius of Radonezh (Russ. Orth.: 25 Sept. OS), founded together with his brother Stephen the Troitsky (Holy Trinity) monastery, which became the greatest religious house in Muscovy; he bestowed his blessing on the Grand Prince Demetrius (see *8 Nov.) before the battle of Kulikovo in 1380. He died in 1392. His translation-feast is 3/16 July.

In 1966, the revolutionary Ernesto Guevara, commonly known as 'Che' (i.e. 'the Argentinian', from the Argentine Spanish for 'mate'), was handed over to the Bolivian army by the peasants of La Higuera, amongst whom he was preaching a political message in which they took no interest. The Western counter-culturalists whose posters proclaim 'Che Lives' may be surprised to learn that he is now honoured on this day at La Higuera as San Ernesto, who never fails to answer prayers for rain.

9 OCTOBER

a.d. VII Idus Octobres   B

ℭ HOLIDAYS AND ANNIVERSARIES Iceland: Leif Erikson Day (Leifr Éiríksson, Viking discoverer of America)
Norway: Leif Erikson Day
Uganda: Independence Day (from Great Britain, 1962)
USA, Wisconsin and Minnesota: Leif Erikson Day

ℭ HOLY DAYS Denys (CofE, RC); John Leonardi (RC); James son of Alphaeus (Orth.; see *1 May)

Denys or Dionysius, bishop of Paris (d. *c*.250, together with Rusticus and Eleutherius); one of the Fourteen Auxiliary Saints. According to Gregory of Tours he was one of Pope Fabian's missionary bishops (*22 Mar.); in later authors he is moved back to the first century and equated with St Paul's Athenian convert Dionysius the Areopagite, the putative author of theological writings (in fact by an early 6th-c. Monophysite Neoplatonist) that became the foundation of medieval mysticism (John Lydgate refers to him as 'Blissed Denys, of Athenys cheef sonne, | Sterre of Grece, charboncle of that contre'). Denys is patron saint of France, and also of archers. Over his tomb was built the great abbey of Saint-Denis; having reputedly carried his head there from Montmartre, guided by an angel, he is invoked against headaches. Olaus Worm, writing in the seventeenth century, states that his day had formerly been the start of the herring-fishing season in Denmark. In symbolic calendars it may be marked with a fish, crosier, or flag.

John Leonardi (*c*.1542–1609), founder of the Clerks Regular of the Mother of God, a congregation of diocesan priests. Feast-day formerly 10 October.

October

My ornaments are fruits; my garments leaves,
    Woven like cloth of gold, and crimson dyed;
I do not boast the harvesting of sheaves,
    O'er orchards and o'er vineyards I preside.
Though on the frigid Scorpion I ride,
    The dreamy air is full, and overflows
With tender memories of the summer-tide,
    And mingled voices of the doves and crows.

Henry Wadsworth Longfellow (1807–82), *The Poet's Calendar*

10 OCTOBER

a.d. VI Idus Octobres   C

❦ HOLIDAYS AND ANNIVERSARIES Fiji: Fiji Day (independence from Great Britain, 1970)
Japan: Health-Sports Day (national holiday)
Kenya: Moi Day
USA, Oklahoma: Oklahoma Historical Day (first white settlers in Oklahoma Territory, 1802)
Taiwan: National Day or Double Tenth Day (proclamation of Chinese Republic, 10/10/1911)

❦ HOLY DAYS Paulinus of York (CY); formerly John Leonardi (see *9 Oct.)

Paulinus of York (d. 644) was sent by Gregory the Great to England in 601 to reinforce St Augustine of Canterbury. Upon the marriage of King Edwin of Northumbria to the Christian Ethelburg of Kent in 625, Paulinus was created bishop of York and converted Edwin and his followers, but upon Edwin's death (see *12 Oct.) he returned with Ethelburg to Kent, where he became bishop of Rochester. The RC Church commemorates him on this day as well.

Gereon (d. *c*.304) and companions, martyrs of Cologne. Gregory of Tours makes him and his companions soldiers of the Theban legion, martyred for being Christian. Their popularity stems from a thirteenth-century legend; warrior saints appear to have been particularly useful in a chivalric age. Like other saints who were beheaded, Gereon is invoked by sufferers of headaches.

Francis Borgia (Francisco Borja, 1510–72). Great-grandson of Pope Alexander VI, he succeeded his father as Duke of Gandía in 1543; after his wife died he resigned in favour of his eldest son and became a Jesuit. He returned to Spain, was ordained, and from 1554 to 1560 was head of the Jesuit provinces of Spain and Portugal. Later he went back to Rome, where he was General of the Society from 1565 till his death and did much to further Jesuit missions in the New World. Under his leadership the Roman College (later Gregorian University) was founded and the church of the Gesù begun. He is a patron saint of Portugal; Benedict XIV declared him patron of Portuguese earthquakes in the year following the devastation of Lisbon in 1755.

Old Michaelmas (1752–99): several Michaelmas fairs are still celebrated on or from this day, known as 'Goose Fairs' or 'Mop Fairs', the latter because Michaelmas was the time for hiring servants and farm labourers. In some places 'Runaway' fairs were held in the following week, originally for those who disliked their new situations.

11 OCTOBER

a.d. V Idus Octobres   D

❦ HOLIDAYS AND ANNIVERSARIES USA, Indiana: General Pulaski Memorial Day (Revolutionary War hero, 1779; Count Kazimierz Pułaski died in 1779 from wounds received at the siege of Savannah on 9 September)

❦ ANCIENT ROME This was the Meditrinalia, on which, after a solemn libation, the new wine was tasted along with the old; it was believed to have curative virtue, attested by the verses recited on this occasion:

Novum vetus vinum bibo,	I drink new and old wine,
novo veteri morbo medeor.	I cure new and old disease.

❦ HOLY DAYS Philip, one of the Seven (Orth.; RC 6 June); formerly Motherhood of Our Lady (RC)

Philip was one of the seven men of honest report appointed to serve at the communal table in Acts 6: 3–6, the first deacons, for *diakonos* means 'servant'; it was also he who baptized Simon Magus and the eunuch treasurer of the Ethiopian queen Candace. He preached along the coast of the Holy Land, and lived at Caesarea Maritima (where Pilate and his successors resided) with four virgin daughters, all prophets in the manner of the early church. In this context he is called 'Philip the evangelist' (Acts 21: 8); he was subsequently identified with the youth bidden to let the dead bury their dead and himself preach the Kingdom of God (Luke 9: 60). Later tradition makes him bishop of Tralles in Lydia.

Tarachus, Probus, and Andronicus, martyrs at Pompeiopolis in Cilicia (304). They were thrown to wild beasts in the amphitheatre, but the beasts refused to eat them; the disappointed spectators began to leave, but the governor blocked the exits and had the prisoners dispatched by gladiators, who were less susceptible to sanctity.

Nectarius, archbishop of Constantinople (397), a father of a family who was named bishop in succession to Gregory of Nazianzus (*25 Jan.) although not baptized; having repaired that omission, he proved a popular bishop, not least for his lavish entertaining. He was remembered the more fondly on this account during the reign of the next bishop, John Chrysostom, who had ruined his stomach with excessive fasting, and who understood full well that praise of his predecessor was intended as censure of himself.

12 OCTOBER

a.d. IV Idus Octobres   E

(HOLIDAYS AND ANNIVERSARIES Canada: Thanksgiving Day (observed on nearest Monday)
Equatorial Guinea: Independence Day (from Spain, 1968)
Spain: National Day

(ANCIENT ROME Fortuna Redux, celebrating Augustus' re-entry into Rome from the East, 19 BC; this day was the last of the Ludi Augustales. (The altar by the Porta Capena, in the precinct of Honos et Virtus, was dedicated on 15 December.)

(HOLY DAYS Wilfrid of Ripon (CY)

Wilfrid, abbot of Ripon, bishop of York, after 705 of Hexham, d. 709. His is still a popular name in Yorkshire, where strong-mindedness is much admired; this was already manifest when as a young man he fell out with his companion Benedict Biscop (see *12 Jan.) at Lyon on the pilgrimage to Rome, where he learnt Dionysius Exiguus' rules for finding Easter. This was one of the subjects of dispute determined at the synod of Whitby in 664, where, speaking on behalf of the West Saxon bishop Æthelberht, he caused the Roman usage to prevail over Celtic in the English Church. When Bishop Colman of Lindisfarne (*18 Feb.) invoked the authority of St Columba, Wilfrid affected not to know whether the Lord would recognize Columba and his followers on the Day of Judgement; but even granted they were holy men who had kept the wrong Easter only out of ignorance, their successors had no such excuse. In any case St Peter was of more account, since the Lord had given him the keys of heaven; at that time 'St Peter' often meant the Pope, but Wilfrid claimed to know how the apostle himself had celebrated Easter. King Oswiu (his head no doubt swimming from the technical arguments) seized on that point, which poor Colman could not deny, and declared that, rather than offend the celestial gatekeeper, he would obey the Roman rules.

Soon afterwards Wilfrid was made bishop of York; refusing to be consecrated by upholders of the Celtic Easter he travelled to Compiègne. During his absence St Chad (*2 Mar.) was elected and consecrated in his place; he was eventually put in possession by Theodore (*19 Sept.), who however divided his see into three parts. The rest of Wilfrid's life is a tale of quarrels with king and fellow-bishops leading to deposition, imprisonment, banishment, and reinstatement. During one period of exile he founded the monastery of Selsey, later removed to Chichester. His life was written by his admiring chanter, Eddius Stephanus; Bede, whose world chronology he had allowed an ignorant monk to call heretical, is noticeably cooler, in particular omitting nearly all his miracles, and in his far fuller account of Whitby, though himself passionately committed to Wilfrid's side, putting some obviously false arguments into his mouth (aptly so, for Wilfrid lies under suspicion of tampering with documents for Dionysius' sake). The RC Church commemorates him on this day as well.

Edwin, son of Ælla, king of Deira and from 616 of all Northumbria, was converted to Christianity by Paulinus (see *10 Oct.) and baptized at Easter 627 along with his council, after a debate in which (as Bede tells the story) the chief priest complained that the heathen gods had given him nothing for all his years of service, and a lay noble likened life on earth to the flight of a bird through the king's hall in winter, a moment of calm between storms; likewise human beings knew something about this life, but nothing about what came before or after it. 'Hence if this new teaching has brought any surer knowledge, it deserves to be followed.' Six years later the Welsh prince Cadwallon, supported by Penda of Mercia—Welsh Christian and English heathen—attacked and defeated him at Hatfield Chase near Doncaster on 12 October 633. His head was taken to St Peter's, York (York Minster), which he had founded; his body, supposedly revealed by miracle, became the focus of a martyr's cult at Whitby.

Our Lady of the Pillar (Nuestra Señora del Pilar). It is said in Spain that while St James (*25 July) was preaching at Zaragoza, he saw a vision of the Virgin and Child, followed by angels carrying a pillar to signify that a church should be built on the spot. She is patron saint of the Spanish Guardia Civil; 'Pilar' is a frequent woman's name in Spain.

Old Georgian manuscripts record a commemoration of the Good Thief (cf. *25 Mar.).

Columbus Day (many countries, observed on different days; in USA observed on second Monday in October). On this day in 1492 the Italian explorer Christopher Columbus, sponsored by Ferdinand of Aragon and Isabella of Castile, made landfall on an island he named San Salvador.

An Irish missionary priest views Columbus Day in Boston in 1870:

Oct. 12 [1870]. This is the anniversary of the discovery of America by Christopher Columbus, and the Italian residents of Boston have celebrated the event with due *éclat*. At 9 o'clock, a.m., a procession of Italians, numbering a hundred, with a band and a banner—the latter representing the landing of Columbus at San Salvador—proceeded through the principal streets, and stopped at the City Hall, where they paid their respects to the mayor, and made him a suitable address. His honor replied appropriately. Will I be accused of hypercriticism if I comment unfavourably upon one passage of his honor's speech, or rather upon a quotation from an American poet, which he adopted.

'If I could have my say', said his honor, 'I would give your illustrious countryman his true deserts, and call our beloved country by its real name—Columbia. I think we could all exclaim in harmonious feelings, in the language of Barlow, the Yankee poet:—

> Columbia, Columbia, to glory arise,
> The queen of the world and the child of the skies.

I only ask, what is the meaning of saying that Columbia is the 'child of the skies'? Were she called 'child of the ocean', there would be sufficient *vraisemblance* in the idea to divest the hearers from too rigid an examination of the words; but 'child of the skies' is too absurd, too inconceivable, or, if conceivable, too prosaic to awaken a poetic sensation. The idea of America, a large continent, falling from the boundless skies, and settling in an ocean small in comparison to the firmament, is an anticlimax annihilative of all poetry.

There was a good deal of cannonading in Boston Common commemorative of the great event, and festivities and convivialities crowned the joyous celebration.   Buckley, 162–3

13 OCTOBER

a.d. III Idus Octobres   F

❦ ANCIENT ROME Fontanalia or Fontinalia: in honour of Fons, god of springs; on that day garlands were cast into springs and placed on well-tops.

❦ HOLY DAYS Edward the Confessor, translated 1163 (CofE, RC England; see also *5 Jan.)

Translation of Edward the Confessor, 1163 (cf. *5 Jan.). Son of Ethelred II and Emma of Normandy, who became King on the extinction of Cnut's line in 1042 and ruled with some skill, except when he tried to break the greatest magnate of the realm, his father-in-law, Earl Godwin. A mighty huntsman, remembered in Scandinavia as a king of valiant warriors, he rebuilt St Peter's monastery outside London, known as 'Westminster' by contrast with St Paul's to the east. Known as a good man, that is not bloodthirsty, and credited with healing powers, he acquired a reputation for piety; the legend that his marriage to Godwin's daughter Edith was chaste from the outset (for a like tale see *3 Mar.) is not supported by the first book of the *Vita Ædwardi regis*, completed just after his death by an author in Edith's confidence, nor by the testimony of other persons who might have known the truth, but it suited Westminster schemes for making a saint of him, and assuaged regret that Edith had not borne a son to inherit the kingdom. On his succession by Godwin's son Harold, Duke William of Normandy asserted (with what truth is still disputed) that King Edward had made him his heir in 1051, and that Harold had subsequently sworn to support him; the claim was made good at the battle of Hastings. In Domesday Book pre-Conquest conditions are registered as *TRE* (*tempore regis Edwardi*, 'in King Edward's time'), Harold's usurpation being ignored; but the English also looked back on his reign as a golden age. His translation, one day before the anniversary of Hastings, marked a stage in the national fusion of Norman and Saxon.

14 OCTOBER

❦ HOLY DAYS Callistus I (RC)

Pope Callistus I (mart. *c.*222); his name, the Greek *Kallistos* ('Handsomest'), was commonly corrupted to Calixtus. As a youth (and slave), he worked in a sort of bank, and lost the money deposited with him; after many adventures he returned to Rome and was elected pope, whereupon he was attacked by St Hippolytus for believing, inter alia, that commission of mortal sin was not in itself sufficient reason for deposing a bishop. According to some, he died after being thrown down a well during a popular uprising. In Norway, where his day was the beginning of winter ('Winternight'), he is represented on primestaves with a leafless tree, a papal staff, or a mitten; this last, though derived from the papal glove, also symbolizes winter, for the old plural of *vott*, 'mitten', is *vetter*, which in some dialects is also the word for winter.

Battle of Hastings, 1066, in which Harold Godwinson king of England was killed and the entire kingdom conquered by William duke of Normandy. John Gibbon, Bluemantle Pursuivant at the College of Heralds and an erudite ass wrongly claimed as great-great-uncle by the historian, wrote a treatise, *Day-Fatality: or Some Observations on Days Lucky and Unlucky* (London, 1678, rev. edn. 1686), designed to show that this was England's lucky day, as the date of the Norman conquest, Edward III's safe return after taking Calais despite a storm at sea in 1347, the Peace of Brétigny in 1360, and the birth in 1633 of James duke of York, afterwards James II. In fact, Edward III returned on 12 October, the 14th being his entry into London; the treaty of Brétigny was concluded on 8 May and ratified 24 October; other factual errors abound, as that Saturday was Henry VII's lucky day, because he defeated Richard III at Bosworth on 22 August 1485 and entered the City on the 29th. Tradition had it so (see **Week: Saturday*), but both days that year were Mondays. Scarcely less remarkable are the Tory sentiments and the gestures towards James's religion: the aggressive Counter-Reformers Sixtus V and Carlo Borromeo are praised, Becket is called a saint and not a traitor. These views are expressed not merely in the second edition, when James was king, but even in the first, when he was under concerted attack, and are the sincere opinions of the author, of whom we read:

He never received further promotion, as he injured himself by his arrogance towards his less learned superiors in the college, whose shortcomings he had an unpleasant habit of registering in the margins of the library books, which he also filled with calculations of his own nativity. He firmly believed his destiny so fixed by the stars which presided at his birth that good or ill behaviour could never alter it.   *DNB*

At the Revolution he was suspended until he could bring himself to swear allegiance to the king who had upset not only his principles but his predictions.

The work is prefaced (p. 4) by a letter from Sir Winston Churchill (father of Marlborough), who observes that Friday had always been his lucky day, on which he was born, christened, married, and knighted, 'and, I believe, will be the Day of my Death'; alas, he died on Monday, 26 March 1688 OS.

In Russia on this day (*1 Oct. OS) is celebrated the Protecting Veil of the Theotokos; the so-called St Basil's in Moscow (see *2 Aug.) is properly the Cathedral of the Protection (*Pokróvskiĭ sobór*), to which in 1554 Ivan the Terrible dedicated a wooden church commemorating his conquest of Kazan'. It stands to the south of *Krásnaya plóshchad'*, so called long before the Communist interlude and meaning not 'Red Square' but 'Beautiful Square', 'Fair Place'.

15 OCTOBER

Idus Octobres   A

❦ ANCIENT ROME *October equus.* The right-hand horse of the winning pair in a race for two-horse chariots was sacrificed to Mars in the Campus Martius; its head was fought over by the inhabitants of the Subura (who sought to nail it to the Turris Mamilia) and the Via Sacra (who intended it for a wall of the Regia), but the tail was whisked off at top speed to the Regia so that the blood could drip onto the hearth. The popular explanation, discounted by the experts, was that the Romans, as descendants of the Trojans, were taking vengeance on the Wooden Horse; but horse sacrifices were known in several ancient cities.

❦ HOLY DAYS Teresa of Ávila (CY, RC)

Teresa of Ávila (1515–82), foundress of the Discalced Carmelites. She joined a rather relaxed Carmelite house in 1535, and only in 1555 was converted to stricter observance while praying before a statue of Christ being scourged. From that point she began to experience ecstasies, vividly portrayed by Bernini in his sculpture-group of St Teresa and the Spear-Bearing Angel in S. Maria della Vittoria in Rome. Her desire to found a stricter Carmelite house met with great opposition, but she succeeded in 1562; the 'Discalced

Carmelites' (who wear sandals instead of shoes), for both men and women, resulted. In her convent of St Joseph in Ávila she wrote her spiritual autobiography, a manual for her nuns, *The Way of Perfection*, and numerous other works, including poetry. Forceful and capable as an administrator, she was also a mystic writer of the first importance.

She was declared a Doctor of the Church in 1970. Paul VI named her patron of Spanish Catholic writers in 1965 as a model to be followed. In 1961 she became patron of the Spanish Military Commissariat.

> *Upon the Book and Picture of the Seraphicall Saint Teresa*
>
> O thou vndaunted daughter of desires!
> By all thy dowr of Lights & Fires;
> By all the eagle in thee, all the doue;
> By all thy liues & deaths of loue;
> By thy larg draughts of intellectuall day,
> And by thy thirsts of loue more large than they;
> By all thy brim-fill'd Bowles of feirce desire,
> By thy last Morning's draught of liquid fire;
> By the full kingdome of that finall kisse
> That seiz'd thy parting Soul, & seal'd thee his;
> By all the heav'ns thou hast in him
> (Fair sister of the Seraphim!);
> By all of Him we haue in Thee;
> Leaue nothing of my Self in me.
> Let me so read thy life, that I
> Vnto all life of mine may dy.
>
> Richard Crashaw (*c*.1613–49), from *The Flaming Heart*

Samuel Isaac Joseph Schereschewsky (1831–1906), Episcopalian bishop of Shanghai, a dedicated missionary who translated the Bible into several Chinese dialects, which over many years he typed with the one finger that had not been paralysed by a stroke. Some Anglican communities have, unofficially, made him patron of the Internet.

On this day in 70 BC (the Ides of October, Gnaeus Pompeius and Marcus Licinius Crassus being consuls) was born the poet Vergil.

16 OCTOBER

a.d. XVII Kalendas Novembres   B

❦ HOLY DAYS Hedwig (RC); Margaret Mary Alacoque (RC); Richard Gwyn (RC Wales); Longinus (Orth.; see *15 Mar.)

Hedwig (*c*.1174–1243). She was born at Andechs (Bavaria) and was the aunt of St Elizabeth of Hungary (see *17 Nov.). Educated by Benedictine nuns, at the age of 12 she married the duke of Silesia and together with him helped spread Christianity in the kingdom of Poland. Her birthplace, where some of her relics are preserved, is a place of pilgrimage.

Margaret Mary Alacoque (1647–90). Childhood illness kept her confined to bed for years, but in 1671 she became a Visitandine at Paray-le-Monial, rising to become Assistant Superior. A series of visions (1673–5) revealed to her the form of devotion to the Sacred Heart; not formally recognized until 1765, it became one of the most popular devotions of the eighteenth and nineteenth centuries. Feast-day formerly the 17th.

Richard Gwyn (1537–84), a native of Llanidloes, Powys, educated at Cambridge. Executed in 1584, he is one of the Forty Martyrs of England and Wales.

Gallus, b. *c.*550 in Ireland. A monk at Bangor, he accompanied Columban (*23 Nov.) to France *c.*590, and then to present-day Switzerland; after many adventures with hostile natives, Columban went on to Italy, but Gallus, who had fallen ill, founded a hermitage on the Steinach, to which, having successively refused the bishopric of Konstanz and the abbacy of Columban's foundation at Luxeuil, he returned in 625 with twelve companions, governing them in accordance with Columban's rule. He died on 16 October 645; his foundation, which *c.*720 adopted the milder Rule of St Benedict, became the great monastery of Sankt Gallen or Saint-Gall. Legend has it that he caught a bear about to eat his dinner and sent it off to fetch firewood; his portraits sometimes show the bear returning with its load. The saint himself is represented with a pilgrim's staff and a loaf of bread, or as a hermit with a simple cross. Where two bishops had failed, Gallus freed a girl from an evil spirit that departed in the form of a black bird (perhaps a crow). He is patron of poultry because *gallus* is Latin for a cock, and of geese. Olaus Worm marks him with an axe, 'for then one must hang up one's nets and attend to the slaughter of cattle'.

Dedication of Mont-Saint-Michel, commemorating St Michael's apparition (see *29 Sept.). In medieval calendars called 'the feast of St Michael in *Monte Tumba*'.

17 OCTOBER

a.d. XVI Kalendas Novembres   C

❡ HOLY DAYS Etheldreda (Audrey) (BCP, properly her translation; CY *23 June); Ignatius of Antioch (CY, RC since 1969); formerly Margaret Mary Alacoque (see *16 Oct.)

Translation of Audrey, formerly celebrated by a fair at which 'tawdry' lace was sold; for the reduction of *Saint* to its final consonant before a vowel, cf. 'tantony' (St Antony, *17 Jan.) and the local pronunciation of St Osyth (see *7 Oct.). This had a certain appropriateness, since she had reportedly accepted the painful swelling of her neck in her last illness as just punishment for having in her youth frivolously weighed it down with necklaces; though that is the kind of thing that saints are expected to say.

She hath given name to a Causeway in the Isle of *Ely*, where there is a Fair kept, and much ordinary Lace sold there, which makes the Country Girls seem finer than they are, whence the word Taudry came.   Dove (1697)

Ignatius, bishop of Antioch, conveyed under guard to Rome during the reign of the emperor Trajan (98–117). The letters he wrote en route (six to various churches, one to St Polycarp of Smyrna, see *23 Feb.) demonstrate his exalted view of the episcopal office and his ardent desire for martyrdom (he urges the Church at Rome not to intercede on his behalf); his wish was granted, as tradition has it in the Amphitheatrum Flavium (as the Romans called the Colosseum), his relics being preserved at San Clemente. He was also called Theophóros, 'God-bearer', which being misinterpreted as Theóphoros, 'God-borne', led to his identification in pious legend with the child that Jesus held in his arms at Capernaum (Mark 9: 36). His letters attest the monarchical episcopacy at an earlier date than the sixteenth-century Reformers cared to contemplate; accordingly Protestants denied their authenticity and Roman Catholics defended it, till in 1672 the Anglican Bishop Pearson definitively distinguished the genuine and the spurious matter in them. Feast-day formerly 1 February; since 1969 the RC Church has honoured him on the traditional Antiochene date of 17 October; the Orthodox do so on 20 December.

Justus of Beauvais (d. 287), supposedly a 9-year-old boy martyr whose bones were 'rediscovered' in the early eleventh century by a trafficker in bogus relics; the rogue took in not only the faithful peasantry but also Ulric-Manfred, marquess of Turin, who coveted them for a monastery he was then building (San Giusto di Susa). Rodulfus Glaber, a contemporary chronicler, puts the story in his *Histories* as a warning against fraudulent relic-mongers. He places the translation on 17 October, but Justus' date in the *Acta Sanctorum* is 18 October.

At dead of night, in his usual way, he dug out the bones of some obscure man from their humble grave, put them in a box on a bier, and said that by an angelic vision a holy martyr, Justus by name, had (as he pretended) been revealed to him. Soon the vulgar crowd and the idle amongst the rustic population came flocking together at the news, as they are wont to do in such cases, even regretting if they had no illness from which they could ask to be cured. They brought the sick, gave miserable little presents, and kept watch all night expecting sudden miracles . . .

    Meanwhile Manfred, wealthiest of the marquesses, hearing news of this business, sent some of his men to seize and bring back to him the pretended relic which people were worshipping, believing it to be that of the venerable martyr. The marquess had begun the construction of a monastery at Susa, the oldest of the Alpine towns, which was to be dedicated to God Almighty and His Mother, the ever-Virgin Mary; he wanted the supposed martyr to be placed there along with the relics of many other saints after the completion of the work. After a while, when the work on the church was finished and the day of consecration fixed, he invited the neighbouring bishops; with them came Abbot William (of whom we have so often spoken) and some other abbots. The pedlar was also present; he was held in high esteem by the marquess because he had promised that soon he would reveal far more precious relics of saints, whose acts, names, and passions he used to invent just as he invented all the rest. When some learned elders asked him how he had come by such knowledge, he made loud protestations of an unconvincing kind. Now I was there, having travelled in the company of the abbot. The pedlar said: 'An angel appears to me at night and he teaches and tells me all that he knows I wish to learn. He stays with me until I force him to go.' When we replied by asking whether he saw all this while he was awake or asleep, he added: 'Almost every night the angel snatches me from my bed without my wife's knowing; after a long conversation he leaves, saluting and embracing me.' We knew this for a polished and cunning lie, for this creature was no frequenter of angels, but rather a minister of treachery and evil.

The bishops, while celebrating duly the rite of consecration for which they had come, put the bones discovered by that cunning impostor in with the other relics of saints, to the great joy of both kinds of people [clergy and laity] who had gathered there in large numbers. All this happened on 17 October. This date was chosen because the partisans of this pretended relic asserted that these were the bones of St Justus, who suffered martyrdom on that day in the city of Beauvais in Gaul. His head was taken to Auxerre, where he was born and bred, and is kept there. I, who knew the truth of the matter, treated what they said as rubbish. The more discerning recognized this as a trick and supported what I said. The following night some of the monks and other religious saw monstrous visions in the church, black Ethiopians coming out of the box in which the bones were kept and leaving the church. Although many men of sound judgement denounced the detestable invention as an abomination, the mass of the rustic population, corrupted by the pedlar, venerating the name of the unjust for Justus persisted for a long time in their error. We have recounted all this to give a warning against the many deceits of demons and men which abound all over the world, especially in springs and trees that are rashly venerated by the sick.   Glaber, 181–5

18 OCTOBER

On Saint Luke's day
the oxen have leave to play.

San Luca, El ton va in te la zuca
(Venetian saying: 'pumpkins go stale')

❦ HOLIDAYS AND ANNIVERSARIES USA, Alaska: Alaska Day (transfer from Russia to USA, 1867)

❦ ANCIENT ROME In AD 17 restoration work was completed on the temple of Janus near the theatre of Marcellus, originally built during the First Punic War; the dedication-day, previously 17 August, became 18 October.

❦ HOLY DAYS **Luke the Evangelist** (CofE, RC); red-letter day

Luke, 'the beloved physician' (Col. 4: 14), companion of St Paul, and author of the third Gospel and (as almost universally agreed) the Acts of the Apostles. He was not one of Jesus' original followers, but a highly educated Gentile convert, certainly the best Greek stylist in the New Testament; he is credibly said to have come from Antioch, the Greek city where the word *Christianós* was first coined (he is well informed about the Church there). His profession is evident in his description of Christ's healing miracles, in which he uses the correct medical terminology. Of all the evangelists, he shows the most human insight into the characters whom he describes, and has the most to say about the Virgin; in particular it is he who relates the Visitation, the Annunciation, and the Purification. Later tradition, beginning from the controversies over icons in eighth-century Byzantium, made him a painter, especially of Christ (of whom he reputedly painted an icon for his dedicatee Theophilus) and the Virgin; from the eleventh century extant icons were attributed to him, beginning with the Hodigítria, the Virgin of the Hodigón monastery at Constantinople. He was also credited with the friezes of the Parthenon, dedicated to Mary since the sixth century. The tradition reached Rome, where several images were said to be his handiwork, and spread thence to important towns and cities along the main pilgrim routes; he was sometimes credited with painting Christ's image for St Veronica (see *4 Feb.). He is patron of physicians, surgeons, painters, and notaries. His symbol, the ox, has made him patron of butchers; it has also, through the post-classical implication of horns, caused him to be associated with cuckolds, even though according to Jerome he never had wife or children.

St Luke's little summer: a period of warm weather following cold; cf. St Martin's summer (*11 Nov.) and the halcyon days (*14 Dec.).

St Luke's Day fair, Charlton, Kent, as described by Daniel Defoe:

Charlton is noted for the Fair held in its Neighbourhood on St. *Luke's* Day, *Octob.* 18, called *Hornfair*; the Rudeness of which, in a civilized, well-governed Nation, may well be said to be unsufferable. The Mob at that time take all kinds of Liberties, and the Women are eminently impudent that Day; as if it was a time that justified the giving themselves a Loose to all manner of Indecency without any Reproach, or without incurring the Censure which such Behaviour would deserve at another.

And this in a Circumstance, which (far from being to be gloried in) ought to be discountenanced by the Sex, as fixing the Brand of Incontinence on too many of them, which they have little Reason to be proud of.

A vulgar Tradition gives the following Origin to this disorderly Fair; namely, That one of the Kings of *England*, some say King *John*, who had a Palace in this Neighbourhood, at *Eltham*, being hunting near *Charlton*, then a pitiful Hamlet only, and separated from his Attendants, entered into a Cottage, and found the Mistress of it alone; and she being handsome, the King took a Liking to her; and, having prevailed over her Modesty, just in the critical Moment her Husband came in; and, threatening to kill them both, the King was forced to discover himself, and to compound with Gold for his Safety, giving the Man moreover all the Land from thence as far as the Place now called *Cuckold's Point*; and, making him Master of the whole Hamlet, established a Fair in favour of his new Demesne; and in Memory thereof, Horns, and Wares and Toys of all Sorts made of Horn, are sold at this Fair.   Defoe, i. 134–5

Whip-dog day in York:

St. *Luke's* day is also known in *York* by the name of *whip-dog-day*, from a strange custom that school-boys use here of whipping all the dogs that are seen in the streets that day. Whence this uncommon persecution took its rise is uncertain: yet, though it is certainly very old, I am not of opinion with some that it is as antient as the *Romans*. The tradition that I have heard of its origin seems very probable, that in times of popery, a priest celebrating mass at this festival in some church in *York*, unfortunately dropped the *pax* after consecration; which was snatched up suddenly and swallowed by a dog that laid under the altar table. The profanation of this high mystery occasioned the death of the dog, and a persecution begun and has since continued, on this day, to be severely carried on against his whole tribe in our city.   Drake, 219

19 OCTOBER

❦ HOLY DAYS Paul of the Cross (RC); John de Brébeuf and Isaac Jogues (RC); Henry Martyn (CY)

Paul of the Cross (1694–1775), founder of the Passionists, an order devoted to the Passion of our Lord, approved in 1741. He was famous as a preacher and miracle-worker. Feast-day formerly 28 April.

John de Brébeuf and Isaac Jogues and companions, also known as the 'North American Martyrs'. Named the patron saints of Canada in 1940, they were John de Brébeuf, Isaac Jogues, Antony Daniel, Gabriel Lalemand, Charles Garnier, Noel Chabanel, René Goupil, and John Lalande, canonized in 1930. All were French Jesuits; Canada was a French colony at the time they undertook their missionary work, in the seventeenth century. The hardships they endured in the Canadian wilderness, living among Indian tribes (principally the Hurons), were nothing compared with the gruesome tortures they underwent when captured by the Hurons' traditional enemies, the Iroquois.

Henry Martyn (1781–1812), Anglican missionary in India and Persia. At the age of 24 he went to India as chaplain of the East India Company. In the remainder of his short life he translated the New Testament into Hindustani, Persian, and Arabic, the BCP into Hindustani, and the Psalms into Persian.

Frideswide, patron saint of the city and University of Oxford, d. 727. She was a Mercian princess who (it was said), having vowed perpetual chastity, refused to make a dynastic marriage but fled to Oxford, where she founded a nunnery. The town grew up around her shrine; a priory, or monastery church, in her name was reputedly burnt down in 1102 when the local Danes took refuge there during the St Brice Day massacre (see *13 Nov.), being rebuilt by Ethelred II. It was originally occupied by secular clerks, a practice that fell into disfavour after the Norman conquest; by 1122 it belonged to Austin canons. St Frideswide's supposed relics were translated on 12 February 1180 (and again in 1289); her shrine became a place of pilgrimage, solemnly visited twice a year by the university, whose patroness she was declared by Archbishop Chichele in 1434. The monastery was suppressed in 1525 when Wolsey was planning his new 'Cardinal's College', which after his fall was partially realized as 'King's College' and in 1546 renamed Christ Church; the church took the place of the suppressed Osney Abbey as the cathedral of the Oxford diocese (created four years earlier). The shrine had been despoiled in 1538, but her purported bones were reburied on the site. Close by, in 1553, was buried Catherine Dammartin, the first wife of the Protestant reformer and Regius Professor of Divinity Peter Martyr or Pietro Martire Vermigli; under Mary, St Frideswide's remains were exhumed and placed in silk bags, Catherine's also exhumed but cast out on a dunghill. In 1561, at the north-east end of the cathedral, Canon James Calfhill solemnly reburied the two sets of relics so commingled as nevermore to be told apart: 'Here lies true religion with superstition.'

At St Margaret's church in Binsey, near Oxford, there is a well that legend associated with Frideswide; it is said that, pursued by her suitor Ælfgar, she prayed for deliverance to St Margaret of Antioch, who blinded him with a flash of lightning and cured him of his lust; when Frideswide prayed again that he should be healed, a spring burst forth, in which she bathed his eyes. It is said to be the origin of Lewis Carroll's treacle well.

20 OCTOBER

a.d. XIII Kalendas Novembres   F

❲ HOLY DAYS Formerly St John Cantius (RC, now *23 Dec.)

Bertilla Boscardin (1888–1922). Overcoming the low opinion of her parish priest as to her suitability for a religious vocation, she entered the convent of the Sisters of St Dorothy at Vicenza at the age of 16. However, she was always assigned to kitchen tasks, until she was allowed to train as a nurse in Treviso; even so she could not escape the pots and pans until she made her profession in 1907. She then devoted herself to nursing sick children, and acted heroically during the First World War in protecting her patients. She herself became seriously ill and died three days after surgery. Miracles were attested at her grave in Treviso and then her tomb in Vicenza; she was canonized in 1961.

October

Bending above the spicy woods which blaze,
Arch skies so blue they flash, and hold the sun
Immeasurably far; the waters run
Too slow, so freighted are the river-ways
With gold of elms and birches from the maze
Of forests. Chestnuts, clicking one by one,
Escape from satin burs; her fringes done,
The gentian spreads them out in sunny days,
And, like late revelers at dawn, the chance
Of one sweet, mad, last hour, all things assail,
And conquering, flush and spin; while, to enhance
The spell, by sunset door, wrapped in a veil

Of red and purple mists, the summer, pale,
Steals back alone for one more song and dance.

Helen Hunt Jackson (1830–85)

21 OCTOBER

a.d. XII Kalendas Novembres   G

❦ HOLIDAYS AND ANNIVERSARIES Marshall Islands: Compact Day (Compact of
Free Association between the USA and the Republic of the Marshall Islands,
1986) (national day)

❦ HOLY DAYS

Hilarion (*c.*291–371). A hermit of extreme asceticism, he spent two months with St
Antony in the Egyptian desert before returning to his native Palestine. His fame as a
miracle-worker soon spread, forcing him to flee to the desert to escape the crowds of
visitors. He lived to the age of 80 despite (or because of) his diet, detailed in Dove's
almanac for 1699 after Jerome's life of the saint:

> his clothing was Sackcloth, and which he never shifted [i.e. changed; but Jerome says 'washed']
> so long as it would last, and over that a skin which S. *Anthony* had given him; his Food, which he
> never took till Sun-set, was dry figs, and juice of herbs; for 6 years his dayly food was only a pint
> of Lentiles, softned in cold water, the next 3 years he eat dry bread with salt and water, the next
> 3 years wild herbs, and the roots of young plants, the next 5 years 6 ounces of Barley-bread and
> a little Colewort; after he was 35 years old, perceiving himself decay, he was forced to add a lit-
> tle Oyl to his former diet, and so he continued till 63 years, and then left off eating bread. Under
> *Julian* they would have put him to death, but he fled, and lurking up and down, at last died.

Ursula (formerly St Ursula and the 11,000 Virgins). Around AD 400 there was a church
in Cologne on the site of some virgins' martyrdom; in the eighth century we hear of
several thousand, led by one Pinnosa. Subsequent accounts vary between a few and a
great many; one calendar lists eleven names, headed by Ursula. By the early tenth century these eleven, including Ursula, had become 11,000 excluding her; the notion that
'XI M.V.', supposedly *undecim martyres virgines*, 'eleven virgin martyrs', was misinterpreted
as *undecim milia virginum*, 'eleven thousand virgins', is as implausible as the rationalization
that gives her a companion Undecimilla, but $\overline{\text{XI}}$ might have been taken for 11,000. In
any case, 11,000 quickly became canonical, being apparently confirmed by the discovery
of a burial-ground in 1106. Ursula became a British princess who, having vowed perpetual virginity, evaded a match with the heathen Aetherius by demanding his conversion to Christianity and a three-year wait. Obtaining from her father ten noble
companions and 1,000 (surely 999?) attendants each for herself and them, she set sail;
after several adventures the party arrived in Rome. Pope Cyriac, the nineteenth after St
Peter, having had a vision that he would be martyred with the virgins, abdicated after

reigning one year and eleven weeks to accompany them on their return, naming one Ametos his successor. The disgusted clergy erased his name from the records; two pagan officers betrayed the pilgrims to their kinsman Julius, ruler of the Huns currently besieging Cologne. They slaughtered the 11,000 but reserved Ursula for Julius; refusing his commands, she was slain by an arrow, whereupon 11,000 angels appeared and drove away the Huns (which must be why no such siege is known to history). The events were dated 238, which not even Jacobus de Voragine could believe; but there may be a confused recollection that in 235 Pope Pontianus (see *13 Aug.) abdicated before his deportation to the mines and was succeeded by Anteros, the nineteenth pope by the inclusive count. Marked in primestaves with an arrow, or a ring, taken to mean that no task performed with wheels, such as spinning or grinding, was to be done on her day.

Trafalgar Day, commemorating Nelson's victory over the French and Spanish fleets in 1805, purchased at the price of his own death.

22 OCTOBER

a.d. XI Kalendas Novembres   A

❦ HOLIDAYS AND ANNIVERSARIES Vatican City and Holy See: Anniversary of the installation of John Paul II (1978)

❦ HOLY DAYS
Seven Holy Children (Orth.; see *27 July)

Mary Salome, one of the three Marys, wife of Zebedee, and mother of St James the Greater and St John the Evangelist. She asked Jesus that her two sons might sit, 'the one on thy right hand, and the other on the left, in thy kingdom' (Matt. 20: 21), witnessed the Crucifixion (Matt. 27: 56), and with the other Marys found his empty tomb on Easter morning (Mark 16: 1–8).

Philip, Severus, Eusebius, and Hermes, martyred in 304. Philip was bishop of Heraclea on the Black Sea, Severus his deacon; Eusebius and Hermes were of the inferior clergy. Arrested under Diocletian, they refused to hand over sacred books and were burnt at Adrianople (now Edirne). Knowledge of the case is derived, not from the improving tales of a later age, but from a record of the proceedings.

Donatus of Fiesole (d. 876), an Irish monk who while returning home from a pilgrimage to Rome *c.*829 happened to pass through Fiesole while the people were assembled in the square to elect a new bishop; the bells starting to ring at his appearance, he was chosen, remaining as bishop till his death. He was devoted to St Brigid, of whom he wrote a life, and founded a hospice for Irish pilgrims.

Cordula, one of St Ursula's 11,000 virgins, hid while the rest were being martyred, but emerged the next day to share their fate. Many years later, she appeared to a nun with instructions that she should be culted the day after the rest.

According to James Ussher, Archbishop of Armagh, God created the world on this day in 4004 BC at 6 p.m.; by ecclesiastical reckoning this is the beginning of Sunday the 23rd. On that basis the luminaries were created on the 26th, Adam and Eve on the 28th. All these dates are Old Style.

23 OCTOBER

❡ HOLIDAYS AND ANNIVERSARIES Hungary: Anniversary of Declaration of Independence, 1956
   Thailand: Chulalongkorn Day (death of King Chulalongkorn, 1910)

❡ HOLY DAYS John of Capistrano (RC); James the brother of the Lord (Orth.; see *11 May); formerly St Anthony Mary Claret (now *24 Oct.)

John of Capistrano (1386–1456). While a Franciscan friar he was appointed governor of Perugia by King Ladislaus of Naples; he married, but after being taken prisoner by the Malatesta reconsidered his life, was dispensed of his marriage, and rejoined the Franciscans. Active in reforming his order, he also undertook missions to convert the Hussites and even raised an army against the Turks. In Capistrano, California, swallows traditionally depart on this day from his mission. John Paul II named him patron saint of military chaplains in 1984. Feast-day formerly 28 March.

Anicius Manlius Severinus Boethius (*c.*480–*c.*525) was born into a senatorial family at a time when imperial rule was no longer exercised over Italy, but the upper class lived as comfortably as ever under Germanic kings, first Odoacer, and after 493 Theoderic the Ostrogoth. Boethius rose in public life, becoming consul in 510 and master of the offices in 522. In this latter post he lost favour with Theoderic for protecting his senatorial friends against royal officials, and was suspected of treasonable correspondence with Constantinople; he was imprisoned, tortured, and executed. A man of great learning, he set out to preserve in Latin all the higher disciplines that had traditionally been read and taught in Greek: his writings on logic, arithmetic, and music became classics in the Middle Ages, but the treatises on geometry and astronomy that Gerbert of Aurillac (the future Pope Sylvester II) claims to have seen at Bobbio are lost. He also wrote theological tractates, including one that prepared eventual Western acceptance of the statement that Christ was 'of two natures', hitherto considered Monophysite, as well as 'in two natures' as laid down at Chalcedon in 451. His greatest and most famous work, however, is the *Consolation of Philosophy*, written while he was in prison; the absence of explicit reference to Christianity has caused some modern readers to regard it as a pagan work, reflecting disillusion with his previous religion, but others observe that there is nothing incompatible with Christianity, and Chadwick has detected some hints that could be recognized by Christians without offending pagans. Unlike the technical writings, it still speaks to modern readers concerned with the problem of accounting for evil in a world governed by providence, and of responding wisely to their own undeserved sufferings.

Having died a Catholic under an Arian king, Boethius was regarded as a martyr, even though at no time was he invited, or commanded, to adopt the king's religion. The religious element was, however, as Chadwick has shown, inseparable from the charge of treason. Under the emperor Justin (518–27), Constantinople had returned from its Monophysite flirtations to communion with Rome, thus providing the Catholics of Italy with another focus of secular loyalty than their Arian king. In 525 Justin—or rather his nephew Justinian, the power behind the throne—instituted a persecution of Arians designed to provoke Theoderic into taking counter-measures; these in their turn induced more Catholics to see their protector in the emperor and not the king. If Boethius had not already been executed, his death was now assured; Justinian will have foreseen it, and found it useful. For that reason his martyr's cult at Pavia, confirmed in 1883 by Pope Leo XIII, is well grounded; his day, however, is properly that of Severinus of Cologne (said to have seen St Martin's soul being borne to heaven in 397). His shrine in the crypt of San Pietro in Ciel d'Oro, directly below St Augustine, is mentioned by Dante; it was restored in 1921, six hundred years after the poet's death.

According to Olaus Worm, this is the day for ploughing rye-fields.

24 OCTOBER

a.d. IX Kalendas Novembres   C

(HOLIDAYS AND ANNIVERSARIES United Nations Day (Charter, 1954)
    Zambia: Independence Day (from Federation of Rhodesia and Nyasaland, 1964)

(HOLY DAYS Anthony Mary Claret (RC); formerly Raphael the Archangel (see *29 Sept.)

Anthony Mary Claret (1807–70). Of Catalan origin, upon ordination he undertook missionary work, forming the Missionary Sons of the Immaculate Heart of Mary (Claretians). Later he became bishop of Santiago de Cuba, where he narrowly escaped assassination at the hands of a man whose mistress he had converted. Returning to Spain in 1857, he became confessor of Queen Isabella II and went into exile with her during the revolution of 1868. His contribution to education extended to establishing a science laboratory and natural history museum, as well as schools of language and music. Feast-day formerly 23 October.

Last Week in October

The trees are undressing, and fling in many places—
On the gray road, the roof, the window-sill—
Their radiant robes and ribbons and yellow laces;
A leaf each second so is flung at will,
Here, there, another and another, still and still.

A spider's web has caught one while downcoming,
That stays there dangling when the rest pass on;
Like a suspended criminal hangs he, mumming
In golden garb, while one yet green, high yon,
Trembles, as fearing such a fate for himself anon.

Thomas Hardy (1840–1928)

25 OCTOBER

a.d. VIII Kalendas Novembres   D

❦ HOLIDAYS AND ANNIVERSARIES Kazakhstan: Republic Day
  Taiwan: Retrocession Day (restoration by Japanese to China, 1945)
  Virgin Islands: Thanksgiving Day (end of the hurricane season)

❦ HOLY DAYS Crispin and Crispinian (CofE); Forty Martyrs of England and Wales (RC England); Six Welsh Martyrs and Companions (RC Wales)

Crispin and Crispinian (d. *c*.285). Roman martyrs, although the translation of their relics to Soissons made them more famous in France; St Eligius rebuilt their shrine. An English tradition has it that they came to England and worked at Faversham in Preston Street, a site of pilgrimage as late as the seventeenth century. They are patrons of shoemakers and all those who work with leather.

The battle of Agincourt was fought on this day in 1415:

This day is called the Feast of Crispian.
He that outlives this day and comes safe home
Will stand a-tiptoe when this day is named
And rouse him at the name of Crispian.
He that shall see this day and live t'old age
Will yearly on the vigil feast his neighbours
And say, 'Tomorrow is Saint Crispian.'
Then will he strip his sleeve and show his scars
And say, 'These wounds I had on Crispin's day.'
Old men forget; yet all shall be forgot,

> But he'll remember, with advantages,
> What feats he did that day. Then shall our names,
> Familiar in his mouth as household words—
> Harry the King, Bedford and Exeter,
> Warwick and Talbot, Salisbury and Gloucester—
> Be in their flowing cups freshly remembered.
> This story shall the good man teach his son,
> And Crispin Crispian shall ne'er go by
> From this day to the ending of the world
> But we in it shall be rememberèd,
> We few, we happy few, we band of brothers.
>
> King Harry, in *Henry V*, IV. iii. 40–60

Dr Johnson commented, in his edition:

It may be observed that we are apt to promise to ourselves a more lasting memory than the changing state of human things admits. This prediction is not verified; the feast of Crispin passes by without any mention of Agincourt. Late events obliterate the former: the civil wars have left in this nation scarcely any tradition of more ancient history.   Johnson, *Shakespeare*, ii. 557

Although the name Agincourt is still recognized, whereas St Crispin's day would be entirely forgotten but for this speech, Johnson's general statement is true; however, there is one noble exception. The poet Horace concluded his first collection of odes (bks. 1–3), probably in 23 BC, with the prediction that his renown among posterity would be renewed so long as the Pontifex climbed the Capitol with the silent Vestal Virgin:

> usque ego postera
> crescam laude recens, dum Capitolium
> scandet cum tacita virgine pontifex.

Pontifex and Virgin have ceased to climb, but the fame of Horace lives.

26 OCTOBER

a.d. VII Kalendas Novembres   E

❦ HOLIDAYS AND ANNIVERSARIES Austria: National Day (national holiday)

❦ ANCIENT ROME First day of Ludi Victoriae Sullanae, celebrating Sulla's victory over the Samnites at the Colline Gate in 82 BC, which saved Rome from her vengeful allies, turned enemies (as Roman writers do not conceal) by long years of ill-usage; they continued till 1 November, the anniversary of the battle. They were instituted the very next year, in 81 BC, as Ludi Victoriae; 'Sullanae' was added after Caesar had founded his own victory games in 46 BC.

❦ HOLY DAYS Alfred the Great (CY); Demetrius (Orth.); Cedd (CY commem.)

Alfred the Great, fifth and youngest son of Æthelwulf king of Wessex, who, not expecting that he would become king, did not give him an 'Æthel' name like his brothers, but called him Ælfred, 'counselled by the elves'; but natural mortality and Viking war had eliminated them all by 871. Almost immediately, Alfred was compelled to fight the invaders against overwhelming odds and buy them off; when a few years later, having conquered Northumbria and East Anglia and put a tame king in charge of Mercia, they set about subjugating Wessex, Alfred rallied his forces at Athelney in 878, defeated the enemy at Edington, besieged the Viking stronghold, and starved it into surrender. Their leader, Guthrum, became a Christian, Alfred himself being his sponsor; Wessex remained untroubled for fourteen years, during which Alfred strengthened the kingdom's defences and reorganized the army.

In 886 he consolidated the alliance of southern and central England by marrying his daughter Æthelflæd to the ealdorman Æthelred, who had taken power in Mercia. When another army landed in 892, it was defeated after four years of war; marauders from Northumbria and East Anglia were countered with longships of Alfred's own design, 'neither on the Frisian model nor the Danish, but as he himself deemed might be most serviceable'. For this he has been popularly called the founder of the Royal Navy. His peacetime administration was notable for his deep concern with justice, and the strict control he exercised over his officials.

He died on 26 October 899, leaving behind a strong and firmly governed kingdom capable in the next two generations of uniting England under its own crown; he was remembered long afterwards as 'England's darling', the model king and model patriot. In the eighteenth century, when 'patriot' implied ostentatious opposition to the government (it was this 'patriotism' that Dr Johnson called the last refuge of the scoundrel), Alfred was duly enrolled amongst the radical heroes; he was especially admired for having hanged forty-four unjust judges in a single year, a medieval fiction no less absurd than the tale that, taking refuge at Athelney in a peasant's hut, he was too preoccupied with planning the coming battle to notice that the cakes the goodwife had bidden him watch were burning, for which she scolded him in Latin verse.

Equally false is the notion that he founded a college at Oxford (see *8 July); but his determination to revive the Christian learning in which England had abounded before the Viking invasions has won him as much approval as his military prowess and political achievements: he also undertook, both in person and through others, English translations of essential texts: he himself translated Gregory the Great's *Pastoral Care* (*Cura pastoralis*), Augustine's *Soliloquies*, Boethius' *Consolation of Philosophy*, and the first fifty psalms; other hands translated Gregory's *Dialogues*, Orosius' *Anti-Pagan History*, and Bede's *History of the English Church*. The famous Alfred Jewel, found near Athelney (where Alfred built a fortress and a monastery) and now kept at the Ashmolean Museum in Oxford, inscribed +AELFRED MEC HEHT GEWYRCAN ('Alfred ordered me to be wrought'), has been identified as the head of a pointer for marking the place in a book; Alfred tells us that, in distributing the *Pastoral Care* to every bishopric in his kingdom, he sent such a pointer with each copy.

Demetrius, martyred at Sirmium (Sremska Mitrovica) *c.*305; in the fifth century a basilica was erected to him at Thessalonica (Saloniki). On his day the Greek shepherd drives his flocks from their summer pastures on the mountains to their winter folds on the plain. The new wine is opened and tasted amid much hilarity. 'St Demetrius' summer' is the Greek equivalent of St Martin's summer in the West. On St Demetrius' Eve masquerades were held, especially in Thrace, to ensure prosperity; thus at Tsando a mock camel would be paraded round the village, accompanied by peasants with vine-leaves in their hair, wishing good luck to every house and receiving gifts in return. In 1919 his city of Saloniki was liberated from Ottoman rule.

Cedd (pronounced Chedd), brother of Chad (see *2 Mar.), bishop of the East Saxons, died on this day in 664. Educated at Lindisfarne in Northumbria, he evangelized the Middle Angles with three companions at the invitation of their newly converted king Peada, son of the Mercian king Penda; Penda himself was the last great pagan king in England, but tolerated preaching, reserving his wrath for nominal Christians who did not live according to their faith. Cedd took his mission to Essex, which had accepted Christianity and then rejected it; but its ruler, King Sigebert, had recently been persuaded by King Oswiu of Northumbria to be baptized. Some time later, Sigebert was assassinated by members of his kindred who thought him too merciful to his enemies; by no means all Christian kings were open to such reproach, but Sigebert extended his forgiveness even to offences against God, continuing to accept the hospitality of a man whom Cedd had excommunicated for an unlawful marriage. This was quite another matter: 'I tell thee,' said the bishop, 'that because thou hast refused to keep away from the house of that lost and damned man, in that house thou shalt die,' and so it proved.

27 OCTOBER

a.d. VI Kalendas Novembres   F

❦ HOLIDAYS AND ANNIVERSARIES Saint Vincent and the Grenadines: Independence Day (from Great Britain, 1979)
   Turkmenistan: Independence Day (from the USSR, 1991)
   USA: Navy Day

❦ HOLY DAYS
Frumentius (d. *c.*380), Tyrian sailor captured along with his brother Aedesius in a Red Sea port, the rest of the party being slaughtered; they were sold as slaves to the king of Axum in Ethiopia, becoming respectively his secretary and his seneschal, but freed before his death. Aedesius returned home to become a priest; Frumentius became tutor to the late king's sons; he instituted Christian colonies, was consecrated bishop by Athanasius, and with the help of his former pupil, now king, thwarted the emperor

Constantius' attempt to depose him in favour of an Arian in 357. His feast used to be celebrated in the state of Louisiana, as a gesture towards the African slaves.

Michael Servetus, physician and scholar, whose theological position rejecting the doctrine of the Trinity was denounced by Catholics and Protestants alike, was burnt as a heretic at Champel near Geneva on this day in 1553 before he could complete his researches into the circulation of the blood.

Servetus: October 27th, 1553

Grey morning, clear October day,
As from the cell of four long weeks
Of doubt, privation, fear of death,
They dragged the living, dying husk.
And where the crowds defined his way
The last leaves were received by earth.

So through the city streets he passed,
Weak with his fear and fever; but
Thrown down before the City Hall
And asked if he would not retract,
Held firm, addressed himself to Christ;
And in the fire at Champel.

Poor mortal, martyred in the fall
Of seasons, cities, centuries,
How like your killers, unaware
Of this event as history:
Each man's own ministry, and all
That protest, blazing in this fire.

And Calvin, in his narrow room,
Against his scorned, spurned body's pain
Cast all his faculties on God
(Though still presiding on that scene)
And rendered final praise to Him;
Then turned to work too long deferred.

Evan Jones (1931–)

28 OCTOBER

a.d. V Kalendas Novembres   G

Simon and Jude
all the ships on the sea home they do crowd.

❦ HOLIDAYS AND ANNIVERSARIES Czech Republic: National Day (anniversary of proclamation of independence, 1918)

Greece: Day of the No (refusal of Italian ultimatum in 1940, followed by invasion; the Greek Prime Minister Ioánnis Metaxás quoted Aeschylus' words from his *Persians*: 'Now the struggle is for all')

Turkmenistan: Independence Day (second day)

❨ HOLY DAYS **Simon and Jude, Apostles** (CofE, RC); red-letter day

Simon and Jude, Apostles. In the New Testament Simon never appears outside the catalogues of apostles. Mark and Matthew call him a *Kananaios*; in the Authorized Version this is mistranslated 'Canaanite' (in Greek *Chananaios*), as if he had been a Gentile from Phoenicia. In fact it represents the Aramaic word *qan'ān*, for which St Luke characteristically substitutes the correct Greek equivalent, *Zēlōtēs*, 'Zealot'; during the Jewish revolt this was to denote an extremist faction among the rebels, but there is no evidence for a political sense in Jesus' day. After the Resurrection tradition sends him preaching to Egypt; Western writers make him travel to Parthia in the company of St Jude to work miracles and be martyred.

The identity of Jude is hardly less problematic; no less than Hardy's character does he deserve the name Jude the Obscure. The shortest book in the New Testament is the Epistle of 'Jude, the servant of Jesus Christ, brother of James'; this James is the brother of the Lord (see *11 May). It is an attack on arrogant heretics, which makes references to Jewish apocrypha; the author bids his readers remember the words of the Apostles, of whom he speaks in the third person, like one not of their number. Nevertheless, he has traditionally been identified, especially in the West, with the *Ioudas Iakōbou*, literally 'Judas of James', listed among the Twelve Apostles by St Luke, both in his Gospel and in Acts; but this is standard Greek idiom for 'Judas son of James', and is so translated in modern (and some older) versions, rather than 'Judas the brother of James', a libel upon the learned evangelist's powers of expression. Luke reports no speech or action on this Apostle's part; at John 14: 23 'Judas not Iscariot' asks Jesus why he will reveal himself after death to the disciples, not to the world, but Mark and Matthew do not so much as mention him, giving his place to an apostle variously called in the manuscripts Thaddaeus and Lebbaeus, of whom they too have nothing else to say. Some early Latin versions of St Matthew substitute 'Iudas Zelotes', attesting to the Western association with Simon, which is not found in the East. Many Christians, especially in the West, have called the disciple Judas Thaddaeus, and identified him with the Thaddaeus of the Abgar legend, in which, however, he is one of not the Twelve but the Seventy (see *4 Jan.); the Orthodox, though not rejecting the identification out of hand, honour St Jude author of the Epistle on 19 June and Thaddaeus on 21 August.

As the namesake of the traitor, St Jude received little cult. For that reason, he has since the eighteenth century been considered the saint most likely to welcome the prayers of the truly desperate, the patron of lost causes.

Traditionally it rains on this day:

s. ALEX. The same; dost thou know her, then?

TRAP. As well as I know 'twill rain upon Simon and Jude's day next.

Middleton, The Roaring Girl, I. i

J. DAPPER. Now, a continual Simon and Jude's rain
  Beat all your feathers as flat down as pancakes.

ibid. II. i

An American in London in 1822:

Almost the first thing that strikes an American, used to the clear skies and glowing sunshine of his own country, is the humidity of the atmosphere, and the frequent absence of the god of day. St. Simon and Jude's day is almost every other day here. It rains or snows about one hundred and fifty days in the year; and of the remainder, between fifty and sixty are cloudy.   Paulding, 12–13

In Venice San Simon Squarzavele (Tearsail) is said to bring with him the winter winds.

This was the original election-day for the Lord Mayor of London, and down to 1751 remained the day on which he was admitted to office, being presented to the King or the Barons of the Exchequer for swearing-in on the 29th. In 1752, after the reform of the calendar, the then Lord Mayor continued in office till 8 November (28 Oct. OS); thereafter the swearing-in, with its great parade, took place on 9 November, except when a Sunday had to be avoided. Since 1960 the parade has taken place on the second Saturday of the month, after a swearing-in the day before. See *Other Holidays: Lord Mayor's Show*.

29 OCTOBER

a.d. IV Kalendas Novembres   A

❦ HOLIDAYS AND ANNIVERSARIES Turkey: Republic Day (anniversary of founding of Republic, 1923) (national day)

❦ HOLY DAYS James Hannington (CY)

James Hannington (1847–85). After missionary work in Zanzibar, he was made bishop of East Equatorial Africa in 1884; he was murdered in October of the following year in Uganda.

Ida of Leeuw (early 13th c.). She entered a Cistercian convent near Mechelen at the age of 13, and became known not only for her mystic experiences but also her passion for copying and correcting liturgical books; under her leadership a scriptorium was established in her convent.

30 OCTOBER

❦ HOLY DAYS

Alfonso Rodríguez (1531–1617). Abandoning his career as a merchant after the death of his wife and children, he became a Jesuit at the age of 44; he spent much of the rest of his life as doorkeeper of the college of Montesión in Palma de Mallorca.

In honour of St. Alphonsus Rodriguez
Laybrother of the Society of Jesus

Honour is flashed off exploit, so we say,
And those strokes that once gashed flesh or galled shield
Should tongue that time now, trumpet now that field,
And, on the fighter, forge his glorious day.
On Christ they do and on the martyr may;
But be the war within, the brand we wield
Unseen, the heroic breast not outward-steeled,
Earth hears no hurtle then from fiercest fray.
Yet God (that hews mountain and continent,
Earth, all, out, who, with trickling increment,
Veins violets and tall trees makes more and more)
Could crowd career with conquest while there went
Those years and years by of world without event
That in Majorca Alfonso watched the door.

Gerard Manley Hopkins (1844–89)

31 OCTOBER

Halloween bairns see far.
Sir Walter Scott, *The Monastery*

❦ HOLIDAYS AND ANNIVERSARIES Germany: Reformationsfest
Taiwan: Chiang Kai-shek Day (born 1887)
USA, Nevada: Admission Day (36th state, 1864)

❦ HOLY DAYS Martin Luther (CY commem.)

Martin Luther (1483–1546), a miner's son who after a university education became an Augustinian monk at Erfurt; in 1508 he was appointed professor of moral philosophy at Wittenberg, in 1511 doctor of theology and professor of biblical exegesis, in 1515 vicar of his order. About this time, he became convinced that salvation depended entirely on faith, and not the good works emphasized by contemporary teaching. This made all the more offensive to him the assertion of Johann Tetzel, who was preaching the indulgence for Leo X's rebuilding of St Peter's, that souls could be freed from Purgatory simply by payment on their behalf even by persons not in a state of grace; on 31 October 1517 Luther nailed his famous ninety-five theses on indulgences to the church door. This action was intended as a challenge to an academic disputation; instead, it unleashed a German anti-papalism originating in the dealings of popes with Holy Roman Emperors (in particular their destruction of the Hohenstaufen dynasty in the thirteenth century) and kept alive by current grievances. Roman attempts at imposing discipline merely drove him into ever more radical rejection of Catholic doctrine; when Leo X issued a Bull against his writings he publicly burnt it, for which he was excommunicated in 1521. He enjoyed broad support amongst the German princes, to whom he addressed an appeal for reform of the Church, the north European humanists, who themselves sought reform and identified his concerns with theirs, and the masses, to whom as never before the controversy was brought by the printing-press; this support inhibited the emperor Charles V in his attempts to silence Luther, who nevertheless, after being put to the ban of Empire, judged it prudent to take refuge with the Elector of Saxony.

It was under the Elector's protection, at the Wartburg near Eisenach, that Luther began his translation of the Bible, whose significance for Germany is even greater than that of the Authorized Version for English-speaking countries; but in May 1522 he had to return to Wittenberg, where religious radicalism was getting out of hand. He introduced a new rite, along with many other reforms, laid aside his monk's habit, and married a former Cistercian nun, Katherina von Bora, in 1525. By this time certain of his tenets, such as the priesthood of all believers, had been given unwelcome interpretations by political radicals, in particular by the peasants who rose against their lords. Luther, having first attempted to mediate, when forced to take sides chose, like the other Reformers, to support authority; but being a master of vivid prose, he expressed this support in violent language, encouraging the princes to cut down the 'predatory and murderous hordes', as indeed they were already doing. (This has earned him much opprobrium, not least in the Marxist classics; nevertheless, he was rehabilitated by the East German regime in time for his quincentenary.) In the ensuing years, Luther and other Reformers proved unable to agree on the nature of the Eucharist; as in other matters, Luther was the more conservative. As a result, the Lutheran Church remained separate from the Reformed churches influenced by such men as Zwingli, Calvin, and Knox. (It was the Lutherans who were first called 'Protestant', after their minority protest at the Imperial Diet of Speyer in 1529; later, when this term had been extended to the Reformed churches and the English middle way, the preferred epithet was *evangelisch*.)

Besides his theological writings, and his biblical translation, Luther composed both the text and the music of numerous hymns, of which the most famous is *Ein feste Burg ist unser Gott* ('A safe stronghold our God is still'). His love of music saved that art from the suspicion with which it was viewed by Reformers of a more humanistic stamp.

All-Hallows Eve, the eve before All Saints Day. In Scotland and Ireland Hallowe'en, a night when spirits walk abroad, *Oidhche* [in modern Irish *Oíche*] *Shamhna*, properly 'the night of Samhain', i.e. of the first day of winter (see *1 Nov.), taken to begin with nightfall. Originally the entire day from sunset on 31 October till sunset on 1 November belonged to the spirits, but the emphasis shifted to the night; in this form the observance passed to Wales and Cornwall, and to border areas of England, as witness the 'souling' or cake-begging rhyme at Knutsford by the Welsh border:

> Soul! soul! for a soul cake!
> I pray, good missus, a soul-cake!
> An apple or pear, a plum or a cherry,
> Any good thing to make us merry.
> One for Peter, two for Paul,
> Three for Him that made us all.
> Up with the kettle and up with the pan.
> Give us good alms and we'll be gone.

Hallowe'en also crossed the ocean with the Scots and Irish to North America; in the USA, despite objections from Christian clergy to its 'diabolical' characteristics, it has become the chief non-sectarian children's festival, a virtual feast of obligation for parents, who complain when other commitments are scheduled to conflict with it. Children dress up as ghosts and witches or more fashionable characters, demanding sweets, or rather 'candy', with the cry 'trick or treat'; pumpkins are carved with strange faces and put on display outside the house. At Delta, Pa., there is an underwater pumpkin-carving competition. In most of England, however, Hallowe'en was even more alien than Hogmanay until the late twentieth century, when it began to encroach on Guy Fawkes Day (see *5 Nov.) as both safer for children than domestic fireworks and more profitable than the collection of near-worthless pennies.

Many of the customs practised on this eve were recorded by Robert Burns. They include:

Nut-crack night (oracle of the nuts). A lad and lass each place a nut in the fire; the course of their courtship is predicted by the behaviour of the nuts, whether they burn quietly together or jump apart:

> The auld Guidwife's weel-hoordet nits
>   Are round an' round divided,
> An' monie lads and lasses fates
>   Are there that night decided:
> Some kindle, couthie, side by side,
>   An' *burn* thegither trimly;
> Some, start awa, wi' saucy pride,
>   An' jump out owre the chimlie
>   Fu' high that night.
>   Robert Burns (1759–96)

Divination by cabbage-pulling:

The first ceremony of Halloween is, pulling each a *Stock* or plant of kail. They must go out, hand in hand, with eyes shut, and pull the first they meet with: its being big or little, straight or crooked, is prophetic of the size and shape of the grand object of all their Spells—the husband or wife. If any *yird*, or earth, stick to the root, that is *tocher*, or fortune; and the taste of the *custoc*, that is, the heart of the stem, is indicative of the natural temper and disposition. Lastly, the stems, or, to give them their ordinary appellation, the *runts*, are placed somewhere above the head of the door; and the christian names of people whom chance brings into the house, are, according to the priority of placing the *runts*, the names in question.   Burns, 153–4 n.

Divination by bonfire:

On All-Saints Even, they set up bonfires in every village. When the bonfire is consumed, the ashes are carefully collected in the form of a circle. There is a stone put in, near the circumference, for every person of the several families interested in the bonfire; and whatever stone is moved out of its place, or injured before next morning, the person represented by that stone is devoted, or *fey*; and is supposed not to live twelve months from that day.

Sinclair, xi. 621–2 (Callander, Perth.)

Divination with a smock or shift:

The last Halloween I was waukin   *watching*
    My droukit sark-sleeve, as ye ken;   *wetted*
His likeness cam up the house staukin,
    And the very grey breeks o' Tam Glen!

Burns, 'Tam Glen' (1790)

Hallow Eve in Ireland in 1828:

A fast day, that is, Hallow Eve, that is, the Eve of all Saints, that is Calcannon Night. . . . There are many pounders crushing 'coimhbleidhe' or calcannan [colcannon, a dish of potatoes and cabbage]. Many apples are being eaten, and nuts being roasted as the Midnight Court has it.

O'Sullivan, ii. 47 (31 Oct. 1828)

NOVEMBER

November take flaile,
Let ships no more sail.

If there's ice in November to bear a duck
there'll be nothing after but sludge and muck.

❦ NAMES OF THE MONTH Latin *November*, French *novembre*, Spanish *noviembre*, Portuguese *Novembro*, Italian *novembre*, German *November*, Welsh *Tachwedd*, Scots Gaelic *an t-Samhainn, an t-Samhuin*, Irish *Samhain*

The Latin name indicates that this was originally the ninth month of the year. The Welsh name means 'slaughter'; similarly, the Dutch used to call this month *slachtmaand*, since beasts were slaughtered in it, and Old English preserved the heathen variant *blōtmōnaþ*, 'sacrifice month'. Another Welsh term is *y mis du*, 'the black month', also recorded for Scots Gaelic (*am mìos dubh*). For the Scots Gaelic and Irish names, see *1 November.

❦ HOLIDAYS AND ANNIVERSARIES
Last Sunday USA, Massachusetts: John F. Kennedy Day

First Monday Northern Tasmania, Australia: Recreation Day

Second Monday Cayman Islands: Remembrance Day

Third Monday Fiji: Prince Charles's Birthday

First Tuesday after first Monday USA: Election Day

First Thursday Liberia: Thanksgiving Day

Third Thursday Beaujolais Nouveau is flown from France in order to please wine-bibbers' palates and augment vintners' profits; connoisseurs make a point of disdain

Fourth Thursday USA: Thanksgiving (see *Other Holidays*)

First Friday Western Samoa: Arbor Day

First Saturday USA: Sadie Hawkins Day (invented by Al Capp in his 'Li'l Abner' comic strip: girls and women may take the initiative in inviting men for a date)

Sweden: All Saints' Day

Second Saturday. UK (London): Lord Mayor's Procession and Show. The incoming Lord
Mayor of London, having been sworn in at the Guildhall the previous day, is presented to the Lord Chief Justice at the Royal Courts of Justice to make the final
declaration of office; the procession is popularly known as the Lord Mayor's Show
(see *Other Holidays: Lord Mayor's Show*); red-letter day

> Next was *Nouember*, he full grosse and fat,
> As fed with lard, and that right well might seeme:
> For, he had been a fatting hogs of late,
> That yet his browes with sweat, did reek and steem,
> And yet the season was full sharp and breem;
> In planting eeke he took no small delight:
> Whereon he rode, not easie was to deeme:
> For it a dreadfull *Centaure* was in sight,
> The seed of *Saturne*, and faire *Nais, Chiron* hight.
>
> Spenser, *The Faerie Queene*, VII. vii. 40

It is now Nouember, and according to the old Prouerbe, Let the Thresher take his flayle, and the
ship no more sayle: for the high winds and the rough seas will try the ribs of the Shippe, and the
hearts of the Sailers: Now come the Country people all wet to the Market, and the toyling
Carriers are pittifully moyled: The yong Herne and the Shoulerd are now fat for the great Feast,
and the Woodcocke begins to make toward the Cockeshoot: the Warriners now beginne to plie
their haruest, and the Butcher, after a good bargaine drinks a health to the Grasier: the Cooke
and the Comfitmaker, make ready for Christmas, and the Minstrels in the Countrey, beat their
boyes for false fingring: Schollers before breakefast haue a cold stomacke to their bookes, and a
Master without Art is fit for an A. B. C. A red herring and a cup of Sacke, make warre in a weake
stomacke, and the poore mans fast, is better then the Gluttons surfet: Trenchers and dishes are
now necessary seruants, and a locke to the Cubboord keepes a bit for a neede: Now beginnes the
Goshauke to weede the wood of the Phesant and the Mallard loues not to heare the belles of the
Faulcon: The winds now are cold, and the Ayre chill, and the poore die through want of Charitie:
Butter and Cheese beginne to rayse their prices, and Kitchen stuffe is a commoditie, that euery
man is not acquainted with. In summe, with a conceit of the chilling cold of it, I thus conclude
in it: I hold it the discomfort of Nature, and Reasons patience. Farewell.   Breton (1626)

In this Moneth *Melancholy* much increaseth, and blood decreaseth; its good to vomit sometimes,
Eggs and Honey now are very wholsome, Salt powdred meats are good; this is the most perillous time in the Year to Bath in . . . the eating of *Honey* this moneth, Ginger, Pulse, and Goats
Milk are very wholsome, and profitable to the body, for that they increase blood, and cause a
good colour, and Cinnamon and Ginger drunk often this Moneth give health, and are commendable, and beware you do not go early forth of doors this Moneth (those that can avoid it)
because of Foggs and Mists, which greatly offend the Head and Stomack, but let the Sun have
first some power on the Horizon.   Saunders (1665)

1 NOVEMBER

Kalendae Novembres   D

> *All Saints doe laie for porke and souse,*
> *for sprats and spurlings for their house.*

> *If ducks do slide at Hollantide,*
> *at Christmas they will swim;*
> *if ducks do swim at Hollantide,*
> *at Christmas they will slide.*

> *On allhallow-day cut a chip from the beach tree;*
> *if it be dry the winter will prove warm.*

❧ HOLIDAYS AND ANNIVERSARIES Algeria: Revolution Anniversary (beginning of the struggle for independence from France) (national day)
Antigua and Barbuda: Independence Day (from Great Britain, 1981)
Mexico: first of the Días de los Muertos or Days of the Dead (beginning on night of 31 Oct.)

❧ ANCIENT ROME Last and culminating day of Ludi Victoriae Sullanae (see *26 Oct.), on which games took place in the Circus Maximus.

❧ HOLY DAYS **All Saints' Day** (CofE, RC); red-letter day

All Saints (Allhallows day, Hollantide, Hallowmas). Sporadic references to a Sunday of All Martyrs, later of All Saints, are found before the seventh century; it was kept, as still in the Orthodox Church, on the Sunday after Pentecost until in 609 or 610 Pope Boniface IV dedicated the Pantheon as the church of *Sancta Maria ad martyres* on *13 May, which for a time became the Western date. The present date was the dedication-date of a chapel in St Peter's dedicated to 'all the saints' by Pope Gregory III (731–41); it was made universal by Gregory IV (827–44). CY permits All Saints' Day to be celebrated on the Sunday between 30 October and 5 November.

from *All Saints Day*

On Champions blest, in Jesus' name,
    Short be your strife, your triumph full,
Till every heart have caught your flame,
    And lighten'd of the world's misrule
Ye soar those elder saints to meet,
Gather'd long since at Jesus' feet,
No world of passions to destroy,
Your prayers and struggles o'er, your task all praise and joy.

John Keble (1792–1866), *The Christian Year*

Pagan celebrations. The 1st of November is the Irish *Samhain* and the Scottish *Samhuin*, celebrated with bonfires, a festival of the dead (Irish *Féile na Marbh*), marking the end of the harvest and the beginning of the winter half-year with heightened activities by the fairies (*aos sídhe*, now spelt *sí*); this is the origin of Hallowe'en, but extended throughout the day. The day is also called in Irish *Féile Moingfhinne*, the feast of the demoness Moingfhionn (Whitehair).

Remnants of pagan customs, curiously admixed with Christianity, can be found well into the seventeenth century, and beyond:

> The Inhabitants of this Island [one of the islands off Lewis] had an antient Custom to sacrifice to a Sea-God, call'd *Shony*, at Hallowtide, in the manner following: The Inhabitants round the Island came to the Church of St. *Mulvay*, having each Man his Provision along with him; every Family furnish'd a Peck of Malt, and this was brew'd into Ale: one of their number was pick'd out to wade into the Sea up to the middle, and carrying a Cup of Ale in his hand, standing still in that posture, cry'd out with a loud Voice, saying, *Shony, I give you this Cup of Ale, hoping that you'll be so kind as to send us plenty of Sea-ware, for inriching our Ground the ensuing Year:* and so threw the Cup of Ale into the Sea. This was perform'd in the Night time. At his Return to Land, they all went to Church, where there was a Candle burning upon the Altar; and then standing silent for a little time, one of them gave a Signal, at which the Candle was put out, and immediately all of them went to the Fields, where they fell a drinking their Ale, and spent the remainder of the Night in Dancing and Singing, *etc.*
>
> The next Morning they all return'd home, being well satisfy'd that they had punctually observ'd this Solemn Anniversary, which they believ'd to be a powerful means to procure a plentiful Crop. Mr. *Daniel* and Mr. *Kenneth Morison*, Ministers in *Lewis*, told me they spent several Years, before they could persuade the vulgar Natives to abandon this ridiculous piece of Superstition; which is quite abolish'd for these 32 Years past.   M. Martin, 28–9 (1716)

In Shakespeare's time, All Saints' Day Old Style corresponded to St Martin's Day New Style, and could appropriate his summer: 'Farewell, the latter spring; farewell, All-hallown summer' (*1 Henry IV*, I. ii. 156–7). It was one of those feasts that only a comic half-wit would not know:

SLENDER. You have not the book of riddles about you, have you?
SIMPLE. Book of riddles? Why, did you not lend it to Alice Shortcake upon All-
hallowmas last, a fortnight afore Michaelmas?   *The Merry Wives of Windsor*, I. i. 184–8

2 NOVEMBER

> Why then All-Souls' Day is my body's doomsday . . .
> This, this All-Souls' Day to my fearful soul
> Is the determined respite of my wrongs.
> That high all-seer which I dallied with

Hath turned my feignèd prayer on my head,
And given in earnest what I begged in jest.
Buckingham, in Richard III, v. i. 12–22

❦ HOLIDAYS AND ANNIVERSARIES Many countries: All Souls' Day
Mexico: second of the Días de los Muertos
USA, North Dakota: Admission Day (39th state, 1889)
USA, South Dakota: Admission Day (40th state, 1889)

❦ HOLY DAYS **Commemoration of all the Faithful Departed or All Souls** (RC);
Commemoration of the Faithful Departed (All Souls' Day) (CY)

All Souls' Day, also known as 'Soul-mass Day'. From the early ninth century onwards, monasteries began to commemorate their dead as well as the souls of their benefactors. This was formalized by Odilo of Cluny in 998 as a day of psalm-singing and alms-giving, but above all the celebration of masses in memory of all those who rest in Christ, to be observed on the day following All Saints. There was a tradition at Cluny that a traveller from southern Gaul had been informed by an African hermit that the monastery was especially proficient at the saving of souls, owing to the frequency with which mass was said there; such was the multitude of brethren that mass was said continuously from dawn to dinner. In one version it is the traveller's report that moved Odilo to institute the feast. It was further promoted by a story found in the thirteenth-century canonist William Durandus (7. 35): 'One may read that a certain abbot forbade his monks to celebrate masses for the dead on Sundays; but the deceased afflicted him for this with very hard blows, and therefore he revoked his prohibition.'

In Mexico the second Día de los Muertos is a very solemn festivity corrupted (so parents complain) in states bordering the USA by Hallowe'en.

Upon All Souls' Day children went begging for soul-cakes. As early as 1696 the decline of this custom is lamented:

Upon the second day of this Moneth, on which is commemorated The Feast of ALL SOULS, it hath been a Custom, time out of mind, for good People to set on a Table-Board a high heap of SOUL-CAKES, lying one upon another, like to the SHEW-BREAD in the Bible.

They were in form about the bigness of a *Two-Penny Cake*: And every Visitant took one of them. And, there is an Old Rhyme, or Saying, which alludes to this, *viz.*

A SOUL-CAKE!
A SOUL-CAKE!
Have mercy on all Christen Souls, for
A SOUL-CAKE!

This Pious Custom, (for such it is) is still in use in some Parts of *Cheshire, Lancashire, etc.* And, were it, together with sundry other Innocent Ones, revived in all Places, we should have more true RELIGION, and less FRAUD and ENVY in the World.   Gadbury (1696)

Rumwold (Rumwald, Rumbald, Rumbold), a miracle of a saint who died at the age of three days; nonetheless he appears in the *Acta Sanctorum* and his cult was fairly widespread in England (in some places on 3 Nov.). Thomas Lambard, in his *Perambulations of Kent* (1576), discusses the cunning contrivance of his statue in Boxley Abbey and the infant saint's legend:

If you minded to haue benefit by the Roode of Grace, you ought firste to be shryuen of one of the Monkes: Then by lifting at this other Image (which was untruly of the common sorte called Sainct Grumbald, for Sainct Rumwald) you shoulde make proofe whether you were in cleane life (as they called it) or no: and if you so founde your selfe, then was your waye prepared, and your offering acceptable before the Roode, if not, then it behoued you to be confessed of newe, for it was to be thought, that you had concealed somewhat from your ghostly Dad . . .

. . . this Sainct Rumwald was a preatie shorte picture of a Boy Sainct standing in the same Churche, of it selfe so small, hollow, and light, that a childe of seuen yeares of age might easily lift it, and therefore of no moment at all, in the hands of suche persons as had offered frankly: But by means of a pyn of wood, stricken through it into a poste (whiche a false knaue standing behinde, coulde put in, and pull out, at his pleasure) it was to such as offered faintly, so fast and unmoueable, that no force of hande could once stirre it: In so muche, as many times, it moued more laughter, then deuotion, to beholde a great lubber to lift at that in vayne, which a young boy or wenche had easily taken up before him.

. . . I my selfe can not coniecture, what reason shoulde moue them, to make this Sainct Rumwald the Touchstone of cleane life and innocencie, unlesse it be upon occasion of a myracle that he did, in making two holy Priestes to lift a greate stone easily, whiche before diuers laye persons coulde not stirre, with all their strength and abilitie . . . as in the worke called *Noua Legenda Angliae*, I finde reported.

A Pagan or unchristened King of Northumberland, had married a Christian woman, daughter to Penda, the King of Midle Englande, who would not (by any meanes) be known carnally of her husband, til such time as he had condescended to forsake Idolatrie, and to become a Christian with her. The husband (with much to doe) consented to the condition, and she not long after waxed great with chylde, and as (upon a time) they were ryding towarde their Father King Penda, she fell into trauayle of chylde byrthe, and was deliuered by the waye (in a faire medowe) at Sutton of a man childe, whiche so soone as he was come out of his mothers belly, cried with a loude voice, three seueral times, *Christianus sum, Christianus sum, Christianus sum.* I am a Christian, I am a Christian, I am a Christian. And not ceassing thus, made foorthwith plaine profession of his faith, desired to be baptised, chose his Godfathers, named himselfe Rumwald, and with his finger directed the standers by to fetche him a great hollowe stone, that he would haue to be vsed for the Fonte: hereupon sondrie of the Kings seruaunts, assayed to haue brought the stone, but it was so farre aboue al their strengthes, that they could not once moue it: when the Childe perceaued that, he commaunded the two Priestes (his appointed Godfathers) to goe and bring it, whiche they did forthwith moste easily. This done he was Baptised, and within three dayes after (hauing in the meane while discoursed cunningly sundrie misteries of Popishe religion, and bequeathing his bodie to remaine at Sutton one yeare, at Brackley two, and at Buckingham for euer after) his Spirit departed out of his bodie, & was by the hands of the Aungels conueied into heauen.   Lambard, 186–9

An almanac of 1664 calls the second of November a critical day for forecasting the weather:

It is common among the countrey people, to judge of the following winter by the quarter wherein the winde shall be on the first of *November*. But that which is more observable is the second of *November*, which to the Arabian Astrologers was a Critical day, from whence they could know something in general concerning the disposition of the aire in rain, thunder and lightning.

For if *Jupiter, Venus,* and *Mercury* were then Occidental, or retrograde, they judged much rain to be in that year. They also had an eye to *Saturn* and *Mars,* whether of them were the stronger; as also what society they had with the other Planets, chiefly with *Mercury;* that so they might judge the better concerning the following changes of the aire.   Dove (1664)

3 NOVEMBER

a.d. III Nonas Novembres   F

❨ HOLIDAYS AND ANNIVERSARIES Dominica: Independence Day (from Great Britain, 1978)
Japan: Culture Day (national holiday)
Panama: National Day (independence from Colombia, 1903)

❨ HOLY DAYS Richard Hooker (CY); Martín de Porres (RC; CY commem.); Winifred (RC Wales)

Richard Hooker (*c.*1554–1600), apologist of the Anglican Church and author of *Of the Laws of Ecclesiastical Polity,* arguing that Scripture did not supersede natural law, which is God's supreme reason.

Martín de Porres (1579–1639), born in Lima, Peru, the illegitimate son of a Spanish knight and a Panamanian mother of Indian or Negro descent (he described himself as a 'mulatto dog'). Trained as a barber, he became a Dominican at the age of 15, and devoted his life to caring for the sick and poor, especially Negro slaves. He also took care of abandoned cats and dogs. An ideal candidate for the patron saint of racial harmony, he was canonized in 1962. In 1965 Paul VI named him patron of public education and television in Peru. John Paul II added the public health service of Peru to his patronage in 1982. He is also patron saint of Italian hairdressers and barbers.

Winifred (Gwenffrewi) (7th c.), supposedly a member of a noble family from North Wales who, having devoted herself to God, was overtaken and beheaded by her jilted lover, Prince Caradog of Hawarden, who was swallowed up by the earth on the spot; where her head fell there arose a stream with red-streaked pebbles; resuscitated by her uncle St Beuno (see *20 Apr.), she established the convent of Gwytherin in Clwyd, and died on this day in 660.
    St Winifred's Well, Holywell, Treffynnon, was a place of pilgrimage for centuries. The indefatigable traveller Celia Fiennes visited Holywell in the late seventeenth century and noted the following description in her journal:

St. Winfreds Well is built over with stone on pillars like a tryumphall arch or tower on the gates of a Church; there is a pavement of stone within ground 3 sides of the Well which is joyn'd on the fourth side by a great arch of stone which lies over the water that runs of from the Well, its many springs which bubbles up very fast and lookes cleane in a compass which is 8 square walled in with stone; in the bottom which you see as clear as Chrystall are 9 stones layd in an oval on which are dropps of red coullour some almost quite covering the top of the stone, which is pretended to be the blood of this holy saint whose head was struck off here, and so where her body laid this spring burst forth and remaines till now, a very rapid current, which runs off from this Well under a barre by which there are stone stepps for the persons to descend which will bathe themselves in the Well and so they walke along the streame to the other end and then come out, but there is nothing to shelter them but are exposed to all the Company that are walking about the Well and to the little houses and part of the streete which runs along by it; but the Religeuse are not to mind it; it seemes the Saint they do honour to in this place must beare them out in all things, they tell of many lameness's and aches and distempers which are cured by it; its a cold water and cleare and runs off very quick so that it would be a pleasant refreshment in the summer to washe ones self in it, but its shallow not up to the waste so its not easye to dive and washe in; but I think I could not have been persuaded to have gone in unless I might have had curtains to have drawn about some part of it to have shelter'd from the streete, for the wett garments are no covering to the body . . . they come also to drinke of the water which they take up in the first square which is walled round and where the springs rise, and they say its of wonder full operation; the taste to me was but like good spring water which with wine and sugar and leamons might make a pleasant draught . . .   Fiennes, 180

The cure was not necessarily efficacious:

In the year 1634, I taught sir *George Peckham*, Knight, astrology, that Part which concerns Sickness, wherein he so profited, that in two or three Months he would give a very true Discovery of any Disease . . . he . . . unfortunately died in 1635 at St *Winifred*'s Well in *Wales*; in which Well he continued so long mumbling his *Pater Noster*s and *Sancta Winifrida ora pro me*, that the Cold struck into his Body; and, after his coming forth of that Well, never spoke more.   Lilly, 32

Hubert (*c.*655–727), reputedly the son of the duke of Aquitaine and of Merovingian blood, certainly kinsman of Pippin, mayor of the palace, to whom he fled from Ebroin. A devoted pupil of St Lambert (*17 Sept.), he became bishop of Maastricht by 708; he transferred the see in 717/18 to Liège, where he founded St Lambert's cathedral. From the fourteenth century onwards we find it said that he was a worldly youth who was converted while hunting by the sight of a cross between a stag's antlers; this became a favourite subject for painters. With St Eustace (*20 Sept.) the patron saint of hunters, he is invoked against rabies.

Malachy O'More (1094–1148, canonized 1190), bishop of Down from 1124, was elected and consecrated archbishop of Armagh in 1132; his installation was delayed till 1134 by opponents of his reforms. Two years later he resigned, but in 1139 he was appointed papal legate, in which capacity he effected the definitive substitution of the Roman liturgy for the Celtic. He became a friend of Bernard of Clairvaux, whose Cistercian order he introduced into Ireland, and who wrote his life at some length.

St Bernard credited him with prophetic powers; in 1595 predictions in his name were published (Wion, i. 307–11), briefly describing future popes (including certain antipopes) beginning with Celestine II (1143–4), 'from the fortress of the Tiber' (*ex castro Tiberis*); he came from Tifernum on the Tiber, now Città del Castello. Down to Urban VII (15–27 Sept. 1590)—called 'from the dew of heaven' (*de rore caeli*) because he had been archbishop of Rossano in Calabria, 'where manna is collected' from the manna-ash—they are annotated by Alonso Chacón, OP, who relates the prophecies to the family name, birth-place, arms, or other known circumstance of the pontiff in question; the next three popes down to the reigning Clement VIII are identified without comment; from 'the man of the waves' (*undosus vir*) onwards no annotation is made.

Urban's immediate successor was Gregory XIV, elected after a long and unedifying conclave; he is described as 'from the antiquity of the city' (*ex antiquitate urbis*). That has usually been taken as a puff for Girolamo Simoncelli of Orvieto (*Urbs Vetus*, 'Old City'), but he was not a candidate. The prophecies are regularly exhumed during conclaves, but make only random matches with the popes elected since. Pius VI, who in 1782 journeyed to Vienna in fruitless protest against Joseph II's Edict of Toleration, is described as the 'apostolic traveller' (*peregrinus apostolicus*), and the intellectual Leo XIII as 'light in heaven' (*lumen in caelo*); but Pius VII's title of 'rapacious eagle' (*aquila rapax*) more aptly fits his antagonist Napoleon, and the Venetians Clement XIII and Gregory XVI are respectively the 'rose of Umbria' (*rosa Umbriae*) and 'from the baths of Tuscany' (*de balneis Etruriae*), which suggests that the prophet had never learnt geography. He did better with John Paul II, 'from the travail of the sun' (*de labore solis*), for on the day of Karol Wojtyła's birth, 18 May 1920, there was a partial solar eclipse; but it was visible only in the southern hemisphere.

The next pope (we are told) will be 'the glory of the olive' (*gloria olivae*), after which 'in the ultimate persecution of the Holy Roman Church Peter II shall sit: he shall feed his sheep amid many tribulations, after the accomplishment whereof the City of the Seven Hills shall be destroyed and the awful Judge shall judge His people.' Readers disturbed by this prospect may be comforted to know that in the great Roman basilica of San Paolo fuori le Mura, where a portrait-frieze depicts every pope from St Peter onwards, there are eight roundels still vacant in the main sequence and another twenty available on the east and west walls of the interior church. The 334 years and 13 days of the last twenty-eight completed reigns, from the election of Innocent X on 15 September 1644 to the death of John Paul I on 28 September 1978, suggest that ample time will be available to make any further arrangements.

In Greece, the 'drunken' feast of St George: on Skyros the great jar buried in the ground before his church is uncovered and filled with wine, which the saint miraculously multiplies.

The Taurids, an annual meteor-shower, peak about this day.

4 NOVEMBER

pridie Nonas Novembres   G

❦ HOLIDAYS AND ANNIVERSARIES Australia, Melbourne: Melbourne Cup Day
    USA, Oklahoma: Will Rogers Day (American humorist, cowboy-philosopher, and actor, b. 1879)

❦ ANCIENT ROME Ludi Plebeii began, lasting till the 17th; they are first recorded for 216 BC, but may have been founded four years earlier; they were the plebeian counterpart to the Ludi Romani. As usual they grew over time, eventually comprising nine days of stage performances from the 4th to the 12th, the Epulum Iovis on the 13th, the Equorum Probatio on the 14th, and three days of Circus games from the 15th to the 17th.

❦ HOLY DAYS Charles Borromeo (RC)

Charles (Carlo) *Borromeo* (1538–84), archbishop of Milan and patron saint of the city. Made cardinal in 1560 by his uncle Pope Pius IV, he was a leading Counter-Reformer whose zeal met with considerable hostility: his insistence that all clergy should be clean-shaven dumbfounded those who considered a beardless man to be decadent. He was canonized in 1610; if the official Church saw in him a model of the reforming church-man, the people loved him for the courage and energy with which, during the Milanese plague of 1576, he ministered to the physical and spiritual needs of a population abandoned by its civil authorities. Pius XI named him patron of catechists and catechumens in 1932. On this day in 1958 Angelo Giuseppe Roncalli, who revered Borromeo and had published five volumes of studies about him, was crowned Pope John XXIII.

Henry James reflects on the experience of viewing the relics in Milan Cathedral:

This holy man lies at his eternal rest in a small but gorgeous sepulchral chapel, beneath the boundless pavement and before the high altar; and for a modest sum of five francs you may have his shrivelled mortality unveiled and gaze at it with whatever reserves occur to you. . . . The performance in question, of which the good San Carlo paid in the first instance the cost, was impressive certainly, but as a monstrous matter or a grim comedy may still be. The little sacristan, having secured his audience, whipped on a white tunic over his frock, lighted a couple of extra candles and proceeded to remove from above the altar, by means of a crank, a sort of sliding shutter, just as you may see a shop-boy do of a morning at his master's window. In this case too a large sheet of plate-glass was uncovered, and to form an idea of the *étalage* you must imagine that a jeweller, for reasons of his own, has struck an unnatural partnership with an undertaker. The black mummified corpse of the saint is stretched out in a glass coffin, clad in his mouldering canonicals, mitred, crosiered and gloved, glittering with votive jewels. It is an extraordinary mixture of death and life; the desiccated clay, the ashen rags, the hideous little black mask and skull, and the living, glowing, twinkling splendour of diamonds, emeralds and sapphires. The collection is really fine, and many great historic names are attached to the different offerings. Whatever may be the better opinion as to the future of the Church, I can't help thinking she will make a figure in the world so long as she retains this great fund of precious 'properties', this precious capital decoratively invested and scintillating throughout Christendom at effectively-scattered points. You see I am forced to agree after all, in spite of the sliding shutter and the profane swagger of the sacristan, that a certain pastoral majesty saved the situation, or at least made irony gape.   James, 127–8

5 NOVEMBER

Nonae Novembres   A

❦ HOLIDAYS AND ANNIVERSARIES UK: Guy Fawkes Day

Guy Fawkes Day, or Bonfire Night, formerly known as 'Gunpowder Treason Day', commemorating the failure of the Gunpowder Plot, a conspiracy by a few Roman Catholic
desperadoes to blow up James I and the two Houses of Parliament on the occasion of
the State Opening in 1605; when a peer reported a warning from his nephew to absent
himself from the ceremony, a search of the Commons cellars revealed several barrels of
gunpowder, and a conspirator called Guy Fawkes. An Act of Parliament passed the following year required the laity to attend church on the morning of 5 November and the
clergy to read special prayers and the Act itself (with justification of anti-papist measures); by King James's death in 1625 this day of deliverance, which could be kept alike
by supporters of royal prerogative and of parliamentary rights, had become a popular
festival. Under Charles I this Protestant celebration took on a new meaning, namely dislike of his marriage to the Roman Catholic Henrietta Maria; it increased in popularity,
attention shifting from the morning sermon to the evening bonfires and fireworks.
(Bonfires recall Hallowe'en and Midsummer; but there is no trace for such usages at this
time in England, outside areas neighbouring the Celts, until the Gunpowder Plot.)

In 1647, after the king's defeat in the Civil War, it was the only festival not abolished
by Parliament; during the Interregnum it was almost the only day on which church bells
were regularly rung. It not only survived the Restoration, but was kept with still more
fervour after 1673, when the heir presumptive, James duke of York, became a Roman
Catholic; from this time the burning of the pope in effigy, sporadically attested beforehand, became a conspicuous part of the London celebration. (John Evelyn remarked in
his diary under 5 Nov. 1673: 'This night the youths of the Citty burnt the *Pope* in *Effigie*
after they had made procession with it in greate triumph; displeased at the D[uke of
York] for altering his Religion, & now marrying an *Italian Lady* &c.') During and after
the Exclusion Crisis, when Whigs unsuccessfully attempted to debar James from the
succession, Tory corporations reacted by suppressing it; but when he came to the throne
in 1685, far more parishes adopted than abandoned it despite attempts at government
regulation. It was on Gunpowder Treason Day in 1688 that William of Orange landed
to effect another deliverance, the Glorious Revolution that overthrew James (much
assisted by his own cowardice; cf. *12 July) and ended both royal absolutism and the
danger of reimposed Roman Catholicism; thereafter, festivities were inhibited only (but
not ineffectively) by the damage to be feared from uncontrolled bonfires and fireworks.

Guy Fawkes Day was a statutory holiday till 1859 (see *29 May), and continues in
popular observance with fireworks and the burning of a human effigy, sometimes representing an unpopular individual (at Edenbridge in Kent, in 1994, Major James Hewitt,
who had written a book about his amours with the Princess of Wales) and at Lewes in

East Sussex still a generic pope, but normally an indeterminate figure known as a guy. This is usually made by children; it was traditionally exhibited in the street during the previous weeks with the request 'Penny for the Guy' (see Pl. 9), but went into de-cline during the 1980s when inflation made even the decimal penny (equivalent to 2.4 pre-1971 pence) no longer worth collecting. (To some extent it has been replaced by trick-or-treating at Hallowe'en, not subject to the same financial cap.) The traditional rhyme associated with this day runs:

> Remember, remember
> The fifth of November,
> Gunpowder, Treason, and Plot,
> I see no reason
> Why Gunpowder Treason
> Should ever be forgot.

A contemporary report on the Gunpowder Plot, noted in the diary of Sir Roger Wilbraham:

The 5 of *Nov.* 1605: the Lords & Commons attended to expect the King's coming the begynning of this parliament then to be held by prorogation: A week before, the Lord Mountegle imparted to the King & Council, a letter sent to his hands by one unknowen & fled: wherein he was ad-vised to be absent from the parliament, for that undoutedlie, some great calamitie wold happen soddainlie by unknowen accident, which wold be as soddaine as the fyring of the letter: wherupon the king after one serch about Parliament Howse grew so ielouse he caused a secrett watch, & discovered one Johnson practizing about midnight to make a traine to fyre 34 barrels powder, hidden under billettz in a vault iust under the Upper Howse of Parliament, confessed by one Johnson servant to Thomas Percy, a pentioner, to have ben preparing 8 moneth to blow up the King, his Queen, children, nobles, bishops, iudges & all the commons assembled, if it had not been so happelie discovered.   Wilbraham, 70–1

In New England, this day was called 'Pope Day' and was the only English holiday ob-served by the Puritans: effigies of Guy Fawkes, the pope, and the devil were carried in procession, then burnt and dismembered. It was often the occasion of violence, even-tually beyond the ability of the civil and religious authorities to control. In 1752 the Massachusetts General Court, stating that such 'practices have been found by experi-ence to encourage and cultivate a mobbish Temper and Spirit in many of the inhabit-ants', forbade the evening processions and bonfires in the streets. When the Stamp Act was passed in 1765, protestors modelled their demonstrations on Pope Day customs, with an effigy of the stamp distributor paraded through the streets, then burnt, along with bonfires and general destruction. The succeeding Pope Day in turn imported elements of the protest against the Stamp Act; the threat to civil disorder was sufficient to alarm the British, who repealed the Act less than five months after it took effect.

In the eighteenth century, at the instigation of William Hogarth, artists exhibited their work on this day at Thomas Coram's Foundling Hospital, since 1954 the Thomas Coram Foundation for Children (founded 1739, housed in Guildford Street 1753–1926, since then 40 Brunswick Square); from these exhibitions was born the Royal Academy of Art.

6 NOVEMBER

a.d. VIII Idus Novembres   B

❰ HOLIDAYS AND ANNIVERSARIES Sweden: Gustavus Adolphus Day, the OS date
of his heroic death at Lützen in 1632 (16 Nov. NS). Special cakes, topped with
marzipan and the Swedish flag, are eaten.

❰ HOLY DAYS Leonard of Noblac (CofE); Illtud (RC Wales); All Saints of Ireland
(RC Ireland)

Leonard of Noblac (d. *c*.559) was largely unremarked until his cult developed in the eleventh
century, when his life was written. This makes him a Frankish noble and godson of
Clovis, who refused a bishopric to become a monk and then a hermit at Noblac. His
patronage of women in childbirth stems from the tale that one day as the king was
hunting in the forest, accompanied by his wife, she suddenly went into labour, with no
one to help her. Leonard came out of his cell and prayed for her, and she was successfully delivered. In Germany, where his cult is still strong today, he is the patron saint of
farm animals. But his most famous patronage is of prisoners, especially those bound in
chains; the Golden Legend tells a number of stories in which those fettered unjustly,
upon praying to him, found their chains broken. The RC Church commemorates him
on this day as well.

> But Leonerd of the prisoners doth, the bandes asunder pull,
> And breakes the prison doores and chaines, wherwith his Church is full.
>
> Naogeorgus, fo. 39

Wroxall Abbey in Warwickshire was reputedly founded by Hugh de Hatton, twelfth-
century lord of the manor of Wroxall, delivered from imprisonment upon praying to
the patron saint of his parish, St Leonard. The story is told by Sir William Dugdale in
the seventeenth century, in terms strongly reminiscent of Odysseus' return:

That one *Richard*, shortly after the Norman Conquest . . . had issue a son called *Hugh*, who was
a person of great stature . . . Which *Hugh* going to warfare in the *Holy Land*, was there taken Prisoner; and so continued in great hardship there for the space of seven years: But at length considering, that S. *Leonard* was the Saint to whom his Parish-Church had been dedicated, and the
many miracles that God had often wrought by the merits of that his glorious Confessor, made
his addresses by earnest Prayers to him for deliverance. Whereupon S. *Leonard* appeared to him
in his sleep, in the habit of a black Monk, bidding him arise and go home, and found at his
Church a House of Nuns of S. *Benet's* Order: But the Knight awakening took this for no other
than a dream, till that the same Saint appeared to him a second time in like manner: Howbeit,
then, with much spirituall gladnesse rejoycing, he made a Vow to God and S. *Leonard*, that he
would perform his command. Which Vow was no sooner made, than that he became miraculously carryed thence, with his Fetters, and set in Wroxhall woods, not far distant from his own
House; yet knew not where he was, untill a Shepherd of his own, passing through those thick-
ets, accidentally found him; and after some communication (though he was at first not a little

affrighted in respect he saw a person so overgrown with hair) discovered all unto him. Whereupon his Lady and Children, having advertisement, came forthwith to him, but believed not that he was her husband, till he shewed her a piece of a Ring, that had been broken betwixt them; which, so soon as she applied to the other part in her own custody, closed therewith. And shortly after, having given solemn thanks to God, our Lady and St *Leonard*; and praying for some divine revelation where he should erect that Monastery, so promised by his said vow; he had speciall direction where to build it, by certain stones picht in the ground, in the very place where the Altar was afterwards set. After the structure whereof, two of his daughters were made Nuns therein, a Lady from the Nuns of Wilton being fetcht to direct them in that their rule of S. *Benedict*.   Dugdale, 489 (under Wroxall)

Illtud or Illtyd, abbot, said to have been a cousin of King Arthur (some have purported to identify him with Sir Galahad), ordained by St Germanus of Auxerre, and renowned for his wisdom and learning. He is not mentioned in liturgical texts before the eleventh century, but the *Historia Britonum* (early 9th c.) relates that while Illtud was praying at Llwynarth on the Gower peninsula in a cave overlooking the sea, a ship pulled up with two sailors transporting the corpse of a holy man over whose face an altar was suspended in mid-air, 'held up by the will of God'; claiming to have been sent by God to bury the corpse with Illtud's help, they charged him not to reveal the name lest men should swear by it. Their duty discharged they departed; St Illtud founded a church on the spot. The suspended altar (says the *Historia*) 'remains to this day'; a chieftain who tested it by pulling it towards him with a stick died within the month, as did another who peered underneath it and was struck blind.

Christine of Stommeln (d. 6 Nov. 1312), a beguine in Cologne, who had visions of Christ from the age of 11 and suffered the stigmata. Legend had her whisked away by demons to distant mountain-tops, fields, and forests, or else from town to town (up to 300 miles a night) to be displayed naked in the public square; the demons also flung dung at her and her visitors. Her biographer, Peter of Dacia, witnessed many incidents and recorded them with horrified fascination.

Paul the Confessor (Orth.; RC 7 June), anti-Arian bishop of Alexandria (d. 350), supported by the Western emperor Constans but persecuted by the Eastern emperor Constantius; he died in exile. On the Sunday before this day the story of Dives and Lazarus is read: see **Orthodox Church Year*.

7 NOVEMBER

a.d. VII Idus Novembres   C

❮ HOLIDAYS AND ANNIVERSARIES Russia: Day of Accord and Reconciliation (see below)

❮ HOLY DAYS Willibrord of York (CY)

Willibrord (658–739), archbishop of Utrecht and apostle of Frisia. Born in Northumbria and educated at Ripon under St Wilfrid (see *12 Oct.), he then went to Ireland for study, where he was ordained. At the time of Frankish domination he was sent to Frisia by Pippin II to establish Christianity, which he did with some success, despite setbacks. Upon being consecrated bishop of Utrecht by Sergius I in Rome he vigorously extended his diocese with new churches and in 698 he founded a monastery at Echternach (now in Luxembourg), where he retired, and which is still a place of pilgrimage. A rare survival of medieval liturgical dance takes place at his tomb on the Tuesday after Whitsunday. He is patron saint of Utrecht, also the Netherlands and Luxembourg. The RC Church commemorates him on this day as well.

On this day in 1468 the Florentine humanist and philosopher Marsilio Ficino held a celebration for Plato's birthday. When Plato was born *c.*428 BC, Greeks did not celebrate their birthdays (Herodotus thought it worth remarking that Persians did), only those of gods and heroes; these were kept monthly, but a particular month might be considered that of the actual birth. In Hellenistic times kings and other godlike figures enjoyed similar honours; the philosopher Epicurus (d. 270 BC), deified by his followers, was honoured alive and dead with a birthday sacrifice on 20 Gamelion (Dec.–Jan.) and a feast on the 20th of every month. Platonists determined that their master too must have a birthday, and so must his own master Socrates, assigning that of Artemis, goddess of childbirth, to the self-styled midwife Socrates, and of Apollo, god of wisdom and high culture, to Plato, whom current legend made his son. In those deities' native Delos their respective birthdays were 6 and 7 Thargelion; this was the fifth month of the year, in our calendar roughly late April to early May. The corresponding month was also called Thargelion at Athens, but occupied eleventh place; Ficino therefore equated it with the eleventh Roman month, November.

The New Style date of the Bolshevik coup in Petrograd (now St Petersburg) on 25 October OS 1917, formerly celebrated in the USSR as the Great October Socialist Revolution. In 1997 President Yeltsin proclaimed it the Day of Accord and Reconciliation; not all participants concurred.

8 NOVEMBER

a.d. VI Idus Novembres   D

(HOLIDAYS AND ANNIVERSARIES USA, Montana: Admission Day (41st state, 1889)

(ANCIENT ROME Mundus patet (cf. *24 Aug.).

(HOLY DAYS Saints and Martyrs of England (CY); All Saints of Wales (RC Wales); St Michael and All Angels (Orth.)

The dedication of this day to all saints of England and of Wales replaces the former Octave of All Saints, declared by Pope Sixtus IV (d. 1484) but suppressed in 1955.

The Four Crowned Ones (*Quattuor Coronati*), Castor, Symphorianus, Claudius, and Nicostratus, honoured in a famous Roman church on the Coelian Hill; their birthplace, and even their original number, is disputed. Owing to the story that they were condemned to forced labour in the stone-quarries of Pannonia, they are patrons of sculptors and stonemasons; hence the title of the English Freemasons' journal, *Ars Quattuor Coronatorum*.

Synaxis of the Archistrategos [Supreme Commander] *Michael and the Other Incorporeal Powers*. Michael and Gabriel are held in particular awe on this day, as being angels of death; at Ainos in Thrace it was the custom, on Archangels' Eve, to keep one's shoes hidden in the house, in order that Michael might overlook one's existence. Albanians tell the story that Michael once yielded to a family's pleas not to take a soul he had been sent to collect; God sent him to the bottom of the sea to fetch a stone, in which were a worm and a leaf: 'If I care for a worm, how much better shall I care for my children on earth!' He then deafened St Michael with a thunderbolt, lest he should again be swayed by prayers.

In Russia, this is the New Style dating of St Demetrius' day (see *26 Oct.); the preceding Saturday is kept as *Dmítrievskaya subbóta*, 'Demetrius' Saturday', commemorating those who fell in the victory over the Tatars won at Kulikovo on the upper Don in 1380 by Grand Prince Demetrius of Muscovy (known as *Dmítrii Donskói*, 'Demetrius of the Don'). The battle was in fact fought on 8 September, which was a Saturday; Demetrius chose the Saturday nearest his own name-day for the commemoration.

Tysilio or Suliau (7th c.?). Abbot of Meifod, he was forced to flee from a widowed sister-in-law who wished to marry him; he went to Brittany, near Saint-Malo, where he died. In the nineteenth century the name of Llanfairpwllgwyngyll ('The Church of Mary of White Hazel Pool') in Anglesey (now officially Ynys Môn even in English) was extended to 58 letters, proudly displayed on the railway platform:

LLANFAIRPWLLGWYNGYLLGOGERYCHWYRNDROBWLLLLANTYSILIOGOGOGOCH

The added items mean 'quite near the rapid whirlpool, the church of Tysilio under a red cave'. This feat provoked imitation: a gift-shop in Llangollen bears the sign

YSIOPFACHGARDIAUWRTHYBONTDROSYRAFONDDYFRDWYYNLLANGOLLEN

or 'The little card shop by the bridge over the river Dee in Llangollen'.

9 NOVEMBER

a.d. V Idus Novembres   E

❰ HOLIDAYS AND ANNIVERSARIES Cambodia: Independence Day (1953)

❰ HOLY DAYS **Dedication of the Lateran Basilica** (RC); Margery Kempe (CY commem.)

Dedication of the Lateran Basilica. S. Giovanni in Laterano, not St Peter's, is the cathedral church of Rome; it is formally titled 'Archbasilica of the Most Holy Saviour', but has taken on the name of John the Baptist from the dedication of its baptistery, and from being served by monks from an adjoining monastery of John the Baptist and John the Divine; when the church was rebuilt after the earthquake of 896, Pope Sergius III (904–11) made the Baptist and St John the Evangelist its patrons.

Margery Kempe (*c.*1373–after 1438). Married to a burgess of Lynn, Norfolk, to whom she bore fourteen children, her life changed drastically after a series of visions following an attack of madness; she and her husband vowed chastity, and she embarked on an astonishingly independent life, pilgrimaging alone to the Holy Land, Rome, Compostela, and other places. She recorded her 'revelations' and her life in a book, which relates in detail the anger she aroused for her criticism of the laxness of the clergy (she was formally accused of Lollardy) and the exasperation occasioned by her copious weeping; her steadfast mystical communion with Christ upheld her strength, as did her numerous supporters.

Theodore of Euchaita (RC): see *17 February.

After the calendar reform of 1752, the Lord Mayor's Day was changed from 28 October to 9 November. Now the Lord Mayor is sworn in on the second Friday in November, and his Show follows on the next day. See *Other Holidays: Lord Mayor's Show.*

Death of Charles de Gaulle (1970); his grave is visited by Gaullist politicians and many humble folk.

On this day in 1989 the government of the German Democratic Republic, by accident under pressure and not design, opened the Berlin Wall, thus setting in motion the collapse of the East German state. A proposal to celebrate this as the Day of German Unity in place of 17 June came to naught upon the recollection that it was also the anniversary of the *Reichskristallnacht* pogrom in 1938, the most serious concerted physical attack on Jews under the Third Reich before the outbreak of war; in any case, the achievement of unity in 1990 soon afforded a definitive date (see *3 Oct.).

10 NOVEMBER

a.d. IV Idus Novembres   F

> *If the 10. day be cloudy, it denunciates a wet; if dry, a sharp winter.*
> (Stevenson)

❡ HOLY DAYS Leo I the Great (CY, RC, formerly 11 Apr.; 18 Feb. Orth.)

Pope Leo I (440–61), the first Pope to be buried at St Peter's, earned his name of 'Great' by the energy with which he imposed his jurisdiction on all the Western provinces, and by the 'Tome', a letter sent to Flavian (see *18 Feb.) stating the Western Church's two-nature Christology with all the clarity and finality for which Latin is renowned. The Tome, which had not been so much as read to the Robber Council (see *18 Feb.) at Ephesus, was declared at Chalcedon to accord with sound doctrine: 'Peter has spoken through Leo.' (This was Leo's view of all papal pronouncements; the Eastern Christians meant only that he happened to be right.) The Council adopted a formulary in which the Tome was quoted. Leo's sermons include an early reference to the Ember fasts, and an admonition against sun-worship on the steps of St Peter's. In 452 he led an embassy to dissuade Attila from marching on Rome; Attila made peace, which since Italy was stricken with plague and famine, and since the forces he had left north of the Danube had been routed, was the only prudent course.

> *Officer of the Papal Guard*
>
> Of course, nobody knows
> What Leo said to him.
> All we could hear was muttering.
>
> The more pious among us,
> His chaplains and so on,
> Believe he put the fear
>
> Of the one true God into
> The Barbarian. Perhaps he did,
> Leo's a saintly man.
>
> But shrewd too. There's a rumour
> One of us brandished a sword
> And the Hun visibly paled.
>
> Take my word, that's rubbish.
> More likely, the old man said
> Something to this effect:
>
> 'You are the Scourge of God?
> But God has other scourges.
> Have you heard, there's plague in Rome?
>
> Some of your men I see
> Have had a taste of it.
> And food's hard to come by,

> For all of us, isn't it?'
> Who knows? But the muttering stopped.
> So did Attila.
>
> Philip Martin (1931–   )

Martinmas Eve in Germany:

On the tenth of *November* (being the eve of S. *Martin*) the *Germanes* use to feast themselves with geese; and as *Olaus Magnus* reporteth, the Northern people use by the breast-bone thereof to prognosticate of the following winter. For if the breast-bone of the goose be fair and clear when the flesh is eaten off, the winter is like to be cold and rigid, full of hard frosts. But if it be thick and dark, then is the winter like to be full of snow, rain and sleet, and yet warm enough.

Dove (1664)

For Protestants, this day is best remembered as the birthday of Martin Luther (see *31 Oct.).

On this day in 1938, at 9.05 a.m., died the founder of modern Turkey, Mustafa Kemal Atatürk; his death is commemorated in Turkey by a minute's silence at that time each year.

11 NOVEMBER

a.d. III Idus Novembres   G

> *At Saint Martin's day*
> *winter is on his way.*
>
> *Between Martinmas and Yule*
> *water's wine in every pool.*
>
> *His Martinmas will come, as it does to every hog.* (i.e. there's no escaping death)

❦ HOLIDAYS AND ANNIVERSARIES Angola: Independence Day (from Portugal, 1975) (national day)
  Australia, Canada: Remembrance Day
  Belgium, France, and other countries: Armistice Day
  Bermuda: Remembrance Day
  Canada: Remembrance Day
  USA: Veterans Day, honouring all men and women who have served in the armed forces; formerly Armistice Day (established 1926), commemorating the signing of the Armistice ending the First World War in 1918
  USA, Washington: Admission Day (42nd state, 1889)
Scottish term day till 1990.

❦ HOLY DAYS Martin of Tours (CofE, RC); Menas (Orth.)

Martin (d. 397), born to pagan parents at Sabaria in Pannonia (now Szombathely in Hungary); his father was a soldier from Pavia, who brought him up there and made him join the army at the age of 15. It was as a soldier, not yet baptized, that he performed the deed that has made him a household name:

Hence, at a certain time, when he had nothing but his armour and a simple military cloak, in the middle of a winter colder and harsher than usual, so that many people froze to death, at the gate of Amiens he met a poor man with no clothes; he was praying to the passers-by to have pity on him, but they all passed by. The God-filled man understood that he had been reserved for himself, since the others were showing no pity; but what was he to do? He had nothing but the cloak he was wearing, having already spent everything else on similar actions. He therefore grasped the sword at his side and cut it down the middle, gave one half to the poor man, and put the other back on. Some of the bystanders began to laugh, thinking he looked grotesque with his cropped cloak; but many, whose judgement was sounder, groaned deeply that they had done nothing of the kind; especially since, being better provided, they could have clothed the poor man without unclothing themselves.

That night, when he had gone to sleep, he saw Christ wearing the half-cloak with which he had clad the poor man. He was bidden to look very carefully at the Lord, and at the garment he had given; next he heard Jesus saying in a loud voice to the multitude of angels standing round: 'Martin, still a catechumen, has clothed me in this cloak.'

Sulpicius Severus, *Life of St Martin*, ch. 3

After baptism in 354, he remained a soldier for a while, then visited St Hilary at Poitiers; he undertook an unsuccessful mission to Illyricum preaching against Arianism. After a period of retreat, he founded a monastery at Ligugé near Poitiers, from which in 371 he was called to be the third bishop of Tours. He translated the body of the first bishop, St Gatianus (see *18 Dec.), to the church built by the intervening bishop, Litorius; this is now the cathedral of Saint-Gatien. A little outside the city, he founded a monastery dedicated to SS Peter and Paul, later to be the great Benedictine house of Marmoutier (*Maius Monasterium*, 'Greater Monastery'). He died on 8 November 397, and was buried on the 11th. Over his tomb his successor Britius (see *13 Nov.) built a church, in which he himself was buried; this became the basilica of Saint-Martin de Tours, of which only fragments remain. Martin's devoted follower Sulpicius Severus wrote a narrative of his life, and dialogues concerning his merits; these helped to spread his cult. There are well over fifty extant Latin *vitae* and related sources dealing with St Martin; the oldest extant church in England bears his name. He is patron saint of soldiers, horses, riders, geese, and wine-growers. His cloak (*cappa, cappella*), the prized relic of the Frankish kings, was kept in a sanctuary or *cappella* from which our word 'chapel' is derived.

Menas, a legendary Egyptian soldier martyred in Phrygia under Diocletian; in Greece said to reveal lost or stolen property, from the word-play *Minás* ~ *minái*, 'indicates'. He also protects sheep against the wolf; on his day the shepherd's wife will not use her scissors, but bind the blades together as if to shut wolves' jaws and gossips' mouths.

Martinmas or St Martin's Day. November was the month when cows and pigs were slaughtered, the beef to be preserved by salting, and the gammon and bacon smoked:

> Now Tenants at their Landlords Courts pay due,
> And Country Huswives strongest pieces chuse,
> To stuff their Powdring-Tubs with well-fed Beef,
> (In starving weather excellent relief)
>   This thrift is taught us by the Bee and Ant,
> Which those that slight, will pinched be with Want.
>
> *Country Almanack* (1675)

This is a great day in many countries; in Cologne, where figures of Christ, the Virgin (a man, except in the Nazi period), and a Peasant take part in the festivities, it is accounted the first day of carnival. A widespread usage is the eating of goose, as in England at Michaelmas; Olaus Worm takes the opportunity, in the best antiquarian spirit, to list classical references to stuffed goose.

Norwegian primestaves may mark this day with crosier, goose, drinking-horn, or pig; one explanation of the drinking-horn is that, on being pledged by the emperor (called by the legend Maximinius), after drinking he passed the horn to his priest instead of returning it to the secular prince. On the other hand St Martin's Day is also a new wine day, marked in parts of Central Europe by the 'baptism of young wine', a colourful and merry occasion at which 'Bishop Martin' and his ministers 'transform' must into wine in numerous vineyard cottages. Venetians say *Samartin, El mosto va in vin*; in sixteenth-century France *Saint Martin boit le bon vin, Et laisse l'eau courre au molin* ('St Martin drinks the good wine and lets water run to the mill'). Beaujolais Nouveau arrives close to Old St Martin's Day.

St Martin's summer: 'a season of fine mild weather occurring about Martinmas':

> Expect Saint Martin's summer, halcyon's days
> Since I have enterèd into these wars.
>
> *1 Henry VI*, 1. ii. 110–11

In parts of Italy this is the traditional date for moving house.

Armistice Day, commemorating the armistice that ended the fighting in the First World War 'at the eleventh hour of the eleventh day of the eleventh month'; until 1939 it was solemnly observed, all sound and movement ceasing for two minutes at 11 a.m. In Britain, after the Second World War, it was replaced by Remembrance Sunday, on the Sunday nearest the 11th; the Sovereign lays a wreath at the Cenotaph; the Union flag is flown. The two minutes' silence is observed at this and at local ceremonies, but has largely ceased to be kept outside them; however, since 1995 the original silence on 11 November has been revived, with increasing success, by the Royal British Legion, with the support of politicians and journalists. It is the custom, on this day and those preceding, to wear a paper replica of a red poppy; the day itself is commonly called Poppy Day.

Douglas Macleane records the first anniversary, 1919:

On the Feast last month of the soldier-saint Martin, for the space of two minutes, there fell on the whole Empire, as it were from heaven, a sacred silence and cessation from action. It was the moment at which, a year earlier, the roar of cannon had been hushed. Men and women seemed to be going about their business on their lawful occasions, expecting nothing particular, but now and then looking up. No especial preparations had been made, except that services had begun in the churches. Suddenly a church bell or two is heard; then the detonation of a rocket; policemen's hands go up; and in a moment 'streaming London's central roar' is hushed, and myriads stand with bowed heads; some kneel. Soldiers come to attention; trains, omnibuses, vessels, stop. It is the same in ten thousand other cities all the globe over; on the high seas; and in a million villages. In warehouse, shop, bank, field, mine or railway all is stilled. . . . It was the man in the street's solemnity; the silence was the hush of a multitude which no man could number, a pause in the midst of turmoil and hubbub, of business and pleasure.   Macleane, 1202

For the Fallen (September 1914)

With proud thanksgiving, a mother for her children,
England mourns for her dead across the sea.
Flesh of her flesh they were, spirit of her spirit,
Fallen in the cause of the free.

Solemn the drums thrill: Death august and royal
Sings sorrow up into immortal spheres.
There is music in the midst of desolation
And a glory that shines upon our tears.

They went with songs to the battle, they were young,
Straight of limb, true of eye, steady and aglow.
They were staunch to the end against odds uncounted,
They fell with their faces to the foe.

They shall grow not old, as we that are left grow old:
Age shall not weary them, nor the years condemn.
At the going down of the sun and in the morning
We will remember them.

They mingle not with their laughing comrades again;
They sit no more at familiar tables of home;
They have no lot in our labour of the day-time;
They sleep beyond England's foam.

But where our desires are and our hopes profound,
Felt as a well-spring that is hidden from sight,
To the innermost heart of their own land they are known
As the stars are known to the Night;

As the stars that shall be bright when we are dust,
Moving in marches upon the heavenly plain,
As the stars that are starry in the time of our darkness,
To the end, to the end, they remain.

Laurence Binyon (1869–1943)

12 NOVEMBER

❦ HOLY DAYS Josaphat (RC); formerly Martin I, Pope (now *13 Apr.)

Josaphat (Józefat Kuncewicz; *c*.1580–1623), born to Orthodox parents in the Volhynian town of Vladimir (now Volodymyr-Volyns'kyĭ in Ukraine) and baptized Ivan Kuntsevich. Volhynia belonged to the Grand Duchy of Lithuania, which in 1569 had entered into full political union with Poland; in 1596 the Orthodox Church in the Polish Commonwealth was officially united with Rome. So long as Polish rule lasted, the 'Greek Catholic' or Uniate Church was the ally of the secular power against Orthodox resistance (under Russian rule the positions were reversed); Kuntsevich, induced by a Jesuit education to become a monk under the name of Josaphat, was a zealous champion of the Union, known to its opponents as *dushokhvát*, 'Soul-snatcher'. Having risen to become archbishop of Polotsk in 1618, he was killed in an anti-Union revolt at Vitebsk in 1623. In 1687 he was canonized as the first RC saint of the Eastern rite. Feast-day formerly 14 November.

Lebuin (Northumbrian *Leafwini*), Benedictine monk from Ripon who built the first church at Deventer and died there *c*.780. At Ghent his name, corrupted to Livinus (Lieven, Liévin), was appropriated for a fictitious seventh-century Irish martyr, invented as part of an aggressive campaign by the Benedictine abbey of St Bavo to outdo in sanctity the rival Benedictine abbey of St Peter of Blandigny. Allegedly baptized and ordained by Augustine of Canterbury, Livinus became bishop of Dublin before evangelizing Brabant, where he got his head chopped off at Eschen near Alost (in Dutch Aalst). Nevertheless, he became sufficiently popular to receive four separate feasts: his *elevatio* was celebrated on 28 June, his *adventio* on 16 August, his *translatio* on 2 October; the main feast, however, also kept in Bruges, Brussels, and Tournai, was the *depositio* or *passio* on 12 November.

Hollantide (*Sauin, Laa Souney*) in the Isle of Man, being the New Style counterpart of Old Allhallows between 1752 and 1799, and not adjusted thereafter (cf. *5 July).

On the Hebridean island of Scarp Hallowe'en continued to be observed on this day; it was strictly reserved for the girls, who in turn left Hogmanay to the boys. Wearing short pinafores and 'head-dresses' (small kerchiefs), they took part in fortune-telling rituals relating to their marriage prospects: each girl dug a hole to which she returned in the daylight, hoping to find a worm in it; each dipped her hand blindfold into one of four saucers, of which three contained oatmeal, salt, and water, signifying respectively wealth, widowhood, and marriage, and the fourth was empty, meaning that she would stay a spinster. There was no procession or traditional rhyme as there was for Hogmanay, but they feasted and stayed up all night singing songs and playing games.

13 NOVEMBER

Idus Novembres   B

❡ ANCIENT ROME On this day Roman senators assembled for a feast of Jupiter, *Iovis epulum*; freed slaves celebrated the goddess Feronia in the Campus Martius.

❡ HOLY DAYS Britius (BCP); Charles Simeon (CY); John Chrysostom (Orth.; see *13 Sept.)

Brice (Lat. Britius), a turbulent priest, who despite quarrelling with St Martin succeeded him as bishop of Tours and reigned there from 397 till his death in 444, despite accusations of various offences including adultery. (He is also said to have claimed that his master was insane; eventually he begged Martin's forgiveness, which was granted with the words, 'If Christ could tolerate Judas, surely I can put up with Brice.') His cult was spread to Italy and England. His day is notorious in English history for the massacre of all Danes within the kingdom, ordered in 1002 by King Ethelred II, on the pretext of a plot against his life: men, women, and children were slaughtered with gleeful savagery (cf. *19 Oct.). Among the victims is said to have been the sister of the Danish king Svend ('Swein Forkbeard'), who invaded Wessex the next year by way of reprisal and in 1013–14 conquered the whole country.

Charles Simeon (1759–1836), vicar of Holy Trinity, Cambridge; a leader of the Evangelical Revival, and active in the Missionary Movement.

Homobonus (d. 1197). A devout merchant of Cremona, notable for his charity towards the poor, he was canonized two years after his death. He is patron saint of Cremona as well as of tailors, merchants, and businessmen in general. His church at Rome in Vico Iugario (built in 1482, rededicated in 1700) stands over remains from the regal period (see *11 June); the site is known as the *Area sacra di Sant'Omobono*.

Stamford bull-running. Thomas Fuller explains the meaning of the proverb 'As mad as the baiting bull of Stamford':

William earl *Warren* Lord of this Town in the time of King *John*, standing upon the *Castle Walls* of *Stamford*, saw *two Bulls* fighting for a *Cow* in the *Meadow*, till all the *Butchers Dogs, great* and *small*, persued one of the Bulls (being madded with Noyse and Multitude) clean through the Town. This Sight so pleased the said Earl, that he gave all those Meadows (called the *Castle Meadows*) where first the *Bull Duel* began, for a Common to the Butchers of the Town (after the first Grasse was eaten) on condition that they find a Mad Bull, the day Six *weeks* before *Christmas day*, for the continuance of that sport every year. Some think that the *Men* must be *mad* as well as the *Bull*, who can take delight in so dangerous a *Wast-Time*; whereby that no more Mischeif is done, not *mans care*, but *Gods Providence* is to be praised.   Fuller, *Worthies*, 153 (1662)

Fuller's sentiments notwithstanding, the custom continued into the nineteenth century:

About a quarter to eleven o'clock, on the festal-day, the bell of St Mary's commenced to toll as a warning for the thoroughfares to be cleared of infirm persons and children; and precisely at eleven, the bull was turned into a street, blocked up at each end by a barricade of carts and wagons. . . . The bull, irritated by hats being thrown at him, and other means of annoyance, soon became ready to run; and then, the barricades being removed, the whole crowd, bull, men, boys, and dogs, rushed helter-skelter through the streets. One great object being to 'bridge the bull', the animal was, if possible, compelled to run upon the bridge that spans the Welland. The crowd then closing in, with audacious courage surrounded and seized the animal; and, in spite of its size and strength, by main force tumbled it over the parapet into the river. The bull then swimming ashore, would land in the meadows, where the run was continued; the miry, marshy state of the fields at that season of the year, and the falls and other disasters consequent thereon, adding greatly to the amusement of the mob. The sport was carried on till all were tired; the animal was then killed, and its flesh sold at a low rate to the people, who finished the day's amusement with a supper of bull-beef.   Chambers

The sport was continued, against the opposition first of local authorities, then the Society for the Prevention of Cruelty to Animals, and finally of the Home Secretary, until at last, in 1840, the townsfolk decided that the expenses for the police force were not worth the candle, and the race was not run thereafter.

14 NOVEMBER

a.d. XVIII Kalendas Decembres   C

HRH the Prince of Wales born 1948; red-letter day; the Union flag is flown

❨ ANCIENT ROME This day was marked by a cavalry review or Equorum Probatio.

❨ HOLY DAYS Dyfrig (RC Wales); formerly St Josaphat (now *12 Nov.)

Dubricius or Dyfrig (6th c.), a shadowy or more likely legendary figure said to have been bishop of Llandaff; according to Geoffrey of Monmouth, he crowned King Arthur at Colchester.

Philip the Apostle (Orth.; BCP *1 May); so near the onset of winter, farmers cannot afford to lose a working day, but recount the legend that St Philip himself was a poor ploughman, who worked all day and came home tired and hungry; his wife was cooking beans, but with the words 'It's Carnival' (alluding to the Orthodox Advent fast beginning the next day), he slaughtered an ox and shared it with the poor. Next morning, on entering the stable, he found the ox alive.

No!

No sun—no moon!
No morn—no noon—
No dawn—no dusk—no proper time of day—
No sky—no earthly view—
No distance looking blue—
No road—no street—no 't'otherside the way'—
No end to any Row—
No indications where the crescents go—
No top to any steeple—
No recognitions of familiar people—
No courtesies for showing 'em—
No knowing 'em!
No travelling at all—no locomotion,
No inkling of the way—no notion—
'No go'—by land or ocean—
No mail—no post—
No news from any foreign coast—
No Park—no Ring—no afternoon gentility—
No company—no nobility—
No warmth, no cheerfulness, no healthful ease,
No comfortable feel in any member—
No shade, no shine, no butterflies, no bees,
No fruits, no flowers, no leaves, no birds,—
November!

Thomas Hood (1799–1845)

15 NOVEMBER

a.d. XVII Kalendas Decembres   D

❦ HOLIDAYS AND ANNIVERSARIES Brazil: Republic Day (proclamation of the Republic, 1889)

❦ HOLY DAYS Machutus (BCP); Albert the Great (RC)

Machutus (Maclou, Malo) (d. *c.*564), a Welsh saint who travelled to Brittany and founded near Alet a monastery that has given its name to the town of Saint-Malo; in turn the Falkland Islands, having been observed by sailors from Saint-Malo, are known in French as the *Îles Malouines*, whence the Spanish name *Islas Malvinas*.

Albert the Great (Albertus Magnus) (*c.*1193–1280), Dominican theologian who taught Thomas Aquinas in Cologne; in 1260 he became bishop of Regensburg, but resigned two years later. One of the most learned men of his age, he is known as the *Doctor universalis*; he was particularly strong in the natural sciences, and played his part in the integration of Aristotle's writings into the Western Christianity of the later Middle Ages. He was beatified in 1622, but not canonized till 1931; ten years later Pius XII declared him the patron saint of scientists.

Leopold III, margrave of Austria, died on this day in 1136; remarkable not only for refusing the imperial crown in 1125, but for a piety and closeness to the Church that won him the title 'son of St Peter' from the Pope. In 1114 he laid the foundation-stone of Klosterneuburg near Vienna; over twenty years later he founded two abbeys in the Wienerwald, Heiligenkreuz of the Cistercian order and Klein-Mariazell of the Benedictine. Leopold was canonized in 1485; in 1663 he was declared patron of Austria by his namesake, the Holy Roman Emperor Leopold I. In Austria this is *Leopoldstag*, also called *Gänsetag*, 'Geese Day', from the traditional dinner of roast goose; it is the official beginning of *Heurigen*, the new wine season. Pilgrims visit Leopold's tomb in the crypt at the Stiftskirche Klosterneuburg and perform the *Fasselrutschen*, a slide down the great cask (completed 1704; holds 46,500 litres of wine) in the cellar; the bumpier one's landing, the better one's luck in the forthcoming year.

Among the Orthodox this day, the fortieth before Christmas, is the beginning of 'Little Lent' (*Mikra Tesserakostē*), a fast that continues down to Christmas Eve, Saturdays and Sundays excepted.

16 NOVEMBER

a.d. XVI Kalendas Decembres   E

❆ HOLIDAYS AND ANNIVERSARIES USA, Oklahoma: Admission Day (46th state, 1907)

❆ HOLY DAYS Margaret of Scotland (CY, RC); Gertrude (RC); Edmund of Abingdon (CY commem.)

Margaret of Scotland (*c.*1046–93), granddaughter of Edmund Ironside, wife of one Scottish king (Malcolm III), mother of two more (Duncan II and Edgar), and mother-in-law of King Henry I of England. Well educated in Hungary, where her family was in exile, she was noted for her personal piety and charity, and took an active interest in reform of the Church in Scotland. Feast-day formerly 10 June.

Gertrude the Great (*c.*1256–1302), Benedictine nun at Hefta in Saxony. She began to have mystical visions of Christ in 1281, which continued throughout her life. Through her writings, begun in 1289, she popularized the devotion to the Sacred Heart. She is patroness of the West Indies.

Edmund of Abingdon, archbishop of Canterbury (*c.*1180–1240). As a schoolboy in Oxford, he had a vision of the boy Jesus, who told him that whoever should before sleeping trace the words 'Jesus of Nazareth' on his or her forehead should be preserved that night from sudden and unshriven death; this was supposedly the origin of a custom of tracing the initials INRI on the forehead while praying. In the late 1220s he was commissioned by Pope Gregory IX to preach the crusade against the Saracens; later, as archbishop of Canterbury, he had many troubles with monks of his diocese as well as with King Henry III, going into exile in France, where he stayed with Cistercian monks of Pontigny; he was canonized in 1246. St Edmund Hall, Oxford, is named after him. The RC Church commemorates him on this day as well.

17 NOVEMBER

a.d. XV Kalendas Decembres   F

❧ HOLY DAYS Hugh, Bishop of Lincoln (CofE); Hilda, Abbess of Whitby (ASB; CY on *19 Nov.); Elizabeth of Hungary (RC; CY on the 18th)

Hugh (*c.*1140–1200), bishop of Lincoln. Born of noble stock in Burgundy, and intended for an order of Canons Regular, he found the greater austerity of the Carthusian Order more to his liking. He was made third prior (the first two having proved incompetent) of the Carthusian house set up by Henry II at Witham in Somerset; from then on he enjoyed close personal relations with Henry (who in 1186 pressed the bishopric of Lincoln on him) and with his sons Richard I and John, even when he stood up to them with a blend of firmness and humour. He had a pet swan that guarded him so zealously that none could approach the bishop without being attacked; so reports his chaplain Adam of Eynsham, who also relates that Hugh, in order to translate a relic of Mary Magdalene to Lincoln, bit a piece out of her arm. The RC Church commemorates him on this day as well.

Elizabeth (Erszébet) *of Hungary* (or Thuringia) (1207–31). Hers was a short but very eventful life. Daughter of King András II of Hungary, she married Ludwig IV, Landgrave of Thuringia, at the age of 14; when he died on crusade six years later, his brother banished her for undue generosity to the poor. Under the influence of a harsh confessor, Conrad of Marburg (who flogged her for disobedience), she gave up her children and practised great austerity, while devoting herself to caring for the sick. She died on 17 November 1231, and was buried in the chapel of St Francis' hospital; miracles were soon reported, and she was canonized only four years later. Such was her fame that she was one of the few saintly women of her time to be included in the Golden Legend, with a full and admiring account. She is patron of the Franciscan Third Order. In many calendars, and the *cisioianus*, her day is the 19th; she must be distinguished from the Blessed Elizabeth of Hungary, daughter of András III, commemorated on 31 October, the anniversary of her death at the Dominican convent of Toess near Winterthur in Switzerland.

Accession of Elizabeth I, 1558. Beginning with the tenth anniversary, in 1568, bells were rung in London and Worcester, and the custom spread in the next decades; it was added to the list of holy days in 1576 (but was not a day of rest), with a special set of prayers. In other places (apparently at local initiative) the day was observed with sermons, music, fireworks, bonfires, and pageants.

The commemoration of Elizabeth's accession long outlived the monarch herself; Protestants in particular cherished her memory, and the elevation to sainthood in 1712 of the pope who had excommunicated her, Pius V, occasioned the following sentiments in *A Protestant Memorial for the Seventeenth of November, being the Inauguration Day of Queen Elizabeth* (1713):

In a grateful remembrance of God's mercy in raising up, continuing, and prospering this most illustrious benefactor of England, the good Protestants of this nation (those especially of LONDON and WESTMINSTER) have annually taken notice (and not without some degree of decent and orderly solemnity) of the 17th of November, being the day on which her Majesty Queen Elizabeth began her happy reign. And at present such decent and orderly observation of it seems to me not only warranted by former motives, but also enforc'd by a new and extraordinary argument. For this present Pope, call'd Clement XI., has this very year canoniz'd the forementioned enemy of England, Pope Pius the Fifth, putting him into the number of heavenly saints, and falling down and worshipping that image of a deity, which he himself has set up. Now the good Protestants of England, who well consider that this present Pope has, so far as in him lies, exalted that Pope who was so bold and so inveterate an adversary of Queen Elizabeth and all her subjects, as also that he is an avowed patron of the Pretender, will think it behoves them to exert their zeal now, and at all times, (tho' always in a fit and legal manner,) against the evil spirit of Popery which was cast out at the Reformation, but has ever since wandered about seeking for a remittance, which I verily hope the good providence of God, at least for his truth's sake, will never permit.   quoted in Brand, i. 223

These sentiments explain why it was customary to burn the Pope and the Devil in effigy on this day; during Queen Anne's reign, the figure of the Pretender was added to the bonfire.

The Leonids, an annual meteor-shower, peak about this day.

18 NOVEMBER

a.d. XIV Kalendas Decembres   G

℄ HOLIDAYS AND ANNIVERSARIES Latvia: Independence Day (from Germany and Russia, 1918)
    Oman: National Holiday

℄ ANCIENT ROME This day was appointed by the Roman emperor Licinius, colleague and enemy of Constantine the Great, for the worship of the sun-god; some scholars infer that, under its Macedonian name of 1 Dios, it was regarded in certain parts of the

Roman East as New Year's Day. Clement of Alexandria's date for the Nativity, 194 years 1 month 13 days before the death of the emperor Commodus (31 December AD 192), works out at 18 November 3 BC; but his calculations are too confused for any deduction to be sure.

❦ HOLY DAYS Elizabeth of Hungary (CY; RC on *17 Nov.); Dedication of the Basilicas of SS Peter and Paul (RC)

St Peter's Basilica, as we see it today, was consecrated by Urban VIII on 18 November 1626; the new basilica of San Paolo fuori le Mura, built after the primitive one was destroyed by fire, was consecrated by Pius IX on 10 December 1854, but the annual commemoration was appointed for 18 November.

A tale of two Cornish saints, Keverne (6th c., on this day) and Just or Ust (12 Aug., to whom a church is dedicated near Penzance):

St. Just it appears, went in a friendly manner to pay a visit to St. Keverne, in whose house he was entertained with the greatest hospitality for several days. It seems however, that soon after his departure, St. Keverne having missed a piece of plate, began to suspect the honesty of his guest; and to bring this matter to an issue, he pursued him, resolving to make him restore the stolen article, or to give proof of his honesty. Anticipating a combat, on crossing Crowsaz Downs, he took up three stones, each weighing full 300 pounds, and put them into his pocket; and being thus armed, pursued his brother saint, whom he overtook in the parish of Germoe, and charged immediately with the robbery. St. Just denied the charge, and a contest immediately ensued; but St. Keverne being armed with his three stones, soon obtained a complete victory; and having recovered his plate, returned. His stones however, being now of no further use, and being rather cumbersome, he sunk triangularly into the ground, in a little nook on the right hand side of the road between Breage and Marazion, where they continue to the present day, as monuments of what ancient saints could accomplish. Many times they are said to have been removed for buildings; but to what place soever they have been carried, they have always found their way back again during the night. It is somewhat remarkable, that these are actually of the same grit with the iron stone of Crowsaz Downs, and that none besides of this kind are to be found in Breage or Germoe. *Hitchins, i. 714–15 (1824)*

19 NOVEMBER

a.d. XIII Kalendas Decembres A

❦ HOLIDAYS AND ANNIVERSARIES Monaco: National Day

❦ HOLY DAYS Hilda (CY); Barlaam (Orth.); formerly Elizabeth of Hungary (RC, now *17 Nov.)

Hilda, abbess of Whitby, is said by Bede to have died on 17 November 680. Ignored by the BCP, she was commemorated on the 17th in the ASB, but moved to the 19th in CY, as Elizabeth of Hungary was to the 18th, in order to separate her feast from St Hugh's.

She was head of a double monastery of monks and nuns at *Streanaeshalch*, also known as Whitby, where the great synod of 664 was held; her name appears in the calendar of St Willibrord, written at the beginning of the eighth century. The American BCP puts her on the 18th.

Barlaam, martyred at Antioch perhaps under Diocletian, an ill-educated but strong-minded Christian who resisted tortures described in detail by Basil the Great and St John Chrysostom. In Russia this day (OS = 2 Dec.) is associated rather with his namesake, Varlaam of the Pechersky monastery, and with Barlaam and Josaphat (see *27 Nov.).

Mechtild of Hackeborn (d. 1298), a German mystic known for her singing as a 'nightingale of Christ'; her revelations were written down by her abbess as the *Book of Special Grace*; some have identified her with the Donna Matelda in Dante, *Purgatorio* 27–8. Another Mechtild, of Magdeburg, was her contemporary in the same nunnery and was even more famed as a mystic writer.

20 NOVEMBER

a.d. XII Kalendas Decembres   B

Set garlike and pease,
saint Edmund to please.

(HOLIDAYS AND ANNIVERSARIES Mexico: Anniversary of the Revolution of 1910 (national holiday)

Wedding-day of HM the Queen 1948; the Union flag is flown

(HOLY DAYS Edmund the Martyr (CofE)

Edmund, born *c*.840, was king of the East Angles by 865. In 869 he was captured by the Vikings, who offered to spare his life if he would share his kingdom with their leader, Ingvarr the Boneless; refusing to associate with a heathen, he was set up as a practice-target for the Danish archers, till he resembled 'a hedgehog whose skin is closely set with quills, or a thistle covered with thorns'; he was then beheaded. Almost at once he was culted as a martyr; in the tenth century his remains were translated to Bury St Edmunds. Before the promotion of St George he was regarded as the patron of England: although the story that the rebel barons pledged themselves on his altar to extract a charter from King John is not supported by local evidence, it is certain that in 1222 his feast was decreed a holy day of obligation for all England. The RC Church commemorates him on this day as well.

21 NOVEMBER

❦ HOLY DAYS Presentation of the Blessed Virgin Mary (RC); **Entry of the Theotokos into the Temple** (Orth.)

This feast, originating with the dedication of New St Mary's in Jerusalem on this day 543, is associated with the story in the Protevangelium of James that Mary was brought to the Temple by her parents, Joachim and Anne, at the age of 3. It is attested at Constantinople by the eighth century, and was made a public holiday in 1166. The earliest observance in the West was in the eleventh century; Sixtus IV introduced it into Rome in 1472. Pius V removed it from the calendar in 1570 as being based on legend, but in 1585 Sixtus V restored it.

Gelasius I, pope (492–6), a zealous champion of ecclesiastical power, active defender of Chalcedonian Christianity and foe of heretics; so intransigent was his resistance to Constantinople that he alienated the Eastern Church. He insisted that communion be taken in both kinds in order to show up Manichees who refused to drink wine. Modern scholars deny him authorship of the Gelasian Sacramentary (an 8th-c. Frankish liturgical book) and the *Decretum Gelasianum* (a 6th-c. account of doctrine and church government including a list of books to be read, or not read, in church); some have reassigned the attack on the Lupercalia (see *15 Feb.) to his predecessor, Felix III; but there is no doubting his letters or his theological treatises, including a defence of Chalcedon against its enemies.

In Greece it is said that the good farmer has sown at least half his field by this day; whence the name 'Our Lady Halfsower' (*Mesosporítissa*) or 'Muchsower' (*Polisporítissa*). On her day one eats a dish made of several kinds of grain, called 'manyseed' (*polispermía*) or in some places 'allseed' (*panspermía*), the name used in ancient Athens for a similar dish honouring the corn goddess Demeter offered on the third day of the Anthesteria festival (the 13th day of the month Anthesterion, in late February or early March).

22 NOVEMBER

❦ HOLIDAYS AND ANNIVERSARIES Lebanon: Independence Day (from France, 1941)

❦ HOLY DAYS Cecilia (CofE, RC)

Cecilia, legendary virgin martyr of patrician birth, who converted her husband Valerian and his brother Tiburtius (*14 Apr.), martyred under Severus Alexander in the time of Urban I, *c*.223, by being suffocated with the steam of a hot bath in her own mansion (later converted into a church). The likely cause of death in such instances would be heatstroke rather than suffocation; but the legend insists that, although she was kept in the bathhouse, with a great fire under it, for more than 24 hours, she proved so impervious to the heat that, as Chaucer puts it, 'It made hir not a drope for to swete'. In frustration, the persecutor ordered her to be beheaded; but not even the executioner's axe could finish her off—at least, not immediately. She lived three more days, with her head half-severed, still teaching her followers and encouraging them in the faith. Chaucer says:

> Thre strokes in the nekke he smoot hire tho,
> The tormentour, but for no maner chaunce
> He myghte noght smyte al hir nekke atwo;
> And for ther was that tyme an ordinaunce
> That no man sholde doon man swich penaunce
> The ferthe strook to smyten, softe or soore,
> This tormentour ne dorste do namoore,
>
> But half deed, with hir nekke ycorven there,
> He lefte hir lye, and on his wey he went.
> 'The Second Nun's Tale', 526–34

At a translation of her supposed remains in 1599, her body was seen to be complete and incorrupt (although in an earlier translation, her head had been enshrined separately); in the basilica of Santa Cecilia in Trastevere, under the high altar, there is a beautiful statue of her reclining body by Stefano Maderno.

Near the site of the basilica, Roman women had worshipped the Bona Dea Oclata or Restitutrix, who gave protection against eye-disease and blindness (*caecitas*); local Christians appear to have transferred this belief to a Caecilia (in one source a male Caecilius), and then identified her with the Caecilia buried in a crypt built next to that of the popes, in the catacomb of Callistus, after the persecutions had ceased. Jewish-Christian influence has been suggested by Connolly (the chief source for this paragraph and the next), not only because Trastevere had a large Jewish population: St Cecilia's cult drew on the Book of Esther, held in very little regard by Gentiles, and early texts record as her 'station' day—that on which the Pope said mass in her church—the Wednesday after the second Sunday in Lent, which is as many days before Good Friday as 13 Adar, the Fast of Esther, before the biblical Passover on 14 Nisan. Since Esther's other name, 'Hadassah' (Esth. 2: 7), means 'Myrtle', a saint who in some sense was Esther had by her presence defied the pagan ban on bringing myrtle, sacred to Venus, to the place of Bona Dea, her chaste opposite; on the other hand, the lesson attested for her station mass is the Prayer of Mordechai (Esth. 13: 8–17 Vulg.), but put in Esther's mouth instead, as if recalling the exclusion of men from the cult of Bona Dea.

In some places Cecilia is a healing saint, but she is mainly known as the patron saint of music. This is commonly thought a fifteenth-century misunderstanding of the tale that on her wedding-day she ignored the playing instruments but sang to God in her heart; the truth seems to be more complex. The *Passio*, composed in the late fifth century to give her legend a definitive form, represents her as possessing, through her virginity, an angelic vision that contrasts with the spiritual blindness of her persecutors. It is as a virgin, sharing in the *vita angelica* as a member of a celestial choir, that she sings to God in her heart, and hears the music of heaven, easily identified with the Neoplatonic music of the spheres. In this she transcends Esther, whose deliverance of her people is celebrated at Purim by drinking till one can no longer tell the difference between 'Accursed be Haman' and 'Blessed be Mordechai'; but at Eph. 5: 18–19 making melody in one's heart to the Lord is preferred to being drunk with wine. Hence in the later Middle Ages Cecilia is symbolically depicted carrying (not at first playing) a portative organ; however, as the Neoplatonic world-view faded, and earthly music regained its inheritance from the spiritual interloper, the musical Cecilia became its patron.

Purcell's ode 'Welcome to all the pleasures' was published in 1684 by John Playford: the title-page proclaimed: 'A Musical Entertainment PERFORM'D ON NOVEMBER XXII. 1683. IT BEING THE Festival of St. Cecilia, a great Patroness of Music; WHOSE MEMORY is ANNUALLY Honour'd by a Public Feast made on that Day by the MASTERS and LOVERS of Music, as well in England as in Foreign Parts.'

At Christ Church in Oxford it is the custom, on St Cecilia's day, for grace before dinner to be sung; so one of us heard it in 1963, and then on sitting down, learnt that President Kennedy had been assassinated.

23 NOVEMBER

a.d. IX Kalendas Decembres   E

> *Cattern and Clement comes year by year,*
> *some of your apples and some of your beer.*

❦ HOLIDAYS AND ANNIVERSARIES Japan: Labour Thanksgiving Day or *Kinrōkansha no Hi* (national holiday)

❦ HOLY DAYS Clement (CofE, RC); Columban (RC)

Clement, apparently of Jewish origin, is traditionally counted as the third pope (*c*.91–*c*.100) after St Peter, who is said to have ordained him; he is chiefly remembered for the much-admired letter sent *c*.96 from the Roman to the Corinthian church, which was riven by internal dissensions. Although Clement's name nowhere appears in the text, other evidence indicates that he wrote it, but as corresponding secretary not as bishop: Rome had not yet adopted monarchical bishops such as existed at Antioch (see *17 Oct.), and the text, like the New Testament, makes no distinction between bishops (in Greek *epískopoi*, 'overseers') and presbyters (*presbýteroi*, 'elders'). The beautiful church of San Clemente in Rome was built *c.*1100, after Robert Guiscard's Normans had ravaged the city in 1084 (see *25 May), above one dedicated in the late fourth century and erected on the site of two first-century houses (of which the smaller contained a second-century Mithraeum or temple of Mithras) standing over the remains of houses destroyed in the fire of AD 64. This site was called the *area Clementis*; it is known that by the third century Christian worship had been conducted in a *titulus Clementis*, a building owned or formerly owned by a Clemens—possibly T. Flavius Clemens (see *22 June), in whose household the saint was sometimes thought to have been a freedman. This seems improbable: although Clemens was a common name for slave and free alike— also borne by St Paul's 'fellow labourer' at Phil. 4: 3—a slave would not be called by the same name as his master, nor would he take his master's *cognomen* when freed; but this notion underlies both the dedication of the church to the bishop in the late fourth century and the belief that he was a martyr. By further confusion with Pontia or Ponza, the island in the Tyrrhenian Sea to which Flavius Clemens' wife Domitilla had been banished, Clement was said to have been exiled to the Pontus or Black Sea area, specifically to the Crimea, and thrown into the sea with an anchor round his neck. In the winter of 860/1 the missionary diplomat Constantine (later Cyril; see *11 May) found what he took to be his relics, complete with anchor, and brought them back to Constantinople; when he and his brother Methodius were sent to Moravia, they carried the relics with them, and in 867/8 brought them back to Rome for solemn interment in the basilica.

His day was long kept in England by processions of children mimicking churchmen and begging for money, till the feast, along with those of SS Catherine, Nicholas, and the Holy Innocents, was suppressed by proclamation on 22 July 1541 (see *6 Dec.).

How Clement became the patron saint of hatters:

Hatters have a tradition that while St. Clement was fleeing from his persecutors his feet became blistered, and to afford him relief he was compelled to put wool between his sandals and the soles of his feet. On continuing his journey, the wool, by the perspiration, motion, and pressure of the feet, assumed a uniformly compact substance, which has since been denominated *felt*. When he afterwards settled at Rome, it is said, he improved the discovery; and from this circumstance has been dated the origin of *felting*. Hatters in Ireland, and other Catholic countries, still hold their festival on St. Clement's day.   Hone, *Year*, 693

Columban, abbot of Luxeuil and Bobbio, died on this day in 615. Born *c.*543 in Leinster, he became a monk *c.*560 in Bangor (Co. Down), and spent thirty years as a teacher before travelling with twelve companions, including St Gallus (see *16 Oct.), by way of England to Austrasia and Burgundy (roughly, eastern France and western Germany); he founded numerous monasteries, in particular Luxeuil, with a rule of his own, based on Irish practices, that proved too austere for Continental tastes and had to be replaced by St Benedict's. His Irish mode of reckoning Easter also gave offence; he defended himself in a letter to Pope Gregory the Great, in which apparent humility peels off to reveal a studied insolence. Expelled from Burgundy in 610 after rebuking King Theuderic or Thierry II for concubinage, he travelled up-Rhine to Bregenz, and thence to northern Italy, where he founded the abbey of Bobbio, south-west of Piacenza, in which he is buried.

24 NOVEMBER

a.d. VIII Kalendas Decembres   F

❦ HOLIDAYS AND ANNIVERSARIES Democratic Republic of Congo (national day)

❦ HOLY DAYS Formerly St John of the Cross (now *14 Dec.)

Chrysogonus, said to have been martyred under Diocletian at Aquileia, but patron of a Roman church (San Crisogono) in Trastevere as well as of a Venetian church (San Grisogono) near the house of Marco Polo.

In the Byzantine Empire this was the beginning of the new wine festival of Brumalia, which lasted until the winter solstice (Latin *bruma*); being essentially a pagan celebration in honour of Dionysos, it was condemned by church councils, but observed by the Byzantine court and popularly until at least the twelfth century. Small cakes were sent as presents.

November
Impression

A weft of leafless spray
Woven fine against the gray
Of the autumnal day,
And blurred along those ghostly garden tops
Clusters of berries crimson as the drops
That my heart bleeds when I remember
How often, in how many a far November,
Of childhood and my children's childhood I was glad,
With the wild rapture of the Fall,
Of all the beauty, and of all
The ruin, now so intolerably sad.

William Dean Howells (1837–1920)

25 NOVEMBER

a.d. VII Kalendas Decembres   G

❦ HOLIDAYS AND ANNIVERSARIES Suriname: Independence Day (from the Netherlands, 1975)

❦ HOLY DAYS Catherine of Alexandria (CofE, RC until 1969)

Catherine of Alexandria, in Greek *Aikateríne*, whence the Church Slavonic *Ekaterína*, used in Russian for the two empresses of that name. Latin form *Katharina* by false etymology from the Greek *katharós*, 'pure'. She was one of the major female saints in the Middle Ages, always portrayed with the spiked wheel on which she was to have been broken but which itself was broken by a thunderbolt from heaven—whence derives her patronage of wheelwrights and millers. According to her legend, dramatically retold in the Golden Legend but now considered pure fiction, she was a fourth-century virgin, noble and of exceptional intelligence, who bested fifty philosophers in a debate ordered by the emperor Maxentius; disgusted, he had them all burnt. The legend also has her body transported to Mount Sinai by angels (slow ones: the trip took twenty days). Artists often portrayed the 'mystic marriage' of St Catherine, where she is shown accepting a ring from the Christ Child, after a vision she once had; the antiphon for Virgins, 'Come, Bride of Christ', perpetuates this theme. She is one of the Fourteen Auxiliary Saints, and patron of philosophers, students, and librarians:

> Saint Cathern favours learned men, and gives them wisedome hye:
> And teacheth to resolve the doubtes, and always giveth ayde,
> Unto the scolding Sophister, to make his reason stayde.
>
> Naogeorgus, fo. 38

She is also the patron saint of young women (her voice was one of the heavenly voices heard by St Joan), and especially of spinsters:

> St Catherine, St Catherine, O lend me thine aid,
> And grant that I never may die an old maid.
>
> A husband, St Catherine,
> A good one, St Catherine;
> But arn-a-one better than
> Narn-a-one, St Catherine.   *any; none*
>
> Sweet St Catherine,
> A husband, St Catherine,
> Handsome, St Catherine,
> Rich, St Catherine,
> *Soon*, St Catherine.
>
> H. Pentin, *Old Dorset* (1907), 105–6

On her day in France women have the right to ask men in marriage. Unmarried women in their twenty-fifth year were expected to give her statue a new bonnet on her day; hence their name of *catherinettes*, especially applied to milliners.

Mercurius (d. *c*.250), a warrior saint, who appeared in a vision with SS George and Demetrius to help the Christians recapture Antioch during the First Crusade (see *23 Apr.).

Evacuation Day in New York City: in 1783 General Knox and his troops entered the city from Harlem, as the last British troops were embarking. Governor Clinton hosted a dinner for General Washington and other army officers at Fraunce's Tavern, and the citizens celebrated with bonfires and rockets. John Pintard, founder of the New-York Histori-cal Society, was instrumental in securing the anniversary celebration.

New York, 25th November, 1820. This is the 37th Anniversary of the evacuation of this city by the British forces which consummated the American revolution, a day that restored our citizens to their desolated dwellings after a long & tedious exile of 7 years, during which many a patriot had died & left their remains in distant lands. . . . This day so dear to us, has long been celebrated by military honours, and I think that I have heretofore told you that the celebration was owing to my suggestion when a young member of the Corporation of this city before my going to Newark.   Pintard, i. 348

Anniversary of the Great Flood?

According to the most experienced chronologists the deluge commenced this day 2348 years be-fore Christ, and in the year 1656 of the world.   *Time's Telescope* (1830), 398

26 NOVEMBER

❦ HOLY DAYS

Siricius, pope (384–99), the first to issue decretals (formal edicts of church law). At a synod in 391/2 he secured the condemnation of the monk Jovinian, who having turned against asceticism had denied that Mary had remained a virgin after bearing Jesus; later, he condemned the opinion expressed by Bonosus, bishop of Niš, that Mary had borne children to Joseph. Although Jovinian had been the target of Jerome's *Iovinianum*, a clas-sic of misogyny, Jerome had no love for Siricius, who had permitted his expulsion from Rome and who showed favour to men whom he detested; his adverse comments, and others from Paulinus of Nola, who found Siricius haughty, caused him to be omitted from the Roman Martyrology of 1584 despite his earlier status as a saint; he was re-stored in 1748 by Benedict XIV, who wrote a treatise in support of his sanctity.

Excellence of St Genevieve. In 1129 an epidemic of ergotism at Paris ended after the popu-lation had besought St Genevieve (see *3 Jan.) to intercede; the annual festival com-memorating the miracle, instituted by Pope Innocent II in the following year, is still observed in Parisian churches.

In Russia, this day was a second feast of St George: Parkinson (58) notes on Friday, 7 December 1792 (NS = 26 Nov. OS): 'This being St George's Day the Knights of that Order dined with the Empress.' The tale was told of a district whose people died every year on this day, having exposed wares for sale, and revived on 23 April to receive pay-ment.

27 NOVEMBER

a.d. V Kalendas Decembres   B

(HOLY DAYS

Barlaam and Josaphat. The ascetic Barlaam converted the young prince Josaphat and eventually his father, the persecuting King Abenner; all three left the world and lived as hermits. The story has been a favourite in the Christian world for many centuries; it was especially popular with the Cathar heretics of southern France, and also caused Tolstoy, as he relates in *A Confession*, to renounce worldly pleasures. Yet it is not originally Christian at all, but Buddhist. Stories of the Bodhisattva's (the future Buddha's) education became very popular with the Manichees of Central Asia, believers in an amalgam of Buddhism, Christianity, and Zoroastrianism whose asceticism is often thought to underlie Catharism and related movements. Of the numerous Manichaean versions of the tale, one was translated into Arabic (and given an Islamic tinge) as the Book of Bilawhar and Yūdāsaf; Bilawhar was a new character, but Yūdāsaf was a corruption of *Bodhisattva* (in Arabic script *b* and *y* are almost the same).

In this form it reached Georgia, where it was turned into a Christian romance entitled *Balahvariani*, the main characters being called Balahvar and Iodasap; this was translated into Greek by Euthymius (see *26 May) and reworked into a highly polished narrative, later ascribed to St John Damascene, in which the chief characters were renamed Barlaám (see *19 Nov.) and Ioásaph. This was translated into numerous Christian languages; in the Latin version, *Ioasaph* became the biblical name *Iosaphat* (Jehoshaphat). One component is a tale of four caskets, two gilded but containing dead men's bones, two covered with pitch but containing gems and perfumes; in the medieval storybook known as the *Gesta Romanorum* they became the three caskets, gold, silver, and lead, that Shakespeare incorporated in *The Merchant of Venice*.

James the Persian served Shah Yäzdegird I (399–420), who was well disposed towards Christians until, in the last year of his reign, some of them launched violent attacks against the Persian national religion of Zoroastrian fire-worship. Persecution was renewed; James apostatized, but was reconverted by his mother and his wife; for this the new shah, Bahram V, ordered his execution. First his fingers, then his toes, then his arms, then his legs were cut off; his thighs were ripped out of his hips; all the while James continued to praise God. He is known as St James Intercisus ('chopped to pieces'). A head said to be his reached Cormarey in the diocese of Tours in 1103 and the Vatican *c.*1440.

Virgilius or Fergil of Salzburg, the Apostle of Carinthia, died on this day in 784. A highly educated Irishman, known at home as the Geometer, he left home *c.*742 and stayed for two years at Compiègne, at the court of the future King Pippin, who sent him on to Duke Odilo of Bavaria. Odilo's territory included Salzburg, which was without a bishop; Virgilius was appointed to administer the diocese, but did so as abbot of

St Peter's through a suffragan, a fellow Irishman called Dubh of the Two Countries (Dubh dá gCríoch). This arrangement, normal in Ireland, offended the Englishman St Boniface, who also complained to Pope Zacharias (see *15 Mar.) that Virgilius had accepted as valid a baptism administered in bad Latin, and that he taught the existence of another world beneath the earth with its own sun and moon; evidently Virgilius (or Boniface) blended the Antipodes of ancient geography with his poetical namesake's abode of the blessed, who have a sun and stars of their own. The Pope avoided a decision on the last question, upheld Virgilius over the baptism, but insisted that he should be properly consecrated as bishop. After Odilo's son and successor Tassilo III had conquered the Carinthian Slavs Virgilius sent missionaries to convert them. His tomb was discovered in 1181; miracles were reported, leading to canonization in 1233. The learned but tongue-in-cheek cosmography of 'Aethicus Ister' is commonly thought to be his work.

28 NOVEMBER

a.d. IV Kalendas Decembres   C

❦ HOLIDAYS AND ANNIVERSARIES Albania: Flag Day (Dit'e Flamurit), commemorating revolt of 1443 and independence (from Turkey) in 1912; the date is the New Style equivalent of the 15th (national day)
Mauritania: Independence Day (from France, 1960)
UK, Scotland: Martinmas Term Day since 1990; previously Removal Day

❦ HOLY DAYS Day of Intercession and Thanksgiving for the Missionary Work of the Church (CofE)

Symeon Metaphrastes (Orth.), hagiographer, flourished *c*.960, who compiled a collection of saints' lives known as the *Mēnologion*, 'Tale of Months'; he is called *Metaphrastēs*, 'Reteller', for adapting most of the lives to the literary style of the age.

Come bleak november in thy wildness come
Thy mornings clothd in rime thy evenings chill
Een they have powers to tempt me from my home
Een they have beautys to delight me still
Tho nature lingers in her mourning weeds
& wails the dying year in gusty blast
Still added beauty to her end proceeds
& wildness triumphs when her bloom is past . . .
    John Clare (1793–1864), 'The Last of Autumn'

29 NOVEMBER

❦ HOLY DAYS

Saturninus (Sernin), bishop of Toulouse, one of Pope Fabian's missionaries (*22 Mar.*), martyred *c.257* by being tied to the heels of a wild bull; deserted by the two priests he had begged to stand by him, he prayed that the city might never have a bishop from its own citizens. His day also belongs (but since 1969 only in local calendars) to a Carthaginian priest of the same name martyred at Rome (*c.262? c.309?*).

St Andrew's Eve. In Germany it was Andrew rather than St Valentine who was the patron saint of lovers, and we find similar divinations on his eve:

> To Andrew all the lovers, and the lustie wooers come,
> Beleeving through his ayde and certaine ceremonies done,
> (While as to him they presentes bring, and coniure all the night)
> To have good lucke, and to obtaine their chiefe and sweete delight.
>
> Naogeorgus, fo. 55

Luther reports that young maidens stripped themselves naked, flung themselves to the ground, and prayed:

Deus, Deus meus, Du lieber Sanct Andreas, gieb mir eynen frommen man, tzeige mir hintte den an, der mir tzuteilt werden sol.

O God, my God, O St Andrew, give me a godly husband; show me tonight what manner of man shall wed me.   *Tischreden*, no. 6186

One girl, he adds, was nearly frozen to death, but no man came.

The UN resolution on the partition of Palestine, 1947, accepted by Jews but not by Arabs, led to the creation of the State of Israel (15 May 1948); it is remembered in Israel as *Kaftet be-November*, where *Kaftet* comprises the names of the numeral letters for 29. Palestinians commemorate a resolution on their rights passed on the same day in 1977.

Almanacs came on sale in November:

Nov. 29 (1654). I bought Wharton's Almanacke wherin are amazing perticulars.   Josselin, 108

30 NOVEMBER

❦ HOLIDAYS AND ANNIVERSARIES Barbados: Independence Day (national holiday) Benin: National Day

❦ HOLY DAYS **Andrew, Apostle** (CofE, RC, Orth.); red-letter day

Andrew, brother of St Peter, patron saint of Scotland; unlike the English (see *23 Apr.), the Scots are well aware of their patron saint's day, which also receives official recognition in Scotland by the flying of the Union flag. However, St Andrew is also patron of Patras and Russia; in the Anglican community St Andrewstide is widely observed by intercessions for foreign missions. For the Orthodox he is 'Andrew the First-Called' and in Greece 'Frying-pan-holer', from the punishment inflicted on those who fail to make pancakes on his day. He was martyred and buried at Patras, but some of his relics were translated to Constantinople (which, feeling the lack of an apostolic founder, half-heartedly tried to cast him in that role), and thence in 1204 to Amalfi by the Crusaders. His head, however, was thought to have remained in Patras; in 1460 Thomas Palaeologus took it with him into exile, and acceded to Pope Pius II's request that it should join the bodies of Peter and Paul in Rome. In his Commentaries Pius describes in great detail the arrival of the head in April 1462; with tears of joy he prayed that 'through his merits and intercession the insolence of the faithless Turk may be crushed' (Constantinople had fallen to the Turks only nine years earlier). The first representations of Andrew's martyrdom on an X-shaped cross (saltire, *crux decussata*) date from the tenth century.

In 1788 forty-five gentlemen of the St Andrews Society of Philadelphia consumed in his honour 38 bottles of Madeira, 27 of claret, 8 of port, 26 of porter, 2 of cider, and 2 bowls of punch. The observance continued in later years, if more soberly, then not without ceremony: diners were led in by pipers, followed by the sword of Gen. Hugh Mercer (who fell at the battle of Princeton), and a ram's head; the top of the snuffbox was ornamented with a large cairngorm. Proceedings concluded with a loving-cup.

DECEMBER

O dirtie December
For Christmas remember.
Forgotten month past,
Do now at the last.

(Tusser)

❧ NAMES FOR THE MONTH Latin *December*, French *décembre*, Spanish *diciembre*, Portuguese *Dezembro*, Italian *dicembre*, German *Dezember*, Welsh *Rhagfyr*, Scots Gaelic *an Dùdlachd*, *an Dùbhlachd*, Irish *Mí na Nollag*

The Latin name indicates that this was originally the tenth month of the year. The Welsh name means 'before the shortest day', the Scots Gaelic 'the darkness', the Irish 'Christmas month'.

❧ HOLIDAYS AND ANNIVERSARIES

Second Saturday Massachusetts: Army and Navy Union Day

Third week Mexico: Nine days of Posada

> And after him, came next the chill *December*
>   Yet he through merry feasting which he made,
>   And great bonfires, did not the cold remember;
>   His Sauiours birth his mind so much did glad:
>   Vpon a shaggy-bearded Goat he rade,
>   The same wherewith *Dan Ioue* in tender yeares,
>   They say, was nourisht by th'*Idæan* mayd;
>   And in his hand a broad deepe boawle he beares;
> Of which, he freely drinks an health to all his peeres.
>
> Spenser, *The Faerie Queene*, VII. vii. 41

Now doth the Lawyer make an end of his harvest, and the clyent of his money, and he that walks the streets shall find dirt on his shooes, except he walk all in boots. Now Capons and Hens, besides Turkyes, Geese and Duckes, with Beefe and Mutton, must all dye as a memoriall and sacrifice to the Feast of the sacred, the great and the sole sacrifice; for in 12 dayes a multitude of people will not be fed with a little. The Asse that hath borne all the yeare must now take a little Rest. The Oxe and the Cow, and the Horse and the Mare shall have their christmasse provant. Now Plumbes and Spice, Sugar and Honey, square it among Pies and broath; and Gossip I drink to you, and how doe you, and you are heartily welcome, I pray be merry, and I thank you. Now are the Taylors and the Tyre-makers full of work against the Hollidayes, and a journey man cares not a rush for his Master, though he beg his Plum-pottage all the 12 dayes. Now or never must the Musick be in tune, for the youth must dance and sing to get them a heat, while the aged set by the fire; Nature hath made it a Law, and reason finds no contradiction. The fat Oxe must dye, and the leane one live till he be more worthy the slaughter. The Footman now shall have many a fowle step; and the Ostler have work enough about the heels of the horses, while the talkative Tapster (if he looks not to his hits) will lye drunk in the Cellar. The Country maid leaves half her Market, and must be sent againe, if she forgets a pair of cards on christmasse Even. Great is the contention of Holly and Ivy, whether Master or Dame weares the breeches. The price of meat riseth apace, and the Aparrell of the proud makes the Taylors rich, and as proud as themselves. Dice and the cards benefit the Butler; and if the cook doe not lack wit he will sweetly lick his fingers. Now Starchers and Laundresses have their hands full of work, and periwigs; and paintings will not be a little set by; strange Stuffs will be well sold, strange tales well told, strange sights much sought, strange things much bought, and what else as falls out. To conclude, I hold it the costly purveyer of excesse, and the after-breeder of necessity; the practise of folly, and the purgatory of Reason.   Stevenson, 48–9 (1661)

In *December* Melancholy and Phlegm much increase, which are heavy, dull, and cold, and therefore it behoves all that will consider their healths, to keep their heads and bodies very well from cold, and to eat such things as be of a hot quality. Therefore now Broth made of Colworts and Onions are good; Cabbage is very good; roasted Onions of themselves, or in Sauce, very good; roasted Apples or Pears after Meats are greatly commended: the Flesh of Weathers, Rams and Goats, excellent Food: Capons, and all manner of Land Fowl, very wholsom, but not Water-Fowl. Bleed but little, and for necessity, for in no month in the year the body has less blood than now. Drink often Wine this month; and Honey, Cinnamon, Mace, Nutmegs, Ginger, Grains, Cloves, Galingale, or such often drunk or eaten this month, do cherish the blood, the heart, and all the body.   Saunders (1679)

Now to see a Plumb-Pudding as big and as long as a Cable-rope: oh how it would make a hungrie mans chaps to water at it! The Grocers have several *Reasons* for Plum-puddings; and there is not a Sectarie, though he rail never so much on *Christmas*, yet loves *Christmas*-Pies well enough. Now as pan cakes and fritters are most proper in *February*, and tansies in *April* and *May*, so Minc'd-pies are most seasonable in this Moneth. I tell you (my friends) much good matter may be squeezed out of a Minc'd-pie: they are good hot, and good cold; and though they are most seasonable at *Christmas*, yet without scruple of Conscience, you may eat them at any other time.   *Poor Robin* (1670)

1 DECEMBER

Kalendae Decembres   F

€ HOLIDAYS AND ANNIVERSARIES Central African Republic: Anniversary of the
    Proclamation of the Republic (1958) (national day)
    Romania: National Day

€ ANCIENT ROME About this time, though not always on this day, women honoured
Bona Dea (cf. *1 May); men were strictly excluded from the rites, which were conducted
by the Vestal Virgins in the house of a leading magistrate under the presidency of his

wife. Since Roman women were not supposed in earlier centuries to drink wine, the wine taken into her temple had to be called milk; the vessel was called a 'honey-pot'. In 62 BC the irresponsible young aristocrat Publius Clodius Pulcher attended in disguise; the ensuing scandal resulted in a trial, at which he was acquitted through blatant bribery. The decision by Cicero, whom he had supported in his hour of need against Catiline (see *5 Dec.), to give evidence against him led to a lasting breach between the two; Clodius embarked on a political career of ultraradicalism supported by armed toughs that ended only with his assassination in 52 BC.

❦ HOLY DAYS

Eligius (Fr. Éloi) of Noyon (*c.*590–660). His professional skill as a goldsmith led to service at the court of Clothar II, who named him Master of the Mint at Marseille. Soon his administrative abilities were recognized by appointment as counsellor to Clothar's son Dagobert I; their friendship is commemorated by a ribald French ballad in which 'le bon roi Dagobert' puts his breeches on back to front, runs away from a rabbit, and makes his bemused way through life only with the help of 'le grand saint Éloi'. (In fact Dagobert was a highly effective king.) Eligius, who founded numerous churches and monasteries, was made bishop of Noyon in 641 on the same day as his friend St Ouen (see *24 Aug.) was made bishop of Rouen. He is sometimes called 'the Apostle of Flanders' for his active role in evangelizing there. He is patron saint of goldsmiths, silversmiths, and all workers in metal, including jewellers; also of horses and veterinarians (his emblem is a horseshoe), blacksmiths, and garage and petrol-station attendants (undoubtedly as the modern successors of farriers). He is also patron saint of collectors of coins and medals.

> And Loye the smith doth looke to horse, and smithes of all degree,
> If they with Iron meddle here, or if they Goldesmiths bee.
>
> Naogeorgus, fo. 39

The 'greeteste ooth' of Chaucer's Prioress was 'by Seinte Loy'.

Edmund Campion (1540–81). While a fellow at St John's College, Oxford, where he was famed as an orator, he welcomed Queen Elizabeth to the University in 1566. Although he was ordained in 1569 in the Church of England, his increasing Catholic sympathies caused him to move to Ireland, where he helped found what is now Trinity College Dublin. In 1571 he returned clandestinely to England and then went to the Jesuit college at Douai; he became a Jesuit in 1573 and a priest in 1578. After a few years teaching in Prague he returned to England in 1580, where his eloquent preaching and, more pointedly, his pamphlet challenging the Privy Council caused political alarm; he was arrested, refused to recant, and was then charged with rebellion. Despite his refutation of all the charges he was found guilty by a jury that dared not otherwise. With two companions he was hanged, drawn, and quartered at Tyburn. He is one of the Forty Martyrs of England and Wales, canonized in 1970.

2 DECEMBER

a.d. IV Nonas Decembres G

❦ HOLIDAYS AND ANNIVERSARIES Laos: National Day
United Arab Emirates: National Day (independence from Great Britain, 1971)

❦ HOLY DAYS

Bibiana (a misspelling of Vibiana), Roman virgin martyr; according to legend, she was killed by being whipped with scourges loaded with lead, and her corpse was left exposed so that dogs would eat it, but they did not. She has a basilica on the Esquiline; relics were sent to Los Angeles in 1853. This is a critical day in Catalonia: if it rains then, it will rain for forty days or even longer.

3 DECEMBER

a.d. III Nonas Decembres A

❦ HOLIDAYS AND ANNIVERSARIES USA, Illinois: Admission Day (21st state, 1818)

❦ HOLY DAYS Francis Xavier (RC, CY commem.)

Francis Xavier (1506–52), one of the first Jesuits, 'Apostle of the Indies' as well as of Japan. Having met Ignatius of Loyola while studying in Paris, he joined with him and five like-inclined friends in a vow of poverty and obedience to the Pope. Accordingly, he was posted to the East, arriving in Goa in 1542, where he made his headquarters. By 1549 he had reached Japan, and founded a church there, despite persecution. He died on a mission to China. In 1904 Pius X named him patron saint of missions. He is patron saint of India and Pakistan, and a decree of 1914 made him patron of Mongolia. When it came time to choose a patron saint of tourism, Francis Xavier was the natural choice; he was so proclaimed by Pius XII in 1952. Thinking that, because of his Basque origin, he must have played pelota as a child, the Argentinian *pelotaris* requested that he become their patron; Paul VI obliged in 1978.

Lucius, supposed king of Britain, son of Coill (better known as 'Old King Cole'); said to have requested missionaries from the *Divi Fratres*—the brother emperors Marcus Aurelius Antoninus (161–80) and Lucius Verus (161–9)—and from Pope Eleutherius (*c.*174–89). At that date Britain was not a kingdom, but (as far as the Antonine Wall) a Roman province; the story has sometimes been ascribed to confusion with Lucius Aelius Septimius Abgarus, otherwise known as King Abgar IX of Osrhoene (176/7–211/12), often said (but some find the evidence inadequate) to have been a Christian convert; nevertheless, Lucius and Eleutherius are depicted in the south window over the choir of York Minster. The story is told at length by that engaging fraudster Geoffrey of Monmouth, who makes Lucius die in 156 and be buried at Rome. Lucius is also credited with the foundation of St Peter's, Cornhill.

Birinus (d. *c.*649), sent in 634 by Pope Honorius I to continue the conversion of England; finding the Gewisse (subsequently called West Saxons) to be thoroughly pagan, he remained amongst them, converted their king, Cynegils, and baptized him in 635, King Oswald of Northumbria being sponsor. He became their first bishop; his see, bestowed on him by Cynegils with the support of Oswald, was Dorchester-on-Thames. The modern visitor, who, while admiring the beauty and antiquity of this town, is amazed that a place so small should have been a cathedral city, does no more than echo William of Malmesbury in the twelfth century. CY commemorates him on 4 September.

In the early thirteenth century Bishop Henry of Avranches versified Birinus' life; he digresses to describe England with the true French distaste as perpetually ice-bound, with foul food, heavy air, a sea full of monsters, sterile soil, a faithless people, a barbarous language, but above all a lethal drink begotten in unnatural wedlock between the goddesses of water and corn, Tethys and Ceres, with the Fury Tisiphone for bridesmaid:

> cervisiam plerique vocant. Nil spissius illa
> dum bibitur, nil clarius est dum mingitur, unde
> constat quod multas feces in uentre relinquit.
>
> The many call it beer. Naught thicker else
> The body enters, clearer naught departs;
> What filth must in the belly then remain!

The joke was not original; the relative merits of wine and beer, as of the French and English nations, had become a subject for literary polemic amongst clerics. However, although ethnic slurs were already a time-honoured tradition, these debates were a kind of sporting contest; the point was not to bring the other nation into hatred and contempt, but to display superior literary talent and have fun.

4 DECEMBER

pridie Nonas Decembres   B

Barbara makes bridges (i.e. of ice)

❆ HOLY DAYS John Damascene (RC, CY commem.); Nicholas Ferrar (CY commem.); formerly St Peter Chrysologus (now *30 July)

John Damascene (*c.*675–*c.*749). Like his father before him, he served as Logothete or official spokesman of the Christians to the Caliph in Damascus; however, he left his riches to the poor and made a pilgrimage to Jerusalem, eventually settling in the lavra of St Sabas (see *5 Dec.). He is known for his theological treatises (so eloquent as to win him the nickname *Chrysorrhóas*, 'Goldenstream': cf. John Chrysostom, *13 Sept.), including defence of images against the iconoclasts. He was declared a Doctor of the Church by Pope Leo XIII. He was credited till recently with writing the romance of Barlaam and Ioasaph (Josaphat); see *27 November. Feast-day formerly 27 March in the West.

Nicholas Ferrar (1592–1637). After study at Cambridge and five years travelling abroad, he began what promised to be a brilliant career in business and as an MP. In 1625 he gave everything up and founded Little Gidding, where families lived in a community based on prayer and work. He was ordained deacon in 1626 and practised a life of austerity. The community met Puritan disapproval and worse, and a raid in 1646 destroyed most of his manuscripts and ended the community.

Barbara of Nicomedia (İzmit). According to her legend she was a Christian locked in a tower by her pagan father, first because of her beauty and then because she refused all suitors. He then handed her over to the Roman authorities under the emperor Maximinus and she was martyred in 306; her father was struck by lightning, against which in Spain she protects pious Christians. In Poland she is patron of miners. In Greece she protects against smallpox; honey-cakes are left at cross-roads as in pagan times they had been left for Hecate, *kóllyva* (boiled wheat sprinkled with cinnamon and almonds), or *varvára* (Modern Greek pronunciation of 'Barbara'; boiled wheat broth). As one of the Fourteen Holy Helpers (see *8 Aug.), she is invoked against lightning and fire, and is patron of gunners, miners, architects, builders, and stonemasons. Before it was decided to remove her from the calendar, in 1951 Pius XII confirmed her as the patron of Italian marines, military engineers, and firemen. Her emblem is the tower.

5 DECEMBER

Nonae Decembres   C

❲ HOLIDAYS AND ANNIVERSARIES Thailand: The King's Birthday and National Day

❲ ANCIENT ROME 'The Immortal Nones of December'. A Senate debate in 63 BC on Catilinarians caught in treasonable conspiracy ended with a motion (of moral but not legal force) calling for the death penalty; Cicero, as consul, immediately executed them, announcing the fact in a one-word sentence, *Vixerunt*, 'They have lived.' Depending on the danger they posed, this was either a salutary extinction of public enemies or an unwarrantable slaughter without trial of citizens, many of whom were Cicero's social superiors; in the next few years, both the highest and the lowest in Rome were swung

towards the latter opinion (in consequence of which he was temporarily exiled), not
only by his enemies, but also for his own insufferable boasting of what Seneca was to
call 'his consulate praised not without cause but without end'.

Horace (*Odes* 3. 18) records a rustic celebration in honour of the god Faunus.

❦ HOLY DAYS

Sabas (439–532; RC, Orth.), a Cappadocian monk who founded a still-extant lavra or
hermit-colony in Palestine, now known as Mar Saba; having been reluctantly ordained
priest (not then the norm for monks, and still not in the East) in 490, two years later
he was made superior of all hermits in Palestine. He is especially honoured by the
Orthodox, being called Savvas in Greek, Savva in Russian; proverbs, however, noting
that Barbara, Sabas, and Nicholas occur in succession at the start of winter, represent
them as confederates in the destruction of fine weather.

St Nicholas' Eve in London, 1557:

The v day of Desember was sant Necolas evyn, and sant Necolas whent a-brod in most plases,
and all Godys pepull received ym to ther howses and had good chere, after the old custum.

Machyn, 160

6 DECEMBER

a.d. VIII Idus Decembres   D

> *St Nicholas in winter sends the horses to the stable,*
> *St Nicholas in spring (9 May) makes them fat.*
> (Russian proverb)

❦ HOLIDAYS AND ANNIVERSARIES Finland: Independence Day (from Russia, 1917)
Spain: Constitution Day

❦ HOLY DAYS Nicholas (CofE, RC)

Nicholas, fourth-century bishop of Myra; his authentic life is very obscure but his
legendary life spectacular, making him one of the most popular patron saints. His cult
in the West dates only from the eleventh century, when his relics were carried off to Bari
(see *9 May). As an exceedingly pious baby Nicholas declined his mother's breast on
Wednesdays and Fridays. From the legend that he resuscitated two or three boys whom
a wicked innkeeper had chopped into small pieces and cast into a brine-tub to sell as
pickled pork, he is the patron saint of children.

And the Schoole-boies in the west [of England]: still religiously observe Sᵗ Nicholas day
(Decemb. 6ᵗʰ), he was the Patron of the Schoole-boies. At Curry-Yeovill in Somersetshire, where
there is a Howschole (or schole) in the Church, they have annually at that time a Barrell of good

Ale brought into the church; and that night they have the priviledge to breake open their Masters Cellar-dore.   Aubrey, 40–1

The gift-giving associated with him stems from another legend, where he gave a secret gift of three bags of gold to a poor man whose only prospect of making ends meet had been to put his three daughters to prostitution. This legend is also responsible for his patronage of pawnbrokers; the three balls of their traditional sign are thought to represent the three bags of gold. Having abated an ocean storm, he is also invoked by those in peril on the sea; indeed, in Greece he is the protector of mariners, who carry his icon in their ships and make and redeem vows to him as formerly to Poseidon, god of the sea. (Much posthumously, Nicholas himself made a lengthy sea voyage in 1087 when his body was translated across the Adriatic to Bari.)

> Saint Nicolas keepes the Mariners, from daunger and diseas
> That beaten are with boystrous waves, and tost in dredfull seas.
>
> Naogeorgus, fo. 38ᵛ

The Golden Legend tells a tale of a Jew who put a statue of St Nicholas in his house to protect his goods against theft. Nevertheless, thieves entered and stole everything except the statue. Enraged, the Jew beat it black and blue, whereupon St Nicholas appeared to the robbers, exhibiting his bruises, and appealing to their sympathy, urged them to return the loot; startled at this appearance, they quickly restored the property. The moral, of course, is that they forthwith reformed and the Jew converted. From this story comes the appellation of thieves as 'St Nicholas' clerks':

Thei are no Churchemen, they are masterlesse men, or rather S. Niclas Clarkes that lacke liuyng, and goyng in procession takes the Churche to be an Hospitall for waie fairers.

T. Wilson, fo. 81ᵛ (1553)

The custom of electing a boy bishop on this day was widespread, especially in England; an account is given by Rimbault. He held office until Holy Innocents' Day (*28 Dec.); if he died within that term he was buried in full pontificals. John Aubrey remarks on the monument in Salisbury cathedral of one of these short-lived boy bishops:

Under the arch, between two pillars on the north side of yᵉ nave of yᵉ cathedrall church of Sarum, is a little monument in Purbec marble of an Episcopus Puerorum, who died, in his honour. . . . The tradition of yᵉ Choristers, and those that show the Church is, yᵗ this Childe-bishop being melancholy, the Children of yᵉ Choire did tickle him to make him merry, but they did so overdoe it that they tickled him to death: and dyeing in his office and Honour, here was this little monument made for him, wᵗʰ the episcopal ornaments, e.g., mitre, crosse, and cope.

Aubrey, 171

At the abbey of Montserrat in Catalonia the boy bishop (*bisbetó*) serves on St Nicholas' day, assisted by a vicar-general, a master of ceremonies, a secretary, and two pages, and issues a pastoral letter.

The laxity of church ceremonial that would allow a boy bishop naturally led to other irregularities. Durandus (see *2 Nov.) reports (7. 39) that in one church the prior refused to let the brethren sing St Nicholas' miracles: 'Be off with you! I won't let such minstrels' songs be sung in *my* church!' On St Nicholas' eve, the saint (or one of the brethren?) appeared to him, haled him out of bed by the hair, flung him down on the flagstones, and sang the antiphon *O pastor aeterne* right through, beating him with a rod at every note. After that, the prior gave in. Perhaps Durandus was complaining about musical plays of St Nicholas, four of which are found in the Fleury Playbook of the twelfth century and are the earliest non-biblical liturgical dramas.

Henry VIII, many centuries later, was also vexed by customs on this and other days, issuing a proclamation on 22 July 1541 that they 'should be nowe againe celebrated and kept holie days':

And whereas heretofore dyverse and many superstitious and childysshe observations have been usid, and yet to this day are observed and kept in many and sondry parties of this realm, as upon sainte Nicolas, sainte Catheryne, sainte Clement, the holye Innocentes, and such like; children be strangelye decked and apparelid to counterfaite priestes, bysshopps, and women; and so ledde with songes and daunces from house to house, bleassing the people, and gatherynge of monye; and boyes doe singe masse, and preache in the pulpitt, with suche other unfittinge and incon-venyent usages, rather to the derision than to any true glory of God, or honour of his saints, the kynge's majestie therefore myndinge nothing so moche, as to advaunce the true glorye of God without vayne superstition, willith and commaundeth, that from henceforth all suche super-stitions be loste and clyrleye extinguisshed throughowte all this his realmes and dominions, forasmoche as the same doe resemble rather the unlawfull superstition of gentilitie, than the pure and sincere religion of Christe.   Wilkins, 860

An eyewitness report on the feast of St Nicholas at Bari in the mid-nineteenth century:

On the festa of St Nicholas . . . the city is absolutely invaded by an army of pilgrims. With staves bound with olive, with pine, or with palm, each bearing a suspended water-bottle formed out of a gourd, frequently barefoot, clothed in every variety of picturesque and ancient costume, de-votees from every province of the kingdom of Naples seek health or other blessings at the shrine of the great St Nicholas. . . . The bones of the saint are deposited in a sepulchre beneath the magnificent crypt, which is in itself a sort of subterranean church, of rich Saracenic architecture. Through the native rock which forms the tomb, water constantly exudes, which is collected by the canons on a sponge attached to a reed, squeezed into bottles, and sold to the pilgrims, as a miraculous specific, under the name of the 'Manna of St Nicholas'. As a proof of its supernat-ural character, a large bottle was shewn to me, in which, suspended from the cork, grew and floated the delicate green bladder of one of the Adriatic *ulvae*. I suppose that its growth in fresh water had been extremely slow, for a person, whose word I did not doubt, assured me that he re-membered the bottle from his childhood, and that the vegetation was then much less visible. . . . I trust that all the water that was sold to the pilgrims was really thus afforded by St Nicholas, if its efficacy be such as is asserted to be the case; but on this subject the purchasers must rely im-plicitly on the good faith of the canons, as mere human senses cannot distinguish it from that of the castle well.

The pilgrims, on entering the Church of St Nicholas, often shew their devotion by making the circuit once, or oftener, on their knees. Some are not content with this mark of humility, but actually move around the aisles with the forehead pressed to the marble pavement, being gener-ally led by a child, by means of a string or handkerchief, of which they hold the corner in the mouth. It is impossible to conceive anything more calculated to stir the heart with mingled feel-ings of pity, of admiration, of sympathy, and of horror than to see these thousands of human beings recalling, in their physiognomy, their dialects, their gesticulations, even their dresses, the *Magna Graecia* of more than two thousand years ago . . .

The mariners of Bari take their own part . . . Early in the morning, they enter the church in procession, and receive from the canons the wooden image of the saint, attired in the robes and mitre of an archbishop, which they bear in triumph through the city . . . and carry him out to sea, where they keep him until nightfall. They then return, disembark under the blaze of illumination, bonfires, and fireworks, and the intonation, by the whole heaving mass of the population, of a Gregorian Litany of St Nicholas; parade the town, visit by torchlight, and again leave, his own church; and finally, and late in the night, return the image to the reverend custody of the canons, who, in their purple robes and fur capes turned up with satin, play only a subordinate part in the solemnity. . . .   Chambers

St Nicholas' patronage of children made him a giver of presents. In the German world he makes his rounds arrayed as a bishop, distributing sweets and nuts to good children, and accompanied by his black-faced servant, Knecht Ruprecht (also known by other names), who spanks bad ones. In Flanders and the Netherlands, 'Sinterklaas' performs similar duties. On the evening of the 5th, children put their shoe in front of the fire, for Sinterklaas, traversing the roof on his white horse, may drop presents down the chimney. A carrot, turnip, or lumps of sugar are put in the shoe for the horse; in the morning the lucky child finds sweets and toys. The saint has a slave, *Zwarte Piet* (Black Pete), who accompanies him to carry off the naughty children; some commentators are dismayed, but the threat is still found useful.

Like other immigrants to the USA, Sinterklaas changed his name to Santa Claus; he also changed his working day to Christmas, and after trying a variety of outfits, notably black with ermine trimmings, consented to wear the red and white Coca-Cola uniform bestowed on him by the company's Christmastide advertisements in the *National Geographic*. He has opened a British branch under the name of Father Christmas, having acquired the goodwill of the feast's medieval personification Syr Cristemas; it expanded into Brazil, where Papai Noel must wear his thick fur in temperatures of 35 °C (95 °F).

7 DECEMBER

a.d. VII Idus Decembres   E

❦ HOLIDAYS AND ANNIVERSARIES Ivory Coast Republic: Independence Day (from France, 1960)
USA: Pearl Harbor Day
USA, Delaware: Delaware Day

❦ HOLY DAYS Ambrose (RC, Orth., CY; BCP on 4 Apr., the day of his consecration)

Ambrose or Ambrosius (*c*.339–97), son of the praetorian prefect (civil governor) of the Gauls, a highly educated man who became governor (*consularis*) of Aemilia and Liguria, his seat being at Milan. In 374 the bishop of that city, Auxentius, a fervent Homoian (see *2 May), died after nineteen years in office; there broke out a struggle over the election of his successor between those who supported this position and those who favoured the Nicene *homoousios*. Unwilling to see a repetition of the bloodshed that had marred the papal election eight years earlier (see *11 Dec.), the praetorian prefect of Illyricum, Italy, and Africa sent Ambrose (who was his protégé) to quell the troubles; while he was urging the people gathered in the church to keep the peace, voices from the crowd (improved by his hagiographer to a child) called out *Ambrosius episcopus*, whereupon, though not yet baptized, he was elected on the spot. He was expected to be a compromise candidate, and at first behaved as such; but political events drove him into conflict with the Homoians, a conflict that was not won till the pro-Homoian imperial court at Milan was driven out in 386/7 by Magnus Maximus, like the eastern emperor Theodosius (who first recognized and then eliminated him) a staunch Nicene.

In 384, when Symmachus, the much-admired pagan prefect of Rome, petitioned the Western court to restore the Altar of Victory in the Roman senate-house, arguing that not by one path alone could the great secret of universal truth be attained, Ambrose successfully replied there was one such path, that of the Christians; later he would intimidate Theodosius out of rebuilding a synagogue destroyed by a Christian mob, and excommunicate him for a massacre by his soldiers. It was Symmachus who procured Augustine the post of professor of rhetoric at Milan; there he encountered Ambrose, who made a great impression on him, at first for his eloquence, then for his doctrine. When conversion followed it was Ambrose who baptized him.

Ambrose's writings have made him a Doctor of the Church along with Augustine, Jerome, and Gregory the Great; but more influential than his theological works were his hymns, written in a simple metre previously marginal in Latin poetry and capable (as many imitations show) of being adapted to a post-classical language in which syllabic quantity was no longer perceived. One of these, 'Deus creator omnium', comforted Augustine on his mother's death.

St Ambrose is the patron of Milan, and also of bees and beekeepers, being portrayed with a hive in token of his learning. In 1981 John Paul II named him patron of the French army commissariat, evidently alluding to his efficiency as an administrator.

Pearl Harbor attacked, 1941, initiating the entry of the USA into the Second World War; in Japan the year was the 16th of the Shōwa or Bright Peace era.

8 DECEMBER

a.d. VI Idus Decembres   F

❨ HOLY DAYS Conception of the Blessed Virgin Mary (CofE); **Immaculate Conception of the Blessed Virgin Mary** (RC)

The feast, instituted in the East (see *9 Dec.) during the seventh century as being nine months before the Virgin's nativity, spread to certain Western churches, including by the early eleventh century that of Anglo-Saxon England (Winchester, Canterbury, and Exeter); it was popularly associated with the belief (not then accepted by serious theologians) that she was free not merely—as all agreed—from actual sin ('immaculate'), but even of original sin ('immaculately conceived'). After the Norman Conquest, the feast was expelled from the calendar by the new archbishop of Canterbury, Lanfranc (*28 May), contemptuous of Anglo-Saxon peculiarities; his successor, Anselm (*21 Apr.), though far more sympathetic to English piety, also rejected immaculate conception as negating the need for the Incarnation. However, his pupil Eadmer defended it according to Anselm's own manner of reasoning; his treatise circulated under Anselm's name and for that reason (together with the story of a miraculous vision originally beheld by Abbot Elsi of Ramsey but reassigned to the more convincing Anselm) played a large part in spreading the doctrine against the opposition of most schoolmen, and later the Dominicans, its main champions being the Franciscans.

Under Spanish pressure the Council of Basle on 17 September 1439 declared the doctrine compulsory on all Catholics, forbade teaching and preaching against it, decreed obligatory observance of the feast, and prescribed readings from the treatise for Matins; but the Council was in schism with the Pope, who did not ratify its acts. In 1449 the Sorbonne imposed the doctrine on its candidates; on 27 February 1477 the Franciscan Pope Sixtus IV approved the feast without quite using the term 'immaculate conception' (his words were *de ipsius immaculatae Virginis mira conceptione*, 'on the wondrous conception of the said immaculate Virgin'); on 4 September 1483 he condemned those (the Dominicans) who maintained that the doctrine was heretical, 'since no decision has yet been taken by the Roman Church and the Apostolic See'. In 1708 Clement XI imposed the Conception as a Feast of Obligation on the universal Church; on 8 December 1854 Pius IX (Bull 'Ineffabilis Deus') proclaimed the Immaculate Conception as a dogma. See too *16 April.

The Virgine Maries conception

Our second *Eve* puts on her mortall shroude,
Earth breeds a heaven, for Gods new dwelling place,
Now riseth up *Elias* little cloude
That growing, shall distill the showre of grace:
Her being now begins, who ere she end,
Shall bring the good that shall our ill amend.

Both Grace and Nature did their force unite,
To make this babe the summe of all their best,
Our most, her least, our million, but her mite:
She was at easiest rate worth all the rest,
What grace to men or Angels God did part,
Was all united in this infants heart.

Four only wights bred without fault are namde
And al the rest conceived were in sinne,
Without both man and wife was *Adam* framde,

Of man, but not of wife did *Eve* beginne,
Wife without touch of man Christs mother was,
Of man and wife this babe was bred in grace.

Robert Southwell (?1561–95)

The opera season begins on this day in Milan, the day after St Ambrose's day.

9 DECEMBER

a.d. V Idus Decembres   G

(HOLY DAYS

Abel, son of Adam and Eve (see *24 Dec.), slain by his brother Cain. He has been considered not only a prototype of the martyr (Jesus names him as the first of the prophets who were killed, Matt. 23: 35) but also a type of Christ, since he was a shepherd and suffered a violent death. His name occurs in the Canon of the mass.

Budoc or Beuzec, abbot (6th c.), a Celtic saint after whom Budock and Budoc Vean in Cornwall and St Budeaux in Devon are named; he is also venerated in Brittany, especially at Plourin, which preserves his relics. Some of the many miracles related in his *Vita* deal with his mother, Azenor, daughter of the king of Brest; in order to distract a snake that was biting her father, she smeared her breast with milk and aromatic oil; the snake bit her breast and would not let go, so she had to cut her breast off; God, in recognition of her piety, gave her back a breast of gold (evidently this appealed to the writer of the legend; Azenor cannot have found it very useful or comfortable). She was supposed to have given birth to Budoc in a barrel in the English Channel, where her wicked stepmother had thrown her on suspicion of infidelity; visions of St Brigid ensured that she reached Ireland, and became a washerwoman near Waterford, where Budoc was raised. This is his feast-day at Vannes; elsewhere his day is the 8th, but at Dol on 18 November.

In the Orthodox Church this is the Conception of St Anne, meaning the day on which she conceived the Mother of God. It was formerly sacred to her in Scandinavia: Olaus Worm marked it with a pitcher, 'for the peasants say it is time to pour water on the barley in order to brew the beer for Christmas cheer'.

10 DECEMBER

a.d. IV Idus Decembres   A

(HOLIDAYS AND ANNIVERSARIES   United Nations: Human Rights Day
USA, Mississippi: Admission Day (20th state, 1817)

❡ ANCIENT ROME This was the day on which Roman tribunes of the plebs assumed office.

❡ HOLY DAYS John Roberts (RC Wales)

John Roberts (1576–1610), a native of Trawsfynydd; after study at Oxford he went to Paris, where he converted to Catholicism, subsequently becoming a Jesuit and then a Benedictine. In 1603 he arrived as a missionary in England; implicated in the Gunpowder Plot, he was acquitted and banished, becoming prior in Douay. Returning to England, he was arrested in 1610, tried for high treason for functioning as a priest, and executed on 10 December.

Translation of the Santa Casa di Loreto. Never sanctioned in the Universal Calendar, and now strongly doubted, even by the most pious Catholics, the story of the miraculous wafting by angels to Loreto of the house in which the Virgin received the Annunciation had a firm hold on the imagination of believers from the late fifteenth century on; although the first translation was supposed to have taken place in 1291, the earliest record dates from *c*.1470. It was a famous place of pilgrimage, tokens of which were not only hung up (by the humble) but displayed (by the magnificent).

A seventeenth-century traveller recounts the peregrinations of this house with a mind of its own, and the efficacious intervention of the Madonna of Loreto at the plea of James II's queen, Mary of Modena:

They pretend, that this House was transported by Angels, from *Nazareth* to *Dalmatia*, and there plac'd on a little Mountain called *Tersatto, May* 10. 1291. It had remain'd there but three Years and seven Months, when the Angels took it away again, and brought it to the Middle of a Forest, in the Territory of *Recanati*, which is in the *Marche* of *Ancona*. The celestial Melody awakened the Inhabitants of the Neighbourhood, who flock'd together from all Parts, and saw the Miracle, by the favour of a great Light, with which the little House was surrounded. . . . After this House had continu'd there Eight whole Months, it cou'd not endure the Thieveries and Murders that were continually committed about that Place; so that it was taken up a third time, and carried a Mile further to the same Hill, on which it stands at present: But it was no sooner come thither, than a Controversie arose between two Brothers, to whom the Land belonged, each desiring to have it in his Share. This was the Cause, that four Months after the Angels lifted it up a fourth Time, and set it down some Paces from thence, in the Midst of the High-way; from whence it has never stirred since. 'Tis true, to prevent the Inconveniencies to which this Place, as well as the others exposed it; and perhaps also to prevent the Misfortune of a new Change, they built in the same Place a magnificent Church, in the Midst of which remains the *Santa Casa*, free from all manner of Insults or Injury. . . .

The last rich Offering is always left for some time, in a Place fram'd on purpose, before the Eyes of our Lady. That which at present occupies that honourable Place, is an Angel of Gold, holding a Heart bigger than an Egg, all covered over with Diamonds of great Value. The *English* Jesuite who conducted us, told us, it was a Present of the Queen of *England*. This Reverend Father inform'd us also of a great Piece of News, of which, you ought, in my Opinion, to have given us some Advice. He assured us, that that Princess was big with Child, and added, that undoubtedly it was by a Miracle; since they had calculated, that the very Moment in which the Present entred, was the happy Minute in which she Conceived.

Misson, *Italy*, i. 332–3, 337–8 (in Loreto, in letter dated 26 Feb. 1688)

A postscript, in a letter of 29 June 1688, confirms the birth:

Just as I was going to seal my Letter, I heard a great Noise in the House, occasion'd by the Rejoicing of the People upon the Advice of the Birth of a Prince of *Wales*. . . . That precious Infant
being a Present from Heaven, and a free Gift of the Holy Virgin of *Loretto*, from whom the King
and the Queen had begg'd a Son with great Zeal and Devotion, there was no great Reason to fear
that she wou'd put 'em off with a Girl, especially since the *Jesuits*, who are the principal Favourites
of that Queen of Paradise, had very earnestly interceded in their behalf.   ibid. ii. 405

Up till then, loyal Anglican Tories whose own principles of passive obedience and non-
resistance had been turned against them could console themselves that, if they endured
the reign of this popish king, he would be succeeded by his daughter Mary, who was
devoted to the Church of England; the birth, by depriving them of that comfort, made
them readier to reconsider their position. On the other hand James, exulting in the prospect of Catholic succession, had let only his own supporters witness the event; in consequence, it was alleged by his enemies and widely, though wrongly, believed that the
child was not his or the Queen's at all, but had been smuggled into the bedchamber in
a warming-pan. A few months later, James prepared on this day to flee the country; the
boy grew up to be the Old Pretender, or as he put it, King James III and VIII.

In April 1581 Michel de Montaigne visited the Santa Casa and hung up his *ex voto*:

This is the spot of the highest sanctity. There may be seen on the upper part of the wall the
image of Our Lady, made, so the story goes, of wood. All the residue of the shrine is so thickly
covered with rich *ex votos* given by divers cities and princes that, right down to the ground, there
is not an inch of space which is not covered with some device of gold or silver. With great difficulty and as a high favour done to me, I was able to find a place whereon I could fix a memorial
device, in which were set four silver figures, that of Our Lady, my own, my wife's, and my daughter's. On the base of mine was engraved on the silver the inscription, 'Michael Montanus Gallus
Vasco, Eques Regii Ordinis, 1581.' On my wife's, 'Francisca Cassaniana, uxor,' and on my daughter's, 'Leonora Montana, filia unica.' These three are all kneeling in a row before Our Lady, who
is set somewhat higher. The chapel has another entrance besides the two of which I have spoken,
and any one entering it thereby will find my tablet on the left-hand side, opposite the door in
the corner, the same having been very carefully fixed and nailed to the wall. I had caused a chain
and ring of silver to be fitted thereto, so as to let it hang from a nail, but the chapel officials preferred to fasten it to the wall itself.   Montaigne, *Journal*, ii. 197

The shrine was pillaged by the French—Montaigne's *ex voto* is not mentioned in the
catalogue of 1792—and by 1802 everything was gone.

Eulalia of Mérida (in Roman times called Emerita), martyred in 304; according to the
Spanish poet Prudentius a century later, having as a baby refused her rattle, at the age
of 12 she ran away from home, burst in upon the governor's tribunal at Emerita, declared
herself a Christian, insulted the gods and the emperor, and challenged the authorities
to martyr her; upon their compliance, as the pyre crackled she struck fear into the trem-
bling executioners by finding her torture sweet. Prudentius' poem fairly bounces along
in its dactylic metre, as when Eulalia declares:

> Isis Apollo Venus nihil est,   Isis, Apollo, and Venus are naught,
> Maximianus et ipse nihil: Nor is Maximian anything more;

| illa nihil, quia factu manu; | Nothing are *they*, for by hands they were wrought, |
| hic, manuum quia facta colit. | *He*, for of hands he the work doth adore. |

The Nobel Prize award ceremony is held on this day, the birthday of Alfred Bernhard Nobel.

11 DECEMBER

a.d. III Idus Decembres   B

❦ HOLIDAYS AND ANNIVERSARIES Burkina Faso: National Holiday (independent within French community, 1958)
   United Nations: UNICEF Anniversary Day
   USA, Indiana: Admission Day (19th state, 1816)

❦ ANCIENT ROME Agonia (see *9 Jan.) in honour of Sol Indiges (see *9 Aug.); also Septimontium, recorded only in late calendars but clearly very ancient, being celebrated by the inhabitants of the original Seven Hills.

❦ HOLY DAYS Damasus I (RC); Daniel the Stylite (Orth.)

Damasus I (*c.*304–84), pope 366–84. Upon the death of Pope Liberius, during whose temporary exile he had supported the imperially sponsored antipope Felix II, clergy loyal to the late pope elected and consecrated his former deacon Ursinus, but the antipope's men elected Damasus; the latter hired a gang of thugs and won the month-long struggle, which culminated in a massacre of 137 Ursinians (so a pagan historian reports; a Christian source says 160) in the church that would become Santa Maria Maggiore. Thereafter Damasus, though harried by his enemies, proved a vigorous leader in the West, albeit too domineering and unsubtle for the East; realizing that apostolic poverty was no way to win the upper class to Christianity, he set out to show with grand banquets that the new religion was fit for gentlemen. (He was particularly successful in showing that it was fit for ladies: in many senatorial families whose male members held to the old ways, the womenfolk turned Christian, and Damasus became notorious for enjoying their company.) In a similar spirit, he restored the catacombs, and devised epitaphs for martyrs and previous popes, in order to claim that Rome's true glories were its Christian, not its pagan antiquities. He built several churches, including San Lorenzo in Damaso, to which his remains were translated.

Daniel the Stylite (409–93). One of the greatest pillar-saints, he was buried at the foot of the pillar he had been ordained on and had lived upon for thirty-three years, with one brief interval, when he thought it necessary to get down and protest against the emperor Basiliscus' support of Monophysitism.

12 DECEMBER

(HOLIDAYS AND ANNIVERSARIES Kenya: Jamhuri Day (Independence from Great
    Britain, 1963) (national day)
    Mexico: Our Lady of Guadalupe Day (patron saint of Mexico)

(HOLY DAYS Jane Frances de Chantal (RC); Spyridon (Orth.)

Jane Frances de Chantal (1572–1641) with St Francis de Sales founded the Order of the
Visitation (1610), for those nuns who wished a less ascetic life. Feast-day formerly
21 August.

Spyridon (*fl.* 325), shepherd and bishop of Trimithus in Cyprus, participated in the
Council of Nicaea; he was much revered in the Greek world, where many associations
are named after him and his day is much celebrated, in particular with processions.

Our Lady of Guadalupe, Nuestra Señora de Guadalupe, is the patron of Mexico (formally
confirmed in 1962) as well as of Central and South America. There are two: the Virgin
who appeared to a shepherd in Guadalupe (Estremadura, Spain) and the more famous
apparition on the hill of Tepeyac just north of Mexico City in 1531 to an Indian named
Juan Diego, instructing him to have a church built on the spot, which was the cult-site
of the Aztec mother-goddess Tonantzin. The bishop disbelieved him, until the Virgin
appeared for the third time and miraculously produced some roses, which Juan Diego
presented to him; as he did so, her portrait was revealed on the Indian's cloak—black,
unlike the images brought from Spain. The shrine is a famous place of pilgrimage.

Old Shortest Day, hence in some parts of Norway called *sjursmessdagen*, 'the magpie's
mass-day' (in others the 23rd); not even the magpie can tell the difference between day
and night, but oversleeps; whoever wakes her will be woken by her every morning thereafter.

13 DECEMBER

        Lucy Light,
        the shortest day and the longest night.

(HOLIDAYS AND ANNIVERSARIES Japan: Sosuharai or Soot Sweeping Day

Malta: Republic Day (1974) (national holiday)
St Lucia: St Lucia Day
Sweden: St Lucia Day

❰ ANCIENT ROME This day was marked by the worship of Tellus in Carinae (a district at the south-west of the Esquiline) and a *lectisternium*, or spreading of a table with food and drink in front of a dining-couch, in honour of Ceres.

❰ HOLY DAYS Lucy (CofE, RC)

Lucy, virgin martyr in Syracuse in 304; according to (doubtful) acts she defiantly proclaimed her Christianity and gave away her goods, refusing the suitor chosen by her parents; her eyes were torn out but miraculously restored (in representations she often bears them on a plate) before she was put to death. Her cult was important from early times. In Syracuse her martyrdom is celebrated annually with a great procession in which her bier is carried through the streets. Her reputed corpse, taken to Constantinople in 1038, seized by the Venetians in the Fourth Crusade, and reburied in S. Giorgio Maggiore, now lies in the church of S. Geremia at the junction of the Grand Canal with Canareggio (the nearby railway station is called Santa Lucia); however, she has another, reportedly translated to Corfinium (in the Pescara valley, near Pentima) in the eighth century and thence to Metz in 970.

Under the old calendar hers became the longest night; cf. the Venetian saying *Santa Lucia, La note più longa che ghe sia*; also *Santa Lúcia, El fredo crussia* ('the cold torments'); in Denmark, according to Worm, cattle are said to be so hungry during her night that if they could they would eat their own hooves. (This recalls the ancient Greek belief that the octopus eats its tentacles in winter.) Because light, in Latin *lux*, returns after her day, in Sweden she is patroness of harvest and of light; all threshing, spinning, and weaving for the year must be done by her day. Indeed, although Swedish calendars, alone among the Lutheran churches, still retain a daily saint, only she is still celebrated, and with great enthusiasm, especially by children. The churches are full, and *Luciatåg* ('Lucy processions') are held in which all participants dress in white and sing in her honour: one girl is appointed to be St Lucy, with a red sash and a crown of lighted candles, the others wearing silver sashes and silver crowns; the boys wear pointed white caps and carry stars in their hands. The girls bring food to the table, typically saffron buns, ginger biscuits, and *glögg*, a hot spiced wine with aquavit. Her feast-day marks the beginning of the twelve days before Christmas, which in some countries are more important than the twelve that follow. She is patron of the blind and of glaziers.

> Tis the yeares midnight, and it is the dayes,
> *Lucies*, who scarce seaven houres herself unmaskes,
> The Sunne is spent, and now his flasks
> Send forth light squibs, no constant rayes;
> The worlds whole sap is sunke:
> The generall balme th'hydroptique earth hath drunk,
> Whither, as to the beds-feet, life is shrunke,

> Dead and enterr'd; yet all these seeme to laugh,
> Compar'd with mee, who am their Epitaph. . . .
>
> John Donne (1572?–1631), 'A nocturnall upon S. Lucies day, Being the shortest day'

Judoc (Josse) (d. *c*.668). Son of a king of Brittany, he renounced his inheritance and became a priest, made a pilgrimage to Rome, then lived as a hermit in Ponthieu at the modern Saint-Josse-sur-Mer. In Charlemagne's time his dwelling-place became a guest-house for English travellers; a century later some of his relics were brought to Winchester. He is the name-saint of the composer Josquin ('little Josse') Lebloitte (d. 1521), better known as Josquin des Prez, and the printer Josse Bade (1462–1535), better known as Iodocus Badius Ascensius. The Dutch form is 'Joost', a name borne by the greatest Dutch poet Joost van den Vondel (1587–1679), and classicized to 'Justus' by the humanist Joost Lips or Justus Lipsius (1547–1606).

The Geminids, an annual meteor-shower, peak about this day.

14 DECEMBER

a.d. XIX Kalendas Ianuarias   E

❆ HOLIDAYS AND ANNIVERSARIES USA, Alabama: Admission Day (22nd state, 1819)

❆ HOLY DAYS John of the Cross (CY, RC); Thyrsus and his Companions (Orth.)

John of the Cross (Juan de la Cruz, 1542–91), founder with Teresa of Ávila of the Discalced Carmelites and a mystical writer. The movement for reform within the Carmelite Order met considerable opposition, and John, the Confessor of St Teresa's Convent of the Incarnation at Ávila, was imprisoned in Toledo in 1577–8 by the Visitor General, escaping after nine months of harsh treatment; in 1579–80 the Discalced separated from the Calced Carmelites. After serving as prior in Granada and Segovia, he came into conflict with the Vicar-General of the Discalced Carmelites, and was banished to Andalusia in 1591. Several of his mystical writings take the form of poems with commentaries on the progress of the soul towards God; the best-known are the *Spiritual Canticle*, the *Ascent of Mount Carmel*, and the *Dark Night of the Soul*. He was declared a Doctor of the Church in 1926. Feast-day formerly 24 November.

Thyrsus and his companions *Lucius* (in Greek Leukios) and *Callinicus*, martyred in Bithynia. 'San Tirso' was sufficiently popular in Spain to have basilicas dedicated to him at Mérida and Toledo; 'Tirso de Molina' was the pen-name adopted by Fray Gabriel Téllez (1583–1648), the author of the first important play on the Don Juan theme (*El burlador de Sevilla y convivado de piedra*, 'The Practical Joker of Seville and the Stone Guest'), and probably of *El condenado por desconfiado*, 'Damned for Despair', in which a hermit is damned for the tragic flaw of not believing that he can be saved—a play that disproves the canard that Christianity is incompatible with tragedy, once it is recognized that for the Christian the ultimate evil is not death but damnation.

Venantius Fortunatus (*c.*530–*c.*610). A native of Treviso educated at Ravenna, he made a pilgrimage to Tours *c.*565 to thank St Martin for curing him of an eye-disease; on the way he stopped for some time at the court of Sigebert, king of Austrasia. Later he served as chaplain to the community established by the former Queen Radegunde (see *13 Aug.); he became a friend of Gregory of Tours and subsequently bishop of Poitiers. He was a prolific author in both prose and verse, best known for his hymns 'Pange lingua gloriosi proelium certaminis' ('Sing, my tongue, the glorious battle') and 'Vexilla regis prodeunt' ('The royal banners forward go').

According to a Mediterranean folk belief, seven days before the winter solstice the halcyon—a mythical bird with the body of a kingfisher, also and more correctly spelt 'alcyon'—begins to build her nest; this takes her seven days, after which for another seven she lays and hatches her eggs. During this period, known as 'the halcyon days', the sea is calm and can be sailed, almost always off Sicily and frequently elsewhere. Aristotle quotes the lyric poet Simonides of Ceos: 'when in the winter month Zeus brings calm to fourteen days that earthlings call the time when the wind is forgotten, the holy breeding-season of the many-coloured alcyon'.

15 DECEMBER

a.d. XVIII Kalendas Ianuarias   F

❦ HOLIDAYS AND ANNIVERSARIES United States: Bill of Rights Day (commemorating ratification in 1791 of first ten amendments to the US Constitution)

❦ ANCIENT ROME At Rome this was another day of Consualia (see *7 July, *21 Aug.).

❦ HOLY DAYS
Wunibald (701–61), son of Richard of England (*7 Feb.). After serving as a missionary in the Upper Palatinate and spending four years discharging the cure of souls in Mainz, he joined his brother Willibald (*7 July), with whom he founded the abbey of Heidenheim; he became its first abbot, his sister Walburg being first abbess (*25 Feb.). Willibald is said to have raised his incorrupt body in 777.

This month, commonly called the Black Month, is subject to every sort of weather which is fatal to plants of a tender Nature. All Vegetables of our climate seem now to sleep; the Days are short, and every little warmth from the Sun makes every Curious Lover of Gardens wish for the Spring; though indeed 'tis now an ingenious Gardener will show his skill in helping Nature by Artifice.

The Gentleman's and Gardener's Kalendar (1724)

16 DECEMBER

a.d. XVII Kalendas Ianuarias   G

❡ HOLIDAYS AND ANNIVERSARIES Bahrain: Independence Day (national holiday)
South Africa: Day of National Reconciliation. This holiday, proclaimed in 1995, replaces the most divisive of the old South African holidays, the *Geloftedag* (Day of
the Covenant) or *Dingaansdag*, on which Afrikaners, in fulfilment of a solemn vow,
commemorated the defeat by Boer Voortrekkers of the encircling Zulu army
under Dingaan at the battle of Blood River, 1838

❡ HOLY DAYS O Sapientia (BCP; CY on the 17th); formerly St Eusebius (now *2
Aug.)

O Sapientia. The first of the 'O' antiphons preceding Christmas; they began on this day
in the Sarum calendar (and the BCP, though they were dropped between 1549 and 1661),
on 17 December in other calendars. See *Western Church Year.*

Adelaide, the empress Adelheid, wife of Otto the Great, and crowned with him on 2 February 962 by Pope John XII (a vicious youth whom Otto was later obliged to depose);
having been on bad terms with her son Otto II and his Byzantine empress, Theophano,
she was regent for her grandson Otto III from 983 to 994; she founded monasteries,
supported the Cluniac reforms, and died in her own foundation of Selz in 999.

Haggai (Orth.): Russians say that if there is a severe frost on this day (OS = 29 Dec. NS)
it will last till Epiphany.

With Christmas only nine days away, preparations for the festal season become more
intense. But mincemeat and plum puddings should already have been made by now; the
traditional day in England is 'Stir-up Sunday' (the last Sunday before Advent).

Today Sister prepares her mince meat. 'Shall auld acquaintance be forgot.' Keep up my beloved
daughter these little anniversary memorials of the olden times, which serve to revive family customs & the memory of departed friends, and moreover prove that we are not of yesterday and
that had hospitable good livers before us. When every thing was cheap & plenty, & less glitter &
more substance, good cheer was the universal order of the day, & all vied, not so much in the re-
dundant variety as in the superior excellence of the dishes. Every female was instructed in the art
of cooking preserves, & pastry, as well as the more ordinary duties of house keeping. . . . Music
was confined to the voice accompanied, now & then by the Flute. No whole hours, days, weeks
& years, wasted in fingering a harpsichord.   Pintard, ii. 320 (16 Dec. 1826)

17 DECEMBER

a.d. XVI Kalendas Ianuarias   A

❡ HOLIDAYS AND ANNIVERSARIES Bhutan: National Day
  USA: Wright Brothers Day, commemorating the first successful flight by Orville and
  Wilbur Wright, 1903

❡ ANCIENT ROME If many of the Roman festivals recorded here were little regarded
even by Romans, this was emphatically not the case with the Saturnalia, the most
beloved of them all. The celebrations originated as the dedication-day of a temple to
Saturnus, possibly a god of seed or sowing, but equated with the Greek Kronos, father
of Zeus and supreme god in the age of the Golden Race; Saturn, it was said, had been
king of Italy in a time of equality and plenty. (Sacrifice was conducted in the Greek
fashion, with bare head, not covered as was Roman practice.) In this temple (which also
served as state treasury), there was a statue of the god, whose feet were bound in wool
except on this day. Proceedings began with a sacrifice, at which the upper classes wore
the toga; from 217 BC onwards a great banquet for all comers was held, at which informal
clothes were worn, ending with the cry of *Io Saturnalia!* Courts, shops, and schools were
closed; gambling was permitted, and jollification reigned, extended by the end of the
Republic for seven days down to the 23rd. Presents were exchanged; when Catullus'
friend, the high-born politician, poet, and orator Calvus, gave him as a booby-present
an anthology of poets whose old-fashioned style they both despised, Catullus rose to
the occasion with a delightful poem of mock indignation at receiving such stuff 'on Saturnalia, best of days'. At home, masters waited on their slaves, who were permitted to
speak their minds; Horace represents his slave Davus as availing himself of this
freedom to address home truths to him (and through him to his readers). A 'king' or
master of the revels was appointed by lot, as later at Twelfth Night; faces might be
blackened by soot and lewd dances performed.

  Naturally, some straitlaced persons disapproved: Seneca has no desire to join the
drunken crowds in their party hats; the younger Pliny hid himself away in his study
while the household frolicked. Others permitted themselves to be cheerful while remaining intellectual: the Roman students at Athens of whom Aulus Gellius was one in
the mid-second century AD met in the baths during the day for a game of forfeits in
which each in turn propounded a logical fallacy, requiring a comrade to point out the
catch; if he succeeded he won a small sum of money, if not he contributed it to the
dinner-fund. At dinner they posed each other problems concerning difficult (but not
too difficult) passages in ancient poets, or philosophical doctrines frequently misunderstood, or unusual words and idioms; the prize for solution was a garland, which
if no one succeeded was dedicated to Saturn. But the supreme literary celebration of
the festival is that by Macrobius in the fifth century AD, who lovingly recreates an imaginary discussion amongst the great pagan intellectuals of Rome on the night before

Saturnalia, probably in 383, and the first three days of the festival: the daytime was given
to serious topics and the evening to lighter, including food and drink. In the first book,
set on the Saturnalia proper, much information is given on the day itself and on the
Roman calendar.

❨ HOLY DAYS O Sapientia (CY; BCP on *16th Dec.)

Lazarus. There are two men named 'Lazarus' in the New Testament. One is the subject
of the parable of the rich man and the beggar (Dives and Lazarus, Luke 16: 19–31), a
leper 'full of sores' who gave his name to the *lazzaretto* or lepers' hospital. The other
Lazarus is the brother of Mary and Martha, raised from the dead (John 11: 1–44); the
effect on public opinion convinced the chief priests that Jesus must be disposed of. A
late legend makes him bishop of Marseille, with relics there and at Andlau in Lower
Alsace, by confusion with a fifth-century bishop of Aix (see *29 July). His feast was
moved to this day in the Roman Martyrology from the fifth Sunday in Lent (Milan and
Spain) and Palm Sunday (Gaul). In the Orthodox Church he is culted on the Saturday
before Palm Sunday (a procession from Jerusalem to Bethany on that day is attested in
the fourth century).

Tydecho (6th c.), Welsh saint, brother of St Cadfan. Thomas Pennant visited a church
dedicated to him:

After riding some time along the bottom of the vale [of Mowddwy], pass by the village and
church of *Llan y Mowddwy*; the last is dedicated to *St. Tydecho*, one of our most capital saints. His
legend is written in verse, by *Dafydd Llwyd ap Llewelyn ap Gryffydd*, lord of *Mathafarn*; a person who
had a great hand in bringing in *Henry* VII. by feeding his countrymen with prophecies, that one
of them was to deliver *Wales* from the *English* yoke, by which means thousands of them were induced to rise, under Sir *Rhys ap Thomas*, and join *Henry*, then earl of *Richmond*, at *Milford*.
    This illustrious bard informs us, that *Tydecho* had been an abbot in *Armorica*, and came over
here in the time of king *Arthur*; but after the death of that hero, when the *Saxons* over-ran most
of the kingdom, the saint retired, and led here a most austere life, lying on the bare stones, and
wearing a shirt of hair: yet he employed his time usefully, was a tiller of the ground, and kept
hospitality. *Malgwyn Gwynedd*, then a youth, took offence at the saint, and seized his oxen; but wild
stags were seen the next day, performing their office, and a grey wolf harrowing after them. *Malgwyn*, enraged at this, brought his milk-white dogs to chace the deer, while he sat on the blue
stone, to enjoy the diversion; but when he attempted to rise, he found his breech immoveably
fixed to the rock, so that he was obliged to beg pardon of the saint, who, on proper reparation,
was so kind as to free him from his aukward pain.   Pennant, *Snowdon*, 79–80 (1781)

In churches that celebrated Epiphany but not Christmas, including that of fourth-
century Spain, this was the first day of a fast; the placing of the antiphon O *Sapientia* on
this day may be a relic of this practice, which in early Christian times had made a fast
of the Roman Saturnalia.

Sow Day in Orkney, when a sow was always killed; this might be a survival of sacrifice
before Yule.

18 DECEMBER

a.d. XV Kalendas Ianuarias B

❦ HOLIDAYS AND ANNIVERSARIES Niger: Republic Day (autonomous republic within the French Community, 1958; independence 3 Aug. 1960)

❦ HOLY DAYS

Gatianus or *Gatien* (d. *c.*337), sent as missionary to Gaul by Pope Fabian (see *20 Jan.); first bishop of Tours. It is to him, not to St Martin, that the cathedral is dedicated.

Modestos (d. 630 or 634), patron of farmers (Greece). It is said that when an evil spirit sent a snake to lurk in water that beasts were to drink in order to poison them, the saint revived the animals, killed the snake, and conjured the demon never to appear when his own name was invoked.

In Spain, up to the eleventh century, this day, not 25 March, was kept as Annunciation. It was observed that this saved the feast from falling in Lent; however, when in 1032 Odilo of Cluny permitted visiting monks from Spain to celebrate the Annunciation on 18 December, two elderly Cluniacs reported a dream in which one of the Spaniards, finding a boy on the altar, cast him with a pitchfork into a pan of hot coals. They added, for the benefit of slower wits, that the boy cried out 'Father, Father, what thou gavest these take away'; whereupon all sympathy for the Spanish custom ended. However, in Spain the feast persisted as the Expectation of the Confinement of the Virgin Mary.

Fragment: December 18, 1847

Oft through the silent air descend the feathery snow-flakes;
White are the distant hills, white are the neighboring fields;
Only the marshes are brown, and the river rolling among them
Weareth the leaden hue seen in the eyes of the blind.

Henry Wadsworth Longfellow (1807–82)

19 DECEMBER

a.d. XIV Kalendas Ianuarias C

❦ ANCIENT ROME Opalia, a feast at a shrine in the Forum in honour of Ops (cf. *25 Aug.); the Ludi Iuventatis may have been held in honour of Iuventas or Youth by young men who had come of age, but the theory depends on the restoration of a fragmentary inscription.

❧ HOLY DAYS There is no St Munditia (whose name means 'cleanliness' or 'elegance of taste'), but the poem in her honour by Kate Jennings is too good to leave out, so we assign her to this day.

Saint Munditia

Saint Munditia (the patron saint
of lonely women) is a relic bound
to inspire affection. Her bones
are barnacled with gold and jewels.
Her skull is stuck in a perpetual grimace.
Cat-yellow eyes start out of sockets.
And in her right hand, fixed at the ready, a writing quill.
Her elaborate hideousness made me laugh,
and, in my mind, her image prospered.
Sometimes I petition her.

Saint Munditia,
they broke your legs to fit you in your showcase,
and I am broken, too.
There's nobody to whom either of us can address a letter.
My humour is as brittle as you.

Saint Munditia,
why don't we sell your jewels
and go see the world, live it up big?
We would make a striking couple.
People are sure to befriend us
for our money and our enthusiasm for life.

Saint Munditia,
damn this loneliness. Damn my seedy guilt,
my laziness, my fears. Damn my cracked mind.
Tell me why it should be so.
Saint Munditia, comfort me.

Kate Jennings (1948–   )

20 DECEMBER

a.d. XIII Kalendas Ianuarias   D

❧ HOLY DAYS Ignatius of Antioch (Orth.; see *17 Oct.)

Domingo de Silos (RC). A herdsman's son who entered the Benedictine abbey of San Millán de la Cogalla in Logroño; having restored to flourishing monastic life a decayed house to which he had been sent, he returned to become prior of San Millán until King García IV of Navarre (1035–54) drove him out for refusing his financial demands. On further pursuit by the king he fled to Castile, where with the help of King Fernando the Great (1037–65) he entered the ancient monastery of San Sebastián de Silos and turned it into a great religious and cultural centre; he also began the construction of its Romanesque cloister. On his death in 1073 he was at once recognized as a saint; having obtained the release of numerous Christians from Moorish captivity, he is portrayed holding fetters. His staff is given to Spanish queens at confinement; it was after him that the noblewoman Juana de Aza, having prayed for his intercession during a difficult pregnancy, named her son, St Dominic (see *8 Aug.). His monastery was subsequently renamed Santo Domingo de Silos; after secularization in 1835 it was resettled in 1880 by monks from Solesmes, which is why its best-selling records are of Gregorian chant and not the Mozarabic liturgy it had previously retained.

December

Riding upon the Goat, with snow-white hair,
     I come, the last of all. This crown of mine
Is of the holly; in my hand I bear
     The thyrsus, tipped with fragrant cones of pine.
I celebrate the birth of the Divine,
     And the return of the Saturnian reign;—
My songs are carols sung at every shrine,
     Proclaiming "Peace on earth, good will to men."

Henry Wadsworth Longfellow (1807–82), *The Poet's Calendar*

21 DECEMBER

a.d. XII Kalendas Ianuarias   E

St Thomas grey, St Thomas grey,
The longest night and the shortest day.

Saint Thomas divine,
brewing, baking, and skilling of fat swine.

❦ HOLIDAYS AND ANNIVERSARIES USA, New England: Forefathers' Day, commemorating the landing at Plymouth 11 December (OS) 1620

❦ ANCIENT ROME Divalia or Angeronalia, to Diva Angerona, allegedly so called for prescribing remedies against angina. She was represented with sealed lips, as a warning that the secret or taboo name of Rome, used in certain secret ceremonies, should not be divulged; a late antiquarian alleges that it was *Amor*, i.e. *Roma* backwards. There was also a sacrifice to Hercules and Ceres of a pregnant cow, baked goods, and honeyed wine.

❦ HOLY DAYS Thomas, Apostle (BCP) (see also translation on *3 July, now also RC and CY date); Peter Canisius (RC)

Thomas the Apostle. Thomas and Didymus being respectively Aramaic and Greek for 'twin', he was popularly supposed to have been Jesus' twin brother. He is known as 'Doubting Thomas' because he refused to believe in the Resurrection 'Except I shall see in his hands the print of the nails, and put my finger into the print of the nails, and thrust my hand into his side' (John 20: 25). In the Abgar legend (see *28 Oct.) he is 'Judas, also called Thomas'; it is a neat touch that he who had refused to take the Resurrection on trust should send Abgar a letter beginning 'Blessed art thou who hast believed in me though thou hast not seen me.' Tradition makes him the Apostle who spread the Gospel to Parthia and then to India; after converting the numismatically attested King Gundaphar he was martyred at 'Calamina', perhaps—as the 'Christians of St Thomas' on the Malabar coast maintain—Mailapur near Chennai (formerly Madras), where the Portuguese claimed to have found his tomb in 1522; a church was built in 1547, on whose altar stands a cross discovered in 1574 with an inscription in Pahlavi script. According to the apocryphal Acts of Thomas, King 'Gundaphorus' commissioned him to build a palace, since Thomas was a carpenter, and from this derives his status as patron saint of architects; he is sometimes portrayed with a T-square. According to the Acts, Thomas greatly impressed the king with his architectural drawings; money was given him and he ostensibly set about constructing the palace. However, he distributed the money to the poor instead, and when the king wished to see the completed palace, he was told that he would find it in heaven; miraculously, the king's dead brother returned thence to describe it to him. Thomas is also invoked by the blind because of his spiritual blindness in refusing to recognize Christ without proof. The Orthodox date is 6 October.

Peter Canisius (1521–97), Jesuit theologian active in Germany, Vienna, and Prague, best known for his catechisms; the Great Catechism was first published in 1554, with many later editions. He became Provincial of Upper Germany in 1556, founding Jesuit colleges at Augsburg, Munich, and Innsbruck, and helped spread the influence of the Jesuits in Poland. Exceptionally, he was canonized and declared a Doctor of the Church at the same time (1925). Feast-day formerly 27 April.

St Thomas Day. Giving to the poor was a custom associated with this day:

Fri. 21 Dec. (1759). About 3.10 we arose to perform our task, *viz.*, some of the ancestors of the Pelham family have ordered that on this day (forever) there should be given to every poor man or woman that shall come to demand it 4*d.* and also to each a draught of beer and a very good piece of bread. My business was to take down their names while Mr. Cotes paid them, and I believe there were between 7 and 8 hundred people relieved, of all ages and sexes, and near £9 distributed, besides a sack of wheat made into good bread and near a hogshead and a half of very good beer. I came home about 11.20, having received my groat amongst the rest. . . . Relieved [30] poor persons today with 1*d.* each and a draught of beer.   T. Turner, 195–6

From this custom St Thomas Day was also known as 'Doleing Day' or 'Mumping (= begging) Day' and children were said to 'go Thomasing', 'go a corning', or 'go a gooding'.

The annual stag hunt in Oxfordshire goes awry in 1820:

On Tuesday the 21st. ult. (St. Thomas's Day), as usual a stag was turned out from Blenheim Park, the property of the Duke of Marlborough. It directed its course towards Wickham, and from thence it took the high road and proceeded to Oxford; and then formed one of the most beautiful and picturesque sights that can be imagined. The stag and dogs, in close pursuit, followed by a great number of well-known and experienced sportsmen, proceeded up the High Street, as far as Brasenose College, when, to the no small astonishment of hundreds of spectators, the stag took refuge in the chapel, during divine service, where it was killed, sans ceremonie, by the eager dogs.   *County Chronicle* (Oxon.) (18 Jan. 1820), quoted in Morsley, 215

Anniversary of the landing of the *Mayflower* on Plymouth Rock, 1620. William Bradford, later Governor of Massachusetts, was on board and described the perilous last stages of the journey and the landing of the shallop party on 11 December OS (21 Dec. NS):

After some houres sailing, it begane to snow and raine, and about the midle of the afternoone, the wind increased, and the sea became very rough, and they broake their rudder, and it was as much as 2. men could doe to steere her with a cupple of oares. But their pillott bad them be of good cheere, for he saw the harbor; but the storme increasing, and night drawing on, they bore what saile they could to gett in, while they could see. But herwith they broake their mast in 3. peeces, and their saill fell over bord, in a very grown sea, so as they had like to have been cast away; yet by God's mercie they recovered them selves, and having the floud with them, struck into the harbore. . . . And though it was very darke, and rained sore, yet in the end they gott under the lee of a smalle iland, and remained there all that night in saftie. But they knew not this to be an iland till morning . . . the next day was a faire sunshining day, and they found them sellvs to be on an iland secure from the Indeans, wher they might drie their stufe, fixe their peeces, and rest them selves, and gave God thanks for his mercies, in their manifould deliverances. And this being the last day of the weeke, they prepared ther to keepe the Sabath. On Munday they sounded the harbor, and founde it fitt for shipping; and marched into the land, and found diverse cornfeilds, and litle runing brooks, a place (as they supposed) fitt for situation; at least it was the best they could find, and the season, and their presente necessitie, made them glad to accepte of it. So they returned to their shipp againe with this news to the rest of their people which did much comforte their harts.   Bradford, 103–5

22 DECEMBER

a.d. XI Kalendas Ianuarias   F

❨ HOLIDAYS AND ANNIVERSARIES Japan: Tōji or Winter Solstice

❨ HOLY DAYS

Frances Xavier Cabrini (1850–1917), founder of the Missionary Sisters of the Sacred Heart. She was the youngest of thirteen children, born to a farmer near Lodi; the family was devout, and thought that the Annals of the Propagation of the Faith made appropriate reading for their children. It inspired the young Maria Francesca to become a foreign missionary, but it was many years before she achieved this goal. She qualified as a school-teacher, then was put in charge of an orphanage with the instruction to turn it into a religious community, a task made all the more difficult by the obstruction of the foundress.

The bishop finally gave her leave to fulfil her childhood dream; not knowing any institution of missionary sisters, he gave her leave to found one herself. She began with a house at Codogno, and soon expanded, eventually to Rome, where a children's home and a school were founded. In 1889, with the Pope's instruction that she should go west rather than east, and overcoming her fear of water, she and several sisters sailed to New York to found an orphanage for Italian children. The beginning was difficult: there were children but no housing, owing to a falling-out between Archbishop Corrigan and the benefactress. The Archbishop wished her to return to Italy, but Mother Cabrini was determined to stay, and within a short time had made all the necessary arrangements. Under her energetic direction the Missionary Sisters spread to Central and South America; when the constitutions of the Order were finally approved in 1907 there were over 1,000 members, in eight countries. She was the first American citizen to be canonized, in 1946. At the request of bishops in the United States and Canada Pius XII declared her patron of emigrants.

23 DECEMBER

a.d. X Kalendas Ianuarias   G

❨ HOLIDAYS AND ANNIVERSARIES Japan: The Emperor's Birthday (national day)

❨ ANCIENT ROME Larentalia or Larentinalia, funeral rites at the tomb of Acca Larentia, said by some to have been the wife of the herdsman Faustulus, and to have nursed Romulus and Remus, by others to have been a highly successful courtesan who made Romulus, or the Roman people, her heir. The stories are not in fundamental contradiction either with each other or even with the legend of the she-wolf who suckled Romulus and Remus, for in the Latin of the late Republic *lupa* means 'prostitute'; an author of that period referring to the she-wolf will write *lupus femina*, not, as an Augustan does, *lupa*.

❨ HOLY DAYS John Cantius (RC)

John Cantius (Jan Kanty, b. Kęty 23 June 1390, d. 24 Dec. 1473), professor of theology at Kraków; he reputedly made four pilgrimages to Rome and one to Jerusalem. He was a man of many charitable works; it is said that he saw a beggar go by while he was eating, rushed out to give him his food, and on returning to his table he found his plate again full; this was commemorated for many years in the university by a ritual involving the feeding of a poor man. It was also said that, on being robbed by highwaymen and asked if he had anything else, he said no, then remembered some gold coins sewn in his cloak and ran after the robbers with them; in sheer amazement they returned their booty. No such tales are told of modern muggers. He was canonized in 1747. Feast-day formerly 20 October.

Thorlac son of Thorhall (1133–93), in Icelandic þórlákr helgi þórhalsson, patron saint of Iceland. Ordained priest at the age of 18, he studied at Paris and Lincoln before returning to Iceland as bishop of Skálholt. The account of twelfth-century Icelandic bishops known as *Hungrvaka* ('Hungerwatch') ends by saying of him: 'He may truly be called the apostle of Iceland even as the holy bishop Patrick is called the apostle of Ireland, for they performed the work of veritable apostles in their preachings and patience towards both the disobedient and the unrighteous.' In 1198 the Althing declared him a saint; elsewhere in the West the papacy was wresting control of canonization from popular devotion, but in Iceland the matter was decided (like the adoption of Christianity itself) by democratic vote. In 1984 Pope John Paul II acknowledged his patronage of Iceland in an Apostolic Letter. In Norway this day (also known as 'Little Christmas Eve') is called *tollesmesse*; but in the county of Rogaland 'Torlak' has turned into a goblin to frighten children.

24 DECEMBER

a.d. IX Kalendas Ianuarias   A

❲ HOLY DAYS Christmas Eve

Adam and Eve. Adam, patron of gardeners and tailors, is placed on the day before the Nativity as the forerunner of Christ, the 'second Adam'. Similarly, Mary is regarded as the 'second Eve', her role in the Redemption reversing Eve's in the Fall, having eaten the forbidden fruit of the tree of the knowledge of good and evil; in the Latin world Gabriel's *Ave*, 'Hail', was understood as the palindrome of *Eva*.

One of Adam's main tasks was the naming of the animals in the Garden of Eden (Gen. 2: 19–20):

> *Naming the Animals*
>
> Having commanded Adam to bestow
> Names upon all the creatures, God withdrew
> To empyrean palaces of blue
> That warm and windless morning long ago,
> And seemed to take no notice of the vexed
> Look on the young man's face as he took thought
> Of all the miracles the Lord had wrought,
> Now to be labelled, dubbed, yclept, indexed.
>
> Before an addled mind and puddled brow,
> The feathered nation and the finny prey

> Passed by; there went biped and quadruped.
> Adam looked forth with bottomless dismay
> Into the tragic eyes of his first cow,
> And shyly ventured, 'Thou shalt be called "Fred." '
>
>   Anthony Hecht (1922–   )

Immediately afterwards, God finds a helpmeet for Adam. In the dialogue *Dives and Pauper* (1405–10), Pauper explains why God created Eve out of Adam's rib rather than another bone:

For the rybbe is nexst the herte, in tokene that God made hyr to ben mannys felawe in loue & his helpere. And as the rybbe is nexst the herte of alle bonys, so schulde the wyf ben nexst in loue of alle women & of alle men. God made nout woman of the foot to ben mannys thral ne he made hyr nout of the hefd to ben hys maystir but of his syde & of his rybbe to ben his felawe in loue & helper at nede. But whan Eue synnyd, than was woman maad soget to man, that the wyf schulde ben rewlyd be hyr housebonde & dredyn hym & seruyn hym as felaw in loue & helper at nede & as nest solas in sorwe, nout as thral & bonde in vyleyn seruage, for the housebonde owyth to han his wyf in reuerence & worchepe in that they ben bothin on flesch & on blood.

                                    Dives and Pauper 6. 4 (ii. 66–7)

Mark Twain, no stranger to foreign lands and customs, purports to have discovered Adam's diary, which he 'translated from the original MS.' In this excerpt Adam complains about his new companion:

Monday
This new creature with the long hair is a good deal in the way. It is always hanging around and following me about. I don't like this; I am not used to company. I wish it would stay with the other animals. . . . Cloudy to-day, wind in the east; think we shall have rain. . . . *We?* Where did I get that word? . . . I remember now—the new creature uses it.

                                    Mark Twain, *The Diaries of Adam and Eve* (1904), 3

A German printer's wife is said to have crept into his workshop at night and corrected God's pronouncement to Eve at Gen. 3: 16, *und er soll dein Herr sein*, 'and he shall be thy lord', by altering *Herr* to *Narr*, meaning 'fool'; she was put to death, and the few copies that reached the market fetched extravagant prices.

Christmas Eve. The night of 24–5 December is known as 'Christmas Eve' or 'Christmas Night', as in the carol 'On Christmas night all Christians sing | To hear the news the angels bring', and in German as *die heilige Nacht*, the Holy Night: *Stille Nacht! Heilige Nacht!*, familiar in English as 'Silent night! Holy night!'

The main Christmas festivities in many countries take place on the Eve. In France, the midnight feast or *réveillon* may begin with oysters and champagne; among the favoured main courses are roast pork, pheasant, or wild boar. It ends with a chocolate log-cake called *bûche de Noël*. Children find presents placed by the Christmas crib, brought by *l'Enfant Jésus* in person. In northern Germany, the traditional dish is blue carp (the colour comes from hot vinegar poured over it before cooking), with a sauce of sour cream, horseradish, and apples. From the beginning of Advent, there are Christmas markets, selling a wide range of food and ornaments, along with Glühwein; like the placing of coloured lights in windows, these are scorned by some as vulgar innovations. In America, children hang up their stockings by the fireplace in preparation for Santa's visit, immortalized in Clement Moore's 1822 poem 'A Visit from St. Nicholas'. In some families the children leave a glass of milk and a cookie for Santa. If the Christmas tree has not already been decorated, parents do it after the childen have gone to bed.

Where the secular spirit has not entirely pre-empted Christmas Eve, it is customary to go to church. In the RC Church the first of the three masses of Christmas Day is celebrated at midnight. Protestant churches often have carol services.

The carol was originally a secular round dance. By the fifteenth century it had become associated with popular religious poetry, and musical settings became more elaborate. Carols are sung, often by groups standing in the street, throughout the twelve days of Christmas; a token of appreciation is expected. This is a remnant of the begging customs associated with many days, especially in Advent. The Revd William More, Prior of Worcester, entered the following expenses in his journal in 1518:

Item rewarded to syngars of carralls at cristmas day at ny3t 16d.
Item rewarded for carralls 4d. 4d. 2d. 1d. 4d. 2d. 2d. W. More, 76

Many will feel sympathy with this report of carolling in 1832:

In the day-time our ears are saluted with the dissonant screaming of Christmas Carols, which the miserable creatures sing who travel from house to house with the *vessel cup*. This is a small chest, which incloses an image, intended to represent the sacred person of our Saviour Jesus Christ . . . It is reputed unlucky to dismiss the singer without a present. This custom is rapidly falling into disuse. *Gentleman's Magazine*, 102 (1832), pt. 2, 491

Robert Burton, in *The Anatomy of Melancholy*, remarks on contemporary and ancient problems of persuading young people who prefer secular carolling to come to church on Christmas Eve:

They will be still singing amorous songs and ditties (if young especially) and cannot abstaine though it be when they goe to, or should bee at Church. We have a pretty story to this purpose in *Westmonasteriensis*, an old writer of ours (if you will beleeve it) *An. Dom. 1012. at Colewiz in Saxony*, on Christmas Eve a company of young men and maids, whilst the Priest was at Masse in the Church, were singing catches and love songs in the Churchyard, hee sent to them to make lesse noyse, but they sung on still; and if you will, you shall have the very song it selfe,

> Equitabat homo per sylvam frondosam,
> Ducebatque secum Meswinden formosam,
> Quid stamus, cur non imus?
> A fellow rid by the greenewood side,
> And faire *Meswinde* was his bride,
> Why stand we so, and doe not goe?

This they sung, he chaft, till at length impatient as he was, hee prayed to Sᵗ *Magnus* patron of the Church, they might all there sing and dance 'till that time twelvemonth, and so they did, without meat and drinke, wearisomnesse or giving over, till at yeares end they ceased singing, and were absolved by *Herebertus* Archbishop of *Colen* [= Cologne]. III. II. iii. 1

The story is already found in William of Malmesbury, *Gesta regum Anglorum*, ii. 174, who does not name the village or quote the song; for Heribert, see *16 March. Burton also speaks of '*Cromnyomantia* [*sic* for *Cromm.*], a kind of Divination with onions laid on the altar on Christmas Eve', inscribed with the names of potential husbands. Luther reports that maidservants would bang on the door of the pigsty; if a large pig grunted, the girl would marry an old man, if a small pig, her husband would be young.

On Christmas Eve the oxen are said to kneel in their stall (see also *5 Jan.):

A superstitious notion prevails in the western parts of Devonshire, that at twelve o'clock at night on Christmas Eve the Oxen in their stalls are always found on their knees, as in an attitude of devotion; and that (which is still more singular) since the alteration of the style they continue to do this only on the Eve of old Christmas Day. An honest country-man, living on the edge of St. Stephen's Down, near Launceston, Cornwall, informed me, October 28th, 1790, that he once, with some others, made a trial of the truth of the above, and watching several oxen in their stalls at the above time, at twelve o'clock at night, they observed the two oldest oxen only fall upon their knees, and as he expressed it in the idiom of the country, make 'a cruel moan like Christian creatures'. I could not but with great difficulty keep my countenance: he saw, and seemed angry that I gave so little credit to his tale, and walking off in a pettish humour, seemed to 'marvel at my unbelief'. There is an old print of the Nativity, in which the oxen in the stable, near the Virgin and Child, are represented upon their knees, as in a suppliant posture. This graphic representation has probably given rise to the above superstitious notion on this head.

Brand, i. 250

Especially in northern countries a Yule log was burnt. In some places it was not a log but a bundle of ash branches; as each hoop binding the faggot was broken a round of cider was due. The festivities often accompanied a ball; the Ashen Faggot Ball at Taunton, still held in the nineteenth century, supposedly commemorated the pleasant discovery by King Alfred's men, cold and hungry on campaign, that ash trees would burn even though green.

> Thy welcome *Eve*, lov'd CHRISTMAS, now arriv'd,
> The parish bells their tuneful peals resound;
> And mirth and gladness, ev'ry breast pervade.
> The pond'rous ASHEN FAGGOT, from the yard,
> The jolly *Farmer*, to his crowded *hall*
> Conveys, with speed; where, on the rising flames
> (Already fed with store of massy brands)
> It blazes soon;—nine bandages it bears,
> And, as they each disjoin (so Custom wills),
> A mighty jug of sparkling *cyder's* brought,
> With *brandy* mix'd, to elevate the guests.
> Romaine Joseph Thorn, *Christmas, a Poem* (1795)

Since pagan times it had been customary to decorate with greenery on festivals, especially holly, ivy, and mistletoe; after some debate, the church authorities permitted it to be done on Christian festivals, at least from the early seventh century in England. Holly and ivy, familiar from the Christmas carols 'The holly and the ivy' and 'Deck the halls with boughs of holly', were associated with good and evil, or male and female, and so were often combined. Sometimes the proportion between holly and ivy denoted whether the master or mistress was dominant in the household:

Great is the Contention of Holly and Ivy, whether Master or Dame weares the breeches.

Stevenson, 50

Others judged the balance of power by the type of holly used:

It depends upon the kind of holly that comes into a house at Christmas which shall be master
during the coming year, the wife or the husband. If the holly is smooth, the wife will be the master; if the holly is prickly, the husband will be the master.   N & Q, 4th ser., viii (1871), 506

Mistletoe in particular has pagan associations: the druids of Gaul regarded mistletoe
growing on oak-trees as sent from heaven; on the rare occasions when they found it,
they used numerous ceremonies in cutting it. They were responsible for belief in its
curative properties, but not for the custom (apparently of eighteenth-century origin)
that shocked Nathaniel Hawthorne, when American consul at Liverpool in 1856:

On Christmas eve, and yesterday, there were little branches of mis[t]letoe hanging in several parts
of our house, in the kitchen, the entries, the parlor, and the smoking room—suspended from
the gas-fittings. The maids of the house did their utmost to entrap the gentlemen-boarders, old
and young, under these privileged places, and there to kiss them, after which they were expected
to pay a shilling. It is very queer, being customarily so respectful, that they should assume this
license now, absolutely trying to pull the gentlemen into the kitchen by main force, and kissing
the harder and more abundantly, the more they were resisted. A little rosy-cheeked Scotch lass—
at other times very modest—was the most active in this business. I doubt whether any gentlemen but myself escaped. I heard old Mr. Smith parleying with the maids last evening, and
pleading his age; but he seems to have met with no mercy, for there was a sound of prodigious
smacking, immediately afterwards. Julian [his young son] was assaulted, and fought most vigorously, but was outrageously kissed—receiving some scratches, moreover, in the conflict.

Hawthorne, *English Notebooks*, 270

As with the eves of major saints' days, where fasting was enjoined, Christmas Eve has
its share of superstitions. It has been reported that it is unlucky to snuff the Yule candle
before the meal is finished, to fail to tip mummers or wassailers, to walk near a cross-
roads, to be first wished a 'Merry Christmas' or a 'Happy New Year' by a red- or fair-
haired man (see First-footing, *1 Jan.), and for spinners to leave yarn on their
spinning-wheels ('rocks'). According to a widespread German superstition a man was
rendered invulnerable, and a woman in labour assured of easy childbirth, by a *Nothemd*
or 'shirt of travail', spun, woven, and sewn on this night by an unsullied virgin who invoked the infernal powers as she worked and dedicated the shirt to them; on the breast
of the waist-length garment were two heads, that on the right having a long beard and
wearing a helmet, that on the left having a demonic face and wearing a crown; on either
side the sign of the cross was depicted. As an indignant sixteenth-century observer
commented, men who counted themselves good Christians boasted of wearing this diabolical amulet, since the crime had been committed not by them but by the girl who
had woven it; nevertheless, the *Nothemd* was highly popular during the Thirty Years War,
and even afterwards was not unknown, being sometimes thought to procure victory in
lawsuits. If the girl was not a virgin, the protection failed; in Ludwig Uhland's ballad
Das Nothemd the duke bids his daughter make him such a shirt, but in the battle he is
challenged by a young man who fights him till both are mortally wounded. His daughter, visiting the battlefield, screams for grief; it was her lover who had slain her father.

Thomas Hardy looks back:

Yuletide in a Younger World

We believed in highdays then,
    And could glimpse at night
        On Christmas Eve
Imminent oncomings of radiant revel—
    Doings of delight:—
    Now we have no such sight.

We had eyes for phantoms then,
    And at bridge or stile
        On Christmas Eve
Clear beheld those countless ones who had crossed it
    Cross again in file:—
    Such has ceased longwhile!

We liked divination then,
    And, as they homeward wound
        On Christmas Eve,
We could read men's dreams within them spinning
    Even as wheels spin round:—
    Now we are blinker-bound.

We heard still small voices then,
    And, in the dim serene
        Of Christmas Eve,
Caught the far-time tones of fire-filled prophets
    Long on earth unseen. . . .
    —Can such ever have been?

25 DECEMBER

a.d. VIII Kalendas Ianuarias   B

*If Christmas day be bright and clear
there'll be two winters in the year.*

Those who are born on Christmas day cannot see spirits.

(HOLIDAYS AND ANNIVERSARIES UK (except Scotland): Quarter Day
Christmas

(ANCIENT ROME After Julius Caesar's reform of the calendar, this was the conventional date of the winter solstice, and could therefore be regarded as the birthday of the Sun. By the third century AD many people considered the Sun to be the true godhead, of which other gods were mere facets, and the authentic guarantor of the Empire; in

274 the emperor Aurelian gave the day official recognition as *Natalis Solis Invicti*, 'the Birthday of the Unconquerable Sun'.

❦ HOLY DAYS **Christmas Day** (CofE); **The Nativity of Our Lord** (RC, Orth.)

In the first three Christian centuries Jesus' birth had been speculatively assigned to various dates (see II: *Christian Chronology: Christian Era*), but not celebrated as a festival, except as subordinate, in the Eastern churches, to His baptism, or birth in the spirit, on 6 January. The Roman Church, however, having previously despised the divine birthdays familiar in the pagan world, responded to the Arians of the East, who made the Son inferior to the Father, by adopting the solar feast of 25 December as Christ's Nativity, on which the Sun of Righteousness (Mal. 4: 2) was born; in an age when the emperor Constantine could come to Christianity through the solar cult, this was both a natural and a profitable identification. From Rome the new feast spread throughout the Western church, and then to Egypt (where there is some evidence that, as 29 Choiak, it was celebrated long before Aurelian as the birthday of the Sun); in the late fourth century it was established at Constantinople and Antioch. By contrast, the church at Jerusalem long resisted the new festival, which is still not observed by the Armenians.

Although theologically the most important Christian festival is Easter, in much of Christendom Christmas has long taken over from it amongst the laity. The lines in 'God rest you merry, gentlemen'

> This holy tide of Christmas
> All other doth deface

are no more than the truth in England and other north European countries, though not in Mediterranean countries or among the Orthodox.

For many centuries a feast of the Church, Christmas is now well on its way to becoming a global secular holiday whose main embodiment is Santa Claus or Father Christmas. Even cultures little influenced by Christianity have absorbed many of the customs and paraphernalia associated with this holiday. Its commercialization has long been deplored, as has its eclipse of older traditions, but Christmas remains impervious. Our coverage of this day is necessarily restricted to highlights of the Anglo-American holiday and the traditions that contributed to it.

There are of course those who dislike Christmas festivities. Ebenezer Scrooge, having uttered his famous Bah! Humbug!, is bidden by his nephew not to be cross:

'What else can I be', returned the uncle, 'when I live in such a world of fools as this? Merry Christmas! Out upon merry Christmas! What's Christmas time to you but a time for paying bills without money; a time for finding yourself a year older, but not an hour richer; a time for balancing your books and having every item in 'em through a round dozen of months presented dead against you? If I could work my will,' said Scrooge indignantly, 'every idiot who goes about with "Merry Christmas" on his lips, should be boiled with his own pudding, and buried with a stake of holly through his heart. He should!'   Dickens, *A Christmas Carol* (1843), Stave 1

It is a stock theme of humorous writers and debaters to maintain that Scrooge was right. But all to no avail, as Scrooge himself recognizes:

At length the hour of shutting up the counting-house arrived. With an ill-will Scrooge dismounted from his stool, and tacitly admitted the fact to the expectant clerk in the Tank [his 'dismal little cell'], who instantly snuffed his candle out, and put on his hat.

'You'll want all day to-morrow, I suppose?' said Scrooge.

'If quite convenient, sir.'

'It's not convenient,' said Scrooge, 'and it's not fair. If I was to stop half-a-crown for it, you'd think yourself ill-used, I'll be bound?'

The clerk smiled faintly.

'And yet', said Scrooge, 'you don't think *me* ill-used, when I pay a day's wages for no work.'

The clerk observed that it was only once a year.

'A poor excuse for picking a man's pocket every twenty-fifth of December!' said Scrooge, buttoning his great-coat to the chin. 'But I suppose you must have the whole day. Be here all the earlier next morning.'

Despite his logic, and his resentment, Scrooge not only allows his clerk the day off, but spares him the embarrassment of raising the subject; in England (though not Scotland) Christmas Day leave was a common-law right that even a heartless miser must accept.

Midwinter, Yule, Mothers' Night.   Before the Norman Conquest this day was normally called 'Midwinter' in Old English; it was not called 'Yule', which represents Norse *júl* (cf. the Scandinavian 'Merry Christmas' greeting, *god jul*) and is more Scots than English, save in the term 'Yule-log' for a large log placed on the fire at this time (contrast the edible French *bûche de Noël*, see *24 Dec.). Bede states that the heathen English had called it, or rather the winter solstice, *modranect*, i.e. *Mōðraniht*, 'the Mothers' Night', 'presumably because of the ceremonies they stayed up all night to perform in it'; in Roman times there were in Sicily, Germany, and Britain goddesses called 'the Mothers', who inspired a hair-raising scene in Goethe's *Faust II*. Nevertheless, Tille (152–7) supposes a misunderstanding of folk rituals in which women baked cakes in honour of the Virgin; such 'care-cakes', to be eaten in bed, were prepared on Christmas morning in Scotland *c*.1800. Christmas cake, though baked and eaten at a more regular time, is still normal fare in England.

Weather prognostications.   Since Christmas was supposed to coincide with the Shortest Day and the rebirth of the sun, it was held that the weather on this and the next eleven days would determine that for each month in the coming year: the weather on 25 December foretold that of January; on the 26th, of February; on the 27th, of March, and so down to 5 January, critical for December. Worm noted that Danish farmers would record the weather on each of these days with a chalk circle, left blank on a fine day, filled in on a cloudy one, and part-filled on a mixed one; but they complained that this Yule mark (*julemærke*) no longer worked, since Christmas did not fall on the solstice. Another belief, recorded by Buchler, was that a waxing moon at Christmas foretold a good year, a waning moon a bad one.

Other prognostications, not only of the weather, were based on the day of the week on which Christmas fell:

Sunday

If the natiuity of our Lorde come on Sunday, Winter shall be good, the spring windy, sweet, & hot, Vintage flourishing, Oxen, and Sheepe multiplied: Hony & milke plentifull, peace, and accord in the Land, yea, all the Sundayes in the yeere following profitable: They that bee borne shall be strong, great, and shining: and he that flieth shall be found.

Monday

If it fall on the Monday, Winter shall bee indifferent, Sommer dry, or cleane contrary, so that if it be rainy and tempestuous, vintage shall be doubtfull: in each Munday of the said yeere, to enterprise any thing it shall bee prosperous and strong. Who that flieth shall soone be found: theft done shall be proued, and hee that falleth into his bed, soone recouer.

Tuesday

If it come on the Tuesday, Winter shall be good, the spring windy, Summer fruitfull, Vintage laboursome, Weomen die, and shippes perish on the Seas. In each Tuesday of this same yeere, to beginne a worke, it will prosper: hee that is borne shall be strong and couetous, dreames pertaine to age. Hee that flieth shall soone bee found; theft done shall be proued.

Wednesday

If it come on the Wednesday, Winter shall be sharpe and hard, the Spring windy and euill, summer good, Vintage plentifull, good wit easily found, young men die, hony sparing, men desire to trauell, and ship-men saile with great hazard that yeere. In each Wednesday to begin a worke is good.

Thursday

If it come on the Thursday, Winter shall bee good, the Spring windy, Summer fruitfull, Vintage plentifull. Kings and Princes in hazard. And in each Thursday to beginne a new worke, prosperous. Hee that is borne shall be of faire speech and worshipfull, hee that flieth shall soone be found: theft done by weomen shall be proued. Hee that falleth in his bed shall soone recouer.

Friday

If it come on the Friday, winter shall be maruellous, the Spring windy and good, Summer dry, Vintage plenteous: There shall be trouble of the aire, Sheepe and Bees perish, Oates deare. In each Friday to begin a worke it shall prosper; hee that is borne shall be profitable and lecherous. Hee that flieth shall soone be found; theft done by a Childe shall bee proued.

Saturday

If it come on the Saturday, Winter shall be dark, snow great, fruit plentious, the spring windy, Summer euill, Vintage sparing in many places: Oates shall be deare, Men waxe sicke, and Bees die. In no Saturday to begin a worke shall be good, except the course of the Moone alter it: Theft done shall be found, hee that flieth shall turne againe to his owne; those that are sicke, shall long waile, and vnneath they shall escape death.   'Godfridus', *The knowledge of things vnknowne*, 1–3

There is a similar text, falsely ascribed to Bede, known as the *Prognostica temporum*, which links the predictions to 1 January (always on the same day of the week as the preceding Christmas). It also exists in an Old English translation, which sometimes varies the details: most drastically in respect of Tuesday, which promises a dry summer in Latin and a rainy one in English.

Christmas in England. The anonymous poet of *Sir Gawain and the Green Knight*, a contemporary of Chaucer, imagines Christmas at King Arthur's court:

> This king held Christmas court in Camelot
> With many lovely lords, all likely lads,
> The Round Table's band of noble brothers,

Joined in carefree joy and jolly play.
At times the heroes hammered at each other,
Jousting as such gentlemen are wont,
Then came into the court to do the carol.
For round them reigned the revels fifteen days
With all the meat and mirth that men could think of;
Such giddy noise, such glorious-sounding laughter,
Delightful din by day, all night the dance,
That happiness rose high in hall and chamber,
Dukes and dames indulging their desires.
With worldly weal complete they dwelt together,
The most accomplished knights, save Christ himself,
The loveliest ladies who have ever lived,
The comeliest king who ever called a court.
For they were fair in all the flush of lovely youth's first age,
   Fortune's favored kind,
   Their sovereign in fine rage.
   In few courts now you find
   A band of like courage.

          trans. Theodore Silverstein

John Stow describes London's Christmas pastimes in the sixteenth century, especially the Lord of Misrule, who held sway over the whole Christmas season:

In the feast of Christmas, there was in the king's house, wheresoever he was lodged, a lord of misrule, or master of merry disports, and the like had ye in the house of every nobleman of honour or good worship, were he spiritual or temporal. Amongst the which the mayor of London, and either of the sheriffs, had their several lords of misrule, ever contending, without quarrel or offence, who should make the rarest pastimes to delight the beholders. These lords beginning their rule on Alhollon eve, continued the same till the morrow after the Feast of the Purification, commonly called Candlemas Day. In all which space there were fine and subtle disguisings, masks, and mummeries, with playing at cards for counters, nails, and points, in every house, more for pastime than for gain.

 Against the feast of Christmas every man's house, as also the parish churches, were decked with holm, ivy, bays, and whatsoever the season of the year afforded to be green. The conduits and standards in the streets were likewise garnished . . .   Stow, 122–3 (1598)

Christmas at court in 1604, where the main feature was masques, allegorical plays with singing and dancing put on by and for the nobility:

The first *Christmas* of worthy king James was at his court at Hampton, A° 1603: wher the French, Spanish & Polonian Ambassadors were severallie solemplie feasted: manie plaies & daunces with swordes: one mask by English & Scottish lords: another by the Queen's Maiestie & eleven more ladies of her chamber presenting giftes as goddesses. These maskes, especialli the laste, costes 2000 or 3000ˡ, the aparells: rare musick, fine songes: & in iewels most riche 20000ˡ, the last to my iudgment: & her maiestie 100 000ˡ: after Christmas was running at Ring by the King & 8 or 9 lords for the honour of those goddesses & then they all feasted together privatelie.

          Wilbraham, 66

 After the Reformation, Christmas was open to attack as wanting scriptural authority; in Scotland and New England this objection was far more effective than in England, where many of the godly continued to keep the day, though for tender conscience' sake they might call it 'Christ-tide' to avoid the hated 'mass'; records in household accounts of payments to minstrels at Christ-tide symbolize the characteristic reluctance to take things to extremes. Nevertheless, during the Civil War Parliament prohibited the celebration; in John Taylor's *Complaint of Christmas* of 1646 the personified feast laments:

After I had walk'd through every Streete, Lane, and Alley (with other by places) the weather being cold, and my entertainment colder, I went to a Cobblers stall, and demanded of him what harme old *Christmas* had done them, and wherefore he was banished so suddainly? the Cobler replied, that it was pitty that ever Christmas was borne, and that I was a Papist, and an Idolatrous Brat of the Beast; an old Reveller sent from *Rome* into *England*, and that the latter (or last syllable of my name) was Popish, as other superstitious daies were.

John Evelyn, with other communicants, was arrested in church on Christmas Day in 1657 and interrogated:

When I came before them they tooke my name & aboad, examind me, why contrarie to an Ordinance made that none should any longer observe the superstitious time of the *Nativity* (so esteem'd by them) I durst offend, & particularly be at *Common prayers*, which they told me was but the *Masse* in *English*, & particularly pray for *Charles stuard*, for which we had no Scripture: I told them we did not pray for *Cha: Steward* but for all *Christian Kings, Princes & Governors*: They replied, in so doing we praied for the K. of *Spaine* too, who was their Enemie, & a *Papist*, with other frivolous & insnaring questions, with much threatning, & finding no colour to detaine me longer, with much pitty of my Ignorance, they dismiss'd me. . . . These wretched miscreants, held their muskets against us as we came up to receive the Sacred Elements, as if they would have shot us at the Altar . . .   Evelyn, *Diary*, iii. 204

With the Restoration in 1660, Christmas returned as before. Samuel Pepys records various Christmas customs:

25 [Dec. 1662]. *Christmas day.* Up pretty early, leaving my wife not well in bed . . . By and by down to the Chappell again, where Bishop Morly preached upon the Song of the Angels—'Glory to God on high—on earth peace, and good will towards men.' Methought he made but a poor sermon, but long and reprehending the mistaken jollity of the Court for the true joy that shall and ought to be on these days. Perticularized concerning their excess in playes and gameing, saying that he whose office it is to keep the Gamesters in order and within bounds serves but for a second rather in a Duell, meaning the Groome porter [who supervised the gaming during the 12 days of Christmas]. Upon which, it was worth observing how far they are come from taking the Reprehensions of a Bishop seriously, that they all laugh in the chapel when he reflected on their ill actions and courses. . . . I walked home again with great pleasure; and there dined by my wife's bedside with great content, having a mess of brave plum-porridge and a roasted Pullett for dinner; and I sent for a mince-pie abroad, my wife not being well to make any herself yet.

Pepys, iii. 292–3

At the Christmas season Londoners who had country homes commonly went back to them; it was the custom to invite one's neighbours for dinner and provide musical entertainment. Thomas Isham of Lamport, writing in his diary in 1671, makes it clear that they were invited according to their social class, with the poorest first, lest they should expect to be given only leftovers:

25 The poor of Lamport and Houghton came to dinner. 26 The Daventry musicians came, being hired to practise their skill. . . . The labourers of Lamport and Houghton were asked to

dinner. 27 The more substantial inhabitants were asked to dinner. 31 The Daventry musicians
went away.   Isham, 71, 75

A Frenchman observes English Christmas customs in 1698:

From *Christmass*-Day 'till after Twelfth-Day, is a Time of Christian Rejoycing; a Mixture of Devotion and Pleasure: They wish one another Happiness; they give Treats, and make it their whole
Business to drive away Melancholy. Whereas little Presents from one another are made only the
first Day of the Year in *France*, they begin here at *Christmass*; and they are not so much Presents
from Friend to Friend, or from Equal to Equal, (which is less practis'd in *England* now than formerly) as from Superior to Inferior. In the Taverns the Landlord gives Part of what is eaten and
drank in his House that and the two next Days; for Instance, they reckon you for the Wine, and
tell you there is nothing to pay for Bread, nor your Slice of *Westphalia*. Every Family against *Christmass* makes a famous Pye, which they call *Christmass* Pye: It is a great Nostrum the Composition
of this Pasty; it is a most learned Mixture of Neatstongues, Chicken, Eggs, Sugar, Raisins,
Lemon and Orange Peel, various Kinds of Spicery, &c. They also make a Sort of Soup with
Plums, which is not at all inferior to the Pye, which is in their Language call'd Plum-porridge.
                                                              Misson de Valbourg, 34–5

Horace Walpole describes his Christmas at Strawberry Hill in a letter of 26 December
1748 to Sir Horace Mann:

Did you ever know a more absolute country-gentleman? Here am I come down to what you call
keep my Christmas! indeed it is not in all the forms; I have stuck no laurel and holly in my
windows, I eat no turkey and chine, I have no tenant to invite, I have not brought a single soul
with me.   Walpole, 141

By the second half of the eighteenth century Christmas was becoming moribund; some
writers blamed the calendar reform of 1752, others the popular resistance to it. Uneducated persons, says our first author, complain that it is popish; on the contrary, it is
they who are serving papal subversion by civil disobedience:

> The late establish'd *Christmas* don't refuse,
> 'Tis what the ancient Church did strictly use;
> Then Virtue flourish'd, Holiness was Fame;
> To seem and be a Christian was the same:
> Shall Smiths, Mole-Catchers, th'unlearned Rabble,
> True Time oppose with inconsistent Babble?
> Cease idle Prate, who act in Pop'ry's Cause,*
> Those that obey or break our Sov'reign's Laws?
>
> *As the Non-observers of new Time do.
>   Season (1754)

Sat. 25 Dec. [1756]. At home all day. No churching here the whole day. James Marchant and the
widow Caine dined with us on a sirloin of beef roasted in the oven with a batter pudding under
it, a plum suet pudding, boiled potatoes and some bullace [wild plum] pies.   T. Turner, 75

The American Samuel Curwen views Christmas in Exeter in 1777:

25 [December 1777]
No shops fully opened nor business publicly and generally carried on, appearance in some
measure saved though the day otherwise negligently enough observed, nor indeed can more be

expected considering the low ebb of religion here. Passed Eve at home. Eat minced pye at
dinner.   Curwen, i. 421

William Gladstone reflects on Christmas:

Monday—Christmas day [1826]

Our Christmas times are not now what they used to be. Sic visum supero ['So One above or-
dains'].   Gladstone, 90

Christmas could be a trial to country parsons, especially those who did not enjoy bell-
ringing. Here is the Somerset parson John Skinner, writing in his diary on Christmas
Day 1827:

I was awakened early by the ringing of the bells, and could not help thinking how much sound
overpowers common sense in all we have to do in the present day. I lay awake last night thinking
of these things, and soon after I had closed my eyes they were again opened by the loud peals
these thoughtless people among whom I dwell chose to ring, in honour of the day. They had better retire within themselves, and commune with their hearts, and be still.   Skinner, 305

The traditional festivities of Christmas began to be revived in the early nineteenth
century; this process was greatly furthered by Charles Dickens, especially but not exclusively in *A Christmas Carol*, which was not only read but dramatized.

Nathaniel Hawthorne, American consul in Liverpool, turns a jaundiced eye on English Christmas preparations in 1856:

Christmas-time has been marked by few characteristics. For a week or so, previous to Christmas
day, the newspapers contained rich details respecting market-stalls and butchers' shops, what
magnificent carcasses of prize oxen and sheep they displayed; for Englishmen really like to think
and talk of butcher's meat, and gaze at it with artistic delight, and they crowd through the
avenues of the market-houses, and stand enraptured around a dead ox. They are very earthy
people. They love to eat, and to anticipate good fare, and even to hear the details of other
people's good dinners.

The Christmas Waits [musicians] came to us on Christmas eve, and on the day itself, in the
shape of little parties of boys or girls, singing wretched doggrel, rhymes, and going away well-
pleased with the guerdon of a penny or two. Last evening came two or three elder choristers, at
pretty near bedtime, and sang some carols (they were psalm-tunes, however) at our door. Every-
body, with whom we have had to do, in any manner of service, expects a Christmas-box; but, in
most cases, a shilling seems to be quite a satisfactory amount.

Hawthorne, *English Notebooks*, 441

Quarter Day. However, we should not forget, amidst all these festivities, that Christmas
is also Quarter Day, when rents are due. In 1289 a cleric of Well, near Richmond in
Yorkshire, did so with disastrous results, as Richard of Durham (who, since he reckons
the year from Christmas, makes the event his first entry for 1290) records both for fun
(*causa ludi*) and as illustrating the old proverb that gamblers and lechers always lose their
wealth. The rector of the parish was a royal clerk, who lived at court and left the rich
estates in the hands of the cleric, a sound man of business but unchaste (*prudens sed im-
pudicus*), who had induced a local widow's daughter to live in the rectory, 'since there was
no one to stop him'; the bed was set up in the great soler or upper chamber. Suddenly
his master's seneschal arrived to collect the rents of the local churches, expecting to stay

overnight and transact his business the next day. It was one thing to move the bed, but there was no suitable place for the cleric to hide his lady-friend (*lecatricem suam*). He hastily shoved her into the strong-room, which was full of money; recognizing the opportunity of a lifetime, she stuck a purse containing 10 marks (£6. 13s. 4d.) down her robe and, once the visitor was out of earshot, begged to be let out on the pretext that she needed to relieve herself. 'He, suspecting no evil, permitted the daughter of fraud to depart; and next day, when he was summarily compelled to render account and pay in his receipts, he discovered he had been cheated by the harlot, for which he at once lost his employment' (*Chronicon de Lanercost*, 134).

Christmas in Scotland. In Scotland, where the Protestant objection to unscriptural festivities struck deep root, Christmas was long a working day like any other. On 24 December 1642 the negotiations between the Scottish commissioners and their counterparts from the English parliament were suspended for a day so that the English might celebrate what the irritated Scots called 'their Christmas'. This rejection was not to pass unchallenged: in 1722 a pamphlet war broke out over a sermon preached on the Sunday before Christmas by Thomas Blackwell senior, professor of divinity and principal of Marischal College, 'to disswade your Hearers from the Observation of that high and holy Festival as unlawfull'; but Aberdeen was not a Presbyterian stronghold. Even after the Second World War Christmas was widely regarded as a children's celebration, although it had been made a Bank Holiday in 1871.

Christmas in Wales. Thomas Pennant reports the North Welsh custom of *plygain*, singing by candlelight before dawn on Christmas Day, in the late eighteenth century:

Upon *Christmas*-day, about three o'clock in the morning, most of the parishioners assembled in church, and after prayers and a sermon, continued there singing psalms and hymns with great devotion till broad day; and if, through age or infirmity, any were disabled from attending, they never failed having prayers at home, and carols on our SAVIOUR's nativity. The former part of the custom is still preserved; but too often perverted into intemperance. This act of devotion is called *Plygan*, or the *Crowing of the Cock*. It has been a general belief among the superstitious, that instantly,

> at his warning,
> Whether in sea or fire, in earth or air,
> Th' extravagant and erring spirit hies
> To his confine.

Pennant, *Snowdon*, 339–40

Christmas in Wales in modern times would not be complete without Dylan Thomas's *A Child's Christmas in Wales*. Here is an extract; having wandered away from the all-important description of the presents when he starts reminiscing about the postman, the narrator is interrupted by the child:

> 'Get back to the Presents.'
>
> 'There were the Useful Presents: engulfing mufflers
> of the old coach days, and mittens made for giant
> sloths; zebra scarfs of a substance like silky gum
> that could be tug-o'-warred down to the galoshes;

blinding tam-o'-shanters like patchwork tea cosies
and bunny-suited busbies and balaclavas for victims
of head-shrinking tribes; from aunts who always
wore wool next to the skin there were moustached and
rasping vests that made you wonder why the aunts
had any skin left at all; and once I had a little
crocheted nose bag from an aunt now, alas,
no longer whinnying with us. And pictureless books
in which small boys, though warned with quotations
not to, *would* skate on Farmer Giles' pond
and did and drowned; and books that told me
everything about the wasp, except why.'

'Go on to the Useless Presents.'

'Bags of moist and many-coloured jelly babies
and a folded flag and a false nose and a tram-
conductor's cap and a machine that punched tickets
and rang a bell; never a catapult; once, by mistake
that no one could explain, a little hatchet;
and a celluloid duck that made, when you pressed it,
a most unducklike sound, a mewing moo that an
ambitious cat might make who wished to be a cow;
and a painting book in which I could make the grass,
the trees, the sea and the animals any colour
I pleased, and still the dazzling sky-blue sheep
are grazing in the red field under the
rainbow-billed and pea-green birds.
Hardboileds, toffee, fudge and allsorts, crunches,
cracknels, humbugs, glaciers, marzipan, and
butterwelsh for the Welsh. And troops of
bright tin soldiers who, if they could not fight,
could always run. And Snakes-and-Families
and Happy Ladders. And Easy Hobbi-Games
for Little Engineers, complete with instructions.
Oh, easy for Leonardo! . . .'

Christmas in Puritan Boston. Judge Samuel Sewall, a Puritan, reports on a debate in 1722 whether business should be transacted at Christmas:

Friday, Decr 21. p. m. The Govr . . . spake to me again about adjourning the Court to next Wednesday. I spake against it; and propounded that the Govr would take a Vote for it; that he would hold the Balance even between the Church and us. His Excellency went to the Board again, and said much for this adjourning; All kept Christmas but we; I suggested K. James the first to Mr. Dudley, how he boasted what a pure church he had; and they did not keep Yule nor Pasch.

Mr. Dudley ask'd if the Scots kept Christmas. His Excellency protested, he believ'd they did not. Govr said they adjourned for the Commencement and Artillery. But then 'tis by Agreement. Col. Taylor spake so loud and boisterously for Adjourning, that 'twas hard for any to put in a word; Col. Townsend seconded me, and Col. Partridge; because this would prolong the Sessions. . . . I said the Dissenters came a great way for their Liberties and now the Church had theirs, yet they could not be contented, except they might Tread all others down. Govr said he was of the Church of England.

Sewall, 1000–1

Christmas in New York in the 1820s, by which time the good bishop St Nicholas of 6 December had become Santa Claus of the 25th. John Pintard, a founder of the New-York Historical Society, was a firm believer in holding on to old customs, which in New York's case were of Dutch origin:

Wednesday [Dec.] 24th [1828]. Mother & Sister are preparing for St Claas' arrival tonight. Pintards eyes sparkled, at breakfast, when I told him that their *Gude Heylig Man* was expected. He is to provide some Hay to feed the Horses. . . . In former days when the children each brought their stockings to be suspended over their Mothers fireplace, they also brought a little parcel of Hay, for the Horses & repeated a Dutch Hymn in praise of St Claas. I think I sent you a picture of this benevolent Saint which I had cut at my own expense, containing the Hymn at the bottom of the picture. It was difficult to obtain the words at the time it was executed, some 15 years ago, and would be almost impossible now. Judge Benson procured them from Mrs Hardenbrook, an ancient lady 87 years of age. Several, grandma Brasher & others knew some lines, but none except Mrs H. remembered the whole.

　　Friday, [Dec.] 26th. . . . Gude Heylig Man . . . came accordingly, during the night, with most elegant Toys, Bon bons, Oranges, &ca, all which after filling the stockings suspended at the sides of Mothers Chimney, were displayed in goodly order on the mantle to the extatic joy of Pintard & Boudy in the morning, whose exultations resounded thro' the house. . . . The Toys are arranged on the back of the sideboard & make quite a display. The most acceptable gift was a Drum, which Pintard promises to beat only in the nursery, not to disturb poor grandma.　　　Pintard, iii. 53–4

Christmas on a slave plantation, as recalled by Harriet Jacobs in 1861:

Every child rises early on Christmas morning to see the Johnkannaus. Without them, Christmas would be shorn of its greatest attraction. They consist of companies of slaves from the plantations, generally of the lower class. Two athletic men, in calico wrappers, have a net thrown over them, covered with all manner of bright-colored stripes. Cows' tails are fastened to their backs, and their heads are decorated with horns. A box, covered with sheepskin, is called the gumbo box. A dozen beat on this, while others strike triangles and jawbones, to which bands of dancers keep time. For a month previous they are composing songs, which are sung on this occasion. These companies, of a hundred each, turn out early in the morning, and are allowed to go round till twelve o'clock, begging for contributions. Not a door is left unvisited where there is the least chance of obtaining a penny or a glass of rum. They do not drink while they are out, but carry the rum home in jugs, to have a carousal. These Christmas donations frequently amount to twenty or thirty dollars. It is seldom that any white man or child refuses to give them a trifle. If he does, they regale his ears with the following song:—

> 'Poor massa, so dey say;
> Down in de heel, so dey say;
> Got no money, so dey say;
> Not one shillin, so dey say;
> God A'mighty bress you, so dey say.'

Christmas is a day of feasting, both with white and colored people. Slaves, who are lucky enough to have a few shillings, are sure to spend them for good eating; and many a turkey and pig is captured, without saying, 'By your leave, sir.' Those who cannot obtain these, cook a 'possum, or a raccoon, from which savory dishes can be made.　　　　　　　　　　　　　　H. Jacobs, 179–81

Christmas trees. The setting-up and decoration of a Christmas tree was a German custom known to several generations of the Royal Family, and sporadically mentioned in

England during the 1830s, before the Prince Consort attracted public attention in 1840 for continuing it.

The young Quaker Barclay Fox describes the wonder of the new custom, observed in Falmouth (Cornwall), in 1841, but does not neglect the quarterly accounting:

24. Christmas eve festivities. We were amongst a select few invited by Sterling's little people to witness the unfolding of a mighty mystery which has occupied their small brains for the last week. The folding doors of the drawing room being thrown open, the inner room appeared like a blaze of light & luxury. In the centre stood a fir tree reaching nearly to the ceiling, covered in all directions with lighted tapers & various gay & glittering symbols, while pendant from the lower branches were numerous presents for children and guests. Papa's ingenious irony had placed a foolscap on the top, immediately overshadowing the man in the moon & the Pope of Rome; crowns & helmets, paper flags & necklaces sparkled amongst the foliage & we all, old children and young, gave ourselves up to the enthusiasm of the moment. My present was a beautiful ivory pen tipped with silver & wreathed with laurel, a most elegant compliment. A.M. & C. were given some very fine engravings. The excitement having somewhat subsided I put off a volcano in the garden. The abandon of the children to their supreme delight was beautiful.

25. Whether this really was the day of Christ's birth is very doubtful yet I would not give up the annual festival for something. As my custom is I joined the Evanses at a good English roast-beef & plum pudding dinner at my cottage. Betsey was able to join us. Tom & I wound up the year's accounts & were mutually pleased at the profitable result.   Fox, 254

The English writer and social observer Harriet Martineau witnesses the introduction of the Christmas tree in New England in 1834 (in fact a German professor at Harvard had put one up in 1832):

I was present at the introduction into the new country of the spectacle of the German Christmas-tree. My little friend Charley, and three companions, had been long preparing for this pretty show. The cook had broken her eggs carefully in the middle for some weeks past, that Charley might have the shells for cups; and these cups were gilded and coloured very prettily. I rather think it was, generally speaking, a secret out of the house; but I knew what to expect. . . . We were sent for before dinner, and we took up two round-faced boys by the way. Early as it was, we were all so busy that we could scarcely spare a respectful attention to our plum-pudding. It was desirable that our preparations should be completed before the little folks should begin to arrive; and we were all engaged in sticking on the last of the seven dozen of wax-tapers, and in filling the gilt egg-cups, and gay paper cornucopiæ with comfits, lozenges, and barley-sugar. The tree was the top of a young fir, planted in a tub, which was ornamented with moss. Smart dolls, and other whimsies, glittered in the evergreen; and there was not a twig which had not something sparkling upon it. . . .

It really looked beautiful; the room seemed in a blaze; and the ornaments were so well hung on that no accident happened, except that one doll's petticoat caught fire. There was a sponge tied to the end of a stick to put out any supernumerary blaze; and no harm ensued. I mounted the steps behind the tree to see the effect of opening the doors. It was delightful. The children poured in; but in a moment, every voice was hushed. Their faces were upturned to the blaze, all eyes wide open, all lips parted, all steps arrested. . . . At last, a quick pair of eyes discovered that it bore something eatable, and from that moment the babble began again. They were told that they might get what they could without burning themselves; and we tall people kept watch, and helped them with good things from the higher branches. When all had had enough, we returned to the larger room, and finished the evening with dancing. By ten o'clock, all were well warmed for the ride home with steaming mulled wine, and the prosperous evening closed with shouts of mirth. . . . I have little doubt the Christmas-tree will become one of the most flourishing exotics of New England.   Martineau, iii. 182–5

Gift-giving. In earlier times, gifts were commonly given at the New Year (see *1 Jan.). But Giles Moore, rector of Horstead Keynes in Sussex, notes several gifts exchanged on Christmas Day:

25th Dec.ʳ [1674]. I sent to Mr. Hely a ribspare and hoggs puddings, for which hee returned mee a boxe of pills and sermons.   Moore, 117

However, in New York, a former Dutch colony, St Nicholas, having been transformed into Santa Claus, brought toys for children at Christmas. John Pintard, in 1830, says that many of them were imported from the Old World:

Friday 24th December [1830]. It is amusing, as I pass along, to look at the Toy Shop windows & see the endless variety of European Toys that attract the admiration & empty the pockets of parents friends & children. . . .

Monday 27th December. It would have delighted you on Friday evening to have witnessed the joy that beamed in Pintard's eyes when I read in the paper the report of 'the arrival of the Dutch Ship, alder lievert (best beloved) vrow, Capt. Wouter Van Twiller, freighted as deep as she could swim with all sorts of Toys, Cakes, fruits & books, for Sᵗ Claas to bestow his annual presents to the good children of the antient city of New Amsterdam, now called N. York'. With what ecstacy did they exhibit next morning, Christmas, the profusion of Toys, Oranges, & bon bons left by Sᵗ Claas for our 3 children, displayed on Mothers Table for their stocking crammed with cakes could not contain the splendid articles left by Sᵗ Claas. For good children, Christmas morn is a perfect Jubilee in this city.   Pintard, iii. 206

Christmas cards. The tradition of sending cards at Christmas goes back only as far as 1843, when, upon the suggestion of Sir Henry Cole, the London artist Joseph Cundall lithographed a drawing by J. C. Horsley, coloured it, and sold some 1,000 copies. Within twenty years the custom of sending cards had become widespread. In the United States, cards first began to be imported from England in the 1870s; they proved so popular that a Boston company started holding competitions for designs, with substantial prizes. Today Christmas cards are sold in the millions.

Christmas crackers. These too are a nineteenth-century invention, and one that has not caught on in the USA, where crackers feature only at children's birthday parties. They were invented by Tom Smith of Norwich in 1884 and modelled on Parisian sweets wrapped in paper, to which he added love verses. Then he was inspired to produce a miniature and relatively safe imitation of the firecracker, using a strip of cardboard with gunpowder that snapped when pulled; the sweet was replaced with a small gift and (now) horrible jokes. Earlier, however, they were very topical, drawing on the events and scandals of the day. The following rhyme was enclosed in a 'Suffragette Crackerette' of 1911:

> Tho' man may baulk us now in our endeavour
> To gain the franchise, we ignore his ban!
> We'll go on pleading till we prove forever
> That we are worthy MATES for any man!

An odd Christmas custom. Goose-dancing in the Isles of Scilly, as reported in 1750:

At *Christmas* Time, the young People exercise a Sort of *Gallantry* among them called *Goose-dancing*; when the Maidens are dressed up for young Men, and the young Men for Maidens. They visit their Neighbours in Companies, where they dance, and make their Jokes upon what has happened in the Islands, when every Person is humorously told of their own, without Offence being taken. By this sort of Sport according to yearly Custom and Toleration, there is a spirit of *Wit* and *Drollery* kept up among the People. The Maidens, who are sometimes dressed up for *Sea-Captains* and other Officers, display their alluring Graces to the *Ladies*, who are young Men equipped for that Purpose; and the *Ladies* exert their Talents to them in courtly and amorous Addresses: Their Hangers are sometimes drawn, &c. after which, and other Pieces of Drollery, the Scene shifts to Music and Dancing; which being over they are treated with Liquor, and then go to the next House of Entertainment.

The Custom of *Goose-dancing* was formerly encouraged by the Military Officers living in these Islands, who distinguished themselves by it among the Ladies. They used to go in party-coloured Dresses, half of one Colour to the Right and Left, or above and below; exercising drawn Swords, in their Dancing, at the Houses, where they entered and retired by Procession of two and two. There was a *Serjeant Kite* who acted his Part in Company, which was repeating Verses in Praise of a military Life, and laughing People out of their Money. At this Time Serenades in the Night were in Practice under the Windows of the fair Islanders, which at this Day are not quite forgot.

Heath, 125–6

Pantomimes. Christmas in England brings the annual round of pantomimes, which have long outgrown their origin in narrative dance in the early eighteenth century; comic and fantastic elements soon predominated, and sung and spoken words belie the name 'pantomime'. David Garrick deplored their popularity at the expense of serious drama:

> They in the drama find no joys,
> But doat on mimicry and toys.
> Thus, when a dance is in my bill,
> Nobility my boxes fill;
> Or send three days before the time,
> To crowd a new-made pantomime.

Chambers, in the mid-nineteenth century, viewed with disdain 'the grotesque performances associated with our English Christmas', but the pantomime shows no sign of waning in popularity. Today's pantomime has lost the harlequin and pantaloon aspects that characterized it originally, and now is more often based on fairy tales. Stock characters are the 'dame' (played by a man), the leading boy (played by a woman), and all sorts of animals.

Traditional Christmas foods. Foods traditional at Christmas have changed over the ages, and differ from country to country, but they are always plentiful; just as Easter breaks the Lenten fast, Christmas breaks the Advent fast. In earlier times it was customary for landowners to feast their tenants. The well-known custom of serving a boar's head dates from as early as 1289, when it is recorded in the expenses of the bishop of Hereford. John Aubrey mentions the ceremony at Queen's College, Oxford (which still continues, though now it is held on a Saturday before Christmas), and reprints the song:

This song is sung on Christmas-day in the Hall at Queen's Coll. in Oxford, by one of the Taberders: but in the chorus all the Company doth assist.

> The Boars Head in hand bear I
> Bedeckt wth Bays and Rosemary,
> And pray my Masters merry be
> Quot estis in convivio.   *All you who are at the feast*
>   CHORUS.—Caput apri defero,   *I bring the boar's head*
>   Reddens laudes Domino.   *Giving due praises to the Lord*
>
> The Boars head as I understand
> Is the bravest dish in all our land,
> And thus bedeckt wth a gay Garland
> Let us servire cantico.   *see to the song*
>   CHOR.—Caput apri, &c.
>
> Our Steward hath provided this
> In honour of the King of Bliss,
> Which on this day to be served is
> In Reginensi atrio.   *in Queen's hall*
>   CHOR.—Caput apri, &c.

Aubrey, 142

A charming legend has grown up to explain the institution of the ceremony. In medieval times, a student of the college, walking near Shotover Hill and immersed in reading Aristotle, was attacked by a wild boar. Not having any other means of defence, he thrust the book down the animal's throat, crying 'Graecum est!' ('It's Greek!'). This did for the boar, and its head was brought back as a trophy.

Boar's head not being easily attainable, a beast still exotic in the sixteenth century, and considerably more edible, came into favour—the turkey:

This kind of Poultry we have not long had amongst us: for before the yeere of our Lord 1530 they were not seene with us, nor I beleeve knowen to the olde wryters. . . . But because this kinde of Foule, both for the rarenesse, and also the greatnesse of theyr body, is at this day kept in great flockes, it shall not be much amisse to speake of them: for in daintynesse and goodnesse of meate, the Hennes may compare with eyther the Goose, or the Pehenne, and the Cocke farre excell them.

Googe, fos. 166^v–167 (1577)

Puritans would have none of the traditional Christmas feasting:

We have never been witnesses of animosities excited by the use of minced pies and plumb porridge, nor seen with what abhorrence those who could eat them at all other times of the year would shrink from them in December. An old Puritan, who was alive in my childhood, being at one of the feasts of the church invited by a neighbour to partake his cheer, told him that if he would treat him at an alehouse with beer, brewed for all times and seasons, he should accept his kindness, but would have none of his superstitious meats or drinks.

Johnson, 'Life of Samuel Butler', Lives, 215

In 1770 Sir Henry Grey, evidently tired of the same old Christmas dinner, conceived and had executed a grandiose Christmas pie:

Monday last was brought from Howick to Berwick, to be shipp'd for London, for sir Hen. Grey, bart., a pie, the contents whereof are as follows: viz. 2 bushels of flour, 20 lbs. of butter, 4 geese,

2 turkies, 2 rabbits, 4 wild ducks, 2 woodcocks, 6 snipes, and 4 partridges; 2 neats' tongues, 2 curlews, 7 blackbirds, and 6 pigeons: it is supposed a very great curiosity, was made by Mrs. Dorothy Patterson, housekeeper at Howick. It was near nine feet in circumference at bottom, weighs about twelve stones, will take two men to present it to table; it is neatly fitted with a case, and four small wheels to facilitate its use to every guest that inclines to partake of its contents at table.   *Newcastle Chronicle*, 6 Jan. 1770, quoted in Hone, *Table Book*, 667

But by far the more common pie at Christmas—indeed, during the whole Christmas season—is mince pie:

As many *mince pies* as you taste at Christmas, so many happy months will you have.

Denham, 62

> Mince-pies grant Wishes: let each name his Prize,
> But as for us, we wish for more Mince-Pies.
> G. K. Chesterton, 'Some Wishes at Xmas', *New Poems* (1932)

In Scotland, where oats are not to be missed out even at Christmas, Yule brose was a delicacy:

Another prelude to the approach of Christmas, was the appearance of flocks of geese, driven from the south to be massacred and eaten on this day. These, however, were chiefly destined for the solace of gentle stomachs, the prevailing Christmas dish among the common people and peasantry, being the national one of *fat brose*, otherwise denominated *Yule brose*. The large pot in almost every family of this description, well provided with butcher meat (if bullocks' heads or knee bones may be so called) was put on the fire the previous evening, to withdraw the nutritive juices and animal oil from the said ingredients. Next day after breakfast, or at dinner, the brose was made, generally in a large punch-bowl, the mistress of the ceremonies dropping a gold ring among the oatmeal upon which the oily soup was poured. The family, or party, (for on these occasions there was generally a party of young people assembled) provided with spoons and seated round the bowl, now began to partake of the half-boiling brose, on the understanding that the person who was so fortunate as to get the ring was to be first married.

Blackwood's Edinburgh Magazine (Dec. 1821), 692

An eighteenth-century Irish Christmas dish:

To roast a Pound of Butter or more the Irish Way.—Take a Pound of Butter, season it well with Salt, and put it on a wooden Spit; place it at a good Distance from the Fire, let it turn round, and as the Butter moistens or begins to drip, drudge it well with fine Oatmeal, continuing so to do till there is any Moisture ready to drip, then baste it, and it will soon be enough. A certain *Irish* Woman told me this eats vere nicely, insomuch that she has done on a *Christmas* Eve twenty-seven different Pounds so, at a Farmer's House in her Country, where it has been kept all the Holidays, to accommodate a Friend with a Slice or two, as we do Cakes or minced Pies here.

Ellis, 365–6

Christmas dinner menus:

1. Timothy Burrell, barrister-at-law, of Ockenden House, Cuckfield, invited his neighbours for Christmas dinner on 1 and 2 January 1707. He listed the following menus in his diary (a clod is the coarse part of an ox neck nearest the shoulder):

1st January (13 guests)	2d January (12 guests)
Plumm pottage,	Plumm pottage,
Calves' head and bacon,	Boiled leg of mutton,
Goose,	Goose,
Pig,	Pig,
Plum pottage,	Plumm pottage,
Roast beef, sirloin,	Roast beef,
Veale, a loin,	Veal, leg, roasted,
Goose,	Pig,
Plumm pottage,	Plumm pottage,
Boiled beef, a clod.	Boiled beef, a rump.

Two baked puddings,	Two baked puddings,
Three dishes of minced pies.	Three dishes of minced pies.

Two capons,	Two capons,
Two dishes of tarts,	Two dishes of tarts,
Two pullets.	Two pullets. Blencowe, 153

2. Parson Woodforde's 1773 Christmas Day dinner at New College, Oxford, when he was Sub-Warden and ordered the meals:

We had for dinner, two fine Codds boiled with fryed Soals round them & Oyster Sauce, a fine Surloin of Beef rosted, Some Peas Soup & an Orange Pudding for the first Course, for the Second we had a Lease of Wild Ducks rosted, a fore Q^r of Lamb & Sallad & Mince Pies. . . . After the second Course there was a fine Plumb Cake brought to the Senr Table as is usual on this Day, which also goes to the Batchelors after.   Hargreaves-Mawdsley, 199–200

The Wassail bowl was brought out every Chrismastide; customs associated with it continue to Twelfth night.

The drinking the Wassail Bowl or Cup was in all probability owing to keeping Christmas in the same manner they had before the Feast of Yule. There was nothing the northern nations so much delighted in as carousing ale; especially at this season, when fighting was over. It was likewise the custom at all their feasts for the master of the house to fill a large bowl or pitcher, and drink out of it first himself, and then give it to him that sat next, and so it went round. One custom more should be remembered; and this is, it was usual some years ago in Chrismas time for the poorer people to go from door to door with a wassail cup adorned with ribbons and a golden apple at the top, singing and begging money for it; the original of which was, that they also might procure lamb's wool to fill it, and regale themselves as well as the rich.

Gentleman's Magazine, 54 (May 1784), 347

A recipe for a Wassail bowl is given under 1 January. Lamb's wool, another seasonal hot punch, is a concoction of brown ale and wine; the 'wool' is produced by the pulp of roasted apples.

Lamb's Wool

4 large eating apples	½ teaspoon nutmeg
2 pints (1.25 l) brown ale	½ teaspoon ginger
1 pint (500 ml) sweet white wine	thin strip of lemon rind
3 in (7.5 cm) cinnamon stick	soft dark brown sugar to taste

Slit skin around the centre of each apple. (A comparable amount of crabapples can also be used.) Bake in oven at 350 °F (180 °C) until soft and pulpy.

Heat brown ale, wine, spices, and lemon rind in a large saucepan gently; do not allow to boil. Remove apple flesh from skins and mash. Stir into liquid. Remove cinnamon stick and lemon rind, then pass the mixture through a sieve, pressing down well. Reheat, adding brown sugar to taste.

Serve steaming from a punch bowl, into earthenware mugs or glass tankards.

after The National Trust Book of Christmas and Festival Day Recipes

For those abroad, Christmas is always a time of nostalgia, and the attempt is often made to recreate the feast with local ingredients. An English admiral in Cádiz in 1695 decided that he could not do without a Wassail bowl on Christmas Day. An eyewitness records Admiral Russel's 'Noble Treat':

There was in the middle of a Garden of Lemons and Oranges (which Garden belonged to *Don Pedro Valasco*, Governor of *Cales*) a Fountain which was set with *Dutch* Tiles in the Bottom and Sides, and was made as clean as a Japan Punch-Bowl.

In this Fountain, on *Christmas-day*, was pour'd six Butts of Water, half a Hogshead of Strong Mountain Malaga Wine, Two hundred Gallons of Brandy, Six hundred weight of Sugar, Twelve thousand Lemons, and Nutmegs and Sugar in Proportion. The Admiral hired the Governor's House belonging to the Garden, and Resided there all the Winter.

He invited all the *English* and *Dutch* Merchants and Officers belonging to the Fleet to Dine with him; There was One hundred Dishes of Flesh-Meat, besides many other Dishes of Rarities; but such a Flesh-Feast was never seen in *Spain* before; he also Roasted an Ox for the Entertainment of the Company.

Dinner being ended, they marched in Order to the Fountain or Punch-Bowl, where on the Punch was floating a little Boat with a Boy in it, and Cups to serve it out to the Company. The Admiral began the Allies Healths; and having drank what they thought fit, they drew off, and in went the Mob, with their Shoes and Stockins and all on, and had like to have turned the Boat with the Boy over, and so he might have been drowned in Punch: but, to prevent further danger, they suckt it up, and left the Punch-Bowl behind. This is a Comical, but a very true Relation, and worth noting, etc.

F. Moore (1711)

Christmas verse

Ther is no rose of swych vertu
As is the rose that bare Jhesu;
   Alleluya.

For in this rose conteynyd was
Heuen and erthe in lytyl space,
   Res miranda.   *A wondrous thing*

Be that rose we may weel see
That he is God in personys thre,
   Pari forma.   *With the same form*

The aungelys sungyn the sheperdes to:
'Gloria in excelcis Deo.'
   Gaudeamus.   *Let us rejoice*

Leue we al this worldly merthe,
And folwe we this joyful berthe;
   Transeamus.   *Let us pass over*

fifteenth-century carol from Trinity College, Cambridge, MS O. 3. 58

The burning Babe

As I in hoarie Winters night stoode shivering in the snow,
Surpris'd I was with sodaine heate, which made my hart to glow;
And lifting up a fearefull eye, to view what fire was neare,
A pretty Babe all burning bright did in the ayre appeare;
Who scorched with excessive heate, such floods of teares did shed,
As though his floods should quench his flames, which with his teares were fed:
Alas (quoth he) but newly borne, in fierie heates I frie,
Yet none approach to warme their harts, or feele my fire, but I;
My faultlesse breast the furnace is, the fuell wounding thornes;
Love is the fire, and sighs the smoake, the ashes, shame and scornes;
The fewell Justice layeth on, and Mercie blowes the coales;
The metall in this furnace wrought, are mens defiled soules:
For which, as now on fire I am to worke them to their good,
So will I melt into a bath, to wash them in my blood.
With this he vanisht out of sight, and swiftly shrunk away,
And straight I called unto minde, that it was Christmasse day.

                                        Robert Southwell (?1561–95)

26 DECEMBER

a.d. VII Kalendas Ianuarias   C

Blessed be Saint Stephen,
there's no fast at his Even.

❰ HOLIDAYS AND ANNIVERSARIES South Africa: Day of Goodwill
UK, Australia, New Zealand: Boxing Day

❰ HOLY DAYS **Stephen, First Martyr** (CofE, RC; Orth. 27 Dec.)

Stephen (d. *c*.35), the first martyr (*protomartyr*), also counted the first deacon, since his name heads the list at Acts 6: 5 (see *11 Oct.). He was stoned by the Jews for preaching that Christ was the Messiah, haranguing them as 'stiffnecked and uncircumcised in heart and ears' (Acts 7: 51). The discovery of his body, supposedly by the priest Lucian in 415, gave him in older calendars another feast, the Invention, on *3 August. Stephen may be recognized in paintings by the stone perched on his head or carried in his hands; the stones are sometimes called 'St Stephen's loaves'. He is the patron saint of bricklayers and all those in the building trade, as well as of deacons; he is also invoked against headache.

In some churches it was the custom, after vespers on Christmas Day, for the deacons to sing an antiphon in honour of St Stephen, whose day, in canonical terms, began at that moment; in turn, at vespers on St Stephen's day priests would pay the like honour to St John the Divine, and at vespers on his day the boys would honour the Holy

Innocents. Subdeacons, whose order had not been defined in apostolic times, celebrated variously at Circumcision, Epiphany, and the octave of the latter, 'which is called the Feast of Fools' (Durandus 7. 42).

Synaxis of Theotokos (Orth.). See *Orthodox Church Year.

St Stephen's Day. This was the traditional day for bleeding horses:

> Then followeth Saint Stephens day, whereon doth every man,
> His horses iaunt and course abrode, as swiftly as he can.
> Untill they doe extreemely sweate, and than they let them blood,
> For this being done upon this day, they say doth do them good,
> And keepes them from all maladies and sicknesse through the yeare,
> As if that Steven any time tooke charge of horses heare.
>
> Naogeorgus, fo. 45

In some Carinthian villages, young men would ride unsaddled round the parish church; in Norway and Sweden one 'rode Stephen', competing in a race to an open spring to water the horses.

'Good King Wenceslas looked out on the feast of Stephen.' Did he? It is a pretty story, but the King (see *28 Sept.) was not known for his charity. The tune, which dates back to the fourteenth century, was printed in *Piae cantiones* of 1582 with the Latin text of a spring song, 'Tempus adest floridum'; but the words were written in the nineteenth century by the liturgist J. M. Neale, probably to illustrate what one ought to do on Boxing Day ('Ye who now will bless the poor | Shall yourselves find blessing').

Wren Day. St Stephen's Day in Ireland is called Wren Day and was a day when children went begging; according to legend, St Stephen's hiding place was thought to have been revealed by the chattering of wrens. O'Sullivan calls it the day of the wren in the holly branch (*lá an dhreolín san graoibh gcuilinn*) and he did not approve the practice:

St. Stephen's Day. . . . The rabble of the town going from door to door, with a wren in a holly bush, asking for money, in order to be drunk late this evening. It is a bad custom to give it to them.   O'Sullivan, ii. 77 (26 Dec. 1828)

Part of the wren-boys' song runs:

> The wren, the wren, the king of all birds,
> St. Stephen's Day was caught in the furze,
> Although he is little, his family's great,
> I pray you, good lady, give us a treat.
>
> My box would speak if it had but a tongue,
> And two or three shillings would do it no wrong;
> Sing holly, sing ivy—sing ivy, sing holly,
> A drop just to drink, it would drown melancholy.
>
> And if you draw it of the best,
> I hope in Heaven your soul may rest;
> But if you draw it of the small,
> It won't agree with the wren-boys at all.
>
> Croker, 233

England too knew the same begging custom, but it was called 'Stephening'.

Boxing Day. Under the Bank Holidays Act 1871 'the day after Christmas Day', described in the schedule as 'the twenty-sixth day of December, if a week day' (i.e. not Sunday), was made a bank holiday in England (in the usage of the time including Wales) and Ireland; in the schedule to the Banking and Financial Services Act 1971 the holiday is assigned to '26th December, if it be not a Sunday', but to '27th December in a year in which 25th or 26th December is a Sunday'. Moreover, since most people now work a five-day week, if Boxing Day is a Saturday, the 28th is proclaimed a bank holiday; if Christmas Day is a Saturday and Boxing Day a Sunday, both the 27th and the 28th are bank holidays. (The *name*, however, should not be transferred: to call Monday the 27th—let alone the 28th—'Boxing Day' is as absurd as to call it 'Christmas', should the 25th be a Saturday.)

Boxing Day is celebrated in New South Wales with a picnic on Bondi Beach. It is unknown in the USA, although a few states treat the 26th as a holiday.

The earliest reference to the term Boxing Day in the *OED* dates back only to 1833. Brady (ii. 343–4) proposes the following explanation of the origin of giving Christmas boxes, a custom he deemed in 1812 as 'nearly forgotten' (together with the 'now almost exploded practice of making New Year's Gifts'):

. . . in the middle and more superstitious ages, the then profligate ministers of religion took advantage of this spirit of liberality, to fill their own coffers.—Masses, or Prayers, as hath already been explained, were appropriated to every purpose that could best answer the ends of religious avarice; and it became, among other practices of the Monks, customary to offer masses for the safety of all ships that undertook long voyages. To quicken the pious gratitude, therefore, of those who embarked in such ships, or were connected with their safety, a Box was regularly appropriated to each ship, and kept in the custody of the priest, into which, money, or other valuable considerations might be put, to secure efficacy to the prayers of the Church.—These boxes were opened at *Christmas*, in each year, and thence got their names of *Christmas-Boxes*, which readily came to be understood as the title also of the presents themselves; and that no person interested in the several vessels, however poor, might neglect these oblations, they were encouraged to beg of their richer neighbours *Box Money*, or, in other words, *Money to enable them to supply the Priest's Box*, that they might be entitled to partake of the virtue and efficacy of the prayers, which *otherwise* they could not reasonably expect.

Another explanation:

Christmas Boxes or Presents.—The custom of annual donations at Christmas and on New Year's Day is very antient, being copied by the Christians from the Polytheists of Rome, at the time the public religion was changed . . . These presents, nowadays, are more commonly made on the morrow of Christmas. From this circumstance the festival of St. Stephen has got the nickname of Christmas Boxing Day, and by corruption Boxing Day.   Forster, 742 (1824)

Although in early times and later Christmas boxes were given freely, in the eighteenth century 'vails', or tips to servants—and not so much one's own as those of others—could become extortionate. A Swiss visitor to England observed in February 1727:

Besides these wines [i.e. vails], you are expected to give Christmas boxes at the end of the year. An acquaintance of mine, one of Mr. [Robert] Walpole's most intimate friends, assured me that the latter's porter receives near on £80 as Christmas boxes. Truly this is a prodigious sum; but if you consider that his master is first minister, it is not incredible, for some persons go to his house so often and pay him so much court that they are obliged to give his porter at least a guinea.

Saussure, 195

A footman's view from the other side, in 1837:

26th [Dec. 1837]. This is what is called about here [London] Boxing Day. It's the day the people goe from house to house gathering their Christmas boxes. We have had numbers here today— sweeps, beadles, lamplighters, waterman, dustmen, scavengers (that is the men who clean the mud out of the streets), newspaper boy, general postmen, twopenny postmen and waits. These are a set of men that goe about the streets playing musick in the night after people are in bed and a sleepe. Some people are very fond of hearing them, but for my own part, I don't admire being roused from a sound sleep by a whole band of musick and perhaps not get to sleep again for an houre or two. All these people expect to have a shilling or half a crown each. . . . Miss P. gave me half a sovering for a Christmas box, one of the trades people gave me half a crown, another gave me a shilling. I mite get fuddled two or three times a day if I had a mind, as all the trades people that serve this house are very pressing with their glass of something to drink their health this Christmas time.

Tayler, 61–2

Kwanzaa. Kwanzaa (Swahili for 'first'), begins on this day and lasts till New Year's. Neither a religious celebration nor a replacement of (secular) Christmas, it is an Afro-American festival invented in 1966 by Maulana Karenga, then chairman of Black Studies at California State University in Long Beach. He devised it around elements of African harvest festivals as a celebration of the African heritage. During the seven days seven principles are discussed: Unity, Self-determination, Collective Work and Responsibility, Cooperative Economics, Purpose, Creativity, and Faith. Fulfilling an obvious lack, and increasingly successful, it combines symbolism with ritual as a family and community festival; there is a feast (Kwanzaa Karamu) on the penultimate day, 31 December.

27 DECEMBER

Never rued the man
that laid in his fuel before St. John.

(HOLY DAYS **John, Apostle and Evangelist** (CofE, RC; 26 Sept. Orth.); Stephen (Orth.; see *26 Dec.)

John was the son of Zebedee, the brother of St James the Greater; the two were close, zealous enough for Jesus to call them 'Sons of Thunder', and with a high view of their own merits, asking to sit on either side of Jesus in His Kingdom. Nevertheless, they, together with St Peter, were permitted to view the Transfiguration (*6 Aug.), and John is generally identified with the Beloved Disciple who leant against Jesus' bosom at the Last

Supper, and into whose care He gave His mother Mary at the Crucifixion. According to tradition he settled in Ephesus, but under Domitian was exiled to Patmos, where he wrote the Apocalypse or Revelation; on the emperor's death he returned to Ephesus, and there wrote the Fourth Gospel and the three Epistles that bear his name. The Eastern Church was slow to accept his authorship of Revelation, written in the worst Greek of the entire New Testament; the second and third Epistles speak in the name of 'the Elder', whom some suppose to be a different person; only the most conservative scholars now ascribe any biblical book to the Apostle. Nevertheless, these writings have won him the name of 'John the Divine' (that is, the Theologian); the Fourth Gospel in particular, largely given to long discourses by Jesus, is doctrinally far in advance of the other three Gospels (called Synoptic because in essentials they share a common point of view). John is patron of writers, theologians, and publishers, and also (among Christians) of Turkey. He is invoked against poison, for according to legend the high priest of Artemis at Ephesus ('Diana of the Ephesians'), Aristodemus by name, undertook to become a Christian if John survived a draught from a poisoned chalice whose deadliness was demonstrated upon two convicts; he did so, and when Aristodemus imposed a second test of raising the dead, gave him his tunic to put on the corpses of the convicts, who promptly rose. Artists add a viper curling round the edge of the cup; in Germany it became the custom to drink a loving-cup in his honour. John's emblem is the eagle; in Byzantine art he is a bearded elder, in the West a beardless youth.

28 DECEMBER

a.d. V Kalendas Ianuarias   E

❨ HOLIDAYS AND ANNIVERSARIES Nepal: The King's Birthday (national day)
USA, Iowa: Admission Day (29th state, 1846)

❨ HOLY DAYS **Innocents' Day** (BCP); **Holy Innocents** (RC, CY)

Holy Innocents' Day or Childermas commemorates the Massacre of the Innocents. According to St Matthew, within two years of Jesus' birth the appearance of a new star drew some Magi ('wise men') to Jerusalem (see *6 Jan.), desirous of worshipping the King of the Jews whose birth they took it to mark; an alarmed King Herod, having ascertained from the Sanhedrin that (on a literal interpretation of Micah 5: 2) the Messiah would be born at Bethlehem, sent them there with instructions to report back so that he too might worship him. Having found the house, and presented gold, frankincense, and myrrh, they were warned by an angel to go home by another way without telling Herod, who meant not to worship but to kill the boy; he, angry at their betrayal, had all boys of 2 or under in the Bethlehem area put to death. The Innocents are patron saints of foundlings.

The star has been associated with astronomical phenomena such as the manifestation of Halley's Comet in 12 BC and the planetary conjunction of 7 BC (see *15 Sept.);
since Jewish culture at the time was not altogether hostile to astrology, Christian Jews
might retrospectively interpret an event of that nature as portending the birth of the
Messiah and claim for it certification by the acknowledged experts. Sceptics ask why
Magi should relate celestial phenomena to the Roman client-kingdom of Judaea rather
than to the Parthian empire in which they lived, why Herod did not put them under
military escort on the pretext of honour and protection, and why Jewish writers, little
as they love King Herod, mention neither such a massacre nor the unrest that must have
followed; but by the early fifth century the story was so well established that the pagan
Macrobius took it for granted, writing in a review of the emperor Augustus' witticisms:

When he heard that among the boys under two whom Herod king of the Jews ordered to be
killed in Syria, Herod's son was slain too, he said: 'It's better to be Herod's pig than his son'.

Saturnalia 2. 4. 11

This joke must originally have been told in Greek (where 'pig', *hus*, and 'son', *huios*, are
similar), about the execution of Herod's disloyal son Antipater.

Martyrs of Nicomedia (Orth.). Nicomedia (İzmit), the emperor Diocletian's residence, was
the base from which the Great Persecution was launched on 23 February 303; when a few
months later the emperor's palace caught fire twice within a fortnight, for which the
Christians were blamed, the attempt to divide the more zealous from the rest gave way
to indiscriminate repression, enforced by the tortures of the age.

Boy bishops. On Holy Innocents' Day in the Middle Ages it was customary in a number
of churches, and especially English churches, for one of the choirboys to represent a
bishop, carrying out many of his functions (though not, of course, the Canon of the
Mass). In some places he was elected on St Nicholas' Day (see *6 Dec.) and ruled till
this day. He blessed the people, preached, and sometimes conducted a visitation. Two
English sermons of boy bishops have survived, one from the early 1490s at St Paul's
printed by Wynkyn de Worde, the other from 1558 at Gloucester, 'pronownsyd by John
Stubs, Querester'; they express the most laudable zeal for virtue and learning. Boy
bishops were forbidden by Henry VIII in 1541 (see *6 Dec.) but revived under Mary.

Childermas Day. Childermas Day was considered an unlucky day (Edward IV's coronation was postponed to the next day, 1460), which infects the day of the week on which
it falls with its own ill-fortune throughout the coming year:

Friday, quoth a, a dismall day, Childermasse day this yeare was friday.

Anthony Munday, Sir John Oldcastle (1619), pt. 1

The same held true in France:

You have heard of the English mens great cheere in Amiens, but one euening Monseur de Torcy
came to the King and told him, that so great a number of them were in the towne, that it stood
in some danger. But the King was displeased with his message: wherefore euery man forbare
to bring him any more such newes. The next morrow was one of the daies that represented

Childermas day that yeere, on the which the King vsed not to debate any matter, but accounted it a signe of some great misfortune towards him, if any man communed with him of his affaires, and would be maruellously displeased with those that were neere him and acquainted with his humor, if they troubled him with any matter whatsoeuer.

Commynes, *Historie*, bk. 4, ch. 9 (trans. Danett, 137)

Nevertheless Commynes had to inform Louis XI that 9,000 Englishmen were roister-ing in the city; the king listened, and gave the appropriate orders. The event was on Wednesday, 23 August 1475, the same weekday as the previous Childermas.

It was considered unlucky to commence a new undertaking on Childermas Day:

It is not good to put on a new sute, pare ones nailes, or begin any thing on a Childermas day.

Melton, 46 (1620)

A little Boy at the lower end of the Table told her, that he was to go into Join-hand [cursive hand-writing] on *Thursday*: Thursday? says she *No, Child, if it please God, you shall not begin upon* Childermas-day; *tell your Writing-Master that* Friday *will be soon enough.*

Spectator, 8 Mar. 1711 (28 Dec. 1710 OS had been a Thursday)

This was a bad-luck day in Scotland in 1879, when the Tay railway bridge collapsed while a train from Edinburgh was passing over it; all lives were lost:

It continued its way onwards, entered the high girders in the middle of the Bridge, and when just about to emerge from them at the north end, a fearful blast, with a noise like thunder, swept down the river. At that moment two intensely brilliant sheets of flame and showers of sparks were seen to rise from the high girders, evidently resulting from the friction of the ponderous ironwork as it crashed and tumbled into the river below from the horrible height of about 100 feet. Simultaneously with the disappearance of the sparks and flashes of light the train also dis-appeared; and before they had time to realise their fearful position, the whole of the 200 pas-sengers were ushered into eternity.

Dundee Courier and Argus, 29 Dec. 1879, quoted in Murison, 168

The event is commemorated in a notorious poem by William McGonagall, and a beau-tiful ballad by Theodor Fontane, in which Shakespeare's three witches induce the storm.

29 DECEMBER

❦ HOLIDAYS AND ANNIVERSARIES USA, Texas: Admission Day (28th state, 1845)

❦ HOLY DAYS Thomas Becket (CY, RC) (see also translation, *7 July); Holy Inno-cents (Orth.; see *28 Dec.)

Thomas Becket (?1120–70); the form 'à Becket' is erroneous. Born to a Norman family in London, Becket served Archbishop Theobald of Canterbury before becoming chan-cellor to Henry II, in which position his love of pomp was no less remarkable than his zeal in his master's interest, often directed against the Church. Their friendship induced Henry in 1162 to press an unwilling Becket to become Archbishop of Canterbury; this was a grave miscalculation on the king's part, for Becket now displayed the same commitment in the service of the Church, asserting rights and privileges that it did not enjoy in practice, above all jurisdiction over all tonsured persons charged with any offence ('criminous clerks'). Lacking support amongst the bishops, he submitted in 1164 to the 'ancient customs of the realm' as codified in the Constitutions of Clarendon, but soon repented; called to account for moneys received as Chancellor, he fled to France and appealed to Pope Alexander III, who was then at Sens. Thereafter both Louis VII of France and Pope Alexander, though dismayed by his extremism, gave him their support while attempting to bring about a reconciliation; in 1170 their efforts appeared to be successful, but the settlement broke down when Becket refused to absolve the bishops who had assisted in the coronation of Henry's son Henry ('the Young King') by the archbishop of York, in breach, as Becket saw it, of Canterbury's privileges. Henry's angry outburst, 'Will no man rid me of this turbulent priest?', induced four knights to kill Becket in his own cathedral. The crime caused indignation throughout Europe; little over two years later Alexander canonized Becket, and in 1174 Henry did public penance at his shrine.

Having been the 'hooly blisful martir' of the Middle Ages, Thomas Becket became a traitor under Henry VIII and remained so (but see *14 Oct.) so long as England considered itself Protestant. Nowadays he is popularly misrepresented as the champion of free conscience, a heresy of which not even Henry II accused him.

Trophimus of Arles, one of Pope Fabian's missionaries (*22 Mar.), but identified in legend with St Paul's Ephesian companion of that name (Acts 20: 4, 21: 29).

30 DECEMBER

a.d. III Kalendas Ianuarias   G

Pope Felix I (*c*.269–*c*.274), of whom almost nothing is known; the tradition that he was a martyr rests on confusion with genuine martyrs of the same name, for during his reign Christians still enjoyed the toleration proclaimed by the emperor Gallienus *c*.260. His importance in church history derives from a dispute concerning the bishopric of Antioch. Paul of Samosata, deposed for heresy and general misconduct (he suppressed hymns to Jesus, but encouraged praises of himself), continued to occupy the church building; in order to regain their property, the local Christians sought justice from its earthly fount, the emperor Aurelian, who awarded the building to those whom the bishops in Italy and Rome should address in writing. Thus the pagan emperor who unwittingly invented the Western Christmas also recognized the unity of the Christian Church with its head at Rome.

Egwin (Ecgwine), bishop of Worcester, founder of Evesham abbey, d. 717; he is portrayed with fish and keys in allusion to the legend that he vindicated himself against slander by fettering his feet and throwing the key into the River Avon; a fish swallowed it and carried it to Rome, where Egwin bought it in the market (had he released himself with the duplicate?). After the Norman Conquest, Archbishop Lanfranc, contemptuous of Anglo-Saxon saints he had never heard of, had the other relics at Evesham burnt, but St Egwin's were taken on tour. Miracles multiplied and contributions ensured the building of their new church. See too *30 January.

For some Orthodox this is the day of the Magi, following the Holy Innocents in their flight from Herod; for the majority it is the 25th. In this case it is the West that has kept the older day, *6 January, but allowed it to become the day of their Adoration to the exclusion of all else.

If any wood be cut on either of the two last days of this month, or on the first of January, it shall not rot, or be full of worms, but always wax harder the longer it is kept.

Lilly's New Erra Pater, 8

31 DECEMBER

pridie Kalendas Ianuarias   A

If New Year's eve night wind blows South,
it betokeneth warmth and growth;
if West, much milk and fish in the sea;
if North, much cold and storms there will be;
if East, the trees will bear much fruit;
if North-east, flee it, man and brute.

❡ HOLIDAYS AND ANNIVERSARIES Japan: Ōmisoka or Grand Last Day
   Scotland: Hogmanay

❡ HOLY DAYS Sylvester I (BCP, RC; 2 Jan. Orth.); John Wyclif (CY commem.)

Sylvester I, bishop of Rome 314–35, who established the Lateran as the cathedral of Rome. Being pope in the time of Constantine the Great, he was falsely credited by later Western writers with baptizing the emperor (see *21 May); legend improved the tale by making Sylvester cure the emperor of leprosy. Far more significant was the fiction recorded in the eighth-century document known as the Donation of Constantine, that Constantine had conferred on Sylvester, his clergy, and their successors primacy over all other churches, made the Pope supreme judge of the clergy, and granted him temporal dominion over Rome and the West (even offering him the imperial crown, which he had refused). This forgery was used by medieval popes against the Byzantine Church and the Holy Roman Empire; in the West, even stout Ghibellines, as the imperial party were known, accepted its truth, much as they deplored Constantine's misjudgement; it took the growth of historical criticism in the fifteenth century to demonstrate that the text could not be genuine.

John Wyclif (*c.*1330–84), probably from the North Riding of Yorkshire, became a leading philosopher and theologian at Oxford, being successively a fellow of Merton, Master of Balliol, and Warden of Canterbury Hall (now incorporated in Christ Church) until in 1367 he was expelled to make way for a monastic establishment. Rebelling against both scholastic scepticism and the current state of the Church, he began to deny the latter any right or authority that was not founded in the Bible, attacking the religious orders, the claims of the Pope, and the doctrine of transubstantiation; he called on the king's government to reform the entire church in England. His teachings were condemned by the Pope and the University of Oxford; he was blamed for the Peasants' Revolt of 1381, as intellectuals often are for disorders among those who have never read them. In the next year, many of his teachings were condemned at the Blackfriars Council, also known as the Earthquake Synod from a tremor that interrupted it; but Wyclif continued to defend his views in both Latin and English until his death in 1384. His chief friend at Court was John of Gaunt; he also had some loyal supporters among scholars, who increasingly preached among the less educated. Wyclif's English followers, rather than himself, appear to be responsible for the English translations of Scripture ascribed to him; they were contemptuously known as 'Lollards' (apparently 'mumblers'), a term extended as such things are to any critic of the Church, but in the sixteenth century they were claimed as forerunners by Protestants. Wyclif's writings were especially influential in Bohemia after King Václav IV's sister Anna ('Anne of Bohemia') married Richard II in 1382; they greatly influenced the national reformer Jan Hus.

A contemporary, Henry Knighton, reports in his chronicle under the year 1382:

The Gospel, which Christ gave to the clergy and the doctors of the church, that they might administer it to the laity and to weaker brethren, according to the demands of the time and the needs of the individual, as a sweet food for the mind, that Master John Wyclif translated from Latin into the language not of angels but of Englishmen, so that he made that common and open to the laity, and to women who were able to read, which used to be for literate and perceptive clerks, and spread the Evangelists' pearls to be trampled by swine. And thus that which was dear to the clergy and the laity alike became as it were a jest common to both, and the clerks' jewels became the playthings of laymen, that the laity might enjoy now forever what had once been the clergy's talent from on high. Knighton, 243–5

Hogmanay. In Scotland, and by Scots in exile, New Year's Eve is celebrated with much drinking and revelry as Hogmanay, a word originally used by children begging from door to door for oatmeal cakes and reputedly derived from an Old French cry of *au gui l'an neuf*. The theory that the French cry perpetuates the Celtic cult of mistletoe (in French *gui*) is no longer believed, for *au gué* or *ô gué* is an exclamation in ballads. The festivities continue after midnight with the first-footing on 1 January, and often for long afterwards; Hogmanay traditionally lasts for a day or more into the New Year, but the Scottish Bank Holiday on 2 January has now been abolished. The Gaelic name is *Oidhche Challainn*, 'the Eve of the Kalends'.

Samuel Johnson learns of Hogmanay in the Hebrides in 1775:

Mr. Maclean informed us of an odd game, of which he did not tell the original, but which may perhaps be used in other places, where the reason of it is not yet forgot. At New-year's Eve, in the hall or castle of the laird, where, at festal seasons, there may be supposed a very numerous company, one man dresses himself in a cow's hide, upon which other men beat with sticks. He runs with all this noise round the house, which all the company quits in a counterfeited fright: the door is then shut. At New-year's Eve there is no great pleasure to be had out of doors in the Hebrides. They are sure soon to recover from their terrour enough to solicit for readmission; which, for the honour of poetry, is not to be obtained but by repeating a verse, with which those that are knowing and provident take care to be furnished.   Johnson, *Journey*, 133

New Year's Eve. The end of the year brings reflection on the past, hope for the future; many people make New Year's resolutions:

31 [Dec. 1661]. I have newly taken a solemne oath about abstaining from plays and wine, which I am resolved to keep according to the letter of the oath, which I keepe by me.   Pepys, ii. 242

It is traditional to stay up and see the old year out. Its exit is usually noisy, whether through ringing of church bells, setting off of fireworks, cheering in Trafalgar Square or Times Square, or the revelry of a New Year's party. Charles Estienne gives advice on how to drink without becoming drunk (partly derived from Marcus Cato, *De agricultura*, 46. 1):

To drinke great store of wine and not to be drunke, you must eate of the rosted lungs of a goate: or otherwise, eate sixe or seuen bitter almonds fasting: Or otherwise, eate raw colewoorts before you drinke, and you shall not become drunke. Some say that a great drinker shall neuer become drunke, if he weave a wreath of *Iua moscata* about his head: Or, if at his first draught he repeate this verse of *Homers: Iupiter his alta sonuit clementer ab Ida*: which is to say. *Iupiter* was heard speaking in a soft and gentle manner from the high mount of Ida.

More normally, the common result on New Year's Day is a hangover, which may lead to a new resolution. Here are some of Estienne's suggestions of how to cure drunkards:

To provoke hatred of wine, you must take the thin licour which droppeth from the branches after they be cut, and put it in the drunken mans glasse against such time as he shall drinke, but so as that he know not any thing of it, and thereupon his appetite and lust to drink wine will depart quite away from him: or else, cause him to drinke with white wine the blossomes of rie, gathered at such time as the rie bloometh: or else, take three or fower eeles alive, and let them lie in wine till they die, and afterward cause this wine to be drunke off by such as are given to be drunke: Or else, take a greene frog, which is ordinarily found in fresh springs, and let the same lie in wine till he die. Otherwise, marke diligently where the owle haunteth, that so you may get some of her egs: frie them and give them the drunken gallant to eate.   Estienne and Liebault, 761 (1600)

More drink than food is associated with New Year's Eve, but in Italy one must eat lentils at midnight, to ensure wealth in the coming year.

Nathaniel Hawthorne, while the American consul in Liverpool, welcomes New Year in but not the old year out in 1856:

Last night, at Mrs. Blodgett's, we sat up till 12 °clock, to open the front-door, and let the New Year in. After the coming guest was fairly in the house, the back-door was to be opened, to let the Old Year out; but I am tired, and did not wait for this latter ceremony. When the New Year made its entrance, there was a general shaking of hands, and one of the shipmasters said that it was customary to kiss the ladies all round; but, to my considerable satisfaction, we did not proceed to such extremity. There was singing in the streets; and many voices of people passing; and when twelve had struck, all the bells of the town, I believe, rang out together, I went up to bed, sad and lonely.   Hawthorne, *English Notebooks*, 270–1

New Year's Eve superstitions:

On New Year's Eve, in many of the upland cottages, it is yet customary for the housewife, after raking the fire for the night, and just before stepping into bed, to spread the ashes smooth over the floor with the tongs in the hope of finding in it, next morning, the track of a foot; should the toes of this ominous print point towards the door, then it is believed a member of the family will die in the course of that year; but should the heel of the fairy foot point in that direction, then, it is firmly believed, that the family will be augmented within the same period.

J. Train, ii. 115–16

Little Christmas Eve in Ireland:

. . . housewives say on 'Little Christmas' Eve: 'See starvation [going] out from tonight till a year from tonight, tonight included', as they throw a loaf of bread at the door.

O'Sullivan, ii. 99 (1829)

This is the day on which Scottish Highlanders begin to prognosticate weather for the coming year, according to Thomas Pennant's report of 1772 (see *25 Dec. for a similar reckoning):

The Highlanders form a sort of *almanack* or presage of the weather of the ensuing year in the following manner: They make observation on twelve days, beginning at the last of *December*, and hold as an infallible rule, that whatsoever weather happens on each of those days, the same will prove to agree in the correspondent months. Thus, *January* is to answer to the weather of *December* the 31st. *February* to that of *January* 1st; and so with the rest. Old people still pay great attention to this augury.   Pennant, *Scotland 1772*, 48

Ringing out the old year and ringing in the new:

Of all sound of all bells—(bells, the music nighest bordering upon heaven)—most solemn and touching is the peal which rings out the Old Year. I never hear it without a gathering-up of my mind to a concentration of all the images that have been diffused over the past twelvemonth; all I have done or suffered, performed or neglected—in that regretted time. I begin to know its worth, as when a person dies.   Lamb, 'New Year's Eve' (written in 1821)

Ring out, wild bells, to the wild sky,
    The flying cloud, the frosty light:
    The year is dying in the night;
Ring out, wild bells, and let him die.

Ring out the old, ring in the new,
    Ring, happy bells, across the snow:
    The year is going, let him go;
Ring out the false, ring in the true.

Ring out the grief that saps the mind,
   For those that here we see no more;
   Ring out the feud of rich and poor,
Ring in redress to all mankind.

Ring out a slowly dying cause,
   And ancient forms of party strife;
   Ring in the nobler modes of life,
With sweeter manners, purer laws.

Ring out the want, the care, the sin,
   The faithless coldness of the times;
   Ring out, ring out thy mournful rhymes,
But ring the fuller minstrel in.

Ring out false pride in place and blood,
   The civic slander and the spite;
   Ring in the love of truth and right,
Ring in the common love of good.

Ring out old shapes of foul disease;
   Ring out the narrowing lust of gold;
   Ring out the thousand wars of old,
Ring in the thousand years of peace.

Ring in the valiant man and free,
   The larger heart, the kindlier hand;
   Ring out the darkness of the land,
Ring in the Christ that is to be.

          Alfred, Lord Tennyson (1809–92)

SEASONS

We are accustomed to dividing the year into four seasons; this, like much else, is an inheritance from the Romans, whose *ver*, *aestas*, *autumnus*, and *hiems* we effortlessly translate as 'spring', 'summer', 'autumn', and 'winter'; the same is true for speakers of other modern European languages. The Chinese take the same view; but not all other cultures do. India knows of six seasons; classical Greek writers often assume three, treating autumn as late summer, but four are found in Alcman (7th c. BC) and later became standard. Thucydides, in his account of the Peloponnesian War, recognizes two seasons, a campaigning season called 'summer' and a quiet time called 'winter'; the Germanic peoples originally reckoned only with these two, a system perpetuated in the Nordic calendars and also underlying the medieval English use of Hockday and Michaelmas as term days (see *Days: Quarter Days, Term Days, Removal Days*). Indeed, whereas the words 'summer' and 'winter' are found in all the Germanic languages, the terms for 'spring' and 'autumn' vary from language to language, and sometimes even within the same language: British 'autumn' is US 'fall', in German the *Frühling* of eastern central dialects competes in the literary language with the *Frühjahr* of most other regions. In poetry one also finds *Lenz*; this is the same word as English 'Lent', which is now confined to the Christian fast.

Different principles have been adopted for defining the seasons, and not only because of differences in climate: even within a particular culture or country there need be no agreement on when seasons begin and end, unless a particular day has been set aside by convention, as in Scandinavia, where summer was taken to start on 14 April (St Tiburtius) and winter on 14 October (St Callistus). One method is to count from equinox to solstice, and from solstice to equinox; from the Roman dates for these cardinal points come the dates of the Annunciation, the Nativity of John the Baptist, his Conception, and Christmas. Astronomical usage favours this principle, but with current dates, so that spring usually begins on 21 March, summer 21 June, autumn 21 September, and winter 21 December.

However, as the Venerable Bede observed, writers disagree ('diverse ponunt diversi'). The Elder Pliny began the seasons about halfway between the cardinal points, on 8 February, 10 May, 11 August, and 11 November. Similar dates are found in post-classical texts; but Isidore of Seville gives 22 February, 24 May, 23 August, and 23 November. Bede asserts that 'the Greeks and Romans' count from *VII Idus*, 7 February, 9 May, 7 August, and 7 November; many calendars mark (with minor variations) both Bede's date, as the beginning (*initium*) of each season, and Isidore's, as that on which it arises (*oritur*; see Pl. 11 under *viii k*). But Irish tradition reckoned from the Kalends of February, May, August, and November; and many churchmen went by the Ember fasts.

Mnemonics using saints' days show corresponding disagreements. One follows Isidore:

> Dat Clemens hiemem, dat Petrus uer cathedratus,
> aestuat Vrbanus, autumnat Bartholomaeus.

St Clement [23 Nov.] gives winter, Peter in his Chair [22 Feb.] spring, Urban [25 May] sweats in summer, Bartholomew [24 Aug.] is autumnal.

but another follows the astronomical reckoning:

> Ver Benedicte tibi comes, Albano datur aestas;
> Matthaeo autumnus iunctus, hiemsque Thomae.

Spring is given for companion to you, Benedict [21 Mar.], summer to Alban [22 June]; autumn is attached to Matthew [21 Sept.], and winter to Thomas [21 Dec.].

The Meteorological Office in the UK begins the seasons with March, June, September, and December; yet the *Oxford English Dictionary* contrasts this 'North American' scheme with a 'British' scheme that begins them Irish fashion with February, May, August, and November. In practice, however, most people either follow the astronomical rule or relate the seasons to the weather, or to plant or animal behaviour.

In the southern hemisphere, spring, summer, autumn, and winter correspond respectively to the northern autumn, winter, spring, and summer. Nevertheless, many customs and conceptions imported from the north are incongruously maintained, such as the association of Christmas with snow, and of St John the Baptist's Day with midsummer.

Ovid represents Pythagoras expounding the similarity between the seasons of the year and the Ages of Man:

> Quid? non in species succedere quattuor annum
> adspicis, aetatis peragentem imitamina nostrae?
> nam tener et lactens puerique simillimus aevo
> vere novo est; tunc herba recens et roboris expers
> turget et insolida est et spe delectat agrestes.
> omnia tunc florent, florumque coloribus almus
> ludit ager, neque adhuc virtus in frondibus ulla est.
> transit in aestatem post ver robustior annus
> fitque valens iuvenis; neque enim robustior aetas
> ulla nec uberior nec quae magis ardeat ulla est.
> excipit autumnus posito fervore iuventae
> maturus mitisque inter iuvenemque senemque
> temperie medius, sparsus quoque tempora canis.
> unde senilis hiems tremulo uenit horrida passu
> aut spoliata suos aut quos habet alba capillos.
>
> Ovid, *Metamorphoses* 15. 199–213

> Perceiv'st thou not the process of the Year,
> How the four Seasons in four Forms appear,

Resembling human Life in ev'ry Shape they wear?
Spring first, like Infancy, shoots out her Head,
With milky Juice requiring to be fed:
Helpless, tho' fresh, and wanting to be led.
The green Stem grows in Stature and in Size,
But only feeds with hope the Farmer's Eyes;
Then laughs the childish Year with Flourets crown'd,
And lavishly perfumes the Fields around,
But no substantial Nourishment receives,
Infirm the Stalks, unsolid are the Leaves.
    Proceeding onward whence the Year began
The Summer grows adult, and ripens into Man.
This season, as in Men, is most repleat,
With kindly Moisture, and prolifick Heat.
Autumn succeeds, a sober tepid Age,
Not froze with Fear, nor boiling into Rage;
More than mature, and tending to decay,
When our brown Locks repine to mix with odious Grey.
    Last Winter creeps along with tardy pace,
Sour is his Front, and furrow'd is his Face;
His Scalp if not dishonour'd quite of Hair,
The ragged Fleece is thin, and thin is worse than bare.

                    trans. John Dryden (1631–1700),
                    'Of the Pythagorean Philosophy', ll. 296–319

An American, visiting England in January 1776 and having been snowed in for four days 'by such a Snow as was not remembered by the oldest Man', compares the English and American seasons:

The People in England seldom meeting with this kind of inclemency are not prepared to encounter it and of course suffer much more than we do in America. But England in the Winter Season has greatly the advantage of us for while we are buried in Snow and a Frost so severe and for many weeks together that our Sheep Cattle and horses must be fed within doors, while here the Verdure is so fine (in general) and the Air so temperate that they may graze unhurt and unattended.

    Nor are the Advantages they reap in Summer over us inferior to these. While we are all parched and burnt with excessive heat our Meadows dressed in Russet brown and our Pastures in Mourning, their repeated rains chear and enliven the whole vegetative Class and all Nature blooms afresh. But our Fall and Spring by no means yield to them. We have much more Sky, less rain and fog and Mist and after a long cold Winter when the whole Face of the Earth has been covered with Snow and all Vegetation disrobed of its Beauty, 'tis impossible to say how pleasing and acceptable is the Spring. And in the Fall while they have nothing but Rain and Mists . . . We have a pure serene Sky and frequently Weeks together without a Drop of Rain, the Dew yielding sufficient Moisture to paint the Fields.

    And though on the whole it must be granted the Advantages of Winter here over us are considerable yet ours are more healthy. Though we have it keen and piercing, they have it raw and damp and . . . seldom can see the Sun. He hides behind the Clouds, or skulks beneath the mist ashamed of himself.   Fisher, 119–20

SPRING

That doeth blossome in the spring will bring forthe fruit in the autumn.

When there is a spring in winter and a winter in spring the year is never good.

It ain't Spring till you can plant your foot on twelve daisies.

Pond's *Almanack* of 1664 describes spring, the 'vernal quarter', according to the old calendrical reckoning, then ten days behind the New Style, and repeats an ancient but fanciful etymology:

The *Vernal* quarter derives his name à *virendo*, from flourishing; *quia tunc omnia virent & florent*, because all things then flourish: this being the first quarter in the year, as appeareth by the old distich.

> *Omnia cùm vireant, tunc est nova temporis aetas:*
> *Sic annus per Ver incipiendus erit.*

> [Since all things flourish, then the season's new;
> A spring beginning gives the year his due.]

This quarter beginneth *March* the 10, the Sun then entring into the first degree of *Aries*, producing the first *Equinox*; and continueth till *June* the 10: in which time the Sun runneth through *Aries*, *Taurus*, & *Gemini*. It is a Quarter naturally (though accidentally it sometime prove otherwise) hot and moist, resembled to the Meridian-region of the world, the South-wind, the Air, the Sanguine complection, and to infancy. The ordinary diseases (according to the common course) of this quarter be Leprosies, Red-spots, Feavers of bloud, small pox, with other infirmities proceeding of bloud.

Spenser and Breton describe the season in more poetic terms:

> So, forth issew'd the Seasons of the yeare;
> First, lusty *Spring*, all dight in leaues of flowres
> That freshly budded and new bloosmes did beare
> (In which a thousand birds had built their bowres
> That sweetly sung, to call forth Paramours):
> And in his hand a iauelin he did beare,
> And on his head (as fit for warlike stoures)
> A guilt engrauen morion he did weare;
> That as some did him loue, so others did him feare.
>
> Spenser, *The Faerie Queene*, VII. vii. 28

It is now Spring: a Time blest of the Heauens for the comfort of the Earth, now begins the Sunne to giue light vnto the Ayre, and with the replexion of his beames to warme the cold earth: the Beasts of the woods looke out into the plaines, and the fishes out of the deepe run vp into the shallow waters, the breeding fowles fall to building of their nests, and the senselesse creatures gather life into their bodies, the Birds tune their throats to entertaine the Sunne rising, and the little flies begin to flocke in the ayre: now Cupid begins to nocke his Arrowes and sharpe their heads: and Venus, if she be, will be knowne what she is: Now Pallas and her Muses try the Poets in their Pamphlets, and Diana, if shee bee to bee seene, is a grace to her fayrest Nymph: Time is now gracious in Nature, and Nature in time: the Ayre wholesome, and the earth pleasant, and the sea not vncomfortable: the Aged feele a kind of youth, and Youth, the Spirit ful of life: it is the messenger of many pleasures: the Courtiers progresse, and the Farmers profit: the Labourers Haruest, and the Beggers Pilgrimage. In summe, there is much good to be spoken of this time: but to auoyd tediousnes, I will thus conclude of it: I hold it in all that I can see in it, the Jewell of time, and the Joy of Nature. Farewell.   Breton (1626)

Spring verse:

> Spring, the sweete spring, is the yeres pleasant King,
> Then bloomes eche thing, then maydes daunce in a ring,
> Cold doeth not sting, the pretty birds doe sing,
> Cuckow, iugge, iugge, pu we, to witta woo.
>
> The Palm and May make countrey houses gay,
> Lambs friske and play, the Shepherds pype all day,
> And we heare aye birds tune this merry lay,
> Cuckow, iugge, iugge, pu we, to witta woo.
>
> The fields breathe sweete, the dayzies kisse our feete,
> Young louers meete, old wiues a sunning sit;
> In euery streete, these tunes our eares doe greete,
> Cuckow, iugge, iugge, pu we, to witta woo.
>   Spring, the sweete spring.
>   Thomas Nashe (1567–1601), 'Summer's Last Will and Testament'

> Spring is the Period
> Express from God.
> Among the other seasons
> Himself abide,
>
> But during March and April
> None stir abroad
> Without a cordial interview
> With God.
>
>   Emily Dickinson (1830–86)

Spring Song

> I know why the yellow forsythia
> Holds its breath and will not bloom,
> And the robin thrusts his beak in his wing.
>
> Want me to tell you? Think you can bear it?
> Cover your eyes with your hand and hear it.
> You know how cold the days are still?
> And everybody saying how late the Spring is?
> Well—cover your eyes with your hand—the thing is,
> There isn't going to be any Spring.
>
> *No parking here! No parking here!*
> *They said to Spring: No parking here!*
>
> Spring came on as she always does,
> Laid her hand on the yellow forsythia,—
> Little boys turned in their sleep and smiled,

Dreaming of marbles, dreaming of agates;
Little girls leapt from their beds to see
Spring come by with her painted wagons,
Coloured wagons creaking with wonder—
Laid her hand on the robin's throat;
When up comes you-know-who, my dear,
You-know-who in a fine blue coat,
And says to Spring: No parking here!

No parking here! No parking here!
Move on! Move on! No parking here!

Come walk with me in the city gardens.
(Better keep an eye out for you-know-who)
Did you ever see such a sickly showing?—
Middle of June, and nothing growing;
The gardeners peer and scratch their heads
And drop their sweat on the tulip-beds,
But not a blade thrusts through.

Come, move on! Don't you know how to walk?
No parking here! And no back-talk!

Oh, well,—hell, it's all for the best.
She certainly made a lot of clutter,
Dropping petals under the trees,
Taking your mind off your bread and butter.
Anyhow, it's nothing to me.
I can remember, and so can you.
(Though we'd better watch out for you-know-who,
When we sit around remembering Spring).

We shall hardly notice in a year or two.
You can get accustomed to anything.

Edna St. Vincent Millay (1892–1950)

SUMMER

So long as the dog-rose appears before Midsummer,
so long before Michaelmas the harvest will commence.

An English summer: three fine days and a thunderstorm.

Put off flannel on Midsummer night and put it on again next morning.

Pond's etymology of 'summer' is more modern, but no more accurate than that of *ver* from *vireo*.

The *Æstival* quarter is next. It beginneth *June* the 11, the Sun then entring into the first degree of *Cancer*: and continueth till *September* the 12: during which time the Sun runneth through these three celestial constellations, viz. *Cancer*, *Leo* and *Virgo*. It deriveth the name *ab æstu*, from the exceeding heat which useth to be now, as also the English word Summer doth: for it is called Summer, *quasi* sunne mehr, as the Germains speak; that is, *plus solis*, because we have more of the sun then, then at any other time.

This quarter is naturally hot and dry, resembled to the Oriental region of the World, to the East, to Choler, to Youth. The sicknesses agreeing hereunto be Stomach-aking, Aposthumes, pestilent Feavers, Jaundise, with other infirmities proceeding of choler. According to the *Arabians* this is the first quarter of the year, who hold that the Sun was made in *Leo*: and their reason is, because the *Lion* is the house of the *Sun*. *Mercator* in his Chronologie is of the same minde, but backs his opinion very weakly.

> Then came the iolly *Sommer*, being dight
>   In a thin silken cassock coloured greene,
>   That was vnlyned all, to be more light:
>   And on his head a girlond well beseene
>   He wore, from which as he had chauffed been
>   The sweat did drop; and in his hand he bore
>   A boawe and shaftes, as he in forrest greene
>   Had hunted late the Libbard or the Bore,
> And now would bathe his limbes, with labor heated sore.

Spenser, The Faerie Queene, VII. vii. 29

It is now Summer, and Zephirus with his sweet breath cooles the parching beames of Titan: the leaues of the trees are in whisper talkes of the blessings of the aire, while the Nightingale is tuning her throat to refresh the weary spirit of the Trauayler: Flora now brings out her Wardrop, and richly embroydreth her greene Apron: the Nymphes of the Woodes in consort with the Muses sing an *Aue* to the Morning, and a *Vale* to the Sunnes setting: the Lambes and the Rabbettes run at base in the sandy Warrens, and the Plow landes are couered with corne: the stately Hart is at Layre in the high wood, while the Hare in a furrow sits washing of her face: The Bull makes his walke like a Master of the field, and the broad-headed Oxe beares the Garland of the market: the Angler with a fly takes his pleasure with the fish, while the little Merline hath the Partridge in the foot: the Hony-dewes perfume the Ayre, and the Sunny-showers are the earths comfort: the Greyhound on the plaine makes the faire course: and the wel-mouthed Hound makes the Musicke of the woods: the Battaile of the field is now stoutly fought, and the proud Rye must stoupe to the Sickle: The Carters whistle cheeres his forehorse, and drinke and sweat is the life of the Labourer: Idle spirits are banished the limits of Honour, while the studious braine brings forth his wonder: the Azure Sky shewes the Heauen is gracious, and the glorious Sunne glads the spirit of Nature: The ripened fruits shew the beauty of the earth, and the brightnesse of the aire the glory of the heauens: In summe, for the world of worth I find in it, I thus conclude of it: I hold it a most sweet season, the variety of pleasures, and the Paradise of loue. Farewell.

Breton

Despite the poets, English summers are often cold, and it is not only foreigners who notice this:

There were four very hot days at the end of last month [July], which you know with us Northern people compose a summer.

Horace Walpole, letter to the Earl of Strafford, 25 August 1771 from Paris

> The English winter—ending in July,
>   To recommence in August—now was done.

Byron, Don Juan, xiii. 42

The older two-season calendar makes summer begin directly after winter, as in the 'roundel' sung by Chaucer's birds (to French music, for the rondeau, beloved of French composers, never caught on in England):

> Now welcome, somer, with thy sonne softe,
> That hast thes wintres wedres overshake,
> And driven away the longe nyghtes blake!
>
> Saynt Valentyne, that art ful hy on-lofte,
> Thus sungen smale foules for thy sake:
>   Now welcome, somer, with thy sonne softe,
>   That hast thes wintres wedres overshake!
>
> Well han they cause for to gladen ofte,
> Sith ech of hem recovered hath hys make,
> Ful blissful mowe they synge when they wake:
>   Now welcome, sommer, with thy sonne softe,
>   That has thes wintres wedres overshake,
>   And driven away the longe nyghtes blake!
>
> *The Parliament of Fowls*, 680–92

Summer verse:

> Chear'd by the milder Beam, the sprightly Youth
> Speeds to the well-known Pool, whose crystal Depth
> A sandy Bottom shews. A while he stands
> Gazing th' inverted Landskip, half afraid
> To meditate the blue Profound below;
> Then plunges headlong down the circling Flood.
> His ebon Tresses, and his rosy Cheek
> Instant emerge; and thro' th' obedient Wave,
> At each short Breathing by his Lip repell'd,
> With Arms and Legs according well, he makes,
> As Humour leads, an easy-winding Path;
> While, from his polish'd Sides, a dewy Light
> Effuses on the pleas'd Spectators round.
>
> James Thomson (1700–48), *The Seasons*, 'Summer', 1244–56

> A something in a summer's Day
> As slow her flambeaux burn away
> Which solemnizes me.
>
> A something in a summer's noon –
> A depth – an Azure – a perfume –
> Transcending ecstasy.
>
> And still within a summer's night
> A something so transporting bright
> I clap my hands to see –
>
> Then veil my too inspecting face
> Lest such a subtle – shimmering grace
> Flutter too far for me –
>
> The wizard fingers never rest –
> The purple brook within the breast
> Still chafes its narrow bed –

Still rears the East her amber Flag –
Guides still the Sun along the Crag
His Caravan of Red –

So looking on – the night – the morn
Conclude the wonder gay –
And I meet, coming thro' the dews
Another summer's Day!

> Emily Dickinson (1830–86)

AUTUMN

If on the trees the leaves still hold,
the winter coming will be cold.

Pond calculates the Jewish New Year by the civil reckoning:

The *Autumnal* quarter beginneth *September* the 13, the Sun entring into the first degree of *Libra*, producing the second *Equinox*; and continueth till the 11 of *December*: in which time the Sun runneth through *Libra*, *Scorpio*, and *Sagittarius*.

This quarter the *Jews* own for the first quarter of the year: and their reason is, *quia tempus est fructuosum*, because it is a time of fruit; according to that in the Scripture, *Et protulit terra herbam virentem facientem fructum juxta genus suum*, And the earth brought forth the green herb yielding fruit according to its kind. It is a quarter naturally cold and dry, resembled to the Septentrional-region of the world, to the North wind, to the Earth, to Melancholy, and to the declining age of man.

Hippocrates calleth this Quarter the Mother and Nurse of deadly diseases, because of the Intemperature and variable Constitution of the Weather: And Galen saith it is the most pestiential and dangerous Time of all the Year. Now the Pores of the Body are opened by a false Spring Heat, then suddenly closed again by Autumnal Colds, so that many dangerous Distempers are now ingender'd; such as sharp Fevers, Vertigoes, Apoplexies, Lethargies, Palsies, Innatious Madness, windy Distempers, Obstructions, and the like. Which to preevent, proper Evacuations must be used, also comfortable and wholsome Diet. Avoid Excess of Liquors of any Kind, and beware of taking cold.   Saunders (1754)

> Thus we see how Fall of th' leaf
> Adds to each condition grief;
> Only two there be whose wit
> Make hereof a benefit.
> These conclusions try on man
> Surgeon and Physician,
> While it happens now and than   *then*
> Kill than cure they sooner can.

> Richard Brathwait (1588–1673), 'The Fall of the Leaf' (*Odes*)

Then came the *Autumne* all in yellow clad,
  As though he ioyed in his plentious store,

Laden with fruits that made him laugh, full glad
That he had banisht hunger, which to-fore
Had by the belly oft him pinched sore.
Vpon his head a wreath that was enrold
With eares of corne, of euery sort he bore:
And in his hand a sickle he did holde,
To reape the ripened fruits the which the earth had yold.

Spenser, *The Faerie Queene*, VII. vii. 30

Two sharply contrasting views of autumn:

It is now Haruest, and the Larke must lead her yong out of the nest: for the Sithe and the Sickle will down with the grasse and the corne: Now are the hedges ful of Berries, and the highwayes full of Rogues, and the lazy Limmes must sleepe out their dinner: The Ant and the Bee worke for their winter prouision, and after a frost, the Grashopper is not seene: Butter, milke, and cheese, are the Labourers dyet, and a pot of good Beere, quickens his spirit. If there be no plague, the people are healthy, for continuance of motion is a preseruation of nature: The fresh of the morning, and the coole of the Euening are the times of Court walkes; but the poore traueller treads out the whole day: Malt is now aboue wheat with a number of mad people, and a fine shirt is better then a Frize Jerkin: Peares and Plummes now ripen apace, and being of a watry substance, are cause of much sicknesse: The pipe and the taber now follow the Fayres, and they that haue any money, make a gaine of their markets. Bucks now are in season, and Partridges are Rowen-taild, and a good Retriuer is a Spaniell worth the keeping. In sum, it is a time of much worth, when, if God bee well pleased, the world will thriue the better. And to conclude, this is all that I will say of it: I hold it the Heauens Bounty, the Earths Beauty, and the Worlds Benefit. Farewell.   Breton

Of Autumne or the fall of the leafe
Autumne, the Barber of the yeare, that shaves bushes hedges and trees; the ragged prodigall that consumes al and leaves himselfe nothing, the arrantest beggar amongst al the foure quarters, and the most diseased, as beeing alwaies troubled with the falling sicknesse, and (like a frenchman) not suffring a hair to stay on his head: this murderer of the spring, this theef to summer, and bad companion of Winter, scornes to come in according to his old custome, when the Sun sits like Justice with a pair of scales in his hand, weying no more houres to the day then he does to the night, as he did before in his Vernall progresse, when he rode on a Ram; but this baldpate Autumnus, wil be seen walking up and down groves, medows, fields, woods, parks and pastures, blasting of fruites, and beating leaves from their trees, when common highwayes shall be strewed with boughes in mockery of Summer, and in triumph of her death; and when the dores of usurers shall be strewed with greene hearbs, to doe honour to poor brides that have no dowrie (but their honestie) to their marriage; when the world lookes like the olde Chaos, and that plentie is turned into penurie, and beautie into uglinesse: when Men ride (the second time) to Bathe . . . and when unthrifts fly amongst hen sparrowes, yet bring home all the feathers they carried out. Then say that Autumne raignes, then is the true fall of the leafe, because the world and the yeare turne over a new leafe.   Dekker, sig. D2 (1609)

Autumn verse:

Spring and Fall:
to a young child

Márgarét, áre you grieving
Over Goldengrove unleaving?
Leáves, líke the things of man, you
With your fresh thoughts care for, can you?
Áh! ás the heart grows older
It will come to such sights colder
By and by, nor spare a sigh
Though worlds of wanwood leafmeal lie;
And yet you *will* weep and know why.
Now no matter, child, the name:
Sórrow's spríngs áre the same.
Nor mouth had, no nor mind, expressed
What heart heard of, ghost guessed:
It ís the blight man was born for,
It is Margaret you mourn for.

Gerard Manley Hopkins (1844–89)

Autumn Refrain

The skreak and skritter of evening gone
And grackles gone and sorrows of the sun,
The sorrows of sun, too, gone . . . the moon and moon,
The yellow moon of words about the nightingale
In measureless measures, not a bird for me
But the name of a bird and the name of a nameless air
I have never—shall never hear. And yet beneath
The stillness of everything gone, and being still,
Being and sitting still, something resides,
Some skreaking and skrittering residuum,
And grates these evasions of the nightingale
Though I have never—shall never hear that bird.
And the stillness is in the key, all of it is,
The stillness is all in the key of that desolate sound.

Wallace Stevens (1878–1955)

Song at the Beginning of Autumn

Now watch this autumn that arrives
In smells. All looks like summer still;
Colours are quite unchanged, the air
On green and white serenely thrives.
Heavy the trees with growth and full
The fields. Flowers flourish everywhere.

Proust who collected time within
A child's cake would understand
The ambiguity of this—
Summer still raging while a thin
Column of smoke stirs from the land
Proving that autumn gropes for us.

But every season is a kind
Of rich nostalgia. We give names—
Autumn and summer, winter, spring—
As though to unfasten from the mind
Our moods and give them outward forms.
We want the certain, solid thing.

But I am carried back against
My will into a childhood where
Autumn is bonfires, marbles, smoke;
I lean against my window fenced
From evocations in the air.
When I said autumn, autumn broke.

Elizabeth Jennings (1926–)

WINTER

A green winter makes a fat churchyard.

If the blackbird sings before Christmas he will cry before Candlemas.

A mild winter makes a cold summer,
A long winter maketh a full ear.

Onion's skin very thin,
mild winter coming in;
onion's skin thick and tough,
coming winter cold and rough.

Lastly, came *Winter* cloathed all in frize,
    Chattering his teeth for cold that did him chill,
    Whil'st on his hoary beard his breath did freese;
    And the dull drops that from his purpled bill
    As from a limbeck did adown distill.
    In his right hand a tipped staffe he held,
    With which his feeble steps he stayed still:
    For, he was faint with cold, and weak with eld;
That scarse his loosed limbes he hable was to weld.

Spenser, *The Faerie Queene*, VII. vii. 31

It is now Winter, and Boreas beginnes to fill his cheekes with breath, shaketh the tops of the high Cedars, and hoyseth the waues of the Sea, to the danger of the Saylers comfort: Now is the Earth nipt at the heart with a cold, and her Trees are disrobed of their rich apparell: there is a glasse set vpon the face of the Waters, and the Fishes are driuen to the bottomes of the deepe: The Usurer now sits lapt in his furres, and the poore makes his breath, a fire to his fingers ends: Beautie is maskt for feare of the ayre, and youth runnes to Physicke for Restoratiues of Nature: The

Stagge roares for losse of his strength, and the Flea makes his Castle in the wooll of a blanket:
Cards and Dice now begin their haruest, and good Ale and Sack are the cause of ciuill warres:
Machiauil and the Deuill are in counsell vpon destruction, and the wicked of the world make
hast to hell: Money is such a Monopoly, that hee is not to be spoken of, and the delay of suits
is the death of hope. In it selfe it is a wofull Season, the punishment of natures pride, and the
play of misery. Farewell.   Breton

Winter, like an angry *Old man*, worn out with Cares, perplex'd with Grief, and impatient in
Suffering, with a waspish, fretful and phlegmatick Countenance, looks upon the Face of the
Earth: For now the blustring *Winds* break forth, the Billows of the *Ocean* mount aloft, threatening to swallow up the Sea-tost Mariner. *Floods* are up, and the cold *Air* taketh away the Strength
and Vigour of all *Creatures*. The *Pores* of the Earth are shut by the extream *Coldness* of the *Air*. *Beasts*
and *Cattel* seek for Shelter. *Fowls* betake themselves to *warmer Regions*, and *Fishes* to the *deepest Waters*.
So that whatsoever the chearful Spring, and Summer *did bring forth and nourish*, this Quarter doth
destroy and *vanish*.   *Great Britain's Diary: or, the Union-Almanack For the Year of our Lord 1711*

Winter thunder:

Thunder and lightning in Winter . . . in these Northern Climates it is held ominous, portending factions, tumults, and bloody wars, and a thing seldome seen, according to the old Adigy,
Winters thunder, is the Sommers wonder.   Willsford, 113 (1658)

9 December 1638, Sounday. This day, about 8 at nycht, thair wes a gret thunder; quhilk wes
thoucht prodigious, being in wynter.   Hope, 81

Winter verse:

> Blow, blow, thou winter wind,
> Thou art not so unkind
>   As man's ingratitude.
> Thy tooth is not so keen,
> Because thou art not seen,
>   Although thy breath be rude.
> Hey-ho, sing hey-ho, unto the green holly.
> Most friendship is feigning, most loving, mere folly.
>   Then hey-ho, the holly;
>   This life is most jolly.
> Freeze, freeze, thou bitter sky,
> That dost not bite so nigh
>   As benefits forgot.
> Though thou the waters warp,
> Thy sting is not so sharp
>   As friend remembered not.
> Hey-ho, sing hey-ho, unto the green holly.
> Most friendship is feigning, most loving, mere folly.
>   Then, hey-ho, the holly;
>   This life is most jolly.
>   *As You Like It*, ii. vii. 275–94

> O Winter! ruler of th'inverted year,
> Thy scatter'd hair with sleet like ashes fill'd,
> Thy breath congeal'd upon thy lips, thy cheeks

Fring'd with a beard made white with other snows
Than those of age; thy forehead wrapt in clouds,
A leafless branch thy sceptre, and thy throne
A sliding car, indebted to no wheels,
But urged by storms along its slipp'ry way;
I love thee, all unlovely as thou seem'st,
And dreaded as thou art. Thou hold'st the sun
A pris'ner in the yet undawning East,
Short'ning his journey between morn and noon,
And hurrying him impatient of his stay
Down to the rosy West. . . .
I crown thee King of intimate delights,
Fireside enjoyments, home-born happiness,
And all the comforts that the lowly roof
Of undisturb'd retirement, and the hours
Of long uninterrupted evening, know.

William Cowper (1731–1800), 'The Winter Evening', ll. 120–43

Two Decisions

I must go back to Winter,
The dark, confiding tree,
The sunflower's eaten centre
That waved so tenderly;
Go back, break fellowship
With bud and leaf,
Break the loud branch and strip
The stillborn grief.
I must restore the thorn,
The naked sentinel,
Call lash of hail, wind-scorn
To laughter's lintel;
End argument in a way
Sudden and swift,
Leave stillness, go away
Beyond this leaf-drift,
Leave the ten-windowed house
And merely remark,
The ivy grew too close:
That house was dark.

Then I look out:
Rut, road and hill I see.
Tracks turn about.
Winter must come to me.
I shall not go.
I shall wait here
Until the snow
Bury the old year,
Until the swallows are gone
And the lintels wet

Tell that the rain that has blown
Is blowing yet.
Let me be nowhere
A melodramatic guest
Since here as anywhere
The light is best.
Though distant things entreat
The afraid, the fanciful,
The near is faithful:
Do not deny it.

    Vernon Watkins (1906–67)

TERMS
(OXFORD, CAMBRIDGE, LAW)

Note. Throughout this section, all dates are inclusive.

UNIVERSITY TERMS

At Oxford and Cambridge, the three periods during which instruction is given are commonly known as 'terms', and the interval between them as 'vacations'. In strict usage, however, 'term' denotes a longer period during which the university is active, the 'term' of everyday speech being correctly Full Term. The dates of the latter are appointed a few years in advance; the dates of term, in the proper sense, are laid down by university enactments.

At Oxford, the statutory terms are currently defined as follows:

Michaelmas Term: 1 October to 17 December
Hilary Term: 7 January to 25 March or the Sunday before Palm Sunday, whichever is the earlier
Trinity Term: 20 April or the Wednesday after Easter, whichever is the later, to 6 July

Within each term, eight weeks, running from a Sunday to a Saturday, are appointed as Full Term. In certain subjects there are extended terms, which may begin before, or end after, Statutory Term.

At Cambridge, there are two terms of eighty days followed by one of seventy, defined by the civil calendar without regard to the date of Easter:

Michaelmas Term: 1 October to 19 December
Lent Term: 5 January to 25 March (24 March in leap year)
Easter Term: 10 April to 18 June, but if Full Term begins on or after 22 April, term is 17 April to 25 June

Full Term is required to occupy three-quarters of each term, consisting respectively of sixty, sixty, and fifty-three days, beginning on a Tuesday and ending on a Friday.

Although 'term' has nothing to do with 'three', the threefold division of the academic year caused the word to be adopted for the thirds into which, about 1865, the English school year was divided instead of the previous halves; however, the name 'half' re-mained (it is in use at Eton), giving rise to the anecdote that a boy translated the open-ing words of Caesar's *Gallic War* as 'All Gaul is quartered into three halves.'

LAW TERMS

Until the reign of Queen Victoria the courts of King's (or Queen's) Bench, Common Pleas, and Exchequer could sit *in banco* (i.e. to determine questions of law) only during four brief periods known as 'terms'; they were modified from time to time by statute, but at the time of their abolition were: Hilary, 11–31 January; Easter, 15 April–8 May; Trinity, 22 May–12 June; Michaelmas, 2–25 November. Successive acts of 1838 and 1854 authorized sittings at other times; but the Judicature Acts of 1873–5, which reformed the entire English system of higher courts, abolished the terms, and substituted much longer sittings (sometimes loosely called 'terms'). These are currently:

Hilary: 11 January to Wednesday before Easter
Easter: Tuesday after Easter week to Friday before Whit Sunday
Trinity: Tuesday after Whitsun week (i.e. after Trinity Sunday) to 31 July
Michaelmas: 1 October to 21 December

The Inns of Court have retained the old terms for computing the time required for call to the Bar, and enforce 'dining terms' during which students are required to eat a pre-scribed number of dinners.

The listing of terms is a regular feature of English almanacs. *Poor Robin* generally adds verses; the following are for 1665:

Hilary Term

Annoint thy Lawyer, grease him in the fist,
And he will plead for thee even what thou list;
Hee'l make thy cause strong though the same were weak,
But if thy purse be dumb, his tongue can't speak.

Easter Term

The Term's the Lawyers Fair, 'tis known full well,
At Westminster 'tis kept, and breath they sell;
Then, Clyent, since thou know'st the time o' the Fair,
Bring mony if thou wouldst buy Lawyers ware.

Trinity Term

Westminster is a mill that grindes mens causes,
But grinde his cause for me there who that list,
For oftentimes what with demurs and clauses
The tole is made far greater then the grist.

Michaelmas Term

Two finds an Oyster, which they will not part,
Both will have all or none, the Lawyers art
Must end the strife; he fitts their humour well,
Eats up the fish, and gives them each a shell.

MONTHS

The main unit of time intermediate between a year and a day is commonly known either by a word meaning 'moon', as in old-fashioned English, or by one derived from such a term, such as English 'month', whether or not the month as determined by the calendar keeps pace with the real moon: even the twenty-day sequences of the Mesoamerican calendars are called by names of this type in the local languages. In lunar and lunisolar calendars, months are of either thirty days (full) or twenty-nine days (hollow), approximating the mean length of the lunation or synodic month, the moon's orbital period from new moon to new moon = 29.530 59 d. = 29 d. 12 h. 44 m. 2.98 s. (Astronomers also recognize other types of month, anomalistic, draconic, sidereal, and tropical, with which we are not concerned)

Before the adoption of formal calendars, portions of the year were commonly known by the natural phenomena, or the human activities, with which they were associated, as when we speak of 'harvest time'. Such 'farmer's year' names might be applied to a particular full moon, as in English 'harvest moon' and 'hunter's moon', respectively the full moon of September and October, or a particular lunation, as when Greek poets speak of the 'leaf-shedding month', the October–November lunation. When the solar calendar was introduced, churchmen would naturally use the Latin month names, but the laity often applied such 'farmer's year' names to the new months; in the late tenth century, the learned Abbot Ælfric speaks of 'the month that we [clergy] call March, which you [layfolk] call *Hlȳda*'; the latter name (probably meaning 'roarer', from the March winds) survived for many centuries as 'Lide'. In some countries these names became widespread: medieval documents from the Low Countries, when they give the date in Dutch and not in Latin, use vernacular names that may still be found in modern dictionaries, though not in modern use. Such names naturally varied from place to place; indeed, the same name might be applied to different months. In Dutch *herfstmaand*, 'harvest month', meant September, which was *Herbstmonat* in German almanacs; Charlemagne, however, is said to have used *herbistmanoth* for November, and older Estonian texts give the corresponding name *lõikuskuu* to August.

Although in some languages such local terms have given way to the international Latin names, this is not universally the case; in particular, some or all months are known by vernacular names in the Celtic languages and some Slavonic ones. The particular names vary from language to language, and in Slavonic may apply to different months: *listopad* ('leaf-fall') is October in Croatian, but November in Czech and Polish; April in Croatian is *travanj*, from *trava* 'grass' (cf. Dutch *grasmaand*), and May in Czech is *květen*, from *kvĕt* 'flower' (cf. Dutch *bloeimaand*, 'flowering month'), but in Ukrainian *traven'* is May, and *kviten'*, like Polish *kwiecień*, is April. By contrast, Russians, Serbians, and Bulgarians, like their fellow Orthodox in Greece and Romania, use only the Latin names.

At common law a month was traditionally understood as four weeks unless otherwise indicated, but in the United Kingdom it has been taken to be a calendar month in statutes since 1850, in deeds since 1925; this is the regular use in commercial relations, and also in the United States.

The rhyme for remembering the number of days in each month goes back to the Middle Ages:

> Thirti dayes hath Novembir,
> April, June, and Septembir;
> Of xxviii^{ti} is but oon,
> And all the remenaunt xxx^{ti} and .i.
>
> Harley MS 2341

Medieval man (as confirmed by many calendar illustrations in manuscripts and printed books) remembered the months by their typical occupations, the so-called 'labours of the month'. A versified form appears in a fifteenth-century manuscript in the Bodleian Library (Digby 88):

Januar	By thys fyre I warme my handys;
Februar	And with my spade I delfe my landys.
Marche	Here I sette my thynge to sprynge;
Aprile	And here I here the fowlis synge.
Maii	I am as lyght as byrde in bowe;
Junii	And I wede my corne well inow.
Julii	With my sythe my mede I mowe;
Auguste	And here I shere my corne full lowe;
September	With my flayll I erne my brede;
October	And here I sawe my whete so rede.
November	At Martynesmasse I kylle my swyne;
December	And at Cristesmasse I drynke redde wyne.

Other descriptions of the months will be found at the beginning of each month in the section on the calendrical year.

The ages of man are often calibrated in units of seven years; in this example from the *Kalendar* of *Sheepehards* of *c.*1580 the span of life is divided by twelve and likened to the months of the year—not beginning in spring but with January:

The fyrste moneth is Januarye, the childe is without might tyll hee bee vi. yeere olde, he can not helpe him selfe.

The vi. yeere that is the first time of the springinge of all flowres, and so the childe till xii. yeere groweth in knowledge and learning, and to doo as he is taught.

Marche is the buddinge time, and in that vi. yeere of Marche the Childe waxeth bygge and apte to doo seruice, and learne scyence from xii. to xviii. such as is shewed hym.

Aprill is the springing tyme of flowres, and in that vi yeere he groweth to mans state in heyght and bredthe, and waxeth wise and bolde, but then beware of sensualitie, for he is xxiiii.

Maye is the season that flowers byn spreade, and bee then in theyr vertue with sweet odours. In these vi. yeeres he is in his most strength, but then let him geather good maners betyme, for if he tary past that age it is an hap if euer he take them, for then he is xxx. yeare.

In June he beginneth to close his mynde, and then hee waxeth rype, for then he is xxxvi. yeere.

In July he is xlii, and he begynneth a lyttle to declyne, and feeleth hym not so prosperous as he was.

In August he is by that vi. yeere xlviii. yeere and then he goeth not so lustely as he dyd, but studieth howe to geather to fynde him in his olde age to liue more easely.

In September he is liiii. yeere he then purueyethe against the winter to cherish himselfe withall and keepe neere together the goods yᵗ he gat in his youth.

Then is a man in October lx. yeere full, if he haue ought he gladdeth, and if he haue nought he weepeth.

Then is man lxvi. in Nouember, he stoupeth and goeth softly, and leeseth all his beauty and fayrnesse.

In December is man lxxii. yeeres, then had he leuer haue a warme fire then a fayre lady, and after this age he goeth into decrepitie to waxe a childe again, and can not welde him selfe, and then young folkes be wery of his company but if they haue much good they beene full lytell taken heede of.   *Kalendar*, cap. xlvi

THE WEEK

The week is the oldest known human institution still functioning without a break, combining the Jewish cycle of six working days and a rest-day or Sabbath adopted by the Christian Church with the planetary doctrines of the astrologers. It has survived attempted abolition by French Republicans (see II: *Other Calendars: French Republican*) and Soviet Bolsheviks (see II: *Modern Calendar: Twentieth-Century Reforms: Soviet Union*), and proposed dilution by calendar reformers (see II: *Modern Calendar: Unsuccessful Proposals*).

THE JUDAEO-CHRISTIAN WEEK

The Jewish week revolves around the Sabbath (see II: *Jewish Calendar*); in Hebrew the six working days are called 'first day' to 'sixth day', but in the Aramaic increasingly spoken by the Jews after their return from Babylonian exile they are commonly called one to six 'in the Sabbath', and Friday may also be 'Sabbath eve' or 'the day of preparation'. This reflects the importance of the Sabbath, and also the similarity of its name *shabbāt* to *shabbūa* 'week' (lit. 'group of seven'); periods of time may be described in biblical Hebrew as so many Sabbaths instead of weeks. In New Testament Greek 'the first day of the week', that on which Jesus rises, is '(day) one of the Sabbath(s)'; but when the Church adapted the Jewish week for its own purposes, the first day became 'the Lord's day' (Rev. 1: 10), and constituted a weekly celebration of the Resurrection. (In Russian it is *voskresen'e*, a Russianized and therefore more popular form of *voskresénie*, 'Resurrection', which retains its learned Church Slavonic guise.) The Sabbath retained its name, though not its nature; the other days were in Greek called 'second' to 'fifth', followed by *Paraskeuē* ('Preparation', now pronounced *Paraskeví*), but in Latin 'second' to 'sixth' *feria*, a new singular created out of classical *feriae* 'holiday'.

THE PLANETARY WEEK

The astrologers of Ptolemaic Egypt, whose discipline spread all over the Greek and Roman world, held that each hour was subject to a planet in descending order of distance from the Earth, namely Saturn, Jupiter, Mars, Sun, Venus, Mercury, Moon, and each day to the planet controlling its first daytime hour; since the day consists of $3 \times 7 + 3$ hours, each day was governed by the third planet from that which governed the day before, giving the cycle Saturn, Sun, Moon, Mars, Mercury, Jupiter, Venus. This is explained in many sources, from the historian Cassius Dio (3rd c. AD) to Chaucer's *Treatise on the Astrolabe*; the astronomy and time-reckoning on which it is based are Greek.

In the reign of Augustus (31 BC–AD 14) the week is attested both in an inscription (see II: *Sunday Letters*) and in a poem by Tibullus (d. 19 BC), who adopts the belief that Saturday, belonging to the most malevolent of the planets, was a day of ill omen, on which it was best to be inactive. The coincidence of unlucky Saturday with restful Sabbath did not go unobserved; Greek and Roman writers misrepresent the Sabbath as a fast, and treat abstention from activity on Saturday as a sign of Jewish sympathies. Moreover, the increasing importance of solar cults caused pagans such as the astrologer Vettius Valens in the second century AD to reckon the planetary week from Sunday instead of Saturday, though a reference to Sabbaths in his text is clearly an interpolation.

The Judaeo-Christian system was pitted against the astrological: when in AD 321 the Christian emperor Constantine decreed that lawsuits were not to be heard on Sunday, he called it not the 'Lord's Day' but 'the day on which its sun is venerated' (*diem solis ueneratione sui celebrem*). He has frequently been suspected of taking Christianity for a form of sun-worship, but laws of later reigns sometimes use the pagan name, or couple the two ('On the Lord's Day, commonly called Sunday'); on the other hand, in a papyrus of AD 325, the record of a trial held in a pagan temple, the court is adjourned at nightfall because the 'Lord's Day' has begun.

Eventually, in the Greek-speaking half of the Empire the Christian terms prevailed; but in the Latin half the pagan names proved more tenacious. Although Portuguese conforms in full to the Christian style (*domingo, segunda-feira, terça-feira, quarta-feira, quinta- -feira, sexta-feira, sábado*), in other Romance languages only 'Lord's Day' (*dimanche/domingo/ domenica*) and 'Sabbath' (*samedi/sábado/sabato*) have ousted the planetary names, though *kenápura* (*cena pura*, alluding to the Last Supper) is attested for the dialect of Logoduro in Sardinia. Speakers of other languages proved even more resistant, above all in Britain, where both Welsh and English have preserved the pagan names intact, Welsh directly (*dydd Sul, dydd Llun, dydd Mawrth, dydd Mercher, dydd Iau, dydd Gwener, dydd Sadwrn*; similar forms in Cornish and Breton), English with the Germanic deities Tiw, Woden (the god of eloquence and wisdom), Thunor, and Frig substituted respectively for Mars, Mercury, Jupiter, and Venus, but Saturn, for whom no counterpart was recognized, left unchanged. Dutch similarly has *Zaterdag*; Tuesday is *Dinsdag*, from a god of the Germanic warrior-assembly or *thing* known from Latin inscriptions as Mars Thincsus. German too has *Dienstag*, but deviates from the pagan pattern in calling Wednesday *Mittwoch* ('midweek') and Saturday *Sonnabend* ('Sun[day]eve') or *Samstag* ('sabbath-day'); Bavarian and Austrian dialects, more exposed to Greek influence, turned the pagan *Areōs*, 'Ares's [day]' (i.e. Tuesday) into *Ertag* and the Christian *Pemptē*, 'Fifth [day]' (Thursday) into *Pfinztag*. In the Nordic languages Saturday is 'bath-day' (e.g. Danish *lørdag*); Icelandic has gone some way to accepting the church names (see II: *Other Calendars: Icelandic*).

Just as Christianity adopted the Jewish week, with its numbered days and Sabbath, so did Islam. Here it is not the first day but the sixth that was renamed, becoming *jumʿa*, from the Arabic root meaning 'gather'; Friday is the Muslims' day of prayer and assembly, but not of rest, except under Western influence. (The word is also used to mean 'week'.) The planetary week, meanwhile, had taken root in the cultures of India and China long before the Europeans came.

Short cycles, often of markets, are found in other cultures, e.g. the Roman eight-day *nundinum*, and various African market-weeks.

THE MONDAY START

As the start of the planetary week was moved during classical antiquity from Saturday to Sunday, so the start of the Christian week has sometimes been moved to Monday. In Lithuanian the days of the week are called 'first day' to 'seventh day', running from Monday to Sunday; the same is true of Latvian, except that Sunday is 'holy day'. The Slavonic languages designate Tuesday, Thursday, and Friday by derivatives of 'two', 'four', and 'five'; however, Sunday is 'not-work' (but in Russian this now means 'week', and Sunday is 'Resurrection'), Monday 'after not-work', and Wednesday 'middle', Saturday being 'Sabbath'. The Orthodox liturgical week begins with Monday except between Easter and Pentecost. In the West, however, the Monday start is a purely secular notion; as Abbot Ælfric complained:

Many people too are ensnared in such great error that they govern their journeying by the [age of the] moon, and their actions by [specific] days; they will not part with anything [*nellað heora ðing wanian*] on Monday, as being the start of the week; but Monday is not the first day of the week, but the second. Sunday is first in creation, sequence, and dignity.

Catholic Homilies, no. vi, p. 100

Nevertheless, the Old English translation of Pseudo-Bede, *Prognostica temporum* (see *25 Dec.), alters the order of its original to start from Monday; this is also the first day in rhymes of the 'Monday's child' type. In such contexts, Sunday is postponed to form a climax; but in the modern secular world, which privileges work over worship, Monday is often counted as the first day. It so appears in some diaries and calendars; the International Organization for Standardization numbers the Monday–Sunday weeks throughout the year from that in which 4 January falls. Monday is also the first day of the cycle for the methodical breaker of hearts in a Spanish ditty:

El lunes me enamoro	On Monday I fall in love,
martes lo digo,	On Tuesday I say so.
miércoles me declaro,	On Wednesday I make my declaration,
jueves consigo;	On Thursday I succeed.
viernes doy celos	On Friday I make her jealous,
y sábado y domingo	And on Saturday and Sunday
busco amor nuevo.	I look for new love.

DATE OR DAY?

I have had the experience, which doubtless you have had also, when the day and date did not agree in the invitation. Wednesday, April 3, was not correct, and we wondered whether Wednesday, April 2, or Thursday, April 3, was meant. It is humorously said that a woman will always decide on the weekday and the man on the month-date in such a dilemma.

Achelis, World Calendar, 116

We commend experiments with cross-dated invitations to social scientists with enough friends and enough money to hold parties on both days; but it is not incredible that the man who goes to work every day and transacts business should be more aware of dates, but the housewife should think of things that happen on given days of the week. If the humorists are right, the women have the better of it; for the eminent historian C. R. Cheney declares: 'When we are presented with a date in which the day of the week and the day of the month do not harmonize, it is generally the day of the week which is right' (*Handbook of Dates*, p. ix). This applies even more to conversions from the Muslim to the Western calendar (see II: *Muslim Calendar*).

BIRTHDAYS AND THE DAY OF THE WEEK

Many will be familiar with the rhymes linking personality traits with the day of the week on which one is born. These exist in several (and often contradictory) versions; one set is given below under the individual days (all begin with Monday, not Sunday), and may be compared with the prognostications of the Babylonian Talmud (completed by the 6th c.), according to which:

One born on	will be	because on that day
Sunday	either completely virtuous or completely wicked	light and darkness were created
Monday	bad-tempered	the waters were divided
Tuesday	wealthy and unchaste	herbs divided (they grow rapidly and intermingle)
Wednesday	wise and of retentive memory	the luminaries were suspended
Thursday	benevolent	fish and birds created, which are fed by God's loving-kindness
Friday	a seeker	one seeks to complete things necessary for observance of the Sabbath

A person born on the Sabbath will die on the Sabbath (but only, said one authority, if very holy), because it was desecrated on his account by his being born.

OTHER PROGNOSTICATIONS

In addition to forecasting the year's weather from the twelve weekdays beginning on Christmas or New Year's Day (see *25 Dec., *31 Dec.), one could also predict future events from thunder on a particular weekday—a safe enough prediction in any case, since the timing of the result is not specified, but one which indicates that thunder was not all that frequent (as is the case in England). Winter thunder was thought to be particularly ominous (see *Seasons).

Somme wryte (theyr grounde I see not) that Sonnedayes thundre, sholde brynge the deathe of learned men, Judges, and others: Mundayes thundre, the deathe of women: Tuesdayes thundre, plentie of grayne: Wedensdayes thundre, the deathe of harlottes, and other blodshede: Thursdayes thundre, plentie of shepe, and corne: Frydayes thundre the slaughter of a great man, and other horrible murders: Saterdayes thundre a generall pestilent plage and great deathe.

Digges, fo. B2^{r-v} (1555)

Week-rhymes exist on sneezing, cutting nails, and washing laundry. A ninth-century Irish book of triads, the *Trecheng Breth Féni*, designates Monday, Tuesday, and Wednesday as days for women: 'If women go to men on those days, the men will love them better than they the men, and the women will survive the men.' On Thursday, Friday, and Sunday it is the other way about: the husbands will not love their wives, and will survive them. Saturday is equally fortunate for both sexes. (It is also noted that Monday is a good day to undertake any business; as we shall see, this was a peculiarly Irish view.) Once again we offer comparison with other cultures.

The Roman chronological compendium of 354, in which pagan and Christian elements sit unproblematically side by side, lists under the seven planets the quality of the days and hours over which they presided, grouped according as they were harmful (N for *noxius*: Saturn, Mars), neutral (C for *communis*: Mercury, Moon, Sun), or good (B for *bonus*: Jupiter, Venus). On Saturday, and in Saturn's hour by night or day, all things become dark and difficult: newborn babies have a poor chance of life, absconders will not be found, those who take to their bed will be in danger, theft will not be discovered. Tuesday, and Mars's hour, is a good day for enrolling in the army and purchasing weapons; but other prospects are no better. Wednesday, and Mercury's hour, is good for installing bailiffs, agents, and shopkeepers; moreover, on this and the remaining days and hours, babies will live, absconders be caught, the sick soon recover, and theft will come to light. Monday, and the Moon's hour, is good for manuring the farm, and making wells and water-tanks; Sunday, and the Sun's hour, for beginning a journey or voyage and launching a ship; Thursday, and Jupiter's hour, for seeking a favour, conversing with the powerful, and rendering account; Friday, and Venus' hour, for betrothals, and sending boys and girls to school.

Nineteenth-century almanacs state that in Cairo:

Sunday is generally considered an unfortunate day, as preceding that on which the Prophet died.

Monday is considered by some unfortunate, by others fortunate.

Tuesday is inauspicious, called 'the day of blood', from the death of many martyrs, but is a favourable day for being bled.

Wednesday is generally considered a good day for travelling, but some among the upper classes deem it unfortunate. This is the day for starting to read books; books begun on any other day are not likely to be finished. Milk should not be drunk.

Thursday is an auspicious day, favourable for all undertakings.

Friday is the most auspicious of days. One should take a bath, put on perfumes, and wear clean clothes, but no sweeping and no sewing should be done.

Saturday is the most inauspicious day, whether for voyages or almost any undertakings. Fish must not be eaten, nor milk drunk. No baths should be taken.

SUNDAY

The child that is born on the Sabbath day
is great, and good, and fair, and gay.

Sneeze on a Sunday, your safety seek:
The devil will have you the whole of the week.

Cut your nails on a Sunday, you cut them for evil,
For all the next week you'll be ruled by the devil.

Sunday is an unlucky day to:

pare one's nails

> But alas! who can look into Fate's book of laws?
> Mr. Lowe would have married Miss Cundy;
> He lost her! he lost her! and only because,
> He cut his toe nails on a Sunday!
> Thomas Hudson, *Comic Songs* (1824), 9

SIR SAMPSON. Ha! thou'rt melancholy, old Prognostication; As melancholy as if thou hadst spilt the Salt, or par'd thy Nails of a Sunday.   Congreve, *Love for Love*, III. i

Sunday is a lucky day to:

get married

PETRUCCIO. And to conclude, we have 'greed so well together
     That upon Sunday is the wedding day.

KATE. I'll see thee hanged on Sunday first.   *The Taming of the Shrew*, II. i. 292–4 *go to sea*

Hee will never set to Sea but on a Sunday; neither ever goes without an *Erra Pater* in his pocket.

J. Hall (1608), 89

Although Christians retained the Jewish name of 'Sabbath' for the seventh day of the week, they regarded the Jewish observance of that day, like other points of the Mosaic law, as superseded; Jesus, after all, had cured on the Sabbath and defended His disciples for plucking ears of corn on it, maintaining that 'The sabbath was made for man, and not man for the sabbath' (Mark 2: 27). They met to break bread on the first day of the week, which was a feast to celebrate the Resurrection, and as a feast was in principle not a day for work. From the fourth century this abstinence from work was increasingly prescribed by Church and State; but it was neither called 'Sabbath' (this being Saturday) nor regulated by Jewish law. The equation of Sunday with the Sabbath is a peculiarity of sixteenth-century Protestantism in the British Isles (Calvin himself had insisted they were not the same), which was taken by Puritans to the New World. Henceforth, in English as spoken by strict Protestants, 'Sabbath' would mean Sunday (although Seventh-Day Adventists retain the original meaning).

Sabbatarianism, the strict observance of the Sabbath thus defined, soon made its mark as Puritan influence extended. When James I, with his *Book of Sports* of 1618, allowed certain recreations as lawful on Sunday, the keeping of the Sabbath became a political question. Under the Commonwealth various acts were published enjoining strict observance of rest, and although some relaxation followed with the Restoration, the English Sunday long remained subject to legal and social restrictions beyond those observed on the Continent. It was much remarked upon by foreign visitors, as our excerpts show; the English, for their part, regarded the 'Continental Sunday' as the last word in immorality and irreligion. During the twentieth century, and especially in its last quarter, more liberal notions spread; but only in 1994, after a Government-abetted campaign of disobedience, were the Sunday trading laws (which went back to Saxon times) repealed. In other parts of the United Kingdom, Sabbatarianism was even stronger—so much so that the Scottish Sunday did not need to be enforced by laws; in Wales, local communities voted every ten years whether to permit the public houses to open on Sundays. Strict Sabbatarianism was also a feature of Puritan New England.

Here a Puritan rails against the abuse of the Sabbath in England in 1583 (though he, or his printer, confused Sabbath with *Sabaoth*, 'of Hosts'):

The Sabaoth day, of some is well sanctified, namely in hearing the Word of GOD read, preached and interpreted, in privat and publique Prayers, in singing of Godly Psalmes, in celebrating the sacraments, & in collecting for ye powre & indigent, which are the true uses and ends wherto the sabaoth was ordained. But other some spend the Sabaoth day (for the most part) in frequenting of baudie Stage-playes and enterludes, in maintaining Lords of mis-rule (for so they call a certaine kinde of play which they use) May-games, Church-ales, feasts and wakesses: in pyping, daunceing, dicing, carding, bowling, tennisse playing: in Beare-bayting, cock-fighting, hawking, hunting, and such like. In keeping of Faires, and markets on the sabaoth. In keeping Courts and Leets: In foot-ball playing, and such other devilish pastimes: reading of lacivious and wanton bookes, and an infinit number of such like practises and prophane exercises vsed upon that day, wherby the Lord God is dishonoured, his Sabaoth violated, his Word neglected, his sacraments

contemned and his People mervelously corrupted, and caryed away from true vertue and god-
lynes.   Stubbes, sig. L2ʳ⁻ᵛ

New Haven, Connecticut, was settled by strict and vindictive Puritans in 1637. The 'Blue
Laws' they imposed have become legendary; they were in fact never published as such,
and are known only from the report of the Connecticut historian Samuel Peters in 1781.
With respect to the Sabbath

No one shall run on the Sabbath-day, or walk in his garden or elsewhere, except reverently to and
from meeting. No one shall travel, cook victuals, make beds, sweep house, cut hair, or shave, on
the Sabbath-day. No woman shall kiss her child on the Sabbath or fasting-day. . . . No one shall
read Common-Prayer, keep Christmas or Saints-days, make minced pies, dance, play cards, or
play on any instrument of music, except the drum, trumpet, and jews-harp. . . .   Peters, 65–8

A tythingman, appointed to ensure strict observance of the Sabbath in church ('meeting'), does his work in Lynn, Massachusetts, in 1646:

Allen Bridges hath bin chose to wake ye sleepers in meeting. And being much proude of his place,
must needs have a fox taile fixed to ye ende of a long staff wherewith he may brush ye faces of
them yt will have napps in time of discourse, likewise a sharpe thorne whereby he may pricke
such as be most sound. On ye last Lord his day, as hee strutted about ye meeting-house, he did
spy Mr. Tomlins sleeping with much comfort, hys head kept steadie by being in ye corner, and
his hand grasping ye rail. And soe spying, Allen did quickly thrust his staff behind Dame Ballard and give him a grievous prick upon ye hand. Whereupon Mr. Tomlins did spring upp much
above ye floore, and with terrible force strike hys hand against ye wall; and also, to ye great wonder of all, prophanlie exclaim in a loud voice, curse ye woodchuck, he dreaming so it seemed yt
a woodchuck had seized and bit his hand. But on coming to know where he was, and ye greate
scandall he had committed, he seemed much abashed, but did not speak. And I think he will not
soon again goe to sleepe in meeting.

                    A. Train, 118 (source: Journal of Obadiah Turner, 3 June 1646)

A Frenchman observes English Sunday customs in 1698:

The *English* of all Sects, but particularly the Presbyterians, make Profession of being very strict
Observers of the Sabbath Day.
    I believe their Doctrine upon this Head does not differ from ours, but most assuredly our
Scruples are much less great than theirs. This appears upon a hundred Occasions; but I have
observ'd it particularly in the printed Confessions of Persons that are hang'd; Sabbath-breaking
is the Crime the poor Wretches always begin with. If they had kill'd Father and Mother, they
would not mention that Article, till after having profess'd how often they had broke the Sabbath.
One of the good *English* Customs on the Sabbath-day, is to feast as nobly as possible, and especially not to forget the Pudding. It is a common Practice, even among People of good Substance,
to have a huge Piece of Roast-Beef on *Sundays*, of which they stuff till they can swallow no more,
and eat the rest cold, without any other Victuals, the other six Days of the Week.

                                        Misson de Valbourg, 310–11

A German describes Sunday in London in June 1710:

In the afternoon we went to St. James Park to observe the prodigious crowds of people who walk
up and down there of a Sunday; on this day no genteel persons come there, but only those who
cannot get there in the week or who live too far from Westminster have much pleasure to go there
on Sundays. Moreover no one can amuse himself here on Sundays, which are observed as strictly

as in any place in the world, so that, not only is all play and frequenting of inns forbidden, but also only a few boats and hackney-coaches are allowed to ply. Thus one is forced to stay at home, and our hostess would not even permit her foreign guests to play to themselves on the viol de gamba or flute, so that she should run no risk of punishment. All this indeed is the only sign that the English are a Christian people, for it is not very apparent from the rest of their dealings.

Uffenbach, 36

An Englishman unwittingly breaks the colonial New England Sabbath, suffers the consequences, and devises an exquisite revenge:

Some years ago, a commander of one of [his] majesty's ships of war being stationed at this place [Massachusetts Bay], had orders to cruise from time to time, in order to protect our trade, and distress the enemy. It happened unluckily that he returned from one of his cruises on a Sunday; and as he had left his lady at Boston, the moment she heard of the ship's arrival, she hasted down to the waters side, in order to receive him. The captain, on landing, embraced her with tenderness and affection: this, as there were many spectators by, gave great offence, and was considered as an act of indecency, and a flagrant profanation of the Sabbath. The next day, therefore, he was summoned before the magistrates, who, with many severe rebukes and pious exhortations, ordered him to be publicly whipped. The captain stifled his indignation and resentment as much as possible, and as the punishment, from the frequency of it, was not attended with any great degree of ignominy or disgrace, he mixed with the best company, was well received by them, and they were apparently good friends. —At length the time of the station expired, and he was recalled: he went, therefore, with seeming concern to take leave of his worthy friends; and that they might spend one more happy day together before their final separation, he invited the principal magistrates and select men to dine with him on board his ship, upon the day of his departure. They accepted the invitation, and nothing could be more joyous and convivial than the entertainment which he gave them. At length the fatal moment arrived that was to separate them: the anchor was apeak, the sails were unfurled and nothing was wanting but the signal to get under way. The captain, after taking an affectionate leave of his worthy friends, accompanied them upon deck, where the boatswain and crew were in readiness to receive them. He there thanked them afresh for the civilities they had shown him, of which, he said, he should retain an eternal remembrance; and to which he wished it had been in his power to have made a more adequate return. One point of civility only remained to be adjusted between them, which, as it was in his power, so he meant most justly to recompense to them. He then reminded them of what had passed, and ordering the crew to pinion them, had them brought one by one to the gang-way; where the boatswain stripped off their shirts, and with a cat of nine tails laid on the back of each forty stripes save one. They were then, amidst the shouts and acclamations of the crew, shoved into their boats: and the captain immediately getting under way, sailed for England.

A. Burnaby, 85–7

Carling Sunday = Passion Sunday
Fig Sunday = Palm Sunday
Green-wood Sunday = Palm Sunday
Little-Easter Sunday = Low Sunday
Mothering Sunday = Mid-Lent Sunday, the fourth Sunday in Lent
Saint Sunday = St Dominick (Sanctus Dominicus, confused with *dies dominica*, the Latin
    for Sunday, the Lord's Day)
Yew Sunday = Palm Sunday

MONDAY

Monday's child is fair of face.

If you sneeze on Monday you sneeze for danger.

Cut your nails on a Monday, cut them for news.

Monday is an unlucky day to:

move house or change employment

They will depart from their olde services, any day in the weeke, but theire desire (hereaboutes [Yorkshire, 1641]) is to goe to theire newe masters eyther on a Tewsday, or on a Thursday; for on a Sunday they will seldome remoove, and as for Munday, they account it ominous, for they say— Munday flitte, Neaver sitte.   Best, 135

give money away

Some, who might well be supposed more enlightened, will not give away money on this day of the week, or on the first day of the Moon.   Jamieson, Supplement, s.v. 'Mononday'

die

HIP. Shee died on monday then.

MAT. And thats the most villainous day of all the weeke to die in: and she was wel, and eate a messe of water-grewl on monday morning.

Thomas Dekker, *The Honest Whore* (1604), i. 1

In 'The Miller's Tale', Chaucer makes the wily clerk Nicholas bamboozle the ignorant and superstitious carpenter whose wife he wishes to seduce into expecting a flood greater than Noah's (against God's express promise, Gen. 9: 15) on the following Monday, a day he already distrusts for its ill luck. Nicholas in turn comes to grief at the hands of the clerk Absolon, who has gone a-wooing by the light of the moon; Monday, as the moon's day, shares in its fickleness, which may account for its evil reputation.

Though all Mondays were doubtful, three during the year were thought to be particularly unlucky. Medieval Latin and Old English texts specify the first Monday in April, the first in August, and the last in December: anyone who lets blood of man or beast on them will not last the week, anyone who accepts a drink, or eats goose, will die within the fortnight, and any child, male or female, born on them will come to a bad end. In time reasons were invented:

Though I thinke no day amisse to undertake any good enterprise, or businesse in hande; yet have I observed some, and no meane Clerks, very Cautionarie, to forbeare these three Mundayes in the yeare, which I leave to thine owne consideration, either to use or refuse, *viz.* 1. The first Munday in April, which day *Caine* was born, and his brother *Abel* slaine. 2. The second Munday in August, which day *Sodome* and *Gomorrah* were destroyed. 3. Last Monday in December, which day *Iudas* was born, that betrayed our *Saviour Christ*.

William Cecil, Lord Burleigh (1520–98), to his son

The second day has been shifted a week, but variations are normal in writings of this kind; the Bodleian Library MS Ashmole 59 (fo. 133ʳ) gives 'The fyrst Munday of Feverrer and þe last Munday of May and the last Munday of Decembr'. Some texts confuse these Mondays with the Egyptian days.

Monday is a bad day for starting things in Wales: work begun on Monday will never be a week old. One should avoid marriages and loans. But Monday is a lucky day to commence an enterprise in Ireland:

> No great undertaking can be auspiciously commenced in Ireland on any morning but *Monday morning*. 'Oh, please God we live till Monday morning, we'll set the slater to mend the roof of the house. On Monday morning we'll fall to, and cut the turf. On Monday morning we'll see and begin mowing. On Monday morning, please your honour, we'll begin and dig the potatoes,' etc.   Edgeworth, 74 (editorial glossary)

Ogden Nash (1902–71) on Monday:

Every Day is Monday

Monday is the day that everything starts all over again,
Monday is the day when just as you are beginning to feel peaceful you have to get up and
      get dressed and put on your old gray bonnet and drive down to Dover again,
It is the day when life becomes grotesque again,
Because it is the day when you have to face your desk again;
When the telephone rings on Saturday or Sunday you are pleased because it probably means
      something pleasing and you take the call with agility,
But when it rings on any other day it just usually means some additional responsibility,
And when in doubt,
Why the best thing to do is to answer it in a foreign accent or if you are a foreigner answer it
      in a native accent and say you are out.
Oh, there is not a week-day moment that can't wring a sigh from you,
Because you are always being confronted with people who want to sell you something, or if
      they don't want to sell you something, there is something they want to buy from you,
And every shining hour swaggers arrogantly up to you demanding to be improved,
And apparently not only to improve it, but also to shine it, is what you are behooved.
Oh for a remedy, oh for a panacea, oh for a something, oh yes, oh for a coma or swoon,
Yes indeed, oh for a coma that would last from nine A.M. on Monday until Saturday noon.

Black Monday = Easter Monday, or the day on which schoolboys returned to school
   (also called Bloody Monday)
Collop Monday = the day before Shrove Tuesday
Fat Monday = the day before Shrove Tuesday
Handsel Monday = the first Monday in the New Year
Hock Monday = the second Monday after Easter
Plough Monday = the Monday after Epiphany
Rope Monday = Hock Monday
Saint Monday = idleness at work on Monday owing to drinking the previous day

TUESDAY

Tuesday's child is full of grace.

Sneeze on a Tuesday, kiss a stranger.

Cut your nails on a Tuesday, a new pair of shoes.

Tuesday is an unlucky day to:

meet

Skir or kir-handed people, *i.e.* left-handed ones, are not safe for a traveller to meet on a Tuesday morning. On other days it is fortunate to meet them.   Henderson, 86

Tuesday is a lucky day to:

sow corn

In the Island of Mull . . . Tuesday is the most lucky day for sowing their corn.

Hampson, i. 387

In modern Greece Tuesday is unlucky: it is the day on which Constantinople fell; the day on which a ballad tells us that the hero Digenis Akritas was born and will die. It was also thought unlucky in Spain, particularly for marriages; but in Jewish tradition it is lucky, since the words 'And God saw that it was good' occur twice in the Creation account for that day (Gen. 1: 10, 12). In Wales too it is lucky, good for journeys and marriage.

A tradition at Canterbury held that Tuesday played a remarkable part in and after the life of Thomas Becket: he was born on St Thomas's Day (21 Dec.) when that was a Tuesday (if so, the year was 1120); the Council of Northampton, at which he was cited to answer the charge of denying justice to John fitzGilbert, was summoned for Tuesday, 6 October 1164; he fled the Council, under indictment for treason and perjury, on Tuesday the 13th; he had a vision at Pontigny in which God said to him 'Thoma, Thoma, ecclesia mea glorificabitur in te' on a Tuesday; he returned to England on Tuesday, 1 December 1170; he was assassinated on Tuesday the 29th; and he was translated on Tuesday, 7 July 1220. It was also on a Tuesday, 11 June 1538, that he was posthumously condemned to death as a traitor.

Hock Tuesday = the second Tuesday after Easter

WEDNESDAY

Wednesday's child is full of woe.

Sneeze on a Wednesday, sneeze for a letter.

Cut your nails on a Wednesday, cut them for health.

Wednesday is the day on which the luminaries were created, and hence the first day of the Jewish sectarian calendar (see II: *Jewish Calendar*); it is the starting-point of the Alexandrian astrologers' weekday count (see II: *Egyptian Calendar*), and also the day proposed by some early Christian writers for the birth of Christ (see II: *Christian Chronology*), the Sun of Righteousness (Mal. 4: 2). It was a fast-day from early times (whence its Irish name of *Céadaoin* 'first fast'), and is so still in the Orthodox Church; the West substituted Saturday, but later contented itself with fasting on Friday.

Wednesday is a witch day in Wales; new enterprises should be avoided.

Spy-Wednesday = Wednesday before Easter

THURSDAY

Thursday's child has far to go.

Sneeze on a Thursday something better.

Cut your nails on a Thursday, cut them for wealth.

Evidence from Roman Egypt suggests that public offices were closed on Thursdays. The keeping of Thursday as a holiday long persisted in Gaul, to the annoyance of the Church: Caesarius of Arles (early 6th c.) complains that men and women (he specifies both sexes) are transferring to Jupiter the honour they should be giving to God, 'nor do I doubt that they are not ashamed or afraid to work on the Lord's day'. More probably, if we may trust the analogy of the 1790s in France and the 1930s in the Soviet Union, some folk kept both days holy; nevertheless St Eligius in the mid-seventh century is reported by his friend and contemporary St Ouen or Audoenus to have urged: 'Let no (Christian) observe Thursday at leisure, neither in May nor at any time, except on holy feasts.' The Thursday holiday was revived in the state schools of the French Republic, though it has recently been changed to Wednesday.

The Cornish town of Marazion, which prospered greatly before the rise of Penzance in the seventeenth century, owes its name to a misreading of a late Cornish form *Mara-jiou* or *Marha Jou* from an earlier *Marghas Dêth-Yow* (Marhasdeythyow, Marghasyewe), 'Thursday Market', in Latin *Forum Iovis*, granted among other liberties to St Michael's

Mount by Robert, Count of Mortain. The name also survives in Market Jew Street, which runs between Marazion and Penzance; it has nothing to do with Jewish traders.

The custom of fasting on Wednesdays and Fridays gives this day its Irish name of *Déardaoin* = 'day between two fasts' (*dia eadar dá aoin*).

In Wales Thursday is not good for moving house, since birds never carried anything to their nests on that day, but is good for christenings.

Bounds Thursday = Ascension Day (from the custom of beating the parish boundaries)
Carnival Thursday or Fat Thursday = the Thursday before Lent
Grand Thursday = Corpus Christi
Great Thursday = Maundy Thursday
Green Thursday = Maundy Thursday
Holy Thursday = Ascension Day or Maundy Thursday
Maundy Thursday = the Thursday before Good Friday
Sheer Thursday = Maundy Thursday

FRIDAY

Friday's child is loving and giving.

Sneeze on a Friday, sneeze for sorrow.

Cut your nails on a Friday, cut them for woe.

Friday is an unlucky day to:

pare one's nails

MISTRESS WATER-CAMLET. What a cursed wretch was I to pare my nails to-day! a Friday too; I looked for some mischief.

Middleton, Any Thing for a Quiet Life (1662), IV. ii. 128

be born

If he be born on Friday or its night, he shall be accursed of men, silly, and crafty, and loathsome to all men, and shall ever be thinking evil in his heart, and shall be a thief and a great coward, and shall not live longer than to mid age.

Bodleian Library, MS Hatton 115 (11th c.), fo. 149^r, trans. Cockayne, iii. 163

undertake anything new

> Now Friday came, your old wives say,
> Of all the week's the unluckiest day,
> Journey to take, or work to do,
> And I for my part found it true;

Being day, on which't might well be sed
No butter'd stick upon my bread.

Flecknoe (1656), VIII. Jornada

I knew another poor woman, who lost half her time in waiting for *lucky* days, and made it a rule never to begin any work, write a letter on business, or set out on a journey on a Friday—so her business was never done, and her fortune suffered accordingly.   C. Smith, 50 (1863)

Among the superstitions in which he [Byron] chose to indulge, the supposed unluckiness of Friday, as a day for the commencement of any work, was one by which he, almost always, allowed himself to be influenced. Soon after his arrival at Pisa, a lady of his acquaintance happening to meet him, on the road from her house as she was herself returning thither, and supposing that he had been to make her a visit, requested that he would go back with her. 'I have not been to your house,' he answered, 'for, just before I got to the door, I remembered that it was Friday; and not liking to make my first visit on a Friday, I turned back.' It is even related of him that he once sent away a Genoese tailor, who brought him home a new coat on the same ominous day. With all this, strange to say, he set sail for Greece on a Friday.   T. Moore, ii. 668

go courting

In East Lancashire Friday evening is not considered a correct or suitable time for courtship. The first person spying a couple so engaged enters the house, seizes the frying-pan, and beats on it a tattoo. This arouses the neighbours, who give a warm reception to the offending couple if they do not withdraw hurriedly.   Ditchfield, 199

move house

A few days ago Mr H. MacPherson, Inspector of Poor, visited Aharacle in order to superintend the removal of the ten selected female paupers to the new cottages. They all occupied houses which were in a wretched state of disrepair, yet each of them resolutely . . . refused to 'flit' . . . The aged dames were invincibly proof against all argument . . . threats . . . and . . . warrants . . . At length it was elicited that the disinclination to remove was based simply on superstition. The day of the week happened to be Friday.

Scotsman, 6 September 1900 (quoted in Opie and Tatem, 169)

Friday is a lucky day to:

get married in Scotland

Nine-tenths of the marriages in Glasgow are celebrated on Friday.   *N & Q*, II. xii. 491

gather St John's wort

S. Johns wort gathered on a friday in the houre of Jupiter . . . hung about the necke, it mightily helpes this affection [melancholy], and drives away all phantasticall spirits.

R. Burton, II. III. i. 5

Friday was Charles Dickens's lucky day:

I was born on a Friday, and it is a most astonishing coincidence that I have never in my life—whatever projects I may have determined on, otherwise—never begun a book, or begun anything of interest to me, or done anything of importance to me, but it was on a Friday.

5 September 1857 (*Letters*, 347)

Ill luck far outweighs good luck on Friday, which is a bad day in general. It is one of the 'dismal' days (in the broader sense) because the Crucifixion occurred on a Friday. But it was also said to be the day on which Adam and Eve ate the forbidden fruit (the same day on which they were created).

LIEU. A plague of Friday mornings, the unfortunate day in the whole weeke.

William Rowley, A Match at Midnight (1633), I. i

Friday dreams:

Her dreames are so chaste, that shee dare tell them; only a Fridaies dream is all her superstition: that she conceals for feare of anger.   'A faire and happy Milk-mayd', in Overbury, Characters

> When first she saw him, o! Quoth she,
> This is the Man!—The Man for me!
> The Sage describ'd him to a T—
> I fasted Friday, had my Dream,
> And dreamt of none but perfect him.

'Progress of Matrimony', in The Palace Miscellany (1733), 32

Friday's feast = fast:

10. Doe you straine curtesies? Had I it in fingering
    I'd make you both make but a Fridayes feast;
    Oh how the steame perfumes my Nostrils.

Robert Davenport, A New Tricke to Cheat the Divell (1639), III. i

According to MS Ashmole 59 (fo. 132ᵛ), there are three Fridays in the year on which anyone who fasts devoutly, being out of mortal sin and fully shriven, will be saved before God and never go to Hell: they are the first Friday in March, the last in June, and the last in November, being referred to the Crucifixions of Jesus Christ, St Peter, and St Andrew.

Friday is the worst day in Wales, because Adam and Eve were expelled from Paradise. Fruit-trees pruned on it would not blossom for three years; the fairies controlled lakes, streams, and rivers.

Black Friday = the Friday after Thanksgiving, at one time the start of the Christmas shopping season

Good Friday = the Friday before Easter Day

SATURDAY

Saturday's child works hard for his living.

Sneeze on a Saturday, see your sweetheart to-morrow.

Cut your nails on a Saturday, a journey to go.

Saturday is the first day of the astrological week, the last of the Judaeo-Christian. It is treated by the Eastern Church as a festival, but by Latins as a day of abstinence.

Saturday is an unlucky day to:

hire a servant

> Saturday's servants never stay;
> Sunday's servants run away. (Northampton)

move house

To flit on Saturday betokens a short term of residence in the place to which one removes.

Jamieson, Supplement, ii. 333

begin an enterprise or journey

Nother can thai excuse thame self fra transgression of the first command, yat superstitiously obseruis ane day mair than ane other, as certane craftis men quhilk will nocht begin thair warke on the saterday, certane schipmen or marinars will nocht begin to sail on the satterday, certane trauelars will nocht begin thair iornay on ye satterday, quhilk is plane superstition, be cause that God almychty made the satterday as well as he made all other dayis of the wouke.

Hamilton (1552), pt. 1, fo. 22ᵛ

Saturday is a lucky day to:

choose a wife

Who will have a handsome wife let him choose her upon Saturday and not upon Sunday. (Spanish proverb)

Saturday was supposedly Henry VII's lucky day (but see *14 Oct.):

> K. HEN. VII.　　Let dinner cheerefully
> 　　　　　　　　Be serv'd in; this day of the weeke is ours,
> 　　　　　　　　Our day of providence, for Saturday
> 　　　　　　　　Yet never fayl'd in all my vndertakings,
> 　　　　　　　　To yeeld me rest at night. . . .
> 　　　　　　　　　　John Ford, *Perkin Warbeck* (1634), III. i

Hee entred the Citie upon a *Saturday*, as hee had also obtayned the Victorie [at Bosworth] upon a *Saturday*, which day of the Weeke, first upon an Observation, and after upon Memorie and Fancie, hee accounted and chose as a day prosperous unto him.　　　　Bacon (1622), 7

Saturday is a fortunate day in Wales, especially for the market in poultry, butter, cheese, and meat; newly-weds' property was always conveyed to their new house on this day, but the marriage itself was never contracted on a Saturday lest the couple not live out the year.

Egg Saturday = the Saturday before Lent
Holy Saturday = the Saturday before Easter Day

DAYS

In this section we offer general considerations regarding the observations of days within the calendar; for the day as a unit of time-measurement, see II: *Days and Times*.

HOLY DAYS, HOLIDAYS, FEASTS

Most religions attach particular significance to certain days; these may be auspicious or inauspicious, but are in either case holy. In many cases work is not permitted, and at least the auspicious days or 'feasts' are marked with revelry; it is for this reason that, in English, the term 'holiday', a compound of *holy* and *day*, has acquired the sense of a time when work gives way to pleasure, so that the original sense has to be expressed by separating the components into 'holy day'.

Not all holy days are of equal status. For Christians (other than those who reject all except Sunday as unscriptural) the greatest feasts are Easter, which commemorates the Resurrection (as do all the Sundays in the year), followed by Pentecost or Whit Sunday and feasts marking the major events in the life of Christ, above all Christmas, and (outside strict Protestantism) of the Virgin Mary. In the Church of England, the Book of Common Prayer includes a table of 'all the feasts that are to be observed in the Church of England throughout the year': they comprise all Sundays, the Monday and Tuesday in Easter and Whitsun week, and:

Circumcision	1 January
Epiphany	6 January
Conversion of St Paul	25 January
Purification	2 February
St Matthias	24 February
Annunciation	25 March
St Mark	25 April
SS Philip and James	1 May
Ascension	6th Thursday after Easter
St Barnabas	11 June
St John the Baptist	24 June
St Peter	29 June
St James	25 July

St Bartholomew	24 August
St Matthew	21 September
St Michael and all Angels	29 September
St Luke	18 October
SS Simon and Jude	28 October
All Saints	1 November
St Andrew	30 November
St Thomas	21 December
The Nativity of Our Lord	25 December
St Stephen	26 December
St John the Evangelist	27 December
The Holy Innocents	28 December

These feasts, provided with their own collect, Gospel, and Epistle, were formerly printed in red letters, and called 'red-letter days'; in general they commemorated persons or events mentioned in the Bible, though they include All Saints and not the Transfiguration or the Beheading of St John the Baptist. Other feasts were printed in black, for that reason being known as 'black-letter days'. More recent editions of the BCP use italic for the red-letter days and roman for the rest. There was also a table of 'Vigils, Fasts, and Days of Abstinence'.

The ASB imposed a threefold division of 'Principal Holy Days' (Easter, Ascension, Pentecost, Christmas, Epiphany, Maundy Thursday, Good Friday, and every Sunday in the year), 'Festivals and Greater Holy Days' (the other BCP red-letter days, with some changes), and 'Lesser Festivals and Commemorations' (including a few of the BCP black-letter days). There were also 'Special Days of Prayer and Thanksgiving' and 'Days of Discipline and Self-Denial'.

In CY the use of red ink was revived for 'Principal Feasts and other Principal Holy Days', printed in capitals (the other Principal Holy Days being Ash Wednesday, Maundy Thursday, and Good Friday) and 'Festivals', printed in lower case; black is used for lesser festivals (with a special collect, psalm, and readings), printed in roman, and commemorations (with mention in prayers of intercession and thanksgiving), in italic—the same face being thus used for the higher festivals in BCP and the lowest in CY. The Principal Feasts and Holy Days are:

Christmas Day
The Epiphany
The Presentation of Christ in the Temple
The Annunciation of our Lord to the Blessed Virgin Mary
Easter Day
Ascension Day
Pentecost (Whit Sunday)
Trinity Sunday
All Saints' Day
Ash Wednesday

Maundy Thursday
Good Friday
all Sundays of the year

Festivals agree with the BCP's list of feasts, with the following exceptions:

Additions (those marked † were black-letter days in the BCP)

St Joseph of Nazareth	19 March
†St George	23 April
Visit of the Blessed Virgin to Elizabeth	31 May (or 2 July)
†St Mary Magdalene	22 July
†Transfiguration	6 August
Blessed Virgin Mary	15 August (or 8 Sept.)
†Holy Cross Day	14 September
Christ the King	Sunday next before Advent

Omissions

Monday and Tuesday of Easter and Whit week

Transferred to other days (but BCP dates permitted)

St Matthias	14 May
St Thomas	3 July

Renamed

Purification now called Presentation of Christ in the Temple
St Peter, now SS Peter and Paul

Optional

Day of Thanksgiving for the Holy Communion	Thursday after Trinity Sunday (RC Corpus Christi)

The RC Church, before the liturgical reform of 1960, honoured at least one saint on nearly every day, and divided the feasts into Duplex of the first and second class, Semi-duplex, and Simplex. In 1960 they were reclassified as I, II, III, and Commemorations; since 1969 they have been ranked as Solemnities, Feasts, and Memorials (some of the latter are optional). These may differ between countries and dioceses. The General Roman Calendar lists the following Solemnities, in addition to all Sundays of the year:

Solemnity of Mary, Mother of God	1 January
Epiphany	6 January (in some countries on a Sunday)
St Joseph, Husband of the BVM	19 March
Annunciation of the Lord	25 March
Birth of St John the Baptist	24 June
SS Peter and Paul	29 June
Assumption of the BVM	15 August

All Saints	1 November
Immaculate Conception of the BVM	8 December
Nativity of Our Lord	25 December
Ascension	6th Thursday (40 days) after Easter
Holy Trinity	First Sunday after Pentecost
Body and Blood of Christ (Corpus Christi)	Thursday after Holy Trinity (in some countries on a Sunday)
Sacred Heart of Jesus	Saturday following Second Sunday after Pentecost
Christ the King	Last Sunday in Ordinary Time

In addition, St David (1 Mar.), St Patrick (17 Mar.), and St Andrew (30 Nov.) are Solemnities in Wales, Ireland, and Scotland respectively.

The Feasts are as follows:

Baptism of the Lord	Sunday after 6 January
Conversion of St Paul	25 January
Presentation of the Lord	2 February
Chair of St Peter	22 February
St Mark	25 April
SS Philip and James	3 May
St Matthias	14 May
Visitation of the BVM	31 May
St Thomas	3 July
St James	25 July
Transfiguration of the Lord	6 August
St Lawrence	10 August
St Bartholomew	24 August
Birthday of the BVM	8 September
Triumph of the Cross	14 September
St Matthew	21 September
SS Michael, Gabriel, and Raphael	29 September
St Luke	18 October
SS Simon and Jude	28 October
Dedication of the Lateran Basilica	9 November
St Andrew	30 November
St Stephen	26 December
St John	27 December
Holy Innocents	28 December
Holy Family of Jesus, Mary, and Joseph	Sunday within the octave of Christmas or 30 December

In addition, the national calendars of England, Wales, Scotland, and Ireland have the following Feasts:

England

St David	1 March
St Patrick	17 March
St George	23 April
Beatified Martyrs of England and Wales	4 May
St Augustine of Canterbury	27 May
SS John Fisher and Thomas More	22 June
St Gregory the Great	3 September
Forty Martyrs of England and Wales	25 October
Thomas Becket	29 December

Wales

St Patrick	17 March
St George	23 April
Six Welsh Martyrs and Companions	25 October
All Saints of Wales	8 November

Scotland

St John Ogilvie	10 March
St Patrick	17 March
St Margaret of Scotland	16 November

Ireland

St Brigid	1 February
St Columba	9 June
St Oliver Plunkett	1 July
All Saints of Ireland	6 November
St Columban	23 November

The Catholic Church in America has one additional Feast:

Our Lady of Guadalupe	12 December

RED-LETTER DAYS (JUDICIAL)

In Great Britain, on certain days of ecclesiastical or civil significance, should they occur within the law sittings, the judges of the Queen's Bench Division wear scarlet robes. The ecclesiastical days are the BCP red-letter days (but with SS Matthias and Thomas transferred to their ASB and CY days), together with St David's Day (still only a black-letter day for the Church of England); the civil days, apart from Lord Mayor's Day, are connected with the Sovereign and the Royal Family. The full list is:

Conversion of St Paul	25 January
Purification	2 February
Accession of HM the Queen	6 February

Ash Wednesday	
St David's Day	1 March
Annunciation	25 March
Birthday of HM the Queen	21 April
St Mark	25 April
SS Philip and James	1 May
St Matthias	14 May (since 1984)
Ascension	
Coronation of HM the Queen	2 June
Birthday of HRH the Duke of Edinburgh	10 June
St Barnabas	11 June
Official Birthday of HM the Queen	As appointed
St John the Baptist	24 June
St Peter	29 June
St Thomas	3 July (since 1984)
St James	25 July
Birthday of Queen Elizabeth the Queen Mother	4 August
St Luke	18 October
SS Simon and Jude	28 October
All Saints	1 November
Lord Mayor's Day	2nd Saturday in November
Birthday of HRH the Prince of Wales	14 November
St Andrew's Day	30 November

QUARTER DAYS, TERM DAYS, REMOVAL DAYS

When rents, interest, or other charges are paid quarterly, custom in England has decreed that they shall fall due on Lady Day (25 Mar.), Midsummer Day (24 June), Michaelmas (29 Sept.), and Christmas (25 Dec.). The date of Lady Day is not affected by the recent practice in the Church of England of celebrating the Annunciation on a different day when 25 March falls in Holy Week or Easter Week.

When most housing was rented, these Quarter Days were also the normal time for moving:

> What is it quarter daie that you remoue
> And carrie bag and baggage too?
>
> *The Raygne of King Edward the third*, sig. [E4]ʳ

These days may also be specified for half-yearly (but see Hocktide, under *Western Church Year*) or annual payments:

xij. d. of rente yerely . . . to be resceived of Raf Marchaunte and his heires at ij. termes of the yere, that is to say, vj. d. at the fest of oure Lady in Marche and vj. d. at the fest of seynt Michell.

Godstow Register, 104 (*c*.1450) (cited in *OED*, s.v. 'term')

It was, in fact, the twenty-fifth of March, which, as most people know to their cost, is, and has been time out of mind, one of those unpleasant epochs called quarter-days. On this twenty-fifth of March, it was John Willet's pride annually to settle, in hard cash, his account with a certain vintner and distiller in the city of London; to give into whose hands a canvas bag containing its exact amount, and not a penny more or less, was the end and object of a journey for Joe, so surely as the year and day came round.

Dickens, *Barnaby Rudge*, ch. 13

(Joe is John Willet's son, who attempts to combine his errand with a wooing.) Christmas was the occasion for a merrier form of payment, till it was commuted in the interests of propriety and the Exchequer to a money rent:

Rowland le Sarcere, held one hundred and ten Acres of land in Hemingston in Com. Suffolk, by Sergeanty, for which on Christmas day, every year before our Sovereign Lord the King of England he should perform simul & semel, unum Saltum, unum Sufflum, & unum Bombulum, or as we read elsewhere in French, un saut, un pet, & un Syflet, simul & semel; that is, he should dance, puff up his Cheeks, making therewith a sound, and let a Crack, Et quia indecens servitium, ideo arrentatur, (sayes the Record) ad xxvi. s. viij d. per annum ad Scaccarium Regis.

Blount (1679), 10–11

In Scotland the equivalent days, usually called 'term days', were fixed by Acts of 1690 and 1693 as Candlemas (2 Feb.), Whitsunday (15 May, always), Lammas (1 Aug.), and Martinmas (11 Nov.); however, after 1752 they continued, in most parts of the country, to be observed according to the Old Style, eleven days later. In 1886 Removal terms for change of houses were fixed on 28 May and 28 November; rent and interest continued to be due on the old term days till 1990, when they were transferred, without change of name, to the 28th of their respective months.

The 25th of May, as the Whitsunday term (old style), is a great day in Scotland, being that on which, for the most part, people change their residences. For some unexplained reason the Scotch 'remove' oftener than their southern neighbours. They very generally lease their houses by the year, and are thus at every twelve-month's end able to shift their place of abode. Whether the restless disposition has arisen from the short leases, or the short leases have been a result of the restless disposition, is immaterial. That the restlessness is a fact, is what we have mainly to deal with.

It haps, accordingly, that at every Candlemas a Scotch family gets an opportunity of considering whether it will, in the language of the country, sit or flit. The landlord or his agent calls to learn the decision on this point; and if 'flit' is the resolution, he takes measures by advertising to obtain a new tenant. The two or three days following upon the Purification, therefore, become distinguished by a feathering of the streets with boards projected from the windows, intimating 'A House to Let'. Then comes on a most lively excitement for individuals proposing to remove; you see them going about for weeks, inspecting the numerous houses offered to them. Considerations of position, accommodation, and rent, afford scope for endless speculation. The gentleman deliberates about the rent—whether it will suit his means. The lady has her own anxious thoughts about new furniture that may be required, and how far old carpets can be made to suit the new premises. Both have their reflections as to what the Thomsons and the Jacksons will say on hearing that they are going into a house so much handsomer, more ambitiously situated, and dearer than their last. At length the pleasing dream is over—they have taken the house, and the only thing that remains to be done is to 'flit'. Chambers (25 May)

UNLUCKY, 'EGYPTIAN', OR DISMAL DAYS

In the ancient Egyptian calendar, many days were considered auspicious or inauspicious, for mythological reasons; in the Middle Kingdom some third of the year was deemed unlucky. Such beliefs persisted: the Elder Pliny (*Natural History* 27. 105) records the belief that if one anoints oneself in the morning of 28 Thoth with the juice of myosotis, before one has said a word, one will be free of eye-disease all year round. Indeed, they have outlasted the mythology on which they were based: according to a Coptic calendar published in 1900, on 27 Thoth one should avoid medicines altogether; unlucky days of the Muslim lunar month are attested, though the details vary.

Unlucky days are also found in Babylonia, for example the 7th, 14th, 21st, and 28th of the lunar month (the term was *shabattum*, to which speculative writers have referred the Jewish sabbath), again with mythological explanations (thus the 19th of the month is made sinister by the 'wrath of Gula'). In Greece too, Hesiod's *Works and Days* from the seventh century BC invoke mythology; Byzantine *selēnodromia* ('moon-courses') continue the tradition, sometimes adding Old Testament justifications. Another tradition, notably represented by Plutarch, relates the character of days to the historical events said to have fallen on them; some manipulation of the evidence can be detected, more suspected. The Romans traditionally believed (see *18 July) that certain days in their own calendar were unsuitable for public business, because the gods would not accept the preliminary sacrifices required before battles or other actions of state; such days were called *religiosi* or *atri*. In particular the days after the Kalends, Nones, and Ides were deemed unlucky, not only for affairs of state but also for private travel.

From the fourth to at least the seventeenth centuries AD certain days, or at least a specified hour in them, were considered inauspicious for any enterprise, and above all blood-letting. These days were marked in calendars (first in that of 354) as *dies Aegyptiaci*, not because they coincided with the many days held to be unlucky in the Egyptian calendar, but because the Egyptians were considered experts in such matters. The lists vary both in the number of such days and in their identification, but the normal medieval belief was that there were two in each month, and the most common account made them 1 and 25 January, 4 and 26 February, 1 and 28 March, 10 and 20 April, 3 and 25 May, 10 and 16 June, 13 and 22 July, 1 and 30 August, 3 and 21 September, 3 and 22 October, 5 and 28 November, 7 and 22 December. Some lists vary in a few particulars, others more radically; only a minority record the unlucky hours, and those do not agree, as if it were wiser to play safe by abstaining from action all day. It was especially important that doctors should not let blood on an Egyptian day since the moon, in its rising and setting, was subject to the influence of a malign planet. Sometimes the Egyptian days are confused with the three unlucky Mondays in the year (see *Week: Monday*).

The Fathers of the Church condemned this superstition: all days were good, because God had made them all. Nevertheless, they were registered by medieval churchmen in their calendars; sometimes by 'dies Egipt.' or the like against the day, sometimes by mnemonic verses written above the respective months. In these, the first day is counted from the beginning, but the second from the end, according to the style commonly called *consuetudo Bononiensis* because in other contexts it was mainly used by notaries trained in the law school of Bologna. More than one set of such verses existed, but the most widespread ran as follows (with minor variations):

> Iani prima dies et septima fine timetur,
> Ast Februi quarta est; praecedit tertia finem.
> Martis prima necat, cuius sub cuspide quarta est.
> Aprilis decima est, undena et fine minatur.
> Tertius in Maio lupus est et septimus anguis.
> Iunius in decimo quindenum a fine salutat.
> Tredecimus Iulii decimo innuit ante kalendas.
> Augusti nepa prima fugat de fine secundam.
> Tertia Septembris uulpis ferit a pede denam.
> Tertius Octobris pullus decimum ordine nectit.
> Quinta Nouembris acus, uix tertia mansit in urna.
> Dat duodena cohors septem inde decemque Decembris.

> The first day of Janus and the seventh from the end are feared,
> but it is the fourth of Februus; the third precedes the end.
> Mars' first kills; the fourth is under his spear-point.
> Of April it is the tenth, and the eleventh from the end threatens.
> The third in May is a wolf and the seventh a snake.
> June in the tenth salutes the fifteenth from the end.
> The thirteenth of July nods to the tenth before the Kalends.
> The first scorpion of August chases the second from the end.
> The third wolf of September smites the tenth from the foot.
> The third chicken of October attaches the tenth in order.
> The fifth of November is a needle, the third has barely remained in the urn.
> The twelfth company then gives seven and ten of December.

Under July, 'decimo ante Kalendas' does not mean X *Kal. Aug.*, 23 July, but the 22nd; the verse for December was often misunderstood as meaning the 12th from the beginning and the 17th from the end, i.e. the 15th of the month. But other verses will be found, including a set published from 'an Old *Romish MSS*. Prayer-Book' by John Gibbon (see *14 Oct.), who finds political applications for them, unfortunately without knowing anything of the *consuetudo Bononiensis*, so that he counts the second day in each line forwards instead of backwards. Correctly interpreted, they agree with those given above.

Yet another set of verses, partly Latin but mainly nonsense, recorded by John of Holiwood (de Sacrobosco) in the thirteenth century, encoded not only the Egyptian days but the dangerous hours, with the following results (a change of spelling would restore the normal 26 Feb.):

Month	Day	Hour	Day	Hour	Month	Day	Hour	Day	Hour
January	1	11	25	6	July	13	11	22	11
February	4	8	20 (26?)	10	August	1	1	30	7
March	1	4	28	2	September	3	3	21	4
April	10	20	20	11	October	3	8	22	9
May	3	6	25	10	November	5	8	28	5
June	10	6	16	4	December	7	1	22	6

Dismal day

A synonym for 'Egyptian day', also found in calendars, was 'evil day', *dies mala*. The Itinerary of Richard I notes that his coronation on 3 September 1189 caused speculation because it was so marked; William of Newburgh, describing the pogrom that broke out on that occasion, notes that the day was 'from an ancient heathen superstition called evil or Egyptian', and proved so for the Jews. Roger of Hovedon records that in 1194 the archbishops of Mainz and Cologne handed Richard over to his mother Eleanor after payment of his ransom on Friday, 4 February, 'an Egyptian day, which the moderns call an evil day; and thus the Lord delivered him in the evil day' (Vulgate Ps. 40: 2 = AV Ps. 41: 1 'in time of trouble'). This term is the origin of English 'dismal', originally a noun; it is so used by Chaucer, but reinterpreted as if Old French *li dis mal*, 'the ten evils', meaning the ten plagues of Egypt:

> And eke, as helpe me God withal,
> I trowe hyt was in the dismal,
> That was the ten woundes of Egipte.
> *The Book of the Duchess*, ll. 1205–7

('Woundes' represents Latin *plagae*, French *plaies*.) The name was further corrupted to 'dismold'; even a St Disemore was invented:

> Is't not a wonder, *Quintius* should so dread,
> To see a Hare runne crossing his way,
> The Salt fall t'wards him, or his Nose to bleed,
> Beginne a iourney vpon *Disemores* day;
> Yet feares not things more ominous than these . . .
> Thomas Freeman, *Rubbe and a Great Cast* (1614), pt. ii, ep. 25

However, two unlucky days in the month were not enough for some writers: we may cite

Maisters of Astronomie and Phisicke that this craft first found, telleth the most perillous and the most dangerous dayes in the yeare. In which if any man or oman be let blood of wound or veine, they shall dye the xxi. dayes following. Or who so falleth into sicknesse on any of these dayes, they shall never escape it till they be dead. And who so taketh any great iourney in any of these dayes, to goe from home hee shall be in danger to dye ere he come againe. And who so weddeth a wife in any of these dayes they shal soone be parted, or else shall liue together with much sorrow. And who so beginneth in any of these dayes any great worke, it shall neuer come to good end: and these are the dayes following: Erra Pater, sig. A5ᵛ–6ᵛ

The days are: 1, 2, 4, 5, 10, 15, 17, 19 January; 8, 10, 17 February; 15, 16, 19 March; 15, 21 April; 7, 15, 20 May; 4, 7 June; 15, 20 July; 19, 20 August; 6, 7 September; 6 October; 6, 10 November; 6, 7, 11 December 'Et alij dicunt, the xv. and the xvi.'

The list was still being published, with minor variations, in the eighteenth century. It bears some resemblance to one found in a fifteenth-century manuscript in the Bodleian Library, MS Ashmole 59 (fo. 132ᵛ), said to be the work of 'notable clerkes' who met together before the birth of Christ. Olaus Worm gives two different lists of unlucky days in Danish folklore.

According to the humanist Lodovico Ricchieri of Rovigo, better known as Caelius Rhodiginus:

Sailors too have their suspect days: 1, 7, 15, 17, 19, 25 March; 5, 6, 12, 20 April; 6, 12, 15, 17, 19, 20 February. They observe them without fail, explaining that it is generally on these days that the sea is subject to extreme change, either for calm or for storm; hence, in so complex and utterly uncertain a matter, they think it safer not to sail. *Lectiones antiquae* (1542), 14. 9

However, none of these texts has an authority to match that claimed in France for the parallel lists of lucky and unlucky days allegedly 'revealed by the angel to good St Job' (*10 May) (Joubert 269–70):

	Lucky	*Unlucky*		*Lucky*	*Unlucky*
January	3, 13	1, 2, 4, 6, 8, 15	July	2, 13, 16	15, 17
February	5, 25	6, 17, 18	August	12	19, 20
March	1, 8, 30	6, 16, 17, 18	September	1, 7, 23, 27	16, 17
April	5, 22, 29	6, 15	October	4, 15	6
May	4, 27	7, 15, 17	November	14, 20	15, 17
June	3, 8	6	December	18, 26	6, 7, 11

Lucky and unlucky lunes

In addition to these days of the calendar month, days of the moon were considered lucky or unlucky; such beliefs, attested in Roman *lunaria* and briefly touched on in Vergil's *Georgics*, survived into and beyond the Middle Ages, being found in England till the eighteenth century. Some expositions are very long and detailed; a simpler instance is a poem in a Bodleian Library manuscript (Digby 88, fo. 60ʳ⁻ᵛ):

> God made Adam the fyrst day of yᵉ moone
> And the secunde day Eve good dedis to doon
>
> The iij. day then was Caym borne
> Begynne not on that day till over yᵉ morne
>
> The iiij.th day as I you say ys right good for man
> For Abel in certayn he was borne thanne.
>
> The v. day ys right good and selle   *blessed*
> And on the vj. day was borne danyel.
>
> The vij. day Caym Abel sloe yᵗ day ys good I nowe   *that day is good enough*
> The viij. day and the ix.ᵗʰ good dedis may be doo.
>
> The x. day goo noo pilgremage
> But the xj. day do thy vyage
>
> The xij. day goo uppon noo floode
> And the xiij. ys yet not so good

The xiiij. ys good to cary
And the xv. yt ys contrary

The xvj. day w^towten stryve   *without contest*
And the xvij. sanke cyteis v   *cities five*

The xviij. ys good all thynge to do
And the xix. ys not soo

The xx. day as I you say
And the xxj. good dedes do y^u may

The xxij. and xxiij. as I rede w^towte drede   *advise without fear*
In all good werke may men spede

The xxiiij. and xxv. day
Thow mayste well take thy Journay

The xxvj. day of ye moone
Good dedys may be doon

The xxvij. day and xxviij. bygynne noo thynge
But loke y^u a byde a better tymynge

The xxix. true it ys
That thy worke shall tend to blysse

And the xxx. day for to spede
Begynne noo werke as I the rede.   *advise thee*

Some prognostics relate to the reliability of dreams: thus we read that a dream on the 12th or 13th lune will be fulfilled within three days, but one on the 14th will come to naught. Others relate to the character of a person born on a particular lune: the 12th lune's child will be honoured in all respects (*on eallum þingum wurðfull*), but one born on the 23rd will be a thieving scoundrel (*þeofsceaða*). Yet others concern the patient's prospects for recovery, with disturbing disagreements; one old text assures us that a person who falls sick on the 6th lune will live, another in both Latin and English that he will not escape.

Unlucky lunes in calendar months
To make matters worse, it was sometimes said that particular lunes were unlucky within each calendar month; thus according to an Old English text now in the British Library,

There are two days in the month such that whatever one begins on those days will never be accomplished: in January, when the moon is 3 nights old and 4, in February 5 and 7, in March 6 and 7, in April 5 and 8, in May 8 and 9, in June 5 and 17, in July 3 and 13, in August 8 and 13, in September 5 and 9, in October 5 and 15, in November 7 and 9, in December 3 and 12; and so take heed who will.

A reassurance
It will be clear even from the texts cited that those who maintained the existence of unlucky days were not agreed on which days they were; moreover, the usual carelessness of scribes and printers, especially where numbers are concerned, subject any given list to unintended variations. It would therefore be unwise to be deterred from any business

by prognostication; furthermore, as John Aubrey observes, the differences between calendars make nonsense of superstitions concerning unlucky days:

Now, the Calendars of these computers are very different; ye Greekes dissenting from the Latins, & the Latins from each other, y^t one observing ye Julian, the other ye Gregorian account; now this latter account by ten dayes at least anticipateth the others: yet in the several calculations ye same events seeme true, and men with equal opinion of verity, expect, and confesse a confirmation from them all. Whereby is evident the oraculous authority of tradition, and the easie seduction of Men, neither enquiring into ye verity of the substance, nor reforming upon repugnance of circumstance. And thus may divers be mistaken who superstitiously observe certain times, or set down unto themselves an observation of unfortunate months, or daies, or houres; as did the Ægyptians, two in every month, and the Romans the days after the Nones, Ides, and Calends. And thus the Rules of Navigators must often fail, setting down, as Rhodiginus observeth, suspected and ominous daies in every Month, as the first and seventh of March, the fifth and sixth of April, the twelfth and fifteenth of February. For the accounts hereof in these months are very different in our daies, and were different with several nations in ages past.   Aubrey, 94

We shall do better to follow William Horman, *Vulgaria* (1519), fo. 19^r, 'I set nat a button by dismolde dayes', and reckon all days to be lucky, and the luckiest time of all to be pudding-time:

The *Pudding* is a Dish very difficult to be describ'd, because of the several Sorts there are of it; Flower, Milk, Eggs, Butter, Sugar, Suet, Marrow, Raisins, &c. &c. are the most common Ingredients of a *Pudding*. They bake them in an Oven, they boil them with Meat, they make them fifty several Ways: BLESSED BE HE THAT INVENTED *PUDDING*, for it is a Manna that hits the Palates of all Sorts of People; a Manna, better than that of the Wilderness, because the People are never weary of it. Ah, what an excellent Thing is an *English Pudding! To come in Pudding-time*, is as much as to say, to come in the most lucky Moment in the World. Give an *English* Man a *Pudding*, and he shall think it a noble Treat in any Part of the World.

Misson de Valbourg, 315 (1719)

When George in pudding-time came o'er.
'The Vicar of Bray', st. 5, l. 1

DOG DAYS

These days were notable as the hottest days of the year, when dogs were 'most ready to run mad' (Philemon Holland, translating the Elder Pliny). There is no agreed account, ancient or modern, of their beginning or ending: Pliny in one place speaks of Sirius entering Leo on 18 August, in another of its rising on 4 July in Egypt, and the 17th in Italy; sometimes they are reckoned from the heliacal, sometimes from the cosmical rising (see *3 July), and sometimes the star used is not Sirius but Procyon. Nevertheless, the name is regularly used for the hottest time of the year:

Also there are fifty Canicular or dog daies, that is to say, from the fifteenth Kalender [*sic*] of August, to the Nonas of September, in the which daies it is forbidden by Astronomy to all manner of folkes to let blood, or take physicke, yea, it is good to abstaine from women: for why, all that time raigneth a starre, that is called Caniculacanis [*sic*] in Latin, a Hound in English: now of the foresaid starre Canicula, the foresaid fifty dayes are called Canicular dayes, and biting as a Bitch: for the kind of the star Canicula is boyling, and brenning as fier, and biting as a bitch whelpe: that time the heate of the Sunne, and of the Starre is so feruent and violent, that mens bodies at midnight sweat as at mid-day, and swelleth lightly, gloweth and brenneth: and if they then be hurt, they be more sicke than at any other time, very neere dead. In these daies all venimous serpents creepe, flie, and gender, and so they ouerset hugely the aire in seeding of their kind; so that many men are dead thereby. In these dayes a fier is good, night and day, and wholsome: seeth your meates, and take heed of feeding violently.

'Godfridus', The knowledge of things vnknowne, 20

> Husband give me my due, the woman saies;
> The man replies, 'Tis naught Wife these Dog daies;
> But she rejoyns, Let women have their rights,
> Though there be Dog daies, there are no Dog nights.
>
> Poor Robin (1675)

Writing in 1864, Robert Chambers views the dog days with scepticism, especially since at that time the mean temperature during July was 61 °F (16 °C):

The great heat of the month led to a superstition among the Romans: they conceived that this pre-eminent warmth, and the diseases and other calamities flowing from it, were somehow connected with the rising and setting of the star Canicula—the Little Dog—in coincidence with the sun. They accordingly conferred the name of DOG-DAYS upon the period between the 3d of July and the 11th of August. . . . The utter baselessness of the Roman superstition has been well shewn by the ordinary processes of nature, for Canicula does not now rise in coincidence with the sun till the latter end of August, while, of course, the days between 3d July and 11th August are what they have ever been. Dr Hutton, remarking how the heliacal rising of Canicula is getting later and later every year in all latitudes, says that, on the Roman principle, the star may in time come to be charged with bringing frost and snow. Yet the *Dog-days* continues to be a popular phrase, and probably will long continue so. It is undoubtedly under some lingering regard for the old notion, as much as from a consideration of the effect of extreme heat upon canine flesh and blood, that magistrates of towns so often order dogs to be muzzled about the beginning of July.

Chambers (July)

THE WESTERN CHURCH
YEAR: MOVEABLE FEASTS

The Western church year begins with Advent Sunday and focuses on two major feasts: Christmas, based on the solar calendar, and Easter, based on the lunar calendar. Although the date of Christmas is fixed, the beginning of Advent varies, according to the day of the week, or 'feria', on which Christmas falls. Similarly, the number of Sundays that follow the last feast based on the Easter cycle, Trinity Sunday, is variable. We include in this section all events in the Church Year that cannot be fixed to an exact day, and also secular events, such as Plough Monday and Carnival, that depend on the date of Church feasts.

The liturgical year prescribed in the Book of Common Prayer is a simplified form of the English medieval rite, developed at Salisbury Cathedral and known as the Use of Sarum: Sundays that are not themselves feasts are numbered within their period, as 'in Advent', 'after Christmas', 'after the Epiphany', 'in Lent', 'after Easter', and 'after Trinity'. In the Middle Ages they were frequently identified by their introits at mass (see also App. C). Moreover, the day falling one week after most important feasts (though not Trinity) was called the 'Octave' (i.e. eighth day, counting inclusively) of the feast; any day falling between feast and Octave, whether a Sunday or not, was known as '[day of the week] within the Octave of [feast]'. (The next seven days are referred to as the 'quindene'; however, the quindene of Easter is sometimes the fortnight comprising Holy Week and Easter Week.) Before the reform of 1969, the RC Church retained the medieval Roman rite as modified after the Council of Trent; the main difference from Sarum practice was that, except in some Orders, Sundays were numbered after Pentecost rather than Trinity, a feast not made universal till 1334. Since 1969, however, it has designated the periods from the first Sunday after Epiphany to Lent, and from Pentecost to Advent, as 'Ordinary Time'; those Sundays falling within Ordinary Time and not being feasts in their own right (the first Sunday, for example, is the Baptism of Our Lord) are called the so-manyeth Sunday in Ordinary Time, or 'of the Year' (see also below, *The Pre-Lenten Season*, *Sundays after Trinity or after Pentecost*). In addition, the Sundays after Easter have now become Sundays 'of Easter', and are therefore numbered from second to seventh; CY follows suit.

The ASB introduced a new system beginning at the fifth Sunday before Advent; this and the following four Sundays were styled the ninth to fifth 'before Christmas'. This has not been retained in CY. Other peculiarities of those books are noted in the appropriate place.

The Lutheran church year is similar to that of the BCP, but designates Sundays from *Estomihi* (Quinquagesima) to *Exaudi* (the Sunday after Ascension) by Latin names. These are mostly the same as the mass introits; differences will be pointed out below.

ADVENT

Advent (from *Adventus*, 'coming') is the beginning of the Western Church year. Formerly a fast season, it is a period of penitence leading up to Christmas, and is sometimes called 'St Martin's Lent'. It begins on the Sunday nearest 30 November (the feast of St Andrew), at the earliest 27 November, at the latest 3 December, and ends with Christmas. (In the Ambrosian rite, Advent begins the Sunday after 11 November.) An old rule for finding the first Sunday in Advent runs:

> Saint Andrew the king,
> Three weeks and three days before Christmas comes in;
> Three days after, or three days before,
> Advent Sunday knocks at the door.

More precisely, the date of Advent in the Roman rite (retained by the CofE) depends on the feria of 1 January:

1 January	Advent	
	Common year	Leap year
Sunday	3 December	2 December
Monday	2 December	1 December
Tuesday	1 December	30 November
Wednesday	30 November	29 November
Thursday	29 November	28 November
Friday	28 November	27 November
Saturday	27 November	3 December

In Germany, according to Naogeorgus, the Thursdays in Advent were considered unlucky days. Children went carolling and girls undertook divinations to learn their future husbands (cf. *29 Nov.):

> Three weekes before the day whereon was borne the Lorde of grace,
> And on the Thursday Boyes and Girles do runne in every place,
> And bounce and beate at every doore, with blowes and lustie snaps,
> And crie, the advent of the Lorde not borne as yet perhaps.
> And wishing to the neighbours all, that in the houses dwell,
> A happie yeare, and every thing to spring and prosper well:
> Here have they peares, and plumbs, and pence, ech man gives willinglee,
> For these three nightes are always thought, unfortunate to bee:

Wherein they are afrayde of sprites, and cankred witches spight,
And dreadfull devils blacke and grim, that then have chiefest might.
In these same dayes young wanton Gyrles that meete for mariage bee,
Doe search to know the names of them that shall their husbandes bee.
Foure Onyons, five, or eight, they take and make in every one,
Such names as they do fansie most, and best do thinke upon.
Thus neere the Chimney them they set, and that same Onyon than,
That first doth sproute, doth surely beare the name of their good man.
Their husbandes nature eke they seeke to know, and all his guise,
When as the Sunne hath hid himselfe, and left the starried skies,
Unto some woodstacke do they go, and while they there do stande,
Eche one drawes out a faggot sticke, the next that commes to hande,
Which if it streight and even be, and have no knots at all,
A gentle husband then they thinke shall surely to them fall.
But if it fowle and crooked be, and knottie here and theare
A crabbed churlish husband then, they earnestly do feare.

> Naogeorgus, fo. 44ᵛ

Bible Sunday. The BCP collect for the second Sunday in Advent is a prayer so to hear all holy Scriptures, 'read, mark, learn, and inwardly digest', as to 'embrace and ever hold fast the blessed hope of everlasting life'; the Epistle (as in the Roman service) is on the same theme, from Rom. 15: 4–13. This has earned it the name of 'Bible Sunday'. The collect is retained in ASB, but CY recommends that Bible Sunday be kept on some other day, such as the Last Sunday after Trinity.

The Greater or 'O' Antiphons. On 17 December (16 Dec. in the Sarum rite, 15 Dec. in medieval Paris and Tours) the Greater or 'O' Antiphons begin; one is sung each evening before and after the Magnificat at vespers in the seven days preceding Christmas Eve (eight days in the Sarum rite, nine in the Parisian). Each of the antiphons begins with the word 'O':

	Roman	Sarum	Parisian	Tours (*Bibl. Mun.*, MS 150, Breviary 14/15 c.)
15			O Sapientia	O Sapientia
16		O Sapientia	O Adonai	O Adonai
17	O Sapientia	O Adonai	O Radix Jesse	O Radix Jesse
18	O Adonai	O Radix Jesse	O Clavis David	O Clavis David
19	O Radix Jesse	O Clavis David	O Oriens	O Oriens
20	O Clavis David	O Oriens	O Rex gentium	[nothing]
21	O Oriens	O Rex gentium	O Sancte sanctorum	O Rex gentium
22	O Rex gentium	O Emmanuel	O Emmanuel	O Emmanuel
23	O Emmanuel	O Virgo virginum	O Domine fac mirabilia	O Virgo virginum

Reading the second letters of the original seven antiphons backwards yields the acrostic ERO CRAS: 'I shall be [with you] tomorrow.'

Ember Week of Advent. Three days of fasting were set down for Ember Week of Advent: the Wednesday, Friday, and Saturday after St Lucy (13 Dec.). These form the first group of Ember Days, of which there are four in the year, marking the *Quattuor Tempora* or Four Seasons: these were ordained by Pope Callistus I (*c*.220), and the dates defined by the Council of Piacenza in 1093, and in BCP, as the Wednesday, Friday, and Saturday:

(in winter)   on or after St Lucy (13 Dec.)
(in spring)   after the first Sunday in Lent
(in summer)   after Whit Sunday
(in autumn)   on or after Holy Cross Day (14 Sept.)

They were fast-days, hence the composer Josquin des Prez's inscription *Vous jeûnerez les quatre temps*, denoting a rest of four breves (*tempora*) before the canonic voice enters in his *Missa de Beata Virgine*. The Ember Days, like the Rogation Days, are included among the 'Days of Fasting, or Abstinence' in BCP, but not among the 'Days of Discipline and Self-Denial' in ASB or CY; in 1969 the RC Church replaced them with days of prayer at times and purposes to be determined regionally. Fasting apart, Embertide has been the traditional season for ordinations, which in RC tradition were conducted on Ember Saturdays, and in the Church of England on the following Sundays. Owing to changes in ordination practice the ASB reallocated the winter, summer, and autumn Ember Days to the weeks respectively preceding the third Sunday in Advent, the Sunday nearest SS Peter and Paul (29 June), and the Sunday nearest Michaelmas; CY designates these as the traditional dates, but 'encourages' the diocesan bishop to set them in the week before ordination.

Although fasting at first meant abstaining from food throughout the day, in later times it was satisfied if one ate no more than one main meal a day and abstained from flesh. In the RC Church fasting, now obligatory only on Ash Wednesday and Good Friday, was distinguished from abstinence (not eating meat) in 1781. Not everyone regarded fasts as an unpleasant obligation. For Montaigne it was more of a penance to eat meat:

I am a great lover of Fish, and consequently make my *Fasts Feasts*, and my *Feasts Fasts*; and I believe what some People say, that it is more easie of digestion than Flesh. As I make a Conscience of eating Flesh upon Fish-days, so does my Taste make a Conscience of mixing Fish and Flesh, the difference betwixt them seems to me to be too great to do so. From my Youth I have us'd sometimes to be out of the way at Supper, either to sharpen my Appetite against the next Morning, (for as *Epicurus* fasted and made lean Meals to accustom his Pleasure to make shift without abundance, I on the contrary do it to prepare my Pleasure to make better and more chearful use of abundance) or else I fasted to preserve my Vigour for the Service of some Action of Body or Mind or to cure my sick Stomach, and for want of fit Company. For I say as the same *Epicurus* did, that a Man is not so much to regard what he eats, as with whom; and commend *Chilo*, that he would not engage himself to be at *Periander's* Feast, till he first was inform'd who were to be the other *Guests*.   Montaigne, *Essays*, 3. 13 (iii. 535–6)

THE CHRISTMAS SEASON

The following feasts are discussed under the Calendar Year:

25 December	Christmas Day
26 December	St Stephen's Day
27 December	St John the Evangelist's Day
28 December	Holy Innocents' Day
1 January	Circumcision (RC since 1969 Solemnity of Mary, Mother of God)
6 January	Epiphany

Sundays after Christmas (CY 'of Christmas'). When Christmas falls on any day but Sunday, there is a Sunday after Christmas, between it and 1 January; when it falls on any day from Wednesday to Saturday there is a second preceding Epiphany. Since 1969 the Sunday between Christmas and 1 January has been dedicated in the RC Church to the Holy Family, a feast originally instituted by Benedict XV in 1921 for the Sunday after Epiphany; when Christmas falls on Sunday, the Holy Family is feasted on Friday, 30 December.

Monday after Epiphany ('Plough Monday'). Twelfth Night marked the end of the Christmas season for farmers; the all-important task of ploughing the land began immediately afterwards. In the thirteenth century the return to work was often begun with a plough race, or—reminiscent of pagan customs—drawing a plough around a fire. By the mid-fifteenth century the holiday season did not end until the Sunday after Epiphany, and the following Monday became 'Plough Monday'. It developed into an occasion for raising money and for tomfoolery, and took the specific form of mumming, sometimes accompanied by a sword-dance. One ploughman dressed as a woman ('Bessy') and was accompanied by Beelzebub or a fool; various localities had their own characters, and texts of many of the plays have been recorded. A collection box was passed; if no appreciation was shown, in coin or refreshment, the plough ceased being a prop and was pressed into action.

Plough Monday was vigorously celebrated into the nineteenth century and has experienced revivals in the twentieth. Chambers records the reminiscences of a Lincolnshire man in 1864:

Rude though it was, the Plough procession threw a life into the dreary scenery of winter, as it came winding along the quiet rutted lanes, on its way from one village to another; for the ploughmen from many a surrounding thorpe, hamlet, and lonely farm-house united in the celebration of Plough Monday. It was nothing unusual for at least a score of the 'sons of the soil' to yoke themselves with ropes to the plough, having put on clean smock-frocks in honour of the day. There was no limit to the number who joined in the morris-dance, and were partners with 'Bessy', who carried the money-box; and all these had ribbons in their hats and pinned about them wherever there was room to display a bunch. . . . The rubbishy verses they recited are not worth preserving beyond the line which graces many a public-house sign of 'God speed the plough'. At the large farm-house, besides money they obtained refreshment, and through the quantity of ale they thus drank during the day, managed to get what they called 'their load' by night. Even the poorest cottagers dropped a few pence into Bessy's box.

But the great event of the day was when they came before some house which bore signs that the owner was well-to-do in the world, and nothing was given to them. Bessy rattled his box and the ploughmen danced, while the country lads blew their bullocks' horns, or shouted with all their might; but if there was still no sign, no coming forth of either bread-and-cheese or ale, then the word was given, the ploughshare driven into the ground before the door or window, the whole twenty men yoked pulling like one, and in a minute or two the ground before the house was as brown, barren, and ridgy as a newly-ploughed field.... We are not aware that the ploughmen were ever summoned to answer for such a breach of the law, for they believe, to use their own expressive language, 'they can stand by it, and no law in the world can touch 'em, 'cause it's an old charter'; and we are sure it would spoil their 'folly to be wise'.   Chambers (11 Jan.)

THE PRE-LENTEN SEASON

Sundays after Epiphany. The Sundays between Epiphany and Septuagesima are numbered in the Church of England and by Lutherans as Sundays after Epiphany; depending on the date of Easter, there are between two and six Sundays if 1 January falls on Sunday, Monday, Friday, Saturday, or in leap year also on Thursday, between one and five if it falls on Tuesday, Wednesday, or, in a common year, Thursday. Before 1970 the RC Church used a similar reckoning, though the first Sunday was called the 'Octave of Epiphany' when it fell on 13 January, and otherwise 'Sunday within the octave of Epiphany'. Since 1969 the Sundays 'in Ordinary Time' begin with the Sunday after Epiphany, or Baptism of Our Lord, and continue to the last Sunday before Lent, formerly called 'Quinquagesima'. Depending on the date of Easter, the number of Sundays in Ordinary Time ranges from five to nine if 1 January falls on Sunday, Monday, Friday, Saturday, or in leap year also on Thursday, four to eight if it falls on Tuesday, Wednesday, or, in a common year, Thursday.

CY divides the pre-Lenten period into two at the Presentation (2 Feb.). Before that date Sundays are counted 'of', not 'after', so that when 6 January is a Sunday, the 13th is 'the second Sunday of Epiphany'; there are three such Sundays when Epiphany falls on a Monday, otherwise four. After the Presentation, Ordinary Time is said to begin, and last till Ash Wednesday before resuming on the Monday after Pentecost; pre-Lenten Ordinary Time may be as little as one day, when Easter falls on 22 March and consequently Ash Wednesday is on 4 February. However, the term is not used for designating Sundays, which are counted 'before Lent'; the number ranges from none to five.

Septuagesima, the third Sunday before Lent, sometimes known from the mass introit as *Circumdederunt*. The word is Latin for 'seventieth (day)'; like Sexagesima ('sixtieth') it is arithmetically false, but was imposed to make a series with Quinquagesima and Quadragesima. Like these terms, it is no longer officially used in the RC Church, which simply reckons them as Sundays in Ordinary Time; the ASB reckoned this as the ninth Sunday before Easter, Sexagesima and Quinquagesima being respectively the eighth and seventh. In CY these days have no set name.

Sexagesima, the second Sunday before Lent (introit *Exsurge Domine* or *Commovisti Domine terram*).

Carnival is celebrated in the days before Lent, though a more extended carnival season begins or has begun earlier, especially in Italy: on St Antony Abbot's day (17 Jan.) or (in the theatre) on St Stephen's day (26 Dec.); in Cologne on St Martin's day (11 Nov.). It is mainly a southern European institution, spectacularly exported to Trinidad and Rio de Janeiro. The Italian name *carnevale* is shortened from *carnelevale*, a corruption of Italian *carne levare*, 'to take away meat'; in the same sense Latin has *carniprivium*, Spanish *carnestolendas* for 'Shrovetide', from Latin *ad carnes tollendas*. A synonym *carnasciale*, from *carne lasciare*, 'to leave off meat', gave its name to the *canti carnascialeschi* or carnival songs of fifteenth-century Florence. The licensed misrule was assisted by masks, and by an etiquette that forbade recognition of the wearers; elaborate carnival masks are still seen in Venice. In Cologne, *Karneval* became associated with political satire against the unwelcome Prussian rulers; further south, in Alemannic territory, it is an expulsion of winter. The corresponding term in Bavaria and Austria is *Fasching*, from *Fastschank*, 'pour(ing) of the fast(-tide drink)'. It never reached England or northern France even before the Reformation; but the seven days from Wednesday after Sexagesima to Shrove Tuesday were called *duivelsweek* in Flemish. Because the experience of carnival on the Continent was so different from Shrovetide in England and northern countries, visitors to Italy often remark on it in detail.

As observed by the Baron de Pollnitz in Rome in 1731:

Thanks to God, the Carnival is ended; I say, Thanks to God, because it was to me very tiresom, tho' it lasted here, according to an establish'd Custom, but a Week. During all that Time, from Two o'Clock in the Afternoon till Sun-set, all the Streets were full of Masquers, some on Foot, and some in open Chaises: The former say a thousand silly Things, and the latter throw Meslin in one another's Eyes by Handfuls; but the best on't is, that either by their Cloaths, or their Equipage, every body is known. Besides, the Pageantry of the *Romans* is always the same, even in Masquerades; they dress up their Domestics like Harlequins, and make them follow them with their Faces bare. They thus take the Air gravely in open Chariots made like Gondolas. Their Horses are adorn'd with Plumes of Feathers, and loaded with little Bells like ours in the Sled Races. In the Evening the Coaches range themselves in two Rows in the Street *del Corso*, which is besides pretty narrow, and there they see the Race of Barbs, which are five or six Horses, that are suffer'd to run loose without a Rider, from the Gate *del Popolo* to a Place beyond the *Venetian* Palace. The poor Beasts gallop thro' the Shouts and Cries of the Populace, and are often crippled by striking themselves against the Coaches. The first of these Horses that reaches the Goal wins a Prize for his Master, which generally consists of a Piece of Cloth of Gold, and at Sun-set every body retires. Mean time a *Roman* will tell you, that the Carnival of Rome is the finest in the World.   Pollnitz, ii. 59–60

As observed by Horace Walpole in Florence in 1740:

Florence, February 27, 1740, N.S.
I have found a little unmasqued moment to write to you; but for this week past I have been so muffled up in my domino, that I have not had the command of my elbows. But what have you been doing all the mornings? Could you not write then?—No, then I was masqued too; I have done nothing but slip out of my domino into bed, and out of bed into my domino. The end of

the Carnival is frantic, bacchanalian; all the morn one makes parties in masque to the shops and coffee-houses, and all the evening to the operas and balls. *Then have I danced, good gods! how have I danced!* The Italians are fond to a degree of our country dances: *Cold and raw* they only know by the tune; *Blowzybella* is almost Italian, and *Buttered peas* is *Pizelli al buro*. There are but three days more; but the two last are to have balls all the morning at the fine unfinished palace of the Strozzi; and the Tuesday night a masquerade after supper: they sup first, to eat *gras*, and not encroach upon Ash-Wednesday. What makes masquerading more agreeable here than in England, is the great deference that is showed to the disguised. Here they do not catch at those little dirty opportunities of saying any ill-natured thing they know of you, do not abuse you because they may, or talk gross bawdy to a woman of quality. I found the other day, by a play of Etheridge's, that we have had a sort of Carnival even since the Reformation; 'tis in '*She would if She could,*' they talk of going a-mumming in Shrove-tide.   Horace Walpole to Richard West (Walpole, 15–16)

Carnival in Rome in 1843, as seen by a young English Quaker:

The afternoon & evening was devoted to the magnificent fooling of the Carnival. Being the last day it was at its wildest pitch of excitement, amidst all, however, I saw no blackguardism, no drunkenness, no quarrelling. All was abandon & revelry. Garofalini's kindness procured me an excellent place in a balcony on the Corso at the house of Signr. Cecci, a Banker. Sham sugar plums, consisting of grains of corn with a coating of flour baked hard, were flying in showers from the windows on the unlucky carriage loads of English aristocracy & Italian figurantes. Nosegays were thrown to the donnas, who honoured the cavaliers with the same attention. Devils walked the street, arm in arm; harlequins with blown bladders banged passengers between the shoulders indiscriminately. One figure was in scale armour of laurel leaves, another as Hercules in a flesh coloured light suit, apparently quite naked with a club & a garland of flowers, & an Indian chief. All were mingling together in the same spirit of unrestrained hilarity. . . . The imaginative character of the Italians peculiarly fits them for a thing of this sort. I leaned against a column & watched the motley movement, & thought I could have sustained a character better than some bungling Englishmen I saw there. At 11 all was quiet. The Carnival was over.

Fox, 310–11

In some places in southern France, on Ash Wednesday the trial and condemnation of Carnival (a stuffed figure, along the lines of the Guy) took place:

His advent has been celebrated by songs, and cries of joy; but, woful example of the fluctuations of popular favour, he is now exposed to the hatred of the same persons who exalted him to the skies a few days ago. He is a fallen monarch, and his reign is ended. At a fixed hour, which has been loudly announced beforehand, a crowd of masks throng into a theatre prepared the previous day. The judges take their seats, the advocates are at their posts. The unhappy *Carnival* arrives on a cart drawn by an ass, and surrounded by *gendarmes*, and most grotesquely dressed. He is lifted into his place—the accusation is made—the witnesses against him examined; he is defended by his lawyers, but in vain. He is condemned to an ignominious death—usually to the double torture of fire and water. Some of the by-standers address him in mocking songs, others deplore his fate. In this manner he is conducted to the bridge, when, after a harangue suited to the gravity of his function, the president of the court executes the sentence he has himself pronounced, by setting fire to the accused's clothes, and precipitating him thus flaming into the river.

Eyre, 218–19 (from F. Rivarès, *Chansons et airs populaires de Béarn*)

SHROVETIDE

Shrovetide is the period immediately preceding Lent, commonly Shrove Tuesday and the two preceding days, although in some places it extends back to the previous Thursday. 'Shrove' comes from 'shriving'—confession and absolution—that took place before Ash Wednesday. Different days in different places were regarded as the appropriate day on which to eat up non-Lenten food. Some of the names given to the days preceding Ash Wednesday are the following:

Fat Thursday (French *jeudi gras*). The Irish diarist Humphrey O'Sullivan records Fat Thursday of Shrovetide, *Déardaoin mhéith na hInide*; *Inid* from Latin *initium* originally denoted the beginning of Lent (see below), but was later extended to Shrovetide. At Cologne it is *Weiberfastnacht*, when women are allowed to indulge in horseplay; a favourite activity is cutting men's ties.

Egg-Saturday, formerly at Oxford the Saturday before Quinquagesima, and still recorded in the Oxford Almanack as the *Festum Ovorum*.

Quinquagesima, the Sunday before Lent (introit *Esto mihi*, and still called *Estomihi* by Lutherans), the fiftieth (Lat. *quinquagesima*) day before Easter, counted inclusively according to the ancient custom. The day was formerly known as *carniprivium clericorum*, 'Clerics' Carnival', in medieval German *der herren vassnacht*, because the clergy indulged themselves before beginning Lenten fast two days earlier than the laity; Irish names are 'Whispering Sunday' (*Domhnach na Cogarnaí*), from the matchmaking that took place at this time, or 'Tippling Sunday' (*Domhnach na Diúgaireachta*, lit. 'Sunday of draining to the last drop'). Around this time the Roman festival on Monte Testaccio took place. The English cleric Adam Usk, who was in Rome in 1405, describes the barbarous custom with some distaste:

Around Quinquagesima Sunday the Romans assemble for their games, drawn up in armed bodies under the heads of the districts, all eagerly competing to win the prize—for, as St Paul said, 'they which run in a race run all,' etc. Three large silver rings are fastened to a rope high off the ground, and they charge their horses at them trying to run their lances through the rings and thus win them. The senator, the two conservators, and the seven regents of the city are also present at the games, attended by much pomp, standing behind the block and axe used for beheading those guilty of sedition. During these games the Romans indulge, like the sons of Belial and Belphegor, in incessant drinking and bestial licentiousness, so that it is in truth an orgy of misery. Then on the Sunday itself, at the Jews' expense, four carts, covered with scarlet cloth and containing eight live boars, are yoked to eight wild bulls and taken to the top of 'the mountain of all earth'—so-called because it is made of earth brought from every part of the world, as a sign of universal lordship—and when the carts come down the hill they break up, and the animals are set free, whereupon it all becomes spoil for the Romans to fight over, and everyone rushes about madly attacking the beasts with whatever weapon he has. Anybody who fails to bring home a piece of the spoil for his wife is regarded as a failure and a fool, and is not allowed to lie with her until the feast of St Pancras [12 May]. And all this commotion is accompanied by a great deal of killing and beating, especially of the courtiers, whom the Romans hate because of what they do to their wives and daughters. Following this three cloths are fastened to the points of lances, the first made of gold for the best horses, the second of silver for the second best, and the third of silk for the fastest mares; and whichever rider gets to each of them first carries it away as his prize. And then eventually they all leave off attacking the animals and swagger off pretentiously to see their wives, some with little bits of animal, and others with innards or dung, on the ends of their swords.   Usk, 195–7

Collop Monday or Fat Monday, the Monday before Lent (collop = bacon and eggs: 'from the primitive custom of regaling with eggs on *collops* or *pieces of bread*, which the less scrupulous, and more luxurious moderns, have extended to *collops of meat*': Brady, i. 211–12); also called *Egg Monday*, *Rosenmontag* ('Rose Monday').

Shrove Tuesday, *Mardi Gras*, *Veilchendienstag* (Violet Tuesday), the Tuesday before Western Lent. An old name is 'Gut-tide', from 'good tide', but popularly associated with the guts, this being the last chance to eat well till Easter:

And this furnishyng of our bellies with delicates, that we vse on fastingham tuiesday, what tyme some eate tyl they be enforsed to forbeare all again, sprong of Bacchus feastes, that were celebrated in Rome with great ioy and deliciouse fare.   Polydore Vergil, v. ii (1546)

In Irish called *Máirt na Smut*, 'Sulky Tuesday', from the discontent of girls who had failed to find a husband before Lent, a closed season for marriage (cf. under *Quinquagesima* and *Quadragesima*).

Shrove Tuesday was formerly celebrated with cock-fighting and cock-throwing, against which cruelties, already in decline, Brady fulminates at length (i. 212–13); similar atrocities appear to have occurred in the Spanish carnival, at which a *rey de gallos* was appointed to ride in front of the revellers. Cock-fighting was often carried out surreptitiously:

A Cock-Pit is the very Model of an *Amphi-Theatre* of the Antients; the Cocks fight in the *Area* as the Beasts did formerly amongst the *Romans*; and round the Circle above, sit the Spectators in their several Rows. It's wonderful to see the Courage of these little Creatures, who always hold fighting on 'till one of them drops, and dies on the Spot. . . .

There is always a continued Noise amongst the Spectators, in laying Wagers upon every Blow each Cock gives; who, by the way, I must tell you, wear *Steel Spurs*, (called, I think, *Gafflets*) for their surer Execution. And this Noise runs fluctuating backwards and forwards during each Battel, which is a great Amusement; and, I believe, abundance of People get Money by taking, and laying Odds on each Stroke; and find their Account in the end of the Battel; but these are People that must nicely understand it.   from a letter dated 17 October 1713, in Macky, i. 93–4

Shrove Tuesday was also the day when traditionally the apprentices ran wild through the city, raiding brothels and theatres:

> You doe abuse the *Time*. These are fit freedomes
> For lawless Prentices, on a Shrove tuesday,
> When they compell the *Time* to serve their riot:
> For drunken Wakes, and strutting Beare-baytings,
> That savour only of their owne abuses.
>
> Ben Jonson, *Time Vindicated*, 253–7

When Shrove Tuesday was still a time for shriving, or confessing, a bell was rung to summon all to church. With the passage of time this was transmuted into the 'pancake bell', the signal to begin making pancakes, to use up eggs and milk before the long Lenten fast.

ALL. The Pancake bell rings, the pancake bel, tri-lill my hearts . . .

FIRKE. O musical bel stil! O Hodge, O my brethren! theres cheere for the heavens, venison pasties walke up and downe piping hote, like sergeants, beefe and brewesse comes marching in drie fattes, fritters and pancakes come trowling in wheele baurowe, hennes and orenges hopping in porters baskets, colloppes and egges in scuttles, and tartes and custardes comes quavering in in mault shovels.

Thomas Dekker, *The Shoomakers Holy-day* (1610), v. ii

Pancake races still take place in several towns. Most are of recent origin, but that in Olney (near Milton Keynes in Buckinghamshire) traces its origins back to 1445. Women, who must have lived in the town for at least three months, wear aprons and bonnets, and must toss their pancakes at least three times during the dash from Market Square to the church. The prize is a new prayer-book, and the race is followed by a church service.

The Pancake Greaze at Westminster School, reported in the *Gentleman's Magazine*, 1790, was still going strong more than seventy years later, and indeed continues today in much the same form (but the pancake is inedible):

At Westminster School, the following custom is observed to this day [1864]:—At 11 o'clock a.m. a verger of the Abbey, in his gown, bearing a silver bâton, emerges from the college kitchen, followed by the cook of the school, in his white apron, jacket, and cap, and carrying a pancake. On arriving at the school-room door, he announces himself, 'The cook'; and having entered the school-room, he advances to the bar which separates the upper school from the lower one, twirls the pancake in the pan, and then tosses it over the bar into the upper school, among a crowd of boys, who scramble for the pancake; and he who gets it unbroken, and carries it to the deanery, demands the honorarium of a guinea (sometimes two guineas) from the Abbey funds, though the custom is not mentioned in the Abbey statutes: the cook also receives two guineas for his performance.

Chambers (9 Feb.)

In the Isles of Scilly in the mid-eighteenth century all three customs were combined:

On a *Shrove Tuesday* each Year after the throwing at *Cocks* is over, the Boys of this Island have a Custom of throwing Stones, in the Evening, against the Doors of the Dwellers Houses; a Privilege they claim Time immemorial, and put in Practice without Controul, for finishing the Day's Sport. I could never learn from whence this Custom took its Rise, but am informed that the same Custom is now used in several Provinces of *Spain*, as well as in some parts of *Cornwall*. The Terms demanded, by the Boys, are *Pancakes*, or *Money*, to capitulate. Some of the older Sort, exceeding the Bounds of this whimsical Toleration, in the Dusk of the Evening, set a bolted Door, or Window-shutter at Liberty, by battering in Breach with large Pieces of *Rock Stones*; which sometimes makes a Job for the *Surgeon*, as well as for the *Smith*, *Glazier*, and *Carpenter*. And the Way of making *Reprisal*, in such Cases, is by a *Rope* drawn cross the Way of these mischievous and masked Batteries, by which they dismount their heavy Artillery, making them ascend off their Carriages, into the Air, to return with their own Weight.

Heath, 127–8 (1750)

Skipping is one of the odder Shrovetide customs that survive. In Scarborough, on Shrove Tuesday, residents flock to the foreshore bearing ropes. Skipping, which used to take place on the beach, now occupies the whole road, and motorists must be patient.

Another long-standing custom is the Shrove Tuesday ball game in Sedgefield (Co. Durham), where rival teams struggle for control of a cricket ball, which must be 'alleyed' in one of the village springs before 5 p.m.; the holder of the ball is then entitled to free beer in every pub. The 'Goteddesse Day' (cf. 'Gut-tide's Day') football match in Chester was converted to a runners' race after excessive violence.

Carnival to most Americans means Mardi Gras, a festival with a grand parade of floats, elaborate costumes, and dancing in the streets. New Orleans is the most famous venue, reflecting the French inheritance of Louisiana. A similar and much-loved celebration takes place in Trinidad. Rio de Janeiro's carnival is even more spectacular, and attracts visitors from around the world in search of exoticism and excess.

LENT

Lent: the Old English *lencten*, 'spring'; German *Fastenzeit*; French *carême*, etc. = Quadragesima, 'fortieth', cf. Greek *Megalē Tesserakostē*, a name commemorating the forty days for which Moses, Elijah, and Jesus are said to have fasted. 'Forty', however, was originally intended as an indefinite term for 'many'; correspondingly, the name was already in use by the fourth century for the pre-paschal fast, which, though longer than the one or two days attested for the second century, might last only a fortnight or three weeks. By late antiquity the prevailing Western custom was to keep six weeks of fast (excepting Sundays) between Quadragesima and Easter, amounting to thirty-six days (the tithe of the year); the Insular Easter calendar or Latercus (see App. J) placed the *initium* or beginning of Lent two days later, on the Wednesday forty days (inclusively) before Easter, but when the Roman calculation was accepted it was moved back to Quadragesima. This six-week fast remained the Mozarabic practice, and also survived in the Ambrosian rite of Milan (the four extra days of carnival being known as *il Carnevalone*), but in the eighth-century 'Gelasian Sacramentary' (see *21 Nov.) the forty days were made up by beginning on Ash Wednesday (a week before the original Celtic *initium*). It is this practice that became the norm.

A Spanish proverb runs:

La cárcel y la cuaresma   Prison and Lent
para los pobres es hecha.   are made for the poor.

The original rule was to eat only one meal a day, after vespers, and that without fish, meat, eggs, or milk products (*lacticinia*, also called 'whitemeats' in English) such as butter and cheese. In the West many of these restrictions were set aside, especially the prohibition on fish; by the end of the Middle Ages food was taken at noon (vespers having been celebrated in the morning) and milk products were generally permitted (but see below under *Ash Wednesday*). Elizabethan parliaments in England attempted simultaneously to suppress the doctrine of abstention as a popish superstition and to enforce the practice in behalf of the fishing-fleet; they were more successful in the former than the latter. Nevertheless Lent survives in BCP, ASB, and CY.

A seventeenth-century writer views Lent:

It is now Lent, and the poore Stockfish is sore beaten for his stubbornesse: the Herring dominiers like a Lord of great Seruice, and the fruit of the Dairy makes a hungry Feast: Fasting and mourning is the life of the poore, and the Dogges grow leane, with the lacke of bones, while the Prisoners heart is nipt with penury: the Beasts of the Forests haue a bare feed, and the hard crusts try the teeth of the Begger: The Byrd hath a little shelter in the Bush, and a bitter frost makes a backward Spring: The Sunne giues but little warmth, and the March wind makes the Ayre cold: The Fishermen now are the Rakers of the Sea, and the Oyster gapes, to catch hold of the Crab: Solitarinesse and Melancholy breed the hurt of Nature, and the nakednesse of the Earth is the eyes discomfort: Idle people sit picking of Sallets, and necessity of exercise is an enemy to study: the winds grow dangerous to the Sayler, and the Rockes are the ruine of the Merchant: the Sentinell now keeps a cold watch, and the Sconce is nothing comfortable to the Souldier: the shepheard hath little pleasure in his Pipe, and Age hath but a dead feeling in loue: the Colt hath a ragged coat, and the halfe mewed head disgraceth the Deere: the Faulcons wing is but young feathered, and the deepe fallow wearies the Huntsman: there is nothing pleasing but hope, that the dayes will lengthen and time will be more comfortable. I conclude, in it selfe, it is an vncomfortable season, the Heauens frown, and the Earths punishment. Farewell.

Breton (1626)

Lenten fare, as suggested by Robert May (1665):

A Bill of Fare formerly used on Fasting Dayes and in Lent

The first Course
Oysters if in season
1 Butter and eggs
2 Barley Pottage, or Rice pottage
3 Stewed oysters
4 Buttered eggs on toasts
5 Spinage sallet boild
6 Boild Rochet, or gurnet
7 A jole of ling [jowl of ling, a fish similar to cod]
8 Stewed Carp
9 Oyster Chewits
10 Boild pike
11 Roast eels
12 Hadducks, fresh Cod, or whitings
13 Eel or carp pie
14 Made dish of spinage
15 Salt eels
16 Souc't turbut

A second Course
1 Fried Soles
2 Stewed oysters in Scollop shells
3 Fried smelts
4 Congers head broild
5 Baked dish of potatoes, or oyster pie
6 A spitch-cock of eels
7 Quince pie, or tarts royal
8 Buttered crabs
9 Fried flounders
10 Jole of fresh salmon
11 Fried turbut
12 Cold salmon pie
13 Fried skirrets
14 Souc't conger
15 Lobsters
16 Sturgeon

Ash Wednesday, the first day of Western Lent. For the Irish in O'Sullivan's time, 'Ash Wednesday it is a great worry to drink milk' (*Céadaoin na Luaithre is mór an buaidhreadh bainne d'ól*) for troubled conscience; one abstained even from whitemeats (*báinbhiadh*).

In England the ceremony of marking a cross of ashes on the congregants' foreheads, with the words *Memento homo quia pulvis es, et in pulverem reverteris* ('Remember man, for dust thou art, and to dust shalt thou return', Gen. 3: 19), was replaced at the Reformation with the Commination, in which curses on various kinds of sinner were pronounced that (perhaps because they did not prove effective) modern clergy do not care to utter or modern sinners to hear.

James Howell's story is surely invented, but it is not hard to imagine how strange the custom of going around with smudged faces on Ash Wednesday might appear to a non-Christian:

The Christian Church hath a longer and more solemn Way of fasting than any other Religion, take *Lent* and *Ember-weeks* together. In some Churches the Christian useth the old Way of Mortification, by Sackcloth and Ashes, to this Day; which makes me think on a facetious tale of a *Turkish* Ambassador in *Venice*, who being returned to *Constantinople*, and asked what he had observed most remarkable in that so rare a City? He answered, that among other Things, the Christian hath a Kind of *Ashes*, which thrown upon the Head doth presently cure Madness; for in *Venice* I saw the People go up and down the Streets (said he) in ugly antic strange Disguises, as being in the Eye of human Reason stark mad; but the next Day (meaning *Ash-Wednesday*) they are suddenly cured of that Madness by a Sort of Ashes which they cast upon their Heads.

Letter to Richard Baker, 1654, in Howell, 452

Until 1715 it was the custom during Lent for an officer designated the King's Cock Crower or Cockerel to announce the hour within the palace by imitating a cockcrow, in commemoration of St Peter; but in that year, when the crower entered the apartment where the Prince of Wales, afterwards George II, was sitting down to supper, and announced that it was past ten o'clock:

Taken by surprize, and imperfectly acquainted with the English language, the astonished prince naturally mistook the tremulation of the assumed crow, as some mockery intended to insult him, and instantly rose to resent the affront: nor was it without difficulty that the interpreter explained the nature of the custom, and satisfied him, that a compliment was designed, according to the court etiquette of the time. From that period we find no further account of the exertion of the imitative powers of this important officer; but the court has been left to the voice of reason and conscience, to remind them of their errors, and not to that of the cock, whose clarion called back *Peter* to repentance, which this fantastical and silly ceremony was meant to typify.

Brady, i. 225

Not all tomfoolery was over with the beginning of Lent. The Jack of Lent, a puppet with fish emblems, was used as a target during Lent and destroyed on Palm Sunday:

> When Jakke a' Lent comes justlynge in,
>   With the hedpeece of a herynge,
> And saythe, repent yowe of yower syn,
>   For shame, syrs, leve yowre swerynge:
> And to Palme Sonday doethe he ryde,
>   With sprots and herryngs by his syde,
> And makes an end of Lenton tyde!

The ceremony of the Dunmow bacon flitch, which still takes place off and on, is attested as early as Chaucer:

The bacon was nat fet for hem, I trowe,   *not fetched for them*
That som men han in Essex at Dunmowe.

'The Wife of Bath's Prologue,' III (D) 217–18

The prior of Dunmow was required, if a married couple came to him and swore the following oath, to give them a gammon or flitch of bacon:

> You shall swear by the Custom of our Confession,
> That you never made any Nuptial Transgression
> Since you were marri'd Man & Wife
> By Household Brawls or Contentious Strife
> Or otherwise in Bed or at Board
> Offended each other in Deed or in Word
> Or since the Parish Clerk said Amen
> Wish'd yourselves unmarri'd agen
> Or in a Twelve Moneth & a day
> Repented not in thought any way
> But Continued true & in desire
> As when you join'd hands in Holy Quire
> If to these Conditions without all fear
> Of your own Accord you will freely Swear
> A Gammon of Bacon you shall receive
> And bear it hence with Love & good Leave
> For this is our Custom at Dunmow well known
> Though the Sport be ours, the Bacon's your own.

An American visitor duly recorded the oath and story on his visit to Dunmow in March 1776, with the following comment:

The words of this place mention no less than three Matrimonial Heroes who in the Space of 5 hundred Years laid Claim and carried off the Prize. Tradition says several hundreds did intend to get possession of it, but disqualified themselves by some act in the preparation. One good Man whose wife was coming with him took it into head that She knew the way better than her husband, which brought on such a Contention, as did permit their [i.e. Dunmow] saving their bacon.   Fisher, 133

A similar ceremony is reported in Whichnour (Staffs.); both descriptions are found in Thomas Blount, *Fragmenta Antiquitatis. Antient Tenures of Land, and Jocular Customs of some Mannors Made publick for the diversion of some, and instruction of others* (London, 1679).

Lent was also one of the numerous occasions for children to go begging. John Aubrey reports an example in Oxfordshire:

It is the custom for the Boys and Girls in Country Schools in several parts of Oxfordshire (as Blechingdon, Weston, Charlton, &c.) at their breaking-up in the week before Easter to goe in a gang from house to house with little clacks of wood and when they come to any door they fall a beating their clacks, and singing [the following] song, and expect from every house some eggs or a piece of bacon, wch they carry baskets to receive, and feast upon them at the week's end. At first coming to ye door they all strike up, very loud,

> Harings Harings white and red
> Ten a penny Lent's dead
> Rise dame and give a Negg

> Or else a peice of Bacon
> One for Peter two for Paul
> Three for Jack a Lents all
> Away Lent away

often repeated.

As soon as they recieve any largess, they begin the chorus,

> Here sits a good wife
> Pray God save her life
> Set her upon a hod
> And drive her to God.

But if they loose their expectation, and must goe away empty, then wth a full cry,

> Here sits a bad wife
> The devil take her life
> Set her upon a swivell
> And send her to y^e Devill.

And, in farther indignation, they commonly cut the latch of y^e door, or stop the keyhole wth dirt, or leave some more nasty token of displeasure. [W. K.] [W. K. = White Kennett, who wrote notes into the MS of Aubrey's book]   Aubrey, 161–2

Quadragesima, the first Sunday in Lent (introit *Invocavit*); originally used for Lent itself (cf. French *carême*), from Latin *quadragesima*, 'fortieth'. In medieval Germany called 'white Sunday', a name now applied to Low Sunday. Bonfires were lit in the Ardennes; children collected wood and smeared the faces of those who did not provide it. Other activities included dancing round fires, jumping over embers, with wishes for good crops, fortunate marriage, and freedom from colic. Seeing seven Lenten fires protects against witches; children may be promised as many Easter eggs as they can count fires. Those who fail to light a fire find God has done it himself, with the house as fuel. In Irish it is sometimes known as 'Chalk Sunday', *Domhnach na Cailce*, from the mischievous practice of making chalk marks on the clothes of unmarried men and women; it also bore several other names referring to these unhappy people's scowls and tears.

The spring Ember Days (see above): Wednesday, Thursday, and Saturday after Quadragesima.

Second Sunday in Lent (introit *Reminiscere*). At Seville, in the sixteenth century, parish churches were closed to encourage attendance at the cathedral, where the Inquisition attended mass and delivered an *edicto de fe*, denouncing the latest heresy and giving the congregation a period of grace to repent; the Gospel was Matt. 15: 21–8, concerning the Canaanite (Syrophoenician) woman who persuaded Jesus to cure her daughter; since Spain admitted polyphony even during Lent, but with texts based on the respective Gospels, we have several settings of *Clamabat autem mulier*.

Third Sunday in Lent (introit *Oculi*).

Mid-Lent, Refreshment, or Mothering Sunday, the fourth Sunday in Lent (introit *Laetare*), often treated as a cheerful day (*Laetare* means 'Rejoice') breaking up the fast: in Flanders, de

Graaf van Halfvasten ('the Count of Mid-Lent') gives good children presents. This is reflected in the name 'Refreshment Sunday' (*Dominica Refectionis*), which also alludes to the Gospel read at Mass before 1970 (and in the BCP Communion service), John 6: 1–14, on the Feeding of the Five Thousand; after the service the priest blessed loaves of bread (hence the German name *Brotsonntag*), which were distributed to the poor and sold by them to persons with means. The Epistle included the words 'Jerusalem . . . which is the mother of us all' (Gal. 4: 26); it was therefore a day for visiting the cathedral or mother church of the diocese in procession and offering *denarii quadragesimales*. Such processions might lead to quarrels over precedence, and even bloodshed, as Robert Grosseteste, Bishop of Lincoln, complained in 1236 (*Epistolae*, no. 22, p. 75); in time they were discontinued, the money commuted to the Easter offerings, and the visits were paid and presents given instead to one's human mother.

Upon midlent Sunday, Every good child is said to dine with his father & mother.

Crosfield, 59 (11 Mar. 1631)

Mothering Sunday as experienced by an American, 5 March 1780:

[After church] Met Miss E., declined her invitation to tea, being preengaged to partake of Mrs. Bearpacker's mothering cake. It is a custom here in midlent Sunday for a cake or cakes to be brought to Mothers and dine with her in conformity with which custom, some persons, meaning Females make a large one and present to their friends and acquaintance. This custom still continues in Gloucester, and is said to be derived from Joseph making himself known to his brethren.

Curwen, ii. 598

The traditional food on Mothering Sunday was the simnel cake, brought to the mother as a gift:

> I'le to thee a Simnel bring,
> 'Gainst thou go'st a *mothering*,
> So that, when she blesseth thee,
> Half that blessing thou'lt give me.

Robert Herrick (1591–1674), 'To Dianeme'

It is an old custom in Shropshire and Herefordshire, and especially at Shrewsbury, to make during Lent and Easter, and also at Christmas, a sort of rich and expensive cakes, which are called *Simnel Cakes*. They are raised cakes, the crust of which is made of fine flour and water, with sufficient saffron to give it a deep yellow colour, and the interior is filled with the materials of a very rich plum-cake, with plenty of candied lemon peel, and other good things. They are made up very stiff, tied up in a cloth, and boiled for several hours, after which they are brushed over with egg, and then baked. When ready for sale the crust is as hard as if made of wood, a circumstance which has given rise to various stories of the manner in which they have at times been treated by persons to whom they were sent as presents, and who had never seen one before, one ordering his simnel to be boiled to soften it, and a lady taking hers for a footstool. They are made of different sizes, and, as may be supposed from the ingredients, are rather expensive, some large ones selling for as much as half-a-guinea, or even, we believe, a guinea, while smaller ones may be had for half-a-crown.

Chambers (6 Mar.)

A modern recipe for simnel cake:

Simnel Cake

British	American
8 oz. (230 g) unsalted butter, softened	2 sticks unsalted butter, softened
6 oz. (170 g) caster sugar	¾ c. granulated sugar
grated zest and juice of two lemons	grated zest and juice of two lemons
3 eggs and one extra yolk	3 eggs and one extra yolk
8 oz. (230 g) plain flour	2 c. all-purpose flour
½ tsp. salt	½ tsp. salt
1 tsp. ground mixed spice	1 tsp. ground mixed spices
½ tsp. baking powder	½ tsp. baking powder
4 oz. (110 g) dried fruits (apricots, mangoes, etc.), chopped	½ c. dried fruits (apricots, mangoes, etc.), chopped
4 oz. (110 g) chopped mixed peel	¾ c. chopped mixed peel
4 oz. (110 g) raisins	¾ c. raisins
4 oz. (110 g) sultanas	¾ c. golden raisins

Almond paste

4 oz. (110 g) ground blanched almonds	1 c. ground blanched almonds
4 oz. (110 g) caster sugar	½ c. finely granulated sugar
4 oz. (110 g) icing sugar	1 c. confectioner's sugar
grated zest of ½ lemon	grated zest of ½ lemon
1 tsp. lemon juice	1 tsp. lemon juice
1 egg white, lightly beaten	1 egg white, lightly beaten

Glaze

1 egg, beaten	1 egg, beaten

1. Make the almond paste first. Mix all the ingredients together thoroughly, using only as much egg white as is needed to bind the mixture. Knead lightly and put to one side, loosely covered.

2. Preheat the oven to 170 °C/325 °F/gas mark 3. Grease and line an 8 in. (20.5 cm) cake tin with parchment paper. Cream the butter and sugar together until light, add the lemon zest, then beat in the eggs, one at a time. Sift the dry ingredients together and fold into the mixture. Stir in the dried fruit and lemon juice, mixing thoroughly but gently.

3. Transfer the mixture to the prepared cake tin and smooth the top of the cake, pushing down slightly in the centre. Bake in the centre of the oven for 1 hour to 1 hour 10 min. (longer baking gives a more cakelike texture). Allow the cake to cool in the tin before removing it.

4. Preheat the grill/broiler to high. Roll out two-thirds of the almond paste and cover the surface of the cake with it so that it overlaps the edge by about ½ in. (1 cm). Brush with beaten egg. Roll the remaining almond paste into 11 balls (to represent the 11 Apostles, omitting Judas) and arrange in a circle on top. Brush again with beaten egg. Place under the grill until golden brown.

Store the cake at room temperature, tightly covered. Like all fruitcakes, it improves with ageing.

Not everyone likes simnel cake, which can be somewhat heavy and dry (not the above recipe, however). William Gunter, a nineteenth-century professional confectioner and author of *Gunter's Confectioner's Oracle* (1830), began his book by lamenting that the art of confectionery was so arcane that 'an Amateur who should hope to satisfy a delicate tooth by his calorific experiments, for instance, would infallibly see his labours end in having reduced good materials to a mass resembling *chalk*, and quite as digestive', appending the footnote:

Or bearing a resemblance to a cake much in vogue at Shrewsbury, called a *simnel-cake*, which itself resembles, more exactly than any thing else I can imagine, the *mortar* of some antique *prison*, mixed up with gingerbread. It is *grating* in the extreme,—at least to a London palate,—but the inhabitants of the Welsh borders may require it as a digester, in the same way that rabbits do sand.

Gunter, p. iv

In recent times Mothering Sunday has, in both Britain and Ireland, taken on the name and character of the US Mother's Day, which is celebrated on the second Sunday in May (as proposed by Anna Jarvis of Philadelphia in 1907).

Mid-Lent Sunday is sometimes called *der Rosentag* in Germany, stemming from the papal gift of the Golden Rose on this day to favoured persons or communities, an institution already called ancient by Pope Leo IX in 1049. Adam Usk saw the ceremony in Rome in 1405:

On the Sunday in mid-Lent on which 'Laetare Ierusalem' is sung—for some relief, now that it is half way through Lent—the pope during mass holds up in his hands a very valuable and astonishingly ornate gold and silver rose, which has been rubbed with fresh myrrh [actually musk] and balsam so that it fills the air with a fragrance of the utmost sweetness, and when the mass is over he makes a gift of it to the most noble knight who has been present at mass; then later that same day this knight, accompanied by his friends, there to honour him, rides about in great state carrying it in his hand.

Usk, 199

Fifth Sunday in Lent, and second before Easter (introit *Judica*), also called 'Passion Sunday' (but after 1969 this has been the RC name for Palm Sunday, and is identified with it in CY). It is also called 'Carling Sunday' (esp. Northumberland), from peas eaten with meals that day (also 'Care Sunday', 'Caring Sunday'); at Newark-on-Trent, Caring Fair was held the previous Friday. Soft beans were formerly distributed upon this Sunday.

HOLY WEEK

Holy Week is the week before Easter, commemorating events in the last days of Christ's life. Since these were very dramatic, the custom arose of re-enacting them in theatrical form, at first as enhancements of the liturgy, where biblical readings in dialogue form were distributed among the clerics, and later as fully staged plays. These were especially favoured in the fourteenth and fifteenth centuries; the most famous modern example is the Passion Play performed at Oberammergau in Upper Bavaria, to discharge a vow made in time of plague in 1633. The first performance was in 1634; it was again staged every ten years up to 1674, thereafter (with a few exceptions) in the decennial years from 1680 onwards with occasional other performances, such as that to celebrate the 200th anniversary in 1984. The text is revised for each performance; controversy was aroused after the Second World War by anti-Jewish emphases introduced during the nineteenth century and much relished by Hitler.

Palm Sunday (RC now Passion Sunday; Lutheran *Palmarum* or *Palmsonntag*), the Sunday before Easter. The name recalls Jesus' triumphal entry into Jerusalem ('others cut down branches from the trees, and strawed them in the way', Matt. 21: 8) when he went to celebrate Passover in the Holy City; palms were blessed on this day and carried in procession. In England, where palms were not to be had, yew, willow, or similar greens were substituted, whence the alternative names 'Branch' (cf. French *les Rameaux*), 'Sallow', 'Willow', 'Yew', and 'Fig Sunday'; willow is commonly used in other European countries, and sometimes placed in the fields to ensure good crops. The custom gave rise to the Latin name *Pascha Floridum*, 'Flowery Easter', in French *Pâques fleuries*, in Spanish *Pascua florida*. The land sighted on Palm Sunday, 20 March 1513 by the expedition of Ponce de León was given the name 'Florida', which in Spanish is stressed on the *i*, but was reinterpreted by English-speakers as Latin, with stress on the *o*, and understood of the local vegetation. In Welsh this day is *Sul y Blodau*, 'Sunday of the Flowers'; when the Reformation ended the carrying of foliage to church, it became the custom to place flowers on family graves. Other Latin names are *Dominica Competentium*, 'Candidates' Sunday', of the catechumens seeking leave of the bishop to be baptized at Easter, and *Capitiluvium*, 'Headwashing', since those successful in this plea washed their heads. An Irish name is *Domhnach na hImsíne* ('Riding Sunday').

   In Spain, and especially in Seville, during Holy Week splendid processions take place, with life-size statues carried on platforms portraying episodes from the Passion. The most famous Holy Week ceremonies, however, are those in Rome, described in several extracts below.

Tenebrae. The last three days of Holy Week are often called 'Tenebrae' ('darkness'), after the particular services that formerly took place on the eves, where the candles before the altar were extinguished one by one, at the end of each psalm.

   It was during these services that Allegri's famous *Miserere* was sung. Dating from the seventeenth century (and enchanting modern listeners), it did not please some nineteenth-century ears. Lady Morgan reports on the first service of Tenebrae, on the Wednesday preceding Easter, in the papal chapel:

. . . the Sistine chapel is unequal to accommodate the numbers who applied for admittance on the Wednesday, to hear the first performance of the *Miserere*. The service of the day, called by the French, *Ténèbres*, has always been celebrated for the magnificence of its music, being of the most solemn and soothing cast, and sung by the whole of the Pope's choir, unaccompanied by instruments. On this occasion the utmost effect of vocal music has been supposed to be attained. There were parts in which the strains resembled the deep-toned mellowness of the diapason stop of the organ; and they fell upon the ear, and died away, like the sighing of the winds on the Æolian lyre. As the music proceeds in solemnity and sadness, light after light is extinguished, and the service finishes in the deep twilight gloom, as the last candle goes out. In the combination of these circumstances, and of the awful mystery to which they allude, there is much to captivate the imagination, and mislead the judgment; but either the execution of the music is greatly fallen off, or the accounts given by authors of its effects are exaggerated. Though a considerable portion of it has all the sublimity of extreme simplicity, some of the pieces are excessively rude; and as the voice dwells upon the protracted breves and semibreves, unsustained by an instrumental accompaniment, it falls by a physical necessity, and few passages finish accurately in tune. Some of the voices also are of a coarse and disagreeable quality. There are few good tenors, and the boys scream most disagreeably in holding notes in the alto parts. The effect likewise is too artificial and theatric; and when the freshness and susceptibility of inexperience have passed off, the mind rejects, as an attempted imposition, such studied contrivances; still, however, if they do not edify, they attract; and the opportunities are so few of hearing the music of Jomelli, of Pergolese, and of the old masters in Italy, that the Sistine Chapel is visited with curiosity and perseverance on all the three nights of performance.

Morgan, iii. 35–7 (1821)

Whatever limitation of taste the lover of this music may discern, the blame must lie mainly with the execution: the standard of the choir (though not its self-esteem) had declined dramatically in the late sixteenth century and not recovered.

Maundy Thursday. The Thursday before Easter, from *Mandatum novum do vobis* (John 13: 34), the beginning of the first antiphon in the ceremony of foot-washing. In England, as formerly in many countries, the sovereign distributes Maundy money: one silver penny to one poor man and one poor woman for each year of the sovereign's age. It is also known as 'Sheer', 'Char', 'Shrift', and 'Sharp' Thursday (said by John Mirk in the fourteenth century to derive from cutting of hair or beards before Easter); in Germany it is *Gründonnerstag*, 'Green Thursday', after green branches given penitents who had confessed on Ash Wednesday. Maundy Thursday is sometimes called 'Holy Thursday', but this name is also given to Ascension Day.

The custom of monarchs' washing poor people's feet dates from as early as the early thirteenth century (Bede says that churchmen had done it before 700 in Lindisfarne); French kings performed it from the early eleventh century. The first English king to do it was John, after his excommunication; the number of paupers was thirteen until Edward III, who made it the number of years he had reigned. After James II the monarchs showed little enthusiasm for foot-washing, but the gift of food and money remained. The Queen now distributes small coins specially minted for the occasion.

Maundy Thursday ceremonies at the English court, as reported by a Frenchman in 1698:

On *Maundy Thursday* the King gives Alms to as many poor People as he is Years old. These poor People are carry'd into the Banquetting-House, where they find a Table spread for them: There is upon each Plate three great Pieces of Fish, a Six-penny Loaf, a Bottle of Wine, a great Jugg of Beer, two Ells of Cloth, Linnen for two Shirts, Stockings, Shoes, as many Shillings and as many Silver Pence as the King is Years old. This Treat was formerly given after that the King, out of a ridiculous Affectation of Humility, had wash'd and wip'd the Feet of those poor People with his own Hands. Misson de Valbourg, 185

In the mid-nineteenth century in Rome it was the Roman nobility who washed the feet. Mary Crawford Fraser (b. 1851) recalls viewing the ceremony in Rome in her childhood:

By Holy Thursday many thousands of pilgrims from all parts of Italy, but more especially from the South, had arrived in Rome; foreigners from all over the world flocked to the hotels, but little notice was taken of them. The housing and caring for the poor peasants, some of whom had walked two hundred miles or more, in great companies, praying and singing hymns all the way, occupied all the attention of the authorities. They were the personal guests of the Holy Father, and were made to feel that they were his very beloved children. The vast building of the 'Santo Spirito', which ran all the way from the Castel' Sant' Angelo to the Piazza of St. Peter's, was portioned out into dormitories and refectories where food and lodging was provided for all who had brought the necessary recommendation from their Parish Priest. . . .

The greatest ladies in the world, in Court dress of black velvet and a long black veil, and wearing their most magnificent family jewels, came to do honour to the Pope's guests. They received the contadine and their babies and led them to the tables loaded with good things which ran down the hall, guiding them to their places, where each found her supper separately laid out. But before enjoying this, the poor dusty feet that had travelled so far must be washed, and the Princesses, following Christ's example, went round from one to another on their knees to perform this kindly act. The first time I witnessed it I found myself beside the group under Princess Massimo's care, and I shall never forget my amazement when I saw that dear and holy lady stagger forward with a tub of steaming hot water, and then kneel down and gently remove the sandals and stockings of a young woman who carried a tiny baby in her arms and who, as I knew by her costume, must have come from the further fastnesses of the Apennines. The Princess was wearing the famous Massimo pearls, string after string of enormous shimmering globes, which hung so far below her waist that they kept getting hopelessly mixed up with the hot water and soapsuds. Talking kindly to the dazzled contadina, she made a very thorough job of her distasteful task, and when it was accomplished carried away her tub like any hospital nurse and prepared to attend to the next on the bench. For three nights, from Holy Thursday to Easter Eve, she and her peers rendered this tribute to poverty and faith, while their husbands and sons did the same for the men on the other side of the building.   Fraser, i. 75

Good Friday. The Friday before Easter, commemorating the Crucifixion. In the Latin rite the altars are stripped bare or covered with a black cloth, mass is not said, and the ceremonies include the Passion of St John, the *Improperia* or Reproaches, the Veneration of the Cross, and Communion using a wafer presanctified on the day before. In medieval England this service included the Creeping to the Cross, where the clergy and laity crept barefoot to the crucifix, placed on a step of the altar, and kissed it. This ceremony disappeared at the Reformation, together with the imposition of ashes on Ash Wednesday and the blessing of palm or other branches on Palm Sunday; however, these and other medieval usages, sometimes in moderated form, have been revived in recent times, not only among Anglo-Catholics.

The lovely Corpus Christi Carol, despite its knightly imagery, may refer to the Crucifixion:

> *Lully, lulley; lully, lulley*
> *The fawcon hath born my mak away.*   mate, love
>
> He bare hym up, he bare hym down;
> He bare hym into an orchard brown.
>
> In that orchard ther was an hall,
> That was hangid with pu rpill and pall.   rich cloth

And in that hall ther was a bede:
Hit was hangid with gold so rede.

And yn that bed ther lythe a knyght,
His wowndes bledyng day and nyght.

By that bedes side ther kneleth a may,   *maid*
And she wepeth both nyght and day.

And by that beddes side ther stondith a ston,
'*Corpus Christi*' wretyn theron.

In Rome, pilgrims creep up the Holy Stairs (*Scala Santa*), near St John Lateran, traditionally identified with those mounted by Christ when summoned by Pilate in
Jerusalem. Captain John Smith, speaking of himself in the third person, observed in
1601:

he came to *Rome*, where it was his chance to see Pope *Clement* the eight, with many Cardinalls,
creepe up the holy Stayres, which they say are those our Saviour Christ went up to *Pontius Pilate*,
where bloud falling from his head, being pricked with his crowne of thornes, the drops are
marked with nailes of steele, upon them none dare goe but in that manner, saying so many *Ave-
Maries* and *Pater nosters*, as is their devotion, and to kisse the nailes of steele: But on each side is a
paire of such like staires, up which you may goe, stand, or kneele, but divided from the holy
Staires by two walls: right against them is a Chappell, where hangs a great silver Lampe, which
burneth continually, yet they say the oyle neither increaseth nor diminisheth.   J. Smith, 5–6

Good Friday has its fair share of superstitions. Bread baked on this day was considered
a curative, especially for children. The custom of eating hot-cross buns, however, is not
attested before the eighteenth century.

> Good Friday comes this Month, the old Woman runs
> With one or two a Penny, hot cross Bunns,
> Whose Virtue is, if you believe what's said,
> They'll not grow mouldy like the common Bread.
>
> *Poor Robin* (1733)

For Good Friday, hot buns marked with a cross for breakfast . . . These buns will keep for ever
without becoming mouldy, by virtue of the holy sign impressed upon them . . . in the province
of Herefordshire a pious woman annually makes two upon this day, the crumbs of which are a
sovereign remedy for diarrhœa.   Southey, *Letters from England*, xx

Good-luck superstitions:

The English and Irish think it good to plant anything on this day, because it was the day when
our Savior lay in the grave. Seeds, therefore, are certain to rise again.

                                        Hawthorne, *English Notebooks*, 59

To wean children on this day is deemed very lucky. Many people then begin to till their gardens,
as they believe, to use their own words, that all things put in the earth on a good Friday will grow
goody, and return to them with great increase.   Bray, ii. 286 (1836)

I used to suffer very much from toothache many years ago, till a neighbour told me how to cure
it. I got up on Good Friday before the sun rose, and cut all the nails on my hands and my feet,

and wrapped it all up in a bit of writing paper, and put it in my pocket, and I've never had the toothache since.   *N & Q*, 3rd ser., xi (1867), 233 (Gloucestershire)

Ill-luck superstitions, some quite contrary to the good-luck ones:

I learn from a clergyman familiar with the North Riding of Yorkshire, that great care is there taken not to disturb the earth in any way; it were impious to use spade, plough, or harrow. He remembers, when a boy, hearing of a villager who shocked his neighbours by planting potatoes on Good Friday, but they never came up.   Henderson, 61–2 (1866)

To bake or brew on Good Friday. The house will be burnt down during year.

To wash clothes on Good Friday: In Cleveland, it is said, clothes so washed and hung out to dry will become spotted with blood.

No iron on that day must be put into the fire. For the poker, a piece of ashwood is used. (Manx)

Samuel Pepys rarely observes fasting, but does so on Good Friday:

17 [Apr. 1663]. Our dinner, it being Goodfriday, was only sugar sopps and fish; the only time that we have had a Lenten dinner all this Lent.   Pepys, iv. 104

8 [Apr. 1664]. So home to dinner, and had an excellent Good friday dinner of pease porridge—and apple pie.   ibid., v. 117

Lenten fasts come to an end, however, and the victuallers have already started their preparations:

It is now Good Friday, and a general Fast must be kept among all Christians, in remembrance of Christs Passion: Flesh and Fish must bee vanished all stomackes, strong or weake: Now beginnes the Farewell to thin fare, and the Fishmongers may shut vp their shops till the Holy-dayes be past: the Butchers now must wash their Boords, make cleane their Aprons, sharpen their kniues, and sort their prickes, and cut out their meat for Easter Eue market: Now must the Poulters make ready their Rabbets and their Fowle, the Cookes haue their Ouens cleane, and all for Pies and Tarts against the merry Feast: Now the Maids bestir them about their houses, the Launders about their Linen, the Taylors about Apparell, and all for this holy time: Now young Lambs, young Rabbets, and young Chickens dye for fine appetites, and now the Minstrell tunes his Instruments, to haue them ready for the yong people: but with the aged and the religious, there is nothing but sorrow and mourning, confession, contrition, and absolution, and I know not what: few that are merry, but children that breake vp schoole, and wenches that are vpon the mariage. In summe, it is such an odde day by it selfe, that I will onely make this conclusion of it: it is the Bridle of Nature, and the Examiner of Reason. Farewell.   Breton (1626)

Holy Saturday. Easter Eve, Holy Saturday, the Saturday before Easter, called 'Easter Saturday' by the unchurched, commemorating the day that Christ lay in the tomb. It is Judas Day in Mexico: he is hanged and burned in effigy. In Greece, the priest and congregation make loud noises during the service to drive away demons; a Czech custom on *Bílá sobota* ('White Saturday') is to rattle keys, and also to burn out Judas by burning the last of the holy oil before the church door.

The Paschal Vigil Service inaugurates the Easter celebrations. The ceremonies are elaborate; Naogeorgus (one must always keep in mind his anti-Catholic bias) reports the ritual in the sixteenth century:

On Easter eve the fire all, is quencht in every place,
And fresh againe from out the flint, is fetcht with solemne grace:
The Priest doth halow this against great daungers many one,
A brande whereof doth every man with greedie minde take home,
That when the fearefull storme appeares, or tempest blacke arise,
By lighting this he safe may be, from stroke of hurtfull skies:
A Taper great, the paschall namde, with musicke then they blesse,
And franckensence herein they pricke, for greater holynesse:
This burneth night and day as signe, of Christ that conquerde hell,
As if so be this foolish toye, suffiseth this to tell.
Then doth the Bishop or the Priest, the water halow straight,
That for their baptisme is reservde: for now no more of waight
Is that they usde the yeare before, nor can they any more,
Yong children christen with the same, as they have done before.
With woondrous pompe and furniture, amid the Church they go,
With candles, crosses, banners, Chrisme, and oyle appoynted tho:
Nine times about the font they marche, and on the saintes doe call,
Then still at length they stande, and straight the Priest begins withall,
And thrise the water doth he touche, and crosses thereon make,
Here bigge and barbrous wordes he speakes, to make the devill quake . . .
The people staring hereat stande, amazed every one:
Beleeving that great powre is given to this water here,
By gaping of these learned men, and such like trifling gere.
Therefore in vessels brought they draw, and home they carie some,
Against the grieves that to themselves, or to their beastes may come.
Then Clappers ceasse, and belles are set againe at libertee,
And herewithall the hungrie times of fasting ended bee.

Naogeorgus, fo. 52

One of the rituals on Holy Saturday was the 'burial' of the third Host consecrated on Maundy Thursday. The pyx containing the Host and a Crucifix were wrapped in cloth and placed in a special sepulchre on an altar or in the wall, and watch kept all night, symbolizing Christ's burial.

EASTER DAY

The name 'Easter' (like German *Ostern*) originally denoted a spring festival in honour of a Germanic dawn-goddess called *Ēostræ* in Bede's Old Northumbrian and *Ēastre* in standard West Saxon. Greek and Latin use *Pascha*, from Hebrew *Pesaḥ* (Pesach), for Jewish Passover and Christian Easter alike; the name survives with the double sense in most European languages from Irish *Cáisc* to Russian *Páskha*, though French distinguishes *Pâque* 'Passover' from *Pâques* 'Easter'. In English, and more especially Scots, it appeared as *Pace*—whence the term 'pace-eggs' for Easter eggs. Even now, although 'Easter' and 'Passover' are used attributively, the only true adjective is 'Paschal'.

Easter commemorates the Resurrection of Christ on the third day (counted inclusively in the ancient manner) after His crucifixion:

And when the sabbath was past, Mary Magdalene, and Mary the mother of James, and Salome, had bought sweet spices, that they might come and anoint him. And very early in the morning the first day of the week, they came unto the sepulchre at the rising of the sun. And they said among themselves, Who shall roll us away the stone from the door of the sepulchre? And when they looked, they saw that the stone was rolled away: for it was very great. And entering into the sepulchre, they saw a young man sitting on the right side, clothed in a long white garment; and they were affrighted. And he saith unto them, Be not affrighted: Ye seek Jesus of Nazareth, which was crucified: he is risen; he is not here: behold the place where they laid him. (Mark 16: 1–6)

Easter is the greatest feast of the Church year, celebrating the Resurrection of Christ and the salvation of man; at the corporeal level it is the release from the long period of Lenten penitence, and a joyous festivity after the sombre re-enactment of the events of Holy Week. In Paschaltide, the period after Easter, the acclamation 'Alleluia' is incorporated in many liturgical texts.

On the mode of finding Easter, see II: *The Date of Easter and Appendix H: *Julian and Gregorian Easter.

Strict Puritans would have nothing to do with Easter, as a merely human institution; when in 1647 Charles I declared it to be as scriptural as Sunday, Parliament contradicted him in print, and abolished it along with all other church festivals. In Scotland, it was not observed at all. But Easter had long been a day associated with secular if not pagan customs. Coming at the end of the long period of abstinence in Lent, it was a time for feasting:

Easter Sunday and Christmas Day: the two best days for the stomach.

O'Sullivan, i. 245 (6 Apr. 1828)

Nicholas Breton pays very little attention to the sacred side of Easter:

It is now Easter, and Jacke of Lent is turned out of doores: the Fishermen now hang vp their nets to dry, while the Calfe and the Lambe walke toward the Kitchin and the Pastry: the veluet heads of the Forrests fall at the loose of the Crosse-bow: the Samman Trowt playes with the Fly, and the March Rabbit runnes dead into the dish: the Indian commodities pay the Merchants aduenture: and Barbary Sugar puts Honey out of countenance: the holy feast is kept for the faith-full, and a knowne Jew hath no place among Christians: the Earth now beginnes to paint her vpper garment, and the trees put out their young buds, the little Kids chew their Cuds, and the Swallow feeds on the Flyes in the Ayre: the Storke clenseth the Brookes of the Frogges, and the Sparhawke prepares her wing for the Partridge: the little Fawne is stolne from the Doe, and the male Deere beginne to heard: the spirit of Youth is inclined to mirth, and the conscionable Scholler will not breake a holy-day: the Minstrell cals the Maid from her dinner, and the Louers eyes doe troule like Tennis balls. There is mirth and ioy, when there is health and liberty: and he that hath money, will be no meane man in his mansion: the Ayre is wholsome, and the Skye comfortable, the Flowers odoriferous, and the Fruits pleasant: I conclude, it is a day of much delightfulnesse: the Sunnes dancing day, and the Earths Holy-day. Farewell.   Breton

A particular dish associated with Easter is tansy pudding. It is flavoured with the juice of tansy (*tanacetum vulgare*), a green plant that grows wild and has a rather bitter taste. Thomas Cogan, in his *Haven of Health* (1584), p. 65, says: 'It is much used among us in Englande about Easter with fryed egs, not without good cause, to purge away the flewme engendred of fish in the Lent season, whereof wormes are soone bred in them that be thereto disposed, though the common people understande not the cause, why Tansies are more used after Lent, than at any other tyme of the yere.' (Popular lore still holds it efficacious for expelling worms.) Flavouring with tansy juice recalls the custom of eating bitter herbs at Passover; the modern equivalent is mint sauce. A medieval recipe calls for eggs, pepper, tansy, butter, and lard. A more appetizing version is the following, adapted from John Nott, *The Cook's and Confectioner's Dictionary* (3rd edn., London, 1726):

Tansy Pudding

½ pt (275 ml) milk
½ oz (15 g) butter
3 oz (75 g) fresh white breadcrumbs
1 oz (25 g) sugar or honey
2 tsps (10 ml) finely chopped tansy leaves (1 tsp finely chopped fresh sage may be substituted)
2 eggs, beaten
honey and cream, to serve

Boil the milk and butter together and pour over the breadcrumbs. Set aside for 30 minutes. Add the sugar or honey and the tansy leaves to the eggs, then mix with the breadcrumbs and bake the mixture in a moderate oven, gas mark 4, 350 °F (180 °C), until set. Eat cold with honey and cream.

At Gaeta, one eats *ciambelle*, pastries in ring shape, with eggs; those for men have the form of a dove (*la colomba*), but women eat *la femmina pregna*, where the egg is in the belly. Taken together, these symbolize Mary's impregnation by the Holy Spirit.

Easter is rich in well-known and long-lived customs. We single out only a few:

Putting on a new garment

The farmer that was contented in times past with his Russet Frocke & Mockado sleeues, now sels a Cow against Easter to buy him silken geere for his credit.   Lodge, 14 (1596)

In 1641 I sent from London against Easter a suite of cloaths for my son Thomas, being ye first breeches & doublet y^t he ever had, & made by my tailor M^r. Miller; it was too soon for him to wear y^m being but 5 years old, but y^t his mother had a desire to see him in y^m, how proper a man he would be.   Slingsby, 71–2

Decorating Easter eggs. The custom of making and giving decorated eggs at Easter is very old. Eggs, with their promise of new life, are particularly suited to the Resurrection. Moreover, they were forbidden during Lent. Since the hens did not stop laying, it was necessary to hard-boil the eggs to preserve them. Come Easter, even those who could not afford meat were able to set a feast with eggs. In many countries Easter breads are made, with decorated eggs filling in the hollows.

The Easter Bunny. Rabbits, famously fertile creatures, have become an Easter version of Santa in the United States: they hide coloured candy eggs in little nests for children to search out on Easter morning. More obliging rabbits bring large chocolate baskets filled with candy eggs. The custom was imported from Germany by the Pennsylvania Dutch, who called the hare the 'Oschter Haws' (= German *Osterhase*). Easter-egg hunts are also organized by communities. Another activity is egg-rolling; the most famous site is the White House lawn.

Observing the sun dancing. It was commonly believed in England that the Sun danced on Easter morning to celebrate the Resurrection; if human eyes could not see him do so, it was because the Devil blocked the view.

> Quhy wes my birth on Eister day at morne?
> Quhy did Apollo then appeir to dance?
> Quhy gaiv he me good morou with a glance?
> > why leugh he in his golden chair and lap,
> > Since that the Hevins are hinderers of my hap?
>
> Alexander Montgomerie (*c.*1545–*c.*1598), from *Complaint of his Nativity*

To this pool the people used to come [in the 18th c.] on Easter morning to see the sun dance and play in the water and the angels who were at the Resurrection playing backwards and forwards before the sun. Kilvert (1870), i. 247

The Greek writer Diodorus Siculus (1st c. BC) relayed from Hecataeus of Abdera (*c.*300 BC) a tale of a northern island the size of Sicily inhabited by the Hyperboreans (the People beyond the North Wind), who were devotees of Apollo: the god was said to visit them every nineteen years, and during his visit 'to play the kithara and dance continuously every night from the vernal equinox to the rising of the Pleiades [about mid-May], rejoicing in his own triumphs' (2. 47. 6). Whatever underlies this story, the duration of Apollo's visit very roughly matches that between Easter and Pentecost; and Diodorus remarks on the astronomical significance of the nineteen-year cycle.

In the Gnostic Acts of John, Jesus leads off a round dance before the Passion.

Spital sermons. Five sermons, mostly on charity, given at Eastertime in Spital Square, Spitalfields, attended by Bluecoat boys of Christ's Hospital, with representatives from the four other royal hospitals:

2 [Apr. 1662]. Mr. Moore came to me and he and I walked to the Spittle, an hour or two before my Lord Mayor and the Blewe coate boys came, which at last they did, and a fine sight of charity it is endeed. We got places and stayed to hear a sermon; but it being a presbyterian one, it was so long, that after above an hour of it we went away. Pepys, iii. 57–8

Banned under the Puritans, but reinstated in 1660, the sermons had a long tradition; now there is only one, at St Lawrence Jewry, close to Guildhall; it takes place on the second Wednesday after Easter.

Pace-egg plays are a survival of medieval mummers' plays, featuring St George, various adversaries, and Old Toss Pot. A notable one is performed in Mytholmroyd (West Yorkshire) and surrounding villages by the boys of the Calder Valley School.

THE POST-EASTER SEASON

Easter Monday. The day after Easter, formerly observed along with Easter Tuesday with much solemnity by the Church but now a secular celebration; it was formerly regarded as unlucky, and called 'Black Monday' ('White Monday' in Greece). Several historical sources attribute the expression 'Black Monday' to great losses of life on military expeditions (1357, 1360, 1633), but Monday itself was generally considered unlucky (see * *Week: Monday*). For schoolboys it meant returning to school after the Easter recess, and was also called 'Bloody Monday'.

In medieval England women were entitled to haul out of bed any man they found there; even Kings Edward I and II underwent this ritual. In northern England it was the custom for men to lift women thrice by the arms and legs; next day the women returned the compliment. The custom was also known in Wales, where an Englishman reported on it in 1732:

They have a Custom at Bangor, & at Caernarvon too, on an Easter- & Whit-Monday, on May-day, &c. for ye Young fellows, y^t can get up soon in ye Morning, to come & pull y^ir Comrades out of bed, put them in Stocks, & holding up one of y^ir legs, pour a Pail of Water down it.

Loveday, 25–6

It died out only around the mid-nineteenth century:

'Heaving' or 'lifting' at Easter has not long been discontinued at Worcester, the locality where the writer last heard of its performance being in Bridport and Dolday. On Easter Monday the women would surround any man who happened to be passing by, and, by their joint efforts lift him up in the air, and on the next day the men did the same to the women. The only mode of escaping this kind of elevation was by 'forking out' (as they term it in the classical phraseology of that neighbourhood) a certain sum to be spent in drink. At Hartlebury, a few years back, the farmhouse mistress would give the male servant a treat on Easter Tuesday, to heave the female servant, for she superstitiously believed that it would prevent the female servant from breaking the crocks during the ensuing year. . . . Heaving was no doubt originally designed to represent the resurrection.

Noake, 211–12 (1856)

Such customs were also observed at Hocktide (see below).

In Ireland, Easter Monday was called *lá na Cúbóige* ('Day of the [Easter Egg] Bundle') or *lá cóisir* ('Day of Feasts'):

Easter Monday . . . There was no parcel of Easter eggs being consumed by youths and maidens in one another's company. There was neither sport nor laughter, drinking nor dancing. Most [of the young people] stayed at home, for Easter Monday is no longer a Holiday of obligation. The bishops removed the double obligation from it; for their Lordships think that a Holiday of obligation is rather harmful in a heretical land like Ireland: as the Protestants put fairs and markets on Catholic Holidays, of set purpose to bring them into disrepute.

O'Sullivan, ii. 263 (12 Apr. 1830)

Easter Tuesday in Headington, 1727:

Last Tuesday (being Easter Tuesday), there being a Bull baiting at Heddington near Oxford, a Quarrel arose between some Scholars that were there, & two or three of Heddington, about a

Cat, that the Scholars would have had tied to the Bulls Tayl. The Scholars being worsted, at which time one Walters . . . & one Laun . . . were sadly beat and bruised, so as not to be able to come home, but were fetched back in a chair, notice was given to other Scholars at Oxford, whereupon a great Number (some say five hundred, others about two hundred) of them went immediately with Clubs to Heddington, and committed such strange disorders, as have hardly been heard of. They broke almost all the windows in the Town, (pulling down the very window bars) got into Houses, opened Chests, beat & bruiz'd several people in an intolerable manner, were going to break all the windows of the Church, and they would have proceeded to worse mischief had not Mr Newland the Proctor of Magd. Coll. been sent for, who coming in the evening, with great difficulty put an end to the unhappy Riot. . . . Heddington looked very strange after this disaster.

Hearne, 295

Popular revelries in the Middle Ages might take strange forms: Richard of Durham reports that at Inverkeithing in Fife, during Easter week of 1282 (29 Mar.–5 Apr.), the parish priest, called John,

preparing the blasphemies of Priapus, gathered the young girls of the manor, and compelled them to execute round dances in honour of Liber Pater [the normal Roman name for the god Dionysus or Bacchus]; just as Bacchus had women in his army, so John, to induce shamelessness, bore a pole topped with the organs of generation at the head of the procession, joining in the dance and inviting all the onlookers to lechery with mummerly movement and indecent speech.

excerpted in *Chronicon de Lanercost*, 109

The outraged burgesses assassinated him in the churchyard.

Low Sunday, the Sunday after Easter, in Irish *Mioncháisc*, 'Little Easter'; also traditionally known in the West as *Dominica in albis* (sc. *deponendis*), 'Sunday in (taking off) white robes', since those baptized at Easter took off their white robes (whence the modern German *weißer Sonntag*) or *Quasimodo* (from the introit at Mass, *Quasi modo geniti*, 'As newborn babes', 1 Pet. 2: 2; the Lutheran name is *Quasimodogeniti*), in the East as 'Thomas Sunday'. Originally on this day, but later on others, satires were attached in Rome to the base of an ancient statue (originally of Menelaus rescuing the corpse of Patroclus) popularly known as *Pasquino* ('Little Easter') between the sixteenth century and the fall of papal government in 1870; in recent years poems in Roman dialect commenting on local affairs have been posted there. Since 1970 the RC Church has designated this day the Second Sunday of Easter, in which it is followed by CY.

On this day the Pope, in the first year of his reign and every seven years thereafter, distributes wax images of the Lamb of God, the *Agnus Dei*. A German visitor observed both the manufacture and the distribution of these images in 1731, during the papacy of Clement XII:

Within the Rails, which were cover'd with red Damask, there was a square Pit, and in the Middle of it four large Cisterns of solid Silver, full of Water, placed on Pedestals of Wood, silvered and gilt, admirably carv'd by *Bernini*. When the Pope, accompanied by ten Cardinals, whom he had invited to this Ceremony, was entered into the Hall, and seated on his Throne, two Chamberlains of Honour placed a Cistern before him of the same Kind as the four that were in the Hall. The Pope, who had a Mitre upon his Head, of silver Brocade, and a Cope of the same, struck-up the *Veni Spiritus Sancte*, which the Music carry'd on. Afterwards the Holy Father read some Collects, and blessed the Water that was in the Cistern before him, into which he poured Holy Oil, and Holy Chrism. Then came four Cardinals with silver Ladles, who dipp'd them into the Holy Water, and carry'd it to mix with the Water that was in the four Cisterns. This done, the Pope and the Cardinals put on great white Aprons, and the Cardinals sat two and two upon Joint-stools at each Cistern, while two other Cardinals supported the Pope. The *Chamberlains of Honour*, and the Prelates of the Houshold, brought the *Agnus Dei's* in wooden Tubs, wash'd with Silver; and as fast as they threw them into the Cisterns fill'd with Holy Water, the Pope and the Cardinals fish'd them up again with great Skimmers of Silver, and put them into other Tubs, which the Prelates deliver'd to the Sextons. This lasted near two Hours, till the Pope, being quite fatigued, rose up, read some more Collects, and then retired. The same Ceremony was repeated next Day, and in these two Days they made threescore thousand *Agnus Dei's*, which they say cost the Chamber twelve thousand Crowns.

Upon *Quasimodo Sunday*, the Pope distributed the *Agnus's* with very great Ceremony in the Chapel of *Monte-Cavallo*. He was carry'd in his Processional Chair from his Apartment to the Chapel, where, being seated on his Throne, and the *Agnus Dei* having been perform'd by the Music, one of the Apostolical Subdeacons, carrying the *Agnus's* in a Silver Bason, preceded by the Cross, and by the Acolytes, or Assistants at Mass, bearing Wax Candles in great Silver Candlesticks, and the Censer, enter'd the Chapel, and kneeling down, said to the Pope with a loud Voice, *Pater Sancte, isti sunt Agni novelli, qui annunciaverint nobis Alleluja; modo venerunt ad fontes, repleti sunt charitate; Alleluja.* To which the Choir answered, *Deo Gratias; Alleluja.* Then the Sub-deacon rose, and went and kneel'd down in the Middle of the Chapel, where he repeated the same Words as before. He did the same Thing at the Foot of the Pope's Throne, to whom he presented a Bason full of *Agnus Dei's*, in little Packets, wrapp'd up in Cotton, which the Holy Father distributed to the Cardinals, and all the Standers-by, who receiv'd them on their Knees.   Pollnitz, ii. 100–2

Monday and Tuesday after Low Sunday are also known as 'Hocktide' or the 'Hockdays'; the singular 'Hockday' properly refers to the Tuesday, when spring payments were due, especially to church and parish. In rural England above all, Hockday and Michaelmas (occasionally Martinmas) were often the term days for half-yearly payments, marking the respective beginnings of summer and winter in the ancient two-season system. The date is often given as 'after the quindene of Easter' (see the introduction to this section).

On Hock Monday, from the fourteenth century, the men of the parish would way-lay the women, tie them up, and release them only against a ransom; on the Tuesday the women did likewise to the men. In some places the women had first turn, and the men sought their revenge on Tuesday. The money thus raised was given to the church, and duly recorded in the accounts: it appears that in general the women proved the better fund-raisers. Proceedings were further enlivened by specially brewed 'hock ale'.

The origin, both of the festival and of the word 'hock', is unknown. Some old books suggest that Hocktide is an anti-Danish festival commemorating either the St Brice Day massacre or the death of King Hardicanute; since the first of these took place on Friday, 13 November 1002 and the latter on Sunday, 8 June 1042, it is evident that neither has anything to do with the case, although in Coventry the play of 'Hocks tuesday' was performed annually celebrating 'the destruction of the Danes in King Ethelred's time' (Dugdale, *Warwickshire*, 1656, ed. 1730, 249/2, from *OED* s.v. 'Hock Tuesday').

Friday after Low Sunday is still kept in some parts of Germany as the Feast of the Holy Lance, or rather of that Holy Lance which, fashioned to serve some eighth-century Frankish or Lombard warrior but successively assigned by legend to Constantine the Great, St Maurice, and St Longinus, was allegedly presented *c.*922 by King Rudolf II of

Burgundy to the Holy Roman Emperor Conrad, and thereafter used in coronations and carried into battle; for other Holy Lances, see *15 March. Charles IV took it from Nuremberg to Prague in 1350; the feast was instituted three years later. In 1424, during the Hussite wars, it was moved to Nuremberg, as requiring, rather than conferring, protection; in 1800 it was translated to Vienna.

Second Sunday after Easter (Third Sunday of Easter), sometimes known from its introit *Misericordia Domini* (Lutheran *Misericordias Domini*).

Third Sunday after Easter (Fourth Sunday of Easter); introit *Jubilate*.

Fourth Sunday after Easter (Fifth Sunday of Easter); introit *Cantate*.

Fourth Friday after Easter. In Denmark, Store Bededag, decreed by Christian VII on advice of Struensee to replace the various penitential days. Shops are closed; special services are held. On its eve in Copenhagen one dons one's new spring clothes, strolls along the Langelinie waterfront, and eats wheatbread.

Fifth Sunday after Easter (Sixth Sunday of Easter); introit *Vocem iocunditatis*; also called 'Rogation Sunday' (Lutheran *Rogate*).

ROGATION DAYS

The Monday, Tuesday, and Wednesday after Rogation Sunday were originally the Minor Rogations (the Major Rogation was on *25 Apr., a Christian appropriation of the Robigalia, when Romans proceeded through the cornfields praying against mildew, *robigo*). Formerly they were fasting days, on which intercessory processions took place; the name (*rogare* means 'to ask') comes from the litanies that were chanted on the processions. They originated *c.*470 in the Gallic diocese of Vienne, which suffered volcanic eruptions, and were later adopted in the Roman liturgy. A Flemish name was *Kruisdagen*, 'Cross Days'. Like the Ember Days, they have been discarded by the RC Church; they remain in the Church of England, but only the BCP treats them as fasts.

The Rogation Days were also called 'Gang Days', after the custom of going (i.e. walking) round the boundaries of the local parish (this also takes place on *Ascension Day*). At various points the procession would stop and the curate would say a prayer, especially for the abundance of fruits on the face of the earth. Since the perambulation might last longer than a day, it was also the custom to serve refreshments along the way. Some parishioners, whose houses straddled two parishes, had to suffer an invasion of men and boys every year. The processions were discontinued at the Reformation, but have been revived.

Particularly [the country Parson] loves Procession, and maintains it, because there are contained therein 4 manifest advantages. First, a blessing of God for the fruits of the field: Secondly, justice in the Preservation of bounds: Thirdly, Charity in loving walking, and neighbourly accompanying one another, with reconciling of differences at that time, if there be any: Fourthly,

Mercy in releeving the poor by a liberall distribution and largesse, which at that time is or ought to be used. Wherefore he exacts of all to bee present at the perambulation, and those that withdraw and sever themselves from it, he mislikes, and reproves as uncharitable, and unneighbourly, and if they will not reforme, presents them.   Herbert, 'A Priest to the Temple', in *Works*, 284

ASCENSION DAY

Ascension Day is the fortieth day (inclusively) after Easter, the Thursday after Rogation Sunday, commemorating Christ's last appearance to the Apostles after the Resurrection, after which he ascended to Heaven in a cloud. To their question 'Lord, wilt thou at this time restore again the kingdom to Israel?' he responded:

It is not for you to know the times or the seasons, which the Father hath put in his own power. But ye shall receive power, after that the Holy Ghost is come upon you: and ye shall be witnesses unto me both in Jerusalem, and in all Judaea, and in Samaria, and unto the uttermost part of the earth. And when he had spoken these things, while they beheld, he was taken up; and a cloud received him out of their sight. (Acts 1: 7–9)

This day was called 'Holy Thursday' in English from Anglo-Saxon times, a name more recently given to Maundy Thursday. In some RC dioceses the feast has been moved to the following Sunday.

The ceremony of beating the bounds is sometimes performed on Ascension Day:

Holy Thursday, 25 May [1876]
    When service was over [at Merton Chapel, Oxford] and the very small congregation had passed out we sauntered through the quadrangle till we came to the iron gate of the college gardens. It was open and we went in. I had never been in Merton Gardens before. They are very beautiful and the famous Terrace Walk upon the old city walls and the lime avenue are most delightful. . . . We suddenly became aware that the peace of this paradise was being disturbed by the voices and laughter and trampling of a company of people and immediately there came into sight a master and a bachelor of arts in caps and gowns carrying a ladder on their shoulders assisted by several men, and attended by a number of parish boys. Every member of the company bore in his hand a long white peeled willow wand with which they were noisily beating and thrashing the old City walls and the Terrace Walk. 'They are beating the bounds', exclaimed Mayhew. . . . The ladder was let down over the city walls at two places where the walls were crossed by the parish bounds and at certain important points which it was desired that the boys should keep in mind they were made to scramble for sweetmeats. We determined to follow the procession and see the end. We came down into Deadman's Walk and then passed up a flight of steps and through an iron gate into Corpus Gardens. Here we were stopped by a gate of which the key could not be found for some time. In this quarter the parish boundary ran through an outhouse where used to be an ancient wheel for raising water. In this outhouse a cross was scratched upon a particular stone to mark where the boundary passed through the wall. By this time the missing key had been found and we found ourselves in the private garden of the President of Corpus, Matthias Wilson. It seemed to be an ancient custom here that those who beat the bounds should be regaled with bread, cheese and ale from the private buttery of the President of Corpus. Accordingly we gathered under an old archway while the customary dole was handed out to us over the buttery hatch. . . . The bounds now led us through an outer court where the parish boys

were liberally splashed with cold water by undergraduates from the windows of the upper rooms. Eventually we emerged close by Canterbury Gate and went into Oriel. Here there was a grand uproar in the quadrangle, the men threw out to the boys old hats (which were immediately used as footballs), biscuits were also thrown out and hot coppers, and the quadrangle echoed with shouting and laughter and the whole place was filled with uproar, scramble, and general licence and confusion . . . at length we went up the hall steps, down through the cloisters into the kitchen precincts where there was a Hogarthian scene and a laughable scrimmage with the young flat-white-capped cooks that might have furnished a picture for the Idle Apprentice. The procession passed next up Oriel Lane and here we left them.   Kilvert, iii. 315–17

Various superstitions are associated with Ascension Day:

In some countries they runne out of the doores in time of tempest, blessing themselves with a cheese, whereupon there was a cross made with a ropes end upon ascension daie. . . . Item, to hang an eg laid on ascension daie in the roofe of the house, preserveth the same from all hurts.

Scot, xii. xviii (1584)

The whole of Lord Penrhyn's slate quarrymen took a holiday on Ascension Day, because of the universally prevalent superstition that a fatal accident will inevitably cut off those who work during that day.   *N & Q*, 7th ser., ii (1886), 166

Ascension Day water is thought to be particularly efficacious:

On a spot called Nell's Point, is a fine well, to which great numbers of women resort on Holy Thursday, and having washed their eyes at the spring, each drops a pin into it. The landlord of the boarding-house told me, that on cleaning out the well, he took out a pint full of these votive pins.   Hoare, *Itinerary*, i. 133

In the parish of Marston St. Lawrence, Northamptonshire, there is a notion very prevalent, that rain-water collected on Holy Thursday is of powerful efficacy in all diseases of the *eye*. Ascension-day of the present year was very favourable in this respect to these village oculists, and numbers of the cottagers might be seen in all directions collecting the precious drops as they fell.

N & Q, 1st ser., ix (1854), 542

An Oxford tradition long forgotten:

The FELLOWS OF NEW-COLLEDGE OXON, have, time out of mind, every *Holy Thursday*, between 8 and 9 in the Morning, gone to an Hospital called SAINT BARTHOLOMEW a little without the City, Eastward: Where in the Chappel they hear certain PRAYERS READ and an ANTHEM Sung, from thence they go to the upper end of the Grove, adjoyning to the Chappel, (the way being strewed with Flowers) and place themselves ROUND the WELL; where they warble forth melodiously A SONG in 3, 4, or 5 parts, which being performed, they Refresh with a Morning-Draught, and retire back to OXFORD before SERMON.   Gadbury (1696)

On this day (*Sensa*) in Venice the Doge wedded the sea in a ceremony called the *Sposa-lizio del Mar*, commemorating the departure on Ascension Day, 9 May 1000, of the fleet under Doge Pietro Orseolo that pacified the Dalmatian coast and gave Venice command of the Adriatic. In its original form, the Doge and his entourage were sprinkled with holy water; other ceremonies accrued, most notably the casting of a golden ring into the sea, a ceremony of propitiation reinterpreted as a wedding. A tradition grew up, but falsely, that this transformation was made on the occasion of Pope Alexander III's visit in 1177; a painting in the Sala del Maggior Consiglio shows him handing the ring to Doge Sebastiano Ziani. It was one of the great Venetian festivals, much remarked upon by travellers. As reported by the English traveller Sir Thomas Hoby in 1549:

The daye of the Ascension the Duke of Venice with all the Siniorye goethe into this vessell the Bucentoro, and after they are a litle from the land they have a wonderous great ceremonie abowt the marying of the see. For the Duke takethe a ring of his finger and castethe yt into the seea, thinking by this meane to knitt yt so sure that yt shall never depart and leave the citie upon the drie land; as it is like to do in processe of time yf it contineue to diminishe still as yt hathe be-gone sith the memorye of man. Yet have they dailie provisions and officers appointed to the same to see the sandes and what soever is in the bottome in the shalowe places voided.   Hoby, 16–17

A less exalted but still extant custom in certain regions of the Veneto was to eat pig's-tongue sausage, supposed to bring good fortune.

Sunday after Ascension Day (CY Seventh Sunday of Easter, and so RC where not Ascension, before 1970 Sunday within the Octave of the Ascension; introit *Exaudi*). The week introduced by this Sunday was formerly called Expectation Week, from the dis-ciples awaiting the Paraclete, the Holy Spirit promised by Christ before his Ascension. The BCP and pre-1970 RC names reflect the conception, retained by the Lutherans, that Eastertide ends at Ascension, not at Pentecost.

WHIT SUNDAY

Whit Sunday, the seventh Sunday after Easter, also called Pentecost from the Greek for 'fiftieth' (so formerly in Spanish *cincuesma*, and similar forms in Walloon and Flemish). Often misunderstood as 'Whitsun Day', whence 'Whitsun' and 'the Whitsun holiday' for the holiday weekend. The name comes from the white robes worn by those baptized on the vigil; the ceremonies recall those of the Easter vigil.

Whit Sunday is the fiftieth day from Easter (inclusive) and is the day when the Holy Spirit descended on the Apostles:

And suddenly there came a sound from heaven as of a rushing mighty wind, and it filled all the house where they were sitting. And there appeared unto them cloven tongues like as of fire, and it sat upon each of them. And they were all filled with the Holy Ghost, and began to speak with other tongues, as the Spirit gave them utterance. (Acts 2: 2–4)

The disciples will have been assembled to keep the Jewish feast of Shavuot, understood as celebrating the bestowal of the Torah on Moses.

An Irish Whit Sunday superstition:

A child born at Whitsuntide will have an evil temper, and may commit a murder. . . . To turn away ill-luck from a child born at that time, a grave must be dug and the infant laid in it for a few minutes. After this process the evil spell is broken, and the child is safe.

S. Wilde, i. 270 (1887)

On this day still takes place the bread and cheese dole at St Briavels in Gloucestershire, a custom that apparently originated in the twelfth century, when, according to local legend, the Earl of Hereford, who was the Lord High Constable of the Forest of Dean, acquiesced to his wife's plea to rescind his order that the villagers could no longer take wood from the forest; the grateful villagers then subscribed to the dole.

On Whitsunday, at St. Briaval's, in Gloucestershire, several baskets full of bread and cheese, cut into small squares of about an inch each, are brought into the church; and, immediately after divine service is ended, the churchwardens, or some other persons, take them into the galleries, whence their contents are thrown among the congregation, who have a grand scramble for them in the body of the church. This occasions as great a tumult and uproar as the amusements of a village wake; the inhabitants being always extremely anxious to attend worship on this day. The custom is holden for the purpose of preserving, to the poor of St. Briaval's and Hervelsfield, the right of cutting and carrying away wood from 3,000 acres of coppice land, in Hudknolls and the Meend; and for which every housekeeper is assessed 2d. to buy the bread and cheese which are given away.   *The Times* (7 Oct. 1816)

By 1857 it was thought too unseemly for such uproar to take place in church; the ceremony was removed outdoors, and eventually away from the church.

Whit Sunday is a time to wear new clothes:

'My french-hood is bought already, and my silke gowne is a making' . . . 'And when do you meane to weare them Gossip?' 'At Whitsontide (quoth she) if God spare me life.'

Deloney (1630), ch. 8

Whit Monday and Tuesday were formerly observed as days of religious duty (they are among the BCP's feasts to be observed); until 1967 Whit Monday was a Bank Holiday (outside Scotland), now replaced by the Late Spring Bank Holiday on the last Monday in May. Formerly it was a time for revelry, similar to the Monday and Tuesday following Easter and Low Sunday. In Lancashire there was a trick by which one confederate would hold a stick over the victim's head and the other knock it downwards. A somewhat similar custom is reported in Ireland in 1828:

Whit Monday. Ballingarry [in Tipperary], that is, Kilboyne, fair day, that is, the most wicked fair in Munster or Leinster: for there is there many a stealthy stick, many a vicious villain with a big blackthorn, many a captious bully and tricky wight and big-headed rascal with a fierce ash shillelagh there peeling and tearing open skulls without sense, and heads without brains, without ability, without intelligence, without manners.   O'Sullivan, i. 273

Many 'church ales' took place at Whitsuntide. These were occasions for parishes to raise money, and involved dancing and drinking; sacred and secular coexisted precariously, and the revelry often got the upper hand.

A Miller at Churchdowne, neere Glocester, would needs . . . keepe a solemne Whitson ale, for which he had made large preparation and provision, even of threescore dozen of cheesecakes, with other things proportionable; in the Church-house, halfe a mile from his mille, his musical instruments were sett forth on the side of the Church-house, when the Minister and people were to passe to the Church to evening Prayer. When prayer and Sermon were ended, the Drumme is struck up, the peeces discharged, the Musicians play, and the rowt fall a dauncing, till the evening;

where they all with the Miller resort to his mille; where that evening before they had supt, about 9 of the cloke on Whitsunday, a fire took suddainly in his house over their heads, and was so briefe and quicke, that it burnt downe his house and mille, and devoured with all the greatest of all his other provision and housholdstuffe. H. Burton, 4 (1636)

TRINITY SUNDAY

The Sunday after Whit Sunday, or Octave of Pentecost. Celebrations of the Trinity were at first frowned on by popes, since they did not commemorate an event; Alexander III (1159–81), asked by an unnamed archbishop to rule whether he should wear his pallium at this feast, declined, since although some kept it on the Octave of Pentecost, others on the Sunday before Advent, Rome had no special feast, but spoke words in praise of the Trinity every day. However, the Octave of Pentecost was proclaimed the feast of the Holy Trinity for the English Church by Thomas Becket, who had been consecrated archbishop of Canterbury on 3 June 1162, the Octave of Pentecost, in the then cathedral, dedicated to the Holy Trinity; it was made universal by John XXII in 1334. Celebrating a unity in three Persons, it has no octave.

CORPUS CHRISTI

This feast, which the RC Church now officially calls 'Feast of the Body and Blood of Christ' (and in many places, though not in the British Isles, moves to the following Sunday), commemorates the institution of the Holy Eucharist at the Last Supper; it was initiated *c.*1230 by the nun Juliana of Liège after having received a series of visions over twenty years of a full moon with a dark spot; at the end Christ revealed to her that the moon represented the Church and was incomplete because a feast was missing. In 1264 observance was ordered in the bull *Transiturus* by Urban IV (the pope damned to hell in the original ballad of *Danhauser* or Tannhäuser); in 1277 the first Corpus Christi procession took place in Cologne; but it was only after John XXII's bull of 1317 that the feast was widely celebrated. By this time it had already acquired the procession that would increase in size and magnificence through the following centuries; as a summer feast and a joyful one at that, marking the widespread medieval devotion to the Eucharist, it drew together clergy and layfolk. In England before 1547 pageants and plays were customary, often staged by Corpus Christi guilds; the procession has been revived in Oxford. The name implies the RC doctrine that at mass the bread and wine are transubstantiated at consecration to the body and blood of Christ; in Protestant eyes this is 'repugnant to the plain words of Scripture' (Article XXVIII of the Church of England), but ASB and CY include an optional Day of Thanksgiving for the Institution of Holy Communion, which name allows it to be celebrated in good conscience.

Corpus Christi Day was marked in Rome with a solemn and triumphant procession in which the Pope took part. The parade route was tented over, and the finest tapestries of the Pope and the cardinals provided hangings. In 1581 Gregory Martin describes it thus:

The way being thus prepared, the multitude beginneth to goe this procession early in the morning, so that the place is never voyd of thicke rankes marching in modest and devout maner, til the Pope come forth him self. . . . At the Palace gate stand on high from the ground the Trompeters. So then, after the vulgar sort which are going al the morning, the first of accoumpt (bycause this is the Popes Procession) are they that belong to the Court, having living, pension, office, dignitie, or any calling there. Of al which none must be away without urgent cause upon that day, every one with his torche of white waxe light in his hand. So, they goe two and two, beginning of the Juniors and the laitie, a goodly companie, and long in passing, filling al the way with double lightes. Then come forth the gowned men in distinct robes according to theyr Office and profession, pewke, purple, and scarlet couler, the Chamberlaynes very many al in red gownes, the Chaplens, the Protonotaries, the Doctors of the Rota, the Referendaries, other dignities that I can not name. Then beginne the Copes or (as the maner is there) rich Vestiments to appeare, first the Penitentiaries or Ghostly fathers of S. Peters . . . then both vestiments and mitres as Abbottes, Bishopes, Archbishopes, Patriarches, and Cardinals, everie one his man by his side that carieth his torche. The Bishopes, Archebyshopes, and Patriarches were 27, when I saw them . . . Never shalt thou see out of Rome such a ranke of reverent Prelates, marching two and two before the B. Sacrament, which his Holinesse in richer Cope and triple crowne besette with pretious stones, carieth with stedfast hand, and fixed looke, in a pretious monstrant, under a costly Canopie, borne by foure of the noblest persons then present . . .

At the very appearing of him in the Palace gate to come forth the Trompeters play their part with melodious blastes, and the gonnes ar heard thicke and thundering from the Castel of Sainct Angelo. The peale being finished, the Popes quyer continewe all the way with most excellent musicke. The swicers [Swiss Guards] on foote in newe partie Cotes with swordes and halbordes, gard both sides of all the mitres throughout; And when the B. Sacrament is so farre passed, immediately enter the horsemen and followe on garding it behinde, and then goe of the twelve peces at their backe, alwayes standing there before S. Peters. In the middle way by the Cardinal of Trent his palace is there a stage and new musicke of the best, for the time that the Procession resteth there. Then goe they forward to S. Peters Churche, and so to his Chapel and aultar, where the solemne Masse is sung by the Pope him selfe or one of the Cardinals.   G. Martin, 87–8

Corpus Christi in Montreal in 1785, as observed by a young Scotsman:

After breakfast I went with McKindlay and Blanchard to hear Mass, this being the day the *grand fête Dieu* was kept. Half the town put up green trees before their houses for the procession. . . . There were about eighteen black nuns and sixteen gray ones, all the boys belonging to the seminary in their proper dresses, a number of *faux prêtres* (tradesmen, very richly dressed for the day), and a great many women carrying candles. These were followed by most of the ladies and gentlemen of the place of the Catholic religion and the whole formed a pretty *coup d'œil*. There were some very pretty women in the church. I thought the frankincense had a droll smell and could not help laughing when McKindlay told me it was rosin. Their music was quite a farce; we had a solo upon the violin, out of tune, by way of a voluntary. . . . Dobie said *les faux prêtres* were a parcel of butchers, bakers, tailors, etc., and half of them the greatest rascals in Montreal. Some of the women, too, bore infamous characters. I agree with him in thinking they treated their *bon Dieu* very ill to suffer such shabby fellows to walk in such a holy procession. They strewed a few flowers in the streets, but as they did not abound in them they made up the deficiency with different colored cloth. In short it was quite a farce.   Hunter, 34

SUNDAYS AFTER TRINITY OR AFTER PENTECOST

Trinity has no octave, a fact said to be appropriate to the celebration of unity within trinity and trinity within unity. The BCP, following the Sarum missal, counts all Sundays between Sunday and Advent as 'Sundays after Trinity'; of these there may be any number from 22 (if Easter falls on 24 or 25 Apr.) to 27 (if Easter falls between 22 and 26 Mar., inclusive). The same usage is found among Lutherans, and was followed by Dominicans and Carmelites, but the normal RC reckoning before 1969 was of Sundays after Pentecost, which were always one higher than Sundays after Trinity. Services, however, were provided for only 25 Sundays after Trinity in the BCP and for only 24 Sundays after Pentecost in the Roman service-books; in both churches the last service of the sequence was always used on the Sunday before Advent and any extra services needed (a respective maximum of two and four) taken from those not needed after Epiphany.

Since 1970 the RC Church has reckoned these Sundays as being in Ordinary Time, which resumes at Pentecost; the second Sunday before Advent is always the 33rd, the 34th being the feast of Christ the King. In consequence, when the year begins on any day but Sunday or Monday, or in leap year Saturday, the week of Ordinary Time introduced by Pentecost will be higher by two, not one, than that introduced by the last Sunday before Lent. Pentecost and Trinity, however, are referred to by those names (and likewise Corpus Christi, where it is observed on the following Sunday) rather than as Sundays of Ordinary Time.

The ASB introduced numbering after Pentecost, but curtailed it to accommodate its Sundays before Advent; depending on the date of Easter, there were 17–22 Sundays after Pentecost, followed by a Last Sunday after Pentecost six weeks before Advent. CY restores numbering after Trinity, but only down to All Saints, allowing 16–21 numbered Sundays and a Last Sunday after Trinity. It then provides for Sundays before Advent, of which, however, it reckons only four; what happens when (as in 2008) Easter falls on or before 26 March, so that there are 27 Sundays separating Trinity from Advent, is not recorded.

SACRED HEART OF JESUS

An RC feast on the third Friday after Pentecost, granted by Clement XIII for the Polish dioceses, extended to the whole Church by Pius XI in 1856, and given a new liturgy by Pius XI in 1928.

VOLKSTRAUERTAG

A day of national mourning in Germany on the second Sunday before Advent for victims of National Socialism and the dead of both world wars.

DAY OF PRAYER AND REPENTANCE

A Lutheran observance, in German *Buß- und Bettag*, on the Wednesday before the last Sunday before Advent. It is a legal public holiday in Germany, except in the solidly RC state of Bavaria.

STIR-UP SUNDAY, CHRIST THE KING, *TOTENSONNTAG*

Before the recent liturgical reforms, the collect for the last Sunday before Advent included the phrase 'Excita, quaesumus Domine, tuorum fidelium voluntates', in the BCP 'Stir up, we beseech thee, O Lord, the wills of thy faithful people'. This phrase was popularly taken as the signal to the housewife that the time had come to stir up the ingredients for the Christmas pudding; the day was therefore known as 'Stir-up Sunday'. It is now the feast of Christ the King, a festival introduced in the RC Church by Pius XI in 1925 on the last Sunday in October, moved in 1969 to the last (thirty-fourth) Sunday in Ordinary Time, one week before Advent, and adopted by the Church of England in CY, which moved the 'Stir-up' collect to the post-communion prayer. Among Lutherans it has since 1816 been *Totensonntag*, the Sunday of the Dead.

FEAST OF THE DEDICATION OF A CHURCH

This is a yearly feast, celebrated on the anniversary of the consecration of a church. The English Convocations of 1536 laid down that it should be kept on the first Sunday in October; this remains normal practice when the true date is not known (CY also permits the Last Sunday after Trinity). No service is prescribed in the BCP, an omission remedied in ASB and CY. The main dedication feast in the RC Church is that of the Lateran Basilica, on 9 November; see too *5 August, *18 November.

The Westminster Abbey dedicated by Edward the Confessor (see *13 Oct.) on 28 December 1065 replaced a predecessor whose miraculous dedication is narrated by Jerome Porter (1632):

When *Ethelred* king of *Kent* by the preaching of S. Augustin the *Benedictin* monk had receaved the Christian faith, *Sebert* his nephew then king of the *East-Angles* by the same holymans endeavour was purged from *Paganisme* in the sacred font of Baptisme. This *Sebert* erected a famous Church in honour of S. Paul within the walls of *London* (which was esteemed the cheif head of his kingdom) and placed *Mellitus* the Monk therein, honouring him with Episcopall dignitie. But without the walls in the West part of the cittie he founded a goodly Monastery for Monks of S. Benedicts order, in honour of S. Peter the Apostle, enriching it with verie large revenews. When the night before the Dedication of the Church, S. Peter himself in an unknowne habitt appeared to a fisherman on the other side of the river *Thames* running by the sayd Abbey, desiring him to passe him over, and he would reward his paines; which was performed: when goeing out of the boate in sight of the fisherman he entred the new-built Church, where suddenly was seene a strainge light from heaven, that gave such a wonderfull lustre to all therein, as if it would have prevented the sunnes comeing by turning night into day. There was present with the Apostle in the Church a multitude of heavenly burgesses filling it with melodious musick, and most fragrant odours. Having finished all the solemnities and ceremonies due unto the dedication of a Church, he whom our Lord made a famous FISHER of men, returned to the *Fisher* of fishes, whom he found wonderfully amazed, and carried allmost beyond himself with the flashes of the divine splendour, and therefore with a courteous consolation the Apostle restored him to himself againe, reducing his distracted thoughts to the rules of reason; and the two fishers entring into the boate togeather, S. Peter demaunded whether he had taken anie fish or noe? Being suddenly strucken (replied he) with the sight of that unusuall brightnes, and detained with expectation of thy returne, I endeavoured not to fish, but securely attended my promised reward from thee, whereunto the Apostle answered; cast forth thy netts, and trie. He obeyed his commaund, and presently found his nett loaden with store of fish, all of one kind excepting one fish of a mightie greatnes without comparison. Having drawne them on shore the Apostle bad him present that great one to Bishop Mellitus in his name, and the rest (said he) take for thy reward. An aboundance of this kind thou shalt enjoy all thy life time, and thy posteritie a long time after thee; only hereafter dare not to fish on the Sundaies. I am the Apostle Peter who with my heavenly fellow-citizens have allreadie consecrated the Church built in my name, and by the authoritie of my owne dedication, I have prevented the Bishops benediction. Tell him therefore what thou hast seene, and heard, and the markes imprinted in the walles shall give sufficient testimonie to strengthen the truth of thy relation. Let him therefore forbeare from anie further dedication . . . The next morning the fisher with his great fish meets the Bishop Mellitus as he was goeing to dedicate the Church, and makes knownes unto him whatsoever was given him in charge by the Apostle. Whereat the Bishop much astonished entred into the Church, and finds the pavement signed with the inscription of the Greek and Hebrew alphabet, the walls annoynted with holy oyle in twelve severall places, and the remnants of as manie wax candles fastened to twelve crosses, all things being yet moist, with the late springling of holy oyle, and water. Whereuppon togeather with the people he gave prayse, and thanks to allmightie God, for that great remonstrance of his goodnes unto them. The whole posteritie of the fisherman confirmed the truth of this miracle, for as they received by tradition from their father they offered the tenth of all the commoditie gotten afterward by that art to S. Peter, and his servants in that place.

Porter, 16–18

THE ORTHODOX CHURCH
YEAR

By 'Orthodox', here and throughout this book, we mean, as usual in Western par-
lance, those churches that are in communion with the Oecumenical Patriarchate of
Constantinople, not the Church of the East (formerly called Nestorian) or the non-
Chalcedonian churches (Syrian of Antioch, or Jacobite; Syrian of India, Coptic,
Armenian, and Ethiopic), even though they claim this title. It is also assumed for con-
venience that they use the Byzantine rite, though a few churches in the West do not, and
conversely some churches in communion with Rome (the so-called 'Uniate' or 'Greek
Catholic' churches) do.

In all Orthodox countries, Easter, and all moveable feasts and fasts, are determined
according to the Julian calendar, even though the dates thus found are expressed in the
New Style; that is to say, Orthodox Easter is the first Sunday after the ecclesiastical full
moon ('Legal Pascha', i.e. Passover according to the Mosaic Law) on or next after 21
March OS, currently equivalent to 3 April NS. Although the methods used for calculating Easter differ in detail from those used in the West before Pope Gregory's reform,
the result is always the same. For immoveable feasts some countries, notably Greece,
Romania, and Bulgaria, use the New Style, albeit with a different rule for suppressed intercalation (the Revised Julian Calendar; see II: *Modern Calendar: Twentieth-Century
Reforms*); but in Russia, Serbia, Macedonia, and Georgia the Julian calendar is retained
for all ecclesiastical purposes, as also on Mount Athos and among the Orthodox of
Jerusalem and Poland. Thus, although the Orthodox year, like the Byzantine indiction-
year, begins on 1 September, in Russia and the other countries listed with it above the
civil date is currently (and will be down to 2099) the 14th. The same adjustment must
be made to calendar dates given for immoveable feasts.

The feasts of the Orthodox Church are distinguished as being of Our Lord, of His
Mother, or of the Saints; Annunciation partakes of both the first two characters, as
does Hypapante, though originally of Our Lord. The most important feast, in practice
as well as principle, is Easter; next are said to come the Twelve Great Feasts, an informal classification never formally defined and therefore differing from list to list. They
may include, among moveable feasts, Orthodoxy Sunday, the Thursday of the Great
Canon (for both these see below on Lent), Palm Sunday, Ascension, and Pentecost;
among the immoveable:

8 September	Nativity of the Theotokos (Mother of God)
14 September	Exaltation of the Honoured and Life-Giving Cross
21 November	Entry of the Theotokos into the Temple
25 December	The Nativity of Our Lord Jesus Christ
6 January	The Baptism of Christ in the Jordan (Theophany, 'the Lights')
2 February	The Meeting of Our Lord (Hypapante)
25 March	The Annunciation of the Theotokos
6 August	The Transfiguration of Christ
15 August	The Dormition of the Theotokos

Loosely corresponding to the octave attached before 1955 to many RC feasts is the 'apodosis' (Russian *otdánie*), literally 'giving back'; it is not always a week after the feast, in some cases being sooner or later. Apart from Easter, whose apodosis is the Wednesday before Ascension, most major feasts are so extended, but not Annunciation, nor Hypapante when it falls in Lent. (The Entry of the Theotokos was formerly also called her Apodosis; that name is not now used. The apodosis of the feast is 25 Nov.)

There are many other feasts, of which among the moveable we may note the Akathistos on the fifth Saturday of Lent, Thomas Sunday a week after Easter, and All Saints on the Sunday after Pentecost; among the immoveable:

23 September	Conception of John the Precursor
8 November	Synaxis of the Archistrategos Michael and the other Incorporeal Powers
26 December	Synaxis of the Theotokos
30 January	The Three Great Hierarchs
3 February	Synaxis of Symeon the God-Receiver and the Prophetess Anna
26 March	Synaxis of Archangel Gabriel
7 May	Appearance of the Sign of the Honoured Cross in the Heavens
24 June	Nativity of John the Precursor
29 June	The Apostles Peter and Paul
30 June	Synaxis of Holy Apostles
2 July	Deposition of the Honourable Vestment of the Theotokos
1 August	Procession of the Life-giving Cross
29 August	Beheading of John the Precursor
31 August	Deposition of the Honourable Girdle of the Theotokos

The term *synaxis* (Russian *sobór*) means 'assembly'; as used on 26 December, 3 February, 26 March, and 30 June, it denotes a service in honour of figures associated with the subject of the previous day's celebration.

There are four major fasts (dates inclusive):

Little Lent	Christmas fast: 15 November–24 December
Great Lent	Monday of seventh week before Easter–Great Saturday
Fast of the Apostles	Monday after All Saints–28 June
Dormition Fast	1–14 August

Wednesdays and Fridays are fast-days unless they coincide with feasts; but no Saturday is a fast except Great Saturday, the day before Easter, nor is either fasting or kneeling permitted on Sundays or during Pentecost. The Exaltation of the Holy Cross is kept as a fast, since it owes its ultimate origin to the Crucifixion, as are feasts recalling a sad event, such as the Beheading of John the Precursor, and also 5 January, the Vigil of the Theophany.

The liturgical year is divided into three main portions, known from their service books as the Triodion, the Pentecostarion, and the Octoechos or Parakletike. Many Sundays, especially in the Triodion and Pentecostarion, are known by names, generally relating to their Gospel readings; in contrast to Western practice, weeks are reckoned, except between Easter and Pentecost, from Monday to Sunday.

THE TRIODION

The Triodion is so called from the many three-ode canons contained in it, which trope the abbreviated sets of three canticles (instead of the normal eight) sung on most Lenten weekdays at matins. This period begins on the fourth Sunday before Lent, known from its Gospel reading as the Sunday of the Publican and the Pharisee. From this time on, the soul should be prepared for Lent, but many of the faithful are more interested in preparing the body: the next three weeks are widely kept as a carnival, known in Greek as *apókreōs*, demotic *apokriés*, which as in RC countries the Church has accepted as a fact, while attempting to ensure that its own message is still heard. We even read of a time when the priest himself would lead off the dance in church, singing 'The tree was Christ and the All-Holy [Virgin] the root, and its branches the Twelve Apostles'; but more characteristic are songs and masquerades, often of a satirical or licentious nature.

The first week of carnival, beginning on the Monday following the Sunday of the Publican and the Pharisee, is sometimes called Proclamation Week, from such mock proclamations as 'Beggar, sell your bag' enjoining people to get meat at any cost, or 'Release Week', since the prohibition of eating meat on Wednesday and Friday was often waived in order to spite the Armenians, who keep this week as a very strict fast. (From the Armenian name for this fast, *aṙačʿavoṙ*, 'preceding', comes the Greek Artsivourion, used to denote Release Week, or more generally for total licence.) Attested celebrations include the mock trial, in the south-western Peloponnese, of a man charged with killing his pig, found guilty, condemned to death, but saved by a last-minute pardon; and at a higher level, the performance in Crete of scenes from its fine Renaissance dramas. Fatted beasts are slaughtered, ready for the repasts to come. The week culminates in the Sunday of the Prodigal Son, corresponding to the Western Septuagesima.

This is followed by Meat Week, Apokreos proper, a time of hearty feasting. To be sure, Wednesday and Friday are fasted, but between them comes *Tsiknopémpti*, 'Burnt Thursday', when families and friends, even the poorest, eat meat and drink wine; the smell of burning meat gives proof that the day is being kept in the proper spirit. Dinner is followed by a masquerade; in Epirus, it is recorded that master masons and apprentices would eat and drink together on terms of equality. The Saturday is an All Souls' Saturday, on which prayers are offered for the dead; the same applies to the Saturday before Pentecost. The last day for eating meat until Easter is the Sunday of Apokreos, the Western Sexagesima.

The church at Jerusalem used to keep this week as the first week of Lent, fasting an exact forty days spread over eight weeks, Monday to Friday; but the practice that prevailed was to fast thirty-six days, as was also the older Western practice. However, whereas the West fasted Monday to Saturday between Quadragesima and Easter, the Orthodox Church fasts Monday to Friday in the six weeks following Apokreos and Monday to Saturday in Great Week. The passage of the seven weeks would be marked in Greece, in the days before wall-calendars, by tearing off, one at a time, the seven feet of a paper nun called Lady Lent (*Kyrá Sarakostí*) with no mouth and her hands crossed in prayer, or seven hen's feathers stuck into a potato or onion suspended from the ceiling by a string.

Nevertheless, the first of these weeks, known as Cheese Week, during which milk products and eggs may be eaten, is distinguished from the Fast proper, being kept cheerfully, in some places with elaborate masquerades. In Russia the popular name is *máslyanitsa* or *máslenitsa*, 'Butter Week'; this is the carnival week, said to have begun as a pagan feast in honour of the cattle-god Volos (see *11 Feb.). The traditional fare consists of pancakes (*bliný*) dipped in caviar and sour cream, of which the first was anciently offered to the dead; traditional amusements include tobogganing and swings.

This week ends in Cheese Sunday, the Western Quinquagesima, on which, at various places in Greece, children might leap through fires, bachelors call the names of their intended, or a dance be held to appease the North Wind. The remaining whitemeats and eggs are consumed in elaborate meals. A typical family or communal meal consists of no meat, but macaroni, eggs, cheese pies, milk pies, and a broth made of white goat cheese with stewed wild herbs. In Arcadia the eldest member of the family is host; the first dish is the cheese broth. A short prayer is said; the participants then lift the table with their little fingers, saying 'Holy broth, cheese broth: whoever drinks of it and does not laugh shall not be bitten by fleas', and then take three spoonfuls quickly in silence, before all burst out in laughter. A macaroni course follows; the unmarried try to sneak out a piece to put under their pillows in order to dream of their future spouse. The last dish is usually an egg: 'With an egg I close my mouth, with an egg I shall reopen it' (meaning the red hard-boiled Easter egg). In Eastern Roumelia the guests used to roll eggs across the table, saying 'May Lent roll by even as this egg rolls', then stop their mouths with it.

The first Monday of Lent is Clean Monday, a time for cleansing pots and pans with ashes and hot water and sobering up, though it is still kept in Greece as a holiday, with trips to the country to visit family for Lenten meals, and often to fly kites. Carnival mummery sometimes continues until the bells of evening service; at certain places in Crete King Carnival is interred, or Easter fare buried to the burning of incense and laments that 'Broadbean has arrived and sent Macaroni and Meatman into exile.' However, the most pious take nothing at all on the first three days until Wednesday evening, after which not only meat but fish, whitemeats, wine, and oil are forbidden; however, wine and oil are permitted on Saturday, Sunday, 9 March (the Forty Martyrs of Sebasteia), and the patronal feast of a church, and fish as well on the Annunciation. Even with dispensations to take account of modern conditions, the Orthodox laity, as well as the clergy, observe far stricter austerity than Westerners have done.

On the first Saturday honour is paid to St Theodore the Recruit (see *17 Feb.), who reportedly appeared to Patriarch Eudoxius of Constantinople with a warning that on Clean Monday Julian the Apostate intended to put on the market bread offered to idols and sprinkled with sacrificial blood; he recommended that Christians eat only *kóllyva* (a dish of boiled wheat kernels with spices, sugar, raisins, or pomegranate seeds in various combinations), which are distributed on this day. This is also a feature of commemorations of the dead, which are held on most ferial Saturdays in Greece, with prayers for the dead and blessing of *kóllyva*; hence this day is popularly regarded as another All Souls' Saturday. St Theodore having been split into two saints, the day is sometimes dedicated to them both.

The first Sunday of the Fast, the Western Quadragesima, is known as 'Orthodoxy Sunday', commemorating the great feast celebrated on this Sunday, 11 March 843, in honour of the holy icons to set the seal on the final defeat of Iconoclasm, the attack on icons first launched by the emperor Leo III in 726. Although the Seventh Oecumenical Council in 787 had upheld their veneration, the attack was resumed by Leo V in 814 and lasted till the emperor Theophilus' death in 842; his widow reversed the policy.

On the second Sunday of the Fast, honour is given to Gregory Palamas, archbishop of Thessalonica (d. 1359), champion of the 'hesychast' tradition of mystical prayer, particularly developed on Mount Athos, through which the specially chosen are believed to behold of the Divine Light of Mount Tabor (see *6 Aug.). In 1337 he came into conflict with Barlaam of Calabria (Petrarch's would-be teacher of Greek), who asserted the utter unknowableness of God, and denounced the hesychasts' exercises as superstitious navel-gazing; Gregory answered that though God's essence could not be known, His uncreated energies can be directly experienced as deifying grace. Gregory's position was upheld by a council in 1341, condemned in 1344, and reaffirmed in 1347 and 1351.

Third Sunday of the Fast: Adoration of the Cross. The Orthodox Church has never celebrated the Invention on 3 May as the West used to do, but a brief commemoration is made on 6 March; this being always in Lent, a feast was appointed for this Sunday.

Fourth Sunday of the Fast: John of the Ladder (see *30 Mar.).

The following Thursday, in the fifth week of the Fast, honours the Great Canon of St Andrew of Crete, a hymn of 250 strophes composed by Andrew, bishop of Gortyn (d. 740, feast-day 4 July). On the following Saturday, the beautiful alphabetic hymn known as the Akáthistos ('[sung] without sitting'), dating from the sixth century, is sung in honour of the Mother of God. The next day is the fifth Sunday of the Fast, dedicated to Mary of Egypt (see *2 Apr.).

The sixth Saturday of the Fast is that of the Holy and Righteous Lazarus, whose raising is celebrated. Children in Greek villages make wreaths of yellow daisies, symbolizing the pallor of Lazarus' corpse, and go round the houses singing about his resurrection and begging for money or eggs; the latter are sold to raise money for a school outing. The next day is Palm Sunday; in the absence of palms it is celebrated with olive branches in Greece, with willow in Russia (where it is called 'Willow' or 'Flower-Bearing' Sunday, and where willow rituals long antedated Christianity).

There follows Great Week, during which all singing, music, and entertainment are forbidden; so is work, except cleaning and preparing for Easter. The Liturgy of the Presanctified is used on the first three days. Icons are covered in black to signify the Passion; but the Orthodox do not concentrate on His suffering to the exclusion of His triumph, as the West may sometimes seem to do: with the Franciscan *Stabat mater*, in which Christ's pain and the Virgin's grief move the 'I' of the poem to grief and repentance, but not a word is said about the Resurrection, may be contrasted Romanos the Melode's *kontakion*, in which Christ on the Cross bids His mother lay aside her grief and explains the purpose and outcome of His sacrifice. After the elaborate Great Friday service comes the *epitaphios*, in which Christ's bier, covered with flowers, is borne in procession; plates of lentil- and barley-shoots have been thought to recall the Gardens of Adonis, pots of fennel and similar plants laid with his effigy. Indeed, popular devotion has been known to assimilate Crucifixion and Resurrection to the annual death and revival of pagan vegetation gods.

THE PENTECOSTARION: EASTER

Great Lent culminates in the midnight service at which the few lights lit are extinguished, leaving the church in pitch darkness; the priest brings in the New Fire, a candle from which worshippers light their own, then goes out to announce 'Christ is risen' (in Greek *Christós anéstē*, in Church Slavonic *Khristós voskrése*). This becomes the Easter greeting, to which the reply is 'He is risen indeed' (*Alēthôs anéstē, Voístinu voskrése*); the faithful exchange the Resurrection kiss and in many places give each other red-coloured eggs, or strike each other's egg with their own; travellers commented on the uninhibited revelry with which, in Russia, all classes and both sexes discharged the ceremonies of kiss and egg. From now until All Saints' Day the invariable portions of services are recorded in the Pentecostarion; until Pentecost, weeks begin on Sunday.

Greeks, who have had their wild enjoyments during Carnival, are moderate in their Easter indulgence: eggs are cracked, *mayéritsa* soup is eaten after the midnight service, and roast lamb after Paschal Vespers, a relaxed service during which the Gospel is read in as many languages as can be managed. Russian traditions are more exuberant: witness this account of Orthodox Easter in Moscow, 8/20 April 1800, as observed by E. D. Clarke:

Fortune loves chance, and by one of those chances, we arrived here at the season of the whole year in which Moscow is most interesting to strangers. Moscow is in every thing extraordinary—

in disappointing your expectations, and in surpassing them—exciting wonder and derision—pleasure and regret. We are now in the midst of the Pâques; which is here celebrated with a pomp and festivity, unknown to the rest of Europe. The most splendid pageants of Rome do not equal the grandeur and costliness of the church ceremonies; neither can Venice, in the midst of her carnival, rival in debauchery, and parade, and licentiousness, and relaxation, what is now passing in Moscow. . . .

We went at midnight to the cathedral to be present at the ceremony of the resurrection. About two o'clock in the morning the Archbishop, attended by all his bishops and priests, in habits of embroidered satin, covered with gold and silver, and precious stones, bear their consecrated candles to look in the holy sepulchre, and finding that Jesus was risen, announced to the people with a loud voice, '*Christos voskress!*' that is to say, 'Christ is risen!' and at the delivery of those important words, the signal is given, for eating flesh, feasting, drinking, and dancing. To be drunk the whole of Easter week, is as much a religious observance, as to abstain from flesh in Lent, and the Russians are very punctual in religious observances.

from a letter of 25 Apr. 1800, in Otter, 399–401

By contrast, the Russian traveller Peter Tolstoy, in the Ukrainian city of Mohyliw (then in Poland) for the Orthodox Easter on 4/14 April 1697, observed that the inhabitants did not bring eggs to church and after the service (marked by the tolling of bells and firing of cannon) spent the rest of the day at home; on the Monday, however, there was a great procession.

THE PENTECOSTARION: WHITE MONDAY
TO ALL SAINTS

Easter Week is often known as 'Renewal Week', as indicating that by the Resurrection 'all things are become new' (2 Cor. 5: 17); it is also known as 'White' or 'Bright' Week. Wednesday and Friday are not fasted. Attested Greek customs include White Monday services not announced by bells, the last comer being fined, and a dance on White Thursday to appease the North Wind, said to be transferred from Cheese Sunday by homophony of *Péfti* 'Thursday' (standard *pémpti*) and *péfti* 'falls'. Seven of the eight Octoechos tones are used.

The Sundays between Easter and Pentecost are known by names rather than numbers, all but the last relating to the Gospel read in the Liturgy (which in Orthodox usage specifically denotes the Eucharist); these names may also be given to the weeks they introduce, but when they are numbered the count includes Easter week. During the whole period there is no kneeling in church, in token of the Resurrection (which is also the reason for not kneeling on Sundays). There was a widespread belief in Russia that during this period Christ and the Apostles wandered the earth in rags, begging for alms.

The Sunday after Easter is known as Antipascha, New Sunday, or the Sunday of St Thomas, whose doubts are narrated in the Gospel reading; nevertheless it is strictly a feast of the Lord, with its own apodosis on the following Saturday. In Russia, before the Revolution, from this week to the end of June spring would be invoked from the hills with a *khorovód* (a circling dance accompanied by choral song), led by a woman with a loaf in one hand and a red-painted egg in the other.

Sunday of the Myrrh-Bearing Women (Mary Magdalene and her companions, who on coming to anoint Jesus' body found his tomb empty). On this day begins the cycle of the eight tones, a new tone being used each week; for those familiar with the Gregorian psalm-tones, they are the same eight tones but in a different order, the four authentic tones followed by the four plagal. However, the Sundays of the Pentecostarion all differ in certain respects from the normal pattern.

Sunday of the Paralytic (healed on the Sabbath at Bethesda).

Sunday of the Samaritan Woman (who met Jesus at Jacob's well), also known as Mid-Pentecost.

Sunday of the Blind Man (the man born blind whom Jesus healed). The following Thursday is Ascension Day.

Sunday of the Holy Fathers (the Council of Nicaea). In Russia, on the following Thursday, was the *semík*, or 'Seven' (this being the seventh week of Easter); a young birch-tree would be cut down and colourfully dressed (often as a woman); after a feast, it was carried back to the village as an honoured guest, visited on the Friday and Saturday, but thrown into running water on the Sunday.

The Saturday of this week is an All Souls' Saturday; it perpetuates the pagan Rosalia, a festival of the dead held at various dates in May or June when the roses were in flower.

Pentecost in the Orthodox Church is also Trinity Sunday; it is a feast of the Lord outside the normal modal cycle. It is sometimes called 'Kneeling Sunday', after the three invocations for which priest and people kneel following the Liturgy, while the following day's vespers are sung. In Russia, rural churches are decorated with branches of birch; Pushkin records a custom requiring their bearers either to bring flowers with them to church or to bewail their sins with as many tears as there were dewdrops on the branch. Sometimes the flowers were brushed across parents' graves 'to clear their eyes'.

From now on weeks are once more counted from Monday, either 'after Pentecost' or 'of' the evangelist (Matthew or Luke) who is read during them, or on Saturday and Sunday. On the Monday after Pentecost, Matthew begins to be read; this is accordingly the first week of Matthew. Greek churches dedicated to the Holy Trinity (*Ayiá Triádha*) celebrate with the slaughter of a lamb. Wednesday and Friday are not fasted.

The first Sunday after Pentecost is All Saints, still kept on its original day; it is also called the first Sunday of Matthew, because his Gospel has begun to be read on the Monday after Pentecost. This is the last day of the Pentecostarion.

THE OCTOECHOS

For the rest of the year, until Lazarus Saturday, the invariable portions of the service are taken from the Octoechos ('eight-tone') service-book, also called the *Paraklētikē*. The first tone is used on the Sunday after All Saints, on which churches commemorate their local saints. On All Saints itself a cycle of eleven resurrectional Gospel readings at

Sunday matins begins, each with accompanying texts written by the emperors Constantine VII (944–59) and Leo VI (886–912).

The count of Sundays 'after Pentecost', of which there are up to thirty-two, runs continuously down to the second Sunday before Christmas, and resumes on the second Sunday after Theophany down to the eleventh Sunday before Easter. Concurrently, the Sundays of Matthew continue as far as the Sunday between 31 August and 6 September inclusive: in countries that still use the Julian calendar for immoveable feasts, when—and only when—Easter is on 22 March OS (as next in 2010) there are seventeen Sundays of Matthew (17 May–6 Sept. OS), of which the last is known as 'the Sunday of the Canaanite Woman' (whose faith persuaded Jesus to cure her daughter); contrariwise, when Easter is on 20 April or later there are only twelve. Where the Exaltation is observed according to the New Style, the maximum is at present fifteen (Easter 22 or 23 March OS = 4 or 5 April NS), the minimum ten (Easter 21 April = 4 May or later).

The next Sunday is the Sunday before the Exaltation, which has its own Gospel reading (from St John), as has the Exaltation itself on 14 September (also from St John) and the Sunday after it (from St Mark); these Sundays (three when 14 September is a Sunday, otherwise two) are included in the count 'after Pentecost'. The following Sunday, either the day preceding the 'New Year' and Conception of the Precursor on *23 September or the first Sunday after it, is the first Sunday of St Luke, the evangelist who narrates the conception and birth of both John the Precursor and Jesus Christ. The Sundays of St Luke are seventeen in all, the sixteenth being the Publican and Pharisee and the seventeenth the Prodigal; but for the fifteen within the Octoechos the sequence is complicated by requirements that particular texts be read at given dates:

Between	and	Sunday of Luke
22 Sept.	28 Sept.	First
29 Sept.	5 Oct.	Second
6 Oct.	10 Oct.	Third
11 Oct.	17 Oct.	Fourth (Parable of the Sower, in honour of the Fathers of the Seventh Oecumenical Council in 787, or of all seven Councils)
18 Oct.	19 Oct.	Third
20 Oct.	26 Oct.	Sixth
27 Oct.	29 Oct.	Seventh
30 Oct.	5 Nov.	Fifth (The Rich Man, known in the West as Dives and Lazarus, in honour of Paul the Confessor: see *6 Nov.)
6 Nov.	9 Nov.	Seventh
10 Nov.	16 Nov.	Eighth
17 Nov.	23 Nov.	Ninth
24 Nov.	30 Nov.	Thirteenth
1 Dec.	3 Dec.	Fourteenth
4 Dec.	10 Dec.	Tenth (The Woman healed on the Sabbath, read on the Sunday before that of the Holy Forefathers because she is called a daughter of Abraham)
11 Dec.	17 Dec.	Eleventh (Holy Forefathers, known in the West as the Patriarchs of the Old Testament; the Gospel is the parable of the Banquet)

After this Sunday the count 'after Pentecost' is interrupted:

Between	and	Sunday
18 Dec.	24 Dec.	Before Christmas
26 Dec.	30 Dec.	After Christmas
31 Dec.	5 Jan.	Before the Lights
8 Jan.	14 Jan.	After the Lights

If 25 December falls on a Sunday, it is kept as Christmas and 1 January as Circumcision; if 6 or 7 January is a Sunday, it is kept as respectively Theophany or the Synaxis of the Precursor. Between Christmas and Theophany Wednesday and Friday are not fasted; this period is often kept in a carnival-like fashion. (The demonic, sun-hating *kalikátzari* said in Greek folklore to wander abroad at this time have been explained as survivals of Byzantine mummers; but for such beliefs elsewhere see *6 Jan.) These usages evidently perpetuate the Roman festival of the Kalends (see *1 Jan.); in the East Slavonic languages *kolyadý* is used to denote this entire period, or the traditional songs sung in it.

When the Julian calendar is used for immoveable feasts, there can be no Sunday after the Lights if Easter falls on 22–3 March OS (4–5 Apr. NS), or the 24th (6 Apr.) in a common year. If Easter falls on 25–31 March (24–30 in leap year; 7–13 and 6–12 Apr. NS), the Sunday after the Lights is that of the Publican and the Pharisee, which is the sixteenth Sunday of Luke. Otherwise, the count after Pentecost now resumes; the Sundays of Luke are governed by the number of Sundays remaining before the Triodion. In the table below, Easter dates are given in both styles, others in New Style.

Easter OS		Easter NS	Sunday	
Common year	Leap year	Common (leap)	Date	Name
1–7 Apr.	31 Mar.–6 Apr.	14–20 (13–19) Apr.	15–21 Jan.	15th of Luke
8–14 Apr.	7–13 Apr.	21–7 (20–6) Apr.	15–21 Jan.	12th of Luke
			22–8 Jan.	15th of Luke
15–21 Apr.	14–20 Apr.	28 (27) Apr.–4 (3) May	15–21 Jan.	12th of Luke
			22–8 Jan.	15th of Luke
			29 Jan.–4 Feb.	17th of Matthew
22 Apr.	21 Apr.	5 (4) May	20 Jan.	12th of Luke
			27 Jan.	15th of Luke
			3 Feb.	16th of Matthew
			10 Feb.	17th of Matthew
23–5 Apr.	22–5 Apr.	6–8 (5–8) May	21–3 (24) Jan.	12th of Luke
			28–30 (31) Jan.	14th of Luke
			4–6 (7) Feb.	15th of Luke
			11–13 (14) Feb.	17th of Matthew

The twelfth Sunday of Luke is that of the Ten Lepers (healed by Jesus; only the Samaritan gave thanks); the fifteenth, of Zacchaeus. The seventeenth Sunday of Matthew (the Canaanite Woman) is next in priority because, when Easter falls on 22 March OS the next Easter must fall on 11 (leap year 10) April, allowing only two Sundays in this period; it therefore cannot have been reached in the direct sequence. The fourteenth Sunday of Luke is included here only if it has not already fallen in December, that is if the first Sunday of December was the 4th or later.

When the New Style is used for immoveable feasts, similar principles apply, but there are (at present) from one to six Sundays before the Triodion. In the table below, Easter dates are given in New Style, though they are of course calculated in Old.

Easter		Sunday	
Common year	Leap year	Date	Name
4 Apr.		17 Jan.	Fifteenth of Luke
5–8 Apr.	4–7 Apr.	18–21 Jan.	Fifteenth of Luke
9–15 Apr.	8–14 Apr.	15–21 Jan.	Twelfth of Luke
		22–9 Jan.	Fifteenth of Luke
16–22 Apr.	15–21 Apr.	15–21 Jan.	Twelfth of Luke
		22–8 Jan.	Fifteenth of Luke
		29 Jan.–4 Feb.	Seventeenth of Matthew
23–6 Apr.	22–5 Apr.	15–18 Jan.	Twelfth of Luke
		22–5 Jan.	Fourteenth of Luke
		29 Jan.–1 Feb.	Fifteenth of Luke
		5–8 Feb.	Sixteenth of Matthew
		12–15 Feb.	Seventeenth of Matthew
27–9 Apr.	26–8 Apr.	19–21 Jan.	Twelfth of Luke
		26–8 Jan.	Fifteenth of Luke
		2–4 Feb.	Sixteenth of Matthew
		9–11 Feb.	Seventeenth of Matthew
30 Apr.–3 May	29 Apr.–2 May	15–18 Jan.	Twelfth of Luke
		22–5 Jan.	Fourteenth of Luke
		29 Jan.–1 Feb.	Fifteenth of Luke
		5–8 Feb.	Sixteenth of Matthew
		12–15 Feb.	Seventeenth of Matthew
4–6 May	3–5 May	19–21 Jan.	Twelfth of Luke
		26–8 Jan.	Fifteenth of Luke
		2–4 Feb.	Fifteenth of Matthew
		9–11 Feb.	Sixteenth of Matthew
		16–18 Feb.	Seventeenth of Matthew
7–8 May	6–8 May	15–16 (17) Jan.	Twelfth of Luke
		22–3 (24) Jan.	Fourteenth of Luke
		29–30 (31) Jan.	Fifteenth of Luke
		5–6 (7) Feb.	Fifteenth of Matthew
		12–13 (14) Feb.	Sixteenth of Matthew
		19–20 (21) Feb.	Seventeenth of Matthew

OTHER HOLIDAYS

If all the year were playing holidays,
To sport would be as tedious as to work.
1 Hen. IV, i. ii. 201–2

With the slouthfull and idle lubbers that loue not to dooe any werke, euery daye is holydaye.

Udall, fo. 155 (1542)

We place here holidays that are not fixed as to date or in relation to the church year. It is impossible to tell when the word 'holiday' lost its original meaning of 'holy day' (see also *Days: Holy Days, Holidays, Feasts*). William Warner's description of the northern countryman's year in the sixteenth century, though naming the main holy days, shows how far the normal pastimes diverged from the religious observance of the day:

At Ewle we wonten gamble, daunce, to carrole, and to sing,	*Yule*
To haue gud spiced Sewe, and Roste, and plum-pies for a King,	
At Fasts-eue pan-puffes, Gang-tide gaites did alie Masses bring,	*Shrove Tuesday; Rogationtide*
At Paske begun our Morrise: and ere Penticost our May:	*Easter; Whitsuntide*
Tho Roben hood, liell John, Frier Tucke, and Marian deftlie play,	
And Lard and Ladie gang till Kirke with Lads and Lasses gay.	
Fra Masse and Eensong sa gud cheere and glee on erie Greene,	
As, saue our Wakes twixt Eames and Sibbes, like gam was neuer seene.	*uncles and kinfolk*
At Baptis-day with Ale and cakes bout bon-fires neighbors stood.	*St John's Day*
At Martlemasse wa turnde a crabbe: thilke tolde of Roben hood,	*St Martin's Day*
Till after long time myrke, when blest were windowes, dares & lights,	
And pailes were fild, & hathes were swept, gainst Fairie-elues & sprites.	
Rock, & plow Mondaies gams sal gang, with Saint-feast & kirk-sights.	*Rock Monday, Plough Monday*

Warner, v, ch. 24 (1589)

It did not take adherence to Puritan ideals to see the inconveniences caused by so many occasions to abstain from work, whether one considered them holy days or holidays. Henry VIII had already abolished the popular observances on many saints' days (see *6 Dec.), and Puritanism had a far-reaching effect. Since the sixteenth century, the number of holidays in England has always been far inferior to that in Catholic countries, and in the United States, with no state religion or church, there are even fewer holidays. Thus even an Englishman was amazed to discover in 1699 in New England, where Puritanism had a much longer hold than in England, that:

Election, Commencement, and *Training-days*, are their only *Holy-days*; they keep no *Saints-Days*, nor will they allow the *Apostles* to be *Saints*, yet they assume that Sacred Dignity to themselves; and

say, in the Title Page of their Psalm-Book, *Printed for the Edification of the Saints in* Old *and* New-England.
                                                                                        Ward, *Trip,* 5

'Commencement' meant graduation ceremonies at Harvard University. These were public occasions, not university affairs alone. A Frenchman attended one in 1788:

In a free country, every thing ought to bear the stamp of patriotism. This patriotism, so happily displayed in the foundation, endowment, and encouragement of his [Pres. Willard's] university, appears every year in a solemn feast celebrated at Cambridge in honour of the Sciences. This feast, which takes place once a year in all the colleges of America, is called the *commencement*: it resembles the exercises and distribution of prizes in our colleges. It is a day of joy for Boston; almost all its inhabitants assemble in Cambridge. The most distinguished of the students display their talents in presence of the public; and these exercises, which are generally on patriotic subjects, are terminated by a feast, where reign the freest gaiety, and the most cordial fraternity.
                                                                        Brissot de Warville, 109

Training Day, which pertains only to New England, was a day set aside for local militias to gather together and practise drill. At first only military manoeuvres were performed, but in the seventeenth century fortifications were built as well, and later churches and houses. The religious element was supplied by an opening and closing prayer and a sermon. At first companies drilled every week; gradually the number of days decreased, and by 1679 there were four in the year. These increasingly became social occasions as well and took on the aspects of a fair, with booths set up to sell food and drink.

Not all Americans were content with such a restricted number of holidays. John Pintard, a New Yorker, regrets their paucity in 1823:

Our Protestant Faith affords no religious holiday & processions like the Catholics. From the period of the Jews & Heathens down thro the Greeks & Romans, the Celts, Druids, even our Indians all had & have their religious Festivals. England retains numerous red letter days as they are called which afford intervals of rest, together with the Christmas, Easter & Whitsun holidays, for all the public offices Banks &c., but with us, we have only Independence, Christmas & New Year, 3 solitary days, not enough & which causes so much breach of the Sabbath in this city, For youth pent up, Mechanics & labourers will seek fresh air & rural exercise on that day, in spite of all human laws to the contrary.
                                                                        Pintard, ii. 137–8

HANDSEL MONDAY

Handsel Monday is the first Monday in the New Year. 'Handsel' or 'Hansel', originally a 'giving of the hand', came to mean a gift at New Year, often a tip (see *1 Jan. under 'Gift-giving'). Whoever receives anything on Handsel Monday will be lucky for the rest of the year. On the other hand, the person who gives may not fare as well, at least in Ireland:

Never pay away money on the first Monday of the year, or you will lose your luck in gaining money all the year after.
                                                                        S. Wilde, ii. 116 (1887)

The custom was particularly prevalent in Scotland, where it used to be frequently observed on the Old Style date, as Chambers reports in 1864:

Among the rural population, *Auld Hansel Monday*, i.e. Handsel Monday old style, or the first Monday after the 12th of the month, is the day usually held. The farmers used to treat the whole of their servants on that morning to a liberal breakfast of roast and boiled, with ale, whiskey, and cake, to their utmost contentment; after which the guests went about seeing their friends for the remainder of the day. It was also the day on which any disposed for change gave up their places, and when new servants were engaged. Even now, when most old fashions are much decayed, *Auld Handsel Monday* continues to be the holiday of the year to the class of farm-labourers in Scotland.

Chambers (4 Jan.)

HARVEST-HOME

In the summer months there were far fewer church feasts and more communal ones, beginning with sheep-shearing festivals in June. Lammas Day (*1 Aug.) signalled the beginning of the harvest season; from this point to October the communal feasts included rush-bearing (gathering rushes to strew on the floors of parish churches; see *21 July), and church ales or wakes. In July and August agricultural labour intensified in order to provide food for people and livestock through the coming winter. The safe gathering of the harvest was of prime importance, and the tradition arose of celebrating it, both in church and on the farm; the festival came to be known as 'harvest-home'.

From at least the thirteenth century landlords provided a communal feast for their tenants at the end of harvest. The farm labourers celebrated by bringing home the last cartload decked with flowers and surmounted with a figure made of corn. A German traveller remarked on seeing one in 1598:

As we were returning to our inn, we happened to meet some country people *celebrating their Harvest-home*; their last load of corn they crown with flowers, having besides an image richly dressed, by which perhaps they would signify Ceres, this they keep moving about, while men and women, men and maid servants, riding through the streets in the cart, shout as loud as they can till they arrive at the barn: the farmers here do not bind up their corn in sheaves, as they do with us, but directly as they have reaped or mowed it, put it into carts and convey it to their barns.

Hentzner, 79

HIRING FAIRS

Hiring fairs took place after the harvest was in; this was the time to seek new employment. They were held on different days in different places; Samuel Curwen reports on one at Waltham Abbey that was regulated by Parliament:

[London], 26 September [1783]
Mrs. Deberdt and myself . . . proceeded with bag and baggage Londonwards [from Ware] meeting and overtaking multitudes in carriages and on foot bound to the Waltham Abbey Statute for
Servants, a day established by act of parliament following the last day of Fairs for hiring servants
whereto resort all who want to go into, or are out of service, as well as those Familys who stand
in need of servants. The males appear with the tools or insignia of their respective employments,
the females of the domestic kind are distinguished by their aprons, viz. Cooks in coloured, nursery maids in white linnen, and the chamber and waiting maids in lawn or cambrick.

                                                                                    Curwen, 948

LORD MAYOR'S SHOW

The feast of SS Simon and Jude, on 28 October, was the original election day for the
Lord Mayor of London. After the reform of the calendar in 1752 his term of office continued till 8 November to make a full year (28 Oct. OS). On the following day (except
if Sunday) the new mayor was sworn in, and the occasion was marked by a grand parade. In 1960 the parade was moved to the second Saturday of November; the swearing-
in takes place on the previous day. The Lord Mayor's Parade has never failed to impress
visitors, though, like many long-standing customs (it dates back to Tudor times), it has
had its detractors. Traditionally, the Lord Mayor went by water to and from Westminster, where he was sworn in. He was then accompanied from the wharf to Guildhall, with pageantry supplied by the guild to which he belonged. By the end of the
sixteenth century the entertainment had become very elaborate, and writers were drawn
in to devise scripts, often on patriotic themes, heavy in mythology and allegory; many
of these were published. Like other municipal festivities, the show was abolished during the Commonwealth, but regained new life after the Restoration. We present two
representative descriptions.
    Celia Fiennes noted in her journal in the 1690s:

At Fleete Ditch they enter the Barges which are all very curiously adorned, and thus he is conducted, the river being full of Barges belonging to the severall Companyes of London, adorned
with streamers and their armes and fine musick, and have sack to drinke and little cakes as bigg
as a crown piece . . . [After the swearing-in] they being conducted through the Citty with greate
acclamations, their own habits and trappings of their horses being very fine, and they haveing all
the severall Companyes of the Citty, which walke in their order and gowns with pagents to most
or many of their Companyes, which are a sort of stages covered and carryed by men and on the
top many men and boys acting the respective Trades or Employments of each Company . . . and
whatever Company the new Lord Major is off his pageant is the finest and that Company has
the precedency that yeare of all the Companyes except the Mercers Company, which allwayes is
the first and esteemed the greatest, and when there is a Lord Major of that Company their
pageant is a maiden queen on a throne, crowned and with royal robes and scepter and most richly
dressed, with severall ladyes dressed, her attendants, all on the same pageant and with a cannopy
over her head and drawn in an open chariot with 9 horses (the horses goe 3 abreast) very finely
accouter'd and pages that ride them all, with plumes of feathers.   Fiennes, 285–6

The Canadian Thomas G. Ridout, writing to his brother in 1811:

I must give you an account of the Lord Mayor's show, on the 9th of November, which day was ushered in by the ringing of every bell in the city, and bars were placed across the great streets to hinder the coaches from passing. By eleven o'clock the crowd had completely filled up King Street, Cheapside, St. Paul's Churchyard, Ludgate Hill, Fleet Street and Blackfriars. . . . The rich golden banners of the city waving over the multitude, preceded and followed by the different companies of London. Then came a string of coaches, reaching from King Street to Ludgate Hill. . . . Presently we saw the twelve stately barges, glittering with gold, having five or six flags made of cloth of gold, most curiously worked, move past us, followed by hundreds of small boats. There was a covering over each boat, supported by gilt Corinthian pillars, on top of which were several bands of music. The company sat beneath. They were rowed by twenty-four men dressed in white, and so they passed on by the sound of the trumpet, fire of small cannon, and martial music, to Westminster Bridge.

At three o'clock they returned in grand procession to dine at Guildhall . . . In a little while we saw the vanguard, consisting of the West London Regiment, coming round Ludgate Hill, having a very fine band of music. Then came the company of Merchant Tailors, of which the Lord Mayor is a member, dressed in gowns trimmed with fur, and six men bearing their colours; followed by the Apothecaries, Clothiers, Stationers, Goldsmiths, Grocers, and other companies of London, with their colours and two bands of music. Then came the band of the German Legion, mounted on black horses, next the city colours, and a knight equipped in Edward the Black Prince's armour, mounted on a black horse, his two esquires on each side, in half-armour, bearing his ancient shield, sword and lance; a band of music, another knight in shining brass armour on a white horse, esquires as before; immediately after the Lord Mayor, in his coach burnished with gold, very large, drawn by six horses, and covered with carvings of the city arms in a most magnificent manner, having out-riders. The coachman was dressed in green and gold. Two footmen rode behind, and six others walked after the coach, dressed in gold-laced cocked hats, green coats, with gold lace four inches broad, scarlet velvet breeches and white silk stockings. Next came another knight in steel armour, as the first, then my lady Mayoress in coach and six, with a band of music; next came the ex-Lord Mayor in coach and six, and his wife in coach and four. Next a very fine band of music, followed by all the aldermen and common council, in their separate coaches. The judges, nobility, ministry, and foreign ambassadors, gentlemen's carriages, a long list of Hackney coaches, and a London mob, with night coming on, closed this Lord Mayor's show, which was the most splendid that had been for many years.

Ridout, 72–4

By the mid-nineteenth century the Lord Mayor's Show was viewed by many as an embarrassment, and it did not take place every year; in 1857 the water procession ceased. In 1883 the Parade had a series of floats representing some quite unofficial symbols of the colonies:

That of 'India' consisted of natives standing among palm-trees, with a stuffed tiger above, followed by two elephants; that of 'Canada', a backwoodsman, amidst pine-logs and piles of corn-sacks with beavers and bears; that of 'Australia', two red-shirted station-hands, with fleeces of sheep and bags of wool; a kangaroo and an emu, and a species of pelican, being perched a little higher. The vehicles upon which these colonial 'exhibits' were set up passed along the street; and they were succeeded by one which conveyed what was supposed to be meant as a representation of the supply of frozen fresh mutton from New Zealand. This was simply a row of twenty or thirty sheep's carcases, hanging up in much the same way as they do at a butcher's shop.

Illustrated London News (17 Nov. 1883), 478

THANKSGIVING

The first Thanksgiving was celebrated by the settlers at Plymouth in 1621, the year after their arrival (see *21 Dec.); the occasion was the successful gathering in of the harvest, and the feast was shared with the Native Americans. Governor William Bradford proclaimed it a day of prayer and thanksgiving, but did not intend it to be a yearly commemoration. In 1623 the harvest appeared bleak, no rain having fallen from the third week in May to the middle of July; a fast was ordered. The drought was broken, and another day of Thanksgiving was proclaimed:

. . . notwithstand all their great paines and industrie, and the great hops of a large cropp, the Lord seemed to blast, and take away the same, and to threaten further and more sore famine unto them, by a great drought which continued from the 3. weeke in May, till about the midle of July, without any raine, and with great heat (for the most parte), insomuch as the corne begane to wither away, though it was set with fishe, the moysture wherof helped it much. Yet at length it begane to languish sore, and some of the drier grounds were partched like withered hay, part wherof was never recovered. Upon which they sett a parte a solemne day of humiliation, to seek the Lord by humble and fervente prayer, in this great distresse. And he was pleased to give them a gracious and speedy answer, both to thier owne and the Indeans admiration, that lived amongst them. For all the morning, and greatest part of the day, it was clear weather and very hotte, and not a cloud or any signe of raine to be seen, yet toward evening it begane to overcast, and shortly after to raine, with shuch sweete and gentle showers, as gave them cause of rejoyceing, and blesing God. It came, without either wind, or thunder, or any violence, and by degreese in that abundance, as that the earth was thorowly wete and soked therwith. Which did so apparently revive and quicken the decayed corne and other fruits, as was wonderfull to see, and made the Indeans astonished to behold; and afterwards the Lord sent them shuch seasonable showers, with enterchange of faire warme weather, as, through his blessing, caused a fruitfull and liberall harvest, to their no small comforte and rejoycing. For shich mercie (in time conveniente) they also sett aparte a day of thanksgiveing.　　　　　　　　　　Bradford, 152–3

Gradually, giving thanks at the end of harvest became a custom, much as the harvest-home festivals in England, to which Thanksgiving owes its origin, at least in part. In 1632 the Governors of Massachusetts and Plymouth colony joined in observing a day of thanksgiving, and public days of thanksgiving were appointed regularly (but not annually) in October or November of the following years:

[Boston], Sabbath-day, Novʳ 15, 1685.
Mr. Willard mentioned what the Elders had done as to a Thanks-giving, and propounded to the Church that we might have one on the First Thorsday in December: because had Fasted, and God had graciously answered our Prayers; so should meet Him in the same place to give Thanks for that, and any other Providence that hath passed before us. Silence gave Consent, no one speaking.　　　　　　　　　　　　　　　　　　　　Sewall, 84

A perplexing problem at a Thanksgiving dinner at Danvers, Connecticut, in 1714:

When ye services at ye meeting house were ended ye council and other dignitaries were entertained at ye house of Mr. Epes, on ye hill near by, and we had a bountiful Thanksgiving dinner with bear's meat and venison, the last of which was a fine buck, shot in ye woods near by. Ye bear was killed in Lynn woods near Reading.

After ye blessing was craved by Mr. Garrich of Wrentham, word came that ye buck was shot on ye Lord's day by Pequot, an Indian, who came to Mr. Epes with a lye in his mouth like Ananias of old.

Ye council therefore refused to eat ye venison, but it was afterward decided that Pequot should receive 40 stripes save one, for lying and profaning ye Lord's day, restore Mr. Epes ye cost of ye deer, and considering this a just and righteous sentence on ye sinful heathen, and that a blessing had been craved on ye meat, ye council of all partook of it but Mr. Shepard, whose conscience was tender on ye point of ye venison.

quoted in Love, 422 n. 1, from an account by the Revd Lawrence Conant

Thanksgiving continued to be proclaimed locally by state governors. The first national proclamation was made by George Washington in January 1795; in the spirit of the first Thanksgiving, it was to give thanks to God for preserving the nation:

When we review the calamities which afflict so many other nations, the present condition of the United States affords much matter of consolation and satisfaction. Our exemption hitherto from foreign war, an increasing prospect of the continuance of that exemption, the great degree of internal tranquillity we have enjoyed, the recent confirmation of that tranquillity by the suppression of an insurrection [the Whiskey Insurrection in Western Pennsylvania] which so wantonly threatened it, the happy course of our public affairs in general, the unexampled prosperity of all classes of our citizens, are circumstances which peculiarly mark our situation with indications of the divine beneficence toward us. In such a state of things it is in an especial manner our duty as a people, with devout reverence and affectionate gratitude, to acknowledge our many and great obligations to Almighty God, and to implore Him to continue and confirm the blessings we experienced.

Deeply penetrated with this sentiment, I, George Washington, President of the United States, do recommend to all religious societies and denominations, and to all persons whomsoever, within the United States, to set apart and observe Thursday, the 19th day of February next, as a day of public thanksgiving and prayer, and on that day to meet together and render sincere and hearty thanks to the great Ruler of nations for the manifold and signal mercies which distinguish our lot as a nation; particularly for the possession of constitutions of government which united and, by their union, establish liberty with order; for the preservation of our peace, foreign and domestic; for the reasonable control which has been given to a spirit of disorder in the suppression of the late insurrection, and generally for the prosperous condition of our affairs, public and private, and at the same time humbly and fervently beseech the kind Author of these blessings graciously to prolong them to us; to imprint on our hearts a deep and solemn sense of our obligations to Him for them; to teach us rightly to estimate their immense value; to preserve us from the arrogance of prosperity, and from hazarding the advantages we enjoy by delusive pursuits, to dispose us to merit the continuance of His favors by not abusing them, by our gratitude for them, and by a corresponding conduct as citizens and as men to render this country more and more a safe and propitious asylum for the unfortunate of other countries; to extend among us true and useful knowledge; to diffuse and establish habits of sobriety, order, morality, and piety, and finally to impart all the blessings we possess or ask for ourselves to the whole family of mankind.

In testimony whereof, I have caused the seal of the United States of America to be affixed to these presents, and signed the same with my hand. Done at the city of Philadelphia the first day of January, 1795.

GEORGE WASHINGTON
quoted in Deems, 343–4

The states, however, continued the custom of celebrating Thanksgiving in November or December. In 1820 Thanksgiving in New York State fell on St Nicholas's Day. John Pintard of New York City describes the day in a letter to his daughter; already it is clear that it is becoming a family occasion as well:

Wednesday 6th December S' *Class* day. Just returned from Church . . . Aunt Helen & family dine with us on the abundant good things so plentifully & cheaply afforded by the Great Giver of all good gifts whose praises we have been celebrating this day with prayers & thanksgivings. Indeed this State, & this city have great cause to rejoice. Blest with an unprecedented harvest & fruit season, enjoying uninterrupted health, whilst some of our sister cities, with yours [New Orleans] have been swept with the besom of destruction.   Pintard, i. 352

Thanksgiving day normally began with church services. Some clergymen took the opportunity to chide the nation for its moral shortcomings. The English writer Harriet Martineau, visiting Boston in 1834, notes with approval the condemnation of slavery:

This is the occasion chosen by the boldest of the clergy to say what they think of the faults of the nation,—and particularly to reprobate apathy on the slavery question. There are few who dare do this, though it seems to be understood that this is an occasion on which 'particular preaching' may go a greater length than on common Sundays. Yet a circumstance happened in New York on this very day which shows that the clergy have, at least in some places, a very short tether, even on Thanksgiving Day. An episcopalian clergyman from England, named Pyne, who had been some years settled in America, preached a thanksgiving sermon in which he made a brief and moderate, even common-place allusion to the toleration of slavery, among other national sins. For some weeks, he heard only the distant mutterings of the storm which was about to burst upon him; but within three months, he was not only dismissed from his office, but compelled to leave the country, though he had settled his family from England beside him. He was anxious to obey the wishes of his friends, and print verbatim the sermon which had caused his ruin; but no printer would print, and no publisher would agree to sell his sermon. At length, he found a printer who promised to print it, on condition of his name being kept secret; and the sermon was dispersed without the aid of a publisher. Mr. Pyne sailed for England on the following 1st of April.   Martineau, iii. 173–5

Nathaniel Hawthorne's description of Thanksgiving in 1842 has a very modern ring:

Novr 24th, Thursday
    This is Thanksgiving Day—a good old festival; and my wife and I have kept it with our hearts, and besides have made good cheer upon our turkey, and pudding, and pies, and custards, although none sat at our board but our two selves. There was a new and livelier sense, I think, that we have at last found a home, and that a new family has been gathered since the last Thanksgiving Day.   Hawthorne, *American Notebooks*, 172

As late as the 1850s, Thanksgiving was above all a New England holiday, sneered at in Virginia as the Puritan Christmas; but President Lincoln, in 1863, issued a proclamation that Thanksgiving was to be observed as a national holiday on the last Thursday of November. The idea was not his; since 1827 Mrs Sarah J. Hale, at first editor of the *Ladies' Magazine* in Boston, and then of *Godey's Lady's Book* in Philadelphia, had campaigned for a national day in her editorials and in personal letters to state governors and the President. In an editorial of 1863 she urged that the annual proclamation be made by the President himself, and then applied by state governors. President Lincoln did so, adding in his proclamation an appeal that 'with humble penitence for our national perverseness and disobedience' the nation commend to God 'all who have become widows, orphans, mourners or sufferers in the lamentable civil strife in which we are unavoidably engaged, and fervently implore the interposition of the almighty hand to heal the wounds of the nation and to restore it, as soon as may be consistent with the Divine purposes, to the full enjoyment of peace, harmony, tranquility and union'. The country was in the midst of the Civil War.

The change from the last to the fourth Thursday in November was made by President Franklin D. Roosevelt, who decreed in 1939 that Thanksgiving should be observed on the 23rd. Not all states complied: Charles W. Jones, in his edition of Bede's computistic writings, compared the resulting confusion with St Columban's unhappiness at finding the date of Easter determined in Gaul by different rules from those that he had known in Ireland:

As I write these words in New England, Thanksgiving approaches. The President of the United States has set November 23, the Governor of the State of Connecticut November 30. In New England the dogma attached to the observance of Thanksgiving is made sensible by a ritual preserved by tradition from the elders. There is a certain spiritual and mystical element indoctrinated by types and figures, subject to different interpretations in different places. I am a pilgrim from New York State, raised in another tradition. Friends from home may undertake a pilgrimage to Connecticut to share a turkey with me on their Thanksgiving, November 23. But in these waste places in this barbarous land, children must attend school all day and miss the great midday feast which our tradition prescribes. A week later, when our friends from home have gone, children will be observing holiday and keeping me from my work. The newspapers of the two states are printing letters of protest, filled with religious fervour and spiritual allegory. No question that principles and traditions are at stake. Jones, in Bede, *Opera de temporibus*, 81

But Roosevelt, a former governor of New York State, prevailed; the fourth Thursday was adopted by act of Congress in 1941. The next year in which it made a difference was 1944.

Canada too had taken up Thanksgiving, in November 1879, though it is now observed on the second Monday in October.

Thanksgiving is hardly thinkable without turkey and pumpkin pie. Thomas Wolfe, in his autobiographical novel *Look Homeward, Angel* (1930), looks back on Thanksgiving and Christmas dinners in Tennessee of the 1890s:

For the Thanksgiving and Christmas feasts four heavy turkeys were bought and fattened for weeks: Eugene fed them with cans of shelled corn several times a day, but he could not bear to be present at their executions, because by that time their cheerful excited gobbles made echoes in his heart. Eliza baked for weeks in advance: the whole energy of the family focussed upon the great ritual of the feast. A day or two before, the auxiliary dainties arrived in piled grocers' boxes—the magic of strange foods and fruits was added to familiar fare: there were glossed sticky dates, cold rich figs, cramped belly to belly in small boxes, dusty raisins, mixed nuts—the almond, pecan, the meaty nigger-toe, the walnuts, sacks of assorted candies, piles of yellow Florida oranges, tangerines, sharp, acrid, nostalgic odours.

Seated before a roast or a fowl, Gant began a heavy clangour on his steel and carving knife, distributing thereafter Gargantuan portions to each plate. Eugene feasted from a high chair by his father's side, filled his distended belly until it was drum-tight, and was permitted to stop eating by his watchful sire only when his stomach was impregnable to the heavy prod of Gant's big finger. 'There's a soft place there', he would roar, and he would cover the scoured plate of his infant son with another heavy slab of beef. That their machinery withstood this hammer-handed treatment was a tribute to their vitality and Eliza's cookery.

Paul Dunbar has a sympathetic eye for the turkey:

Signs of the Times

Air a-gittin' cool an' coolah,
  Frost a-comin' in de night,
Hicka' nuts an' wa'nuts fallin',
  Possum keepin' out o' sight.
Tu'key struttin' in de ba'nya'd,
  Nary step so proud ez his;
Keep on struttin', Mistah Tu'key,
  Yo' do' know whut time it is.

Cidah press commence a-squeakin'
  Eatin' apples sto'ed away,
Chillun swa'min' 'roun' lak ho'nets,
  Huntin' aigs ermung de hay.
Mistah Tu'key keep on gobblin'
  At de geese a-flyin' souf,
Oomph! dat bird do' know whut's comin';
  Ef he did he'd shet his mouf.

Pumpkin gittin' good an' yallah
  Mek me open up my eyes;
Seems lak it's a-lookin' at me
  Jes' a-la'in' dah sayin' "Pies."
Tu'key gobbler gwine 'roun' blowin',
  Gwine 'roun' gibbin' sass an' slack;
Keep on talkin', Mistah Tu'key,
  You ain't seed no almanac.

Fa'mer walkin' th'oo de ba'nya'd
  Seein' how things is comin' on,
See ef all de fowls is fatt'nin'—
  Good times comin' sho's you bo'n,
Hyeahs dat tu'key gobbler braggin',
  Den his face break in a smile—
Nebbah min', you sassy rascal,
  He's gwine nab you atter while.

Choppin' suet in de kitchen,
  Stonin' raisins in de hall,
Beef a-cookin' fu' de mince meat,
  Spices groun'—I smell 'em all.
Look hyeah, Tu'key, stop dat gobblin',
  You ain' luned de sense ob feah,
You ol' fool, yo' naik's in dangah,
    Do' you know Thanksgibbin's hyeah?
        Paul Laurence Dunbar (1872–1906)

PART II

CALENDARS AND
CHRONOLOGY

DAYS AND TIMES

DAYS: NATURAL, ARTIFICIAL, AND CIVIL

The word 'day' in ordinary language may refer to one of three things: the time taken by the earth to rotate once upon its axis (the *natural* or solar day); the light period between sunrise and sunset (the *artificial* day, or daytime); or a length of time reckoned by law or custom as a day, from one defined point to the next (the *civil* day).

The term 'natural day' also has three meanings: that adopted here is the medieval sense of the period of the earth's rotation relative to the sun, with a mean length of 24 hours. This should be distinguished from the sidereal day, defined as the interval of time between two consecutive transits of the mean equinox = 23^h $56'$ $4''$, which is $0.0084''$ shorter than the earth's rotational period relative to the stars. However, it is nowadays often used to denote the hours of daylight, becoming thus synonymous with 'artificial'; and in relation to calendar reform it is a day defined purely by the passage of time, and hence unaffected by the reform, in contrast to the nominal day or date, which is changed. Thus Shakespeare and Cervantes died on the same nominal day, *23 April 1616, but ten natural days apart; the Oxford Almanack for 1752 recorded the suppression of the eleven nominal days 3–13 September in accordance with the Act of Parliament for correction of the calendar.

The artificial day varies in length according to latitude and (except at the equator) by the time of year; it is longer in summer, and shorter in winter, the further one travels from the equator, being longest at the summer solstice (the Longest Day), shortest at the winter solstice (Shortest Day), and 12 hours of mean solar time at the equinox (though a few minutes less when measured in the apparent solar time shown on a sundial). This is also called the 'vulgar day', since the Elder Pliny observed that all ordinary people (*vulgus omne*) reckoned the day from sunrise to sunset.

The civil day has been reckoned from different points at different times and places. In the modern West, official usage follows ancient Rome in beginning the day at midnight; this has also been the Chinese rule since the Zhou dynasty (1122–255 BC). The ancient Egyptians began the day at dawn (see *Egyptian Calendar*), as did the Persians and the Armenians, and in ordinary conversation we do the same. On the other hand the Greeks, like Jews and Muslims, reckoned the day from sunset, and counted the month from the evening on which the new moon was first seen. In Umbria, so the Roman scholar Varro tells us, the day began at noon, as it seems also to have done in Meso-america; this was the standard practice in ships' logbooks down to the nineteenth century, and of astronomers from Hipparchus in the second century BC till 1925, but with a day's difference: at noon on Sunday of the civil reckoning the nautical Sunday ended and the astronomical Sunday began.

Some languages have a specific term for a period of 24 hours, used for instance in stating the length of a voyage: Greek *nuchthēmeron* (first in St Paul), Danish *døgn*, Russian *sútki*. English has no such word except as a scientific loan from the Greek.

HOURS

In classical Greek *hōra* is either a season of the year or the right time to do something; but from Hellenistic times onwards (the last three centuries BC) it might also denote a mathematical division of the day—the normal sense of Latin *hora* and its equivalent in modern languages—to supplement the traditional marks of time such as cockcrow or the ploughman's dinner. (For the survival of such 'daymarks' in Iceland, see **Other Calendars: Icelandic*.)

The hour was invented in Egypt, where an early division into 12 hours of day, 10 of night, and 2 of twilight gave way to the 12 hours of daylight and 12 of night that remained the norm in antiquity and for most of the Middle Ages; these hours, which vary in length with the seasons, are known as 'unequal hours'. The first hour began at dawn, the sixth ended at midday, the twelfth was the tail-end of daylight; night was similarly divided, from sunset to sunrise, though at Rome, especially in military usage, an alternative division was into four watches, *vigiliae*, of three hours each. Only astronomers and computists divided the natural day into 24 equal or 'equinoctial' hours, so called because they were equal to the sundial hours at the spring and autumn equinoxes.

The situation began to change, outside the monastery, in the fourteenth century, when the development of the mechanical clock and the hourglass introduced the equinoctial hour into daily life. In Italy, and sometimes elsewhere, the entire natural day was divided into 24 hours, beginning half an hour after sunset, clocks being periodically adjusted as sunset advanced and retreated; but the most favoured system was and is the counting of hours from midnight and midday (the 12-hour clock), or from midnight alone (the 24-hour clock). In general, English-speakers, especially in the USA, prefer the former, regarding the latter as pedantic, military, or bureaucratic; in Continental countries the 24-hour clock is more widespread, and in some, such as Italy, it is freely used in ordinary conversation.

In Babylonia and China the natural day was often divided into twelfths, known to modern writers as double hours; but when computists do likewise, it is through confusion with the artificial day, as in John 11: 9: 'Jesus answered, Are there not twelve hours in the day?' Another Babylonian division was into successive powers of 60; thus the length of the synodic month was estimated as $29 + 31/60 + 50/3600 + 8/216\,000 +$

20/12 960 000 days; this is nowadays conventionally written 29;31,50,8,20 days, with a semicolon after the integer and commas after the successive sexagesimal fractions.

❡ CANONICAL HOURS The Divine Office or daily public prayer of the RC Church was divided before 1971 into 'hours': matins (*matutinum*), combined with lauds (*laudes*, 'praises') and in some uses called nocturns (*nocturnum*); the four Little Hours, namely prime (*prima*, 'first [unequal hour]'), terce (*tertia*, 'third'), sext (*sexta*, 'sixth'), and none (*nona*, 'ninth'); vespers (*vesperae*); and compline (*completorium*). Their equivalent in clock-times depends on both latitude and time of year. In many Orders none was celebrated directly after the main mass; from this custom comes the English use of *noon* to mean midday, in contrast to Icelandic *nón* '3 p.m.' The third, sixth, and ninth hours were re-spectively those of the Crucifixion, the darkening of the sun, and Jesus' giving up the ghost. The Church of England simplified the hours into morning and evening prayer, for which in the nineteenth century the old names of 'matins' and 'evensong' were re-vived; in 1971 the RC Church introduced a new 'Liturgy of the Hours' comprising an Office of Readings (which may be said at any time during the day), lauds, a single mid-day office (terce, sext, or none), vespers, and compline. In the Orthodox Church the basic divisions (subject to variations between traditions) are orthros (matins), the Little Hours, hesperinos (vespers), apodeipnon ('after-dinner', the equivalent of compline), and mesonyktion (nocturns).

SUBDIVISIONS OF THE HOUR

Whereas Ptolemy, in the second century AD, had divided the day into 24 equinoctial hours and 360 'equinoctial times' of 4 minutes each, by the seventh century AD the hour had been divided into smaller units according to a bewildering number of systems: it might consist of 4 or 5 *puncti* ('points'), 10 *minuta* ('small units'), 15 *partes* (Ptolemy's 'times'), 40 *momenta* (literally 'impulses'), 60 *ostenta* ('showings', as in a flash), and 480 *unciae* ('ounces', i.e. twelfths of a moment), each equivalent to 7½ seconds in modern usage and comprising 47 or 54 *atomi*. Similar names are found in Byzantine Greek, but not always for the same unit; Bede relates them to the astronomers' 12 zodiacal signs, each sign of 30 parts (the usual Greek and Latin terms for 'degrees'), each part of 12 points, each point of 40 moments, each moment of 60 ostents, used for determining the exact time of birth. 'Which observation being false and foreign to our faith, may we see these disused'; but since most people, and not only layfolk, were more easily con-vinced that astrology was un-Christian than that it was false, these divisions continued to be used.

   Not till the late Middle Ages was the geometrical system of *minutae primae* ('first minute parts', 1/60) and *minutae secundae* ('second minute parts', 1/3600), commonly re-duced to 'minutes' and 'seconds', transferred from degrees of arc to the hour; under this system, one *minuta* is 1/6 of the earlier *minutum*. The second, nowadays divided decimally, was previously taken as containing 60 *minutae tertiae*; thus the Babylonian estimate of the synodic month may be restated as 29 days, 12 hours, 44 minutes, 3 seconds, 11 'third minutes', conventionally written 29^d 12^h 44′ 3″ 11‴.

MEAN AND APPARENT SOLAR TIME

The earth's orbit not being circular, and its axis of rotation not perpendicular to its orbit, the absolute length of the natural day, from noon to noon by the sundial, varies over the year by half an hour; by comparison with the time shown by the mechanical or atomic clock, known as 'mean solar time', that shown on sundials, known as 'apparent solar time', may be as much as 14 minutes behind (in Feb.) or 16 minutes ahead (in Nov.). The difference between the two is known as the equation of time; its value is negative when apparent time is behind mean and positive when it is ahead. About 25 December it is zero, apparent time being equal to mean; from then on it is negative until *c*.15 April, rising to about +3′ 40″ in mid-May before descending to zero *c*.14 June; it reaches −6′ 30″ in late July, is zero again *c*.1 September, and thereafter reaches its peak in early November before descending to 25 December.

STANDARD TIME AND GREENWICH MEAN TIME

As clocks and watches improved in accuracy and declined in price, cities and nations began to adopt mean solar time for purposes of legal definition, Great Britain doing so in 1792. This still varied with the local meridian, the same nominal time arriving one minute earlier or later in one place than another for each 15′ of longitude that the first place lay respectively east or west of the other; inconvenience did not arise until the improvement of communications, and in particular the spread of railways and telegraphs, made first national, then international standards necessary. Greenwich Mean Time, measured from a brass line at the Royal Observatory, was effectively imposed as the national standard by the railway companies, despite opposition from the Astronomer Royal and in some towns and cities, being finally adopted by statute in 1880. At Oxford (longitude 1° 15′W.), the great clock at Christ Church was furnished with an additional minute-hand to record Greenwich time, five minutes ahead of local time; the tradition of the college remains that one is not late till five minutes past the appointed time, that is till one is late by Oxford mean solar time as well as Greenwich.

In October 1884 the International Meridian Conference at Washington, DC, resolved that 'it is desirable to adopt a single prime meridian for all nations, in place of the multiplicity of initial meridians which now exist'; this should be 'the meridian passing through the centre of the transit instrument at the Observatory of Greenwich', from which longitude should be counted eastward (plus) and westward (minus) up to

180°. It further proposed the adoption of a universal day 'for all purposes for which it may be found convenient, and which shall not interfere with the use of local or other standard time where desirable', being a mean solar day 'to begin for all the world at the moment of mean midnight of the initial meridian, coinciding with the beginning of the civil day and date of that meridian' and counted from zero up to 24 hours. It also expressed the hope that astronomers and sailors would begin their days at midnight 'as soon as may be practicable', a hope fulfilled 41 years later, and that study should be resumed into decimal division 'of angular space and of time'; the right angle is sometimes divided into 100 grads, but decimalized time remains a French Revolutionary dream.

Although in the following decades most nations accepted Greenwich Mean Time, France, always as suspicious of things 'Anglo-Saxon' as England of things 'Continental', succumbed only in 1911, and even then with the subterfuge of adopting as legal time Paris Mean Time minus 9 minutes 21 seconds; long afterwards on French maps the prime meridian continued to run through Paris instead of Greenwich.

Projects to impose a single *civil* time on the world naturally foundered, time-zones proving more convenient. Russia has eleven, North America and US possessions eight: Atlantic, Eastern, Central, Mountain, Pacific, Yukon, Alaska-Hawaii, Bering (American Samoa), respectively 4 (but Newfoundland keeps 3½), 5, 6, 7, 8, 9, 10, and 11 hours behind Greenwich (technically UTC, see below); however, Alaska keeps Yukon time and Yukon Pacific. Australia has three zones, 8, 9½, and 10 hours ahead of Greenwich, despite a proposal in 1891 by the Postmaster-General of South Australia to adopt a uniform Australian time of 9 hours in advance of Greenwich—and a quarter of an hour behind mean solar time in Adelaide, the capital of South Australia. But the whole of China keeps Beijing time.

UNIVERSAL TIME AND INTERNATIONAL
ATOMIC TIME

For astronomical purposes Greenwich Mean Time was reckoned until 1925 by the 24-hour clock commencing at noon; since then it has been reckoned from midnight, in which mode it is technically designated Universal Time. This is reckoned not from the brass line at Greenwich but on a notional prime meridian a few metres away, and comes in three varieties: astronomical time as observed (UT0), as corrected for irregularities due to polar motion (UT1), and as further corrected for irregularities due to meteorological factors such as the melting and freezing of the polar ice-cap, and the change over Siberia from high pressure during winter to low in summer, which cause the speed of the earth's rotation to vary by some 1.2 milliseconds between its slowest rate (in the northern spring and early summer) and its fastest (in the northern autumn).

However, even when these corrections have been made, the earth is not as good a timekeeper as the atomic clock, which measures time according to the frequency of current generated by irradiated atoms of caesium-133; the base unit is the second, which is defined by the International Committee on Weights and Measures as 'the duration of 9 192 631 770 cycles of radiation corresponding to the transition between the two hyperfine levels of the ground state of the caesium-133 atom'. For astronomical purposes the day, as a unit of reckoning, is defined as 86 400 seconds; but unpredictable irregularities in the earth's rotation may lengthen or shorten the day by up to 4 milliseconds in 10 years. These are corrected by leap seconds, either positive (23.59.60 added before 00.00.00) or negative (23.59.59 omitted), at the end of March, June, September, or December, by which International Atomic Time (TAI, *Temps atomique international*) is adjusted at the behest of the Bureau International de l'Heure in Paris to produce Co-Ordinated Universal Time, or UTC.

THE INTERNATIONAL DATE LINE

As Phileas Fogg forgot in Jules Verne's story, if all time is measured by local sunrise and sunset, a person travelling eastwards round the world will gain a day, that is come back one day earlier, by home reckoning, than the daily record of the journey would indicate; contrariwise, one travelling westwards will lose a day, that is come back one day later than the perceived passage of time suggests. To correct this irregularity, ships crossing the International Date Line repeat the day when eastward bound and suppress a day when westward; similarly, air travellers must set their calendar watches one day back in the former case and one day forwards in the latter. The International Date Line is the meridian 180° E. of Greenwich, modified for convenience' sake when it would run through land or divide islands within a political entity; in territories lying west of the line the time of day is up to 12 hours (in a few places over 12 hours) in advance of Universal Time, in those to the east it is behind. However, there being no international body charged with its maintenance, its course has been subject to adjustment for political reasons, as when on 11 August 1997 the Republic of Kiribati declared the date line to pass east of Caroline Island, renamed 'Millennium Island', instead of west, so that it should be the first place to see in the third millennium.

DAYLIGHT SAVING (SUMMER TIME)

In the early twentieth century, William Willett (1856–1915), a Chelsea builder, advocated that during the spring and summer months the use of daylight should be maximized by setting clocks forward; his initial suggestion of four successive 20-minute advances upon Greenwich Mean Time gave way to a single advance of an hour, which thereafter became the definitive proposal. Despite some parliamentary discussion, little enthusiasm was shown for the idea until the First World War, when Germany adopted it on 31 March 1916, followed by her ally Austria-Hungary and the neutral Netherlands.

Willett's compatriots reluctantly adopted the enemy measure in an Act of Parliament that lapsed in peacetime; however, the principle was revived in 1922, since when 'British Summer Time' has been in force for at least part of every year; during the Second World War clocks were advanced two hours ('Double Summer Time') between May and August from 1941 to 1945, and again in 1947 from 13 April to 10 August, following a fuel shortage. In 1968 the reversion to GMT due on 27 October was not made; clocks remained ahead, on 'British Standard Time' (much to the convenience of business, which during winter was enabled to keep the same time as its Continental partners), till public disgust at dark winter mornings (particularly in northern Scotland, where darkness might remain till 10 a.m.), the danger to schoolchildren, and the opposition of farmers and builders forced the restoration of GMT on 31 October 1971. The Summer Time Act of 1972 lays down that

the period of summer time for the purposes of this Act is the period beginning at two o'clock, Greenwich mean time, in the morning of the day after the third Saturday in March, or, if that day is Easter Day, the day after the second Saturday in March, and ending at two o'clock, Greenwich mean time, in the morning of the day after the fourth Saturday in October.

We may admire the forethought that provided for a case not arising till 2285 (for the third Saturday in March can be no later than the 21st, but not till that year will it be Easter Eve); however, these provisions have been varied by Order in Council so as to minimize the difference with other West European countries: the hour of change is now 0100 GMT = 0200 West European time, and the introduction of Summer Time is generally delayed till the last Sunday in March. The reversion to GMT remained four weeks later than is normal on the Continent, despite a proposal to compromise on the second Sunday of October, until 1996, when Continental countries accepted the end of October. A Private Member's Bill that year to advance the clocks by one hour in winter and two in summer was blocked by the Government.

In the United States, the Uniform Time Act of 1967 imposed daylight saving from 2 a.m. on the last Sunday in April to 2 a.m. on the last Sunday in October; but states and US possessions could vote to be exempt, and in 1972 those straddling time-zones were permitted to exempt parts of themselves. The oil crisis of 1973 caused Congress to legislate for continuous Daylight Saving Time from 6 January 1974 to 26 October 1975; the Act was not renewed, but in 1986 the start of Daylight Saving Time was moved to the first Sunday in April with effect from 5 April 1987.

COMPARATIVE WORLD TIMES

At 1200 UTC the official time in the following cities and islands, when Summer Time or Daylight Saving is not in operation, is (geography in some cases notwithstanding):

0100	Kiribati; American Samoa; Tonga
0200	Honolulu

0230	Marquesas Islands
0300	Anchorage, Alaska
0330	Pitcairn Island
0400	Whitehorse, Yuk.; Los Angeles
0500	Edmonton, Alta.; Denver
0600	Winnipeg; Chicago; Mexico City; Easter Island
0700	Montreal; New York; Havana; Lima
0800	Halifax, NS; La Paz; Santiago; Falkland Islands
0830	Newfoundland
0900	Nuuk; Recife; Buenos Aires
1000	South Georgia
1100	Scoresbysund
1200	Reykjavík; Dublin; Lisbon; Dakar
1300	Stockholm; Berlin; Lagos
1400	Helsinki; Athens; Jerusalem; Cape Town
1500	Riga; Moscow; Riyadh; Dar es Salaam
1530	Tehran
1600	Volgograd; Tbilisi; Oman; Mauritius
1630	Kabul
1700	Ekaterinburg; Karachi
1730	Delhi and all India
1745	Kathmandu
1800	Tashkent
1830	Yangon (Rangoon)
1900	Novosibirsk; Bangkok; Jakarta
2000	Irkutsk; Beijing (and all China); Perth
2100	Chita
2130	Adelaide
2200	Vladivostok; Sydney
2230	Lord Howe Island
2300	Magadan; Vanuatu
2330	Norfolk Island
2400	Anadyr'; Wellington
0045	(next day) Chatham Islands
0100	(next day) Western Samoa

THE ROMAN CALENDAR

Whereas for the modern world the calendar is primarily a functional or abstract entity, for the Romans it was a vital constituent of their culture, part of what it was to be a Roman for pagan and Christian alike; the months were represented in the visual arts, and calendar poetry ranged from simple couplets on the months to Ovid's *Fasti*, an account of the ceremonial calendar that had not extended beyond June when the poet abandoned the project on being exiled. Written calendars were inscribed in pagan temples and (with modifications) in Christian churches; a lavishly illustrated manuscript calendar for AD 354 combining pagan and Christian festivals was prepared as a gift (perhaps at New Year) for one Valentinus, a Christian aristocrat apparently related to the great pagan orator Symmachus, and written by the calligrapher Furius Dionysius Filocalus who was later to carve Pope Damasus' epitaphs on the martyrs' tombs. Their name of *fasti* was also used for lists of consuls (in the more elaborate *fasti* all consuls, not merely the *ordinarii* after whom the year was named), of commanders who had held triumphs, or other citizens worthy of commemoration; the Calendar of 354 lists imperial birthdays, consuls, and urban prefects (governors of Rome) along with a table of Easter dates, burial dates (*depositiones*) of bishops of Rome and of martyrs, and a list of the former; it also contains astrological matter relating to the planetary week and the zodiac, with chronicles of the world from Adam and of Rome from Romulus.

The latter was reputedly the king who, more skilled at soldiering than stargazing, had given Rome the ten months from March to December; his pious successor, Numa, had added the other two. Macrobius in his *Saturnalia* tells of further developments, which it would be dangerous to take for historical truth. Our firm evidence relates to the calendar as Caesar found it and as he left it, having changed the length of the months and the nature of intercalation; since in the Julian calendar these will already be familiar to the reader, we begin by stating them for the Republican. The numerals 4, 9, etc. will be given in the form *IIII*, *VIIII*, etc., which is more frequent in antiquity and regular in the early Middle Ages; conversely, Romans sometimes wrote *IIX* for 8, but we shall abide by *VIII*.

THE CALENDAR OF THE ROMAN REPUBLIC

The year contained 12 months, *Ianuarius, Februarius, Martius, Aprilis, Maius, Iunius, Quinctilis, Sextilis, September, October, November, December*. March, May, Quinctilis, and October contained

31 days, February 28, and all the rest 29, yielding a regular year of 355 days; the length both of year and of month reflected a belief in the superior auspiciousness of odd numbers. Every so often a board of priests known as *pontifices* (who were active politicians, and often behaved accordingly) would curtail February at the 23rd or 24th and insert an extra month (*mensis intercalaris* or *intercalarius*, also spelt with *k*, 'called between') of 27 days to give a year of 377 or 378 days; statements in late sources that a month of 22 or 23 days was inserted within February are contradicted by better evidence. It follows that Republican dates will seldom correspond to the same nominal day in the retrojected Julian calendar; since the true Julian date can rarely be ascertained except for astronomical phenomena such as eclipses or when it is equated with a date in a better-calculated calendar, historical dates, even in modern authors, should be understood as pertaining to the Republican, not the retrojected Julian calendar: the statement that Cicero was born on 3 January 106 BC refers to *a.d. III Nonas Ianuarias Q. Servilio Caepione C. Atilio Serrano coss.* [= *consulibus*], not to 3 January in the 106th Julian year before the Christian era.

Although in intention lunisolar, the Republican calendar was in practice neither lunar nor solar. Its structure prevented it from keeping in step with the moon: an eclipse identified with that of 21 June 400 BC was recorded as having taken place on the Nones of June, i.e. the 5th of the lunar month, and not the 1st, even though it was new moon. The discrepancy between the calendar and the solar year might have been made up with 11 intercalations in every 24 years, but regularity was sacrificed to political convenience and superstition. In particular, the supposed ill luck attaching to intercalation (as in many other cultures) apparently caused it to be suppressed during the Second Punic War (218–201 BC), when Rome was fighting for her life; at all events, in 190 BC the solar eclipse that according to modern astronomers fell on 14 March was recorded on *a.d. V Eid. Quinct.*, or 11 July. Compensatory intercalations had reduced the discrepancy to two and a half months by 168 BC, when the solar eclipse of 21 June was observed on *a.d. III Non. Sept.*, or 3 September; if ancient sources are right that the consuls' entry into office was moved back in 153 BC from 15 March to 1 January because of a military emergency, the calendar had been overcorrected and was now running behind the sun.

JULIUS CAESAR'S REFORM, AND AFTER

The calendar again fell out of step during the Gallic War of 58–51 BC, since intercalation took place only in those years when the *pontifex maximus*—none other than Julius Caesar—spent February in Rome. However, after winning both the Gallic and the Civil wars, he gave his mind to the matter; having taken advice from the best astronomers, he extended 46 BC (the last year of the confusion, as Macrobius puts it) to 445 days, and ordained that in all subsequent years January, Sextilis, and December should have 31 days, April, June, September, and November 30. In order to minimize disruption to festivals the Nones and Ides were left unchanged and the extra days added immediately before the last of the month, thus keeping festivals in the second half of the month at the same distance from the preceding Ides; the exception was April, when the new day was inserted four days earlier (*a.d. VI Kalendas Maias*) to avoid interrupting the Floralia. For a modern falsehood concerning the reform, see *30 February.

Since the tropical year was some 6 hours in excess of 365 days, Caesar ordained that 24 February, the sixth day before the Kalends of March, should in leap year be counted twice (see *Leap Year*). This intercalation was to take place *quarto quoque anno*, by which he meant what we mean by 'every fourth year'; however, such expressions usually being inclusive in Latin, after his murder in 44 BC the *pontifices* understood him to mean every third year. An inscription of 9 BC, reforming the local calendar of Asia Minor on Roman principles, explicitly prescribes a three-year cycle, 'beginning with this year'; but the emperor Augustus, who upon the death of the *pontifex maximus* Lepidus (Shakespeare's 'slight unmeritable man') in 12 BC had succeeded to his office, was about to correct the error by suppressing the leap day due in 5 BC, 1 BC, and AD 4. Intercalation was resumed in AD 8, and took place every four years thereafter.

This sequence, if retrojected, makes 45 BC a leap year; some scholars suppose that it was in Caesar's calendar, and ought to have been followed by 41 BC, 37 BC, . . . but was in fact followed by 42 BC, 39 BC, 36 BC, . . . There was precedent for a cycle beginning with leap year in the four-year weather cycle devised in the fourth century BC by Eudoxus of Cnidus, beginning with the rising of Sirius; the case of Asia Minor proves less, since the calendar was being adjusted to the Roman. Others note that in the retrojected cycle 2 January 45 BC was the day of visible new moon and also Saturday, the beginning of the planetary week, hence a doubly appropriate day on which to begin the reformed year, deducing that Caesar had intended his leap years to be 42 BC, 38 BC, . . ., that the mistake began not with the first intercalation after his death but the second, and that Augustus too erred by resuming intercalation in AD 8 instead of AD 7. Our sources tell us that after 12 intercalations had been made in 36 years, Augustus ordained 12 common years in a row, after which the current sequence should begin; on the first view 45 BC is excluded from the 36 years 44–9 BC, just as the common years AD 5–7 are excluded from the 12 years 8 BC–AD 4, on the second the 36 years result from multiplying the 12 leap years (the primary fact) by 3 and the intended 9 by 4. Other considerations have been advanced, but too speculatively; there is no irrefutable evidence.

In 44 BC the month *Quinctilis* was renamed *Iulius* in honour of the murdered dictator; in 8 BC *Sextilis* was renamed *Augustus* in honour of his living avenger, who restored his calendar in that year and had added Egypt to the Roman empire in that month. When his successor Tiberius, who as Tacitus tells us 'feared free speech and hated flattery', was offered a similar honour, he asked what would happen if there were 13 Caesars; nevertheless such renamings did take place in later reigns, but did not outlive the emperor or at most the dynasty. In AD 192 the mad Commodus restyled all 12 months after his names and titles (some self-awarded), Amazonius Invictus Felix Pius Lucius Aelius Aurelius Commodus Augustus Herculeus Romanus Exsuperatorius; he was assassinated in the same year on the day before the Amazonian Kalends, but at the Roman garrison in Dura-Europos the anniversary of his sole rule was celebrated the next year on 17 March, designated in the inscription as the 16th before the Kalends of Pius.

TALE OF DAYS

In each month there were three marker-days, from which all other days are counted backwards. The first day of each month was known as the *Kalendae*, in English 'Kalends', from the archaic verb *kalare* 'proclaim'; they were sacred to Juno, to whom sacrifice was offered, originally upon sighting of the new moon. One of the *pontifices* would then announce 'Juno Covella' (the hollow or first-quarter moon), normally for the 5th of the month, but for the 7th in the original 31-day months; this day, on which the people met again to hear the month's festivals announced, was called *Nonae*, 'Nones', as being the ninth day (inclusive) before the third of the three marker-days, on the 13th or 15th respectively. These were the *Eidus* (later spelt *Idus*), 'Ides', named from an Etruscan word meaning 'divide', and notionally the day of full moon, which divides the month in half; although the Etruscans counted days forwards throughout the month in the modern fashion, it is evident from the spread of this term in the Italic languages that special significance was given to this day. It was sacred to Jupiter, whose priest (the *flamen Dialis*) led the 'Ides sheep' or *ovis Idulis* down the Via Sacra to be sacrificed. It was said to be *Iovis fiducia*, the trust of Jupiter, because light from the full moon continued after sunset. All these named days were considered unlucky for marriages.

The month names are adjectives agreeing with the day names, which are feminine plural: 1 January is *Kalendae Ianuariae*, 5 April *Nonae Apriles*, 13 September *Idus Septembres*; 'on' these days is expressed by the ablative case: *Kalendis Ianuariis, Nonis Aprilibus, Idibus Septembribus*. These expressions are commonly abbreviated, e.g. *K.* or *Kal. Ian.* All other days are named by idioms in which the accusative is used: 6 March = *pridie Nonas Martias*, 14 July = *pridie Eidus Quinctileis* or *pridie Idus Iulias*, 31 October = *pridie Kalendas Septembreis* (later spelt *Septembris* or *Septembres*); *pridie* is normally abbreviated *pr.*, but other forms are found. The other days were expressed by an idiom literally meaning 'before the so-manyeth day', again followed by the accusative; they were counted inclusively, the normal method especially with small numbers in the ancient world, and still employed in the statement that Christ rose on the third day, meaning the next day but one after the Crucifixion.

When the Nones were on the 5th of the month (*Nonae quintanae*) the 2nd, by the modern forward count, was the fourth day before them; when they were on the 7th (*Nonae septimanae*) it was the sixth: 2 January = *ante diem quartum Nonas Ianuarias*, commonly written *a.d. IIII Non. Ian.*, 2 March = *a.d. VI Non. Mart.* The day after the Nones was always *a.d. VIII Idus* whether it was the 6th or the 8th of the month; that after the Ides was, in the Republic, *a.d. XVII Kalendas*, the Kalends being those of the next month, except for 14 February, which was *a.d. XVI K. Mart.* (the Republican abbreviation) or *a.d. X Terminalia*, a form necessary until one knew whether intercalation would be ordered, and more specific than *a.d. XI* or *XII K. Interk.* when it was. After the reform 14 February was still *a.d. XVI Kalendas* even in leap year; but in January, August, and December the 14th was *a.d. XVIIII Kalendas*, in April, June, September, and November *a.d. XVIII Kalendas*; *pridie Kalendas* was respectively the 31st or 30th instead of the 29th.

The placement of the extra days changed the nominal date of all festivals in the second half of the month except the Floralia, which remained on *a.d. IIII K. Mai.*, but now 28 April instead of the 27th; but (for instance) the Saturnalia on 17 December, previously *a.d. XIIII K. Ian.* down to 46 BC, thereafter became *a.d. XVI K. Ian.* However, it became the custom to omit *ante diem*, referring to the day by the plain ordinal, *sextus Nonas Martias* '2 March', adjusted to the syntax of the sentence, being read in the ablative when the sense is 'on': *sexto Nonas Martias*. The day and month sometimes appear in the genitive: *sexto Nonarum Martiarum*, 'the sixth of the March Nones'; *II* is occasionally found in place of *pridie*.

When Romans communicated on official business with Greek cities, Latin administrative formulae were translated, often with distressing literalness, from Latin into Greek; Roman dates were no exception. *Nonis Ianuariis* ('on 5 Jan.') became *Nōnais Ianuaríais, pridie Idus Februarias* (12 Feb.) *protérāi Eid(u)ôn Phebrouaríōn, a.d. XVII Kalendas Apriles* (16 Mar.) *pro hēmerôn déka heptà Kalandôn Aprilíōn* (with cardinals not ordinals: 'before 17 days of the April Kalends'). These expressions were adopted by the Greeks themselves when Roman dates needed to be expressed; the prepositional phrases were retained even after they had been superseded in Latin, though the word 'days' (*hēmerôn*) might be omitted, but *protérāi* for *pridie* was replaced by *prò miâs*, 'one before'. After Caesar's reform the *bissextus* was *hē dìs prò héx*, 'the twice before six', leap year being *dísekton étos*, though we also find the direct borrowing *bísextos*.

In the fifth century the forward count ('first of January', etc.) begins to be attested; it became regular in Greek, but long remained rare in Latin outside Merovingian Gaul; even in vernacular texts, dates are commonly given in Latin according to the Roman system, though Irish writers sometimes translate them literally. From the eleventh century the forward count makes increasing inroads, and is not even halted by the Renaissance; on the other hand there is no suggestion that it is somehow more Christian, for papal bulls remain a bastion of Roman dating (not a single forward date sullies Pope Gregory XIII's exposition of his calendar reform). The specifically Christian method of dating was by saints' days and church festivals, which indeed is very frequent even in secular documents (see I: *Western Church Year*).

In the Middle Ages both the use of *II* and the genitive plural of the day are frequent; however, the month is commonly treated as a substantive and put in the genitive: *II Kalendarum Martii, VII Iduum Octobris*. (In both classical and medieval texts, however, scribes and editors often render dates as they see fit; the original author's usage cannot always be determined.) It occasionally happens that a scribe who has not mastered the system (being more used to the forward count in his vernacular, or reference to saints' days) will count the days before the Kalends forwards instead of backwards, or give the name of the current month after *Kalendarum* instead of that following.

THE CHARACTERS OF DAYS

Roman *fasti* included not only the days but the holy days (*feriae*) observed on them; moreover, since Roman markets, known as *nundinae* ('nine days', counted inclusively), were held at eight-day intervals, each day was marked cyclically with one of the letters A–H, so that when the date of any one market-day was known, the rest could be found throughout the year; proposed laws had to be promulgated with three markets' notice (*trinum nundinum*). Under the Republic, 1 January, 28 February (the 57th day of the year), and the 27th of the intercalary month were all A, so that in both intercalated and common years the sequence ran unbroken from *pridie Kalendas Martias* (A) to *Kalendae Martiae* (B); the break came at the intercalary Kalends (G), following either 23 February (D) or the 24th (E). In the Julian calendar 24 February and the *bissextus* were G. Already by Augustus' time a second sequence, A–G, had been devised for the planetary week (see **Sunday Letters*), which becomes regular in later calendars; the Calendar of 354 also marks 1, 4, 7 January and every third day thereafter with a letter from A to K, two days being left unmarked between succeeding letters, except that in the even months E and F are only one day apart. This register was used for determining the age of the moon: if 1 January was new moon, then all other days marked A will be new moon too, all those marked B will have a lunar age of 4, those marked C 7, D 10, E 13, F 16 (in hollow months 15), and so on, intermediate lunes being found by interpolation. This system, but with the single day's space after K, is also found in medieval calendars, but concern with the moon's age was not a Christian innovation: a pagan inscription of AD 205 is dated *X K. Iun. lun. XVIII die Iovis*, 'on Thursday, 23 May, the 18th lune'. The attested dates on such inscriptions agree better overall with modern calculations than with ancient tables.

In addition, each day had a letter noting its character at public law, mostly C (*comitialis*), F (*fastus*), or N (*nefastus*). Only on a *dies comitialis* could the people meet in formal assembly (*comitia*); on a *dies fastus* the praetor was allowed to conduct legal business with the *tria verba*, the formal three words *do dico addico*, 'I grant, I pronounce, I adjudge'. (All ten days added by Caesar were *dies fasti*.) The three words were also permitted on a *dies comitialis*, if no *comitia* were actually held on it, but could not be uttered on a *dies nefastus*; despite a common opinion already attested in Horace this had nothing to do with ill luck, for many of the recognized unlucky days (*dies atri* or *dies religiosi*), such as those following Kalends, Nones, and Ides (*dies postriduani*, 'days after'), were *comitiales* or *fasti* (even 18 July, the day of the Allia disaster, was a *dies comitialis*), and the Senate could meet, and battles be fought, on *dies nefasti*. When a *dies nefastus* coincided with a holy day (including the Ides), a loop was attached to the N, suggesting a fused NP; no ancient source explains this symbol, and modern scholars are reduced to conjecture, the most favoured expansion being *dies nefastus publicus*. A few days were *endotercisi* or 'divided', beginning *nefasti* but becoming *fasti* at a certain point (see **24 Mar., *24 May, *15 June*); they were marked either with EN or with an abbreviation of the specific circumstance.

Some days changed their character over time; for others it is not known, since our evidence is physically incomplete. In the late Empire these indications are suppressed, as no longer relevant in an age when the people had ceased to meet and new judicial procedures had ousted the old; on the other hand, the Calendar of 354 records the days on which the Senate meets, which in earlier times had not been formalized.

YEARS

❦ CONSULAR DATING Under the Republic, the supreme power resided in two consuls, elected annually; under the Empire, the consuls lost most of their power, but not their dignity. The year was regularly designated as 'So-and-so and So-and-so being consuls' (though in Latin *et* is normally used only when the consuls are called by single names); unofficially, one might remember only one of the two, as when the excellent vintage of 121 BC, *L. Opimio Q. Fabio Maximo coss.*, was associated with the energetic and controversial Opimius alone (*vinum Opimianum*, i.e. made *Opimio consule*). Even when a consul died, or otherwise left office, before the end of the year, his name was seldom replaced by that of the *consul suffectus* who succeeded him. Resignation was rare during the Republic, but regular in the early Empire, for much of which consuls served for no more than two months; nevertheless it was the *consules ordinarii*, those entering office on 1 January, who gave their names to the year, whence the joke 'Under what consuls was he consul?'

After the division of the Empire, East and West nominated one consul each, but did not always recognize the other's nominee; and it sometimes happened that no one could be found to undertake the vast expense of giving consular games. In either case the year would be designated as 'after the consulate' of the previous consul or consuls. Other than emperors, the last consul in the West was Paulinus the younger in 535, in the East Basilius in 541; thereafter years were designated by their respective postconsulates, or by that of Justin, the son of the emperor's cousin, who had been consul in 540.

Until the late fourth century, the emperor's full titulature included the number of times he had taken the *tribunicia potestas*, first devised in 23 BC as a legal basis for Augustus' powers, which was renewed every year (originally on the anniversary of the grant, from AD 97 on 10 Dec. with a short-lived change to 1 Jan. in 244–53); but this was not employed in isolation as a date. In unofficial contexts regnal dates are found, mostly for historical or (in Christian authors) computistic purposes; they are liable to be adjusted to the calendar year, with inconsistent treatment of the first and last years of the reign. However, regnal dating is found in provinces so accustomed, reckoned according to local usage (see *Christian Chronology: Nativity*), and regularly so in Egypt (see *Egyptian Calendar*), where the emperors ruled as Pharaohs, until Diocletian abolished its special status; after that normal consular dates appear, though not exclusively.

Only in AD 537 did the emperor Justinian ordain that documents should be dated by regnal year; it was reckoned from the date of accession. (See *Chronology: Regnal Years*.) Upon Justinian's death in 565 his nephew and successor, Justin II, took the next year's consulate on 1 January 566; thereafter each new emperor took the consulate on 1 January following his accession and counted subsequent years as postconsulates, stated immediately after the regnal year. (Sometimes the reckoning is inclusive, so that the year after the consulate is called the second.) A co-emperor's regnal year, counted from his appointment, was stated after the senior Augustus' regnal year and postconsulate; he did not himself take the consulate until he had become sole or senior emperor, but having done so continued to count his regnal years from first appointment.

❦ YEARS FROM THE FOUNDATION Although the Romans sometimes assigned events to such-and-such year from the foundation of the City, they did not agree on when it had been founded. Varro's date of Ol. 6.3 (the third year of the sixth Olympiad; see *Chronology: Cycles*), which in April (see *21 Apr.) corresponds to 753 BC, the most familiar to modern readers, was only one of several guesses; chief among the rest was Ol. 6.4 (752 BC), known as the Capitoline era because it was used in the *Fasti Capitolini*, the list of consuls and triumphs inscribed on a triumphal arch in the Forum under Augustus. Even when, in the late Empire, writers agreed on the Varronian era, their years of the City are often inconsistent with it: this is notably true of the pagan Eutropius and the Christian Orosius, through whom the outlines of Roman history were transmitted to the Middle Ages. Eutropius uses the foundation alongside other datings, but Orosius makes it the basis of his chronology, referring even non-Roman events to so many years before or after it. In this he was followed by early modern scholars, who before the general adoption of BC dating commonly dated Greek events by Olympiads and Roman by the year AVC (*anno urbis conditae*, also read as *ab urbe condita*). Even in the nineteenth and early twentieth centuries it was normal in Germany to say that Cicero was consul in year 691 of the City, rather than in 63 BC; but the system is little used now, being neither convenient nor authentic. For the 'era of the Romans' reckoned from AD 249, see *Chronology: Eras*.

LEAP YEAR

In order to make up the difference of not quite 6 hours between the 365-day civil year and the solar year of 365.2422 days an extra day is added to the former every fourth year, the 366-day year being known as a leap year, in contrast to the common year of 365 days, and the extra day as leap day. The leap day was abortively introduced into the *Egyptian calendar* in 238 BC and successfully by Augustus; it was incorporated in the *Roman calendar* by Julius Caesar, though wrongly administered in the first four decades after his death. Once Augustus had corrected that error, the leap-year cycle has continued unbroken since AD 8 (except that in the Gregorian calendar years divisible by 100 but not by 400 have been common from 1700 onwards); hence it is by happy accident that leap years in the Christian era are divisible by 4, as also in the Byzantine world era as reckoned from 1 September 5509 or from 1 or 25 March 5508 (see *Chronology: Eras*), though not in the various Alexandrian or Ethiopic eras. When the Julian calendar is treated as a universal time-frame, AD 4 is a leap year, as are 1 BC, 5 BC, 9 BC, and all other years BC of the form $4n + 1$, though owing to the early mishandling of Caesar's reform only 9 BC, 21 BC, 33 BC, and (disputedly) 45 BC were Julian leap years.

NAMES

The term 'leap year' is first attested in Icelandic, where *hlaupár* has been used since at least the twelfth century. Although most Christian terms in Old Norse come from English, there is no trace of an Old English counterpart; in Byrhtferth's *Enchiridion* or Handbook of 1010–12, written in both Latin and English, the Latin *bissextus* and *bissextilis* (see below) are retained even in the English portions. Not till 1387 do we find *lepe ȝere*, in John de Trevisa's translation of Bartholomaeus Anglicus' *De proprietatibus rerum*; but the Dutch name *schrikkeljaar*, from *schrikken*, 'to jump' (nowadays 'to start' when frightened, but not originally so), is found in a didactic poem of *c*.1300 besides a more frequent synonym, *lopeliaer*, from *lopen*, the same word as 'leap' but (like German *laufen*) meaning 'to run'. This name would appear to be a formal, and the other a semantic, loan from English; the notion of 'running year' recurs in Hungarian (*szökőév*).

The statement in the Norse Mirror for Princes (*Konungsskuggsjá*) that in every fourth year there are three long hundred (= 360) and six days, 'and that is called leap year, because there is one day more in the 12 months than before', hardly counts as an explanation; but no more authoritative reason is available. It is true that the intercalation causes the feriae of the same date in successive years to differ by two instead of one, or as the seventh-century *De ratione computandi* observed, the Kalends of March leap across (*transiliunt*) from the feria of 1 February to that following; but neither in Hiberno-Latin nor in Irish did this generate any such name as 'leap year'. To this day the Irish term is *bliain bhisigh*, in contrast to the Anglicisms *bliadhna-leum* in Scots Gaelic and *blwyddyn naid* in Welsh. Another suggestion is that the name given to the omission of one lune in each Metonic cycle, *saltus lunae*—meaning that the moon leaps over or skips that lune in order to keep pace with the sun—which remained *salt* in Irish but was rendered *monan hlyp* or *oferhlyp*, 'the moon's (over)leap' by Byrhtferth and *tunglhlaup* in Old Norse, was illogically transferred in English to the addition of one day every fourth year, though that is not a leap but a standstill. But all this is mere guesswork.

The formal English 'bissextile year', and the regular French *année bissextile*, perpetuate Caesar's mode of intercalation by repeating the 'sixth day before the Kalends of March', 24 February. The extra day was known as 'twice sixth', *a.d. bis sextum Kalendas Martias*, or *bissextus* for short; from this was derived *annus bissextilis*. In Greek, the name was translated as *dísekton étos*, in modern demotic *dhísekhtos khrónos*; but we also find the direct loan *bísextos*, in Byzantine pronunciation *vísextos*, which by further adaptation yields the Russian name for leap year, *visokósnyĭ god*. This term is used in a few other Slavonic languages; most, however, speak of an overstepping or transgressive year (e.g. Polish *rok przestępny*, Serbian/Croatian *prestupna godina*), using a pan-Slavonic adjective that in other contexts means 'criminal' (cf. Dostoevsky's title *Prestuplenie i nakazanie*, 'Crime and Punishment'). In Albanian it is the 'brittle year' (*vit i brishtë*); but German *Schaltjahr* means no more than 'insert-year', cf. Continental Scandinavian 'shot-year' (e.g. Danish *skudår*). For Lithuanians it is 'the raising year' (*keliamieji metai*), for Latvians 'the long year' (*garais gads*).

POSITION OF LEAP DAY

An inscription from the Old Casbah at Constantine in Algeria declares: 'Temple dedicated in the consulate of Lucius Venuleius Apronianus for the second time and Lucius Sergius Paulus for the second time [AD 168] on the fifth before the Kalends of March, which day was after the twice sixth before the Kalends of March.' That is to say, the day before 26 March was the *bissextus*, which was therefore on the 25th in accordance with the assertion of the Roman jurist Celsus that 'the second day is intercalated, not the first' (*posterior dies intercalatur, non prior*); a person born on 24 February, *VI Kal. Mart.*, in a common year still had the 24th for birthday under that name in leap year, whereas one born on the 25th in leap year had the 24th for birthday in a common year, the *bissextus* being accounted one day with *VI Kal. Mart.* (The suggestion that in counting back from the Kalends 'earlier' means 'later' and vice versa is disproved by the verses cited below on St Matthias' day.) In 364 Valentinian I, summoned to become emperor at the death of Jovian on 17 February, refused to make an appearance on the *bissextus*, owing to its ill luck, but accepted acclamation on the next day, which chroniclers record as *V Kal. Mart.* in leap year, not the 25th (as the Greek church historian Socrates mechanically converts it) but the 26th; Ammianus Marcellinus, an eyewitness, states that the empire remained without a helmsman for ten days, namely the 17th to the 26th inclusively.

However, two non-legal scholars, Censorinus in AD 238 and Macrobius some 200 years later, tell us the opposite: that the 24th was the leap day, as the logic of the backward count might suggest (*VII, bis VI, VI*); not by coincidence, both assert that the intercalary month of the pre-Julian calendar was added after the 23rd, though in fact it was sometimes added after the 24th. Macrobius' account of the Roman calendar was extracted under the name of *Disputatio Cori* [corrupt for *Hori*] *et Praetextati* to become a stock text with the computists, making the order *bis VI Kal., VI Kal.* predominate, though the other was not unknown. This uncertainty persisted in the Western Church with regard to the feast of St Matthias on *VI Kal. Mart.* (see *24 Feb.), which in leap year was generally celebrated on the 25th; the rule was expressed in the verses:

> Bissextum sextae Martis tenuere Kalendae,
> Posteriore die celebrantur festa Mathiae.

To render doggerel by doggerel:

> *Mars* his *sixth Kalends* have the Leap-day gript;
> On the next Day, *Matthias'* Feast is kept.

In other words, the day called in common years *VI Kal. Mart.* (= 24 Feb.) occupies the *bissextus* position in leap year, St Matthias' feast being deferred to the day after (the 25th); or, as Byrhtferth has it, 'se bissextus his cynestol gesytt on þam forman .vi. kalendas Martii, and on þam æftran .vi. kalendas man sceal healdan Sanctus Mathias mæssedæges freols': leap day sits on his throne on the first *VI Kal. Mart.* and on the latter *VI Kal.* the feast of St Matthias' mass-day must be held.

This, however, was not universal practice. Olaus Worm quotes a breviary at Århus that adds 'Daci tamen celebrant diem VI Kl. Martij' ('but the Danes celebrate the sixth before the Kalends'); this appears to indicate non-postponement, which was certainly prevalent in medieval Norway and Iceland. In a breviary from Nidaros the second verse begins not 'posteriore' but 'ipso quoque' ('And that same day . . .'); the old Icelandic church canons state that from Peter's mass (St Peter's Chair, 22 Feb.) to Matthias' mass there are two nights and from Matthias' mass to St Gregory's (12 Mar.) 16, 'but 17 if it is leap year'. This means that St Matthias' day must always be on the 24th; likewise the computus known as the *Rímbegla* states that leap year's day (*hlaupársdagr*) stands on the next day after St Matthias. On the other hand *bissextus* on 24 February is prescribed by notes in the Irish *Félire Óengusso Céli Dé* (see *11 Mar.) even though it puts the saint on the 23rd.

In 1172/3 Pope Alexander III ruled that provided the vigil immediately preceded it, the feast might lawfully be kept, according to local custom, on either the first or the second day, 'which two are taken so to speak for one' (*qui duo quasi pro uno reputantur*). Nevertheless, the pre-Gregorian use of Rome was to repeat the martyrology for 23 February in leap year on the 24th, St Matthias following on the 25th; and despite a humanistic revival of non-postponement, the order *bis VI Kal., VI Kal.* became canonical, the phrase 'Vigilia sancti Matthiae Apostoli' being deferred from 23 February to the 24th, when it precedes a general commemoration of martyrs, confessors, and virgins.

Postponement was also the rule in England both before and after the Reformation: the two recensions of Edward VI's Book of Common Prayer, in 1549 and 1552, stated, as a matter of fact, that the 'xxv' day was counted twice, and required the same psalm and lessons to be said on the first day as the second. This may have been a misprint for 'xxiv'; but under Elizabeth I the rule was to repeat those of the 23rd upon the 24th. The 1662 book, however, is silent on the matter, taking the rule for granted; but amongst various other tokens of hasty drafting (including a misstatement of the rule for finding Easter), it added a 29th day to February with its own lessons and no Sunday Letter, while failing to indicate the effect of leap year on Sunday Letters, St Matthias, or (in those editions that include them) Roman dates. This apparently misled Archbishop Sancroft, in 1684, to ordain that St Matthias should always be kept on 24 February even in leap year, and thus in effect that leap day should be the 29th, as in civil and Orthodox usage.

THE 'STATUTE OF LEAP YEAR'

In the reign of Henry III uncertainty arose whether a person impleaded by a writ of right who had been granted an essoin or delay of a year and a day by reason of illness, should appear at the Tower on the 366th or 367th day when leap day intervened. The great jurist Henry Bracton held that he should appear on the 366th; his exposition, an exceedingly confused parade of second-hand and ill-digested learning, identifies the extra day (*dies excrescens*) of leap year with the 366th day accorded the essoinee by virtue of the six hours by which the natural year exceeds the civil common year. In leap year the *dies excrescens* is called the *bissextus*, as being recorded *sexto kalendas Martii*, when two days are reckoned to the same letter F; this *bissextus* is the lawful time for appearance, and not the other day with the same letter beginning the next four years. This seems to mean that if the essoin was granted on 23 February in a pre-leap year, the defendant should appear on the 24th, even though it is the *bissextus*, and not on the other F day the 25th; in any other circumstances the day of appearance will be the same nominal day as that on which in the preceding year the essoin had been granted, and not, as in a common year, the day after. (Hence leap year is a consideration to be taken into account when the justices check that the grant is for a lawful day.) However, his view did not prevail: a writ of 9 May 40 Henry III (1256), reissued four years later and commonly known as the Statute of Leap Year, instructs the justices of King's Bench that the *dies excrescens* shall be reckoned in the year, as part of the month in which it excresces, 'and it and the day immediately preceding shall be counted as a single day' (*et computetur ille, et dies proxime precedens pro unico die*). The text does not specify whether the *dies excrescens* is a particular day in February or the 366th day from the essoin, merely establishing that it does not count against the defendant, who will thus appear on the next nominal day in leap year as in common year.

LEAP YEAR SUPERSTITIONS

Valentinian's fear of the *bissextus* was no private quirk. Leap year, and in particular leap day, has often been accounted unlucky. (There are similar superstitions concerning leap months in lunisolar calendars; see *Chinese Calendar; *Roman Calendar.) The Norman church historian Orderic Vitalis records under both 1124 and 1136, apropos respectively of rebel traitors and of king and people, that the *bissextus* is popularly said to fall or crash on those who come to grief in leap year. In Greece, leap year is thought bad for marriage, planting vines, and laying the foundations of houses; a song speaks of 'leap years and angry months'. In Denmark the ill luck of leap year was extended to married women, who were thought likelier to die in childbirth than in other years. As a result, terms for 'leap year' may be applied to unlucky years in general, as was the case with French *bissêtre*; as Cotgrave wrote, 'Bissestre. *Ill lucke*; (*from* Bissexte, *which is held vnluckie.*)'; in modern Greek *dhísekhtos khrónos* may have this sense. In nineteenth-century Norway, the peasants of Gudbrandsdalen, asked when the last leap year was, would nominate the last bad year.

Churchmen naturally combated such notions. Byrhtferth, ever the expansive school-master, rubs his hands and instructs his readers 'about the venerable leap day' (*ymbe þone arwyrðan bissextum*). Five centuries later Mantuan (see*20 Mar.: Battista Spagnoli), on coming to St Matthias in his account of the Christian year, explains the intercalation, and then records the superstitions attached to it: crops and all human endeavours will be blasted; vines ought not to be planted or seeds sown; beasts will bear sickly young; fruit-trees will grow upside down (may we suspect the beatified author of burlesque?); in short, no business should be begun in leap year.

> Nil tamen interpres caeli, nil Tuscus aruspex,
> Nil magus inuenit, quod dici debeat huius
> Causa mali, quod virus agat tam triste per orbem.
> Quo fit ut errorem nugis vulgaribus istum
> Attribui debere putem; felicior iste
> Iudice me credi debet, quia longior, annus.
>
> Mantuanus, sig. g4^r

> Yet naught could e'er the watcher of the skies,
> The Tuscan seer or Persian mage devise,
> Why such infection should the earth o'erspread;
> Nay, of mere fable is this fancy bred:
> Would men but judge as things to me appear,
> The longer should be deemed the luckier year.

Thus, he observes, bigger is better in trees, bulls, and corn. He would be glad to know that in Irish *biseach* has become a general term for increase and prosperity.

THE MODERN CALENDAR

The modern international calendar, in the names and length of its months, though not in its designation of days, is the Roman calendar as amended with effect from 45 BC by Julius Caesar (see *Roman Calendar*) and further adjusted in AD 1582 by Pope Gregory XIII. Adjustment was necessary because the Julian year, consisting of 365 days, with a 366th day added every fourth year, has an average length of 365 days 6 hours, which is some 11 minutes 12 seconds too long, causing Julian dates to fall progressively further behind the sun. Even more inaccurate was the lunar calendar (see *Computus*), used not merely for calculating Easter but for determining the age of the moon throughout the year: whereas after 76 years the solar calendar was about three-quarters of an hour behind the sun, the lunar calendar was nearly 6 hours behind the moon.

EARLY PROPOSALS FOR REFORM

Discrepancies between the calendar and the true sun and moon became evident during the early Middle Ages; the facts were at first merely noted, but in the thirteenth century several clerics included proposals for reform in their writings on the computus. About the year 1232 John Holiwood (Sacrobosco) proposed omitting one leap day every 288 years; Giovanni Campano, in a treatise addressed to Pope Urban IV (1261–4), called for astronomical determination of the equinox and full moon; Robert Grosseteste and Roger Bacon also considered the problem. From the next century onwards we find treatises specifically devoted to such proposals, and popes who took an interest; but no action was taken. In 1437 the Council of Basle, on the verge of schism with Pope Eugenius IV, considered a proposal from his supporter Nicholas Cusanus to omit the last seven days of May 1439, later amended in discussion to 21–7 October 1440, but forbore to issue the decree. The astronomical genius Johann Müller of Königsberg, known in Latin as Regiomontanus, having published a calendar for 1475–1534 that contrasted the dates of Easter 'according to the usage of the Church' and 'according to the decrees of the Fathers', was in 1476 invited to Rome by Pope Sixtus IV to assist with a reform, but died shortly after his arrival. Pope Leo X intended the subject to be discussed at the Lateran Council, but made the mistake of seeking advice from the universities, which dawdled to no purpose.

Proposals continued to be made by various writers; Luther too observed that the cal-endar was out of joint, and in particular that in 1538 Easter ought to have been kept not on 21 April but five weeks earlier, on 17 March. This was before the nominal, but after the real, equinox; had the Gregorian calendar already been in force, Easter would have fallen on that day, redesignated the 27th. For Jews, it was 16 Nisan 5298, the second day of Passover; unlike some of his later followers Luther was not disturbed by that co-incidence, but took it as supporting evidence for his case. However, he regarded reform as a matter not for the Church, since it had nothing to do with the Faith, but for the Christian princes, who must act together or not at all, since otherwise great confusion would result in respect of markets, fairs, and other secular business.

THE GREGORIAN REFORM

The Council of Trent, with many other matters to consider, did not discuss the calen-dar; however, in the final session (4 Dec. 1563) it referred reform of the breviary and the missal to the Pope. Both were revised by Pius V (1566–72); but in 1578 Pope Gregory XIII, deriving from the decree an implicit charge to correct the calendar on which they were based, set about reform in earnest. The new calendar, drawn up by Aloysius Lilius and revised by Christopher Clavius, was promulgated in the bull *Inter gravissimas* of 24 February 1582, which ordained that 4 October in that year should be followed by the 15th, and that centennial years should be common unless divisible by 400. Thus 1600 (re-assuringly) remained a leap year, and likewise 2000, but 1700, 1800, and 1900 became common. The purpose of this reform was to restore the vernal equinox, not to its the-oretical date in Caesar's calendar, which was 25 March, but to 21 March, the date pre-supposed by the existing rules for calculating Easter (see *The Date of Easter*), then believed to have been laid down by the Council of Nicaea in AD 325. Although some previous reformers had argued for replacing the lunar calendar with astronomical tables, this was thought too radical; instead the principle of calculation was retained, but with a corrected (and far more complex) calendar.

❨ ACCEPTANCE AND REJECTION Even in Roman Catholic countries the reform re-quired enactment by the civil power; Spain, Portugal, and the Italian states implemented it at the stated time; in France there were objections in the Paris *parlement* (which could invalidate a decree by refusing to register it), but the death of one opponent and the ab-sence of another enabled Henri III to order the omission of 10–19 December. Other Roman Catholic or confessionally mixed states and regions had accepted reform within a few years: the last was Transylvania, which omitted 15–24 December 1590.

In the Low Countries the Duke of Anjou issued a *plakkaat* on 10 December 1582 for the Netherlands that 15–24 December should be omitted. This was followed by the Staten-Generaal and some provinces—including the Protestant provinces of Holland and Zeeland, which were in revolt against Spanish power—though the days omitted were sometimes later than those specified, so that Christmas had to be kept on 4 January 1583 NS. Other Protestants, however, rejected the reform; the city of Groningen, which, at loggerheads with the surrounding territories or Ommelanden, had stayed in the Spanish camp, adopted the reform by omitting 1–10 March 1583, but upon its capture by Maurice of Nassau reverted to the Julian calendar (sometimes confusingly called *nieuwe stijl*) by repeating 10–19 November 1594.

A reform, however salutary, proposed by the Pope stood little chance of being accepted by the Orthodox, or generally by Protestants. The former, who venerated the 318 Holy Fathers at Nicaea, would do nothing without an Oecumenical Council; Patriarch Jeremias II of Constantinople refused Pope Gregory's request to introduce the reform. In certain Venetian possessions, Roman Catholics were granted dispensation to follow the Julian calendar rather than come into conflict with the Greek Orthodox majority. By contrast Protestants, taking a low view of church councils, objected that the vernal equinox should have been restored to 25 March (as in New Testament times) instead of the supposed Nicene date of the 21st. With the exception of Holland and Zeeland, Protestant Europe rejected the reform; denial of the Pope's authority apart, it was all too easy to show that the Easter tables were astronomically inexact.

The coexistence of Julian and Gregorian calendars in Germany often made it necessary to date by both; a satirical poem, alluding to the custom that during Holy Week wives should not prevent their husbands from visiting the tavern, makes a woman complain that men have now obtained two weeks of freedom, in other words that they claim this privilege during both the new Holy Week and the old. It is entitled 'Der Weiber Krieg wider den Bapst, darumb das er zehen tage aus dem Calender gestollen hat' ('Women's war against the Pope for stealing ten days from the calendar').

Introduction of the new calendar annoyed the peasantry, whose traditional calendar lore, expressed in so many weather proverbs, was upset by the 10-day shift: another satire accuses the Pope of so confusing poor folk 'That we can now no longer know | When we should plough and delve and sow' (*Das wir nun mehr kein wissen haben, | Wenn man soll pflantzen, seen, graben*) and wishes that he may face the Last Judgement 10 days earlier than other people. His blackest crime, however, was to interfere with established drinking habits, in particular the celebration on a fine St Urban's day, portending a bumper wine-harvest (see *25 May).

However, more reflective minds were also disturbed, in particular Montaigne:

I will here declare, by way of example, that the late ten days diminution of the *Pope*, have taken me so low, that I cannot well recover my self. I follow the Years wherein we kept another kind of account, so antient, and so long a *Custom*, challenges and calls me back to it; so that I am con-strain'd to be a kind of Heretick in that point, impatient of any, tho corrective Innovation. My Imagination, in spite of my teeth, always pushes me ten days forward or backward, and is ever murmuring in my Ears.   *Essays*, 3. 10 (iii. 373–4)

'Tis now two or three Years ago that they made the Year ten days shorter in *France*. How many Changes may we expect should follow this Reformation! This was properly removing *Heaven* and *Earth* at once; and yet nothing for all that stirs from its Place: my Neighbours still find their Seasons of Sowing and Reaping, the Opportunities of doing their Business, with the hurtful and propitious days, just at the same time, where they had time out of mind assign'd them. There was no more Error perceiv'd in our old Usance, than there is Amendment found in this new Alteration. So great an Incertainty there is throughout; so gross, obscure and dull is our Understanding. *ibid. 3. 11 (iii. 398)*

During the seventeenth century a few Protestant states accepted reform, most notably the Duchy of Prussia (the later East Prussia, not Brandenburg), which omitted 23 August–1 September 1610; but the Easter tables remained a stumbling-block, and in particular the coincidence of Easter and Passover, which had not disturbed Luther. However, as the year 1700 approached, bringing with it an increase in the difference between the calendars, Protestants reconsidered their position. The Lutheran states of the Holy Roman Empire were finally persuaded to accept the New Style by omitting 19–29 February 1700; nevertheless, they spurned the Gregorian Easter tables, adopting instead a so-called 'Improved Calendar', in which the date of Easter was astronomically determined (see *The Date of Easter*). In this they were joined by Denmark, and most but not all Protestant cantons in Switzerland; those Dutch provinces that had held out against the papal reform voted to adopt it under the name of 'Improved Julian Calendar', but thereafter in practice observed the Gregorian Easter.

❡ ENGLAND When Pope Gregory promulgated the reform, Queen Elizabeth I was sufficiently intelligent and enlightened to favour adopting it, but desisted upon advice; national hostility was not abated even by the partial example of the Dutch, whom the more advanced Protestants took as their model. Nevertheless, at the end of the seventeenth century the Archbishop of Canterbury, Thomas Tenison, contemplated change, but nothing was done. The great mathematician John Wallis, in a letter of 30 June 1699 to the Bishop of Worcester, set out grounds against: the Gregorian calendar was inferior (since astronomers had 'first to adjust their calculations to the Julian Year, and thence transfer them to the Gregorian'); to adopt it would be to readmit papal supremacy. It would put England out of step with other Protestant countries; apparently he did not know of Continental developments, but his chief concern was with Scotland, then a separate kingdom:

'Tis happy they did comply with us upon the late Revolution (to be under the Same King with us.) We cannot presume they will be so fond of Compliance in all the Modes of Rome· as is very evident in their not admitting Episcopacy nor the Observation of Easter; (which latter was the only Pretense of first introducing the Gregorian Year.) . . .

Furthermore, it would require a new Act of Parliament, and alteration to the Book of Common Prayer; moreover, Easter could be found astronomically:

If yet your Lordship think it necessary that the Seat of Easter should be rectified, that may easily be done, without altering the Civil Year. For if in the Rule of Easter, instead of saying, next after the one & twentieth of March, you say, next after the Vernal Equinox, the work is done· For then Every Almanack will tell you when it is Equinox and when it is Full Moon for the present Year without disturbing the Civil Account, and this Pope Gregory might as well have done without troubling the Civil Account of Christendom.

Bodleian Library, MS Tanner 21, fos. 110ʳ–111ʳ

Besides, if the civil calendar were to be changed, Pope Gregory's reform was incorrect: 'most certain it is that at our Saviours Birth the Vernal Equinox was not on the one and twentieth of March (as this New Account would suppose) but nearer to the Five and Twentieth'. However, he would rather that the Pope issued a new bull reversing the reform; the same line was taken, with similar arguments, by John Willes DD, who argued that 'such alteration as this is not likely to produce good, but mischief to our Church, and occasion new differences, as it hath already done in the *Palatinate* Churches' (p. 16); he too had retrospective advice for Gregory XIII:

There need have nothing else been done, but declaring the 11th of *March* to be the *Paschal Equinox*, and that in every 120 Years, it should have advanc'd one day farther, for its [*sic*] not material what day of our *Solary Month* we call the *Equinox*, so that we be agreed of the time. And then, instead of introducing perplex'd and difficult *Tables of Epacts*, the *New-Moons* might be discover'd for ever by the *Old Tables*, only going backward one Day in 312 Years, from the Time of the *Nicene Council*, at this time 4 Days . . .   Willes, 23–4

By the mid-eighteenth century polite society was less superstitious, and Scotland, being under the same parliament as England, could be included in the reform. To be sure the notion of independent reform continued to find adherents (see below); but serious people understood that it was the Gregorian New Style that ought to be adopted. In 1750 Lord Macclesfield, a fine mathematician, submitted to the Royal Society his preliminary 'Remarks on the Solar and Lunar Year'. Lord Chesterfield, never a man to be inhibited by vulgar prejudices, introduced a bill to adopt the New Style. As he wrote to his son on the day of the Second Reading debate (18 Mar. 1751 OS):

It was notorious, that the Julian calendar was erroneous, and had overcharged the solar year with eleven days. Pope Gregory the 13th corrected this error; his reformed calendar was immediately received by all the Catholic powers of Europe, and afterwards adopted by all the Protestant ones, except Russia [*sic*], Sweden, and England. It was not, in my opinion, very honourable for England to remain in a gross and avowed error, especially in such company; the inconveniency of it was likewise felt by all those who had foreign correspondences, whether political or mercantile. I determined, therefore, to attempt the reformation; I consulted the best lawyers, and the most skilful astronomers, and we cooked up a bill for that purpose. But then my difficulty began; I was to bring in this bill, which was necessarily composed of law jargon and astronomical calculations, to both which I am an utter stranger. However, it was absolutely necessary to make the House of Lords think that I knew something of the matter; and also, to make them believe that they knew something of it themselves, which they do not. For my own part, I could just as soon have talked Celtic or Sclavonian to them, as astronomy, and they would have understood me full as well: so I resolved to do better than speak to the purpose, and to please instead of informing them. I gave them, therefore, only an historical account of calendars, from the Egyptian down to the Gregorian, amusing them now and then with little episodes; but I was particularly attentive to the choice of my words, to the harmony and roundness of my periods, to my elocution, to my action. This succeeded, and ever will succeed; they thought I informed, because I pleased them; and many of them said, that I had made the whole very clear to them; when, God knows, I had not even attempted it. Lord Macclesfield, who had the greatest share in forming the bill, and who is one of the greatest mathematicians and astronomers in Europe, spoke afterwards, with infinite knowledge, and all the clearness that so intricate a matter would admit of: but as his words, his periods, and his utterance, were not near so good as mine, the preference was most unanimously, though most unjustly, given to me.   Chesterfield, ii. 117–18

In consequence the Act of 24 George II, c. 23, ordered that in 1752, throughout Great Britain and all lands under the British Crown, the 11 days 3–13 September should be omitted; in place of the Gregorian Easter tables, new tables were adopted that reached the same result by a different and more convenient means (see *The Date of Easter*). This act also provided that from 1752 the year should be reckoned from 1 January in England and the colonies, as it was already in Scotland.

As usual there were complaints about the adoption of a Continental and popish reform; some complained it had been done behind the King's back, for George II had been in Hanover at the time (though since the Improved Calendar was used there, he could hardly disapprove). It was observed that the Glastonbury thorn flowered on Old Christmas Day and not according to Act of Parliament (cf. *5 Jan., *26 Feb.). For the supposed calendar riots, see *14 September.

(SWEDEN In his complaints about Pope Gregory's reform, Montaigne recollected Augustus' correction of the *Roman calendar*:

'Tis said, that this Regulation might have been carried on with less Inconvenience, by subtracting, according to the Example of *Augustus*, the *Bissextile*, which is in some sort a Day of Trouble, till we had exactly satisfied that Debt; which is not perform'd neither by this Correction, and we yet remain some Days in arrear: And yet by the same means such Order might be taken for the future, ordering, That after the Revolution of such a Year, or such a number of Years, the supernumerary Day might be always thrown out, so that we could not henceforward err above four and twenty Hours in our Computation.   *Essays*, 3. 11 (iii. 398–9)

Precisely this plan was adopted in Sweden, the intention being to omit all leap days between 1700 and 1744 inclusive; however, although 1700 was made a common year, 1704 and 1708 were not, and the reform was undone in 1712 by adding a second leap day to February (see *30 Feb.). New Style was finally adopted in 1753, by the omission of 16–28 February. See too *Sunday Letters* and Appendix I.

(LATER SPREAD OF THE NEW STYLE By 1798 the only Swiss Protestants still using the Julian calendar were in Graubünden (Grisons); the French-imposed Executive Directorate of the Helvetic Republic ordered them to adopt the Gregorian calendar, but the commune of Süs held out till force of arms was used in 1811. In 1875 the Khedive of Egypt, Ismail Pasha, introduced the Gregorian civil calendar over the Muslim, Julian, and Coptic calendars in use; in the twentieth century most of the Orthodox have had the New Style forced on them for civil purposes: in Bulgaria on 1/14 April 1916, in Russia on 1/14 February 1918, in Serbia on 14/27 January 1919, in Greece on 16 February/1 March 1923. In Greece the Church was pressed into accepting the reform, except with regard to Easter, on 10/23 March 1924; in Romania both Church and State adopted it on 1/14 November 1924. Reform did not take place in either country without protests that ranged from the cutting-off of a Metropolitan's beard to full-scale riots quelled by the police; nevertheless in 1926 Romania even kept the Gregorian Easter on 4 April rather than the Julian 19 April/2 May, which appeared to lie outside the limit of 25 April. The Bulgarian Church accepted the reform from 7/20 December 1968.

❨ OLD DAYS Even when the New Style had been accepted, many days that had their place in popular consciousness, or government administration, continued to be kept according to the Old Style. In England the Old Style was remembered for certain purposes: the start of the financial year was postponed from 25 March to 5 April, and Lord Mayor's Day from 29 October to 9 November. The former was again adjusted in 1800 to 6 April, but not in 1900; the latter was left at 9 November, though nowadays the following Saturday is kept. In Friesland, where the New Style was adopted by omitting 1–11 January 1701, many contracts were reckoned to the New Style date corresponding to their traditional Old Style incidence, e.g. *Oude Mei* (1/12 May) or *Oude Sint Petri* (St Peter's Chair, 22 Feb./5 Mar.); the New Style equivalent was adjusted in 1800, when the nature of the reform was still remembered, Old May Day becoming the 13th, but not in 1900, so that *Oude Mei* remained the 13th and not the 14th. In Norway, which received the New Style in 1700 as part of the Danish kingdom, the Old Style was still used alongside it in the mid-nineteenth century; in the rural calendar, days may be kept on 'old' dates at 11, 12, 13, or even 14 days' distance from the new according to locality.

TWENTIETH-CENTURY REFORMS

❨ REVISED JULIAN CALENDAR In May 1923 a congress of some but not all Orthodox churches at Constantinople adopted a Revised Julian Calendar under which 1–13 October of that year should be omitted, Easter determined astronomically according to the meridian of Jerusalem, and leap days suppressed not according to the Gregorian rule but in any centennial year whose hundredth part did not, when divided by 9, leave a remainder of 2 or 6; the first divergence from the Gregorian system will thus be in making 2800 a common year and 2900 bissextile. (This is more accurate than the Gregorian rule, giving an average year of $365^{d}\ 5^{h}\ 48'\ 48''$; but see below, 'Considerations for the Future'.) The proposal was made by the Serbian scientist Milutin Milanković (1879–1958), best known for his work on the Ice Ages; but not even national pride persuaded the Serbian Orthodox Church to adopt his calendar. However, certain other churches accepted it except in regard to Easter: from 2800 onwards they will therefore be ahead of the old Julian calendar by $S - 2Q - T - 2$ days, and of the Gregorian by $[S/4] - 2Q - T$ days, where $S = [Y/100]$, $Q = [S/9]$, $R = S \bmod 9$, $T = [(R + 2)/4]$.

❨ THE SOVIET UNION Eleven years after Lenin had signed a decree (26 Jan./8 Feb. 1918) introducing the New Style, a rationalized and anti-religious calendar was introduced in the Soviet Union with effect from 1 October 1929. All 12 months had 30 days, with five extra days distributed as national holidays: after 30 January came Lenin Day (31 Jan. Gregorian), after 30 April the two-day Workers' First of May (2–3 May Gregorian); after 7 November two Industry Days (7–8 Nov. Gregorian). In leap year 30 February was to be followed by Leap Day (2 Mar. Gregorian). The consequence was that the Soviet months began respectively on Gregorian 1 January, 1 February, 3 March, 2 April, 4 May, 3 June, 3 July, 2 August, 1 September, 1 October, 31 October, and 2 December.

The seven-day week was replaced by a five-day cycle from Monday to Friday; propaganda posters showed the bourgeois idlers Saturday and Sunday being pitched out of doors. Each day was a rest day for one-fifth of the population, symbolized by the slip in one of five colours (yellow, pink, red, purple, and green) given to each citizen; the national holidays and leap day remained outside the cycle. This arrangement was meant to combine generous individual leisure with continuous industrial production (hence its name of *neprerývka*, 'non-interruption'), but also to interfere with religious observance and family reunions; in the latter aim it succeeded so well as to cause widespread discontent, in the former it failed, proving disruptive and inefficient.

With effect from 1 December 1931 the Western months were restored, but with a six-day week of five working days followed by a rest-day on the 6th, 12th, 18th, 24th, and (except in February) 30th of the month; the 31st was outside the cycle, being sometimes a holiday, sometimes overtime. This system was in turn abandoned on 26 June 1940, ostensibly to increase production, but actually because the peasants, even under collectivization, had sabotaged the new system by taking Sundays off as well as the new free days; indeed, despite reports that urban workers had forgotten the old weekdays, they had never been entirely lost to view even in official documents, and when the seven-day week was restored there was no question of selecting a different rest-day.

The assertion in some Western sources that the Soviet Union adopted the Revised Julian Calendar for its civil reckoning is quite false.

UNSUCCESSFUL PROPOSALS

Whereas previous Protestant proposals for calendar reform had essentially been debating counters against the Pope, in the eighteenth century British writers suggested independent reforms in earnest. Thus in 1737 the compiler of *Gadsbury's Almanack* proposed that the 14 days 11–24 March should be omitted, so as to restore Lady Day to its proper astronomical place and strengthen its position as the first day of the year. But a more radical suggestion was advanced in the *Gentleman's Magazine*, 15 (1745), 377–9, by one 'Hirossa Ap-Iccim' of Maryland, who proposed a '*Georgian* account' or era, named after George II, reckoned from 11 December 5 BC (11 Dec. Julian was the Shortest Day; 5/4 BC was the last year of Herod the Great). Accepting Sir Isaac Newton's estimate of the tropical year as $365^d \ 5^h \ 48' \ 57''$, he proposed that one intercalation in 33 should be suppressed, every 132nd year being common, with an error of less than one day in 10 000 years. (This would yield a mean calendar year of $365^d \ 5^h \ 49' \ 50.5''$) He also wished to divide the year into 13 four-week months, for preference numbered in sequence (and the weekdays likewise); but if the existing names were to be retained the thirteenth month should be called Georgy (by analogy with July, which was still stressed on the first syllable). To the 52 weeks contained in these months a 365th day should be added, 'sequester'd by *Christians* out of the year' and kept as Christmas, followed in leap year by 'the *British Lustrum, Olympiad,* or the *national day*'; neither this nor Christmas Day should form part of the week, but every month of every year should begin on Sunday. (Since the new reckoning was to be adopted from 1750 Georgian, which would begin on Wednesday, 11 Dec. 1745 OS, the break with the historic week would be immediate.) He also proposed that Easter should be 'fixt on the *Sunday* nearest to that day, on which the sun comes to the very same degree in the ecliptic, where it was on the resurrection, which might easily be calculated'; and further that money, weights, and measures should be reckoned 'in an octave proportion', each unit eight times the next. An expanded revision of these proposals, *The Pancronometer* 'by H.J.', was published at London in 1753.

The principle of the blank day, without a place in the sequence of feriae, in order to remedy the mismatch of year and week, was independently hit on by the Abate Marco Mastrofini (1763–1843). In his treatise on calendar reform, *Sul calendario gregoriano perpetuo opuscoli due* (Rome, 1834), he devoted Part I to the proposal that 1 January should be permanently fixed as a Sunday, 31 December being excluded from the sequence of weekdays, and likewise in leap year the extra day, which would immediately follow it; in Part II he argued that in such a calendar Easter should be fixed on 2 April, only here deeming it necessary to anticipate ecclesiastical objections. The work was published under Pope Gregory XVI (who though a notorious conservative bore the same throne-name as the previous reformer), with three *nihil obstat*s and two *imprimatur*s.

Unlike 'Hirossa Ap-Iccim', Mastrofini did not touch the irregular length of the months; but the 13-month plan, with blank days, was again proposed by other reformers such as Auguste Comte, in whose Positivist Calendar every month and every day was dedicated to an eminent man (or occasionally woman), the 365th day to all the dead, and the leap day to holy women. Positivist calendars continued for several decades to be issued in France and Brazil.

The Yorkshire-born Canadian Moses B. Cotsworth (1859–1943) obtained the financial backing of George Eastman, the president of the Eastman Kodak Company, for an International Fixed Calendar, commonly known as the Eastman Plan: the year consisted of thirteen months of 28 days, all beginning on a Sunday; the thirteenth month, called Sol, was to come between June and July; Leap Day (29 June) and Year Day (29 December) were not to be counted in the week. Several businesses had already adopted such a calendar for their internal accounts.

Concurrently, the League of Nations had adopted the cause of calendar reform; proposals were considered by the Advisory and Technical Committee for Communications and Transit in 1923. In 1926, the League assembly voted in favour of stabilizing Easter on the Sunday following the second Saturday in April and empowering the chairman of the Committee to set up national committees on further reform of the civil year; a recommendation that such committees should be established was officially communicated to member states in the following year. In the USA, which was not a member of the League, Eastman seized the initiative by setting up a National Committee on Calendar Simplification that duly found in favour of the International Fixed Calendar.

Not all would-be reformers were happy with a year in which there would be 13 Friday the 13ths. To be sure, certain native peoples of North America have reckoned 13 months to the year, and in Mesoamerican cultures 13 was a number of cosmic as well as calendrical significance; Eastman's party declared it to be the lucky number of a country founded by the rebellion of 13 colonies. But such arguments, even if they could satisfy Americans, were of no comfort abroad; it was also objected that the months could not be formed into quarters, and that landlords would charge an extra month's rent each year at the same rate as before. An alternative proposal provided for four equal quarters of 91 days, in each of which the first month, beginning on Sunday, consisted of 31 days and the second and third, beginning respectively on Wednesday and Friday, of 30; Leap Day, following 30 June, and Year Day, following 30 December, were to be international holidays or World Days not included in the week. This project was given the name of World Calendar, and championed by the World Calendar Association founded by Elisabeth Achelis.

A Congressional resolution introduced on 5 December 1928 inviting the President of the United States to convene or attend an international conference to simplify the calendar died in the Committee on Foreign Affairs. Nevertheless, the League Committee, at its session of June 1931, considered nearly 200 proposals from such interested parties as the Chicago Lumber Retail Dealers' Association (which favoured the 13-month year, with the equal-quarter year as fall-back); most attention was given to the Eastman Plan and the World Calendar. Both schemes, however, were fervently opposed by Orthodox Jews (and also Seventh-Day Adventists) as interrupting the regular succession of Sabbaths, which they would be obliged to continue observing every seventh day, on whatever feria it fell, and thereby incur civil and economic disabilities; the Chief Rabbi of Great Britain went in person to Geneva to speak against the proposals. Jews had no objection to reforms that respected the Sabbath, for instance by reducing the regular year to 364 days (52 weeks exactly) and adding a leap week whenever the deficit reached seven days; but this found no favour with the Committee or with reformers at large, even though such a calendar, with five weeks added over 28 years, had been in use for centuries in Iceland (see *Other Calendars: Icelandic*), and could be made compatible with the Gregorian reckoning by adding 71 weeks in 400 years. Accountants blenched at a week's difference in length of year, astronomers at the variation in the date of the vernal equinox.

Although the Committee did not adopt a single plan, the League continued to take an interest, soliciting the views of member and non-member governments. The 13-month year, regarded in much of the world as unlucky, impious, or both, lost all favour, especially after Eastman's suicide in 1932; many of the enterprises that conducted their own affairs on that basis abandoned it. Supporters of reform rallied behind the World Calendar; but although 14 out of 45 states pronounced in its favour to the League of Nations Council in 1937, none was a major power and nothing was done, on the traditional pretext that the time did not seem ripe.

In the early 1950s the government of India, engaged in the search for a new civil calendar of its own (see *Hindu Calendar*), invited the United Nations Organization to adopt the World Calendar. Few countries gave support; the United States recommended that all study of the question should cease, and in 1956 the Economic and Social Committee voted to postpone all further consideration *sine die*. The Holy See announced in 1962 that it would oppose any interruption to the week in the absence of compelling reasons, of which it alone would be the judge; since then the advantages that might result from the equalization of months have seemed less than the trouble of persuading the world to adopt it.

CONSIDERATIONS FOR THE FUTURE

In due course another reform will be needed to correct the excessive mean length of the Gregorian year, 365.2425 days ($365^d\ 5^h\ 49'\ 12''$). If the tropical year remained at its 1900 length of 365.242 198 781 25 days ($365^d\ 5^h\ 48''\ 45.9747'$), the Gregorian calendar would after 10 000 years be $3^d\ 17'\ 33''$ behind the sun (so that omitting leap day in 4000 and 8000 would not be enough); but since the tropical year is currently decreasing and the natural day increasing at current approximate rates per 100 tropical years of respectively $0.53''$ and $0.0015''$, the discrepancy will in fact be greater, so that not only the Gregorian calendar but the 132-year cycle and the Revised Julian Calendar, which also make the average year longer than tropical 1900, err on the wrong side. More accurate, for the time being, would be the rule, more than once proposed, of suppressing intercalation in every 128th year (or for convenience' sake in the nearest centennial year), with a mean year of 365.242 187 5 days ($365^d\ 5^h\ 48'\ 45''$); even better, though more complicated, would be the Iranian solar cycle of 2820 years (see *Muslim Calendar: Iran*), which falls short of 2820 tropical years by less than 2 minutes. But since in the longer term, when the tropical year approaches 365.242 days ($365^d\ 5^h\ 48'\ 28.8''$), it will be necessary to make four centennial years common out of five, a simpler reform would be to omit intercalation in 3200, when the calendar will be nearly a day behind, keep 3600 and 4000 as leap years, and thereafter substitute 500 for 400 in the Gregorian rule, making all centennial years common except 4500, 5000, 5500, 6000, etc., until such time as further adjustment should be needed. More precise proposals are impossible, since the rate of change in the length of day and year cannot be predicted.

THE BAHĀ'Ī CALENDAR

In the Bahā'ī calendar, known as *Badī'* (unprecedented), the year contains 19 months of 19 days, with 4 epagomenal days, 19 being the Bahā'ī mystical number; 19 years make a cycle or *vaḥīd* (One [God]), 19 cycles *kull-i-shay* ('all things'). These terms are Persian, though many are derived from Arabic. The first day of the year falls on the same day (reckoned from sunset) as the vernal equinox; usually 21 March, which is assumed below, but when the equinox will fall later than sunset on that day 2 March is a fifth epagomenal day and the new year begins on the 22nd. The week begins on Saturday; the era is reckoned from 1844.

The days of the week are:

Saturday	Jalāl	Glory
Sunday	Jamāl	Beauty
Monday	Kamāl	Perfection
Tuesday	Fiḍāl	Grace (Mercy)
Wednesday	'Idāl	Justice
Thursday	Istijlāl	Majesty
Friday	Istiqlāl	Independence

The days and months bear identical cyclical names:

Bahā'	Splendour	21 March–8 April
Jalāl	Glory	9–27 April
Jamāl	Beauty	28 April–16 May
'Aẓamat	Grandeur	17 May–4 June
Nūr	Light	5–23 June
Raḥmat	Mercy	24 June–12 July
Kalimāt	Words	13–31 July
Kamāl	Perfection	1–19 August
Asmā'	Names	20 August–7 September
'Izzat	Might	8–26 September
Mashiyyat	Will	27 September–15 October
'Ilm	Knowledge	16 October–3 November
Qudrat	Power	4–22 November
Qawl	Speech	23 November–11 December

Masāʾil	Questions	12–30 December
Sharaf	Honour	31 December–18 January
Sulṭān	Sovereignty	19 January–6 February
Mulk	Dominion	7–25 February
ʾAyyām-i-Hāʾ	'H Days'	26 February–1 March
ʿAlāʾ	Loftiness	2–20 March

The most important Bahāʾī celebration is the first day of each month, called the 'Nineteenth Day's Feast' since it is 19 days from the last occasion, when the faithful gather together for prayers, readings, consultation on the community's affairs, and a communal meal. Other holidays are:

1 Bahāʾ (21 Mar.)	Nawrūz (New Year)
13 Jalāl–5 Jamāl (21 Apr.–2 May)	Riḍvān (Paradise), commemorating the last twelve days that Bahāʾuʾllāh (Mīrzā Ḥusayn ʿAlī Nūrī, 1817–92) spent in Baghdad in the garden of Najīb Pasha, known to Bahāʾīs as the *Bāgh-i Riḍvān* or 'Garden of Paradise', before departing from the city. It was on this occasion that he proclaimed himself the new messenger from God whose coming had been foretold 19 years earlier by the Bāb; the special holy days are 13 Jalāl/21 April, 2 Jamāl/29 April, and 5 Jamāl/2 May. Elections are held at this period.
7 ʿAẓamat (23 May)	Commemorates the recognition of Sayyid ʿAlī Muḥammad Shīrāzī by his devotee the Mullah Ḥusayn as the Bāb or Gate through whom a messenger of God would come, 5 Jumādā I 1260 = 23 May 1844; this year is the starting-point of the Bahāʾī Era. On the very same day was born ʿAbbās Efendī, who as ʿAbduʾl-Bahāʾ greatly expanded the religion founded by his father Bahāʾuʾllāh, laid the foundation-stone of the great temple at Wilmette, Ill., in 1912, died in 1921 as a Knight of the British Empire, and was buried on Mount Carmel in British-mandated Palestine, now in Israel. Bahāʾīs gather to recite prayers and hear passages from their scriptures.
13 ʿAẓamat (29 May)	Ascension of Bahāʾuʾllāh, 13 ʿAẓamat 49 BE = 29 May 1892. Bahāʾīs gather for prayers at the hour of his passing.
16 Raḥmat (9 July)	Martyrdom of the Bāb by firing-squad at Tabrīz barracks in 1850.
5 ʿIlm (20 Oct.)	Birth of the Bāb, 1 Muḥarram 1235 = 20 October 1819. Feasting and devotion.

9 Qudrat (12 Nov.) Birth of Bahā'u'llāh, 2 Muḥarram 1233 = 12 November 1817. Celebrated with public or private gatherings.

4 Qawl (26 Nov.) Day of the Covenant, in honour of 'Abdu'l-Bahā' as the perfect exemplar of his father's teachings.

6 Qawl (28 Nov.) Ascension of 'Abdu'l-Bahā', 1921, observed with prayers at the hour of death.

The 'Ayyām-i-Hā' (26 Feb.–1 Mar., in leap year also the 2nd) are devoted to hospitality, charity, and service, also to preparing for the fast-month of 'Alā', observed by abstinence from food and drink between sunrise and sunset (ages 15–70, except travellers, the sick, and pregnant or nursing women).

In the United States, further days are observed according to the Gregorian calendar:

Third Sunday in January: World Religion Day
Second Sunday in June: Race Unity Day (est. 1957)
21 November: World Peace Day

THE CHINESE CALENDAR

The Chinese calendar is a lunisolar calendar based on the 'Metonic' cycle of 235 lunations distributed over 19 years, seven of which contain 13 months and the rest 12. The month may be either full (*dà*, 'large') or hollow (*xiǎo*, 'small'), but there is no rule of alternation. In contrast to other moon-based calendars, the day begins not at sunset but at midnight, and the month is determined by the astronomically calculated conjunction; the first day is that on which the conjunction takes place, even if in the last minute before midnight Beijing time. A conversion table for the years 1997/8–2020/1 is given at the end of this section. Similar calendars are or have been used in Korea, Japan, and Vietnam; also in Tibet, but reckoned from full moon instead of the conjunction.

Every year, month, day, and double hour or *shí* (1/12 day) has its place in the sexagenary cycle formed by combining the 10 Heavenly Stems (*tiāngān*) with the 12 Earthly Branches (*dìzhī*). Each successive pair of stems is associated with one of the five elements (each with a yang and a yin manifestation), five cardinal points, and five planets; each branch with an animal, an element, a double hour, a point of the compass, and a sign of the zodiac.

Stems	Element			Cardinal point	Planet
		yang	yin		
jiǎ *yǐ*	wood	fir	bamboo	east	Jupiter
bǐng *dīng*	fire	kindling	lamp-flame	south	Mars
wù *jǐ*	earth	hill	plain	centre	Saturn
gēng *xīn*	metal	weapons	kettle	west	Venus
rén *guǐ*	water	waves	brooks	north	Mercury

Branches	Animal	Element	Double hour	Compass point	Sign of zodiac
zǐ	rat	water	2300–0100	north	Aries
chǒu	ox	earth	0100–0300	N 30° E	Taurus
yín	tiger	wood	0300–0500	N 60° E	Gemini

Branches	Animal	Element	Double hour	Compass point	Sign of zodiac
mǎo	hare	wood	0500–0700	east	Cancer
chén	dragon	earth	0700–0900	S 60° E	Leo
sì	snake	fire	0900–1100	S 30° E	Virgo
wǔ	horse	fire	1100–1300	south	Libra
wei	sheep	earth	1300–1500	S 30° W	Scorpio
shēn	monkey	metal	1500–1700	S 60° W	Sagittarius
yǒu	fowl	metal	1700–1900	west	Capricorn
xū	dog	earth	1900–2100	N 60° W	Aquarius
hài	pig	water	2100–2300	N 30° W	Pisces

Stems and branches combine in the sequence 1 *jiǎzǐ* 2 *yǐchǒu* 3 *bǐngyín* . . . 9 *rénshēn* 10 *guǐyǒu* 11 *jiǎxū* 12 *yǐhài* 13 *bǐngzǐ* . . . 20 *guǐwèi* 21 *jiǎshēn* . . . 30 *guǐsì* 31 *jiǎwǔ* . . . 40 *guǐmǎo* 41 *jiǎchén* . . . 50 *guǐchǒu* 51 *jiǎyín* . . . 59 *rénxū* 60 *guǐhài*.

The year is commonly known by the animal associated with its branch; hence a person born in 1984/5, 1996/7, 2008/9, or 2020/1 is said to have been born in the Year of the Rat. (The Year of the Donkey, *lǘzinián*, is the Chinese counterpart of latter Lammas and the Greek Kalends.) This cycle is found in great parts of Asia from Turkestan eastwards; in some countries the ox is replaced by the buffalo, and also in Vietnam the hare by the cat (*mèo*, the branch being called *mǎo*). It was officially used in Iran between 1911/12 (Pig) and 1924/5 (Rat). Fiery Horse (*bǐngwǔ* or *dīngwǔ*) is an unlucky year to be born in: many Japanese girls born in 1966 remain unmarried.

The Chinese year running from 1 BC to AD 1 was the 57th year of the sexagenary cycle, *gēngshēn*, that beginning in AD 1 was the 58th, *xīnyǒu*. Hence to find the cyclical year corresponding to a date AD (supposing the Chinese new year to have begun), subtract 3, and divide by 60; the unit-figure of the remainder will indicate the stem. Divide this remainder by 12; the new remainder will indicate the branch. Thus, for 1999:

$$1999 - 3 = 1996 = 33 \times 60, \text{ remainder } 16$$
Unit-figure of 16 is 6; sixth stem is *jǐ*
16 = 12 + 4; fourth branch is *mǎo*
year beginning in 1999 is *jǐmǎo*

In imperial times, each year also had its numbered place in an auspiciously named era (*niánhào*); until 1368 new eras were proclaimed at the emperor's whim, but under the last two dynasties, the Míng (1368–1643 and recognized longer in the south) and the Qīng (1644–1911), the emperor proclaimed a single era at the start of his reign, beginning from the New Year after his accession, and was known by its name after death: the emperor who reigned during the Celestial Prosperity era (1736/7–1795/6) is therefore properly not the emperor Qiánlóng (formerly transliterated Ch'ien-lung) but the Qiánlóng emperor.

In astronomical usage the first month is the lunation during which the winter solstice occurs; this lunation is allocated the first branch, being called the *zǐyuè* (*yuè* = 'moon' or 'month'). The civil year has since 104 BC (with a few exceptions, the last in AD 761) begun two months later with the *yínyuè*; the first civil month has the special name *zhēngyuè*, the others are numbered 2–12, though literary and colloquial synonyms abound. The branch of the civil month will always correspond to its place in the sequence *yín* (1st month)–*chǒu* (12th month); the stem of the 1st month is determined by that of the year:

Year	First Month
jiǎ or *jǐ*	*bǐng*
yǐ or *gēng*	*wù*
bǐng or *xīn*	*gēng*
dīng or *rén*	*rén*
wù or *guǐ*	*jiǎ*

For most of the imperial period, days were far more often dated by the sexagenary cycle than by *quantième* and month; 1 January AD 1 was the 14th cyclical day, *dīngchǒu*.

The first double hour (*shí*) begins at 2300 or 11 p.m. on the previous civil day, and is assigned the branch *zǐ*; its stem is determined by that of the day:

Day	First shí
jiǎ or *jǐ*	*jiǎ*
yǐ or *gēng*	*bǐng*
bǐng or *xīn*	*wù*
dīng or *rén*	*gēng*
wù or *guǐ*	*rén*

Hence 11 p.m. on 31 December 1 BC began the double hour *gēngzǐ*. Until 104 BC there were 10 *shí* to the day, thereafter 12; but until 1670 the day was also divided into 100 *kè*, of which the first and seventh *shí* each contained ten, the rest eight each. In 1670 a Western system was introduced: each *shí* contained two 'small hours' (*xiǎoshí*) of four *kè*, each *kè* being divided into 15 *fēn* (corresponding to the minute). Times were stated, e.g.

11 p.m.	*yèzǐchūchūkè*	'night, *zǐ*, first (half), first quarter-hour'
11.01 p.m.	*yèzǐchūchūkèyīfēn*	'night, *zǐ*, first, first quarter, one minute'
11.15 p.m.	*yèzǐchūyīkè*	'night, *zǐ*, first, one quarter'
midnight	*zǐzhèngchūkè*	'*zǐ*, main, first quarter'

The *fēn* comprised 60 *miǎo* of 60 *wēi*; beyond that one said that the time stated was *jiáng* ('strong', i.e. a little bit past) or *rè* ('weak', a little bit less).

The time of birth is traditionally designated by the 'eight characters' (*bāzì*), or cyclical signs of the year, month, day, and double hour; at betrothal the respective families exchange the eight characters of bride and groom. A Chinese born at 8 p.m. on the 9th day of the 12th month of Dàoguāng 9 (26 Dec. 1829) would have had the eight characters *jǐchǒu dīngchǒu jǐsì jiǎxū*.

The embolismic month (*rùnyuè*) is treated as a repetition of the regular month that preceded it, and does not take a stem or branch of its own; the embolismic year (*rùnnián*) is thought unlucky, as affording more days of toil, especially when the repeated month is the eighth, even though 8 is normally an auspicious number. (One such *rùnbāyuè* or 'repeated eighth month' year was 1911/12, when the Empire was overthrown; another 1976/6, marked by the Tangshan earthquake, in which 240 000 people died, floods, drought, a meteorite, and the death of Mao Zedong; another 1995/6, in which there were severe floods, earthquakes, and reputedly showers of frogs. One leading party elder, Chen Yun, died, but not, contrary to widespread expectation, Deng Xiaoping.) It is said that the *wútóng* or *Sterculia platanifolia*—the only tree on which the phoenix will alight—knows when there will be a *rùnnián*, and grows an extra leaf in consequence.

The intercalary cycle begins in the Christian year that by Western reckoning has the Golden Number 10; although other systems have obtained in the past, the current rule is to repeat a month in years 3, 6, 9, 11, 14, 17, and 19 of the cycle (= Golden Number 12, 15, 18, 1, 4, 7, 9) subject to the following conditions:

(i) The vernal equinox, summer solstice, autumnal equinox, and winter solstice must fall respectively in the 2nd, 5th, 8th, and 11th civil months.

(ii) The sun must spend the whole of the embolismic month within the same sign of the zodiac; hence it can contain only one change of solar term (see below), and that not a principal term.

(iii) The 1st, 11th, and 12th months must not be repeated, since the solar terms about the winter solstice are shorter than the others.

(iv) If intercalation would cause the winter solstice to fall before the 11th month, contrary to (i), intercalation is postponed till after the 2nd month of the following year.

The detailed application of these rules was the responsibility of the Board of Mathematics, which was not immune to error even after the improved calendar presented to the Shùnzhì Emperor in 1644 by Father Adam Schall von Bell SJ (in Chinese Tāng Ruòwàng): every year, during the tenth month, there was published a *Shíxiànshū* or 'Book of Constant Conformity' (before 1644 *Lìrì*, 'Ordering of Days') giving: the cyclical signs of the year, months, and days; the long, short, and intercalary months; the designation of the day according to the 5 elements, 28 constellations, and 12 happy presages; the day and hour of the moon's quarters; that of the sun's position in the 24 solar terms calculated for the various Chinese capitals, Manchuria, Mongolia, and the tributary kingdoms; sunrise, sunset, and length of day or night, ditto; and (over the protests of the learned) various astrological assertions about lucky and unlucky days, these last not being the responsibility of the Board. There was also a *Wànniánshū* or 'Myriad Year Book' for 1624/5–2020/1; the starting-point being chosen because 1624/5 (Tiánqǐ, 4) began a new sexagenary cycle. It contained the cyclical signs of the year, the long, short, and intercalary months, the cyclical signs of the 1st, 11th, and 21st of each month, and the day and hour at the meridian of Beijing at which each solar term began.

On the overthrow of the monarchy in Xuāntǒng 3 (1911/12), the Republican government introduced the Gregorian calendar, numbering the months from 1 (*yīyuè*, January, as against *zhēngyuè* for the first lunar month) to 12. It did not, however, introduce the Christian era, but proclaimed a new Mínguó ('Republic') era, reckoned from 1 January 1912, still used on Taiwan, where 1999 is Mínguó 88; in the People's Republic and over-seas, the Western year is designated according to the Christian era (introduced by the Communists in 1949), and the Chinese year by the sexagenary cycle, or popularly by its animal.

The chief festivals of the Chinese year are or were:

❲ 1ST MONTH (HOLIDAY MOON)

1   *Yuándàn* (New Year's Day); to be spent indoors with the extended family, though in imperial times officials had first to offer their congratulations to the court, and then visit their close relatives and friends to wish them New Year's Happiness (*xīnxǐ*). Food (in particular boiled dumplings called *bōbo*) should already have been prepared; it is very unlucky to use a sharp instrument. Fireworks are lit, wells are closed for the first two days of the year. Also named *Jīrì* (Fowl Day), the first 10 days of the year being named after members of the animal or vegetable kingdom. In the Gregorian calendar, it is the first new moon (as calculated for the appropriate longitude) after 20 January. In Vietnamese the day is known as *tết*, properly 'festival'; the full form, incorporating the Chinese name, is *tết Nguyên-dán*).

2   *Quǎnrì* (Dog Day).

3   God of Wealth (*Cáishén*) honoured. After this people begin to go out, though bet-ter form was to stay indoors till the 5th. *Zhūrì* (Pig Day).

4   *Yángrì* (Sheep Day).

5   *Niúrì* (Cattle Day). Resumption of normal life (*pòwǔ*, 'breaking the fifth').

6   *Mǎrì* (Horse Day).

7   *Rénrì* (Human Day).

8   *Gǔrì* (Grain Day). In some places the *Shùnxīng* or Homage to the Stars (see the 18th).

9   *Márì* (Hemp Day).

10 *Dòurì* (Pulse Day).

15 *Dēngjié* (Feast of Lanterns): lanterns are displayed and fireworks are let off. The fes-tival lasted for three days, of which the second, on the 16th, was known as *hàumórì*, 'wasting day'.

18 *Shùnxīng* in most provinces (cf. the 8th): 108 lamps of paper tapers soaked in oil were lit, incense burnt and offered. Women were expected to keep out of the way.

19 Rats' Wedding Day; one retires to bed early so as not to disturb the rats. Also Gathering of the Hundred Gods; newly married daughters may visit their parents only on this day during the month. The Emperor attended a sports festival and received the Mongolian nobles; this was called the *Yànjiǔ* ('Entertaining Ninth'), being the 9th day of the second *décade*. Those officials who had the right to wear sable robes exchanged them for silver-fox furs. On this day or one of the next two, as seemed propitious, official seals were brought out and administration ceremonially resumed.

25 *Tiáncāng* (Filling the Granary): sacrifice by grain- and rice-merchants to Granary God (Cāngshén); in former times celebrated by feasting on pork, beef, and mutton, of which guests must eat their fill before leaving.

☾ 2ND MONTH (BUDDING MOON)
 1 Sun-cakes (*tàiyánggāo*) sacrificed to the sun. Fires were put out in Beijing.
 2 *Lóngtáitóu* (Dragon Raises Head): dragon-scale cakes (*lónglínbǐng*) and dragon-whisker noodles (*lóngxūmiàn*) are eaten, and needlework is suspended lest the needle injure the dragon's eyes. Earlier called *Zhōnghé* (Mid[-spring] Harmony).
15 Birthday of Lǎozǐ; *nirvāṇa* of Buddha.
19 Birthday of Guānyīn, the Goddess of Mercy.
21–end of month   Sale of spring chickens and ducks.

☾ 3RD MONTH (SLEEPY MOON)
1–15 Clear-Pool and Wild-Mulberry Monastery (Tánzhèsì) was opened; in its grounds was an ancient gingko tree called Emperors' and Kings' Tree (Dìwángshù), thought to put forth a new shoot on the accession of the emperor, which died in forewarning of his death.
1–3 *Pántáogōng* (Trained Peach Temple) Festival, in honour of the Mother of the Western Heaven.
18 Exalted Heaven Monastery (Tiāntáisì) was opened; it held the so-called Demon King (Mówáng), an image of an elderly man in imperial robes, falsely identified with the Shùnzhì Emperor (1644–61), but perhaps a mad monk who died in 1710.
28 *Dǎnchénhuì* ([Image-]Dusting Meeting); birthday of the Emperor of the Eastern Peak (the god of Tàishān), whose temple was opened on the 1st and 15th of each month, and stayed open till the end of the first month.

☾ 4TH MONTH (PEONY MOON) Pilgrimages to sacred places are especially frequent.
 8 Birthday of the Buddha, celebrated by distribution of beans.
14 Fire-god (Huǒshèng).

☾ 5TH MONTH (DRAGON MOON) Evil Month (Èyuè), dangerous (red threads tied round boys' wrists).
 5 Duānwǔjié (Upright Fifth Festival) or Duānyáng (Upright Sun); celebrated by eating *zòngzi* (pyramidal dumplings of glutinous rice or millet wrapped in bamboo or reed leaves), also by 'dragon-boat' (*lóngchuán*) races, whence the name 'Dragon-Boat Festival'. Settlement day. Foreheads, noses, and ears of small children were painted with realgar mixed with wine and dried in the sun, to ward off poisonous creatures; their foreheads might also be painted with the character for *wáng*, 'king', supposed to appear in the markings of the supreme dispeller of evil, the tiger; among other charms, one hung at one's gate leaves of mugwort (*àizi*), thought to resemble a tiger, and calamus (*chāngpú*), thought to resemble a sword. In Vietnamese the Chinese name becomes *tết Doan-ngo*.

13 Sacrifice to War-god (Guāndì), a deified warrior (d. AD 219) who on this day in 215 was reportedly invited to a banquet by the leader of a rival state, who hoped to murder him. Before going he ground his sword sharp; hence rain on this day was known as 'sword-grinding rain'.

25 *Fēnlóngbīng* (Dividing Dragon Hosts), because the phenomenon during rainy season of rain falling on one cart-rut but not another was supposed to be due to division among the dragons.

◖ 6TH MONTH (LOTUS MOON), HOT MOON (SHǓYUÈ)

1 A temple fair was held at the temple of the Coloured Clouds Princess at Central Peak (Zhōngdǐng).

6 Airing the Classics: books and clothes were shaken out and aired; imperial elephants were washed till 1884, when one of them ran amok and injured a spectator.

23 Horse-god (Mǎwáng).

24 Thunder-god (Léigōng) or God of War worshipped with fireworks; Birthday of the Lotus.

25 Five Tiger Spirits (Wǔhǔshén), patrons of artillery.

◖ 7TH MONTH (HUNGRY GHOST MOON)

7 *Diūzhēn* (Laying down Needles): girls would lay a needle in a bowl of water in the sunlight; the fineness, coarseness, or other quality of the shadow at the bottom was understood to foretell by analogy the character of their needlework. Also known as *Niú nǚ dù hé*, 'Cow(herd) and (Weaving) Maiden Cross the River' (the Milky Way). About 2900 BC the two stars known to the Chinese as the Cowherd (Altair, α Aquilae) and the Maiden (Vega, α Lyrae) had the same right ascension and in early June culminated together about midnight; when in later ages this was no longer so, the story was told that the two were given in marriage, but that the Maiden forgot her weaving in the contemplation of her happiness. In consequence, the Sun-god ordered a flock of magpies to bridge the Heavenly River, and banished the Cowherd across it; the pair now meet only once a year, on the 7th of the 7th month, when the magpies form a bridge once more for the Maiden to cross. But she cannot do so if there is rain; therefore women would pray for fair skies as well as skill in handiwork, and offer such gifts as cakes and watermelons.

15 *Guǐjié* (Festival of the Ghosts), also called *Zhōngyuán* (Mid-year Renewal), which in Vietnamese becomes *tết Trung-nguyên* and *Yúlánpénhuì*, adapted to Chinese phonetics from Sanskrit *avalambana*, 'support'; ancestors' graves are swept clean and offerings made. Buddhist temples made a long paper 'boat of the law' (*fǎchuán*) and burnt it in the evening to help wandering spirits (with no descendants, or drowned) to cross the sea of punishment; each temple formed a society (*huì*) to light lanterns and recite sūtras on such souls' behalf, offerings being collected in a bowl (*pén*).

◖ 8TH MONTH (HARVEST MOON)

1 Birthday of the Kitchen God Zàoshén, also called the Black Lord (Zàojūn), whose

temple was opened for the first three days of this month, and was visited especially by cooks.

15   *Zhōngqiūjié* (Mid-Autumn Festival), in Vietnamese *tết Trung-thu*, a Festival of the Living (*rénjié*) like the New Year and the Dragon Boats. Also Moon Feast; 13 mooncakes (*yuèbǐng*) were offered, stacked in a pyramid. This was a women's ritual; no man could take part save the Moon's celestial brother, the Emperor, whence the saying 'Men do not bow to the moon, women do not sacrifice to the Kitchen God'. Cakes were also eaten, some with images of the Three-Legged Toad (a moon-dweller said to be a metamorphosis of Cháng'é, who stole the elixir of immortality) and the Moon-Rabbit Tùryé; also with little paper squares said to date from the end of the Yuán dynasty, when they were used to smuggle secret messages preparing the Chinese uprising past the Mongol spies. Settlement day.

17   God of Thieves.

27   Birthday of Confucius.

☽ 9TH MONTH (CHRYSANTHEMUM MOON)

9   *Chóngyángjié* (Double Yang Festival), also called *Dēnggāo* (Mounting the Heights), celebrated by feasting on a hill, flying kites, and distributing 'flower-cakes' (*huāgāo*), of which the better kind was made of sugar and flour with fruits within, the other a steamed cake dotted on top with dates and prunes. At one time wives went back to eat flower-cakes with their own parents, and chrysanthemums were displayed.

11   Anniversary of Yánzǐ, the favourite disciple of Confucius.

15   Veneration of sage Zhū Xī; temple of God of Wealth (Cáishén) was opened for three days.

☽ 10TH MONTH (KINDLY MOON)

1   *Sònghányī* (Delivering Winter Clothes), third festival of the dead; clothes were burnt for the dead and graves visited. Fires were lit in Beijing.

5   Anniversary of Dàmó (the Buddhist missionary Bodhidharma).

6   The Five Mountain Spirits (Wǔyuèshén).

15   In Qīng times, the Manchu Eight Banners were drilled.

☽ 11TH MONTH (WHITE MOON)

1   Stuffing up Windows; all cracks are sealed against cold. *Fānguàzi* (Turning Jackets): those officials who had the right to wear sable furs put them on.

15   *Yuèdǎngtóu* (Moon Overhead), the full moon nearest winter solstice; children would stay awake till the moon was overhead and then look for a shadow.

☽ 12TH MONTH (WINTER SACRIFICE MOON) In Chinese *Làyuè*, also understood as Bitter Moon, with a different character for *là*.

8   *Làbāzhōu* (Sacrifice Eighth Gruel) to Buddha and Ancestors, in morning also given to friends and relations along with pickled cabbage ('big cabbage'), whose quality portends the master's fortune.

19–22   On whichever of these days was determined to be auspicious by the Imperial Board of Astronomy, officials would put away their seals, and each department would hold a party; after which schoolboys were released from their studies, and the theatres would decide upon a closing day, give the proceeds from their last perform- ance to their employees, and not reopen till the New Year performance of *Cìfú* ('Conferring Happiness').

20   Sweeping the Ground: houses are thoroughly cleaned.

23 (24 in south)   Head of household makes sacrifice to the Kitchen God before he re- ports to heaven; only men are allowed to participate. His mouth is stuffed with sweet foods (so that he will say only sweet things, or nothing at all), his portrait is burnt, fireworks are let off. 'Little New Year' (*Xiǎonián*).

Day before New Year's Eve: visits are made to relations not under the roof; pupils visit teachers; charity is distributed.

Chúxī (Removal Evening). New Year's Eve. Settlement day. A feast is prepared. A new picture of the Kitchen God is put up, Household gods are feasted, then the ances- tors, and then the family sits up to see out the old year. Wine and refreshments are laid out; lamps and candles are lit; during *hài* and *zǐ* double-hours (last of the old year and first of the new), as fireworks explode outside, incense is burnt to meet the de- scending spirits; the family then sleeps with its clothes on.

Besides the lunar calendar, China recognizes a sequence of 24 solar terms (*jiéqì*) on which the sun enters, or reaches the mid-point of, a 30° sector of the ecliptic (corre- sponding to a sign of the Western zodiac). Their lunar dates varied from year to year; their approximate Gregorian dates, and the signs entered at the principal terms, are as follows:

Lìchūn	Rise of spring	4 February	
Yǔshuǐ	Rain-water	19 February	(Pisces)
Jīngzhé	Awakening insects	6 March	
Chūnfēn	Vernal equinox	21 March	(Aries)
Qīngmíng	Pure and bright	5 April	
Gǔyǔ	Grain rains	20 April	(Taurus)
Lìxià	Rise of summer	6 May	
Xiǎomǎn	Little full (grain formed)	21 May	(Gemini)
Mángzhǒng	Awn seed (grain in ear)	6 June	
Xiàzhì	Summer solstice	21 June	(Cancer)
Xiǎoshǔ	Little heat	7 July	
Dàshǔ	Great heat	23 July	(Leo)
Lìqiū	Rise of autumn	8 August	
Chǔshǔ	Suppression of heat	23 August	(Virgo)
Báilù	White dews	8 September	
Chiūfēn	Autumnal equinox	23 September	(Libra)
Hánlù	Cold dews	8 October	
Shuāngjiàng	Frost falls	23 October	(Scorpio)

Lìdōng	Rise of winter	7 November	
Xiǎoxuě	Little snow	22 November	(Sagittarius)
Dàxuě	Great snow	7 December	
Dōngzhì	Winter solstice	22 December	(Capricorn)
Xiǎohán	Little cold	5 January	
Dàhán	Great cold	20 January	(Aquarius)

Festivals connected with the solar terms:

Yíngchūn: Welcoming Spring, last day of Dàhán.

Dǎchūn: Beating Spring, first day of Lìchūn: spring cakes and turnips are eaten, clay ox broken (replacing an actual sacrifice).

Hánshí: Cold Food, eve of Qīngmíng: last day of Chūnfēn: nothing hot should be eaten, and the hearth should be left cold for a natural day before being relit on Qīngmíng, as formerly in England the fire was allowed to go out on Easter Day and rekindled on Easter Monday.

On the first day of the solar term Qīngmíng is held the festival of that name at the graves of ancestors; it is also a day for planting trees, and the last day for flying kites.

At Xiàzhì one eats noodles.

The third *gēng* day after Xiàzhì began the *shǔfú* ('heat-prostration days'), lasting till Chǔshǔ, during which the Emperor distributed ice to the yamens. Officials wore yellow silk gauze hats and yellow silk crêpe gowns.

At Dōngzhì the Emperor sacrificed to Heaven, and was congratulated on the forthcoming increase in the male principle or yang as the days lengthened. The common people ate wonton. It was the custom to paint a plum-branch with 81 petals in outline and mark off one each day with a symbol representing its weather; one might also draw nine sets of nine circles each in three rows of three, or a poem of nine characters each containing nine strokes, drawn in hollow outline. Such symbolic representations of the winter days on the 'nine nines' principle (*jiǔjiǔ*) were known as Lessening Cold Charts (*xiāohántú*).

For the first 27 days after Dōngzhì ice was cut up at night; this was known as Smiting the Ice (*dǎbīng*). The ice was then stored for use in the summer.

In early China, on the third day after Dōngzhì, the ruler would sacrifice for bounteous harvests to his ancestors and to the five guardian spirits (of door, main gate, kitchen stove, impluvium, and well or alley). This sacrifice was known as *là*.

THE CHINESE CALENDAR 1997/8–2020/1

Table shows for each month the Western date of the 1st day.
Cyclical signs of 1st month of 1997/8 are *rényín*
Cyclical signs of 1st day are *gēngchén*.

Year:	1997/8	1998/9	1999/2000	2000/1	2001/2	2002/3
Signs:	*dīngchǒu*	*wùyín*	*jǐmǎo*	*gēngchén*	*xīnsì*	*rénwǔ*
Animal:	Ox	Tiger	Hare	Dragon	Snake	Horse
1	7 Feb.	28 Jan.	16 Feb.	5 Feb.	24 Jan.	12 Feb.
2	9 Mar.	27 Feb.	18 Mar.	6 Mar.	23 Feb.	14 Mar.
3	7 Apr.	28 Mar.	16 Apr.	5 Apr.	25 Mar.	13 Apr.
4	7 May	26 Apr.	15 May	4 May	23 Apr. / 23 May	12 May
5	5 June	26 May / 24 June	14 June	2 June	21 June	11 June
6	5 July	23 July	13 July	2 July	21 July	10 July
7	3 Aug.	22 Aug.	11 Aug.	31 July	19 Aug.	9 Aug.
8	2 Sept.	21 Sept.	10 Sept.	29 Aug.	17 Sept.	7 Sept.
9	2 Oct.	20 Oct.	9 Oct.	28 Sept.	17 Oct.	6 Oct.
10	31 Oct.	19 Nov.	8 Nov.	27 Oct.	15 Nov.	5 Nov.
11	30 Nov.	19 Dec.	8 Dec.	26 Nov.	15 Dec.	4 Dec.
12	30 Dec.	17 Jan.	7 Jan.	26 Dec.	13 Jan.	3 Jan.

Year:	2003/4	2004/5	2005/6	2006/7	2007/8	2008/9
Signs:	*guǐwèi*	*jiǎshēn*	*yǐyǒu*	*bǐngxū*	*dīnghài*	*wùzǐ*
Animal:	Sheep	Monkey	Fowl	Dog	Pig	Rat
1	1 Feb.	22 Jan.	9 Feb.	29 Jan.	18 Feb.	7 Feb.
2	3 Mar.	20 Feb. / 21 Mar.	10 Mar.	28 Feb.	19 Mar.	8 Mar.
3	2 Apr.	19 Apr.	9 Apr.	29 Mar.	17 Apr.	6 Apr.
4	1 May	19 May	8 May	28 Apr.	17 May	5 May
5	31 May	18 June	7 June	27 May	15 June	4 June
6	30 June	17 July	6 July	26 June	14 July	3 July
7	29 July	16 Aug.	5 Aug.	25 July / 24 Aug.	13 Aug.	1 Aug
8	28 Aug.	14 Sept.	4 Sept.	22 Sept.	11 Sept.	31 Aug.
9	26 Sept.	14 Oct.	3 Oct.	22 Oct.	11 Oct.	29 Sept.
10	25 Oct.	12 Nov.	2 Nov.	21 Nov.	10 Nov.	29 Oct.
11	24 Nov.	12 Dec.	1 Dec.	20 Dec.	10 Dec.	28 Nov.
12	23 Dec.	10 Jan.	31 Dec.	19 Jan.	8 Jan.	27 Dec.

Year:	2009/10	2010/11	2011/12	2012/13	2013/14	2014/15
Signs:	*jǐchǒu*	*gēngyín*	*xīnmǎo*	*rénchén*	*guǐsì*	*jiǎwǔ*
Animal:	Ox	Tiger	Hare	Dragon	Snake	Horse
1	26 Jan.	14 Feb.	3 Feb.	23 Jan.	10 Feb.	31 Jan.
2	25 Feb.	16 Mar.	5 Mar.	22 Feb.	12 Mar.	1 Mar.
3	27 Mar.	14 Apr.	3 Apr.	22 Mar.	10 Apr.	31 Mar.
4	25 Apr.	14 May	3 May	21 Apr. 21 May	10 May	29 Apr.
5	24 May 23 June	12 June	2 June	19 June	9 June	29 May
6	22 July	12 July	1 July	19 July	8 July	27 June
7	20 Aug.	10 Aug.	31 July	17 Aug.	7 Aug.	27 July
8	19 Sept.	8 Sept.	29 Aug.	16 Sept.	5 Sept.	25 Aug.
9	18 Oct.	8 Oct.	27 Sept.	15 Oct.	5 Oct.	24 Sept. 24 Oct.
10	17 Nov.	6 Nov.	27 Oct.	14 Nov.	3 Nov.	22 Nov.
11	16 Dec.	6 Dec.	25 Nov.	13 Dec.	3 Dec.	22 Dec.
12	15 Jan.	4 Jan.	25 Dec.	12 Jan.	1 Jan.	20 Jan.

Year:	2015/16	2016/17	2017/18	2018/19	2019/20	2020/1
Signs:	*yǐwei*	*bǐngshēn*	*dīngyǒu*	*wùxū*	*jǐhài*	*gēngzǐ*
Animal:	Sheep	Monkey	Fowl	Dog	Pig	Rat
1	19 Feb.	8 Feb.	28 Jan.	16 Feb.	5 Feb.	25 Jan.
2	20 Mar.	9 Mar.	26 Feb.	17 Mar.	6 Mar.	23 Feb.
3	19 Apr.	7 Apr.	28 Mar.	16 Apr.	5 Apr.	24 Mar.
4	18 May	7 May	26 Apr.	15 May	5 May	23 Apr. 23 May
5	16 June	5 June	26 May	14 June	3 June	21 June
6	16 July	4 July	24 June 23 July	13 July	3 July	21 July
7	14 Aug.	3 Aug.	22 Aug.	11 Aug.	1 Aug.	19 Aug.
8	13 Sept.	1 Sept.	20 Sept.	10 Sept.	30 Aug.	17 Sept.
9	13 Oct.	1 Oct.	20 Oct.	9 Oct.	29 Sept.	17 Oct.
10	12 Nov.	31 Oct.	18 Nov.	8 Nov.	28 Oct.	15 Nov.
11	11 Dec.	29 Nov.	18 Dec.	7 Dec.	26 Nov.	15 Dec.
12	10 Jan.	29 Dec.	17 Jan.	6 Jan.	26 Dec.	13 Jan.

Source: Hoang, *Notice*, 117–24.

THE EGYPTIAN CALENDAR (INCLUDING COPTIC AND ETHIOPIAN)

PHARAONIC

The civil year of Pharaonic Egypt was an *annus vagus* consisting of 12 30-day months, grouped into three seasons called respectively '(Nile) flood', 'winter', and 'summer', with five extra days 'upon the year' (*ḥryw rnpt*) between the fourth month of summer and the first of flood; days began at dawn, and were numbered from 1 to 30. The year was at first designated by an event that occurred in it, then by the number of times the biennial cattle census had been held in the reign; by the Middle Kingdom (*c.*2040–*c.*1786 BC) the regnal year had been adopted. The period between accession and the fifth day 'upon the year' were counted as the king's first year, and the second and subsequent years were reckoned from the regular New Year, the first day of the first month of flood; however, in the New Kingdom (*c.*1575–*c.*1087 BC) the regnal year was reckoned from accession to anniversary as in England.

According to Parker, the solar calendar was derived by averaging the years of a lunisolar religious calendar, in which the month was reckoned from the morning on which the old moon was no longer visible. In the lunisolar calendar the months were known by the names of festivals occurring within them; only in the sixth century BC, which by Egyptian standards is very late, were these names transferred to the solar months. They are most familiar to Western readers in Greek transcription as (flood) Thōth, Phaōphi, Hathyr, Choiak; (winter) Tybi, Mecheir, Phamenōth, Pharmouthi; (summer) Pachōn, Payni, Epeiph, Mesorē. The days 'upon the year' are known in Greek as *epagómenai*, in the genitive as in *epagoménōn pémptēi*, 'on the fifth of the epagomenal days'.

Since in the civil calendar there was no leap year, 1461 Egyptian years corresponded to 1460 Julian; this is known as a Sothic period, from the Egyptian name for Sirius, the Dog-star, whose heliacal rising *c.*19 July was recognized as the theoretical New Year. The actual New Year coincided with it in 2782 BC, 1322 BC, and AD 139, when it fell on 20 July in the Julian calendar; at the opposite extreme, in 2052 BC and 592 BC it fell on 18 January, so that the 'summer' months coincided with winter and vice versa.

In the fourth century BC the lunar calendar was correlated with the solar calendar by a cycle in which 25 solar years = 9125 days were matched by 309 lunations, nine of them embolismic; in Parker's reconstruction every fifth year a normally hollow month was made full, and when 1 Thoth lunar was due to precede the civil new year the month was taken as embolismic. In contrast to Western practice, the lunar month normally began in its solar namesake.

PTOLEMAIC

The Macedonian kingdom of the Ptolemies that emerged from the conquests of Alexander the Great at first attempted to retain its own calendar beside the Egyptian civil reckoning by applying Macedonian names (see *Greek Calendar*) to the Egyptian lunar months, but reckoning them from the evening when the new moon was first visible. However, by adding a second Peritios every other year they fell behind the seasons; attempts to remedy this led to calendrical chaos, besides which outside Alexandria other methods were in use. By the second century BC the Ptolemies contented themselves with using Macedonian names as equivalents to the Egyptian, so that Thoth was called Dystros; but towards the end of that century it was equated instead with Dios, with whose notional place in the year (Sept.–Oct.) it then corresponded.

In 238 BC Ptolemy III, in the 'Canopus Decree' that also ordained divine honours for his late daughter Berenice, attempted to reform the Egyptian calendar by decreeing that a sixth epagomenal day should be added every four years, but the native priests refused to comply.

ROMAN: THE 'ALEXANDRIAN' YEAR

In August of 30 BC Cleopatra VII took her own life and Ptolemy XV was executed at Roman command; on the following 1 Thoth Imperator Caesar, soon to be Augustus, became king of Egypt. Within a few years Ptolemy III's reform had been imposed for all official purposes, although the old calendar remained in use for a long time among astronomers and the native Egyptians; it is sometimes called the 'Egyptian' year in opposition to the reformed 'Alexandrian' year (for strictly speaking Alexandria was 'by Egypt', not in it). Nevertheless, the Alexandrian year is the rule in the many Greek papyrus documents from Roman Egypt. The day was reckoned in the Greek fashion, from the preceding sunset; but the month names were normally Egyptian. For conversion between the Alexandrian and Western calendars, see Appendix F.

At the time of the reform, the Roman calendar was out of step with Julius Caesar's plan (see *Roman Calendar*). Since 1 Thoth 1 Augustus was 31 August 30 BC true, but the 29th as observed, many scholars have supposed that the first Alexandrian leap day was added in 28 BC, half a year before the mistaken *bissextus* at Rome, after which there was intercalation every third year down to 10 BC and again in AD 7 and every fourth year thereafter, to match the state of affairs in Rome; but the alternative view, that the first intercalation took place in 22 BC on 29 August true (the 27th as observed) and thereafter the correct four-year cycle was employed from the outset, draws confirmation from a document in which 'XIIII K. August.', i.e. 19 July observed, is equated with 27 Epeiph, i.e. 21 July true. Had the Egyptian calendar adopted the Roman error, the day called 27 Epeiph would have been the day called 21 July (or rather *XII K. August.*) whatever the true date was; the discrepancy requires the Egyptian calendar to be correct and the Roman two days behind it, which it was between 5 and 2 BC (an earlier date being precluded by the month name *Augustus*). However, once the Roman calendar was back on course the Egyptian year began on 29 August three years out of four, but on 30 August in the Roman pre-leap year.

For the first three centuries of Roman rule, Egypt stood administratively apart from the rest of the empire, being ruled through a prefect by the emperor as king of Egypt. Years were reckoned by his reign, the first year running from accession, or recognition in Egypt, the second from the following 1 Thoth; thus 2 Augustus began in 29 BC, 2 Tiberius in AD 15. When Diocletian introduced the normal dating by consuls, in which the new year was 1 January, astronomers and astrologers, having at last adopted the reformed calendar, preferred to count by his regnal years, reckoned from 1 Thoth in AD 284, and continued doing so after his death.

The fourth-century astrologer Paul of Alexandria gives a rule for finding the feria of any day. Take the year of Diocletian, add a quarter (ignoring fractions), and a constant parameter of 2, divide the total by 7, and call the remainder 'the [number of the] days of the gods'; this tells you *pósai tôn theôn hēmérai gínontai*, 'how many days of the [planetary] gods there occur'. To this add the *quantième* and twice the serial number of the month, take the remainder to 7, and you have your feria ('to which of the gods the day belongs'). He gives as example 'today', 20 Mecheir 94 Diocletian (14 Feb. AD 378): 94 + 23 + 2 = 119 = 16 × 7 + 7; 7 + 2 × 6 + 20 = 39 = 5 × 7 + 4; therefore 20 Mecheir 94 Diocletian is a Wednesday. Rather than reckon from Friday, 1 Thoth 1 Diocletian, which would entail restating the date as 93 years plus 5 months plus 19 days after the epoch, Paul in effect counts 94 years 6 months and 20 days after Monday, 6 Mesore 1 Carus = 30 July 283, that is to say 1 year 1 month and 1 day before the epoch.

CHRISTIAN

The Alexandrian year was adopted by the Christians of Egypt and is still in use amongst the Christians both of that country and of Ethiopia. In Egypt the traditional month names survive in Coptic or Arabic guise; the epagomenal days are known in one dialect of Coptic as the 'little month' (*koudi pabot*) but in Arabic as *khams al-nasī*, 'the five of oblivion', reflecting the belief persisting throughout Egyptian history that they are very unlucky. In Ethiopia the month names have been changed, but otherwise the calendar is the same.

The era of Diocletian was retained by Egyptian and Ethiopian Christians alongside three others of their own devising: of the World (epoch 2943/2 BC), of the Incarnation (AM 5501 = AD 8/9), and of Grace (AM 5853 = Inc. 353 = Diocl. 77 = AD 360/1), beginning with the 12th 532-year Paschal cycle since the Creation. The term 'Year of Grace' is occasionally applied to the Era of Diocletian, renamed 'of the Martyrs' in the seventh century; year 1 is equivalent to AM 5777 = Inc. 277. Years are sometimes stated modulo 532, that is as the year of the current Paschal cycle as reckoned from the epoch of the era in question; thus year 257 of the Martyrs may be not AD 540/1 but 1072/3 or 1604/5. The era of the Martyrs now predominates amongst the Copts, that of the Incarnation in Ethiopia; years are assigned to the four evangelists in turn, Matthew, Mark, Luke (leap year), and John. In the lunar reckoning used at Alexandria, and ultimately at Rome, for calculating Easter, the eras of the World, Diocletian, and Grace all begin with a new Metonic cycle; that of the Incarnation does not, nor was that era used in Alexandrian Easter tables.

The ferial formula recorded above was adapted to Christian use (see *Computus) for finding the feria of 1 Thoth, which was also that of 1 Pharmouthi and hence normally of the Easter month; one could either stop at *pósai tôn theôn* and count the feria from Wednesday, the day on which sun and moon were made, or complete the calculation, finding the feria of 1 Thoth as reckoned from Sunday by adding another 3, so that the parameters became 5, 2, and 3 respectively. The Wednesday count was known in Christian Ethiopia by the pagan name, corrupted to *ṭentyon*; the Sunday count as the 'day of John'.

The structure of the Egyptian calendar, 12 30-day months plus five epagomenai, was also that of the Iranian and Armenian calendars; in its reformed or Alexandrian guise it was adopted in the calendar of the Roman province of Arabia, which used Macedonian month names and reckoned from 22 March AD 106, and again in the French revolutionary calendar (see *Other Calendars: French Republican).

THE GREEK CALENDAR

The characteristic of the ancient Greek city-states is that within a common culture each ran its affairs as it saw best, with minimal regard for uniformity with other cities; this applied to the calendar as to other things. In principle, all Greek cities employed a lunisolar year of 30- and 29-day ('full' and 'hollow') months, with extra months as needed to keep in touch with the seasons; however, different cities called the same month by different names, and applied the same names to different months; each community had its own New Year; and both days and months were frequently out of step from one city to the next, owing to discrepancies in intercalation, irregular sequences of full and hollow months, or even adjustments made for political convenience. Documents quoted by Thucydides with both Athenian and Spartan dates indicate that in 422 BC 14 Elaphēboliōn at Athens was 12 Geraistios at Sparta, but that in 421 BC 25 Elaphēboliōn was 27 Artamisios; therefore, not only has there been intercalation in one city but not the other (nor do we know which), but the Spartan calendar, from being two days behind the Athenian, has moved two days ahead. Hence, when Plutarch begins a list of days and months that have brought good or ill fortune to the Greeks with two victories by Boeotian forces (he himself was a Boeotian) 'on 5 Hippodromios, which the Athenians call Metageitniōn', we cannot be sure that an Athenian in either year would have called that day the 5th, or even (given the possibility of intercalation) that month Metageitniōn; indeed, he himself tells us in another place that the battle of Plataea, in 479 BC, was fought on 4 Boēdromiōn in the Athenian calendar, but 27 Panamos in the Boeotian.

DAYS

The tale of days differed from city to city: the forward count was normal down to the 20th, but not necessarily by plain ordinals: at Athens the 1st was *noumēnía* (New Moon), the 2nd to 10th were 'of the rising month' (*histaménou*), and the 13th to the 19th were the third to ninth 'upon ten' (*epì déka*). At Argos the 1st was *pratomēnía* (First of Moon), the 2nd *husteraía pratomēnías* ('the day after First of Moon'), the 3rd to 10th were the 'first' (*práta*) 3rd to 9th, and the 13th to 19th the middle (*mésa*) 3rd to 9th; the names for 11th, 12th, and 20th are not known. In most, but not all, cities days after the 20th were counted backwards down to the '3rd of the waning moon' (or some similar expression), i.e. the 28th; the last day of the month, whether full or hollow, was usually called *triakás* ('30th'), the intervening day in a full month being *protriakás* ('day before the 30th'). However, at Athens the last day was *héné kaì néa* ('old and new'), preceded in a full month by *deutéra phthínontos* ('2nd of waning'), from the late fourth century BC renamed *deutéra met' eikádas*, '2nd after the 20th'; most scholars accept that this was still the day omitted in a hollow month, but the question has been bitterly disputed. In the second century AD the Athenians are said to have adjusted their calendar to remove from it the day on which the plutocrat Herodes Atticus' daughter Panathenais died; presumably she died in a full month that thereafter was always hollow.

MONTHS

The names of months varied so much from city to city that the same name might be attached to different lunations: it is never safe to infer that a month occupies the same place in the calendar one is trying to reconstruct as it does in another that one already knows. This will be clear from the (very small) selection of known calendars given below, in which Panamos and Panēmos, Metageitniōn and Pedageitnuos, Boēdromiōn and Badromios, are dialectal variants of the same name. The lists begin with the month immediately following the summer solstice; in each list an asterisk indicates the first month of the calendar in question, a dagger the month repeated in embolismic years. This latter is not indicated for the Macedonian calendar, which is known almost entirely as assimilated to those of Babylon (see *Other Calendars: Babylonian* and *Egyptian Calendar*).

Athens	Miletus	Boeotia	Delphi	Rhodes	Macedon
Hekatombaiōn*	Panēmos	Hippodromios	Apellaios*	Panamos†	Lōios
Metageitniōn	Metageitniōn	Panamos	Boukatios	Karneios	Gorpiaios
Boēdromiōn	Boēdromiōn	Pamboiōtios	Boathoos	Dalios	Hyperberetaios
Pyanopsiōn	Pyanopsiōn	Damatrios	Hēraios	Thesmophorios*	Dios*
Maimaktēriōn	Apatouriōn	Alalkomeniost†	Daidaphorios	Diosthuos	Apellaios
Poseideōn†	Poseideōn	Boukatios*	Poitropiost†	Theudaisios	Audnaios
Gamēliōn	Lēnaiōn	Hermaios	Amalios	Pedageitnuos	Peritios
Anthestēriōn	Anthestēriōn	Prostatērios	Busios	Badromios	Dystros
Elaphēboliōn	Artemisiōn	Agriōnios	Theoxenios	Sminthios	Xandikos (Xanth-)
Mounychiōn	Taureōn*†	Thiouios	Endusipoitropios	Artamitios	Artemisios
Thargēliōn	Thargēliōn	Homolōios	Herakleios	Agrianios	Daisios
Skirophoriōn	Kalamaiōn	Theilouthios	Ilaios	Huakinthios	Panēmos

At both Athens and Miletus Pyanopsiōn was later written Pyanepsiōn; in the Milesian colony of Olbia the name was Kyanepsiōn. The use of names in *-iōn* is characteristic of the Ionian peoples, and not found among Dorians or Aeolians.

This variety of month names explains the rarity of their use in Greek poetry, in contrast to Latin or English; in the seventh century BC Hesiod, in the agricultural precepts of his *Works and Days*, names only one month: 'Avoid the month of Lēnaiōn, evil days that can all take the hide off an ox', followed by a marvellous description of icy winter when the north wind blows from Thrace. Although Hesiod composed his poem in Boeotia, Lēnaiōn was not a Boeotian month; but it existed in several of the Ionian cities where he had sung for a living, generally beginning about the winter solstice. (The Attic festival of the Lēnaia, in honour of Dionysos, was celebrated in this month, though it was called Gamēliōn, being sacred to Hera, goddess of marriage, *gámos*.) A month is also named in a poorly preserved stanza by Anacreon of Ceos (6th c. BC), of which we have the paraphrase 'It is the month of Posidēiōn: the clouds are heavy with rain and fierce storms are beating down.' If Posidēiōn on Ceos corresponded to Poseideōn at Athens, it ran from late November to mid-December, in the wet Mediterranean winter. Several poets speak of the 'leaf-shedding month', but that is a description, not a name (see I: *Months).

The cultural prestige of Athens made the Athenian names normative (albeit in competition with the Macedonian) for theoretical or astronomically calculated lunations, as when Troy was said to have fallen on 23 Thargēliōn, 17 days before the summer solstice. Eventually the Attic names were given by literary affectation to Julian months, sometimes even reckoned from January (cf. *7 Nov.).

THE ATHENIAN PRYTANY CALENDAR

Athens also had a second calendar, used for official purposes, under which, in the fifth century BC, a solar year of 366 days (according to some scholars sometimes 365) was divided into ten periods of 37 or 36 days known as 'prytanies', during each of which the councillors from one of the ten major citizen groups (the so-called tribes) performed various functions; in the fourth century the solar year was abandoned, the prytanies being divisions of the lunisolar year; further adjustments followed from the third century in accordance with changes in the number of tribes.

INTERCALATION

Various intercalary cycles are recorded by ancient writers, but none seems to have been used anywhere in public life with the possible exception (but even that is contentious) of an eight-year cycle, with embolisms in years 3, 5, and 8; this would need correction by omitting one embolism every 160 years. The Athenian astronomer Meton (*fl.* 432 BC) is credited with a 19-year cycle, containing seven embolisms; we are told that the succession of 125 full and 110 hollow months was established by first treating all 235 months as provisionally full, then omitting every 64th day. About a century later, Callippus of Cyzicus combined four of these cycles into a 76-year cycle, containing 28 embolisms; this required 499 full months and 441 hollow, of which 440 were found as before and the 441st was the last of the cycle (since there were not 64 days left after the previous omission).

HELLENISTIC AND ROMAN DEVELOPMENTS

The armies of Alexander the Great brought with them the Macedonian calendar, with a year beginning about the autumnal equinox; although little is known about it in its homeland, it is amply attested in Asia and Egypt, with days numbered continuously (in figures rather than words) from 1 to 30 (29 being omitted in hollow months), without the backward count found in most other Greek calendars. The Seleucid kings in the Near East applied Macedonian names to the months of the Babylonian calendar, itself lunisolar, but adopted the Metonic cycle of intercalations; the Macedonian names could also be used to designate months of the Jewish calendar or the Christian Paschal calendar derived from it. By contrast the Ptolemaic kings in Egypt, having first made various attempts to relate Macedonian and Egyptian calendars, by the end of the third century BC simply applied Macedonian month names to the Egyptian solar calendar (see *Egyptian Calendar*); in Roman times the Egyptian names prevail. When under the Roman Empire many cities of Asia Minor adopted calendars of Julian type, Macedonian month names were often used; these calendars do not use the Roman dating system by Kalends, Nones, and Ides, but sometimes treat the first day outside the numbered sequence, or reckon the last ten days backwards as 30th, 29th, 28th, etc. Macedonian names, like Attic, were also applied to the Roman months themselves, as when the *Chronicon Paschale* of the seventh century AD assigns the Annunciation to 25 Dystros, dates the beheading of John the Baptist to 29 Lōios, and declares that indictions are counted from 1 Gorpiaios.

YEARS

Greek particularity is also seen in the designation of the year: since the normal period of service for city magistrates was a year, in most cities the year was called by the name of a particular office-holder. Thus at Athens the year was named after one of the nine magistrates called archons, who in the early fifth century BC were reduced to mere administrators; most of the 'eponymous archons' on record are mere names, even for periods in which we have some idea of political history. (Our list is continuous for 480/79–292/1 BC, but before then there are gaps, and afterwards few archons are known by name and fewer by date.) At Sparta the eponymous magistrate was one of the five 'ephors' or 'overseers', who during their year in office ran public affairs at discretion rather than under law. However, at Argos, the especial city of the goddess Hera, dating was by her current priestess's length of service, in the manner of a regnal year. The disadvantage was that dates meant nothing to people from other cities, which made history difficult to write; Thucydides, writing for all Greeks and not merely his fellow Athenians, dates the first action of the Peloponnesian war in spring 431 BC as follows: 'when Chrysis had been priestess at Argos for 48 years, Aenesias was ephor at Sparta, and Pythodoros had two months to serve as archon at Athens'; for further clarity he states that it occurred in the 15th year of the 30-year truce that followed the Athenian reconquest of Euboea.

ERAS

The cities created by Alexander and his successors characteristically dated by eras, taking as epoch their foundation or some other significant event; Roman provinces might commemorate their incorporation into the empire, or a decisive battle in the civil wars. Examples are the eras of Antioch (1 Oct. 49 BC, the beginning of the local year in which the battle of Pharsalus was fought) and the Roman province of Arabia (22 Mar. AD 106), which used Macedonian month names but a calendar of Egyptian type, comprising 12 months of 30 days and five epagomenal days or in leap year six. The most important era, however, was the Seleucid (see *Chronology: Eras*).

THE HINDU CALENDAR

The calendars officially used for civil purposes in modern India are the international Gregorian calendar and the National Calendar, introduced with effect from 1 Chaitra SE (= Saka Era) 1879 = 22 March 1957. The Saka Era is reckoned in elapsed years from AD 78; the month names are taken from the traditional lunar calendar. In the official English spelling, which will be used throughout, they are:

Chaitra	30 days	22 March–20 April; in leap year 31 days, 21 March–20 April
Vaisakha	31 days	21 April–21 May
Jyaistha	31 days	22 May–21 June
Asadha	31 days	22 June–22 July
Sravana	31 days	23 July–22 August
Bhadra	31 days	23 August–22 September
Asvina	30 days	23 September–22 October
Kartika	30 days	23 October–21 November
Agrahayana	30 days	22 November–21 December
Pausa	30 days	22 December–20 January
Magha	30 days	21 January–19 February
Phalguna	30 days	20 February–21 March; in Gregorian leap year 20 February–20 March

Leap year in the National Calendar begins on 21 March of the Gregorian leap year, e.g. in SE 1918 = AD 1996/7; the year of the Saka Era, divided by 4, leaves a remainder of 2.

National holidays:

24 Sravana	= 15 August	Independence Day
10 Asvina	= 2 October	Mahatma Gandhi's Birthday
6 Magha	= 26 January	Republic Day

However, most religious festivals are observed according to the traditional Indian calendars, which are highly complex and vary greatly from place to place. Whole books have been written on the calendars themselves and on the conversion of historical dates (see Bibliography s.n. Sewell); the *Rashtriya Panchang* or official almanac published annually by the Government of India gives details of six different regional calendars, four solar and two lunar (strictly lunisolar), but reckons those in current use at more than thirty. Only a simplified account of the main calendars can be offered here.

Until 1957, the solar calendar was not tropical but sidereal, the month beginning from the sun's entry into a new *rasi*; this term may be translated 'sign of the zodiac', but denotes the actual constellation, not as in the Babylonian and Greek tradition a 30° arc of the ecliptic reckoned from the equinoctial point. As a result, the equinoctial and solstitial festivals fell behind the true dates. This slippage, due to the precession of the equinoxes, has now been frozen (at a little over three weeks) but not reversed; the *rasi* is taken to begin at $(30a + 23)° 15'$, $0 \leq a \leq 11$. Solar days are reckoned from sunrise, and correlated with days of the week: in some places, the first day of the civil month is that on which the sun enters the new sign, in others the day after or even in some circumstances the next but one. The months are generally named after the *rasi*, but in Bengal and Tamil Nadu the lunar names are used.

In the lunar calendar, the months bear the names that were adopted for the National Calendar. Each month is divided into two halves (called *paksha*, 'wing'), 'bright' (Sukla in the south, Sudi in the north) from new moon to full, and 'dark' (Krishna in the south, Vadi in the north) from full moon to new; in the north the month begins on the day after full moon with the dark half unless it is embolismic, in the south on the day after new moon with the bright half. Since theoretical astronomy uses the southern system, the bright half bears the same month name everywhere, determined in accordance with the *rasi* in which the sun stands on the day after new moon, whereas during the dark half the north is always one month name ahead of the south. For example, Chaitra is defined in theoretical astronomy, and in southern practice, as the month beginning while the sun is in Mina (Pisces, now mid-Mar.–mid-Apr.); but whereas northern Chaitra Sudi is the same as southern Chaitra Sukla, northern Chaitra Vadi is southern Phalguna Krishna, and southern Chaitra Krishna is northern Vaisakha Vadi. If the sun is in the same *rasi* at the start of two successive months (reckoned from new moon), the first is embolismic, and takes the same name as the second, the two months being distinguished as *adhika* (additional) and *nija* (regular); in the north, where the dark half of the regular month has already run its course, the embolismic month is inserted at the same place, still beginning with its bright half, and is followed by the bright half of the regular month. On the other hand, if, as occasionally happens in winter, the sun enters two successive *rasi*s in one month (again reckoned from the new moon), the following month will be designated according to the second *rasi*, the intervening name being passed over; in this case the name omitted is the same in both north and south.

Each *paksha* is divided into fifteen *tithi*s, the *tithi* being the time taken by the moon to travel 12° from the sun; its value is 1/30 of the true (before the 12th c. the mean) synodic month. The day is usually numbered according to the *tithi* current at sunrise, so that dates are occasionally omitted (when the *tithi* begins after one sunrise and ends before the next) or repeated (when it incorporates two sunrises); either case is inauspicious. The planetary week is not affected: Sunday the 7th is followed by Monday even when it is the 9th, or the 7th again, and not the 8th. (Some festivals, however, have their own determination of the day.) Time is also measured by the *nakshatra* (the time taken by the moon to traverse 1/27th of the ecliptic), the *karana* (one of 11 half-*tithi*s), and the *yoga* (the time during which joint longitudinal motion of sun and moon is 13° 20′).

There are many different eras in use, most of which reckon in elapsed years. The most widely used, with both solar and lunar calendars, is the Saka era, reckoned in elapsed years from AD 78; in the solar calendar the year begins with the sun's entry into Mesha (Aries, now fixed at mid-Apr.), in the lunar calendar with Chaitra bright in the south (about the time of Passover or the Gregorian Easter) and with Chaitra dark in the north (about a fortnight earlier). Other systems noted in the *Rashtriya Panchang* are:

The Vikram Samvat, reckoned in elapsed lunar years from 58 BC, beginning with Chaitra bright in much of central India, but with Kartika bright (the new moon of Oct.–Nov.) in Gujarat (also favoured as the start of the commercial year).

The Bengali San, reckoned in elapsed solar years from AD 594, beginning with the sun's entry into Aries (now mid-Apr.).

The Saptarshi Kala of Kashmir, reckoned in elapsed lunar years from 3177 BC, beginning with Chaitra bright.

The Kollam era of Kerala, reckoned in current solar years from AD 825, beginning with the sun's entry into Simha (Leo, now mid-Aug.).

The Fasli era of northern India, reckoned in current lunar years from AD 593, beginning with Asvina dark (northern reckoning = mid-Sept.); the days of the month are numbered continuously without division into *pakshas*.

The Kaliyuga era, reckoned in elapsed solar years from 3102 BC, beginning with the sun's entry into Aries.

The Buddha Nirvana era, reckoned in elapsed lunar years from 544 BC, beginning with 15 Vaisakha bright.

The Mahavira Nirvana era, reckoned in elapsed lunar years from 527 BC, beginning with Kartika dark; used by Jains.

The Kaliyuga is the last and shortest of the world's ages or *yugas*, beginning on 18 February 3102 BC, and due to last 432 000 years; it was preceded, in descending order of length, by three other *yugas*, respectively four times, thrice, and twice as long, combining with it to form a *mahayuga* or Great Yuga of 4 320 000 years. A thousand *mahayugas* make a *kalpa*.

Besides the solar and lunar calendars, there is a Jovian calendar known as the Barhaspatya Varsa based on a cycle of five revolutions of Jupiter, which amount to about 60 solar years; the mean motion of Jupiter from one *rasi* to the next takes 361.626 721 days. It is reckoned according to three different systems: northern, southern lunar, southern solar.

The *Rashtriya Panchang* also records, for each day of the National Calendar, the times of sunrise and sunset in four cities, the apparent midday, moonrise, and moonset Indian Standard Time (5 hours 30 minutes ahead of Greenwich), the end of the *tithi*, *nakshatra*, and *yoga* obtaining at sunrise, the *karana* obtaining at sunrise, the *rasi* in which the moon is situated, and any festivals falling on that date. A selection of these festivals is given, along with a few secular and non-Hindu holidays, in a preliminary list.

There are naturally far more festivals celebrated in various parts of India than can conveniently be listed. In the following list, those falling in the dark half are given the southern month name followed by the northern.

Ram Navami (Rama's 9th) = Chaitra bright 9 (Birth of the Lord Rama).

Rathayatra (Chariot Pilgrimage) = Asadha bright 2 (shortly after new moon of June–July); the festival at Puri in Orissa in honour of Vishnu as Jagannatha, 'Lord of the World' (formerly Anglicized as 'Juggernaut'), in which three wooden images are drawn in procession on wooden carts by teams of over 4000 men.

Teej = Sravana bright 3 (shortly after new moon of July–Aug.); women undergo austerities for the sake of their husbands.

Naga Panchami (Naga Fifth) = Sravana bright 5, kept mainly in southern India in honour of the cobra as guardian.

Raksha Bandhan = Sravana bright 15 (full moon of July–Aug.); sisters tie coloured threads round brothers' wrists to make them their protectors; wrist-threads are also tied to renew friendships.

Janmashtami (Birth 8th) = Sravana Krishna/Bhadra Vadi 8 (about third quarter of July–Aug. lunation); birth of Lord Krishna celebrated at midnight after a day's fast.

Ganesh Chaturthi (Ganesh's 4th) = Bhadra bright 4 (shortly after new moon of Aug.–Sept.); birth of the Lord Ganesh, the cheerful elephant-god of wealth who rides on a rat; tools of trade are laid before him to be blessed.

Onam = Bhadra bright 12 (shortly before full moon of Aug.–Sept.); kept in Kerala as the birth of Vamana, avatar of Vishnu (see under Diwali).

Dusshera, Durga Puja (Durga homage), Navaratri (Nine Nights) = Asvina bright 1–10 (from new moon of Sept.–Oct.), honouring the warrior goddess Durga and her victory over the buffalo demon Mahisha; in some places the first seven nights are fasts. On the last day her statue is ceremonially washed, a celebration marked by dancing, theatrical performances, and the giving of gifts; in some places the day is also called Vijaya Dasami ('Victory Tenth'), celebrating Rama's victory with his monkey allies over the ten-headed demon king Ravana, but in others this celebration takes place on the last day of Diwali.

Diwali, Dipavali (light strings) = Asvina Krishna/Kartika Vadi 13–15 + Kartika bright 1 (about the new moon of Oct.–Nov.); light is carried from waning to waxing fortnight; presents are exchanged. On the first day the image of Lakshmi, goddess of wealth, is bathed, often in milk, in honour of her creation when Vishnu churned the sea; women bathe and put on perfume. On the second the men bathe in honour of Vishnu's victory over the filth-demon Narkasur, who dragged beautiful women to live in his disgusting den. On the third the year's accounts are closed; gambling is frequent. The story is told of frenetic gambling by Siva, his wife Parvati, and their sons Kartik and Ganesh, stopped only when Vishnu turned himself into a set of dice: Parvati, having lost, was restrained just in time from cursing him and instead blessed all those who felt the urge to gamble at this time. On the fourth day presents are exchanged. Especially in Mumbai, flour models are made of the demon Bali, who was tricked out of his wealth by Vishnu in his guise of the dwarf Vamana, as many think unfairly: the prayer is said, 'May all evil disappear and Bali's empire be restored.'

Bhratri Dvitiya (Brotherly Second) = Kartika bright 2; sisters honour their brothers.

Vasanta Panchami, Sri Panchami = Magha bright 5 (soon after new moon of Jan.–Feb.), celebrated as the first day of spring; the auspicious colour is yellow, from the mustard in flower at the time. It is also Sarasvati Puja, the worship dedicated to Sarasvati, goddess of learning and the arts; her day is often observed by family celebrations, rather than in larger groups. Nothing may be eaten between daybreak and the ceremony, at which the goddess is offered food and flowers; if a child is about to begin its education, the priest will trace the word *Om* on its tongue with a reed pen. On the next day Sarasvati's image is immersed in a nearby pond or river. In some parts of Bengal, the *hilsa* fish may not be eaten between Durga Puja and Sarasvati Puja, so that it may have a chance to grow; in others, students offer goats to Sarasvati for success in examination.

Maha Sivaratri (Great Siva Night) = Magha Krishna/Phalguna Vadi 14 (about new moon of Feb.–Mar.); said to be the blackest night of the year; Siva is worshipped, and the lingam anointed.

Holi = Phalguna bright 15 (full moon of Feb.–Mar.), a spring festival at which restraint is abandoned, bonfires are lit, dirty songs are sung, and there is role-changing and mocking of superiors; people are sprinkled with coloured powder and doused with water. According to one myth, the festival celebrates the defeat of the sorceress Holika, who attempted to make her brother Prahlad worship their wicked father instead of Vishnu; but since in much of northern India the following day (Chaitra Vadi 1) begins the new year, the story is also told that Holika was the sister of the year-god Sambat, who by throwing herself on his funeral pyre caused him to be restored to life. In southern India the day is associated with the impudent love-god Kama, who like Eros is armed with a bow; one day, seeing Siva deep in meditation, he made to shoot an arrow at him, but was burnt to ashes with one glance from the great god's third eye. Kama's wife Rati persuaded Siva to let him be reborn, but is never permitted to see him.

In the solar calendar, the main festivals are those of the sun's entry into Mesha (Aries) in mid-April and into Makara (Capricorn) in mid-January; the day differs from place to place in accordance with the rules of the local calendar. The entry into Makara is celebrated in southern India as Pongal; the festival lasts for three days, on the first of which visits are made and presents exchanged, on the second rice is boiled in milk in the open air, and on the third the men sprinkle the cattle with flavoured water and perform prostrations before them. The women have no part in this, but it was they, during the preceding month, who had laid out pellets of cow-dung to appease Siva. The abbé J. A. Dubois, who described the festival in the early nineteenth century, observed that the month before Pongal consists entirely of unlucky days, that following it of lucky ones.

The Sikhs honour the birthday of their founder Guru Nanak on Kartika bright 15 (the full moon of November), and the martyrdom of Guru Tegh Bahadur on Margasirsha bright 5; they also celebrate the solar new year (Vaisakhi), which begins on 1 Vaisakha solar (*c.*13 Apr.), with a three-day festival including continuous reading of the Holy Book (Guru Granth Sahib). It was on this day in 1699 (30 Mar. OS) that Gobind Singh Guru declared to the Sikhs the code of discipline by which they live.

THE JEWISH CALENDAR

The Jewish calendar is a lunisolar calendar, in which months run from new moon to new moon, and a thirteenth, 'embolismic', month is added to the year when it begins to run ahead of the seasons. Its original basis in direct observation, increasingly modified by ritual restrictions, has now given way to a highly sophisticated mathematical plan.

ANCIENT, BY OBSERVATION

In the Bible, months are usually numbered rather than named; but occasionally Phoenician names are used in the books written before the Exile and the modern names, which come from the Babylonian calendar, in those written after it. The first month is normally that beginning at the spring equinox, called Abib in Exodus and Nisan in Nehemiah; this was also Babylonian usage. However, at Exod. 23: 16, 34: 22 the harvest is said to come at the end of the year, implying a new year in the autumn; the two systems were long in competition. (It was said that the regnal years of kings of Israel were counted from Nisan, of other kings from Tishri; but exceptions were adduced.) Eventually 1 Tishri became the standard usage; 'Nisan is the beginning of the months, but Tishri of the year.' It has remained so ever since.

If on the 30th night from the start of the month a sighting of the new crescent was reported by reliable witnesses and confirmed by the Sanhedrin before nightfall, the new moon was 'sanctified' and the day (beginning at sunset) counted as the first of the next month; the news being broadcast by beacons and by couriers sent from Jerusalem (or after its capture in AD 70, from Jamnia). If no such report was received or upheld, the day counted as the 30th and the next month began the following day. Since messengers could not always reach outlying communities, Jews of the Diaspora added a second day to festivals. Observation would sometimes be made from a favourable outpost, or discussion of the witnesses' reports deliberately prolonged, in order to hasten or delay the sanctification, so that fasts, and in particular Yom Kippur, should not fall on Friday or Sunday, that is on the day before or after the Sabbath; last came a rule that 1 Tishri must not fall on a Sunday so that Hoshanah Rabbah, with its energetic ritual, should not fall on a Sabbath. In order that Passover should not fall in winter, an embolismic month was inserted whenever any two of three conditions held: that the crops were still young; that the fruit-trees were still young; that the equinox was not yet due. (However, it was preferred to intercalate before, rather than during or after, a sabbatical year, during which the land was not cultivated.) A rule was formulated that no year should have fewer than four or more than eight—in embolismic years nine—full (30-day) months.

Besides this calendar, some Jews in the Second Temple period (5th c. BC–1st c. AD) used a different, pseudo-solar calendar, expounded or presupposed in the Book of Jubilees, the First Book of Enoch, and the writing of the Qumran community (the 'Dead Sea Scrolls'), in which the year, beginning on a Wednesday (the day on which the luminaries were created), consisted of 364 days, divided into 52 weeks and 12 numbered 30-day months grouped into four seasons, spring to winter, each season separated from the next by an additional 'day of remembrance'. Such a calendar would have required intercalation of five weeks in 28 years if the year were not to become detached from the seasons even during a single lifetime; but no intercalation is attested, and certain passages in 1 Enoch suggest that it was the seasons, not the calendar, that received the blame for the discrepancies. Other sectarian groups had usages of their own.

The dispersal of Jews in the Roman Empire, both before and after the reprisals that followed failed rebellions, broke the unity of Temple-directed worship; in the fourth century the Jews of Antioch were defining Passover by the full moon of March (locally called Dystros). At Alexandria it depended in common years on the full moon of Phamenoth, in embolismic years on that of Pharmouthi. The sources for this are Christian, but may be believed in a matter of observable fact even though their complaint that Passover sometimes fell too early, or too late, was based on the misapprehension that it ought always to follow the equinox; the nearest approach was a rule that the Omer on 16 Nisan should not precede it. The confusion was not ended before the publication of calendrical calculations; the traditional date is AD 359 (AM 4119, AS 670), the emperor Constantius having impeded the dispatch of messengers, but some writers suggest that no more was established then than the principle of cyclical intercalation, and that not till the tenth century was the calendar given its final modern form.

Mention should be made of the Karaite sect, which rejects rabbinic traditions (or, as it would say, 'innovations'); it governs the months by the real lunar phases, keeps Shavuot always on Sunday (see below) but allows other festivals to fall on any other feria, does not allow a second day even to Rosh Hashanah, and rejects Chanukah as un-biblical.

MODERN, BY CALCULATION

The Jewish calendar, in its calculated form, is based on the Metonic cycle, with an underlying mathematical structure that needs to be exposed before the surface dating system can be understood.

The day begins at sunset, which for mathematical purposes only is normalized as 6 p.m. Jerusalem time (= 3.39 p.m. GMT); it is subdivided into 24 equal hours each containing 1080 'minims', each equivalent to 1/18 minute = 3⅓ seconds and itself divided into 76 'moments', each of 5/114 second. For other purposes, and in particular for the observation of the Sabbath or of holidays, sunset is defined as the moment when three stars of second magnitude become visible (the sun, under average conditions, being 7° below the horizon), and hours are unequal.

The synodic month or lunation is taken to comprise 29 days 12 hours 793 minims (44 minutes 3⅓ seconds), less than half a second more than the present estimate. Twelve synodic months make a common year of 354 days 8 hours 876 minims; 13 months an embolismic year of 383 days 21 hours 589 minims.

The year begins with the first *molad* or calculated conjunction of sun and moon in autumn, which may be up to 14 hours before or 7 hours after the actual conjunction, itself in the region of Jerusalem between 20 and 72 hours before the first sighting of the crescent. Nineteen years make a Metonic cycle, of which 12 are common and seven embolismic, yielding a total of 235 lunations = 6939 days 16 hours 595 minims, compared with 6939 days 18 hours for 19 mean Julian years and 6939 days 14 hours 626 minims 30.4 moments for 19 mean Gregorian years. The seven embolismic months are assigned to years 3, 6, 8, 11, 14, 17, and 19 of the cycle, these being the years in which the accumulated excess of solar over lunar years would otherwise exceed or most nearly approach 30 days. The mean length of the lunisolar year is thus 365 days 5 hours 997 minims 48 moments (365^d 5^h $55'$ $25\,^{25}/_{57}''$), or approximately 365.246 822 2 days, as against the Gregorian year of 365.242 5 days (365^d 5^h $49'$ $12''$).

This mathematical calendar is converted to a practical calendar as follows. The common year contains 12 months of 30 or 29 days:

Tishri or Tishrei	30	
Cheshvan	29	(30 in abundant years, see below)
Kislev	30	(29 in deficient years, see below)
Tebet	29	
Shebat	30	
Adar	29	
Nisan	30	
Iyar	29	
Sivan	30	
Tammuz	29	
Ab	30	
Elul	29	

In embolismic years a 30-day month called Adar Rishon ('First Adar') or simply 'Adar' precedes the normal 29-day Adar, which is then called Ve-Adar (or Adar Sheni, 'Second Adar'); it is in the latter that Purim (see below) is celebrated, though there is a Little Purim (Purim Katan) on 14 Adar I. Cheshvan was formerly called Marcheshvan.

The minimal length of the common year is 353 days, of the embolismic 383; such years are called 'deficient'. Years may also be regular, of 354 or 384 days, or abundant (or perfect), of 355 or 385 days, according to the incidence of the *molad* of Tishri in the next year. In principle, 1 Tishri is the day during which the *molad* falls; however:

(i) If the *molad* falls at or after noon, an extra day is added to Kislev in the current year, making it regular and postponing the following New Year to the next day (since there is thought to be no chance of the new moon's being observed on the same day).

(ii) The same happens if the feria of the *molad* is Sunday, Wednesday, or Friday, on which 1 Tishri is not permitted to fall (respectively so that Hoshanah Rabbah shall not fall on the Sabbath, nor Yom Kippur immediately precede or follow it).

If adding a day under (i) would set the following 1 Tishri on one of the feriae forbidden under (ii), an extra day is also added to Cheshvan, making the year abundant.

However, since the year may not be longer than abundant or shorter than deficient,

(iii) If the *molad* of a common year occurs on a Tuesday at or after 9 hours 204 minims (3 h. 11 m. 20 s. a.m.), the previous year will be abundant, so that 1 Tishri is postponed to Thursday; for it were allowed to fall on Tuesday, there would be 356 days till the next New Year, which under rule (iii) will be a Monday.

(iv) If the *molad* of the year immediately following an embolismic year occurs on a Monday at or after 15 hours 589 minims (9 h. 32 m. 43⅓ s. a.m.), 1 Tishri must be postponed to Tuesday; for since the previous *molad* fell after noon on a Tuesday, 1 Tishri was a Thursday, the Monday is only 382 days later.

Years are counted according to the Era of the World, beginning at 5 hours 204 minims on Monday 7 October (= 11 h. 11 m. 20 s. p.m. on Sunday 6 October) 3761 BC. For many centuries, however, Jews employed the Seleucid era (see *Chronology: Eras*); with the exception of certain dates in 1 Maccabees, it is reckoned in the Greek manner, from autumn 312 BC = AM 3450.

Besides the lunisolar year described above, there is a theoretical solar year of 365 days 6 hours, by which the *tekufot*, or beginnings of the seasons, are governed; at the beginning of each solar cycle, when the year AM, divided by 28, leaves a remainder of 1, the sun is deemed to have reached the equinoctial point of spring—the '*tekufah* of Nisan'— at the same time, 6 p.m. on Tuesday, as in the first year of creation; the event is marked with the ceremony of *birkat hahammah* or Blessing of the Sun, held however on the first Wednesday of lunisolar Nisan. Since the solar year, equivalent in length to the Julian, is slightly longer than the mean lunisolar year, the *tekufah* of Nisan comes progressively later with respect to the lunar calendar, sometimes following the 16th in contravention of the older rule.

The observance of the seventh day in every week as a day of rest or Sabbath, is traced back to Creation itself: having created the universe in six days God made an end 'and he rested on the seventh day from all his work which he had made. And God blessed the seventh day, and sanctified it: because that in it he had rested from all his work' (Gen. 2: 2–3). As God rested, so must man; hence follow the numerous prohibitions, designed to ensure that no action changing the physical nature of the world should be performed on the Sabbath, which thus becomes a day free from mundane concerns, a delight (Isa. 58: 13), welcomed as a bride in the poem *Lekhah Dodi* ('Come my beloved') by Shelomoh Alkabets (16th c.) sung as part of the Friday evening liturgy.

Apart from the Sabbath, there are many other Jewish holy days; in biblical Hebrew some are called sabbaths without reference to feria, in the etymological sense of 'rest day', as at Lev. 23: 32, where the term is used of Yom Kippur. The most important are:

1 Tishri	Rosh Hashanah ('Head of the Year'), marked especially by the blowing of the *shofar* or ram's horn, and by white covers on the synagogue ark and the Torah scroll. This feast begins the Ten Days of Repentance, or Days of Awe, also known in English as the High Holy Days, lasting until Yom Kippur.
3 Tishri	Tsom Gedalyah, Fast of Gedaliah (on 4th if 3rd is a Sabbath). Having conquered Judah, Nebuchadnezzar appointed a Jewish governor, Gedaliah; however, he was murdered by a member of the old royal house. Some Jews fled to Egypt, others were deported.
10 Tishri	Yom Kippur, Day of Atonement: technically a festival, though observed with a 25-hour fast during which eating and drinking are forbidden, preceded and concluded with a festive meal. While the Temple stood, this was the one day on which the high priest entered the Holy of Holies. The prayers in synagogue, begun with Kol Nidrei, renounce all vows between man and God.
15 Tishri	First day of Succoth, Sukkot (Feast of Tabernacles) (Lev. 23: 34). The feast lasts until 21 Tishri; the tradition is to eat, drink, and sleep in a booth or *sukkah* covered with vegetation. At services, one waves the 'four species': palm branch (*lulav*), citron (*etrog*), myrtle twigs (*hadasim*), and willow twigs (*aravot*); worshippers make procession in a circle around the synagogue, holding *lulav* and *etrog* and chanting prayers known as *hoshanot*.
21 Tishri	Hoshanah Rabbah: climax of Succoth. Worshippers circle the synagogue seven times, and beat their *aravot* as if to drive away sins, so energetically that the calendar rules ensure the day shall not fall on Sabbath.
22 Tishri	Shemini Atseret (Eighth Day of Assembly), marked by the prayer for rain; in Israel it also serves as Simchat Torah.
23 Tishri	In the Diaspora this is Simchat Torah (Rejoicing of the Law); the reading of the Torah reaches the end and at once resumes; it is a day of much merriment.
25 Kislev	Chanukah (Encaenia: Dedication of the Temple Lights): Judas Maccabaeus' rededication of the Temple in AM 3598 (164 BC); candles, increasing in number on successive evenings from one to eight, are lit by the window or front door for passers-by to see.
10 Tebet	Asarah be-Tevet. This is the Fast of Tebet, commemorating the start of the Babylonian siege of Jerusalem *c.* AM 3175 (the end of 587 BC).

15 Shebat	(Tu bi-Shvat) New Year for Trees, at the end of the rainy season, when tithes of fruit were determined. It being forbidden to eat the crop of a fruit-tree under 3 years old, a tree is deemed to have entered a new year of its life on this day; therefore, if it was planted on 14 Shebat one year, the third year begins on 15 Shebat in the next. It became a time of study, especially among mystics, but even more a feast for children; in Jerusalem it is a school holiday, on which the pupils go into the fields to plant trees.
13 Adar	Ta'anit Esther, Fast of Esther (on 11th if 13th is a Sabbath).
14 Adar	Purim, celebrating the thwarting of an intended pogrom under the Persian king Ahasuerus (Xerxes), as related by the Book of Esther, which is read publicly from a scroll. Food and charity are distributed; above all there is revelry; students mimic their teachers, and at the late-afternoon feast one is expected to drink till one cannot distinguish between 'cursed be Haman' and 'blessed be Mordecai'. (The numerical values of the Hebrew phrases are identical; it was Haman's jealousy of Mordecai that began the crisis.)
15 Adar	Shushan Purim. The Jews of Susa (Shushan), still engaged in fighting on the 14th, celebrated on the 15th instead; this day was adopted for cities already walled in Joshua's time, so that in Israel Purim is kept on the 15th at Jerusalem, but the 14th at Tel Aviv.
14 Nisan	Ta'anit Bekhorim, fast of firstborn males (on the 12th if the 14th is a Sabbath), to commemorate the saving of the Israelite firstborn before the Exodus; it became the custom to end the study of a Talmudic tractate on this day, an occasion for festivity that broke the fast. In biblical usage this is the day of 'Passover', the slaughter of the paschal lamb 'between two evenings'; the Sadducees (whose power ended with the destruction of the Second Temple) had interpreted this of the twilight period, but the Pharisees referred the phrase to the entire afternoon, and also, again contrary to the Sadducees, ruled that the slaughter should take place even on the Sabbath.
15–21 Nisan	Pesach (Passover), but in the Bible called the feast of Unleavened Bread (*matzot*, 'azymes'). Since 15 Nisan is 23 weeks and two days before 1 Tishri, it cannot fall on Monday, Wednesday, or Friday.
16 Nisan–5 Sivan	Sefirat ha-Omer: the counting of the sheaf of barley (*omer*) formerly waved in the Temple 'on the morrow after the

sabbath [of Passover]' (Lev. 23: 11). The Sadducees took this to be the Sabbath within the seven days of Unleavened Bread, but the Pharisees understood the word in the sense of 'holy day' and applied it to 15 Nisan itself, so that the sheaf was waved on the 16th. From this day on the days are counted, e.g. 'Today is 25 days, which makes three weeks and four days of the Omer'; the period has characteristics of mourning, such as a ban on weddings and haircuts that amongst the Ashkenazim lasts throughout the seven weeks except on 18 Iyar, amongst the Sephardim is lifted on 19 Iyar and not reimposed.

14 Iyar   Pesach Sheni, 'Second Passover'; originally observed by those who owing to impurity or absence could not attend Temple on the proper day; when King Hezekiah, son of the polytheist Ahaz, restored the Temple worship, Passover was kept in this month because the restoration was not far enough advanced in that before. *Matzot* are kept back to be eaten on this day.

18 Iyar   Lag ba'Omer, the 33rd day in the Omer (see above). One explanation, both for the mourning characteristics of the Omer weeks and for the relaxation, is that a plague, having killed 24 000 students of Rabbi Akiva during the Omer period, ceased on this day; other stories make this the day on which the Great Flood began, and manna fell from heaven, or the day on which Rabbi Shimon bar Yochai, the supposed author of the Zohar, died. At the site of his reputed grave bonfires are lit and songs sung in his honour; in modern Israel this has become a bonfire day even amongst the non-observant.

6 Sivan   Shavuot (Feast of Weeks), marking the first-fruits of summer, but also taken to commemorate the giving of the Torah. The Book of Ruth is read, since it mentions harvest and its heroine accepted the Torah; her great-grandson King David was reputedly born and died on this day. It is also called Pentecost ('50th') in English, being the 50th day (inclusively counted) after the Omer; hence the Sadducees (and Samaritans) always kept it on the eighth Sunday after 14 Nisan.

17 Tammuz   Shiva Asar be-Tammuz. This day is observed as the Fast of Tammuz (on the 18th if the 17th is a Sabbath), commemorating the first breaches of the walls by the Babylonian army c. AM 3175 (586 BC), and the cessation of sacrifice under Roman siege in AM 3830 (AD 70). It begins three weeks of mourning, culminating on 9 Ab.

9 Ab   Tisha be-Av. This fast (on the 10th if the 9th is a Sabbath), the only one besides Yom Kippur to begin at nightfall, commemorates

the Babylonian capture of the First Temple *c.* AM 3175 (on 7 Ab) and the Roman capture of the Second Temple in AM 3830. The book of Lamentations is read. By tradition the Messiah will be born on this day.

15 Ab Tu be-Av: a summer festival of the Second Temple era, when marriageable girls danced in the vineyards wearing borrowed white clothes and young men chose their wives amongst them. It was also the last day for bringing wood to be offered at the Temple altar. Some people have revived it in modern Israel.

Of these Rosh Hashanah (as 'the day of blowing the *shofar*'), Yom Kippur, Passover, Shavuot, and Sukkot are laid down in the Torah; on the last three, male Israelites were expected to make the pilgrimage to Jerusalem.

The first day of each month (Rosh Chodesh) was observed with festivities in First Temple times, before the Babylonian conquest; it remained a holiday, on which fasting and mourning were forbidden, but has become a favourite with Jewish women in America. When the preceding month is full, the 30th is added to the festival, which thus comprises two days; this goes back to the days of observation, when the sanctification of the moon might not be reported in time. For the same reason, the custom grew up in the Diaspora of extending major festivals by an extra day, so that 2, 16, 23 Tishri, 16, 22 Nisan, 7 Sivan are a second holiday. In Erets Yisrael this second day (*yom tov sheni*) is not kept except at Rosh Hashanah; contrariwise, Yom Kippur is a single day even in the Diaspora.

Although the reason for adding the *yom tov sheni*, namely the doubt as to the incidence of new moon, has not existed since the reduction of the calendar to fixed and public rules, it was determined, and repeatedly stated with the utmost emphasis, that the day should continue to be observed; that a hostile government might suppress Jewish learning was only one of the reasons given. Thus doubt was not eliminated but canonized.

Moreover, modern communications have created problems in respect of the *yom tov sheni* for Jews domiciled in Erets Yisrael who travel *chuts la-arets* ('outside the Land'), or vice versa; the consequences have been worked out in great detail. In general, a Jew domiciled in the Diaspora is held by majority opinion to be bound by *yom tov sheni* even in Erets Yisrael, whereas a Jew domiciled in Erets Yisrael is bound by it when abroad, except in a place without Jewish inhabitants. Thus a *ben chuts la-arets* visiting Erets Yisrael may not travel in a car driven by a *ben Erets Yisrael* on that day, nor board a bus even if a *ben Erets Yisrael* pays the fare; he must not ask the *ben Erets Yisrael* to perform actions for him that he is not allowed to do himself, such as cooking, and if he does the latter must refuse, though he is free to do them on his own initiative. When it is the *ben Erets Yisrael* who is the guest, he may not offer to perform such services for the host.

Another difference between Erets Yisrael and Diaspora concerns the prayer for rain, which in Erets Yisrael is said from 7 Cheshvan until Pesach; elsewhere it is not said till 4 December in a common year and 5 December in leap year, according to the custom of the Babylonian Diaspora. Authorities do not always agree on which day a traveller should begin saying it.

The twentieth century has added the following observances:

27 Nisan   Yom ha-Shoah, Holocaust Memorial Day; this was the day on which Buchenwald was liberated (27 Nisan 5705 = 10 April 1945).

4 Iyar   Yom ha-Zikaron, Memorial Day, commemorating those who have died defending the State of Israel; at sunset a siren sounds, marking the transition to the rejoicing of Independence Day.

5 Iyar   Independence Day (Yom ha'Atsmaut), commemorating Israel's proclamation of independence (5 Iyar 5708 = 14 May 1948).

28 Iyar   Jerusalem Day (Yom Yerushalayim), commemorating the liberation of the Old City (28 Iyar 5727 = 7 June 1967).

Many Jews also commemorate the *Reichskristallnacht* pogrom of *9 November 1938, but on that date and not its Jewish equivalent.

For conversion of Jewish dates to Christian, or vice versa, see Appendix F; for Rosh Hashanah and 15 Nisan till 2020, see Appendix K, Table 2.

THE MUSLIM CALENDAR

The Muslim calendar is a pure lunar calendar, of 12 months to the year, without the embolisms of the lunisolar calendar used by the Arabs before Islam; a few years before his death, the Prophet announced that embolism entailed an impious postponement of the sacred months (Qur'ān, *Sūra* 9, v. 37), and none is now thought to have taken place since his arrival in Medina. As a result, 33 Muslim years are roughly equivalent to 32 Christian ones.

Soon afterwards it was decided to replace the Seleucid era, till then in common use, reckoned from the Byzantine New Year on 1 September, with a new era dating from the Prophet's departure, or *Hijra*, from Mecca; years so counted are when necessary marked *h.* in Arabic, for *hijrī*, and AH in the West, for *anno Hegirae*. Although some early writers reckoned from the Hijra day itself, Monday, 1 Rabī' al-'awwal = 13 September AS 934/AD 622, the preferred epoch was the first day of the Arab year, 1 Muḥarram, which fell in the previous Seleucid year on Friday, 16 July AS 933/AD 622. However, since the Arab civil day began at sunset, the Hijrī era runs in Western terms from the evening of Thursday, 15 July; much early Muslim usage sets 1 Muḥarram AH 1 on the Thursday, as astronomers (who reckon the day from noon) still do.

As set out in handbooks, the Muslim calendar is one of the simplest as well as most accurate in the world. However, since the month properly begins not on any pre-calculated day but when the new moon has been observed by reliable witnesses in the night sky, and since cycles of intercalation have varied both as to their length and to the distribution of leap years within them, the theoretical pattern may not correspond to the actual. In particular, Ramaḍān is still very widely determined by observation, made either locally or at some recognized place within the Islamic world; some British Muslims await reports from Saudi Arabia sent by email or fax. Hence the Christian equivalent of a Muslim date given in a text cannot be established for certain unless (as it often is) the feria is added; in case of conflict between feria and conversion table, the feria should be believed.

The Muslim year consists of 12 months, with Arabic names that like the Latin names of our own calendar are variously modified in other languages; but their correct forms, with their handbook lengths, are:

Muḥarram	30 days
Ṣafar	29 days
Rabī' al-'awwal	30 days
Rabī' al-'ākhir	29 days

Jumadā 'l-ʾūlā	30 days
Jumadā 'l-ʾukhrā	29 days
Rajab	30 days
Shaʿbān	29 days
Ramaḍān	30 days
Shawwāl	29 days
Dhū 'l-qaʿda	30 days
Dhū 'l-ḥijja	29 or 30 days

In the calculated, though not the observed, calendar, a 30th day is added to Dhū 'l-ḥijja in 11 years out of every 30; as a result, the average length of the calendar month over the 30-year cycle, 29 days 12 hours 44 minutes, is only some 3 seconds short of the synodic month (from new moon to new moon) of 29.530 59 days. A leap year is called *sana kabīsa*, a common year *sana basīṭa*. The standard rule is to intercalate those years which when divided by 30 leave a remainder of 2, 5, 7, 10, 13, 16, 18, 21, 24, 26, and 29; but variations are found, in particular year 15 instead of 16 when the epoch is taken as Thursday, 15 July 622. In classical (though not modern) Arabic, dates from the 1st to the 15th are expressed as 'at so many nights past', those from the 16th as 'at so many nights remaining', from 14 nights in a full month, 13 in a hollow month, down to one night on the 29th or 28th respectively, the last night or (artificial) day being described as such.

The month names go back to the pre-Islamic calendar: Muḥarram means 'sacred', Rabīʿ denotes the rainy season, Jumadā the dry, their appended epithets meaning 'Former' and 'Latter'; Rajab is 'forbidden'. Dhū 'l-ḥijja is 'that of pilgrimage', namely to the Kaʿba in Mecca, the sanctuary housing the black stone adopted by Islam but previously associated with the sun.

The first, seventh, eleventh, and twelfth months are sacred, warfare against other Muslims being prohibited, and the ninth is observed by fasting throughout the hours of daylight. The only holy days enjoined by the Qurʾān are the fast of Ramaḍān and the Ḥājj; but many other days are observed by Muslims of one community or another. Many are purely local; a selection of Sunnī festivals and commemorations is given, with no suggestion that they are of equal prominence or prevalence. Those marked with an asterisk, together with the nights preceding the two ʿīd feasts, are called *mubāraka*, 'blessed'.

1 Muḥarram	New Year.
10 Muḥarram	*yawm al-ʿāshūrāʾ* (voluntary) fast-day, borrowed from Yom Kippur; commemoration of the landing of Noah's ark after the flood, celebrated by a pudding of figs, raisins, dates, and nuts as made by his wife.
12 Rabīʿ I*	*mawlid al-nabiy* (Birth of the Prophet), also *laylat al-mawlūd*, but properly the date of his death. In some countries candles are lit (in Turkey the day is Mevlût Kandili), though stricter circles disapprove of this and any other observance of the day except readings from the Qurʾān.

3 Rabī' II	Burning in AH 63 (10 Dec. 682) of the Ka'ba during a civil war.
1st Fri. of Rajab*	*laylat al-rāghā'ib* ('night of desires'), conception of the Prophet by 'Amina.
27 Rajab*	*laylat al-mi'rāj* (night of the Prophet's ascent from Jerusalem to the seven heavens); another *kandil* in Turkey, with daytime fast.
15 Sha'bān*	*laylat al-barā'a* ('diploma', Persian *šäb-e barāt*), also *laylat al-ṣakk* ('document'): God places on record all the deaths that will take place in the coming year; in principle one should fast, watch, and pray, but in many places, especially on the Subcontinent, it is an occasion for illumination and fireworks. The night of the Prophet's triumphant entry into Mecca.
16 Sha'bān	Mecca made *qibla* (the direction in which prayers are addressed) instead of Jerusalem, AH 2 (11 Feb. 624).
1–30 Ramaḍān	Fast from the moment each morning when white threads may be distinguished from black till the sun has completely set, when the believer eats an odd number of dates and drinks some water before performing the evening prayer.
19 Ramaḍān	Battle of Badr, AH 2 (15 Mar. 624), defeat of Meccans by Muslims.
27 Ramaḍān*	*laylat al-qadr* ('Night of Power'): first revelation of the Qur'ān, 'better than a thousand months' (*Sūra* 97. 3). After prayers, much festivity; a second meal is taken before dawn.
1–3 Shawwāl	*'īd al-fiṭr* ('feast of fast-breaking'): end of Ramadan fast; also *'īd al-ṣadaqa* ('feast of almsgiving'), *'īd al-ṣaghīr* ('the little feast'). In Turkey called Feast of Sugar, *Şeker Bayramı*, from the distribution of sweets, or simply *Bayram*.
1 Shawwāl	*yawm al-raḥma* ('day of mercy').
5 Dhū 'l-qa'da	Descent of Ka'ba, the stone building at Mecca to which the Ḥājj is made.
7 Dhū 'l-ḥijja	Preaching at Ka'ba to pilgrims, who on arrival in Mecca will already have performed the *ṭawāf* or sevenfold anticlockwise walk round the Ka'ba and the *sa'y* or sevenfold run (four out, three back) between Ṣafā and Marwa.
8 Dhū 'l-ḥijja	*yawm al-tarwiya* ('day of watering'). If pilgrims had relaxed their state of ritual purity or *'iḥrām* they must now resume it before departing for the plain of Arafat by way of Minā

and Muzdalifa. There are many ritual actions (some varying from one juridical school to another) that pilgrims must perform during the Ḥajj; but fasting is strictly forbidden.

9 Dhū 'l-ḥijja   *yawm ʿArafāt* ('day of Arafat'), where pilgrims spend this day; whoever has reached it before nightfall is deemed to have participated in the Ḥajj. The central event is the station (*wuqūf*) before a hill known as Jabal al-Raḥma, 'the Mountain of Mercy'. At sunset the pilgrims depart at a run for Muzdalifa, where they spend the night.

10–12 Dhū 'l-ḥijja   *ʿīd al-ʾaḍhā* ('feast of immolation') or *ʿīd al-ḥājj* ('feast of pilgrimage'); also *al-ʿīd al-kabīr* ('the great feast').

10 Dhū 'l-ḥijja   *yawm al naḥr* ('day of slaughter'), *yawm al-ʾaḍhā* ('day of blood sacrifice)', *yawm al-qurbān* (day of offering). After a service before sunrise, the pilgrims depart for Minā, where each throws seven stones at the easternmost of three pillars said to represent Satan. There follows the sacrifice, usually of a sheep or a goat, also conducted on this day all over the Muslim world; the pilgrims then have their heads shaved and come out of *ʾiḥrām*, though not all everyday activities are yet permitted. They return to Mecca, where they perform another *ṭawāf* around the newly bedecked Kaʿba; they drink the waters of Zamzam before departing for Minā.

11–13 Dhū 'l-ḥijja   *ʾayyām al-tashrīq* ('days of eastening', i.e. departure). The pilgrims relax in Minā, no longer wearing ritual garments: every day they throw seven stones at each of the three pillars, unless they have left for Mecca on the 12th; there they perform a farewell ritual, and repeat the *ṭawāf*.

The main Shīʿī festivals observed in Iran are:

9 Muḥarram   *yawm al-tāsūʿāʾ*, eve of the following.

10 Muḥarram   *yawm al-ʿāshūrāʾ*, anniversary of Battle of Karbalāʾ AH 61 (10 Oct. 680), elaborately observed as the martyrdom of the Prophet's grandson Ḥusayn; in Persian called *ruz-e qätl*, 'Day of the Slaughter'.

20 Ṣafar   *ʾarbaʿīn* ('Forty'): fortieth day after above.

28 Ṣafar   Death of the Prophet and martyrdom of Ḥasan.

17 Rabīʿ I   Birthday of the Prophet and the Sixth Imām (the last recognized by both Ismaʿīlī and Twelver Shiites), Jaʿfar al-Ṣādiq.

13 Rajab	Birth of ʿAlī.
27 Rajab	*laylat al-miʿrāj* (night of the Prophet's ascent from Jerusalem to the seven heavens); Persian name *ʿīde mābaʿs̱*.
15 Shaʿbān	Birth of the Twelfth Imām, Imām Mahdi.
21 Ramaḍān	Martyrdom of ʿAlī.
1 Shawwāl	*ʿīd al-fiṭr*.
25 Shawwāl	Martyrdom of Imām Jaʿfar al-Ṣādiq.
11 Dhū 'l-qaʿda	Birthday of Imām Reżā.
10 Dhū 'l-ḥijja	*ʿīd-e qurbān*.
18 Dhū 'l-ḥijja	*ʿīd-e ghadīr-e Khumm*, day when the Prophet invested ʿAlī as his successor (caliph) by the stream Khumm.

The inconvenience of the unintercalated lunar year does not need to be pointed out by Westerners; for civil and astronomical purposes Muslims have readily used other calendars, or even devised them. Two cases are considered below.

IRAN

At the time of the Muslim conquest the Iranian year was an *annus vagus* of 365 days, consisting of twelve 30-day months and five epagomenal days added after the eighth month; days were not numbered but named. It was reckoned either by regnal year or according to an era; Muslim astronomers continued the regnal years of the last Sasanian king, Yäzdegird III, thus acquiring an era with epoch 16 June 632. (This era is also used by the Parsis of India; see *Hindu Calendar*.) In 1006 (AY 375) the epagomenal days were returned to the end of the year.

To convert the *annus vagus* into a true solar calendar, astronomers said to have included the young Omär Khäyyam proposed, at the behest of the Selçuk ruler Celâleddin Melik Şah (Pers. Jälal-äd-din Mälek Shah; 1073–92):

(i) that the year should begin at the vernal equinox on the day in which the sun should have passed the First Point of Aries before midday;

(ii) that a sixth epagomenal day should be added every four years, provided that on it the Sun would pass the First Point of Aries after noon; if it would still do so before midday, then intercalation should be postponed to the following year.

No cycle of postponements was laid down, although our sources make various attempts to devise one: the most commonly repeated view in modern writers is that every eighth intercalation should be postponed for a year, giving an average year of $365\frac{24}{99}$ days, but the statement in one account that Omär provided for seven intercalations in 29 years or eight in 33 has led to surmise that he intended the even more accurate rule of adding 31

days in 128 years, with an average year of 365.242 187 5 days, by successive postponements of the 7th, 15th, 23rd, and 31st intercalation in each cycle. A new era was declared,
called Jälali or Mäleki after the sultan; the first day of the first month, Färvärdin, in 1 Jäl.
corresponded to 19 Färvärdin AY 448 = Friday, 15 March 1079. However, this calendar
was discontinued; before 1925, Iran used for financial purposes a solar calendar in which
the years were designated according to the Turkic and Chinese animal cycle (see *Chinese Calendar*) together with the lunar (later the solar) Hijrī date, and the months named
after the constellations, corresponding every year in length to the time the Sun spent in
them, from 29 days to 32.

The solar calendar of modern Iran (*täqvim-e hejri-ye shämsi*), introduced by vote of the
Mäjles on 31 March 1925 (11 Färvärdin 1304), is reckoned from the year of the Hijra,
restoring the traditional month names; the New Year festival of Nouruz falls at the vernal equinox on or about 21 March. Days are numbered with the normal ordinals; the
months, with their most frequent date of commencement, are:

Färvärdin	31 days	21 March
Ordibehesht	31 days	21 April
Khordad	31 days	22 May
Tir	31 days	22 June
Mordad	31 days	23 July
Shährivar	31 days	23 August
Mehr	30 days	23 September
Aban	30 days	23 October
Azär	30 days	22 November
Dei	30 days	22 December
Bähmän	30 days	21 January
Esfänd	29 days	20 February
	(30 in leap year)	

The length of the months is determined by the speed of the earth's revolution round
the Sun: from spring equinox to autumn is 186 days, from autumn to spring 179.

Intercalation is theoretically dependent on the time of the equinox as in Omär's calendar; but in order to avoid variation between longitudes a grand cycle of 2820 years
has been devised: in it there are 21 cycles of 128 years, each comprising an initial small
cycle of 29 years and three of 33 years, followed by a 132-year cycle comprising an initial 29-year small cycle, two of 33 years, and a final small cycle of 37 years. Within each
small cycle there is a leap year in year 5 and every fourth year thereafter up to year 29,
33, or 37 as the case may be, i.e. when $Y > 1$ and $Y \bmod 4 \equiv 1$. There are thus 7, 8, or 9
leap years in each small cycle, yielding 31 leap years in each 128-year cycle and 32 in the
132-year cycle, or 683 in the grand cycle, which thus contains 1 029 983 days; if the length
of the tropical year is taken to be 365.242 199 days throughout, then 2820 tropical years
exceed 2820 Iranian solar years by 1 minute 41.952 seconds.

The current grand cycle is taken to have begun with AH 475 = AD 1096/7; the calendar was introduced within the seventh 128-year cycle, which began on 1243 (1864/5), and

in the last year of the second small cycle, which was therefore a leap year; so, in the third small cycle, was 1309 (1930/1) and every fourth year thereafter to 1337 (1958/9), and in the fourth small cycle 1342 (1963/4) and every fourth year after that to 1370 (1991/2). The present 128-year cycle began in 1371 (1992/3); leap years are 1375 (1996/7) and every fourth year to 1399 (2020/1), the first in each subsequent small cycle being 1404 (2025/6), 1437 (2056/7), and 1470 (2087/8).

On 24 Esfänd 1354 = 14 March 1976, Reza Shah's son Mohammad Reza substituted a new Shahänshahi ('Imperial') era for that of the Hijra, reckoned from Cyrus the Great's accession to the Persian throne in 559 BC; AH solar 1354 = 1975/6 was thus followed by Shahänshahi 2535, beginning on 21 March 1976. This affront to Islam was one of the many popular grievances manifested during the next year, Shahänshahi 2536; the new era was discontinued as from 5 Shährivar 1357 = 27 August 1978, the last *shämsi* year of the Shah's reign. Despite a proposal in the early days of the revolutionary regime to abolish the solar calendar, it remains the civil calendar of the Islamic Republic of Iran.

The main public holidays and celebrations are:ah

		Usual Gregorian equivalent
1–4 Färvärdin	Nouruz, a joyous feast: seven objects whose names begin with *s* must be on the table	21–4 March
12 Färvärdin	Islamic Republic Day (proclaimed 1 April 1979/1358)	1 April
13 Färvärdin	Thirteenth day of Nouruz (Public Outing Day)	2 April
14 Khordad	Death of Imam Khomeini 1989/1368	4 June
15 Khordad	Riots of 6 June 1963/1342 against Shah's White Revolution and arrest of Imam Khomeini	5 June
17 Shährivar	Martyrs of Islamic revolution	8 September
12 Aban	Seizure of US Embassy 1979/1358	3 November
22 Bähmän	Islamic Revolution Day, commemorating the collapse of the government left behind by the Shah 11 February 1979/1357 and the seizures of power by the Islamic revolutionaries. The Arabic words '*Alläbu 'akbar*, 'God is most great', are reproduced in Küfic script 22 times along the edges of the outer (green and red) stripes on the national flag in honour of this date	11 February
29 Esfänd	Nationalization of the oil industry, 1951/1329	20 March

TURKEY

From the late seventeenth century onwards Ottoman documents are sometimes dated according to the so-called financial year (*sene-i maliye*), which in the later reigns was frequently, though not exclusively, also used for dating books. It was based on the Julian calendar, reckoned from 1 March OS, the count being known as *marti*; the choice of March as the first month, perhaps copied from Venice, permitted the leap day, as in the lunar calendar, to occupy the most convenient place, at the end of the year. This always coincided with the Julian leap day, irrespective of the irregularities about to be described in the numbering of the years.

The years were designated according to the lunar (*kameri*) Hijrī year current on 1 March OS; but since it is possible for a lunar year to be entirely contained within a solar one, there were occasional gaps in the sequence: thus 1 March 1676 OS fell on 25 Dhū 'l-ḥijja (in modern Turkish spelt *zilhicce*) AH 1086 lunar, but 1 March 1677 on 6 Muḥarram (*muharrem*) 1088, so that *marti* 1086 was followed directly by *marti* 1088, passing over 1087. This was known as *siviş* (= 'slippage'); for the same reason there was no *marti* 1121, 1154, 1188, 1221, or 1255; but when *siviş* was next due, the consolidated debt bonds for the slip year, 1288, had by inadvertence been already printed. It was therefore decided to abandon the principle of keeping up with the lunar year and count the year 3 Muḥarram 1289–12 Muḥarram 1290 lunar as *maliye* 1288 (1872/3); similarly, *maliye* 1320 (1904/5) began on 26 Dhū 'l-ḥijja 1321 lunar and ended on 6 Muḥarram 1323.

In 1917 the New Style was adopted by the omission of 16–28 February 1332; with effect from 1 March 1333/1917 the official Turkish calendar was the NS *marti* year, under the name of *Takvim-i Garbî* or 'Western Calendar', the days being omitted, until by law of 25 December 1341/1925 the Christian (*milâdî*, 'Nativity') era with modern style was adopted with effect from 1 January 1926.

OTHER CALENDARS

ANGLO-SAXON

The Venerable Bede, in his *De temporum ratione* of 725, describes a heathen English luni-solar calendar in which the year began at or near the winter solstice, called 'Mothers' Night' (see *25 Dec., 'Midwinter, Yule, Mothers' Night'); it was divided about the equinoxes into two seasons, summer and winter, with 12 months in common years and 13 in embolismic. He lists the names of the months, which were subsequently trans-ferred to those of the Roman calendar: thus Bede states that the first month of the year, which followed the winter solstice, was the second of two called *giuli*, and later writers call the Church's January *se æfterra geōla*, 'the latter Yule'. Next came *solmōnaþ*, on the face of it 'mud-month', but conjectured by Bede to be named after the cakes offered to the gods, and *hreþmōnað*, named according to Bede after the goddess worshipped in it; this name was generally displaced by *hlȳda*, 'Lide' (see I: *March). The first month of spring, *ēastermōnað*, was also named after a goddess still lurking under our term 'Easter'; there followed *þrimilce*, 'three milkings (a day)', and two months called *līþa*, 'gentle'. In em-bolismic years there was a third, causing such a year to be called *þrilīþe*, 'three-Lithe'; un-fortunately we are not told on what principle it was added. These months were followed by *wēodmōnað*, 'weedmonth', and *hālegmōnaþ*, 'holy month', which concluded summer. The tenth month was *winterfylleþ*, 'winter fullness'; winter was deemed to begin at the full moon. The eleventh was *blōtmōnaþ*, 'sacrifice month'; finally came *se ærra geōla*, 'the former Yule'. How far calculation had displaced observation in the ordering of the calendar we do not know.

ARMENIAN

The Armenian calendar was an *annus vagus* of 12 30-day months: *nawasard hoṙi sahmi trē k'aloç araç mehekan areg arekan mareri margaç hrotiç*, plus five epagomenal days called *aweliaç*. The era began on 11 July 552, when the Easter table then in use ran out (see *Chronology: Eras*); the lack of a leap day caused the beginning of the year to move ever earlier with respect to the Julian calendar, till in Armenian year 766 it fell on 1 January 1317; it remained on

1 January for the next three years, but since AD 1320 was a leap year Armenian 770 began
on 31 December. Unfortunately not only Western but some Armenian writers have lost
sight of this fact, so that years after 1320 may be found with a *millésime* one too low.
Whereas many saints' days were determined according to the *annus vagus*, the liturgical
year began and begins with *Haymut'iwn* (Epiphany including Christmas) on 6 January
according to the Julian calendar; the need to reconcile the two calendars led to various
expedients, the most important of which was a fixed calendar, reckoned from 1084, in
which the year always begins on 11 August.

During the nineteenth century the Julian calendar displaced other reckonings; but in
1892 it was in turn supplanted by the Gregorian, except for the calculation of Easter and
the dependent feasts and fasts. These are reckoned according to a Metonic cycle (see
*Chronology: Cycles) that for 528 years out of 532 yields the normal Julian Easter, but in
the remaining four causes Easter to be kept on 13 April instead of the 6th. This happened in 570 (Arm. 18), 665 (113), 760 (208), 1007 (456), 1102 (551), 1197 (646), 1292 (741),
1539 (988), 1634 (1083), 1729 (1178), 1824 (1273); the next instance will be 2071. These
'false Easters' have been a subject for discord between the Armenians and the 'Greeks
and Georgians' (the Georgian Church, previously at one with the Armenians, entered
into communion with Byzantium by the early 7th c.). In 1634 and 1729 there were fierce
battles in Jerusalem between Greeks and Armenians; in 1824 the peace was kept through
the intervention of the Russians, who concur with the Greeks on the date of Easter but
are well disposed towards Armenians.

BABYLONIAN

The Babylonian year, which began at the first new moon after the spring equinox, had
12 months, each beginning at the first sighting of the crescent, called Nisanu, Aiaru,
Simanu, Duzu, Abu, Ululu, Tashritu, Ahrasamnu, Kislimu, Tebetu, Shabatu, Addaru.
The years were grouped into cycles of 19 years, within which in years 3, 6, 8, 11, 14, and
19 the month Addaru was repeated, in year 17 Ululu; such cycles can be traced back at
least into the fourth century BC, but in all probability originate far earlier. When Alexander the Great conquered Babylonia, this calendar was retained, as being more accurate than anything known in Greek practice (as opposed to theory); the months were
given Macedonian names, so that Nisanu became Artemisios. The spring beginning was
retained, so that the years of the Seleucid era remained six months behind those used
in other parts of the Near East, being reckoned from 1 Artemisios/Nisanu 311 BC (2/3
Apr.); as 1 Babylonian was year 19 of an intercalary cycle. Days were counted forward
from 1 to 30 or 29. This calendar was retained when Babylonia fell under Parthian domination; however, from AD 17 onwards we find the Macedonian names running one
month behind, Nisanu now being Xandikos instead of Artemisios. The change, if uniform, had only just taken place, for coins from another city show the old system still in
use in 15/16; but the new equivalences are general even outside Parthian territory and are

used by Josephus when giving Greek names for Jewish months, which bore the Baby-lonian names (see *Jewish Calendar*).

CELTIC

The pagan Celtic peoples of the Continent have left behind them some inscriptions, mostly Gaulish but a few Celtiberian; the surviving Celts of the British Isles (and their offshoot in Brittany) have abundant literatures, but none pre-Christian. Evidence for pagan beliefs and practices is easiest to find in Ireland, but even when it may be taken at face value it makes no claim to be pan-Celtic. We know for a certainty that Ireland had four seasonal feasts, which as correlated with the Roman calendar were *Imbolc* or *Oímelc* on 1 February, considered the first day of spring, *Bealtaine* on 1 May, *Lughnasadh* on 1 August, and *Samhain* on 1 November, of which the last, the beginning of winter, was the most important and *Bealtaine* the next; but early Welsh writers recognize only *Calan Mai*, 1 May, investing it with the supernatural qualities that *Samhain* had for the Irish. An underlying two-season system, as in Germanic culture, in which winter and summer made the year, may reasonably be posited, but it had no relation to the solstices, even though midsummer was long celebrated in Ireland and Celtic Britain with particular fervour, and midwinter was the beginning of the year in early calendars. (The monu-ments in Britain and Ireland aligned on the midwinter, midsummer, or equinoctial sun-rise belong to far earlier ages.) Nor has a pre-Christian calendar survived, though legal texts recognize intervals of five days (*cóicde*) and fifteen days (*cóicthiges*); the latter is half a month, an entity recognized in the name *faoillidh* for 1–15 February. (It hardly needs saying that Robert Graves's Celtic Tree Calendar is a literary figment.)

By contrast, a pre-Christian Gaulish calendar inscribed on bronze in Roman script at the end of the second century AD was discovered at Coligny (Ain) in 1897. It covers a five-year cycle of 62 months, comprising (so the most recent study has determined) 1832 days, beginning with an intercalary month Quimonios, of 30 days; the 12 regular months are Samonios (30 days), Dumannios (29), Rivros (30), Anagantio(n) (29), Ogronnios (30), Qutios (30), Giamonios (29), Semivisonns (30), Equos (30 days in odd years of the cycle, 28 in the 2nd, 29 in the 4th), Elembivios (29), Aedrinios (30), Cantlos (29); after Qutios in the third year was added a 30-day intercalary month (R?)antaronos. It appears that the year began at the winter solstice, with the month Samonios (cf. *Samhain*); it marked the ascent to summer, as Giamonios (related to Latin *hiems*) the des-cent to winter. Each month was divided into two halves, the first always comprising 15 days; as in the Hindu calendar, the days of each half were numbered separately, but by the forward count. However, certain days changed places within or even between the months; for details of this, and the devices used to keep track of the sun and the moon, see Olmsted, who also finds that a 30-year cycle was changed into a 25-year cycle shortly before Caesar's conquest, at a time when the calendar was five days out of true. Al-though the 30 years are attested by the Elder Pliny (d. AD 79), his ultimate source is agreed to be Caesar's contemporary Posidonius; the displacement of the calendar is proved by the statement (*Natural History* 16. 251) that months, years, and cycles begin on the sixth lune. Olmsted suggests that the Irish (or their ancestors) had a similar calendar, but allowed the nominal dates of the solstices to slip backwards through the year till they reached their present positions, being then fixed by the adoption of the Roman calendar.

FRENCH REPUBLICAN

At the height of the French Revolution, the zeal to replace Christian and monarchical culture with new institutions of a rational and republican nature attacked not only the Christian era, but the entire Roman calendar. A new calendar was devised, consisting of twelve 30-day months with five epagomenal days, or six in leap year, reckoned from the establishment of the Republic on 22 September 1792. It was based on the Egyptian calendar as reformed by Augustus, according to the Masonic enthusiasms of the revolutionaries: 'Les traditions sacrées de l'Égypte, qui devinrent celles de tout l'Orient, faisoient sortir la terre du chaos sous le même signe que notre République, et y fixoient l'origine des lois et des temps.'

Each month was divided into three 10-day periods called *décades*; the original plan, set out in the report of the Comité d'Instruction Publique to the Convention Nationale on 5 October 1793, was to number the months and *décades*, making that day the 4th day of the 2nd *décade* of the 1st month of year 2. This was too cumbersome; the Convention preferred to number the days of each month from 1 to 30, and name the months according to a system devised by the poet Philippe-François-Nazaire Fabre d'Églantine to reflect the French climate and the French agricultural year. Within this geographical limitation, the names are both attractive and ingenious, being distinguished according to season by suffixes admirably matching sound to sense. The autumn months end in *-aire*:

vendémiaire	wine harvest
brumaire	mist
frimaire	hoar frost

The winter months in *-ôse*:

nivôse	snow
pluviôse	rain
ventôse	wind

The spring months in *-al*:

germinal	shoots
floréal	flowers
prairial	fields

The summer months in -*dor* (from the Greek for 'gift', but to a French ear suggesting *d'or*, 'golden'):

messidor	harvest
thermidor	heat
fructidor	fruits

It was in this form that the Republican calendar was enacted by the Convention on 4 frimaire year II = 24 November 1793. It is distressing to record that Fabre d'Églantine was guillotined on 16 germinal year II = 5 April 1794.

The decree also envisaged a decimal division of the day into 10 hours each of 100 minutes themselves each of 100 seconds, with effect from 1 vendémiaire year III. This proved impractical, but ten-hour clock-faces are found, and even in 1884 France persuaded the International Meridian Conference at Washington to adopt a resolution supporting decimal division of angles and time.

In each *décade* the days were styled *primidi, duodi, tridi, quartidi, quintidi, sextidi, septidi, octidi, nonidi, décadi*, the last a day of rest in place of Sunday; to celebrate it *fêtes décadaires* were devised in honour of various collectivities and abstractions such as the French people (30 vendémiaire) and misfortune (10 thermidor). As in the old calendar every day had its saint, so in the new every day was dedicated to an animal, a vegetable, or an implement of agriculture; a few anti-Christian hotheads renamed themselves according to the item honoured on their old name-day, but such names were less popular than those taken from classical antiquity, for the most fiery François would rather call himself Brutus after the Roman tyrannicide or Aristide after the just Athenian than Potiron, or pumpkin, after the vegetable to which St Francis's day (4 Oct.) had been reassigned as 13 vendémiaire; nor, on finding that 5 frimaire (*ci-devant* 25 Nov.) was consecrated to the pig, was Catherine likely to call herself Cochon.

The epagomenal days, whose original name of *sans-culottides* became *jours complémentaires* after Thermidor, were dedicated to Virtue, Genius, Work, Opinion (on which free speech was permitted), and Rewards, with a sixth, dedicated to the Revolution, added in every fourth year; the period from one leap year (*année sextile*) to the next being called a *franciade*. As in the model, the leap year was that which terminated in the Julian pre-leap year: III in 1795, VII in 1799, XI in 1803; since 1800 was not a Gregorian leap year, from 10 nivôse year VIII = 1 March 1800 the equivalences onwards differ by one day from those four or eight years earlier in the previous two *franciades*.

The Convention did not prohibit the old calendar, even under the Terror; during the Thermidorian reaction the cultural battle between Citizen Décadi and Monsieur Dimanche was fought out in pamphlets. But after the coup of 18 fructidor year V (4 Sept. 1797) had delivered the Directoire into Republican hands, fresh emphasis was laid on the use of the new calendar: attempts were even made to coerce the Church into transferring Sunday worship to *décadi*. On 14 germinal year VI (3 Apr. 1798) the Directoire issued an *arrêté* laying down, among other things, that newspapers in which the old date appeared alongside the new should be suppressed, and that employees in the public works who absented themselves on Sundays or the old feast days should be dismissed. The only permissible free days were *décadi* and Republican holidays, though if workers should request *quintidi* afternoon off as well, managers were empowered (not required) to accede.

The Republican calendar was introduced by force of arms to Italy, the month names being translated as *vendemmiaio, brumaio, frimaio* (or *glaciale*); *nevoso, piovoso, ventoso; germinale, floreale, pratile; messidoro, termidoro, fruttidoro*. By contrast, an Englishman of the John Bull persuasion satirized the poetic (or as he thought namby-pamby) names: 'Autumn: wheezy, sneezy, freezy. Winter: slippy, drippy, nippy. Spring: showery, flowery, bowery. Summer: hoppy, croppy, poppy' (Brady, i. 39).

When Napoleon Bonaparte overthrew the Directoire on 18 brumaire year VIII (9 Nov. 1799), many people hoped or feared that he would abolish the metric system and the Republican calendar. The former expectation was completely mistaken; the latter, though ultimately correct, left out of account an attachment to the calendar, not as revolutionary or Republican, but as French. To be sure, there was a retreat from extremes: on 3 nivôse year VIII (24 Dec. 1799) all purely Republican festivals except 14 July, 1 vendémiaire, and the *fêtes décadaires* were abolished; on 7 thermidor year VIII (26 July 1800) the coercive measures were repealed, but public servants' rest-day remained *décadi* till the Concordat with Pius VII, signed 26 messidor year IX (15 July 1801), proclaimed 28 germinal year X (18 Apr. 1802); Sunday was finally restored for the publication of marriage banns on 13 floréal year XI (3 May 1802). However, Napoleon scrupulously employed the French calendar (though he often added the Gregorian date in parentheses) in all correspondence except with the Pope, and even on 6 fructidor year XIII (24 Aug. 1805), when abolition was imminent, complained to Talleyrand when his minister in Salzburg dated a letter 12 August instead of 24 thermidor. So long as the law was in force it ought to be obeyed, and ministers should set an example; next thing the fellow would be writing in German (*Correspondance*, xi. 153). On the 15th (2 Sept.) the formal proposal was made before the Senate to abolish the *calendrier français*, 'à partir du 11 nivôse prochain' (i.e. 10 nivôse year XIV should be followed by 1 January 1806); it was passed on the 22nd (9 Sept.).

French laws and decrees from the period when the Republican calendar was in force are still cited by it: thus the use of forenames and surnames other than those in the birth certificate is forbidden by the law of 6 fructidor year II, and till 1993 forenames were still restricted to those found 'dans les différents calendriers' (the Catholic and the Republican) and names of persons known from ancient history by the law of 11 germinal year XI. Historians generally use the normal calendar; nevertheless, certain turning-points (*journées révolutionnaires*) from the factional struggles of the period are still known by their dates in the revolutionary calendar. The most important are:

9 thermidor year II = 27 July 1794 (fall of Robespierre)
1–3 prairial year III = 20–2 May 1795 (Jacobin rebellion in Paris)
13 vendémiaire year IV = 5 October 1795 (royalist rebellion in Paris)
18 fructidor year V = 4 September 1797 (Republicans seize control of Directoire)
18 brumaire year VIII = 9 November 1799 (Directoire overthrown by Bonaparte)
28 floréal year XII = 18 May 1803 (Bonaparte proclaimed emperor)

To convert between the French and Gregorian calendars, see Appendix F.

Attempts at revival by a few enthusiasts upon the establishments of the Second Republic in 1848 and the Third Republic in 1870 came to naught. There were ephemeral notions of introducing the *dekada* in the early days of Bolshevik rule; some Nazi neopagans renamed the months, not by the traditional German names, but by neologisms that in form and sometimes meaning recalled those of Fabre d'Églantine, so that March became not *Lenzmonat* but *Lenzing*, November not *Windmonat* but *Nebelung*, an obvious calque on *brumaire*. However, these extravagances remained unofficial.

ICELANDIC

Although the Roman calendar was known in Christian Iceland and used by the Church, the civil calendar, recognized by law as well as custom into the modern period, was an adaptation of a pre-Christian Germanic reckoning by summer and winter: these two, known as *misseri*, combined to form a year of 364 days, nominally divided into 11 months of 30 and one of 34 days, but in practice reckoned in weeks. In five years out of every 28 an extra week was added to restore parity with the sun.

Summer began *at sumarmálum*, 'at the summer marks', on the Thursday between 9 and 15 April inclusive; in the first year of the Church's solar cycle this was the 11th. *Sumarmál* constituted the first day of the first month. Thereafter till midsummer weeks were counted as elapsed weeks of summer: thus the *fardagar* in which contracts, leases, etc., were terminated or renewed began with the Thursday between 23 and 29 May, called 'that Thursday on which there are six weeks of summer' = sixth Thursday after *sumarmál*. The following Thursday, seven weeks of summer, was the legal term for payment if no other arrangement had been made. Other weekdays were expressed in relation to the summer weeks completed on the nearest Thursday; e.g. 'that Wednesday on which there are six weeks of summer, but on the next day after'. The third summer month, beginning on the Monday between 8 and 14 June, had four extra days (*aukadagar*, 'eke-days'), after which in the 3rd, 8th, 14th, 20th, and 25th years of the solar cycle an extra week (called *aukavika* or *sumarauki*) was added. The fourth month of summer began on *miðsumar*, the Sunday between 13 and 19 July; however, in the eighth year of the cycle it fell on the 20th, thus disrupting the relation of church festivals to the weeks of the year; this was known as *rímspillir*, 'count-spoiler', and the year was called *varnaðar ár*, 'warning-year'.

Although one might count up to 14 nights, or half a month, after *miðsumar*, from then on reckoning was by remaining weeks of summer: 'that Saturday when ten weeks of summer are left', or for short 'at ten weeks of summer'; similarly 'till that Monday at which on the preceding Saturday there were four weeks of summer left'; 'not till after that Sunday before which there were four weeks of summer left'. However, 'at eight weeks of summer' was often expressed as *at tvímánaði*, 'at two-month', reflecting a notion that four weeks made a month; for that reason the fifth month of summer was sometimes called Tvímánaðr.

Winter began on a Saturday, the first day of the first winter month; this and the next two days were called *vetrnætr*, 'winter-nights'; thereafter, in principle, days were reckoned on the same principle as in summer, forwards for the first three months, backwards for the last three, but such dates are rarely mentioned in records, since less business was done then. The last three months of winter, the *útmánaðir* or 'outmonths', were the only ones commonly called by their names, or indeed to have fixed names: þorri, Gói, and Einmánaðr. The first two names remain obscure; the last, 'one-month', reflects the concept noted for Tvímánaðr.

When in 1700, under Danish rule, New Style dating was adopted for the church calendar, the civil reckoning remained unchanged, so that *sumarmál* became the Thursday between 20 and 26 April; however, the backward count was ultimately abandoned and the weeks in each *misseri* counted continuously.

Despite the independence of civil and church calendars, churchmen had more success than among other Germanic peoples in imposing ecclesiastical names on the weekdays: although *dróttinsdagr* (Lord's day) and *annarr dagr* (second day) have lost out to *sunnudagur* and *mánudagur* (where *-r* is the ancient and *-ur* the modern spelling), the next four are still *triðjudagur* (third day), *miðvikudagur* (midweek day), *fimmtudagr* (fifth day), *föstudagr* (fastday). Saturday is *laugardagur* (washday; earlier called by the synonym *þváttdagr*).

As was the old Germanic custom, lapse of time was normally counted in nights and winters rather than days and years; and just as the two *misseri* of winter and summer were conceptually prior to the year, so the two *dægr* (in modern Icelandic *dægur*) of *nátt* and *dagr* were prior to the 24-hour day or *sólarhringr* ('sun-ring'). Time was normally measured in 'daymarks' (*dagsmörk*) at three-hour intervals: *rismál* (rising-mark) or *miðrmorgun* 6 a.m., *dagmál* (day-meal, the other sense of *mál*) 9 a.m., *hádegi* (highday) or *miðdegi* 12 noon, *nón* (Latin *nona*) 3 p.m., *miðaptan* (mid-evening) 6 p.m., *náttmál* (night-meal) 9 p.m., *miðnætti* 12 midnight, *ótta* (last part of the night) 3 a.m. At each daymark the sun was at one of eight points in the sky from east at *dagmál* to north-east at *ótta*, indicated for each farm by physical markers called *eyktarmörk*, either prominent natural features or piles of stones; many such markers still survive.

MESOAMERICAN

The many calendars used in pre-Columbian Central America, of which the first was reckoned from the summer solstice of 739 BC, were united in their fundamental principles, the determination of each day by its place in a uniform cycle of 260 days common to the entire region throughout its recorded history, and in a 365-day year whose beginning was subject to local determination. The 260-day cycle or 'day-count'—known as *tonalpohualli* in Nahuatl (the language spoken by the Aztecs), *tzol kin* in the language of the Yucatec Maya, and by other names elsewhere—was formed by two concurrent cycles respectively of 13 and 20 days, which modern writers call by their Spanish names of *trecena* and *veintena*. The *trecena* was a numerical cycle from 1 to 13 (in two calendars 2–14); the *veintena* was a sequence of sacred signs after which the days were named. These names varied from calendar to calendar; in the two calendars most familiar to modern readers they were:

Nahuatl	Yucatec
(1) Cipactli (alligator)	Imix (alligator)
(2) Ehecatl (wind)	Ik (wind)
(3) Calli (house)	Akbal (night)
(4) Cuetzpallin (iguana)	Kan (iguana)
(5) Coatl (serpent)	Chicchan (serpent)
(6) Miquitzli (death)	Cimi (death)
(7) Mazatl (deer)	Manik (deer)
(8) Tochtli (rabbit)	Lamat (rabbit)
(9) Atl (water)	Muluc (rain)
(10) Itzcuintli (dog)	Oc (foot)
(11) Ozomatli (monkey)	Chuen (monkey)
(12) Malinalli (grass)	Eb (tooth)
(13) Acatl (cane)	Ben (cane)
(14) Ocelotl (jaguar)	Ix (jaguar)
(15) Quahtli (eagle)	Men (eagle)
(16) Cozcaquautli (buzzard)	Cib (owl)
(17) Ollin (quake)	Caban (quake)
(18) Tecpatl (flint)	Etz'nab (flint)
(19) Quiahuitl (rain)	Cauac (storm)
(20) Xochitl (flower)	Ahau (lord)

Despite the differences not only in language but in sense, these two sequences are identical just as our January and February are identical with the Poles' *styczeń* and *luty* or the Czechs' *leden* and *únor*; the first day of the cycle was the same whether called 1 Cipactli or 1 Imix. It was followed by 2 Ehecatl and 2 Ik respectively, and these in turn by 3 Calli and 3 Akbal; 13 Acatl/Ben was followed by 1 Ocelotl/Ix, 7 Xochitl/Ahau by 8 Cipactli/Imix.

In addition, there was a year (Nahuatl *xihuitl*, Yucatec *haab*) of 365 days (*tonalli, kin*) comprising 18 months (*meztli, uinal*) each of 20 days and a highly unlucky sequence of five epagomenal days at the end. Days were numbered, in some calendars (e.g. the Aztec) from 1, in others (e.g. the most important Maya calendar) from 0; months were sometimes numbered, more often named. The Nahuatl-speakers' month names were not uniform; even those of the Aztec calendar vary in the sources, and they were often omitted in giving the date; the prevailing list is Izcalli, Cuahuitleua, Tlacaxipehualiztli, Tozoztontli, Hueitozoztli, Toxcatl, Etzalcualiztli, Tecuilhuitontli, Hueitecuilhuitl, Tlaxochimaco, Xocotlhuetzi, Ochpaniztli, Teotleco, Tepeilhuitl, Quecholli, Panquetzaliztli, Atemoztli, Tititl, the epagomenal days being known as Nemontemi. The Yucatec months, by contrast, are fixed and well known: Pop, Uo, Zip, Zotz', Tzac, Xul, Yaxkin, Mol, Ch'en, Yax, Zac, Ceh, Mac, Kankin, Muan, Pax, Kayab, Cumku, and the epagomenal Uayeb.

Unlike the *veintenas*, which were the same days under different names, the Nahuatl and Yucatec months do not coincide, for whereas the day-count was universal, the year was local; although New Year's Day always began the first month, and was immediately preceded by the epagomenal days of the previous year, the day so functioning in one calendar might not be New Year's Day, or even begin the month, in another. Thus the Aztec New Year of 1 Izcalli corresponded to 7 Yax in the Tikal calendar used from the first century AD by the Eastern Maya, whose own New Year, 0 Pop, was 14 Hueitecuilhuitl in the Aztec calendar. On the other hand, the equivalent in any one calendar of a date in another remained constant, since there was no leap year until the Spanish conquest; though new calendars were sometimes substituted for those previously in force either by adding 1 day or by *omitting* 20 days so as to speed up the return of the New Year to its astronomically appropriate place, during the lifetime of each calendar the year remained an *annus vagus* of 365 days. The equivalence of 1507 tropical years to 1508 *anni vagi* was discovered in 433 BC, one year before Meton of Athens made his observation of the summer solstice (see *Greek Calendar*).

In some calendars, including nearly all those used by the Maya, the year took its name from the place in the day-count of New Year's Day; in others, including the Aztec, it was named according to the 360th day (that is, the last before the epagomenal days, which one preferred to ignore). Thus, if 0 Pop fell on 6 Ik (as happened on 14 July 1549), the Tikal year was called 6 Ik; but when 1 Izcalli fell on 11 Atl (as on 17 Jan. 1550) the Aztec year was called 6 Tochtli, corresponding to the place in the day-count of 20 Tititl. Whichever method was adopted, the name-day occurred on one other occasion during the year (respectively the first day of the 14th month, e.g. in the Tikal calendar 0 Kankin, or the last day of the fifth, e.g. in the Aztec calendar 20 Hueitozoztli), and was greeted with celebrations as a lesser version of the New Year.

From year to year, the name-day advanced by 1 as to its numerical part, but by 5 as to the day-name in the *veintena*, called the year-bearer; thus 5 Calli was followed by 6 Tochtli, 6 Ik by 7 Manik. In consequence, while in any given calendar the year-numbers ran through the full *trecena*, only four bearers of the 20 were available; among the Aztecs these were Calli, Tochtli, Acatl, and Tecpatl, in the Tikal calendar Ik, Manik, Eb, and Caban. The possible combinations yield a cycle of 52 years (or 73 day-counts) called the 'calendar round' (Nahuatl *xiuhmolpilli*, Yucatec *hunab*); it generally began when the year-number was 1 and the bearer was that considered senior by the community in question (e.g. Caban in the Tikal calendar), though among the Aztecs it began on 2 Acatl. The beginning of the new calendar round was marked by solemn ceremonies, in which all fires were extinguished and New Fire ignited.

The Tikal calendar, however, was more complex. Beside the day, month, day-count, year, and calendar round, it recognized the *tun* of 18 months or 360 days, always ending on a day Ahau; 20 *tun* made a *katun*, of which 13 made a *may* and 20 a unit called *baktun* by modern scholars; 20 *may* or 13 *baktun* constituted a Long Count. This latter, instituted by the Olmec (probably in 355 BC), began on the completion of the last *tun* of its predecessor; within it the day was identified by the number of elapsed *baktun*, *katun*, *tun*, months, and days, by its place in the day-count, and finally by the date in the year. The

current Long Count began with the ending of its predecessor on the day called
0 0 0 0 0 4 Ahau 8 Cumku, corresponding to 5 September 3114 BC, and will end on
13 0 0 0 0 4 Ahau 3 Kankin = 21 December 2012, the winter solstice. (The starting-date
is sometimes given as '11 August 3113 BC Gregorian', that is by a hybrid reckoning in which
Gregorian rules of intercalation are applied retrospectively; even so '3113 BC' is an error
for –3113, i.e. 3114 BC stated in astronomical reckoning, which calls 1 BC 0 and 2 BC –1.
Furthermore, when the equivalences are stated in Julian days, 1 January 4713 BC is
counted as JD 1, so that the Long Count is reckoned from JD 584 283 and ends on JD
2 456 283.)

For certain purposes, the Tikal calendar recognized even longer units of time: the
pictun of 20 *baktun*, the *calabtun* of 20 *pictun*, the *kinchiltun* of 20 *calabtun*, and the *alautun* of
20 *kinchiltun* or 23 040 000 000 days. The current Long Count was reckoned from 1
(*kinchiltun*) 11 (*calabtun*) 19 (*pictun*) 0 0 0 0 0 4 Ahau 8 Cumku.

There is no room here to consider the many other calendars of Central America, nor
the impact on them of the Julian calendar and the Gregorian reform (see Edmonson).
From time to time revised native calendars are promulgated in popular Spanish-
language booklets to inculcate a national spirit.

❦

ZOROASTRIAN (INCLUDING PARSI)

The Iranian year, perhaps since Achaemenid times and certainly by the end of the
Sasanian empire, was an *annus vagus* of 365 days, comprising 12 months each of 30 days
and five epagomenal days, originally added after the last month, Spandarmad, but subsequently after the eighth month, Ābān, apparently after the freezing of a cyclical trans-
position intended to return the coincident feast to its rightful position in the seasons;
within each month the days were not numbered but named after the presiding spirit.
Chronology was either by regnal year or according to an era: under the Parthians from
22 January 248 BC, by the Sasanians from 26 September AD 226 (Nawrūz or New Year's
day in the first years of their respective empires), and by Zoroastrian survivors of the
Muslim conquest either from 11 June 652 (the 'Magian era'), the year after that in which
the last Sasanian monarch, Yāzdegird III, was killed, or from 16 June 632, the year of his
accession. The latter reckoning, which outlasted the other, is also used by their Parsi
co-religionists in India, who restored the epagomenal days to the end of the year; however, they fell a month behind the Zoroastrians of Iran, reportedly through adding an
extra month in the belief that such an embolism ought to take place once in 120 years.
A proposal in 1744 to adopt the Iranian calendar by subtracting a month at the end of
AY 1114, advancing the new year from 11/22 October to 11/22 September, provoked a
schism, in which the majority held to their own traditions; the disagreement was all the
more significant in that a Parsi is required, when praying, to include the day, month, and
year. In 1906 a third system, reckoning from the spring equinox, produced another
schism. The Government of India lists among the principal festivals in its *Rashtriya*

Panchang only the unreformed Parsi New Year, which in AY 1366–9 is 22 August AD 1996–9, in AY 1370–3 will be the 21st (AD 2000–3), in AY 1374–7 will be the 20th (AD 2004–7) and so backwards through the year; between AY 1466 and AY 1473 it will remain on 28 July AD 2096–2103.

CALENDARS AS WRITTEN
OBJECTS

Besides denoting the system of time-reckoning as an abstract pattern, or as lived experience, the term *calendar* may also be used for a written tabulation of the days and months throughout the year; in everyday modern usage a calendar is specific to a particular year, giving the feria of each day and such festivals and commemorations as its publisher sees fit to record, but it may also in ecclesiastical use be a permanent table of immoveable feasts, the feria being found through Sunday Letter or by other means (see below, *Liturgical Calendars*). In this sense the word was formerly spelt *kalendar*.

An *almanac* is a calendar for a particular year recording for each day not merely its feria but the rising, setting, and position of the sun and moon, often including much other matter as well, both astronomical and other. Although it is a species of calendar, it is rarely so called in English; but in German *Kalender* is the standard term, and similar forms are used in some other languages.

A synonym is *ephemeris* (plural *ephemerides*, which is the subject-heading under which almanacs are listed in the printed catalogue of the British Library), which now normally denotes an almanac providing advanced astronomical information (or if intended for sailors, also on tides). It is derived from the Greek *ephémeros*, which meant 'daily' as well as 'ephemeral' (*hēméra* = 'day'); *ephēmerídes* were daily records or logbooks, either financial or military, and most notably those kept during the campaigns of Alexander the Great. The term was translated into Latin as *diarium*.

A *diary*, in both British and US English, is a record of a person's daily thoughts and actions, or the book in which they are noted; an older term was *journal*, which although derived from the same root, and in French used for the daily newspaper, in modern English normally denotes a weekly, monthly, or even annual magazine. Diaries or journals were originally kept on blank pages bound into one's almanac, allowing each entry to be as short or as long as one wished; the custom became widespread in the seventeenth century. (The Protestant journal of the seventeenth century, with its daily spiritual accounting, stands in contrast to the more matter-of-fact journals of Roman Catholics, who took such concerns to their confessors.) Nowadays the book is already bound, the days of the year being printed in sequence with space left for the user to fill. In Britain the word is also used of such a book when intended to record forthcoming appointments and dates that must not be forgotten; in the United States this is an *engagement calendar* or simply *calendar*.

ALMANACS

The word 'almanac' was formerly spelt with a final *k*, which is still usual in the titles of British, though not of US, almanacs. It first appears, as Latin *Almanach*, in Roger Bacon's writings from the later thirteenth century; both form and sphere of reference would suggest an Arabic loanword mediated through Spanish, but no such Arabic word exists apart from the unsupported and presumably back-formed *manākh* found in Pedro de Alcalá's dictionary of 1505. It has been speculatively connected with the *almenichiaká* in which, according to Porphyry (late 3rd c.) as reported by Eusebius (early 4th c.), the astrological lords of the ascendant are named; the word is not Greek, and perhaps belongs no more to any real language than 'hocus-pocus'. However, it is not clear how the term should have reached the medieval West, bypassing the Arab world; nor does it denote the astronomical tables to which the word *almanach* was first applied.

From the *almanach*, thus defined, the data for any given year could be calculated; tables of such calculations were prepared, either for so many years ahead, as by Regiomontanus (see **Modern Calendar*), or, combined with the church calendar, for the coming year alone. It is this latter that in the sixteenth century became the modern printed almanac, giving solar, lunar, and sometimes planetary data for each day along with feasts, fasts, and public commemorations. These were augmented with useful information of various kinds: in England we may expect the dates of law terms, high water at major ports, and eclipses in the coming year, the reigns of kings and queens (essential not only for patriotism but for interpreting dates by regnal year), and a list of historical events often going back to the Creation. There may be other useful facts such as the year's fairs, the chief town and other characteristics of the English shires, the distances between major cities, descriptions of foreign kingdoms, tables of annuities, interest, and wages, model legal and financial documents such as wills and bills, together with practical advice, especially for farmers ('Rules Concerning Husbandry'), and moral advice of a traditional and commonsensical nature. Many attempted to predict the weather; in parts of Norway this function was so important that the almanac was popularly known as *verboki*, 'the weather-book'. They also carried advertisements, especially for quack medicines; some have been suspected of being little more than vehicles for such matter.

Almanacs were generally pocket-size and printed on poor paper, in common with much ephemeral literature. Printing was not all it might be: one may easily find wrong or missing Sunday Letters, even (to the glee of rivals) errors in the solar and lunar times. A study of German almanacs (Pfaff, 20) finds five different saints on one day, and the same saint on eight different days, though closer inspection reveals that these are three different saints of the same name. Sometimes almanac-makers forgot to shift St Matthias in leap year from 24 to 25 February; the Oxford Almanack, which was first printed in 1674, under the auspices of John Fell, bishop of Oxford, having for 1676 correctly given the 25th, gave the 24th for 1680 and again for 1684. Conversely, when the Church of England had determined that the feast should remain on the 24th, we several times find the 25th, and once the 23rd. The almanac-maker Henry Season nearly gave up his profession in despair at the misprints gleefully pointed out by his competitors:

Errors, I confess, Humanity will always be liable to, no Writer or Printer can possibly avoid them; but Errors deliberate, or designed Blunders, are too provoking to be winked at. . . . in a lying Advertisement two Years past . . . [my Adversary] burlesqued on the Word *Onion*, which was *Orion* in my Copy; the next Year on *Damabitur*, as many may remember. There was the same Occasion on the front Page last Year.

He that would set up for a Critick, ought to have a good stock of Learning and Sense, which my Detracters are but meanly supplied with, therefore I may predict their Trade will not last long. I laid them a small Bait last Year, to set the Covy of them a nibbling and snarling at me and my SPECULUM, for leaving Bishop *Blaze's Day* out, *Good Friday, Holy Thursday, Dog Days*, and *St. Thomas's Day*, and perhaps some other Festivals not printed. I appeal to any Man of Genius and Honesty, a little to reflect how silly and ill-natured it was to cavil, or begin a Sneer, at finding such a common Fault, as a few Days not printed; or would any Man, that has but a slender Share of Sense, accuse me of being ignorant of not knowing these Days, or that I would wilfully omit them? There were some other Errors that might have employed my would-be Criticks, as the inserting old *Christmas*, old *Candlemas*, and old *May Day*, the other Days repeated, which were all a Day wrong; but this Fault was to be found in other Almanacks . . .   *Speculum Anni . . . 1754*

The most popular, and notorious, feature of almanacs, however, was the astrological lore that most (though not all) imparted, both in general, as the government of particular regions of the body, from head to foot, by individual signs of the zodiac, and in particular, namely their predictions, especially political, for the coming year. This was a risky enterprise, should the almanac-maker be too specific, and not only because of the obvious ridicule if the predictions did not come to pass; it was a long-standing rule that one must never predict a ruler's death, only danger.

Some almanac-makers avoided political statements beyond the conventional expressions of loyalty; others took sides, especially in time of conflict. William Lilly ('Merlinus Anglicus'), the most eminent astrologer of the seventeenth century, supported Parliament in the Civil War; this brought him into conflict with a rival almanac-maker, the committed royalist George Wharton (alias Naworth, easily mocked as 'No-worth'). In 1644 he hinted at the King's death and the overthrow of monarchy; in 1648 he was summoned to boost Army morale with his prophecies, though he is also said to have supplied Parliament with news from France and the King with a saw to break prison. His predictions for January 1649 spoke of 'Justice', the slogan of the army at Charles's show trial; despite his expression of surprise, he seems to have had some involvement with the preparations. Having rashly asserted that monarchy would not be restored, in 1652 he more accurately foretold the speedy overthrow of the Rump Parliament, but escaped with a brief imprisonment by doctoring the texts he submitted for examination; having learnt discretion from this misfortune, he failed in his almanac for 1660 to predict the Restoration. His adopted son and successor, Henry Coley, learnt a different lesson when he predicted of November 1688:

This Month is ushered in with a Malevolent *Conjunction* of *Saturn* and *Mars* in the very beginning of the sign *Scorpio*, and it affords us the fewest *mutual Aspects* of the *Planets* of any *Month* in the year: thence we may expect little or nothing in Action of any kind . . .

Conjunction or no, in November 1688 William of Orange landed in England and the Glorious Revolution began. Having failed to foresee any of the year's turmoil, Coley changed the motto on the title-page of the 1689 edition from *Agunt non cogunt. Quod supra nos nihil ad nos* ('They [the stars] act, but do not compel. What is above us is nothing to us') to *Alius alio plura invenire potest, nemo omnia* ('One man may discover more things than another, but no one everything'). About the same time, in his *Nuncius Syderius: or the Starry Messenger* for 1689—published in the previous November—he wrote: 'I find the Month of *December*, 1688, moderately calm, and in all probability may produce very healing Actions in General Affairs.' This was the month in which James II fled from England— twice, for the first time he was captured and brought back, much to William's annoyance. For February 1689 'Merlinus Anglicus Junior' predicted:

THIS Month is accompanied with a Crowd of *Aspects* of the *Planets*, and all of a *benevolent* Nature, which, in *Starry Dialect*, promises much Quietness and Satisfaction among the People. Now all matters tend to Unity, or great Endeavours us'd to that purpose.

The escape-clause at the end was but prudent: the Convention Parliament that offered William and Mary the joint crown certainly used great endeavours to unite Whigs and Tories, but by no means all the nation was quiet and satisfied. Once more Coley's stars had failed him, for his harmless wish under May, 'Heavens bless the English Affairs, and direct the great Councils of his Majesty!', ought to have read 'their Majesties'.

Nevertheless, almanacs did not cease to flourish: many continued to be published long after their nominal authors' death, and new ones came on the scene. Some were directed to the public at large, others to particular interests, such as chapmen and travellers. In the reign of Queen Anne (whose portrait remained on the title-page even after her death), John Tipper published *The Ladies Diary: Or, The Womens Almanack*, which instructed the 'Fair-Sex' in astronomy and the 'Nature of Love', with riddles, mathematical puzzles, and a serial 'Story of the Vnfortunate Lover'; he also celebrated the Union of England and Scotland by founding *Great Britains Diary: Or, the Union-Almanack*.

The almanac form was ripe for parody; from 1664 *Poor Robin*, while providing the serious data that readers demanded, included mock saints' days, mock prophecies, and mock chronologies. The genuine saints are accompanied, on different days in different years, by such famous or infamous figures of fact and fiction as Edward IV's mistress Jane Shore, Ovid and Corinna (the lady-love of his *Amores*), the Fair Rosamund, Charles I's enemy Pym, Henry VII's tax-gatherers Empson and Dudley, the tyrannical duke of Alva who had provoked the Dutch Revolt, the Knave of Spades, Don Quixote, Mother Shipton the bawd, Robin Hood, Jack Falstaff, Cesare Borgia, Tarquin, Sejanus, and Moll Cutpurse. As to predictions, in 1689 we learn that:

Sol is in a Biquintile with *Mars* [i.e. the Sun and Mars are 144° apart], therefore if there be no Deceit among Tradesmen, no Bribery among Officers, no Banquerant out of *Ludgate* [i.e. all bankrupts are in prison], nor Whore out of *Bridewel*; Then will there be no Wit among Knaves, no Want among Scholars, nor no Unquietness in Marriage.

(A bankrupt, at the time, was not an unfortunate or incompetent trader, but a fraudulent or reckless one, and hence a criminal.) In the same issue, the list of years elapsed under 'A brief Chronology of Other things' includes the entry:

Since *R.P.* proffer'd his Neighbours Wife a bushel of Wheat for a close Embrace, or Familiar Hug; which her Husband blamed her for refusing, since it would have made a great many Dumplings and Hasty Puddings   1 [year]

The name inspired Benjamin Franklin's *Poor Richard*.

Naturally each almanac-maker would have the reader shun his rivals; many took the opportunity to abuse each other in their pages for errors in their figures or their predictions. A zealous combatant, at the turn of the eighteenth century, was John Partridge, the author of *Merlinus Liberatus*, in which the author's merits were extolled, and his Whig sympathies proclaimed, with unremitting clarity, but in the matter of prediction 'the phraseology of equivocation was carried to a pitch of rare perfection' (*DNB*). His almanac for 1708, after listing the planetary aspects of January, continues:

These are strange kind of Rays to make Peace upon, which is the Thing mightily press'd, and as much expected at this time. Consider the Trine of the *Sun* and *Jupiter* at this New Moon. There are great Councils in most Kingdoms, and weighty Matters of State under their Considerations, especially in *Germany, Hungary, Spain*, and other Countries nearer Home.

Is peace going to be made, or not? This very almanac, however, was accompanied into the bookshelves by *Predictions for the Year 1708. Wherein the Month and Day of the Month are set down, the Persons named, and the great Actions and Events of next Year particularly related, as they will come to pass. Written to prevent the People of England from being further impos'd on by vulgar Almanack-makers. By* ISAAC BICKERSTAFF *Esq.* Having demolished the loosely worded prophecies and self-protecting ambiguities in which almanac-makers dealt, the author offered his own highly specific prognostications:

My first Prediction is but a Trifle, yet I will mention it, to shew how ignorant these Sottish Pretenders to Astrology are in their own Concerns: It relates to *Partridge* the Almanack-maker; I have consulted the Star of his Nativity by my own Rules, and find he will infallibly dye upon the 29th of *March* next, about Eleven at night, of a raging Feaver; therefore I advise him to consider of it, and settle his Affairs in time.

This Isaac Bickerstaff was none other than Jonathan Swift, who had taken offence at Partridge's attacks on High Churchmen such as himself; Swift's own character apart, it must be remembered that the reign of Queen Anne was a time of exceptionally bitter partisan feeling in Church and State. He had appropriated the name of Bickerstaff from a locksmith; in turn it was adopted by his friend Richard Steele in his new-founded journal the *Tatler*.

Partridge hit back in an *Answer to Esquire Bickerstaff's Strange and Wonderful Predictions*, mocking him as a charlatan: 'for 'tis plain, he knows no more of the Art of *Astrology* (in Comparison) than he knows when his Wife will make him a Cuckold.' Since Swift was not married, the shot flew wide; so far was Partridge from identifying his tormentor that in a letter to a false friend who published it he blamed someone else.

On 30 March 1708 there appeared a pamphlet entitled *The Accomplishment of the First of Mr. Bickerstaff's Predictions. Being an Account of the Death of Mr. Partrige, the Almanack-maker, upon the 29th Inst.* Before expiring, so it was reported, Partridge had confessed that astrology was a fraud and he himself an impostor even in medicine; but 'when looking upon my

Watch, I found it to be above five Minutes after Seven: By which it is clear, that Mr. *Bickerstaff* was mistaken almost four Hours in his Calculation.' This pamphlet, which of course was also Swift's, sold in great quantities, and was followed by its author with a ballad upon Partridge's death. The Stationers' Company struck the astrologer off its rolls, and sought an injunction against further publications of his purported almanac; the Portuguese Inquisition ordered Bickerstaff's predictions to be burnt, as obviously supplied him by the Devil.

Partridge was in fact still alive, and used the pages of *Merlinus Liberatus* for 1709 'to inform the World that I am Living, contrary to that base Paper said to be done by one *Bickerstaff*'; his predictions were as evasive as ever, in particular one for autumn: 'There is some great Matter in Expectation, and so it is like to be for ought I see without any Effect.' But a fresh blow was struck by *A Vindication of Isaac Bickerstaff Esq; against What is Objected to Him by Mr. Partridge, in his Almanack for the present Year 1709,* a systematic demonstration that Partridge must be dead as the anonymous report had stated; not even the evidence that Partridge was still writing almanacs proved anything, since '*Gadsbury, Poor Robin, Dove, Wing,* and several others, do yearly publish their Almanacks, although several of them have been dead since before the *Revolution.*' Bickerstaff, evidently a man of the most sensitive feelings, not only complained of Partridge's discourtesy in personally insulting him for mere disagreement, but defended himself against the hurtful statement that he had been nearly four hours out in the time (it was half an hour at the most).

Poor Partridge was now the target of ridicule and abuse: mock-Tudor verses purported to translate a prophecy of the original Merlin's against him, and a new Bickerstaff, this time not Swift, taking the form of a regular almanac for 1710, includes a letter from 'Jeremy Wagstaff' dated 3 September 1709, accusing *Merlinus Liberatus* of giving that day as new moon: '*Now I having been abroad last Night, and seeing a pretty large broad-faced Moon, no more like a New Moon than an* Owl *is like a* Partridge, *do conclude, that* No Man alive *cou'd assert a New Moon on* Sept. 3.' This is a puzzle; Merlin had given that date, not for 1709, but for 1708, when it had been correct.

Partridge was crushed; not for four years did he venture to publish another Merlin. At last, however, he discovered his enemy's name: allusions to Swift are unmistakable in the letter 'To *Isaac Bickerstaffe,* Esq;' prefaced to *Merlinus Redivivus* for 1714, beginning 'Sir, There seems to be a kind of fantastical Propriety, in a *Dead Man's* Addressing himself to a Person not in Being.' In 1715 he died in earnest; but (as Bickerstaff might have predicted) that did not curtail the appearance of his almanac, with an assurance 'To the Protestant Reader' that 'it is Printed from a Transcribed Copy, written with the Doctor's own Hand'. (Roman Catholics were unlikely to read an almanac that had regularly vilified them, or they might have asked who had been guiding that hand.)

Another almanac of the period, *Vox Stellarum,* first published in 1697 over the name of a possibly fictitious Dr Francis Moore, still appears annually as *Old Moore's Almanack;* it contains predictions of world events and horse-races, in which connoisseurs will not fail to observe the frequency of 'may' and 'could'. Times of sunrise and sunset, high water, and the moon's rising, setting, and quarters are given; but the other useful information (what Merlinus Anglicus Junior called 'variety of other Furniture, proper for such a Work') is omitted, as commonly sought elsewhere. By contrast, such publications as *Whitaker's Almanack* in Britain and the *World Almanac and Book of Facts* in the United States pay no heed to astrology, but are major works of reference for public facts of many kinds. The *Old Farmer's Almanac*, first published in 1793, still relates the moon's position for every day not to a sign of the zodiac, but to the part of the body that sign governs, an important consideration in the days of bloodletting and still to certain readers; however, it also provides feature articles, advice, advertisements, and weather forecasts (called 'indications' during the Second World War to evade censorship).

Long-standing almanacs have their devoted followers, who are quick to take offence at changes to content or format. This reinforces the natural conservatism of publications that deal in recurrence, a conservatism that in Germany, a great almanac country, attracted the hostility of Nazi and then of Communist authorities, who saw in their failure to move with the respective times a sign of political recalcitrance. The Oxford Almanack, a single sheet whose top half is occupied by a picture (formerly an engraving), has over the centuries changed its ferial indications from Sunday Letters to abbreviated names of days, converted the years of kings and queens who reigned before 1752 from the Lady Day style to the modern and dropped them altogether, and suppressed the table of high tides; but the calendar, after a brief flirtation with ASB in 1993 and 1994, remains based on the Book of Common Prayer.

LITURGICAL CALENDARS

The liturgical calendar regularly prefixed to medieval breviaries, missals, and books of hours sets out at the head of each month the number of days it contains, and the number of days in the corresponding lunar month. According to computistic principle, each lunar month took the name of the solar month in which it ended: the odd months had 30 days and the even 29 (lunar February having 30 days in leap year). This principle was consistently applied in MS Auct. D. 2. 6, from which Pl. 6 is taken. However, another principle applied by some copyists was to assign 30 days to all those months that in solar reckoning had 31 days and 29 to the rest; thus in MS Douce 135 (Pl. 10) lunar October is shown with 30 days instead of the correct 29. Even when followed consistently, as in that book or in the calendar prefixed to the English Bible of 1611, this makes the lunar year a day too long (one month needs to be solar minus 2, as March was in the old Celtic computus); but so little were many scribes' minds engaged in this part of the business that they switch from one principle to the other and back again. Even the solar months may be inaccurately described. A book of hours at Tours (Bibliothèque Municipale 218) gives 31 days to solar June and 29 to lunar September; in the famous and beautiful Hours of Mary of Burgundy, solar September is said to have 31 days, October 30, and 'November habet dies' with no number at all.

The heading (Pl. 6) or the foot (Pl. 3) may also include the length of night and day in (equinoctial) hours; 16 and 8 in January, falling and rising 2 hours a month to 12 and

12 in March, 6 and 18 in June, 18 and 6 in December; for this the *Très Riches Heures* of the duc de Berry substitutes a column giving the hours and minutes of daylight for each day. There may also be, at either the head or the foot, verses setting out the Egyptian days of the month, or the zodiacal sign in which it begins or ends. Pl. 6 shows a page beginning:

> Tredecimus [*sic*] mactat iulij, decimus labefactat
> Solsticio ardentis cancri fere iulius astrum.
>
> The thirteenth of July slaughters, the tenth [from the end] topples.
> July is largely the constellation of Cancer, burning with the solstice.

In the second verse (from a poem composed by Ausonius in the late fourth century AD) the sign is that in which the month begins; other calendars give that which the sun enters during its course, which in the case of July is Leo. Illustrations characteristically represent the activity of the month, such as reaping in July or the grape-harvest in October.

The first column in the table indicates the new moons; Pl. 10 shows the Golden Numbers XVI, V, XIII, and II against the first four days of October, meaning that in the 16th year of the decemnovenal cycle new moon will be on 1 October, in the fifth year on 2 October, and so on; similarly Pl. 6 shows XIX against the 1st and VIII against the second. Books differ in the treatment of the *saltus*, which Douce 135 places in November and Auct. D. 2. 6 in July. These dates had long since lost all pretensions to accuracy; new calculations were made, and sometimes inserted in addition to the old (as in the 'Nombre dor nouel' column of the *Très Riches Heures*) or instead (as in the 1611 Bible), although they were of no use for finding Easter.

Next, especially in the later Middle Ages, we may find the cycle of characteristic letters from A to G used for finding Sunday (see *Sunday Letters*); see Pl. 10. Pl. 6 shows instead a column of civil days stated in the Roman manner, by Kalends, Nones, and Ides, which is often absent in late medieval books of hours; when it is present, it immediately precedes the saints' days. Its absence facilitates errors, as when Mary of Burgundy's hours put the vigil of St Matthew on 19 September instead of the 20th and all subsequent feasts one day early down to St Jerome, leaving the 30th unmarked except for the letter G. On the other hand, the civil-day column might itself go astray, as when the breviary of Meyer van den Bergh in Antwerp miscounts the number of days before the Kalends of August as 18 instead of 17, so that the 31st is still *iii kl* instead of *ii*.

The days are then listed according to the saint's day or other feast, fast, or vigil of each, sometimes with appended remarks concerning the equinox, the solstice, the sun's entry into a new sign, the beginning of a new season, the Paschal limits, the *saltus lunae*, or the *bissextus*; thus English calendars record that in leap year St Matthias is on the fourth day (inclusive) from St Peter's Chair. Pl. 3 bids the user remember that in leap year the moon of February is 30 days, without affecting the normal 30 of the March moon, so as to keep the Paschal moon on course.

These calendars are simplified forms of the calendars found in computistic manuscripts such as those illustrated in Pls. 11 and 12. In Pl. 11 the first column gives in Greek numerals the lune of every day in the first year of the decemnovenal cycle, the second the Golden Numbers against their respective new moons. The third, fourth, sixth, seventh, and eighth all indicate, when read in conjunction with a table, the lune of the day throughout the decemnovenal cycle; thus in the eighth column all days are marked with a sequence of 59 letters (A to V, A· to V·, ·A to ·T) correlated with a table illustrated in Pl. 12, indicating that in GN 1 the new moon falls on days marked C· and ·M. The fifth column indicates the position of the moon within the zodiac, according to a table set forth in chapter 19 of Bede's *De temporum ratione*; the ninth gives the Sunday Letters, and the tenth the civil date.

SYMBOLIC CALENDARS

In the Middle Ages and even afterwards, the church calendar was not always recorded in Latin or vernacular manuscripts or printed books: it might be carved on wood or some other suitable substance, with symbols instead of words. In England such calendars are called 'clog calendars' or simply 'clogs', i.e. lumps of wood; although some were made of brass, most were wooden, box being favoured, though there were specimens in oak and fir. Some were large enough to hang from the mantelpiece for all the family to use, others fitted into pockets. Being a northern phenomenon, they appear to be derived from the Scandinavian 'runic calendars', which were the means by which the Nordic farmer was apprised of the church calendar and reminded of his tasks.

The name 'runic calendar' is most appropriate for those calendars in which both Golden Number and (where recorded) Sunday Letter were represented by runes (see Pl. 13), which were for long the script of the people, Latin letters being for the learned. Such true runic calendars (like runic monuments in general) are especially characteristic of Sweden, where they are called *runstavar* (runestaves), and her former possessions Finland and Estonia. Other Nordic countries (except Iceland) also used carved calendars, but often dispensed with runes for the Golden Numbers, or altogether; hence a better generic term than 'runic calendar' would be 'primestaff', from Norwegian *primstav*, where 'prime' means 'Golden Number' (as in the BCP: 'the Golden Number, or Prime') or 'rimestock' from Danish *rimstok*, where 'rime' is the old Germanic word for 'count'. The term 'symbolic calendar' is used here in an even broader sense to include clogs.

'Runic' calendars are first discussed in print by Worm (pp. 88–106), who illustrates several types and proposes a modernized symbolic calendar, his *Fasti restituti*; soon afterwards a Norwegian primestaff was illustrated by Christen Jenssøn in *Den Norske Glossarium eller Glosebog* of 1646, and an English clog by Robert Plot in *The Natural History of Stafford-shire* (see Pl. 14), preserved in the Ashmolean Museum in Oxford together with a larger clog of almost identical design dated 1644 and two small clogs that resemble each other but not those. Calendars of similar type are also found in manuscripts, often brightly coloured.

The basic principle of symbolic calendars is that every day is marked either by its Sunday Letter (see below) or else by a notch, which is made larger, or otherwise distin-

guished, for the days corresponding to Sunday Letter A and sometimes for the first of
the month. The principal feasts of the church year as locally observed are indicated on
the appropriate day with an emblem of the saint or event to be commemorated, or the
manner in which the day is celebrated, or the task to be performed: thus Plot's clog
marks St Clement (23 Nov.) with a pot, 'from the ancient custom of going about that
night, to begg drink to make merry with', and St Barnabas (11 June) with a rake, denoting the hay harvest. Every A day has a broader notch, the 1st of each month a curling one; all feasts of the Virgin are symbolized with a heart (cf. Luke 2: 19); the small
clogs in the Ashmolean use a vertical, and many of Worm's calendars a crown.

Even within particular cultures, there is a wide variety in the number and choice of
feasts to be illustrated: moreover, since the calendars were carved by layfolk with only
rudimentary knowledge of matters ecclesiastical, many symbols were distorted or reinterpreted (see *12 Mar., *25 July), or even defy recognition. Some saints defeated the
pictorial imagination, being represented by crosses or verticals; Plot's clog favours initial letters, though it sometimes portrays objects with similar-sounding names, a mallet
for St Matthias (24 Feb.), a lute for St Luke (18 Oct.).

In order to accommodate the year to the writing surface it was necessary to divide it
into smaller units, normally not months but halves or quarters. Sweden favoured half-
years beginning on 1 January and 1 July, but Norway remained faithful to the ancient
summer and winter marks on 14 April and 14 October. Nevertheless, these were not the
only patterns: the runic calendar illustrated in Pl. 13 sets out the year in book form on
11 boxwood leaves, not divided into either months or seasons, but ending on 1 July;
although the first of the leaves is lost, it must have run from the Visitation on 2 July to
St Margaret on the 20th. Similarly, one of Worm's calendars is divided into half-
years beginning on 2 January and 2 July; each face is divided into two bands, the lower
bands beginning on 3 April and 2 October, so that the quarters begin with Sunday
Letter B and end with A (written with runes *ur* and *Frey* respectively). Plot's clog is divided into quarters, beginning on 1 January, 1 April, 1 July, and 1 October; the smaller
Ashmolean clogs begin each quarter on an A day (1 Jan., 26 Mar., 25 June, 1 Oct.).
Quarters are also used besides half-years in Denmark and south-western Sweden (which
belonged to Denmark till 1667), but in those countries the favoured beginning was
Christmas.

The new moons are recorded according to their Golden Number, either, as in Pl. 13,
by an expanded runic alphabet, or in pentadic symbols based on roman numerals, 1–4
being represented as so many dots or cross-strokes on a downward prolongation of the
notch, 5 and 10 by special symbols combined with each other for 15 and with the others
as need be; 19 sometimes by counterparts of XVIIII or XIX, sometimes as 20. Worm
finds a whalebone calendar in which arabic numerals were used, as also on some Norwegian primestaves.

Some calendars also recorded the Sunday Letters; especially on Swedish *runstavar* the
first seven letters of the runic alphabet, representing the sounds *f u th o r k h*, were substituted for the day-notches, as in our Pl. 13; an alternative sequence of runes and quasi-
runes is found in some calendars, notably a whalebone primestaff illustrated by Worm.

The solar cycle may be set out in a circular diagram, sometimes accompanied by the Golden Number cycle similarly displayed.

We conclude with a brief note on the ancient Egyptian 'diagonal calendars'. About the time of the Middle Kingdom, coffin lids may display a diagonal band of 36 columns each portraying 12 of 36 constellations corresponding to ten-day portions of the year; by means of this layout, one could determine the hour of the night from the constellation that had last risen. These calendars, or rather star clocks, make provision for the epagomenal days, but not for the deficit of the Egyptian civil year, which caused the constellations to be reallocated; by the New Kingdom they had degenerated into pure decoration, being replaced by more elaborate (but no more accurate) representations of the heavens. However, the principle of 36-fold division was taken over into classical astrology: the ecliptic was divided into 10° arcs known in Greek as *dekanoí* and Latin as *decani*, a word apparently coined in the camp to mean the officer in charge of ten men, which by way of French *doyen* has yielded the English *dean*.

CHRONOLOGY

The oldest method of identifying years, found in early records from Egypt and Mesopotamia and still surviving in rural communities, is by some memorable event that took place in them: a military conquest, the foundation of a temple, or a great frost; we too use it when we call AD 69 (during which power at Rome was held successively by Galba, Otho, Vitellius, and Vespasian) 'the Year of the Four Emperors'; in England 1665 is the Plague Year and 1666 the Year of the Great Fire; in Ireland 1798 is *bliain na bhFrancach*, 'the Year of the French', from the French troops who landed in support of the Irish Rebellion. Cultural advance, however, leads to the adoption of more systematic systems, of which there are four main types: the eponymous year, the regnal year, the era, and the cycle.

EPONYMOUS YEARS

The Greek word *epōnumos* means either 'giving one's name (to something)' or 'named after (someone)': the eponymous year is identified by the name of the person (or persons) holding a particular office with an annual term. This method is especially characteristic of the ancient city-state; the most familiar examples are Athenian dates *ep' archontos tou deina*, 'when So-and-so was archon' (in fact one of a board of nine) and Roman dates *illo et illo consulibus*, 'So-and-so and So-and-so being consuls'. The magistrates might have as much power as Spartan ephors or as little as Athenian archons; the mighty consuls of the Roman Republic declined into mere dignitaries under the Empire, but the year continued to bear their names and not the emperor's, unless he chose to take the consulate himself. Outside the Graeco-Roman world, whereas Babylon dated by regnal years, at Ashur, subject to the same king, years were designated according to the city *limmu*, who took office on 13 Aiaru (the April–May lunation). The disadvantage of this system is that the date means nothing to foreigners, and even natives need to have a list of magistrates; the embarrassment that eponymous dating caused is illustrated by Thucydides (see *Greek Calendar*). Complete lists of Roman consuls exist; but the church writers who attempt to date the life of Christ, or compile their Easter tables, by consuls are led by corrupt sources into crass errors.

REGNAL YEARS

When the term of office is longer than a year, dates may be given according to length of service. This method was used in the ancient Greek city of Argos, with respect to the priestess of Hera. It is particularly favoured by kings and other rulers to designate the year according to their length of reign. Naturally the dates do not always correspond to *de facto* power: for most of his reign Edward III added his purported year as king of France, and Charles II counted his regnal years from his father's execution not only in respect of Scotland, where he had been proclaimed king six days after that event, but of England, where his writ did not run till 1660.

In order to make sense of regnal dates, royal canons or king-lists may be drawn up, stating the length of each king's reign; in pre-modern times these are as liable to corruption as lists of magistrates, and are in any case of chronographic rather than historical inspiration: whereas historians need to know in what year of our reckoning King X actually began to reign, chronologists and astronomers need to know in what year of our reckoning year Y of King X was counted as beginning by those who compiled the records. Hence in cultures where regnal years begin with the new year, the first and last months of a reign must be somehow fitted into the scheme, and joint rule (e.g. by the king and the son he has chosen to succeed him) is likely to cause confusion.

The Venerable Bede ingeniously, though wrongly, suggests that the cycle of indictions (see below, *Cycles: Indictions*) was invented for the benefit of historians faced with conflicting reign-dates; in fact Roman emperors had not dated by regnal years until 537. Nevertheless, thereafter they did so regularly, and from 566 they added their postconsulates (see *Roman Calendar*). This system was employed by the papal chancery until the late eighth century, the last known example being a letter of Pope Hadrian II on 21 February 772, the tenth before the Kalends of March 53 Constantine [V], 33rd postconsulate, 21 Leo [IV], 10th indiction. Of the three imperial dates only the last is compatible with the indiction, for Constantine V became co-emperor on 31 March 720, sole emperor on 18 June 741, and consul on 1 January 742; he made his son Leo IV co-emperor on 23 September 751. However, on 1 December 781, the same pope dates by the tenth year of his own pontificate, the 5th indiction; since he had been consecrated on 9 February 771 he has miscounted his regnal year, but the 'Greek' 5th indiction ran from 1 September 781 to 31 August 782.

Regnal dating did not immediately become the papal norm. In 798 Pope Leo III dated 'of the lord Karl, most exalted king of the Franks and Lombards, from his conquest of Italy, the 25th year'; Charlemagne had defeated the Lombard King Desiderius in 774. After the coronation of 25 December 800, Leo began to date by Charlemagne's years as emperor, adding a postconsulate with the same number as the regnal year; neither Charlemagne nor his successors ever used postconsulates, but the papal chancery mechanically perpetuated a system it did not understand. The last instance is a letter of Sergius III of 23 February 904, dated to 4 Louis III (crowned emperor in 901) 'and the fourth year after his consulate', in the 7th indiction.

Whereas Byzantine emperors continued to reckon their regnal years from the anniversary of their accession, as did Frankish kings before Charlemagne, and German kings not yet crowned emperor, kings of France and Holy Roman Emperors generally dated from their coronation; the emperor Charles IV, crowned on Easter Day, 5 April 1355, thereafter treated Easter as the beginning of a new regnal year. Similarly, popes generally date by regnal years counted from consecration, though the total length of a pope's reign is reckoned from his election. (For the regnal years of popes since 999, see App. B.) In all such matters, however, the vagaries of clerks must be attended to, and even of their superiors; under Robert II of France (996–1031) the chancery, amidst other confusions, used three different starting-points for the regnal year.

❦ ENGLAND, GREAT BRITAIN, UNITED KINGDOM In England, despite the early use of the Christian era, the regnal year, already attested since the eighth century, became the regular mode of civil dating for official documents from 1189, and for private charters from the reign of Edward I. Down to the time of Henry III it was counted from the date of coronation, which in the case of John, who was crowned on Ascension Day, 27 May 1199, was taken to be Ascension Day and not the calendar date. But, when Henry III died on 16 November 1272, his heir, Edward I, was in the Holy Land; the new king's peace was proclaimed on the 20th, from which day his regnal years were counted. Subsequent reigns have been reckoned from accession, except that Henry VII, having come to power by defeating Richard III at the battle of Bosworth on 22 August 1485, dated his first year from the 21st, thus making Richard, not himself, the rebel. The practice was continued after the Union of England and Scotland in 1707 and that with Ireland in 1801; neither Queen Anne's nor George III's regnal year was thereby affected. However, between the reigns of Henry I (1100–35) and William IV (1830–7), the clerks of the Exchequer, in dating the Great Roll of the Pipe (though not other documents), adjusted the monarch's regnal year to the end of their fixed account year on Michaelmas, 29 September; in some reigns the first year was curtailed, in others prolonged until the second Michaelmas.

Dating by regnal year remained the official rule for Acts of Parliament down to 1962. Thus the Statute of the Supreme Head 1534, which ousted the papal supremacy in England and Ireland, is correctly 25 Hen. VIII c. 3, the third chapter of the statute (all the Acts of a single session being originally counted as a single statute) of the Parliamentary session of the 25th year of Henry VIII (22 Apr. 1533–21 Apr. 1534), and British Summer Time was introduced in 1925 by 15 and 16 Geo. V c. 64, since the session spanned the anniversary of George V's accession on 6 May. Until 1837, Parliament was automatically dissolved by the demise of the Crown; only in the twentieth century can one find such sessions as 16 Geo. VI and 1 Eliz. II (1951/2). Acts passed since 1963 are known by short title and calendar year of their enactment, as earlier Acts are unofficially. (For regnal years of English and British sovereigns, see App. A.)

❦ REGNAL YEAR AND NEW YEAR Whether counted from accession or coronation, the Western regnal year runs till the day preceding the anniversary, without regard to either New Year's Day or the date at which the year AD is changed; the Pipe Roll practice noted above is exceptional. In other cultures, however, it is quite normal for the regnal year to change with the civil new year, which leaves chanceries with the problem of the period between accession and new year. In ancient Egypt (except in the New Kingdom, which used the anniversary principle), the time between accession and the end of the calendar year was the king's first year, his second year running from the 1 Thoth after his accession; the same system was used in Sasanian Iran and is also used in modern Japan, where the second year of the regnal era begins on 1 January following the emperor's accession. (This is also the method for stating the age of a horse.) It is sometimes known as the 'non-accession-year' system, to distinguish it from the 'accession-year' of Sumer and Babylon, by which the days between the king's accession and the new year on 1 Nisanu (the Mar.–Apr. lunation) were counted as the 'beginning of the reign', or as completing the last year of the previous reign, so that the next civil year is his first; the regnal eras of Míng and Qīng China always began with the new year.

ERAS

The term *era* is first attested in Roman Spain; the etymology is unknown, but a borrowing from a native language seems likelier than a subliterary corruption of the neuter plural *aera*, 'moneys'. Besides the meaning 'era' it is used for 'number in a sequence'; this explains the form of dates in the Hispanic era, *era MCC*, as it were 'no. 1200'. The reckoning of years in sequence from a starting-point or epoch is the characteristic modern method of identifying years; the most widespread are the Christian era (see *Christian Chronology*) and the Jewish and Muslim eras, treated under those calendars.

Many eras were used in the Greek world during Hellenistic and Roman times; of these the most important is the Seleucid era, also known as that 'of Alexander' or 'the Greeks' or 'the Syromacedonians' and to Jews as 'the reckoning of contracts', variously reckoned from autumn 312 BC and spring 311 BC. However, the dating by the 'year of the foundation of the city' (AUC), with epoch 753 BC, often ascribed to the ancient Romans, is essentially a modern construct: the Romans occasionally use a similar language, but very rarely as a formal dating system, and not always with that epoch (see *Roman Calendar*). Whereas the 800th anniversary of the foundation was celebrated in AD 47 in agreement with this reckoning, the 1000th was kept in 248; the next year, 249, was subsequently taken as the epoch for a so-called 'era of the Romans' used in a Byzantine Paschal computus with a 200-year table beginning in 353, soon abandoned at Byzantium, but retained in Armenia, whose own era begins with its expiry in 552.

❴ WORLD ERAS Several widely different eras are reckoned from the date of the Creation, as determined from study of the Bible; there is a considerable difference between those based on the Hebrew text of the Old Testament, either directly or through the

Latin Vulgate, and those based on the Greek translation (the Septuagint), in which many of the Patriarchs are 100 years older when they beget their firstborn sons. The *Jewish calendar* sets Creation in 3761 BC, but Sextus Julius Africanus (*c.*221) placed the conception of Christ on 29 Phamenoth = 25 March, the first day of AM 5501; since he dates the Roman conquest of Egypt in 30 BC to AM 5472, the year will be 1 BC/AD 1. A century later, Eusebius of Caesarea dated Creation to 5200 BC, Christ being born in AM 5199; this era became so well entrenched in the West through Jerome's translation that Bede created a scandal by reducing the period between Creation and Nativity to 3952 years. In time Bede's calculation was rounded to the 'four thousand winters' of the Christmas poem 'Adam lay ybounden', perpetuated in the Masonic era but refined to 4004 BC by Archbishop Ussher (see *22 Oct.).

World eras may be further divided into those calculated purely out of sacred history and those adjusted computistically, in particular so that the first day of Creation might be a Sunday, which neither Africanus nor Eusebius had achieved, and begin a cycle (see Grumel and Strobel). In the early fifth century, the Egyptian monk Annianus proposed Sunday, 29 Phamenoth = 25 March 5492 BC, with the Incarnation in AM 5501 = AD 9/10. Although his contemporary Panodorus countered with a Creation date of Sunday, 23 Phamenoth = 19 March 5493 BC, the Incarnation being AM 5494 = AD 1, Annianus' calculation became the canonical Alexandrian era, but with the beginning of the year moved back to the civil date of 1 Thoth; his AM 1 was the first year of a Metonic cycle.

In the Byzantine empire, where such eras were mainly in learned use, several different epochs were tried. The *Chronicon Paschale*, still supposing a spring Creation, used Sunday, 25 March 5509 BC; some later writers used an epoch one year later, but the date eventually chosen was the intervening civil New Year, 1 September 5509 BC. In Russia, where the year of Creation was the regular dating system, this epoch took over from 1 March 5508 BC during the fourteenth century. Under the Polish crown, the West Russian territories in the Grand Duchy of Lithuania adopted the Christian era; but in Muscovy the era of the World remained in use till by decree of Peter the Great 31 December AM 7208 was followed by 1 January 1700 OS.

❰ OTHER BIBLICAL ERAS Besides years of the world and of Christ's Incarnation or Nativity (see *Christian Chronology*), the most important biblical dating-systems used by Christian writers were the era of Abraham with epoch 2016 BC, devised by Eusebius and brought to the Latin world by Jerome's adaptation of his chronicle, and that of the Passion, which varied according to the date adopted for the epoch: for those who follow Victorius of Aquitaine, AP 1 = AD 28; at Rome in Bede's day it was AD 34; other dates are found in the East. The computist of 243, whose Easter cycles were calculated back to the first Passover kept by the Children of Israel in the wilderness, counted in elapsed years (unusual for the Graeco-Roman world) from the Exodus the year before, which turns out to be 1552 BC. (In his view Christ was born in 1548 *ab Exodo.*)

❰ ERA OF DIOCLETIAN, OR THE MARTYRS Until the reign of Diocletian, Roman Egypt stood administratively apart from the rest of the empire, ruled through a prefect by the emperor as king of Egypt; dates were reckoned by his regnal years, counted from 1 Thoth. When Diocletian abolished this special status, normal consular years, beginning with 1 January, were introduced; astronomers, who found this inconvenient, continued to count by Diocletian's regnal years, of which the first was 284/5, even after his abdication in 305; this was the method used to designate years in Alexandrian Easter tables. The connection with the notorious persecutor induced Dionysius Exiguus to calculate his Easter tables from the birth of Christ instead; but the Diocletianic era was retained by the Coptic Church and extended to general dating purposes; the hated name of Diocletian was replaced by 'the Martyrs', first attested in a document of 19 Choiak 360 = 15 December 643. Another term was the Year of Grace, although this properly denotes an era beginning on 1 Thoth AM 5853 = 353 Incarnation = 77 Diocletian = AD 360, the first year of the eleventh Paschal cycle since Creation.

❡ HISPANIC ERA Whether the Hispanic era (*era hispánica*), reckoned from 1 January 38 BC, is of Christian or pagan origin is a matter of dispute. It is indubitably attested in Christian inscriptions from *era* 409 = AD 371 onwards, and in written texts from the fifth century; a writer of that period asserted that the era was so counted 'because Octavianus Augustus, in the fifth year of his reign, appears to have discovered the moon's course that makes the era', and modern scholars have produced competing accounts of the era's origin in a miscalculated Nativity. However, dating by an era, sometimes specified as consular, is found in much earlier pagan or secular inscriptions from northern Spain, for which those who regard the Hispanic era as a Christian invention have failed to account, but neither have their opponents convincingly explained why 38 BC should have been adopted as an epoch. Isidore of Seville, deriving *aera* from *aes*, declared that the epoch was Augustus' first imperial census, which in fact took place ten years later; taxation ordered in 39 BC but perhaps not collected till the next year has been invoked, as has a hard-fought victory over a Pyrenaean tribe won on Octavian's behalf by the proconsul Gnaeus Domitius Calvinus, beginning the 20-year conquest of those very peoples, the Astures and Cantrabri, on whose territory the first examples of era-dating were discovered. At all events, the Hispanic era became the standard chronology in much of Visigothic Spain, and remained so in Castile and León till 1383 and in Portugal till 1422. It is not found in the more easterly parts before the *Reconquista*, but thereafter was employed in Navarre till 1234, in Aragon till 1350, and in Valencia till 1358; but in Catalonia it was seldom used, and then only together with regnal years of Frankish or French kings, till in 1180 the Christian era was made compulsory by the Council of Tarragona. Dates are indicated with *era* and the number, not *anno* except in a pagan inscription (*anno CCLI*). It is also known as the 'Era of Augustus' and in Muslim sources as the Era of the Magi.

❡ JULIAN PERIOD, JULIAN DAY, JULIAN YEAR The Julian Period was proposed in 1583 by Joseph Justus Scaliger, *De emendatione temporum* (198) as a standard era to which dates in non-Julian calendars could be referred; the common assertion that he named it in honour of his father Julius Caesar Scaliger is not true. It was a cyclical era of 19 × 28 ×

15 = 7980 years, thus combining within itself the lunar cycle of 19 years, the solar cycle of 28 years, and the indictional cycle of 15 years; since the next 15th indiction ending an Easter cycle in the unreformed calendar was 3267, Scaliger made that year JP 7980, so that JP 1 was 4713 BC. For any year AD, the year JP is obtained by adding 4713; its place in each of the cycles will be the remainder to 19, 28, and 15 respectively. Thus (to use Scaliger's example) AD 1582 = JP 6295; since 6295 = 331 × 19 + 6, 224 × 28 + 23, and 419 × 15 + 10, its Golden Number is 6, it is the 23rd year of the solar cycle, and down to 23 September the 10th (Bedan) indiction.

This convenience (except as regards the indiction, which is of little practical significance) is lost in the Gregorian reckoning, which was promulgated in the year before Scaliger published and against which he sustained a protracted war of words; however, astronomers continue to make use of the epoch as the basis for a continuous count of Julian Days *elapsed* from noon Universal Time on Monday, 1 January JP 1, or as it may also be written −4712 I 1; the 24 hours from then till noon on 2 January JP 1 are thus Julian Day 0, midnight being JD 0.5; 6 a.m. GMT on 3 January JP 1 = JD 1.75. (Non-astronomers sometimes count 1 Jan. 4713 BC as JD 1.)

The Julian Period is not to be confused with the Julian year, an obsolete mode of reckoning first found in Censorinus (*fl.* AD 238) from the introduction of the Julian calendar in 45 BC = JP 4669, and used in early modern discussions of New Testament chronology.

❦ OTHER ERAS Despite Spanish Muslim usage, the Era of the Magi is properly that of the Zoroastrian calendar reckoned from 11 June 652, as opposed to the Era of Yäzdegird III, reckoned from 16 June AD 632 (see *Other Calendars: Zoroastrian*). This latter was widely used by astronomers, as were the Era of Nabonassar, king of Babylon, reckoned from 1 Thoth = 26 February 747 BC, and the Era of Philip Arrhidaeus, from 12 November 324 BC (i.e. 1 Thoth following the death of Alexander the Great 10/11 June). These systems use *anni vagi* of 365 days, as did the Armenian calendar (epoch 11 July AD 552).

Many eras are in use in India (see *Hindu Calendar*); but for official purposes the Christian era coexists with the Saka era, in which the epoch is 22 March AD 78 and the date is counted in years elapsed.

Under Mussolini the year AD was often accompanied by that of the Fascist Era, in roman numerals (I = 1923), and occasionally by that of the Italian Empire (I = 1937). See too *Other Calendars: French Republican*.

CYCLES

In cyclical chronology, a fixed number of years are grouped into a longer period known as a cycle, the individual year being numbered according to its position within the cycle. The cycle itself is numbered in some systems, but more usually is not; respective examples are afforded by the two most familiar cycles, the Olympiad and the indiction. Some Christian chronologies use the 532-year Paschal cycle, combining the 19-year lunar and 28-year solar cycles; in Western writers this is a sign that a computist is showing off, but this is not the case in Coptic or Ethiopic sources (see *Egyptian Calendar*). Georgian dates, from the ninth to the nineteenth century, were stated as 'such-and-such a year of the *kronik'oni*', reckoned from AD 781 (= year 533 'of the Romans') or 1313, the Creation being dated 12 cycles earlier to 5604 BC. In the 12-year animal cycle used in much of Asia, and the 60-year Chinese cycle incorporating it, the years are not numbered but named; the cycle is not specified (see *Chinese Calendar*).

❦ OLYMPIADS From the third century BC, dates were made comprehensible to all readers of historical and scholarly writing by reference to the most important Pan-hellenic institution, the Olympic Games, first celebrated according to the record in 776 BC and thereafter at four-year intervals called 'Olympiads' in July or August. Olympiads were numbered continuously, the years within them cyclically; hence 432/1 BC, so labori-ously identified by Thucydides, was the first year of the 87th Olympiad, written by modern scholars Ol. 87.1, and AD 1 is Ol. 195.1. Confusion was not entirely abolished, for writers might extend an Olympic year to comprise a whole campaigning season, or equate it with a civil year that began in a different lunation, even with a Roman year reckoned from 1 January; a reference to 'the so-manyeth Olympiad' by itself may denote an unspecified year within that period, or the first, or the fourth. Olympiads are occa-sionally found in late inscriptions at Elis, where the Games were held, but were never employed in everyday life; yet within its own sphere the system remained in use even after the suppression of the Olympic Games in AD 393. However, the revived Olympics do not respect the ancient cycle: the 669th Olympiad would have begun in summer 1897, but the first modern Games were held in 1896.

❦ INDICTIONS In medieval records, the year, whether reckoned by the Christian era or the ruler's reign, is often accompanied by the indiction. This term, derived from the Latin *indicere*, to declare or impose, in the late Roman Empire denoted the annual as-sessment of levies in kind; from 287 the reforming emperor Diocletian regulated these on a five-year basis, which gave way to a 15-year cycle. (The Greek term *epinémēsis*, 'allo-cation', fought a losing battle with *indiktíōn* or *índiktos*.) The normal practice was to num-ber only the year and not the cycle; the year was regularly known as the '*n*th indiction', so that 312/13 and 1347/8 are equally the first indiction, 686/7 and 1121/2 equally the fifteenth. A rare exception is an Egyptian papyrus dated 10 Epeiph in year 649 of the Martyrs (4 July 933) 'in the 43rd cycle', which would require the first to have begun in 297; most scholars, however, prefer to follow the *Chronicon Paschale*, which designates 312 'the beginning of Constantine's indictions', although Constantine was in no posi-tion to institute indictions in 297 and the chronicler dates the absolute 'beginning of the indictions' to 42 BC. Similar dates appear elsewhere in Byzantine sources; West-ern exponents of Dionysius' computus assert that the Incarnation took place in the fourth indiction, as if the system already existed. Since it was more important to most people than the official dating system by consuls, it was very soon used in non-fiscal contexts.

Dionysius Exiguus, in his Easter tables, gives the indiction alongside the year of Diocletian or the Incarnation; he also gives a rule for finding the year AD from the indiction or vice versa. The latter is that which we still use, to add 3 and divide by 15; the former, to find a suitable multiple of 15 and add the indiction and a constant 12, implies that one already knows the approximate year AD. (If one does, a notice dated by indiction can be recorded against the right year in one's Easter table without the need to ask how long this or that potentate has reigned.) An Irish commentator asserts that the rule was given because both wise and foolish—meaning the learned and the ignorant—knew their indictions. This was true in the Byzantine empire, where the indiction was the most familiar dating system, the Year of the World being largely a plaything of the learned; when a Byzantine date exhibits conflict between the indiction and the Year of the World it is normally the former that should be believed. In the West, however, indictions declined into a mere affectation of notaries; a notorious French charter is dated '1023, in the 21st indiction'. In consequence the year AD or the regnal year will generally deserve more credit, but the indiction may serve to indicate the date from which the year is counted, provided we know when the indiction year begins.

The indiction year was reckoned at Alexandria from 6 Pachon = 1 May, elsewhere in Egypt from 1 Thoth; at Constantinople it began at first on 23 September, but from (probably) 462 onwards on 1 September, thus coinciding with the civil year. This 'Greek' or 'Constantinopolitan' indiction was also used in many parts of Italy, even after the fall of the Roman empire, in particular at Milan and in the Lombard territories; it was favoured by the papal chancery till 1087, after which a period of confusion set in.

St Ambrose states that March was properly the first month of the year because the vernal equinox fell in it, as the Romans think, 'on the eighth before the Kalends of April'; September is the seventh month even though the year seems to start with it 'as the present usage of indictions shows'. Either because he took this to mean that the indiction began *VIII Kal. Oct.*, or because he found the 23rd in a Greek calendar and adjusted it to a more meaningful date, Bede states without argument in *De temporum ratione* that indictions were counted from 24 September; in this he is followed by the Holy Roman Emperors as well as in England and France. This 'Bedan', 'Caesarean', or 'Imperial' indiction was established as the norm in the papal chancery under Alexander III (1159–81).

There were also local indictions at Siena, beginning on 8 September a week after the Greek, at Cologne, beginning on 1 October, and at Genoa, beginning on 24 September, one year behind the Bedan; but despite the favour shown to 25 March as the change of year, it was rarely used for indictions. It is attested when they are related to Alexandrian years of the world, and was used by Pope Nicholas II (1058–61), who had been bishop of Florence since 1045, in fourteenth-century Dauphiné, and occasionally elsewhere; it is misleadingly known as the 'Papal indiction'.

This 'Papal' indiction must not be confused with the 'Roman' or 'Pontifical' indiction, reckoned from 1 January (in some cases perhaps 25 Dec.); like the Egyptian, Greek, and even 'Papal' indictions in their own territories, it had the advantage of coinciding with the civil year. An inscription of the year 619 at Santa Cecilia in Trastevere reckons not only the indiction but the regnal year from 1 January (see *Dating: Year*); other suspected cases in sixth- and seventh-century inscriptions are less secure. Under Urban II (1087–99) the 'Roman' indiction competed at the papal chancery with the Greek and Bedan indictions, and in the thirteenth century it spread over much of Europe. It outlasted the other two, being still found in some modern almanacs even though it is no longer in practical use.

The Roman indiction for the year, and the Greek, Bedan, and Sienese indiction current on 1 January, may be found by adding 3 to the year AD and dividing by 15; if there is no remainder the indiction is 15, otherwise it is the remainder. Thus 1399 + 3 = 1402; 1402 ÷ 15 = 93, remainder 7; therefore 1399 was the seventh indiction. For the Genoese and 'Papal' indictions, add 2 instead of 3; for a Byzantine year of the world reckoned from 1 September 5509 BC, add nothing, but divide directly by 15.

CHRISTIAN CHRONOLOGY

The era by which most of the world reckons most of its dates is counted from a calculation of the year in which Jesus Christ was born; very few if any who have studied the question, whether Christians or not, regard this calculation as correct, nor does any church insist on it, but neither faith nor scepticism has found an agreed alternative. Those who hold the statements of worldly fact in the Bible to be literally true have failed to resolve the conflict between the two Gospel datings in a manner satisfactory even to each other; those who do not, having made short work of the biblical accounts, have no evidence to put in their place. We shall first consider the historical problem, and then review the history of the Christian era.

NATIVITY AND CRUCIFIXION

❨ THE GOSPEL DATA   St Matthew dates the birth of Jesus to at least two years before the death of Herod the Great, which took place shortly before Passover in 4 BC; St Luke sets the Annunciation during the pregnancy of Elizabeth, who had conceived John the Baptist 'in the days of Herod, the king of Judaea' (1: 5), but assigns the Nativity to the time when 'there went out a decree from Caesar Augustus, that all the world should be taxed' (2: 1), that is to say a general census of the Roman Empire. This cannot be the citizen census of 8 BC, for Herod's kingdom was not part of the Roman Empire, and neither Joseph nor Mary was a Roman citizen; in any case, Luke continues: 'this taxing was first made when Cyrenius was governor of Syria', namely Publius Sulpicius Quirinius, who as legate of Syria in AD 6 supervised the thorough survey of the new Roman province that Judaea proper had just become, and suppressed the resulting insurrection. Moreover, Luke's Joseph, unlike Matthew's, is a resident of Nazareth in Galilee, which remained outside the Empire under Herod Antipas, and was not subject to the census; if it had been, Joseph would have been required to register in his normal place of residence, not in his ancestral town.

Luke also states (3: 1–2) that John the Baptist embarked upon his mission 'in the fifteenth year of the reign of Tiberius Caesar, Pontius Pilate being governor of Judaea, and Herod being tetrarch of Galilee, and his brother Philip tetrarch of Ituraea and of the region of Trachonitis, and Lysanias the tetrarch of Abilene, Annas and Caiaphas being the high priests'. Since the evangelist in all probability came from Antioch (see *18 Oct.), the regnal year should be interpreted according to the Antiochene reckoning, in which the emperor's first year ran from accession to 30 September and his second began on 1 October; since Tiberius accepted full power on 17 September AD 14, his 15th year ran from 1 October 27 to 30 September 28. Pontius Pilate was prefect of Judaea from AD 26 to early 37; Herod Antipas was tetrarch from 4 BC to AD 39, Philip from 4 BC to AD 34; Lysanias' dates are unknown; Annas, or rather Hanan, had been appointed high priest by Quirinius and deposed in AD 15, but upon the appointment of his son-in-law Joseph Caiaphas in 18 appears to have exercised power jointly with him and retained it till the latter's deposition in 36. Hence none of these names adds precision.

Having narrated the progress of John's mission down to his imprisonment, Luke relates Jesus' baptism (3: 20–1); he does not explicitly date the event to 15 Tiberius, though he has traditionally been so read. He adds that Jesus was beginning to be about 30 years of age (3: 23); this expression, no less awkward in the original Greek though penned by the best stylist of the New Testament, evidently confesses ignorance of the exact age, though some ancient writers understood it to mean that Jesus was baptized on his 30th birthday. On the other hand the reproach at John 8: 57 'Thou art not yet fifty years old, and hast thou seen Abraham?' is most naturally said to a man in his late 40s, which lends credence to the suggestion that at John 2: 20–1 Jesus, like the temple, was 46 years old by the next Passover after baptism. This interpretation has generally been dismissed, as it was by Augustine, as an error due to ignorance of the consuls in whose years Jesus was born and crucified, but some recent writers take it more seriously.

Jesus was crucified on a Friday while Pilate was governor; no evangelist specifies the length of Jesus' mission between baptism and crucifixion explicitly, but the Synoptic Gospels are normally taken to imply one year and St John two or three. There is another discrepancy between the Synoptic Gospels, which make the Last Supper a Passover meal, eaten after the sunset beginning 15 Nisan ('the first day of unleavened bread'), and John, who puts the Crucifixion on the 14th.

❦ EARLY CHRISTIAN CONJECTURES ON THE NATIVITY Early Christians, who like their pagan counterparts had to correlate dates for themselves, were so far from being troubled by the conflicting dates for the Nativity as to propose dates incompatible with both evangelists at once. Tertullian asserted that Christ had been born 52 years and 6 months before the fall of the Temple in AD 70, hence in January or February 18; the Computist of 243 sets the Nativity 1548 years after the Exodus, which since he counts AD 243 as year 1794 after the Exodus is equivalent to 4 BC, on the 14th lune, corresponding to Wednesday, *28 March. Since the *Roman calendar, still in the process of correction, was two days behind the sun, the day called V Kl. April. was a Friday, by rights the 30th, but both ancient and modern chronologists operate with the calendar as it ought to have been and not as it was; we shall do likewise.

Alexandrian writers at first favoured the 28th year of Augustus, which in their calendar was the leap year 29 August 3 BC–29 August 2 BC; non-Egyptians speak of his 42nd year, which they reckon from 1 January in the year of his first consulate, 43 BC, and therefore equate with 2 BC. Clement of Alexandria, in the early third century, dates the Nativity 194 years 1 month 13 days before the death of the emperor Commodus; since Commodus was assassinated on 31 December AD 192, by either Roman or Alexandrian reckoning the date comes to 18 November 3 BC = 22 Hathyr 28 Augustus. Some writers (see *18 Nov.) have seen in this the appropriation of an Asian solar festival; others, taking the years to be the unreformed *anni vagi* still used in outlying areas, give the date as 6 January 2 BC, but an Alexandrian was unlikely to reckon so, nor does the hypothesis rescue his confused chronography, in particular with respect to the lengths of emperors' reigns. He notes that others give the date as 25 Pachon 28 Augustus = 20 May 2 BC, and yet others (without year) as 24 or 25 Pharmouthi = 19 or 20 April. At Rome, Clement's near-contemporary Hippolytus gives Wednesday, 2 April in his Easter table and also in his commentary on Daniel, where he specifies 42 Augustus = 2 BC. In the latter place a later scribe has intruded 25 December (which in 2 BC was a Thursday); the next sentence, purporting to date the Crucifixion, fuses three dates into one.

In the early fourth century Eusebius of Caesarea put the Nativity in Ol. 194.3, namely 2 BC, which for him was also year 5199 of the world and 2015 of Abraham; these dates gained currency in the West through St Jerome's translation of his chronicle. Later in that century the heresy-hunter Epiphanius, who grossly overestimated his intellectual powers, declared that according to his careful researches Christ was born on 6 January 2 BC, baptized on 8 November in his 30th year (hence in AD 28, though he gives the wrong consuls from his faulty list), and crucified on 20 March in AD 30 (wrongly identified as 18 Tiberius), which was in fact a Monday.

The Calendar of 354—the first to record the celebration of Christmas on 25 December—adds in its list of consuls against the entry corresponding to AD 1: 'In this consulate the Lord Jesus Christ was born on the eighth before the Kalends of January, on Friday, the 15th lune.' To be sure feria and lune are wrong, for 25 December was a Sunday and the lune, according to the system used by the compiler, was the 17th; but no year in his table will fit those data. In the early fifth century Sulpicius Severus asserted that Christ was born on 25 December 'Sabino et Rufino consulibus', i.e. 4 BC; at Alexandria Annianus set the Incarnation in AD 9 (see *Chronology: Eras). A tradition known from Irish sources, which purports to derive at two removes from the manuscripts of the Apostles, and which designates the years by garbled names of consuls, sets the Nativity on 25 December AD 9, the Baptism on 6 January 46, and the Crucifixion on 23 March 58 (which was a Thursday), with Resurrection on the 25th and Ascension on 3 May; the first two dates are repeated in a work wrongly ascribed to Alcuin and identified with 42 Augustus and 15 Tiberius; a variant puts the Crucifixion on its Western date of 25 March, which in 58 was a Saturday.

The Alexandrian era, adjusted to begin on the civil new year of 1 Thoth/29 August 5493 BC, gave Conception on Sunday, 29 Phamenoth AM 5500 = 25 March AD 8 and Nativity on Tuesday, 29 Choiak AM 5501 = 25 December AD 8 = Inc. 1; this era is still used in Ethiopia, where the year 1993 will begin on 29 August/11 September 2000.

The feriae of Sunday for the Annunciation and Tuesday for the Nativity are also propounded in a calendar rule appended to those of Dionysius Exiguus but making nonsense of his era, for they imply 4 BC, AD 3, or AD 8. Panodorus, correcting Annianus, gave AD 1, as the Calendar of 354 had done and as Irish computists would implicitly take Dionysius to have done; in the seventh century the Byzantine *Chronicon Paschale* put the Nativity on Wednesday, 25 December 3 BC. Certain Georgian and Armenian texts count from 2 BC or 1 BC.

❡ EARLY CHRISTIAN CONJECTURES ON THE CRUCIFIXION Clement of Alexandria reported that some dated the Crucifixion to 25 Phamenoth 16 Tiberius, others to 25 or 19 Pharmouthi; at Alexandria the regnal year was understood as 29 August AD 29 to 28 August 30, the alternative dates being Monday, 21 March AD 30, Thursday, 20 April, or Friday, 14 April, though Passover in AD 30 was probably about 3 April. The Computist of 243 dates the Crucifixion to Friday, 9 April, 1579 years after the Exodus, i.e. in AD 28, which he miscalls 16 Tiberius, Jesus being 31; most Western and Byzantine writers appear to count the emperor's second regnal year from 1 January, after accession, but often work with the wrong date for the latter. The main Western tradition, however, set the Crucifixion on 25 March in the consulate of the two Gemini (Lucius Rubellius Geminus and Gaius Fufius Geminus), AD 29; the day was the vernal equinox by Roman reckoning as well as the Annunciation, but in 29 it was at best the Friday after Passover, and that only if spring weather had set in early.

Another view, particularly favoured in Gaul and Alexandria, regarded 25 March as the Resurrection, the Crucifixion being the 23rd. During Pilate's governorship 23 March was a Friday in 31 and 36, but in both years too soon for Passover; Alexandrians mostly favoured 42, when Pilate was out of office. Lactantius (*c*.300) gives a date of 23 March 15 Tiberius, in the consulate of the two Gemini, not realizing that in 29 it was a Wednesday. Little better is the date proposed by Victorius of Aquitaine, 26 March AD 28, which he takes to be at the beginning of AM 5229 and 14 Nisan in the year of the two Gemini; like several other writers he finesses the Gospels by reckoning the lune from sunset and the Roman date and feria from midnight, but again like other writers (even Bede) he imagines that the moon obeyed his tables in Christ's time as in his own. The *Chronicon Paschale*, apparently completed in 630, amidst manifold confusions gives Nativity on 25 December 3 BC, Baptism on 6 January AD 28, and Crucifixion on 23 March 31.

As with the Nativity, and the early Easter tables, chronological and arithmetical confusions abound. The interpolated passage from Hippolytus' commentary on Daniel continues: 'and he suffered in the thirty-third year on Friday 25 March in the eighteenth year of Tiberius Caesar in the consulate of Rufus and Rubellio and Gaius Caesar for the fourth time and Saturninus.' Jesus' age (assuming birth in 2 BC) and Tiberius' regnal year (if counted from his first full Roman year, AD 15) indicate 32; the first two consuls are those of 29 in light disguise, the other two those of 41; but only in 29 was 25 March a Friday. Rufus and Rubellio turn up elsewhere, sometimes separated from the 'two Gemini'; regnal years of Tiberius are numbered at haphazard. The Christian historian Orosius dates an event of AD 17 to his 4th year and one of 27 to his 12th; but his Crucifixion year of 17 Tiberius may denote 33, for he alludes, albeit vaguely, to a report by the pagan Greek author Phlegon of Tralles, cited more exactly by Eusebius, that in the year Ol. 202.4 = AD 32/3 a solar eclipse took place at noon on the same day as an earthquake at Nicaea. Some Christians equated these events with the eclipse and the earthquake said to have accompanied the Crucifixion; but since there was a total eclipse of the sun on 24 November 29, in the first year of that Olympiad, we may suppose that either in Phlegon's text or in that of his source A′ ('1st') had been corrupted to Δ′ ('4th'). Later, the belief that Jesus was born in 2 BC and died at the age of 33 renewed the credit of AD 33, which has survived the adoption of a Christian era incompatible with such reasoning, though the Roman Passion era with years 33 less than those AD attested by Bede should imply the year 34. The Anglo-Saxon Chronicle dates the Crucifixion to AD 33, but also to AM 5226.

❦ MODERN THEORIES ON THE NATIVITY Those who accept St Matthew's problematic story of the Massacre of the Innocents (see *28 Dec.) sometimes associate the star that led the Magi with the planetary conjunction of *15 September 7 BC, though the appearance of Halley's comet of 12 BC has also been invoked; but even historians who treat the Massacre as a legend beneath their notice accept birth under Herod as a tradition older than the written Gospels. Older too is the first statement (Rom. 1: 3) that Jesus was descended from King David; if a birth in that line at Bethlehem aroused messianic speculations that attracted the hostile attention of Herod, it is credible that Joseph should leave for the safety of Roman Egypt, and on Herod's death settle at Nazareth in Galilee because he felt safer under its tetrarch, Herod Antipas, than under Archelaus, who had succeeded in Judaea proper.

St Luke raises greater difficulty. Since Nativity in AD 6 is impossible unless Jesus was under 30 at baptism and no more than 30 at crucifixion, attempts have been made to conjure up an earlier governorship for Quirinius; they have not been successful, and in any case would have detached the Nativity from the Roman census. Most critics therefore discard Luke; some have rehabilitated John, who seems to imply that Jesus was born c.18 BC.

❦ MODERN THEORIES ON THE CRUCIFIXION Both Synoptic and Johannine Crucifixion dates have had their partisans. The doctrine that since all things were perfect at Creation the moon must have been created full, on the 15th lune, encouraged acceptance of 15 Nisan for the Crucifixion, so that the 17th should be at once the day on which Adam fell and Christ rose. On the other hand, Crucifixion on the 14th makes Jesus himself the Paschal sacrifice, the Lamb of God; that date passed not only into the apocryphal Gospel of Peter but into hostile Jewish accounts of 'Yeshu the Nazarene' in the tractate Sanhedrin of the Babylonian Talmud and the counter-gospel known as the Toledot Yeshu. Since the latter assigns Yeshu's execution to the reign of Alexander Jannaeus' widow Queen 'Helen' (correctly Shalom-Tsiyon Alexandra, 76–67 BC), and other Talmudic tractates represent him as a former disciple of Yehoshua ben Perachyah (1st c. BC), these texts make no contribution to historical fact; nevertheless they attest the wide acceptance of the Johannine date. Moreover, Jews knew, even if Christians did not, that execution on 15 Nisan would have been a serious and public profanation of a holy day (cf. Exod. 12: 16, Lev. 23: 7).

Scaliger (*De emendatione temporum*, 263) declared the date to be 23 April 34, which was 15 Nisan provided the year was embolismic; the Jesuit Petavius, anxious to differ from his Huguenot predecessor, gave 23 March 31 (*De doctrina temporum*, ii. 666), which was in all likelihood only the 10th. Modern writers, however, generally adopt either 7 April 30 or 3 April 33, both of which had been shown to be almost certainly 14 Nisan even before Shaefer's work on lunar visibility; despite his advanced theology and his greater hostility to 'the Jews', John is now taken more seriously by both historians and theologians than was fashionable in the early twentieth century. Of these two dates, the former has often been championed by Protestant scholars, the latter is generally favoured by Roman Catholics.

Against 7 April 30 it has been objected that a date after the execution of Tiberius' lieutenant Sejanus (18 Oct. 31) has the advantage of explaining the normally despotic Pilate's uncharacteristic surrender to Jewish pressure, not merely in crucifying Jesus but in releasing the rebel and murderer Barabbas. On the one hand Tiberius, having contrived his over-powerful minister's downfall, reversed the latter's anti-Jewish policies, which conflicted with his personal sympathies; on the other Pilate, appointed during Sejanus' ascendancy, lived in fear of malicious denunciation, as an accomplice in his treasonable designs, to a ruler only too prone to believe it. This is the threat underlying the words ascribed to the Jews at John 19: 12, 'If thou let this man go, thou art not Caesar's friend.'

Several writers have related the partial lunar eclipse of 3 April 33 to the 'darkness over the whole land from the sixth to the ninth hour' reported at Mark 15: 33, Luke 23: 44, and to the blood moon of Acts 2: 20; however, Shaefer finds that it was unlikely to have been observed in Jerusalem. Luke adds a reference to a solar eclipse (in some manuscripts a darkening of the sun, which might relate to an earthquake, cf. Matt. 27: 51); since as an educated man he must have known that solar eclipses happen only at new moon, we are evidently to infer a miracle (portents are to be expected in narratives of terrible events), yet one that failed to convince either Jews or Romans of divine displeasure at their proceedings. However, 33/4 (reckoned from 1 Tishri) has been shown to be a sabbatical year (see *Jewish Calendar*), during which the land lay fallow; such years were not normally embolismic, which would exclude 23 April 34, but the preceding year often was, which would exclude 3 April 33.

Recently 30 March 36 has been proposed, not least because it would allow Herod Antipas' defeat, later in that year, by the father of the wife he had discarded in favour of Herodias, to follow soon after his execution of John the Baptist, which took place during Jesus' lifetime and for which the rout of Herod's army was viewed as punishment. This is historically attractive, but Shaefer's calculations indicate that it was only 13 Nisan.

Some scholars still prefer to follow the Synoptics in making the Last Supper a Passover meal, eaten by Roman reckoning on a Thursday but by Jewish on Friday, 15 Nisan (not yet an impossible date as in the modern Jewish calendar); however, since the only plausible dates are 11 April 27, which is too early for 15 Tiberius, and 23 April 34, which requires an improbable intercalation, it seems necessary to discard the traditional inference that the entire process from Last Supper to Crucifixion was completed within a single day, thus also avoiding the outrage of execution on the first day of Unleavened Bread. If the Friday of the Crucifixion fell after 15 Nisan, allowing more time for the legal processes, other dates and even other years come into consideration, as is also the case if John's 'preparation of the passover' (19: 14) is reinterpreted as meaning not Friday, 14 Nisan but the Friday within the seven days of Unleavened Bread.

Some commentators have attempted to deny that the Gospels disagree, but themselves disagree on the manner of reconciling them. It has even been supposed that Jesus and his disciples followed a sectarian calendar and kept Passover a few days ahead of other folk; but why are no comments by other Jews recorded in texts that justify Jesus' teaching and practice against his enemies' objections, and why was this calendar abandoned without trace by a Church increasingly divorced from mainstream Jewry? The suggestion seems all the less tenable in the light of the importance that John ascribes to the Jewish holy days in Jesus' life.

THE CHRISTIAN ERA

❡ THE TABLE OF DIONYSIUS EXIGUUS In 525 the monk Dionysius Exiguus drew up, at the behest of papal functionaries dissatisfied with the Easter tables of Victorius (see *The Date of Easter* and *Computus*), a new table based on Alexandrian principles to continue one that had only six more years to go. However, whereas the Alexandrians had designated the years according to the era of Diocletian, Dionysius declined to perpetuate the persecutor's memory, dating instead 'from the Incarnation of our Lord Jesus Christ, in order that the beginning of our hope should be better known to us and the cause of our recovery, that is the Passion of our Redeemer, should shine forth more clearly'. This last phrase is a studied insult to Victorius, whose own tables were dated from the Passion.

The existing Alexandrian table being due to expire in 247 Diocletian (AD 530/1, hence current at Easter 31), Dionysius began with 532, thus instituting the era that we use today. However, nowhere in his exposition of his table does Dionysius relate his epoch to any other dating system, whether consulate, Olympiad, year of the world, or regnal year of Augustus; much less does he explain or justify the underlying date, or even claim it for his own discovery, but treats it as an unproblematic fact, corresponding to current knowledge or belief. Yet the general opinion in the West was, and long remained even among authors who used his era, that Christ had been born in AM Eus. 5199 = 2015 Abraham = 42 Augustus = 2 BC (see below); if Dionysius, whose calendrical rules or *argumenta* make September, not January, the beginning of the year, treated incarnation as synonymous with birth (as his early followers, including Bede, do) rather than conception (as in the later 25 Mar. styles), and (like the Computist of 243) counted in elapsed, not current years, then the first year after the incarnation ran from 1 September 1 BC to 31 August AD 1, so that at Eastertide (which alone concerned him) it matched the January–December year *Caesare et Paullo coss.* that subsequent Western computists took as the first year of his era. The alternative, and not improbable, explanation is error due to an inaccurate list of consuls, or confused summations of emperors' regnal years, such as constantly confront us in chronographers.

In his covering letter Dionysius equates year 525 from the Incarnation with the consulate of Probus Junior, which certainly began on 1 January AD 525, and the third indiction, which properly began on 1 September 524, but two-thirds of which fell in 525. The southern Irish computists and their great pupil Bede supposed him to have set the Incarnation in a 4th indiction, with concurrent 5 (i.e. 24 Mar. a Thursday), epact 11 (i.e. the moon 11 days old on 22 Mar.), being year 2 of the decemnovenal cycle; all four characteristics belonged in his table to 533, which had the same position in the Paschal cycle as AD 1. Bede, in *De temporum ratione*, ch. 47, carefully avoids saying that Dionysius was right, and when later in the chapter he deduces from the Passion era used at Rome that Christ, having lived a little over 33 years, was crucified in AD 34, the arithmetic implies Nativity in 1 BC. However, his concern is not to date Christ's birth, but (both here and in ch. 61) to undermine with gentle irony his predecessors' attempts at dating the Crucifixion.

❰ THE SPREAD OF DIONYSIUS' ERA Dionysius' Incarnation era was intended purely for his tables; he had no design of replacing indictions or consulates. Although his rules for Easter calculation (*argumenta Paschalia*) include worked examples with the current Incarnation date of 525, he does not use it in his covering letter, which he dates by consul, indiction, and place in the decemnovenal and lunar cycle. At the end of the sixth century Victor, bishop of Tonnenna in North Africa, continued the chronicle of Prosper of Aquitaine, dating first by consuls and then by regnal years. Towards the end these go wrong: the final entries, including the death of Justinian and succession of Justin II, are assigned to 40 Justinian, indiction 15. In fact Justinian had died on 13 November 565; but had he survived to his 40th regnal year it would have been 567, and this was a 15th indiction. Victor then reckons the years from Adam to the Nativity as 5199, from the Nativity, 'which took place in the 43rd year of power of Augustus Octavianus Caesar', to the first year of Justin as 567, and the total as 5766; it would appear that Victor has taken the current year from his Easter table and set the Nativity—of which he speaks explicitly, and not of Incarnation—on 25 December 43 Augustus = 1 BC, just before the beginning of the first Christian year, rather than in AD 1, when it was nearly over. Unfortunately, he has combined it with Eusebius' Nativity date of AM 5199 = 2 BC; so does his own continuator, John, abbot of Biclarum in Spain, who dates his work to year 592 from the Nativity and 5791 from Adam, again with Imperial and Spanish reigns two years behind.

Neither Victor nor John had used Dionysius' era in his running dates; and to count years passed from the Nativity, or Adam, no more entails a formal era than to count those passed since the Norman Conquest or the Declaration of Independence. Spanish datings to '$(Y-38)$' are still of this class. However, monks who used the blank spaces to the right of entries in their Easter tables to record events of the year might begin to associate the era date with chronicle as well as computus, and hence to think of the year as the so-manyeth since the Passion, or of the World, if they used Victorius' tables, since the Incarnation or the Nativity if they used Dionysius. Some era dates have been found, sometimes encoded, in Celtic sources, though the normal Irish manner of identifying the year was by feria and lune of 1 January, the lune being taken from the Latercus, Victorius, or Dionysius according to local usage. In England there are seventh-century charters dated by the Incarnation; but the turning-point came with Bede. Whereas in the chronicles attached to *De temporibus* (703) and *De temporum ratione* (725), he dated his annals by his own world era, in which Christ came to earth in the year 3952, clearly identified as the traditional 2 BC (and is crucified in 3984 = AD 32), in his *Historia ecclesiastica gentis Anglorum* of 731, dates are given from the Incarnation; thereafter this became the norm in England, and spread to Western Europe, where it supplemented or supplanted regnal years, Passion eras, and eventually the Hispanic era reckoned from 1 January 38 BC.

Although Bede the computist equates Dionysius' Incarnation year with AD 1, Bede the chronicler had set the Incarnation in 2 BC; theories making Bede the historian count his years AD from 24 September or 25 December 1 BC are no longer favoured, but reckoning from Christmas 1 BC was subsequently adopted in pre-Conquest England and in many Continental chanceries. Such years are properly called *a nativitate Domini*, but are often called years of the Incarnation, or even the Passion; however, a stricter definition of incarnation as equivalent to conception gave rise to two competing Incarnation styles, the *calculus Pisanus* reckoned from 25 March 1 BC, and the more widespread method, known as the *stilus Florentinus* and normal in England from the thirteenth century, reckoned from 25 March AD 1. Incarnation in that year is also implied by the *mos Venetus* and the *mos Gallicus* (see **Dating: Year*).

Despite finding Dionysius' era useful, Bede rather accepted than justified it; there was, and is, no evidence either sacred or profane in its support. Regino of Prüm, compiling his chronicle in the ninth century, found that it would not fit his other information, but suggested that miscopied figures might be to blame; he too had hampered himself by equating Dionysius' first year with 42 Augustus. Indeed, this traditional date died so hard that Cardinal Baronius' Roman Martyrology still dated the Nativity in Eusebian fashion to year 5199 of the world, 2015 of Abraham, 752 of Rome, and 42 of Augustus.

In 982 the computist Abbo of Fleury observed that Dionysius' chronology afforded no year in Jesus' lifetime in which 15 Nisan, the Synoptic date of the Crucifixion, was 25 March, the traditional Western date; since, as Bede had observed, they came together when the thirteenth year of the decemnovenal cycle had five concurrents, the true year must have been AD 12, which he renumbered 33. The same year, but renumbered 34, was the basis, some decades later, of the dates in the chronicle of Marianus Scotus, the Irish monk of Fulda. In the one form or the other this chronology *secundum evangelicam veritatem*—a 'gospel truth' that makes nonsense of the Gospels, and exonerates Pontius Pilate more efficaciously than any handwashing—became quite fashionable for a time, though other writers proposed the Alexandrian date instead. The author of the Icelandic *Hungrvakr* (see *23 Dec.) consistently gives dates 'from Christ's Nativity' (*frá hingatburði Christi*) seven years lower than the Dionysian, as if he were using an Alexandrian era adjusted to begin on 25 December AD 7; some of his copyists correct to the normal dating. More recent objections have been not computistic but historical, based on the date of Herod's death (see e.g. *The Modern Calendar: Unsuccessful Proposals*).

In modern times, the universal acceptance of 1 January as the first day of the year, and the supremacy in popular culture of Christmas over Lady Day, have caused the Christian era to be understood as celebrating the Nativity and dating it to 25 December 1 BC. It is of course easier to count from a week after the event commemorated than from almost a year before it; yet a richer fabric of meaning could have been woven from Incarnation on 25 March AD 1, a Friday and *luna XIV*—the same feria, the same lune, and in Western tradition the same date as the Crucifixion—and Nativity on Sunday, the Lord's day, feria as well as date being wrested from the pagan sun-god by the Sun of Righteousness. This would be no more obscurantist than citing 'on earth peace, good will toward men', which is a false reading of Luke 2: 14 not preserved in modern translations, or regarding the 'millennium' of AD 2000 as the 2000th anniversary of Christ's Nativity.

❡ DATING 'BEFORE CHRIST' Given the importance of the Incarnation in Christian thought, it may now seem strange that once a date had been found for it, dating 'before Christ' was not in widespread use before the late eighteenth century, though sporadic instances are known much earlier, in particular the *Flores temporum* of an anonymous Franciscan writing *c*.1292; however, other eras, even that of the Hijra, have not been made retrospective. Just as when Roman writers say that this or that happened so many years before (or indeed after) the foundation of Rome, this is rather a statement of relative chronology than a formal date; so it is when Isidore of Seville dates the supposed arrival of a Gothic contingent in Pompey's camp in the 12th year before the Hispanic era was established (*ante aeram conditam*), or Bede states (inaccurately) that Julius Caesar was consul 'in the 60th year before the Lord's incarnation'. By contrast, a BC date is now considered on the same footing as an AD date, and not even historians of Rome use anything else.

Dates BC are normally reckoned according to the Julian calendar; since the year preceding AD 1 was not 0 but 1 BC, four years before AD 4, the leap years BC are of the form $4n + 1$, i.e. 1, 5, 9, etc. There are two exceptions:

(i) in references to Roman history, dates BC are to be understood as straight translations from the *Roman calendar* as actually used, not as Julian dates (which can rarely be established);

(ii) occasionally one finds a 'Gregorian' system used, in which years BC of the form $100x + 1$ are leap only if x is a multiple of 4, but years AD (normally) remain Julian till 1582; this should never be done without explicit statement.

The absence of a year o must be borne in mind when one is finding anniversaries (which are counted in elapsed years) and converting eras (which outside India are counted in current years).

❡ ASTRONOMICAL RECKONING In astronomical usage the era is not specified. Years AD are designated by *millésime* alone, or for clarity's sake preceded by a plus sign; 1 BC is year o, and all other years BC are negative, the absolute value of their *millésime* being one lower than in BC reckoning: 2 BC is −1, 3 BC is −2, and so on. Leap years are thus those divisible by 4 whether negative or positive, including o. The year precedes the month (which may be given in Roman numerals) and the month the day: thus Julian Day o begins at noon on −4712 I 1 (see *Chronology: Eras: Julian Period*) and the lunar eclipse during Cicero's consulate in 63 BC fell on −62 V 3.

❡ CHRISTIAN OR COMMON ERA? In modern times Dionysius' era has become the standard world reckoning, even in countries that have calendars of their own and do not profess Christianity; in China it was officially adopted by the Communists, in place of the Republican era still used on Taiwan. In consequence, those who wish to use it without acknowledging its basis sometimes call it the 'Common Era', replacing BC by BCE and AD by CE; 'our era' is favoured in other languages, and was standard in the Soviet bloc. Some Christians have followed suit, either from their modern fear of giving offence (though some other communities prefer convinced Christians to secular humanists) or because the era, considered as Christian, is historically inaccurate; but if it is not an era of the Incarnation it is an era of nothing at all, for there is no known event in either 1 BC or AD 1 deserving universal commemoration, though the Georgian king Aderk'i, who reigned from AD 1 to 58, is said by the native chronicle to have ruled well. A truly secular chronology would adopt some other era, such as the institution of the Julian calendar in 45 BC; such Julian years were indeed used by early modern chronologists.

❡ A NOTE ON TERMINOLOGY Whereas one may correctly speak of the 'fifth century BC', the corresponding 'fifth century AD' is logically unjustified, since AD stands for *anno Domini*, 'in the year of (Our) Lord'. Nevertheless, it is established usage, not least because both BC and AD are commonly pronounced as letter-names: 'before Christ' is sometimes said in full, but *anno Domini* is chiefly used as a jocular expression for advancing age, and 'in the year of Our Lord' is largely confined to legal usage. The abbreviation AC, for *anno Christi*, found in older writers who did not expect it to be read as *ante Christum*, is nowadays legitimate only with reference to chronologies in which the Nativity is dated to a different year.

DATING

In this section we are concerned only with dating by day, month, and year of the Christian era; for dating according to the feasts of the Church, see I: *Western Church Year* and Appendix D; for dating by the introits at Sunday Mass, see Appendix C; for dating by regnal years see *Chronology* and Appendices A and B.

DAY AND MONTH

The modern method of stating the date counting the days of each month consecutively from the first is found in the Egyptian, Jewish, and Chinese calendars. It was also used in the Macedonian calendar, and therefore in the Hellenistic kingdoms; but most of the ancient Greek cities counted the last ten days of the month backwards (see *Greek Calendar*). Rome rejected it until well after the fall of the Western empire (see *Roman Calendar*); however, as the East Roman or Byzantine empire became more Greek and less Latin in its official culture, it abandoned the Roman system of inclusive backward reckoning from Kalends, Nones, and Ides in favour of the forward count.

In the Western Middle Ages, the Roman method competed for centuries with the forward count in Latin texts; even in vernacular texts Roman dates were often used, mostly expressed in Latin. Another practice, known as the *consuetudo Bononiensis* or 'custom of Bologna' since it was mainly used by notaries trained there, was to reckon the first 15 days (or in 31-day months the first 16) forwards, *intrante mense*, and the remainder backwards (*stante* or *exeunte mense*); this count (attested in England from 1268) is also regular in statements of 'Egyptian days' (see I: *Days*). A similar system is employed in classical Arabic, though not the modern language; on the other hand the Gaulish calendar, which also divided the month into halves, counted days forwards in the waning as well as in the waxing half (see *Other Calendars: Celtic*), as do *Hindu* lunar calendars. For dating by syllable of the *cisioianus*, see Appendix D.

The most formal manner of stating the date in English is 'the fourth day of May'; less formal are 'the fourth of May' or 'May the fourth', in the USA 'May fourth' or 'May four'; in writing one may find '4 May' (especially in modern British usage, but not unknown in the USA), '4th May', 'May 4' (US and older British), 'May 4th'. Often the month too is expressed by its number in the sequence from January (1) to December (12); in Continental countries it is normally given in roman numerals ('4.v.'), but

English-speakers prefer arabic. Unfortunately, whereas British usage in this case is to put the day before the month, in the USA the month precedes the day: hence '4. 5' or '4/5' is 4 May in the UK and 5 April in the USA, and '5. 4' vice versa. The only safe rule is to avoid this form in any text likely to be read in both countries. A proposed international system in which the year comes first, followed by month and day always with two digits apiece (2000–05–04), is little used in practice, except among astronomers as 2000 V 4.

Some Puritans, refusing to give pagan names for months, simply numbered them from first to 12th; before 1752 in England and America the first month was March. Such numbering, as also of weekdays, was long maintained by the Society of Friends, who in 1752 recognized the Act reforming the calendar by transferring the name of first month from March to January; however, it had previously been more general. Increase Mather (1639–1723, Rector of Harvard College 1685–1701), a bitter enemy of the Quakers, begins his diary for 1675: '1ᵐ 25ᵈ 1675 And is it so indeed? Doe I live to write any thing in yᵉ year 1675?' The 1675–6 diary is almost but not quite consistent in using this style, the numbered month preceding the numbered day; the extracts from his other journal, even those relating to the same period, sometimes name the months in the conventional fashion, and when they number them sometimes put the day first. This may be the fault of Dr Jeremy Belknap, who transcribed them in the late eighteenth century; but the day is regularly put first by Mather's older contemporary John Fiske, e.g. '2ᵈ of 1ˢᵗ 45 This day being Lords day', i.e. Sunday 2 March 1644/5 (Fiske always changed the year on 1 March).

YEAR

Whereas the term 'New Year' and its equivalents in other languages, when used with reference to the Western calendar, should in default of other evidence be understood of 1 January, the date on which the number of the year changed varied from one country to another:

  1 *January* ('Circumcision style' or 'Modern style'): Roman consular year from 153 BC; retained in the Hispanic era and for Irish dating by kalend and lune; disapproved but never suppressed by the Church, and presupposed in Western computus; increasingly frequent from thirteenth century under influence of Roman law and subsequently humanism; adopted in much of Europe during sixteenth century; in France from 1563, in Scotland from 1600, in Russia from 1700, in England and the American colonies from 1752, but often found before then in printers' colophons (an example in 1553) and private usage; regular in almanacs.

  1 *March*: prehistoric Rome according to tradition (and month names); the Franks till the eighth century; Venice (the *mos Venetus*, used for official and sometimes—not always—for private purposes); Turkish *maliye* year; Russian Year of the World (reckoned from 5508 BC) until fourteenth century and sometimes later.

25 *March*, reckoned from 1 BC (*calculus Pisanus*): earliest example from ninth-century Burgundy; 'Sunday, 6 June 897, indiction 14', i.e. 896; taken to Lombardy when Hugh of Arles became king in 926; thereafter rare except at Pisa, where it was used up to and including 1749; also found in fourteenth-century Lucca, but the norm was Nativity up to 1509, Circumcision from 1510; some Byzantine writers (from 5508 BC).

25 *March*, reckoned from AD 1 (*calculus Florentinus*, also called the 'custom of the English Church'): Florence up to and including 1749, papal bulls, England and the American colonies up to and including 1751. The *calculus Florentinus* may have originated at Fleury, and been brought thence to England by St Oswald along with dedication of churches to the BVM (to whom he rededicated St Peter's cathedral church at Worcester). Adopted by French chancery from 1112 (earlier usage varied); reaches Trier and Cologne; sometimes under Italian influence in imperial chancery from Philip of Swabia to Frederick II. Apparently used in south-east (Lyon 1201, Arles 1249). Adopted in papal chancery from Urban II till the thirteenth-century reaction in favour of Nativity.

Both Florentine and Pisan styles presuppose that years 'from the Incarnation' should be reckoned from the Annunciation, not the Nativity; they were abolished by a decree of the Grand Duke Francesco Stefano, who was also the Holy Roman Emperor Francis I.

Easter (*mos Gallicus*): France at least from 1215 down to 1564, which edict of Roussillon (9 August) curtailed at 31 December. Not in all parts.

29 *August* (30 August in year preceding Julian leap year): Coptic and Ethiopic churches, but according to Julian reckoning.

1 *September*: Byzantium from (probably) 462; Russia (from 5509 BC) increasingly from fourteenth century, retained down to 1699 and unofficially even thereafter.

23 *September*: several calendars of the Greek East; Constantinople till 462.

24 *September*: Bede, but only when he converts an indiction to a year AD: early tenth-century entries in Anglo-Saxon Chronicle.

29 *September*: Adam Murimuth's chronicle (1303–36); but the continuation counts from 25 December.

30 *September*: English Exchequer Pipe Rolls.

1 *October*: Antioch; Seleucid era in Roman and Muslim times.

25 *December*: pre-Conquest England, retained in Benedictine houses till the fourteenth century; Holy Roman Empire; Iberia after abandonment of Hispanic era; Roman curia.

In principle, a writer dating by calendar year, regnal year, and indiction might have three different days from which to reckon them. In practice, however, they tended to be assimilated, even as Olympiad years and Roman consular years had been assimilated by Diodorus Siculus in the first century BC. On the front wall of Santa Cecilia in Trastevere at Rome is an inscription recording the burial of Theodorus, a Greek from Byzantium, 'on the fifteenth day of the month of August in the seventh indiction' and of his son Theodoracus, 'on the Ides of October under the emperors our most pious lords, the Augusti Heraclius in his ninth year, the eighth after the consulate of the same our lord, and Heraclius the New Constantine his son in his seventh year, in the seventh indiction' (all these numbers are spelt out). One supposes that the son was buried three months after the father, not nine months before, and therefore that the indiction was counted from 1 January not 1 September. The seventh indiction, on that basis, will be 619, which is confirmed by the regnal year of Heraclius Constantinus Novus, made co-emperor on 22 January 613. It follows that the regnal year of Heraclius senior, who had acceded on 5 October 610, has also been assimilated to the Roman calendar year as used for his postconsulate (the eighth year after 611); we should therefore be chary of supposing 'seventh indiction' in the later date to be an error induced by the preceding regnal year.

Similar complications confront readers of histories and chronicles from both the Western and the Byzantine Middle Ages, which may combine different dating systems (such as regnal years, indictions, and Olympiads), or draw on sources that reckon the year on a different basis from that used by their compilers, who may or may not correct the dates they find there. The year AD and the indiction found on the same line in the Easter table may be equated (even by Bede); we do not always know which is correct. These difficulties are additional to those caused by the easy miscopying of numerals, and the slippage due to the physical structure in which years were tabulated and events written against them (that is why, in the Anglo-Saxon Chronicle, 'in this year' is expressed as *hēr*, 'here, in this space'). Not only might a subsequent scribe insert an event in the wrong space, but the record might overflow the space available; the danger was especially great when the annal was entered in Easter tables, but Eusebius' world chronicle exhibits the same phenomenon. The Greek original is largely lost, but it survives in St Jerome's Latin adaptation and in an Armenian translation, which often differs in its dates; St Jerome's account of the Crucifixion spans the 18th and 19th years of Tiberius, the Armenian version puts it in the latter, quotations in later Greek authors vary. The 19th year, Ol. 202.4, better suits the quotation from Phlegon of Tralles (see *Christian Chronology: Nativity and Crucifixion*).

CENTURIES AND MILLENNIA

Since the first year of the Christian era is AD 1, the first century must be AD 1–100 and the first millennium AD 1–1000; similarly the second century is AD 101–200 and the second millennium AD 1001–2000. That is to say, century and millennium begin respectively in the 01 and 001 year, end in the 00 and 000 year, and are known by the multiple of 100 or 1000 they will attain in the latter. Hence the 21st century, and the third millennium, will begin in 2001, albeit celebrations will be held in much of the world in 2000; those who know better will join in for sociability's sake, then hold their own celebrations in 2001. Those who side with the ignorant are bringing forward the day when a twentieth-century view of the world will be not perceptive and progressive but bigoted and reactionary.

Such divisions are by their nature arbitrary; if we called the twentieth century the 'nineteen hundreds', we should naturally count from 1 January 1900 to 31 December

1999. (Swedes speak of *1900-talet*, 'the number 1900', Italians of *il Novecento*, also written '900.) For converting Julian dates to Gregorian, or vice versa, centuries begin in the centennial year (that ending in 00), but only from the Julian leap day onwards; similarly, it is from the centennial year that they are reckoned in calculating the Gregorian Easter.

The Book of Revelation predicts a thousand-year reign of Christ, followed by the loosing of the Devil and the final battle of the world; since 'one day is with the Lord as a thousand years, and a thousand years as one day' (2 Pet. 3: 8), the six days of Creation and the following Sabbath were taken to signify that the world would last 6000 years before the reign of Christ began, which since Julius Africanus had set the Creation 5500 years before the birth of Christ did not give it very long to last. In 397 Quintus Julius Hilarianus, who followed the Computist of 243 in dating the Passion to AD 28 and took that year to be AM 5530, but adjusted the date to the normal Roman and African 25 March, declared that of the 470 years left to the world 369 had expired on 24 March; there were therefore only another 101 remaining, unless the ten kings of the Apocalypse should appear sooner and make away with the daughter of Babylon.

Other Westerners followed Eusebius and his translator Jerome in dating the Nativity to AM 5199 (or thereabouts; see p. 809); as late as 727 a Merovingian computist declared: 'Again, from the beginning of the world to the present year all told there are 5928 years; there yet remain of this sixth thousand 72 years.' On this footing, Charlemagne was crowned emperor by the pope in AM 6001; but neither party chose to say so. Chiliasm, as belief in a millennium is called, had long since ceased to be respectable; nevertheless it could not be suppressed (particularly among the discontented) by condemnation even from an Augustine, who had interpreted the texts symbolically, or a Bede, who had made the world only 3952 years old at the Nativity and denied that there was a prescribed term for the sixth or current age, which had begun with it. (The previous five had ended respectively with the Flood, the Tower of Babel, the reign of King Saul, the Babylonian captivity, and the Roman conquest of Judaea.)

Nor was it discredited even by the failure of a prophecy: if one end of the world had not come, that proved only that the count must begin from a different epoch. When the year 6000 was past, and reckoning from the Incarnation had displaced that from Creation, the end of the first millennium caused a turbulence in Western Christendom that, having been exaggerated by romantic historians, was for long belittled or even denied by their rationalist successors, who assumed that the élite were too intelligent to believe such twaddle and the masses were too ignorant to know the date. This involved ignoring or explaining away the numerous treatises and sermons on Antichrist, the great peace rallies, the Easter tables ending or beginning in 1000, Abbo of Fleury's revision of the Christian era in 982, which it called 1003, the charters dated so many years before 1000, and much else (see Landes). When the fatal year was passed relief was manifested, the Burgundian chronicler Rodulfus Glaber tells us, over all the world, especially Italy and Gaul, in the building of churches: 'For it was as if the world, shaking itself free, had sloughed off its old skin and were everywhere donning a white cloak of churches.' Fresh discoveries of relics were made; there also began that wave of pilgrimages to Jerusalem that eventually led to the Crusades, reinforced around the millennium of the Passion in

1033. This, according to Glaber, was a year of abundance preceded by famine and disaster.

In the Greek-speaking world, when AM 6000 had passed without incident, Anastasius of Sinai (7th c.) interpreted the mysterious heading of Ps. 6, 'for the eighth' (probably a musical direction), as referring to the life to come after the seventh millennium of the world should have been completed. Some 40 years before the fateful day, Constantinople fell to the Turks, bereft of the Western help for whose sake, as most in the East believed, the emperor and the patriarch had betrayed Orthodoxy by signing the Union of Florence with the Pope; in Russia apprehension could be detected as the year 7000 aproached. Many Russian Easter tables end at 7000, which was the last year of the solar cycle but year 8 of the lunar cycle and year 84 of the (14th) Paschal cycle. However, a monastic exposition of the Easter computus translates Anastasius' exegesis, but observes that the Easter cycle went on for ever (*Poslanie po povodu sporov*); on 1 September 7001 = AD 1492 human life continued as before.

In our own day the approaching end of the twentieth century has encouraged fears, first of nuclear winter, then of global warming; but on 1 January 2000, a year before the third millennium begins, we shall learn whether civilization is about to collapse through the failure of computers to recognize the change in thousand and hundred.

OLD STYLE AND NEW STYLE

The term 'Old Style' (abbreviated OS), appended to a date, is correctly used to indicate that it is given according to the Julian calendar, which continues that of the Roman Empire with no change except in the numbering of the year, and in which every year AD divisible by 4 is a leap year without exception. 'New Style' (NS) indicates that the date is given according to the Gregorian calendar, in which 15 October 1582 corresponds to 5 October OS and centennial years thereafter are not leap years unless divisible by 400. The distinction needs to be made because the reform was not universally accepted; in Great Britain and her American colonies dates remained Old Style down to 2 September 1752.

The difference between the two calendars, originally ten days, increases from century to century, whenever the centennial year in the Gregorian year is common; it is therefore sometimes known as the secular difference (from Latin *saeculum*, 'century'), or else the Gregorian correction. In any non-centennial year (i.e. any year not ending in 00), the difference is found by omitting the last two figures of the year, dividing the rest by 4, ignoring the remainder, subtracting the answer, and then taking away another 2; this may be written $S - [S/4] - 2$, where $S = [Y/100]$. Thus

Secular difference

1582–99	$15 - 3 - 2 = 10$
1600s	$16 - 4 - 2 = 10$
1700s	$17 - 4 - 2 = 11$

1800s   18 − 4 − 2 = 12
1900s   19 − 4 − 2 = 13
2000s   20 − 5 − 2 = 13

The secular difference must be added to an Old Style date to obtain the corresponding New Style date, or subtracted from the New Style date to obtain the Old. Thus in the seventeenth century, when the calendars were ten days apart, 23 April 1623 OS (the death of Shakespeare) was 3 May 1623 NS; 23 April 1623 NS (the death of Cervantes) was 13 April 1623 OS.

When the centennial year is a leap year even in the Gregorian calendar, the secular difference remains constant; but when the centennial year is common, the difference increases by 1 at the point where the Gregorian calendar suppresses 29 February:

Julian (OS)	Gregorian (NS)				
	1600	1700	1800	1900	2000
1 January	11 January	11 January	12 January	13 January	14 January
1 February	11 February	11 February	12 February	13 February	14 February
15 February	25 February	25 February	26 February	27 February	28 February
16 February	26 February	26 February	27 February	28 February	29 February
17 February	27 February	27 February	28 February	1 March	1 March
18 February	28 February	28 February	1 March	2 March	2 March
19 February	29 February	1 March	2 March	3 March	3 March
20 February	1 March	2 March	3 March	4 March	4 March
28 February	9 March	10 March	11 March	12 March	12 March
29 February	10 March	11 March	12 March	13 March	13 March
1 March	11 March	12 March	13 March	14 March	14 March

Similarly, from 16 February/1 March 2100 to 14/28 February 2200 the secular difference will be $21 − 5 − 2 = 14$.

When dates in both styles are given, they are often represented in fractional form: thus we may say that George Washington was born on 11/22 (or $^{11}/_{22}$) February 1731; it is normal to make the Julian date the numerator (before or above the line) and the Gregorian the denominator (after or below the line), but in the seventeenth century some Roman Catholic chanceries adopted the opposite procedure.

NEW STYLE VS. MODERN STYLE

The term 'New Style' should be distinguished from Modern Style, in which the year (whether Old or New Style) changes its number on 1 January: Scotland, which did not adopt the New Style till 1752, had used Modern Style since 1600; conversely Florence and Pisa, which had adopted the New Style in 1582, continued to count from 25 March (respectively following and preceding the Nativity) down to 1749. Unfortunately, since in England and the American colonies the reckoning from 1 January began in the same year as the New Style was adopted, the Modern Style is sometimes called New, and the reckoning from 25 March (in Florentine fashion) called Old Style; this leads to confusion especially when applied to other countries, although in French the term *nouveau style* was already in use before the Gregorian reform to denote the counting of years from 1 January rather than Easter.

The fractional notation is also used to convert years to Modern Style, as when Washington's birth is dated 11 February 1730/1, or the capture of Pisa by Florence 9 October 1407/6; here again the modern reckoning follows.

THE DATE OF EASTER

Both the definition of Easter and the means of calculating it have varied over the centuries; we give below a brief account of the former question, the more technical matters being considered under *Computus*. Since the early Middle Ages all churches have agreed to define Easter as the first Sunday after the full moon falling on or after the vernal equinox; in turn the equinox is defined as 21 March, and the full moon as the 14th lune or day of the lunar month (*luna XIV*), which is determined by calculation and not observation. If the full moon is itself a Sunday, it is kept as Palm Sunday and Easter observed on the Sunday following; the earliest possible date for Easter is 22 March, the last 25 April. Tables for finding Easter are given in Appendices H and I and under *Computus*.

THE EARLY CHURCH

Whereas Passover is now held to begin on 15 Nisan, in the Bible the name is applied to the 14th, on which the Paschal lamb is slaughtered, and on which according to St John Jesus was executed (see *Christian Chronology: Nativity and Crucifixion*). In the second century the Christians of Asia Minor kept it on 14 Nisan irrespective of feria; as Greek-speakers, they supposed that *pascha* came from *paschein*, 'to suffer', and therefore denoted the Passion. For this 'Quartodeciman' Easter they claimed the authority of the apostles Philip and John, John's pupil the martyr Polycarp, and other great luminaries; even those who rejected it allowed that it was the older practice. The paradox of a Jewish-Christian practice abandoned by the Church in Jerusalem but maintained in a province where relations between Christians and Jews were strikingly bad has engendered the suggestion that it was an innovation of St Polycarp's; such a view presupposes bad faith in Asia and ignorance at Rome. Whether Gentile Christians elsewhere observed Easter in Apostolic times besides celebrating Christ's Resurrection every Sunday remains controversial; by the reign of Pope Victor I (189–98) the feast was general, but most churches took it to commemorate the Resurrection, and hence kept it on Sunday. Provoked by the Quartodeciman campaign that one Blastus launched in Rome, Victor attempted to impose the rule of Sunday on the Asians on pain of excommunication as heretics, but incurred a devastating rebuke from Irenaeus of Lyon, who pointed out that St Polycarp and Pope Anicetus (*c.*155–*c.*166) had agreed to differ in peace. He is frequently understood to mean that Rome had not kept the feast at all before Pope Soter (*c.*166–*c.*174).

Apart from Quartodecimans, from Montanist sectarians who kept Easter on 6 April
or the following Sunday, and from churches in Cappadocia and Gaul which celebrated
on 25 March irrespective of feria, all Christians agreed that Easter should be kept on
the Sunday after the 14th lune of the First Month, and most that this applied even when
luna XIV was itself a Sunday; not only were they unwilling to keep Easter on the Jewish Passover, but since the liturgical Sunday began on Saturday evening, if they broke
their fast before moonrise they would be feasting on *luna XIII* and if they did not they
would be fasting on Easter Sunday. However, from the third century onwards, most
churches were no longer content to regulate Easter by the Jewish date of 14 Nisan, but
preferred to calculate it for themselves; but they disagreed on when the First Month fell,
and how to find *luna XIV*.

PASCHAL CONTROVERSIES

By the end of the third century the Church in Alexandria had adopted a 19-year
Metonic cycle, with seven embolismic months. The fundamental rules were that the
14th lune should not precede the vernal equinox, defined as 25 Phamenoth = 21 March,
and must not be kept as Easter even when it was a Sunday; in consequence, the first
lunar month was that beginning between 12 Phamenoth = 8 March and 9 Pharmouthi
= 5 April, and Easter fell between the 15th and 21st lunes, on 26 Phamenoth = 22 March
at the earliest and 30 Pharmouthi = 25 April at the latest (all dates inclusive). This
Easter would ultimately triumph throughout Christendom.

In the East many Christians were content to take the date of 14 Nisan from the Jews
(some observed Easter itself on that day if it was a Sunday) until, following the Council of Nicaea in 325, the emperor Constantine wrote a letter exalting uniformity and
condemning dependence on Jews, but prescribing neither the basis on which uniformity
was to be established, nor the method to be used in calculation. The Eastern churches
in time adopted the principle of the Metonic cycle, and the Alexandrian limits; two
slight divergences in the placing of *luna XIV* were abolished in the 560s, though one was
retained by churches not in communion with Constantinople. These were in any case
slight beside the differences between Alexandria and Rome.

At Rome a stringent rule laid down that Easter should never fall later than *21 April,
the Parilia or birthday of Rome, lest Christians should fast while pagans feasted; this
prohibition, observed even by other Westerners who followed Roman calculations, remained until the mid-fifth century. The feast was deferred not only when the 14th lune
was a Friday but even when it was a Saturday, the lunar limits being thus *XVI–XXII*; in
consequence, Good Friday never preceded *luna XIV*. In principle, the First Month was
that beginning between 5 March and 2 April; there was no rule preventing the 14th lune
from preceding the equinox, but by the early fourth century it was thought wrong to
keep Easter itself before the equinox, which was taken to be 25 March as in Julius
Caesar's day. The impracticality of this rule caused the limit to be moved back in

mid-century to the 22nd. Romans were also concerned that their Easter tables should repeat in respect not only of the moon but of the sun, and therefore of Easter dates; for this reason they based them on multiples of 28 years, at first 112 years, but by the late third century 84 years. Others too used 84-year cycles; indeed the earliest, that of Augustalis, seems to be African. It is decidedly un-Roman in not postponing Easter when *luna XIV* falls on a Sunday; it allows celebration as early as 21 March.

In practice the dates observed were less often different than those of *luna XIV*, either because of the leeway created by the following-Sunday rule, or because one church gave way to another for the sake of uniformity (see **Computus*); but by the later fourth century Alexandria was asserting that Nicaea had entrusted it with finding Easter, a claim accepted by St Ambrose at Milan. Even the Popes came to accept it, but still resisted celebrating later than 21 April. In 417 Alexandria kept 22 April, but Rome 25 March; however, before the next late Alexandrian Easter on 23 April 444 Pope Leo, seeking advice from Bishop Paschasinus of Lilybaeum (Marsala in Sicily), was informed not only that the latest table, beginning in 437, gave 23 April, but that on the previous occasion a font that always filled miraculously for the Easter Day baptisms had observed the Alexandrian, not the Roman date. The Pope submitted to science or to superstition, for as Paschasinus noted Good Friday still lay within the Roman limit, on the 21st; the circus games for the City's birthday were cancelled. This palliation was unavailing for 24 April, the date that Alexandria was due to keep in 455 when the Roman tables prescribed the 17th. Leo pestered the emperor Marcian and Bishop Julian of Constantinople to intervene; the political circumstances were not in his favour, for despite his theological victory at the Council of Chalcedon he had objected to the canon declaring Constantinople second in status after Rome. Marcian referred the question to Bishop Proterius of Alexandria, who, affecting to misunderstand the Romans as objecting to deferment from *luna XIV*, instructed the Pope in his duty to inform all doubters that 24 April was right. Leo gave way for unity's sake.

These crises provoked computists to construct new 84-year cycles, and Leo's archdeacon (later his successor) Hilarus to charge Victorius of Aquitaine with drawing up a table to resolve disagreements and establish uniformity; he responded in 457 with a perpetual cycle of 532 Easters, running from AD 28 to 559 and repeating thereafter. It is vitiated by his attempt to moderate Alexandrian rigour with residual Roman prejudices: when *luna XIV* falls on Saturday, he generally gives both *luna XV* and *luna XXII*, leaving the Pope to choose; *luna XIV* falls between 20 March and 17 April, Easter between 22 March and 24 April, but still not the 25th. Moreover, in 13 years out of 19 his Paschal term is a day earlier than the Alexandrian. His incompetence was apparent as early as 482, for which he gave a Latin date of 18 April on *luna XV*, and a Greek of 24 [*sic*] April on *luna XXII*, violating both parties' lunar limits and condemning the 'Greeks' to keep Easter on a Saturday.

The church in Africa had not been consistent in its Easter reckoning: although St Augustine at Hippo had followed Alexandria (or perhaps rather Milan), 84-year tables had continued to be composed at Carthage as late as 455; one Quintus Julius Hilarianus, apparently an African, had even written a treatise dated 5 March 397 upholding the eight-year cycle (see pp. 801–2) with arguments largely taken from the Computist of 243 (see *28 Mar.). But Victorius' blunder concentrated minds: all other tables were cast aside and the Alexandrian adopted, which made Easter 25 April on *luna XXI*.

Others were not so particular; shakier mathematicians preferred Victorius' tables, which had the twin advantages over the Alexandrian of being perpetual, and of using the familiar Roman New Year of 1 January. However, in the early 520s Pope John I demanded a new study, perhaps because the impending Easter on 19 April 526, although shared with Alexandria, was designated *luna XXII*. The expert called in was the Scythian monk Dionysius Exiguus ('Tiny', a pretension to humility rather than a statement of stature), who prepared a table for the 95 years 532–626 based on Alexandrian principles and dated by the Incarnation (see *Christian Chronology: Christian Era*). His only concession to Western convention was to translate the Egyptian dates into the Roman calendar: he not only ignored the 'Latin' rules, but took no account of 1 January for either epact or feria. That greatly simplified his task, which cannot (it has been estimated) have taken him more than one hour's work; it did not encourage acceptance of his tables, nor did he explain how his results were arrived at.

There is no proof that Rome had committed herself to Dionysius' tables (which in 616 were continued for 627–721) until in 654 St Wilfrid (12 Oct.) learnt it there; it was certainly not imposed on churches that followed Victorius, whose tables were made binding in his native Gaul in 541, just in time for an even more egregious error, a 'Greek' date for year 516 (AD 543) on *luna XXIII* (his 'Latin' date agreed with Dionysius); nevertheless, they remained in force till the time of Charlemagne. In 577, when the Alexandrian Easter fell on 25 April, Gregory of Tours kept the 18th; the Spaniards, evidently following some modification of Augustalis or even Hippolytus, kept 21 March, but Gregory records with glee that certain miraculous springs in Spain, which always flowed at Easter, ran on *his* date. As usual, more than one party has its miracles; but these springs were all the dearer to Gregory for having confounded the Arian king Theudegisil (548–9), who had tried to find out how the 'Romans', i.e. Catholics, worked the trick. In 590 the Alexandrian date was 26 March, *luna XV*, but Gregory kept the 'Latin' day of 2 April; the Spanish springs did likewise. In Italy there is evidence for use of Victorius' tables and even a form of the 84-year cycle; disagreement is attested in Spain even after the adoption of Dionysius' table, for so little were these matters understood that Isidore of Seville could suppose that it was cyclical, though Dionysius himself had warned that it was not.

INSULAR EASTER

Although Victorius' tables were known in Ireland by the sixth century, and the Alexandrian reckoning was known there in the seventh, both the British and Irish churches calculated Easter on quite other principles, not fully understood till the rediscovered cycle was published in 1987. The fundamental difference was that Easter was kept between *luna XIV* and *luna XX*; since the lune was taken as beginning half an hour after midday there was no question of feasting on *luna XIII*, but celebration on *XXI* and *XXII*, moons that did not rise till after midnight, was anathema, since darkness prevailed over light. It was found from an 84-year cycle, the so-called Latercus, in which *luna XIV* might fall between 21 March and 17 April, Easter itself between 26 March and 23 April (for details, see App. J).

The Insular Easter often differed from that required either by the Alexandrian reckoning or by Victorius'; when under Gregory the Great papal missionaries brought Roman methods to England, and St Columban took Insular methods to the Continent, bitter controversies broke out. About 600 Columban, in a letter equally remarkable for baroque Latinity and studied insolence, informed the Pope that Victorius' tables, used by the Franks and at least tolerated by Rome, were held in disdain by 'our teachers and the ancient Irish scholars and the most skilled computists', and denounced the wickedness of keeping *luna XXI* or *XXII*; in 597 Victorius' 'Latin' date was 14 April on *luna XXII*, in 600 he gave 10 April on *luna XXI*. A few years later Augustine of Canterbury tried and failed to browbeat the British bishops into adopting Roman methods.

About 629 Pope Honorius I urged the Irish to conform to the universal usage of Christendom; a conference of southern communities summoned by one Cummian, probably Cuimine Fota (Cummianus Longus) of Clonfert Brendan, sent a delegation to Rome in 631, which found everyone else in the hostel celebrating on 24 March, four weeks ahead of the Insular date. The southerners thereupon adopted Victorius' tables; but the northerners in Bangor, Iona, and Lindisfarne held fast to their tradition and rebuked the southerners for abandoning it. This rebuke was answered by Cummian; in 640 the pope-elect wrote to the northerners condemning *luna XIV*, again to no avail.

The conflict spread to Northumbria, where King Oswiu (642–71), obedient to the Irish bishops of Lindisfarne, sometimes celebrated Easter on the day that Queen Eanfled, having lived in Kent, kept as Palm Sunday. In 664 the Insular Easter was 14 April, *luna XIV*, but both Victorius and Dionysius gave the 21st; on 1 May following there was a solar eclipse, total for the Northumbrian monasteries, followed by aurorae at a time of advancing plague. As McCarthy has shown, it was these omens of divine displeasure over the disputes between Roman and Celtic usage, of which the Paschal question was only one, that caused Oswiu to hold a synod at Whitby to settle them. Proceedings were dominated by St Wilfrid, who brought about the triumph of Rome, including the Dionysian Easter he had learnt there ten years earlier; its status, and the consequential disowning of Victorius, were confirmed by Pope Vitalianus in a letter to Oswiu of 667. It was imposed on all England by Theodore of Tarsus (19 Sept.) after his arrival as archbishop of Canterbury in 669.

Adomnán (see *23 Sept.) persuaded many of the northern Irish to abandon the Latercus *c.*686, though not his own monks at Iona or its dependent monasteries; he may have been helped by the ascription to St Patrick, already attested by Cummian, of a treatise based on Alexandrian principles, though Victorius was generally preferred to Dionysius in Ireland for many generations. Some Britons in Strathclyde and Cornwall adopted Dionysius' Easter about this time, the Picts *c.*710, Iona in 716, but the Welsh were more obdurate. Bishop Elfoddw of Bangor Fawr imposed the Roman usage on Gwynedd in 755, and persuaded others to adopt it in 768, but the bishops of Llandaff and Menevia, which claimed to be older than Bangor, refused to submit (which King Offa of Mercia made a pretext for invading South Wales in 777–8), and some diehards put their case to Patriarch Methodius I of Constantinople (843–7).

While both parties appealed to principle and authority, the subject of the quarrel was the range of permissible Easters, by sun and by moon; the mode of calculation came second, its astronomical accuracy not even third. In 664 Dionysius' table put new moon on 4 April, Victorius' on the 3rd, the Latercus on 30 March; the true conjunction took place at 6.18 a.m. GMT on 2 April. This was the last year of an Alexandrian cycle, or as a later age would say, Golden Number 19, in which such discrepancies were frequent; but though Bede answers a hypothetical claim to have seen the new moon in such a year on the evening of 2 April, the tone suggests the most recent instance in 721, and no such comment is reported from the debate at Whitby. However, the next new moon, at 3.52 p.m. GMT on 1 May 664, was made memorable by the eclipse; but the Dionysian lunar age is 28, with new moon on the 3rd. The Latercus was even less accurate, putting the new moon on 28 April; nevertheless, the eclipse must have been recorded in Wilfrid's Easter table on 3 May, in order to show the perfection of the Roman reckoning, for Bede gives that day but the right time ('about the tenth hour of day').

THE VENERABLE BEDE

The Synod of Whitby is described, and the Easter question treated at length, in Bede's *Historia ecclesiastica gentis Anglorum*, which was known in Continental Europe within a few years of composition and gave general currency to reckoning AD. Whereas in modern times this is the work for which he is chiefly honoured, in the Middle Ages the fame of 'Beda computista' rested above all on his classic account of calendar and computus, *De temporum ratione* (based, as he does not say, on southern Irish materials acquired by Wilfrid) with a 532-year Easter table constructed on Dionysius' principles, which secured their triumph over Victorius' tables throughout the Western Church.

The monks of Iona who came to Northumbria aroused in him the sincerest admiration; he felt nothing of the kind for Wilfrid. Nevertheless, he detests the Insular Easter with a passion that dismays modern readers given to supposing that only the enemies and not the upholders of uniformity are capable of speaking from the heart. Yet both parties were united in their belief that truth was in combat against error: the treatise on which the Celts most relied declared that those who kept Easter on *luna XXI* or *XXII* 'not only cannot support it with the authority of Holy Writ but incur both the charge of sacrilege and disrespectfulness and the peril of their souls, in asserting that a dominance of darkness is a possible time for sacrificing the true Light that dominates over all darkness'. Long before then, St Jerome had asserted that those who kept a separate

Easter ate the flesh, not of the Lamb, but of the Psalmist's dragon; in a law issued by the emperor Theodosius II in 413 persons celebrating on a different day from the orthodox are said to 'honour almost another Son of God, not Him whom we worship'.

Allowance too must be made for Bede's personal interest, and special competence, in computus; the Roman party was no less offended by the Celtic tonsure, which seemed too druidical and was tarred with the name of Simon Magus, but Bede, though aware that it is to be condemned, has no intellectual interest in the matter. Wilfrid's biographer, Eddius Stephanus, who knows no bounds in his hero worship, reports the debate far more briefly, and completely obscures the browbeating style in which it had been won.

GREGORIAN EASTER

The Gregorian reform of the calendar in 1582 did not affect the definition of Easter, but the inaccuracy of the Julian lunar calendar caused the reformers to devise new Easter tables, embodying a new principle. The epacts, which were now once more calibrated to 1 January, became the direct basis of determining the date of Easter. The first step is to determine, from a centennial table (see *Computus, Table 7), the epact for each Golden Number within the century, defined for this purpose as running from 00 to 99; one then seeks its first recurrence after 7 March in a table of epacts for each day of the year (*Computus, Table 8); that will be the new moon of the Paschal month, to which 13 days must be added to obtain the Paschal term, and the following Sunday found by the *Sunday Letter, itself calculated according to the appropriate century. In Appendix H the date of Easter corresponding to any Golden Number and Sunday Letter is given for the years 1583–2199 inclusive.

An alternative reform, using the annual epact to reallocate the Golden Numbers within each century to the appropriate lunar dates, had been rejected because the need to know the moon's age all year round, so as to announce it at the daily reading from the martyrology, would have entailed preparing 30 different calendars. When Great Britain adopted the New Style in 1752, the Church of England accepted the Pope's Easter dates but not his tables; having no use for the martyrology and needing the moon's age only to find Easter, it took up the rejected method, but simplified it by assigning the Golden Numbers directly to the Paschal term or 'Ecclesiastical Full Moon'. The necessary tables are printed in the BCP, but not in ASB or CY, confirming their status as alternatives, not replacements.

PASSOVER AND EASTER

The deferment of Easter when the Paschal term fell on a Sunday, inasmuch as intended to save Christians from celebrating their *pascha* on the same day as the Jews kept theirs, was rendered otiose by the Jewish rule that 1 Tishri must not be a Wednesday lest Yom Kippur immediately precede the Sabbath, which entails that the preceding 14 Nisan cannot fall upon a Sunday; however, the sentiment reattached itself to those days that count in the Diaspora as Passover, 15 and 16 Nisan. In the Julian calendar, Easter last coincided with 15 Nisan on 23 March 783 (other cases being 31 March 614 and 14 April 743), and with 16 Nisan on 23 March 1315; but the correction of the calendar made such coincidences inevitable. Although the reformers knew that it was neither forbidden nor unprecedented, they so far accommodated themselves to the prejudice as to write the epacts a day or two later in the calendar than in the original draft so as to minimize the chance of the two feasts' coinciding. Nevertheless, as early as 19 April 1609 Easter fell on 15 Nisan, and again on 14 April 1805, 3 April 1825, 12 April 1903, 1 April 1923, 17 April 1927, 18 April 1954, 10 April 1981. It will next do so on 3 April 2072, and for the last time on 19 April 7485; after 8948 Passover will always be later than 25 April. However, at present the Gregorian Easter generally falls on the 16th almost every time that 15 Nisan is a Sabbath, beginning with 3 April 1589 and five cases in the 1590s.

ASTRONOMICAL EASTER

Although Protestants were not disposed to accept any reform promulgated by the Pope, they found an easy target in the astronomical inaccuracies presented from time to time by the tables—whose defenders admitted them, while rightly insisting that no better tables of equal simplicity could be devised on a cyclic basis. In 1699 the Lutherans of Germany voted to accept the New Style from 1 March 1700, but to determine Easter by the real full moon and the real equinox (*calculus astronomicus*); this 'Improved Calendar' was adopted by Denmark and most of the Protestant cantons in Switzerland. (It was also adopted, as the 'Improved Julian Calendar', by those Dutch provinces that had kept the Old Style; but in practice they observed the Gregorian Easter.) Having failed to notice that in that very year they ought to celebrate Easter a week earlier than the Gregorian date, when the case next arose in 1724 they discovered to their embarrassment that their astronomical Easter would coincide with the second day of Passover; this had not troubled Luther himself (see *Modern Calendar: Early Proposals for Reform*), but his followers, having made much of the matter in their anti-Gregorian polemics, found that when their astronomical Easter diverged from the Gregorian, it was likely to coincide with Passover. After much debate the Protestants of Germany and Switzerland, but not Denmark, kept Easter a week earlier than the rest of Christendom (for Julian and Gregorian Easter coincided); it was thus on the astronomical Good Friday, 7 April, that Bach's *St John Passion* received its first performance.

In 1740 the astronomical Easter was adopted by Sweden, albeit with Old Style dating down to 1752, and in 1744 German and Swiss Protestants, Danes, and Swedes all kept Easter on 29 March (called the 18th in Sweden), a week ahead of the rest of Europe, even though it was the second day of Passover. The next case would have been in

1778, but by then the prejudice thus flouted had been exploited by Frederick the Great to persuade the German Protestants in 1776 to give up the *calculus astronomicus* and adopt the Gregorian calendar in full, under the face-saving name (agreed in advance with the emperor Joseph II) of 'Improved Imperial Calendar'. (Frederick, it hardly needs saying, cared nothing about either Easter or Passover, but found the divergence an unwelcome complication, especially after acquiring Roman Catholic subjects from partitioned Poland.) The Danes and Swiss followed suit, but the *calculus astronomicus* remained in force in Sweden till 1823 (though overridden on account of Passover in 1778 and 1798), and in Finland (which Sweden had ceded to Russia in 1809) till 1867; for the resulting Easter dates, see Appendix I.

SURVIVAL OF JULIAN EASTER

The Julian Easter is still used by all Orthodox outside Finland and a few communities in the West. If no further reform is undertaken by either party, between 6700 and 6799 inclusive the Orthodox Easter will coincide with the Western Pentecost; the nominal dates will be the same in the civil calendar, but one day ahead in the Revised Julian Calendar of the Orthodox Church. The congress at Constantinople in 1923 that adopted this latter also voted to celebrate Easter on the astronomical principle, defining equinox and full moon by the meridian of Jerusalem; a few such dates were kept by certain churches in the 1920s, a time of political upheaval also marked by civil imposition of the New Style, after which the proposal lapsed. It was revived in 1997 at a meeting in Aleppo attended by various churches from the World Council of Churches and Middle East Council of Churches, being proposed to take effect from 15 April 2001, the first Easter of the new millennium by Orthodox and Western reckoning alike.

FIXED EASTER

Recalling those sects and churches that had kept Easter either on a fixed day of the civil calendar or on a Sunday defined by it, Luther recommended the Christian princes to make Easter an immoveable feast like Christmas. Others suggested a definite Sunday: in 1723, when Protestants were preparing to keep the next year's Easter a week ahead of the Roman Catholics, the Swiss mathematician Jean Bernoulli proposed that it should always be the first Sunday after 21 March; in 1834 Marco Mastrofini set Easter on 2 April in his fixed calendar (see *Modern Calendar: Unsuccessful Proposals*). In 1926 the League of Nations endorsed the keeping of Easter on the Sunday after the second Saturday in April, that is (assuming no more general reform) between the 9th and the 15th; an Act of Parliament to this effect was passed by the UK Parliament in 1928, to come into force once general agreement should have been reached among the churches. However, the

Vatican will not move without the Orthodox, and the Orthodox cannot accept such a reform except through an Oecumenical Council; in 1962 the Vatican restated its position that such a change ought not to be made without urgent need, which has not been felt. Easter therefore continues to be kept, in many countries as a public as well as a religious holiday, according to rules that not even many Christians understand.

COMPUTUS

GENERAL

Computus is calculation, especially of the calendar, in particular but not exclusively for the determination of Easter. The following account is intended only as an introduction; much more is to be found in computistic manuscripts than can be expounded here.

From the theological point of view, the essential rules are those determining on what days of the solar year, and the lunar month, Easter may be celebrated; these are discussed under *The Date of Easter*. By the third century, most Christians agreed that Easter should be kept on the Sunday after the 14th lune (*luna XIV*) of the first lunar month, a date known in the West as the Paschal term and in the East as the Legal [i.e. Old Testament] or Hebrew Pascha; but they agreed on little else except that the age of the moon was not to be determined by watching the skies. Some Eastern Christians watched the Jews, to see when they kept Passover; but the dominant practice was to calculate the date of Easter in advance. This was done by determining the interval of recurrence, or cycle, of the epact, or age of the moon, on a given day, and the feria of the same or another given day. It was therefore necessary to construct a lunar calendar, which especially in the Latin world became more than a mere Easter-finding device; the pagan interest, demonstrated by inscriptions from the third century onwards, in stating the lune as well as the date of an event (see *Roman Calendar*) was matched by Christians who prefaced the daily reading from the martyrology at prime with the date and lune: thus on 5 May under Golden Number 6 in the Julian calendar and epact 2 in the Gregorian, *Tertio Nonas Maii, luna decima*. This was still required in RC religious houses till the later twentieth century.

❦ METONIC CYCLES The mean length of the synodic month or lunation, from new moon to new moon, is 29.530 59 days; the traditional approximation of 29½ days, taken over by the Christian computists, entails an alternation of 30-day 'full' months and 29-day 'hollow' months. On this footing, 12 months amount to 354 days, 11 days fewer than the calendar year of 365 days; the deficit is made up by adding extra 'embolismic' months of 30 days at various points in a cycle designed to correlate the lunar with the solar year. In accordance with a tradition that Jews, Greeks, and early Romans had kept their calendar in touch with the sun by intercalating three months in every eight years, the earliest Easter computus was based on the eight-year cycle or *oktaetēris*, which inserted an embolism in years 3, 6, and 8; but a more accurate device is the 19-year cycle or *enneakaidekaetēris*, known as the Metonic cycle after the Athenian astronomer Meton (*fl.* 432 BC), based on the near-equivalence of 235 synodic months = 6939.688 65 days and 19 tropical years = 6939.6018 days. Depending on the starting-point, embolisms will occur at three- and two-year intervals, combining into subcycles of eight years (intercalated 3, 3, 2) and eleven (intercalated 3, 3, 3, 2); these are known respectively as the *ogdoad* and the *hendecad*, terms of no practical use, but often flaunted by computists.

This was the cycle adopted at Alexandria, followed by the rest of the Greek-speaking world; but in Roman eyes it had the disadvantage of requiring too great a spread between the first and last legitimate date of Easter, for since 7 is incommensurate with 19, every possible Paschal term must over time fall on each day of the week, yielding some 35 different Easter dates. That did not disturb the Greeks, but many Latins objected that late Easters entailed celebrating in the second month; moreover, at Rome it was vital not to let the feast be later than 21 April. For this reason, Alexandrian methods were resisted as long as possible.

❡ SOLAR CYCLES Since the common year contains $365 \equiv 1 \bmod 7$ days, in any two consecutive common years any given date will fall one feria later in the second than the first; since leap year contains $366 \equiv 2 \bmod 7$ days the difference will be two feriae if leap day intervenes. It is therefore possible, knowing the feria of a given date in a particular year, to find its feria in any subsequent year by adding one day for each year elapsed and one day for each leap year; that is to say, dividing the number of years by 4, ignoring the remainder, and adding the quotient to the dividend. In an era reckoned by current years, as is normal outside India, the feria of the first day in any year can be determined by the ferial formula $Y + [Y/4] + P \pmod 7$: add to the year of the era its quarter, ignoring fractions, and a parameter corresponding to the feria of the day *preceding* the first day of the era (since 1 will be added for year 1), and take the remainder to 7. However, in the Julian calendar the ferial cycle of 7 days and the bissextile cycle of 4 years have a combined periodicity of 28 years, known as the solar cycle; one may therefore apply the ferial formula not to the *millésime* of the year, but to its place in the solar cycle of the calendar in question.

❡ PASCHAL CYCLES The 19- and 28-year cycles combine to form a 532-year sequence, devised by Annianus in the early fifth century and stumbled into a few decades later by Victorius of Aquitaine, variously known as a 'Great Cycle', a 'Great Year', a 'Paschal cycle', *alpha* (because in Greek the numerical value of the constituent letters is 532), and in Russian as a 'Great Indiction'. In the Julian calendar, though not the Gregorian, Easter in any year falls on the same date as it did 532 or 1064 years previously.

HISTORICAL

❡ ALEXANDRIA: 19-YEAR CYCLES Dionysius bishop of Alexandria (d. *c.*264) drew up an Easter table based on the *oktaetēris*; but it was swiftly superseded by the Metonic cycle. An extract cited by the church historian Eusebius from the Paschal canon of Anatolius (*fl.* 278), an Alexandrian who became bishop of Laodicea, appears to advocate a 19-year cycle beginning with new moon on 22 March (defined as 26 Phamenoth = 22 Dystros = *XI Kal. Apr.*), said to be the sun's fourth day in Aries, the sign of the vernal equinox, before which Jews ought not to celebrate Passover. He was understood by later writers to mean that 22 March was the equinox, as it had been for Ptolemy in AD 140; the text does not say so, but does make plain that this was *luna XIV* in the first year of his cycle, which in consequence was either AD 258 or 277.

Within a generation, however, the Alexandrian Church had adjusted the cycle to take account of the civil year; the reform is commonly thought to have been instituted with effect from the observed new moon of the post-leap year 1 Thoth 20 Diocletian (= 30 Aug. 303). The basis was the Jewish lunar calendar as adapted to the Alexandrian civil reckoning and, so the Christians maintained, operated more accurately than by the Jews themselves. To ensure that the lunar new year should not begin before 15 Thoth, or the Paschal month before 12 Phamenoth, an embolismic month of 30 days was added to the end of years 2, 5, 7, 10, 13, 16, 18. In cycle 19 the lunar new year began on 12 Phaophi, and hence the penultimate lunar month on 7 Mesore; the *saltus* made it hollow, ending on 5 Epagomenon, so that the last lunar month began on 1 Thoth in the first year of the new cycle and the lunar new year began on 30 Thoth. Leap year was dealt with by repeating the lune of 5 Epagomenon on the 6th.

The epact remains *de facto* the lune of 26 Phamenoth = 22 March, but is not so defined except in Western sources; it is understood rather as the lune of 5 Epagomenon in the preceding year. Epact 1 no longer began the cycle but belonged to year 12. The day before, 25 Phamenoth = 21 March, was defined as the equinox, which *luna XIV* was permitted to coincide with but not to precede; if the latter is Sunday, Easter was postponed, but Alexandria, unlike Rome, was willing to celebrate on *luna XV*. In consequence, Easter always follows the equinox, but provided *luna XIV* is no earlier than 25 Phamenoth the next Sunday is always Easter, with no recourse to the forbidden Second Month. The First Month begins no earlier than 12 Phamenoth = 8 March and no later than 10 Pharmouthi = 5 April; *luna XIV* falls between 25 Phamenoth = 21 March and 23 Pharmouthi = 18 April inclusively, Easter between 26 Phamenoth = 22 March and 30 Pharmouthi = 25 April, also inclusively. The limits are thus *XV–XXI*, though they may be stated as *XIV–XXI* out of respect to the biblical distinction between Passover on the 14th of the First Month and the Feast of Unleavened Bread from the 15th to the 21st; in every year there is one possible date for Easter and one only.

Cycle 19 having ended in a hollow month on 5 Epagomenon, cycle 1 began without epact; in early sources the epact was written as 29, or even 30 (since Greeks liked to call the last day of hollow months *triakás*; see **Greek Calendar*), but Ethiopic tables give 'nothing', which Dionysius Exiguus made the standard Western practice. Thereafter, if c is the place of the year in the Metonic cycle, the epact $\equiv 11(c-1)$ mod 30. The Paschal term is painlessly found by subtracting the epact from 10, or if greater than 10 from 40; the remainder will give the correct day in Pharmouthi, or if over 23 in Phamenoth. The feria of 1 Pharmouthi, which is always that of 1 Thoth, is found from the ferial formula with parameter 2 for the Diocletianic era, 6 for those of the World and Grace, 0 for the Incarnation; the remainder is the feria reckoned from Wednesday, known by the pagan term *tôn theôn*, 'of the [planetary] gods'. If it is preferred to count from Sunday, the parameters are increased by 3; the result is the 'day of John'.

Of the four eras in use, those of the World, Diocletian, and Grace marched in step with the Metonic cycle but that of the Incarnation did not: 1 Incarnation (AD 8/9) = AM 5501 = cycle 10. For that reason the Incarnation era is never used in Alexandrian computus, even though it begins the solar cycle; to find the place of the year in this, take the remainder to 28 directly if it is a year of the Incarnation, but first subtract 4 if it is a year of Diocletian and 12 if it is a year of Grace or the World.

Early in the fifth century the monk Annianus devised the Paschal cycle of 532 years; but more often the Alexandrians were content with shorter tables, of 95, 100, or 114 years. The 95-year table reflected the fact that after five Metonic cycles *luna XIV* returned to its original feria (so that Easter was on the same day) except in leap year, when it fell on the feria before.

In the Alexandrian cycle the years divisible by 4 are post-leap years; their solar epacts correspond to those required for the same place in the Byzantine cycle from March, whereas those of other years are identical with the concurrents (see below) for the same place in the Western cycle. They indicate the place of 1 Thoth in a sequence beginning on Wednesday (the feria of 1 Thoth in year 1 of the Incarnation). In the Paschal computus, the Alexandrian solar epact will be the same as the Western concurrent for the actual year.

The Alexandrian Paschal cycle is normally counted for computistic purposes from Year of Grace 1 = 77 Diocletian = 353 Incarnation = 5853 World (AD 360/1), notionally the first year of the 12th cycle; it is therefore out of step with the solar cycle, which begins in Paschal year 13 mod 28. Tables sometimes begin with Paschal 153 (229 Diocletian = AD 512/13, 761 = 1044/5, etc.), since only then do both a new Metonic and a new solar cycle begin.

The elaborate tables preserved in Ethiopic sources (see Neugebauer, *Ethiopic Astronomy and Computus*) set forth for every civil year: its place in the 532-year and 19-year cycle; the 'beginning of the epact' (the civil date of the last new moon in the previous year); the number of epagomenal days (which for ease of computation were counted with the following year); the evangelist of the year (see **Egyptian Calendar: Christian*); the day of John; the day of the gods (*tentyon*); the epact; the civil date of the Jewish New Year (this sometimes with its feria), Day of Atonement, and Tabernacles according to the adapted calendar, each accompanied by its lunar date (1, 10, and 15 respectively); the 'day of Nineveh' (Monday 69 days before Easter); the 'beginning of the Fast' (Monday 55 days before Easter, sometimes with its lunar date); the civil and lunar date (the latter always 14) of Passover (sometimes also its feria); and the civil date of Easter.

❦ ROME: 112-YEAR TABLES The first known Easter table, that of Hippolytus, prepared at Rome and preserved in the Vatican Library (see *13 Aug.), purports to give the dates of *luna XIV* and of Easter for 112 years (i.e. four solar cycles), from 222 to 333, divided into seven 16-year cycles each comprising two *oktaetērides* in which the Paschal term falls successively on 13 April, 2 April, 21 March (leap year), 9 April, 29 March, 18 March, 5 April (leap year), and 25 March, with embolisms (implicitly preceding the Paschal month) in years 1, 4, 7. The double cycle was adopted as the basis because, 16 Julian years being one day less than 835 weeks, the feriae of corresponding dates run smoothly in reverse sequence from column to column: 13 April, a Saturday in column 1 (222), is a Friday in column 2 (238), a Thursday in column 3 (254), and so on. After 112 years the table would repeat, 13 April being a Saturday in 334 as in 222. According to Roman practice, when *luna XIV* is a Sunday, Easter is the next Sunday, and when a Saturday, Easter is deferred to the Sunday eight days after it, the permissible lunes being *XVI–XXII*; in consequence the earliest Easter on Hippolytus' table is 20 March, the latest 21 April.

Unfortunately, while eight years of 354 days with an additional three full months, making 2922 days, are equivalent to eight solar years including two leap days, 99 synodic months are 2923.528 41 days, eight tropical years 2921.937 6 days. The discrepancy soon became apparent, though not all understood its cause. In 243 another computist—who conducts a polemic against his rivals—revised the table to run from 242 to 353, displacing Hippolytus' period by 20 years, or one year more than a Metonic cycle; in consequence, the 14th lunes, and the embolisms, are set one cyclical year earlier. Moreover, all but those originally in Roman leap years are shifted to the previous day, so that the Paschal term in the Computist's year 1, namely 1 April, is 12 days earlier than in Hippolytus' year 1, the 13th; since 247 synodic lunations are 7294.055 73 days and 20 tropical years 7304.844 days, the difference ought to have been 10 days, not 12. Thus, whereas in Hippolytus' table *luna XIV* fell on 18 March in years 6 and 14 of each 16-year cycle, in the revised tables it fell on 17 March in years 5 and 13. Since Roman theory allowed the first month of the lunar year to begin between 5 March and 2 April inclusive, some sleight-of-hand is needed in the exposition, and duly provided. None of this addressed the inherent fault of the cycle, that whereas 112 solar years are 40 907.344 8 days, and 112 Julian years 40 908 days, the 1386 synodic months supposedly emulated by Hippolytus' and the Computist's calendar are 40 929.397 74 days, some three weeks in excess.

❦ ROME: 84-YEAR CYCLES (SUPPUTATIO ROMANA) The fundamental inaccuracy of these tables, in which the Paschal term rapidly slipped back towards new moon, was apparent even to Roman churchmen of the third century, men of very limited scientific understanding. However, they still wished their tables to repeat as to feriae as well as lunes; but this could be achieved by cycles of 84 years (comprising three 28-year solar cycles instead of Hippolytus' four) with 31 embolisms. Astronomically, this was somewhat more accurate than the Hippolytan tables, but still inadequate: the difference of 1.938 21 days between 1039 lunations = 30 682.283 01 days and 84 solar years = 30 680.344 8 days caused the epacts in successive cycles to run ahead of their true values. However, it was not this that caused trouble in practice, but the impractical Roman Paschal limits.

The tables, which indicate the feria and lune of 1 January and of Easter, presuppose a lunar calendar in which all months ending in an odd solar month were full and all ending in an even month were empty; but whereas Hippolytus and the Computist of 243 had allowed *luna XIV* to fall one nominal day earlier in leap year, the authors of 84-year cycles assigned an extra day to lunar February, which thus became full instead of hollow. This, together with the 31 embolisms, would have given 30 687 days as opposed to the 30 681 days of 81 Julian years; to avoid this excess, six days were omitted in the course of the cycle. This is known to computists as the *saltus lunae* or 'moon's leap'; it appears to have been achieved by advancing two lunes instead of one from 31 December to 1 January. The earliest known (perhaps African) 84-year cycle, that of Augustalis, whose 100-year table or *laterculus* for 213–312 was continued by other hands, places the *saltus* every 14 years; Roman practice favoured 12-year intervals between cycles 12 and 72 inclusive.

The epact or lune of 1 January is also that of 1 March; for the other Kalends, add 1 for February and April, 2 for May, 3 for June, 4 for July, 5 for August, 7 for September and October, 9 for November and December, subtracting 30 when the total exceeds that figure; the epact of the following January will be higher by 11, but by 12 after a *saltus*. However, when the epact in January is 29 or 30 February and April have the same epact as May, respectively 1 or 2.

Years with epact 20 or higher were embolismic; the dates of the embolisms are not recorded, but subsequent practice shows concern that the relation between the monthly epacts shall be constant, that lunar months shall end in the like-named solar months, and that the embolism shall end either on Kalends whose epact is 30, or on *pridie Kalendas* when the next month's epact is 1. On this footing the embolism under annual epact 20 began on 2 December, under 21 on 2 November, under 22 on 2 October, under 23 on 2 September, under 24 on 2 August, under 25 on 3 July, under 26 on 2 June, under 27 on 3 May, and under 28 on 2 April. Under epact 29, however, when lunar January ended on 2 January solar, 'February' was 3–31 January, and 'March' 1 February–2 March; had the embolism been called on 3 March, the epact of April would have been 30, as against 1 in February. More seriously, there would be two years (epacts 28 and 29) on which *luna XIV* fell on 15 April, an extremely inconvenient date given Roman Paschal limits. To overcome this disadvantage 3–31 March were assigned to lunar April, and solar April taken as the embolism. Similarly, under epact 30, lunar 'February' was 2–30 January, 'March' 31 January–1 March, 'April' 2–30 March, and the embolism 31 March–29 April. Thus in contrast to other tables the embolisms never preceded the First Month, which might follow either lunar March (full) or lunar April (hollow); to be sure, epacts 1 and 30 shared the same date for *luna XIV*, namely 13 April, but that date always gave a valid Easter. In other years, *luna XIV* was $(14 - E)$ under epacts 2–13, thereafter $(45 - E)$ March, with an alternative from epact 24 onwards of $(43 - E)$ April.

More than one set of tables was drawn up on this basis, differing both in their starting-points and in the epacts assigned to any given year; but the most important are those used at Rome in the fourth and early fifth centuries, beginning with epact 1 in 298 and 382. The *saltus* is taken in years 12, 24, 36, 48, 60, and 72, embolism in years (modulo 19) 3, 6, 9, 11, 14, 17, and 19, with a final embolism in year 84 (381, 465). No notice is taken of the notional First Month dates, provided the date of Easter is itself acceptable; in cycle 55 (352 and 436; leap year, epact 29, 1 January Wednesday), the table offers 22 March on *luna XX* (implying a Paschal term of 16 March) besides 19 April on *luna XIX*, the choice being left to the Pope.

However, in some years there were no good dates for Easter. The strictest of prohibitions enforced the lower solar limit of 21 April; the lunar limits of *XVI–XXII* were still upheld; but in the early fourth century Rome had become reluctant to celebrate before the vernal equinox, which as in Julius Caesar's day was taken to be 25 March. This reluctance—perhaps due to a misunderstanding of Alexandrian doctrine—could be overcome in case of need, as when in cycle 3 (300 and 384; leap year, epact 23, 1 January Monday) Easter is set down for 24 March, *luna XVI*: had that date been spurned, the alternative would have been 21 April on *luna XV*. By the mid-century the Popes had realized that the restrictions could not all be upheld; the upper limit, which was the newest, was moved back to 22 March, matching the Alexandrian rule. (After all, there had been three days before the luminaries were created on the first equinox.) However, even this was not enough. In cycle 6 (AD 303 and 387; epact 26, 1 January Friday), *luna XIV* was either Friday, 19 March or Saturday, 17 April; this entailed violating either the new solar limit, by celebrating on 21 March, or the Roman lunar limit, by keeping 18 April even though it was *luna XV*. Even worse, in cycle 63 (AD 360 and 444; leap year, epact 28, 1 January Saturday) *luna XIV* was either Friday, 17 March or Saturday, 15 April, requiring Easter to be either 19 March or *luna XV*.

❦ THE CONFLICT BETWEEN ROME AND ALEXANDRIA The Alexandrian reckoning, though in the long run it would prove defective, was the most accurate devised by the Christians of antiquity. Nevertheless, Romans objected, not only that it ignored the solar limit of 21 April, but that the Alexandrians, by refusing to accept a Paschal term earlier than 21 March, were liable to celebrate in the second month instead of the first; in turn they were accused by the Alexandrians of celebrating in the 12th month of the preceding lunar year, and hence of keeping Easter twice in one year. (The converse was true when Alexandria accepted, and Rome rejected, a date before 25 March.) These charges amounted to the observation that one party's date broke the other's rules. No doubt the Alexandrian computus also suffered in Roman eyes for ignoring both the Roman calendar and the week.

In the second quarter of the fourth century, Rome and Alexandria sometimes deferred to each other for the sake of unity: Rome accepted *luna XV* on 19 April 330, thus avoiding the premature 22 March prescribed by the 84-year table, Alexandria *luna XXII* on 25 March 333, since Rome would not keep 22 April. On 30 March 340 Rome again kept *luna XV* for Alexandria's sake; in 343, during a serious schism, Alexandria kept *luna*

XV on 27 March, Rome *luna XXII* on 3 April; but in 346, when both cities agreed that *luna XIV* was 22 March, Rome persuaded Alexandria to celebrate on the 30th, even though it was *luna XXII*, rather than on the 23rd, and in 349 to keep 26 March, the Alexandrian 23 April being too late for Rome (which alleged St Peter's personal authority for the rule).

However, Alexandrian compliance, due in large part to Athanasius' need for support against the Arians of Constantinople (see *2 May), endured no longer; for its part Rome adopted the Alexandrian upper limit of 22 March. Indeed, when in 357 the Alexandrian date was 23 March, *luna XVI*, Rome had little choice but to accept this date (though the Chronographer of 354 had predicted the 30th), for the next 14th lune, on 19 April, was a Sunday, entailing a completely impossible Easter on the 26th. By then, the inadequacy of Roman methods was evident in Milan, for St Ambrose records that in 76 Diocletian = AD 360, 14 years before he became bishop, 'we' kept 28 Pharmouthi = 23 April when the Paschal term fell on Sunday the 16th; at Rome, where after a hollow lunar April it fell on the 15th, the choice lay between the 16th, *luna XV*, and the 23rd, *luna XXII*, the one too early and the other too late. The Chronographer predicts the 16th; given the importance of the 21st in Roman eyes he was probably correct. St Ambrose cites 360 as his precedent for keeping the Alexandrian Easter on 25 April 387, *luna XXI*; at Rome, where the 14th lunes fell on 19 March and 17 April, 21 March on *luna XVI* breached even the new solar limit, 18 April on *luna XV* breached the lunar limit, and 25 April on *luna XXII* was after the Parilia. The Chronographer predicted 18 April, but a writer in 381 had supposed the choice to lie between 21 March and the 28th, commending the former as incurring only mild reproach and damning the latter, which was *luna XXIII*, as a serious offence. We may be sure only that Pope Siricius did not keep the 25th, for even after accepting that Alexandria had been charged at Nicaea with determining the date of Easter the papacy attempted to preserve the limit of 21 April. It succeeded in 417, but not in 444 or 455 (see *The Date of Easter*). It was the latter débâcle, when Pope Leo was compelled to celebrate on 24 April though not even Good Friday was within the Roman limit, that caused a new computus to be commissioned from Victorius of Aquitaine.

❡ VICTORIUS OF AQUITAINE Victorius had the merit of understanding that Alexandrian rules were superior to Roman both in accuracy and in certainty, and that Easter dates would repeat after 532 years; had he presented this cycle in Roman fashion by correlating Easter to the epact and feria of 1 January, he would have deserved the highest praise. However, he lacked the mental clarity to see—or perhaps the authority to insist—that the pill must be swallowed whole; instead he attempted, by violating the integrity of the Alexandrian computus, to preserve the Roman lunar limits and to save the Popes from the remaining humiliation of celebrating on 25 April. The result was confusion and uncertainty.

His Easter tables, drawn up in 457, introduced to the West the 532-year Paschal cycle already known at Alexandria; however, he does not appear to understand why it repeats. They are reckoned in years of the Passion, all past years being also designated by consuls; however, his consular tables were so inaccurate that he placed the year of the Gemini, to which the West dated the Crucifixion, a year too early, in the leap year we know as AD 28, from which they run down to AP 532 = AD 559. Since Eusebius put the Passion at the beginning of AM 5229, Victorius' implicit Creation year was 5201 BC, from which date he reckoned his Metonic cycles; on this basis AP 1 was the fourth year of a cycle, or cycle 4 as computists say, but at Alexandria it was cycle 10. In consequence the *saltus* in cycle 19 of the Creation fell in cycle 16 of the Passion but cycle 6 Alexandrian; it was achieved by curtailing lunar November on the 17th. For the next 13 years, and altogether in 364 years out of 532, the Paschal term was one day too early; its overall limits were 20 March and 17 April.

In the Roman 84-year table, the succession of full and hollow lunar months from January to April had not been interrupted by the embolism: when the epact was 30, lunar April ended with the 29th lune on 30 March and *luna XIV* was 13 April in the embolismic month, 18 days after its date in the previous year under epact 19 and on the same day as under epact 1, when it fell in lunar April. However, Victorius, like the Alexandrians, required *luna XIV* to fall (except after the *saltus*) either 11 days earlier or 19 later than in the previous year, and on a different day each year; hence under epacts 27, 28, and 30 an embolism was needed to prevent lunar April from preceding the Paschal month.

It is Victorius' stated policy, when the Paschal term falls on a Saturday, to give *luna XV* in the main column, but to add *luna XXII* in the margin as the Latin date, leaving the choice to the Pope; he generally does so even when his Paschal term is a day too early for Alexandria, so that the true Alexandrian date is his 'Latin' *luna XXII*. Nevertheless, he occasionally promotes *XXII* to be the main date with a 'Greek' *XV* in the margin; in a number of instances he gives only *luna XXII*, as always when *luna XV* would be 21 March; on the other hand, when *luna XV* is 17 April he gives 24 April as the Greek date and when it is the 18th refuses to mention the 25th at all, though in AP 360 and 455 = AD 387 and 482 he gives a 'Greek' *luna XXII* on the 24th, which was a Saturday. In the land of the computistically blind—some of whom entered 'Greek' dates on *luna XXIII* in his tables—his one eye made him king; he was even described as a 'painstaking mathematician', which provoked his most recent editor to declare: 'The *calculator scrupulosus* was a man of very limited intellect and not even honest either.'

THE DEFINITIVE WESTERN COMPUTUS:
DIONYSIUS AND BEDE

In 525 Dionysius Exiguus attached to the last cycle of a 95-year table ascribed to Cyril of Alexandria, which was due to expire in 247 Diocletian (AD 530/1), another five cycles for the 95 years 532–626, dated from the Incarnation (see *Christian Chronology: Christian Era*). Whereas 1 Diocletian was year 1 of an Alexandrian Metonic cycle, so that the cyclical place of the year was its remainder to 19, Dionysius' first year, 532, was exactly divisible without remainder. Now since $248 = 13 \times 19 + 1$, this year was the first of a new cycle; since $532 = 28 \times 19$ without remainder, the place of a year AD is found by adding 1, dividing by 19, and taking the remainder (treating 0 as 19). This was later known in the West as the Golden Number, in which 'Golden' means 'especially important', as in Golden Rule and Golden Section; the modern tale that Meton's cycle was publicly displayed in gold letters is a baseless fiction. In calendars the Golden Number is written (sometimes in gold ink) against the dates on which new moon falls in the relevant year of the cycle (whence its other name of 'prime', from *luna prima*).

Dionysius' table, and subsequent Latin tables based on Alexandrian principles, comprised eight columns, indicating respectively: (i) the year; (ii) the indiction; (iii) the epact; (iv) the concurrent; (v) the position of the year in the lunar cycle; (vi) the date of *luna XIV*; (vii) the date of Easter; (viii) its lune. Of these, the epact, concurrent, and lunar cycle require more explanation than Dionysius saw fit to give; he explains how to find them, but not what they are. Since the last cycle of the Cyrillan table exhibits the same data except that it counts its years from Diocletian, it is likely that there were some who already understood the principles of Alexandrian computus, at least in Westernized form; but a reader would be hard put to develop the principles, as opposed to the outcome, of Easter reckoning from Dionysius' tables and text alone.

The epact is not, as any Latin might have expected, the age of the moon on 1 January, but the Alexandrian epact; Western computists redefined it as the age of the moon on 22 March (the *sedes epactarum*), since that was the nearest date to the equinox for which the epact was correct. It is found by taking the remainder of the year AD to 19 (or, which comes to the same thing, subtracting 1 from its place in the cycle); if the remainder is 0, so is the epact by virtue of the *saltus*; if not, it is multiplied by 11, and the remainder taken to 30. The concurrent is found by the ferial formula with parameter 4; even if Westerners had known it was the Egyptian 'day of the gods', they could have done little with that knowledge. It was far more usefully taken as the feria of 24 March (hence also of 31 March, 7, 14, 21 April); this *sedes concurrentium* had the advantage of being four weeks after *a.d. VI Kal. Mart.*, and hence after the disruption of leap year was past. The lunar cycle is not Dionysius' own 'decemnovenal' or 19-year cycle, but the Byzantine cycle, which ran three years behind it; if he knew what it was doing in an Alexandrian Easter table, he did not condescend to explain, and later readers were reduced to guesswork. Nevertheless, it remained in the table.

Once the epact is known, *luna XIV* can easily be found, though not so handily as in the Alexandrian calendar: the epact being E, the date of *luna XIV* is $5 - E$ April when E is less than 5, $36 - E$ March when E is between 5 and 16, otherwise $35 - E$ April. The next Sunday is found by adding to the concurrent the Paschal regular, or number of feriae by which *luna XIV* is in advance of 24 March. The Paschal regular for each year of the decemnovenal cycle was recorded in barbarous Latin verses found in virtually all computistic manuscripts and said to have been dictated by an angel to St Pachomius (14 May); it is noted in Table 1 below. Thus, to find the date of Easter in 729:

$729 + 1 = 730 = 19 \times 38 + 8$, ∴ Golden Number $= 8$, ∴ epact $= 17$

(or: $729 = 19 \times 38 + 7$; $7 \times 11 = 77$; $77 = 30 \times 2 + 17$, ∴ epact $= 17$)

∴ *luna XIV* = 18 April.

729 = 4 × 182 + 1; 729 + 182 + 4 = 915 = 7 × 130 + 5, ∴ concurrent 5.

Paschal regular of 18 April = 4

∴ feria of 18 April 729 = 5 + 4 = 9 ≡ 2 mod 7 = Monday,

∴ Easter Sunday 729 was 24 April.

Concurrents recur in a solar cycle of 28 years, after which years must repeat in respect both of intercalation and the feria of 1 January. In order that the first four years of the cycle should have concurrents 1, 2, 3, and 4, a new cycle was taken to begin in 9 BC; AD 1 is solar cycle 10, and the cyclical place of any year is found by adding 9 and dividing by 28; the ferial formula may then be applied without addition of a parameter. Thus 729 + 9 = 738 = 28 × 26 + 10; $\lceil 10/4 \rceil$ = 2; 10 + 2 = 12 ≡ 5 mod 7, ∴ concurrent = 5. In the later Middle Ages the concurrent was discarded in favour of the Sunday Letter; the relation between solar cycle, concurrent, and Sunday Letter is set out in Table 2.

The feria of the monthly Kalends is found by adding to the concurrent correctives known as 'solar regulars'. Bede lists them from January, with the warning that in leap year those of January and February will be one lower; Abbo of Fleury preferred to evade this difficulty by reckoning from the following 1 March.

Month	Regular	(from March)
January	2	(3)
February	5	(6)
March	5	
April	1	
May	3	
June	6	
July	1	
August	4	
September	7	
October	2	
November	5	
December	7	

Thus in AD 1000, concurrent 1, by Bede's rule the feria of 1 January will be 1 + 2 − 1 = 2, i.e. Monday; by Abbo's rule the year is taken as 999, concurrent 6, and the feria of 1 January calculated as 6 + 3 = 9 ≡ 2 mod 7. Abbo himself would have denied that the year was either 999 or 1000 (see *Christian Chronology: Christian Era*), but his computistic tables were found useful by people who ignored his redating of the Incarnation; they are combined with Bedan and pre-Bedan materials in such tables as that illustrated in Pl. 12.

❦ CLAVIS TERMINORUM The 'key of the limits', *clavis terminorum*, is the number of days to be counted *inclusively* from the *clavis* of particular moveable feasts, which would fall on the Sunday after the date thus found (even if it was itself a Sunday). It is found by subtracting the epact from 26 in common years, but from 56 in embolismic years and also in year 9 (since the epact, namely 28, is greater than 26); the *claves* of the moveable feasts are:

clavis Septuagesimae	7 January
clavis Quadragesimae	28 January
clavis Paschatis	11 March
clavis Rogationum	15 April
clavis Pentecostes	29 April

Thus, when the Golden Number is 1, epact 0, *clavis terminorum* 26, Septuagesima will fall on the Sunday next after 1 February (the 26th day inclusively, or 25th exclusively) from 7 January, Quadragesima on the Sunday next after 22 February, Easter on that after 5 April, Rogation Sunday on that after 10 May, and Whitsun on that after 24 May. The Sunday may be found in the normal fashion by the concurrent or the Sunday Letter: in leap year the first Sunday Letter is used for Septuagesima, the second for Easter, Rogations, and Whitsun; for Quadragesima the rule was to take the first letter, but if the resulting date is 25 February or later to subtract a day (which amounts to using the second letter).

The epact, Paschal term, Paschal regular, and *clavis terminorum* for each year of the decemnovenal cycle are set out in Table 1; Egyptian dates are included because the cycle was of Alexandrian origin, and because its structure is more easily performed from them. The lune of 1 January (which is also that of 31 Mar.) is noted for ease of comparison with other cycles; some Irish computists used it in preference to Dionysius' epact, and Irish annalists combined it with the feria of 1 January to identify the year.

❆ THE PASCHAL CYCLE If Easter falls on a given day in year Y, it must also do so in Y + 532, Y + 1064, and so on. It is therefore easy to compile an Easter table valid for all years in which the Julian calendar is valid; Victorius, no great intellect, had stumbled into one by accident, and although Dionysius had not devised one, many of Bede's contemporaries possessed that skill as well as Bede himself, who prefixed such a table, from 533 to 1064, to his classic work *De temporum ratione*, and thus secured the final victory of Alexandria over Aquitaine.

Table 3 gives a complete Paschal cycle of 532 years; the columns represent Golden Numbers, the rows the solar cycle. It begins at GN 1, solar cycle 1 = AD 76, 608, 1140, 1672 (OS) ≡ 76 mod 532. The table may be used to find Easter without recourse to concurrents or Sunday Letters by those who find the solar cycle easier to calculate than the ferial formula. For example, to find Easter 1436:

$$1436 = 1064 + 372 \equiv 372 \bmod 532; 372 - 75 = 297; 297 \equiv 12 \bmod 19 \equiv 17 \bmod 28;$$
∴ Golden Number = 12, solar cycle = 17
Column 12 and row 17 intersect at 8 April,
∴ Easter fell on 8 April 1436.

❦ THE BEDAN LUNAR CALENDAR So little did Dionysius care about the lunar calendar for its own sake that in his most detailed exposition each year of the cycle begins on the day after one Paschal term and ends on the next, except that the first, 18 April–5 April, runs from the Paschal term of GN 19 to that of GN 1, so that 18 April belongs to both the 19th year and the first; he specifies neither the day of *saltus* nor the beginnings of the embolisms, being concerned only with the number of days in the year. The West, however, adapted to it the lunar calendar inherited from the Supputatio Romana, with full lunar months ending in odd solar months and hollow in even, summed up in the mnemonic *Impar Luna pari, par fiet in impare mense*. However, as in Victorius' calendar irregularities were unavoidable; these were known as 'contrary rules' (*contrariae regulae*) by the Irish computists.

A complex and subtle arrangement was set out in the mid-seventh century by an unknown author (perhaps Cummian) in a treatise *De ratione conputandi* and subsequently copied into a manuscript (the so-called *Liber Commonei*) owned by St Dunstan; it borrows solutions for some problem years from the Latercus reckoning (see App. J), freely admits 'abortive moons' that begin after the Kalends of one month without reaching those of the next, and restricts the term 'embolism' to the period between a *luna XIV* in March preceding the 21st and the Paschal term in April. However, the decisive treatment was that set out in Bede's *De temporum ratione*; the solutions were as follows.

(i) Whereas *De ratione conputandi* and other Irish sources understood the *saltus* to be a leap from *luna XXVIII* on 21 March to *luna XXX* on the 22nd, and therefore wrote the epact of 1 January in GN 1 as 8, Bede, though in principle deeming this the most appropriate place, in practice gave the epact as 9, and noted that some put the *saltus* in November, to get it out of the way before the new year, 'obviously after the example of the Egyptians, who are said to do this in their penultimate month, which is our July'. In fact, as we have seen, the Alexandrian *saltus* was taken in the penultimate month not of the solar, but of the quasi-Jewish year, cut short at 28 August; nevertheless, later Western calendars curtailed either lunar July at the 29th or lunar November at the 24th.

(ii) Whereas *De ratione conputandi* had overcome leap year by assigning no age to the moon on the *bissextus*, Bede declared that lunar February was to be full, whether it ended before or after the intercalation.

(iii) The allocation of embolisms, attributed by Bede to the Romans, was as follows: 2–31 December in GN 2; 2 September–1 October in GN 5; 6 March–4 April in GN 8; 4 December–2 January in GN 10–11; 2 November–1 December in GN 13; 2–31 August in GN 16; and 5 March–3 April in GN 19. The embolism in GN 10–11 (for which some writers give 3 January–1 February) was preferred to the 3 March–1 April of *De ratione conputandi* so that February lunar should end on 1 February solar rather than 31 January.

Three of these embolisms cause irregularities in the monthly epacts: in GN 8, May has epact 27 instead of 28, July 29 instead of 30; in GN 11, March has 28 instead of 29; in GN 19, May has 28 instead of 29. Moreover, in these years some lunar months begin in the like-named solar months but end in the next: in GN 8 and 19 May and June, in

GN 11 January, February, and March, so that in leap year the epact of 1 March reverts to 29. In leap year, all three years exhibit four full months in succession (Jan., Feb., Mar., and the embolism). No such irregularities were introduced by the remaining embolisms; however, some computists began the embolism of GN 13 on 1 December to avoid putting the new moon of lunar January on the same day, 2 December, as that of the embolism in GN 2, this being the only case of two new moons on one day.

The lunes of the Kalends are obtained by adding 'lunar regulars' (i.e. corrections) to the epact of the year, subtracting 30 as necessary. These regulars were in origin the *katholikaí*, 'general [days]', calculated for a Byzantine year beginning on the previous 1 September; the corresponding values are sometimes given in Western tables, even after Bede had based his regulars on January.

Month	Regular	(from September)
January	9	
February	10	
March	9	
April	10	
May	11	
June	12	
July	13	
August	14	
September	16	(5)
October	16	(5)
November	18	(7)
December	18	(7)

Thus in GN 3, the epact is 22; the lunar regular of January is 9; 22 + 9 = 31; 31 − 30 = 1; therefore the new moon falls on 1 January. In GN 19 the epact is 18; 18 + 9 = 27; therefore 1 January is the 27th lune. This entails a lunar January beginning on 6 December, and hence a lunar December ending on the 5th; since this is a hollow month, the epact of 1 December will be 25. By Bede's reckoning this is given by the epact of GN 18, which is 7, added to the lunar regular for December, which is 18; the Byzantine system achieves the same result by adding a lunar regular of 7 to epact 18. These regulars take no account of contrary rule, which epact tables often ignore, or acknowledge only in a footnote (e.g. Pl. 17), nor of the *saltus*.

The most frequent distribution of new moons (understood as first visibility of the crescent, not as conjunction) throughout the cycle is given in Table 4; italics indicate embolismic months. Underlining indicates lunations named after the solar month in which they begin; all others are named after that in which they end except for embolisms, which are nameless. The corresponding monthly epacts, or lunar ages for the Kalends, are set out in Table 5. At Fleury, where several indices of lunar age were devised (see *Calendars as Written Objects: Liturgical Calendars*), a table of epacts for every day of the cycle was drawn up. Throughout the Middle Ages, artistic as well as mathematical ingenuity was applied to devising novel expositions of familiar facts (see Pl. 15); these facts, moreover, were integrated into a comprehensive understanding of time, man, world, and God (see Pl. 16).

Chroniclers as well as computists will often define a year not merely by its *millésime* AD, but by the number of concurrents and epacts; they may also append the lune to the date. Errors are not unknown: Rodulfus Glaber, having stated that the moon's eclipse of 8 November 1044 took place on the 14th lune, adds that there were no epacts and 7 concurrents. Unfortunately, the correct indications were 18 epacts and 5 concurrents *cum bissexto*; the null epact belonged to 1045 and 7 concurrents to 1046. Presumably the learned chronicler's Easter table was askew.

The increasing inaccuracy of the lunar tables did not go unnoticed; in some calendars the Golden Numbers are reassigned to other days. By the end of the Middle Ages, the true new moons were recognized as falling four days earlier than in the inherited tables; in Latin this was said to be the fifth day before by the usual inclusive reckoning, and located through five-syllable mnemonics such as *in caelis est hic* ('in the skies 'tis here').

❦ BYZANTIUM AND THE ORTHODOX CHURCH In its first two and a half centuries Byzantium experimented with various ways of finding Easter, including a Metonic cycle beginning with the new moon of 1 January, corresponding at Eastertide to the third year of the Alexandrian; it put the *saltus* in year 19, so that the Paschal terms of years 18 and 19 were 6 April instead of the 5th and 26 March instead of the 25th, causing Easter to fall on 13 April 475 instead of the 6th and on 2 April 495 instead of 26 March. When in the mid-sixth century Constantinople adopted the Alexandrian dates, the Armenians, the Syrian Jacobites, and the Church of the East, though willing to accept 25 March, insisted on retaining 6 April, so that when that day is a Sunday they postpone Easter till the 13th; the *saltus* is thus in year 18 of their cycle. The Georgians, however, who had previously been in communion with the Armenians, broke with them and entered into full communion with Constantinople; they therefore accepted 5 April, moving the *saltus* to year 17 of the cycle (= year 16 in the definitive Byzantine cycle and year 19 in the Alexandrian). Much ill feeling between the Armenians and their neighbours resulted from these 'false Easters'; which date was false naturally depended on whether one asked the Armenians or the 'Greeks and Georgians'.

The Metonic cycle eventually adopted by the Orthodox Church runs three years behind the Alexandrian, yet putting the *saltus* in the same year, its own 16th, so that the 'Legal Pascha' agrees with the Western *luna XIV*; this is the 'lunar cycle' given for reference purposes in Dionysius' tables. In the world era as reckoned from 1 September 5509 BC, the cyclical value is found by taking the remainder of the year to 19. The epacts of 22 March and 1 September gave way to that of 1 January (and 31 Mar.), known as the 'foundation' (*themélios*, in Russian *osnovánie*). This was at one time calculated by the formula $11c + 1 \pmod{30}$ when c (the cyclic value of the year) is less than 17 and $11c + 2$ $\pmod{30}$ when c is 17 or more; the result for each year was thus the same as in post-Bedan Western tables. However, a computistic reform increased the value of the *themélios* by 2; one then found the next full moon (*luna XV* not *XIV*) by subtracting the *themélios* from 16 (mod 30) and added 60 days to obtain the Legal Pascha, or 90 if full moon were earlier than 20 January. Another method, used in Russia, is to subtract the *osnovanie* from 21 (mod 30), thus obtaining the number of days (*epákty*) after 13 March that the Paschal new moon falls. But one may also find the Legal Pascha directly from the cycle by taking $11c + 6$ (mod 30)—increased by 1 for $c > 16$—from 50; the result will be the day in March (or, minus 31, in Apr.) of the Legal Pascha.

However the Legal Pascha has been established, one will next find its feria from the solar cycle. This is identical with the Alexandrian cycle, running 11 years ahead of the Western, and begins in 5509 BC; one will thus find the 'solar epacts' of a year AM by adding a quarter of a quarter of its *millésime*, ignoring fractions, and taking the remainder to 28. They are thus identical with the concurrents for the same place in the Western cycle (not of course for the year itself), but indicate the feria of 30 September (a Sunday in 5509 BC), to which the feria of any day from 1 October onwards may be found by adding the *quantième*, plus 3 for every 31-day month elapsed since September, 2 for every 30-day month other than September itself, and in leap year 1 for any date after 29 February, then taking the remainder to 7.

ℂ RUSSIA Until the fourteenth century, Russian dates were reckoned from 1 March 5508 BC; even afterwards for computistic purposes the year was taken as beginning on 1 March, the most convenient date for calculation. Slavonic Church calendars employed a device for finding feriae similar to the Western Sunday Letter. Each day was labelled with one of the numbers 1–7, represented (as all numbers were before Peter the Great) by a letter of the Cyrillic alphabet having the numerical value of its Greek prototype: 1 March is labelled 3, 2 March 2, 3 March 1, 4 March 7, and so on in descending sequence down to 28 February 3, 29 February 2; it made no difference that the year, and the physical calendar, began with 1 September, which was labelled 1 not because it was New Year but because it came exactly 26 weeks after 3 March.

The 'Sunday number' for each year, known as *vrutseléto* (Church Slavonic, 'the year in [your] hand'), indicates the number of days (inclusively) to the next Sunday. To find it, apply the ferial formula with parameter 0 to the year AM: all days against which the resulting number is written will be Sundays from March to August, and in the older reckoning all year round, but once the year was reckoned from 1 September 5509 BC, as was normal from the fourteenth century, for dates between September and February the year must be reduced by 1. Thus to find the *vrutseleto* for AM 7136 (AD 1627/8), between 1 September and 29 February, take the year as $7135 = 4 \times 1783$ (rem. 3); $7135 + 1783 = 8918 = 7 \times 1274$; call remainder 7, ∴ *vrutseleto* is 7; all days marked 7 will be Sundays, beginning with 2 September, down to 24 February. From 1 March to 31 August, reckon directly with $7136 = 4 \times 1784$; $7136 + 1784 = 8920 = 7 \times 1274 + 2$, ∴ *vrutseleto* is 2; all days marked 2 will be Sundays, starting with 2 March.

If we call the *vrutseleto* V, the first Sunday of March is $4 - V$ (mod 7); but if we call this Q, then 3 March is feria $4 - Q$ (mod 7) $= 4 - 4 + V$. Since the feria of 3 March is also that of the 24th, the March–September *vrutseleto* of any year is the same as the Western concurrent. For confirmation, call the year AD y, the year AM Y: the concurrent $= y + [y/4] + 4$ (mod 7), the *vrutseleto* $= Y + [Y/4]$; but $Y = y + 5508$; ∴ $[Y/4] =$

$[y/4] + 1377;$ $5508 + 1377 = 6885 = 7 \times 983 + 4;$ $\therefore$ $Y + [Y/4] \equiv y + [y/4] + 4$ (mod 7).

The feria of the first of each month may also be found directly from the solar cycle using Table 6, in which again the year begins with March. Hence, in year 12 of the Byzantine solar cycle, reckoned from March to February, the feria of 1 March is 6, i.e. Friday.

Russian church reckoning also knows a 'key of limits' (*klyuch graníts* or *graníchnyĭ*), which is not the same as the Western *clavis terminorum* but the number of days, from 1 to 35, by which Easter is subsequent to 21 March; if we call it K, Meatfare Sunday (Western Sexagesima) = K + 24 January (K + 25 in leap year); Clean Monday (the Monday after the Western Quinquagesima) = K + 1 February (K + 2 in leap year), Ascension = K + 29 April, Pentecost = K + 9 May, the Eve of St Peter's Fast = K + 16 May, and the length of St Peter's Fast (to 28 June) = 43 − K days. See I: *Orthodox Church Year* for the significance of these days.

THE GREGORIAN LUNAR CALENDAR

When Pope Gregory XIII changed the style in 1582, he did not change the definition of Easter, which remained the Sunday after the 14th lune on or next after 21 March, but advanced 21 March nominal by 10 days to the natural day previously called the 11th, with provision for further transference to the 10th, the 9th, the 8th, and so forth. As a result, 14th lunes that had hitherto preceded 21 March now followed it, and constituted Paschal terms. The 532-year cycle therefore needed to be replaced; the opportunity was also taken to compensate for the excess of the true synodic month. Moreover, since the Golden Numbers could no longer be written against the new moons in the calendar unless a new calendar were prepared from century to century, they were confined to the ancillary function of indicating the epact, which became once more the basis of the computus; its seat was moved from 22 March to 31 December in the previous year, so that Gregorian epact e corresponds to pre-Dionysian E − 1.

In each century (defined for this purpose as running from 00 to 99) the 19 Golden Numbers, still equivalent to Y + 1 (mod 7), correspond to 19 different epacts, increasing by 11 with a *saltus* at the end of the cycle; but the epacts change from century to century (see Table 7). Every time an intercalation is suppressed, the epact is reduced by one; for ease of reckoning, the reduction, known as the 'solar correction', is made with effect from 1 January instead of 25 February. However, to compensate (a little too much) for the excess of the true synodic month over 29.5 days, the epact is increased eight times in 2500 years; this 'lunar correction' is made seven times after 300 years and the eighth after 400. Only in centennial leap years does it actually increase the epact; otherwise it cancels the solar correction, as when it was first made in 1800, which was deemed the last in a 2500-year cycle. Of the future corrections, due every 300 years up to and including 3900 but not again till 4300, only those of 2400 and 3600 will actually augment the epact; in all other cases (2100, 2700, 3000, 3300, 3900, 4300) the solar correction will be cancelled. Hence in years divisible by 400 the epact rises if there is a lunar correction and otherwise remains the same; in other centennial years it remains the same if there is a lunar correction and otherwise diminishes by 1.

Each set of epacts is set out in a line with an index-letter, also used in the Roman Martyrology (see App. E). The epacts from 15 October 1582 to 31 December 1599 stand on line D; thereafter the lines are:

1600 D (no correction)
1700 C (solar correction only)
1800 C (solar correction cancelled by lunar)
1900 B (solar correction only)
2000 B (no correction)
2100 B (solar correction cancelled by lunar)
2200 A (solar correction only)
2300 u (solar correction only)
2400 A (lunar correction only)

Hence the epacts of 1900 will remain in force down to 2199.

The annual epacts are then assigned to the 365 days of the year to indicate the new moons (see Table 8). When the moon is 30 days old on 31 December, the next year's epact is stated as *; it is written against 1 January, and again against 31 January, 1 March, 31 March, and so on down to 21 December, indicating that those are the days of new moon under epact *. Other epacts are stated in the normal way, but in older books they are set in roman numerals (and frequently printed in red ink), with the exception of two special epacts to be considered. Thus 2 January is marked 29 (formerly XXIX), meaning that when that day is new moon, 31 December solar was 29 January lunar, and 1 January the 30th; 3 January is marked 28 (formerly XXVIII), and so on backwards throughout the year. The new moon of the First Month is the first incidence of the annual epact after 7 March; 13 days later comes the Paschal term. The following Sunday is then found by the Sunday Letter (the concurrent being obsolete in Pope Gregory's day); however, once epact and Sunday Letter are known, the date of the festival may be found directly from Table 9.

From one year to the next the epact of each year increases by 11 (mod 30), except that from GN 19 to GN 1 it increases by 12 (mod 30) owing to the *saltus* at 31 December; under epact 18 this causes the embolism beginning on 3 December, which normally ends on 1 January under epact 29, to become a hollow month, ending on the 31st, the next year having epact $* \equiv 18 + 12$ (mod 30); under epact 19 the embolism that would normally have ended on the 31st ends on the 30th, so that the next year's epact may be 1; new moon therefore falls on 31 December. That happened in 1595 and at 19-year intervals to 1690; failing further reform, the next instance will be in 8511. The case is covered in the table by writing against 31 December a special form of the epact number: in the older books, which gave epacts in roman figures and often in red, this was arabic 19 in black; in modern books, which use arabic throughout, it is 19′. This marked 19 stands to the left of the normal epact for 31 December, 20, indicating the new moon of lunar January that under that epact follows the embolism of 1 December.

In the odd months of the year, epact 25 is written twice, in older books as 25 XXV (the 25 being black), in modern as 25′ 25; in even months the marked form is written before 26 and the normal form before 24. The explanation is as follows.

(i) Since there are 30 possible lunar ages on 21 December, but only 29 possible dates for the Paschal term, two epacts must share the same term (as under the Supputatio Romana 30 and 1 shared 13 Apr.).

(ii) In order to obtain successive Paschal terms of 30 March and 18 April, as provided by Dionysius for epacts 6 and 17, Gregorian epact 14 must be followed by a year with Paschal term on 5 April. This is the regular term under epact 24 (new moons 7 Jan., 5 Feb., 7 Mar., 5 Apr.), but the year following epact 14 must have epact 25; therefore epact 25 must be fictionally equated for the purpose with epact 24.

(iii) However, in certain Golden Number cycles epact 24 occurs in its own right; since no two years of the Metonic cycle may have the same Paschal term, epact 25 will have to have its proper new moon of 4 April, with Paschal term on the 17th. This is indicated by distinguishing the epact either in style or with the stroke.

(iv) A Paschal term on 17 April is also required in the year after epact 15, which has it on 29 March; but the epact will be 26. Hence epact 26 must be fictionally equated with epact 25′.

In no Metonic cycle do epact 24, 25, and 26 all occur, only 24 and 25 or 25 and 26; the former pair only when 25 is under a Golden Number of 11 or less, the latter only when the Golden Number is 12 or more. Therefore one writes 25 under Golden Numbers 1–11 and 25′ under 12–19.

The equation of 25 with 24 and 25′ with 26 applies only in hollow months; in full months both epacts function identically with their proper value of 25. In consequence, under epact 25 there is *contraria regula* throughout the year, full lunar months beginning in the odd solar months and hollow in the even, whereas epact 25′ obeys the normal rule, with an embolism beginning on 26 November. Epact 26 has *contraria regula* to 1 June, after which the hollow month from the 2nd to the 30th restores the normal pattern; so has epact 27 down to 1 May, 28 to 1 April, and 29 to 1 March. In all these cases, the month ending in solar January is taken as embolismic; embolisms are also required on 2 December under epact 19 and progressively 1 day earlier under epacts 20 (1 Dec.) to 24 (27 Nov.). Under epacts 5–24, the *bissextus* causes the current lunation to comprise 31 days in leap year, though the counted lune remains the same from 24 to 25 February.

❡ TO FIND GREGORIAN EASTER 1998

     1998 + 1 = 1999; 1999 = 19 × 105 + 4; GN = 4

     1900 is on line B

     ∴ epact of GN 4 = 2 (Table 6)

     ∴ Paschal new moon is 29 March (Table 7)

     ∴ *luna XIV* = 29 + 13 March = 11 April, Sunday Letter C

Sunday Letter of 1998 = D
∴ Easter is 12 April.

Or, using Table 8, epact is 2, Sunday Letter is D, ∴ Easter is 12 April.

℃ TO FIND THE LUNE OF 27 NOVEMBER 1869

1869 + 1 = 1870; 1870 = 19 × 98 + 8; ∴ GN = 8

1800 is on line C

∴ epact of GN 8 = 17 (Table 6)

∴ last new moon before 27 November was the 5th (Table 7)

∴ 27 November was the 23rd lune.

In fact, the conjunction was at 11.36 p.m. on 3 November at Greenwich, or 26 minutes after midnight on the 4th at Rome.

TABLE 1. *Principles of Julian Easter*

Golden Number	Epact	Paschal term		Paschal regular	Lune 1 Jan.	Clavis terminorum
		Egyptian	Roman			
1	0	10 Pharmouthi	5 April	5	9	26
2	11	29 Phamenoth	25 March	1	20	15
3	22	18 Pharmouthi	13 April	6	1	34
4	3	7 Pharmouthi	2 April	2	12	23
5	14	26 Phamenoth	22 March	5	23	12
6	25	15 Pharmouthi	10 April	3	4	31
7	6	4 Pharmouthi	30 March	6	15	20
8	17	23 Pharmouthi	18 April	4	26	39
9	28	12 Pharmouthi	7 April	0	7	28
10	9	1 Pharmouthi	27 March	3	18	17
11	20	20 Pharmouthi	15 April	1	29	36
12	1	9 Pharmouthi	4 April	4	10	25
13	12	28 Phamenoth	24 March	0	21	14
14	23	17 Pharmouthi	12 April	5	2	33
15	4	6 Pharmouthi	1 April	1	13	22
16	15	25 Phamenoth	21 March	4	24	11
17	26	14 Pharmouthi	9 April	2	5	30
18	7	3 Pharmouthi	29 March	5	16	19
19	18	22 Pharmouthi	17 April	3	27	38

TABLE 2. *Solar cycle, concurrents, Sunday Letter*
An asterisk denotes leap year

Solar cycle	Concur-rents	Sunday Letter	Solar cycle	Concur-rents	Sunday Letter	Solar cycle	Concur-rents	Sunday Letter	Solar cycle	Concur-rents	Sunday Letter
1*	1	GF	8	2	E	15	4	C	22	6	A
2	2	E	9*	4	DC	16	5	B	23	7	G
3	3	D	10	5	B	17*	7	AG	24	1	F
4	4	C	11	6	A	18	1	F	25*	3	ED
5*	6	BA	12	7	G	19	2	E	26	4	C
6	7	G	13*	2	FE	20	3	D	27	5	B
7	1	F	14	3	D	21*	5	CB	28	6	A

TABLE 3. *Julian Paschal cycle*

Leap years are noted in bold

Solar cycle	Golden Numbers																		
	1	2	3	4	5	6	7	8	9	10	11	12	13	14	15	16	17	18	19
1	**7A**	**31M**	**14A**	**7A**	**24M**	**14A**	**31M**	**21A**	**14A**	**31M**	**21A**	**7A**	**31M**	**14A**	**7A**	**24M**	**14A**	**31M**	**21A**
2	6A	30M	20A	6A	23M	13A	6A	20A	13A	30M	20A	6A	30M	13A	6A	23M	13A	30M	20A
3	12A	29M	19A	5A	29M	12A	5A	19A	12A	29M	19A	5A	29M	19A	5A	22M	12A	5A	19A
4	11A	28M	18A	4A	28M	11A	4A	25A	11A	28M	18A	11A	28M	18A	4A	28M	11A	4A	18A
5	**9A**	**26M**	**16A**	**9A**	**26M**	**16A**	**2A**	**23A**	**9A**	**2A**	**16A**	**9A**	**26M**	**16A**	**2A**	**26M**	**16A**	**2A**	**23A**
6	8A	1A	15A	8A	25M	15A	1A	22A	8A	1A	22A	8A	25M	15A	8A	25M	15A	1A	22A
7	7A	31M	14A	7A	24M	14A	31M	21A	14A	31M	21A	7A	31M	14A	7A	24M	14A	31M	21A
8	6A	30M	20A	6A	23M	13A	6A	20A	13A	30M	20A	6A	30M	13A	6A	23M	13A	30M	20A
9	**11A**	**28M**	**18A**	**4A**	**28M**	**11A**	**4A**	**25A**	**11A**	**28M**	**18A**	**11A**	**28M**	**18A**	**4A**	**28M**	**11A**	**4A**	**18A**
10	10A	27M	17A	3A	27M	17A	3A	24A	10A	3A	17A	10A	27M	17A	3A	27M	10A	3A	24A
11	9A	26M	16A	9A	26M	16A	2A	23A	9A	2A	16A	9A	26M	16A	2A	26M	16A	2A	23A
12	8A	1A	15A	8A	25M	15A	1A	22A	8A	1A	22A	8A	25M	15A	8A	25M	15A	1A	22A
13	**6A**	**30M**	**20A**	**6A**	**23M**	**13A**	**6A**	**20M**	**13A**	**30M**	**20A**	**6A**	**30M**	**13A**	**6A**	**23M**	**13A**	**30M**	**20A**
14	12A	29M	19A	5A	29M	12A	5A	19A	12A	29M	19A	5A	29M	19A	5A	22M	12A	5A	19A
15	11A	28M	18A	4A	28M	11A	4A	25A	11A	28M	18A	11A	28M	18A	4A	28M	11A	4A	18A
16	10A	27M	17A	3A	27M	17A	3A	24A	10A	3A	17A	10A	27M	17A	3A	27M	10A	3A	24A
17	**8A**	**1A**	**15A**	**8A**	**25M**	**15A**	**1A**	**22A**	**8A**	**1A**	**22A**	**8A**	**25M**	**15A**	**8A**	**25M**	**15A**	**1A**	**22A**
18	7A	31M	14A	7A	24M	14A	31M	21A	14A	31M	21A	7A	31M	14A	7A	24M	14A	31M	21A
19	6A	30M	20A	6A	23M	13A	6A	20A	13A	30M	20A	6A	30M	13A	6A	23M	13A	30M	20A
20	12A	29M	19A	5A	29M	12A	5A	19A	12A	29M	19A	5A	29M	19A	5A	22M	12A	5A	19A
21	**10A**	**27M**	**17A**	**3A**	**27M**	**17A**	**3A**	**24A**	**10A**	**3A**	**17A**	**10A**	**27M**	**17A**	**3A**	**27M**	**10A**	**3A**	**24A**
22	9A	26M	16A	9A	26M	16A	2A	23A	9A	2A	16A	9A	26M	16A	2A	26M	16A	2A	23A
23	8A	1A	15A	8A	25M	15A	1A	22A	8A	1A	22A	8A	25M	15A	8A	25M	15A	1A	22A
24	7A	31M	14A	7A	24M	14A	31M	21A	14A	31M	21A	7A	31M	14A	7A	24M	14A	31M	21A
25	**12A**	**29M**	**19A**	**5A**	**29M**	**12A**	**5A**	**19A**	**12A**	**29M**	**19A**	**5A**	**29M**	**19A**	**5A**	**22M**	**12A**	**5A**	**19A**
26	11A	28M	18A	4A	28M	11A	4A	25A	11A	28M	18A	11A	28M	18A	4A	28M	11A	4A	18A
27	10A	27M	17A	3A	27M	17A	3A	24A	10A	3A	17A	10A	27M	17A	3A	27M	10A	3A	24A
28	9A	26M	16A	9A	26M	16A	2A	23A	9A	2A	16A	9A	26M	16A	2A	26M	16A	2A	23A

TABLE 4. *Julian New Moons*

Bold = embolisms. Underline = lunar months named after solar months in which they begin but do not end.

GN	Jan.	Feb.ᵃ	Mar.	Apr.	May	June	July	Aug.	Sept.	Oct.	Nov.	Dec.
1	23	21	23	21	21	19	19	17	16	15	14	13
2	12	10	12	10	10	**8**	**8**	6	5	4	3	**2**
3	1, 31	—	1, 31	29	29	27	27	25	24	23	22	21
4	20	18	20	18	18	16	16	14	13	12	11	10
5	9	7	9	7	7	5	5	3	**2**	2, 31	29	29
6	28	26	28	26	26	24	24	22	21	20	19	18
7	17	15	17	15	15	13	13	11	10	9	**8**	7
8	6	4	6	<u>5</u>	<u>4</u>	<u>3</u>	2	**1, 30**	29	28	27	26
9	25	23	25	23	23	21	21	19	**18**	17	16	15
10	14	12	14	12	12	10	10	8	7	6	5	**4**
11	<u>3</u>	<u>2</u>	<u>3</u>	2	1, 31	29	29	27	27	25	24	23
12	22	20	22	20	20	18	18	16	15	14	13	12
13	11	9	11	9	9	**8**	7	5	4	3	**2**	2,ᵇ 31
14	30	28	30	28	28	26	26	24	23	22	21	20
15	19	17	19	17	17	15	15	13	12	11	10	9
16	8	6	8	6	6	4	4	**2**	1	1, 30	29	28
17	27	25	27	25	25	23	23	21	20	19	**18**	17
18	16	14	16	14	14	12	12	10	9	8	7	6
19	5	3	5	<u>4</u>	<u>3</u>	2	1, 30ᶜ	28ᶜ	27ᶜ	26ᶜ	25	24

ᵃ In leap year lunar February is full; all new moons in this column will therefore be 1 day later except in GN 11; in GN 6, 14, and 17 the Roman date remains unchanged (respectively *IV, pr.*, and *V Kal. Mart.*).

ᵇ The 1st in some calendars to avoid coincidence with GN 2.

ᶜ Some calendars give new moons on 31 July, 29 Aug., 28 Sept., and 27 Oct.

TABLE 5. *Julian monthly epacts*

GN	Jan.	Feb.	Mar.	Apr.	May	June	July	Aug.	Sept.	Oct.	Nov.	Dec.
1	9	10	9	10	11	12	13	14	16	16	18	18
2	20	21	20	21	22	23	24	25	27	27	29	29
3	1	2	1	2	3	4	5	6	8	8	10	10
4	12	13	12	13	14	15	16	17	19	19	11	21
5	23	24	23	24	25	26	27	28	30	30	2	2
6	4	5	4	5	6	7	8	9	11	11	13	13
7	15	16	15	16	17	18	19	20	22	22	24	24
8	26	27	26	27	27^d	29	29^d	1	3	3	5	5
9	7	8	7	8	9	10	11	12	14	14	16	16
10	18	19	18	19	20	21	22	23	25	25	27	27
11	29	30	28$^{a,\,b}$	30	1	2	3	4	6	6	8	8
12	10	11	10	11	12	13	14	15	17	17	19	19
13	21	22	21	22	23	24	25	26	28	28	30	30
14	2	3	2	3	4	5	6	7	9	9	11	11
15	13	14	13	14	15	16	17	18	20	20	22	22
16	24	25	24	25	26	27	28	29	1	1	3	3
17	5	6	5	6	7	8	9	10	12	12	14	14
18	16	17	16	17	18	19	20	21	23	23	25	25
19	27	28	27	28	28^d	30	1	2^c	4^c	4^c	6^c	7^d

[a] The lunar regular gives a figure 1 higher, often recorded in tables despite Bede's caveat.
[b] But 29 in leap year.   [c] If the *saltus* is taken in July, these epacts should be 1 higher.
[d] This is the correct epact whether the *saltus* be taken in July or Nov.; but tables often give 6.

TABLE 6. *Feriae of first day of month in Byzantine solar cycle*

Year of cycle (as reckoned from 1 March 5508 BC)

	1	2	3	9	4	5	6
	7	13	8	15	10	11	17
	12	19	14	20	21	16	23
	18	24	25	26	27	22	28
March	6	7	1	2	3	4	5
April	2	3	4	5	6	7	1
May	4	5	6	7	1	2	3
June	7	1	2	3	4	5	6
July	2	3	4	5	6	7	1
August	5	6	7	1	2	3	4
September	1	2	3	4	5	6	7
October	3	4	5	6	7	1	2
November	6	7	1	2	3	4	5
December	1	2	3	4	5	6	7
January	4	5	6	7	1	2	3
February	7	1	2	3	4	5	6

TABLE 7. *Gregorian epacts by century*

Year	Index	Golden Number 1	2	3	4	5	6	7	8	9	10	11	12	13	14	15	16	17	18	19
1700 1800 8700	C	*	11	22	3	14	25	6	17	28	9	20	1	12	23	4	15	26	7	18
1900 2000 2100	B	29	10	21	2	13	24	5	16	27	8	19	*	11	22	3	14	25'	6	17
2200 2400	A	28	9	20	1	12	23	4	15	26	7	18	29	10	21	2	13	24	5	16
2300 2500	u	27	8	19	*	11	22	3	14	25	6	17	28	9	20	1	12	23	4	15
2600 2700 2800	t	26	7	18	29	10	21	2	13	24	5	16	27	8	19	*	11	22	3	14
2900 3000	s	25	6	17	28	9	20	1	12	23	4	15	26	7	18	29	10	21	2	13
3100 3200 3300	r	24	5	16	27	8	19	*	11	22	3	14	25'	6	17	28	9	20	1	12
3400 3600	q	23	4	15	26	7	18	29	10	21	2	13	24	5	16	27	8	19	*	11
3500 3700	p	22	3	14	25	6	17	28	9	20	1	12	23	4	15	26	7	18	29	10
3800 3900 4000	n	21	2	13	24	5	16	27	8	19	*	11	22	3	14	25'	6	17	28	9
4100	m	20	1	12	23	4	15	26	7	18	29	10	21	2	13	24	5	16	27	8
4200 4300 4400	l	19	*	11	22	3	14	25	6	17	28	9	20	1	12	23	4	15	26	7
4500 4600	k	18	29	10	21	2	13	24	5	16	27	8	19	*	11	22	3	14	25'	6
4700 4800 4900	i	17	28	9	20	1	12	23	4	15	26	7	18	29	10	21	2	13	24	5
5000 5200	h	16	27	8	19	*	11	22	3	14	25	6	17	28	9	20	1	12	23	4
5100 5300	g	15	26	7	18	29	10	21	2	13	24	5	16	27	8	19	*	11	22	3
5400 5500 5600	f	14	25	6	17	28	9	20	1	12	23	4	15	26	7	18	29	10	21	2
5700 5800	e	13	24	5	16	27	8	19	*	11	22	3	14	25'	6	17	28	9	20	1
5900 6000 6100	d	12	23	4	15	26	7	18	29	10	21	2	13	24	5	16	27	8	19	*
6200 6400	c	11	22	3	14	25	6	17	28	9	20	1	12	23	4	15	26	7	18	29
6300 6500	b	10	21	2	13	24	5	16	27	8	19	*	11	22	3	14	25'	6	17	28
6600 6800	a	9	20	1	12	23	4	15	26	7	18	29	10	21	2	13	24	5	16	27
6700 6900	P	8	19	*	11	22	3	14	25	6	17	28	9	20	1	12	23	4	15	26
7000 7100 7200	N	7	18	29	10	21	2	13	24	5	16	27	8	19	*	11	22	3	14	25'
7300 7400	M	6	17	28	9	20	1	12	23	4	15	26	7	18	29	10	21	2	13	24
7500 7600 7700	H	5	16	27	8	19	*	11	22	3	14	25	6	17	28	9	20	1	12	23
7800 8000	G	4	15	26	7	18	29	10	21	2	13	24	5	16	27	8	19	*	11	22
7900 8100	F	3	14	25	6	17	28	9	20	1	12	23	4	15	26	7	18	29	10	21
8200 8300 8400	E	2	13	24	5	16	27	8	19	*	11	22	3	14	25'	6	17	28	9	20
1600 8500 8600	D[a]	1	12	23	4	15	26	7	18	29	10	21	2	13	24	5	16	27	8	19

[a] This line applies from 15 Oct. 1582 to 31 Dec. 1699.

Note: After 8700 move one line down at each centennial year not divisible by 400, and one line up at each centennial year that, after subtraction of 1800, leaves a remainder to 2500 of 0, 300, 600, 900, 1200, 1500, 1800, or 2100; when both cases apply, remain in same line as previous century. Hence 8800 will remain on line C, 9000 will be on line B, 9100, 9200, and 9300 on line A, 9400 on line u, 9500 on line t, 9600 back on line u, 9700 again on line t, 9800, 9900, and 10000 on line s, and so on.

TABLE 8. *Gregorian new moons with Sunday Letters*

Against each day is shown the epact of the years in which that day is new moon. Throughout the year, use epact 25 when Golden Number is 11 or less, epact 25′ when Golden Number is 12 or more.

Day	January Epact	Let.	February Epact	Let.	March Epact	Let.	April Epact	Let.	May Epact	Let.	June Epact	Let.
1	*	A	29	D	*	D	29	G	28	B	27	E
2	29	B	28	E	29	E	28	A	27	C	26 25′	F
3	28	C	27	F	28	F	27	B	26	D	25 24	G
4	27	D	26 25′	G	27	G	26 25′	C	25′ 25	E	23	A
5	26	E	25 24	A	26	A	25 24	D	24	F	22	B
6	25′ 25	F	23	B	25′ 25	B	23	E	23	G	21	C
7	24	G	22	C	24	C	22	F	22	A	20	D
8	23	A	21	D	23	D	21	G	21	B	19	E
9	22	B	20	E	22	E	20	A	20	C	18	F
10	21	C	19	F	21	F	19	B	19	D	17	G
11	20	D	18	G	20	G	18	C	18	E	16	A
12	19	E	17	A	19	A	17	D	17	F	15	B
13	18	F	16	B	18	B	16	E	16	G	14	C
14	17	G	15	C	17	C	15	F	15	A	13	D
15	16	A	14	D	16	D	14	G	14	B	12	E
16	15	B	13	E	15	E	13	A	13	C	11	F
17	14	C	12	F	14	F	12	B	12	D	10	G
18	13	D	11	G	13	G	11	C	11	E	9	A
19	12	E	10	A	12	A	10	D	10	F	8	B
20	11	F	9	B	11	B	9	E	9	G	7	C
21	10	G	8	C	10	C	8	F	8	A	6	D
22	9	A	7	D	9	D	7	G	7	B	5	E
23	8	B	6	E	8	E	6	A	6	C	4	F
24	7	C	5	F	7	F	5	B	5	D	3	G
25	6	D	4	G	6	G	4	C	4	E	2	A
26	5	E	3	A	5	A	3	D	3	F	1	B
27	4	F	2	B	4	B	2	E	2	G	*	C
28	3	G	1	C	3	C	1	F	1	A	29	D
29	2	A			2	D	*	G	*	B	28	E
30	1	B			1	E	29	A	29	C	27	F
31	*	C			*	F			28	D		

Day	July Epact	Let.	August Epact	Let.	September Epact	Let.	October Epact	Let.	November Epact	Let.	December Epact	Let.
1	26	G	25 24	C	23	F	22	A	21	D	20	F
2	25'25	A	23	D	22	G	21	B	20	E	19	G
3	24	B	22	E	21	A	20	C	19	F	18	A
4	23	C	21	F	20	B	19	D	18	G	17	B
5	22	D	20	G	19	C	18	E	17	A	16	C
6	21	E	19	A	18	D	17	F	16	B	15	D
7	20	F	18	B	17	E	16	G	15	C	14	E
8	19	G	17	C	16	F	15	A	14	D	13	F
9	18	A	16	D	15	G	14	B	13	E	12	G
10	17	B	15	E	14	A	13	C	12	F	11	A
11	16	C	14	F	13	B	12	D	11	G	10	B
12	15	D	13	G	12	C	11	E	10	A	9	C
13	14	E	12	A	11	D	10	F	9	B	8	D
14	13	F	11	B	10	E	9	G	8	C	7	E
15	12	G	10	C	9	F	8	A	7	D	6	F
16	11	A	9	D	8	G	7	B	6	E	5	G
17	10	B	8	E	7	A	6	C	5	F	4	A
18	9	C	7	F	6	B	5	D	4	G	3	B
19	8	D	6	G	5	C	4	E	3	A	2	C
20	7	E	5	A	4	D	3	F	2	B	1	D
21	6	F	4	B	3	E	2	G	1	C	*	E
22	5	G	3	C	2	F	1	A	*	D	29	F
23	4	A	2	D	1	G	*	B	29	E	28	G
24	3	B	1	E	*	A	29	C	28	F	27	A
25	2	C	*	F	29	B	28	D	27	G	26	B
26	1	D	29	G	28	C	27	E	26 25'	A	25'25	C
27	*	E	28	A	27	D	26	F	25 24	B	24	D
28	29	F	27	B	26 25'	E	25'25	G	23	C	23	E
29	28	G	26	C	25 24	F	24	A	22	D	22	F
30	27	A	25'25	D	23	G	23	B	21	E	21	G
31	26 25'	B	24	E			22	C			20 19'ᵃ	A

[a] Use epact 19' on 31 Dec. when Golden Number is 19; this case arose in 1595, 1614, 1633, 1652, 1671, and 1690, but will not arise again till 8511.

TABLE 9. *Perpetual Gregorian Easter table*

Epact	Sunday Letter (March–December)						
	A	B	C	D	E	F	G
*	16 April	17 April	18 April	19 April	20 April	14 April	15 April
1	16 April	17 April	18 April	19 April	13 April	14 April	15 April
2	16 April	17 April	18 April	12 April	13 April	14 April	15 April
3	16 April	17 April	11 April	12 April	13 April	14 April	15 April
4	16 April	10 April	11 April	12 April	13 April	14 April	15 April
5	9 April	10 April	11 April	12 April	13 April	14 April	15 April
6	9 April	10 April	11 April	12 April	13 April	14 April	8 April
7	9 April	10 April	11 April	12 April	13 April	7 April	8 April
8	9 April	10 April	11 April	12 April	6 April	7 April	8 April
9	9 April	10 April	11 April	5 April	6 April	7 April	8 April
10	9 April	10 April	4 April	5 April	6 April	7 April	8 April
11	9 April	3 April	4 April	5 April	6 April	7 April	8 April
12	2 April	3 April	4 April	5 April	6 April	7 April	8 April
13	2 April	3 April	4 April	5 April	6 April	7 April	1 April
14	2 April	3 April	4 April	5 April	6 April	31 March	1 April
15	2 April	3 April	4 April	5 April	30 March	31 March	1 April
16	2 April	3 April	4 April	29 March	30 March	31 March	1 April
17	2 April	3 April	28 March	29 March	30 March	31 March	1 April
18	2 April	27 March	28 March	29 March	30 March	31 March	1 April
19	26 March	27 March	28 March	29 March	30 March	31 March	1 April
20	26 March	27 March	28 March	29 March	30 March	31 March	25 March
21	26 March	27 March	28 March	29 March	30 March	24 March	25 March
22	26 March	27 March	28 March	29 March	23 March	24 March	25 March
23	26 March	27 March	28 March	22 March	23 March	24 March	25 March
24	23 April	24 April	25 April	19 April	20 April	21 April	22 April
25	23 April	24 April	25 April	19 April	20 April	21 April	22 April
25'	23 April	24 April	18 April	19 April	20 April	21 April	22 April
26	23 April	24 April	18 April	19 April	20 April	21 April	22 April
27	23 April	17 April	18 April	19 April	20 April	21 April	22 April
28	16 April	17 April	18 April	19 April	20 April	21 April	22 April
29	16 April	17 April	18 April	19 April	20 April	21 April	15 April

SUNDAY LETTERS

The ancient Romans, who observed market-days at eight-day intervals, labelled the days in their calendars with the eight-letter cycle A–H so that, once one market-day was known, the corresponding letter would indicate all other market-days in the same year. When the seven-day week became significant, a second cycle of letters, from A to G, was sometimes appended; the first known example dates from the reign of Augustus. The cycle was a regular feature of liturgical calendars and of almanacs; the appropriate letter is given for each day in Part I. The year begins with A on 1 January and ends with A on 31 December; in leap year 24 and 25 February are both marked F.

February	Leap year	Common years
24	F	F
25	F	G
26	G	A
27	A	B
28	B	C
29	C	

If in a common year the first Sunday of a year falls on 5 January, or in leap year if the first Sunday of March falls on the 2nd, both which days are labelled E, then all subsequent E days will be Sundays. The year is therefore said to have the *littera dominicalis* or Sunday Letter E; by extension, the characteristic letters in the calendar are also called Sunday Letters.

In order to find the Sunday Letter of a common year, first find the displacement, or number of days by which 1 January is later than Sunday, from the ferial formula $Y + [Y/4] + P \pmod 7$; in the Julian calendar the parameter P is always 5, in the Gregorian it varies according to the formula $P \equiv [S/4] - S \pmod 7$, where $S = [Y/100]$, or in words, strike off the last two digits of the *millésime*, divide by 4, ignore the remainder, take away the dividend from the quotient, and add 7 as many times as is needed for a positive answer. Thus for the 1900s, $19 \div 4 = 4$ (rem. 3); $4 - 19 + 21 = 6$.

Gregorian years	Parameter
15 October 1582–31 December 1699	2
1700–99	1
1800–99	0
1900–2099	6

Gregorian years	Parameter
2100–99	5
2200–99	4
2300–99	3
2400–2599	2

Then read off the Sunday Letter as follows:

Displacement	1 January	First Sunday	Sunday Letter
0	Sunday	1 January	A
1	Monday	7 January	G
2	Tuesday	6 January	F
3	Wednesday	5 January	E
4	Thursday	4 January	D
5	Friday	3 January	C
6	Saturday	2 January	B

In leap year the letter found by this rule applies from 25 February to 31 December; from 1 January to 24 February the valid letter, written in front of the other, is one place ahead in the alphabet, A being treated as next after G.

To find the Gregorian Sunday Letter of any year between 1900 and 2099:

(i) *In common years*

Take the year AD, say		1999
Divide by 4	$1999 = 4 \times 499 + 3$	
Ignoring the remainder, add the quotient to the year:		499
Add the parameter		6
Total		2504
Divide by 7	$2504 = 7 \times 357 + 5$	

The displacement being 5, the Sunday Letter of 1999 is C.

(ii) *In leap years*

Take the year AD, say		2000
Divide by 4	$2000 = 4 \times 500$	
Ignoring the remainder, add the quotient to the year:		500
Add the parameter		6
Total		2506
Divide by 7	$2506 = 7 \times 358$	

The displacement being 0, the second Sunday Letter of 2000 is A; therefore the first is B; therefore the Sunday Letters of 2000 are BA.

Since in the Julian calendar P is always 5, in the examples given above the Julian Sunday Letters (required for calculating the Orthodox Easter from Western tables) are 1999 D, 2000 CB. Up to 2099 the Julian letters will be alphabetically one ahead of the Gregorian; in 2100 the Gregorian letter will be C, the Julian letters DC; thereafter, since the two calendars will be exactly two weeks apart, there will be no difference in Sunday Letter till 2200 Gregorian E, Julian ED.

Having obtained the Sunday Letter of the year, one may find the nearest Sunday to a given date from any calendar (such as Part I above) in which the days are provided with their Sunday Letters, and then count forwards or backwards in feriae to the day itself. Thus to find the feria of 3 February 2000:

> Sunday Letter of 1 January–24 February 2000 is B
> Nearest B day to 3 February is the 6th
> ∴ 6 February 2000 will be a Sunday,
> ∴ 3 February 2000 will be a Thursday.

See too Appendix G.

The Sunday Letters were applied in the later Middle Ages to the calculation of Easter, as being more intuitive than the previous concurrents, and were retained in the Gregorian calendar and its BCP adaptation: if the Sunday Letter of a common year, or the second Sunday Letter of a leap year, is E, Easter is the first E day after the Paschal term. From 21 March (the notional equinox) to 25 April (the 'last Easter') the day letters are:

	A	B	C	D	E	F	G
March			21	22	23	24	25
March	26	27	28	29	30	31	1 April
April	2	3	4	5	6	7	8
April	9	10	11	12	13	14	15
April	16	17	18	19	20	21	22
April	23	24	25				

PERPETUAL TABLE OF SUNDAY LETTERS

Find the column whose heading includes the century of the year in question, and the line of the tens and units; the Sunday Letter (or in leap year Letters) of the year will stand at the intersection. Thus for 1342, find the column with 1300 in the heading and the line of 42; they intersect at F, which is the Sunday Letter. From 15 October 1582 onwards, take the Julian or Gregorian column as appropriate: thus for the leap year 1688, the Julian (Old Style) Sunday Letters are AG, where the Julian column of 1600 crosses the line of 88; the Gregorian (New Style) Sunday Letters are DC. For the purpose of this table the century begins in the 00 year: the New Style Sunday Letter of 1900 was G.

				Julian							*Gregorian*			
				1–99	100	200	300	400	500	600			1582	1600
				700	800	900	1000	1100	1200	1300	1700	1800	1900	2000
				1400	1500	1600	1700	1800	1900	2000	2100	2200	2300	2400
0				DC	ED	FE	GF	AG	BA	CB	C	E	G	BA
1	29	57	85	B	C	D	E	F	G	A	B	D	F	G
2	30	58	86	A	B	C	D	E	F	G	A	C	E	F
3	31	59	87	G	A	B	C	D	E	F	G	B	D	E
4	32	60	88	FE	GF	AG	BA	CB	DC	ED	FE	AG	CB	DC
5	33	61	89	D	E	F	G	A	B	C	D	F	A	B
6	34	62	90	C	D	E	F	G	A	B	C	E	G	A
7	35	63	91	B	C	D	E	F	G	A	B	D	F	G
8	36	64	92	AG	BA	CB	DC	ED	FE	GF	AG	CB	ED	FE
9	37	65	93	F	G	A	B	C	D	E	F	A	C	D
10	38	66	94	E	F	G	A	B	C	D	E	G	B	C
11	39	67	95	D	E	F	G	A	B	C	D	F	A	B
12	40	68	96	CB	DC	ED	FE	GF	AG	BA	CB	ED	GF	AG
13	41	69	97	A	B	C	D	E	F	G	A	C	E	F
14	42	70	98	G	A	B	C	D	E	F	G	B	D	E
15	43	71	99	F	G	A	B	C	D	E	F	A	C	D
16	44	72		ED	FE	GF	AG	BA	CB	DC	ED	GF	BA	CB
17	45	73		C	D	E	F	G	A	B	C	E	G	A
18	46	74		B	C	D	E	F	G	A	B	D	F	G
19	47	75		A	B	C	D	E	F	G	A	C	E	F
20	48	76		GF	AG	BA	CB	DC	ED	FE	GF	BA	DC	ED
21	49	77		E	F	G	A	B	C	D	E	G	B	C
22	50	78		D	E	F	G	A	B	C	D	F	A	B
23	51	79		C	D	E	F	G	A	B	C	E	G	A
24	52	80		BA	CB	DC	ED	FE	GF	AG	BA	DC	FE	GF
25	53	81		G	A	B	C	D	E	F	G	B	D	E
26	54	82		F	G	A	B	C	D	E	F	A	C	D
27	55	83		E	F	G	A	B	C	D	E	G	B	C
28	56	84		DC	ED	FE	GF	AG	BA	CB	DC	FE	AG	BA

Notes

(i) Years BC are commonly reckoned according to the Julian calendar; to find the Sunday Letter, subtract 1, and take the result away from 700 (or a multiple thereof) to obtain a positive remainder: thus 207 BC = − 206 + 700 will conform to the pattern of AD 494, Sunday Letter B. Note that leap years BC are those that when divided by 4 leave a remainder of 1, e.g. 1 BC, 5 BC, 9 BC.

(ii) The change of Sunday Letter in leap year takes place between the two days *a.d. VI Kal. Mart.*, 24 and 25 Feb., which are both characterized F.

(iii) In Sweden, where the leap day of 1700 was suppressed and a 30th day added to Feb. 1712, the Sunday Letters are 1700 G, 1701 F, 1702 E, 1703 D, 1704 CB, 1705 A, 1706 G, 1707 F, 1708 ED, 1709 C, 1710 B, 1711 A; 1712 GFE (G Mon. 1 Jan.–Sat. 24 Feb., F Sun. 25 Feb.–Fri. 30 Feb., E Sat. 1 Mar.–Wed. 31 Dec.).

APPENDICES

APPENDIX A. REGNAL YEARS OF ENGLISH AND BRITISH SOVEREIGNS

	First year	Last year
William I	1 Will. I 25 Dec. 1066*–24 Dec. 1067	21 Will. I 25 Dec. 1086–9 Sept. 1087
William II	1 Will. II 26 Sept. 1087*–25 Sept. 1088	13 Will. II 26 Sept. 1099–2 Aug. 1100
Henry I	1 Hen. I 5 Aug. 1100*–4 Aug. 1101	36 Hen. I 5 Aug.–1 Dec. 1135
Stephen	1 Steph. 22 Dec. 1135*–21 Dec. 1136	19 Steph. 22 Dec. 1153–25 Oct. 1154
Henry II	1 Hen. II 19 Dec. 1154*–18 Dec. 1155	35 Hen. II 19 Dec. 1188–6 July 1189
Richard I	1 Ric. I 3 Sept. 1189*–2 Sept. 1190	10 Ric. I 3 Sept. 1198–6 Apr. 1199
John	1 John 27 May 1199*ᵃ–17 May 1200	18 John 19 May–19 Oct. 1216
Henry III	1 Hen. III 28 Oct. 1216*–27 Oct. 1217	57 Hen. III 28 Oct.–16 Nov. 1272
Edward I	1 Edw. I 20 Nov. 1272ᵇ–19 Nov. 1273	35 Edw. I 20 Nov. 1306–7 July 1307
Edward II	1 Edw. II 8 July 1307–7 July 1308	20 Edw. II 8 July 1326–20 Jan. 1327ᶜ
Edward III	1 Edw. III 25 Jan. 1327ᵈ–24 Jan. 1328	13 Edw. III 25 Jan. 1339–24 Jan. 1340
	14 & 1 Edw. IIIᵈ 25 Jan. 1340–24 Jan. 1341	34 & 21 Edw. III 25 Jan.–8 May 1360
	34 Edw. III 9 May 1360–24 Jan. 1361	43 Edw. III 25 Jan.–10 June 1369
	43 & 30 Edw. III 11 June 1369–24 Jan. 1370	51 & 38 Edw. III 25 Jan.–21 June 1377
Richard II	1 Ric. II 22 June 1377–21 June 1378	23 Ric. II 22 June–29 Sept. 1399ᵉ
Henry IV	1 Hen. IV 30 Sept. 1399–29 Sept. 1400	14 Hen. IV 30 Sept. 1412–20 Mar. 1413
Henry V	1 Hen. V 21 Mar. 1413–20 Mar. 1414	10 Hen. V 21 Mar.–31 Aug. 1422
Henry VI	1 Hen. VI 1 Sept. 1422–31 Aug. 1423	39 Hen. VI 1 Sept. 1460–4 Mar. 1461ᶠ
Edward IV	1 Edw. IV 4 Mar. 1461–3 Mar. 1462	10 Edw. IV 4 Mar. 1470–3 Mar. 1471
	49 & 1 Hen. VI 9 Oct. 1470–14 Apr. 1471	
	11 Edw. IV 4 Mar. 1471–3 Mar. 1472	23 Edw. IV 4 Mar.–9 Apr. 1483ᵍ
Edward V	1 Edw. V 9 Apr.–25 June 1483	
Richard III	1 Ric. III 26 June 1483–25 June 1484	3 Ric. III 26 June–22 Aug. 1485
Henry VII	1 Hen. VII 22 Aug. 1485ʰ–21 Aug. 1486	24 Hen. VII 22 Aug. 1508–21 Apr. 1509
Henry VIII	1 Hen. VIII 22 Apr. 1509–21 Apr. 1510	38 Hen. VIII 22 Apr. 1546–28 Jan. 1547

Edward VI	1 Edw. VI 28 Jan. 1547–27 Jan. 1548	7 Edw. VI 28 Jan.–6 July 1553
Jane	1 Jane 6–19 July 1553	
Mary	1 Mary 19 July 1553'–5 July 1554	2 Mary 6–24 July 1554
Philip & Mary	1 & 2 P. & M. 25 July 1554'–5 July 1555	5 & 6 P. & M. 25 July–17 Nov. 1558
Elizabeth I	1 Eliz. I 17 Nov. 1558–16 Nov. 1559	45 Eliz. I 17 Nov. 1602–23 Mar. 1603
James I	1 & 36 Jac. I* 24 Mar.–23 July 1603	23 & 58 Jac. I 24–7 Mar. 1625
	1 & 37 Jac. I 24 July 1603–23 Mar. 1604	
	2 & 37 Jac. I 24 Mar.–23 July 1604	
Charles I	1 Car. I 27 Mar. 1625–26 Mar. 1626	24 Car. I 27 Mar. 1648–30 Jan. 1649
Charles II	[1 Car. II 30 Jan. 1649'–29 Jan. 1650]	37 Car. II 30 Jan.–6 Feb. 1685
James II	1 Jac. II 6 Feb. 1685–5 Feb. 1686	4 Jac. II 6 Feb.–11 Dec. 1688
Interregnum	11 Dec. 1688–12 Feb. 1689	
William III & Mary II	1 Wm. & Mar. 13 Feb. 1689–12 Feb. 1690	6 Wm. & Mar. 13 Feb.–27 Dec. 1694
William III	6 Wm. III 28 Dec. 1694–12 Feb 1695	14 Wm. III 13 Feb.–8 Mar. 1702
Anne	1 Anne 8 Mar. 1702–7 Mar. 1703	13 Anne 8 Mar.–1 Aug. 1714
George I	1 Geo. I 1 Aug. 1714–31 July 1715	13 Geo. I 1 Aug. 1726–11 June 1727
George II	1 Geo. II 11 June 1727–10 June 1728	25 Geo. II 11 June 1751–10 June 1752
	26 Geo. II 11 June 1752–21 June 1753'''	
	27 Geo. II 22 June 1753–21 June 1754	34 Geo. II 22 June–25 Oct. 1760
George III	1 Geo. III 25 Oct. 1760–24 Oct. 1761	60 Geo. III 25 Oct. 1819–29 Jan. 1820
George IV	1 Geo. IV 29 Jan. 1820–28 Jan. 1821	11 Geo. IV 29 Jan.–26 June 1830
William IV	1 Wm. IV 26 June 1830–25 June 1831	7 Wm. IV 26 June 1836–20 June 1837
Victoria	1 Vic. 20 June 1837–19 June 1838	64 Vic. 20 June 1900–22 Jan. 1901
Edward VII	1 Edw. VII 22 Jan. 1901–21 Jan. 1902	10 Edw. VII 22 Jan.–6 May 1910
George V	1 Geo. V 6 May 1910–5 May 1911	26 Geo. V 6 May 1935–20 Jan. 1936
Edward VIII	1 Edw. VIII 20 Jan.–11 Dec. 1936	
George VI	1 Geo. VI 11 Dec. 1936–10 Dec. 1937	16 Geo. VI 11 Dec. 1951–6 Feb. 1952
Elizabeth II	1 Eliz. II 6 Feb. 1952–5 Feb. 1953 WHOM GOD PRESERVE	

* Date of coronation.

ᵃ Ascension Day; subsequent years run from Ascension Day: (2) 18 May 1200, (3) 3 May 1201, (4) 23 May 1202, (5) 15 May 1203, (6) 3 June 1204, (7) 19 May 1205, (8) 11 May 1206, (9) 31 May 1207, (10) 15 May 1208, (11) 7 May 1209, (12) 27 May 1210, (13) 12 May 1211, (14) 3 May 1212, (15) 23 May 1213, (16) 8 May 1214, (17) 28 May 1215, (18) 19 May 1216.

ᵇ Date of proclamation.

ᶜ Date of deposition; murdered 21 Sept. 1328.

ᵈ When Edward III claimed the throne of France, he added his French regnal years to his English, but counted them from his English accession, so that 25 Jan. 1340 begins '14 and 1 Edward III'. This lasted down to 8 May 1360 (year '34 and 21'), and resumed on 11 June 1369 ('43 and 30') down to Edward's death on 21 June 1377 ('51 and 38').

ᵉ Date of deposition; died of starvation 14(?) Feb. 1400.

ᶠ Date of deposition. He was restored 1 Oct. 1470–11 Apr. 1471, 'the 49th year from the beginning of Our reign and the first of Our readeption of the royal power', and murdered on 21 May 1471.

ᵍ Edward IV's regnal years were not affected by Henry VI's readeption.

[b] Henry VII dated the first year of his reign from 21 Aug., to make Richard the rebel.

[i] Her succeeding regnal years date from 6 July, ignoring Jane.

[j] Philip was king only during Mary's lifetime, but takes precedence in dating: 25 July 1554–5 July 1555 is 1 and 2 Philip and Mary, 6–24 July 1555 1 and 3 Philip and Mary.

[k] English documents are normally dated by James's Scottish year as well as his English; he acceded in Scotland as James VI on 24 July 1567.

[l] Charles counted his regnal years from the death of Charles I but his *de facto* reign begins with his restoration on 29 May 1660.

[m] This regnal year spanned the omission of the 11 days 3–13 Sept. 1752.

APPENDIX B. PAPAL REGNAL
YEARS FROM 999

The first date for each pope given below is that of consecration where known, otherwise of election. From Innocent III onwards, regnal years have been officially counted from consecration; between election and consecration popes issue 'half-bulls' (*dimidiae bullae*). Irregularities are found in the first year's dating, but from the second year on the pope's regnal year always begins on the anniversary of the coronation. There are no surviving papal documents before 384, when dating is by consulate; from 537 to 800 it is by indiction and regnal year of the Byzantine emperor; from 800 to the twelfth century the regnal years of Western emperors are used. From the later tenth century the year AD is added. The pope's regnal year, first attested in 781 of the pontificate, is not normally used till the eleventh century, and then for papal privileges; from February 1188 it is extended to other papal documents as well. Antipopes' throne-numbers are given in parentheses if they were reused; but those of the precipitately elected Benedict X and the Conciliar Pope Alexander V were recognized by the next bearers of their names.

Silvester II	2 or 9 Apr. 999–12 May 1003
John XVII	?June–6 Nov. 1003
John XVIII	2 Jan. 1004–June or July 1009
Sergius IV	?31 July 1009–12 May 1012
Benedict VIII	18 May 1012–9 Apr. 1024
Gregory (VI)	?May–Dec. 1012 (antipope)
John XIX	Apr.–May 1024–20 Oct. 1032
Benedict IX	?17 Dec. 1032–Sept. 1044; 10 Mar.–1 May 1045; 8 Nov. 1047–16 July 1048 (deposed)
Silvester III	13 or 20 Jan.–10 Mar. 1045 (deposed)
Gregory VI	?5 May 1045–20 Dec. 1046 (deposed)
Clement II	25 Dec. 1046–9 Oct. 1047
Damasus II	17 July–9 Aug. 1048
Leo IX, St	12 Feb. 1049–19 Apr. 1054
Victor II	16 Apr. 1055–28 July 1057
Stephen IX (X)[a]	3 Aug. 1057–29 Mar. 1058
Benedict X	5 Apr. 1058–Jan. 1059 (antipope)[b]
Nicholas II	24 Jan. 1059–19 or 26 July 1061

Alexander II	30 Sept. 1061–21 Apr. 1073
Honorius (II)	28 Oct. 1061–31 May 1064 (antipope)
Gregory VII, St	29 or 30 June 1073–25 May 1085
Clement III	(25 June 1080); 24 Mar. 1084–8 Sept. 1100 (antipope)
Victor III, Bl.	(24 May 1086); 9 May–16 Sept. 1087
Urban II, Bl.	12 Mar. 1088–29 July 1099
Paschal II	14 Aug. 1099–21 Jan. 1118
Theoderic	Sept. 1100–Jan. 1101 (antipope)
Albert or Adalbert	Feb.–Mar. 1101 (antipope)
Silvester IV	18 Nov. 1105–12 Apr. 1111 (antipope)
Gelasius II	10 Mar. 1118–29 Jan. 1119
Gregory (VIII)	8 Mar. 1118–Apr. 1121 (antipope)
Callistus II	9 Feb. 1119–14 Dec. 1124
Celestine (II)	15/16 Dec. 1124
Honorius II	21 Dec. 1124–13 Feb. 1130
Innocent II	23 Feb. 1130–24 Sept. 1143
Anacletus II	23 Feb. 1130–25 Jan. 1138 (antipope)
Victor (IV)	mid-Mar.–29 May 1138 (antipope)
Celestine II	26 Sept. 1143–8 Mar. 1144
Lucius II	12 Mar. 1144–15 Feb. 1145
Eugenius III, Bl.	18 Feb. 1145–8 July 1153
Anastasius IV	12 July 1153–3 Dec. 1154
Hadrian IV	5 Dec. 1154–1 Sept. 1159
Alexander III	20 Sept. 1159–30 Aug. 1181
Victor IV	4 Oct. 1159–20 Apr. 1164 (antipope)
Paschal III	26 Apr. 1164–20 Sept. 1168 (antipope)
Callistus (III)	Sept. 1168–29 Aug. 1178 (antipope)
Innocent (III)	29 Sept. 1179–Jan. 1180 (antipope)
Lucius III	6 Sept. 1181–25 Nov. 1185
Urban III	1 Dec. 1185–19/20 Oct. 1187
Gregory VIII	25 Oct.–17 Dec. 1187
Clement III	20 Dec. 1187–late Mar. 1191
Celestine III	14 Apr. 1191–8 Jan. 1198
Innocent III	22 Feb 1198–16 July 1216
Honorius III	24 July 1216–18 Mar. 1227
Gregory IX	21 Mar. 1127–22 Aug. 1241
Celestine IV	?27 Oct.–10 Nov. 1241
Innocent IV	28 June 1243–7 Dec. 1254
Alexander IV	20 Dec. 1254–25 May 1261
Urban IV	4 Sept. 1261–2 Oct. 1264
Clement IV	15 Feb. 1265–29 Nov. 1268
Gregory X, Bl.	27 Mar. 1272–10 Jan. 1276
Innocent V, Bl.	22 Feb.–22 June 1276

Hadrian V	11 July–18 Aug. 1276
John XXI[c]	20 Sept. 1276–20 May 1276
Nicholas III	26 Nov. 1277–22 Aug. 1280
Martin IV	23 Feb. 1281–28 Mar. 1285
Honorius IV	20 May 1285–3 Apr. 1287
Nicholas IV	22 Feb. 1288–4 Apr. 1292
Celestine V, St Peter	29 Aug.–13 Dec. 1294 (resigned)
Boniface VIII	23 Jan. 1295–11 Oct. 1303
Benedict XI, Bl.	27 Oct. 1303–7 July 1304
Clement V	15 Nov. 1305–20 Apr. 1314
John XXII	5 Sept. 1316–4 Dec. 1334
Nicholas (V)	22 May 1328–25 July 1330 (antipope)
Benedict XII	8 Jan. 1335–25 Apr. 1342
Clement VI	19 May 1342–6 Dec. 1352
Innocent VI	30 Dec. 1352–12 Sept. 1362
Urban V, Bl.	6 Nov. 1362–19 Dec. 1370
Gregory XI	5 Jan. 1371–27 Mar. 1378
Urban VI	18 Apr. 1378–15 Oct. 1389
Clement (VII)	31 Oct. 1378–16 Sept. 1394 (antipope)[d]
Boniface IX	9 Nov. 1389–1 Oct. 1404
Benedict (XIII)	11 Oct. 1394–26 July 1417 (antipope)[e]
Innocent VII	11 Nov. 1404–6 Nov. 1406
Gregory XII	19 Dec. 1406–4 July 1415 (resigned)
Alexander V	7 July 1409–3 May 1410 (antipope)[f]
John (XXIII)	25 May 1410–29 May 1415 (antipope)[g]
Martin V	21 Nov. 1417–20 Feb. 1431
Clement (VIII)	10 June 1423–26 July 1429 (antipope)
Benedict (XIV)	12 Nov. 1425–? (antipope)
Eugenius IV	11 Mar. 1431–23 Feb. 1447
Felix V	5 Nov. 1439–7 Apr. 1449 (antipope) (crowned 24 July 1440)
Nicholas V	19 Mar. 1447–24 Mar. 1455
Callistus III	20 Apr. 1455–6 Aug. 1458
Pius II	3 Sept. 1458–15 Aug. 1464
Paul II	16 Sept. 1464–26 July 1471
Sixtus IV	25 Aug. 1471–12 Aug. 1484
Innocent VIII	12 Sept. 1484–25 July 1492
Alexander VI	26 Aug. 1492–18 Aug. 1503
Pius III	8 Oct.–18 Oct. 1503
Julius II	26 Nov. 1503–21 Feb. 1513
Leo X	11 Mar. 1513–1 Dec. 1521
Hadrian VI	31 Aug. 1522–14 Sept. 1523
Clement VII	26 Nov. 1523–25 Sept. 1534

Paul III	1 Nov. 1534–10 Nov. 1549
Julius III	22 Feb. 1550–23 Mar. 1555
Marcellus II	10 Apr.–1 May 1555
Paul IV	26 May 1555–18 Aug. 1559
Pius IV	6 Jan. 1560–9 Dec. 1565
Pius V, St	17 Jan. 1566–1 May 1572
Gregory XIII	25 May 1572–10 Apr. 1585
Sixtus V	1 May 1585–27 Aug. 1590
Urban VII	15–27 Sept. 1590
Gregory XIV	8 Dec. 1590–16 Oct. 1591
Innocent IX	3 Nov.–30 Dec. 1591
Clement VIII	9 Feb. 1592–5 Mar. 1605
Leo XI	10–27 Apr. 1605
Paul V	29 May 1605–28 Jan. 1621
Gregory XV	14 Feb. 1621–8 July 1623
Urban VIII	29 Sept. 1623–29 July 1644
Innocent X	4 Oct. 1644–1 Jan. 1655
Alexander VII	18 Apr. 1655–22 May 1667
Clement IX	26 June 1667–9 Dec. 1669
Clement X	11 May 1670–22 July 1676
Innocent XI, Bl.	4 Oct. 1676–12 Aug. 1689
Alexander VIII	16 Oct. 1689–1 Feb. 1691
Innocent XII	15 July 1691–27 Sept. 1700
Clement XI	18 Dec. 1700–19 Mar. 1721
Innocent XIII	8 May 1721–7 Mar. 1724
Benedict XIII	4 June 1724–21 Feb. 1730
Clement XII	16 July 1730–6 Feb. 1740
Benedict XIV	22 Aug. 1740–3 May 1758
Clement XIII	16 July 1758–2 Feb. 1769
Clement XIV	4 June 1769–22 Sept. 1774
Pius VI	22 Feb. 1775–29 Aug. 1799
Pius VII	21 Mar. 1800–20 July 1823
Leo XII	5 Oct. 1823–10 Feb. 1829
Pius VIII	5 Apr. 1829–30 Nov. 1830
Gregory XVI	6 Feb. 1831–1 June 1846
Pius IX	21 June 1846–7 Feb. 1878
Leo XIII	3 Mar. 1878–20 July 1903
Pius X, St	9 Aug. 1903–20 Aug. 1914
Benedict XV	6 Sept. 1914–22 Jan. 1922
Pius XI	12 Feb. 1922–10 Feb. 1939
Pius XII	12 Mar. 1939–9 Oct. 1958
John XXIII	4 Nov. 1958–3 June 1963
Paul VI	30 June 1963–6 Aug. 1978

| John Paul I | 3 Sept.–28 Sept. 1978 |
| John Paul II | 22 Oct. 1978– |

[a] In Mar. 752 an elderly presbyter was elected pope, but died before he could be consecrated, and was not considered to have reigned; a deacon, also called Stephen, was thereupon elected, consecrated, and known throughout the Middle Ages as Stephen II (for Stephen I, see *2 Aug.). Subsequently, it was held that election sufficed to make a pope even without consecration; from the 16th c. onwards the presbyter was accounted Pope Stephen II, and the deacon Stephen III. Since 1961 the presbyter Stephen has been omitted, and subsequent Stephens given a double numeration.

[b] Irregularly elected while the reform party was awaiting the return of Hildebrand (later Gregory VII) from the imperial court.

[c] The absence of a Pope John XX is due to a misreading of the notice that John XIV had been pope for eight months, four of them in prison, as referring to two consecutive Popes John, so that Popes John XV–XIX were wrongly counted as XVI–XX.

[d] First Avignon pope of the Great Schism.

[e] Second Avignon pope of the Great Schism; deposed by the Council of Constance, but in his own eyes pope till his death on 23 May 1423.

[f] Elected by the Council of Pisa to replace both rival popes, who refused to accept their deposition.

[g] Elected by the Council of Pisa as Alexander's successor, but deposed by the Council of Constance.

APPENDIX C. DATING BY INTROITS AT SUNDAY MASS

Dates, especially in the Middle Ages, are sometimes given according to the first words of the introit at Mass on Sundays and major feasts in the Church year. From Whitsun onwards the Sundays are numbered in different ways in different rites. In the Sarum rite, and in some religious orders, they are numbered after Trinity as in the BCP. In the Roman Rite, since the Feast of the Trinity (the Sunday after Whit Sunday or Pentecost) was not universally enjoined until 1334, Sundays were numbered after Pentecost; but in 1570 the reformed Missal of Pius V placed the introits on Sundays after Pentecost one week earlier than in medieval practice. Therefore between 1570 and 1969 the same introit was sung on, say, the 16th Sunday after Pentecost as had been sung on the 16th Sunday after Trinity in the Sarum rite. The number of Sundays between Epiphany and Lent and between Whit Sunday and Advent differs according to the date of Easter. If Easter is early, the extra Sundays after Epiphany are transferred to the end of the series of Sundays after Whit Sunday. In 1969 the RC Church renumbered the Sundays after Epiphany as 'in Ordinary Time' up to Lent, resuming the numbering on the Sunday after Trinity. (See I: *Western Church Year*.)

Since dating by introit is most often to be found in medieval sources, here follows a list of introits according to the liturgical calendar before 1570; Sundays are numbered from Trinity. Some introits differ in the Sarum rite.

Adorate deum	3rd to 6th Sundays after Epiphany
Ad te levavi	1st Sunday in Advent
Benedicta sit	Trinity Sunday
Cantate domino	4th Sunday after Easter
Cibavit eos	Corpus Christi
Circumdederunt me	Septuagesima
Cum (Dum) clamarem	10th Sunday after Trinity
Da pacem	18th Sunday after Trinity
Deus in adiutorium	12th Sunday after Trinity
Deus in loco sancto	11th Sunday after Trinity
Dicit dominus	23rd and 24th Sunday after Trinity, 1st Sunday before Advent
Domine, in tua misericordia	1st Sunday after Trinity

Domine, ne longe	Palm Sunday (Sarum)
Dominus fortitudo	6th Sunday after Trinity
Dominus illuminatio mea	4th Sunday after Trinity
Dum (Cum) clamarem	10th Sunday after Trinity
Dum medium silentium	Sunday within octave of Christmas
Ecce deus adiuvat	9th Sunday after Trinity
Esto mihi	Quinquagesima
Exaudi domine	Sunday within octave of Ascension, and 5th Sunday after Trinity
Exaudi nos domine	Ash Wednesday
Exsurge quare obdormis	Sexagesima
Factus est dominus	2nd Sunday after Trinity
Gaudete in domino	3rd Sunday in Advent
Inclina domine aurem tuam	15th Sunday after Trinity
In excelso throno	1st Sunday after Epiphany
In illo tempore vidit Johannes	Sunday within octave of Epiphany (Sarum)
Invocabit me	Quadragesima (Sarum: Invocavit me)
In voluntate tua	21st Sunday after Trinity
Jubilate deo omnis terra	3rd Sunday after Easter
Judica me	Passion Sunday
Justus es domine	17th Sunday after Trinity
Laetare Jerusalem	4th Sunday in Lent
Memento nostri	4th Sunday in Advent (Sarum)
Miserere mihi	16th Sunday after Trinity
Misereris omnium	Ash Wednesday (Sarum)
Misericordia domini	2nd Sunday after Easter
Nos autem gloriari	Maundy Thursday (Sarum)
Oculi	3rd Sunday in Lent
Omnes gentes	7th Sunday after Trinity
Omnia quae fecisti	20th Sunday after Trinity
Omnis terra	2nd Sunday after Epiphany
Osanna	Palm Sunday
Populus Sion	2nd Sunday in Advent
Protector noster	14th Sunday after Trinity
Quasimodo	1st Sunday after Easter (Low Sunday)
Reddite quae sunt	23rd Sunday after Trinity (Sarum)
Reminiscere	2nd Sunday in Lent
Respice domine	13th Sunday after Trinity
Respice in me	3rd Sunday after Trinity
Resurrexi	Easter Sunday
Rorate caeli	4th Sunday in Advent
Salus populi	19th Sunday after Trinity
Si iniquitates	22nd Sunday after Trinity

Sitientes	Saturday before Passion Sunday
Spiritus domini	Pentecost
Suscepimus deus	8th Sunday after Trinity
Viri Galilaei	Ascension Day
Vocem jucunditatis	5th Sunday after Easter

APPENDIX D.
DATING BY CISIOIANUS

One method by which the medieval monk, especially in Central Europe, learnt the immoveable feasts by heart was a sequence of doggerel verses, apparently originating in
Poland; French and German texts are found, but usually the language is (roughly) Latin
and the measure (even more roughly) the hexameter, with one syllable for each day and
two verses for each month; the feasts of importance in the particular community were
represented by one or more syllables of their name, beginning in the place appropriate
to the day; the other syllables were used as fillers, along with the name of the month
and anything else that might serve. It was known as *Cisioianus*, from the first five syllables, indicating that Circumcision fell on the 1st of the month and the month was
January. In the most widespread form the January verses ran:

> Cisio Ianus Epi sibi vendicat Oc Feli Mar An.
> Prisca Fab Ag Vincen Ti Pau Po nobile lumen.

That is 'Janus [i.e. January] claims [*vendicat* is medieval Latin for *vindicat*] for himself the
Circumcision [*Ci* in syllabic place 1], Epiphany [*E* at 6], the Octave [*Oc* 13], Felix [*Fe* 14],
Marcellus [*Ma* 16], Antony [*An* 17], Prisca [*Pri* 18], Fabian [*Fab* 20], Agnes [*Ag* 21], Vincent [*Vin* 22], Timothy [*Ti* 24], (Conversion of) Paul [*Pau* 25], Polycarp [*Po* 26], glorious
light.' The rest of the year was similarly given by:

> Bri Pur Blasus Ag Dor Febru Ap Scolastica Valent
> Juli conjunge tunc Petrum Matthiam inde.
> Martius Adria Per decoratur Gregorio Cyr
> Gertrud Alba Bene iuncta Maria genetrice.
> April in Ambrosii festis ovat atque Tiburti
> et Valer sanctique Geor Marcique Vitalis.
> Philip Crux Flor Got Joha latin Epi Ne Ser et Soph
> Maius in hac serie tenet Urban in pede Cris Can
> Nic Marcelle Boni dat Iun Primi Ba Cyrini
> Vitique Mar Protas Al sancti Iohan Io Dor Le Pe Pau
> Iul Proces Udal Oc Wil Kili Fra Bene Margar Apost Al
> Arnolfus Prax Mag Ap Christ Jacobique Sim Abdon
> Pe Steph Steph proto Six Don Cyr Ro Lau Tibur Hip Eus
> Sumptio Agapiti Timo Bartholo Ruf Aug Coll Aucti.
> Egidium Sep habet Nat Gorgon Protique Crux Nic
> Eu Lampertique Mat Mauricius et Da Wen Mich Ier

> Remique Franciscus Marcus Di Ger Arteque Calix
> Galle Lucas vel Und Se Seve Crispine Simonis Quin.
> Omne Novembre Leo Qua Theo Martin Briciusque
> Post haec Elisa Ce Cle Crys Katharina Sat An.
> December Barba Nico Concep et alma Lucia
> sanctus abinde Thomas modo Nat Step Io Pu Thomae Sil
> syllaba quaeque diem, duo versus dant tibi mensem.

In April, 'Valer' is not a saint pertaining to the 18th, but the companion of Tiburtius; similarly Peter and Paul occupy the last two places in June, though their joint day is the 29th, and 'Cyr Ro' in August stands for Cyriacus Romanus. Some saints are on their medieval German days: the Seven Sleepers ('Dor' = *Septem Dormientes*) 27 June, Margaret 13 July. Albanus (19 Mar.) is a martyr also culted in Trento and Copenhagen but unknown to the Bollandists; Vitalis and Valerius (on 28 Apr.) were second-century martyrs; 'Oc' (6 July) is the octave of SS Peter and Paul; Justus (11 Oct.) and his companions were saints too fictitious for the Golden Legend, 'Pu' (28 Dec.) is the feast of the Holy Innocents, called the *Pueri innocentes*, the Innocent Boys. The other feasts can all be found in Part I.

This mnemonic was also used for dating. In a Polish chronicle we find 5 November 1370 recorded thus: 'Tuesday before St Martin, and it was on the syllable *bre*, that is *omne Novembre*.' In fact, had the chronicler simply said 'the day on *bre*', without saint's day or even feria, the date would have been uniquely determined; but had it been *pi*, which might be 7 January, 20 August, or 26 October, more information would have been needed.

APPENDIX E.
MARTYROLOGY LETTERS

In some pre-Gregorian martyrologies the lune of each day is stated according to the Golden Numbers, represented by the first nineteen letters of the alphabet; e.g. for 1 January:

A	b	c	d	e	f	g	h	i	k	l	m	n	o	p	q	r	s	t
9	20	1	12	23	4	15	26	7	18	29	10	21	2	13	24	5	16	27

In the official Roman Martyrology published immediately after the reform (and subsequently revised by Cardinal Baronius) a similar principle was employed to designate the epact: the lower-case letters a to u (o being omitted to avoid confusion with arabic o) were assigned to epacts 1–19, followed by the capitals A to E for epacts 20–4, F for 25 (written f for 25'), G for 27, H for 28, N for 29, and P for *. These same letters are used in the Gregorian epact table as indices for the lines of epacts; whereas in the Julian calendar 1 January had been new moon in GN 3, in the Gregorian calendar the index of the century corresponded to the epact of GN 3. If the letters are set out in the order of the successive epacts from * to 29, P = *, l = 11, C = 22, c = 3, p = 14, F/f = 25/25', f = 6, s = 17, M = 28, i = 9, A = 20, a = 1, m = 12, D = 23, d = 4, q = 15, G = 26, g = 7, t = 18, N = 29, k = 10, B = 21, b = 2, n = 13, E = 24, e = 5, r = 16, H = 27, h = 8, u = 19, one finds the second letter (called 'third' in Latin) before the index, assigns it to Golden Number 1, and the next eighteen in order to GN 2–19, reverting from u to P as necessary. Thus between 1900 and 2199, index B, the epact of GN 1 will be N = 29; then GN 2 will have k = 10, GN 3 will have B = 21, GN 4 will have b = 2, and so on down to GN 19, epact s = 17, which is 12 less than the epact of GN 1, but between 2200 and 2299, index letter A, the epact of GN 1 will be M = 28, followed by GN 2 with i = 9, GN 3 with A = 20, and so on down to GN 19 with r = 16.

Above each day in the Martyrology, the lune of the day is set out for each Martyrology Letter: e.g. for 1 January:

a	b	c	d	e	f	g	h	i	k	l	m	n	p	q	r	s	t	u
2	3	4	5	6	7	8	9	10	11	12	13	14	15	16	17	18	19	20
A	B	C	D	E	f	F	G	H	M	N	P							
21	22	23	24	25	26	26	27	28	29	30	1							

Thereafter the lunes are increased by 1 every day, subject to the leap from 29 to 1 after a hollow month; note that f = 25' precedes F. The *saltus* is taken, not on 31 December, but on the last day of the lunar month current on 1 January; hence under Golden Number 1 the lune must, under any Martyrology Letter but P, be reduced by 1 until the first new moon. For example, in 1957, GN 1, epact 29, Martyrology Letter N, the lune of 1 January was called not 30, as the above table indicates, but 29, since in 1956, GN 19, epact 17, the lunar month, having begun on 4 December, had reached only the 28th lune by New Year's Eve; on the other hand, when as in 1862 the Martyrology Letter was P, indicating epact * and new moon on 1 January, it was called *luna prima*; the previous lunation, beginning on 3 December under epact 18, ended with *luna XXIX* on the 31st. However, the refinement of Epact 19′ was not used; instead, according to explicit prescription, the last lunation of 1595, having begun on 2 December, was continued down to *luna XXX* on the 31st, so that 1 January 1596, with Martyrology Letter a, was called *luna prima* and not *secunda*.

APPENDIX F.
THE CONVERSION OF DATES

I. TO CONVERT BETWEEN ROMAN AND MODERN DATES

In order to convert a Roman date expressed as the so-manyeth day before the Nones or Ides into the modern form, add 1 to the date of the Nones or Ides and subtract the number of days before; thus *a.d. III Non. Ian.* is (5 + 1 − 3 =) 3 January, *a.d. VI Id. Oct.* is (15 + 1 − 6 =) 10 October. To convert a day before the next month's Kalends, add 2 to the number of days in the current month and subtract the days before: thus since *a.d. XVI Kal. Nov.* falls in October, take 31 + 2 − 16 = 17, and you have the date 17 October. In February, count 28 + 2 = 30 days even in leap year unless the number of days is 5 or less: *a.d. VIII Kal. Mart.* is always 30 − 8 = 22 February, but *a.d. III Kal. Mart.* is 30 − 3 = 27 February in common years, 31 − 3 = 28 February in leap year. For pre-Julian dates (e.g. in Livy, and in most of Cicero's speeches and letters), subtract from 29 + 2 = 31 in all months except February, March, May, Quinctilis, and October: *a.d. VIIII Kal. Oct.* = 31 − 9 = 22 September.

The same method may be used to convert modern dates into Roman when writing in Latin; but every day in Part I is accompanied by its Roman date according to the Julian calendar.

To find any anniversary AD of an event BC

> Let the event have taken place in Y BC; let the anniversary be the *n*th.
> Then the anniversary will fall in AD *n* + 1 − Y.

Example. What year will be the 2500th anniversary of the battle of Marathon, which was fought in 490 BC?
Answer. AD 2500 + 1 − 490 = 2011.

Similarly, the 2000th anniversary of Vergil's death in 19 BC fell in 1982, though it was observed in 1981.

To find the interval between a year BC and a year AD

> Let the year BC be Y_1 and the year AD be Y_2.
> Then Y_2 is $Y_1 + Y_2 − 1$ years after Y_1.

Example. How many years will have elapsed between the murder of Julius Caesar on 15 March 44 BC and the anniversary on 15 March AD 2000?

Answer. 44 + 2000 − 1 years = 2043 years.

To find the year AD *corresponding to a date in an era whose epoch is* BC

Let the epoch of the era be Y_1 BC and the date in the era be Y_2.

Then the equivalent AD of Y_2, up to 31 December, is $Y_2 − Y_1$.

Example. What year AD corresponds to Hispanic era 1173, reckoned from 1 January 38 BC?
Answer. 1173 − 38 = 1135.

When the year to be converted does not begin on 1 January, the date found by this formula will need to be increased by 1 if the corresponding day falls on or after 1 January.

Example. What date AD corresponds to 29 May in the Byzantine year of the world 6961, reckoned from 1 September 5509 BC?
Answer. 1 September AM 7061 corresponded to 1 September AD 6961 − 5509 = 1452, but 29 May is later than 1 January, therefore the date required is 29 May 1453.

To convert a date AD *into an era whose epoch is* BC

Let the epoch of the era be Y_1 BC and the date AD be Y_2.

Then the equivalent in the era of Y_2, from 1 January to the end of the year in the other calendar, will be $Y_1 + Y_2 − 1$; but from the new year of the other calendar to 31 December $Y_1 + Y_2$.

Example. What years of the Jewish era, reckoned from 3761 BC, will correspond to AD 2000?
Answer. Between 1 January 2000 and 29 Elul, AM 3761 + 2000 − 1 = 5760; between 1 Tishri and 31 December, AM 3761 + 2000 = 5761. We may then establish that 1 January 2000 = 23 Tebet 5760, 1 Tishri 5761 = 30 September 2000, 31 December 2000 = 5 Tebet 5761.

II. TO CONVERT DATES BETWEEN THE ALEXANDRIAN (REFORMED EGYPTIAN) AND MODERN CALENDARS

1st of Alexandrian month	Modern date	
1 Thoth	29 August	(30 Aug. in Julian pre-leap year)
1 Phaophi	28 September	(29 Sept. " " " ")
1 Hathyr	28 October	(29 Oct. " " " ")
1 Choiak	27 November	(28 Nov. " " " ")
1 Tybi	27 December	(28 Dec. " " " ")
1 Mecheir	26 January	(27 Jan. in Julian leap year)
1 Phamenoth	25 February	(26 Feb. " " " ")
1 Pharmouthi	27 March	
1 Pachon	26 April	
1 Payni	26 May	
1 Epeiph	25 June	
1 Mesore	25 July	
Epagomenai	24–8 August	(24–9 Aug. in Julian pre-leap year)

1st of modern month	*Alexandrian date*	
1 January	6 Tybi	(5 Tybi in Julian leap year)
1 February	7 Mecheir	(6 Mecheir ″ ″ ″)
1 March	5 Phamenoth	
1 April	6 Pharmouthi	
1 May	6 Pachon	
1 June	7 Payni	
1 July	7 Epeiph	
1 August	8 Mesore	
1 September	4 Thoth	(3 Thoth in Julian pre-leap year)
1 October	4 Phaophi	(3 Phaophi ″ ″ ″ ″)
1 November	5 Hathyr	(4 Hathyr ″ ″ ″ ″)
1 December	5 Choiak	(4 Choiak ″ ″ ″ ″)

III. TO CONVERT DATES BETWEEN THE FRENCH REPUBLICAN AND MODERN CALENDARS

French Republican to modern

	I (1792–3)		VIII 1799–1800	
	II 1793–4		IX 1800–1	
	III 1794–5*		X 1801–2	
	V 1796–7		XI 1802–3*	
	VI 1797–8		XIII 1804–5	
	VII 1798–9*	IV 1795–6	XIV 1805	XII 1803–4
1 vendémiaire	22 Sept.	23 Sept.	23 Sept.	24 Sept.
1 brumaire	22 Oct.	23 Oct.	23 Oct.	24 Oct.
1 frimaire	21 Nov.	22 Nov.	22 Nov.	23 Nov.
1 nivôse	21 Dec.	22 Dec.	22 Dec.	23 Dec.
1 pluviôse	20 Jan.	21 Jan.	21 Jan.	22 Jan.
1 ventôse	19 Feb.	20 Feb.	20 Feb.	21 Feb.
1 germinal	21 Mar.	21 Mar.	22 Mar.	22 Mar.
1 floréal	20 Apr.	20 Apr.	21 Apr.	21 Apr.
1 prairial	20 May	20 May	21 May	21 May
1 messidor	19 June	19 June	20 June	20 June
1 thermidor	19 July	19 July	20 July	20 July
1 fructidor	18 Aug.	18 Aug.	19 Aug.	19 Aug.
jour de la Vertu	17 Sept.	17 Sept.	18 Sept.	19 Sept.
jour du Génie	18 Sept.	18 Sept.	19 Sept.	20 Sept.
jour du Travail	19 Sept.	19 Sept.	20 Sept.	21 Sept.
jour de l'Opinion	20 Sept.	20 Sept.	21 Sept.	22 Sept.
jour des Récompenses	21 Sept.	21 Sept.	22 Sept.	23 Sept.

*In leap year also

| jour de la Révolution | 22 Sept. 1795, 1799 | | 23 Sept. 1803 | |

Modern to French Republican

1793 I–II				1800 VIII–IX		
1794 II–III				1801 IX–X		
1797 V–VI	1795 III–IV			1802 X–XI		
1798 VI–VII	1799 VII–VIII	1796 IV–V		1805 XIII–XIV	1803 XI–XII	1804 XII–XIII
1 Jan.	12 nivôse	12 nivôse	11 nivôse	11 nivôse	11 nivôse	10 nivôse
1 Feb.	13 pluviôse	13 pluviôse	12 pluviôse	12 pluviôse	12 pluviôse	11 pluviôse
1 Mar.	11 ventôse	11 ventôse	11 ventôse	10 ventôse	10 ventôse	10 ventôse
1 Apr.	12 germinal	12 germinal	12 germinal	11 germinal	11 germinal	11 germinal
1 May	12 floréal	12 floréal	12 floréal	11 floréal	11 floréal	11 floréal
1 June	13 prairial	13 prairial	13 prairial	12 prairial	12 prairial	12 prairial
1 July	13 messidor	13 messidor	13 messidor	12 messidor	12 messidor	12 messidor
1 Aug.	14 thermidor	14 thermidor	14 thermidor	13 thermidor	13 thermidor	13 thermidor
1 Sept.	15 fructidor	15 fructidor	15 fructidor	14 fructidor	14 fructidor	14 fructidor
1 Oct.	10 vendémiaire	9 vendémiaire	10 vendémiaire	9 vendémiaire	8 vendémiaire	9 vendémiaire
1 Nov.	11 brumaire	10 brumaire	11 brumaire	10 brumaire	9 brumaire	10 brumaire
1 Dec.	11 frimaire	10 frimaire	11 frimaire	10 frimaire	9 frimaire	10 frimaire

IV. TO CONVERT JEWISH AND CHRISTIAN DATES

In order to convert a Jewish date into a Christian, or vice versa, it is not enough to know when 1 Tishri falls; whether the year is common or embolismic may be determined by taking the remainder to 19, but in order to establish whether it is deficient, abundant, or perfect, one needs to calculate the *molad* for that year and the next from the number of cycles and years that have elapsed from the epoch in 3761 BC, and then apply the rules for determining 1 Tishri. However, the Julian equivalent (midnight to sunset) for 15 Nisan in any year AM may be found from a formula published by the great mathematician C. F. Gauss (cf. App. H); he did not reveal his workings, but an explanation will be found in S. B. Burnaby, 219–39. Since 1 Tishri is always 163 days (23 weeks 2 days) after 15 Nisan, the date of Rosh Hashanah in any Christian year may be deduced from that of the previous Passover, and its characteristics established by counting the days to 1 Tishri following. That done, any other date may be found by counting the number of days between it and 1 Tishri previous or following according to Section VI, Tables 1 and 2 below.

Let the year AM be Y; year AD at Passover = $Y - 3760$.

Take: $a \equiv 12Y + 17 \pmod{19}$

$\qquad b \equiv Y \pmod 4$

$\qquad M$ and m = respectively the integer and decimal part of

$$32.044\ 093\ 2 + 1.554\ 218a + 0.25b - 0.003\ 177\ 794Y$$

$\qquad c \equiv M + 3Y + 5b + 5 \pmod 7$, where for Y we may substitute $Y \bmod 7$

Then 15 Nisan = M March (Julian), the feria being c,

except that:

if $c = 2, 4,$ or $6,$

or if $c = 0$, $a > 11$, $m \geq 0.897\ 723\ 765$

$\qquad$ 15 Nisan = M + 1 March (Julian), the feria being $c + 1$;

if $c = 1$, $a > 6$, $m \geq 0.6328\ 70\dot{3}$

$\qquad$ 15 Nisan = M + 2 March (Julian), the feria being $c + 2$.

The date thus found may be converted to the Gregorian calendar (see p. 788). In either calendar, to find 1 Tishri following, when 15 Nisan is day P of the Christian month:

$\qquad$ If P falls in March, 1 Tishri = P + 10 August = P − 21 September

$\qquad$ If P falls in April, 1 Tishri = P + 10 September = P − 20 October

Thus, for Passover AM 5298 (AD 1538)

$\qquad$ $5298 \times 12 + 17 = 63\ 576 + 17 = 63\ 593 = 3347 \times 19$ without remainder;

$\qquad$ $\therefore a = 0$, $b = 2$,

$\qquad$ $M + m = 32.044\ 093\ 2 + 0.5 − 16.835\ 952\ 612 = 15.708\ 140\ 588$

$\qquad$ $c \equiv 15 + 18 + 10 + 5\ (\mathrm{mod}\ 7) = 48\ (\mathrm{mod}\ 7) \equiv 6$

$\therefore$ 15 Nisan 5298 = Saturday, 16 March 1538; $\therefore$ 1 Tishri 5299 = Monday, 26 August 1538

$\therefore$ In AM 5297, $a = 7$, $b = 1$, $M + m = 26.340\ 844\ 382$, $c = 2$

$\therefore$ 15 Nisan 5297 = Tuesday, 27 March 1537; $\therefore$ 1 Tishri 5298 = Thursday, 6 September 1537. This is 354 days before 26 August 1538; $\therefore$ AM 5298 was common regular.

$\qquad$ Hence, to find the Christian equivalent of 25 Kislev 5298:

Days elapsed before 1 Kislev	59
Add *quantième*	25
Total	84

$\qquad$ $\therefore$ 25 Kislev = 84th day of Jewish year = 83rd day after 1 Tishri.

But 1 Tishri 5298 = 6 September 1537:

Days elapsed before September	243
Add *quantième*	6
Add days after 1 Tishri	83
Total	332

$\qquad$ $\therefore$ 25 Kislev = 332nd day of Christian year = 28 November

For Passover in AM 5760 = AD 2000

$\qquad$ $a = 15$, $b = 0$, $M + m = 37.053\ 269\ 76$, $c = 4$

$\qquad$ $\therefore$ 15 Nisan = Thursday 7 April 2000 OS = 20 April NS.

$\qquad$ Hence, to find the Jewish equivalent of 15 August 2000 NS, argue as follows. In leap year, 213 days have elapsed before 1 August, $\therefore$ 15 August is 228th day; 91 days have elapsed before 1 April, 20 April is 111th day; but $228 − 111 = 117$, $\therefore$ day required is 117 days after 15 Nisan; on 15 Nisan there are inclusively 163 days remaining in the year; $163 − 117 = 46$; on 1 Ab there are 59 days remaining; $59 − 46 = 13$; $1 + 13 = 14$; $\therefore$ day required is 14 Ab.

If the calendar is not reformed, the value of $M + m$ will eventually become negative; it must then be restated in the form $-(M + 1) + (1 - m)$; e.g. for AM 11245 = AD 7485:

$$a = 11\,245 \times 12 + 17 \,(\text{mod } 19) = 134\,957 \,(\text{mod } 19) \equiv 0,\, b = 1,$$
$$M + m = 32.044\,093\,2 + 0.25 - 35.734\,293\,53 = -3.440\,200\,33 = -4 + 0.559\,799\,67$$
$$c = 1,\text{ but } a < 6;$$

$\therefore$ 15 Nisan 11245 = -4 March = Sunday, 25 February 7485 Julian.

But the Gregorian correction = $74 - [74/4] - 2 = 54$,

$\therefore$ 15 Nisan 11245 = Sunday, 19 April 7485 Gregorian (the last occasion on which it will coincide with the Gregorian Easter).

The value of a may be found directly from the following table, which correlates the value of a with the place of the year in the Metonic cycle, $Y \,(\text{mod } 19)$.

Y mod 19	1	2	3	4	5	6	7	8	9	10	11	12	13	14	15	16	17	18	19
a		10	3	15	8	1	13	6	18	11	4	16	9	2	14	7	0	12	5	17

In embolismic years (indicated in bold) $a > 11$; in pre-embolismic years $a \leq 6$. When $c = 0$, $a > 11$, $m \geq 0.897\,723\,765$, the embolismic year precedes a common year with *molad* on Monday at or after 15 hours 589 minims; when $c = 1$, $a > 6$, $m \geq 0.6328\,\dot{7}0\dot{3}$, the following year will be a common year with *molad* on Tuesday at or after 9 hours 204 minims.

V. TO CONVERT MUSLIM AND CHRISTIAN DATES

Method 1

Since 33 computed Muslim years, assuming 12 intercalations, comprise 11 693 days and 32 Julian years 11 688 days, subtract 1 from the Muslim *millésime* and divide by 33; add the remainder and 32 times the quotient to 622; multiply the quotient by 6, and add the product to 197; from the sum subtract 11 times the remainder, and you will have the number of the Christian day corresponding to 1 Muḥarram according to the Julian calendar. Using Section VI, Table 1 below, add the number of days from 1 Muḥarram to the date in question, convert the resulting day of the Christian year to the month and *quantième*, and correct to the Gregorian date where appropriate. The margin of error caused by non-coincidence of intercalation may be corrected by finding the Christian *feria* from Appendix G and the Muslim as follows:

Find the number of 'collected years' AH (complete cycles of 30) and read off the corresponding tricennial parameter from the following table:

Collected years								Parameter
0	210	420	630	840	1050	1260	1470	5
30	240	450	660	870	1080	1290	1500	3
60	270	480	690	900	1110	1320	1530	1
90	300	510	720	930	1140	1350	1560	6
120	330	540	750	960	1170	1380	1590	4
150	360	570	780	990	1200	1410	1620	2
180	390	600	810	1020	1230	1440	1650	0

Add the annual parameter corresponding to the remainder:

Remainder	0	1	2	3	4	5	6	7	8	9	10	11	12	13	14
Parameter	3	0	4	2	6	3	1	5	3	0	4	2	6	3	1

Remainder	15	16	17	18	19	20	21	22	23	24	25	26	27	28	29
Parameter	5	2	0	4	2	6	3	1	5	2	0	4	2	6	3

Add the monthly parameter:

Muḥarram	0	Rabīʿ II	5	Rajab	2	Shawwāl	0
Ṣafar	2	Jumādā I	6	Shaʿbān	4	Dhū 'l-qaʿda	2
Rabīʿ I	3	Jumādā II	1	Ramaḍān	5	Dhū 'l-ḥijja	5

Add the *quantième*, and divide by 7; the remainder (counting 0 as 7) will be the feria.

Thus, to find the Christian equivalent of 24 Jumādā I AH 531:

$531 - 1 = 530 = 33 \times 16 + 2$; $32 \times 16 = 512$; $622 + 512 + 2 = 1136$.

$6 \times 16 = 96$; $197 + 96 = 293$; $293 - 2 \times 11 = 271$.

$\therefore$ 1 Muḥarram 531 = (provisionally) AD 1136 (a leap year), day 271.

Days elapsed before 1 Jumādā I	118
Add *quantième*	24
Total	142

$\therefore$ 24 Jumādā I 1136 is provisionally AD 1136, day $271 + 142 - 1 =$ day $412 = 1137$, day $(412 - 366) = 46 = 15$ February.

It remains to check the feria. By Appendix G, 15 February 1137 was a Monday; $531 = 510 + 21$; tricennial parameter for $510 = 6$; annual parameter for $21 = 3$; monthly parameter for Jumādā I = 6; $6 + 3 + 6 + 24 = 39 \equiv 4 \pmod 7$; $\therefore$ 24 Jumādā I 531 was a Wednesday; $\therefore$ Christian equivalent was 17 February 1137.

Method 2 (*for Gregorian dates only*)

The mean length of the computed Muslim year is 354.36; that of the solar year 365.242 2 days; hence the former is 0.970 224 of the latter. The date of the Hijra, 16 July 622, would have been the 19th had the Gregorian calendar been in operation; 19 July is the 200th day of the civil year, which falls when the solar year is at some 0.5476 parts of its course. Since both Muslim and Christian years are counted on the current not the elapsed basis, we may call the epoch 622.547 6; adding this to $0.970\,224(Y - 1)$, where $Y - 1$ is the number of complete Muslim years from the Hijra to the date we intend to convert, we obtain $0.970\,224Y + 621.577\,4$. The integral part will give the Christian year; the decimal, multiplied by 365, will give a provisional Christian date of 1 Muḥarram subject to a day's margin of error, which can be corrected as above.

To find the Gregorian date of 11 Ramaḍān 1419:

$1419 \times 0.970\,224$	1376.747 856
Add	621.577 4
Total	1998.325 256

∴ 1 Muḥarram AH 1419 = AD 1998 day (provisionally) 118 (0.325 256 × 365 ≈ 118.718)

∴ 11 Ramaḍān 1419 = (provisionally) 1998 day 118 + 236 + 11 − 1 = 364 = 30 December 1998, which is a Wednesday;

but 1419 = 1410 + 9; parameter for 1410 = 2; parameter for 9 = 0; parameter for Ramaḍān = 5; 2 + 0 + 5 + 11 = 18 ≡ 4 (mod 7); ∴ 11 Ramaḍān 1419 was a Wednesday; ∴ provisional Christian equivalent is correct.

However, it must be remembered that these equivalences work only for the computed, not the observed, Muslim calendar.

To convert Christian dates into Muslim, subtract 621 from the year AD, divide the difference by 32, add the quotient, find 1 Muḥarram in the year resulting, and proceed from there; thus to find the theoretical equivalent of 6 August 2040:

$$2040 − 621 = 1419 = 44 × 32 + 11; 1419 + 44 = 1463$$
$$1463 × 0.970 224 + 621.577 4 = 2041.015 112$$
$$015 112 × 365 = 5.515 88$$

∴ 1 Muḥarram AH 1463 = (provisionally) 5 January 2041.

But 5 January 2041 is a Saturday, the feria of 1 Muḥarram 1463 (= 1440 + 23) 0 + 5 + 0 + 1 = 6 = Friday; ∴ correct Christian equivalent is 4 January. Since this is later than 6 August 2040, the date sought will be in AH 1462, a common year.

From Section VI, Table 2, the number of days remaining at the end of July is 153; hence on 6 August the number of days remaining inclusively to the end of the Christian year is 153 − 6 + 1 = 148, and to the end of the Muslim year (3 Jan. 2041) 151. At the end of Jumādā, the number of days remaining in a common year is 177; hence the day on which there are 151 days (inclusively) remaining is (171 − 151 + 1 =) 27 Rajab.

VI. DAYS ELAPSED AND REMAINING IN THE YEAR

TABLE 1. *Cumulative total of days in preceding months*

Christian			Muslim	
	Common year	Leap year		
January	0	0	Muḥarram	0
February	31	31	Ṣafar	30
March	59	60	Rabīʿ I	59
April	90	91	Rabīʿ II	89
May	120	121	Jumādā I	118
June	151	152	Jumādā II	148
July	181	182	Rajab	177
August	212	213	Shaʿbān	207
September	243	244	Ramaḍān	236
October	273	274	Shawwāl	266
November	304	305	Dhū ʾl-qaʿda	295
December	334	335	Dhū ʾl-ḥijja	325
January	365	366	Muḥarram	354 (leap year 355)

TABLE 1 *(cont.)*

Jewish

	Common			Embolismic		
	Deficient	Regular	Abundant	Deficient	Regular	Abundant
Tishri	0	0	0	0	0	0
Cheshvan	30	30	30	30	30	30
Kislev	59	59	60	59	59	60
Tebet	88	89	90	88	89	90
Shebat	117	118	119	117	118	119
Adar	147	148	149	147	148	149
Adar II				177	178	179
Nisan	176	177	178	206	207	208
Iyar	206	207	208	236	237	238
Sivan	235	236	237	265	266	267
Tammuz	265	266	267	295	296	297
Ab	294	295	296	324	325	326
Elul	324	325	326	354	355	356
Tishri	353	354	355	383	384	385

TABLE 2. *Total days remaining in the year at end of previous month*

Christian   *Muslim*

	Christian		Muslim	Common year	Leap year
January	365 (366)	Muḥarram	354	355	
February	334 (335)	Ṣafar	324	325	
March	306	Rabīʿ I	295	296	
April	275	Rabīʿ II	265	266	
May	245	Jumādā I	236	237	
June	214	Jumādā II	207	208	
July	184	Rajab	177	178	
August	153	Shaʿbān	147	148	
September	122	Ramaḍān	118	119	
October	92	Shawwāl	88	89	
November	61	Dhū ʾl-qaʿda	59	60	
December	31	Dhū ʾl-ḥijja	29	30	

Jewish

	Common			Embolismic		
	Deficient	Regular	Abundant	Deficient	Regular	Abundant
Tishri	353	354	355	383	384	385
Cheshvan	323	324	325	353	354	355
Kislev	294	295	295	324	325	325

Jewish

	Common			Embolismic		
	Deficient	*Regular*	*Abundant*	*Deficient*	*Regular*	*Abundant*
Tebet	265	265	265	295	295	295
Shebat	236	236	236	266	266	266
Adar	206	206	206	236	236	236
Adar II				206	206	206
Nisan	177	177	177	177	177	177
Iyar	147	147	147	147	147	147
Sivan	118	118	118	118	118	118
Tammuz	88	88	88	88	88	88
Ab	59	59	59	59	59	59
Elul	29	29	29	29	29	29

APPENDIX G.
HOW TO FIND THE DAY OF THE
WEEK FOR ANY KNOWN DATE

METHOD I

From the Perpetual Table of Sunday Letters under II: *Sunday Letters*, find the Sunday Letter of the year; then calculate the feria of the given date from the Month and Day tables below.

Month

January October	A	B	C	D	E	F	G
February March November	D	E	F	G	A	B	C
April July	G	A	B	C	D	E	F
May	B	C	D	E	F	G	A
June	E	F	G	A	B	C	D
August	C	D	E	F	G	A	B
September December	F	G	A	B	C	D	E

Day

1	8	15	22	29	Sun.	Sat.	Fri.	Thu.	Wed.	Tue.	Mon.
2	9	16	23	30	Mon.	Sun.	Sat.	Fri.	Thu.	Wed.	Tue.
3	10	17	24	31	Tue.	Mon.	Sun.	Sat.	Fri.	Thu.	Wed.
4	11	18	25		Wed.	Tue.	Mon.	Sun.	Sat.	Fri.	Thu.
5	12	19	26		Thu.	Wed.	Tue.	Mon.	Sun.	Sat.	Fri.
6	13	20	27		Fri.	Thu.	Wed.	Tue.	Mon.	Sun.	Sat.
7	14	21	28		Sat.	Fri.	Thu.	Wed.	Tue.	Mon.	Sun.

To find the feria (day of the week for any date):

In the line of the month, find the Sunday Letter of the year. (NB. In leap year take the first letter for 1 Jan.–24 Feb., the second for 25 Feb.–31 Dec.) Run down the column in which you have found the Sunday Letter until it meets the line of the day; the feria required will be at the intersection.

To find the feria of 27 August 1521 (death of Josquin des Prez)

Calendar is Julian: therefore the Sunday Letter of the year is F.
In line of August, F stands in the fourth column.
Fourth column intersects line of 27 at Tuesday,
therefore 27 August 1521 was a Tuesday.

To find the feria of 23 April 1616 New Style (death of Cervantes)

> Sunday Letters of Gregorian 1616 are CB; in April take B.
> In line of April, B stands in the third column.
> Third column intersects line of 23 at Saturday,
> therefore 23 April 1616 NS was a Saturday.

To find the feria of 23 April 1616 Old Style (death of Shakespeare)

> Sunday Letters of Julian 1616 are GF; in April take F.
> In line of April, F stands in the seventh column.
> Seventh column intersects line of 23 at Tuesday,
> therefore 23 April 1616 OS was a Tuesday.

To find the feria of 11 February 1732 Old Style (birth of Washington)

> Sunday Letters of Julian 1732 are BA; in February take B.
> In line of February, B stands in the sixth column.
> Sixth column intersects line of 11 at Friday,
> therefore 11 February 1732 OS was a Friday.

To find the feria of 26 March 1827 (death of Beethoven)

> Sunday Letter of Gregorian 1827 is G.
> In line of March, G stands in the fourth column.
> Fourth column intersects line of 26 at Monday,
> therefore 26 March 1827 was a Monday.

For a year BC reckoned according to the Julian calendar, find the Sunday Letter as explained in note (i) to the Perpetual Table of Sunday Letters, then proceed as above.

To find the feria of 15 March 44 BC (murder of Julius Caesar)

> 44 BC corresponds to AD 700 − (44 − 1) = 700 − 43 = 657, Sunday Letter A.
> In line of March, A stands in the fifth column.
> Fifth column intersects with line of 15 at Wednesday,
> therefore 15 March 44 BC was a Wednesday.

METHOD 2

If you have no table to hand, but have memorized the ferial formula for determining the Sunday Letter, you can find the feria of any date from the relation between the Sunday Letter of the year and the cyclical letter for the 1st of the month, supplied by the mnemonic rhyme:

> At Dover Dwells George Brown Esquire,
> Good Christopher Fitch And David Friar.

That is, 1 January A, 1 February D, 1 March D, 1 April G, 1 May B, 1 June E, 1 July G, 1 August C, 1 September F, 1 October A, 1 November D, 1 December F. The letter of the 1st will also be that of the 8th, 15th, 22nd, and 29th.

The first Sunday of each month may be found by counting inclusively from the letter of the month to the Sunday Letter of the year, and subsequent Sundays by adding 7 or a multiple. If the Sunday Letter of the year is F, the first Sunday of January will be the 6th (count A B C D E F), and the others will be the 13th, 20th, and 27th; the first Sunday of February will be the 3rd (count D E F), followed by the 10th, 17th, and 24th. Having found the first Sunday, one may if convenient count back to the feria of the 1st: if 6 January is Sunday, count back six days, Sunday, Saturday, Friday, Thursday, Wednesday, Tuesday; 1 January will be a Tuesday.

METHOD 3

If the feria of any date in the year is known, find the number of days between it and the date whose feria is to be sought by adding the *quantième* of each date to the cumulative total of days in the preceding months according to the following table.

Month	Cumulative total of days in preceding months	
	Common year	Leap year
January	0	0
February	31	31
March	59	60
April	90	91
May	120	121
June	151	152
July	181	182
August	212	213
September	243	244
October	273	274
November	304	305
December	334	335

Subtract the smaller figure from the larger, take the remainder to 7, and count so many feriae forwards if the known date is earlier than the unknown, backwards if it is later. Thus, if we know that 24 March of a common year is a Thursday, we may find the feria of 15 October as follows:

Dates	24 March	15 October
Total days in preceding months	59	273
Add the *quantième*	24	15
Total	83	288
Subtract smaller figure from larger		− 83
Difference		205
Divide by 7		29, remainder 2

Therefore 15 October is 2 feriae later than 24 March.
But 24 March is a Thursday.
Therefore 15 October is a Saturday.

Or, to find the feria of 12 January:

Dates	12 January	24 March *
Total days in preceding months	0	59
Add the *quantième*	12	24
Total	12	83
Subtract smaller figure from larger		− 12
Difference		71
Divide by 7		10, remainder 1

Therefore 12 January is 1 feria earlier than 24 March.
But 24 March is a Thursday.
Therefore 12 January is a Wednesday.

In leap year, assuming the same feria for 24 March, the day-total will be 60 + 24 = 84, the difference 72 = 7 × 10 + 2, so that 12 January will be two feriae earlier, on Tuesday.

APPENDIX H.
JULIAN AND GREGORIAN EASTER

The following tables are designed for finding the date of Easter, Julian and Gregorian, for any year until 2199 if you already know the Sunday Letter (from an almanac or diary, from the Table given under II: *Sunday Letters*, or by calculation). Table 1 may be used indefinitely; for Gregorian dates between 1583 and 1899 inclusive use Table 2, between 1900 and 2199 use Table 3; in other centuries use II: *Computus*, Tables 7 and 9.

Method. Add 1 to the year and divide by 19; the remainder is the Golden Number (treat 0 as 19); Easter will be at the intersection of the Golden Number line and Sunday Letter column. In leap year, the Sunday Letter to be applied is the second of the pair.

TABLE 1. *Perpetual Julian Easter table*

| GN | Sunday Letter | | | | | | |
	A	B	C	D	E	F	G
1	9 April	10 April	11 April	12 April	6 April*	7 April	8 April
2	26 March	27 March	28 March	29 March	30 March	31 March	1 April
3	16 April	17 April	18 April	19 April	20 April	14 April	15 April
4	9 April	3 April	4 April	5 April	6 April	7 April	8 April
5	26 March	27 March	28 March	29 March	23 March	24 March	25 March
6	16 April	17 April	11 April	12 April	13 April	14 April	15 April
7	2 April	3 April	4 April	5 April	6 April	31 March	1 April
8	23 April	24 April	25 April	19 April	20 April	21 April	22 April
9	9 April	10 April	11 April	12 April	13 April	14 April	8 April
10	2 April	3 April	28 March	29 March	30 March	31 March	1 April
11	16 April	17 April	18 April	19 April	20 April	21 April	22 April
12	9 April	10 April	11 April	5 April	6 April	7 April	8 April
13	26 March	27 March	28 March	29 March	30 March	31 March	25 March
14	16 April	17 April	18 April	19 April	13 April	14 April	15 April
15	2 April	3 April	4 April	5 April	6 April	7 April	8 April
16	26 March	27 March	28 March	22 March	23 March	24 March	25 March
17	16 April	10 April	11 April	12 April	13 April	14 April	15 April
18	2 April	3 April	4 April	5 April	30 March	31 March	1 April
19	23 April	24 April	18 April	19 April	20 April	21 April	22 April

* 13 Apr. in Armenian, Jacobite, and Nestorian churches.

Note: If you know the concurrent, there is a fixed correspondence between it and the Sunday Letter as follows: 1 = F, 2 = E, 3 = D, 4 = C, 5 = B, 6 = A, 7 = G.

TABLE 2. *Gregorian Easter table, 1583–1899*

GN	1583–1699 Sunday Letter							1700–1899 Sunday Letter						
	A	B	C	D	E	F	G	A	B	C	D	E	F	G
1	16 A	17 A	18 A	19 A	13 A	14 A	15 A	16 A	17 A	18 A	19 A	20 A	14 A	15 A
2	2 A	3 A	4 A	5 A	6 A	7 A	8 A	9 A	3 A	4 A	5 A	6 A	7 A	8 A
3	26 M	27 M	28 M	22 M	23 M	24 M	25 M	26 M	27 M	28 M	29 M	23 M	24 M	25 M
4	16 A	10 A	11 A	12 A	13 A	14 A	15 A	16 A	17 A	11 A	12 A	13 A	14 A	15 A
5	2 A	3 A	4 A	5 A	30 M	31 M	1 A	2 A	3 A	4 A	5 A	6 A	31 M	1 A
6	23 A	24 A	18 A	19 A	20 A	21 A	22 A	23 A	24 A	25 A	19 A	20 A	21 A	22 A
7	9 A	10 A	11 A	12 A	13 A	7 A	8 A	9 A	10 A	11 A	12 A	13 A	14 A	8 A
8	2 A	27 M	28 M	29 M	30 M	31 M	1 A	2 A	3 A	28 M	29 M	30 M	31 M	1 A
9	16 A	17 A	18 A	19 A	20 A	21 A	15 A	16 A	17 A	18 A	19 A	20 A	21 A	22 A
10	9 A	10 A	4 A	5 A	6 A	7 A	8 A	9 A	10 A	11 A	5 A	6 A	7 A	8 A
11	26 M	27 M	28 M	29 M	30 M	24 M	25 M	26 M	27 M	28 M	29 M	30 M	31 M	25 M
12	16 A	17 A	18 A	12 A	13 A	14 A	15 A	16 A	17 A	18 A	19 A	13 A	14 A	15 A
13	2 A	3 A	4 A	5 A	6 A	7 A	1 A	2 A	3 A	4 A	5 A	6 A	7 A	8 A
14	23 A	24 A	25 A	19 A	20 A	21 A	22 A	26 M	27 M	28 M	22 M	23 M	24 M	25 M
15	9 A	10 A	11 A	12 A	13 A	14 A	15 A	16 A	10 A	11 A	12 A	13 A	14 A	15 A
16	2 A	3 A	4 A	29 M	30 M	31 M	1 A	2 A	3 A	4 A	5 A	30 M	31 M	1 A
17	23 A	17 A	18 A	19 A	20 A	21 A	22 A	23 A	24 A	18 A	19 A	20 A	21 A	22 A
18	9 A	10 A	11 A	12 A	6 A	7 A	8 A	9 A	10 A	11 A	12 A	13 A	7 A	8 A
19	26 M	27 M	28 M	29 M	30 M	31 M	1 A	2 A	27 M	28 M	29 M	30 M	31 M	1 A

Note: In leap year, the Sunday Letter to be applied in the above table is the 2nd of the pair.

TABLE 3. *Gregorian Easter table, 1900–2199*

GN	*Sunday Letter*						
	A	B	C	D	E	F	G
1	16 April	17 April	18 April	19 April	20 April	21 April	15 April
2	9 April	10 April	4 April	5 April	6 April	7 April	8 April
3	26 March	27 March	28 March	29 March	30 March	24 March	25 March
4	16 April	17 April	18 April	12 April	13 April	14 April	15 April
5	2 April	3 April	4 April	5 April	6 April	7 April	1 April
6	23 April	24 April	25 April	19 April	20 April	21 April	22 April
7	9 April	10 April	11 April	12 April	13 April	14 April	15 April
8	2 April	3 April	4 April	29 March	30 March	31 March	1 April
9	23 April	17 April	18 April	19 April	20 April	21 April	22 April
10	9 April	10 April	11 April	12 April	6 April	7 April	8 April
11	26 March	27 March	28 March	29 March	30 March	31 March	1 April
12	16 April	17 April	18 April	19 April	20 April	14 April	15 April
13	9 April	3 April	4 April	5 April	6 April	7 April	8 April
14	26 March	27 March	28 March	29 March	23 March	24 March	25 March
15	16 April	17 April	11 April	12 April	13 April	14 April	15 April
16	2 April	3 April	4 April	5 April	6 April	31 March	1 April
17	23 April	24 April	18 April	19 April	20 April	21 April	22 April
18	9 April	10 April	11 April	12 April	13 April	14 April	8 April
19	2 April	3 April	28 March	29 March	30 March	31 March	1 April

EASTER WITHOUT TABLES

Readers with a facility for mental arithmetic may prefer to find Easter by a formula derived from the celebrated mathematician Carl Friedrich Gauss (1777–1855), directed at determining first the number of days by which *luna XV* (not *luna XIV*) falls later than its earliest possible date, 22 March, and then the number of days from *luna XV* to Sunday; when both are 0, Easter falls on 22 March. Let year AD be *Y*; take the remainder of *Y* to 19, 4, and 7 respectively:

$$a \equiv Y \bmod 19$$
$$b \equiv Y \bmod 4$$
$$c \equiv Y \bmod 7$$

For the Julian calendar, put:

$$d \equiv 19a + 15 \ (\bmod\ 30)$$
$$e \equiv 2b + 4c + 6d + 6 \ (\bmod\ 7)$$
Easter = 22 + *d* + *e* March, or *d* + *e* − 9 April.

As always, things are not so simple in the Gregorian calendar. Put

$$S = [Y/100] \ \text{(i.e. divide by 100 and ignore the remainder)}$$
$$s = [(S - 17)/25] \ (= 0 \text{ down to } 4299)$$

$$M \equiv 15 + S - [S/4] - [(S-s)/3] \pmod{30}$$
$$d \equiv 19a + M \pmod{30}$$

except that:

if M = 0, 3, 6, 8, 11, 14, 17, 19, 22, 25, 27, and $19a + M \pmod{30}$ = 29, d = 28.

if M = 2, 5, 10, 13, 16, 21, 24, 28, and $19a + M \pmod{30}$ = 28, d = 27.

$$N \equiv S - 3 - [S/4] \pmod 7$$
$$e \equiv 2b + 4c + 6d + N \pmod 7.$$

Then, as before,

Easter = $22 + d + e$ March, or $d + e - 9$ April.

Century	M	N
1500–1699	22	2
1700–99	23	3
1800–99	23	4
1900–2099	24	5
2100–99	24	6
2200–99	25	0
2300–99	26	1
2400–99	25	1

To find Western (Gregorian) and Orthodox (Julian) Easter 2003

2003 = 105 × 19 + 8 = 500 × 4 + 3 = 286 × 7 + 1

∴ a = 8, b = 3, c = 1

In Gregorian calendar:

19 × 8 + 24 = 176 = 5 × 30 + 26, ∴ d = 26

2 × 3 + 4 × 1 + 6 × 26 + 5 = 171 = 24 × 7 + 3, ∴ e = 3

∴ Easter = 26 + 3 − 9 April = 20 April

In Julian calendar:

19 × 8 + 15 = 167 = 5 × 30 + 17, ∴ d = 17

2 × 3 + 4 × 1 + 6 × 17 + 6 = 118 = 16 × 7 + 6, ∴ e = 6

∴ Easter = 17 + 6 − 9 April = 14 April OS = 27 April NS.

To find Western and Orthodox Easter 7485

7485 = 393 × 19 + 18 = 1871 × 4 + 1 = 1069 × 7 + 2

∴ a = 18, b = 1, c = 2

In Gregorian calendar:

S = 74 = 18 × 4 + 2, s = [57/25] = 2, $S - s$ = 72

15 + 74 − 18 − 24 = 47 = 30 + 17, ∴ M = 17

74 − 3 − 18 = 53 = 7 × 7 + 4, ∴ N = 4

19 × 18 + 17 = 359 = 11 × 30 + 29, but M = 17, ∴ d = 28

2 × 1 + 4 × 2 + 6 × 28 + 4 = 182 = 26 × 7, ∴ e = 0

∴ Easter = 28 + 0 − 9 April = 19 April

In Julian calendar:

$$19 \times 18 + 15 = 357 = 11 \times 30 + 27, \therefore d = 27$$
$$2 \times 1 + 4 \times 2 + 6 \times 27 + 6 = 178 = 25 \times 7 + 3, \therefore e = 3$$
$$\therefore \text{Easter} = 27 + 3 - 9 \text{ April} = 21 \text{ April OS};$$

but Gregorian correction (p. 788) $= 74 - [74/4] - 2 = 54$,

and Revised Julian correction (p. 688) $= 74 - 2 [74/9] - [4/4] - 2 = 55$,

$\therefore$ Orthodox Easter 7485 $= 75$ April $= 14$ June NS $= 15$ June Revised Julian.

DATES OF FEASTS AND FASTS DEPENDENT ON EASTER

Once the date of Easter is known, the other feasts and fasts dependent on it may be found in Table 4.

TABLE 4. *Moveable feasts and fasts dependent on Easter*

Listed are Clean Monday (beginning of Orthodox Lent), Ash Wednesday (beginning of Western Lent), Mothering Sunday, Good Friday, Ascension, and Whit Sunday. All Orthodox dates must be understood according to the Julian calendar.

Clean Monday[a]	Ash Wednesday[a]	Mothering Sunday	Good Friday	**Easter Sunday**	Ascension	Whit Sunday
2 Feb.	4 Feb.	1 Mar.	20 Mar.	**22 Mar.**	30 Apr.	10 May
3 Feb.	5 Feb.	2 Mar.	21 Mar.	**23 Mar.**	1 May	11 May
4 Feb.	6 Feb.	3 Mar.	22 Mar.	**24 Mar.**	2 May	12 May
5 Feb.	7 Feb.	4 Mar.	23 Mar.	**25 Mar.**	3 May	13 May
6 Feb.	8 Feb.	5 Mar.	24 Mar.	**26 Mar.**	4 May	14 May
7 Feb.	9 Feb.	6 Mar.	25 Mar.	**27 Mar.**	5 May	15 May
8 Feb.	10 Feb.	7 Mar.	26 Mar.	**28 Mar.**	6 May	16 May
9 Feb.	11 Feb.	8 Mar.	27 Mar.	**29 Mar.**	7 May	17 May
10 Feb.	12 Feb.	9 Mar.	28 Mar.	**30 Mar.**	8 May	18 May
11 Feb.	13 Feb.	10 Mar.	29 Mar.	**31 Mar.**	9 May	19 May
12 Feb.	14 Feb.	11 Mar.	30 Mar.	**1 Apr.**	10 May	20 May
13 Feb.	15 Feb.	12 Mar.	31 Mar.	**2 Apr.**	11 May	21 May
14 Feb.	16 Feb.	13 Mar.	1 Apr.	**3 Apr.**	12 May	22 May
15 Feb.	17 Feb.	14 Mar.	2 Apr.	**4 Apr.**	13 May	23 May
16 Feb.	18 Feb.	15 Mar.	3 Apr.	**5 Apr.**	14 May	24 May
17 Feb.	19 Feb.	16 Mar.	4 Apr.	**6 Apr.**	15 May	25 May
18 Feb.	20 Feb.	17 Mar.	5 Apr.	**7 Apr.**	16 May	26 May
19 Feb.	21 Feb.	18 Mar.	6 Apr.	**8 Apr.**	17 May	27 May
20 Feb.	22 Feb.	19 Mar.	7 Apr.	**9 Apr.**	18 May	28 May
21 Feb.	23 Feb.	20 Mar.	8 Apr.	**10 Apr.**	19 May	29 May
22 Feb.	24 Feb.	21 Mar.	9 Apr.	**11 Apr.**	20 May	30 May
23 Feb.	25 Feb.	22 Mar.	10 Apr.	**12 Apr.**	21 May	31 May
24 Feb.	26 Feb.	23 Mar.	11 Apr.	**13 Apr.**	22 May	1 June
25 Feb.	27 Feb.	24 Mar.	12 Apr.	**14 Apr.**	23 May	2 June
26 Feb.	28 Feb.	25 Mar.	13 Apr.	**15 Apr.**	24 May	3 June

Clean Monday[a]	Ash Wednesday[a]	Mothering Sunday	Good Friday	**Easter Sunday**	Ascension	Whit Sunday
27 Feb.	1 Mar.	26 Mar.	14 Apr.	**16 Apr.**	25 May	4 June
28 Feb.	2 Mar.	27 Mar.	15 Apr.	**17 Apr.**	26 May	5 June
1 Mar.	3 Mar.	28 Mar.	16 Apr.	**18 Apr.**	27 May	6 June
2 Mar.	4 Mar.	29 Mar.	17 Apr.	**19 Apr.**	28 May	7 June
3 Mar.	5 Mar.	30 Mar.	18 Apr.	**20 Apr.**	29 May	8 June
4 Mar.	6 Mar.	31 Mar.	19 Apr.	**21 Apr.**	30 May	9 June
5 Mar.	7 Mar.	1 Apr.	20 Apr.	**22 Apr.**	31 May	10 June
6 Mar.	8 Mar.	2 Apr.	21 Apr.	**23 Apr.**	1 June	11 June
7 Mar.	9 Mar.	3 Apr.	22 Apr.	**24 Apr.**	2 June	12 June
8 Mar.	10 Mar.	4 Apr.	23 Apr.	**25 Apr.**	3 June	13 June

[a] In leap year, add 1 to all dates in February.

APPENDIX I. EASTER DATES SINCE 1582 DIFFERING FROM BOTH JULIAN AND GREGORIAN DATES

I. ARMENIAN ORTHODOX CHURCH, SYRIAN ORTHODOX CHURCH (JACOBITES), CHURCH OF THE EAST (NESTORIANS)

These follow an older Constantinopolitan cycle, in which the Paschal term of the year 18 (= GN 1) falls on 6 April and not the 5th; consequently, when that day is a Sunday, Easter is 13 April. This happened in 570, 665, 760, 1007, 1102, 1197, 1292, 1539, and again in 1634 (23 April NS), 1729 (24 April NS), and 1824 (25 April NS); the next case will be 2071 (26 April NS).

II. ASTRONOMICAL EASTER

On the history of the *calculus astronomicus*, or keeping of Easter according to the equinox and full moon at the longitude of Uraniborg, see II: *The Date of Easter: Astronomical Easter.* Even when theoretically in force it was by no means always observed in practice: in 1700 through inadvertence, in subsequent years because of the prejudice against coincidence of Easter and Passover.

Year	Easter			Passover	Astronomical Easter observed[a]			
	Astronomical	Gregorian	Julian[b]		Ger.[c]	Den.	Sw.	Fin.[d]
1700	4 April	11 April	31 March	4 April	No	No	—	—
1724	9 April	16 April	5 April	8 April	Yes	No	—	—
1744	29 March	5 April	25 March	28 March	Yes	Yes	Yes[e]	Yes[e]
1778	12 April	19 April	8 April	12 April	—	—	No	No
1798	1 April[f]	8 April	28 March	1 April	—	—	No	No
1802	25 April	18 April	7 April	17 April	—	—	Yes	Yes
1805	21 April	14 April	3 April	14 April	—	—	Yes	Yes
1818	29 March	22 March	14/26 A.	21 April	—	—	Yes	Yes
1825	10 April	3 April	23 March	3 April	—	—	—	Yes
1829	26 April	19 April	8 April	18 April	—	—	—	Yes
1845	30 March	23 March	15/27 A.	22 April	—	—	—	Yes

[a] 'Yes' means that the astronomical date was accepted, 'No' that it was rejected, a dash that the *calculus astronomicus* was not in force.

[b] Given in Old Style only unless different from Gregorian Easter.

^c Protestant states, also most Protestant cantons in Switzerland (a few kept to the Julian calendar).

^d Finland was part of Sweden till 1809, and thereafter belonged to Russia till 1917.

^e Designated 18 March in Old Style (see Section III below).

^f So for the meridian of Uraniborg; for most of Sweden 8 April was correct.

III. SWEDEN

In 1700 Sweden omitted the leap day (see II: *Modern Calendar: Gregorian Reform: Sweden*), without making further adjustment, so that between 1 March 1700 and 30 February (*sic*) 1712, when the change was reversed, the same nominal day fell one day earlier than in the Julian calendar. In 1705, 1709, and 1711 a Paschal term that in the Julian calendar fell on Sunday was a Saturday in Sweden, allowing Easter to be celebrated the next day (italicized in the table below); in the other years Easter was kept on the same natural day as under the Julian calendar, but the next nominal day or calendar date. In 1705 and 1711 the Swedish Easter agreed with the Gregorian against the Julian; in 1709 the Gregorian Easter went its own way, as also in 1701, 1704, and 1708. In the other years Easter was kept on the same day under three different dates.

Year	GN	Sweden		Julian		Gregorian		
		Letter	Easter	Letter	Easter	Letter	Easter	Same day as
1700	10	G	1 April	GF	31 March	C	11 April	Sw. and Jul.
1701	11	F	21 April	E	20 April	B	27 March	—
1702	12	E	6 April	D	5 April	A	16 April	Sw. and Jul.
1703	13	D	29 March	C	28 March	G	8 April	Sw. and Jul.
1704	14	CB	18 April	BA	17 April	FE	23 March	—
1705	15	A	*2 April*	G	8 April	D	12 April	Sw.
1706	16	G	25 March	F	24 March	C	4 April	Sw. and Jul.
1707	17	F	14 April	E	13 April	B	24 April	Sw. and Jul.
1708	18	ED	5 April	DC	4 April	AG	8 April	—
1709	19	C	*18 April*	B	24 April	F	31 March	—
1710	1	B	10 April	A	9 April	E	20 April	Sw. and Jul.
1711	2	A	*26 March*	G	1 April	D	5 April	Sw.

In 1740, Sweden adopted the *calculus astronomicus* for Easter, but down to 1752 with Old Style dating. The astronomical Easter agreed with the Gregorian except in 1744, but the dates were 11 nominal days earlier:

Year	Swedish	Gregorian	Year	Swedish	Gregorian
1740	6 April	17 April	1747	22 March	2 April
1741	22 March	2 April	1748	3 April	14 April
1742	14 March	25 March	1749	26 March	6 April
1743	3 April	14 April	1750	18 March	29 March
1744	*18 March*	5 April	1751	31 March	11 April
1745	7 April	18 April	1752	22 March	2 April
1746	30 March	10 April			

For astronomical Easter after 1752, see Section II above.

APPENDIX J. THE INSULAR EASTER
OF THE LATERCUS

The Greek *plinthíon*, diminutive of *plínthos*, 'brick', is sometimes used for a mathematical table divided into squares. The corresponding Latin diminutive *laterculus*, from *later*, acquired this sense by loan-translation, and among Christians became a term for an Easter table such as the 84-year table devised by Augustalis in the third century. However, the computists of the British Isles, not recognizing the formation, took it to be the normal diminutive in -*lus* of a principal *latercus*; this barbarous, allegedly Egyptian, word became the specific name for the Insular 84-year Easter cycle.

Since Bede did not describe, and probably did not know, the detailed rules of the Insular Easter, modern scholars until the 1980s had to base conjectural reconstructions on inadequate hints in scattered sources. All these were rendered obsolete by the discovery of a complete Latercus in a manuscript at Padua, first published by McCarthy and Ó Cróinín, 'The "Lost" Irish 84-Year Easter Table', but definitively set forth by McCarthy, 'Easter Principles'. It comprises six columns: the feria of 1 January (marked B in leap year), its lune, the date and lune of Easter, and the date and lune of the Initium, or first day of Lent, which in the Insular Church was the Wednesday 40 days (counted inclusively) before Easter, one week after the modern Ash Wednesday. Although many of the figures are miscopied, the structure of the system enables errors to be corrected, and the absolute values of the cyclical years determined.

The cycle begins in AD 354, 438, 522, 606, 690, etc., on Saturday, 1 January, epact 19; the *saltus* is taken at 14-year intervals, beginning with the leap from epact 12 in cycle 14 to epact 24 in cycle 15. However, the lunar calendar of the Latercus differed sharply from the Roman model: a full January was followed by three consecutive hollow months (with the usual filling of February in leap year); the remaining eight months all had one day fewer than their solar counterparts. As a result, between April and the following February inclusive the monthly epacts advance steadily by 1.

Month	Jan.	Feb.	Mar.	Apr.	May	June	July	Aug.	Sept.	Oct.	Nov.	Dec.
Solar	31	28	31	30	31	30	31	31	30	31	30	31
Roman lunar	30	29	30	29	30	29	30	29	30	29	30	29
Epact = Jan +	0	1	0	1	2	3	4	5	7	7	9	9
Latercus	30	29	29	29	30	29	30	30	29	30	29	30
Epact = Jan +	0	1	0	2	3	4	5	6	7	8	9	10

The next January will have an epact 11 ahead, just as in the Roman system, and February 12 ahead. Even in the 1850s a verse mnemonic in Irish for finding the lune of the day was being recited in West Cork that presupposed the lunar calendar of the Celtic Easter cycle, which had been abandoned over 1200 years earlier in favour of another scheme itself rendered obsolete by the Gregorian reform (O'Leary, 1; cf. McCarthy, 'Easter Principles', 212). The rule is: count the months from March (inclusively, thus taking care of the leap between March and April), add the *quantième* less 1 (since the epact belongs to the Kalends), add the epact, and take away 30 or 60 if need be. Whether the *saltus* was taken at the end of lunar or solar December is not clear; a confused statement in one source indicates lunar November, but that was already hollow.

When the epact was 20 or higher, an embolism of 30 days was added, up to epact 27 one month earlier than in the Supputatio Romana and always ending on the Kalends, from 2 November–1 December under epact 20 to 2 May–1 June under epact 27. (It is possible, however, that Insular computists, or some of them, would have said that the normal month ended on the Kalends, being given a 30th day if it lacked one, and an abortive moon followed from the 2nd to *pridie Kalendas*.) Under epact 28, however, this monthly advance would require the embolism to coincide with lunar April, after the hollow lunar March had ended on the 31st solar; but for the April epact to be 28 + 2 = 30 according to rule, the embolism would have to be 3 March–1 April. In the two years under this epact (10 and 75), the surviving table shows the Easter lune corrected from that implying monthly epact 1 to that for epact 30; the date of Easter was not affected. Under epact 29, it is evident from the table that lunar March began on the 3rd solar, and lunar April on the 1st; since an embolism 3 January–1 February would fall out of sequence and reduce the March epact to 28, there must have been a full month 1 February–2 March, with monthly epacts February 1, March 29, April 1. Under epact 30 we have express evidence for a full month 31 January–1 March, giving epact 2 in both February and April.

The solar limits were 26 March, the day after the Roman equinox, and 23 April; but it was the lunar limits that scandalized outsiders, *XIV–XX*, for when *luna XIV* fell on Sunday it was celebrated as Easter and not as Palm Sunday. This was vigorously defended in the treatise *De ratione paschali* discussed below, cited by St Columban in a letter to Gregory the Great and exploited by all parties to the Irish and English polemics of the seventh century: since on *luna XXI*, let alone *XXII*, the moon did not rise till after midnight, darkness prevailed over light, contrary to the meaning of the festival. Celebration on the Jewish *luna XIV* was simply not seen as a problem: as Columban observed, it was the Lord's Passover (Exod. 12: 11) and not the Jews'.

Luna XIV is 12 April under epact 1, one day earlier than in the Supputatio Romana, and moves to the previous day with each increase of 1 in the epact up to 21 March under epact 23; in cycle 80, 1 January being Sunday, this gives Easter on 26 March, *luna XIX*. Under this epact, however, *luna XIV* may also be 19 April; in cycle 61, 1 January being Thursday, this is a Sunday and therefore Easter. Under epact 24, *luna XIV* is 18 April (we shall see why 20 Mar. is excluded); under 25, the 17th; under 26, the 16th; under 27, the 15th. Under epact 28, it was (at least according to the correction) also the 15th; under

29 and 30 it is respectively the 14th and 13th, falling on the same days owing to the embolism as in the Supputatio Romana owing to the lack of embolism.

Whereas the Alexandrian rules, which define the Paschal term as the first *luna XIV* within an upper solar limit, of necessity give one and only one Easter date for every year, Paschal limits based on the date of Easter run the risk that some years will have two or none. On the other hand, whereas the Alexandrian system obliges every *luna XIV* to fall on every feria, in an 84-year table it is possible by careful choice of initial epact to avoid those combinations of feria and epact that would lead to this result; the Supputatio Romana does not, but the Latercus does. Under epact 19, if 1 January had been Monday in a common year or Tuesday in a leap year, Sunday, 25 March would have been too early for *luna XIV* and Monday, 23 April too late; similar considerations apply under epacts 20 to 23. On the other hand, under epact 24, had 1 January been a Sunday in a common year or Saturday in leap year, the *luna XIV* on Monday, 20 March would have pointed to Easter on the 26th, and that on Tuesday, 18 April to Easter on the 23rd, these being respectively the first and the last lawful dates. None of these cases occurs; whatever theological judgement may be passed on the Paschal limits, the Latercus is a well-constructed table subject only to the discrepancy between the real lengths of 84 years and 1039 lunations.

The Latercus appears to modify the *laterculus* of Augustalis, which uses the standard alternation of full and hollow months but has *saltus* every 14 years and lunar limits *XIV–XX*, and also began with epact 19; Augustalis' epact for 270, and therefore 354, is 20, but the difference in the length of lunar March causes *luna XIV* in both tables to fall on 25 March. Under epact 25 on Friday (AD 219, 303) it set Easter on 21 March, which a later computist treated as justification for allowing this date in 387; if (as is not certain) this was the earliest date admitted, then under epact 26 on Saturday (AD 276, 360) Easter must have been 23 April as in the Latercus, but it never needed to be later.

According to Aldhelm, the rules of the Latercus were devised by Sulpicius Severus, the chronologist and hagiographer of St Martin who was tempted by Pelagianism; in support of this assertion McCarthy cites Columban's statement, in his letter to Pope Gregory I, that Victorius compiled his tables 103 years after St Martin: 457 − 103 = 354, the beginning (at least retrospectively) of a Latercus cycle and the year of St Martin's baptism, for Sulpicius an auspicious starting-point. He would thus have applied to Augustalis' *laterculus* (rather than the Supputatio Romana) the solar limits 26 March–23 April exhibited, along with the unusual distribution of full and hollow months, by the unworkable 19-year cycle with only two leap years of the treatise *De ratione paschali* ascribed to Anatolius of Laodicea; it has commonly been regarded as an Irish or British forgery of the sixth century, but McCarthy and Breen argue that it draws on genuine Anatolian material, a case they will set out at greater length in their forthcoming edition.

The table of Latercus dates below is translated from the Paduan table as corrected by McCarthy, 'Easter Principles', but with the years AD added for the five cycles during which it had at least some currency.

Latercus Easter and Initium dates, 354–773

Cycle	Year					1 Jan.	Epact	Easter	Lune	Initium	Lune
1	354	438	522	606	690	Sat.	19	27 Mar.	16	16 Feb.	6
2	355	439	523	607	691	Sun.	30	16 Apr.	17	8 Mar.	7
B 3	356	440	524	608	692	Mon.	11	7 Apr.	19	28 Feb.	9
4	357	441	525	609	693	Wed.	22	20 Apr.	14	12 Mar.	4
5	358	442	526	610	694	Thu.	3	12 Apr.	16	4 Mar.	6
6	359	443	527	611	695	Fri.	14	4 Apr.	19	24 Feb.	9
B 7	360	444	528	612	696	Sat.	25	23 Apr.	20	15 Mar.	10
8	361	445	529	613	697	Mon.	6	8 Apr.	15	28 Feb.	5
9	362	446	530	614	698	Tue.	17	31 Mar.	18	20 Feb.	8
10	363	447	531	615	699	Wed.	28	20 Apr.	*19	12 Mar.	10
B 11	364	448	532	616	700	Thu.	9	4 Apr.	14	25 Feb.	4
12	365	449	533	617	701	Sat.	20	27 Mar.	17	16 Feb.	7
13	366	450	534	618	702	Sun.	1	16 Apr.	18	8 Mar.	8
S 14	367	451	535	619	703	Mon.	12	1 Apr.	14	21 Feb.	4
B 15	368	452	536	620	704	Tue.	24	20 Apr.	16	12 Mar.	6
16	369	453	537	621	705	Thu.	5	12 Apr.	18	4 Mar.	8
17	370	454	538	622	706	Fri.	16	28 Mar.	14	17 Feb.	4
18	371	455	539	623	707	Sat.	27	17 Apr.	16	9 Mar.	6
B 19	372	456	540	624	708	Sun.	8	8 Apr.	17	29 Feb.	7
20	373	457	541	625	709	Tue.	19	31 Mar.	20	20 Feb.	10
21	374	458	542	626	710	Wed.	30	13 Apr.	14	5 Mar.	4
22	375	459	543	627	711	Thu.	11	5 Apr.	17	25 Feb.	7
B 23	376	460	544	628	712	Fri.	22	27 Mar.	19	17 Feb.	9
24	377	461	545	629	713	Sun.	3	16 Apr.	20	8 Mar.	10
25	378	462	546	630	714	Mon.	14	1 Apr.	16	21 Feb.	6
26	379	463	547	631	715	Tue.	25	21 Apr.	18	13 Mar.	8
B 27	380	464	548	632	716	Wed.	6	12 Apr.	19	4 Mar.	9
S 28	381	465	549	633	717	Fri.	17	28 Mar.	15	17 Feb.	5
29	382	466	550	634	718	Sat.	29	17 Apr.	17	9 Mar.	7
30	383	467	551	635	719	Sun.	10	9 Apr.	20	1 Mar.	10
B 31	384	468	552	636	720	Mon.	21	21 Apr.	14	13 Mar.	4
32	385	469	553	637	721	Wed.	2	13 Apr.	16	5 Mar.	6
33	386	470	554	638	722	Thu.	13	5 Apr.	19	25 Feb.	9
34	387	471	555	639	723	Fri.	24	18 Apr.	14	10 Mar.	4
B 35	388	472	556	640	724	Sat.	5	9 Apr.	15	1 Mar.	5
36	389	473	557	641	725	Mon.	16	1 Apr.	18	21 Feb.	8
37	390	474	558	642	726	Tue.	27	21 Apr.	20	13 Mar.	10
38	391	475	559	643	727	Wed.	8	6 Apr.	15	26 Feb.	5
B 39	392	476	560	644	728	Thu.	19	28 Mar.	17	18 Feb.	7
40	393	477	561	645	729	Sat.	30	17 Apr.	18	9 Mar.	8

Latercus Easter and Initium dates (cont.)

Cycle	Year					1 Jan.	Epact	Easter	Lune	Initium	Lune
41	394	478	562	646	730	Sun.	11	2 Apr.	14	22 Feb.	4
S 42	395	479	563	647	731	Mon.	22	22 Apr.	16	14 Mar.	6
B 43	396	480	564	648	732	Tue.	4	13 Apr.	18	5 Mar.	8
44	397	481	565	649	733	Thu.	15	29 Mar.	14	18 Feb.	4
45	398	482	566	650	734	Fri.	26	18 Apr.	16	10 Mar.	6
46	399	483	567	651	735	Sat.	7	10 Apr.	18	2 Mar.	8
B 47	400	484	568	652	736	Sun.	18	1 Apr.	20	22 Feb.	10
48	401	485	569	653	737	Tue.	29	14 Apr.	14	6 Mar.	4
49	402	486	570	654	738	Wed.	10	6 Apr.	17	26 Feb.	7
50	403	487	571	655	739	Thu.	21	29 Mar.	20	18 Feb.	10
B 51	404	488	572	656	740	Fri.	2	17 Apr.	20	9 Mar.	10
52	405	489	573	657	741	Sun.	13	2 Apr.	16	22 Feb.	6
53	406	490	574	658	742	Mon.	24	22 Apr.	18	14 Mar.	8
54	407	491	575	659	743	Tue.	5	14 Apr.	20	6 Mar.	10
B 55	408	492	576	660	744	Wed.	16	29 Mar.	15	19 Feb.	5
S 56	409	493	577	661	745	Fri.	27	18 Apr.	17	10 Mar.	7
57	410	494	578	662	746	Sat.	9	10 Apr.	20	2 Mar.	10
58	411	495	579	663	747	Sun.	20	26 Mar.	16	15 Feb.	6
B 59	412	496	580	664	748	Mon.	1	14 Apr.	16	6 Mar.	6
60	413	497	581	665	749	Wed.	12	6 Apr.	19	26 Feb.	9
61	414	498	582	666	750	Thu.	23	19 Apr.	14	11 Mar.	4
62	415	499	583	667	751	Fri.	4	11 Apr.	16	3 Mar.	6
B 63	416	500	584	668	752	Sat.	15	2 Apr.	18	23 Feb.	8
64	417	501	585	669	753	Mon.	26	22 Apr.	20	14 Mar.	10
65	418	502	586	670	754	Tue.	7	7 Apr.	15	27 Feb.	5
66	419	503	587	671	755	Wed.	18	30 Mar.	18	19 Feb.	8
B 67	420	504	588	672	756	Thu.	29	18 Apr.	18	10 Mar.	8
68	421	505	589	673	757	Sat.	10	3 Apr.	14	23 Feb.	4
69	422	506	590	674	758	Sun.	21	26 Mar.	17	15 Feb.	7
S 70	423	507	591	675	759	Mon.	2	15 Apr.	18	7 Mar.	8
B 71	424	508	592	676	760	Tue.	14	30 Mar.	14	20 Feb.	4
72	425	509	593	677	761	Thu.	25	19 Apr.	16	11 Mar.	6
73	426	510	594	678	762	Fri.	6	11 Apr.	18	3 Mar.	8
74	427	511	595	679	763	Sat.	17	27 Mar.	14	16 Feb.	4
B 75	428	512	596	680	764	Sun.	28	15 Apr.	14†	7 Mar.	5
76	429	513	597	681	765	Tue.	9	7 Apr.	17	27 Feb.	7
77	430	514	598	682	766	Wed.	20	30 Mar.	20	19 Feb.	10
78	431	515	599	683	767	Thu.	1	12 Apr.	14	4 Mar.	4
B 79	432	516	600	684	768	Fri.	12	3 Apr.	16	24 Feb.	6
80	433	517	601	685	769	Sun.	23	26 Mar.	19	15 Feb.	9

Latercus Easter and Initium dates (*cont.*)

Cycle	Year					1 Jan.	Epact	Easter	Lune	Initium	Lune
81	434	518	602	686	770	Mon.	4	15 Apr.	20	7 Mar.	10
82	435	519	603	687	771	Tue.	15	31 Mar.	16	20 Feb.	6
B 83	436	520	604	688	772	Wed.	26	19 Apr.	17	11 Mar.	7
S 84	437	521	605	689	773	Fri.	7	11 Apr.	19	3 Mar.	9

* Corrected in MS from 20.   † Corrected in MS from 15.

APPENDIX K.
CHRISTIAN, JEWISH, AND MUSLIM
CALENDARS, 1997–2020

TABLE 1. *Western and Orthodox Easter 1997–2020*

Year	Easter		Golden No.	Epact (Greg.)	Sunday Letter	
	Western	*Orthodox*			*Gregorian*	*Julian*
1997	30 March	27 April	3	21	E	F
1998	12 April	19 April	4	2	D	E
1999	4 April	11 April	5	13	C	D
2000*	23 April	30 April	6	24	BA	CB
2001	15 April	15 April	7	5	G	A
2002	31 March	5 May	8	16	F	G
2003	20 April	27 April	9	27	E	F
2004*	11 April	11 April	10	8	DC	ED
2005	27 March	1 May	11	19	B	C
2006	16 April	23 April	12	*	A	B
2007	8 April	8 April	13	11	G	A
2008*	23 March	27 April	14	22	FE	GF
2009	12 April	19 April	15	3	D	E
2010	4 April	4 April	16	14	C	D
2011	24 April	24 April	17	25'	B	C
2012*	8 April	15 April	18	6	AG	BA
2013	31 March	5 May	19	17	F	G
2014	20 April	20 April	1	29	E	F
2015	5 April	12 April	2	10	D	E
2016*	27 March	1 May	3	21	CB	DC
2017	16 April	16 April	4	2	A	B
2018	1 April	8 April	5	13	G	A
2019	21 April	28 April	6	24	F	G
2020*	12 April	19 April	7	5	ED	FE

Orthodox dates are calculated by the Julian calendar but stated by the Gregorian.

* (in left-hand column) Leap year.

TABLE 2. *Jewish calendar,* AM *5758–5781*

	Rosh Hashanah	Chanukah	Pesach
5758	Th 2 Oct. 1997	We 24 Dec. 1997	Sa 11 Apr. 1998
5759⁺	Mo 21 Sept. 1998	Mo 14 Dec. 1998	Th 1 Apr. 1999
5760*⁺	Sa 11 Sept. 1999	Sa 4 Dec. 1999	Th 20 Apr. 2000
5761⁻	Sa 30 Sept. 2000	Fr 22 Dec. 2000	Su 8 Apr. 2001
5762	Tu 18 Sept. 2001	Mo 10 Dec. 2001	Th 28 Mar. 2002
5763*⁺	Sa 7 Sept. 2002	Sa 30 Nov. 2002	Th 17 Apr. 2003
5764⁺	Sa 27 Sept. 2003	Sa 20 Dec. 2003	Tu 6 Apr. 2004
5765*⁻	Th 16 Sept. 2004	We 8 Dec. 2004	Su 24 Apr. 2005
5766	Tu 4 Oct. 2005	Mo 26 Dec. 2005	Th 13 Apr. 2006
5767⁺	Sa 23 Sept. 2006	Sa 16 Dec. 2006	Tu 3 Apr. 2007
5768*⁻	Th 13 Sept. 2007	We 5 Dec. 2007	Su 20 Apr. 2008
5769	Tu 30 Sept. 2008	Mo 22 Dec. 2008	Th 9 Apr. 2009
5770⁺	Sa 19 Sept. 2009	Sa 12 Dec. 2009	Tu 30 Mar. 2010
5771*⁺	Th 9 Sept. 2010	Th 2 Dec. 2010	Tu 19 Apr. 2011
5772	Th 29 Sept. 2011	We 21 Dec. 2011	Sa 7 Apr. 2012
5773⁻	Mo 17 Sept. 2012	Su 2 Dec. 2012	Tu 26 Mar. 2013
5774*⁺	Th 5 Sept. 2013	Th 28 Nov. 2013	Tu 15 Apr. 2014
5775	Th 25 Sept. 2014	We 17 Dec. 2014	Sa 4 Apr. 2015
5776*⁺	Mo 14 Sept. 2015	Mo 7 Dec. 2014	Sa 23 Apr. 2016
5777⁻	Mo 3 Oct. 2016	Su 25 Dec. 2016	Tu 11 Apr. 2017
5778	Th 21 Sept. 2017	We 13 Dec. 2017	Sa 31 Mar. 2018
5779*⁺	Mo 10 Sept. 2018	Mo 3 Dec. 2018	Sa 20 Apr. 2019
5780⁺	Mo 30 Sept. 2019	Mo 23 Dec. 2019	Th 9 Apr. 2020
5781⁻	Sa 19 Sept. 2020	Fr 11 Dec. 2020	Su 28 Mar. 2021

* Embolismic year. ⁻ Deficient year. ⁺ Abundant year.

TABLE 3. *Muslim calendar,* AH *1418–1442*

	1 Muḥarram	1 Ramaḍān
1418	Fr 9 May 1997	We 31 Dec. 1997
1419	Tu 28 Apr. 1998	Su 20 Dec. 1998
1420*	Sa 17 Apr. 1999	Th 9 Dec. 1999
1421	Th 6 Apr. 2000	Tu 28 Nov. 2000
1422	Mo 26 Mar. 2001	Sa 17 Nov. 2001
1423*	Fr 15 Mar. 2002	We 6 Nov. 2002
1424	We 5 Mar. 2003	Mo 27 Oct. 2003
1425	Su 22 Feb. 2004	Fr 15 Oct. 2004
1426*	Th 10 Feb. 2005	Tu 4 Oct. 2005
1427	Tu 31 Jan. 2006	Su 24 Sept. 2006
1428*	Sa 20 Jan. 2007	Th 13 Sept. 2007

TABLE 3 *(cont.)*

	1 *Muḥarram*	1 *Ramaḍān*
1429	Th 10 Jan. 2008	Tu 2 Sept. 2008
1430	Mo 29 Dec. 2008	Sa 22 Aug. 2009
1431*	Fr 18 Dec. 2009	We 11 Aug. 2010
1432	We 8 Dec. 2010	Mo 1 Aug. 2011
1433	Su 27 Nov. 2011	Sa 20 July 2012
1434*	Th 15 Nov. 2012	Tu 9 July 2013
1435	Tu 5 Nov. 2013	Su 29 June 2014
1436*	Sa 25 Oct. 2014	Th 18 June 2015
1437	Th 15 Oct. 2015	Tu 7 June 2016
1438	Mo 3 Oct. 2016	Sa 27 May 2017
1439*	Fr 22 Sept. 2017	We 16 May 2018
1440	We 12 Sept. 2018	Mo 6 May 2019
1441	Su 1 Sept. 2019	Fr 24 Apr. 2020
1442*	Th 20 Aug. 2020	Tu 13 Apr. 2021

* Leap year.

GLOSSARY

Annunciation style: the Christian era with years counted from 25 March. See 'Florentine style', 'Pisan style'.

annus vagus: a year of fixed length not adjusted by intercalation to keep pace with the sun or moon: e.g. the ancient Egyptian, Iranian, Armenian, and Mesoamerican years of 365 days.

apparent solar time: time measured by sun's position relative to earth, e.g. by a sundial.

Arianism: properly the doctrine, propounded by the presbyter Areios or Arius but condemned at the Council of Nicaea in AD 325, that the Son was created by the Father; the term is applied polemically by supporters of the council to any Christology with which they disagreed, in particular the Homoian.

artificial day: the period of light between sunrise and sunset.

backward count: the counting of days (in the Roman calendar and the *consuetudo Bononiensis*), weeks (in the Icelandic calendar: see II: **Other Calendars: Icelandic*), or years (in BC dating) before a given point.

calculus astronomicus: the calculation of Easter according to the best available astronomical information in preference to cyclical tables (see 'Improved Calendar').

calculus Florentinus: see 'Florentine style'.

calculus Pisanus: see 'Pisan style'.

calendar month: the period from a *quantième* in any month to the same *quantième* in next month.

Calendar of 354: a collection of chronological information, Christian and pagan. See II: **Roman Calendar.*

cardinal days: the summer and winter solstices and the spring and autumn equinoxes.

century: period of 100 years, counted in any era from the year ending 01: thus the first century is 1–100, the second 101–200. This also applies in backward reckoning: the first century BC is 100–1 BC, the second 200–101 BC.

Circumcision style: same as 'modern style'.

civil day: the period of time defined as a day by law or custom, a calendar day.

clavis: 'key', the date from which a moveable feast is to be found by counting forwards, inclusively, a number of days known as the *clavis terminorum* and varying with the annual epact.

common year: a year without intercalation; opp. *embolismic, leap year.*

computus: the calculations pertaining to the calendar, in particular for finding Easter.

concurrent: the feria of a given day, especially in Easter computus of 24 March; from Latin *dies concurrentes,* 'days running with [the sun]', i.e. in excess of a complete week.

consuetudo Bononiensis: the counting of days up to full moon as 'when the month is entering' (*intrante*), after full moon as 'when the month is departing' (*exeunte*).

current years: dating that includes the year in progress; opp. *elapsed.*

custom of the English Church: same as 'Florentine style'.

cycle: any sequence of years (or other units of time) that repeat themselves in a particular respect after a fixed interval; also a year within a cycle ('cycle 3', i.e. the third year of the given cycle).

decade, *décade:* respectively English for a period of ten years and French for a period of ten days; both from Greek *dekás,* 'the number ten', 'group of ten'. The French for a decade is *une décennie.*

decemnovenal cycle: the Metonic cycle used to calculate Easter at Alexandria, ultimately adopted by the Western Church, reckoned from 1 BC.

depositio: a saint's burial-feast.

Diocletian, era of: Alexandrian era reckoned from 29 August AD 284.

dog days: supposedly the hottest of the year; for an explanation of the term see I: **Days: Dog Days.*

ecliptic: the path of the sun's apparent annual course through the heavens, so called because eclipses occur only when the moon crosses it; see also 'zodiac'.

elapsed years: dating that excludes the year in progress; opp. *current.*

embolism: intercalation of a month, or the month so intercalated (from Greek *embolismós,* 'intercalation').

embolismic year: a year with an intercalary month.

enneakaidekaetēris: a Metonic cycle, in particular the Alexandrian cycle (called 'decemnovenal' in the West) and the 'Byzantine' lunar cycle (q.v.).

epact: the age of the moon on a given day of the solar year, especially in Easter computus that on 1 January, 22 March, or 31 December; from Greek *epaktaì hēmérai,* 'additional days', ought strictly to be plural.

epagomenal days: days not counted within any month but added to the year in order to make up the right length.

epoch: the date from which an era is reckoned.

era: reckoning of years in continuous numerical sequence from an epoch; the years may be either current or elapsed (qq.v.), the former being more usual outside India.

feria: the day of the week on which any given date falls, expressed either by its name or by a number: 1 = Sunday, 2 = Monday, 3 = Tuesday, 4 = Wednesday, 5 = Thursday, 6 = Friday, 7 = Saturday.

ferial formula: the general rule for finding the feria of any date in a calendar of Julian or Gregorian type, by adding to the year of the era a quarter of itself, not counting fractions, together with the appropriate parameter, and taking the remainder to 7; it may be written $F \equiv Y + [Y/4] + P \pmod 7$. See II: **Computus; *Egyptian Calendar; *Sunday Letters.*

Filioque: Latin for 'and the Son', the phrase added to the Creed in the Western Church to assert that the Holy Spirit proceeds from the Son as well as the Father.

Florentine style: the Annunciation style reckoned from 25 March following the beginning of the modern year.

forward count: the reckoning of days within the month as 1st, 2nd, etc. till the end.

full month: in a lunar or lunisolar calendar, a month of 30 days; opp. *hollow.*

Gnostic: any of several Christian and other sects claiming a special knowledge (in Greek *gnôsis*) either handed down in secret from the Apostles or divinely revealed to their founders, and typically distinguishing the supreme God from the inferior Demiurge or creator.

Golden Legend: the collection of saints' lives and other church traditions collected by Jacobus de Voragine.

Golden Number (abbrev. GN): the number indicating the place of the year in the decemnovenal cycle as used by the Western Church, found by adding 1 to the year AD and dividing the sum by 19; the remainder is the GN, or if there is no remainder, the GN is 19.

Grace, era of: Alexandrian (Coptic, Ethiopic) era calculated from 1 Thoth 77 Diocletian = 29 August AD 360; but the term 'year of Grace' was sometimes applied to the era of Diocletian. It is also a common synonym for the year AD.

Gregorian calendar: the reformed calendar promulgated in 1582 by Pope Gregory XIII, comprising the New Style (q.v.) and the Easter tables of Aloysius Lilius.

historical year: the year reckoned in modern fashion from 1 January, irrespective of the system in use at the time and place under discussion.

hollow month: in a lunar or lunisolar calendar, a month of 29 days; opp. *full.*

Homoian: the formula that the Son is 'like' the Father, avoiding talk of 'substance' (see *homoiousios, homoousios*).

homoiousios: the formula that the Son is 'of like substance' with the Father.

homoousios: the formula that the Son is of the same substance (in Latin *consubstantialis*) with the Father.

Improved Calendar: the calendar adopted by German, Swiss, and Scandinavian Protestants in the 1700s, accepting the New Style (q.v.) but not the Gregorian Easter table (see *calculus astronomicus*). Accepted in principle by Dutch Protestants under the name of Improved Julian Calendar, though in practice they followed the Gregorian calendar.

Incarnation era: an era reckoned from the supposed date of Christ's Incarnation; usually that of the year AD, otherwise called the Nativity, Christian, or Common era, but in an Alexandrian, Coptic, or Ethiopic context an era reckoned from 29 August AD 8. (The distinction between Incarnation and Nativity was not drawn until the late ninth century, when in some places the Incarnation epoch was identified with Christ's conception, i.e. the Annunciation on 25 March; see 'Annunciation style'.)

indiction: a 15-year cycle devised in the later Roman empire for taxation purposes, and long maintained as a dating formula (see II: **Chronology: Cycles*).

intercalation (adj. **intercalary**): the addition of one or more days or months to the year beyond its normal length in order to keep pace with the moon or sun. The Greek name *embolism* is sometimes used for the addition of a month.

Jacobite: (in politics) a supporter of the exiled James II or his descendants; (in religion) a Syrian Monophysite, so called after Jacob Baradaeus (*c.*500–78), who created an underground clergy in opposition to the official Church.

Julian calendar: the Roman calendar as reformed by C. Julius Caesar and adopted by the Christian Church, but not subjected to the Gregorian reform, i.e. retaining Old Style and the unreformed Easter computus.

Lady Day style: same as 'Florentine style'.

Latercus: the Insular (British and Irish) 84-year Easter table.

leap year: a year containing an intercalary day.

luna XIV: the 14th day of the first lunar month of spring, also called the 'Paschal term' because Easter is the Sunday after it.

lunar calendar: a calendar based on the moon: it may be either pure, taking no notice of the sun (see II: **Muslim Calendar*), or lunisolar.

lunar cycle: a Metonic cycle: specifically that used by the Byzantine Church, which runs three years behind the decemnovenal (q.v.).

lunar month: a month of a lunar calendar.

lunar regulars: numbers that when added to the epact yield the lune of the 1st of a given month.

lunation: the synodic month from conjunction to conjunction.

lune: a day of the lunar month.

lunisolar calendar: a lunar calendar adjusted by embolisms to take account of the sun: e.g. the Jewish, Chinese, and some Hindu calendars.

Manichaeism: an ascetic religion invented in Persia *c.*240, named after its founder Mani, and blended out of Zoroastrian, Buddhist, and Gnostic Christian beliefs.

mean solar time: time reckoned according to the average length of the apparent solar day.

Metonic cycle: a 19-year cycle of 235 lunar months, including seven embolisms; named after the Athenian astronomer Meton (*fl.* 432 BC).

millésime: the number of the year in an era.

modern style: the year reckoned from 1 January; same as 'Circumcision style'.

modulo: 'to the modulus of (a number)', i.e. dividing by that number and taking the remainder. Thus 365 is equivalent ('congruent') to 1 modulo 7 (notated $365 \equiv 1 \bmod 7$), since on being divided by 7 it leaves a remainder of 1.

Monophysitism: the doctrine that Christ had only one nature, the divine.

Monotheletism: the doctrine that Christ, in His two natures, had only one will.

mos Gallicus: the Christian era with years counted from the Easter following the beginning of the modern year.

mos Venetus: the Christian era with years counted from the 1 March following the beginning of the modern year.

Nativity style: the Christian era with years counted from the 25 December before the beginning of the modern year; also called 'the style of the Roman curia'.

natural day: the time taken for the earth to rotate once on its axis relative to the sun; also the day defined by the passage of time as against a nominal day. Now sometimes used for 'artificial day'.

Nestorian: the Christology of Nestorius (*27 June under Cyril), who refused to call Mary *Theotokos*, and was accused by his enemies of teaching that He existed in two persons as well as two natures. The term has traditionally been applied to the Mesopotamian Christians, who now prefer to be called the Church of the East.

new moon: (i) the conjunction of sun and moon; (ii) the first sighting of the crescent.

New Style: the date according to the Gregorian calendar; cf. II: *Modern Calendar. Sometimes used for *modern style* (a usage already attested in French before the Gregorian reform, but best avoided as ambiguous), and in Groningen of the Julian calendar restored in 1594.

nominal day: the verbal expression of a date, irrespective of its relation to an actual day.

Old Style: the date according to the Julian calendar. The term is often misapplied to the Lady Day year used in England and her American colonies before 1752, by confusion of the two reforms; in the 1790s it was sometimes used in France of the Gregorian calendar in contrast to the Republican.

Paschal cycle: period of 532 years after which, in the Julian calendar, Easter dates repeat themselves.

Paschal limits: the lunar or solar (i.e. civil) dates within which Easter is allowed to fall.

Paschal regular: number added to the concurrent to give the feria of Paschal term.

Paschal term: same as *luna XIV*.

Pelagianism: the doctrine that man is free by his God-given nature to choose the good, and thereby take the first steps to salvation, without the need for divine grace.

Pisan style: the Annunciation style reckoned from the 25 March before the beginning of the modern year.

primestaff, pl. **primestaves:** a symbolic calendar (Norwegian *primstav*), usually called 'runic calendar' in English but not necessarily using runes (see II: **Calendars as Written Objects*).

quantième: the serial number of the day in the month, or the day so numbered.

Quartodeciman: one who keeps Easter on *luna XIV* irrespective of feria; polemically extended to those who did not defer Easter when *luna XIV* was a Sunday.

red-letter day: a major feast, recorded in church calendars with red ink; in Great Britain also a day on which the judges of the Queen's Bench Division wear scarlet robes. (See I: *Days: Red-Letter Days (Judicial)*.)

retroject: to apply a calendar, especially the Julian, to the period before its inception.

Revised Julian Calendar: the reform adopted for reckoning immoveable feasts by some Orthodox churches, in which centennial leap years after 1800 are omitted unless they leave a remainder to 900 of 200 or 600.

Roman count: reckoning by Kalends, Nones, and Ides, and days before them. See II: *Roman Calendar*.

runic calendar: properly a calendar in which Golden Numbers (and sometimes Sunday Letters) are indicated by runes, but sometimes extended to other Scandinavian symbolic calendars (cf. 'primestaff').

saltus lunae: the omission of a day in the lunisolar calendar in order to keep in step with the solar calendar. (The plural of *saltus* is *saltus* with long *u*, sometimes written *saltûs*.)

sedes: lit. 'seat', the day to which a computistic parameter is calibrated; *sedes concurrentium*, 24 March; *sedes epactarum*, variously 1 January, 22 March, 31 December.

sidereal year: the earth's orbital period relative to the stars = 365.256 36 d. = $365^d\ 6^h\ 9'.\ 9.5''$.

solar calendar: a calendar taking note of the sun but not of the moon: e.g. the Julian and Gregorian calendars, based on the tropical year, and certain Hindu calendars based on the sidereal year.

solar regulars: numbers that when added to the concurrent of a given year yield the feria of the first of a given month.

style of the Roman curia: same as 'Nativity style'.

Supputatio Romana: the Easter computus based on an 84-year cycle and Roman Paschal limits.

symbolic calendar: general term for English clogs and Scandinavian 'runic calendars', in which important days are marked with symbols.

synodic month: the moon's orbital period from new moon to new moon = 29.530 59 d. = $29^d\ 12^h\ 44'\ 3''$.

tale of days: the manner of counting the days within the month.

Theotokos: Greek for 'She who bore God', title of the Virgin Mary (in Latin *Deipara*).

translation: (of a saint or a relic) removal in a different church, or a more honourable place within the same church.

tropical year: the earth's orbital period from vernal equinox to vernal equinox = 365.242 19 d. = $365^d\ 5^h\ 48'\ 45.2''$. It is decreasing by about 0.53 seconds in a century.

zodiac: a celestial belt some 16° wide centred on the ecliptic, so called after the twelve 'little beasts' (*zodia*) or star-signs into which it is divided; although these constellations no longer occupy the places they held when the 30° sectors were named after them, the 'signs' (except in Hindu astronomy) remain unchanged.

SOURCES AND
BIBLIOGRAPHY

ACHELIS, ELISABETH, *The Calendar for Everyone* (New York, 1941).
—— *The World Calendar* (New York, 1937).
ADAMS, JOHN, *Familiar Letters of John Adams and his Wife Abigail Adams, during the Revolution*, ed. Charles Francis Adams (Boston and New York, 1875).
ADAMS, THOMAS, *Heaven Made Sure*, in *The Workes of Thomas Adams* (London, 1630).
Ælfric's Catholic Homilies: The First Series, Text, ed. Peter Clemoes (EETS, ss 17; Oxford, 1997).
ALVER, BRYNJULF, *Dag og merke: folkeleg tidsrekning og merkedagstradisjon* (Oslo, 1970).
AMADES, JOAN, *Costumari català: el curs de l'any*, 5 vols. (Barcelona, 1930–6).
Aristotle's Last Legacy: or, his Golden Cabinet of Secrets Opened, for Youth's Delightful Pastime . . . Translated into English by Dr. Saman, Student in Astrology (London, 1711).
Arrêté du Directoire exécutif qui prescrit des mesures pour la stricte observation du Calendrier Républicain. Du 14 Germinal, an VI de la République française, une et indivisible (Paris, 1798).
AUBREY, JOHN, *Remaines of Gentilisme and Judaisme* (1686–7), ed. James Britten (London, 1881).
AUSTEN, JANE, *Jane Austen's Letters*, ed. Deirdre Le Faye (Oxford, 1995).
The Babylonian Talmud Translated into English with Notes, Glossary and Indices, ed. I. Epstein, 36 vols. (London, 1935–62).
BACON, FRANCIS, *Historie of the Raigne of King Henry the Seventh* (London, 1622).
BAILLIE, MARIANNE, *Lisbon in the Years 1821, 1822, and 1823* (London, 1824).
BALE, JOHN, preface to *The Laboryeuse Journey and Serche of John Leylande for Englandes Antiquitees*, repr. in *The Lives of those Eminent Antiquaries John Leland, Thomas Hearne, and Anthony à Wood*, 2 vols. (Oxford, 1772).
BANKS, M. MACLEOD, *British Calendar Customs: Scotland*, ii (The Folk-Lore Society, 104; London, 1939).
BARTRUM, PETER C., *A Welsh Classical Dictionary: People in History and Legend up to about A.D. 1000* (Cardiff, 1993).
BAUER, R. W., *Calender for Aarene fra 601 til 2200 efter Christi Fødsel* (Copenhagen, 1868; repr. Viborg, 1968).
BECKWITH, ROGER T., *Calendar and Chronology, Jewish and Christian: Biblical, Intertestamental and Patristic Studies* (Leiden, 1996).
BECON, THOMAS, *The Reliques of Rome, contayning all such matters of Religion, as have in times past bene brought into the Church by the Pope and his adherents* (London, 1563).
BEDE, the Venerable, *Bedae opera de temporibus* (Cambridge, Mass., 1943).
—— *Opera didascalica*, ed. Charles W. Jones, fascs. 2–3 (Corpus Christianorum, ser. Latina 123 B–C; Turnhout, 1977–80).
BEERBOHM, MAX, 'Enoch Soames', in *Seven Men* (London, 1919).

Bertholdi Annales, ed. G. H. Pertz (Monumenta Germaniae Historica, Scriptores, v; Hanover, 1844), 264–326.

BEST, HENRY, *Rural Economy in Yorkshire in 1641* (Surtees Society, 33; Durham, 1857).

Bibliotheca Sanctorum, 12 vols. and index (Rome, 1961–70); appendix vol. (Rome, 1987).

BICKERMAN, E. J., *Chronology of the Ancient World* (London, 1968; rev. 1980).

BILFINGER, GUSTAV, *Untersuchungen über die Zeitrechnung der Germanen: i. Das altnordische Jahr* (Stuttgart, 1899).

AL-BĪRŪNĪ, MUḤAMMAD B. AḤMAD, *The Chronology of Ancient Nations*, trans. C. E. Sachau (London, 1879).

BLACKBURN, BONNIE J., 'Music and Festivities at the Court of Leo X: A Venetian View', *Early Music History*, 11 (1992), 1–37.

BLAKE, ROBERT, *The Conservative Party from Peel to Thatcher* (London, 1985).

BLENCOWE, ROBERT WILLIS, 'Extracts from the Journal and Account-Book of Timothy Burrell, Esq., Barrister-at-Law, of Ockenden House, Cuckfield, from the Year 1683 to 1714', *Sussex Archaeological Collections*, 3 (1850), 117–72.

BLOUNT, THOMAS, *Fragmenta Antiquitatis: Antient Tenures of Land, and Jocular Customs of some Mannors. Made publick for the diversion of some, and instruction of others* (London, 1679).

BOECE, HECTOR, *Heir Beginnis the Hystory and Croniklis of Scotland*, trans. John Bellenden (Edinburgh, 1536).

The Book of Saints, comp. by the Benedictine monks of St Augustine's Abbey, Ramsgate (6th edn., London, 1989).

BOSWELL, JAMES, *Boswell's London Journal 1762–63*, ed. Frederick A. Pottle (London, 1985).

BOURGEOIS OF PARIS, *A Parisian Journal 1405–1449. Translated from the Anonymous Journal d'un Bourgeois de Paris* by Janet Shirley (Oxford, 1968).

BRADFORD, WILLIAM, *Bradford's History of Plymouth Plantation 1606–1646*, ed. William T. Davis (Original Narratives of Early American History; New York, 1908).

BRADY, JOHN, *Clavis Calendaria*, 2 vols. (3rd edn., London, 1815).

BRAND, JOHN, *Observations on Popular Antiquities: Chiefly Illustrating the Origin of our Vulgar Customs, Ceremonies, and Superstitions*, rev. Henry Ellis, 2 vols. (London, 1841).

BRATHWAIT, RICHARD, *Brathwayte's Odes; or Philomel's Tears*, ed. Sir Egerton Brydges (Lee Priory, Kent, 1815).

—— *The Whimzies, or a New Cast of Characters* (London, 1631).

BRAY, A. E., *A Description of the Part of Devonshire Bordering on the Tamar and the Tavey*, 3 vols. (London, 1836).

BREDON, JULIET, and MITROPHANOW, IGOR, *The Moon Year* (1927, repr. Hong Kong, 1982).

BRETON, NICHOLAS, *Fantasticks: Serving for a Perpetuall Prognostication* (London, 1626).

Brewer's Dictionary of Phrase and Fable, 14th edn., ed. Ivor H. Evans (London, 1989).

BRINCKEN, ANNA-DOROTHEE VON DEN, 'Beobachtungen zum Aufkommen der retrospektiven Inkarnationsära', *Archiv für Diplomatik*, 25 (1979), 1–20.

BRIND'AMOUR, PIERRE, *Le Calendrier romain: recherches chronologiques* (Collection d'études anciennes de l'Université d'Ottawa, 2; Ottawa, 1983).

BRISSOT DE WARVILLE, J. P., *New Travels in the United States of America. Performed in 1788, translated from the French* (London, 1792).

BRYDONE, PATRICK, *A Tour through Sicily and Malta. In a Series of Letters to William Beckford, Esq. of Somerly in Suffolk*, 2 vols. (London, 1773).

BUCHLER, JOHANNES, Γνωμολογία, *sive Memorabilium cum primis Germanicae, Gallicaeque linguae, sententiarum, Latino carmine descriptio facta* (Cologne, 1602).

BUCKLEY, MICHAEL BERNARD, *Diary of a Tour in America* (1870–1), ed. Kate Buckley (Dublin, 1886).

BURLEIGH, WILLIAM CECIL, LORD, *Precepts or, Directions for the Well Ordering and Carriage of a Man's Life, through the Whole Course thereof: Left by William, Lord Burghly, to his Sonne* (London, 1636).

BURNABY, ANDREW, *Travels through the Middle Settlements in North-America, in the Years 1759 and 1760, with Observations upon the State of the Colonies* (London, 1775).

BURNABY, SHERRARD BEAUMONT, *Elements of the Jewish and Muhammadan Calendars* (London, 1901).

BURNEY, CHARLES, *Dr. Burney's Musical Tours in Europe*, ed. Percy A. Scholes, i: *An Eighteenth-Century Musical Tour in France and Italy* (London, 1959).

BURNS, ROBERT, *The Letters of Robert Burns*, ed. J. De Lancey Ferguson (2nd edn., ed. G. Ross Roy), 2 vols. (Oxford, 1985).

—— *The Poems and Songs of Robert Burns*, ed. James Kinsley, 3 vols. (Oxford, 1968).

BURROWS, MONTAGU, *Worthies of All Souls: Four Centuries of English History Illustrated from the College Archives* (London, 1874).

BURTON, HENRY, *A Divine Tragedie, lately Acted, or a Collection of Sundry Memorable Examples of Gods Judgements upon Sabbath-breakers* (London, 1636).

BURTON, ROBERT, *The Anatomy of Melancholy*, ed. Thomas C. Faulkner, Nicolas K. Kiessling, and Rhonda L. Blair, with an introduction by J. B. Bamborough, 3 vols. (Oxford English Texts; Oxford, 1989–94).

Butler's Lives of Patron Saints, ed. and with additional material by Michael Walsh (Tunbridge Wells, 1987).

BUTTES, H., *Dyet's Dry Dinner* (London, 1599).

Byrhtferth's Enchiridion, ed. Peter S. Baker and Michael Lapidge (EETS, ss 15; Oxford, 1995).

CAELIUS RHODIGINUS, LODOVICUS, *Lectiones antiquae* (Basle, 1542).

Calendrier de la République française (decree of 4 frimaire year II: Paris, 1793).

CAMDEN, WILLIAM, *The Antient and Modern Customs of the Irish*, in *Camden's Britannia* (1586), trans. Edmund Gibson (London, 1695).

CARLYLE, THOMAS, *The French Revolution: A History*, 3 vols. (London, 1837).

CARMICHAEL, ALEXANDER, *Carmina Gadelica* (2nd edn., Edinburgh, 1928).

CARR, WILLIAM, *Remarks of the Government of severall Parts of Germanie, Denmark, Sweedland, Hamburg, Lubeck, and Hansiactique Townes, but more particularly of the United Provinces, with some few directions how to Travell in the States Dominions* (Amsterdam, 1688).

CARTWRIGHT, THOMAS, *The Diary of Dr. Thomas Cartwright, Bishop of Chester*, ed. Joseph Hunter (Camden Society, 22; London, 1843).

CASA, ALFONSO, *Los calendarios prehispánicos* (Mexico City, 1967).

CHADWICK, HENRY, *Boethius: The Consolations of Music, Logic, Theology, and Philosophy* (Oxford, 1981).

CHAMBERS, ROBERT (ed.), *The Book of Days: A Miscellany of Popular Antiquities in Connection with the Calendar*, 2 vols. (London and Edinburgh, 1864).

CHASTELLUX, MARQUIS DE, *Travels in North America in the Years 1780, 1781 and 1782 by the Marquis de Chastellux*, a revised translation with introd. and notes by Howard C. Rice, Jr., 2 vols. (Chapel Hill, NC, 1963).

CHENEY, C. R. (ed.), *Handbook of Dates for Students of English History* (London, 1945; repr. 1991).

CHESTERFIELD, 4th Earl of, *Letters Written by the Late Right Honourable Philip Dormer Stanhope, Earl of Chesterfield, to his Son, Philip Stanhope, Esq., Late Envoy Extraordinary at the Court of Dresden: Together with Several Other Pieces on Various Subjects*, ed. Eugenia Stanhope, 2 vols. (London, 1774).

CHILD, LYDIA MARIA, *Letters from New-York* (New York and Boston, 1843).

Chronicon de Lanercost M.CC.I–M.CCC.XLVI, ed. Joseph Stephenson (Edinburgh, 1836).

Chronicon Paschale, ed. Ludwig Dindorf, 2 vols. (Bonn, 1832).

CHURCHILL, CHARLES, *Poems*, 3 vols. (London, 1776).

CLARENDON, EDWARD HYDE, 1st Earl of, *The History of the Rebellion and Civil Wars in England, Begun in the Year 1641*, 3 vols. (Oxford, 1705).

CLARK, W. G., 'Naples and Garibaldi', in Francis Galton (ed.), *Vacation Tourists and Notes of Travel in 1860* (Cambridge and London, 1861), 1–75.

CLAVIUS, CHRISTOPHORUS, *Romani calendarii a Gregorio XIII. P. M. restituti explicatio S. D. N. Clementis VIII. P. M. iussu edita* (Rome, 1603).

CLEGG, JAMES, *The Diary of James Clegg of Chapel en le Frith 1708–1755*, ed. Vanessa S. Doe (Derbyshire Record Society, 2, 3, 5; Matlock, 1879–81).

COCKAYNE, OSWALD, *Leechdoms, Wortcunning, and Starcraft of Early England*, 3 vols. (Rolls Series; London, 1864–6).

COGAN, THOMAS, *The Haven of Health* (London, 1584).

Coleridge: The Early Family Letters, ed. James Angell (Oxford, 1994).

COLES, WILLIAM, *The Art of Simpling: An Introduction to the Knowledge and Gathering of Plants* (London, 1656).

Combat sanglant entre le dimanche et le décadi (n.p., n.d.).

COMMYNES, PHILIPPE DE, *The Historie of Philip de Commines Knight, Lord of Argenton*, trans. Thomas Danett (London, 1596).

The Complaynt of Scotlande, wyth ane Exortatione to the Three Estaits to be vigilante in the Deffens of their Public veil [= weal] (1549), ed. J. A. H. Murray, 2 pts. (EETS, ES 17–18; London, 1872–3).

CONNOLLY, THOMAS H., 'The Legend of St. Cecilia', *Studi musicali*, 7 (1978), 3–37; 9 (1980), 3–44.

—— *Mourning into Joy* (New Haven, 1995).

—— 'Traces of a Jewish-Christian Community at S. Cecilia in Trastevere', *Plainsong and Medieval Music*, 7 (1998), 1–19.

Consultation sur cette question: doit-on transférer le dimanche au décadi? ('Fait à Paris le 3 Décembre [1797], premier dimanche de l'Avent (13 Frimaire an VI)').

COOKE, EDWARD, *A Voyage to the South Sea, and Round the World, Perform'd in the Years 1708, 1709, 1710, and 1711* (London, 1712).

COOPER, ANTHONY ASHLEY, autograph in the Public Record Office, printed in David Novarr (ed.), *Seventeenth-Century English Prose* (New York, 1967), 384–5.

COOPER, QUENTIN, and SULLIVAN, PAUL, *Maypoles, Martyrs & Mayhem* (London, 1994).

COPAGE, ERIC V., *Kwanzaa: An African-American Celebration of Culture and Cooking* (New York, 1991).

CORYAT, THOMAS, *Coryat's Crudities hastily gobled up in five Moneths travells in France, Savoy, Italy, Rhetia commonly called the Grisons country, Helvetia alias Switzerland, some parts of high Germany and the Netherlands; Newly digested in the hungry aire of Odcombe in the County of Somerset, and now dispersed to the nourishment of the travelling Members of this Kingdome*, 2 vols. (Glasgow, 1905) (orig. publ. 1611).

COUCH, JONATHAN, *The History of Polperro, a Fishing Town on the South Coast of Cornwall* (Truro, 1871).

The Country Almanack for the Year 1675 (London, 1675).

COWPER, MARY, *Diary of Mary Countess Cowper, Lady of the Bedchamber to the Princess of Wales 1714–1720* (London, 1864).

COXE, WILLIAM, *Travels into Poland, Russia, Sweden, and Denmark. Interspersed with Historical Relations and Political Inquiries*, 4 vols. (3rd edn., London, 1787).

CRANE, J. W., 'Historische Verhandeling over den zoogenaamden nieuwen stijl en deszelfs invoering in ons vaderland, bijzonder in Vriesland', in H. W. C. A. Visser and H. Amersfoordt, *Archief voor vaderlandsche, en inzonderheid vriesche geschiedenis, oudheid- en taalkunde* (Leeuwarden, 1824), separate pagination.

CRESWELL, NICHOLAS, *The Journal of Nicholas Creswell, 1774–1777* (New York, 1924).

CROKER, T. CROFTAN, *Researches in the South of Ireland* (London, 1824).

CROSFIELD, THOMAS, *The Diary of Thomas Crosfield*, ed. Frederick S. Boas (London, 1935).

CUOCO, VINCENZO, *Saggio storico sulla rivoluzione napoletana del 1799, seguito dal rapporto al Cittadino Carnot di Francesco Lommaco*, ed. Fausto Nicolino (Bari, 1913).

CURWEN, SAMUEL, *The Journal of Samuel Curwen, Loyalist*, ed. Andrew Oliver, 2 vols. (Cambridge, Mass., 1972).

DANAHER, KEVIN, *The Year in Ireland* (Cork, 1972).

DEEMS, EDWARD M. (comp.), *Holy-Days and Holidays: A Treasury of Historical Material, Sermons in Full and in Brief, Suggestive Thoughts, and Poetry, Relating to Holy Days and Holidays* (New York and London, 1942).

DEFOE, DANIEL, *A Tour Thro' the Whole Island of Great Britain. Divided into Circuits or Journeys. Giving a Particular and Entertaining Account of whatever is Curious and worth Observation . . . by a Gentleman*, 4 vols. (4th edn., London, 1748).

DEKKER, THOMAS, *The Ravens Almanacke Foretelling of a Plague, Famine, and Civill Warre that shall happen in this present yeare 1609* (London, 1609).

DELONEY, T., *The Pleasant History of Iohn Winchcomb, in his Younger Yeares Called Iack of Newbery* (11th edn., London, 1630).

DENHAM, M. A., *A Collection of Proverbs and Popular Sayings Relating to the Seasons, the Weather, and Agricultural Pursuits* (Percy Society; London, 1846).

DERSHOWITZ, NACHUM, and REINGOLD, EDWARD M., *Calendrical Calculations* (Cambridge, 1997).

DICKENS, CHARLES, *Letters from Charles Dickens to Angela Burdett-Coutts, 1841–1865*, ed. Edgar Johnson (London, 1955).

DIGGES, LEONARD, *A Prognostication of Right Good Effect* (London, 1555).

DINNEEN, PATRICK S., *Foclóir Gaedhilge agus Béarla: An Irish–English Dictionary* (Dublin, 1927).

DITCHFIELD, P. H., *Old English Customs Extant at the Present Time* (London, 1901).

Dives and Pauper, ed. Priscilla Heath Barnum (EETS 275, 280; Oxford, 1976–80).

DOUGLAS, GEORGE WILLIAM, *The American Book of Days* (New York, 1938; rev. edn., ed. Helen Douglas Compton, 1948).

DOUGLASS, FREDERICK, 'What to the Slave is the Fourth of July?', repr. in *Black Scholar*, 7 (July–Aug. 1976).

DOVE, *Speculum anni or an Almanack for the Year of our Lord God* (various years).

DRAKE, FRANCIS, *Eboracum: Or the History and Antiquities of the City of York* (London, 1736).

DUFFY, EAMON, *Saints and Sinners: A History of the Popes* (New Haven, 1997).

—— *The Stripping of the Altars* (New Haven, 1992).

DUGDALE, WILLIAM, *The Antiquities of Warwickshire* (London, 1656).

DUMVILLE, DAVID (ed.), *Saint Patrick A.D. 493–1193* (Studies in Celtic History, 13; Woodbridge, 1993).

DUNCAN, ANGUS, *Hebridean Island Memories of Scarp*, ed. A. Duncan (East Linton, 1995).

DURANDUS, GULIELMUS, *Rationale divinorum officiorum* (Lyon, 1612).

EDGEWORTH, MARIA, *Castle Rackrent* (London, 1895).

EDMONSON, MUNRO S., *The Book of the Year: Middle American Calendrical Systems* (Salt Lake City, 1988).

EDWARDS, H., *A Collection of Old English Customs, and Curious Bequests and Charities, extracted from the Reports made by the Commissioners for Enquiring into Charities in England and Wales* (London, 1842).

ELLIS, WILLIAM, *The Country Housewife's Family Companion* (London, 1750).

Encyclopaedia Iranica, 'Calendars': iv (1996), 658–77.

ERRA PATER, *A Prognostication for ever* (London, 1602).

ESTIENNE, CHARLES, and LIEBAULT, J., *Maison rustique or the Countrie Farme* (1570), trans. Richard Surflet (London, 1600).

EVELYN, JOHN, *The Diary of John Evelyn*, ed. E. S. de Beer, 6 vols. (Oxford, 1955).

—— *Kalendarium Hortense; or, the Gardner's Almanac* (10th edn., London, 1706).

—— *Sylva, or a Discourse of Forest-Trees* (London, 1670).

EWALD, JOHANN, *Diary of the American War: A Hessian Journal*, trans. and ed. Joseph P. Tustin (New Haven and London, 1979).

EYRE, MARY, *A Lady's Walks in the South of France in 1863* (London, 1865).

FARMER, DAVID HUGH, *The Oxford Dictionary of Saints* (2nd edn., Oxford, 1987).

FAY, GEORGE E., *Fiesta Days of Mexico* (University of Northern Colorado–Greeley, Museum of Anthropology, Miscellaneous Series, 17; July 1970).

Félire hUí Gormáin: The Martyrology of Gorman, ed. Whitely Stokes (Henry Bradshaw Society, 9; London, 1895).

Félire Óengusso Céli Dé: The Martyrology of Oengus the Culdee, ed. Whitely Stokes (Henry Bradshaw Society, 29; London, 1905).

FIENNES, CELIA, *The Journeys of Celia Fiennes*, ed. Christopher Morris (London, 1947).

FISHER, JABEZ MAUD, *An American Quaker in the British Isles: The Travel Journals of Jabez Maud Fisher, 1775–1779*, ed. Kenneth Morgan (Records of Social and Economic History, NS 16; Oxford, 1992).

FISKE, JOHN, *Extracts from the Notebook of the Rev. John Fiske, 1637–1675*, ed. Samuel A. Green (Cambridge, Mass., 1898).

FLECKNOE, RICHARD, *The Diarium or Journall* (London, 1656).

FLOYER, JOHN, *An Essay to Prove Cold Bathing both Safe and Useful* (London, 1702).

FONER, PHILIP S., *May Day: A Short History of the International Workers' Holiday 1886–1986* (New York, 1986).

FORSTER, T., *The Perennial Calendar, and Companion to the Almanack; illustrating the Events of Every Day in the Year* (London, 1824).

FOVARGUE, STEPHEN, *A New Catalogue of Vulgar Errors* (Cambridge, 1767).

FOX, BARCLAY, *Barclay Fox's Journal*, ed. R. L. Brett (London, 1979).

FRASER, Mrs. HUGH [MARY CRAWFORD], *A Diplomatist's Wife in Many Lands*, 2 vols. (London, 1910).

FRENCH, C. N., *A Countryman's Day Book: An Anthology of Countryside Lore* (London and Toronto, 1929).

FRIED, RAV YERACHMIEL D., *Yom Tov Sheini keHilchaso: The Second Day of Yom Tov in Israel and Abroad*, trans. Moshe Dombey (Southfield, Mich., 1990).

FRIEDRICH, GUSTAV, *Rukověť křesťánské chronologie* (Handbook of Christian Chronology) (Prague, 1934).

FROISSART, JEAN, *The Chronicle of Froissart*, trans. John Bourchier, Lord Berners (1523–5), 6 vols. (London, 1901).

Frostiana: or a History of the River Thames, in a Frozen State; with an Account of the Late Severe Frost; and the Wonderful Effects of Frost, Snow, Ice, and Cold, in England, and in Different Parts of the World; Interspersed with Various Amusing Anecdotes. To Which is Added, the Art of Skating (London: Printed and published on the Ice on the River Thames, February 5, 1814, by G. Davis).

FULLER, THOMAS, *The History of the Worthies of England* (London, 1662).

—— *The Holy State* (Cambridge, 1642).

GACHET, ÉMILE, 'Recherches sur les noms des mois et les grandes fêtes chrétiennes', *Compte-rendu des séances de la Commission royale d'histoire*, 3rd ser., 7/3 (Brussels, 1865).

GADBURY, JOHN, *'ΕΦΗΜΕΡΙΣ or, a Diary Astronomical, Astrological, Meteorological for the Year of Our Lord, 1696 . . . by John Gadbury* (London, 1696).

GEE, JOHN, *Hold fast, a Sermon Preached at Pauls Crosse* (London, 1624).

GEHRTS, HEINO, 'Zur Rattenfängerfrage', *Zeitschrift für deutsche Philologie*, 74 (1955), 191–207.

GIBBON, EDWARD, *The Decline and Fall of the Roman Empire* (London, 1776–88).

—— *Memoirs of My Life*, ed. Betty Radice (Harmondsworth, 1984).

—— *A Vindication of Some Passages in the Fifteenth and Sixteenth Chapters of the History of the Decline and Fall of the Roman Empire*, with a preface by H. R. Trevor-Roper (Kendal, 1977).

GINZEL, F. K., *Handbuch der mathematischen und technischen Chronologie*, 3 vols. (Leipzig, 1906–14).

GLABER, RODULFUS, *Historiarum libri quinque*, ed. and trans. John France (Oxford Medieval Texts; Oxford, 1989).

GLADSTONE, WILLIAM, *The Gladstone Diaries*, ed. M. R. D. Foot and H. C. G. Matthew, i (Oxford, 1968).

'GODFRIDUS', *The knowledge of things vnknowne* (1552?) (London, *c*.1619).

GOETHE, JOHANN WOLFGANG VON, *Italian Journey*, trans. Robert R. Heitner, Introduction and Notes by Thomas P. Saine, ed. Thomas P. Saine and Jeffrey L. Sammons (The Collected Works, 6; Princeton, 1994).

GOLDSTINE, HERMAN H., *New and Full Moons 1001 B.C. to A.D. 1651* (Memoirs of the American Philosophical Society, 94; Philadelphia, 1973).

GOOGE, BARNABY (trans. and ed.), Conrad Heresbach, *Four Bookes of Husbandry* (London, 1577).

G[ORDON], W., *A Letter to Mr Thomas Blackwell, Professor of Divinity in the Marishal-College of Aberdeen, with Other Papers concerning the Observation of Christmas and the Other Festivals of the Church* (Edinburgh, 1722).

Gospelles of Dystaues (Wynken de Worde, London, [1520]).

GRANT STEWART, W., *The Popular Superstitions and Festive Amusements of the Highlanders of Scotland* (Edinburgh, 1823).

Great Britain's Diary: or, the Union-Almanack For the Year of our Lord 1711 (London, 1711).

GREENE, R. L., *The Early English Carols* (2nd edn., Oxford, 1977).

GREGORY, JOHN, *Gregorii Posthuma: or, Certain Learned Tracts Written by John Gregory* (London, 1650).

GRIERSON, WILLIAM, *Apostle to Burns: The Diaries of William Grierson*, ed. John Davies (Edinburgh, 1981).

GROSSETESTE, ROBERT, *Epistolae*, ed. H. R. Luard (Rolls Series, 25; London, 1861).

GROTEFEND, HERMANN, *Handbuch der historischen Chronologie des deutschen Mittelalters und der Neuzeit* (Hanover, 1872).

GRUMEL, VICTOR, *La Chronologie* (Traité d'études byzantines, 1; Paris, 1958).

GUNTER, WILLIAM, *Gunter's Confectioner's Oracle containing Receipts for Desserts on the Most Economical Plan for Private Families, and all Founded on the Actual Experiments of Thirty Years. With an Appendix, containing the Best Receipts for Pastry-Cooks, and an Elucidation of the Principles of Good Cheer. Being a Companion to Dr. Kitchiner's Cook's Oracle* (London, 1830).

HAGEDORN, DIETER, 'Zum ägyptischen Kalender unter Augustus', *Zeitschrift für Papyrologie und Epigraphik*, 100 (1994), 211–22.

HALL, EDWARD, *Hall's Chronicle*, ed. Sir Henry Ellis (London, 1809).

HALL, JOSEPH, *Characters of Vertues and Vices* (London, 1608).

HALLIWELL, JAMES ORCHARD, *Popular Rhymes and Nursery Tales* (London, 1849).

HAMILTON, JOHN, *The Catechisme* (St Andrews, 1552).

HAMPDEN, JOHN (comp.), *An Eighteenth-Century Journal: Being a Record of the Years 1774–1776* (London, 1940).

HAMPSON, R. T., *Medii Aevi Kalendarium; or Dates, Charters, and Customs of the Middle Ages*, 2 vols. (London, 1841).

HARGREAVES-MAWDSLEY, W. (ed.), *Woodforde at Oxford 1759-1776* (Oxford, 1969).

HARRISON, KENNETH, *The Framework of Anglo-Saxon History to A.D. 900* (Cambridge, 1976).

HASKINS, CHARLES HOMER, *Studies in the History of Medieval Science* (2nd edn., Cambridge, Mass., 1927).

HASTRUP, KIRSTEN, *Culture and History in Medieval Iceland: An Anthropological Analysis of Structure and Change* (Oxford, 1985).

—— *Nature and Policy in Iceland 1400–1800: An Anthropological Analysis of History and Mentality* (Oxford, 1990)

HAWTHORNE, NATHANIEL, *The American Notebooks by Nathaniel Hawthorne*, ed. Randall Stewart (New Haven, 1932).

—— *The English Notebooks*, ed. Randall Stewart (New York, 1941).

HEARNE, THOMAS, *Remarks and Collections of Thomas Hearne*, ed. H. E. Salter, ix (Oxford, 1914).

HEATH, ROBERT, *A Natural and Historical Account of the Islands of Scilly* (London, 1750).

HENDERSON, WILLIAM, *Notes on the Folk Lore of the Northern Counties of England and the Borders* (London, 1866).

HENTZNER, PAUL, *A Journey into England. By Paul Hentzner, in the Year M.D.XC.VIII*, ed. and trans. Horace Walpole (Strawberry Hill, 1757).

HERBERT, GEORGE, *Works*, ed. F. E. Hutchinson (Oxford, 1941).

HERTZ, J. H., *The Battle for the Sabbath at Geneva* (London, 1932).

—— *Changing the Calendar: Consequent Dangers and Confusions* (London, 1931).

HITCHENS, FORTESCUE, *The History of Cornwall, from the Earliest Records and Traditions, to the Present Time*, ed. Samuel Drew, 2 vols. (Helston, 1824).

HOANG, PIERRE, *Concordance des chronologies néoméniques chinoise et européenne* (Variétés sinologiques, 29; Shanghai, 1910).

—— *A Notice of the Chinese Calendar and a Concordance with the European Calendar* (Xujiahui ['Zi-Ka-Wei near Chang-Hai'], 1900).

HOARE, RICHARD COLT, *A Classical Tour through Italy and Sicily* (London, 1819).

—— (trans.), *The Itinerary of Archbishop Baldwin through Wales A.D. MCLXXXVIII by Giraldus de Barri*, 2 vols. (London, 1806).

HOBY, THOMAS, *The Travels and Life of Sir Thomas Hoby, Kt. of Bisham Abbey, Written by Himself. 1547–1564*, ed. Edgar Powell (Camden Miscellany, 10; 3rd ser., 4; London, 1902).

HOLE, CHRISTINA, *British Folk Customs* (London, 1976).

HONE, WILLIAM, *The Table Book, of Daily Recreation and Information: Concerning Remarkable Men, Manners, Times, Seasons, Solemnities, Merry-Makings, Antiquities and Novelties, forming a Complete History of the Year* (London, 1827).

—— *The Year Book of Daily Recreation and Information: Concerning Remarkable Men and Manners, Times and Seasons, Solemnities and Merry-Makings, Antiquities and Novelties, on the Plan of the Every-Day Book and Table Book, or Everlasting Calendar of Popular Amusements, Sports, Pastimes, Ceremonies, Customs, and Events, incident to each of the Three Hundred and Sixty-five Days, in Past and Present Times: Forming a Complete History of the Year; and a Perpetual Key to the Almanac* (London, 1832).

HOPE, THOMAS, *A Diary of the Public Correspondence of Sir Thomas Hope of Craighall, Bart. 1633–1645* (Bannatyre Club, 80; Edinburgh, 1843).

HOSPINIANUS, RODOLPHUS, *De origine, progressu, ceremoniis et ritibus festorum dierum Iudaeorum, Graecorum, Romanorum, & Turcarum libri tres* (Zurich, 1592).

—— *Festa Christianorum* (Zurich, 1593).

HOWELL, JAMES, *Epistolae Ho-Elianae: Familiar Letters Domestic and Foreign* (11th edn., very much corrected, London, 1754).

HUMBURG, NORBERT, *Der Rattenfänger von Hameln* (Hameln, 1990).

HUNTER, ROBERT, Jr., *Quebec to Carolina in 1785–1786: Being the Travel Diary and Observations of Robert Hunter, Jr., a Young Merchant of London*, ed. Louis B. Wright and Marion Tinling (San Marino, Cal., 1943).

HUTTON, RONALD, *The Pagan Religions of the Ancient British Isles: Their Nature and Legacy* (Oxford, 1991).

—— *The Rise and Fall of Merry England: The Ritual Year 1400–1700* (Oxford, 1994).

—— *The Stations of the Sun: A History of the Ritual Year in Britain* (Oxford, 1996).

Θρησκευτικὴ καὶ ᾽Ηθικὴ ᾽Εγκυκλοπαιδεία (Encyclopedia of Religion and Ethics), 12 vols. (Athens, 1962–8).

IRVING, WASHINGTON, 'Governor Manco and the Soldier', in *Tales of the Alhambra*, in *Selected Writings* (Modern Library; New York, 1984).

ISHAM, THOMAS, *The Diary of Thomas Isham of Lamport (1658–81) kept by him in Latin from 1671 to 1673 at his Father's Command*, trans. Norman Marlow (Farnborough, 1971).

JACOBS, HARRIET, *The Deeper Wrong: or, Incidents in the Life of a Slave Girl*, ed. L. Maria Child (London, 1862).

JACOBUS DE VORAGINE, *Legenda Aurea, vulgo Historia Lombardica dicta*, ed. Th. Graesse (3rd edn., 1890; repr. Osnabrück, 1969); crit. edn. G. P. Maggioni (Florence, 1998).

JAMES, HENRY, *Italian Hours* (1909) (New York, 1968).

JAMIESON, JOHN, *An Etymological Dictionary of the Scottish Language*, 2 vols. (Edinburgh, 1808); Supplement, 2 vols. (1825).

The Jewish Religion: A Companion, ed. Louis Jacobs (Oxford, 1995).

JOHNSON, SAMUEL, *Johnson on Shakespeare*, ed. Arthur Sherbo (The Yale Edition of the Works of Samuel Johnson, 7–8; New Haven, 1968).

—— *A Journey to the Western Islands of Scotland*, ed. Mary Lascelles (The Yale Edition, 9; New Haven, 1971).

—— *Lives of the English Poets*, ed. George Birkbeck Hill, 3 vols. (Oxford, 1905).

JONES, CHARLES W., *Saint Nicholas of Myra, Bari, and Manhattan: Biography of a Legend* (Chicago and London, 1978).

JONES, FRANCIS, *The Holy Wells of Wales* (Cardiff, 1992).

JOSSELIN, RALPH, *The Diary of the Rev. Ralph Josselin 1616–1683*, ed. E. Hockliffe (Camden 3rd ser., 15; London, 1908).

JOUBERT, LAURENS, *Annotations sur toute la Chirurgie de M. Guy de Chauliac* (Rouen, 1615).

Kalendar of Sheepehards: Newly Augmented and Corrected (London, c.1580).

Kalendarium Ecclesiasticum, being a New Two-fold Kalendar for the Year 1699 (London, 1699).

KALTENBRUNNER, FERDINAND, 'Beiträge zur Geschichte der Gregorianischen Kalenderreform. I. Die Commission unter Gregor XIII. nach Handschriften der Vatikanischen Bibliothek', *Sitzungsberichte der philosophisch-historischen Classe der Kaiserlichen Akademie der Wissenschaften*, 97 (Vienna, 1881), 7–54.

—— 'Die Polemik über die Gregorianische Kalenderreform', *Sitzungsberichte der philosophisch-historischen Classe der Kaiserlichen Akademie der Wissenschaften*, 87 (Vienna, 1877), 485–586.

—— 'Die Vorgeschichte der Gregorianischen Kalenderreform', *Sitzungsberichte der philosophisch-historischen Classe der Kaiserlichen Akademie der Wissenschaften*, 82 (Vienna, 1876), 289–414.

KARAKA, DOSIBHAI FRAMJI, *History of the Parsis*, 2 vols. (London, 1884).

KELLY, J. N. D., *The Oxford Dictionary of Popes* (Oxford, 1986).

KEMBLE, JOHN MITCHELL, *The Saxons in England*, 2 vols. (London, 1849).

KIELMANSEGGE, FREDERICK, *Diary of a Journey to England in the Years 1761–1762 by Count Frederick Kielmansegge*, trans. Countess Kielmansegg (London, 1902).

KIGHTLY, CHARLES, *The Customs and Ceremonies of Britain: An Encyclopaedia of Living Traditions* (London, 1986).

KILVERT, FRANCIS, *Kilvert's Diary: Selections from the Diary of the Rev. Francis Kilvert*, chosen, ed., and introd. by William Plomer (1938), 3 vols. (London, 1969).

KIPRIAKIDOU-NESTOROS, ALKI, *Οι Δώδεκα Μήνες· Τα Λαογραφικά* (The Twelve Months in Folklore) (2nd edn., Athens and Thessaloniki, 1986).

KIRKWOOD, JAMES, *A Collection of Highland Rites and Customes copied by Edward Lhuyd from the Manuscript of the Rev James Kirkwood (1650–1709) and Annotated by him with the Aid of the Rev John Beaton*, ed. J. L. Campbell from MS Carte 269 in the Bodleian Library (Cambridge, 1975).

KITCHINER, WILLIAM, *The Cook's Oracle* (6th edn., London, 1823).

KNIGHTON, HENRY, *Knighton's Chronicle 1337–1396*, ed. and trans. G. H. Martin (Oxford Medieval Texts; Oxford, 1995).

KRUSCH, BRUNO, *Studien zur christlich-mittelalterlichen Chronologie: Der 84jährige Ostercyclus und seine Quellen* (Leipzig, 1880).

—— *Studien zur christlich-mittelalterlichen Chronologie: Die Entstehung unserer heutigen Zeitrechnung* (Abhandlungen der Preußischen Akademie der Wissenschaften, Jahrgang 1937, Philosophisch-historische Klasse, 8; Berlin, 1938).

KUBITSCHEK, WILHELM, *Grundriß der antiken Zeitrechnung* (Handbuch der Altertumswissenschaft, 1/7; Munich, 1928).

LAMB, CHARLES, *Elia and The Last Essays of Elia*, ed. Jonathan Bate (World's Classics; Oxford, 1987).

LAMBARD, WILLIAM, *A Perambulation of Kent: Conteining the Description, Hystorie, and Customes of that Shyre. Collected and Written (for the most part) in the yeare 1570* (London, 1576).

LANDES, RICHARD, 'Giants with Feet of Clay: On the Historiography of the Year 1000', article available on Center for Millennial Studies website (http://www.mille.org/AHR9.html).

—— *Relics, Apocalypse, and the Deceits of History: Ademar of Chabannes, 989–1034* (Cambridge, Mass., 1995).

LANGE, LUDWIG, *'Paradoxe' Osterdaten im Gregorianischen Kalender und ihre Bedeutung für die moderne Kalenderreform* (Sitzungsberichte der Bayerischen Akademie der Wissenschaften, Philosophisch-philologische und historische Klasse, 1928, no. 9; Munich, 1928).

LATIMER, HUGH, *The Syxte Sermon of Maister Hughe Latimer, whyche he preached before the kynges Maiestye . . . the xii. daye of Apriel* (London, 1549).

LEOPOLD, ALDO, *A Sand County Almanac and Sketches Here and There*, introd. by Robert Finch (New York, 1949; repr. 1989).

LILLY, WILLIAM, *History of His Life and Times, from the Year 1602, to 1681*, ed. Elias Ashmole (London, 1715).

Lilly's New Erra Pater; or, A Prognostication for Ever (London, c.1750)

LITWICKI, ELLEN MARIE, 'Visions of America: Public Holidays and American Cultures, 1776–1900' (Ph.D. diss., University of Virginia, 1992).

LLOYD, LODOWICK, *The First Part of the Diall of Daies* (London, 1590).

——*The Triplicitie of Triumphes* (London, 1591).

LODGE, THOMAS, *Wits Miserie* (London, 1596).

LONG, GEORGE, *The Folklore Calendar* (London, 1930).

LOVE, W. DELOSS, Jr., *The Fast and Thanksgiving Days of New England* (Boston and New York, 1895).

LOVEDAY, JOHN, *Diary of a Tour in 1732, through Parts of England, Wales, Ireland and Scotland* (Roxburghe Club; Edinburgh, 1890).

LUPTON, THOMAS, *A Thousand Notable Things of Sundrie Sorts . . . newly corrected* (London, 1595).

LUTHER, MARTIN, *D. Martin Luthers Werke. Kritische Gesamtausgabe: Tischreden*, 6 vols. (Weimar, 1912–21).

Lutheran Cyclopedia, ed. Erwin L. Lucker (St. Louis, 1975).

McCarthy, Daniel, 'The Chronological Apparatus of the Annals of Ulster AD 431–1131', *Peritia*, 8 (1994), 34–79.

—— 'Easter Principles and a Lunar Cycle Used by Fifth Century Christian Communities in the British Isles', *Journal for the History of Astronomy*, 24 (1993), 204–24.

—— 'The Lunar and Paschal Tables of *De ratione paschali* Attributed to Anatolius of Laodicea', *Archive for History of Exact Sciences*, 49 (1996), 285–320.

—— 'The Origin of the *Latercus* Paschal Cycle of the Insular Celtic Churches', *Cambrian Medieval Celtic Studies*, 28 (Winter 1994), 25–49.

—— and Breen, Aidan, 'Astronomical Observations in the Irish Annals and Their Motivation', *Peritia*, 11 (1997), 1–43.

—— and Ó Cróinín, Dáibhí, 'The "Lost" Irish 84-Year Easter Table Recovered', *Peritia*, 6–7 (1987–8), 225–42.

MacGregor, Arthur (ed.), *Tradescant's Rarities: Essays on the Foundation of the Ashmolean Museum 1683* (Oxford, 1983).

Machyn, Henry, *The Diary of Henry Machyn, Citizen and Merchant-Taylor of London, from A.D. 1550 to A.D. 1563*, ed. John Gough Nichols (Camden Society, 42; London, 1848).

Macky, John, *A Journey through England. In Familiar Letters from a Gentleman Here, to his Friend Abroad*, 3 vols. (London 1714–23).

Macleane, Douglas, 'Martinmas 1919', *The Nineteenth Century and After*, 86/514 (Dec. 1919), 1202–6.

Macrae, David, *The Americans at Home: Pen-and-Ink Sketches of American Men, Manners and Institutions*, 2 vols. (Edinburgh, 1870).

Mactaggart, John, *The Scottish Gallovidian Encyclopedia: or, the Original, Antiquated, and Natural Curiosities of the South of Scotland* (London, 1824).

Mahler, Eduard, *Handbuch der jüdischen Chronologie* (Leipzig, 1916).

Malmesbury, William of, *De Gestis Pontificum Anglorum libri quinque*, ed. N. E. S. A. Hamilton (Rolls Series, 52; London and Oxford, 1870).

Mantuanus, Baptista, *Fastorum libri duodecim* (Strasburg, 1518).

Markham, Gervase, *Countrey Contentments, or the English Huswife* (London, 1623).

Marryat, Frederick, *Diary in America*, ed. Jules Zanger (London, 1960).

Martin, Gregory, *Roma sancta (1581)*, ed. George Bruner Parks (Rome, 1969).

Martin, Martin, *A Description of the Western Islands of Scotland* (2nd edn., London, 1716) (orig. publ. 1703).

Martineau, Harriet, *Retrospect of Western Travel*, 3 vols. (London, 1838).

Mather, Increase, *Diary by Increase Mather, March, 1675–December, 1676, together with Extracts from Another Diary by him, 1674–1687*, ed. Samuel A. Green (Cambridge, Mass., 1900).

May, Robert, *The Accomplisht Cook, or the Art and Mystery of Cookery* (London, 1665).

Megas, George A., *Greek Calendar Customs* (Athens, 1958).

Melton, John, *Astrologaster, or, the Figure-Caster* (London, 1620).

Michels, Agnes Kirsopp, *The Calendar of the Roman Republic* (Princeton, 1967).

Milanković (Milankovitch), Milutin, 'Das Ende des julianischen Kalenders und der neue Kalender der orientalischen Kirchen', *Astronomische Nachrichten*, 220/5279 (Kiel, 1924), 379–84.

Millar, Fergus, 'Reflections on the Trial of Jesus', in P. L. Davies and R. T. White (eds.), *A Tribute to Geza Vermes* (Oxford, 1990), 355–81.

Miller, Daniel (ed.), *Unwrapping Christmas* (Oxford, 1993).

MISSON, MAXIMILIAN, *A New Voyage to Italy. With Curious Observations on several Other Countries*, 2 vols. (4th edn., London, 1714).

MISSON DE VALBOURG, HENRI, M. *Misson's Memoirs and Observations in his Travels over England. With some Account of Scotland and Ireland. Dispos'd in Alphabetical Order. Written originally in French, and translated by Mr. Ozell* (London, 1719); orig.: *Mémoires et observations faites par un voyageur en Angleterre* (The Hague, 1698).

MOMMSEN, THEODOR, *Die römische Chronologie bis auf Caesar* (Berlin, 1859).

MONTAIGNE, MICHEL DE, *The Essays of Michael, Sieur de Montaigne . . . made English by Charles Cotton, Esq.* (London, 1700).

—— *The Journal of Montaigne's Travels in Italy by Way of Switzerland and Germany in 1580 and 1581*, trans. and ed. with an Introduction and Notes by W. G. Waters, 3 vols. (London, 1903).

MOORE, FRANCIS, *Vox Stellarum; being an Almanack for the Year of Human Redemption 1711 . . . by Francis Moore* (London, 1711).

MOORE, GILES, *Journal*, in Robert Willis Blencowe, 'Extracts from the Journal and Account Book of the Rev. Giles Moore, Rector of Horstead Keynes, Sussex, from the Year 1655 to 1679', *Sussex Archaeological Collections*, 1 (1848), 65–127.

MOORE, THOMAS, *Letters and Journals of Lord Byron; with Notices of his Life*, 2 vols. (London, 1830).

MORE, THOMAS, *A Dialogue concerning Heresies*, ed. Thomas M. C. Lawler, Germain Marc'hadour, and Richard C. Marius, 2 vols. (The Complete Works of St. Thomas More, 6; New Haven and London, 1981).

MORE, WILLIAM, *Journal of Prior William More*, ed. Ethel S. Fegan (Worcestershire Historical Society; London, 1914).

MORGAN, LADY SYDNEY, *Italy*, 3 vols. (Paris, 1821).

MORSLEY, CLIFFORD, *News from the English Countryside 1750–1850* (London, 1979).

MORTOFT, FRANCIS, Journal, British Library, Sloane MS 2142. There is also a modern edition: *Francis Mortoft: His Book. Being his Travels through France and Italy 1658–1659*, ed. Malcolm Letts (Hakluyt Society, 2nd ser., no. 57; London, 1925).

MURISON, DAVID, *The Scottish Year: A Calendar of Noteworthy Anniversaries in the Story of Scotland* (Edinburgh, 1982).

NAOGEORGUS, THOMAS [KIRCHMEYER], *The Popish Kingdome or Reigne of Antichrist written in Latin Verse by Thomas Naogeorgus and Englyshed by Barnabe Googe 1570*, ed. Robert Charles Hope (London, 1880).

NAPOLEON BONAPARTE, *Correspondance de Napoléon Ier publiée par ordre de l'empereur Napoléon III*, 32 vols. (Paris, 1858–69).

NEALE, JOHN MASON, *A History of the Holy Eastern Church*, 5 vols. (London, 1847–73).

NEUGEBAUER, OTTO, *Ethiopic Astronomy and Computus* (Sitzungsberichte der Österreichischen Akademie der Wissenschaften, Philosophisch-historische Klasse, 347; Vienna, 1979).

—— *The Exact Sciences in Antiquity* (2nd edn., Providence, RI, 1957).

—— 'On the "Spanish Era" ', *Chiron*, 11 (1981), 371–80.

—— ' "Years in Royal Canons" ', in *A Locust's Leg: Studies in Honour of S. H. Taqizadeh* (London, 1962), 209–12.

NICOLL, JOHN, *A Diary of Public Transactions and Other Occurrences, Chiefly in Bannatyne* (Bannatyne Club; Edinburgh, 1836).

NILSSON, MARTIN P., *Primitive Time-Reckoning: A Study in the Origins and First Development of the Art of Counting Time among the Primitive and Early Culture Peoples* (Skrifter utgivna av Humanistiska Vetenskapssamfundet i Lund, 1; Lund, 1920).

NOAKE, JOHN, *Notes and Queries for Worcestershire* (London, 1856).

Ó CRÓINÍN, DÁIBHÍ, 'The Irish Provenance of Bede's Computus', *Peritia*, 2 (1983), 229–47.

—— 'A Seventh-Century Irish Computus from the Circle of Cummianus', *Proceedings of the Royal Irish Academy*, 82 C (1982), 405–30.

O'LEARY, PETER (PÉADAR UA LAOGHAIRE), *Irish Numerals and How to Use Them* (Dublin, n.d.).

OLMSTED, GARRETT, *The Gaulish Calendar* (Bonn, 1992).

OPIE, IONA, and TATEM, MOIRA (eds.), *A Dictionary of Superstitions* (Oxford, 1989).

O'SULLIVAN, HUMPHREY, *The Diary of Humphrey O'Sullivan*, ed. and trans. Michael McGrath, SJ, 4 vols. (Irish Texts Society, 30–3; London, 1936–7).

OTTER, WILLIAM, *The Life and Remains of the Rev. Edward Daniel Clarke, Ll.D., Professor of Mineralogy in the University of Cambridge* (London, 1824).

Our Sunday Visitor's 1996 Catholic Almanac, comp. Felician A. Foy and Rose M. Avato (Huntington, Ind., 1995).

OVERBURY, THOMAS, *Characters*, in *The Miscellaneous Works in Prose and Verse*, ed. Edward R. Rimbault (London, 1856).

The Oxford Dictionary of the Christian Church, ed. F. L. Cross and E. A. Livingstone (3rd edn., Oxford, 1997).

The Oxford Dictionary of the Jewish Religion, ed. R. J. Zwi Werblowsky and Geoffrey Wigoder (New York and Oxford, 1997).

PARIS, MATTHEW, *Gesta abbatum Monasterii S. Albani*, ed. H. T. Riley, *Chronica Monasterii S. Albani* (Rolls Series; London, 1867) and *Chronica majora*, ed. H. R. Luard, 7 vols. (Rolls Series; London, 1872–83).

PARKER, RICHARD A., *The Calendars of Ancient Egypt* (Studies in Ancient Oriental Civilization, 26; Chicago, 1950).

PARKINSON, JOHN, *A Tour of Russia, Siberia, and the Crimea, 1792–1794*, ed. William Collier (London, 1971).

Patrologia Graeca, ed. J.-P. Migne, 166 vols. (Paris, 1857–66).

PATTEN, WILLIAM, *The Expedicion into Scotlande of the most woorthely fortunate prince Edward, Duke of Soomerset, uncle unto our most noble souereign lord yͤ kinges Maiestie Edward the VI. Goouernour of hys hyghnes persone, and Protectour of hys graces Realmes, dominions & subiectes: made in the first yere of his Maiesties most prosperous reign, and set out by way of diarie, by W. Patten Londoner* (London, 1548).

PAULDING, JAMES KIRKE, *A Sketch of Old England, by a New England Man* (London, 1822).

PENNANT, THOMAS, *The Journey to Snowdon* (London, 1781).

—— *A Tour in Scotland, MDCCLXIX* (Chester, 1771).

—— *A Tour in Scotland, and Voyage to the Hebrides, MDCCLXXII, Part II* (London, 1776).

—— *A Tour in Wales MDCCLXX* (London, 1778).

PEPYS, SAMUEL, *The Diary of Samuel Pepys*, ed. Robert Latham and William Matthews, 11 vols. (London, 1995).

PETAVIUS, DIONYSIUS, *De doctrina temporum*, 2 vols. (Paris, 1627).

PETERS, SAMUEL, *A General History of Connecticut . . . by a Gentleman of the Province* (2nd edn., London, 1782; 1st edn. 1781).

PFAFF, ALFRED, *Aus alten Kalendern* (Augsburg, c.1945).

PHILIP, ALEXANDER, *The Calendar: Its History, Structure, and Improvement* (Cambridge, 1921).

PINTARD, JOHN, *Letters from John Pintard to his Daughter, Eliza Noel Pintard Davidson, 1816–1833*, ed. Dorothy C. Barck, 4 vols. (New York, 1940).

PLOT, ROBERT, *The Natural History of Stafford-shire* (Oxford, 1686).

POLLNITZ, CARL LUDWIG, *The Memoirs of Charles-Lewis, Baron de Pollnitz*, 2 vols. (2nd edn., London, 1739).

POMARIUS, JOHANN, *Chronica der Sachsen und Nidersachsen* (Wittenberg, 1588).

Pond, An Almanack for the Year of our Lord God 1664 (Cambridge, 1664).

POOLE, REGINALD LANE, *Medieval Reckonings of Time* (Helps for Students of History, 3; London, 1918).

—— *Studies in Chronology and History* (Oxford, 1934).

Poor Robin (various years).

PORTER, JEROME, *The Flowers of the Lives of the Most Renowned Saincts of the Three Kingdoms England, Scotland, and Ireland* (Douai, 1632).

Poslanie po povodu sporov ob istechenii sed'moĭ tysyachi let ot sotvoreniya mira ('Letter concerning controversies over the expiry of the seventh millennium from the creation of the world'), ed. A. I. Pliguzov and G. V. Semenchenko, in V. I. Vuganov (ed.), *Russkiĭ feodal'nyĭ arkhiv*, 5 vols. (Moscow, 1986–92), iii. 695–6.

PRYNNE, WILLIAM, *Histrio-Mastix: The Players Scourge, or, Actors Tragœdie* (London, 1633).

Rashtriya Panchang for 1911 Saka Era (New Delhi, 1989).

RESTAD, PENNE L., *Christmas in America: A History* (New York and Oxford, 1995).

RICHARDS, E. G., *Mapping Time: The Calendars of the World* (Oxford, 1998).

RICHARDSON, ROBERT, *Travels along the Mediterranean, and Parts Adjacent; in Company with the Earl of Belmore, during the Years 1816–17–18*, 2 vols. (London, 1822).

RICHARDSON, W., *Anecdotes of the Russian Empire. In a Series of Letters, Written, a Few Years ago, from St. Petersburg* (London, 1784).

RIDOUT, THOMAS G., *Ten Years of Upper Canada in Peace and War, 1805–1815; being the Ridout Letters*, ed. Matilda Edgar (London, 1891).

RIMBAULT, EDWARD F., introduction to *Two Sermons preached by the Boy Bishop at St. Paul's, temp. Henry VIII., and Gloucester, temp. Mary*, ed. John Gough Nichols (Camden Miscellany, NS 14/7; London, 1875).

ROGER OF WENDOVER, *Roger of Wendover's Flowers of History*, trans. J. A. Giles, 2 vols. (London, 1849).

RÜHL, FRANZ, *Chronologie des Mittelalters und der Neuzeit* (Berlin, 1897).

SACROBOSCO, JOHANNES DE, *De anni revolutione* (Paris, 1550).

SALZMAN, MICHELE RENEE, *On Roman Time: The Codex-Calendar of 354 and the Rhythms of Urban Life in Late Antiquity* (Berkeley and Los Angeles, 1990).

SAMUEL, ALAN EDOUARD, *Greek and Roman Chronology: Calendars and Years in Classical Antiquity* (Handbuch der Altertumswissenschaft, 1/7; Munich, 1972).

—— *Ptolemaic Chronology* (Münchener Beiträge zur Papyrusforschung und antiken Rechtsgeschichte, 43; Munich, 1962).

SAUNDERS, RICHARD, *Apollo Anglicanus, The English Apollo . . . by Richard Saunders* (various years).

SAUSSURE, CÉSAR DE, *A Foreign View of England in the Reigns of George I. & George II.: The Letters of Monsieur César de Saussure to his Family*, trans. and ed. Madame van Muyden (London, 1902).

SCALIGER, JOSEPH JUSTUS, *Opus novum de emendatione temporum in octo libros tributum* (Paris, 1583).

SCHELLINKS, WILLIAM, *The Journal of William Schellinks' Travels in England 1661–1663*, trans. from the Dutch and ed. Maurice Exwood and H. L. Lehmann (Camden Fifth Series, 1; London, 1993).

SCHMITZ, WOLFGANG, 'Zu den Verzeichnissen der sog. Aegyptischen Tage und Stunden', *Beiträge zur lateinischen Sprach- und Literaturkunde* (Leipzig, 1877), 307–20.

SCHONFIELD, HUGH J., *According to the Hebrews: A New Translation of the Jewish Life of Jesus (the Toldoth Jeshu) with an Inquiry into the Nature of its Sources and Special Relationship to the Lost Gospel according to the Hebrews* (London, 1937).

SCHWARTZ, EDUARD, *Christliche und jüdische Ostertafeln* (Abhandlungen der Königlichen Gesellschaft der Wissenschaften zu Göttingen, Philologisch-historische Klasse, NF 8/6; Berlin, 1905).

SCOT, REGINALD, *The Discoverie of Witchcraft* (1584), ed. Brinsley Nicholson (London, 1886).

SCULLARD, H. H., *Festivals and Ceremonies of the Roman Republic* (London, 1981).

SEASON, HENRY, *Speculum Anni: or, Season on the Seasons; being an Almanack for the Year of our Lord . . . by Henry Season* (various years).

SEWALL, SAMUEL, *The Diary of Samuel Sewall 1674–1729*, ed. M. Halsey Thomas, 2 vols. (New York, 1973).

SEWELL, ROBERT, *Indian Chronography* (London, 1912).

——— *The Siddhantas and the Indian Calendar* (London, 1921).

——— and DÎKSHIT, ŚANKARA BÂLKṚISHNA, *The Indian Calendar* (London, 1896).

SHAEFER, BRADLEY E., 'Lunar Visibility and the Crucifixion', *Quarterly Journal of the Royal Astronomical Society*, 31 (1990), 53–67.

SINCLAIR, JOHN, *The Statistical Account of Scotland: Drawn up from the Communications of the Ministers of the Different Parishes*, 21 vols. (Edinburgh, 1791–9).

SKINNER, JOHN, *Journal of a Somerset Rector 1803–1834*, ed. Howard and Peter Coombs (Bath, 1971).

SLINGSBY, HENRY, *The Diary of Sir Henry Slingsby, of Scriven, Bart.*, ed. Daniel Parsons (London, 1836).

SMITH, CHARLOTTE, *Conversations, Introducing Poetry* (London, 1863).

SMITH, JOHN, *The True Travels, Adventures, and Observations of Captaine Iohn Smith* (London, 1630).

SMOLLETT, TOBIAS, *Travels through France and Italy*, 2 vols. (London, 1766).

The South English Legendary, ed. Charlotte D'Evelyn and Anna J. Mill (EETS 235, 236, 244; London, 1956).

SOUTHEY, ROBERT, *Letters from England*, ed. Jack Simmons (London, 1951).

——— *Letters of Robert Southey: A Selection*, ed. Maurice H. Fitzgerald (London, 1912).

SPICER, DOROTHY GLADYS, *Festivals of Western Europe* (New York, 1958).

STEER, FRANCIS W., *The History of the Dunmow Flitch Ceremony* (Chelmsford, 1951).

STEVENSON, MATTHEW, *The Twelve Moneths* (London, 1661).

STIOUI, ROGER, *Le Calendrier hébraïque* (Paris, 1988).

STOW, JOHN, *A Survay of London Contayning the Originall, Antiquity, Increase, Moderne Estate, and Description of that Citie, Written in the Year 1598*, ed. Henry Morley (London, 1890).

STROBEL, AUGUST, *Texte zur Geschichte des frühchristlichen Osterkalenders* (Liturgiewissenschaftliche Quellen und Forschungen, 64; Munich, 1984).

——— *Ursprung und Geschichte des frühchristlichen Osterkalenders* (Texte und Untersuchungen zur Geschichte der altchristlichen Literatur, 121; Berlin, DDR, 1977).

STUBBES, PHILLIP, *The Anatomie of Abuses* (London, 1583).

SWIFT, EDMUND L., *The Life and Acts of Saint Patrick . . . translated from the Original Latin of Jocelin* (Dublin, 1809).

SWIFT, JONATHAN, *Bickerstaff Papers and Pamphlets on the Church*, ed. Herbert Davies (Oxford, 1940).

——— *Journal to Stella*, ed. Harold Williams, 2 vols. (Oxford, 1948).

TAQIZADEH, S. H., 'Various Eras and Calendars used in the Countries of Islam', *Bulletin of the School of Oriental Studies (University of London)*, 9 (1937–9), 903–22; 10 (1940–2), 108–32.

TAYLER, WILLIAM, *Diary of William Tayler, Footman, 1837*, ed. Dorothy Wise (London, 1962).

TAYLOR, JOHN, *Christmas In and Out* (London, 1652).

——— *Complaint of Christmas* (London, 1646).

——— *Wandering to See the Wonders of the West* (London, 1649).

THISTLETON DYER, T. F., *British Popular Customs, Present and Past* (London, 1876).

THORN, ROMAINE JOSEPH, *Christmas, a Poem* (Bristol, 1795).

TILLE, ALEXANDER, *Yule and Christmas: Their Place in the Germanic Year* (London, 1899).

TORRES RODRÍGUEZ, CASIMIRO, 'La era hispánica', *Revista de archivos, bibliotecas y museos*, 79 (1976), 733–56.

TRAIN, ARTHUR, *Puritan's Progress, an Informal Account: Of Certain Puritans & their Descendants from the American Revolution to the Present Time, their Manners & Customs, their Virtues and Vices* (New York, 1931).

TRAIN, JOSEPH, *An Historical and Statistical Account of the Isle of Man*, 2 vols. (Douglas, Isle of Man, 1845).

TUN LI-CH'EN (DŪN LǏCHÉN), *Yānjīng Suishíjì*, 'Record of a Year's Time at Yenching [= Beijing]' (1900), trans. from Beijing 1906 edn. and annotated by Derk Bodde, *Annual Customs and Festivals in Peking* (1936, rev. edn. Hong Kong, 1965, repr. 1968).

TURNER, DAWSON, *Account of a Tour in Normandy* (London, 1820).

TURNER, THOMAS, *The Diary of Thomas Turner 1754–1765*, ed. David Vaisey (Oxford, 1984).

TUSSER, THOMAS, *Five Hundred Pointes of Good Husbandrie*, ed. W. Payne and Sidney J. Herrtage (London, 1878) (edn. of 1580 collated with edns. of 1573 and 1577).

TWAIN, MARK, *The Diaries of Adam and Eve* (The Oxford Mark Twain; New York, 1996).

—— *The Innocents Abroad* (The Oxford Mark Twain; New York, 1996).

UDALL, NICHOLAS, *Apophthegmes* (London, 1542).

UDOLPH, JÜRGEN, 'Zogen die Hamelner Aussiedler nach Mähren? Die Rattenfängersage aus namenkundlicher Sicht', *Niedersächsisches Jahrbuch für Landesgeschichte*, 69 (1997), 125–83.

UFFENBACH, ZACHARIAS CONRAD VON, *London in 1710 from the Travels of Zacharias Conrad von Uffenbach*, trans. and ed. W. H. Quarrell and Margaret Mare (London, 1934).

UHL, WILHELM, *Unser Kalender in seiner Entwicklung von den ältesten Anfängen bis heute* (Paderborn, 1893).

USK, ADAM, *The Chronicle of Adam Usk, 1377–1421*, ed. and trans. C. Given-Wilson (Oxford Medieval Texts; Oxford, 1997).

VARDAMAN, JERRY, and YAMAUCHI, EDWIN (eds.), *Chronos, Kairos, Christos: Nativity and Chronological Studies Presented to Jack Finnegan* (Winona Lake, Ind., 1989).

VERGIL, POLYDORE, *An Abridgement of the Notable Worke of Polidore Virgile* [*De rerum inventoribus*], trans. Thomas Langley (London, 1546).

VERSTEGAN, RICHARD, *A Restitution of Decayed Intelligence* (Antwerp, 1605).

WALLIS, JOHN, *A Treatise concerning St. Matthias Day, Misplaced in the Oxford Almanack for the Year 1684 (being Leap-Year) at Feb. 24* (Oxford, 1709).

WALPOLE, HORACE, *Selected Letters* (London, 1939).

WALSH, MAURA, and Ó CRÓINÍN, DÁIBHÍ, *Cummian's Letter* De Controversia Paschali *and the* De ratione conputandi (Pontifical Institute of Mediaeval Studies, Studies and Texts, 86; Toronto, 1988).

WALSH, WILLIAM S., *Curiosities of Popular Customs and of Rites, Ceremonies, Observances, and Miscellaneous Antiquities* (London, 1898).

WALTON, IZAAK, *The Compleat Angler, or the Contemplative Man's Recreation* (2nd edn., London 1655).

[WARD, EDWARD,] *A Trip to New-England. With a Character of the Country and People, both English and Indians* (London, 1699).

—— *The Whigs Unmask'd: Being the Secret History of the Calf's-Head-Club* (8th edn., London, 1713).

WARNER, WILLIAM, *The First and the Second Parts of Albions England* (London, 1589).

WASHINGTON, GEORGE, *The Diaries of George Washington 1748–1799*, ed. John C. Fitzpatrick, 4 vols. (Boston and New York, 1925).

WELD, ISAAC, Jr., *Travels through the States of North America, and the Provinces of Upper and Lower Canada, during the Years 1795, 1796, and 1797*, 2 vols. (4th edn., London, 1807).

WHITAKER, W. B., *Sunday in Tudor and Stuart Times* (London, 1933).

WHITE, GILBERT, *Gilbert White's Journals*, ed. Walter Johnson (London, 1931; repr. 1970).

WILBRAHAM, ROGER, *The Journal of Sir Roger Wilbraham, Solicitor-General in Ireland and Master of Requests for the Years 1593–1616*, ed. Harold Spencer Scott (Camden Miscellany, 10; 3rd ser., 4; London, 1902).

WILDE, 'SPERANZA', *Ancient Legends, Mystic Charms, and Superstitions of Ireland*, 2 vols. (London, 1887).

WILDE, W. R., *Irish Popular Superstitions* (Dublin, 1852).

WILKINS, DAVID (ed.), *Concilia Magnae Britanniae et Hiberniae*, iii (London, 1737).

[WILLES, JOHN,] *The Julian and Gregorian Year: Or, the Difference between the Old and New-Stile, Shewing, that the Reformed Churches should not alter the Old Style, and that the Romanists should return to it* (London, 1700).

WILLSFORD, THOMAS, *Natures Secrets* (London, 1658).

WILMOT, MARTHA, *The Russian Journals of Martha and Catherine Wilmot*, ed. the Marchioness of Londonderry and H. M. Hyde (London, 1934).

WILSON, JAMES GRANT, 'The Twelfth of August', *Harper's New Monthly Magazine*, 47 (1873), 567–71.

WILSON, THOMAS, *The Arte of Rhetorique* (London, 1553).

WIMMER, OTTO, and MELZER, HARTMANN, *Lexikon der Namen und Heiligen*, ed. and suppl. by Josef Gelmi (Innsbruck, 1988).

WION, ARNOLD, *Lignum vitae*, 2 vols. (Venice, 1595).

WOOD, ANTHONY, *History and Antiquity of the Colleges and Halls of the University of Oxford*, ed. John Gutch (Oxford, 1786).

WORM, OLAUS, *Fasti Danici, universam tempora computandi rationem antiquitus in Dania et vicinis regionibus observatam libris tribus exhibentes* (Copenhagen, 1643; first publ. 1626).

WRIOTHESLEY, CHARLES, *A Chronicle of England during the Reigns of the Tudors, from A.D. 1485 to 1559. By Charles Wriothesley, Windsor Herald*, ed. William Douglas Hamilton (Camden Society, 116; London, 1875).

ZELZER, MICHAELA, 'Zum Osterbrief des heiligen Ambrosius und zur römischen Osterfestberechnung des 4. Jahrhunderts', *Wiener Studien*, NF 52 (1978), 187–204.

ZERUBAVEL, EVIATAR, *The Seven-Day Circle: The History and Meaning of the Week* (Chicago, 1989).

Zimmerische Chronik, ed. Karl August Barack, 4 vols. (2nd edn., Freiburg im Breisgau and Tübingen, 1881–2).

INDEX

Saints born after 1500 are listed under their surnames. **Boldface** distinguishes the main entry.